A THEOLOGY FOR THE TWENTY-FIRST CENTURY

A THEOLOGY FOR
THE TWENTY-FIRST CENTURY

Douglas F. Ottati

William B. Eerdmans Publishing Company
Grand Rapids, Michigan

Wm. B. Eerdmans Publishing Co.
4035 Park East Court SE, Grand Rapids, Michigan 49546
www.eerdmans.com

Published 2020
Printed in the United States of America

26 25 24 23 22 21 20 1 2 3 4 5 6 7

ISBN 978-0-8028-7811-3

Library of Congress Cataloging-in-Publication Data

Names: Ottati, Douglas F., author.
Title: A theology for the twenty-first century / Douglas F. Ottati.
Other titles: theology for the 21st century
Description: Grand Rapids, Michigan : William B. Eerdmans Publishing Company, 2020. | Includes bibliographical references and index. | Summary: "A systematic theology that expounds Christian understandings of creation and redemption as practical wisdom for twenty-first-century readers"—Provided by publisher.
Identifiers: LCCN 2020003714 | ISBN 9780802878113 (hardcover)
Subjects: LCSH: Theology, Doctrinal—History—21st century. | Creation—History of doctrines—21st century. | Redemption—History of doctrines—21st century.
Classification: LCC BT75.3 .O88 2020 | DDC 230—dc23
LC record available at https://lccn.loc.gov/2020003714

For J. M. G.

Contents

List of Propositions xiii

Preface xxi

Abbreviations xxix

Introduction: Point of View 1

Augustinian 3

Protestant 5

Liberal 8

Augustinian, Protestant, and Liberal 11

Humanist 13

I METHOD 23

1. **A Conception of Christian Theology** 25

Mystery and Sensibility 31

Religious Communities and Interpretive Resources 46

Varieties of Theological Visions (or Wisdoms) 56

Christianity 70

Christian Theology 80

2. **The Formation and Arrangement of Theological Statements** 89

The Formation of Theological Statements 89

The Arrangement of Theological Statements 138

II CREATION 155

3. **The Constitution of the Dynamic World: Cosmic Ecology** 157

The Creator-Redeemer 157

The World as Created 165

4. **The Dynamic Continuation of the World: Cosmic Passage** 194

Providence and Experience 199

Particularity and Plurality 201

The Decalogue and Natural Law 202

Cosmological Implications of Modern Knowledge 203

Rethinking Our Theatrical Imagery 209

Some Characteristics of Cosmic Passage 210

An Unscientific Postscript for a Scientific Age 216

Patterns 217

A Calvinist Vocabulary 219

What's at Stake Practically 221

A Proposal 225

Reenvisioning Destiny 230

5. **Created and Sustained Human Life** 234

Humans Are Socially Inclined 244

Institutions Sustain by Furnishing Critical Goods 249

Distinctive Powers and Capacities 258

Capacity Implies Distinctive Responsibility 261

Limitations 263

Responsive Participants 267

We Apprehend Ourselves as Persons Narratively 268

We Apprehend Ourselves as Persons Practically 269

We Apprehend Ourselves as Persons in the Midst of Encounters 271

Persons before God 273

We Pursue Ends 278

Our Chief End and Calling in the Midst of Cosmic Ecology and Passage 280

How We Participate in the Wider Cosmos 283

Living in the Face of Mystery 286

6. God the Creator 288

Biblical Roots 289

Negative Theology 291

A Proposal 296

Biblical Depictions 302

Theologies of Creation 305

Some Critical Points 309

A More Rough-and-Ready Vocabulary 313

Creation and Governance 317

Cosmic Passage and Emergence 319

A Unifying Reign, or Trajectory 323

The Deity at Work in Cosmic Passage 325

God Is the Real 328

The Encompassing Tendency of the Real Bears on Us as a Dynamic Order of Grace 328

The Dynamic Ordering of Grace Pushes Us toward an Ec-centric Orientation in Life 331

III REDEMPTION 333

7. Jesus Christ and the Covenant of Grace 335

Biblical Themes 338

The Covenant of Grace 340

Further Intricacies 343
Critical Observations 345
Stepping beyond Barth 347
What's New? 348
An Expansion and a Revision 349
Excursus on the Image of God 352
Sensing the Gratuitous Heart of Reality 356
Excursus on Christology and History 361
An Inexhaustible and Multifaceted Theme 365
A Proposal 372
A Cosmic Resonance and Reference 374
The Reconciler Also Judges 379
Hope 382
Excursus on Christological Doctrine 384
8. The Truth, the Way, and the Life 393
Teacher 396
The Kingdom 403
Love God, Your Neighbor, and Even Your Enemies 411
Biblical Texts 458
Crucifixion and Atonement 475
A Proposal 479
9. The Spirit and the Church 498
Some Initial Reflections 499
The Spirit Orients and Directs 501
A Contemporary Restatement 511
Word 536
Sacrament 539

10. **Human Life: Sin and Regeneration** 543

The Fall and Original Sin 545

Radical and Universal 556

Original? 559

Reformed Tradition 579

A Proposal 582

Luther and Calvin 591

Where Luther and Calvin Go Wrong 593

Reinterpreting Justification by Grace through Faith 598

Why the Reinterpreted and Revised Idea Is Relevant, Even Subversive 601

An Alteration in Our Motives 605

Interpreting and Reinterpreting Moral Norms and Commands 607

An Impetus toward Forgiveness 612

Liturgical Expressions 618

Coherence and Complexity 623

Mingling Practices 626

Spouses, Parents, Physicians, and Soldiers 628

Protestant Differences 634

11. **The Fragmentation and Renewal of the World: Civil Government, Church, and Sustainability** 640

Calvin's Reformation Perspective 644

Updating Calvin's View 646

Critical Standards 651

The Demonic 655

Conflicting Dynamics 658

The Church *in* the World 662

The Church *with* the World 664

The Church *against* the World 666

The Church *for* the World 669

The Problem 675

Planetary-Scale Thinking, Human Responsibility and Limits 676

Prospects for Sustainability 678

12. God the Redeemer 688

Jesus as the Christ and the Spirit 693

The Creator, Judge, and Redeemer Is the God of Grace 699

Future Developments 702

Pastoral, Political, and Spiritual Dimensions 706

Some Eschatological Views 710

Epilogue: The Sense the Trinity Makes 741

A Biblically Initiated Exploration 744

The Courage to Live Ec-centrically in God's World 745

A Threefold Apprehension 748

Select List of Works Consulted 751

Index of Names and Subjects 761

Index of Scripture References 765

List of Propositions

PART I: METHOD

Chapter 1
A Conception of Christian Theology

Proposition #1 Christian theology is a practical wisdom that articulates a vision of God, the world, and ourselves in the service of a piety, a settled disposition, and a way of living.

Proposition #2 Life in the world evokes wonder and mystery, and these evocations are integral to religious sensibility.

Proposition #3 A deep basis for religious living and for participating in religious communities lies in affections or emotions that are taken to be responsive to the divine.

Proposition #4 Generally speaking, affections emerge as we interact with other persons, objects, situations, and realities. They are intertwined with our knowledge of and beliefs about the many things with which we interact, and they influence and dispose us. . . .

Proposition #5 Affections associated with a sense for the divine are evoked in the midst of our interactions with objects and others. . . . Unlike secularized people . . . religious people take certain affections to have a further referential element. . . .

Proposition #6 Religious people interpret interactions and affections with the aid of resources furnished by particular communities of language, practice, and belief.

Proposition #7 The interpretive resources furnished by religious communities are mythopoeic. . . . They make analogical and symbolic use of rather ordinary ideas and images . . . to portray the additional felt dimension that lies beyond the threshold.

Preposition #8 The relationship between religious affections and communities is reciprocal and circular. Imaginative resources furnished by religious communities and traditions are . . . instruments by which religious inklings and affections come to expression and media that shape inklings and affections.

Proposition #9 Religions may be distinguished by their organizing and paradigmatic proposals.

Proposition #10 Different kinds of theological visions may be classified according to the ways . . . they portray the divine in relationship to us and to the many objects and others we interact with.

Proposition #11 The mythopoeic discourses of polytheistic communities . . .

Proposition #12 The mythopoeic resources of monotheistic communities . . .

Proposition #13 Pantheistic theological visions . . .

Proposition #14 Christian communities bear monotheistic theological visions in which the event of redemption in Jesus Christ constitutes the paradigmatic proposal for picturing God, the world, and ourselves.

Proposition #15 Christians who internalize the basic image/idea of God as Creator, Judge, and Redeemer find that it shapes and expresses their interpretations of the world and humanity as well as many of their salient attitudes and sensibilities.

Proposition #16 A Christian theology presents a Christian community's theological vision or wisdom and, as such, represents the disciplined development of the interpretive work of preaching.

Proposition #17 As the disciplined development of a vision of God, the world, and ourselves, Christian theology strives to keep in touch with a community's religious affections, symbols, and images. . . . It also tries to achieve a higher level of coherence and precision . . . to formulate a more general wisdom than is indicated by isolated symbols, images, and texts. The result is a kind of "in-between" discourse. . . .

Proposition #18 The disciplined formulation of a contemporary theological vision makes a number of additional reflections and inquiries possible. . . . Even so, Christian theological reflections retain their ecclesial and practical aim.

Chapter 2
The Formation and Arrangement of Theological Statements

Proposition #19 Certain recurrent theological stances represent malformations of the Creator-Judge-Redeemer idea and also shape and express basic dispositions or pieties that have exceedingly negative consequences for faithful living.

Proposition #20 Traditional textbooks do not treat another recurrent malformation of theology and piety: anti-Judaism, a devaluation of Jewish religion that often mixes with anti-Semitism. . . .

Proposition #21 Particular Christian subtraditions may articulate distinctive understandings of God as Creator-Judge-Redeemer that shape and express distinctive variations in piety and faithfulness.

Proposition #22 The theology presented here emerges from the Reformed Christian subtradition.

Proposition #23 The theology presented here is also indebted to an ecumenical and liberal strand of the Reformed tradition in North America that supports a social Christianity, is willing to revise inherited beliefs and practices in the light of new knowledge and inquiries, accepts plurality within both the Reformed tradition and the wider Christian movement, and appreciates the importance of conversations among world religions.

Proposition #24 Theological statements or doctrines will be formulated with reference to the Scripture of the Old and New Testaments, church history or tradition . . . , contemporary knowledge, and consistency with other theological statements.

Proposition #25 This book arranges doctrines systematically in order to pursue greater clarity, depth, and coherence.

PART II: CREATION

Chapter 3
The Constitution of the Dynamic World: Cosmic Ecology

Proposition #26 God the Creator is God the Redeemer, and this equation has important consequences for the way we understand both creation and redemption.

Proposition #27 The world is contingent.

Proposition #28 Creation is a formed and dynamic ensemble, and intricate and vast system, a set of orderings, or cosmic ecology.

Proposition #29 The created world is good.

Chapter 4
The Dynamic Continuation of the World: Cosmic Passage

Proposition #30 Creation and sustenance go together.

Proposition #31 The world and its ordering processes continue.

Proposition #32 We have a place and a time within a vast cosmic passage.

Proposition #33 The image of cosmic passage is compatible with a robust understanding of divine governance, but it encourages us to remain agnostic about what some theologians have meant by particular and special providence.

Proposition #34 The images of creation as cosmic ecology and of divine governance and sustenance manifest in an all-encompassing cosmic passage have implications for a view of redemption.

Chapter 5
Created and Sustained Human Life

Proposition #35 Created and sustained human life is mysterious.

Proposition #36 Created and sustained human life is a gift.

Proposition #37 Created and sustained human life is socially inclined, institutionally sustained, and socially conditioned.

Proposition #38 Created and sustained human life is capable and responsible.

Proposition #39 Created and sustained human life is personal.

Proposition #40 Created and sustained human life is historical.

Proposition #41 The chief end, calling, or vocation of created and sustained human beings in the midst of cosmic ecology and passage is to participate in true communion with God in community with others.

Chapter 6
God the Creator

Proposition #42 Theological language is peculiar because God is not an object alongside other objects—and is not knowable as other objects are knowable.

Proposition #43 Creator and Sustainer or Governor are symbols that point to God with respect to the constitution and continuation of the world.

Proposition #44 God is Creator.

Proposition #45 God is Sustainer.

Proposition #46 God is the Real, whose fundamental tendency or trajectory is to ground, instigate, and shape a process of reality that we encounter as a dynamic order of grace, and that pushes us toward an ec-centric orientation in life.

PART III: REDEMPTION

Chapter 7
Jesus Christ and the Covenant of Grace

Proposition #47 God the Redeemer is God the Creator, and this equation has important consequences for the way we understand both redemption and creation.

Proposition #48 The event of Jesus Christ points to a Trinitarian dynamic.

Proposition #49 Jesus Christ fulfills the covenant of grace.

Proposition #50 Jesus is the Christ, the living Word and wisdom of God in a human life.

Proposition #51 Jesus Christ is reconciler.

Chapter 8
The Truth, the Way, and the Life

Proposition #52 Jesus as the Christ teaches the truth.

Proposition #53 The ministry and mission of Jesus as the Christ embody and display a way or a manner in life that accords with the truth.

Proposition #54 The crucifixion and continuing presence of Jesus as the Christ empower a manner or way in life that aligns with the truth.

Chapter 9
The Spirit and the Church

Proposition #55 The Spirit gives and renews life.

Proposition #56 The Spirit gathers the church and sends it on its mission.

Proposition #57 The church that the Spirit gathers and sends is a community of worship.

Chapter 10
Human Life: Sin and Regeneration

Proposition #58 People stand in need of rehabilitation and renewal because they are mired in and diminished by a persistent fault.

Proposition #59 Sin's corruption is multifaceted, radical, and universal.

Proposition #60 For those who embrace the Word of the gospel, there is a transition from a previous constricted orientation to a new and ec-centric manner of life in Christ and the Spirit, and this transition is called regeneration.

Proposition #61 Before God, sinners may know themselves to be accepted and to have worth by grace through faith. This is justification.

Proposition #62 By the grace of God and in the power of the Spirit, people may be caught up in a lifelong process of rehabilitation, regeneration, and renewal. This is sanctification.

Proposition #63 The idea of calling and vocation helps to clarify the sanctifying formation of persons and communities toward ec-centric piety and existence in the world.

Proposition #64 Hopeful realism names the practical stance in the world that comes to expression (among other places) in this understanding of calling and vocation, and that draws on a strain of piety intertwined with the symbolic ideas of creation, sin, and redemption.

Chapter 11
The Fragmentation and Renewal of the World: Civil Government, Church, and Sustainability

Proposition #65 Civil government is a historical means in and through which God's sustenance and care are mediated to us, but all governments are subject to chronic corruptions, all fall short of the kingdom, and so all stand in need of criticism and reform. Occasionally, they also stand in need of fundamental reconfiguration.

Proposition #66 The church is in, with, against, and for the world.

Proposition #67 Current challenges posed by the effects of human activity on our planetary home and by the prospects for sustainability call for both realism and hope.

Chapter 12
God the Redeemer

Proposition #68 God is Redeemer.

Proposition #69 God is the answer to the question of hope.

Proposition #70 God is love.

Preface

This book presents a theology for the twenty-first century, a time when we confront new and pressing realities and in which, for many in North America and in Europe, Christian believing feels deeply problematic. No genuine Christian theology will try to mitigate or dispel this discomfort; faithful living in God's good, chronically corrupted, but nonetheless hopeful world must always be troubling. But a good theology may at least help us to identify the task at hand.

The twenty-first century has been characterized thus far by heightened interdependencies and pluralities, stunning scientific and technological advances, vast economic systems and disparities, polarized politics, grave environmental threats, and more. Still, the task is not how to meet these and other new realities by demonstrating the instrumental value of Christian faith for resurgent nationalism, a healthy "life balance," progressive cultural agendas, or what-have-you. In fact, for those occasionally tempted by such arguments, I hope this book can be a step toward an unapologetic and more specifically Christian piety. Neither is the task how to bolster defensive, judgmental, and anti-intellectual attitudes that shun new ideas and turn away from pressing realities. For those alienated by these attitudes, including thoughtful evangelicals and searchers raised in conservative churches, I hope my theology can be a step toward a reflective, capacious, and compassionate Christian faithfulness eager to engage a changing world. I hope it will also make sense to people like me who were raised in comparatively flexible religious environments.

The task, I believe, is how to live and move today in relationship with the God who creates and redeems. This is why in the pages that follow I pay careful attention to biblical texts and insights, the kingdom-minded message and mission of the crucified and resurrected one, and classical affirmations concerning the Spirit, the church, sin, grace, sanctification, and hope. It is also why I attend to critical arguments and modern scientific knowledge, recognize that all things (including religious traditions) develop historically, and support robust commitments to social criticism and reform.

When, after twenty-three years, he had finally revised his *Institutes of the Christian Religion* to the point where he was satisfied with it, John Calvin quoted a sentence from Augustine's *Letters*: "I count myself one of the number of those who write as they learn and learn as they write." Though I have not worked quite so long on this more modest volume, it too has changed over time. Earlier versions of parts 1 and 2 were published in 2013 under the title *Theology for Liberal Protestants: God the Creator*. In a quite helpful review of that book entitled "How Liberal Is 'Liberal'?," Professor Christine Helmer of Northwestern University argued that mine, "in fact, is a theology that can speak to all Christians." That point, together with similar comments by former students (among them James Calvin Davis, Roger Gench, and Timothy Allen Verhey), ideas contributed by my editor, James Ernest, and the experience of writing the lengthy third part on redemption, led me to alter my views somewhat, revise certain features of parts 1 and 2, and change the title of the completed work to *A Theology for the Twenty-First Century*. Perhaps, then, I should say that I learn not only as I write but also as (or rather, if and when) I *listen* to critics and companions.

Working on this systematic has, in fact, been a part of my routine for many years while teaching at two different institutions. Faculty and students at Union Theological Seminary in Virginia (now Union Presbyterian Seminary), as well as students at the School of Theology at Virginia Union University, helped me to develop my theology even when they disagreed (sometimes sharply). Five colleagues at Union Seminary were especially supportive: Dawn DeVries, H. McKennie Goodpasture, Matthias Rissi, James H. Smylie, and Charles M. Swezey. I remain indebted also to Fred R. Stair, the president of Union who hired me, for my many years of teaching and learning at that institution. Davidson College, in turn, has provided me with the opportunities of a liberal arts environment, partly in the form of conversation partners who represent different scholarly pursuits as well as different religious traditions, including B. Andrew Lustig, C. Matthews Samson, and Syed Rizwan Zamir.

The Seminary granted me sabbatical leave in 2002–2003, when I also enjoyed a grant from the Louisville Institute. The College granted me sabbatical leave in 2010–2011, when the Louisville Institute awarded me a second grant, and again in 2016–2017, when I benefited from a Senior Scholar Grant at the Center of Theological Inquiry in Princeton. I want to thank the Center and its director, Will Storrar, for a highly enjoyable, productive, and stimulating scholarly experience, during which I was able to work with a fine group of scholars, including Frank Rosenzweig, professor of biology at the Georgia Institute of Technology.

I was given the opportunity to work on theological themes central to this book in preparation for my Orr Lectures at Wilson College in Chambersburg, Pennsylvania, in April 2010, entitled "A Theology for the Twenty-First Century." Many thanks are due to David True and Ellen Crawford True for their hospitality on that occasion. I was invited to deliver the Robert Gunning Lecture in October 2011, entitled "A Reformed Theological Realism," at New College, Edinburgh, where I was very pleased to become reacquainted with my friend from Chicago days, Jay Brown. I presented portions of the chapters on creation and the dynamic continuation of the world to a group of Presbyterian ministers near Grand Rapids, Michigan, and owe thanks to Seth Wheeldryer for that opportunity. I developed portions of chapter 5, on human life, in a lecture entitled "Life Is a Miracle," which I delivered in two different forms during the spring of 2012 at the Center of Theological Inquiry in Princeton and then at the invitation of Hal Breitenberg at Randolph-Macon College in Ashland, Virginia. At the invitation of the Vann Center for Ethics of Davidson College and its director, David Perry, a lecture in January of 2015 entitled "Love Your Enemies: The Teaching of Jesus and Dynamics of Crusading Violence" helped me sharpen an important dimension of my christological reflections. The Department of Religion and Philosophy at High Point University invited me to give a lecture entitled "The Church and a Peculiar Discipline of Grace" in November of 2015, a theme that found its way into chapter 9. In June of 2017, a lecture for the Annual Convocation of the Mercersburg Society at Lancaster Seminary entitled "Grace Alone: Interpreting and Revising a Great and Potentially Subversive Protestant Idea" gave me an opportunity to develop parts of chapter 10. In July of 2017, I outlined themes of chapters 7 and 8 in a lecture entitled "Some Elements of a Liberal Christology" at the Ecumenical Institute of Heidelberg University, and I should like to thank Professor Friederike Nuessel for both the kind invitation to speak and her gracious hospitality on that occasion. My presentation entitled "A Christian Humanism: Wonder, Realism, and Hope," in April of 2019, part of a series of faculty lectures at Davidson College entitled "Being Human: Disciplinary Reflections," helped to formalize themes in part 3, and I should like to thank Professors Jaya Jay and Rizwan Zamir for that opportunity. Ever since I began teaching in Richmond, I have benefited from speaking engagements in Presbyterian churches throughout the United States. These have always been my pleasure, and I should like to thank Grace Covenant Presbyterian Church in Richmond, Virginia, Second Presbyterian Church in that same city, and Davidson College Presbyterian Church for many regular opportunities to teach.

Portions of the early chapters of this book were read and discussed by a group called "the Biblical Theologians," which meets annually at Princeton Theological Seminary. Segments of four or five were read and discussed by members of the Colloquy on Theology and Ethics at meetings of the American Academy of Religion: Terrence J. Martin, Richard B. Miller, William Schweiker, and Charles A. Wilson. Sara Jane Bush, Anne Havard, Lisa Landoe, and Lucy Trumbull—all of them at one time or another students at Davidson College—helped me prepare and refine parts 1 and 2. My special thanks go to Isaac Young Kim, then a doctoral student at Princeton Theological Seminary, for very helpful discussions of theological ideas and for preparing significant portions of part 3. I would also like to thank two very fine editors at Eerdmans Publishing Company, Jon Pott and James Ernest, for their support and skilled guidance of this project.

I am old enough now to thank good friends—some theologically inclined and some not—who have helped to make things both enjoyable and worthwhile. Mine have included John S. Javna, Robin W. Lovin, Douglas Trump, and David L. Bartlett. My family—Pamela, Katherine, and Albert—continue to put up with me on a regular basis and with uncommon grace. I am also increasingly aware of the considerable debts I owe my teachers: James Luther Adams, Martha Borowski, Robert F. Evans, Benjamin Franklin Fisher IV, B. A. Gerrish, Langdon Gilkey, James M. Gustafson, Van A. Harvey, John McDermott, Francis Platt, Joseph Sittler, David Tracy, Louis Visco, and Charles White. Were I a sufficiently prolific writer, I would dedicate a volume to each.

Addendum to Preface

While the page proofs for this book were under review, the world found itself in the grips of the coronavirus pandemic, an event surely to be a defining one for the twenty-first century. (A friend suggested it may have as profound effect on this century as World War I did on the twentieth.) As I recall the faces of undergraduates in my newly virtual classes and imagine those of my son's middle school students in his, I think the pandemic may be powerfully formative. Widespread "social distancing," entire countries and states "sheltering in place," hospitals and care facilities stretched beyond capacity and without sufficient equipment, rising death tolls—these are dark days, and many knowledgeable people expect darker days ahead. No theology can solve the present crisis, but every theology should at least begin to interpret it, and so here I offer some preliminary thoughts while the pandemic and our responses to it have yet to run their course.

The theology I present in this book focuses on our relationship with the God of grace who is Creator, Judge, and Redeemer; these three images therefore drive my interpretation.

We humans are creatures who live within a vast and interdependent cosmic ecology as well as its dynamic continuation (or cosmic passage). We participate in this sweeping ecology and its movement, a creation encompassing all that is from galaxies to microbes, though it is not centered on us. We experience the gift of existence as well as compelling presences and beauty in this world's magnificent theater. We encounter important sustaining regularities, such as the brightness of the sun, genomic sequences, families, and civil governments, many of which are beyond our own doing and control. But we also encounter destructive tendencies and occurrences, including alterations in Earth's climate, the deterioration of our bodies, and the occasional dissolutions of societies and clans. These may furnish materials and conditions for the emergence of new realities and possibilities, but there is no denying their destructive force.

As distinctively equipped and intelligent creatures, we can explore, imagine, and appreciate the cosmos. We clearly also are able to wield significant powers, to understand and to influence environments and courses of events through intentional practices and technologies, including systems of public health, medical research, treatments, and vaccines. Even so, our powers of understanding and action are limited; we are able neither to anticipate nor control all relevant outcomes and consequences. We are significantly dependent, and our actions take the form of responses to conditions and events. Indeed, there is for us no action without risk, whether raising a child, overseeing an institution, altering a river, or "sheltering in place." Human life in the midst of interrelations, conditions, agents, and events is therefore often characterized by uncertainties and anxieties. The present pandemic forcefully reminds us of all this. Caught in the grips of a reality we presently cannot control, we need to try to keep our anxieties from overrunning intelligent responses. If we can, we need to forgo destructive tendencies to overconfidence and overreach as well as to slothful denial and inattention to threatening circumstances.

Do our experiences of the pandemic also have features that can be interpreted under the theological rubric of judgment? They do *if* we understand judgment appropriately. The rubric refers not to random destructive happenings, but to deleterious consequences of our skewed devotions to partial interests and communities, our constricted fields of vision and attention, and the destructive actions and practices they support. Viruses are for us destructive features of cosmic passage. They overmatch us, though today we understand important things about them and can also draw on significant medical research and technology to defend against them. Judgment highlights *not* the emergence of the virus and its destructive force but our own destructive failures, of attitudes and action, to prepare for public health disasters in general and this pandemic in particular.

We need to recognize that persons, communities, and institutions are responding to an unprecedented situation, and missteps and mistakes are inevitable. But we should also consider those loyalties, commitments, attitudes, and practices that, with some frequency, have rendered us inattentive and uncooperative, and so placed many—especially those with fewer resources—at profound risk. I think, for example, of long-term social decisions that make for underdeveloped systems of medical care, political disinclinations to recognize and communicate the danger, leaders who vacillate and sometimes balk at crossing ideological divides and conventional interests in order to obtain needed medical tests and equipment and to devise realistic plans for trials ahead. Again, more than a few persons fail to practice measures of social distancing aimed at slowing the spread of the disease, and it also appears that comparatively little is being done to address the pandemic's potential ravages in the poorer global south, in war zones, and in refugee camps. Judgment properly understood focuses attention on the destructive, sometimes horrific consequences of our attitudes and actions that call us to reconsider and to turn. In this case, these consequences call us to relinquish shortsighted politics as well as individualist and commercial mentalities, and to take up more attentive, responsible, and cooperative postures. They call us to examine ourselves, our attitudes, lifestyles, and commitments, and to turn toward new levels of attention to others and to the general good by strengthening health-care systems as well as international health organizations and agencies. Recall the achievement of establishing the United Nations, an international forum for dialogue and a degree of cooperation, following the destruction of two world wars. When it comes to turning under duress, adopting more other-directed attitudes, and devising more cooperative and responsible structures, humanity's record is ambiguous but also significant.

Finally, then, and not apart from acknowledging anxieties, fears, and terrible sufferings, we may also look and hope for traces of grace and the kingdom. We may achieve a more accurate sense of our place as capable but also limited, dependent, and often anxious creatures, and we may be inspired by glimpses of gracious moral commitment. No doubt, in the face of pandemic, we shall see our share of destructive attitudes and actions—ones that are irresponsible, callous, or xenophobic, ones that are beside the point, and ones that put people at risk. But we may look too for demonstrations, whether small or large, that there is often much to admire in people, in their other-directed sensibilities, their impulses to solidarity, and their responsible courage. My current, incomplete, and anecdotal list includes hospital staff who work long shifts in dangerous circumstances; a divided Congress that manages to enact some relief for persons struggling with layoffs, small businesses and their employees, and large corporations; a preschool superintendent who works with her board to obtain half pay for her teachers in the months of April and May, while the schools are unexpectedly closed; employees in supermarkets and pharmacies who serve a contagious public; police and fire departments; sanitation workers; janitors who clean buildings where people must continue to work; government bureaucrats and news media staff working from home; and schools, businesses, families, and friends learning how to communicate remotely. Are these harbingers? The God of grace willing, we may hope so and also work for better communities and a more humane world.

March 29, 2020

Abbreviations

BOC	The Constitution of the Presbyterian Church (USA), Part I, *Book of Confessions*. Louisville: Office of the General Assembly, 2016.
CD	Karl Barth, *Church Dogmatics*. Edited by G. W. Bromiley, T. F. Torrance, et al. 14 vols. Edinburgh: T&T Clark, 1936–1969.
CF	Friedrich Schleiermacher, *The Christian Faith*. Edited by H. R. Mackintosh and J. S. Stewart. Philadelphia: Fortress, 1976.
Dogmatics	Emil Brunner, *Dogmatics*. Vol. 1, *The Christian Doctrine of God*. Vol. 2, *The Christian Doctrine of Creation and Redemption*. Vol. 3, *The Christian Doctrine of the Church, Faith, and the Consummation*. Translated by Olive Wyon and David Cairns. London: Lutterworth, 1952.
ETP	James M. Gustafson, *Ethics from a Theocentric Perspective*. Vol. 1, *Theology and Ethics*. Vol. 2, *Ethics and Theology*. Chicago: University of Chicago Press, 1981, 1984.
ICR	John Calvin, *Institutes of the Christian Religion*. Edited by John T. McNeill. Translated by Ford Lewis Battles. Louisville: Westminster, 1960.
IFM	Gordon D. Kaufman, *In Face of Mystery: A Constructive Theology*. Cambridge, MA: Harvard University Press, 1993.
LW	*Luther's Works*. Edited by Jaroslav Pelikan et al. American Edition. St. Louis: Concordia, 1958–.
NDM	Reinhold Niebuhr, *The Nature and Destiny of Man*. Vol. 1, *Human Nature*. Vol. 2, *Human Destiny*. Louisville: Westminster John Knox, 1996.
ST	Thomas Aquinas, *Summa Theologiae*. Blackfriars Edition. New York: McGraw-Hill, 1964–1981.
WA	*The Works of Saint Augustine: A Translation for the 21st Century*. John E. Rotelle, OSA, director. Hyde Park, NY: New City, 1997–.
WJE	*The Works of Jonathan Edwards*. General Editors, Perry Miller, John E.

Smith, and Harry S. Stout. 26 vols. New Haven: Yale University Press, 1957–2008.

Introduction

Point of View

Christian theology, as I understand it, is a particular practical wisdom. Enriched by interactions with other traditions, sources of insight, and ideas, it makes use of diverse resources drawn from the Bible and from Christian traditions in order to formulate a vision of God, the world, and ourselves that helps people take up and explore a specific manner in living. There are other practical wisdoms that also furnish visions of the world and ourselves, and that help to guide and orient persons—for example, more than a few philosophies and political ideologies, as well as a number of religious and spiritual teachings. Some of these are theological, but all are historically particular, and many are aligned with specific communities, which is why, when we encounter one, we usually are able to identify quite quickly its particular provenance, for example, conservative Republican, existentialist, or Hindu.

The theology I present here is Christian in the sense that it takes Jesus as the Christ to be paradigmatic for understanding God and human life in appropriately responsive relationship with God, and it works especially (though not exclusively) with the Bible and Christian traditions. Nevertheless, any particular practical wisdom—including a Christian theology—must engage not only inherited devotions, practices, and ideas but also current contexts and circumstances if it is to help order and sustain a manner of living today. My focus then is on the contributions Christian theological wisdom may make to faithful living in a world where scientific findings, new technologies, and complex economic and social systems exert significant influences. I recognize that our present world is very diverse and that these influences are thus hardly uniform. Depending on one's physical, social, and cultural location, the context of one's present experience may be described as postmodern or premodern, market-driven or tribal, globally interconnected, ineluctably local, agricultural, industrial, postindustrial, democratic, oligarchic, monarchic, and more. Even so, I think the current twenty-first-century world is a place where, sooner or later, very many people, including Christians of virtually every stripe, encounter new pluralities, profound scientific and technical advances, powerful markets, and highly structured (often bureaucratic) social systems.

These encounters provoke basic and important questions about meaning as well as about Christian faith and practice. How shall we understand ancient affirmations about Jesus, God, sin, grace, the church, and so on in our contemporary world? What shall we make of the new picture of human beings and the cosmos now emerging from well-attested scientific findings? How shall we come to terms with the many faiths and religious traditions—not only in the world at large but also in our own culture and (frequently secular) societies? How shall we participate responsibly (i.e., both critically and constructively) in modern nation-states during an age of global markets, electronic communications, political interdependencies, extensive immigration, international assemblies, and proliferating technologies of destruction? How, in this environment, can we render an integral witness to God in Christ? How can we find faithful ways to restate, rethink, and revise Christian believing in the face of contemporary knowledge and realities?

Especially once we factor in the plurality of practical wisdoms that offer differing visions of current life and circumstances, a contemporary environment that provokes questions such as these is interpretatively and sapientially quite demanding. This, I think, signals a critical issue. The Christian movement faces a host of important challenges, for example, secular defections, "mainstream Protestant decline," and tensions between Christians in postindustrial and pluralistic societies and Christians in more traditional ones with respect to the place of women and matters of sexuality and family. But a primary danger in many places today is simply a loss of *theological acuity*, a diminishment of our readiness and aptitude to draw on explicitly theological language, ideas, and symbols as we engage a demanding, contemporary world. And, where its theological vocabulary fails, specifically Christian wisdom falters.

In some quarters, this danger is partly the consequence of an exceptional—even laudable—practical energy. Progressive Protestants and Catholics, at least since the time of the Social Gospel, have tended to be socially and politically active. They organize committees, associations, and networks that call attention to injustices, advocate humane causes, and seek to mitigate destructive ills. They try to "be prophetic," they protest, and they work for change. Many appear to know almost intuitively where they stand on important issues of the day, such as economic inequality, racism, Christianity and other religions, migration, gay marriage, the environment, and uses of military power. Their witness is both good and important. Too often, however, they are unable to give strong theological reasons for the stands they take, and some appear to regard theological reflection itself as little more than an ancillary "head trip" that detracts from the real business at hand.

Another development sometimes intensifies the danger. For about four generations now, leading theologians in America and elsewhere have been trained in highly specialized PhD programs where emphasis falls on technical scholarship pursued and written up by academics for other academics. This system furnishes accomplished researchers and professors, but it often leaves educated laypeople, seminarians, and ministers to be addressed by popular writings whose engagements with contemporary knowledge, interpretations of the longer tradition, and constructive reflections lack depth.

In this book I have tried to mitigate the split between scholarly and more accessible theological literature by writing a rigorous yet comparatively uncluttered text that engages piety, ministry, and practice—and that addresses both pastors and professors. To that end, I have placed a number of demanding and detailed scholarly comments in explanatory footnotes. I have tried to enhance the integrity and acuity of a distinctly contemporary Christian stance by presenting a *systematic* theology—by exploring interrelationships among theological symbols, ideas, and arguments—rather than by presenting a history of theology or a series of monographs about discrete themes and figures. My aim is to communicate, sometimes illustratively rather than exhaustively, a more or less complete account of Christian piety and the vision of God, the world, and ourselves that it supports.[1]

Clearly, however, just as there is no generic practical wisdom, there is also no generic Christian theology—only different varieties, each of which articulates a somewhat distinctive version of Christian wisdom. I therefore must write as a Christian theologian of a particular sort. This is a historical necessity to which I willingly consent, and so my immediate task in the balance of this introduction is to describe my particular theological viewpoint by commenting on four terms: "Augustinian," "Protestant," "liberal," and "humanist."

Augustinian

When I use the term "Augustinian," I mean following the theological lead of Augustine (354–430 CE), the bishop of Hippo in northern Africa and probably the most influential Christian theologian in the West. Specifically, I mean three

1. On systematics and other forms of theological literature, see chap. 2, prop. #25 below. An example of a recent and magisterial history of theology in America is Gary Dorrien, *The Making of American Liberal Theology: Imagining Progressive Religion, 1805–1900* (Louisville: Westminster John Knox, 2001); *The Making of Liberal Theology: Idealism, Realism, and Modernity, 1900–1950* (Louisville: Westminster John Knox, 2003); *The Making of Liberal Theology: Crisis, Irony, and Postmodernity, 1950–2005* (Louisville: Westminster John Knox, 2006).

related convictions of Augustine: first, God is Creator, and the world is God's good and gracious gift; second, God is Judge, and all persons, communities, and institutions are fallen, mired in sin's radical and misorienting constriction; third, God is Redeemer, that is, in Jesus Christ God forgives sinners and also rehabilitates or enlarges their corrupted hearts, loves, and life orientations by the renewing gifts of grace and the Spirit. In summary, we belong to the God of grace, who creates the world and life as good gifts, who judges wayward sinners, and who reconciles and renews fallen creatures rather than abandoning them to corruption.

The first point is anti-Manichaean and anti-Gnostic, and Augustine emphasizes it in a number of writings, including portions of *City of God*, his treatise *The Catholic Way of Life and the Manichean Way of Life*, and the final chapter of his *Confessions*.[2] Stated negatively, the one God's good creation is not a field where coequal good and evil powers are locked in conflict, nor is it a snare that entraps good immaterial spirits or souls. The second point, that sin is deeper than bad habits and cannot be addressed merely by joining the right moral standards with exhortations and incentives, is anti-Pelagian (though it sometimes also comes to expression against Donatist claims that the church is holy because it is morally upright and "without spot or blemish"). The third point, that forgiveness and regeneration depend on grace, assumes that people are in bondage to sin and thus cannot rightwise and reorient themselves by their own efforts.

I anticipate points I will make later when I note that this reading of Augustine is essentially a Protestant one that emphasizes the centrality of his doctrine of grace. A different, classically Catholic appropriation emphasizes his doctrine of the church and his anti-Donatist points. It holds that (1) sanctification and a changed life are a condition for justification or forgiveness; (2) genuine faith is faith in the authoritative teaching of the Catholic Church; and (3) saving grace is available only in the sacraments of the true (and visible) Roman Catholic Church.[3]

A practical consequence of the Protestant reading of Augustine is that piety and the life of faith take on certain characteristics. We respond with gratitude to God and God's gifts at every turn, participating in God's good world rather than regarding the world as an evil place to be shunned or escaped. We expect persons, groups, and institutions (including ourselves and our own) to be mired

2. Augustine, *The Manichean Debate*, introduction and notes by Roland Teske, SJ, *WA*, I/19:28–103; *The Confessions*, trans. Maria Boulding, OSB, *WA*, I/1:342–80.

3. The Princeton theologian Benjamin B. Warfield claimed that there are typically Catholic and Protestant readings of Augustine (Warfield, *Calvin and Augustine* [Philadelphia: Breckenridge, 1956], 322). But see below for a distinction that may be drawn between appropriations by Lutherans and Reformed Protestants.

in constricted devotions and skewed by corrupt tendencies and interests. We are thus realists who are not surprised at the persistent train of injustice, malice, and destruction in human history, and we know the importance of rough balances of power, compromises, and restraints that help to check chronic abuses. Nevertheless, because we also recognize that renewing grace abounds, we remain hopeful. We refuse to give up. We continue to criticize the shortcomings and injustices even of needed compromises and partial solutions. We look for promising possibilities, and we are willing to take risks in order to pursue them. Relying on the God of grace, we are hopeful realists who participate faithfully in the ambiguities, sorrows, and promises of God's good, corrupted, and renewed world.[4]

A chief difficulty with Augustinian piety is that, from time to time, this delicate balance of conviction and practical consequence gives way. For example, the emphasis on hope and renewal may overtake the themes of realism and sin. Then there may emerge a naïve Christian idealism that expects injustice, malice, and destruction to be overcome apart from significant tragedy and struggle, and often retreats from worldly taint and ambiguity when (inevitably) this does not happen.[5] The balance may be skewed in the other direction as well, and that, in fact, is a more typical Augustinian malaise. The sense of sin and emphasis on realism may overwhelm hope and anticipations of renewal. The way is then clear for a Christian pessimism that is consumed with restraining corruption, too willing to compromise with worldly powers that promise to check destructive forces, and too timid to take risks in order to make things better.

Protestant

In the hands of Luther and Calvin, Protestant piety meant—as it will also for me—an intensification of the Augustinian theology of sin and grace (*sola gratia*). It was thus characterized by a radical sense of repentance or remorse as well as a radical acknowledgment of our dependence on God for the gift of renewed life and possibilities. (Indeed, as a Reformed Protestant—one who looks especially to a line of reflection that includes Calvin, Swiss Reformed, Puritans, and Pres-

4. See Douglas F. Ottati, *Hopeful Realism: Reclaiming the Poetry of Theology* (Cleveland: Pilgrim, 1999), 1–4.

5. While possible, this particular imbalance is not especially characteristic, since Augustinian appeals to hope and renewal are themselves premised on an apprehension of grace that entails a recognition of sin's radical corruption. Even as they celebrate grace, Augustinian Christians tend to believe that in this life we are never entirely free from sin's misorienting constriction, that we are thus unable to pursue true good on our own, and that the need for compromises and restraints persists.

byterians—I shall affirm one covenant of grace that extends from creation to the end.) But not all Protestants subscribed to an intense Augustinianism, and here I want to point to some typical convictions concerning the Bible, church, and tradition.

What Lutherans, Calvinists, Baptists, and others did share was an emphasis on Scripture (*sola Scriptura*) that signaled an effort to go back behind the accumulated teachings and practices of church traditions to the original sources of Christian faith and believing. This vivifying return to the original sources was something that Protestants also shared with Christian humanists, such as Erasmus.[6] Among other things, it implied a significant revision in the meaning of church—particularly with regard to authoritative teaching and history. Protestants were ready to criticize the received teachings of church councils and authorities in the light of the Bible and its message. They were ready to revise and reject long-standing ecclesiastical practices. Moreover, they insisted that access to the truth (in Scripture) is not the prerogative of an authoritative ecclesiastical hierarchy and its special graces but a gift of the Spirit to the entire people of God. They also denied infallible authority to any person, group, office, or institution (including themselves).[7]

This critical attitude and the protest it engendered against what the church had become presumed that the church has a history. It also presumed that this history is not the untarnished story of an incarnate ideal, nor is it simply the happy tale of divinely inspired and providentially guaranteed positive achievements. Instead, church history is an *actual history*, a story of ups and downs, replete with degenerations, ambiguities, wrong turns, and errors that must be recognized, confessed, criticized, and reformed.

Whatever these ideas may have meant in theory, one practical result was the rejection of a single overarching church and its teachings. Protestantism led to multiple interpretations of Scripture and its message by different individuals and movements, and thus it meant an end to the pretension of a universal and generic Christianity. Protestantism meant schism, but even more fundamentally it also meant a plurality of churches, each deciding its own teachings for itself and each remaining subject (in principle, at least) to criticism—as well as to further schisms.[8]

6. B. A. Gerrish, *The Old Protestantism and the New: Essays in the Reformation Heritage* (Chicago: University of Chicago Press, 1982), 206–7.

7. See, for example, the Scots Confession of 1560, the Second Helvetic Confession, and the Westminster Confession of Faith in *BOC* 3.20; 5.010–5.014; 6.175.

8. This is part of the reason why, even to the present day, there can be no such thing as a generic Protestant theology. Instead, there are Protestant theologies (plural), each responding to particular ecclesiastical contexts and circumstances, as well as to somewhat distinct Chris-

Interestingly, it was with the question of interpretation that many Protestants were willing to acknowledge a revised (if also secondary) role for tradition. Part of the idea was that earlier Christians and their communities were engaged in the same interpretive enterprise that we are. Therefore, we may look to traditional statements and reflections as we try to engage and interpret the classic originals in our own place and time. Indeed, if we do not assume that we alone have escaped with the truth, if we take up a self-critical stance that assumes that we, too, are fallible and prone to errors, then it seems wise to check our own interpretations and statements against those of faithful Christians from other places and times. The net result is not that all discussions of church teaching and theological traditions are dismissed as irrelevant, but rather that appeals to church teaching and theological traditions contribute to discussions of a certain kind. The broader theological conversation is never simply about authoritative church teachings and traditions per se; critical appeals to fallible church teachings and theological traditions are significant to the extent that they help us to get at the truth of the gospel.

A problematic feature of Protestant piety is the (somewhat paradoxical) temptation to false certainty and intolerance. This sometimes follows the potentially anxious realization that, on Protestant grounds, there can be no authoritative guarantee that either one's own or one's church's understanding of the truth is correct. The insecurity can be unbearable. If religion and the life of faith are about ultimate truth and absolute reality, shouldn't one's religious convictions and ideas be absolutely certain? Hence the almost countless Protestant theories of biblical infallibility and authority that are offered in conjunction with descriptions of the "right" method or "surefire" approach to interpreting the Bible correctly. Hence, also, the recurrence in some Protestant communions of unbending and authoritarian denials of disagreement and plurality, for example, efforts to define the "fundamentals" or "essential tenets" on which all right-thinking Christians must agree that effectively reinstate the authoritative church pronouncements to which Protestants objected in the first place. In effect, these attempts at certainty almost always reject a self-critical piety as well as an actual history of grace and accomplishment but also corruption and degeneration. They entail the assertion that a particular Protestant church in history finally has achieved an unambiguous and infallible apprehension of truth.[9]

tian subtraditions, for example, Lutheran, Reformed, Baptist, Episcopalian, and Methodist. See chap. 2, prop. #21.

9. Rubem Alves once objected that the polemic of North American Protestant missionaries against Catholicism in Latin America assumed something like this. "The presupposition was that Protestant theology had completed the codifying of biblical truths. The system of doctrine in harmony with the Scriptures was already perfected" (Alves, "The Protestant Principle

Liberal

"Liberal" is a problematic word because, as anyone who reads the newspapers knows, it means many different things to different people. In addition, liberal theologies have been subjected to important, often trenchant, criticisms for well over eighty years. Do they compromise and dilute Christian believing in order to accommodate it to prevailing cultural preferences and ideas? This is one reason why some look for alternative terms, such as "revisionary" or "progressive." My own judgment, however, is that the most direct way to confront the problem and also take advantage of liberal insights is simply to risk a specific definition. So, by "liberal," I mean a piety and theological stance characterized by (1) appeals to critical arguments and scientific inquiries; (2) a historical consciousness that recognizes that ideas, traditions, practices, institutions, and even species change and develop; and (3) a commitment to social criticism, engagement, and reform.

The first characteristic has roots in the Renaissance and the Enlightenment. Think of Galileo's unfortunate run-ins with the church, Immanuel Kant's encouragement to make use of critical reasoning rather than simply accept whatever is handed down by social authorities, and the attempts of some Deists to promote "freethinking" here in America.[10] During the nineteenth and twentieth centuries, liberal theologians such as Ernst Troeltsch, Henry Nelson Weiman, and James M. Gustafson tried to come to terms not only with contemporary ideas and philosophies but also with well-attested scientific findings.[11] For example, what is the meaning for Christian life and believing of the fact that species rise and fall? What does it mean that the earth is one planet out of billions in a galaxy out of billions of galaxies?

---

and Its Denial," trans. Lewistine McCoy, in *Faith Born in the Struggle for Life: A Rereading of Protestant Faith in Latin America*, ed. Dow Kirkpatrick [Grand Rapids: Eerdmans, 1988], 218). Alves also complained about fundamentalist denials of fallibility (Alves, "From Paradise to the Desert," trans. John Drury, in *Frontiers of Theology in Latin America*, ed. Rosino Gibellini [Maryknoll, NY: Orbis, 1983], 286–87). For an extended discussion, see also Rubem A. Alves, *Protestantism and Repression: A Brazilian Case Study*, trans. John Drury, rev. Jaime Wright (Eugene, OR: Wipf & Stock, 1985), 47–83.

10. It might be argued that, given available evidence at the time, there were good reasons to reject some of Galileo's ideas. But, of course, even if one believes that to be true, one may also argue that church authorities should not penalize inquirers whose ideas conflict with church teaching. See also Immanuel Kant, "What Is Enlightenment?" in *Kant's Political Writings*, ed. Hans Reiss (Cambridge: Cambridge University Press, 1970), 54–60; Anthony Collins, "A Discourse on Free Thinking," in *Deism and Natural Religion: A Source Book*, ed. E. Graham Waring (New York: Frederick Ungar, 1967), 56–65.

11. See esp. James M. Gustafson, *An Examined Faith: The Grace of Self-Doubt* (Minneapolis: Fortress, 2004).

Historical consciousness, which in some respects may be regarded as a further outgrowth of Protestant ideas of history and fallibility, emerged in Europe during the late eighteenth and early nineteenth centuries and is now a feature of very many perspectives on human life and the world. Classical, medieval, and Enlightenment thought patterns often assumed too quickly that certain values, ideas, roles, practices, and institutions were rational, natural, universal, and invariant. But, as voyages of discovery expanded the number of known societies and cultures, and as historical investigations uncovered additional insights into past civilizations and practices, this assumption seemed increasingly flawed. Historically inclined theologians, such as Ferdinand Christian Baur, Friedrich Schleiermacher, Adolf von Harnack, Alfred Loisy, and Ernst Troeltsch, came to regard values, ideas, roles, practices, institutions, and even entire religious traditions as historically and socially particular realities that develop over time and are shaped in response to specific and changing conditions.

With the emergence of modern critical methods, historical inquirers raised questions about the authorship and historical accuracy of certain biblical texts; they also noted the formation and development of practices and ideas in response to particular cultural and social conditions, not only in the church's tradition but also in the Bible itself. The effect was to challenge certain Protestant understandings of the inerrancy of biblical texts, as well as the sharp distinctions that classical Protestants were wont to draw between the Bible and later church history. Over time, liberal Protestants came to understand biblical texts as the literary products of particular human communities that reflect assumptions and ideas of the cultures in which they were written.[12] Again, many classical philosophers and theologians regarded biological forms (or types of plants and animals) as static and permanent, but Charles Darwin and others showed that species (including our own) have histories of development and change. Geologists such as Charles Lyell showed that the earth does, too. One result was that historically minded liberal Protestants increasingly came to recognize the mythological character of biblical creation narratives and ideas. In addition, a number of twentieth-century theologians, such as Teilhard de Chardin and Gordon D. Kaufman, have recognized not only that human societies and cultures are ineluctably historical but also that nature itself has a history, and that human history needs to be viewed within the wider story of nature and the cosmos.[13]

12. This is affirmed by the Confession of 1967, which appears in the *BOC* 9.29, and also by *The Book of Discipline of the United Methodist Church* (Nashville: United Methodist Publishing House, 2000), 78.

13. Almost any one of Teilhard's major works illustrates this point, but surely one of the most impressive is *The Phenomenon of Man*, trans. Bernard Wall (New York: Harper & Row, 1959). In his introduction to this book, Sir Julian Huxley claims that here Teilhard examines

A third characteristic of liberal piety might be called "social Christianity." If we frame critical arguments and think freely, and if we understand current social arrangements and institutions to be neither universal nor invariant but historically particular, then it follows that we may subject these arrangements and institutions to both criticism and reform. This is exactly what happened when industrialization in the West brought about significant social strains and upheavals.[14] Liberal Protestants addressed the "social question," or "social problem," by focusing their attention on modern economic life and its relationship to politics. In Europe, and particularly in Switzerland, Christian socialists tried to bring the work of the church into closer relationship with the interests of labor, political liberalism, and the idea of social democracy. The Christian socialism of many Anglicans in Britain owed much to the theology of F. D. Maurice, with its emphasis on incarnation and the consecration of daily life. In America, theologians like Washington Gladden and economists like Richard T. Ely mounted a critique of laissez-faire capitalism.[15] Walter Rauschenbusch, the leading exponent of the Social Gospel in America, emphasized that Jesus's prophetic message of the kingdom entails the society-making virtue of love as well as a demand for justice that undercuts selfishness and supports "economic democracy."[16] The impetus toward social criticism and reform remained important for Reinhold Niebuhr's Christian realism and for Martin Luther King Jr. as well.[17] Recently it has also been taken up and forcefully developed by some liberation and feminist theologians.[18]

---

every fact and subject with respect to its evolutionary development (11). See also Kaufman, *IFM*, 97–111.

14. Henry F. May, *Protestant Churches and Industrial America* (New York: Harper & Brothers, 1949).

15. See Dorrien, *The Making of American Liberal Theology: Imagining Progressive Religion, 1805–1900*, 313.

16. See Douglas F. Ottati, foreword to *Christianity and the Social Crisis*, by Walter Rauschenbusch (Louisville: Westminster John Knox, 1991), xi–xxxii. Rauschenbusch emphasized Jesus's prophetic message of the kingdom. Vida Dutton Scudder, an Anglican laywoman and professor of English at Wellesley College, supports a similar—but more forthrightly feminist—stance with an incarnational theology reminiscent of the theology of F. D. Maurice. See Elizabeth L. Hinson-Hasty, *Beyond the Social Maze: Exploring Vida Dutton Scudder's Theological Ethics* (New York: T&T Clark, 2006).

17. Reinhold Niebuhr once called Rauschenbusch "not only the real founder of social Christianity in this country but also its most brilliant and generally satisfying exponent to the present day" (Reinhold Niebuhr, preface to *An Interpretation of Christian Ethics* [New York: Seabury, 1979], n.p.). Martin Luther King Jr. drew on the work of both Rauschenbush and Niebuhr. See *A Testament of Hope: The Essential Writings of Martin Luther King Jr.*, ed. James Melvin Washington (New York: Harper & Row, 1986), 35–40.

18. In their social criticism, liberationist and feminist theologians draw on very many cur-

Liberal piety is also not without typical difficulties and degenerations. Consider Van A. Harvey's account of its "pathos." As they attempt to be relevant and to speak to modern culture, says Harvey, liberals make use of current findings, beliefs, ideas, and values. Having thus embraced the spirit of the age, however, they may then find that they no longer have anything especially new or distinctive—and therefore relevant—to say to the current culture.[19] Another difficulty dogs the effort to critique and reform society in the light of contemporary knowledge; some liberals seem tempted to conclude that, as human knowledge and sciences increase, human life, society, and morality are bound to improve. This belief lies at the core of an overly optimistic and naïve idea of progress that may be regarded as a degeneration of the Protestant idea of actual (rather than ideal) history, and it was called into question during the twentieth century by two world wars, the rise of totalitarianism, repeated holocausts, and massive famines.[20]

Augustinian, Protestant, and Liberal

Although significant tensions and ambiguities inevitably remain, there are important respects in which Augustinian, Protestant, and liberal currents can be mutually correcting. The typical degenerations of liberal piety thus called forth an Augustinian and Protestant correction during the 1930s and 1940s by theologians such as Paul Tillich, Reinhold Niebuhr, and H. Richard Niebuhr. The cornerstone of the correction was made up of three insistences that were decidedly realist and

---

rents of thinking. However, a strong historical consciousness seems linked with the impetus to social criticism and reform whenever liberationists offer genetic accounts of current ills and pursue a new society, and whenever feminists point out that it is not nature and biology but culture and socialization that have oppressed women in sexist societies and truncated their roles. See, e.g., Gustavo Gutiérrez, *A Theology of Liberation: History, Politics, and Salvation*, ed. and trans. Sister Caridad Inda and John Eagleson, 15th anniversary ed. (Maryknoll, NY: Orbis, 1988), xvii–xlvi, 13–25. See also Elisabeth Schüssler Fiorenza, *Discipleship of Equals: A Critical Feminist Ekklesia-logy of Liberation* (New York: Crossroad, 1993), 55–58.

19. Van A. Harvey, "The Pathos of Liberal Theology," *Journal of Religion* 56, no. 4 (1976): 382–91, a review of David Tracy, *Blessed Rage for Order: The New Pluralism in Theology* (New York: Seabury, 1975). "The pathos of the liberal theologian is that, if he identifies himself too unqualifiedly with modernity, he runs the risk of alienation from the very community his apologetic is to serve. If, on the other hand, he defines his role primarily in terms of classical Christianity, he runs the risk of being an obscurantist, alienated from the modern intellectual community of which he also wants to be a member" (383). It is primarily the first possibility that I have in mind here.

20. And that was explicitly criticized by Reinhold Niebuhr, *NDM*, 2:164–69; see also Langdon Gilkey, *Reaping the Whirlwind: A Christian Interpretation of History* (New York: Seabury, 1981), 223–24.

also at odds with a good deal of modern culture: (1) human beings, their possibilities and limits, are never adequately understood apart from the apprehension that sin is radical and universal; (2) human history is fraught with possibilities but also with ambiguities and corruptions; and (3) in the final analysis, we depend, not on ourselves, but on the God of grace who creates, judges, and redeems.[21]

While there can be no guarantees, a vital appreciation for Protestant virtues of self-criticism and self-doubt may be reinvigorated with the help of liberal emphases on critical argument and freethinking, as well as by thoroughgoing Augustinian senses for the limitations of finite minds, the radical corruption of human interests, our need for grace, and the incomprehensibility of God. Protestant and liberal insistence not only on the need for criticism but also on the presence of continuing possibilities for positive change and reform may help to mitigate Augustinian temptations to pessimism.

To summarize, then, an *Augustinian* Protestant is one whose understanding of the Bible and the life of faith reaffirms or even radicalizes Augustine's broad theology of grace. This describes the emphasis of Luther and Calvin: persons are good and limited creatures, radically corrupted by sin but nevertheless forgiven, turned, and enabled by grace alone to respond faithfully to God and others. But it does not describe the posture of many Baptist or "left-wing" Protestants, such as Menno Simons during the sixteenth century or John Howard Yoder in the twentieth, both of whom emphasized a strenuous life of radical discipleship and obedience.[22] (I should also note, parenthetically, a characteristic difference among Augustinian Protestants. Lutherans often emphasize justification and grace as free forgiveness; Reformed communities agree, but they also emphasize a changed way of life. That is, they point to *both* reconciliation and renewal. In this they follow John Calvin, who spoke of "a double grace," or both justification—being pardoned by Christ's blamelessness—and sanctification—being regenerated by Christ's spirit—and who emphasized the latter so much that he treated it before the former in his *Institutes*.)[23]

21. See Robin W. Lovin, "Christian Realism: A Legacy and Its Future," *Annual of the Society of Christian Ethics* 20 (2000): 3–18; see also James H. Cone, *A Black Theology of Liberation* (Philadelphia: Lippincott, 1970), 238–49, and Gutiérrez, *Theology of Liberation*, 123–26. Did the (very necessary) correction understate the importance of hope in theology, ethics, and society? Given the typical malaise of Augustinian theologies mentioned above, we should not be surprised if it did. Certainly this was an implication of the theologies of hope and the political and liberation theologies that followed in the wake of Tillich and the Niebuhrs.

22. See *The Complete Writings of Menno Simons*, trans. Leonard Verduin (Scottdale, PA: Herald, 1956), 395–404. Yoder's most impressive statement of the theme of radical discipleship is *The Politics of Jesus: Vicit Agnus Noster*, 2nd ed. (Grand Rapids: Eerdmans, 1994).

23. Indeed, to emphasize the importance of works and a changed life, he treated "regeneration . . . the second of these gifts," before he treated justification (Calvin, *ICR* 3.11.1).

A *liberal* Protestant is one whose piety and sensibility join Protestant convictions about Bible, tradition, church, history, and truth with sustained attention to critical argument and scientific inquiries, a developed historical consciousness, and a commitment to social criticism and reform. This describes the stances of theologians such as Friedrich Schleiermacher, Ernst Troeltsch, and Walter Rauschenbusch. But it does not describe the work of more recent evangelical, "postliberal," and "postmodern" theologians, those who harbor deep suspicions about the Enlightenment and also tend to minimize the significance for theology of the findings of the natural sciences and some other disciplines.[24]

The theology I am presenting here is Augustinian, Protestant, and liberal because it endeavors to combine signal sensibilities and themes indicated by all three terms. This combination also describes, with variations, the contributions of some theologians during the mid-twentieth century, such as Paul Tillich, Reinhold Niebuhr, and H. Richard Niebuhr, as well as more recent contributions by Langdon Gilkey, James M. Gustafson, Douglas John Hall, Robin W. Lovin, William Schweiker, Kristine A. Culp, Paul Capetz, Rebekah Miles, and others. I believe that this particular strand of theology has the resources to help us faithfully engage a world where resigned pessimism, naïve optimism, and authoritarian dogmatism are badly out of place, and where recent scientific inquiries and technological advances as well as market economies and complex social systems do much to shape contemporary life. This is why I believe that it can continue to contribute to the integrity and vitality of a distinctive Christian witness in our own time.

Humanist

Now for a last introductory point. When a theology of the kind I have just described engages our present world, the posture that emerges may be called a *Christian humanism*.[25] Allow me to explain.

24. So many theologians describe themselves as postliberal and postmodern today that it is difficult to know where to begin. But note, for example, the very slight place William C. Placher accords historical studies about Jesus in *Jesus the Savior: The Meaning of Jesus Christ for Christian Faith* (Louisville: Westminster John Knox, 2001), 2–5. Again, the theological method commended by Stanley J. Grenz and John R. Franke—"in a postmodern context"—effectively protects the text of Scripture from being challenged by insights garnered from the wider culture and scientific findings. See Grenz and Franke, *Beyond Foundationalism: Shaping Theology in a Postmodern Context* (Louisville: Westminster John Knox, 2001), 150–63.

25. I have learned much from William Schweiker's understanding of a "theological humanism" that "insists on a wider, more complex reach of value" than do some other kinds of

What are humans for? People raise the question of the meaning of life in every age and culture, but it takes different forms at different places and times.[26] For example, ancient Hellenistic culture pictured people as an amalgam of the spiritual and the material on the boundary of eternity and time. The question of meaning came to reflect experiences of being caught up in the temporal flux of material change, decay, and death. What can be the meaning or the point of rational human spirit enmeshed, exiled, or even imprisoned in a treacherous and tragic bodily existence? This was the form of the question answered by Stoics, mystery cults, Neoplatonists, and Christian theologians. Essentially, the answer they gave was the participation of human spirit in, and its return to, the eternal beyond time and change—a theme that came to varied Christian expressions in the divinizing dimensions of Origenistic theologies, as well as of "one-nature" Alexandrian and "two-natures" Orthodox Christologies.[27]

The question took another form in the Christian culture of medieval Europe, with its emphasis on satisfying the divine will. Humans were thought to occupy a pivotal position in the chain of being: decisively above mere animals and also a little lower than angels. But now they were understood primarily as agents-under-orders, earthly subjects of their heavenly and holy Lord. The dynamics of feudal hierarchies and stations, Roman penance, and monastic attempts at purity all contributed to this picture, and the peculiarly medieval form of the meaning question came to reflect unshakeable experiences of disobedience, moral taint, missing the mark, and guilt.

The response in certain corners of the monastic movement, as well as of the left wing of the Protestant Reformation, was a strenuous commitment to obedience and radical discipleship.[28] But the Augustinian wing of the church claimed that this response failed to appreciate the severity of sin. What can be

---

humanism. See Schweiker, *Theological Ethics and Global Dynamics: In the Time of Many Worlds* (Oxford: Blackwell, 2004), 202–3.

26. Paul Tillich suggests this in a number of places, for example, *The Courage to Be* (New Haven: Yale University Press, 1952), 17, where he says that the Stoic strain of the courage to affirm one's life in spite of fate and death differs from a later form of courage in spite of sin and guilt. See also Tillich, *Existence and the Christ,* vol. 2 of *Systematic Theology* (Chicago: University of Chicago Press, 1957), 21–26, where he discusses the rise of the existentialist problem and its different expressions at different places and times.

27. For the Stoic, says Tillich, one is able to affirm one's personal center because it participates in the universal reason that transcends temporal fate, passions, and anxiety (Tillich, *The Courage to Be*, 13–15).

28. The monastic movement was not uniform in this regard. For example, Bernard of Clairvaux articulated a fairly Augustinian theology. See Dennis E. Tamburello, *Union with Christ: John Calvin and the Mysticism of St. Bernard* (Louisville: Westminster John Knox, 1994), 14, 41–50.

the meaning or the point of life defiled, accused by its own sense of righteousness, chained and in bondage to, or, to mix metaphors, fatally infected by, the debilitating sickness of sin? How can chronically corrupted humans merit or be worthy of communion with the holy God? Surely *not*, said the Augustinians, by recommitting themselves to their own inadequate strength and skewed efforts. Instead, Augustinians insisted that the true answer (dispensed in sacraments and expressed in theories of atonement) was grace, an answer discernible in Thomas Aquinas's contention that divine assistance perfects the soul, most pointedly articulated by Martin Luther's insistence on free justification, and then combined with an emphasis on sanctification in the theology of John Calvin.

What are humans for? What is the meaning or point of human life? Today we ask these questions against a different background. Why? Because scientific knowledge, technological advances, and complex economies and social systems have combined with a soul-numbing history of war, genocide, oppression, and seemingly indiscriminate violence to shatter the classical picture of humanity as the crown of creation standing at the crossroads of heaven and earth.

Consider a partial inventory of current experiences and their implications. Many of us today benefit from dazzling improvements in communications, electronics, information technologies, medicine, and transportation, as well as from dramatically increased capacities for production. We also recognize that humans now have the power not only to change the earth but to destroy it, not only to take life but to extend it, clone it, and (in some instances) manufacture it. Have we thus finally succeeded in our age-old quest to become gods? At the same time, the sciences, as well as increasingly dire consequences of environmental degradation, suggest that, despite our considerable and distinctive capacities, we are animals who have emerged in a long (and continuing) evolutionary process; we remain enmeshed in a welter of interdependent interrelationships; but we have little inclination to look after the long-term welfare of our planetary habitat. We recognize that species rise and fall. We also recognize that the planet we inhabit is a comparatively small one set within an immense cosmos made up of virtually countless galaxies, stars, and planets, a cosmos that has been expanding for billions of years and continues to do so. So perhaps we are neither gods nor cosmically pivotal beings; perhaps we are merely incidental, maladaptive, and beside the point.

Consumerist and secular societies present us with powerful, multiple, and entertaining media, as well as with dramatically increased choices, but they can also seem blandly standardizing, shallow, or even intolerant as they challenge and unhinge traditional communities and identities. Large-scale economic and political structures seem impervious to the actions and concerns of persons and communities. Individuals often feel overwhelmed by industrial and postindustrial economies, adrift in global markets, dwarfed by vast political systems, and lost in highly bureaucratized, routinized, and impersonal institutions. Have we, therefore, relinquished all particularity and become little more than interchangeable cogs? We are routinely, often grudgingly, aware of the horrifying holocausts, terrible weapons, persistent poverty, intolerable injustices, massive starvations, mistreated children, neglected epidemics, recurrent tyrannies, and increasing terrors that characterize our time. We see venerable cultural and religious ideas manipulated to sanctify the partial interests and causes of communities and to demonize opponents. Shall we, therefore, recognize the worth only of those who belong to our own specific groups and concede that human beings as such make no fundamental moral claims on us?

The general result, I believe, is that we live in an age of dislocation. Having dislodged ourselves from our pivotal link in the classical chain of being, we have trouble locating ourselves at all. Too often we estimate human life only disconnectedly. We try to understand human beings in isolation or on their own. We ask what they are for, but only with reference to their own interests, needs, choices, wants, and desires. We raise the question of meaning but without any clear sense of our integral relationships within a wider context.

The theology I wish to present here insists that a fuller and deeper response to the question of meaning, or of what people are for, poses yet another and prior question: What is the place and worth of human beings? Where do we fit, and how does our "location" indicate our true significance?[29] In part, this is simply to underscore an old and classic truth: we humans cannot effectively raise the question of what we are for without also engaging the question of our *context*. We do not understand ourselves apart from a worldview that locates us in response to a wider circumstance.[30]

The psalmist noted that we are moved to put the question of human beings when we look out into the night sky and survey the moon and the many stars in sight (Ps. 8). And we might say that the Bible as a whole encourages us to put the question in a similarly contextual way. In the midst of the heavens and the many creatures, of nature's constancies and threats, and of history's events, promises, and sufferings, what are human beings that they, too, should wield distinctive capacities and also be objects of divine care and concern? Only today we should note that the mundane and cosmic compass, the natural ecologies

29. I take the suggestion from Paul E. Capetz, *Christian Faith as Religion: A Study of the Theologies of Calvin and Schleiermacher* (Lanham, MD: University Press of America, 1998), 201.

30. This idea connects with Clifford Geertz's understanding of religious symbols and the religious perspective as "a particular manner of construing the world." See his famous essay "Religion as a Cultural System," in *The Interpretation of Cultures: Selected Essays by Clifford Geertz* (New York: Basic Books, 1973), 90, 110, 112, 123.

and interdependencies, the historical frames, sequences, and perils seem significantly complicated and expanded in ways that our ancient traditions did not entirely anticipate.

This is where a contemporary Christian humanism comes in. Partly because it is instructed by recent knowledge and experiences, and partly because it is heir to a vibrant religious tradition, this is a posture that does not try to raise the question of meaning disconnectedly. It does not try to reinstate what, under current circumstances, seems impossible to reinstate. It does not say that Earth and cosmos are simply for us humans, or that the value of all other things is only a function of human needs, wants, and desires. It does not simply reassert that we occupy the pivotal position among beings. Instead, a truly *theistic* humanism senses that the Creator-Judge-Redeemer stands in relationship to all things, including ourselves. It is theocentric and thus criticizes reductive anthropocentrisms, including theistic varieties that point to God only to claim that humans alone constitute God's chief end. It locates humans in the context of a divine dynamic whose wider (and largely mysterious) trajectories, activities, and ends extend far beyond the frame of human realities. This is its decentering, or *dis*placing, movement.

At the same time, however, this "displacing" movement is also the beginning of a "relocating" movement, or of a drive toward a theologically situated estimate of the place and worth of humans. A theocentric Christian humanism puts people in their place by recognizing that, in the context of the divine governance, the world beyond humans has value. However, it also senses that, in the context of the divine dynamic, human beings have worth—not as the lone, central, or primary point of God's world but as worthy participants with distinctive qualities and capabilities to whom God stands related as Creator, Judge, and Redeemer.[31] A theocentric Christian *humanism*, especially for those who find Jesus's reconciling ministry and message compelling, affirms that the worth of humans in the context of the divine dynamic is not something that we—whether as individuals, communities, or institutions—either construct or bestow. The worth humans have in relationship to God is a reality that we (as persons and communities) are simply called on to recognize and acknowledge (a point that bears repeating by a socially and politically critical theology written from within the most powerful nation on Earth during a time of global markets, mass migration, and often reductive technical sensibilities).

Historically speaking, a key Christian humanist is Erasmus of Rotterdam—a cosmopolitan Catholic scholar interested in classical philosophical and literary texts, an editor of a Greek edition of the New Testament and a translator of same,

31. This is, as I shall argue, compatible with a detailed reading of Gen. 1; see chap. 3, prop. #28.

a master of irony, satire, and playful dialogues, who challenges princes and popes to abandon their militaristic policies. Erasmus pursued human self-knowledge, knowing full well that we are finally complex, confusing, disappointing, inspiring, and aspiring creatures.[32] But there are other fifteenth- and sixteenth-century Catholic representatives—for example, Jacques Lefevre, who translated the New Testament into French and challenged the sterner views of the theology faculty at Paris.

Reformed Protestantism also has its humanist strand. Ulrich Zwingli preached from Erasmus's Greek New Testament and consulted Cicero to define true piety or religion.[33] John Calvin, who was taught Greek by a Lutheran student of Lefevre, also came to endorse the humanist strategy of reaching back behind medieval scholasticism to reread classic sources. Humanist text interpretation, in fact, formed the basis for Calvin's biblical exegesis, and he strongly endorsed the arts and sciences as God's good gifts. In addition, he harbored broadly philosophical positions and ideas—favoring Stoic over Epicurean ethics and retaining an appreciation for natural law or a generally distributed conception of equity. And then there are the opening lines of his major work, the *Institutes of the Christian Religion*: "Nearly all the wisdom we possess, that is to say true and sound wisdom, consists of two parts: the knowledge of God and ourselves. But, while joined by many bonds, which one precedes and brings forth the other is not easy to discern." Calvin the *Christian humanist* claims that true wisdom is largely a matter of the interrelation of self-knowledge and knowledge of God. His "Christian philosophy," as he sometimes called it, affirms that, in relation to God, all persons have dignity and worth.[34]

This Reformed strand continues with Friedrich Schleiermacher, who, during the nineteenth century, helped to found the University of Berlin, worked extensively in hermeneutics, and understood ethics, or the broad study of human activity, to be the branch of knowledge of which religion and theology are parts. Karl Barth—no fan of Schleiermacher—nevertheless insisted that Christians hold fast to the humanity of God revealed in Jesus Christ rather than capitulate to the alien ideas of National Socialists. H. Richard Niebuhr commended a "radical monotheism" that insists on the value in relation to God of humans and, indeed, of all things.[35] The contemporary antiapartheid South African John

32. Terrence J. Martin, *Truth and Irony: Philosophical Meditations on Erasmus* (Washington, DC: Catholic University of America Press, 2015), 1–33.

33. Samuel Macauley Jackson and Clarence Nevin Heller, eds., *Commentary on True and False Religion* (Durham, NC: Labyrinth, 1981), 56–57.

34. Calvin, *ICR*, "Subject Matter of the Present Work," p. 6; 1.1.1; 3.7.6.

35. H. Richard Niebuhr, *Radical Monotheism and Western Culture, with Supplementary Essays* (Louisville: Westminster John Knox, 1993).

W. de Gruchy, a self-described Christian humanist, emphasizes our common humanity, our tendency to lose the ability to recognize others as human, but also hope and the struggle for justice and peace.[36]

As I see it, then, the following characteristics define Christian humanism in a Reformed vein: an effort to understand ourselves in relation to God that is shaped by the Christ event and engages humanities, sciences, and other sources of insight; an insistence that, in relation to the God of grace, while we humans are not the sole point of everything, all humans have worth; and a biblically attentive and prophetic disposition concerned for justice and the interests of others. With these points in mind, one notes affinities with theological humanists beyond Reformed Protestantism, including Protestant liberals, such as the Christian socialist Walter Rauschenbusch, who contend that we are called to recognize the true worth and vocation of humans in the context of Jesus's teaching about God's wider kingdom purpose; the nonviolent advocate for social justice, Martin Luther King Jr., who claims that all persons have value in relation to God; and the feminist Roman Catholic Rosemary Radford Ruether, who insists on the equality of women in relation to the God of Jesus Christ. In each case the claim is that we know ourselves, and others, our human possibilities and limits, more truly in relationship to God and God's purposes. But the designation is not infinitely elastic. Fundamentalists often decry Christian humanists for engaging plural sources of insight, and Christian humanists, whether of a Reformed or any other variety, criticize movements that limit the grace of God only to the "worthy," and so undercut the value of humans as humans by extolling their worth primarily as Christians, Germans, Americans, women, men, heterosexuals, the strong, the intelligent, the productive, or what-have-you.

That is a hurried review of Christian humanism, which emphasizes the Reformed Protestantism from which I generally work. In broad brushstrokes, its view of humans is captured in the following statement. *To be human is to stand in relationship with the presiding and gracious mystery that meets us at every turn as Creator, Judge, and Redeemer, and thus to understand ourselves as good, distinctively equipped, and limited participants in a compelling and sublime creation, who are chronically and destructively curved in upon ourselves and our partial interests but nevertheless may hope for restraint, redirection, and renewal.*

This inherently relational stance can be skewed or even wrecked by impulses to collapse its basic terms. On the one hand—and ordinarily in the name of humanism—the reality of God may be effectively equated with the human. Consider Walter Rauschenbusch's identification of the will of God with "the

36. See John W. de Gruchy, *Confessions of a Christian Humanist* (Minneapolis: Fortress, 2006). He also notes that Martin Buber once described himself as a "Hebrew humanist" (43).

good of mankind" and the "common good of humanity."[37] There was more to his theology than this, and the equation did indeed support needed efforts at social reform. Even so, there is reason to worry that here we come across a piety where the good for humans threatens to become the touchstone for statements about God and God's purposes; the reality of the deity threatens to be reduced to an aid to human purposes and the human spirit. Despite his strenuous effort to preserve the "otherness" of God, similar worries emerge with Karl Barth's insistence on God's humanity and his christologically based assertion that "God is for man."[38] They emerge more forcefully when Immanuel Kant contends that the requirements of a morality known and valued by humans quite apart from any experienced relationship to God should become the criteria for acceptable theological statements.[39]

The equation of the human with the divine was the radical point of Ludwig Feuerbach's contentions that God represents our projection of the best human qualities on to an imaginary being, that man *is* God, and that hence "the true sense of theology is anthropology."[40] Sigmund Freud developed this idea in a psychological direction when he claimed that religion amounts to wish fulfillment.[41] Indeed, the ready implication of Van A. Harvey's recent work on Feuerbach is

37. Walter Rauschenbusch, *The Social Principles of Jesus* (New York: Association, 1925), 128; Rauschenbusch, *A Theology for the Social Gospel* (Louisville: Westminster John Knox, 1997), 46–47, 98–99.

38. Barth, *CD* IV/1:631ff.; IV/3.2:647ff.; Barth, *The Humanity of God*, trans. John Newton Thomas (Richmond, VA: John Knox, 1960), 37–65. I made a similar point about Barth's theology in *Jesus Christ and Christian Vision* (Louisville: Westminster John Knox, 1996), 102–3.

39. Immanuel Kant, *Religion within the Limits of Reason Alone*, trans. Theodore M. Greene and Hoyt H. Hudson (New York: Harper & Row, 1960), 5, 100–14, 129–38, 179–90; see also H. Richard Niebuhr, "Value-Theory and Theology," in *The Nature of Religious Experience: Essays in Honor of Douglas Clyde Macintosh,* ed. Julius Seelye Bixler, Robert Lowry Calhoun, and H. Richard Niebuhr (New York: Harper & Brothers, 1937), 93–116.

40. Ludwig Feuerbach, *The Essence of Christianity*, trans. George Eliot (New York: Harper & Row, 1957), p. xxxvii.

41. Sigmund Freud, *The Future of an Illusion*, ed. and trans. James Strachey (New York: Norton, 1961), 30–31. Emile Durkheim developed Feuerbach's insight in a sociological direction by viewing ideas of God as representations of the society and its ethos (*The Elementary Forms of the Religious Life*, trans. Joseph Ward Swain [New York: Free Press, 1965], 466, 490–91, 495–96). We could also add Karl Marx's comments about religion to this list. There is much that is right in these ideas, and they have generated highly illuminating perspectives on the study of religion and on theology. Even so, the theology I am presenting here proceeds on the assumption that at least some of the sensibilities and symbols we call religious, while historically, sociologically, and psychologically conditioned, do indeed point beyond to a divine object or reality. It claims further that attention to the divine generates distinctive and illuminating perspectives on the world—on human possibilities and limits.

that every attempt to hold the realities of God and humanity in relationship must finally fail, since human wants and desires are the egoistic touchstone for religious statements about (an imaginary and illusory) God.[42] The true relationship that human religion clings to, then, is not between humans and God but only between humans and their own most fervent interests, wants, and desires. Religion in the end therefore fails to displace humans from their preferred place at the center of things. Despite our God-talk, and despite our encounters with a threatening and indifferent natural world, what we deem good for *us* remains the sole supernaturally and cosmically endorsed standard of value.

A relational and theocentric Christian humanism may also be skewed by theologies that threaten to collapse all into the divine. Particularly in my own Reformed subtradition of the Christian movement, theism and divine governance have sometimes been developed in ways that not only displace and relocate human beings but also threaten the integrity of both the world and human agents. For example, Calvin holds that God's all-determining providence need be no respecter of the integral operations of created realities (natural processes, animals, or human agents), their tendencies and trajectories.[43] Any particular occurrence, a sudden hailstorm, say, or the lack of milk in a mother's breasts, *may* be an act of God—quite apart from, or clean contrary to, the stream of nature and course of history. A hypertheism thus threatens to obliterate the integral reality of all things other than God.

Consider, too, the doctrine of double predestination as stated in the Westminster Confession. "By the decree of God, for the manifestation of his glory, some men and angels are predestined to everlasting life, and others fore-ordained to everlasting death."[44] A rather clear and even salutary effect of this doctrine is that we are kept from simply equating God and God's purposes with the good for human beings or our own wants and desires. Though, if we assume that we are predestined to life while others—and especially our enemies—are predestined to death, the doctrine may be turned toward the satisfaction of rather warped but also somewhat typically human in-group and out-group loyalties. The point I wish to make here, however, is that the doctrine of double predestination finally sculpts a piety that protects the "otherness" and "objectivity" of God only at the price of insisting on an eternal and arbitrary vindictiveness far more terrifying and unrelenting than either retribution in this life or simple extinction. The doctrine does not simply displace and then relocate humanity,

42. Van A. Harvey, *Feuerbach and the Interpretation of Religion* (Cambridge: Cambridge University Press, 1995), 281–309.

43. Calvin, *ICR* 1.16.2; 1.17.

44. The Westminster Confession of Faith, in *BOC* 6.016.

and it does considerably more than reject reductive humanisms. In the end, it seems *misanthropic*: the manifestation of an unbalanced theism that threatens to undermine the fundamental value and worth that humans otherwise may be understood to have in relationship to God the Creator, Judge, and Redeemer.

In summary: the question of the meaning of life, or of what humans are for, takes different forms at different places and times. Today, I think, it cannot be adequately asked apart from revisiting the question of worldview or of the place and worth of human beings in relation to all other things. The Augustinian, Protestant, liberal, and humanist theology that I present here answers this latter query by pointing to the divine dynamism at work in the cosmos. It responds to the question of what we are here for by promoting a piety or theistic sensibility that emphasizes the dynamic interrelationship of God, the world, and ourselves. This piety displaces but also repositions human beings: it criticizes their inveterate tendency to picture themselves as the primary point of all reality, but it also recognizes their inalienable worth as distinctive participants in God's world.

PART I

Method

Chapter One

A Conception of Christian Theology

What conception of Christian theology underlies my reflections? If there were a broad consensus today about what the study of Christian theology is and does, the answer might be comparatively simple. Then I might endorse the prevailing conception or else note where I depart from it. In fact, however, we live at a time of radical plurality (if not downright confusion) in approaches to Christian theology, and so I need to describe my own approach in some detail.[1]

Proposition #1 Christian theology is a practical wisdom that articulates a vision of God, the world, and ourselves in the service of a piety, a settled disposition, and a way of living.

To begin at the beginning, theology is *logos* of *theos*, or discourse and reflection about God (or the gods); inquiry into God (or the gods); and the reflective attempt to understand God (or the gods) more truly. A statement, a set of statements, or a discourse is theological if it has to do with God (or the gods).

1. Today some view theology as the reflective work of particular churches, while others attempt global or world theologies that transcend even the great religious traditions. Many believe theology reflects on revelation, whereas others claim that it is our human effort to fashion imaginative constructs that furnish practical guidance. Some see Christian theology primarily as the task of identifying patterns in biblical narratives; others write theologies that emerge from personal stories, analyses of current circumstances, and conversations with political philosophies. Still others link theology to recent scientific findings and theories. Friedrich Schleiermacher began his work *The Christian Faith* by observing that where there is disagreement and controversy, it is important to begin a treatment of a branch of study with a definition of that branch (*CF*, #1 [pp. 1–2]). More recently, Gordon D. Kaufman writes: "That the contemporary theological scene has become chaotic is evident to everyone who attempts to work in theology. There appears to be no consensus on what the task of theology is or how theology is to be pursued" (Kaufman, *An Essay on Theological Method*, rev. ed. [Missoula, MT: Scholars, 1979], ix). If anything, the scene has become more chaotic since Kaufman wrote that.

Many statements and discourses may be about matters of genuine importance, such as personal fulfillment, politics, economics, or the moon, and not be directly theological. Conversely, statements, sets of statements, and discourses about very many matters, including personal life, politics, economics, and the cosmos, may be theological if they refer to God (or the gods), or if they are made in a context that refers to God (or the gods). The great medieval Catholic Thomas Aquinas said that theology, or holy teaching (*sacra doctrina*), expresses judgments about God and creatures in relation to God.[2] The theological ethicist James M. Gustafson says that he once attended a party where a colleague in chemistry challenged him to say something theological. Gustafson said, "God." And he regards theology (rightly, I think) as an attempt to understand all things in their appropriate relations with God.[3] Relatedness to God is what unifies theological reflections.

Even at this early stage in our explorations, then, we may hazard a generalization. Theology situates human life and the world in relation to a Something More that we do not entirely comprehend or control. It appreciates that we live "in face of Mystery, and it orients life toward a point of reference that lies beyond church, nation, ethnic group, or species."[4] It does not envision what's important and what's possible simply as a function of humanity on its own, and this is one reason why theology may seem troubling from the perspective of some secular humanisms.

As a historical matter of fact, however, most theology is not freewheeling, generic discourse about God (or the gods). It is also discourse and reflection in the service of the teachings of particular religious communities.[5] This is why there is no generic theology and why we may speak of doctrinal reflections among Jewish communities, Islamic communities, and so on that engage the historic teachings and sense-making resources of their respective communities. Likewise, Christians have engaged in theological reflections with the aid of the historic resources of the Christian movement. Christian churches through the centuries have stated their teachings and doctrines in creeds, catechisms, and confessions (and, less formally, in hymns, liturgies, and prayers). Moreover, from Origen of

2. Aquinas, *ST* 1a.1.1–3, 7 (pp. 4–15, 24–27).

3. James M. Gustafson, "Say Something Theological!" (Nora and Edward Ryerson Lecture at the University of Chicago, Chicago, IL, April 25, 1981).

4. Kaufman, *IFM*, 3–17; Kaufman, *God—Mystery—Diversity: Christian Theology in a Pluralistic World* (Minneapolis: Fortress, 1996), 1–12.

5. The word "doctrine" need not be associated exclusively with Christian communities, particularly if we note that it comes from the Latin *doctrina*, meaning teaching and instruction, the knowledge imparted by teaching, and also the habit produced by instruction (Charlton T. Lewis and Charles Short, *A Latin Dictionary* [Oxford: Clarendon, 1907], s.v. "doctrine").

Alexandria to the present day, Christian theologians have regarded themselves as teachers in the church.[6]

The persistent connection between Christian theology and church teaching points to its practical and affectively resonant nature. Broadly speaking, Christian teaching and instruction is training in a Christian piety, fidelity, and way of living. It is teaching intended to elicit, express, and shape affections that orient people toward faithful practices, such as worshiping God and caring for one another. It is training in a devotion that encourages people to interact with persons, objects, situations, and realities in a way that is faithfully responsive to the God disclosed in Jesus Christ. That is, the church has an interest in helping its members interact with families, possessions, governments, forests, animals, and more in a way that is influenced and informed by devotion to God. It teaches because its pastoral aim is the faithful formation of the people of God.[7]

A primary purpose of the church is to deepen, promote, and extend a certain pattern or skein of sensibility (a piety), and thus build up the people of God in a life of faithfulness. It does this by means of a variety of practices, from worship, liturgy, preaching, and instruction to fellowship, care, and mission. The critical point for our purposes here, however, is that the enterprise of pastoral formation, or of building up people in a piety and a faithful way of living, also requires reflective activity. This is true because, generally speaking, the way we envision and interpret an object, situation, or reality influences our emotional responses to it. For example, those who pictured the Soviet Union as an evil empire were disposed to dislike, fear, and oppose its communist regime. Those who envision the current global circumstance with the aid of the image of a clash of civilizations may be disposed to dislike, fear, and oppose particular cultures and religious traditions. Christian theology helps to shape and express our sensibilities and attitudes toward objects and others by encouraging us to envision them with the aid of a particular image: the idea of God. It trains us in a piety or fundamental disposition toward God and other things in relation to God.

Consider our adolescent children. While they are sleeping until noon, talking interminably with friends, challenging authority, and lurching toward questionable decisions about their futures, you and I are called to interact with them in a way that is also faithfully responsive to God. A Christian theological vision helps

6. Not surprisingly, then, a good deal of Christian theology has been undertaken in church-related schools concerned with training leaders for the church. This was true of Origen's Catechetical School in Alexandria, of Thomas Aquinas's University of Paris, and of John Calvin's College of Geneva; it remains true of many church-related colleges, universities, and seminaries today.

7. *Gildas Silvianus: The Reformed Pastor,* vol. 6 of *The Practical Works of Richard Baxter* (Ligonier, PA: Soli Deo Gloria, 1990–1991), 367, 377–91.

us to do this by interpreting them with the aid of an image of God as Creator and thus to envision them as gifts of God who are entrusted to our care for a time. It emphasizes (just in case we are prone to forget) that we never really choose or control the particular children we are given. And it insists, despite occasional appearances to the contrary, that our adolescent children remain *good* gifts for which we should be thankful. It emphasizes that we have responsibility to care for and guide our adolescent children, but it also recognizes that they are not simply our personal projects and possessions. As gifts of God, our children, who routinely remain focal points of a good many of our feelings, are never entirely defined by our own goals and expectations. Indeed, first and foremost, they belong to God, and there is an important sense in which, no matter how old they are, they are never simply our own.

By introducing the images of God the Creator and gifts of God, a Christian theology frames a somewhat distinctive interpretative perspective on our children. (Remember that in many other contexts, if I give you something, then it really is yours to do with as you please.) This perspective gains support from the Bible and Christian tradition, and it expresses and shapes both our gratitude to God and our disposition toward our children. It informs our attempts to interact with our children in a way that is also faithfully responsive to God.

Now for an additional point: It makes a difference whether or not we regard our children as gifts of God, but other images, information, and beliefs can also make a difference in how we picture them, feel about them, and respond to them in a theological frame of reference. For example, there is now a sizable body of evidence to indicate not only that adolescents need a lot of sleep but also that their "biological timers" generally are set to stay up comparatively late and get up comparatively late.[8] Psychological studies also suggest that adolescence is a time when persons' identities are being formed with reference to emerging sexuality and thus significantly redefined personal relationships, as well as by some rather experimental efforts to discern where one fits into a wider social world. Left to my traditional theological images alone, I might judge the sleeping in, the constant attention to friends and peers, the challenges to authority, and the

8. Circadian rhythms (fluctuations that organisms exhibit over twenty-four hours) undergo age-related changes in humans and other animals, particularly with respect to sleep, and some seem hormonally related. See Federica Latta and Eve Van Cauter, "Sleep and Biological Clocks," in *Biological Psychology*, ed. Michela Gallagher and Randy J. Nelson, vol. 3 of *Handbook of Psychology* (New York: Wiley & Sons, 2003), 355–64; Mary Carskadon, "Work, School, Sleep, and Circadian Timing in Adolescents" (presentation given at the International Conference on Contemporary Perspectives on Adolescent Sleep Patterns, Los Angeles, CA, April 18–20, 1997); "Inside the Teenage Brain: An Interview with Mary Carskadon," *Frontline*, accessed August 6, 2019, http://www.pbs.org/wgbh/pages/frontline/shows/teenbrain/interviews/carskadon.html.

questionable decisions as not only a tad exasperating but also the results of a vaguely objectionable and morally corrupting self-absorption.[9] Once I factor in some recent findings and theories, however, I may feel differently. I may come to regard these adolescent traits not simply as chronic irritations but also as classic characteristics of the adolescent human creature—and thus of the gift I have been given. I may even come to recognize that, in the economy of God's creation, and under certain conditions, these simply are some of the things a thankful parent must expect.

To summarize: The pastoral aim of the church is to deepen and shape Christian piety, or fidelity, and thus help people interact with objects, others, situations, and realities in a way that is faithfully responsive to God. A Christian theology serves this aim by furnishing a vision or a picture of things with respect to the God disclosed in Jesus Christ, which expresses and shapes certain feelings and sensibilities. It articulates a vision that is responsive to the symbolic resources of the Christian community, such as the images of God as Creator and creation as gift, and that interprets and shapes affectively resonant experiences, such as our interactions with our adolescent children. Nevertheless, Christian vision and sensibility are not enclosed within a tight circle. They are also responsive to other things we know and believe about objects, others, situations, and realities, such as studies of adolescent sleep needs.

My purpose in this book, then, is to present a Christian theology or practical wisdom that deepens and clarifies a specific piety or settled disposition by helping us envision God, the world, and ourselves. While this wisdom takes account of information and ideas contributed by sources other than the Bible and Christian tradition, it is not a neutral or detached enterprise either. It tries to strengthen and support a faithful orientation in living by making use of interpretive resources furnished by the Bible and ecclesial traditions—for example, God the Creator—and it is closely intertwined with felt senses or inklings of the divine that have been cultivated by Christian communities.

I do not describe what I am doing as a *dogmatics* because the term, while boasting a distinguished history, is also bedeviled by negative connotations. Paul Tillich was essentially correct, I think, to say that negative developments sur-

9. Current developmental thinking emphasizes the critical importance of "the adolescent peer context" and the time adolescents need to interact with their friends (Margaret Kerr et al., "Relationships with Parents and Peers in Adolescence," in *Developmental Psychology*, ed. Richard Lerner et al., vol. 6 of *Handbook of Psychology* [New York: Wiley & Sons, 2003], 402). Laurence Sternberg, professor of psychology at Temple University, notes that the parts of the brain "responsible for things like sensation seeking" get turned on during puberty, while "the parts for exercising judgment are still maturing." See Claudia Wallis, "What Makes Teens Tick," *Time*, September 26, 2008, 61.

rounding orthodoxy, heresy, civil law, criminal charges, and activities directed against theological honesty and scientific autonomy have made the use of the term "dogmatics impossible."[10] Moreover, for reasons clearly associated with the history of Christianity, the adjective "dogmatic" in modern English may be defined as "characterized by or given to unwarranted and arrogant assertion," and dogma may refer to "a point of view or tenet put forward as authoritative without adequate grounds."[11]

I recognize that almost all religious communities engage in (doctrinal) reflections aimed at clarifying and developing their teachings, and that many of them claim special authority for their teachings, but I do not assume that these teachings need be either unwarranted or arrogant. I do not assume that the teaching of only one branch of Christianity, or the teaching of only one religion, can be valid or true. Furthermore, as implied in the illustration above, I also believe that the practical and emotionally freighted wisdom of Christian theology may strive to be responsive to other inquiries and their findings. In these senses, then, my aim is to present a nonauthoritarian and "undogmatic" theology. The liberal theologian Ernst Troeltsch was also uneasy with the term "dogmatics" and, like Schleiermacher, favored the term *Glaubenslehre* ("doctrine of faith" or "faith teaching") because he believed that earlier theologians often treated dogmas as timeless, permanent, and authoritarian statements.[12] Essentially, I agree: Christian theology is "piety-teaching."

Emil Brunner claimed that dogmatics is associated with church teaching because, in the face of disagreements, the church needs to establish sound, standard, or right doctrine. Dogmatics, then, is inherently involved in the formulation of orthodox dogma and "the struggle against false doctrine."[13] I think Brunner was correct to note that divergent doctrines and teachings sometimes call for adjudication. In my view, however, this is true largely because doctrines have to do with something more than beliefs, namely, felt orientations and trajectories in life. *Seriously* divergent doctrines (and not all doctrinal divergences are serious), therefore, train people in divergent pieties, fidelities, and ways of living. Nevertheless, unlike Brunner, I also believe that Christian theological reflections need not presuppose struggles for right doctrine. Even apart from sharp disagreements, the enterprise of pastoral formation itself requires broad

10. This is one reason why he favored "systematic theology," a term he took to embrace apologetics, dogmatics, and ethics (Paul Tillich, *Reason and Revelation, Being and God*, vol. 1 of *Systematic Theology* [Chicago: University of Chicago Press, 1951], 2).

11. *Merriam-Webster's Collegiate Dictionary*, 10th ed., s.v. "dogmatic."

12. Ernst Troeltsch, *The Christian Faith*, translated with an introduction by Garrett E. Paul (Minneapolis: Fortress, 1991), xxiv–xxv, 16.

13. Brunner, *Dogmatics*, 1:4, 9, 51, 56–57.

theological reflections concerning the relationship to God of the very many objects, situations, and realities with which we interact. As a practical and emotionally resonant wisdom, Christian theology does not come into play only when Christians are having a fight—and it is not always polemical. The reflective and practical work of picturing things in their relationship to God is simply part and parcel of trying to build up people in a particular piety and faithful way of living, and, as such, it has deep experiential and communal roots.

Mystery and Sensibility

Proposition #2 Life in the world evokes wonder and mystery, and these evocations are integral to religious sensibility.

Wonder and mystery sometimes seem in short supply, but their persistence is easy to understand if we recall that, as Alfred North Whitehead once observed, "we find ourselves in a buzzing world," or in the midst of interactions and interdependencies.[14] We are cast into a world of objects and interactions that we have not made and do not control. We find ourselves in the midst of things, in the push and shove of dynamic relationships and encounters. We react and respond, but we are also aware that our capacities and possibilities depend on a welter of conditions beyond our doing. We plan and predict, but we also recognize that we are able neither to determine nor to anticipate all relevant outcomes, and so we also hope and fear.

Just because we recognize both our capacity to intervene and our inability to control, we recognize that situational factors shape the consequences of our actions. We thus inquire into our contexts and how our interventions may or may not fit into them. I ask how my professional activities may or may not fit with my interrelationships with my children. A politician asks how her nation's actions and objectives fit within a wider international scene. A county commission asks whether and how a planned industrial park will fit within an area's environmental ecology.

We are also able to raise questions about our place within comparatively expansive contexts. Where, we may ask, do we humans fit within the evolutionary sequences of life on Earth? Perhaps we shall even ask about our *ultimate* and *encompassing* context. These questions connect with additional queries: What is the basis for our immediate and expansive contexts? Why do we find ourselves

14. Alfred North Whitehead, *Process and Reality: An Essay in Cosmology* (New York: Free Press, 1969), 49–50.

here in this particular context? Why are its contours and structures as they are? Where is it going? Indeed, people in almost every age and place raise questions about alpha and omega, first cause and last end, as well as about the forms and the design of things. Today these questions are likely to arise when we ponder the origins of the cosmos and the course of its expansion. The current reigning cosmological theory is that our universe began with a "big bang," is now expanding, and will continue to do so to the point of entropy and dissolution. But it doesn't take a trained astrophysicist to ask, What was before the big bang? And, of course, if once we are able to describe a prior state or condition, we may then also ask what preceded it. We may wonder what is beyond the expanding "edge" of the cosmos. What is it expanding into? We may also ask questions about existence itself. Why is there any context at all? Why is there something rather than nothing?

The most encompassing questions are "limit-questions," those that point beyond the boundaries of what we know and can establish about our contexts on the basis of the usual interrelationships and interactions.[15] They are not easily answered, but the critical thing to emphasize here is simply that they express puzzlement and indicate wonder. They suggest the possibility of Something More.

Limit-questions indicate a persistently religious dimension to human consciousness in the world that seems rather closely associated with some classical "arguments for God." Consider the second of Thomas Aquinas's "five ways." Aquinas notes that "in the observable world causes are found to be ordered in series; we never observe, nor ever could, something causing itself, for this would mean that it preceded itself, and this is not possible." Even so, he says, "A series of causes must stop somewhere," for "if you eliminate a cause you also eliminate its effects, so that you cannot have a last cause, or an intermediate one, unless you have a first." Thus, if there were "no stop in the series of causes, and hence no first cause," there would be nothing at all. But "this would be an open mistake," because things clearly do exist. "One is therefore forced to suppose some first cause, to which everyone gives the name 'God.'"[16]

The argument begins with our experience of causes in the world and then asks about their ground or basis. What is *their* cause? The supposition that they must be caused summarizes our ordinary experience of causation, for we never observe something causing itself. Nevertheless, Thomas insists, the argument

15. See Willem Drees, *Beyond the Big Bang: Quantum Cosmologies and God* (La Salle, IL: Open Court, 1990). On the significance of limit-questions for religion and theology, see Willem Drees, *Religion, Science, and Naturalism* (New York: Cambridge University Press, 1996), 274–83. David Tracy also discusses limit-questions in *Blessed Rage for Order: The New Pluralism in Theology* (New York: Seabury, 1975), 91–118.

16. Aquinas, *ST* 1a.2.3 (pp. 12–19).

finally "forces" us to suppose a first cause causing itself or exactly the kind of reality that, he admits, "we never observe, nor ever could."

This argument for God "from causation," as Thomas calls it, has occupied the attention of philosophers and logicians, and its cogency has been the subject of debate. The point I want to make here, however, is simply that it intimates wonder. It seems as much a way of posing a question or a "what if?" as of furnishing an answer. What if there is a first cause, which causes itself, that we call God? Well, if there is, then what we call God is an ineluctably odd reality (unlike any we observe or could observe). This odd reality is the ground of the realities we do observe and with which we interact. Moreover, if this is true, then the context within which we live and move acquires a dimension of depth; the world of objects and realities connects with a further reality beyond itself that we do not fully comprehend. Indeed, even if we think Aquinas's argument is flawed, we might regard it nonetheless as a rather telling expression of a persistent wonderment. Perhaps we should say that, first and foremost, Aquinas's argument is not really a matter of strict logic but of a reflective inkling of encompassing mystery, an intellectual wonderment about the reality we inhabit or the world to which we belong.[17]

This inkling is hardly the whole of religion and spirituality, but it is a salient feature. Even in modern secular societies that often seem captivated by the merely technical, one regularly encounters scientists in whom the natural world, its processes and structures, evokes similar sensibilities, feelings of mystery, majesty, and sublimity that demand their attention and also provoke awe and respect.[18] Moreover, as many of the world's religions indicate, the felt apprehension that we live in the face of mystery may be nurtured and maintained in a way that lends life a certain quality or even fascination.[19]

17. Compare this with Paul Tillich's contention that the arguments for the existence of God are best understood as expressions of the question of God implied in human finitude. They "analyze the human situation in such a way that the question of God appears possible and necessary" (Tillich, *Reason and Revelation, Being and God*, 204–10).

18. James M. Gustafson, in *A Sense of the Divine: The Natural Environment from a Theocentric Perspective* (Cleveland: Pilgrim, 1994), 11, 30–31, notes the sense of wonder and of the sublime that comes through in Melvin Konner's remarks at the close of *The Tangled Wing: Biological Constraints on the Human Spirit* (New York: Harper, 1982), 435–36. Willem Drees, in *Religion, Science, and Naturalism*, 280, refers to an article by the physicist C. W. Misner entitled "Cosmology and Theology," in *Cosmology, History, and Theology*, ed. W. Yourgrau and A. D. Breck (New York: Plenum, 1977), 96. See also philosopher Mary Midgley's statements about wonder and the sublime at the close of *Beast and Man: The Roots of Human Nature* (Ithaca, NY: Cornell University Press, 1978), 360–63.

19. The point about mystery is made forcefully but also somewhat differently by Kaufman, *IFM*, 54–63.

Proposition #3 A deep basis for religious living and for participating in religious communities lies in affections or emotions that are taken to be responsive to the divine.

Religion is not a matter of puzzlements and wonderments alone. Thus, commenting on multiple interviews with people over a ten-year period, American sociologist of religion Wade Clark Roof observes that "in story after story the quest is for something more than doctrine, creed, or institution, although of course these are usually involved. What is sought after has more to do with feelings, with awareness of innermost realities, with intimations of the presence of the sacred—what amounts to the very pulse of lived religion."[20]

The pulse of lived religion is an emotional sense of the divine. Or, as Jonathan Edwards claimed, "true religion, in great part, consists in holy affections."[21] Humans raise limit-questions and they wonder, but at least some wondering humans also feel themselves to stand in relationship to the divine. And those who do often find this relationship deeply affecting, and so there is in religion what Edwards called a "vigorous engagedness of the heart."[22] Similarly, William James says, "We shall see how infinitely passionate a thing religion at its highest flights can be. Like love, like wrath, like hope, ambition, jealousy, like every other instinctive eagerness and impulse, it adds to life an enchantment which is not rationally or logically deducible from anything else. . . . If religion is to mean anything definite for us, it seems to me that we ought to take it as meaning this added dimension of emotion."[23]

What sort of dimension? Edwards viewed affections in close connection with inclination and will, and he did not believe that they hampered or opposed the exercise and operation of our capacities for reasoning and understanding. Among the "holy affections" mentioned in the Bible, he counted hope in God (which inclines people to steadfastness and courage), joy and delight in God (which incline them to rejoice), gratitude to God (which is exercised in thankfulness and praise), and preeminently love of God (which inclines people to love neighbors). Edwards also claimed that affection signifies "something more extensive than passion": there is a habitual constancy to affections, whereas passions are actions of the will or inclination "that are more sudden" and tend to over-

20. Wade Clark Roof, *Spiritual Marketplace: Babyboomers and the Remaking of American Religion* (Princeton: Princeton University Press, 1999), 33–34.

21. Jonathan Edwards, *Religious Affections*, ed. John E. Smith, vol. 2 of *WJE*, 2:95. The point is echoed by Richard R. Niebuhr, *Experiential Religion* (New York: Harper & Row, 1972), 41–48, and by Gustafson, *ETP*, 1:119.

22. Edwards, *WJE*, 2:99.

23. William James, *The Varieties of Religious Experience* (New York: Signet, 1958), 53–54.

power the mind.[24] Richard R. Niebuhr associates affection with "a phenomenon in the life of the mind in the body" that is more encompassing and less turbulent than passion. An affection, he says, is an attunement, a "basic and all-including frame of mind" that lends a pervasive tone to personal existence.[25]

We note, too, that what Edwards called holy affections and the exercises or activities they prompt often bring people together. Historical religious *communities*—their texts, traditions, structures, and practices—are closely intertwined with affections and emotions. Preaching, worship, faithfulness, duty, prayer, activities of piety and praise that very often are closely connected with communities and institutional structures also prompt and reflect feelings of love, awe, reverence, hope, gratitude, and joy. Therefore, we should modify in a decidedly social direction James's preliminary definition of religion as "the feelings, acts, and experiences of individual men in their solitude, so far as they apprehend themselves to stand in relation to whatever they may consider the divine."[26]

Proposition #4 Generally speaking, affections emerge as we interact with other persons, objects, situations, and realities. They are intertwined with our knowledge of and beliefs about the many things with which we interact, and they influence and dispose us to interact with these things in certain ways.

Affections emerge in the midst of things. They are emotions elicited by interactions, meetings, contacts, and encounters, rather than mere expressions of isolated subjectivity. They are responsive to objects and others that impinge on us. Our affections are concern-based impressions of objects, situations, and circumstances; they register how things are in our experience, and they intertwine

24. Edwards, *WJE*, 2:98.

25. Richard R. Niebuhr, *Experiential Religion*, 44–45.

26. James, *Varieties*, 42. Many commentators have noted the bias toward the individual and the private and against the social and institutional in James's account of religion. James Luther Adams wrote about an exchange of letters between Baron von Hügel and William James concerning *Varieties*. According to Adams, von Hügel appreciated James's openness to mysticism and experience as well as James's refusal to adopt a narrow rationalism that psychologizes religion and renders it merely subjective. But he criticized *Varieties* for being exclusively concerned with personal and private experiences, a point echoed by Reinhold Niebuhr's lament that James exhibits a "lack of interest in the collective experiences of men." Adams agrees, noting that "*Varieties* fails to deal not only with collective and institutional manifestations of religious experience; it fails also to deal with the prophetic and priestly dimensions." See James Luther Adams, "William James: 'No Man for Committees,'" in *An Examined Life: Social Context and Religious Commitment*, edited and introduced by George K. Beach (Boston: Beacon, 1991), 91.

with our knowledge and our beliefs about the things we encounter. They are felt apprehensions, basic elements of our intelligent experiences of the objects and others that impinge on us.[27]

Suppose I see funnel clouds on the horizon. Depending on my knowledge and beliefs about tornadoes, the sight may elicit fear. Similarly, if I believe that I have benefited from the dedicated labors of many teachers, my memories of them may evoke gratitude. Or, again, encountering dire political and social circumstances that take a positive turn—American society during the civil rights movement, for example—may bring out hope in me and a sense of possibilities. We apprehend certain persons, things, circumstances, and events as fearful, awe-inspiring, hopeful, beautiful, attractive, assuring, threatening, repulsive, and so on. These emotions refer to—and also intertwine with—beliefs, judgments, and information about the objects we encounter. They "take" objects and construe them; they are ingredients in our interpretations—in our ways of "seeing" objects and others.

What should be rejected, then, is the idea that emotional life is merely "subjective," in contrast to "objective" knowledge or rational thinking about objects. There is no such bifurcation. We attend to objects that evoke affectivities, and our perceptions, reasoning, and judgments about things are always affectively tinged. At the same time, the kinds of affectivities evoked in us, such as fear and gratitude, also depend partly on how we envision and interpret the objects in question. This account, therefore, implies a kind of philosophical realism: our affections and emotions put us in touch with a world of objects and others, a world of impressive and meaningful presences that "push back" and thus exert influences on us. Our affections register lived human experiences as encounters with felt realities.[28]

It follows, then, that affections are emotions suffused with discernment. They are intelligent responses to how objects, others, and events impinge on us, and they are connected with judgments and interpretations that can be true or false, good or bad.[29] That is, our emotions—in response, say, to the sight of funnel

27. This aligns me with perceptual theories of emotions claiming that certain emotions may involve a mind-to-world fit. See Andrea Scarantino and Ronald de Sousa, "Emotion," in *Stanford Encyclopedia of Philosophy*, September 25, 2018, http://plato.stanford.edu/entries/emotion/.

28. See John E. Smith, *Experience and God* (New York: Oxford University Press, 1968), 31; see also Richard R. Niebuhr on Edwards's "mystical empiricism" in *Streams of Grace: Studies of Jonathan Edwards, Samuel Taylor Coleridge, and William James* (Kyoto, Japan: Doshisha University Press, 1983), 27–35; Douglas F. Ottati, *Hopeful Realism: Reclaiming the Poetry of Theology* (Cleveland: Pilgrim, 1999), 28–31.

29. Martha C. Nussbaum, *Upheavals of Thought* (Cambridge: Cambridge University Press, 2003), 1–2. Nussbaum's masterful discussion has contributed much to my understanding of affections and emotions.

clouds or to a change in political circumstances—are ways of seeing things that are intertwined with our knowledge, images, information, and beliefs (most of which we acquire by being socialized into particular communities). This is why things count for and against them, and also why, on further examination and reflection, we may judge that our emotional responses to the sight of funnel clouds or to certain political circumstances were good or bad, appropriate or mistaken.

Now for another point: Affections generate activity. Edwards maintained that, as vigorous exercises of will or inclination, affections set persons going and move them to activity. Affections dispose. Therefore, they come to expression in humans' activities and practices. So much so that Edwards regarded works, practice, or activity as the surest sign of the presence of truly religious affections.[30] Richard R. Niebuhr notes that affections and temper of mind contribute to the character and direction of one's life. A person's affections, he says, are intimately bound up with her energy, tone, and manner of living.[31] We might say that affections and emotions, which emerge in and are shaped by our intelligent encounters with objects and others, also orient us toward objects and others. They support tendencies: they incline us to interact with persons, situations, and realities in certain ways.

Suppose, then, that I am grateful to my teachers for their dedicated contributions to my education. My emotion is intertwined with positive judgments, interpretations, and beliefs concerning the qualities and benefits of their teaching that dispose me to thank them, and perhaps I will have occasions to repay certain debts of gratitude directly to them. And yet, it is also possible that my beliefs about my teachers and their dedicated teaching will prompt me to extend my understanding of what counts as thanking them beyond direct repayments to their persons. In the light of my knowledge and beliefs, I may very well conclude that I may also be appropriately responsive to my teachers in and through my interactions with my own students. That is, my gratitude to my teachers may dispose me to interact with others in a manner that is appropriately responsive (i.e., grateful) to my teachers.

Or suppose you are gripped by reverence for the Appalachian Mountains in western North Carolina—their beauty and integrity. You may be disposed to treat them with respect, and just what this entails will be connected with your judgments, information, and knowledge about the land. Moreover, you may also be disposed to interact with other persons, institutions, and realities—from farmers and corporations to legislatures—in a way that is appropriately responsive to (i.e., respectful of) the Appalachians.

30. Edwards, *WJE*, 2:383–407.

31. Richard R. Niebuhr, *Experiential Religion*, 45, 47–48.

Affections are perceptual or "apprehensive." They emerge in the midst of our encounters with objects and others, and they are intertwined with knowledge, beliefs, and judgments about the objects and others with whom we interact. They also dispose us to interact with objects and others in certain ways. Indeed, if we say that our experiences amount to interactions with our environments, then we should also say that our experiences involve affections, interpretations, and dispositions.

Proposition #5 Affections associated with a sense for the divine are evoked in the midst of our interactions with objects and others, and they intertwine with our socially conditioned understandings of objects and others. Like other human emotions, they influence and dispose. They get humans going, move them to activities, and are bound up with manners of living. Unlike secularized people, however, religious people take certain affections to have a further referential element. They take them to refer to an encompassing mystery, to a felt presence and reality of Something More in the many objects and realities with which they interact. In turn, they also take these affections to dispose them to interact with objects and others in a way that is appropriately responsive to the divine.

There is no exhaustive catalogue of religious emotions, just as there is not one concerning human emotions more generally. In fact, sensibilities and emotional states are neither inherently religious nor inherently nonreligious, though some sensibilities and affections, such as reverence and awe, have often been associated with religion, religious communities, and spiritual lives. James Gustafson lists senses of dependence, gratitude, obligation, remorse, possibilities, and direction.[32] I am willing to hazard the following incomplete and suggestive (rather than universal and invariant) remarks.

A SENSE OF DEPENDENCE We are often impressed by the contingency of things. We find ourselves in the midst of objects, situations, and realities, and we recognize that much depends on matters beyond our own or anyone else's control. We recognize, as Aquinas observes, that many things (including ourselves) "can be but need not be, for we find them springing up and dying away."[33] Indeed, Paul Tillich claims that this awareness is part and parcel of finite human existence.[34]

32. James M. Gustafson, *Can Ethics Be Christian?* (Chicago: University of Chicago Press, 1975), 91–94; see also Gustafson, *ETP*, 1:129–36.

33. Aquinas, *ST* 1a.2.3 (p. 15).

34. Tillich, *Reason and Revelation, Being and God*, 163, 189, 205–8.

Reinhold Niebuhr notes what seems apparent from a good deal of theological and philosophical literature in the West: the apprehension of contingency and an accompanying sense of dependence relate especially to questions of origins and endings (or how things will ultimately turn out).[35] Think, for example, of how your parents met, how easily (at least in many cases) they might not have, and what their failure to meet might have meant for your identity, existence, or nonexistence. Or I may wonder how my children will turn out, how the Chicago Cubs' baseball season will turn out, or what will become of the United States of America, realizing all the while that these and other outcomes depend on factors and events beyond my own or anyone else's control. We should also observe that apprehensions of contingency and dependence often are accompanied by recognitions of risk and vulnerability. We feel dependent when we acknowledge that we lack self-sufficiency and that life includes what Martha Nussbaum calls "a large measure of uncontrol."[36]

A SENSE OF THANKFULNESS We often encounter benefits—capacities, conditions, and relationships—that enhance and sustain our lives but are not of our own making, and sometimes we regard these benefits as gifts. Consider an athlete who benefits from exceptional physical abilities, a daughter who is nurtured by loving parents, or a spouse whose life is enriched by his wife and children. Think of the educational institutions from which many people benefit or the opportunities that accompany life in a comparatively stable, tolerably just, and prosperous society. If we consider the intricate and expansive cosmic, evolutionary, and historical sequences and time frames involved, perhaps we shall also come to regard human life itself as a benefit and a gift. Perhaps we shall come to regard air, water, earth, and stars as gifts.

We may respond to benefits such as these with feelings of gratitude. If so, our emotional response helps to form our subjectivity, even as it also connects us with certain objects, conditions, and realities. A deep-seated feeling or sense of gratitude disposes us in a particular way toward certain objects, conditions, and realities. Here again, emotion acknowledges our dependence on things we neither create nor control; only now it refers to objects and conditions we judge to be beneficial to our lives and well-being.

A SENSE OF OBLIGATION We often acknowledge responsibilities. Sometimes we understand them in the face of another (whether the other is a person or

35. Reinhold Niebuhr, *NDM*, 1:128.
36. Nussbaum, *Upheavals of Thought*, 12.

not), and we may also find that a disposition to care is evoked in us. Or perhaps a feeling of responsibility will arise in connection with the knowledge that we are enmeshed in interrelationships of interdependence and that, in this circumstance, not only are we vulnerable but others who are similarly vulnerable also depend on us. An apprehension of responsibility may accompany the recognition that we have received gifts or that we have benefited from certain capacities, relationships, and conditions, and thus should make good use of them. In addition, many moralists note that persons often have a sense of equity and feel that important responsibilities follow on their sense of fairness.

Here we come across the rather complex phenomenon called "conscience," and we note that we often experience a sense of obligation.[37] Once more, we are dealing with a feeling or sensibility that refers to external objects and others and that turns or disposes us toward them. Once more, we also have to do with an affective sensibility that is intertwined with judgments, information, and beliefs about ourselves, our capacities, our relationships, and the objects and others we interact with.

A SENSE OF REMORSE Together with conscience and a sense of obligation, the feeling that we have failed to uphold important responsibilities and agreements ordinarily also arises. We feel that we have failed to make entirely positive and effective use of our gifts. We feel that we have acquiesced in or participated in inequitable judgments, practices, institutions, and arrangements. We recognize that we have forfeited and lost opportunities to be trustworthy, to care, to live, and to act in ways that we recognize to be good and right. Perhaps we recognize at times that we have actively violated moral norms and rules. And, of course, in many such instances we also recognize that bad consequences have followed for others, and even for others who generally have remained steadfast toward us. Moreover, in a world of objects, situations, and realities that we do not control, it seems unlikely that we shall have opportunities to put all these things right. Such apprehensions and realizations often are accompanied by feelings of guilt and a sense of remorse.

A SENSE OF POSSIBILITIES It is also not unusual to experience "openings," to encounter possibilities that are not of our own making, opportunities for one or another activity, benefit, and pursuit. In fact, our encounters with certain openings may become so routine that we fail to recognize them unless and until circumstances shift and they are taken away. At times, no doubt, we are

37. Reinhold Niebuhr, *NDM*, 1:129–36.

surprised or even caught off guard by the possible. Occasionally, we also find ourselves released from conditions that threaten, shut off, and destroy. Imposing, destructive, and seemingly incorrigible circumstances or conditions sometimes change. Perhaps the politics of South Africa take a promising turn. Perhaps we are released from a threatening illness by a physician's skillful care. Or perhaps we unexpectedly find ourselves in a position to put something right, for instance, to repay a debt or correct an injustice. Gustafson notes that "within limits, persons can become other than what they are; they can alter some of the external conditions of life; they can see opportunities to alter the course of affairs by their intentional interventions."[38] These experiences may evoke a felt sense of possibilities that furnishes grounds for hope.

A SENSE OF LIMITATIONS We also encounter "closings." We come up against conditions that block one or another activity and pursuit; realities that limit and threaten; circumstances, events, and states of affairs that destroy, deny, and cut off. Perhaps we encounter an intractable illness or injury, an economic crisis that limits or even destroys opportunities for employment, a cultural attitude that needlessly restricts our activities and opportunities. Like our encounters with various openings, our encounters with closings can also be both routine and surprising; but these experiences, so far from evoking a sense of possibilities, are more likely to be accompanied by a sense of limitations, and perhaps also by fear, patience, anger, resistance, or even despair. Indeed, in conjunction with the feeling of the "riskiness" and vulnerability of contingent life, encounters with closings may also make us feel insecure. At times we may even have a sense of being rendered small and insignificant, or of being overwhelmed.

A SENSE OF COMPELLING PRESENCE, GRANDEUR, OR SUBLIMITY We are sometimes gripped by an almost aesthetic appreciation for the compelling presence, excellence, and attractiveness of an action, a mountain range, a microbe, a painting, a mathematical equation, a symphony, or a coastline. (Although I root for the Chicago Cubs, I think particularly of the exuberant artistry of Ozzie Smith playing shortstop some years ago for the St. Louis Cardinals.) We are drawn out from ourselves by realities that capture or grasp our attention. Such encounters connect with senses of reverence, wonder, awe, and respect. Here again, as in the other instances I have mentioned, we have to do with affections and emotions that can turn both our attention and our activity. Here we are dealing with emotions that register how things are, emotions that are intertwined

38. Gustafson, *ETP*, 1:133.

with information, judgments, and beliefs, and that, on further reflection and investigation, may or may not be sustained.

A SENSE OF ASSURANCE May we also say that, in the midst of the dependencies and benefits, the responsibilities and remorse, the openings and closings, risks, vulnerabilities, and gripping excellences, we sometimes have a sense of assurance? May we recognize that, despite our own shortcomings and failures, we can continue to rely on persistent possibilities, responsibilities, limits, and excellences to turn us toward what is worthwhile? May we feel it appropriate that we are and that we are here and now, or that we are well matched with these particular companions, challenges, threats, and promises? May we thus speak (at least occasionally) of a trust or a confidence that we belong in existence and in life at this particular place and time? If so, then here again we come upon an emotion that refers to objects and others and that intertwines with beliefs, judgments, and discernments. Might this feeling also help to dispose us to persevere and to continue to participate in the contingent, risky, demanding, astounding, attractive, and threatening world around us?

Jonathan Edwards also mentions joy and delight. As theoreticians of emotions, maybe we shall conclude that these finally amount to different names for gratitude, wonder, and awe. Then again, maybe not. In any case, a key point is that emotions such as joy and delight are once again not simply disconnected expressions of isolated subjectivity. They are about something going right or fitting into place, something that elevates and buoys our spirits. I repeat: my list is suggestive rather than exhaustive or complete. One might easily go further. For example, if experiences of excellence and of compellingly attractive realities evoke reverence, wonder, awe, and so forth, we certainly also have experiences of brutality, cruelty, ugliness, and waste that evoke anger and revulsion. And surely our revulsions may also be suffused with discernment and may also set us into motion. So might an occasional sense that we are out of place and out of kilter.

Religious Consciousness

To say that these affections (as well as others) are often associated with religious persons, communities, and practices hardly means that they do not emerge in concert with natural and social realities. Consider the awe many people feel at first encountering the Alps or the Grand Canyon. Again, if gratitude ordinarily signals thankfulness in response to a perceived benefit, a son may be grateful to his parents for having cared for him when he was young, which may, in turn, dispose him toward certain activities as debts of gratitude, for example, caring for his parents as they age or caring for his own children.

What is true is that a *further referential element* comes in when religious people and communities take these sensibilities to point toward an encompassing mystery, toward a further felt reality and presence in the many other objects and realities. For example, religious people and communities often take experiences of contingency to indicate not only their dependence on constellations of circumstances and events but also their felt dependence on the divine. A religious sense of gratitude responds to benefits believed to derive not only from one's parents, friends, the larger society, and biological endowment but also—through these many others and realities—from God. Moreover, this "extended" sense of gratitude may also dispose someone toward certain distinctively religious actions and practices, such as singing hymns of praise. A sense of assurance may be taken to respond not only to continuing circumstances, structures, possibilities, and limits but also to the deity, who is believed to be responsible for these conditions, and this sensibility, in turn, may also contribute to one's cast of mind, energy, or temper in living.

Religious consciousness crosses a threshold. It suggests that, in the push and shove of interdependent interactions, we encounter additional forces, influences, powers, and presences. It feels that our lives point toward Something More. Religious persons and communities take certain *emotions*, *sensibilities*, and *affections* to point not only toward more immediate objects and others that push back but also to an additional felt dimension, background, presence, order, matrix, or pattern that impinges on them.[39] In their dependence on constellations of circumstances and events, in their gratitude to parents, teachers, and natural processes, religious people and communities have an inkling of Something More, a sense of the divine. The claim, then, is for deep-seated and pervasive moods in conjunction with a felt reality that lies in, with, and under the many objects and others we interact with.[40] The claim is not for a separate encounter with a discrete divine object alongside other objects but for an emotional overtone or undertone of our many encounters with objects and others that suggests a peculiar Object and Other.[41] The claim is for emotional overtones and undertones that intimate encounters with the divine through our many encounters.[42]

39. Ottati, *Hopeful Realism*, 28–31.

40. See M. Wynn, "Valuing the World: The Emotions as Data for the Philosophy of Religion," *International Journal for Philosophy of Religion* 52, no. 2 (2002): 106, 108–9.

41. Reinhold Niebuhr suggests that "the experience of God is not so much a separate experience as an overtone implied in all experience" (Reinhold Niebuhr, *NDM*, 1:127).

42. John E. Smith speaks of a religious *dimension* of experience rather than religious experience. By doing so he means to emphasize the point that the divine is not encountered in

A Religious Temperament

William James suggests that the divine is a primal and enveloping reality to which we feel compelled to respond, and we should also observe that the added dimension of emotion that he identifies with religion often *inclines* people toward activities of worship and service.[43] Thus, as we have seen, for Jonathan Edwards, gratitude to God may be exercised in thankfulness and praise by saying prayers of thanksgiving or by singing hymns of praise. Moreover, here we note the same dynamic that we did earlier with respect to our affections and the many more mundane objects and others with which we interact. Precisely what counts as praising the deity will depend on what we apprehend, know, believe, or suppose about God and God's purposes. It will depend on how we "see" or envision the deity. And, depending on how one envisions God, it is entirely possible to conclude that thankfulness and praise to God are also important for how we interact with persons, situations, and realities. That is, the affection "gratitude-to-God" may dispose one to interact with other persons, situations, and realities in a way that shows forth thanks and praise to God and is thus thought to be appropriately responsive to God.

A nexus or cluster of affections—such as dependence on God, delight in God, gratitude to God, and obligation before God—may constitute an overall religious temper, cast of mind, or piety. Especially where the various affectivities are interconnected and ordered, they may yield an attuning to the divine and a settled disposition toward the world.

These claims will not be persuasive to everyone, and they often seem out of place in a modern demystified world of surfaces without depths and in cultures focused on manipulated means-ends relationships, as well as technical (and often also reductive) sensibilities. But they are not unusual; they recur throughout human history and even among people who live in modern secular societies. Theologically speaking, modern thinkers such as William James, John E. Smith, and James M. Gustafson seem wise not to dismiss these claims as so much mere and misguided subjectivity. It is a wisdom that often goes missing when modern secularists confront religious persons and communities; and its absence goes

---

the same way that other objects and realities are. The reality of God is always mediated in and through our encounters with other objects and realities, for example, our apprehensions of dependence on particular circumstances, persons, communities, and institutions. Every alleged encounter with the divine is thus also an encounter with something else at the same time. What we are to notice is not simply one particular experience called "the encounter with the divine" in a way that is analogous to an encounter with a wooden desk, Mount Rainier, or the Republic of India, but a depth dimension of many ordinary encounters (Smith, *Experience and God*, 52, 55).

43. James, *Varieties*, 47.

some distance toward explaining their persistent inability to understand religious persons and communities sympathetically and adequately.[44]

In summary, there is an indispensable experiential-emotional dimension to spirituality or religiousness. Some people are more responsive to it than others are; some appear only marginally responsive, if indeed they respond to it at all. But that this is a rather general aspect of human life in the world seems indicated by the fact that it recurs in almost every place and time. Do attempts to repress it or eliminate it lead to a reduction or impoverishment of human sensibility? Do they leave important dimensions of human life and affection unaddressed and unevaluated, and thus render us vulnerable to destructive attachments of religious emotions to inappropriate objects? I think so. Moreover, there is another possibility, one represented by particular religious communities and institutions: rather than repress or eliminate felt religious inklings and sensibilities, we may instead try to interpret them.[45]

44. William James's third lecture in *Varieties*, "The Reality of the Unseen," remains a classic statement; see also his conclusions in lecture 20. Throughout this discussion I have intentionally avoided the word "supernatural," which may be defined as that which is "above nature; belonging to a higher realm or system than that of nature; transcending the powers of the ordinary course of nature" (*The Compact Edition of the Oxford English Dictionary*, vol. 2, s.v. "supernatural"). "It is often implicitly assumed," says William Christian Sr., "and sometimes (as by Marx and Freud) explicitly stipulated, that religion always includes belief in something supernatural. But we encounter cases where we are inclined to say that M is religious even though we are doubtful whether he has any supernatural beliefs at all, for example, Theravada Buddhism, Spinoza, and Einstein" (Christian, *Meaning and Truth in Religion* [Chicago: University of Chicago Press, 1978], 71).

45. Here also I depart from William James's understanding of religion in his *Varieties of Religious Experience.* Smith expresses the objection this way: "The mistake embodied in the idea of religious experience as set forth by James and the so-called empirical theology consists in the acceptance of an absolute distinction between immediacy and mediation, or between immediate experience and inference. On the one hand, it was felt that religion is too intimate an affair to be a matter of rationalistic doctrines supported by a God whose reality is merely inferred without being experienced. On the other, it was believed that the only alternative to the rationalist approach is to be found in immediate data of experience that would represent, in James's expression, the 'cash value' of the divine reality.

"Perhaps there is a third possibility that avoids the difficulties of both points of view, because, if an experiential approach does not mean that God must be a matter of absolutely immediate experience, some third alternative in the form of *interpreted experience* may provide the answer. There must be a way beyond and between absolute immediacy and inference. Absolute immediacy can never deliver what it promises because some form of mediation—concepts, language, symbols—always intervenes and makes it impossible to pass from the experience to the reality of God; inference does not suffice because it always takes the form of necessity, which means not that God is experienced, but that something else is experienced and that hence God 'must' be real. The deficiencies of the two approaches point the way to

Religious Communities and Interpretive Resources

Proposition #6 Religious people interpret interactions and affections with the aid of resources furnished by particular communities of language, practice, and belief.

Whether and how in the midst of one's emotionally resonant interactions with objects and others one is also grateful to God, remorseful before God, and so forth depend in part on what one believes about God, on how one understands and envisions the deity or the encompassing mystery. That is, religious affections and sensibilities such as these are intertwined with religious images, concepts, and beliefs.[46]

Suppose I am ill. I seek out a physician. She makes use of new medical technologies, and I am restored to health. Suppose, too, partly because of socially mediated information and beliefs about my biology, my condition, my physician, and the technologies in question, that I judge my physician and the technologies to have interacted with my body in a beneficial way. I am thus disposed to be grateful for a body that is responsive to medical interventions, to my physician, to the persons and institutions that helped to train her, and to the persons and institutions responsible for devising and distributing the new technologies. Now suppose that, in addition, I also "take" my gratitude to be responsive to the divine. This "taking" includes a further layer of interpretation; that is, I interpret myself and the persons and realities I have encountered in the light of religious images, concepts, and beliefs. This additional layer of interpretation specifies how the divine relates to my body, my physician, the persons and institutions that trained her, the new technologies, and the persons and institutions that devised and distributed them. I am able to engage in it because certain images and beliefs about the divine are mixed in with my socially mediated images and

---

a third approach, that of mediated or interpreted experience in which both experience and interpretation are interwoven" (Smith, *Experience and God*, 52–53).

46. See Wayne Proudfoot's criticism of Schleiermacher's understanding of piety and the feeling of absolute dependence, in Proudfoot, *Religious Experience* (Berkeley: University of California Press, 1985), 1–40. He maintains that when piety is defined as the feeling of absolute dependence, it "is certainly not independent of concepts and beliefs. To say that the religious person is conscious of being absolutely dependent is to attribute to him or her the concept of dependence and that of complete dependence" (19). Paul Capetz notes that "Proudfoot is attempting to correct a simplistic view that language merely expresses an experience that is in no way formed by the language used to interpret it." See Capetz, *Christian Faith as Religion: A Study in the Theologies of Calvin and Schleiermacher* (Lanham, MD: University Press of America, 1998), 143n92.

beliefs about my biology, my condition, my physician, and the relevant technologies and institutions.

For example, a religious apprehension or idea that, as Creator, Sustainer, and Redeemer, God actively orders nature and history may encourage me to construe my encounter with my physician and the new medical technologies as instances of sustenance and renewal that point toward Something More and that take place through the Creator-Sustainer's beneficial orderings of nature and history. If so, it will help to encourage, sharpen, and shape in me a gratitude-to-deity. Moreover, in conjunction with additional encounters and experiences, my belief may also suggest a more generally thankful way of living that is appropriately responsive to the God who sustains and renews. But, of course, this interpretation or construal, which is part and parcel of my thankfulness to God for having been restored to health at the hands of my physician and her skillful use of new technologies, does not take place apart from the language, practices, and beliefs of a particular religious community. The belief that, as Creator, Sustainer, and Redeemer, God actively orders nature and history is a symbolic concept and imaginative resource furnished by a community and its tradition that points toward an additional dimension or presence that is felt by an individual. It is mixed in with the other socially mediated information, images, and beliefs that I bring to my encounter with my physician, and it supports something like my interpretation of adolescent children as gifts of God in conjunction with other information and ideas I have about them (see prop. #1 above).

The interpretation, in relation to the divine, of emotions and interactions in the midst of things thus signals an *indispensable role* for religious communities. Religious communities furnish mythopoeic discourses; they supply images, analogies, stories, ideas, and beliefs that help us portray and interpret the divine in relation to us and to the many objects and others we interact with; they supply imaginative resources that shape our emotionally resonant interactions with those objects and others and gather them into patterns. These imaginative resources have emerged with a community's interpreted and emotionally charged encounters with past circumstances and realities, for example, an exodus or an exile. When we are socialized into these resources, they are mixed in with other things we know and believe about the objects and realities with which we interact. And then they help to interpret and shape our current interactions and emotions. The genius of at least some of these resources is that they succeed in interpreting and shaping our present affections and interactions and so help us portray the depth of reality, our living and emotionally charged encounters with it, and the ways in which our lives may be conducted and adjusted in response to it.

In summary, our affections—whether or not we take them to refer to the divine—are suffused with discernment because they are intertwined with beliefs and information about the objects and others with whom we interact. Images of and beliefs about the divine are mixed in with the beliefs and information that religious people bring to their affecting interactions. The additional interpretive step beyond what others find strictly warranted or required by various inklings and sensibilities in response to more immediate objects and others is an imaginative one that religious people take with the aid of these narrative, symbolic, and conceptual resources furnished by their historic religious communities and traditions, for example, the idea that God is Creator. These resources help to elicit and shape their sense of the divine and circumambient mystery with respect to themselves and the many objects and others they interact with.

We might say that the discernment of religious affections, sensibilities, and inklings remains fragmentary, inchoate, sporadic, and implicit, or that it flickers and wobbles apart from interpretive depiction. The interpretive resources of religious communities offer principles of depiction by taking certain ideas, objects, realities, relationships, and events as clues to the additional reality that we feel in our sensibilities and inklings. They furnish imaginative clues that portray the divine in relationship with us and to the objects and others with whom we interact.

Proposition #7 The interpretive resources furnished by religious communities are mythopoeic in the sense that they make analogical and symbolic use of rather ordinary ideas and images in order to portray the additional felt dimension that lies beyond the threshold.

Mythopoeic discourse makes use of ideas, symbols, and stories to depict patterns and structures in our relationship to the "Mystery" and the Something More that lies beyond us, and hence it functions analogically and symbolically rather than technically or scientifically.[47] It makes imaginative use of natural and historical sequences, relationships, objects, and others in order to portray our affecting interactions with a further and deeper reality that we understand to be both like and unlike the sequences, relationships, objects, and others used to portray it. As such, there is always dissimilarity. Mythopoeic discourse makes use of mountains and seas and people and laws and nations and oppression and liberation and tragedies and joys—things that are not the divine—in order to portray the divine reality with which we interact through all these things and more. Therefore, its delicate and dialectical depictions are always in danger of a kind of reduction, of being understood merely literally, or of being taken to

47. For a suggestive essay on these matters, see Amos Wilder, *Theopoetic: Theology and the Religious Imagination* (Philadelphia: Fortress, 1976), 73–100.

equate the divine (or the Something More) with the mundane sequences, relationships, concepts, objects, and others that are used to portray the divine. Thus, for example, Reinhold Niebuhr claimed that "the Christian religion may be characterized as one which has transmuted primitive religious and artistic myths and symbols without fully rationalising them," and that doctrines sometimes deceive even as they illuminate.[48]

Consider Genesis 1:1–2:4a: the text depicts the divine as both distinct from and related to the world, as separating light and darkness, waters and land, and as making all plants and animals in their kinds. It portrays humans as having been endowed with distinctive powers and having been placed within the expanded matrix of "world-ordered-by-God." If we understand it as mythic poetry, however, the text does not commit us to believing that the deity actually said or enunciated "Let there be light"—precisely as a mundane monarch might have in one or another ancient tongue.

Indeed, we may note that the writers of the passage had no experience of a mundane monarch ordering the existence of light or the fertility of the earth (and neither do we). Genesis 1 depicts God's creating activity by making rather odd use of commanding words and speech. Thus, "the command 'Let there be light' is followed by its execution, 'and there was light,' just as in the case of any potentate who issues a command; but there is this difference: there is nobody there to whom the command is directed, through whom the command can be executed."[49] And it is just this combination of similarity and difference with the commands of earthly monarchs that gives an imaginative, symbolic, and analogical cast to God's creative word in Genesis 1.

48. Reinhold Niebuhr, *Beyond Tragedy: Essays on the Christian Interpretation of History* (New York: Scribner's Sons, 1937), 3–24, esp. 7, 21. Indeed, Niebuhr wrote that he was happy to say the Nicene Creed liturgically but that, in this creed, to which he should not like to commit himself "in cold blood . . . poetry has been transmuted into dogma" (Reinhold Niebuhr, "A Christmas Service in Retrospect," in Reinhold Niebuhr, *Essays in Applied Christianity: The Church and the New World*, ed. D. B. Robertson [New York: Meridian, 1959], 30). Along these lines, it is interesting that, in his dispute over the Trinity with Peter Caroli at Lausanne in 1537, John Calvin refused to sign the Nicene, Athanasian, and Apostles' Creeds. He had a number of reasons for refusing to do so, including that he "wished to retain a measure of freedom in the matter of terminology" and did not "wish to limit the confession of the church in his own time to a formal repetition of earlier creeds." But he also claimed that it would be more suitable to sing the Nicene Creed than to regard it as an exact formula. See E. Nijenhuis, *Ecclesia Reformata: Studies on the Reformation*, trans. Mary Foran (Leiden: Brill, 1972), 86, 91–92. See also François Wendel, *Calvin: The Origin and Development of His Religious Thought*, trans. Philip Mairet (London: Collins, 1963), 53–55.

49. Claus Westermann, *Genesis 1–11: A Commentary*, trans. John J. Scullion, SJ (Minneapolis: Augsburg, 1984), 111.

Genesis 1 imaginatively portrays the deity (somewhat like and somewhat unlike an ancient monarch) as a masterful ordering power in relation to us and to the many objects and others we interact with, and it depicts a world of categories and structures as a coordinated whole rendered from what was originally amorphous.[50] It thereby expresses, encourages, and configures felt senses of dependence, gratitude, and possibilities in the midst of our interactions with ordered objects and others. It interprets these feelings as responses not only to natural endowments, processes, and so on but also to the ordering God. Genesis 1:1–2:4a takes certain aspects or parts of ordinary life (e.g., using distinctive human powers and capacities in the midst of a world of interdependent relationships, dependencies, gifts, possibilities, and limits, a monarchal structure of political sovereignty, and so on) in order to symbolize and depict the primal reality in relationship with us. It is mythopoeic discourse that contributes to the formation of a symbolic concept: in relation to us and to the many objects and others with which we interact, God is the masterful Creator (who nevertheless is not entirely like any other creative agents we know).

To the extent that the scriptural depiction offered in Genesis 1:1–2:4a and the symbolic concept of God as Creator to which it contributes succeed at interpreting or reinterpreting our own present interactions with objects and others, they also dispose us today to live in a thankful manner that is appropriately responsive to the Creator, on whom both we and other creatures rely. They help to shape and inform a contemporary piety attuned to the divine.[51]

This understanding of the function of imaginative resources furnished by religious communities and the way they function may be distinguished from what Stanley Hauerwas says about narrative. Hauerwas emphasizes the idea that

50. Claus Westermann, *Elements of Old Testament Theology*, trans. Douglas W. Stott (Atlanta: John Knox, 1982), 91; Westermann, *Genesis 1–11*, 125; William P. Brown, *The Ethos of the Cosmos: The Genesis of Moral Imagination in the Bible* (Grand Rapids: Eerdmans, 1999), 39; Walter Brueggemann, *Theology of the Old Testament: Testimony, Dispute, Advocacy* (Minneapolis: Fortress, 1997), 528–51.

51. Here I should say that I am *not* claiming that all discourses generated, developed, and handed down by religious communities and traditions are mythopoeic. The collection of literatures we call the Bible, for example, is really very diverse. In it we find legal codes, proverbs, chronicles, hymns, epic poems, oracles, parables, preaching, and more. These literary forms sometimes shade into and overlap with mythopoeic discourse, for example, hymns such as Ps. 8. And indeed, what religious traditions furnish that may not be furnished by legal traditions, traditions of moral discourse, music, or history writing is a mythopoeic discourse that makes proposals about the divine in relationship with us and with objects and others. In fact, when they are associated with religious traditions, items such as legal codes and proverbs often are situated within mythopoeic discourses and their depictions of divine reality in relation to us, for example, Exodus and Deuteronomy.

unity of self and character depends on our formation by narratives. Scripture, then, is primarily a narrative: it tells a story that forms individual and communal identity. Individuals and communities, in turn, act in accordance with their narratively formed characters.[52]

What I am saying here is that varied mythopoeic resources, including narratives, images, and beliefs, portray the divine with respect to a community's past affections in the midst of its interactions with situations, realities, and others, for example, Genesis 1:1–2:4a. We, the continuing religious community, internalize these imaginative resources and use them in order to interpret and make sense of our own affections and interactions in our own place and time. These interpretations, in turn, elicit, shape, and deepen a piety, temper, or fidelity; they help us envision our present life in a way that is faithfully responsive to the divine. The resulting way of life surely involves patterns, practices, and character. But the move is not simply from the mythopoeic resources of a religious community to the formation of identity or character; our pieties and ways of living are not only the result of having internalized our religious community's mythopoeic discourse. The process is more complicated. Imaginative resources furnished by our religious community promise to help us interpret and construe our present affections and interactions in relationship to the divine. We, in turn, internalize these resources, and, in combination with other internalized resources furnished by our additional cultural activities, communities, and involvements, we make use of them to do so. Where the interpretation succeeds, the result is an enlivened piety, temper, and outlook that help to shape our identity and to form our way of living.

Proposition #8 The relationship between religious affections and communities is reciprocal and circular. Imaginative resources furnished by religious communities and traditions are at once both instruments by which religious inklings and affections come to expression and media that shape those inklings and affections.

Emotionally freighted encounters call forth narratives, symbols, ideas, practices, and beliefs; the narratives, symbols, ideas, practices, and beliefs of particular religious communities are thus responsive to people's emotionally freighted encounters and experiences. For example, Genesis 1:1–2:4a expresses felt senses of dependence, wonder, gratitude, and possibility that emerge in encounters with the "world-ordered-by-God." At the same time, however, a community's imagi-

52. Stanley Hauerwas, *A Community of Character: Toward a Constructive Christian Social Ethic* (Notre Dame: University of Notre Dame Press, 1981), 55–67, 131–45.

native resources also help to shape our affections: they influence and sculpt our emotionally freighted encounters and experiences. Hence Genesis 1:1–2:4a also directs our attention toward orderings in the world, interprets those orderings as God's doing, and thus helps to form our senses of dependence, wonder, gratitude, and possibility before God. The text both expresses and shapes religious inklings and affections. This, finally, is a knot that cannot be untied.[53]

This account of the relationship between religious affections and the imaginative resources furnished by religious communities has affinities with historicist understandings of science.[54] During much of the twentieth century, logical empiricists claimed that scientific theories are statements derived by formally logical means from incorrigible neutral observations. They held that our observations constitute raw sensory perceptions from which we logically derive theoretical statements about objects. This position came under attack by thinkers such as Thomas Kuhn and Stephen Toulmin, who rejected formal logic as the primary tool for analyzing science and replaced it with attention to the history of scientific inquiry.[55] According to the historicist view, one internalizes a framework of beliefs and practices through participation in a community of inquirers. One's subsequent observations, therefore, are not neutral but "theory-laden," because one is predisposed by one's interpretive framework to view things in certain ways, to regard some problems as significant and others as trivial, and to attend to some things rather than others.[56] Therefore, "perception is not of raw and uninterpreted sensory data"; the mind makes important contributions to the interpretation of sensory data. Indeed, "perception results from a combination of raw sensory 'input' *and* the categories for its interpretation, as bestowed by socialization, education, or indoctrination, in a particular scientific discipline or culture." Or, again, "perception . . . is not a matter of being presented with 'raw feels' or wholly uninterpreted sensory data. . . . Rather, an observer directly

53. See Nancy Frankenberry, *Religion and Radical Empiricism* (Albany: State University of New York Press, 1987), 143–44.

54. What I say in this paragraph relies heavily on Martin L. Cook's fine but unjustly neglected book *The Open Circle: Confessional Method in Theology* (Minneapolis: Fortress, 1991), 7–27.

55. Thomas S. Kuhn begins *The Structure of Scientific Revolutions*, 2nd ed. (Chicago: University of Chicago Press, 1970), by noting: "History, if viewed as a repository for more than anecdote or chronology, could produce a decisive transformation in the image of science by which we are now possessed" (1). Stephen Toulmin, in the general introduction and part 1 of volume 1 of *Human Understanding* (Princeton: Princeton University Press, 1972), claims that "in science and philosophy alike, an exclusive preoccupation with logical systematicity has been destructive of both historical understanding and rational criticism" (vii).

56. Harold I. Brown, *Perception, Theory, and Commitment: The New Philosophy of Science* (Chicago: University of Chicago Press, 1977), 93, 108–9.

perceives what is produced by a combination of the sensory input and the categorical scheme that provides the context for such perception."[57]

Somewhat similarly, I maintain that our affections are responsive to our encounters with objects and others but that there are no "raw feels" or wholly uninterpreted affections. Instead, our emotional responses are always intertwined with imaginative resources and categories for interpretation obtained by socialization, education, and indoctrination in communities and cultures. Through socialization, education, and indoctrination into *religious* communities, then, we obtain imaginative resources for interpretation having to do with the divine in relation to the world and ourselves. These resources, in turn, are mixed into the interpretive frameworks that we bring to our affecting encounters, and they dispose us to interpret and envision our encounters in relation to the divine.

Where religious interpretation succeeds, inklings and emotions that emerge in the midst of current encounters and are intertwined with varied interpretive resources also become "religious-image- or framework-laden." At the same time, our religious imaginative resources and interpretive frameworks—our beliefs, narratives, images, and ideas of the divine in relation to us—become emotionally resonant and enlivened. They become connected with current felt realities.

Of course, any given religious depiction might *not* succeed at interpreting a particular object or circumstance and our affective response to it in relationship to the divine. This is so because the imaginative religious interpretation or depiction of the divine in relationship to the object or circumstance in question needs to cohere with our actual and current emotional response to that object or circumstance. But, as we have seen, our emotional response is ordinarily also shaped by other interpretive resources or beliefs, theories, images, and ideas obtained by socialization into other communities and discourses. And it may be that, when viewed in the light of these other interpretative resources, the object or circumstance we encounter calls for an emotional response at odds with the response called for by our religious vision.

For example, suppose that, partly because of what I know and believe about tornadoes and their destructive force, I respond to funnel clouds with fear. Suppose, too, that my community's imaginative religious resources encourage me to see all natural occurrences as features of a divine dynamic or creativity that is wholly benevolent and beneficial to all creatures all the time. This would impose a disjunction between my fear at the sight of funnel clouds and the gratitude with which (presumably) I should respond to them according to the interpretation of my religious community.

57. Cook, *The Open Circle*, 10, 11, 13.

This disjunction, together with others like it, may become something of a religious crisis if I am unable to assimilate it into the religious vision into which I have been socialized, or if I am unable to revise the religious vision into which I have been socialized in order to accommodate what I believe to be appropriately fearful emotions in response to tornadoes as well as to other natural disasters and threats. It may even precipitate the disintegration of my religious outlook and its attendant piety or disposition toward the world. Moreover, since my affectively charged and conflicted responses to tornadoes and other natural circumstances will also reflect interpretive images, ideas, beliefs, and frameworks furnished by other communities and discourses (e.g., contemporary sciences, philosophies, or even other religious traditions), contributions from another framework may suggest a different outlook and settled disposition. If so, then perhaps I will exchange the religious vision and piety that encouraged me to affirm a wholly benevolent and beneficial divine creativity for another life orientation and worldview. This would amount to a conversion.

It is also possible, however, that I will successfully address the disjunction by further elaborations or selective retrievals and revisions in the interpretive schema and depictions put forward by my religious community, as well as by other communities and their interpretive discourses. For example, I may come to understand tornadoes and their destructive force within a wider pattern of weather and ecology that brings benefits. I may also revise my religious or theological vision and claim (possibly with the help of a heretofore neglected aspect of my community's mythopoeic discourse and tradition) that the divine dynamism does not always guarantee the needs and interests of every creature. If that is so, the emotional responses called for by my religious vision and by other things I believe about the destructive force of tornadoes and other natural occurrences are no longer at odds. (I should note, however, that my piety or settled disposition has undergone a revision so that, in addition to gratitude, I may also have feelings of awe and fear as I encounter natural occurrences in God's world.)

In any case, then, our imaginative theological reflections and portraits do not express raw and uninterpreted feelings and experiences. They do not merely make statements about objects, situations, and realities. Neither is their only function to influence and condition our experiences or emotional responses. Theology works with experiences that already represent a combination of affections and imaginative resources. It offers reinterpretations of objects, situations, and realities with respect to the divine, for instance, natural processes as aspects of divine ordering, in a reflective attempt to develop and refine a religious piety and vision. This vision, in turn, influences our subsequent affections and responses to the objects, situations, and realities with which we interact.

My position may be compared with the three kinds of theories of religion and doctrine distinguished by George A. Lindbeck in his benchmark book *The Nature of Doctrine*. Lindbeck says that cognitive theories emphasize "ways in which church doctrines function as informative propositions or truth claims about objective realities"; they regard religions somewhat as logically empirical philosophies regarded science. According to Lindbeck, "this is the approach of traditional orthodoxies," and it has affinities with the view of religion in "much Anglo-American analytic philosophy with its preoccupation with the cognitive or informational meaningfulness of religious utterances." Another approach, says Lindbeck, emphasizes "the 'experiential-expressivist' dimension of religion; it interprets doctrine as non-informative and non-discursive symbols of inner feelings, attitudes, or existential orientations." Experiential-expressivist theories highlight "the resemblances of religions to aesthetic enterprises" and are "particularly congenial to liberal theologies influenced by the Continental developments that began with Schleiermacher."[58]

Lindbeck himself favors a third approach he calls "cultural-linguistic" that emphasizes the "respects in which religions resemble languages together with their correlative forms of life and thus are similar to cultures." Here "religions are seen as comprehensive interpretive schemes usually embedded in myths or narratives and heavily ritualized, which structure human experience and understanding of self and world." Religion, a communal phenomenon, thus furnishes "a kind of cultural and/or linguistic framework or medium" that shapes life and thought.

Unlike these three approaches, my position affirms no Archimedean point on which to base a theory of religion and doctrine. Religion, which has a great deal to do with affections, since it both expresses and shapes them, finally cannot be reduced simply to belief, emotion, practices, or linguistic frameworks. A religion is a life that engages the entire person; it is a multidimensional phenomenon replete with experiential, cultural-linguistic, and cognitive aspects.[59]

My attention to affections and emotions signals an experiential aspect. However,

58. George Lindbeck, *The Nature of Doctrine: Religion and Theology in a Postliberal Age* (Philadelphia: Westminster, 1984), 16, 17–18, 33.

59. In a paper on Christian faith, American philosopher Charles Sanders Peirce laments the degeneration in religion from lived perception to belief. He excoriates theologians for rendering belief more and more abstract by means of "fallacious logical disputations" that draw "the narrowing bounds of doctrine" tighter and tighter, "with less and less attention to the living essence of religion, until, after some *symbolum quodcumque* has declared that the salvation of each individual absolutely and almost exclusively depends upon his entertaining a correct metaphysics of the godhead, the vital spark of inspiration becomes finally quite extinct." Then Peirce says: "Yet it is absurd to say that religion is a mere belief. You might as well call society a belief, or politics a belief, or civilization itself a belief. Religion is a life, and can be identified with a belief only provided that belief be a living belief—a thing to be lived rather than said or thought" (Peirce, *Scientific Manuscripts*, vol. 6 of *Collected Papers of Charles*

because I claim that affections and emotions are responsive to objects, I do not reduce them to inner feelings, and I think a theology that attends to religious affections and emotions is not merely attending to expressions of subjectivity. Again, I maintain that religious affections and emotions are suffused with intelligence in the sense that they are intertwined with imaginative resources that help us discern, envision, and make judgments about how the divine relates to the many objects and others we interact with. Thus my emphasis on the proposals, myths, narratives, symbols, ideas, beliefs, and practices furnished by particular religious communities that offer frameworks for interpreting objects in relationship to the divine and also help shape our affections and emotional responses to those objects. This is a cultural-linguistic aspect—but without the claim that language or linguistic frameworks simply produce our affections (since our affections and sensibilities also are responsive to objects). That is, our affections are shaped and influenced by imaginative, cultural, and linguistic forms, but they are not simply constituted by these forms because they are also responsive to the objects with which we interact.

Finally, I also maintain that theology is a reflective enterprise that holds these elements together. To support the pastoral project of helping to faithfully form the people of God, theologians try to interpret or reinterpret the current lives and felt encounters of Christians and their communities. Doctrinal reflections construe objects, situations, and realities with respect to encompassing mystery or the divine as portrayed with the aid of the community's mythopoeic discourse. In doing so, they develop a connected *outlook*, or vision, of God, the world, and ourselves. They develop a *wisdom* that helps to orient persons in their interactions with objects and others. This wisdom disposes us to certain affectivities, but it also makes cognitive claims about objects and realities, such as orderings and processes of nature in relation to human well-being, that both can and should be brought into conversation with interpretations offered by other religions, philosophies, and disciplines. (See chap. 1, props. #4 and #18.)

Varieties of Theological Visions (or Wisdoms)

Proposition #9 Religions may be distinguished by their organizing and paradigmatic proposals.

A paradigmatic proposal is an item in a community's mythopoeic inventory that configures other imaginative resources and makes a decisive contribution to a basic image of the divine. A religious community's mythopoeic resources

---

Sanders Peirce, ed. Charles Hartshorne and Paul Weiss [Cambridge, MA: Harvard University Press, 1978], 6:438–39).

ordinarily include very many (if not virtually countless) symbols, narratives, teachings, and practices. A paradigmatic proposal, therefore, is an especially compelling item that sets these other imaginative resources into a wider pattern and helps a community formulate a basic image/concept of the divine. This basic concept, in turn, promises to interpret and shape in relationship to the divine affectivities and emotions evoked in persons by a wide range of interactions and expectations.

Consider the exodus and the Sinai covenant. Here we come across narratives, codes, songs, and poems that present the liberation of oppressed Hebrew slaves and the establishment of a society governed by laws as a compelling clue or paradigmatic proposal. The proposal depicts what lies beyond the threshold, the deity, or the encompassing mystery freely and faithfully binding itself to the Hebrews as the lawgiver who constitutes Israel and bestows the gift and promise of an ordered, just, and continuing life together. Moreover, this proposal concerning the free faithfulness of the deity helps to configure the mythopoeic resources of Genesis 1:1–2:4a. Indeed, as a paradigmatic proposal, the exodus and the Sinai covenant lend a decisive pattern and texture to the mythopoeic discourse of Israel and Hebrew Scripture more generally. Thus, whether the experience at hand concerns emotionally resonant interactions with natural orderings, the kingship, or captivity in Babylon, Hebrew Scripture interprets it in relation to the gracious and just Deliverer, who brought slaves out of Egypt and constituted them as a people and a nation.

We might say that paradigmatic proposals such as this one are signal gifts to the imagination. They furnish key principles of interpretation that, in conjunction with additional resources, help historic religious communities formulate more or less comprehensive and basic images of and beliefs about the divine with respect to the world and ourselves. Logically speaking, any object, relationship, or event might become the vehicle for a paradigmatic religious proposal and thus might support the development of a basic image of or belief about the divine. In fact, however, promising proposals are contingent and we cannot produce them just when we need them. We have to wait for the illuminating image, experience, or idea. Indeed, when taken together, the broadly illuminating character of paradigmatic proposals and their occasional or contingent quality form an experiential basis for the talk about inspiration and revelation that we often encounter in religious circles. If Judaism looks to the exodus for its organizing and paradigmatic proposal, Christianity looks to Jesus Christ, Islam looks to the prophet Muhammad, Buddhism looks to the Buddha, Neoplatonism focuses on a mystical experience, and Stoicism emphasizes experiences of accepting limitations.[60] These paradigmatic proposals, in turn, organize and configure additional ideas and resources.

60. Christian, *Meaning and Truth*, 99, 102.

As we have seen, the exodus suggests that the divine is the historically active Deliverer who chooses Israel, delivers it from oppression, and establishes and provides for the chosen people. This proposal, in turn, configures additional mythopoeic material concerning the creation of world and humanity (both are envisioned as good and intentionally ordered by the Deliverer), the Deliverer's purposeful governance of history, and its fulfillment in a coming kingdom. By contrast, the mystical experience central to Neoplatonism proposes that the divine is the eternal One absolutely beyond the material world of multiplicity and change. This proposal configures additional resources and yields a picture of the material world and life in the body as degenerations of spiritual perfection. Redemption is thus portrayed, not as the fulfillment of God's governance in history, but as the soul's release from material-temporal imprisonment and its return to the One. In short, here we have two distinct visions or wisdoms concerning life and the world in relation to the divine that express and shape different pieties or configurations of affection and emotion.

This is an important reason why actual religions are historically particular rather than generic. The textures of their theological wisdoms and their basic images, their depictions, orienting visions, and pieties are shaped by specific mythopoeic resources and organizing proposals. There is no such thing as "religion-in-general" partly because actual religions involve particular mythopoeic discourses, symbol systems, and frameworks. They entail specific formations of imagination from which their leading experiences, affections, pieties, and practices cannot be abstracted.[61]

Proposition #10 Different kinds of theological visions may be classified according to the ways in which they portray the divine in relationship to us and to the many objects and others we interact with.

Religions may be classified in different ways, for example, according to patterns of leadership and authority that obtain within their communities, and according to how these communities relate to the wider societies in which they are found.[62] Here I am concerned with a related but distinguishable matter, namely, how

61. This point is like one Schleiermacher made in his fifth speech to "religion's cultured despisers." Religions are definite historical individuals that emerge from their own original facts and particular intuitions, which was the basis on which he criticized the idea of natural religion. See Schleiermacher, *On Religion: Speeches to Its Cultured Despisers*, trans. John Oman (New York: Harper & Row, 1958), 210–53.

62. See, e.g., Max Weber's distinctions between prophets, priests, and magicians as different sorts of religious leaders (*The Sociology of Religion*, trans. Ephraim Fischoff [Boston: Beacon, 1963], 20–59).

to classify different kinds of *affectively resonant theological visions*. The focus is on patterns in their portraits of the divine in relationship to the world, or in relationship to ourselves and the many objects and others we interact with.

Friedrich Schleiermacher distinguished three forms of piety that he also regarded as stages of development. The lowest, the chaotic stage, he said, is fetishism, animism, and idol worship; each idol has influence "only over a limited field of objects or processes" and so "the sense of totality has not yet developed." Religious conceptions are fluid and indeterminate, and religious consciousness remains confused. A second—intermediate—stage is polytheism, where many gods and spirits are organized into a coherent plurality. Although "a presentiment of One Supreme Being behind the plurality of higher Beings" emerges "here and there" at this stage, Schleiermacher says that the essential factor in religion, or the feeling of absolute dependence, "cannot appear in its complete unity" because it is associated with more than one higher being.[63] Finally, there is monotheism, the stage at which we are conscious of ourselves as absolutely dependent and have "a general consciousness of finitude" or the absolute dependence of all parts of the world solely on one Supreme Being.[64]

Schleiermacher then distinguishes two types of monotheism: an aesthetic type, which has a fatalistic character because emphasis falls on the determination of the individual's activity by the whole of finite existence, and a teleological type, where the religious affections refer predominantly to the moral task. He locates Islam as an illustration of the former type, though he also claims that a large influence of sensuous objects on the religious emotions keeps many Muslims on the level of polytheism. Judaism and Christianity, Schleiermacher says, are representatives of the latter type, though Judaism vacillates between fetishism and idol worship until monotheistic faith becomes predominant following the Babylonian exile, and it also reduces the active side of piety to "divine punishments and rewards."[65] By contrast, he says, Christianity is more thoroughly monotheistic and expresses the teleological type more completely.

Schleiermacher's classification was an advance over claims that Christianity is true and all other religions simply false, but there are also significant difficulties—some of which derive from his problematic (and also rather curious) generalizations about Islam, Judaism, and Christianity. (We might have expected a Reformed theologian to point to vacillations in the ways Christian commu-

63. Schleiermacher, *CF*, #8 (pp. 34, 35).

64. See also Julia Lamm, *The Living God: Schleiermacher's Theological Appropriation of Spinoza* (State College: Pennsylvania State University Press, 1996), 120–22; Schleiermacher, *On Religion*, 96; Schleiermacher, *CF*, #8 (p. 34).

65. Schleiermacher, *CF*, #8 (p. 37); #9 (pp. 42, 43).

nities have understood monotheism, not to mention a tendency among some Christians to portray the active side of piety with respect to divine rewards and punishments.) The difficulty I want to emphasize here, however, is that the language of higher and lower stages with respect to animism, polytheism, and monotheism is a direct correlate of Schleiermacher's theory of religion as absolute dependence. Animism and polytheism are judged deficient because they confuse the feeling of absolute dependence, whereas monotheism alone gives it full expression.

William A. Christian Sr. says that this simply goes to show that Schleiermacher's theory of religion itself favors a monotheistic piety that construes the religious object as the single reality on which we and all other things depend absolutely.[66] I agree, and I would note that Christian's point can be stated in the terms I am developing here: Schleiermacher imports a normative theological judgment into his theory of religion, and this is what authorizes much of his language of higher and lower. That is, the idea of religion as the feeling of absolute dependence itself emerges from Schleiermacher's own Christian (and Reformed) theological vision. Specifically, it amounts to a restatement of his theology of sovereign divine causality, or the idea that God alone determines all other causes, agents, and things.

In what follows I will try to distinguish and relate polytheistic and monotheistic patterns of theological wisdom, but I will not use the language of higher and lower. I do not doubt that one may finally prefer monotheistic theological images or visions and thus also judge other kinds of theological visions to be deficient. But this judgment, I think, should not be made at the level of a neutral theory of religion; neither should it be a feature of one's typology of theological visions. If it is offered, it should be offered as a theological judgment or as a feature of a particular theological vision and the way it pictures the divine, the world, and ourselves.

Consider, for example, H. Richard Niebuhr's remarks about radically monotheistic faiths that identify God with the power or principle of being, henotheistic faiths in a closed society or group, and polytheistic faiths in many objects of meaning and value that come into play at different places and times, or else with respect to different activities and areas of life. From the perspective of a radically monotheistic theological wisdom, henotheistic and polytheistic formations of religious affections are idolatrous because they attach themselves to (falsely elevated) finite realities. They also lead to deleterious moral consequences because they fail to support a universal community of moral concern. That is, they leave out some persons, groups, and realities as being of no account because they iden-

66. Christian, *Meaning and Truth*, 43–54.

tify the divine, which bestows value on things, with only a part or a subset of the universal community of all beings. They inappropriately uphold understandings of the divine that indicate that some things do not have value with respect to the divine. (And this inevitably undercuts the theological rather than theistic humanism that my theology supports; see "Introduction: Point of View.")

But to identify the divine as the creator of all things or the principle of being, rather than with a lesser reality such as the nation or the race—to understand the divine in such a way that *all* things have value in relationship to it—is itself a *normative theological judgment*, made and shared by radically monotheistic faiths and the particular traditions that bear them. It is a feature of some particular theological wisdoms or visions of God, the world, and ourselves rather than a judgment required by an adequate understanding of religion per se. From the viewpoint of a henotheistic wisdom, say, a nationalist or racist theological vision, it simply remains the case that some things are appropriately left out of the primary community of moral concern.[67]

Proposition #11 The mythopoeic discourses of polytheistic communities support pieties and theological visions that encourage persons to depict and encounter a number of divine objects; they order and envision life and the world pluralistically. However, the divine objects often are also interrelated and organized, and the patterns that obtain among them correlate with contexts, spheres, and more general patterns of coherence in life and the world.

It is logically possible that encompassing mystery will be both pictured and responded to emotionally as a number of divine objects that are wholly unconnected or independent of one another, and there may be polytheistic traditions that do so. This would verge on what Schleiermacher calls animism, and the question likely to arise is whether such a vision can depict any reliable and workable patterns of coherence in human life and the world and also encourage the awakening of a coherent piety or temper of mind. Most known polytheisms, however, are more complicated than this because they envision a *coherent* plurality.

Thus, where familial, operational, and territorial relationships obtain among the divine beings, these make for an organized collective, assemblage, or ensemble. Indeed, where someone worships more than one object at the same time, then the encompassing mystery, the entity taken as the primary reference

67. H. Richard Niebuhr, *Radical Monotheism and Western Culture, with Supplementary Essays* (Louisville: Westminster John Knox, 1993), 24–37.

point for meaningful life, may be *the gods*. This, says Christian, is "collective polytheism."[68] Moreover, the assemblage or collection itself may be ordered hierarchically in such a way that there is a main or primary god with wide-ranging responsibilities for the cosmos and the other gods. In some instances the organized collective, assemblage, or ensemble may itself begin to take on characteristics of a single, relatively unified divine reality.

For example, despite Olympian bickering and conflicts, the polytheism of the ancient Greeks entailed an organized assemblage. Some commentators note that, notwithstanding "their anthropological appearance," the gods of the Greeks "were not persons so much as powers, ordered and classified" according to a system, each with its own "modes and spheres of operation and their inherent limitations." Indeed, "this diversity of gods . . . was not necessarily incompatible with the idea of a unity of the divine."[69]

Ancient Greek religion, so varied at different places and times and among different classes and groups, also furnishes an illustration of a main or primary god with wide-ranging responsibilities for the cosmos and the other gods. Zeus, of course, was the father and head of the twelve Olympians, who were all related and whose mountain residence towered above other gods, who lived in the underworld. Indeed, "when the Greeks used the singular *ho theos*, 'god,' for the most part they did not mean just any member of the class 'gods,' but rather the highest god, Zeus, who held the world, humans and gods alike, in his hands." In fact, the Stoics, who argued for one god, a benevolent, rational, and providential principle who created all things, interpreted Zeus as "the supreme providential god, on whom the universe depends."[70] In Egyptian polytheism during the Middle Kingdom, the sun god, Amun-Re, accumulated the attributes of a single divinity responsible for the creation, ordering, and continued existence of the cosmos

68. Christian, *Meaning and Truth*, 67.

69. Louise Bruit Zaidman and Pauline Schmitt Pantel, *Religion in the Ancient Greek City*, trans. Paul Cartledge (Cambridge: Cambridge University Press, 1992), 176–77. During the late fifth and fourth centuries BCE, Athenians believed that it was among Zeus's functions to provide rain, and they sometimes turned to Asclepius to cure diseases (Jon Mickalson, *Athenian Popular Religion* [Chapel Hill: University of North Carolina Press, 1983], 4–5, 21, 23). Religion in Greek cities, during the archaic and classical periods (approximately 750–330 BCE), tended to associate one group of divinities with marriage, another with technical production, and so on. Moreover, in the pantheon that operated at the city of Mantineia, Zeus was worshiped "in virtue of five different functions at five different cultic places." In general, then, "the Greek pantheon . . . did not consist of a mere juxtaposition of divinities but a structured ensemble within which each god was defined by his or her relationships with the rest" (Zaidman and Pantel, *Religion in the Ancient Greek City*, 185–91, 196, 212).

70. Jan Assmann, *The Search for God in Ancient Egypt*, trans. David Lorton (Ithaca, NY: Cornell University Press, 2001), 10, 120–21, 189–90.

and its many deities. In this polytheism there emerged a tension between the idea of a "god" responsible for the cosmos, good and evil, and "the gods."[71]

Complex polytheisms envision the many and plural aspects of the world as only relatively independent, all (at some level and to some degree) being ordered in correspondence with an organized *collective* of divine objects or more general and even universal pattern, structure, or reality. Life lived in an appropriately responsive relationship with the divine will thus also be ordered in a way that recognizes a plurality, or variety, of goods and practices within an overall matrix of relationships or a patterned unity.[72]

Proposition #12 The mythopoeic resources of monotheistic communities support a distinctive kind of piety and theological vision that encourages us to depict and encounter the divine as an Other; they interpret sensibilities and affections that emerge within the interactive flux of our experiences to respond to one all-encompassing mystery, or reality.

Charles Sanders Peirce claims that monotheism entails "a sort of sentiment, or obscure perception, a deep recognition of a something in the circumambient All." He also believes that such sentiments are not necessarily best represented by clear and distinct concepts. Indeed, Peirce insists that the vernacular word "God" is very (and appropriately) vague, and that it is not made less so by attributes such as infinity, which are at least as vague.[73] The vagueness is appropriately retained

71. Simon Price, *Religions of the Ancient Greeks* (Cambridge: Cambridge University Press, 1999), 138–39. William K. Powers's study of Oglala Sioux religion in North America from about 1700 to 1975 indicates complexity of a somewhat different sort. Powers says that Oglala religion envisions superhuman beings and powers having to do with everything from the sun, sky, earth, and thunder to the buffalo, the whirlwind, and life (or breath). These benevolent beings and powers are organized and embodied in *Wakantanka* ("*wakan* 'sacred' and *tanka* 'great, large, big'"), which is sometimes rendered into English as "Great Spirit"; it has sixteen aspects hierarchically arranged in four groups of four. *Wakantanka* is the center of everything and, though not itself personified, may be called upon and addressed, and also may be said to manifest itself in the personified beings of the sun, moon, sky, and so forth. In addition, there are other beings and powers, including spirits that inhabit different parts of the world, for example, water spirits, forest spirits, and camp spirits. These are dangerous and may be warded off by rituals (Powers, *Oglala Religion* [Lincoln: University of Nebraska Press, 1977], 45–50, 54, 137, 170–71).

72. According to Christian, there is also "symbolic polytheism," where "in worshiping the gods someone may really be worshiping something else"—perhaps the quality of divinity that the gods exemplify or the whole of nature, each of whose parts the gods personify (Christian, *Meaning and Truth*, 65). This also seems to verge on those forms of monotheism that eschew uniformity, and it may be that Oglala religion counts as an illustration. See prop. #13 below.

73. Peirce, "The Marriage of Religion and Science," in *Collected Papers of Charles Sanders Peirce*, 6:429, 494.

where the word strives to be adequate to the actual experience or obscure inkling as well as to various specifications of it. Somewhat similarly, Christian calls God "an open concept" that is intelligible but not comprehensible, and so leaves room for mystery and wonder.[74]

If monotheism, then, favors comparatively vague theological representations of a mysterious and incomprehensible reality, it may be wise to consider some historical complexities before we settle on too clear and distinct a description of them.[75]

74. Christian, *Meaning and Truth*, 260.

75. Jan Assmann says that the "New Solar Theology," which preceded Akenhaten's revolutionary Amarna religion in Egypt, was at least implicitly monotheistic in that it traced all of life, existence, and reality to the sun god, who continually creates—though it also accepted the context of other deities. Akenhaten radicalized the New Solar Theology, expressly denying the reality of the many deities, suppressing their cults, and insisting that the new god, Aten, take the place of the divine realm as a whole. Following the brief Amarna period, one might say that the many deities return, but with monotheistic overtones that make for theological tensions and complexities. Accordingly, Ramsesside theology portrayed Amun as a single, hidden, and transcendent god who was too mysterious to be revealed but who, nonetheless, was also manifest in many aspects, names, deities, forms, or "immanent refractions" (Assmann, *Search for God*, 205–7, 237–40). That is, it presented a vision that attempted to hold together both unity and plurality (or at least differentiation).

The Hebrew Bible, as Schleiermacher well understood, may be looked upon as "monotheizing literature" that reflects diverse strategies for depicting God, as well as a protracted struggle to portray one God (John J. Scullion, "God in the OT," in *The Anchor Bible Dictionary* [New York: Doubleday, 1992], 2:1042). For example, Yahweh is often called "Lord of Hosts" (YHWH Seba'ot). Commentators note that some texts depict the hosts, including the sun, moon, and stars, as Yahweh's military retinue or heavenly army, for example, Judg. 5:11–21. Elsewhere the hosts are portrayed as Yahweh's heavenly council, a collection of beings that execute the divine will. See Ps. 103:19–21, where Yahweh is enthroned as king over a heavenly court, and Ps. 148:1–5, where the heavenly hosts are extolled to praise Yahweh. In addition, the main Canaanite god, El, is portrayed as the creator who formed all things (including the gods of the council) and sits enthroned in the council as king, while Baal is the primary divine warrior in Canaanite mythology. Thus it appears that the epithet YHWH Seba'ot combines themes and dominant imagery in the El and Baal traditions. However, the Israelites were consistently commanded not to worship the hosts of heaven, as that would amount to worshiping other gods (see E. Theodore Mullen Jr., "Hosts, Host of Heaven," and C. L. Seow, "Hosts, Lord of," in *The Anchor Bible Dictionary*, 3:302, 304, 306).

The idea of a single, transcendent, and mysterious God comes to expression in passages that prohibit making images of Yahweh and also indicate that Yahweh lies beyond human ideas and measure. Again, a number of verses in Deutero-Isaiah declare Yahweh's uniqueness. For example, "God is with you alone, and there is no other; / there is no god besides him" (Isa. 45:14); here, as in a number of other passages in the Hebrew Bible and as in Akenhaten's Amarna religion, we find an explicit denial of other gods.

Calvinist Protestants during the Reformation of the sixteenth century in Europe empha-

In fact, monotheistic theological visions relate the deity to other objects and realities in a variety of ways. For example, the divine may be pictured as entirely determining all objects and others (as appears to be the case in some forms of Calvinism).[76] If so, then the world is clearly unified by the divine all-Sovereignty; but the question that is likely to arise from time to time is whether we and the many objects and others with whom we interact have any real efficacy. Then again, the deity may also be portrayed as interacting with other, relatively independent, objects and realities that it does not entirely determine or control. In this case, the world and its patterns may be unified by the divine activity; nevertheless, it may also exhibit some measure of dynamism and plurality. And this form of monotheism has affinities with those forms of polytheism that recognize many realities and powers but subordinate them to an overarching hierarchy, deity, force, or principle (see prop. #11 above). It is even possible for monotheistic symbolizations simply to stand in tension with portraits of other deities; this may support a view of life and world that portrays a unifying power and process in

sized the idea of one God beyond all images, and they also affirmed God's absolute omnipotence and sovereignty over all the angels. John Calvin himself claimed that the one God rules over all and, indeed, that God's providence "is the determinative principle of all things in such a way that sometimes it works through an intermediary, sometimes without an intermediary, sometimes contrary to every intermediary" (Mullen, "Hosts, Host of Heaven," and Seow, "Hosts, Lord of," 3:302, 304, 306).

76. Calvin, *ICR* 1.7.1–3; 1.14.3–17; 1.16.1–9. Robert Cummings Neville and Wesley J. Wildman note that the religions of West Asia developed monotheistic rhetoric from the polytheism of the Vedas. A case in point is an interesting text by the Hindu theologian Vedanta Desika (1268–1369). Desika, says Francis X. Clooney, rejects the idea of a "three-fold lord—the creator Brahma, the preserver Narayana, the destroyer Siva." Narayana alone is ultimate, the single source of the ordered and finite world, the ontological ground for everything. Nevertheless, Desika also claims that Narayana shares his lordship with his consort, the goddess Sri. Neville and Wildman also say that "the East Asian religions in their intellectual moments are centered in more universalizing and philosophical rhetoric, tending to look on the personifying elements as superstitious, save in a few instances" (Neville, ed., *Ultimate Realities: A Volume in the Comparative Religious Ideas Project* [Albany: State University of New York Press, 2000], 96, 100, 103, 112–13). So, for example, the Tao is sometimes called the reality behind the origin of the universe, the Mother or source of all creatures and life (Isabelle Robinet, *Taoism: Growth of a Religion*, trans. Phyllis Brooks [Stanford, CA: Stanford University Press, 1997], 7–8, 19; Max Kaltenmark, *Lao Tzu and Taoism* [Stanford, CA: Stanford University Press, 1969], 28–29, 36–40). Herrlee G. Crell claims that in the *Chuang Tzu*, a text from about 300 BCE, the Tao is the indivisible totality of all things, the great whole in which all things are treasured and safe (Crell, *What Is Taoism? And Other Studies in Chinese Cultural History* [Chicago: University of Chicago Press, 1970], 2–3). But note that there are disagreements among interpreters over whether and how the Tao is the true ontological ground of things; see Neville, *Ultimate Realities*, 31–32, 130–43, 156–57, 166–67.

conflict with other powers and processes. Some Christian portraits of the relationship between the one God and the devil come close.

Metaphysically speaking, the question here is how to relate categories such as monism and pluralism to monotheism. Does monotheism require a metaphysical monism? Thinkers influenced by process philosophies often claim that monotheism may be framed in a way that is compatible with a pluralistic world. Religiously speaking, a related issue has to do with the relationship between monotheism and polytheism and/or positions that recognize what we might call a plurality of relatively independent principalities and powers (including human agents and social structures) in addition to the one God.

In any case, more than complex polytheisms that envision an organized collective of divine objects, monotheistic theological visions emphasize that our religious sensibilities and affections are responsive to an encompassing and primary reality that we meet at every turn. The many buzzing interdependent processes and realities with which we interact may have their own dynamisms and integrities, but, as a result of divine influence, they are nevertheless linked within a single extensive and interconnected web, fabric, matrix, system, or ecology. The interrelationships and interdependencies in which we participate integrate into a single "background," or whole, and at some level affectivities evoked in our converse with the many others and objects may also be regarded as responses to the deity. Or, to put this point another way, the deity and its dynamism are envisioned as relating to the many in such a way as to be experienced by us in our experiences of the many others. Our inkling or sense for the divine suggests a single interconnected whole, ensemble, or "circumambient All."

This felt sense of being situated in a wider *uni*verse, this recognition of the encompassing interconnectedness in which we live and move, entails a distinctive apprehension of the depth of life, an inkling that all the sinews and surfaces connect with Something More. Monotheism often is said to demystify the world because it denies the many divinities and affectivities associated with discrete natural phenomena and places. But monotheistic sensibilities and depictions may also involve a sacramental awakening to the world because they suggest that the world, or single natural and social ecology, points beyond itself. They suggest that we are enmeshed in a single and extensive web of relationships that opens toward *an* Other. Monotheistic sensibility and theological wisdom encourage us to picture an environment of relationships, forces, and divine presence. They suggest that the radical actuality of things mediates encounters with the deity. They envision a world where, in some sense, the divine reality that cannot be confined to temple or ark is always present in the pragmatic and mundane.

Proposition #13 Pantheistic theological visions encourage people to depict and encounter the divine in close connection with a world order or system and its forces, patterns, and structures. Here we are dealing not with a third kind of theological vision in contrast to polytheism and monotheism but with a tendency, feature, or characteristic of certain polytheistic and monotheistic visions.[77]

Divine reality may be regarded as the only reality; and all things and beings—all other apparent objects—may be understood as manifestations of the divine. Indeed, the divine may be equated with the world in such a way that there are no relatively independent agents or powers. If so, then the world is simply and directly God, or the divine, and the question arises whether the plurality of things and creatures—their efficacious powers and agencies, their possibilities and limits—are merely apparent. Or, again, the divine may be envisioned as the reality or dynamic that is active and influential through all the many agencies, forces, laws, and objects of the universe or the world. If so, then perhaps there may also be relatively independent creatures, powers, and differentiated spheres, and this kind of vision verges on certain forms of both polytheism and monotheism. (See props. #11 and #12 above.)

Admittedly, these are murky waters. We can get at one issue by asking whether there may be both monistic and pluralistic pantheisms. Another important question is this: Is it possible to argue that, strictly speaking, the "middle options" that try to emphasize both unity and plurality—that is, polytheism with an overarching principle of unity and monotheism with relatively independent powers and spheres—are neither simply monistic nor pluralistic?[78]

77. Lamm, *The Living God*, 102, 120–22.

78. Once again, there are historical complexities. There are pantheistic overtones to Oglala Sioux religion, where the sun, moon, sky, and so on are regarded as aspects or manifestations of *Wakantanka*. There are also clear pantheistic implications to Herrlee Crell's claim that, in the *Chuang Tzu*, the Tao is "not merely a substance and a thing. It is the only substance and the only thing, for it is the totality of all things whatsoever" (Crell, *What Is Taoism?*, 2).

Islamic monotheism often insists on a sharp distinction between God and cosmos (world, or creation). But not always. As S. Nomanul Haq points out, "the Qur'an perpetually suggests the utter dependence of everything on God, and the essential nonexistence of everything except Him," and this connects with the pantheistic tendencies of later Muslim mystics, such as Ibn Àrabi: "For Ibn Àrabi, God is the only reality, and the cosmos is this very reality manifested in its attributes. This is the famous *wahdat al-wujud* (ontological monism) doctrine of Ibn Àrabi. Is it pantheism? The Sufi will say no, for once again: The divine Names are the divine Essence itself, but they are *not* identical with divine Essence as such" (Neville, *Ultimate Realities,* 81, 90).

One discerns pantheistic tendencies among medieval Christian mystics, such as Meister Eckhart and Julian of Norwich. And we have had occasion to note that John Calvin's portrait of divine sovereignty makes for questions concerning the relative independence of mundane things and creatures. (See prop. #12 above.) Calvin envisioned a quite close relationship between God's providential activity and the course of nature, claiming that divine wisdom and power are displayed in the ordering of the universe and that, as God governs and directs everything, "there is no such thing as fortune or chance." Indeed, he could write: "I confess, of course, that it can be said reverently, provided that it proceeds from a reverent mind, that nature is God; but because it is a harsh and improper saying, since nature is rather the order prescribed by God, it is harmful in such weighty matters, in which special devotion is due, to involve God confusedly in the inferior course of his works."[79] Here, then, we have a passage where Calvin both relates God to and distinguishes God from the created world.

More recently, Grace M. Jantzen has explored the ideas that God is coextensive with the universe and that all that exists may be understood as God's creative self-manifestation. She claims: "If pantheism is . . . understood as an affirmation that all reality is God's reality, that there can be nothing without God or wholly apart from him or independent of him, then pantheism is not an alternative to Christian theology but ingredient in it." (Of course, one might also say that this is a comparatively broad understanding of pantheism.) Jantzen herself opts for a portrait or "model of the universe as God's body, a body some of whose parts have been given a measure of autonomy in God's gracious self-manifestation."[80]

With respect to polytheistic theological visions, pantheistic depictions include a principle of unity that seems incompatible with the mere affirmation of pluralism or of many unconnected gods. In addition to recognizing the many gods and powers, such depictions may also include some recognition of the totality of the world system (which includes the many gods and powers) as divine. Or, again, they may equate ultimate reality with a more abstract power at work in and through all the lesser gods and powers of the world. Therefore, a "pantheistic polytheism" has a tendency toward unity or toward an ordering principle that is not simply another god alongside the many other gods. It will also bear both similarities and differences with monotheistic visions that affirm a world system or unified whole in relation to one deity.

With respect to monotheistic theologies, pantheistic depictions emphasize

79. Calvin, *ICR* 1.16.2; see also 1.5.2; 1.16.4; and 1.5.5.

80. Grace M. Jantzen, *God's World, God's Body* (London: Darton, Longman & Todd, 1984), 149, 153–54.

the interrelatedness of the deity with nature and the system of nature. That is, a "pantheistic monotheism" emphasizes what Schleiermacher called the All in relationship to the One and the One in relationship to the All. It stands against sharp distinctions and oppositions between God and world. This emphasis remains compatible with monotheism (at least of a certain kind) as long as the All does not replace the One or become simply interchangeable with it. For in a monotheistic frame of reference, the All cannot exist (as single totality) without the One; there can be no All—no differentiated unity of the world—without the One.

A number of Christian theologians have envisioned a rather close relationship between the All and the One, and they have often used the language of being to make this relationship explicit. Consider Augustine's query near the beginning of his *Confessions*: "Or is it rather that I should not exist, unless I exist in you? . . . This, Lord, is the true answer to my question. But if I exist in you, how can I call upon you to come to me? And where would you come from? For you, my God, have said that you fill heaven and earth (Jer. 23:24)."[81]

Thomas Aquinas claimed that "God is the essentially self-subsisting Being," that "all beings apart from God are not their own being, but are beings by participation."[82] Jonathan Edwards sometimes referred to God as "being-in-general," while H. Richard Niebuhr speaks of the universal community of being and God as the "principle of being."[83] Paul Tillich rather famously referred to God as "being-itself" and "the ground of being."[84] Interestingly, in the wider compass of their writings, many of these theologians made use of language to refer to a God who is both nonpersonal and personal, both philosophical and devotional.[85]

This brings us to *panentheism* (literally, "all is in God"). Charles Hartshorne and William L. Reese define it this way: "God is not just the all of (other) things; but

81. Augustine, *Confessions*, translated and introduced by R. S. Pine-Coffin (London: Penguin Books, 1961), 1.2 (p. 22).

82. Aquinas, *ST* 1a.44.1 (p. 229).

83. Jonathan Edwards's striking phrase appears in "The End for Which God Created the World" and "The Nature of True Virtue." He claims that "being in general" is the whole and "the universal system of existence." However, he also claims that "the Divine Being" is eternal and infinite and that "the eternal and infinite Being is, in effect, being in general; and comprehends universal existence" (Edwards, *Ethical Writings*, ed. Paul Ramsey, vol. 8 of *WJE*, 8:461, 540). See also Sang Lee's contention that, for Edwards, "the world is in some sense a further actualization of God's own being" (Lee, *The Philosophical Theology of Jonathan Edwards* [Princeton: Princeton University Press, 1988], 201). See also H. Richard Niebuhr, *Radical Monotheism and Western Culture*, 31–34.

84. Tillich, *Reason and Revelation, Being and God*, 1:235–38; 2:5–12.

85. For example, Augustine uses personal pronouns to refer to God throughout his *Confessions*, and Edwards insists that "the essential qualities of a moral agent are in God, in the greatest possible perfection" (Edwards, *Freedom of the Will*, ed. Paul Ramsey, vol. 1 of *WJE*, 1:166).

yet all other things are literally in him."[86] This is not a pantheism, in which "all is God," because for the panentheist, "God is not reducible to the nondivine individuals, to the universe as a whole, or to the structure of the universe."[87] Panentheism maintains that "God's being includes the world but is not exhausted by it."[88]

A number of theologians who make use of the process philosophies of Alfred North Whitehead and Charles Hartshorne may be characterized as panentheists. Given the definition of panentheism presented by Hartshorne and Reese, however, perhaps it is not surprising—especially in light of their statements about God as "being-in-general" and "being itself"—that some have found panentheistic understandings of God and the world in Jonathan Edwards and Paul Tillich. Indeed, although Hartshorne and Reese include selections from Augustine and Aquinas as illustrations of a classical theism that is not panentheistic, it may be that some statements by Augustine and Aquinas (such as the ones quoted above) at least have panentheistic undertones. In any case, when it comes to ordering life in a way that respects both plurality and unity, there may not be a great deal of difference between panentheism and some forms of pantheism and pantheistic monotheism.

Christianity

Proposition #14 Christian communities bear monotheistic theological visions in which the event of redemption in Jesus Christ constitutes the paradigmatic proposal for picturing God, the world, and ourselves.

For Christians, the event of Jesus Christ is the most important clue to the deity who meets us at every turn, as well as to a faithful life, or to patterns of affectivity and interaction that are appropriately responsive to the divine. Moreover, with respect to this deity, Christians understand the many objects and others we interact with to be linked in a single encompassing and interconnected matrix or world. Therefore, they picture themselves responding to the deity disclosed in Jesus Christ in the midst of their many interactions with objects and others.

We might say that the event of Jesus Christ is the primary contingent occurrence in response to which the Christian community was formed. It casts up a

86. Charles Hartshorne and William L. Reese, eds., *Philosophers Speak of God* (Chicago: University of Chicago Press, 1953), 22.

87. David H. Nikkel, *Panentheism in Hartshorne and Tillich: A Creative Synthesis* (New York: Peter Lang, 1995), 2.

88. Paul E. Capetz, *God: A Brief History* (Minneapolis: Fortress, 2003), 150.

pattern that is taken to illuminate God, the world, and ourselves. The contingency of this event is an experiential basis for talk within Christian circles about the adventitious coming of Jesus Christ and the recognition that we can neither manipulate nor control it. Taken together, the illuminating and contingent characteristics of the event of Jesus Christ indicate that it is *revelatory*; indeed, when Christians speak of revelation in Jesus Christ, much of what they mean is that Jesus Christ is the contingent and illuminating event that renders God, the world, and ourselves intelligible.[89]

An Expansive Account

The New Testament presents an expansive account of the event of Jesus Christ. For example, as if to underscore the fact that this event cannot be understood apart from the longer story of Israel, the Gospel of Matthew (and thus the New Testament itself) opens with a genealogy that presents "Jesus the Messiah" as "the son of David, the son of Abraham" (Matt. 1:1). Jesus the Messiah is the one in whom God's kingdom draws near. A descendant of David, he embodies the promise of God's reign of justice and righteousness for all that is heralded by texts such as Psalm 72. God's covenant with Abraham, of course, establishes Israel as the people of God who enjoy a relationship with the divine that neither falters nor fails. In fact, the promise here is that, through the covenant with Abraham and his descendants, not only Israel but all nations and families of the earth shall be blessed (Gen. 12:2–3; 15:5–6; 22:17–18). Jesus represents the fulfillment of God's promise "that a seed would arise from Abraham in which all nations would find blessing."[90]

The New Testament also presents the event of Jesus Christ in conjunction with the Spirit, or with experiences of new and renewed life and of the gathering and empowering of the church. The association with the Spirit is underscored by stories of Jesus's spiritual conception in Matthew and in Luke, as well as by the descent of the Spirit like a dove at Jesus's baptism (Matt. 3:16; Mark 1:10; Luke 3:22; John 1:32). In the Gospel of John, Jesus promises to send this same Spirit to his disciples (16:7). In Acts, the Spirit becomes the guiding power of the church, gathering a new community that cuts across ethnic, geographic, linguistic, and political boundaries to undertake a worldwide mission. For Paul, the Spirit of

89. H. Richard Niebuhr, *The Meaning of Revelation* (New York: Macmillan, 1941), 32–43, 67–100. See also chap. 8, prop. #54.

90. John Calvin, *A Harmony of the Gospels of Matthew, Mark, and Luke*, trans. A. W. Morrison, vol. 1 of *Calvin's New Testament Commentaries* (Grand Rapids: Eerdmans, 1975), 58. Jack Dean Kingsbury offers a similar interpretation in *Matthew: Structure, Christology, Kingdom* (Philadelphia: Fortress, 1975), 79.

God (which he also calls "the Spirit of Christ") is the motive, principle, and power of new life, of an orientation in living characterized by a new relationship with God as God's children in a community of mutuality and common concern (Rom. 7:6–8:9, 14–17). Indeed, by the Spirit we are baptized into the body of Christ and become members of it.

The Creator Is the Redeemer

The expansive event of redemption in Jesus Christ shows that the one God who creates and sustains all things also redeems. It indicates, in short, that the Creator is the Redeemer. This comes through in Calvin's theology, where redemption in Jesus Christ functions as a broad symbolic image or concept that includes what is meant by such other terms as "atonement," "reconciliation," "regeneration," "justification," and "sanctification." For Calvin, then, redemption refers to what is accomplished by Jesus Christ as well as to the renovating and enlivening work of the Spirit. It means that Christ discloses the grace of God to the sinner, but also that the presence of the Son in the flesh and the work of the Spirit renew a fallen world and restore and elevate persons from death to life.[91] Fundamentally, then, Calvin understands Jesus Christ as the Mediator who communicates and expresses God's love, mercy, and benevolence. Christ is God's loving act, and we participate in the salvation found in Christ by the Spirit. For Calvin, redemption in Jesus Christ shows that God is Redeemer.[92] Thus the title of book 2 of the *Institutes*: "The Knowledge of God the Redeemer in Christ."[93]

The God who covenants with Abraham and Israel is the deity who governs the world and whose dominion we inhabit. Accordingly, Psalm 124 says that, had it not been for Israel's Helper and Deliverer, "our enemies . . . would have swallowed us up alive." It then concludes with the liturgically popular sentence: "Our help is in the name of the Lord, who made heaven and earth." Or consider Psalm 136: the Creator who made the heavens, spread out the earth on the waters, and made the great lights to rule over day and night is also the Deliverer who

91. John Calvin, *ICR* 2.16.1–19; 3.1.2; Calvin, *A Harmony of the Gospels*, xi.

92. Calvin, *ICR* 2.16.2, 4.

93. Calvin, *ICR* 1.1. Friedrich Schleiermacher followed Calvin's lead when he wrote that "the Redeemer assumes believers into the power of his God-consciousness," that this establishes a new life, and that the Spirit animates the common life of believers (Schleiermacher, *CF*, #100 [pp. 425, 428], #123 [p. 569]). Nevertheless, for Schleiermacher, the Redeemer is always Jesus of Nazareth. Calvin affirms that the name "Christ," or "Messiah," signifies Jesus's mission as "one divinely appointed to fulfill the role of Redeemer" and that "the office of Redeemer was laid upon [Jesus Christ] that he might be our Savior" (Calvin, *A Harmony of the Gospels*, 60; *ICR* 2.16.1). But he also insists that God is Redeemer.

brought Israel out of Egypt, divided the Red Sea, led the people through the wilderness, and gave them land.

As presented by the New Testament, the event of Jesus Christ in conjunction with the Spirit further clarifies and specifies the characteristics of the deity. Jesus Christ is "the image of the invisible God" in whom "all the fullness of God was pleased to dwell, and through whom God was pleased to reconcile to [Godself] all things" (Col. 1:15, 19–20). In Jesus Christ, the God who directed Israel through perils and threats was reconciling the world to Godself (2 Cor. 5:18). The Spirit bestows life by adopting the world's many peoples as Christ's sisters and brothers, thus engrafting them into the people of God (Rom. 11:17). Redemption in Christ and the Spirit thus indicates that the faithful reality who creates and then also covenants with Israel is the God of grace whose purpose is reconciliation and renewed life. God the Creator is God the Redeemer.

The Apostles' Creed makes a similar point: "I believe in God the Father Almighty, maker of heaven and earth." That is, the all-governing God is Creator. "And in Jesus Christ his only Son our Lord"—the Christ in whom reconciliation is accomplished is the Son who carries out the Creator's purpose. "And in the Holy Spirit"—who convokes the universal church, sanctifies the faithful, and brings everlasting life. The Trinitarian linkage of Maker, Christ, and Spirit indicates that the God who creates also reconciles and renews (or redeems).

What emerges, then, in connection with the event of redemption in Jesus Christ is a basic image and concept of God, or the divine, that has important consequences for interpreting the world and ourselves. God is Creator, and so, in relationship to God, the world is a good creation, and we humans are good creatures endowed with distinctive capacities and gifts (Gen. 1:1–2:4a). God is Redeemer, and so both we ourselves and the good world in which we participate are beneficiaries of God's reconciling and renewing grace.

God as Judge

Now for a little *theo*-logic. From the idea of God as Creator-Redeemer, it is a short step to a sense of sin and the image of God as Judge. This is true because redemption is a solution to a problem. Reconciliation and renewal indicate that we are caught up and entangled in a difficulty; they imply that we are diminished and corrupted. To say that our help is in the name of the Lord indicates that we are in need of being helped. To call God our Deliverer implies a threatening situation or circumstance from which we need to be delivered. To call God the Redeemer indicates that we *need* redeeming and renewing.

This is where the image of God as Judge comes in. It suggests that God orders the world so that negative consequences attend our entanglement, diminution, and corruption. Trespass leads to punishment. Therefore,

> for three transgressions of Israel,
>   and for four, I will not revoke the punishment;
> because they sell the righteous for silver,
>   and the needy for a pair of sandals. (Amos 2:6)

Diminution leads to dissatisfaction, an accusing conscience, or even despair: "I do not understand my own actions. For I do not do what I want, but I do the very thing I hate. . . . I can will what is right, but I cannot do it . . . wretched man that I am!" (Rom. 7:15–24).

In this way, the basic image of God as Creator-Redeemer also indicates that God is Judge. This accords with New Testament portraits of Jesus Christ, the one who lives a life of love to God and neighbor and is our judgment as well as our hope. Again, all fall short of the law as Christ exposits it in the Sermon on the Mount, and at the foot of the cross, where people become aware of their sin and its destructive consequences.[94] Indeed, the one in whom the blessing of all peoples and nations is fulfilled is also the Son of Man, who returns in power and glory to judge (Matt. 25:31–46; Mark 13:24–27), a point also preserved in the creed.

Therefore, we arrive by fits and starts at the contention that, when configured by the event of Jesus Christ, the mythopoeic resources of the Bible specify the divine as *Creator*, *Judge*, and *Redeemer*. Moreover, this basic concept of God (as Reinhold Niebuhr also emphasizes) stands in close connection with a number of affectivities. For example, the symbol of God as Creator portrays God in conjunction with our felt sense of dependence. The image of God as Judge correlates with feelings of responsibility, obligation, and remorse. And the idea of God as Redeemer correlates with our longing for forgiveness and renewal.[95] Indeed, following Calvin, we might say that the knowledge of God's many benefits evokes a distinctive piety or skein of affections.[96] Feelings of awe, dependence, gratitude, and obligation emerge with the apprehension that God is the Creator and the bestower of gifts. Our senses of gratitude, dependence, possibilities, and direction correlate with the understanding that, in Christ and the Spirit, God redeems and renews. A sense of remorse arises with the recognition that we often fail to use our gifts appropriately and to uphold our obligations—as well as an attendant apprehension of God as Judge.

94. Reinhold Niebuhr, *Essays in Applied Christianity*, 31–33.
95. See Reinhold Niebuhr, *NDM*, 1:131–33.
96. Calvin, *ICR* 1.2.1.

At the same time, we should also note that, when they are configured by the event of Jesus Christ, sin and grace, judgment and redemption go together. When it is set within the overall pattern or dynamic of creation and redemption, judgment is not simply destructive but has its place within an economy or pattern that points to redemption. Judgment seeks to turn misdirected and corrupted persons and communities toward possibilities for renewal.[97] And thus, for Christian piety, feelings of remorse are ordered toward forgiveness. They are part and parcel of a movement toward renewal.

Indeed, the idea that the divine judging is situated within the pattern of creation and redemption comes to striking expression in the Reformed subtradition of the Christian movement. There sin and grace, judgment and redemption, are so closely intertwined that they often are treated together. Thus does Calvin put his discussion of sin near the beginning of book 2 of his *Institutes* under "Knowledge of God the Redeemer in Jesus Christ." The second part of Schleiermacher's *The Christian Faith* explicates "the antithesis of sin and grace." Karl Barth insists that it is only in the light of Jesus Christ that the darkness is revealed as such. "But," says Barth, "this means that there can be no place in dogmatics for an autonomous section *De peccato* constructed in a vacuum between the doctrine of creation and that of reconciliation."[98]

A Trinitarian Account

The Trinitarian character of this account of the event of Jesus Christ and of the divine as Creator-Judge-Redeemer can be understood in the light of a passage such as 2 Corinthians 13:13: "The grace of the Lord Jesus Christ, the love of God, and the communion of the Holy Spirit be with you all." The interconnections of the expansive event of Jesus Christ with the Abrahamic covenant and with Pentecost are critical. In my judgment, the earliest Trinitarian formulae summarize Christians' experiences of reconciliation in Jesus Christ, of the creating and sustaining God of Israel, and of renewal and new community through the Spirit. They point to the Creator, who covenants with Israel (and, through Israel, promises to bless all nations), to the Christ, who reconciles persons to God and one another (and thus opens a way for all to become God's children), and to the Spirit, who engrafts persons into the people of God and enlarges their hearts toward God and neighbor. Moreover, these formulae indicate that the three work

97. For a powerful statement of this point, see H. Richard Niebuhr, "War as the Judgment of God," in *War in the Twentieth Century*, ed. Richard B. Miller (Louisville: Westminster John Knox, 1992), 47–55. Niebuhr's article was originally published in the *Christian Century*.

98. Calvin, *ICR* 2.1.1–11; Schleiermacher, *CF*, ##62–64 (pp. 259–70); Barth, *CD* IV/1:141.

to bring about the same thing, namely, redemption, or a relationship with God that neither falters nor fails.[99]

This clearly is not yet a statement about a common divine nature, being, or substance shared by all three, and, as will become apparent in part 3, I am not convinced that such a statement is required. But when it is more fully developed, it does indicate how God, Christ, and Spirit are related in the experiences of the Christian community. It also makes a statement about divine reality. God creates and provides for the world and creatures. In Jesus Christ, the crucified one who, in the form of a servant, crosses barriers and boundaries, God reconciles the world. By the Spirit, God renews the world, turns persons to new life, and gathers them into communion with God and community with one another. This threefold dynamic summarizes the actuality, tendency, and trajectory of the encompassing mystery, the Creator-Judge-Redeemer.[100]

Proposition #15 Christians who internalize the basic image/idea of God as Creator, Judge, and Redeemer find that it shapes and expresses their interpretations of the world and humanity as well as many of their salient attitudes and sensibilities.

For people who internalize it, the image of God as Creator, Judge, and Redeemer becomes a basic part of the interpretive frame they bring to bear on their emotionally freighted interactions with objects and others. Indeed, within this framework, God, the world, and ourselves are correlative: they refer to one another, and a correct understanding of each requires that they be understood in relationship to each other.

Envisioning Creation

The image/concept of God as Creator encourages us to envision and respond to the world as God's creation. Within this frame of reference, people sense that the extensive and interconnected world is not centered on them but on the

99. Although her Trinitarian reflections are more traditional than are mine, Kathryn Tanner recognizes the difficulty of obtaining a highly developed Trinitarian doctrine out of the New Testament alone, and she also emphasizes that "the story of the gospel" may be read as the three "working a single action of salvation together" (Tanner, *Christ the Key* [Cambridge: Cambridge University Press, 2010], 152).

100. See Ottati, *Hopeful Realism*, 39–50, where I offer a similar interpretation of the economic Trinity. Although he came to a different understanding, Ernst Troeltsch also continued to regard the economic Trinity as a succinct summary of the Christian faith, even when he no longer affirmed an immanent Trinity (see Troeltsch, *The Christian Faith*, 104–7).

deity, who is its true depth and ground. They come to feel that the cosmos is the theater of God's glory. Indeed, they confess that God creates the world and that, apart from this vast interconnected creation, neither humans nor other creatures would exist. They acknowledge that everything depends on the Creator, that the world is itself a good gift and matrix of further gifts bestowed by God, and that this acknowledgment elicits our sense of dependence, gratitude, reverence, and awe.

Psalm 104:10–15 comes to mind: God makes springs gush forth, "giving drink to every wild animal," streams where "the birds of the air have their habitation." Or again, God causes

> the grass to grow for the cattle,
>   and plants for people to use,
> to bring forth food from the earth,
>   and wine to gladden the human heart.

Even so, we do not picture the Creator's good world as a display case in which nothing is to be changed or disturbed. This is true because, within the frame of the Creator-Judge-Redeemer image, we envision ourselves as creatures endowed with distinctive gifts. As creatures, we have reason, no doubt, to note our limitations. Whenever we act, we find ourselves situated within an extensive world of further actions and conditions, and we acknowledge that we neither know nor anticipate all relevant outcomes. Nevertheless, within the frame of the Creator's world, we also sense that we are endowed with distinctive capacities and possibilities for intervention. These, too, are among the good gifts for which we are grateful, and we recognize that they are to be exercised and cultivated. This seems an implication, for example, of the distinctive reference to humankind in Genesis 1:26b and in Psalm 8:5–8 as having been given dominion over things.

Envisioning Corruption

The image/concept of God as Judge encourages us to envision ourselves as well as others as corrupted and at fault. Two main points come into view. We sense that we humans are caught up in the grip of a tendency from which we cannot extricate ourselves, a misorientation that brings with it a train of bad consequences. This is part of the meaning of the relationship that Paul sees between our salvation by grace in Jesus Christ (rather than by our own efforts and works) and Adam's trespass. It is also why the saga of corruption and spiraling violence that occupies Genesis 4:1–11:9 makes a fitting introduction to persistent tendencies and features of human civilization. The symbolic concept of sin or the human fault anchors a profound pessimism, and it presses us to envision the entire human project as chronically skewed. It encourages us to see that persons (including ourselves), communities, and institutions are caught up in corrupting relationships, circumstances, and interests that they cannot easily alter or escape. These apprehensions are tied to experiences of irresponsibility as well as revulsion at the destructive consequences of the human fault, and they evoke in us a persistent sorrow at what we humans have become. They also furnish a basis for a sense of remorse and for a disposition toward confession.

Indeed, the image/concept of God as Judge encourages us to understand that the world at large suffers destructive consequences of the human fault. If the world is a good creation, a gift and a structured matrix of further gifts, it is also a place of corrupted persons, commitments, communities, and institutions, a place of skewed cultures and damaged ecosystems, a place of oppression, injustice, holocausts, and hates. Thus we have the negative picture of the world that comes through in New Testament passages such as James 4:4 and 1 John 5:4–5, which contrast renewed life and community with the world as fallen, apostate, and opposed to God. At the same time, however, at least some recurrent consequences of human corruption may be interpreted as judgments, or as destructive realities and conditions that follow upon our faults, diminish life, and thus call persons and groups to change their ways if they wish to avoid further diminishment and destruction. Consider, for example, Amos's exhortation that Israel

> seek good and not evil,
>   that you may live. . . .
> Hate evil and love good,
>   and establish justice in the gate;
> it may be that the LORD, the God of hosts,
>   will be gracious to the remnant of Joseph. (5:14–15)

Envisioning Renewal

Therefore, despite the sense of fault, those who internalize the symbolic idea of God as Redeemer are also encouraged to acknowledge that corrupted humanity—as well as this chronically diminished world—remain objects of renewing grace. The world is good, and it is a matrix of many gifts. The world is skewed and corrupted, a place of incalculable injustice and destruction. But it is also graced with new possibilities and opportunities. It is also the world that God refuses to give up on, and hence it remains the deity's valued creation.

In fact, despite persistent consequences of the human fault, the cosmic ensemble often continues to enable and sustain. Although caught up in destructive cycles—and sometimes just because they are beset by judgments—persons, communities, and societies often get second chances. Occasionally they find themselves beset by opportunities for reconciliation and renewal. And for people who internalize the symbol of God as Redeemer, these circumstances evoke felt senses of possibilities, gratitude, and hope.[101]

Situated in the midst of circumstances, conditions, and interrelationships, we are thus encouraged not only to envision ourselves as contingent creatures endowed with significant gifts, and as sinners caught up in destructive tendencies; we are also encouraged to recognize that we encounter benefits of redeeming grace. Consider the symbolic pattern of death and resurrection: in the midst of the many circumstances, limitations, and tragedies, and despite the human fault and its destructive consequences, persons and communities sometimes are graced with possibilities for renewed life.

This connects with a classical theological point about regeneration, mortification, and a vivifying newness of life in Christ and the Spirit that we find in the writings of Calvin and others, and it is as old as Paul's epistles. "Therefore we have been buried with him by baptism into death, so that, just as Christ was raised from the dead by the glory of the Father, so we too might walk in newness of life" (Rom. 6:4).[102] By the grace of God human life can be elevated. But there is also a related point about what may happen in the historical situation of human living. "It is an actual fact that human life, which is always threatened and periodically engulfed by the evil which human sin creates, is also marvelously redeemed by the transmutation of evil into good. This transmutation is not a human but a divine possibility. No man can, by taking thought, turn evil into good. Yet in the total operations of providence in history this transmutation occurs."[103]

Those of us who internalize this symbolic pattern in the context of the Redeemer image will be on the lookout for instances of help and deliverance. We note that help sometimes does come, as when we experience release from an illness by new pharmacological products and medical technologies. We discern that—whether because they are blessed with the right nightmares or with compelling glimpses of a better way, like Charles Dickens's Scrooge—people some-

101. This is another implication of some prophetic oracles. Hence, in Jer. 23:3, following the warning that Jerusalem shall go into captivity, we read of restoration: "Then I myself will gather the remnant of my flock out of all the lands where I have driven them, and I will bring them back to their fold, and they shall be fruitful and multiply." It is also an implication of the apostle Paul's insistence on a close connection between the Spirit, reconciliation, renewal, and new community.

102. Calvin, *ICR* 3.3.1–9.

103. Reinhold Niebuhr, *Beyond Tragedy*, 20.

times do relinquish diminishing and constraining postures in favor of more expansive loyalties, affections, and spirits. With an appreciation bordering on astonishment, we may also have noted that, following decades of apartheid and informed by a commitment to reconciliation, South Africa took a new turn. And we may continue to hope for similarly renewing possibilities.

A Piety or Disposition

A point to emphasize here is that, among those who internalize it, the image/concept of God as Creator, Judge, and Redeemer tends to express and sculpt an overall schedule of emotions, a general attitude, disposition, or piety. It encourages us to both interpret and experience life and history as a saga of gifts, capabilities, corruption, fragmentation, and conflict infused, surrounded, and bounded by grace. It encourages us to depict and encounter history as the story of good creatures gone awry but nevertheless also reconciled and renewed. It therefore helps to elicit or provoke in us a temper or deep-seated mood that might be called hopeful realism. As hopeful realists, we acknowledge significant, good, and even wondrous gifts, and thus we have reasons to exercise created capacities, to be grateful, and to give thanks. We acknowledge persistent corruption, are remorseful, and have reasons to expect diminishment, conflict, fragmentation, and death. Nevertheless, we also encounter redemptive possibilities and turnings, and thus we do not fail to hope and to look for enlargement, reconciliation, renewal, and life.[104]

Christian Theology

Proposition #16 A Christian theology presents a Christian community's theological vision or wisdom and, as such, represents the disciplined development of the interpretive work of preaching.

Religious sensibilities and affections may dispose people to interact with objects and others in a way that is appropriately responsive to the divine. These affections are both expressed and shaped by imaginative and mythopoeic resources that include particular clues and proposals and that enable a community to interpret and depict the divine, the world, and ourselves. When a community's portrayals reach an appropriate level of cultivation, they produce theological statements or doctrines. They yield an interconnected vision or practical wisdom that, in

104. See Ottati, *Hopeful Realism*, 34–37.

conjunction with continuing experiences and interactions, helps the community deepen and extend its piety or skein of sensibilities and affections and thus to form a way of life.

Christian doctrines help Christians and their communities interpret themselves and the many objects and others they interact with in relation to the Creator-Judge-Redeemer who is portrayed by the imaginative and mythopoeic resources of Scripture as they are configured by the paradigmatic proposal of redemption-in-Jesus-Christ. A Christ-configured engagement with Scripture, therefore, furnishes a constant baseline for Christian theology. Even so, we should recognize that specific Christian communities formulate theological statements and doctrines at particular places and times. Because their circumstances differ, their visions and portrayals of God, of themselves, and of the many objects and others they interact with also differ. Again, because the particular circumstances and conditions of specific communities constantly change, the work of depicting God in relationship to ourselves and to the many objects and others we interact with goes on in every Christian community in every time and place.

One may, in fact, look on preaching as a continuing attempt to interpret the contemporary life of a particular congregation—its affections, practices, and interactions with many objects and others in relationship to God—as God is understood in the light of the event of redemption-in-Jesus-Christ and the mythopoeic resources of Scripture. If so, then Christian theologies are simply the disciplined continuation of the interpretive work of preaching. As such, they do not merely repeat the imaginative and mythopoeic resources of Scripture. For one thing, a Christian theologian does not reflect on scriptural resources alone. Like a preacher, she also interprets current lives and affections in relationship with God, as God is understood in the light of Scripture's mythopoeic resources. She endeavors to interpret present life in relation to the deity. Therefore, we may say that Christian theology aims to clarify *current* life. It tries to illumine encounters, events, relationships, and structures in our present context, and thus it inevitably relates the mythopoeic resources of Scripture to contemporary knowledge and conditions.

For example, a contemporary Christian theology of creation as "world-ordered-by-God" will draw on the Genesis portrait of God arranging and ordering light, darkness, seas, earth, stars, plants, animals, and humans as male and female, as parts of God's good creation. However, in order to engage and interpret our current encounters with dependencies, benefits, limits, and possibilities, it will also take into account recent knowledge and interactions having to do with ecosystems, natural interdependencies, sexuality, gender, and justice. In fact, precisely by combining and intertwining these classical and current resources, a contemporary theology suggests that here and now there is something more and something other going on than often meets the eye. It suggests that, here and now, the world as we encounter it is God's creation, a "world-ordered-by-God" in which we experience the divine dynamism and creativity.[105]

Another reason why a Christian theology does not merely repeat the church's originating imaginative and mythopoeic resources is that Christian theologians consider these resources in the light of a tradition or subsequent history of interpretations and reflections offered by different Christian communities at different places and times. For example, a contemporary Christian interpretation of creation will be formulated not only in response to symbols, terms, and ideas in the early chapters of Genesis, Proverbs 8, and Colossians 1, and in response to present knowledge and interactions. It will also be formulated in conversation with past articulations of the doctrine (e.g., Thomas Aquinas and Karl Barth), previous interpretations of Genesis (e.g., John Calvin, Gerhard von Rad, and Carol Newsom), defining controversies (e.g., creationism versus evolution), and influential theological movements (e.g., liberation theology and feminist theology).

Again, Christian theology does not simply repeat received imaginative and mythopoeic expressions because it tries to develop more precise statements and to ask how these statements interconnect. Therefore, it is not simply a literary, poetic, and suggestive enterprise. It is also disciplined in the sense that it arranges statements and symbolic resources into an overall framework. This framework, in turn, yields a more or less comprehensive outlook or vision that deepens and extends a community's piety or disposition. And, in doing these things, Christian theology interprets, qualifies, and adjusts various symbols, mythic resources, and ideas so that they fit together as constituent parts of a larger whole.

Consider the scheme for Christian doctrine introduced in propositions 14 and 15 above. The doctrines of creation, sin, and redemption—each of which joins diverse mythopoeic images with interpretations of current situations and realities; each of which may be formulated in conversation with past doctrinal statements; and each of which may be stated in a disciplined and even propositional form—are now fitted together as parts of a single, more capacious framework. If we then ask, What are human beings? the answer will be a function of the entire scheme and the more general outlook it articulates rather than of any single symbol or statement. Humans are good creatures who are corrupted by sin and renewed by redeeming grace.

Proposition #17 As the disciplined development of a vision of God, the world, and ourselves, Christian theology strives to keep in touch with a com-

105. See Ottati, *Hopeful Realism*, 27–28.

> munity's religious affections, symbols, and images. It thus has much in common with hymns, prayers, sermons, liturgies, and the like. At the same time, however, it also tries to achieve a higher level of coherence and precision, to take into account new situations and realities, and to formulate a more general wisdom than is indicated by isolated symbols, images, and texts. The result is a kind of "in-between" discourse—one that emerges in close connection with the attempt to evoke, enrich, and criticize a particular piety, temper, life, and practice.

Consider an extended illustration: "Sin is radical and universal." Within a Christian frame of reference, this statement may be taken to explicate (among other things) certain symbolic ruminations of the apostle Paul, as well as a persistent skewing of human life intimated by narratives in Genesis 2:4b–11:9. It articulates the mythopoeic idea that people are both responsible and yet caught in the grip of a corrupting tendency. It also interprets our sorrow and remorse over ever-present and contemporary incidents of betrayal and misdirection in human interactions, whether these take place in personal relationships, relationships among ethnic groups or nations, relationships between people and nonhuman creatures, or what have you. Moreover, in a way that reflects important insights developed by Augustine and other classical theologians, our statement also indicates that in our experience there is no capacity of the person (reason, feeling, or will) that is not skewed by sin and its consequences, and that there is no person, community, or institution that is exempt from sin's effects. Thus understood, the proposition draws on Scripture, tradition, human history, and current interactions. It strives to keep in touch with and to interpret a community's affections. But it also makes use of the concepts of radicality and universality in order to modify the religious symbol "sin," and it presents a broader, more comprehensive portrayal of human fault than may be available in one or another hymn, prayer, or passage from Scripture.

Now introduce another sentence: "People are capable and good creatures." This elaborates an important aspect of the mythic symbol of God's creation, as well as our experiences of continued dependence on and gratitude toward God for capacities to intervene in the world and to attend responsibly to others. Among other things, it may be taken to mean that, as embodied creatures, persons are endowed with significant, even wondrous abilities, and that they are fitted for a good and abundant life in relationship with God and with others.

How, then, does the statement "people are good creatures" relate to the statement "sin is radical and universal"? To avoid conflict or inconsistency, further doctrinal reflection may emphasize that sin's radical and universal nature does not mean that humans are essentially evil. It may also note that sin or the human fault does not destroy the capacities of persons and communities for interventions and attentive and responsible interrelationships. Therefore, the statement "sin is radical and universal" does not remove all reasons to be grateful in response to our experiences of the good capacities and qualities of humans. Instead, sin and its deleterious effects will be taken to represent a recurrent misdirection and corruption of capacities and also of the good and abundant life for which we are fitted. Taken together, then, our statements about creation and sin encourage us to understand ourselves as "corrupted goods." And this, in fact, is part of the force of John Calvin's claim that "sin is not our nature but its derangement."[106]

This further reflection, then, helps both to qualify and to adjust our understandings of creation and sin so that they fit together into a *larger framework*. The larger framework expresses and shapes a piety that is critical of both an unqualified optimism and an unqualified pessimism about the tendencies and capacities of persons, communities, and institutions. The broader doctrinal wisdom represented by our two propositions links our gratitude and our sorrow, our admiration and our apprehension, at what humans both are and have become.

Proposition #18 The disciplined formulation of a contemporary theological vision makes a number of additional reflections and inquiries possible. These, in turn, suggest a variety of places or roles for theology in contemporary institutions of higher education. Even so, Christian theological reflections retain their ecclesial and practical aim.

A contemporary and disciplined theological vision takes into account questions that emerge as Christians and their communities confront current situations and realities, such as, How does faithfulness to the Creator, Judge, and Redeemer relate to the emergence of nuclear and other weapons of mass destruction, possibilities for fairness and equity in an era of globalization, fragile natural ecologies, the plurality of world religions, and life-extending technologies? Such questions necessarily bring Christian theology into conversations with additional sources of insight, for instance, political movements and the writings of historians, biologists, sociologists, geologists, economists, and philosophers. In fact, new knowledge and theories, for example, in genetics, biology, sociology, astrophysics, and so on, are themselves among the current situations and realities to be addressed as Christians and their communities interpret God, the world, and themselves.[107]

106. Calvin, *ICR* 2.1.10.

107. John Calvin, *The Second Epistle of Paul to the Corinthians and the Epistles to Timothy,*

The formulation of a disciplined theological outlook makes possible a variety of additional inquiries.

- It allows a Christian community to make comparatively clear theological claims and to ask what counts for and against these claims and the larger vision or picture they articulate. For example, what kinds of evidence count for and against the claim that the considerable capacities of persons and groups are persistently misdirected and skewed?
- It becomes possible to compare doctrinal outlooks or wisdoms put forward by different theologians and documents within the same Christian subtradition. For example, one may compare statements of Reformed Christian doctrine put forward by Friedrich Schleiermacher and Karl Barth, or by the Scots Confession of 1560 and the Belhar Confession written during the 1980s in South Africa.
- It allows us to compare theological outlooks and visions that are characteristic of different subtraditions within the broader Christian movement, for example, Augustinian and Pelagian, Roman Catholic and Lutheran.
- It allows people to compare Christian doctrinal outlooks and visions with outlooks and visions that have emerged within different religious movements, for example, Christian and Muslim, Christian and Buddhist.
- It allows us to compare theological outlooks, visions, or wisdoms with outlooks, visions, and wisdoms that arise in contexts and communities we do not ordinarily think of as religious, for example, a novelist's portrayal of the human prospect or a Marxist or Darwinist portrait of human possibilities and limits. (Should a novelist's portrayal of human interactions or a Marxist or Darwinist interpretation of human possibilities and limits be understood as "near equivalents" to theological outlooks, or should theological outlooks be called more or less "near equivalents" to them? The answer makes little difference. What matters is that each presents a vision that interprets human life in the world—and that these visions may be compared.)
- Again, it becomes possible to compare one or another aspect of a theolog-

Titus, and Philemon, trans. T. A. Small, vol. 10 of *Calvin's New Testament Commentaries: A New Translation*, ed. Thomas F. Torrance and David W. Torrance (Grand Rapids: Eerdmans, 1975), see esp. 363–64 on Titus 1:2. See also Calvin's comments on "Science as God's Gift" in *ICR* 2.2.15. The monotheistic bent of Christian piety may intensify a community's commitment to engage additional sources of insight. Consider, for example, Calvin's convictions that "all truth is of God," and that "if we regard the Spirit of God as the sole fountain of all truth, we shall neither reject the truth itself, nor despise it wherever it shall appear, unless we wish to dishonor the Spirit of God."

ical vision with one or another aspect of interpretations of ourselves, objects, and others offered by novelists, philosophers, geologists, biologists, sociologists, psychologists, physicists, politicians, and so on. For example, one might compare views of the modern nation-state offered by a political theorist and a Christian theologian. One might compare a Christian understanding of persons with an evolutionary biological understanding of mind, body, and personal identity. Or one might compare Christian portraits of sin and remorse with psychological understandings of guilt.

These additional inquiries will be understood, first and foremost, as attempts to develop and refine—in a way that engages culture and takes account of recent knowledge and experiences—the piety and practical vision of human life and the world offered by a particular Christian community. They will be understood as reflections that engage and support a particular piety and way of negotiating life. Indeed, we should note that, precisely because the formulation of a theological vision (which is indispensable for ecclesial teaching) enables us to join additional inquiries and pose further questions, the enterprise of ecclesial teaching itself generates further questioning and inquiry. This is one reason why Christian theology seems bound to include dialogical and apologetic dimensions, and why it stands against false dogmatisms that assume that nothing more is necessary for Christian faithfulness than is supplied by received doctrines and creeds. Nonetheless, it is also true that the additional inquiries suggest a variety of places or roles for theological inquiries and reflections in contemporary institutions of higher education.

- A good Christian theologian will be adept at exploring the imaginative and mythopoeic resources of Scripture, ways in which they interact with the patterns of affection and life that the Christian community supports, the history of a Christian community's attempts to interpret and engage current realities and events in the light of these resources, and the contemporary challenges the community faces as it tries to do so today. One or another college or university may have reasons to value such explorations because an affiliation with a Christian communion commits it to bringing resources of Christian faith into conversation with contemporary life and thought, because it offers professional programs for the training of a particular ecclesiastical community's leaders, or because it is a community of learning that invites people to develop, explore, and criticize the worldviews articulated by their religious traditions.
- A Christian theologian may become adept at exploring visions of human life in the world put forward by representatives of different religious

movements in a way that is sensitive to the patterns of sensibility and life they support. That is, she or he may offer nonreductive perspectives on comparative religious teachings.

- A theologian may become adept at identifying and comparing distinctive pieties. She or he may note that the emotionally charged and generally human question of meaning or of orienting vision and wisdom emerges with some frequency, whether in explicitly religious or in other venues, such as political communities and institutions, and contemporary literature. He or she also may note that, in these contexts as well, answers to the question often make use of particular clues and suggestions in order to depict and envision the whole of human life and the world. That is, at some level, other communities also traffic in imaginative and mythopoeic discourse. Moreover, since the question of orienting vision, outlook, or wisdom is difficult to suppress, he or she may also point out that politicians, scholars, novelists, culture critics, political essayists, and so on engage in something analogous to doctrinal reflections more often than some secularists care to admit, especially when they discuss ethics and policy, the nation and its cause, or meaning in life, in the context of pluralistic societies. The point, of course, is not so much to catch politicians, political theorists, pundits, novelists, and scholars doing something that some may not recognize, as to ask what counts for and against their ruminations, to compare them with near equivalents, and thus to inquire about alternative *pieties and visions* of human life and the world.[108]
- Theology, in fact, may be understood as a matter of "worldviewing"—an inquiry that critically analyzes and constructs views of human life in the world in relation to the pieties, attitudes, and dispositions they evoke, their coherence, their practical consequences, and the findings of other disciplines and sciences.[109] And this points to a possible role for theology in contemporary colleges and universities, whether or not they have explicit religious affiliations or missions. Theology may be valued simply as a discipline that critically analyzes and constructs worldviews or orienting visions of human life in the world. Of course, there is no reason why this sort of reflection should be confined to theologians. The critical evaluation and construction of orienting worldviews might be taken up by

108. Theological ethicist Max L. Stackhouse refers to "metaphysical-moral visions" in *Public Theology and Political Economy: Christian Stewardship in Modern Society* (Grand Rapids: Eerdmans, 1987), 142–43, 152.

109. On theology, conceptual outlooks, world pictures, and worldviews, see Julian N. Hartt, *Theological Method and Imagination* (New York: Seabury, 1977), 10, 77; see also Kaufman, *IFM*, 35–41, 70–93.

> philosophers, by scientists interested in the sapiential implications of their own work, and by literary critics interested in interpreting worldviews that emerge, for example, in novels by Charles Dickens or Alice Walker.

For all their diversity and variety, however, and for all their ability to spawn and encourage more general reflections about various pieties and orienting visions, *Christian* theological reflections and inquiries will retain an ecclesial and practical aim, namely, to explicate, promote, deepen, and extend a Christian community's distinctive piety, interactive orientation, wisdom, and way of negotiating life. Christian theology aims to help people live in a way that is appropriately responsive to God as Creator, Judge, and Redeemer.

Chapter Two

The Formation and Arrangement of Theological Statements

My understanding of how to formulate and arrange theological statements reflects two interlocking convictions. First, Christian theology serves the enterprise of building up people in a piety or a basic disposition that supports a faithful way of living. Second, it does so by envisioning the world and ourselves in relation to the Creator-Judge-Redeemer.

The Formation of Theological Statements

Proposition #19 Certain recurrent theological stances represent malformations of the Creator-Judge-Redeemer idea and also shape and express basic dispositions or pieties that have exceedingly negative consequences for faithful living.

An account of these malformations, their distorted pieties and practical consequences, indicates important boundaries, what older textbooks called heresies, that is, teachings contrary to church dogma. I will make use of historical terms such as "Gnosticism," "Manichaeanism," and "Pelagianism" to name recurrent malformations of Christian theology, piety, and faithfulness, but I have abandoned the word "heresy" due to some of its historical associations. Determinations of heresy often have been made by hierarchical and nonrepresentative institutions, and sometimes they have been accompanied by severe penalties, including imprisonment, torture, and execution. One objective of heresy judgments was to enforce agreement; but surely a Protestant is bound to object that all doctrinal judgments are both fallible and subject to challenge.[1] Indeed, ever

1. See the Scots Confession of 1560, the Westminster Confession of Faith, and the Confession of 1967, in *BOC* 3.20; 6.175; 9.03.

since the Reformation of the sixteenth century, it has been painfully evident that one Christian community's heresy may be another's orthodoxy. What may be termed an Enlightenment objection is that judgments and penalties concerning heresy sometimes suppressed significant intellectual inquiries. Anyone familiar with more recent Marxist, liberationist, and deconstructionist discussions will also recognize that historical judgments and penalties concerning heresies often reflected distributions of power and functioned as instruments by which dominant groups oppressed less powerful persons and communities.[2] It is thus hardly surprising that, in contemporary English, the word "heretic" is associated with nonconformity and dissent, while the word "orthodox" implies conservatism, conventionality, and rigidity.[3]

Basically, I agree with Schleiermacher's effort to interpret "heresy" as a distortion of a proposed (and argued for) interpretation of the essence of Christianity.[4] However, I also believe that the language of *formation* and *malformation* is more appropriate to the function of theology, as it contributes to the building up of people in a piety and way of faithful living and it avoids much of the negative baggage associated with the words "heresy" and "orthodoxy."

Spiritualist and Moral Dualisms

Piety and faithful living are distorted by spiritualist and moral dualisms. *Spiritualist dualisms* (of which some forms of Gnosticism furnish historical examples) have devalued the world and our participation in it. Typically, this form of dualism envisions human beings as spirits mired, caught, or entrapped in a physical body, and the redeemer delivers or releases human spirits from a bad

2. See Rosemary Radford Ruether's important discussion of dominant and marginal strands of the Christian tradition in *Sexism and God-Talk: Toward a Feminist Theology*, with a new introduction (Boston: Beacon, 1993), 33–38. Ruether finds important insights articulated by movements that were deemed "heretical," and so do I.

3. *Merriam-Webster's Collegiate Dictionary*, 10th ed., s.v. "heretic." Paul Tillich said that the word "heresy" could not be saved because persecutions have ruined it. See Tillich, *Life and the Spirit, History and the Kingdom of God*, vol. 3 of *Systematic Theology* (Chicago: University of Chicago Press, 1963), 176.

4. Friedrich Schleiermacher, *CF*, #21–#22 (pp. 95–101); Schleiermacher, *A Brief Outline of the Study of Theology*, trans. Terrence N. Tice (Richmond, VA: John Knox, 1970), #54–#62 (pp. 35–38). However, because judgments about the essence or core of Christianity depend significantly on one's particular Christian subtradition and its specific construal of Christian believing, as well as on additional subjective elements, I believe that we simply must learn how to live with a plurality of particular judgments. See also Ernst Troeltsch, "What Does 'Essence of Christianity' Mean?" in Troeltsch, *Writings on Theology and Religion*, ed. and trans. Robert Morgan and Michael Pye (Louisville: Westminster John Knox, 1990).

(or at least inert) material realm. Some classical forms of Gnosticism go so far as to envision two gods at cross-purposes: a creator, who is responsible for the material world, and a deliverer, or redeemer, who returns human spirits to the spiritual realm.[5]

Or consider the Christian theology of Origen of Alexandria, in which, due to their failure to cleave to the one God, good immaterial souls or spirits fall into bodies and the material world. From my perspective, this confounds Creator and Judge in a way that compromises the goodness of creation, and it also misconstrues redemption as release from bad bodies and the material realm. Therefore, even apart from an affirmation of two gods, God the Redeemer, or the faithful God of grace, may be closely associated with spirit and thoroughly distanced from physical reality. The result is that a part of creation (namely, the realm of spirit) will be sharply distinguished from the devalued material world of physical bodies, institutions, and nature, a realm of materiality that faithful persons are counseled to avoid or else to tolerate and endure as a tiresome (but passing) necessity.

The exclusive association of the Redeemer with human spirit and the consequent devaluation of the material world distort piety by undercutting senses of gratitude and thanksgiving in response to the good gifts of the material world and physical embodiment. Occasionally they also support postures in life that are especially uncomfortable with women and the necessarily physical and "earthy" aspects of motherhood.[6] Moreover, in recent as well as classical times, this theo-

5. Robert M. Grant, *From Augustus to Constantine: The Thrust of the Christian Movement into the Roman World* (New York: Harper & Row, 1970), 124–25. For the Gnostic teacher Valentinus, the creator, named Ialdabaoth, made humans, and his mother, Sophia, inserted a divine spirit or spark in them. "In order to redeem both her and mankind, Jesus was sent down to collect the scattered spiritual seeds and restore them to the 'pleroma' (cf. Col. 1:19) or 'fullness' of spiritual being. . . . The Valentinian system is dualistic, but it is less dualistic than that of Saturnus or the *Apocryphon of John*. . . . In the *Apocryphon* there is a primeval struggle between Ialdabaoth [the creator] and Christ." Or, in my terms, there is an overt struggle between Creator and Redeemer.

Marcion of Pontus interpreted the resurrection of the body as the salvation of the soul in the context of a similar struggle: "For it was the purpose of the coming of Jesus to abolish all the works belonging to 'this world' and to its Creator, the 'ruler of the universe.' . . . When he came, 'he did not come into that which was his own, but into that which was alien to him'" (Jaroslav Pelikan, *The Emergence of the Catholic Tradition (100–600)*, vol. 1 of *The Christian Tradition: A History of the Development of Doctrine* [Chicago: University of Chicago Press, 1971], 73). The literature on Gnosticism is immense, and contemporary scholarship is alert to significant variations and diversities. Here I wish only to point to a basic dualism of spirit and matter and indicate some of the difficulties it makes for envisioning God as Creator-Judge-Redeemer.

6. For Marcion, "the natural world was made up of 'beggarly elements,' among which [he] especially included reptiles and insects. Particularly repulsive to him was the 'uncleanliness'

logical posture also often supports a strong identification of faithfulness with "spiritual" experiences or an inner life of contemplation as well as a negative disposition toward social structures and institutions.[7] Spiritualists fail to see the importance of engaging, maintaining, criticizing, and altering institutions and practices that are crucial for human well-being, such as civil government, patterns of economic production, and courts of law.

Loosely defined, Gnosticism emphasizes a spiritual journey or quest for fulfillment and meaning away from and beyond the material world. There are, no doubt, many reasons for the recent popularity in some circles of early Gnostic gospels, not the least of which is that their discovery challenges established forms of Christianity. It may also be that world-transcending spiritual quests seem especially attractive to religiously inclined but ecclesially uninterested intellectuals at a time of intractable cultural, economic, ethnic, and political conflicts. Nevertheless, the attractions of personal serenity and inner spiritual meaning are in danger of spawning fundamental dispositions or pieties of world denial and world escape that come to expression in and are shaped by malformations of the Creator-Judge-Redeemer idea.

I should also mention a more modernist and activist strain. The liberal Protestant Albrecht Ritschl claimed that we are spiritual personalities who are called to overcome ethically irrational nature and to transcend it toward morally universal (and spiritual) ends.[8] Ritschl's theology supported efforts at social reform, and prominent proponents of the Social Gospel took up some of its primary themes. Even so, the emphasis on human spirit over against ethically irrational nature can distort important aspects of creation piety by making common cause with reductively technical sensibilities that fail to appreciate how persons and communities are enmeshed within natural ecologies. More than a tinge of spiritualist dualism is discernible in postures that regard the material world as

---

of sex and of childbirth, none of which could have anything to do with the salvation of man" (Pelikan, *Emergence of the Catholic Tradition*, 73).

7. An interior, largely privatized spirituality may come to characterize the pieties of those who prefer to maintain the status quo (as the focus on spirit generally spares current society from prophetic critiques). Sigmund Freud and Karl Marx pointed out that it may also offer psychic compensations for the poor and oppressed that function to keep these groups satisfied in their dependent social positions. See Karl Marx, *Critique of Hegel's Philosophy of Right*, trans. Annette Jolin and Joseph O'Malley (Cambridge: Cambridge University Press, 1970), 131ff.; Sigmund Freud, *The Future of an Illusion*, trans. W. D. Robson-Scott (Garden City, NY: Anchor, 1964), 47–53.

8. Albrecht Ritschl, *The Christian Doctrine of Justification and Reconciliation*, trans. H. R. Mackintosh and A. B. Macaulay (Clifton, NJ: Reference Book Publishers, 1966), 199, 326, 610–14, 620.

little more than raw material for productive and purposeful manipulation at the behest of the human spirit—thus, in effect, devaluing the goodness and integrity of creation and nonhuman nature.[9]

Moral dualism is a posture represented classically by Manichaeanism and the vision of a cosmic clash or contest between irreducibly good and evil powers. In some more recent and popular forms, good is associated with God, while evil is associated with the devil, Satan, or the "evil one," who, in effect, becomes a second god or metaphysical power and principle independent of God (though quite often this is not explicitly stated). Here evil and good are metaphysically basic or fundamental; they are unalloyed and pure, and they cannot be turned, converted, or changed. Because there is no hope for turning it toward good, evil must be destroyed in the end, or else defeated and forever separated and imprisoned. Because good is and shall remain good, the only question is whether it will prevail.[10]

From the perspective of the theology I am developing here, such a posture harbors both a moralistic pessimism and a moralistic optimism. Moralistic pessimism takes root in the idea that, unlike sinful realities with respect to the Creator-Judge-Redeemer, evil realities are ontologically evil rather than skewed or corrupted goods.

In effect, the Puritan John Milton agreed with me when he portrayed Satan not as an evil god but as a fallen angel who was originally good in *Paradise Lost*, book 1, lines 34–40:

9. Spiritualist malformations of Christian life and vision are sometimes associated with docetic Christologies, which portray Jesus Christ as a redeeming manifestation of eternal and spiritual divinity who only appears in bodily form but does not actually take up a fleshly body. That is, the one through whom God redeems does not really take up the life of the body and is not closely associated with creation or the material realm. Indeed, the denial of the reality of the physical body of Christ may be said to exclude the reality of truly human life and nature in him, and so it becomes difficult to see how he can mediate a transformative grace and renewed and genuinely human life to embodied persons. But, of course, the Nicene Creed, which associates Jesus Christ with the Creator in a most intimate manner, flatly opposes all of this: "We believe in one God the Father Almighty, maker of heaven and earth, and of all things visible and invisible; And in one Lord Jesus Christ, the only-begotten Son of God . . . by whom all things were made; who for us men, and for our salvation . . . was incarnate . . . and was made man."

10. See Peter Brown, *Augustine of Hippo: A Biography* (Berkeley: University of California Press, 1969), 47–51. Classic Manichaeanism assumes that the evil in humans, since it cannot come from a good God, represents an invasion of the good by a hostile force "equal in power, eternal, totally separate." Salvation, then, requires that our baser or evil nature be split off and taken away—or forever discarded.

Th' infernal Serpent; hee it was whose guile
Stirred up with Envy and Revenge, deceiv'd
The Mother of Mankind; what time his Pride
Had cast him out from Heaven, with all his Host
Of Rebel Angels . . .
Him the Almighty Power
Hurl'd headlong flaming from th' Ethereal Sky.[11]

Moralistic optimism follows from the idea that those associated with the forces of good are not subject to persistent corruption. Creation piety is distorted because there is no single, unified world that is valued by the one Creator-Judge-Redeemer and provokes awe and wonder—and for which we are thankful. Instead, there are good realities (an in-group) on the side of goodness that largely escape judgment and are distinguished from bad realities (an out-group) on the side of evil, which remain largely beyond hope for renewal. And here we see two additional results: a severe diminution of the more far-reaching sense of possibilities and renewal in relationship with the Creator-Judge-Redeemer, and, among those identified with the good, truncated senses of judgment and remorse.

The train of deleterious and even terrifying consequences that may accompany stances of this kind is not difficult to imagine, especially if one equates particular political powers and cultural and ethnic communities with good and evil principles. For example, we may note a Manichaean streak in some thinking about the United States and its role in the world. Whether the perceived opponent is the former Soviet Union or Islamic civilizations today, the American nation is sometimes understood to be an unalloyed good on the side of God pitted against an unalloyed and satanic evil.

Manichaeanism is a worldview in black and white, without significant moral ambiguities and shades of gray, where our own virtue goes largely unquestioned and where our enemies make few profound moral claims on us.[12] (Think, for

11. Pelikan, *Emergence of the Catholic Tradition*, 136. Pelikan suggests that, in early Christian contexts, Manichaean views took root in the sharp interest in demons that accompanied the beginnings of monastic piety and emphasized a conflict between a hero, such as Saint Antony, and the demonic powers. At points, Manichaean dualism was closely related to antimaterialist aspects of Gnosticism, teaching that "the god of this world," or the devil, is an independent deity, whereas orthodox church teaching emphasized that the demons are fallen creatures of the one good God, and God exercises dominion over them. Accordingly, "a council at Braga in 563 decreed: 'Whoever denies that the devil was originally a good angel created by God, contending instead that he arose from the chaos and the darkness and has no Creator but is himself the principle and substance of evil . . . let him be anathema.'"

12. By contrast, Peter Beinart, "The Rehabilitation of the Cold-War Liberal," *New York*

example, of the difficulty communities sometimes have recognizing their moral duties to prisoners.) Certainly, there is no place in it for what Reinhold Niebuhr understood to be basic to forgiveness, namely, "the demand that the evil in the other shall be borne without vindictiveness because the evil in the self is known"—a demand borne by the sort of self-knowledge that accompanies a sense of remorse.[13] In short, this is not a theological vision or worldview in which all are God's good creatures, all sin and experience God as Judge, and possibilities for turning and renewal emerge for morally ambiguous persons, communities, and institutions.

I should also mention *double predestinarian* schemes that recur in Reformed Protestantism and sometimes entail an insistence that only some people are the objects of redeeming grace. For example, the Westminster Confession of Faith of 1647 affirms that Jesus Christ dies only for the elect (or those chosen in eternity before the foundation of the world).[14] Significantly, Reformed thinkers are not of one mind about this. The affirmation that Jesus Christ dies only for the elect is not present in another early Presbyterian document, the Scots Confession of 1560. Karl Barth complained that Calvin's doctrine of double predestination truncates the good news of the gospel and threatens to make life "a gloomy affair."[15] H. Richard Niebuhr criticized both Augustine and Calvin for failing to follow through on "the great eschatological possibility" of the transformation of the world and of humanity's ruined life, and instead succumbing to a dualism of an eternal heaven and an eternal hell.[16]

In the end, double predestinarian schemes offer no hope for the reprobate. They suggest a Manichaean-like pessimism about those who cannot be turned and thus must simply be separated from the good or discarded. This, in turn, threatens to distort the Creator-Judge-Redeemer idea and the piety it both expresses and shapes. God creates all, and all are mired in sin. But when compared with the elect, the reprobate appear to have been differently created, brought into being as creatures who live, by definition, beyond the scope of God's redeeming grace. Again, with respect to the reprobate at least, divine judgment loses all rehabilitative significance and reduces to casting-away status those whom it has determined shall

Times Magazine, April 30, 2006, 42, points out that Reinhold Niebuhr emphasized our own moral fallibility and limitations.

13. Reinhold Niebuhr, *An Interpretation of Christian Ethics* (New York: Seabury, 1979), 137.

14. *BOC* 6.014–6.021; 6.071. "God did, from all eternity, decree to justify all the elect, and Christ did, in the fullness of time, die for their sins and rise again for their justification" (6.071).

15. Karl Barth, *The Humanity of God*, trans. John Newton Thomas (Richmond, VA: John Knox, 1960), 49.

16. See H. Richard Niebuhr, *Christ and Culture*, foreword by Martin E. Marty, preface by James Gustafson, 50th anniversary ed. (San Francisco: HarperSanFrancisco, 2001), 215–18.

not be redeemed. The result is a truncated piety in which judgment and remorse no longer are ordered toward renewal and no longer support a good hope for all. Indeed, one finds it difficult to avoid the conclusion that the words "Creator," "Judge," and "Redeemer" have each been assigned a double meaning.

Overconfidence in Human Effort

Piety and faithfulness may also be distorted by theological postures that express and shape an overconfidence in human effort and striving. The classic representative is Pelagianism. Thus, while Augustine maintained that grace and the Spirit must turn human hearts if we are to love goodness for itself, Pelagius could write as follows: "When I have to discuss the principles of right conduct and leading a holy life, I usually begin by showing the strength and characteristics of human nature. By explaining what it can accomplish, I encourage the soul of my hearer to the difficult virtues. To call a person to something he considers impossible does him no good."[17]

From the perspective of the theology I am developing here, one problem with Pelagianism is its comparatively weak appreciation for the radically debilitating effects of human sinfulness and corruption. The less than radical and universal sense of sin correlates with a diminished sense of repentance and a diminished apprehension of God as Judge. A related problem is that Pelagianism envisions people as being able to rehabilitate themselves by their own powers, capacities, and efforts (perhaps with the assistance of a disciplined holy community). This correlates with a diminished idea of God as Redeemer and a diminished sense of our radical dependence, since there is no dire need for redeeming grace. Instead, there is a naïve or unbalanced optimism about the abilities of people to be good and to correct their faults through their own discipline.

Practically speaking, the overly optimistic view of what persons can accomplish often supports a stringent moralism and even a reliance on moral heroism as communities try to form people to do good (with rather limited success). Indeed, in the face of persistent human corruption, backsliding, and recalcitrance, the resulting moral rigorism may give way to a cynical pessimism about the human condition altogether. Or it may support a moralistic outlook that no longer hopes for corrupted or "evil" persons to turn and, at the same time, both overestimates the goodness of "the righteous" and underestimates their being liable to judgment. In these instances the practical consequences resemble those of Manichaean dualism.[18]

17. See Pelagius's "Letter to Demetrias," in *Theological Anthropology*, ed. and trans. J. Patout Burns (Philadelphia: Fortress, 1980), 40.

18. See Douglas F. Ottati, *Hopeful Realism: Reclaiming the Poetry of Theology* (Cleveland:

Schleiermacher argues that, for Manichaeanism, the ability of baser human nature to receive redeeming influences disappears. That is, since evil is metaphysically original and opposed to God, redemption is not possible. For the Pelagian, by contrast, the hindrance is so small that "the need of redemption is reduced to zero," or else merely to the need of persons in their weaker moments for other persons to encourage them in doing good.[19]

Where they are "baptized" by a few stray Christian images and phrases, some forms of American optimism and liberalism, with their notions of the "self-made person" and "pulling yourself up by your own bootstraps," may be regarded as recent variations on Pelagian themes. A related development is modernist overconfidence in science, technology, and economic production (and so also in scientific, technically accomplished, and economically productive humans) to furnish all meaning and value, create better persons and societies, and solve all serious difficulties. Yet another development, I suspect, is the postmodern confidence that we "create" our own worlds—not scientifically, technically, and economically so much as linguistically—since this implies that we alone bestow meaning and value and that, apart from our own efforts and apart from our technical and linguistic constructions, the world has no valence, trajectory, or worth. We thus have no sense of our dependence on a Creator-Judge-Redeemer to confer meaning and value, because we ourselves are exclusively competent to do so. A peril of both the classical and more recent overconfidence in human effort and in human goodness is that, when faced with historic and persistent failures to achieve righteousness, restrain inordinate interests, solve perennial injustices, and overcome destructive hatreds, it may tumble into a despairing cynicism or even moralistic dualism.

Proposition #20 Traditional textbooks do not treat another recurrent malformation of theology and piety: *anti-Judaism*, a devaluation of Jewish religion that often mixes with anti-Semitism, or hatred of the Jewish people.

One might argue that anti-Semitism has already insinuated itself into the New Testament.[20] For example, Matthew 27 portrays Pilate, the Roman governor, as one who recognizes that the Jewish priests and elders have handed over Jesus "out of

Pilgrim, 1999), 29–30. Naïvely optimistic theological stances are often associated with so-called Nazarene or Ebionitic Christologies that portray Jesus as a good man more than a reconciler. He is the teacher of true morality, the embodiment of a new standard whom we are exhorted to follow. We may also be encouraged to follow him by appeals to positive and negative incentives, such as mundane successes and heaven, or mundane sorrows and hell.

19. Schleiermacher, *CF*, #22 (pp. 97–99).

20. See, e.g., Craig A. Evans and Donald A. Hagner, eds., *Anti-Semitism and Early Christi-*

jealousy." Pilate's wife tells her husband to "have nothing to do with that innocent man," and when the crowd calls for Jesus to be crucified, Pilate asks, "Why, what evil has he done?" Then come verses whose consequences have often been cruel and disturbing. "So when Pilate saw that he could do nothing, but rather that a riot was beginning, he took some water and washed his hands before the crowd, saying, 'I am innocent of this man's blood; see to it yourselves.' Then the people as a whole answered, 'His blood be on us and on our children!'" (Matt. 27:24–25).

The question of anti-Semitism is also acute in the Gospel of John, where "the Jews" are presented as hostile to Jesus and his followers. For example, "the Jews" seek to kill Jesus (5:18), they plot against him (11:45–53), and they demand that Pilate hand him over to them for execution (18:28–19:6). When Jesus first appears to the disciples on the day of his resurrection, they are meeting behind locked doors "for fear of the Jews" (20:19). Used in this way, the expression "the Jews" obscures the fact that Jesus and his followers also *were* Jews, and it inculcates highly negative attitudes. Therefore, it is not unusual for scholars to observe that "in its canonical status the Gospel of John has nurtured (if not conceived) repugnant attitudes and evoked abhorrent actions on the part of Christians toward their Jewish colleagues."[21] For centuries, interpretations of the Fourth Gospel have "legitimated some of the most outrageous behavior of European Christians, including pogroms and the attempted genocide of the Holocaust." One might even conclude that "the language used to speak of the Jews is so violently anti-Semitic that the Fourth Gospel should not be used in today's churches."[22]

Patristic and Medieval Theology

Claims about Jews by patristic theologians such as John Chrysostom, Jerome, and Augustine included the following: (1) the Jews have rejected God; God, therefore, has rejected them, and their harsh treatment is God's judgment; (2) the Jews are Christ-killers and guilty of deicide, not only because some called for Jesus's crucifixion long ago but also because the subsequent refusal of Jews to accept Christianity constitutes a continuing acquiescence to Jesus's execution; (3) Jews intend to harm Christians; (4) Jews are immoral. Some Christian writers, Augustine among them, favored comparatively moderate policies toward Jews; others pressured the Roman state to curtail toleration and also condone the

anity: Issues of Polemic and Faith (Minneapolis: Fortress, 1993), 55–211; William R. Farmer, ed., *Anti-Judaism and the Gospels* (Harrisburg, PA: Trinity Press International, 1999).

21. Robert Kysar, "Anti-Semitism and the Gospel of John," in Evans and Hagner, *Anti-Semitism and Early Christianity*, 126.

22. Francis J. Moloney, SDB, *The Gospel of John*, Sacra Pagina (Collegeville, MN: Liturgical Press, 1998), 9. However, Moloney himself does not come to this conclusion.

destruction of Jewish property. Stimulated by polemics, Christian mobs sometimes attacked synagogues and burned them, with the approval of bishops such as Ambrose of Milan.[23]

Medieval church leaders pressed rulers to enact laws and policies that restricted Jewish worship, "quarantined" Jews in ghettos, restricted their contact with Christians, and limited ways that they might earn a living. There were attempts to convert Jews, sometimes forcibly, and when many did not convert, some Christian leaders accused rabbis and others of lying about the content of Scripture.[24] Sporadic violence against Jews continued, for example, in pogroms associated with the Second Crusade, and the "deep-rooted, hate-engendering piety of the Passion . . . turned Holy Week into a time of dreaded horror for the Jews of Christian Europe."[25]

Like nearly all medieval Christian theologians, Thomas Aquinas believed that all Jews, and not just some of Jesus's contemporaries, were guilty of Jesus's death and so deserved to be punished.[26] He claimed that the exile of the Jews from grace (which now is available only in the church's sacraments) is punishment for their part in Jesus's crucifixion and a sign of Christianity's triumph. God's rejection, however, is only temporary: though not every Jew will be saved, in the end the Jewish people will convert. Aquinas argued, too, as had Augustine, that Christianity benefits from the testimony of the Jews to the antiquity of Hebrew prophecies. Practically, he sought to limit social and commercial contact with Jews and claimed they should not be allowed to hold Christian slaves, employ Christian servants, or exercise official authority over Christians. Nevertheless, Aquinas also believed that Jews should be free from forced conversion, free to worship, and free to raise their own children as Jews.[27]

23. Marcel Simon, "Christian Anti-Semitism," in *Essential Papers on Judaism and Christianity in Conflict: From Late Antiquity to the Reformation*, ed. Jeremy Cohen (New York: New York University Press, 1991), 131–73.

24. John Y. B. Hood, *Aquinas and the Jews* (Philadelphia: University of Pennsylvania Press, 1995), 36–37, observes: "The preaching campaign of Pablo Christiani in Provence and Aragon in the late 1250s and early 1260s represented the first serious attempt by the medieval Church to convert the Jews in its midst." Despite this Dominican's lack of success in winning converts, he was authorized by Louis IX to preach in synagogues in and around Paris as late as 1269.

25. Heiko A. Oberman, *The Roots of Anti-Semitism in the Age of Renaissance and Reformation*, trans. James I. Porter (Philadelphia: Fortress, 1984), 124.

26. Aquinas recognized that, at Jesus's crucifixion, some Jews had not known Jesus was the Christ and thus were not guilty of consciously killing the Messiah. However, he reasoned, the miracle of Jesus's resurrection made it clear who he was, and, by refusing the apostles' preaching, persecuting them, and continuing to wait for the Messiah, the Jewish people as a whole deny Christ (Hood, *Aquinas and the Jews*, 62–63, 72–75).

27. Hood, *Aquinas and the Jews*, 77–79, 99–100.

Reformation Theology

Attempts at conversion, expulsion, and quarantine continued during the Reformation.[28] Early in his career, Martin Luther emphasized that Jesus was a Jew, and he also urged toleration because he believed that, with the Protestant rediscovery of the gospel, the Jews might convert. By the 1530s and 1540s, however, and particularly as he believed that the last judgment was near and the devil would be unleashing his final and strongest attacks on the church, the German Reformer regarded Jewish resistance as a stubborn, blasphemous, and intolerable apostasy.[29]

Luther's tract *On the Jews and Their Lies* (1543) argued that (1) "in honor of our Lord and of Christendom," Christians should set fire to synagogues and schools, and bury what will not burn; (2) Jews' houses, "where they pursue the same aims as in their synagogues," should also be destroyed (instead, they can live in barns); (3) their prayer books, talmudic writings, and Bibles should be confiscated; (4) rabbis should be "forbidden to teach . . . on pain of loss of life and limb"; (5) safe conduct for Jews on the highways should be abolished; and (6) young Jews should be forced to earn their living at menial labor. However, Luther judged that even these measures could not guarantee that Jews would not harm "us or our wives, children, servants, cattle, etc." Neither could they keep the Jews' blasphemies from continuing. Therefore, the only solution was to expel the Jews from "our country," as had already been done in "France, Spain, Bohemia, etc."[30]

Calvin claimed, as he commented on Matthew 27:25, that the Jews "commit an irreparable crime" and "wicked error" in demanding Jesus's execution. Even under these circumstances, he said, God proves the fidelity of the promise and the durability of the covenant with Abraham by rescuing from destruction those Jews who are elected by free grace.[31] Commenting on Romans 11:28–32, Calvin notes: "The counsel of God, by which He had once condescended to choose

28. Here is a list of events that Heiko A. Oberman used to outline the condition of Jews in Europe on the eve of the Reformation: Edward I had banished Jews from England, while Erasmus praised France for having outdone all other nations in "nearly cleansing" the Jews from its kingdom; in 1494, King Ferdinand and Queen Isabella expelled Jews from Spain; those who went to Portugal were forced to flee or be baptized in 1499, though even those who converted "were subjected to pogroms that culminated in the dreadful massacre of Lisbon in 1506" (Oberman, *Roots of Anti-Semitism*, 95).

29. Mark U. Edwards, "Against the Jews," in Cohen, *Essential Papers on Judaism and Christianity in Conflict*, 371.

30. Martin Luther, *The Christian in Society IV*, ed. Franklin Sherman, vol. 47 of *LW*, 268–72, 285–88.

31. John Calvin, *Harmony of Matthew, Mark, and Luke*, trans. William Pringle, vol. 3 in *Calvin's Commentaries*, Calvin Translation Society (Grand Rapids: Baker Books, 1998), 288–89.

them for Himself as a peculiar nation, stands firm and immutable."[32] In general, Calvin's theology of grace and election entailed a high appreciation for God's covenant with Israel, the Mosaic law, and the value of the Old Testament, and some believe that, over time, these positions contributed to a comparatively positive attitude toward Jews among many Reformed Christians and communities.[33] Even so, the German Reformed theologian Martin Bucer joined others in urging Landgrave Philip of Hesse to allow Jews to reside in the electorate only under stringent conditions, for example, that Jews pledge not to harm Christians, refrain from religious disputations with Christians, be required to attend Christian sermons, discontinue using the Talmud, and engage only in menial labor.[34]

So much has gone wrong here that one scarcely knows where to begin. Many classical interpreters assumed that the Gospels were simple historical reports, and more recent literary and historical criticism helps us to see features and qualities in the texts that this assumption obscured. For example, the way Matthew 27:24–27 and the Gospel of John portray "the Jews"—not to mention the opposition between Paul and "the Jews" in Acts—appears to reflect conflicting interests associated with changing relationships between Jewish Christians and other Jews, Paul's mission to the gentiles, and more positive emerging relationships between Christian communities and Roman authorities. Other texts seem to interpret Roman suppression of the Jewish revolt of 67–73 CE (including the destruction of the temple at Jerusalem) and the expansion of the church among the gentiles (more so than among Jews) in the Roman world as reflecting those conflicting interests.[35]

32. Indeed, says Calvin, Paul makes Jews and gentiles equal in guilt, and "it is the mercy of God alone which saves, and which may be bestowed on both." Again, "Paul simply means that both Jews and Gentiles obtain salvation from no other source than the mercy of God" (*The Epistles of Paul the Apostle to the Romans and to the Thessalonians,* trans. Ross Mackenzie, in *Calvin's New Testament Commentaries: A New Translation*, ed. Thomas F. Torrance and David W. Torrance [Grand Rapids: Eerdmans, 1973], 257–58).

33. Salo W. Baron, "John Calvin and the Jews," in Cohen, *Essential Papers on Judaism and Christianity in Conflict*, 391–94.

34. Baron, "John Calvin and the Jews," 382; Oberman, *Roots of Anti-Semitism*, 96; Gerhard Falk, *The Jew in Christian Theology* (Jefferson, NC: McFarland, 1992), 85–87.

35. Against this background, the Gospel of John emphasizes that "the Jews were divided" by Jesus's words and actions. See also Dominic M. Crossan, OSM, "Anti-Semitism in the Gospel," *Theological Studies* 26, no. 2 (June 1965): 189–215; Gerald O'Collins, SJ, "Anti-Semitism in the Gospel," *Theological Studies* 26, no. 4 (December 1965): 663–66; Joseph A. Fitzmyer, SJ, "Anti-Semitism and the Cry of 'All the People' (Matt. 27:25)," *Theological Studies* 26, no. 4 (December 1965): 667–71; Daniel J. Harrington, SJ, *The Gospel of Matthew* (Collegeville, MN: Liturgical Press, 1991), 390.

A Malformation of the Creator-Judge-Redeemer Symbol

Christian anti-Semitism and Christian anti-Judaism have roots in a dark human tendency to think ill of divergent groups. Our brief survey also shows that both attitudes were intertwined with interpretations of Jesus's crucifixion as well as of the continuation of the Jewish community and its conversion (or not) to Christianity. The point I want to emphasize here, however, is that anti-Judaism often gains support from the idea that Christianity and the New Testament have to do with a God of grace, love, and forgiveness in Jesus Christ, whereas Judaism honors a God of law, wrath, and judgment portrayed in the Old Testament.

This idea sometimes emerges from misguided attempts to heighten the distinctiveness and originality of Jesus. It can be associated with interpretations of Galatians (apart from Romans) that assume Paul's message of God's adoption or acceptance of the gentiles must also entail God's rejection of the law as a way of salvation for Jews and its replacement by grace in Jesus Christ.[36] It may also be associated with interpretations of 1 John and the "new commandment" given in Christ that we love one another. Indeed, some Christian theologians have understood Christianity to be the antithesis of Judaism: that is, Judaism, as a legalistic religion of obedience, law, and judgment, serves mainly as a negative precondition for the saving truth of the gospel of grace. Consider, for example, Hegel's early insistence that Judaism set itself and the world over against an infinite commanding power, but that Jesus's message amounted to the extinction of law and duty in love. "To the Jewish idea of God as their Lord and Governor, Jesus opposes a relationship of God to men like that of a father to his children."[37]

One may respond to such assertions by pointing to passages in Hebrew Scripture that express the faithfulness, forgiveness, and love of God, as well as to New Testament passages that honor the law and the prophets. One may also observe that the (largely polemical) picture of Judaism as a religion of works righteousness is skewed, since in Hebrew Scripture the covenant with Israel is freely offered and upheld by God, while Israel's obedience to the law is a faithful response to God's life-giving and gracious covenanting deed. If one observes that the justice and the will of God as portrayed in Hebrew Scripture sometimes exact a terrible price and make for considerable theological ambiguities, surely one

36. John G. Gager, *Reinventing Paul* (New York: Oxford University Press, 2000), 27–31, 44–50, offers a helpful account of new views of Paul and also of "Paul-based Christian anti-Judaism."

37. See G. W. F. Hegel, *Early Theological Writings*, trans. T. M. Knox (Philadelphia: University of Pennsylvania Press, 1971), 223, 253. Hegel maintained that "Jesus was opposed to the Jews on the question of their Most High." That is, Jesus directly confronted the underlying principle of the Jewish spirit, or its conception of God, as "infinite Sovereign Lord."

may also observe similar prices and ambiguities in the New Testament regarding God's will, Jesus's crucifixion, the eschaton, sin, and judgment.

For our purposes, it is crucial to recognize that many forms of Christian anti-Judaism entail serious malformations of the Creator-Judge-Redeemer symbol. Indeed, we should take care lest a major theological point gets lost in the shuffle: both Christians and Jews acknowledge the God who creates, judges, and redeems (or delivers). The implied *split* between God as commanding Judge (in Judaism) and God as loving Redeemer (in Christianity) simply suppresses or forgets that, properly understood, judgment and redemption go together: the God who judges redeems and the God who redeems judges.

Christian anti-Judaism insists that, when it comes to understanding the deity, Christianity and Judaism are sharply discontinuous and even opposed. Therefore, if Christianity is right and true, Judaism must be wrong and false. Despite strong indications in the Gospels themselves, such as the genealogies of Jesus and aspects of the Sermon on the Mount, anti-Judaism denies that the event of Jesus Christ stands in an important measure of continuity with Judaism and the Hebrew Scriptures. This denial exerts pressures on the Creator-Judge-Redeemer idea to the point where some conclude that the true, redeeming God made known in Jesus Christ is entirely different from the Creator-Judge-Deliverer who covenants with Israel and the Jews. Or alternatively, it may be supposed that God changes from the vindictive judge allegedly portrayed in the Old Testament to the loving Father allegedly portrayed in the New. But this amounts to the portrait of a God at cross-purposes rather than of a dependably faithful God of grace who is Creator-Judge-Redeemer all along.

The additional point to emphasize is that the theological stances typical of Christian anti-Judaism encourage and express severe malformations of piety and faithfulness. By insisting that apprehensions of divine commands and judgment are restricted to Judaism and superseded in Christianity, they diminish senses of obligation, repentance, and remorse and also invite a sense of superiority and self-righteousness. They truncate the critical appreciation for our human solidarity in sin as well as our common dependence on grace. And they support practical consequences as deleterious and just as terrifying as the worst moral dualism.[38]

38. Consider, e.g., Schleiermacher's remarks in *The Christian Faith* about the relationship between Christianity and Judaism. These are based largely in his insistence that in Jesus of Nazareth there arises a new form of religious consciousness and a new religion, which is in no sense a continuation of Judaism, as well as in his contention that "the Old Testament appears simply a superfluous authority for dogmatics" (Schleiermacher, *CF*, #12 [pp. 60–62]; #27 [p. 115]). The position has the advantage of discouraging some Christocentric Christian traditions of Old Testament interpretation that assume that Jews are unable even to interpret

Proposition #21 Particular Christian subtraditions may articulate distinctive understandings of God as Creator-Judge-Redeemer that shape and express distinctive variations in piety and faithfulness.

The connection between Christian theology and church teaching helps us understand why there is a plurality of historically particular Christian theologies: the rise of distinct subtraditions is endemic to the dynamics of faithful formation. By means of preaching, teaching, and pastoral care, communities try to form the people of God at particular places and times. They train people to interact with things at Antioch in 380, at Paris in 1270, and at Cape Town in 2011 in a way that is faithfully responsive to the God disclosed in Jesus Christ. But at these places and times, the circumstances and realities, the challenges and the intellectual resources with which Christians interact differ, change, and develop. Over time, subcommunities and subtraditions thus emerge that are characterized by distinctive lines of faithful formation, practice, and theological reflection.

Traditional Emphases

In addition, partly because so many biblical texts themselves were written in the service of practical and pastoral aims, there is also plurality within the Bible.[39] Subsequent Christian communities, therefore, find themselves having to formulate normative and characteristic approaches to interpreting Jesus Christ and Scriptures (since there is, for example, no single unified Christology in the New Testament). Under the pastoral pressures of forming faithful persons at particular places and times, they select and develop different themes, images, and ideas from biblical portraits and texts. Consider, for example, Roman Catholic emphases on the Gospel of John, the incarnation, and nature and grace; Lutheran

their own scriptures aright. But one wonders whether it obscures important similarities in Jewish and Christian pieties. We might also look at Schleiermacher's comments in *Speeches* on Judaism's understanding of humanity's relationship to "the Eternal" as "a relation of universal immediate retribution, of a peculiar reaction of the Infinite against every finite thing that can be regarded as proceeding from caprice" (Schleiermacher, *On Religion: Speeches to Its Cultured Despisers*, trans. John Oman [New York: Harper & Row, 1958], 239).

39. This observation is common in current biblical studies, where the theologies of biblical writers and communities often are correlated with specific circumstances and challenges they faced. Consider, for example, the comparatively new reading of Paul on justification, grace, and law that owes more to an estimate of the pastoral challenge of going to the gentiles and expanding the community of God's people to include non-Jews than to later understandings of sin, such as the one developed by Martin Luther. See Gager, *Reinventing Paul*; Stanley K. Stowers, *A Rereading of Romans: Justice, Jews, and Gentiles* (New Haven: Yale University Press, 1994).

emphases on Paul, crucifixion, law and gospel; and Mennonite emphases on the Synoptic Gospels, Jesus's reign, and radical discipleship.

These theological emphases connect with distinctive understandings of God as Creator-Judge-Redeemer. For example, when compared with Lutheran emphases on atonement, sin, and grace, Roman Catholic emphases on incarnation, nature, and grace correlate with an understanding of God that stresses continuity between creating and redeeming as well as a diminished emphasis on sin and God as Judge. The distinctive theologies, in turn, shape and express characteristic variations of Christian piety, especially with respect to senses of remorse and renewal, and judgments as to how reasoning about moral law directs faithful living. Mennonite emphases on radical discipleship and the new law revealed in Jesus correlate with a comparatively sharp understanding of God's judgment on fallen institutions, principalities, and powers that are opposed to Christ's reign. They also accord with an emphasis on God's redeeming activity as a great reversal of the predominant trajectories of history. This, in turn, shapes and expresses a distinctive piety with respect to moral law and a sense of moral direction, as well as a comparatively selective pattern of participation in civil societies and institutions.[40]

Variations such as these help to explain why there is no generic Christian theology and why claims that a particular position is or is not "orthodox," or that a given theology does or does not affirm "the God of Jesus Christ," often do little to advance scholarly debates. We need to know whose theologies, which Christologies, and which strains of piety are at issue, how they compare, and what counts for and against them, because the dynamics of church teaching, faithful formation, and theological reflection make for a historical *plurality* of theologies, characteristic pieties, and patterns in faithful living.[41]

Continued Developments

In addition, subtraditions also continue to develop. This sometimes leads to practically significant emendations of received stances, such as Roger Williams's creative revision of Calvinist ideas of civil society, religious liberty, and fairness in seventeenth-century Rhode Island, or Karl Barth's sharp Christocentric turn

40. I continue to believe that H. Richard Niebuhr offers one of the most helpful accounts of these and other varieties of Christian theology in *Christ and Culture*, and I outline a case for this judgment in "*Christ and Culture*: Still Worth Reading after All These Years," *Journal of the Society of Christian Ethics* 23 (Fall 2003): 121–32.

41. See Douglas F. Ottati, "How Can Theological Ethics Be Christian?" *Journal of the Society of Christian Ethics* 31, no. 2 (Fall/Winter 2011): 3–21; see also Ottati, "Whose Gospel? Which Culture?" *Insight: A Journal of the Faculty of Austin Seminary* 108, no. 2 (Fall 1993): 41–57.

in twentieth-century Europe.[42] Further subdivisions and strands thus emerge *within* longer-standing theological subtraditions, and some of these also connect with significant variations in piety and practice. Compared with earlier Calvinist insistence on creation as the theater of God's wisdom and glory, for example, Barth's Christocentric turn encourages and expresses a less robust creation piety. Moreover, Barth's emphasis on God's humanity in Jesus Christ correlates with his rejection of double predestination, a different portrait of God as Judge, and correspondingly altered senses of obligation, remorse, joy, and gratitude.[43] More recently, feminist varieties of Roman Catholic theology have developed understandings of God as Creator, of sin, and of redemption in Jesus Christ that accord with enhanced senses of gratitude and thanksgiving for embodied human life, and they support revised postures on marriage and family, justice, and religious leadership that some other Catholics do not share. In fact, Rosemary Radford Ruether's classic book *Sexism and God-Talk* might be read as a theological expression of and encouragement to a distinctive strain of Catholic piety and faithfulness.[44]

We should make similar observations about the impact of liberationist emphases and themes. During the late 1960s in North America, black theologians sought a theology more engaged with their experiences of oppression and often-thwarted drives toward freedom. They recognized important connections between their own reflections and the work of liberation theologians trying to join Catholic moral theology with experiences of the poor and marginalized in Latin America. The close association of the gospel with lived experiences of oppression is much of what James H. Cone meant by his assertion that "God is black."[45] J. Deotis Roberts noted that black theology is bound up with experiences of recurrent oppression at the hands of whites and that, in this context, it generates distinct perspectives and insights about the gospel.[46] More recently, James H. Evans Jr. has claimed that "African-American theological development can best be understood as the convergence of an African-derived worldview, the complexities of the experience of slavery, oppression, survival, rebellion, and adjustment in the New World, and their encounter with the biblical text."[47]

42. See *On Religious Liberty: Selections from the Works of Roger Williams*, edited and introduced by James Calvin Davis (Cambridge, MA: Belknap Press of Harvard University Press, 2008), 1–45.

43. Barth, *The Humanity of God*, 37–65.

44. Ruether, *Sexism and God-Talk*.

45. James H. Cone, *A Black Theology of Liberation* (Philadelphia: Lippincott, 1970), 120–25.

46. J. Deotis Roberts, *A Black Political Theology* (Philadelphia: Westminster, 1974), 47–73.

47. James H. Evans Jr., *We Have Been Believers: An African-American Systematic Theology* (Minneapolis: Fortress, 1992), 2.

Womanist theologians and theological ethicists, such as Katie Cannon, insist that oppression among blacks has also been shaped by gender differences and that attention should be paid to a theological and ethical vision that emerges from the experiences and realities of black women.[48] *Mujerista* theologies offered by Hispanic women and *Minjung* theologies offered by Korean activists also emphasize the critical importance of particular experiences of oppression in order to understand Jesus and the Gospels correctly. For our purposes, a crucial point is that each of these groups emphasizes a close link between participation in experiences of oppression and liberation and understandings of Jesus Christ, sin, and grace. These accord, in turn, with distinctive understandings of God as Judge and Redeemer (or Liberator) that sculpt and express senses of gratitude, remorse, solidarity, possibilities (or hope), and direction, and thus lend a distinctive cast to various Catholic and Protestant pieties.

Acknowledging Particularity

An appreciation for historic plurality should not be mistaken for the conviction that anything goes or that one must exempt particular subtraditions, strands, factions, and their views from serious theological criticism. There is, after all, nothing to guarantee that every group that calls itself Christian will be genuinely responsive to the historic symbols of the Christian movement, let alone an adequate and sustained interpretation of God as Creator-Judge-Redeemer. This,

48. Katie G. Cannon, "Hitting a Straight Lick with a Crooked Stick: The Womanist Dilemma in the Development of a Black Liberation Ethic," *Annual of the Society of Christian Ethics* (1987): 165–77, reprinted in Lois K. Daly, ed., *Feminist Theological Ethics: A Reader* (Louisville: Westminster John Knox, 1994), 33–41. Consider, too, James H. Cone's statement that "before the emergence of the literature of Black Theology, Black people's invisibility in white theological deliberation was not challenged." Indeed, Cone observed further that, even after some white theologians began to respond to black theology, "the majority remained adamant in their silence, because they contended that theology is concerned with the *universal* dimension of the gospel, which transcends the particularities of the Black experience." See Gayraud S. Wilmore and James H. Cone, *Black Theology: A Documentary History, 1966–1979* (Maryknoll, NY: Orbis, 1979), 135, 136.

The point about plurality is strengthened further when we realize that, before the emergence of black theology, few whites would ever have considered that there is any such thing as "white theology." And, as Helmut Gollwitzer observed, the recognition that there is such a thing is itself theologically significant. "Whoever belongs to the camp 'white theology,' as soon as he is confronted by 'black theology,' has every reason to become conscious of the specific historical and societal conditioning of his theology and his view of the Christian message. . . . Ideology critique as self-criticism is now required of him, but not merely as an individual; the tradition itself in which he stands and which he tries to develop further is being questioned as a whole" (Gollwitzer, "Why Black Theology?" in Wilmore and Cone, *Black Theology*, 152).

in fact, is the point of propositions #19 and #20 above. Even so, an honest and unflinching appreciation for historic plurality indicates that every developed Christian piety and theology is a view from somewhere in particular within the wider Christian movement.

A contemporary Christian theologian should therefore acknowledge her preference for and indebtedness to a particular subtradition of theology and piety in order to signal to others (both Christians and non-Christians) the particular place from which she views things. In some respects this is simply a matter of practical serviceability and clarity. It allows those who share a theologian's standpoint to estimate her reflections as a contribution to the faithful formation of persons in their common ecclesial community and its current situation. It helps others estimate with greater accuracy (and perhaps also greater appreciation) just where their own visions and subtraditions cohere with or depart from her theological interpretations. But it is also a matter of acknowledging one's own Christian particularity as well as the legitimate particularities of other Christian thinkers and groups, and so of avoiding a kind of imperial overreach by refusing to pass off one's own theological outlook as if it were universal Christian theology plain and simple.

Proposition #22. The theology presented here emerges from the Reformed Christian subtradition.

The origins of the Reformed subtradition, its distinctive piety and pattern of faithfulness, were multiple and intertwined with diverse contexts in sixteenth-century Europe. Although Calvin's work at Geneva proved preeminent from the first, there were also Ulrich Zwingli and Heinrich Bullinger in Zurich, John Oecolampadius in Basel, Martin Bucer in Strassburg and at Cambridge, John Knox in Edinburgh, Zacharias Ursinus and Caspar Olevianus in the Palatinate, and many more. Multiple figures operating in multiple centers, in different languages, and in varied contexts produced multiple theological treatises, confessional documents, liturgies, and polities.

Today, Reformed Christianity is a worldwide movement with about two hundred church bodies in a hundred countries. Compared with Lutheranism, another great Protestant movement, it has not been as concentrated, either in its origins or its subsequent developments, and it can seem rather loosely wound. Its style of piety, theology, and faithfulness has not been as dependent on a single towering figure; neither has it been as tied to a limited number of confessional documents written in the same region over a brief period of time.[49]

49. John H. Leith, ed., *Creeds of the Churches: A Reader in Christian Doctrine from the Bible to the Present*, rev. ed. (Richmond, VA: John Knox, 1973), 62.

Unlike Catholicism, Reformed Christianity has no tradition of a single hierarchical institution and teaching authority. In fact, it exhibits an aversion to centralized structures. For my purposes here, the movement's characteristic strain of piety and faithful living accords with four broad and interconnected theological emphases.

Reformed theology insists on the adjustment of persons to God.

This comes to expression in affirmations articulated by Jonathan Edwards and the Westminster Shorter Catechism. God's chief end in creating the world is God's own glory, and, according to Edwards, the glory of the God who creates and redeems is not God in isolation but God in relationship with all things. The catechism famously claimed that the chief end of the human being is to glorify God and enjoy God forever, or, if we accept Edwards's idea, to be oriented not simply toward ourselves but toward the encompassing reality of God and all things in which we participate. We might call this a "Reformed theological realism," or the fundamental understanding—expressed in different ways by Calvin, Edwards, Barth, H. Richard Niebuhr, and others—that we need to be adjusted to divine reality.

For Calvin, the adjustment entails a true piety that joins reverence for God, or the power on which we and all other creatures depend, with a love of God induced by the knowledge of God's many benefits. It links senses of dependence on and gratitude toward the Creator and Governor, who is the source of every good gift with gratitude to and love for the Redeemer made known in Jesus Christ.[50] The result is a fundamental disposition that, in worship and life, encourages persons and communities to turn away from their own isolated interests toward the deity. Reformed piety presses people to attend to the God who creates and bestows, who judges the inordinately self-centered and contracted postures of persons and groups, and who lures them to refocus their lives. The linchpin is what Edwards called a sense for the excellence of God and of divine things.[51] Reformed piety means *metanoia*, that is, being caught up in the messianic event of Jesus Christ, the Word who discloses the faithful God of grace, the person-for-others who embodies a direction in life oriented by love of God and neighbor. It means a life reordered and reformed by a Christ-configured discernment of the glory of God.

A broad picture emerges. In our relationship to God as Creator, we humans are good creatures, equipped for an abundant and good life in the world, fitted and sustained for responsible interactions with God and others, or for true

50. Calvin, *ICR* 1.2.1; 1.2.2; 1.6.1.

51. Jonathan Edwards, *Religious Affections*, ed. John E. Smith, vol. 2 of *WJE*, 2:240–66.

communion with God in community with others. Caught in the grip of a warping tendency, however, we become narrowed, curved in upon ourselves, irresponsible, and isolated, so that our community with the neighbor and communion with God are broken. We are radically corrupted, diminished, and fragmented, and we fall away from what we are equipped and sustained to be. Nevertheless, the faithful God of grace refuses to abandon creatures to sinful corruption. God as Judge encourages individuals and communities, through the deleterious consequences of their misalignment and fragmentation, to turn from that corruption. Through reconciliation in Christ and renewal in the Spirit, humans encounter God the Redeemer, who forgives and enables them to turn again toward God and the inclusive world of other creatures. That is, regenerating grace brings a new tendency, direction, vocation, and disposition because it entails the conversion and rehabilitation of persons as faithful participants in the divine commonwealth—or their genuine readjustment to God and neighbor.

> *Reformed theology affirms the priority of God's Word, recognizes that church teachings are subject to criticism, and remains open to wisdom and truth wherever those might be found.*

These affirmations shape and express an intellectual attitude that accords with the adjustment of persons to the Creator-Judge-Redeemer as the source of all truth. They accord with a temper of mind that attends to God's truth, is wary of corrupted interests that often skew human insight, but also is thankful for created gifts of intelligence and understanding.

> As we do not rashly condemn what good men, assembled together in general councils lawfully gathered, have set before us; so we do not receive uncritically whatever has been declared to men under the name of the general councils, for it is plain that, being human, some of them have manifestly erred, and that in matters of great weight and importance. So far then as the council confirms its decrees by the plain Word of God, so far do we reverence and embrace them.[52]

These are the opening sentences of the chapter on general councils, their power and authority, in the Scots Confession of 1560. They express not only typical Scottish contrariness but also a classic Protestant idea that Reformed communities share with Lutherans and others: church teaching and tradition are

52. The Scots Confession of 1560, in *BOC* 3.20.

subordinate to Scripture and subject to criticism in light of Scripture.[53] Indeed, as the deliberations and decisions of all persons, communities, and institutions not only draw on limited insight but also are subject to the skewing effects of sin, *all* church statements, including those made by general councils, are fallible, a point that connects with the refusal of Calvin and the company of Genevan pastors to sign the Nicene Creed as a test of orthodoxy in a theological disputation at Lausanne in 1537.[54]

Part of the Protestant idea is that we may go back behind accumulated teachings and traditions to the original documents of the Christian movement as the standard of criticism. Of course, these classic originals also stand in need of interpretation, and thus the Scots' confidence that they will be able to confirm or deny conciliar decrees "by the plain Word of God" may justifiably be regarded as a recurrent Protestant hubris.[55] Even so, the critical regard for church teaching is a feature of a Reformed temper of mind. It not only draws on convictions about the priority of Scripture and the universality of sin but also reflects the humanism of John Calvin and other Swiss Reformers, such as Ulrich Zwingli, who shared Erasmus's concern to work from the best editions of classical texts rather than only from later glosses and interpretations.[56] As is typical of other Reformed Protestants, the writers of the Scots Confession affirm an important role for theological teaching and tradition. (Otherwise, why write a confession at all?) The net result is that appeals to church teaching are understood to contribute to inquiries of a certain kind. The broader theological tradition is never simply about (authoritative) church teaching per se; appeals to church teachings and theological traditions are significant to the extent that they help us to get at the truth of the gospel.

53. Thus did the Scottish divines, in their preface, promise to alter whatever in their confession someone could prove from Scripture to be wrong. "If any man will note [anything] in our Confession contrary to God's Holy Word, that it would please him of his gentleness and for Christian charity's sake to inform us of it in writing; and we upon our honor, do promise him that by God's grace we shall give him satisfaction from . . . Holy Scripture, or else we shall alter whatever he can prove to be wrong." Nevertheless, as the Reformation in Scotland proved rather passionate as well as violent, depending on the nature of the complaint, it may also have been prudent for anyone who posted one to have booked passage to a New World." *Book of Confessions: Study Edition [Part I of the Constitution of the Presbyterian Church (U.S.A.)]* (Louisville: Geneva, 1999), 31.

54. W. Nijenhuis, *Ecclesia Reformata: Studies on the Reformation*, trans. Mary Foran (Leiden: Brill, 1972), 73–96.

55. A point made in some detail by Heinrich Bullinger in chapter 2 of his Second Helvetic Confession, *BOC* 5.010–5.011.

56. François Wendel, *Calvin: Origins and Development of His Religious Thought*, trans. Philip Mairet (Grand Rapids: Baker Books, 1997), 31.

At the same time, Calvin himself regarded the arts and sciences as God's good gifts, maintaining that "if we regard the Spirit of God as the sole fountain of truth, we shall neither reject the truth itself, nor despise it wherever it shall be found, unless we wish to dishonor the Spirit of God." On this basis, he commended the writings of ancient jurists, philosophers (especially the Stoics), mathematicians, and physicians.[57] He also claimed that those who observe the world with the aid of disciplines such as astronomy, medicine, and natural science behold evidences of God's "wonderful wisdom." Jonathan Edwards pondered, drew, and described the movements of spiders partly because he regarded natural philosophy as the study of the manner of God's acting in the world.[58]

Obviously, the Reformed subtradition has had its share of disagreements and conflicts over freethinking and inquiry. Calvin prepared charges against Servetus, even if it is true that Roger Williams's likeness appears on the Reformation wall at the University of Geneva. This is also a subtradition that, in North America anyway, later found itself torn by the fundamentalist-modernist controversy. Even so, if the Reformed disposition of mind routinely points to the Word of God attested in the indispensable biblical witness, it has also been willing to appeal to the church's theological tradition as well as to sources of insight well beyond the confines of both Scripture and historic Christianity.[59] The reason is that we ought to be adjusted to God, and, as Calvin himself insisted, "all truth is of God."[60]

57. Calvin, *ICR* 2.2.15; 1.5.2.

58. Jonathan Edwards, *Scientific and Philosophical Writings*, ed. Wallace E. Anderson, vol. 6 of *WJE*, 6:145–69, 353.

59. The historical episode most likely to keep some contemporary Reformed theologians from recognizing this is the disagreement in twentieth-century Europe between Karl Barth and Emil Brunner over our ability to know God's will. Brunner claimed that revelation furnishes us with knowledge of the good—of personal freedom, responsibility, and community—which, in turn, forms a basis for generalizations about created orders, such as family, labor, and the state. Barth, who lamented vestiges of a natural theology even in the classical Reformers, complained that Brunner had embraced a theology of compromise that threatened the independence of revelation from alien sources of insight. Much might be said about this debate, including that Barth was the more creative theological mind and that his insistence on revelation alone proved decisive for his response to National Socialism and the German Christians who compromised with Hitler's government. Nevertheless, Barth's insistence that theology be based in Jesus Christ or the Word of God alone represents a departure from classical Reformed positions. See Emil Brunner, *The Divine Imperative*, trans. Olive Wyon (Philadelphia: Westminster, 1937), 51–60, 291ff.; Brunner, *Natural Theology*, ed. John Baillie (London: Geoffrey Bles, 1946), 71–72; Barth, *CD* I/1:6, 72. At points, Barth seems confused about the status of appeals to "the law of nature inborn in men" in Luther and Calvin, which, he is concerned to point out, do not ground an "independent ethics" (see *CD* I/2:783).

60. John Calvin, *The Second Epistle of Paul the Apostle to the Corinthians and the Epistles to Timothy, Titus, and Philemon*, trans. T. A. Small, in *Calvin's New Testament Commentaries:*

The Reformed subtradition emphasizes the reordering of both inward disposition and outward action in thankful response to the gifts and the grace of God.

Calvin, like Luther, was concerned about the proper motive for morality. For him, we should not be moral because we believe that we can merit or deserve salvation by our moral commitments and performance. We cannot. Forgiveness is free; election is by the grace of God alone. This is why our typically prudential reasons for being moral, such as to gain God's favor or to be healthy, wealthy, and wise, need reordering. True moral interest and truly good works proceed instead from thankfulness for the goodness and grace of the Creator-Redeemer.

To this fundamental insistence and disposition Calvin joined a distinctive emphasis on moral law. Like Luther, he affirmed that the law restrains evil through threats of punishment, and that it also accuses us or shows us how far short we fall of true righteousness. But he added a "third and principal use which pertains more closely to the proper purpose of the law," namely, to guide and exhort the faithful in their efforts to perform good actions. Thus, for Calvin, the gospel of grace and free forgiveness is not simply the end of the law, and love is not all one needs to lead a faithful life. One also needs standards of justice and fidelity, rules against murder and stealing, and so forth. Law also follows gospel: it remains an essential ingredient of faithful life not only as a tutor in remorse and repentance but also as an indispensable compass or guide for directing faithful practices.[61]

A New Translation, ed. Thomas F. Torrance and David W. Torrance (Grand Rapids: Eerdmans, 1964), 363–64. Calvin makes this statement in his commentary on Titus 1:12: "From this passage we may gather that it is superstitious to refuse to make any use of secular authors. For since all truth is of God, if any ungodly man has said anything true, we should not reject it, for it also has come from God. Besides, since all things are from God, what could be wrong with employing to His glory everything that can be rightly used in that way?"

61. Zacharias Ursinus and Kaspar Olevianus, the young authors of the Heidelberg Catechism, were at one with the Genevan Reformer when they placed their discussion of good works and the law under the rubric of thankfulness. The Puritan casuist Richard Baxter also did a characteristically Calvinist thing when, refusing to reduce the Christian life to dispositions alone, he instructed husbands and wives in their mutual duties, soldiers on the necessity of having a just cause, and physicians on the importance of helping the poor as well as those who were able to pay. Again, Barth's Calvinist understanding of gospel and law and his rejection of Lutheran attempts to separate them were close to the center of his controversy with German Christians. "What those good folk obviously want," he wrote, "—a church that is only inward and not at all outward—is identical with what National Socialism wants of the church" (*BOC* 4.086–4.115). See also *A Christian Directory*, vol. 1 of *The Practical Works of Richard Baxter* (Ligonier, PA: Soli Deo Gloria, 1990), 1:431–38, 740, 743, 771–72, 775.

But, of course, if Reformed piety deems love alone insufficient, if it is unwilling to relinquish specific lawlike standards for conduct, it also understands love to be entirely necessary. Edwards thus maintains that, among other things, regenerating grace extends our love for ourselves and of our groups toward others and so turns us away from what is merely partial and toward what is more truly general or universal. Horace Bushnell believed that persons in Christ are brought to a new reigning love, so that "life proceeds from a new center." Similarly, H. Richard Niebuhr claimed that radical faith in the Creator-Redeemer entails a devotion to God and God's universal community of being that transforms our lesser loyalties to self, nation, race, and so on.[62] Lesser loves are reordered within the expansive frame of love to God and to all things under God. Genuine faithfulness and piety in the Reformed tradition thus entail the adjustment of the whole person to God, or the adjustment of both inward disposition and outward practice.

Reformed theology expresses and shapes a "worldly" faithfulness.

Calvin criticized "certain fanatics" who boast that, once we are in Christ and "transported to God's Kingdom," it is "unworthy" of us "to be occupied with worldly things." Instead, he claimed, the Creator-Judge-Redeemer has established civil government, that "its function among men is no less than that of bread, water, sun, and air," and that "its place and honor is far more excellent." He believed that God has "entrusted [to magistrates] the business of serving him through their office," and that "civil authority is a calling not only lawful before God, but also . . . by far the most honorable of all callings, in the whole life of mortal men." Indeed, he said, it is the responsibility of magistrates "to represent in themselves . . . some image of divine providence, protection, goodness, benevolence, and justice." Turning to civil laws, Calvin noted that God is a lawgiver, that varied historical constitutions are founded on natural equity, and that Christians should not resist the judicial process.[63]

These statements shape and express a fundamental disposition toward participation in civil government and society that differs from the attitude fostered

62. Edwards, "Dissertation II: The Nature of True Virtue," in *Ethical Writings*, ed. Paul Ramsey, vol. 8 of *WJE*, 8:575–88, 609–18; H. Richard Niebuhr, *Radical Monotheism and Western Culture, with Supplementary Essays* (Louisville: Westminster John Knox, 1993), 31–37, 49–77; Horace Bushnell, *The New Life* (London: Richard D. Dickinson, 1885), 69.

63. Calvin, *ICR* 4.20.2; 4.20.3–4, 6; 4.20.16, 19. Calvin commended "restraint and humanity in war," and he claimed that magistrates properly exercise violent means "not only to restrain the misdeeds of private individuals by judicial punishment, but also to defend the dominions entrusted to their safekeeping" (see *ICR* 4.20.11–12).

by Peter Rideman and others, who saw civil government in terms of a fundamental conflict between Christ's rule and the reign of fallen principalities and powers. For Rideman, Christian piety or faithfulness yielded a commitment to follow Jesus rather than other (alien) lords.[64] By contrast, Calvin understood Christian piety and faithfulness as a response to the universal reign of the Creator-Judge-Redeemer that is disclosed in Jesus Christ but in which civil government also may mediate God's providence, goodness, and justice. Therefore, Calvin understood government service, soldiering, the legal profession, and others as legitimate callings and vocations, as avenues for directing us to pursue justice and combat injustice, or as lines of both faithful and public service before God.

Calvin's view of civil society was representative of a spirit of faithful participation in God's world that yields a "worldly Christianity." A participatory piety was also characteristic of later Puritans, such as William Perkins and Richard Baxter, who described the callings of husbands, wives, schoolmasters, doctors, lawyers, ministers, and soldiers.[65] Again, somewhat like Calvin, Abraham Kuyper, the Dutch prime minister in the early twentieth century, held that God's single government of the world takes place by means of relatively independent spheres, such as politics, religion, and scholarship, which are structured by appropriate institutions, such as civil government, the church, and the university. And thus, for Kuyper also, true thankfulness and gratitude, true piety and adjustment to God, dispose us to participate responsibly in all these institutions.[66]

Proposition #23 The theology presented here is also indebted to an ecumenical and liberal strand of the Reformed tradition in North America that supports a social Christianity, is willing to revise inherited beliefs and practices in the light of new knowledge and inquiries, accepts plurality within both the Reformed tradition and the wider Christian movement, and appreciates the importance of conversations among world religions.

This strand is largely made up today of elements within the United Church of Christ, the Presbyterian Church (PCUSA), and elements of the United Church of Canada. By and large, it does not extend to some other communions with Reformed roots, such as the Orthodox Presbyterian Church, established in 1936

64. Peter Rideman, *An Account of Our Religion, Doctrine, and Faith Given by Peter Rideman of the Brothers Whom Men Call Hutterians* (Rifton, UK: Plough, 1970), 105, 107–8, 111–14.

65. See Douglas F. Ottati, *Reforming Protestantism: Christian Commitment in Today's World* (Louisville: Westminster John Knox, 1995), 125–35.

66. Abraham Kuyper, *Lectures on Calvinism* (Peabody, MA: Hendrickson, 2008), 77–79, 85, 92.

in order to uphold biblical inerrancy and other fundamentalist tenets, and the Presbyterian Church in America, which split from the PCUSA in the United States in 1973 in order to reject theological liberalism and the PCUSA's decision to ordain women as deacons, elders, and ministers.

Social Christianity

By "social Christianity" I mean a faithful posture that emphasizes social justice, that intentionally engages and critiques social powers, practices, and realities, and that represents a further development of the worldly emphasis discernible in Reformed Christianity.[67] A pivotal point in this development was the commitment of the Social Gospel movement to address problems associated with urbanization and industrialization during the late nineteenth and early twentieth centuries, though the commitment had roots in the work of earlier abolitionists, such as the Congregationalist Theodore Dwight Weld and the New School Presbyterian Henry Ward Beecher. During the 1880s, Washington Gladden, a Congregationalist minister who supported labor unions, and the Presbyterian-cum-Episcopalian economist Richard T. Ely launched a critique of laissez-faire capitalism.[68] The movement also enlisted the energies of Jane Addams, a Presbyterian suffragette who established Hull House in Chicago to furnish social and educational services to immigrants and to train social workers. A number of denominations founded social service commissions and departments; among the more important of these were the Social Services Department of the Congregational Churches and the Department of Church and Labor that was organized by the Presbyterians.[69]

For our purposes, it is crucial to note that social Christianity involves a variation in piety. Walter Rauschenbusch, the most important exponent of the Social Gospel, described a religiosity refracted through "the medium of solidaristic social feeling" that expands the sense of obligation toward prophetic demands for social justice and differs from the comparatively individualistic and otherworldly piety fostered by older orthodoxies. His prayers and reflections shaped and expressed corresponding expansions of the sense of sin or remorse toward "social repentance" and the sense of possibilities toward "redeeming the social order."[70] For Rauschenbusch, these sensibilities and affections accorded with

67. Reinhold Niebuhr uses the term to refer approvingly to the work of Walter Rauschenbusch (*An Interpretation of Christian Ethics*, preface).

68. Gary Dorrien, *The Making of American Liberal Theology: Imagining Progressive Religion, 1805–1900* (Louisville: Westminster John Knox, 2001), 313.

69. Walter Rauschenbusch, *Christianizing the Social Order* (New York: Macmillan, 1913), 17.

70. Walter Rauschenbusch, *Prayers for the Social Awakening* (Boston: Pilgrim, 1909, 1910),

a theology that takes the kingdom of God, an inherently social and political symbol, as its primary doctrine. In fact, as a portrait of "the supreme purpose of God," the kingdom symbol indicated that God judges and redeems communities, institutions, and societies.

Christian realists such as John Bennett and Reinhold Niebuhr criticized the naïve optimism of the Social Gospel, even as they continued to develop a politically and socially engaged posture.[71] Niebuhr's Christian realism emphasized penetrating analyses of sociopolitical interests and powers, a suspicion of social progress, and an Augustinian appreciation for the radical and persistent nature of sin, though, in contrast to mystical otherworldliness, he also affirmed a prophetic religion that tries to discover meaning in the varied facts and events of history and society. With respect to piety, Niebuhr radicalized a socially sensitive sense of repentance and self-criticism by noting that even our highest achievements are always infected by sin and that the highest moral ideal not only inspires us but also convicts us.[72] (Therefore, "Christ is our judgment as well as our hope.")[73] Hence, while he recognized that tolerable approximations of justice are possible, when humans are inspired by the law of love, Niebuhr also insisted that kingdom fulfillment always remains beyond history. His more realistic social Christianity thus entailed a correspondingly more radical apprehension of God as Judge than did Rauschenbusch's Social Gospel.

Martin Luther King Jr.'s campaigns for civil rights and poor people, as well as his trenchant theological reflections, also made major contributions to social Christianity in America and the extension of feelings of obligation and hope toward social justice. King, who read *Christianity and the Social Crisis* while he was in seminary, accepted Niebuhrian criticisms of Rauschenbusch's belief in progress and "unwarranted optimism." At the same time, he insisted, "Rauschenbusch gave to American Protestantism a sense of social responsibility that it should never lose."[74] King's faithful commitment to nonviolent resistance and the power of unmerited suffering, as well as his hope for the beloved community, intertwine with a realistic strain of social piety that is shaped and expressed by

---

12; *Christianizing the Social Order*, 52; *Theology for the Social Gospel* (Louisville: Westminster John Knox, 1997), 131.

71. See John C. Bennett, "After Liberalism—What?" *Christian Century*, November 8, 1933, 1403–6; see also Reinhold Niebuhr, *Christian Realism and Political Problems* (New York: Scribner's Sons, 1953), 74–115.

72. Reinhold Niebuhr, *An Interpretation of Christian Ethics*, 39–61.

73. Reinhold Niebuhr, *Essays in Applied Christianity*, ed. D. B. Robertson (New York: Meridian, 1959), 31.

74. *A Testament of Hope: The Essential Writings of Martin Luther King, Jr.*, ed. James Melvin Washington (New York: Harper & Row, 1986), 35–38.

his understanding of "cosmic companionship" in the struggle for justice and of God's redemptive love operating in history.[75]

Revisionist

For the liberal wing of Reformed theology in America, a willingness to question and revise inherited beliefs, practices, and ideas was intensified by the historicist recognition that they are shaped by the particular conditions of past cultures and communities as well as by the emergence of modern sciences. Things came to a head with the fundamentalist-modernist controversy, a conflict that led to tensions and factions within "mainline" churches and prompted some groups to establish alternative denominations. Liberals like Charles Briggs and Arthur McGiffert of Union Seminary in New York affirmed the theological import of questions raised by modern historical and literary studies of the Bible.[76] The controversy led Union to sever official ties with the Presbyterians, but the posture of Briggs, McGiffert, and others toward the modern study of biblical texts eventually came to expression in the Confession of 1967 of the United Presbyterian Church.

> The Scriptures, given under the guidance of the Holy Spirit, are nevertheless the words of men, conditioned by the language, thought forms, and literary fashions of the places and times at which they were written. They reflect the views of life, history, and the cosmos which were then current. The church therefore has an obligation to approach the Scriptures with literary and historical understanding.[77]

Over time, theologians, ministers, and laypeople associated with the more moderate and liberal Reformed communions also came to accept the broad outlines of the story of life as told by evolutionary biology and to recognize the mythological character of much of the material in the early chapters of Genesis. More recently, they have engaged in new quests for the historical Jesus, as well as scholarship about early gospels that were not included in the New Testament. James M. Gustafson and others also have argued that theology should take into account well-established scientific findings.[78]

75. King, *A Testament of Hope*, 7, 13, 18–20, 35–36, 41, 230.

76. See Dorrien, *The Making of American Liberal Theology: Imagining Progressive Religion, 1805–1900*, 344–70.

77. *BOC* 9.29.

78. Gustafson, *ETP*, 1:251–72; see also Douglas F. Ottati, "Which Way Is Up? An Experiment in Christian Theology and Modern Cosmology," *Interpretation* 59, no. 4 (October 2005): 370–81.

Modernists clearly did not enjoy immediate and total victories in congregations and educational institutions affiliated with the United Church of Christ, the Presbyterian Church (USA), and the United Church of Canada, and significant tensions remain to the present day. Nevertheless, continued splits and the persistent erosion of membership of those on the right have tilted these churches in more forthrightly liberal and ecumenical directions. I should also note the importance of recent deliberations and decisions about gay ordination and marriage that have pressed those affiliated with progressive churches to become more explicit about critical approaches to the Bible and to acknowledge more openly the importance for theology and ethics of additional sources of insight, such as biological studies of human sexuality.

Generally speaking, the willingness under modern conditions to question and revise inherited beliefs and practices in the light of contemporary inquiries and realities represents a further development of the classic convictions that tradition is fallible and subject to criticism and that the arts and sciences are gifts of God. These convictions, in turn, emerge from fundamental sensibilities that support an appreciative yet critical regard for contemporary inquiries as well as received tradition. An appreciative disposition has roots in piety's sense of dependence on and gratitude to the Creator, the source of all good gifts, including truth, wherever they may be found. A critical regard for received tradition, as well as for contemporary inquiries, has roots in senses of human limitation, sin, and corruption.

Accepting Plurality

An appreciative recognition of and engagement with varieties within Reformed Christianity are apparent from the fact that churches affiliated with the liberal and ecumenical stream have incorporated items and ideas from other Reformed communions into their own lives and institutions. This develops a historical trajectory. Before the end of the seventeenth century, Reformed churches in Switzerland, Germany, France, Holland, Scotland, Hungary, and Poland fashioned a variety of theological treatises, confessional documents, liturgies, and polities. These churches sometimes shared confessions, as when the Heidelberg Catechism became the doctrinal standard for churches in Holland, Germany, and Hungary, and when, in addition to adopting their own confession in 1560, Scottish Presbyterians also used and approved Calvin's Geneva Catechism, the Confession of Faith adopted by the English-speaking congregation at Geneva, the Heidelberg Catechism, and the Second Helvetic Confession. In 1581, Theodore Beza put together *A Harmony of Confessions of Faith*, which was drawn from Reformed churches in Europe, a collection that also included a revised form of the Lutheran Augsburg Confession.

For example, recent hymnbooks published by these churches include entries from historically black congregations in America as well as from Reformed communities in Korea, Latin America, central Europe, and Asia. The *Book of Confessions* of the Presbyterian Church (USA) includes documents produced by Reformed churches in Scotland, England, Switzerland, Germany, and the United States during the sixteenth, seventeenth, and twentieth centuries. Recently the Belhar Confession, written by Reformed Christians in South Africa, has also been included. Denominations such as the United Church of Christ, the PCUSA, and the Cumberland Presbyterian Church support comparatively open seminaries and theological schools, many of which have curricula that expose candidates for ministry to the histories and theologies of different Reformed communities in North America and around the world. Many of the seminaries also maintain programs, institutes, and centers that encourage conversations and exchanges among scholars and ministers who represent different Reformed churches and different Christian traditions. The ecumenical stream of Reformed Christianity in America has also been supportive of international Reformed organizations, such as the World Alliance of Reformed Churches.

Important practices, institutions, and affiliations of churches in the ecumenical Reformed stream also reflect an appreciative recognition of plurality within the wider Christian movement. For example, the *Book of Confessions* of the PCUSA begins, not with a document produced by a Reformed church, but with the Nicene Creed and the Apostles' Creed, documents shared with Roman Catholic, Orthodox, Lutheran, Episcopalian, and Methodist churches. Ecumenical impulses also come through in the recent *Book of Common Worship* of the PCUSA, a resource for worship that is "fully Reformed and catholic" and has roots not only in the Reformation but also "in the earliest liturgical traditions that have characterized Christian worship."[79]

Seminaries supported by the ecumenical stream retain faculty and admit students who belong to a variety of ecclesiastical communities. They offer courses in church history that introduce students to the longer story of the Christian movement as well as to other Christian subtraditions. Courses in Bible and theology routinely engage texts written by scholars and theologians affiliated with other churches. Moreover, many of these schools are members of consortia that include seminaries and divinity schools affiliated with Methodist, Baptist, Lutheran, Unitarian, and Catholic churches. It is also not unusual for churches in the ecumenical stream to allow significant numbers of their own candidates for ministry to be trained at interdenominational schools and in seminaries affiliated with other denominations. The liberal stream participates in ecumenical

79. *The Book of Common Worship* (Louisville: Westminster John Knox, 1993), 8, 9.

associations such as the National Council of Churches and the World Council of Churches, as well as a number of conversations and dialogues with other Christian traditions.[80]

An explicit assumption is that there are many ways of being Christian and that different Christian traditions may stand in meaningful continuity with inherently diverse scriptural witnesses. An additional assumption is that there is more to the gospel than is comprehended by any of our theologies, that no single person or group is the church, "but that there is a church of faith in which we do our partial, relative work."[81] Ecumenically considered, then, good Reformed theology engages its own particular subtradition, its confessions, practices, theological treatises, and so on; but it also enters into conversations with other, equally particular and partial Christian subtraditions. By means of these conversations, ecumenically inclined Reformed theologians expect to encounter productive tensions and also to become more aware of their own tradition's distinctiveness. They do not try to supersede particular Christian subtraditions, nor do they endorse dogmatic isolation. Instead, they engage their own particular subtradition, bring it into conversation with other, equally particular and partial subtraditions, and remain open to the possibility that these conversations will lead to vital and faithful emendations of Reformed theology.

Christianity and Other Religions

Extensive economic and political interdependencies, more frequent international travel, recent patterns of immigration, life in religiously plural societies, the international political significance of religious communities and viewpoints, and increasing information about the religions of the world have combined to render the question of Christianity and other religions virtually inescapable. Perhaps unsurprisingly, then, in recent decades the ecumenical strand has begun to reassess missionary aims and interfaith relations against a backdrop of doubts about Christian absolutism. How shall we witness to the gospel of Jesus Christ when we are not convinced that Christianity alone is true and that all other religions are simply false?

For example, Wilfred Cantwell Smith, a United Church of Canada minister and professor of Islamic studies at McGill and Harvard universities, claims that

80. See Jean-Jacques Bauswein and Lukas Vischer, eds., *The Reformed Family Worldwide: A Survey of Reformed Churches, Theological Schools, and International Organizations* (Grand Rapids: Eerdmans, 1999), 709–16.

81. H. Richard Niebuhr, *Christ and Culture*, 256. Indeed, Niebuhr's entire project in this book indicates that there are a number of ways to be faithfully Christian in the world.

"the first two great challenges to Christian thought, Hellenistic philosophy in the second century and agnostic science in the nineteenth, would prove minor compared to the challenge of religious diversity in the twenty-first century." In Smith's mind, parochialism was "the critical problem . . . [and] the Bible itself did not, on balance, warrant intolerance toward other faiths."[82]

As Smith's career indicates, the ecumenical stream's reassessment of missions and interfaith relations has been associated with the growth of religious studies departments at both church-related and more secular colleges and universities. In addition, there has been increasing emphasis on the question of Christianity and other religions at denominational and ecumenical seminaries.[83] Many offer courses that expose candidates for ministry to other faith traditions, practices, and communities. Some have gone considerably further. Hartford Seminary, a school characterized by concern for "faithful living in a pluralistic and multi-faith environment," offers programs aimed at enhancing diverse Christian ministries, as well as an Islamic chaplaincy program.[84] At Harvard Divinity School, "MDiv students of many faith communities study side by side in order to foster a greater understanding of interreligious dialogue and work."[85] Furthermore, a good share of ecumenical seminary faculty is active in the American Academy of Religion, an association animated in part by the conviction that it is a scholar's responsibility to try to understand the faiths of other persons and communities on their own terms.

There is no detailed theological consensus in this area. Some in the ecumenical stream believe that deep insights of the several great world religions converge, and one occasionally runs across attempts to draw insights from Islam, Buddhism, Hinduism, Judaism, Christianity, and so on, in order to formulate a global or human theology that is not Islamic, Buddhist, Hindu, Jewish, or Christian.

John H. Hick's *Death and Eternal Life* counts as a subtle example of this. Although Hick admits a plurality of "mythic cultic substances" of the religions, he

82. Grant Wacker, "The Protestant Awakening to World Religions," in *Between the Times: The Travail of the Protestant Establishment in America, 1900–1960* (New York: Cambridge University Press, 1989), 266.

83. Max L. Stackhouse points out that globalization raises important issues and difficulties for understanding particular texts and traditions, and also that ministers need to be trained to interpret—in relationship with God—both life and civil society in a global context. See Stackhouse, *Apologia: Contextualization, Globalization, and Mission in Theological Education* (Grand Rapids: Eerdmans, 1988), 29–42; see also Stackhouse, "If Globalization Is True, What Shall We Do? Toward a Theology of Ministry," *Theological Education* 35, no. 2 (Spring 1999): 155–65.

84. The latter is located in the MacDonald Center for the Study of Islam and Christian-Muslim Relations, "Mission Statement" and "Islamic Chaplaincy," https://www.hartsem.edu/mission-statement; https://www.hartsem.edu/islamic-chaplaincy-program/.

85. See http://www.hds.harvard.edu/academics/degree-programs/mdiv-program.

distinguishes these from "central affirmations concerning the nature of reality." These affirmations, while "not identical," make truth claims that may be synthesized. Hick's inquiry, although admittedly undertaken from a "christian" religious standpoint, is not intended "primarily as a contribution to christian theology, but rather as a christian contribution to global or human theology." His "tentative conclusion" is that the theologies of the religions do indeed "converge" and point toward "a common conception of human destiny." Hick's later work *A Christian Theology of Religions: The Rainbow of Faiths* argues that the awareness of religious pluralism, as well as interreligious conversations, offers good reasons why the traditional stance that Christianity is the only true religion is no longer workable. "An undogmatic Christianity, centered on the person and teachings of Jesus, is being heard again, alongside the teachings of Buddhism and of Hinduism and Islam and other traditions."[86]

Others suspect that efforts to construct a world theology fail to estimate with sufficient seriousness the importance of particular traditions for human visions of the divine, the world, and ourselves because they almost inevitably entail attempts to formulate common or genuine concepts that are less than adequate to the doctrines of the historic religious communities.[87] Still others claim that the different faiths, their particular practices, symbol systems, and propositions, are incommensurable.[88]

Interestingly, Mark Heim presents "a more pluralistic hypothesis" than Hick's, but he is not committed to incommensurability. Heim understands religions as irreducible orientations that entail unique perspectives. He recognizes that various religions may be truthful or valid responses to reality in their own terms and that it is possible for adherents of one religious orientation to appreciate the appropriateness of views and doctrines put forward by another. Since there is no generic and universal religious orientation, however, the relationship of the religions can only be apprehended in the specific: "There is no meta-language of a higher order than the religions' languages to express what is authentically represented by the religions." For Heim, we can evaluate the doctrines, practices, and attitudes involved in different religious orientations only from the perspective of a commitment to one of those orientations. The religious aims and fulfillments of Christianity, Buddhism, Taoism, and so on are various (a point reflected in

86. John H. Hick, *Death and Eternal Life* (San Francisco: Harper & Row, 1976), 29, 27, 34; Hick, *A Christian Theology of Religions: The Rainbow of Faiths* (Louisville: Westminster John Knox, 1995), 139.

87. On some of the difficulties that emerge when one tries to articulate generic concepts, see Wilfred Cantwell Smith, *Towards a World Theology: Faith and the Comparative History of Religion* (Philadelphia: Westminster, 1981), 180–94.

88. See Paul Griffiths, *An Apology for Apologetics* (Maryknoll, NY: Orbis, 1991).

the title of Heim's book *Salvations: Truth and Difference in Religion*). Therefore, while we commit ourselves (in practice) to the superior validity (adequacy?) of one religious orientation, we need not condemn others as false. In fact, if we enter into conversations with adherents of other religious traditions, we may well learn to take into account important evidences and also to adjust our own views without relinquishing our own perspectives.[89]

In any case, the ecumenical strand of Reformed Christianity rejects exclusionary theologies that do not recognize the limitations of their own symbols, doctrines, traditions, and subtraditions and that do not allow for the possibility of valid knowledge of the divine and valid orientations toward it beyond the bounds of Christianity. Consider the following prayer entitled "For Muslims," which appears in the *Book of Common Worship* (p. 815) for the PCUSA and the Cumberland Presbyterian Church.

> Eternal God,
> you are the one God to be worshipped by all,
> the one called Allah by your Muslim children,
> descendants of Abraham as we are.
> Give us grace to hear your truth
> in the teachings of Mohammed, the prophet,
> and to show your love as disciples of Jesus Christ,
> that Christians and Muslims together
> may serve you in faith and friendship. Amen.

The late Lewis S. Mudge, a Presbyterian minister and professor of theology at McCormick and San Francisco seminaries, proposed "parallel hermeneutics," or the practice of Jews, Christians, and Muslims interpreting their own sacred texts in a parallel relationship with one another.[90]

The idea is to enter into conversations among representatives of different faith traditions that may help us appreciate distinctive features and doctrines as well as commonalities. From an ecumenical Reformed perspective at least, we can hope that these conversations will also keep us questioning the adequacy of our own doctrines in the light of insights offered by others. The aim is neither a

89. S. Mark Heim, *Salvations: Truth and Difference in Religion* (Maryknoll, NY: Orbis, 1995), 128–57, 224–25. Here he is describing features that he approves of in Shubert M. Ogden's position.

90. Together with Rev. Laird Stuart of Calvary Presbyterian Church in San Francisco, Mudge convened a pilot group to engage in this practice. See Lewis S. Mudge, *The Gift of Responsibility: The Promise of Dialogue among Christians, Jews, and Muslims* (New York: Continuum, 2008), 117–38.

common world theology nor a defense of Christianity, but rather illuminating conversations with worthy partners in our quests to know God more truly.[91]

Humility

The convictions and practices of the liberal and ecumenical stream as it engages diverse Reformed communions, different Christian traditions, and different faith traditions in the contemporary world represent a further development of earlier ecumenical postures under conditions of religious pluralism and more frequent interactions with other Christian and religious communities. For our purposes, it is also important to recognize that these attitudes, convictions, and practices draw on a deep—if also fragile—humility with profound bases in senses of limitation and sin.

Reformed piety nurtures a strong sense of dependence on the only and sovereign God who creates and redeems. This accords, in turn, with the understanding that, as limited creatures, our experience and knowledge are partial; we never achieve an absolute perspective on life, history, faith, or what have you. Indeed, resident in the sense of sin as it intertwines with feelings of repentance and remorse is the recognition that limited persons and communities (ourselves most certainly among them) constantly are tempted to place themselves at the center of things. Human knowledge and faith are thus mired in the chronic pretension to be more than they are. They are finite and limited, gained from particular perspectives at particular places and times; but they pretend to be final and ultimate. Thus, as Reinhold Niebuhr noted, the church itself can become a vehicle for collective egoism and pretension. "Every truth can be made the servant of sinful arrogance, including the prophetic truth that all men fall short of the truth. This particular truth can come to mean that, since all men fall short of the truth and since the church is a repository of a revelation which transcends the finiteness and sinfulness of man, it therefore has the absolute truth which other men lack."[92] The attitudes and practices of the liberal and ecumenical wing of Reformed Christianity toward plurality within the Christian movement and

91. Gordon D. Kaufman claims that everyday conversations among equals and friends can furnish a helpful model for interreligious dialogues, and the conversations that many in the liberal and ecumenical stream of Reformed Christianity have in mind are something like the kind he endorses. "Each participant in the conversation posits the others as substantive contributors in this collective pursuit of (religious) truth, and thus is open in principle to collaboration with those others—instead of these several voices each presuming it is capable of expressing (by itself) what needs to be said" (Kaufman, *God–Mystery–Diversity: Christian Theology in a Pluralistic World* [Minneapolis: Fortress, 1996], 201).

92. Reinhold Niebuhr, *NDM*, 1:217.

toward religious plurality are attempts to keep faith with signal dimensions of its theocentric piety.

Proposition #24 Theological statements or doctrines will be formulated with reference to the Scripture of the Old and New Testaments, church history or tradition (confessions, practices, and past theological formulations), contemporary knowledge, and consistency with other theological statements.

We turn now to some classic methodological questions. To which sources of insight and criteria shall we refer as we formulate Christian theological statements? How shall we understand these resources? How do our appeals to these sources and criteria interrelate?[93]

My approach owes much to the judgment that Scripture, church history (or tradition), and contemporary knowledge function as resources for formulating a theological vision or picture whose purpose it is to advance the church's pastoral aim of building up people in Christian piety. I am also indebted to signal features of Reformed Christianity and theology, particularly as they have developed in the liberal and ecumenical strand in North America. I believe that Christian theology tries to shape and express a living piety and its key sensibilities by formulating a vision of God, the world, and ourselves that is responsive to classical resources as well as to our knowledge and experiences of present realities. Its sources of insight and courts of appeal should thus be understood in the context of an ongoing, dynamic, and pastorally relevant process of interpretation and reflection. And as it engages in this reflective enterprise, Christian theology should be open to critical perspectives on the Bible and Christian tradition as well as to insights and perspectives generated by modern sciences and modes of inquiry.

93. One comprehensive answer to these questions is the "Wesleyan Quadrilateral." *The Book of Discipline of the United Methodist Church* says: "Wesley believed that the living core of the Christian faith was revealed in Scripture, illumined by tradition, vivified in personal experience, and confirmed by reason" (*The Book of Discipline of the United Methodist Church 2000* [Nashville: United Methodist Publishing House, 2000], 77). Even so, just how these four touchstones actually operate in Wesley's writings is a matter of some discussion, and scholars agree that they are not distinctive to him. The Quadrilateral was adopted in 1972 as a supplementary statement on the contemporary theological task of the United Methodist Church when, on the occasion of the merger of the Evangelical United Brethren and the Methodist Church, it became apparent that it would be difficult to write a new creed. In addition to conversations over Wesley's own use of the four guidelines, there has been discussion concerning a priority ordering among the four. See W. Scott Gunter et al., eds., *Wesley and the Quadrilateral: Renewing the Conversation* (Nashville: Abingdon, 1977), 9–13, 17, 129.

Consider, for example, our current interactions with animals, plants, atmospheric temperatures, polar ice caps, weather patterns, and ozone layers. In light of contemporary knowledge and beliefs, many Christians today sense that we depend on all these things—but also that we may influence and alter all of them and more. A contemporary theologian brings a variety of interpretive resources to bear on these current sensibilities, interactions, and beliefs—such as symbolic ideas of God as Creator, Sustainer, and Judge, portraits of humans as active agents and participants, and images of the world as creation-ordered-by-God. These, in turn, have roots in biblical passages, such as Genesis 1:1–2:4 and selected psalms; they are also developed in theological works of the church's history, such as Thomas Aquinas's *Summa Theologiae* and Calvin's *Institutes*, not to mention numerous hymns, prayers, and liturgical forms. Moreover, these symbolic ideas and texts both express and shape senses of dependence on God and gratitude for God's gifts of life in an ordered, dynamic, and sustaining world. Contemporary theologians thus make use of interpretive resources that were developed by earlier persons and communities in conjunction with their own interactions with and ideas and feelings about natural environments.

A current theological statement rarely simply repeats these inherited images, ideas, and sensibilities, because our present interactions with and emotional responses to animals, plants, atmospheric temperatures, polar ice caps, weather patterns, and ozone layers intertwine with current knowledge and beliefs about natural environments and human interventions. Therefore, contemporary theological statements need to account for recent knowledge and experiences of the highly destructive consequences for intricate and vulnerable ecosystems of many human practices. And the effort to do so may well lead us to revise or emend important aspects of biblically and traditionally informed portraits and apprehensions of divine judgment and human capacities for intervention, as well as the responsibilities that accompany them.

Scripture

Scripture refers to the Bible—a particular collection of sacred texts—as a primary resource for theological reflection. Appeals to Scripture are neither esoteric nor strange; other religious traditions also appeal to well-defined sacred writings, such as the Pali Canon and the Qur'an.[94] Indeed, when viewed in the

94. Max L. Stackhouse makes this point about the sacred writings of other traditions, and he also regards the quadrilateral as a "cogent formulation of the key classical criteria by which we assess . . . various proposals for theological meaning" (Stackhouse, *Public Theology and Political Economy: Christian Stewardship in Modern Society* [Grand Rapids: Eerdmans, 1987], 4, 5).

context of the ongoing, emotionally resonant, and reflective process mentioned above, we should also say that these writings continue to orient and guide living pieties of religious communities in much the same way that certain charter documents continue to guide the living sensibilities and conviction of political communities.[95]

For Christian theology, then, Scripture contributes to the interpretation of the present world and the formation of contemporary sensibilities. It furnishes a treasury of imaginative, mythic, and poetic resources (themes, images, stories, codes, chronicles, prophecies, and more) that helps us portray ourselves and the many objects and others we interact with in our relationship to the Creator-Judge-Redeemer. Indeed, precisely as we make use of scriptural images and ideas to reflect on current interactions and experiences, we recognize that the same interplay of experience, imagination, and sensibility was also involved in the formation of Scripture. Accordingly, Genesis 1:1–2:4 uses images, ideas, and myths of creation drawn from longer Near Eastern and Mesopotamian traditions in order to express and interpret in relationship to God certain experiences of dependence, wonderment, and gratitude at living in an ordered and sustaining world. Lamentations uses received ideas and images of divine wrath, judgment, and deliverance in order to reinterpret, with respect to God, the grief, humiliation, and hope that accompanied the destruction of Jerusalem and the exile of its people in Babylon.

When, in the context of the present system, I say that Scripture is the primary source for Christian doctrine, I mean that it is the basic source of images, portraits, and ideas about God, the world, and ourselves that shape and express the Christian community's living piety. More particularly, I mean that Scripture presents the event of Jesus Christ, the paradigmatic suggestion in the light of whom we envision God as Creator-Judge-Redeemer, humans as good but corrupted creatures who benefit from redeeming grace, and the world as good creation mired in consequences of sin but nonetheless governed toward transformation. This particular suggestion and its contours or shape, this paradigmatic gift to Christian interpretive imagination that is so critical for living Christian piety, is unavailable apart from Scripture. Its availability in the Bible distinguishes the testimony of Scripture from other resources and criteria for Christian theological reflection. Stated more traditionally, Scripture constitutes the unique and indispensable witness to the Word of God in Jesus Christ.

As we have seen, the event of Jesus Christ and the affections it engenders are of a piece with the longer saga of God's governance, from the work of creation, through the story of Israel, to the sending of the Spirit, the emergence of the

95. On the analogy with charter documents of political communities, see Douglas F. Ottati, *Jesus Christ and Christian Vision* (Louisville: Westminster John Knox, 1996), 14.

church, and the end at the new Jerusalem. This is why the unique and indispensable witness that attests to God, as God, understood in the light of redemption-in-Christ, is always *both* Hebrew Scripture and the New Testament.[96] This is why the primary and originating treasury of ideas, images, stories, codes, and chronicles with which Christians try to envision God, the world, and themselves is made up of both the Old Testament and the New.[97]

This brings us to a related point. Scripture functions as a primary and indispensable source of insight for a continuing process of reflection, but Scripture itself also needs to be interpreted, and three matters concerning its interpretation call for special emphasis.

First, Scripture will be interpreted as it is configured by the suggestion redemption-in-Jesus-Christ; the Bible will be interpreted in the light of its witness to redemption-in-Jesus-Christ.[98] Understood in this way, the Bible will be construed as the story of the Creator-Judge-Redeemer's dealings with Israel—indeed, with all of humanity and the world—from creation to the end. This is the broad sweep of the Bible, and it indicates that we look to Scripture primarily for *theological* claims about God, the world, and ourselves in conjunction with religious apprehensions and sensibilities.[99]

Second, and as is traditional in Reformed circles, Scripture will be interpreted in the light of Scripture.[100] Particular texts, passages, images, ideas, and the feelings or emotions that they shape and express will be understood in the context of the Bible's broader witness and sweep. Rather than consider them in isolation, I will try to read and interpret them in a way that respects their specific integrity but also keeps this wider frame in view.

Third, Scripture—its texts, images, and ideas—will be understood with the

96. See chap. 1, prop. #14.

97. *BOC* 9.27–28. This is my own way of saying what the Confession of 1967 of the PCUSA also affirms: "The Scriptures are not a witness among others, but the witness without parallel" to Jesus Christ, the Word of God. "The Old Testament is indispensable to understanding the New, and is not itself fully understood without the New." (This last statement, of course, is made from the viewpoint of the *Christian* community, which reads Hebrew Scripture in the light of the New Testament and the New Testament in the light of the Hebrew Scripture, and thus, at least in some important respects, necessarily reads and interprets Hebrew Scripture differently than do Jewish communities.)

98. The Confession of 1967 makes a similar point in *BOC* 9.29.

99. Question 3 of the Westminster Shorter Catechism makes a similar point, I think, when it says that the Scriptures "principally teach what man is to believe concerning God, and what duty God requires of man" (*BOC* 7.003).

100. This point is made by a number of Reformed confessions. See selected passages from the Scots Confession, the Second Helvetic Confession, and the Westminster Confession of Faith, in *BOC* 3.18; 5.010; 6.009.

aid of historical, critical, and literary studies. These studies clearly are subject to error as well as to corrupting interests, but this does not distinguish them from any other form of human reasoning, including more traditional theological arguments, commentaries, and methods of text interpretation (which should also be consulted). Moreover, an especially helpful result of modern historical and literary studies is that they help us understand how the interpretive interplay of experiences, imaginative resources, and emotions very often was involved in the formation of biblical texts and the expression and formation of piety. They help us see that, like our subsequent theological statements, biblical texts often reinterpret, with respect to God, experiences, interactions, events, and emotions that were bound up with the then current knowledge, beliefs, and judgments. In general, then, I regard human competence in historical and literary disciplines as a gift to be used in our interpretations of biblical texts.

This does *not* mean (as is too often the case among modern Bible scholars) that one should either dismiss or neglect insights into biblical resources and ideas generated by more traditional theological arguments and commentaries. Past interpretations of biblical texts—for example, Augustine on Genesis, Martin Luther on Galatians, Peter Rideman on the Ten Commandments and the Sermon on the Mount, or Rosemary Radford Ruether on the portrait of Jesus in the Gospels—offer important insights into Scripture and its meanings. In fact, the value of classical theological perspectives on Scripture increases once we understand that, like us, earlier theologians also were interested in using biblical images and ideas in order to envision present life and cultivate a living piety.

Church History and Tradition

With this last observation, we begin to see how appeals to the Bible connect with appeals to the church's history and theological tradition. The theology that I present here will emphasize the growth and development of the church's theological tradition as a continuing response to its pastoral aim. It will regard past theological statements as the attempts of Christians, at particular places and times, to envision themselves and the many objects, situations, and realities with which they interacted in relationship to the Creator-Judge-Redeemer disclosed in Jesus, and so to deepen and extend a particular Christian piety and fidelity. These attempts made use of scriptural images and ideas to reinterpret emotionally resonant interactions that also were interpreted and understood in connection with then-current information, knowledge, and beliefs. They were previous attempts—in the face of specific opportunities, challenges, and circumstances—to do something like what the biblical writers and communities did, as well as what we are trying to do here and now.

An important difference between the interpretative labors of biblical writers and those of later church theologians is that the latter—for example, the work of Thomas Aquinas—take place in different (postbiblical) places and times, such as thirteenth-century Europe. Therefore, they engage different circumstances and realities than did the biblical writers, such as the Moors in Spain, the medieval papacy, and the rise of European universities, as well as different cultural resources, such as Aristotle, Averroes, and Spinoza. In addition, postbiblical churches and communities continue to develop and support catechisms, creeds, confessions, commentaries, and theological treatises in order to summarize, teach, and regulate their faith and practice, such as Origen's commentaries, the Nicene Creed, and Augustine's *On the Trinity*. These, too, are among the resources available to a church theologian such as Aquinas as he tries to formulate his contemporary vision of humanity and world in relation to God.

Another important difference is that, for later church theologians, the canon or collection of biblical writings is stabilized and accorded a special status as Scripture. Specific theories of this status differ, but a general result is that one particular collection of texts exerts a powerful influence on the church's subsequent theological reflections. Church theologians and communities not only refer to biblical texts, they also strive to frame leading elements of their current visions of God, humanity, and world in accordance with scriptural texts, images, and ideas. And so, at the same time that their theological statements are responsive to emotionally resonant encounters with current situations and realities, encounters with Scripture continually shape ecclesial interpretations of ourselves and the many objects and others we interact with—in relationship to God. The canonical collection and its treasury of evocative and imaginative resources constitute an originating and indispensable baseline for the church's subsequent theological reflections.

The critical matter of the canon also underscores an important relationship between the Bible and church history (or tradition). Elaine Pagels points out that "alternative gospels" to the four that Christian orthodoxy included in the New Testament have been discovered at Nag Hammadi and elsewhere. For example, she argues that the Gospel of Thomas offers a portrait of Jesus and his renewing good news that differs markedly from what we find in Matthew, Mark, and Luke, and is explicitly rejected by the Gospel of John. She adds that Irenaeus and others, who were directly involved in the formation of the orthodox canon, often made their decisions about which texts to include and which to suppress on explicitly theological and political grounds.[101] An inescapable conclusion is

101. Elaine Pagels, *The Gnostic Gospels* (New York: Random House, 1979), xxxv, 142; see also Pagels, *Beyond Belief: The Secret Gospel of Thomas* (New York: Random House, 2003), 50–73,

that the church might have tolerated a wider variety of gospels, or it might have assembled a different canon of New Testament writings than it did. In either case, given what we have just said about the profound influence of the canonical collection, the church's subsequent theological reflections and the particular form of piety that they built up and extended would have been quite different. But this means that the Bible not only influences subsequent theology; the church's theological judgments also contribute to the formation of the Bible.

Indeed, the church closed the canon rather late, and there is no agreement among Christian churches about its exact composition—to the present day. The question of what to include and exclude was reopened by sixteenth-century Protestants: they judged seven books that had been included in the Old Testament by the Roman Catholic Church to be apocryphal. The books were jettisoned partly as a result of an attempt to go back to the earliest sources; the seven had entered the church's canon because they were included in the Septuagint translation of Hebrew writings into Greek, but they were not included in older Jewish Bibles. For his part, Martin Luther, who favored a Pauline emphasis on grace as well as a piety strongly marked by senses of gratitude, remorse, and forgiveness, also indicated that, were the question of the canon to be pursued further, he would favor dropping the Epistle of James.

Observations such as these are enough to raise serious questions about the efforts of an older Protestant orthodoxy to secure the absolute authority of a strictly defined collection of canonical writings by means of supernatural appeals. For example, the Westminster Confession of Faith listed the biblical books that its Puritan authors deemed genuine and inspired, and also insisted that the authority of these books "dependeth not upon the testimony of any man or church, but wholly upon God." Furthermore, it claimed that the apocryphal books, not being inspired by the Holy Spirit, were thus no different from any other human writings.[102] But, of course, on this last point there is disagreement even among different Christian communions. Indeed, the role of theological and other ecclesial judgments in the formation and revision of the canon illustrates a close and inevitably somewhat circular relationship between Scripture and the church.

Might one or more churches decide to reopen the question of the canon? The possibility cannot be ruled out, even if one believes (as I do) that there are strong reasons to be conservative. But the main point I would like to make here is simply

---

111–13. The idea of a lost first-century gospel that might shake the foundations of Christianity is the premise of *Gospel* (New York: Picador, 1993), an immensely entertaining novel by Wilton Barnhardt.

102. The Westminster Confession of Faith, *BOC* 6.002–6.004.

that, like the decision to select certain books and to close the canon in the first place, any decision to reopen it or not may have major implications for piety and faithfulness and must always be the church's theological judgment to make. In any case, churches decide on the canon, and thus any actual church never has a particular canon of Scripture apart from its own theological judgments. Bible, theology, and piety go together, as do canon, creed, and sensibility.

The close relationship between the Bible and the church has considerable significance for theology. What we may call the substantive theological norm (in the present system, knowledge of the Creator-Judge-Redeemer in the event of Jesus Christ) can be said to derive from the Bible, and my proposal is that we should bring it to bear on our subsequent emotionally resonant interactions with situations and realities. As we have seen, however, the substantive theological norm and the way we understand it also influence our judgments as to what counts as Scripture, for example, *both* the Old Testament and the New, as well as how we interpret Scripture. Moreover, the substantive norm and the sensibilities it expresses and shapes do not emerge in a vacuum any more than the canon of Scripture does. They are produced, as Paul Tillich noted, "in an encounter between the church and the biblical message."[103] Indeed, at different places and times the encounter appears to yield somewhat different normative theological emphases and strains of piety, for example, Reformation insistences on remorse, gratitude, and grace alone, liberal attention to Jesus, social obligation, and the kingdom, plus more recent liberationist emphases on solidarity and justice.

Two points follow. First, we never have the Bible apart from normative theological judgments of church history, and we cannot appeal to the Bible apart from also recognizing the importance of church history and tradition as sources of insight. Much as certain forms of Protestantism may wish it were otherwise, there really is no such thing as a simple return to the Bible. Second, though ecclesiastical judgments and decisions influence what counts as Scripture and how Scripture is interpreted, they do not alone determine the substantive norm for Christian theology. Church authorities and traditions are never enough; we must also show how a specific understanding of the norm emerges from our encounter with the Bible.

Accordingly, I will regard past theological statements of Christian communities as affectively resonant attempts to envision the world and humanity in

103. Paul Tillich, *Reason and Revelation, Being and God*, vol. 1 of *Systematic Theology* (Chicago: University of Chicago Press, 1951), 51. Consider also this fuller statement: "The Bible can be called the norm of systematic theology only because the norm is derived from the Bible. But it is derived from it in an encounter of the church with the biblical message. The norm derived from the Bible is, at the same time, the criterion for the use of the Bible in systematic theology" (50).

relationship to the Creator-Judge-Redeemer disclosed in Jesus Christ. I will approach them as earlier and potentially instructive attempts to do what I am trying to do here and now. Operating with a preference for the Reformed subtradition of the Christian movement, I will give special (but by no means exclusive) attention to past doctrinal statements generated by Reformed theologians and communities. I will also appeal to practices, catechisms, confessions, liturgies, hymns, declarations, and the like that articulate the doctrinal visions of particular Reformed churches.

These appeals assume that theological frameworks are shaped and sustained by communities that bear particular heritages of fidelity, practice, and reflection. Symbolic resources that others in the past have both developed and found illuminating, therefore, continue to inform Christian communities, their living pieties, practical orientations, and visions. So, for example, the Scots Confession says that one reason why ecclesiastical councils and assemblies generate theological statements is "to give public confession of their faith to the generations following."[104] A willingness to receive this gift of commitment, sensibility, and reflection across the generations is a willingness to be attentive to tradition and, where appropriate, to be informed by our heritage in our own envisioning, feeling, and living. In that sense, good theology requires respect for those who have gone before, as well as sustained attention to received paradigms, practices, symbols, ideas, arguments, and interpretations. This is why there is always a conservative aspect to Christian doctrine.

At the same time, we also recall that past practices and theological statements necessarily reflect specific limitations in the knowledge, languages, and experiences of Christians and their communities. Therefore, we receive them with gratitude and respect even as we also recognize that they were subject to error as well as to corrupted interests. Like our own statements, they are always "the work of limited, fallible, sinful human beings and churches" that reflect the biases and scientific and cultural limitations of specific persons, communities, and circumstances.[105] This is why, as I have noted earlier, an appropriate respect for tradition must always be a measured and critical respect.

Contemporary Knowledge and Beliefs

Contemporary knowledge and beliefs concerning the many objects, others, situations, and realities with which we interact constitute yet another important

104. *BOC* 3.20.

105. "The Confessional Nature of the Church," in *Book of Confessions: Study Edition* (Louisville: Geneva, 1999), 359.

source of insight for Christian theology. Why this should be true becomes apparent when we consider the ongoing process of interpretation or reinterpretation that lies near the center of the church's pastoral aim. To return to a previous illustration, when we try to reinterpret—in relationship to God—our present interactions with animals, plants, atmospheric temperatures, polar ice caps, weather patterns, and the earth's ozone layer, contemporary knowledge and beliefs are already involved and have already influenced our sensibilities and affections. Therefore, our theological reinterpretation will need to take into account our current knowledge and beliefs about natural environments and human interventions. Indeed, the effort to do so may lead us to amend or revise aspects of our biblically and traditionally informed portraits of divine governance as well as of human powers and responsibilities.

Here, as elsewhere, of course, it is appropriate to be critical. Current knowledge and beliefs arrive in many forms: empirical studies, scientific theories, philosophical assumptions, personal stories, communal histories, cultural images, and so on. These may be more or less well attested, contested, and idiosyncratic. There is nothing to guarantee that one or another study, theory, assumption, story, or image will not be incomplete or even wholly mistaken. Moreover, even well-attested theories and research outcomes yield place to further research and reflection.

It makes sense to be cautious because our knowledge and information remain limited and incomplete. We clearly know many things today that our ancestors did not (for instance, that there *is* an ozone layer). Nonetheless, the sense that there is much we do not know waits only for a thoughtful gaze into the night sky, acquaintance with the cosmological ruminations of a contemporary scientist, or inquiries into the histories of persons and communities. Again, persons and groups are able to attend to only limited selections of factors, circumstances, and events; they are unable to take in everything at once. And as we attend selectively, we sometimes select poorly; occasionally we get sidetracked; quite often we fail to take relevant factors into account. Indeed, as almost any inquiry into recent judgments and debates concerning markets, monetary policies, economic development, and natural environments will likely suggest, more often than we care to admit, our interests and purposes dispose us to neglect relevant information and arguments. For all these reasons and more, any confidence we may have in one or another study, theory, assumption, story, or belief needs to be an appropriately measured and critical confidence.

Even so, appeals to contemporary knowledge, theories, and beliefs are especially important if Christian doctrines are to offer reinterpretations—with respect to God—of our current life and interactions with objects and others, and so contribute to the pastoral aim of the church. The formation of persons, their contemporary affections and sensibilities, in a pattern or piety that is responsive to the Creator-Judge-Redeemer, requires theological reflections that envision the Creator-Judge-Redeemer in relationship to our present lives in our actual world. This cannot be done unless we (critically) take into account what we currently know and believe about the world or about ourselves and the objects, situations, and realities with which we interact and how this influences our emotional responses. Otherwise, our theological vision becomes pastorally anachronistic, an archaeology of imaginative themes, symbols, stories, and ideas that certain persons and communities once found illuminating and compelling but that no longer help to interpret and orient contemporary living. It becomes a museum of imaginative resources that no longer serves to cultivate, express, and shape living religious affections and sensibilities in response to current realities as we know and experience them.

Thus, as I have noted, when one develops a doctrine of creation, it is insufficient simply to engage in sustained and disciplined interpretation of biblical texts. It is also important to develop imaginative resources that are presented in Scripture and developed by subsequent tradition—images of ordering, blessing, generativity, and so on—in a way that takes into account our more recent interactions with and knowledge of intricate natural ecologies. When one develops a doctrine of sin, the human fault and the chronically destructive misorientation of human beings, it is not enough to work with biblical texts and also engage a broad Augustinian line of theological reflection. It is also important to consider contemporary accounts of human agency, responsibility, and emotional constitution informed by evolutionary biology, and also the train of terrifying atrocities and disturbing holocausts that punctuates modern history.[106]

Consistency and Coherence

Finally, in the present work, I will also try to formulate theological statements that are consistent with one another. Even allowing for illuminating tensions and paradoxes in Christian theology, such as Martin Luther's famous statements

106. How should evidences from various sciences be used in theology? James M. Gustafson has raised this difficult question most forcibly, and I essentially agree with his answer. Theological statements that express and shape affections in response to objects are not themselves scientific explanations; neither are they deduced from scientific findings. Therefore, the relationship between them need not be one of simple harmony. Theological statements are imaginative pictures, portrayals, or construals of God, the world, and ourselves that emerge in the interplay of imaginative mythopoeic resources of Scripture and tradition with our current interactions, knowledge, sensibilities, and beliefs. These imaginative pictures, portrayals, or construals should be congruent in some way with relevant and well-established scientific theories and findings (Gustafson, *ETP*, 1:252).

about the freedom and the servitude of a Christian, a modicum of internal consistency seems required if a given vision or picture of God, the world, and ourselves is to be intelligible.[107] Moreover, as the very idea of a system indicates, "a regularly interacting or interdependent group of items forming a unified whole," a significant measure of interrelatedness and coherence, seems to be a requirement for any systematic theology.[108]

For theology as an ecclesial reflection, however, there is an additional and practical reason to value consistency and coherence. Recall that the pastoral aim of the church is to form people in a particular piety or pattern of sensibilities and affections. The church tries to dispose persons toward other persons, objects, situations, and realities in a way that is faithfully responsive to the Creator-Judge-Redeemer disclosed in Jesus Christ. This practical and pastoral aim, in turn, requires a vision or a picture of God in relationship to us and to the many persons, objects, situations, and realities we interact with. A Christian theology formulates this vision. It is a reflective wisdom that a Christian community uses to inform piety and faithful living by picturing ourselves and the many persons, objects, situations, and realities with which we interact in relationship with God the Creator-Judge-Redeemer.

But this is as much as to say that, as a reflective enterprise in the service of the church's pastoral aim, Christian theology formulates a vision, reading, or picture of God, the world, and ourselves in order to inform and guide an orientation, disposition, temper, or stance in life. A theology tries to advance an attitude and a way of living that, even as we make allowances for the messiness and the ambiguities of actual history and experience, has its own integrity. This is why theology tries to furnish a vision that supports a coherent piety or pattern of sensibility. And this is why, more than a single proposition or doctrine, a larger theological vision requires a comparatively ordered collection of statements, propositions, images, and ideas that interrelate and cohere. Because a living piety that is appropriately responsive to the one Creator-Judge-Redeemer disclosed in Jesus Christ has a certain consistency and integrity, a theology that serves the church's pastoral aim should also have a certain consistency and integrity.[109]

107. Luther's statements come at the beginning of his treatise *The Freedom of a Christian* and are as follows: "A Christian is a perfectly free lord of all, subject to none. A Christian is a perfectly dutiful servant of all, subject to all." As Luther explains these propositions, not only are they not contradictory, they fit together. Each has to do with a Christian's life in a distinguishable relationship, that is, in relationship to God, where the governing principle is free grace, and in relationship to other persons, where a Christian is to be a Christ to the neighbor (*Career of the Reformer I*, ed. Harold J. Grimm, vol. 31 of *LW*, 344).

108. *Merriam-Webster's Collegiate Dictionary*, 10th ed., s.v. "system."

109. See the comments on consistency in chap. 1, props. #17 and #18.

The theology presented here affirms that people are capable and good creatures and that sin is radical and universal. At the level of piety and affection, these statements correlate with a feeling of gratitude and thanksgiving to God for the capacities and abilities with which we are endowed, as well as with a sense of remorse and repentance before God at what we have become. They express and shape sensibilities of thanksgiving and remorse that cohere and thus contribute to an integral attitude, disposition, or stance. And this is a major reason why, in much classical Christian theology, statements about creation and sin are fitted into a wider framework. The wider framework makes it clear that sin does not mean persons are essentially evil, and that the goodness of creation does not mean humans have escaped entanglement in a serious and persistent fault. It shapes and expresses a coherent piety in which the apprehension of sin does not remove all reasons for us to be grateful to God for the gift of good qualities and capacities, and in which an appreciation for the goodness of creation is compatible with our feelings of remorse for sinful corruption.

The Arrangement of Theological Statements

Proposition #25 This book arranges doctrines systematically in order to pursue greater clarity, depth, and coherence.

Why write a *systematic* theology? The answer is to pursue clarity, understanding, and coherence by focusing on interrelationships and interconnections in a way that supports an integral piety. There are, of course, other forms of theological literature and discourse that advance understanding and pursue clarity, for example, fragments, monographs, commentaries, and sermons. And each is especially adept at focusing on matters of importance for Christian believing and theology, such as disjunctions and oppositions, expositions of specific ideas and doctrines, encounters with biblical texts, and the interpretation of the gospel within a particular congregation.

Fragments challenge encrusted patterns of reflection and affection. Consider, for example, the following contentions from Blaise Pascal's *Pensées*. "Contradiction is not an indication of falsehood and the absence of contradiction is not a sign of truth." "There is nothing so consistent with reason as the denial of reason." "Reason's last step is to recognize that there is an infinite number of things which surpass it."[110] Nicholas Hammond says that Pascal's fragments make an

110. Blaise Pascal, *Pensées and Other Writings*, trans. Honor Levi, introduction and notes by Anthony Levi (New York: Oxford University Press, 1995), 61–62. Scholars disagree about

important point. "This disorder in itself acts as a persuasive force for the reader as he is made aware of the fragmentariness of his being in a fallen world, pushing him to search for coherence and truth elsewhere."[111]

Systematic theology as an idea or form of theological discourse has been subjected to important criticisms. For example, Karl Barth says it confines theology to a structure determined by philosophical conceptions.[112] Gordon D. Kaufman objects that systematic theology is conservative, atomistic, and insular. My own judgment, however, is that these criticisms themselves should be critically evaluated and that, when they are, they need not expose fatal deficiencies.

Barth's objection is rooted in his rejection of "alien" sources of insight in Christian theology.[113] However, the present work takes systematics to indicate not a theology built on philosophical foundations but one that articulates organic interrelationships and interconnections among images, symbols, and doctrines in order to furnish a Christian community's vision of God, the world, and ourselves. Barth hardly seems against this. And we need only say further that (1) philosophical considerations may enter into a theology without thereby furnishing the "fundamental conceptions" on which an "edifice of thought" is constructed; (2) the extent to which Barth himself successfully avoided *all* philosophical conceptions in his own theology, say, in his conviction that God's being is in God's act, is itself worth a bit of critical discussion; and (3) neither is his the dominant understanding of a theological system put forward by many of those who have tried to write theological systems, or what Origen of Alexandria called connected bodies of doctrine.

Kaufman claims that "projects in systematic theology . . . presuppose that theological 'truth' is dispersed among, and resides in, the many Christian 'doctrines' . . . that have been handed on from generation to generation in the churches," and that the theologian arranges

---

just how Pascal's fragments should be ordered and presented. Were many of them intended as points of a single and continuous apologetic (pp. xxxviii–xxxix)? See also Robert J. Nelson, *Pascal: Adversary and Advocate* (Cambridge, MA: Harvard University Press, 1981), 229–36. Nicholas Hammond, in *Playing with Truth: Language and the Human Condition in Pascal's Pensées* (Oxford: Clarendon, 1994), says that, even if they were so intended, what we have now—namely, a collection of fragments—is what we must attend to (4–5).

111. Hammond also notes that Pascal made use of a Cartesian method of rational demonstration in *De l'espirit geometrique* but explicitly did not do so as he treated religious topics in the *Pensées*, where his approach seems partly directed against theologians who tried to synthesize Descartes and Augustine (Hammond, *Playing with Truth*, 14, 17–18, 77). See also *Pensées de M. Pascal sur la Religion, et sur quelques Autres Sujets*, Images et témoins de l'âge classique 2, Centre Universitaire d'éditions et de rééditions (Université de la Région Rhone-Alpes, n.d.), 20–21.

112. Barth had Tillich in mind; see *Dogmatics in Outline*, trans. G. T. Thompson (New York: Harper & Brothers, 1959), 5.

113. Barth, *CD* I/1:4, 72.

them to give a synoptic view of Christian faith as a whole. This, he says, presupposes "a semi-atomistic conception of theological truth," and it also tends to conservatively pass on the same major doctrines. By contrast, Kaufman himself tries to construct a holistic and rough "Christian world-picture."[114]

Nevertheless, I fail to see why it is necessarily "semi-atomistic" to claim that particular doctrines interact to form a whole that is greater than the sum of its parts. I also do not think Kaufman's drive toward a holistic picture is entirely different from the current project (except, perhaps, in its level of detail). In part, this is because Kaufman's magisterial work is one of the sources for my own approach, which regards Christian doctrines and doctrinal schemes as attempts to connect imaginative symbols and images that yield a particular Christian community's vision of God, the world, and ourselves. I happily admit that there are conservative dimensions to my project—as there are to most systematic theologies. After all, it is necessary to draw on images, symbols, and ideas that have emerged in a longer tradition, a point that Kaufman himself seems bound to concede at some level if he is actually working with a *Christian* categorial scheme. But then, of course, there must also be innovative dimensions to the project of articulating as an interconnected whole a Christian community's vision for its *present* time and place. And this means that, like other systematic theologians, I not only consider inherited ideas, I also assess them and occasionally find reasons to revise inherited ideas as well as some of the broader schemes and patterns into which these ideas and doctrines are set.[115]

Kaufman also claims that systematic theologies tend to focus on dynamics of retrieval and contemporary restatement that are internal to Christian tradition and community and thus neglect comparisons with other points of view.[116] I want to respond rather carefully to this point, since I see no reason to deny that Christian communities concerned with the formation of piety and sensibility have their own practical and pastoral reasons for entering into theological inquiries. Indeed, this hardly distinguishes them from other religious

114. Kaufman, *IFM*, 411, 491.

115. Interestingly, some revisions that have been tried by systematic theologians in the past seem at least as fundamental as Kaufman's. Consider, for example, Thomas Aquinas's willingness to make use of the "new knowledge" represented by Aristotle's philosophy, as well as Schleiermacher's decision to begin his dogmatics with a theory of religion and his reinterpretation of the status of Christian doctrines as an expression of religious affections; not to mention Immanuel Kant's somewhat systematic and rather radical reinterpretation of Christian believing in *Religion within the Limits of Reason Alone*; Schleiermacher's refusal to treat the doctrine of God, as many of his predecessors had done, continuously in a single place, as well as his reinterpretation of the person of Christ; and Ernst Troeltsch's decision to begin his *Glaubenslehre*, not with God or creation, but with his (significantly revised) understanding of Jesus Christ; Tillich's rather radical "reopening of the Trinitarian Problem" (Tillich, *Life and the Spirit, History and the Kingdom of God*, 291–94); and Barth's decision, in his *Church Dogmatics*, to reject all natural theology and "alien" sources of insight.

116. Kaufman, *IFM*, 491–92.

> communities, or from political communities, or from other groups that offer their own guiding visions and worldviews. Any and all of these communities may find that, from time to time, they have important reasons for concentrating on their own understandings and interpretations of their own visions. If I am correct, however, they need not stop there, and there is no reason why a theology that is systematic necessarily encourages one to stop there. In fact, as I argued earlier, the effort to frame a more or less comprehensive Christian vision of God, the world, and ourselves is itself an important step on the way toward comparisons with other visions and worldviews (see chap. 1, prop. #18).

What seems important to recognize is that different kinds of theological literature and discourse inform and challenge one another. A system draws on commentaries and monographs, while a collection of fragments may challenge the patterned consistency of one or another systematic presentation. A commentary may put us in touch with what seems, given the prevailing bent of current theological literature and preaching, the "strange world" of a biblical text.[117] Or, again, it may enrich our understanding of a biblical theme, such as liberation, that initially was lifted up by sermons, essays, or systematic presentations. Sermons that interpret the gospel through the lens of a specific biblical text and for a particular congregation often draw on commentaries. They also may be constructed in such a way that systematic patterns of interconnection among doctrines recede into the background, even as these same patterns continue to inform what is said, how it is said, and what is not said.

One thinks, for example, of Karl Barth's contention that dogmatics, as the self-examination of the church with respect to the content of its proclamation and its preaching, serves church proclamation by criticizing and testing it.[118] Barth insisted that the two be neither equated nor separated, and he noted that if beginners seem tempted merely to preach their favorite textbooks of dogmatics, "older preachers are usually far too confident in removing themselves from the jurisdiction of this critical authority."[119]

117. See, e.g., Barth's well-known address, "The Strange New World within the Bible," in *The Word of God and the Word of Man*, translated, with a new foreword, by Douglas Horton (Gloucester: Peter Smith, 1978), 28–50.

118. Barth, *CD* I/1:75, 78, 83.

119. Barth, *CD* I/1:79. Barth continued: "One cannot and should not expect to hear the content of proclamation from dogmatics. This content must be found each time in the middle space between the particular text in the context of the whole Bible and the particular situation of the changing moment. Dogmatics can only be a guide to the right mastery and the right adaptability, to the right boldness and the right caution, for the given moment when this space has to be found. It can only be a guide to orientation between the two poles of saying what has to be said in all circumstances and not saying what must not be said in any circumstances."

Not surprisingly, then—and especially before increased specialization and fragmentation took hold in theological studies during the modern period—the same theologians often produced different kinds of theological works. Origen of Alexandria wrote a connected body of doctrine but also numerous commentaries, texts on biblical interpretation, and spiritual treatises. Calvin believed that a more or less systematic presentation of theology and biblical commentaries belong together; he presented his *Institutes* as an aid for knowing what to look for while reading and interpreting Scripture, as well as a statement of true piety and religion.[120]

The differentiation of theological studies into exegetical studies, church history, dogmatics, and the like was an important fact for Schleiermacher at the University of Berlin when he wrote his own famous outline of theological studies.[121] While Schleiermacher himself did not write biblical commentaries, as Calvin did, he preached frequently.[122] He also distinguished a number of literary forms for theology as it treats doctrinal propositions: monographs that explicate some single proposition in various relationships; *loci theologici*, or collections of such monographs; and a complete system of doctrine "in which every essential moment of the religious and Christian consciousness is given its developed dogmatic expression, and all the dogmatic propositions are brought into relationship with each other."[123] Converting this last remark into the terms of the present work, we may speak of a system in which essential elements of a Christian community's piety and vision of God, the world, and ourselves are given developed theological expression and theological statements are brought into relationship with each other.

A systematic theology, then, is not the only way to pursue clarity, depth of understanding, and a coherence of sensibility; but it does pursue a kind of clarity, depth, and coherence that would be largely unavailable apart from a systematic arrangement. The greater clarity, understanding, and coherence pursued by systematics are of the kind that accompany an appreciation for and apprehension

120. Over the years, Calvin worked on the many editions of the *Institutes* together with his commentaries. In the second edition, published in August of 1539, just before his first commentary (on Romans) appeared in October, he wrote: "If, after this road has, as it were, been paved, I shall publish any interpretations of Scripture, I shall always condense them, because I shall have no need to undertake long doctrinal discussions" (Calvin, *ICR*, "John Calvin to the Reader," p. 5).

121. Schleiermacher, *A Brief Outline of the Study of Theology*.

122. On continuities between Calvin's understanding of preaching and Schleiermacher's, see Dawn DeVries, *Jesus Christ in the Preaching of Calvin and Schleiermacher* (Louisville: Westminster John Knox, 1996), 2, 95.

123. Schleiermacher, *CF*, #18 (pp. 87–88).

of the interconnectedness, interdependence, and ecology of Christian piety and believing. Additional clarity and coherence come from understanding how different beliefs, information, ideas, and sensibilities interact, and greater depth comes from seeing how the whole is more than the sum of its parts. This is the primary respect in which systematic theology seems indissolubly associated with faithful inquiry, or with faith seeking understanding.

On the Importance of Interrelationships and Wholeness

A drive toward greater clarity, depth, and coherence by presenting Christian believing as an interconnected whole comes through in creeds and confessions that present important teachings in organized summaries for catechumens as well as for ministers and theologians. Although quite brief, the three articles of the early creed function this way: they present believing in God as Creator, Reconciler, and Renewer in a way that sculpts and expresses both gratitude and a sense of possibilities for gifts of creation and redemption. Lengthier Reformation confessions such as the Scots Confession of 1560 and the Westminster Confession of Faith function similarly. They present believing as an interconnected whole in a way that intimates a distinctive cast of fidelity and piety, or a particular stance.

The importance that generally has been attached to interrelation and wholeness also will be apparent from a brief if also selective review of systematic theologies through the ages. In *On First Principles*, which was fashioned to address questions and conflicting opinions at the Catechetical School in Alexandria, Origen appealed to a rule, or tradition, as he treated main topics. Indeed, from "elementary and foundation principles," he tried to construct "a connected body of doctrine," hoping that "by clear and cogent arguments (those interested in enlightening themselves) will discover the truth about each particular point and so will produce, as we have said, a single body of doctrine."[124]

Thomas Aquinas's *Summa Theologiae* tried a synthesis of the main subject matters in theology as a field of knowledge or a science. This work is more than a collection of teachings, sentences, or statements about discrete doctrines, and Thomas organized the material into an ordered discipline, a consistent whole that moved beyond piecemeal analysis and was intended to reduce the "swarm of pointless questions, articles, and arguments" sometimes generated by commentary and academic debate. In fact, "a *summa*, or systematic summary, was a genre of thirteenth-century writing which grew from more loosely knit *sententiae*, or judgments, which themselves had grown out of glosses on Scripture and from patristic passages often collected in anthologies, *florilegia*."[125]

124. Origen, *On First Principles*, trans. G. W. Butterworth (Gloucester: Peter Smith, 1973), 6.

125. *Christian Theology*, ed. Thomas Gilby, vol. 1 of *ST*, Blackfriars ed. (New York: McGraw-Hill, 1964), preface, p. xxi; foreword, p. 3; appendix 1, Structure of the *Summa*, p. 43. See also M. Dominique Chenu, OP, *The Scope of the Summa of St. Thomas*, trans. Robert Edward Brennan, OP, and Albert Marie Landry, OP (Washington, DC: Thomist, 1958), 3–5.

Calvin regarded his *Institutes* as "a sum of Christian doctrine" that articulates true piety as it treats "the chief and weightiest matters comprised in the Christian philosophy" by exploring the interrelated knowledge of God and ourselves.[126]

Schleiermacher believed that system is organic. He claims that it clarifies but does not answer all questions decisively, and he criticizes the "mania for system" behind egregious claims of church authorities to know the entire truth about everything. At the same time, he also maintains that doctrinal propositions communicate true piety and the religious self-consciousness only when they are taken all together, and that each individual proposition implies a striving after all the remaining ones. Accordingly, Christian teaching or doctrine (*Lehre*) uses the didactic form of expression in order to clarify doctrines and ideas in the totality of their predicates. "But manifestly this can only reach a satisfactory conclusion when the system of doctrine has become a complete system, in which every essential moment of religious and Christian consciousness is given its developed dogmatic expression, and all the dogmatic propositions are brought into relation with each other."[127] For Schleiermacher, the felt need for this sort of unity and completeness was closely associated with the need of the ecclesial community for clarity and norms as it teaches and as it tries to rouse and cultivate religious consciousness by preaching.[128]

The nineteenth-century American Presbyterian Charles Hodge wrote that the office of systematic theology is "to collect, authenticate, arrange, and exhibit [in] their internal relation to each other" the truths that the Bible contains.[129] Although his commitment to coherence is clear, Hodge's work does not always match the attention to piety and affection discernible in Calvin and in Schleiermacher. Was this due to a modernist scientism? In any case, Hodge claims that theology is a science that concerns both facts and ideas, and exhibits "the internal relation of those facts to one another, and each to all." Systematics presents an interrelated whole, and "a much higher knowledge is thus obtained than by mere accumulation of isolated facts. . . . We cannot know what God has revealed in his Word unless we understand, at least in some good measure, the relation in which separate truths therein contained stand to each other."[130] Augustus Hopkins Strong, a Baptist whose textbook was widely used in American seminaries for many years, took a similar tack. Strong defined theology as "the science of God and of the relations between God and the universe." And, he wrote, "science = facts + relations." Thus, the aim of the science of theology is to exhibit the facts with respect to God and the relationship between God

126. Calvin, *ICR*, "Subject Matter of the Present Work," pp. 6, 8; 1.1.1.

127. Schleiermacher, *CF*, #18 (pp. 86–87).

128. Schleiermacher, *CF*, #18 (p. 87); see also Julia Lamm, *The Living God: Schleiermacher's Theological Appropriation of Spinoza* (University Park: Pennsylvania State University Press, 1994), 60, 62.

129. Charles Hodge, *Systematic Theology: In Three Volumes* (Grand Rapids: Eerdmans, 1977), 1:1–2.

130. Hodge, *Systematic Theology*, 1:2.

and the universe "in their rational unity, as connected parts of a formulated and organic system of truth."[131]

Paul Tillich took pains to keep in view existential themes and what concerns us ultimately, and he introduced his *Systematic Theology* by saying: "It has always been impossible for me to think theologically in any other than a systematic way. The smallest problem, if taken seriously and radically, drove me to all other problems and to the anticipation of a whole in which they could find their solution."[132] Somewhat similarly, Helmut Thielicke wanted to go beyond theological essays in *The Evangelical Faith* because he believed basic questions had arisen that could be tackled "only by attempting a doctrinal totality." Again, "when problems affect the substance of Christian faith and touch on all its dimensions, then it is challenged as a whole and it must react accordingly." This is why Thielicke attempted what he called "the venture of a system" or "the venture of recapturing the total picture."[133]

In his *Foundations of Christian Faith*, Karl Rahner explicitly does not attempt a systematic or a summa in the sense of a sum of all theological knowledge, because he regards such a work as impossible for any contemporary theologian due to the specialization of theology and the proliferation of subdisciplines. He nevertheless tries a "first level of reflection" that "has a somewhat more comprehensive and systematic character than one might be accustomed to in the other theological writings of the author." Why? Because he believes that something is lost if we simply capitulate to fragmentation, namely, an intellectually honest expression of the Christian faith and Christian self-understanding as a whole that stands in a line with other such attempts, for example, professions of faith such as the Apostles' Creed, Augustine's *Enchiridion on Faith, Hope and Love*, Bonaventure's *Breviloquium*, and Aquinas's *Compendium of Theology to Brother Reginald*. Rahner notes that each of these texts gives "a relatively brief overview of the whole and of the essentials of Christianity," and he claims that "there must always be new attempts at such reflection upon the single whole of Christianity."[134]

My own commitments to the clarity, depth of understanding, and coherence available from a systematic arrangement of theological statements are rooted in the conviction that the church's pastoral aim—the formation of the people of God in a piety, fidelity, or stance—requires an interpretive vision or reading

131. Augustus Hopkins Strong, *Systematic Theology: A Compendium and Commonplace Book Designed for the Use of Theological Students*, 4th ed. (New York: A. C. Armstrong & Son, 1893), 1–2.

132. Tillich, *Reason and Revelation, Being and God*, vii.

133. Helmut Thielicke, *Prolegomena*, vol. 1 of *The Evangelical Faith*, ed. and trans. Geoffrey W. Bromiley (Grand Rapids: Eerdmans, 1974), 16.

134. Karl Rahner, *Foundations of Christian Faith*, trans. William V. Dych (New York: Seabury, 1978), xii, xv, 2.

with respect to God of the many others, objects, situations, and realities we interact with. The church tries to form people in a piety or skein of sensibility and affection that is more than the sum of its parts and that can be communicated, shaped, and expressed in its integrity only by a holistic vision of God, the world, and ourselves. Such a vision can only be obtained when theological statements are taken all together as an organic unity. This is why, as it pursues the church's pastoral aim by means of preaching, teaching, and pastoral care, the leadership of the church has a special interest in the sorts of clarity, understanding, and coherence furnished by systematic theology.[135]

It is not surprising, then, that summary theological statements have been written to further the formation of Christians in a piety or faithful stance and, quite often, in order to contribute to the education of leaders for the church. Summary presentations of Christian believing are didactic or educational products of the church; historically, they have been most at home in catechetical instruction and church-related schools. Indeed, from Origen's Catechetical School at Alexandria onward, we may speak of the ecclesial-scholastic character and setting of systematic theology.

> Up until the beginning of the fourth century, it was the day-to-day life of local congregations in worship, preaching, baptism, instruction, and written correspondence that supplied occasions for the development of creedal statements. The text that has come down

135. Some curricular implications for the training of ministers follow. For example, the purposes and aims of a class where students learn how to interpret one or another biblical text may be distinguished from the purposes and aims of a class in systematic theology, where a high premium will be placed on understanding interconnections and gaining some knowledge of a comprehensive theological vision. Within the field of theology itself, classes that focus on one or another topic or doctrine—for example, the church, sin, grace—are analogous to monographs and have somewhat different objectives than do classes in systematics.

Survey courses that introduce students to different ways of doing theology—for example, fundamentalist, liberal, neoorthodox, process, liberation, feminist—offer important exposures to the increasingly large number of different approaches to the discipline. A danger, however, is that they will never move beyond comparative studies in theological methods and thus will fail to suggest how much and how often, in theology, method and content interact. Moreover, by themselves, they do not furnish an exposure to a comprehensive theological vision, and they do not give students a sense for the organic unity of Christian faith and believing. Survey courses, therefore, do not introduce students to the kinds of clarity, understanding, and coherence that are developed by a systematic theology. For this reason, while they have a role in seminary curricula, survey courses are no substitute for significant study in systematics. Furthermore, where survey courses are substituted for systematics, churches are more likely to suffer pastoral leaders who know a little about many different approaches to Christian theology but are unable to interpret and envision the life of faith as a whole with theological clarity and depth (and who are possibly even unaware that positions of pastoral leadership call on them to do so).

to us as the Apostles' Creed, for example, was originally used by the church at Rome as a formula for summarizing catechetical instruction in the faith on the occasion of baptism. Although no single Eastern formula acquired a preeminent status similar to that of the Roman creed in the West, there is sufficient resemblance among local creeds in the East to speak of "an Eastern type." Here again, a primary function of local creeds was to summarize catechetical instruction on the occasion of baptism.[136]

During the Reformation, Protestant churches sometimes marked their establishment by adopting a confessional statement that took a somewhat systematic form, for example, the Scots Confession of 1560. Churches used these statements not only to communicate their beliefs and to guide clergy, but also for instructional purposes. Indeed, it was not unusual for churches to issue confessions together with catechisms, for example, the Westminster Confession of Faith and the Larger Catechism, and even to issue catechisms as primary doctrinal standards, such as the Heidelberg Catechism.

Emil Brunner was thus quite correct to regard catechetical instruction as a major impetus for theological reflection. For thoughtful people, he said, instruction in doctrines and beliefs naturally raises questions and so leads to the reformulation of the Christian message in intellectual terms. "The thoughtful believer is constantly perceiving new depths and heights in the truth of the Gospel. Thus the Christian catechetical instruction, which was given through the rich intellectual medium of the Greek world of culture, became a method of theological and dogmatic teaching. The instruction of educated catechumens developed into Dogmatics"—that is, theology, or disciplined reflection on church teaching.[137]

Brunner's point is strengthened when we remember that it was the instruction of educated catechumens at Alexandria that gave rise to the first systematic theology, Origen's *On First Principles*. Moreover, it appears that in this work Origen was dealing with questions and topics that were raised and discussed at the Catechetical School even before his time, and that Clement, Origen's predecessor there, also wrote a work on first principles and theology, which is now lost. The ecclesial-scholastic character and context of systematics are further underscored by the probability that "in both works the substance was simply the lectures delivered to students in the School."[138]

In his foreword to the *Summa Theologiae*, Thomas Aquinas says that "the teacher of Catholic truth has not only to develop advanced students but also to shape those who are making a start," and that "we propose in this work to convey the truths of the Christian religion in a style serviceable for the training of beginners." This led M. D. Chenu to claim that the *Summa* "was written . . . for the instruction of freshmen in theology," although he also suggested that the "angelic doctor" may have overestimated his students' abilities!

136. See J. N. D. Kelly, *Early Christian Creeds*, 3rd ed. (New York: McKay, 1972), 131–66, 181–83.

137. Brunner, *Dogmatics*, 1:10.

138. Origen, *On First Principles*, introduction by Henri de Lubac, xxxi.

Thomas himself clearly hoped that the disciplined order of his work would treat essential points according to requirements of "sound educational method" as it had developed in medieval universities and that it would reduce the kind of repetitiveness that "breeds boredom and muddle" in students' minds.[139] Somewhat similarly, Calvin understood himself to occupy "the office of a teacher in the church" as he undertook the task of writing his *Institutes* in 1536 to be something of an extended reflection on the elements of catechism (the Apostles' Creed, the Ten Commandments, and the Lord's Prayer). By 1559, Calvin's treatise had grown into a textbook (with wide margins) "to prepare and instruct candidates in sacred theology for the reading of the divine Word" at the College of Geneva.[140]

The very term "Protestant Scholasticism" "refers specifically to the methods used in classroom disputation or in written works arising out of that context."[141] Indeed, it was not unusual for a theologian during the sixteenth and seventeenth centuries to publish his "theological course," as did the Scot John Sharp, who taught at Die University.[142] However, not every work by a Protestant Scholastic was directed exclusively at formal students; Wollebius's *Compendium of Christian Theology*, for example, was based on popular lectures.[143]

For all its innovations, Schleiermacher's *The Christian Faith* retains the propositional form and at least some vestiges of the "outline-like" organization characteristic of the Protestant Scholastics. He also associated theology quite closely with the training of ministers, and in his *Brief Outline on the Study of Theology* he claims that theology is the special responsibility of "the leadership of the church."[144]

A number of systematic theologies in America emerged directly out of class notes and lectures, as did Robert Lewis Dabney's text *Syllabus of the Course of Systematic and Polemic Theology Taught in Union Theological Seminary, Virginia*. Indeed, the first edition was printed by Dabney's students themselves, and in his preface to the second edition Dabney says that "the main design . . . has been to furnish students in divinity, pastors, and intelligent lay-Christians, a view of the whole field of Christian theology, without swelling

139. Aquinas, *ST* 1:3 (preface); Chenu, *The Scope of the Summa of St. Thomas*, 3.

140. Calvin, *ICR*, "John Calvin to the Reader 1559," p. 4; see also John Calvin, *Institutes of the Christian Religion (1536)*, trans. Ford Lewis Battles (Atlanta: John Knox, 1975).

141. Richard Muller, "The Problem of Protestant Scholasticism—a Review and Definition," in *Reformation and Scholasticism: An Ecumenical Enterprise*, ed. Willem J. van Assekt and Eef Dekker (Grand Rapids: Baker Academic, 2001), 53–54, 62.

142. P. G. Ryken, "Scottish Reformed Scholasticism," in *Protestant Scholasticism: Essays in Reassessment*, ed. Carl R. Trueman and R. Scott Clark (Carlisle, UK: Paternoster, 1999), 200–201.

143. John W. Beardslee III, ed. and trans., *Reformed Dogmatics: Seventeenth-Century Reformed Theology through the Writings of Wollebius, Voetius, and Turretin* (Grand Rapids: Baker Books, 1977), 10.

144. Schleiermacher, *Brief Outline on the Study of Theology*, #3 and #4 (p. 20).

the work to a size too unwieldy and costly for the purposes of instruction."[145] A similarly scholastic context and concern comes through in Augustus Hopkins Strong's *Systematic Theology: A Compendium and Commonplace Book Designed for the Use of Theological Students*, an enlarged and emended edition of the author's "Lectures on Theology," printed in 1876 for the use of students at Rochester Theological Seminary.[146]

Louis Berkhof's *Systematic Theology* owes a good deal with respect to both its organization and its substance to earlier Reformed Scholastics. It was intended as a textbook for students in theology at Calvin Theological Seminary in Grand Rapids, Michigan, and Berkhof himself was gratified that it was also taken up at other seminaries and Bible schools both in the United States and abroad. In fact, Berkhof's work had its beginning when two students transcribed his lectures in 1926–1927 and 1927–1928.[147]

The extraordinary length of Karl Barth's *Church Dogmatics* limits its usefulness for classes that intend to furnish a comprehensive outline of Christian theology.[148] At the same time, Barth's appreciation for the orderliness of Scholastic, orthodox Protestant theology is well known.[149] And, after a fashion, his dogmatics also retains a propositional form and "outline-like" organization.

Karl Rahner's *Foundations of Christian Faith* was occasioned by the call of Vatican II for a reform of ecclesiastical studies. In particular, the Decree on Priestly Formation called for "an introductory course" for students of priestly ministry that would integrate philosophy and theology and present the mystery of salvation in interrelationship with the pastoral intent of theological studies.[150] Hence Rahner's attempt at a disciplined first level of reflection on Christian faith as a whole.

Rosemary Radford Ruether's *Sexism and God-Talk: Toward a Feminist Theology* came

145. Robert Lewis Dabney, *Syllabus of the Course of Systematic and Polemic Theology Taught in Union Theological Seminary, Virginia*, 2nd ed. (St. Louis: Presbyterian Publishing Company of St. Louis, 1878), 4.

146. Strong, *Systematic Theology*, vii.

147. Louis Berkhof, *Systematic Theology*, new edition containing the full text of *Systematic Theology* and the original *Introductory Volume to Systematic Theology* (Grand Rapids: Eerdmans, 1996), vi.

148. Hence the different books that have attempted summary introductions to Barth's approach, including Geoffrey W. Bromiley's introductory exposition for "the ordinary student of theology" who runs into the many and huge volumes of the *Church Dogmatics* (Bromiley, *Introduction to the Theology of Karl Barth* [Grand Rapids: Eerdmans, 1979], ix). See also Karl Barth, *Dogmatics in Outline*, trans. G. T. Thompson (New York: Harper & Brothers, 1959); *Church Dogmatics: A Selection*, trans. and ed. G. W. Bromiley; selected, with an introduction, by Helmut Gollwitzer (New York: Harper & Row, 1961).

149. See "Karl Barth's Foreword" to Heinrich Heppe, *Reformed Dogmatics: Set Out and Illustrated from the Sources*, ed. Ernest Bizer, trans. G. T. Thompson (Grand Rapids: Baker Books, 1978), v–vii.

150. Rahner, *Foundations of Christian Faith*, 3.

> about as a textbook for courses in feminist theology. Says Ruether: "There existed [in the 1970s] very little systematic Christian theology written from a feminist perspective." Therefore, she arranged readings around familiar theological topics, and her work eventually covered "the whole range of topics of systematic theology."[151] Peter C. Hodgson's *Winds of the Spirit: A Constructive Christian Theology*, which tries to reenvision Christian theology as a whole, evolved from lectures in introductory courses in Christian theology at Vanderbilt Divinity School.[152] Christopher Morse's *Not Every Spirit: A Dogmatics of Christian Disbelief* also underscores the ecclesial-scholastic context. Morse refers to a rethinking of the role of dogmatics and the critical study of church doctrines at Union Theological Seminary in New York, as well as to a number of teaching contexts. "But always I have come back to the classrooms of students. . . . There is scarcely a page of this book that does not recall to me some student question, disagreement, or remark."[153]

This brings us to a final point. Associated as it is with the transmission of faithful wisdom by means of catechetics and theological education, systematic theology pursues greater clarity, depth of understanding, and coherence by engaging and answering *questions*. Many of these questions arise as Christians and their communities interact with changing circumstances and thus become involved in attempts to envision or interpret themselves and these changing circumstances and realities in relationship to God.

Christians have made use of theological inquiry and argument in order to address controversies and questions since New Testament times. Consider some issues addressed in Paul's letters, for example, 1 Thessalonians (questions about what happens to those who have died before the Lord returns), 1 Corinthians (questions concerning marriage and food offered to idols, as well as the resurrection of the dead and the kinds of bodies with which the dead are raised), and Romans (questions of the law and faith, the relationship between God's election of Israel and salvation for gentiles). Again, early conciliar creeds and definitions addressed disputed questions—for example, the Nicene Creed and the relationship of Jesus Christ to God, the Chalcedonian Definition and the constitution of Christ's person. Catechisms, of course, have ordinarily consisted of an ordered set of questions and answers.

At the beginning of *On First Principles*, Origen says: "Many of those . . . who profess to believe in Christ, hold conflicting opinions not only on small and

151. Ruether, *Sexism and God-Talk*, xiii, xv.

152. Peter C. Hodgson, *Winds of the Spirit: A Constructive Christian Theology* (Louisville: Westminster John Knox, 1994), xi.

153. Christopher Morse, *Not Every Spirit: A Dogmatics of Christian Disbelief* (Valley Forge, PA: Trinity Press International, 1994), xiv.

trivial questions but also on some that are great and important; on the nature, for instance, of God or the Lord Jesus Christ or of the Holy Spirit, and in addition on the natures of those created beings, the dominions and the holy powers. In view of this it seems necessary first to lay down a definite line and unmistakable rule in regard to each of these."[154] Individual articles in Thomas Aquinas's *Summa Theologiae* are presented according to a *quaestio* form and method of inquiry. That is, they proceed from a question (e.g., Is Christian theology a science?) to a number of initial objections (e.g., Christian theology does not look like a science because it does not advance from self-evident principles). These are followed by a contrasting statement (Augustine calls it a science). Then comes a general answer or reply to the question (Christian theology is a science of a certain kind). Finally, there are specific replies to the initial objections (e.g., the premises of a science need not be self-evident principles; they may also come from a higher science, as is the case with Christian theology).[155]

Schleiermacher claims that the didactic form of expression is most appropriate in dogmatics and that it "arises mainly out of the problem of settling apparent conflicts between individual metaphors and figures" at a less precise level of religious discourse. Many apparent contradictions at this level, he says, can be reconciled by an alternative and more precise expression. This reconciling expression, in turn, cannot contradict itself or other propositions accepted to be true, and thus inevitably branches out into a full systematic inquiry as "certainty on this point can be gained only by the relating of several such expressions to each other, and by ever repeated attempts to connect them together."[156]

Tillich understood his *Systematic Theology* as an answering theology in which existential questions were correlated with theological answers. He says that he was especially interested in the questions asked by the students who heard his lectures as well as the questions that they, in turn, were asked by people both inside and outside their churches. "A help to answering questions: this is exactly the purpose of this theological system."[157]

All in all, it seems worth repeating Brunner's perceptive observation that the thoughtful person cannot receive the doctrinal elements of Christian teaching "without finding that they raise questions in his mind."[158] Systematic theology engages such questions, and it is thus at home in contexts of inquiry, investigation, argument, and discussion. It cannot flourish where questions and disputes

154. Origen, *On First Principles*, pp. 1–2.
155. Aquinas, *ST* 1a.1.1 (p. 11).
156. Schleiermacher, *CF*, #18 (p. 86).
157. Tillich, *Reason and Revelation, Being and God*, viii.
158. Brunner, *Dogmatics*, 1:10.

are suppressed in favor of a merely authoritarian indoctrination (see chap. 1, prop. #1 above).

The basic content of the present work determines its fundamental framework or architecture, and, like the structure of the 1559 edition of Calvin's *Institutes of the Christian Religion*, its general arrangement hinges on the complex image of God as Creator and Redeemer. Calvin himself regards Christian theology as a kind of wisdom having to do with true piety, or the knowledge of God and ourselves. He claims, further, that the sort of knowledge of God that correlates with a true understanding of ourselves is knowledge of God as both Creator (the one who bestows on creatures gifts of existence, capacities, order, and sustenance) and Redeemer (the one who saves and bestows on creatures gifts of reconciliation and new life). In addition, he maintains that this portrait of the deity entails the recognition of human diminution and corruption as well as an apprehension of God as Judge—items Calvin understood in close connection with grace and renewal and thus placed in the initial section of book 2 of his *Institutes* under "Knowledge of God the Redeemer in Jesus Christ."[159]

My system presents a vision of God, the world, and ourselves. It, too, presumes that a true piety, disposition, and understanding of the world and ourselves are helped when we and the many others, objects, situations, and realities with which we interact are depicted in relationship with the Creator-Redeemer, where this specification of the divine also entails the image of God as Judge. Thus, the structure of my theological vision is determined by the substantive norm of God as the Creator-Judge-Redeemer disclosed in the event of Jesus Christ. All other things (the world and ourselves) will be interpreted with reference to this image/idea of God.

Additional layers of complexity derive from the contours of the event of Jesus Christ as it is presented in the New Testament. In its expansive compass, this event gathers up and fulfills the graceful trajectory of God's dealings with Israel and all of humanity, and it also extends to the Spirit that renews life, as well as to the consummation of all things (see chap. 1, prop. #14 above). For these reasons, redemption will be understood to include three closely related aspects: judgment, reconciliation, and renewal.

Accordingly, part 2 of the following system pictures the world and ourselves in relation to God as Creator, and it includes sections on creation and sustenance

159. Calvin, *ICR* 2.1.1–11. Schleiermacher adapted Calvin's schema to his own understanding of theology as an explication of piety or religious self-consciousness, treating creation and the original perfection of humanity in the "First Part" of his system of doctrine, and treating sin, Christ, regeneration, sanctification, the church and its consummation in the "Second Part" (Schleiermacher, *CF*, pp. ix–xii).

(or continuation). Part 3 depicts the world and ourselves in relation to God as Redeemer. It contains sections on the event of Jesus Christ and the covenant of grace, sin and renewal, history, and hope. We therefore obtain the following (rough) organizational schema.

Part I: Method
Part II: God the Creator
—creation
—continuation
Part III: God the Redeemer
—Jesus Christ, the covenant of grace, and the Spirit
—sin and regeneration
—history and hope

Where does the present system set forth the doctrine of God? Schleiermacher notes that his system includes statements about God and divine attributes in each of its parts. Therefore, "the doctrine of God, as set forth in the totality of the divine attributes, can only be completed simultaneously with the whole system: whereas it is usually treated continuously and without break, and before any other points of doctrine."[160] The usual treatments he had in mind were Scholastic writings such as Wollebius's *Compendium of Christian Theology* and Francis Turretin's *Institutes of Elenctic Theology*.[161] The Westminster Confession of Faith of 1647 also treated the doctrine of God in this fashion.[162] The practice persisted in nineteenth-century works, such as Charles Hodge's *Systematic Theology*, and in Emil Brunner's dogmatics in the twentieth century.[163] More recently, Robert W. Jenson has presented a doctrine of God that is highly christologically determined—continuously in a single section, and before his consideration of creation, creatures, the church, and fulfillment.[164] I should note, however, that, like Schleiermacher, Calvin does not present his entire doctrine of God continuously at any one place in the *Institutes*.

Having adopted an organizational scheme that pictures the world and ourselves in relationship to the Creator-Judge-Redeemer, I follow Calvin and Schleiermacher in *distributing* the depiction of God throughout my system. In fact,

160. Schleiermacher, *CF*, #31 (p. 128).

161. Beardslee, *Reformed Dogmatics*, 37–45; Turretin, *Institutes of Elenctic Theology*, trans. George Musgrave Giger (Phillipsburg, NJ: Presbyterian and Reformed, 1992), 1:169–310.

162. See the Westminster Confession of Faith, in *BOC* 6.011–6.013.

163. See Hodge, *Systematic Theology*, 1:366–441; Brunner, *Dogmatics*, 1:117–302.

164. Robert W. Jenson, *The Triune God*, vol. 1 of *Systematic Theology* (New York: Oxford University Press, 1997), 63–236. See also Jenson, *The Works of God*, vol. 2 of *Systematic Theology* (New York: Oxford University Press, 1999), 380.

the same thing may be said of my depictions of the world and ourselves: I have distributed these throughout, and they only come to completion with the system as a whole.

The substantive theological vision of God as Creator-Judge-Redeemer, therefore, comes to articulation only in this work as a unified whole. Indeed, both the vision of God, the world, and ourselves that I shall present and the piety that it shapes and expresses inevitably are distorted if and when symbols such as creation, sin, and redemption are isolated from one another.[165] The point is to pursue clarity, understanding, and coherence by emphasizing interrelationships and interconnections in a way that promotes an integral piety.

165. I should also note that the order of presentation adopted here should not be confused with the order of knowing and experience. It is not true that persons must first come to envision or apprehend God as Creator and then, only later, as Judge and Redeemer. Indeed, for a good many Christians and their communities, the sequence often seems reversed: a compelling experience of being caught up in consequences of corruption but also of being redeemed in Christ and the Spirit is followed by attention to the Creator and Sustainer of nature and history. Of course, it is entirely possible that, for some, there will be no discernible sequence.

PART II

Creation

Chapter Three

The Constitution of the Dynamic World: Cosmic Ecology

Christian theology, I maintain, concerns God, the world, and ourselves, where God is understood as Creator-Redeemer. Accordingly, part 2 of the present system is especially occupied with the world as creation, ourselves as creatures, and God as Creator. It focuses on the relationship of the world and ourselves to the deep ground, source, and ordering power, as well as on the piety or pattern of sensibilities evoked in us by this relationship and how it may inform our living. Part 3 will focus on the world and ourselves in relationship to God as Redeemer. Therefore, the full vision or picture of God, the world, and ourselves will emerge only when both parts are complete.

The Creator-Redeemer

Proposition #26 God the Creator is God the Redeemer, and this equation has important consequences for the way we understand both creation and redemption.

The basic nature of this equation in a Christian context is apparent from the early creeds, which join "God the Father Almighty, maker of heaven and earth" with Jesus Christ, the one who reconciles, and with the Spirit, who gives life. The creeds thereby join the principle or agency of creation by which all things exist with the work of reconciliation and renewal (or redemption).[1]

H. Richard Niebuhr argues that, by referring to "God the Father Almighty," the first article of the Apostles' Creed already suggests that the God who creates is also the faithful Redeemer whom Jesus teaches us to call "our Father"

1. See chap. 2, prop. #19, where I argue that the idea that God is Creator-Redeemer rules out a variety of dualisms.

in the Lord's Prayer.[2] Commenting on the first article of the creed, the Heidelberg Catechism directs the catechumen to say that, through Jesus Christ, I trust God as "faithful Father."[3] That is, for the writers of the catechism, Jesus Christ, the life-giving Word, demonstrates that God is faithful. He discloses that the Creator, the power of reality who makes all things, visible and invisible, is the faithful Redeemer.

The Deliverer Is the Creator

Israel's scriptural witness equates the Deliverer with the Creator. The God of Abraham and Sarah, the God of Miriam, Moses, and Zipporah, who delivers Israel from slavery in Egypt and who covenants at Sinai, the God who blesses David, and the God who returns the people from exile in Babylon is identified with the God who fashions the cosmos, who creates the heavens and stretches them out, and who alone presides over all that is. To examine some consequences of this equation, consider the expression "Yahweh, maker of heaven and earth" as it recurs in the Psalms.

> May you be blessed by the LORD,
>   who made heaven and earth. (Ps. 115:15)
>
> I lift up my eyes to the hills—
>   from where does my help come?
> My help comes from the LORD,
>   who made heaven and earth. (Ps. 121:1–2)
>
> Our help is in the name of the LORD,
>   who made heaven and earth. (Ps. 124:8)
>
> Happy are those whose help is the God of Jacob,
>   whose hope is in the LORD their God,
> who made heaven and earth,
>   the sea, and all that is in them;
> who keeps faith forever,
>   who executes justice for the oppressed;
> who gives food to the hungry. (Ps. 146:5–7)

2. H. Richard Niebuhr, *Radical Monotheism and Western Culture, with Supplementary Essays* (Louisville: Westminster John Knox, 1993), 32–33.

3. See *BOC* 4.026.

Each psalm makes a distinct point. Psalm 115 contrasts the greatness of Yahweh with the impotence of idols, while Psalm 121 gives assurance of God's protection. Psalm 124 gives thanks for Israel's deliverance from enemies, and Psalm 146 contrasts the happiness of those whose help is the God of Jacob with the situation of those who rely on princes and mortals (or even empires). In all four psalms, however, the import of the phrase "'the Lord who made heaven and earth' is to identify Yahweh as the deity who can help and bless the people of the Lord because of Yahweh's power as creator of all that is."[4] This is why Yahweh is unlike other gods and idols; this is why Yahweh rules over princes and mortals; and this is why Yahweh, the faithful one who covenants with Israel, is able to execute justice and feed the hungry.

That Yahweh is the Creator—the cosmic orderer and designer who stretches out the heavens like a tent and sets the earth on its foundations (Ps. 104:2, 5)—indicates that Yahweh is able to bless, help, and deliver. It may even be accurate to say that, in the terms of Israel's mature witness, the deliverer would be unable to deliver were the deliverer not also the creator. In any case, Israel's creation piety claims creation for the God of Israel. It claims that the God who covenants with Israel and keeps faith forever, the one in whom Israel hopes, is none other than the only cosmic creator who presides over the processes of the world and is thus sufficiently powerful to deliver on promises and hopes. Or, to put this same point another way, because Yahweh is able to create life and the conditions for it in the world, Yahweh is also able to transform life and renew it.

Psalm 114 displays a similar logic. Verses 1 and 2 say:

> When Israel went out from Egypt, . . .
> Judah became God's sanctuary,
>   Israel his dominion.

Accordingly, the psalm has to do with Yahweh, the God who resides with Israel and who, in a nation-establishing act of deliverance, brought up "the house of Jacob" from slavery. Next, the psalm says that the sea fled, the Jordan turned back, the mountains skipped like rams and the hills like lambs. Why? Because the exodus, the paradigmatic saving event in the history of Israel, is an act of deliverance performed by the God who presides over the seas, the rivers, the mountains and hills, and all that is. This is why it makes sense to say,

4. James L. Mays, "'Maker of Heaven and Earth': Creation in the Psalms," in *God Who Creates: Essays in Honor of W. Sibley Towner*, ed. William P. Brown and S. Dean McBride Jr. (Grand Rapids: Eerdmans, 2000), 76.

> Tremble, O earth, at the presence of the LORD,
> at the presence of the God of Jacob. (Ps. 114:7)[5]

To equate Yahweh with the maker of heaven and earth is, of course, a monotheizing move. Yahweh becomes something more and something other than just another national deity or local power. Like Amun-Re in ancient Egypt, the God of Israel accumulates the powers of a single divinity responsible for the creation, ordering, and continued existence of the cosmos.[6] Yahweh becomes a God unlike all other gods who do not have such powers and responsibilities. In fact, when compared with Yahweh, the cosmic ruler, these other deities seem not to be real or complete gods at all.[7] But this, in turn, suggests an important respect in which the symbolic idea of the creator influences the symbolic ideas of the redeemer and redemption. Unlike other gods and idols, not only is Yahweh able to deliver because Yahweh is creator of the cosmos, but also—unlike other helpers and deliverers—Yahweh and Yahweh's acts of deliverance may now be understood in a cosmic and universal key.

This becomes explicit in Amos 9:5–7, where once again the God of Israel is the creator who "founds his vault upon the earth," who brings forth the seas and pours them out on the earth. Only here—and perhaps for the first time—Israel's Deliverer claims to deliver others besides Israel.

> Are you not like the Ethiopians to me,
> O people of Israel? says the LORD.
> Did I not bring Israel up from the land of Egypt,
> and the Philistines from Caphtor and the Arameans from Kir?
> (Amos 9:7)

Walter Brueggemann notes that, with these words, "the exclusiveness between Israel as an Exodus people and Yahweh as an Exodus God is broken. . . . This same God has wrought exoduses for the Philistines and for the Arameans, Israel's most persistent enemies. Yahweh is characteristically a God who enacts

5. In his commentary on Ps. 114, John Calvin says: "The sea rendering such obedience to its Creator, sanctified his name; and Jordan, by its submission, put honor upon his power; and the mountains, by their quaking, proclaimed how they were overawed at the presence of his dreadful majesty" (Calvin, *Commentary on the Book of Psalms*, trans. James Anderson, vol. 4 in *Calvin's Commentaries*, Calvin Translation Society [Grand Rapids: Baker Books, 1998], 338).

6. Jan Assmann, *The Search for God in Ancient Egypt*, trans. David Lorton (Ithaca, NY: Cornell University Press, 2001), 120–21, 189–90.

7. See chap. 1, props. #11 and #12.

exoduses, and who does so in many places, perhaps everywhere."[8] There are other passages that paint a different and more exclusive picture of Yahweh the Deliverer, but the universal horizon that emerges at this point in Israel's witness should not be ignored; neither should its roots in the equation of Israel's helper and Deliverer with the *Creator*, who presides over all of history as well as the entire cosmos. In short, to equate Deliverer with Creator suggests a universal horizon for deliverance.

The Redeemer Is the Creator

The New Testament equates the Redeemer with the Creator, and with similar results. One important text is the prologue to the Gospel of John, where the Word, or Logos, who was in the beginning with God, who was God, and through whom all things came into being, is identified with the principle of redemption in whom is life, who became flesh and dwelt among us, and whose light (which darkness attempts to overcome but has not) continues to shine (John 1:1–5, 14). That is, the Creator comes to creatures as Redeemer, and the historically particular work of redemption in Jesus Christ is thus associated with an explicitly cosmic horizon.[9]

For Paul, the symbolic idea of new creation associates redemption with the God who creates, and it also presses the idea of redemption, in turn, toward a universal and cosmic horizon. David L. Bartlett notes that Paul's entire gospel may be regarded as a message of new creation, and that there is a tension in this message between more restrictive and capacious meanings. For example, in Galatians "new creation" is restricted to those who believe in Jesus Christ, while in 2 Corinthians 5 it remains unclear whether the new creation of a "righteous humankind out of sinners" is a gift only for believers or "a hope for all humankind." Again, though the exact term "new creation" is not used in Romans 5 and 1 Corinthians 15:22, Bartlett notes that, in these passages, "Paul . . . holds out the possibility that Christ will overcome death for all of humankind."

Indeed, in Romans 8, where Paul pointedly tells us that "the whole creation has been groaning in labor pains," it is "not just humans who move between creation and new creation, it is the whole universe."[10] Redemption "is no longer considered from an anthropological point of view; it is now recast in cosmic

8. Walter Brueggemann, *Theology of the Old Testament: Testimony, Dispute, Advocacy* (Minneapolis: Fortress, 1997), 178.

9. See chap. 1, prop. #14.

10. David L. Bartlett, "Creation Waits with Eager Longing," in Brown and McBride, *God Who Creates*, 232, 237, 250, 243.

terms" and "is expected to affect not only human beings but all material and physical creation as well."[11]

Bartlett says that the statement in 1 Corinthians 15:28, "all things are subject to [the Son] . . . that God might be all in all," is a poetic expression that intimates redemption for all people or God's coming redemptive relationship with all things. In short, he concludes that, for Paul, "sometimes 'new creation' seems to be a gift for the faithful and sometimes a promise for all humankind, even a promise for the whole cosmos."[12]

The apocalyptic image of a "new heaven and a new earth" in Revelation 21:1 might be taken to indicate a repudiation of God's original creation and thus to complete the discontinuity between creation and redemption. However, a number of commentators note that this motif points to a transformation or renewal of the present world.[13] John T. Carroll says: "It is misleading to suggest that the old world is simply replaced by a new and perfect one." We thus come across yet another image of redemption that strains toward the cosmic scope of creation. The reason is that the God who makes all things new in Revelation 21:5 is, in fact, the God who creates. "For John the visionary, God—the eternal one, the one 'who was and is and is to come'—is the creator of the universe. All of space-time is in the hands of God the *Pantokrator* (Rev. 1:8; 4:8; 11:17; 15:3; 16:7, 14; 19:6, 15; 21:22)."[14]

Creation Piety

If the identification of Creator and Redeemer leads us to entertain images of redemption that strain toward the (cosmic and universal) scope of creation, then it also suggests a piety for which creation is more than merely the prerequisite for the historical drama of human redemption. Paul says that "*creation* waits with eager longing" (Rom. 8:19), and it follows that we must now reckon with the idea that the dynamics of redemption extend well beyond the province of the

11. Joseph A. Fitzmyer, SJ, *Romans: A New Translation with Introduction and Commentary* (New York: Doubleday, 1993), 505–6.

12. Bartlett, "Creation Waits with Eager Longing," 242–43, 250. Brendan Byrne, SJ, *Romans*, Sacra Pagina, vol. 6 (Collegeville, MN: Liturgical Press, 1966), 255, says that Rom. 8:18–22 is "particularly distinctive" in "its apparent inclusion of the nonhuman created world . . . within the sweep of salvation," but also claims that "this is unprecedented in Paul."

13. Wilfrid J. Harrington, OP, *Revelation*, Sacra Pagina, vol. 16 (Collegeville, MN: Liturgical Press, 1993), 210; J. Massyngberde Ford, *Revelation: Introduction, Translation, and Commentary* (Garden City, NY: Doubleday, 1975), 364–65.

14. John T. Carroll, "Creation and Apocalypse," in Brown and McBride, *God Who Creates*, 255–56, 258–59.

human. Indeed, because the Creator of all things is Redeemer, grace (whether creating, redeeming, or renewing) is not foreign to the world but embedded in it. Grace is built into the existence, constitution, and continuation of all things. We may thus envision the nebula, galaxies, geospheres, biospheres, societies, and histories as a cosmos of grace, a region of gifts and occasions in which we encounter tendencies and trajectories of the Creator-Redeemer.[15]

This last point puts us at odds with theologies in which history, understood as the realm of moral interactions among persons as well as salvific interactions between God and humans, is sharply distinguished from nature, understood as raw material for historical transformation and an inert setting for the divine-human encounter. This is because the almost inevitable implication of this distinction is that creation and cosmos exist entirely for the sake of human history and redemption.

The nineteenth-century liberal Protestant Albrecht Ritschl claimed that the human predicament is characterized by a contradiction. On the one hand, we are a part of the world and its natural restrictions. We participate in forms of society, such as marriage, family, and the state, that are conditioned by natural differences in sex, birth, class, and nationality, "and therefore also offer occasions for self-seeking." On the other hand, we are spiritual personalities claiming to dominate nature. God, said Ritschl, is the loving will or power above the world who sustains human spiritual self-consciousness and moral personality by helping us overcome ethically irrational nature and transcend it toward universal moral ends. Indeed, the kingdom of God, or the *telos* of history, "the divinely ordained highest good," is the ultimate triumph of spirit over nature, which presents humanity with this supernatural and supramundane ethical task.[16]

Ritschl's student Wilhelm Hermann continued a sharp distinction between nature and free moral personality, associating the latter with faith, history, communion with God, and the believer as a new creation. Hermann emphasized that faith is awakened through a historical revelation that touches our inner spiritual life. Indeed, he claimed that "God is hidden from us in nature because we do

15. Joseph Sittler, *Evocations of Grace: Writings on Ecology, Theology, and Ethics*, ed. Steven Bouma-Prediger and Peter Bakken (Grand Rapids: Eerdmans, 2000), 83–86, 150–59.

16. Albrecht Ritschl, *The Christian Doctrine of Justification and Reconciliation*, trans. H. R. Mackintosh and A. B. Macaulay (Clifton, NJ: Reference Book Publishers, 1966), 199, 326, 610–14, 620; Ritschl, *Three Essays*, translated with introduction by Philip Hefner (Philadelphia: Fortress, 1972), 157, 222–24. See also Claude Welch, *Protestant Thought in the Nineteenth Century*, vol. 2, *1870–1914* (New Haven: Yale University Press, 1985), 8, 23; H. Richard Niebuhr, *Christ and Culture*, 50th anniversary ed. (New York: Harper & Row, 2006), 94–100.

not find our whole selves there. . . . It is only out of life in history that God can come to meet us."[17]

Is there something of a Ritschlian "hangover" in Karl Barth's theology when he claims that creation makes possible covenant history? For Barth, "creation sets the stage for the story of the covenant of grace" as the story of God's saving interactions with humans. Creation is like a structure, platform, or theatrical stage on which human history plays when the lights come up. Barth claims, "The aim of creation is history," a view that accords with a potentially myopic concentration on the anthropological. "Creation . . . fashions the world as a sphere for man who is to be a participant" in God's grace. Indeed, "the whole cosmos was precisely created in that in it there might be this event and revelation—that man might be what he is by the grace and for the grace of God."[18]

The Confession of 1967 of the Presbyterian Church (USA) makes a similar point: "God created the world of space and time to be the sphere of his dealings with men."[19]

Some liberation theologians emphasize the historical transformation of human nature and society. For example, in *A Theology of Liberation*, Gustavo Gutiérrez focuses on the relationship between salvation and the process of human liberation. When he considers creation, Gutiérrez regards it as the first salvific act because it "initiates history, the human struggle, and the salvific adventure of Yahweh." Creation "is the work of a God who saves and acts in history; since humankind is the center of creation, it is integrated into the history which is being built by human efforts." In sum, Gutiérrez means to emphasize the God of the exodus, and "the God of the Exodus is the God of history and of political liberation more than the God of nature."[20] (The Bible certainly gives us good reason to speak of the God of the exodus. But if we identify this God with a somewhat fuller and more detailed portrait of the maker of heaven and earth—if, like the psalmist, we understand the exodus to be an act of deliverance performed by the God who presides over the seas, rivers, mountains, hills, and all that is—then, without neglecting the importance of social transformation, we may perhaps also endeavor to understand it within a more forthrightly cosmic horizon.)

By contrast, a Christian piety that identifies Creator and Redeemer finds itself

17. Wilhelm Hermann, *The Communion of the Christian with God*, trans. J. S. Sandys Stanton, revised and expanded by R. W. Stewart (London: Williams & Norgate, 1930), 65, 211, 254, 342, 352; Welch, *Protestant Thought*, 48–49.

18. Barth, *CD* III/1:44, 59, 67.

19. *BOC* 9.16.

20. Gustavo Gutiérrez, *A Theology of Liberation: History, Politics, and Salvation*, trans. Sister Caridad Inda and John Eagleson, 15th anniversary ed. with a new introduction (Maryknoll, NY: Orbis, 1988), 83, 89.

in sympathy with the implications for theology of a statement made over half a century ago by the evolutionary anthropologist Loren Eiseley:

> There is something wrong with our world view. It is still Ptolemaic, though the sun is no longer believed to revolve around the earth.
>
> We see ourselves as the culmination and the end, and if we do indeed consider our passing, we think that sunlight will go with us and the earth be dark. We are the end. For us continents rose and fell, for us the waters and the air were mastered, for us the great living web has pulsated and grown more intricate.[21]

The World as Created

Proposition #27 The world is contingent.

"Creation," said Ernst Troeltsch, "is that aspect of the world-concept that expresses the *grounding of the world's existence as a whole in God*."[22] Piety understands that the world as creation (or the whole of reality) is contingent in the sense that it points beyond itself toward what it depends on. Again, "an event, property, or state of affairs is contingent if it is possible but not necessary: it could have been different."[23] Therefore, the world as creation is contingent not only because it is based in or depends on another but also because it might have been different, and the felt sense that this is true remains a basic experiential element of creation piety.

Intensifying an Inkling

Once more we note that wondering humans endowed with imagination ask questions. They ask about human history and, when they do, they often inquire about particular communities, institutions, and events. But they may also be struck by the knowledge that, had certain genetic and environmental factors not developed as they did, there might be no humans, no human history, and no

21. Loren Eiseley, *The Immense Journey* (New York: Vintage Books, 1957), 57. See also Sittler, *Evocations of Grace*, 98.

22. Ernst Troeltsch, *The Christian Faith*, translated with an introduction by Garrett E. Paul (Minneapolis: Fortress, 1991), 198.

23. Willem Drees, *Beyond the Big Bang: Quantum Cosmologies and God* (La Salle, IL: Open Court, 1990), 94.

human culture. When they ask about life on Earth, they investigate particular species and habitats, but they may also be struck by the realization that, had the surface temperature of the sun been different, or had Earth ended up a different distance from the sun, there might be no life on Earth. Given the current knowledge of astrophysics, it is not difficult to imagine a universe without our particular solar system or even without the Milky Way. Wondering humans thus may also ask, "Why this world or this cosmos rather than another?" Or even, "Why is there any cosmos at all?"

Charles Darwin described a line of human descent that runs from ancient marine larva-like progenitors of vertebrates to various fishes, amphibians, reptiles, birds, mammals, and Old World monkeys. Then he wrote two sentences that communicate a sense of the contingency of humanity as well as a profound wonderment. "The world, it has often been remarked, appears as if it had long been preparing for the advent of man; and this, in one sense is strictly true, for he owes his birth to a long line of progenitors. If any single link in this chain had never existed, man would not have been exactly what he now is."[24] But, of course, the sensibility and the wonder might also be extended to the entire present world, which itself appears to have been quite a long time in preparation, from the births of planets, the sun, stars, and the cosmos. At virtually countless junctures, had the sequence of realities and events been different, the present world might not have been what it now is.[25]

The symbol of God as Creator underscores the inkling that the world is contingent, by insisting that, theologically speaking, the world stands in relationship to its ground. It implies that the world is neither self-sufficient nor self-explanatory; as such, the symbol does not offer a technical explanation of how the world comes to be so much as it intensifies, interprets, and illuminates our wonderment at the world and our place in it. "To say that God created the Universe," writes the physicist Charles Misner, "does not explain either God or the Universe, but it keeps our consciousness alive to the mysteries of awesome majesty that we might otherwise ignore."[26]

The symbol of God as Creator encourages us to construe the world as an immense but contingent and thus *derivative* reality. In a Christian theological frame of reference, the world's existence is beyond its own doing. It depends

24. Charles Darwin, *The Descent of Man, and Selection in Relation to Sex* (Princeton: Princeton University Press, 1981), 213.

25. Robert Jastrow offers a widely read and popular account of these matters in *Until the Sun Dies* (New York: Norton, 1977).

26. Charles W. Misner, "Cosmology and Theology," in *Cosmology, History, and Theology*, ed. W. Yourgrau and A. D. Breck (New York: Plenum, 1977), 95 (quoted in Drees, *Beyond the Big Bang*, 101).

on an Other and has its source in an Other. Thomas Aquinas made use of an ontological vocabulary to indicate this, insisting that "all things other than God are not their own existence but share in existence."[27] They subsist in the sense that they have their being or existence *in* God or in radical dependence on God. Friedrich Schleiermacher, who did not use the same vocabulary, emphasized the absolute dependence of all things on God. Process theologians such as John Cobb and Schubert Ogden criticize the ontological approach as well as Schleiermacher's idea of *absolute* dependence; nevertheless, they also claim that the world has its source and ground in God.[28]

Within a Christian frame of reference, then, and despite a certain philosophical variability, to say that the world is God's creation is to say that all is from God. God is the principle of reality. Therefore, where it has been confronted by sharp dualisms, Christian creation theology has rejected other origin stories. God, rather than something or anything else, is the principle of reality. Thus Augustine insists that, because it is from God, rather than, say, an evil and hostile creator, as the Manichaeans taught, all creation is good.[29] The world and human life have their source and ground in the great God of glory and grace. The key scriptural passage is the magnificent poetry of John 1, where "In the beginning . . ." points to a Creator who redeems—as the source beyond all else and beyond which we look no further.

A Precious and Contingent Gift

We rightly understand what is dependent and contingent, or derivative, what might or might not be as it is as being something *precarious*, or vulnerable. Moreover, in the case that what is precarious or vulnerable also seems good to us, its value is thereby intensified; it becomes *precious*. This might be said of life and living. One reason why life seems especially valuable or precious to us is that it is contingent. It might not be as it is. It might change or come to an end at any time. Or, as Jonathan Edwards said in a sermon entitled "The Preciousness of Time and the Importance of Redeeming It," one reason why time appears exceedingly precious to us is that none of us knows just how much or how little of it we have left.[30]

27. Aquinas, *ST* 1a.44.1 (p. 7).

28. See John B. Cobb Jr., *A Christian Natural Theology*, 2nd ed. (Louisville: Westminster John Knox, 2007), 227, and esp. Schubert M. Ogden, *The Reality of God and Other Essays* (New York: Harper & Row, 1977), 62–63.

29. Augustine, *The Confessions*, trans. Maria Boulding, OSB, vol. I/1 of *WA*, 374–75.

30. *The Works of Jonathan Edwards*, revised and corrected by Edward Hickman (Edinburgh: Banner of Truth, 1974), 2:233–34.

Something like this may also be said of the contingent, dependent, and derivative reality of the world as the Christian community construes it with respect to the symbol of God as Creator. The world is rendered the more valuable. It becomes exceedingly precious, as does the contingent opportunity to participate in it. And this, in turn, is closely connected with the inkling or the sense that the world is a gift, something of value that we do not bring about and that does not bring itself about. Thus do wondering humans, whose piety and sensibility are shaped by the symbol of God as Creator, come to regard the world as something dear, as a gift of possibility, habitation, and beauty. The world depends on an Other. It might not be, and yet we find ourselves in it, sustained, and participating.

Many of these points come through in the first article of the Apostles' Creed: "I believe in God the Father Almighty, Maker of heaven and earth." This is a statement about God, but resident or implied in it are a number of statements about the *world*. For example, the world-as-a-whole has a maker, and thus it is not self-sufficient but dependent or derivative. The Swedish theologian Gustav Wingren notes that, in his Small Catechism, Martin Luther explains what "maker of heaven and earth" means by pointing directly "to the fact that he [Luther] is himself alive, with 'all my limbs and senses, my reason and all the faculties of my mind.'"[31] Consider also Luther's sermonic exposition:

> The first article teaches that God is the Father, the creator of heaven and earth. What is this? What do these words mean? The meaning is that I should believe that I am God's creature, that he has given to me body, soul, good eyes, reason, a good wife, children, fields, meadows, pigs, and cows, and besides this he has given to me the four elements, water, fire, air, and earth. Thus this article teaches that you do not have your life of yourself, not even a hair. I would not have a pig's ear, if God had not created it for me. Everything that exists is comprehended in that little word "creator."[32]

There is, of course, considerably more to "heaven and earth" than Martin Luther! But his statements vividly underscore the feeling that creation is God's gift, and that to be is to be in relationship to the God who creates.

The word "creator" indicates that the world-as-a-whole, heaven and earth—or all things visible and invisible—always exists in relationship to God. World *is* in relationship to God. Everything *is* in relationship to God because God makes

31. Gustav Wingren, *Credo: The Christian View of Faith and Life* (Minneapolis: Augsburg, 1981), 38.

32. Luther, *Sermons I*, ed. and trans. John W. Doberstein, vol. 51 of *LW*, 163.

everything and is at work in everything. To exist contingently, then, is to be in relationship with God the Creator, who already stands always in relationship to all. Within the frame of Christian piety, this is the first thing to be said about the world as creation: world, cosmos, all that is made, all things visible and invisible, you and me, are in relationship to God and stand in the presence of God our Creator in whom we live and move (Acts 17:28). This is endemic to what it means to be creation and to exist. This is why, in a Christian perspective, life, world, and existence always point beyond themselves, always have referential valence and depth, because they *are* in relationship to an Other. Theologically speaking, no created and existent reality can ever be entirely alone, and at some level we must also speak of an endemic inkling or sense of companionship. All created and existent realities are creatures, beings-in-relation-with-God, beings inescapably before God.

Gustav Wingren speaks of a relationship that is given in existence. He continues: "When we humans survey our whole situation, including that which we have not gained through our own efforts but have *received* at birth and every day, then we stand at the very boundary of our existence, and therefore we also stand in the presence of God. What is added when one describes all of this in religious language is the word 'God.' But even without that word, we were already standing in the presence of God, without using God's name."[33] George W. Stroup reminds us that, "according to the Bible, human life is lived *coram Deo*—before God." He notes that "the modern self-defining self" may find this difficult to imagine. Nevertheless, a fundamental theological claim is that to be is to be before God.[34]

How, then, shall we understand this emotionally resonant being-in-relation? How shall we respond to it? As a contingent gift to be cherished and to be met with gratitude and thanksgiving, as an existence and a living-in-relationship that is owed and held in trust.[35]

Proposition #28 Creation is a formed and dynamic ensemble, an intricate and vast system, a set of orderings, or *Cosmic Ecology*.

33. Wingren, *Credo*, 38.

34. George W. Stroup, *Before God* (Grand Rapids: Eerdmans, 2004), 1, 34.

35. Something of this comes through in Emil Brunner's insistence that "the Christian statement of Creation is not a theory of the way in which the world came into being—whether once for all, or in continuous evolution—but it is an 'existential' statement." Brunner continues: "The Lord meets me . . . as the Creator, as My Creator and the Creator of all things. . . . I become aware that I who know that I am the servant of this Lord, am His servant, His property, because not only I but all that is, has been created by Him. I, together with my world, am, O God, Thy creation; therefore I too am included in the aim of creation" (Brunner, *Dogmatics*, 2:35).

We interact with a world of processes, patterns, and structures; we know and experience objects, others, situations, and realities within an articulated environment. "World," therefore, means something very different than mere randomness or chaos. The image of God as Creator expresses and shapes these experiences and ideas by insisting that God forms, arranges, and orders the world-as-a-whole.

Genesis 1:1–2:4

This is a fundamental point of Genesis 1:1–2:4, a passage that, as some contemporary commentators point out, construes the writer's *present* world, its structures and dynamics. Indeed, the first chapter of the Bible outlines a vision of God, the world, and ourselves. Allow me to say what I mean.

Classical theological comments on this chapter are varied. Origen of Alexandria read it as an allegory, or symbolic representation, of the fall of good created spirits into material and bodily existence. Genesis 1, he claims, is really about how eternal but created spirits came to be entangled in this material and temporal world. Augustine closed his *Confessions* with a sustained meditation on Genesis 1 and the creation of all things. In contrast to Origen's allegory of entanglement and fall, Augustine notes that God creates not from any necessity but solely out of the abundance of God's own goodness; therefore, whatever is, is good.[36] Nor does he, interestingly, read Genesis 1 as a simply literal account; he observes that the first three days could not be just like the days that we experience, since the sun and moon were not created until day four.

More than a few early theologians understood creation to be a mysterious topic that demands a rather strange kind of literature. For example, John Chrysostom and others claim that no person could have written the opening to the Gospel of John. "In the beginning was the word . . ." Such verses, they maintain, treat things that no human could either witness or know; only the angels could have written them. Of course, a number of classical commentators assumed that Genesis 1:1–2:24 presents historically accurate accounts of the fashioning of the world and the making of the first human pair. Thus, in his lectures on Genesis, Martin Luther criticizes Augustine's "extraordinary trifling in his treatment of the six days" as mystical rather than natural ones. He claims: "We know from Moses that the world was not in existence before 6,000 years ago."[37] When John Calvin commented on Genesis 2:10–14, he drew a map of Eden and its rivers. When he commented on God's fashioning of Adam and then Eve in Genesis 2, he tried to harmonize the episode with Genesis 1:26 so as to

36. Augustine, *Confessions*, 311, 313.

37. Luther, *Lectures on Genesis Chapters 1–5*, trans. George V. Schick, vol. 1 of *LW*, 3–4.

obtain a single, self-consistent—and thus presumably also historically accurate—account.[38] A recent physicist has argued that God's statement "'let there be light' may . . . be understood as designating the creation of the primeval fireball—the big bang."[39] His point is that Genesis fits better with this model of the universe than with ideas of a "steady state universe" or an "alternating universe."

My own view is that many verses in Genesis 1 and 2 connect with readings of facts. It is a fact, for example, that we experience periods of light and darkness (called day and night). It is true that waters are gathered into seas, that animals reproduce in their kinds, and that humans (as a *kind* of animal) reproduce similarly. It is also true that we humans name the animals and birds, and that a special and intimate kind of relationship may obtain between a woman and a man. Moreover, we *can* locate two of the four rivers (the Tigris and the Euphrates) mentioned in Genesis 2:14. Even so, Genesis 1 and 2 do not invite easy equations with scientific theories and historical reconstructions. Indeed, these texts seem to discourage such equations, whether the equations are made by fundamentalists or by more liberal-minded people who want to demonstrate that the Bible somehow anticipates the latest scientific findings and ideas. The early chapters of Genesis present imaginative pictures of God, the world, and ourselves in the form of theological stories, sagas, and mythic poetry. They envision God's world and our place in it. They interpret and construe a community's experiences of an ordered and dependable world with the help of the idea that God creates, and, in turn, they also take these interpreted experiences to offer significant clues about our human predicament and about God the Creator.

In the beginning, etc. (v. 1). Right here, in the Bible's first verse, we run into a translation issue. Should the verse be rendered "In the beginning when God created the heavens and the earth, the earth was a formless void"? Or should it be: "When God created the heavens and the earth, the earth was a formless void"? The first rendering sounds as if it might be an absolute starting point. It implies that "before" the beginning, there was nothing, and *then*, when God began creating, the earth was initially a formless void. The second rendering doesn't sound like an absolute starting point: when God began to create the heavens and the earth, the earth was already there as a formless void. But, in either case, we may say that the Bible opens with an intimation of mystery.[40] Creation means

38. Indeed, he was fond of referring to the accounts in Gen. 1 and 2 as elements of Moses's "history" (Calvin, *Commentaries on the First Book of Moses Called Genesis*, trans. John King, vol. 1 in *Calvin's Commentaries*, Calvin Translation Society [Grand Rapids: Baker Books, 1998], 58, 132).

39. Nathan Aviezer, *In the Beginning . . . Biblical Creation and Science* (Hoboken, NJ: Ktav, 1990), 15, 121.

40. On these opening verses, see more in chap. 6.

something other and something more than the mere continuation of what (if anything) was already the case, and depictions of the origin (as also the end) of things verge on profound limits of human knowledge and experience.[41] In this sense, Chrysostom and the others were right. Texts such as Genesis 1:1 and the opening verses of the Gospel of John depict things we can neither witness nor entirely comprehend.

"When God created the heavens and the earth, the earth was a formless void and darkness covered the face of the deep, while a wind from God swept over the face of the waters." However one might resolve the translation issue noted above, here a main theme emerges: the primary movement of the text will be from formless watery void to formed creation or world. (Many modern commentators add that, in the wind from God sweeping over the waters, there is a residue of an older idea of creation from conflict where the world is fashioned from the dismembered goddess Tiamat.) In any case, we are now prepared for the forming and the organizing to begin.

Then God said, "Let there be light"; and there was light, etc. (v. 3). Light comes first. Is the passage saying that light was made from darkness, that darkness is the material from which light was made? It doesn't seem so, since the very next lines tell us that God separated the light from the darkness to form day and night. Light is created by word, by command. We may say that here God commands in the way that an ancient monarch might have commanded, though not even ancient monarchs were able to bring about things without someone to follow or enact their commands. In Genesis 1:3, God simply speaks light into being. Equally remarkably, God also sees that it is good. "Good for what?" we may ask, since there is as yet nothing else for which it might be useful. Perhaps God is being portrayed somewhat like an artist or a photographer who makes an aesthetic judgment. In any event, the rest of verse 4, and then also verse 5, tell us that God separates the light from the darkness, calling the former day and the latter night. So God makes the light and names it, and God names the darkness and neither makes it nor eliminates it. "And there was evening and there was morning, the first day"—a basic building block for a calendar, a start at organizing time. Indeed, when the entire account is done, we will have seven days, the first week (with days figured as Judaism still does, from sunset to sunset).

Day Two: God separates the waters by means of a dome (the sky), so that some waters are kept above the sky and some below it—a further and critical bit of forming and organizing of the world as we know it is to emerge. (But with which current scientific theory does *this* correspond?) Day Three: God commands the waters below the sky to be gathered into seas so that dry land

41. See Drees, *Beyond the Big Bang.*

appears, and God sees that this is good. God then commands the earth to "green forth" with plants and trees of every kind bearing fruit with the seed in it. So the plants are not random but organized according to kinds that have the ability to generate more of their kinds by means of their distinctive seeds. That is, earth and plants possess an inherent generativity. (In addition, as we now know, new kinds of plants may also emerge.) "And God saw that it was good" (1:12). The fact that plants may be divided into groups that bring forth fruit with different seeds clearly is essential knowledge for rudimentary classification and for agriculture, a point that gives us a clue as to who wrote this. Nevertheless, the text says that God saw the goodness of the land and seas, as well as the goodness of the plants in their kinds and with their seeds, at a point when humans were not yet present. So we probably shouldn't *restrict* the reported divine recognition of the goodness of land and sea and plants in their kinds and their inherent generativity to the utility of these things for agriculturally inclined humans. Day Four involves additional essential patterns and organization. God speaks into being the great lights of the day and the night (the sun and the moon). This also separates the day from the night and light from darkness (didn't God already do this in 1:4–5?), and it installs "signs for seasons and for days and years." Creation now has what is needed for the yearly cycles on which so much on planet Earth depends, and from which humans may devise a full calendar. And once again, "God saw that it was good."

On Day Five, God speaks into being "swarms of living creatures" in the waters (including sea monsters) as well as birds in the sky. These, too, are fashioned in kinds. "And God saw that it was good." Indeed, God blesses them, saying, "Be fruitful and multiply . . ." Thus the animals make their debut, and, like the plants, they are differentiated into kinds that are capable of generating more of their kinds. From God they receive the blessing of life, or the blessing of generativity. We note in these verses, as in others, the rudiments of a classification scheme of living things according to their kinds—that is, the beginnings of biology. But the animals created on the fifth day are not domesticated; people even have reason to fear some of them, for example, the sea monsters. And so, when we compare Day Five to the next day, when God creates both cattle and humans, agriculture appears to take a back seat.

On Day Six the action is divided into two parts. First, God commands and the earth brings forth "living creatures of every kind: cattle and creeping things and wild animals of the earth of every kind." Once again, we note the text's high interest in the fact that creatures are arranged into kinds, and an especially pronounced interest in cattle in their kinds. "Then God said, 'Let us make humankind in our image, according to our likeness; and let them have dominion over the fish of the sea, and over the birds of the air, and over the cattle, and over all the wild animals of the earth, and over every creeping thing that creeps upon the earth." (Have "the great sea monsters" been intentionally dropped from this list?)

In any case, the text obviously means to indicate that we humans are special. Claus Westermann claims that "Let us" amounts to a kind of royal expression that forms a special introduction to the creation of humans and sets it off from the surrounding text.[42] We are made in the image of God (or perhaps of plural divine beings), and this, no doubt, is a significant mark of distinction. It isn't easy to say just what the image consists of. Thomas Aquinas identified it with the rational soul. Others argue that our power of dominion—or even rulership—is Godlike. Still others say the passage shows that humans are created for a special relationship with the divine: humans may image, mirror, or reflect the divine, a distinctive form of praise. It is clear, however, that humans—both male and female—are created in God's image and that this is a matter of dignity and importance, a basis (as many classical theologians, including Calvin, remarked) for according to humans a distinctive worth.[43]

It is significant, too, that humans are accorded *dominion*. This does not mean that humans displace God. Neither here nor elsewhere does God simply abdicate or renounce God's position as ruler or governor. Again, let us note that, by the time humans appear on Day Six, God has already fashioned a patterned world. Hence, whatever human dominion is, it is to be exercised within already existent orderings. Commenting on Psalm 8, James L. Mays says that "the dominion of the human corresponds to and is subordinate to the reign of the creator," and that humans are to use their powers "in a way that serves the purposes and practices of their sovereign."[44] In less definitely hierarchical and monarchic terms, the point seems to be that, for creation piety, humans occupy an office that corresponds to their place as distinctively capable participants in the world. Humans are charged to be stewards or trustees of God's good world. They have a distinct

42. Claus Westermann, *Genesis 1–11: A Commentary*, trans. John J. Scullion, SJ (Minneapolis: Augsburg, 1984), 143–47.

43. Westermann also says that Gen. 1:26–30 originated independently and was later integrated into the larger framework of Gen. 1. Within this larger framework, God creates humanity to rule over the rest of creation, but the narrative of 1:26–30 has other concerns as well. This is where the image of God comes in. Contrary to a good deal of theological tradition, Westermann maintains that 1:26–28 describes neither "the nature of human beings" nor some particular trait or quality of humans. It speaks rather of an action of God by which humans are created in unique relationship to God, to correspond to God, or as God's counterparts, so that "something can happen between creator and creature." And this "relationship to God is not something which is added to human existence; humans are created in such a way that their very existence is intended to be their relationship with God" (Westermann, *Genesis 1–11*, 155, 157, 158).

44. Mays, "Maker of Heaven and Earth," 69.

calling and vocation; they occupy an administrative office within God's wider sets of orderings (a point that, at some level, accords with Holmes Rolston's observation that the question before us today is not whether but how humans shall manage planet Earth).[45] In any case, the Genesis text recognizes that, among creatures, human beings have distinctive and rather impressive capabilities, and it intimates that with these capabilities come distinctive responsibilities (see chap. 6 below).

God blessed them, and God said to them, "Be fruitful and multiply, and fill the earth and subdue it; and have dominion," etc. (v. 28). For our purposes, there are two basic things to note here: (1) "Be fruitful and multiply" is the same blessing of generativity that God gives to the living creatures brought forth in the waters and to the birds of the air in 1:22. It indicates that, like other creatures, humans have the ability to generate more of their kind. The gift and blessing of life, and here particularly of human life, continue a point that comes through in our experience of the succession of generations and that is underscored by the many genealogies that punctuate Scripture. Embedded in the text, then, is a bit of biological knowledge that also came in handy on my uncle Dick's farm outside of Ann Arbor, Michigan: animals of the same kind, or species, are able to reproduce. So, if you want more pigs, you need to put pigs together. And, in fact, humans reproduce in their kind, much as other animals do. As Darwin himself might almost have put it, humans *are* animals who share in the same blessing of generativity given to other creatures. (2) As we had occasion to note in commentary on 1:26, these particular animals have been given something that, in our experience, other animals have not, namely, *dominion*. Humans are endowed with distinctive and highly pronounced powers of intervention. When joined with distinctive abilities for social organization, language, and technological innovation, these powers enable humans to "subdue" the earth. Or, as we might say in language less reminiscent of hierarchy and conquest, they form the basis for capacities to manage, administer, or even oversee the planet.

"See, I have given you every plant yielding seed that is upon the face of all the earth, and every tree with seed in its fruit; you shall have them for food. And to every beast of the earth, and to every bird of the air, and to everything that creeps on the earth, everything that has the breath of life, I have given every green plant for food" (vv. 29–30). Many things might be noted here. Why don't the creatures in the waters come in for more explicit mention? After all, many of them also eat plants. Is the idea that all animals, including humans, were created vegetarian? But a more general theme also comes through in these verses, and it seems to be

45. Holmes Rolston III, *Conserving Natural Value* (New York: Columbia University Press, 1994), 8–9, 223–28.

an important dimension of everything else taking place in Genesis 1. The world that God forms from a formless and watery void is a *sustaining habitat*. To a significant extent and degree, its orderings, processes, and structures—for example, night and day, sea and land, seasons, plants and animals in their kinds—are hospitable to life. So, among other things, Genesis 1 encourages persons of piety to say that God the Creator is the Lord of life, the one who fashions and upholds a habitat that sustains living creatures.

God saw everything that he had made, and indeed, it was very good. And there was evening and there was morning, the sixth day (v. 31). God's work of creation, God's speaking and sculpting things into order and existence, is completed in six days and, when it is completed, God surveys the whole of what God has made and sees that it is *very* good. More on that presently.

On Day Seven, God rests and makes the seventh day holy. Here we have the prototypical Sabbath, the day that the Priestly writer (i.e., the source responsible for Genesis 1:1–2:4) is concerned be set aside for worship and temple observance. This, of course, is one reason why the ordering of time into days and weeks is so important in the passage: it makes possible a regular liturgical observance and calendar. In somewhat more cosmic terms, part of the point is that all things in heaven and on earth are built with a tendency toward Sabbath rest. Embedded in Genesis 1:1–2:4, as in Psalm 148, is the apprehension, feeling, or claim that creation is worshipful and doxological. The chief end, goal, tendency, and purpose of all things individually, as well as of creation regarded as a whole, is to praise and to worship God—a thoroughly religious and *theo*logical point.

World as Ensemble

From here, it is a short step to the idea of the created world as an *ensemble*, a set of realities, relationships, and orderings that work together and cohere. As he comments on Genesis 1, Augustine notes that, in God's sight, the parts of creation are good, but the entire ensemble is *very* good. What it may mean to say that something is good "in God's sight" is a point that shall occupy us in proposition #29 below, but let us simply note here that the language of ensemble indicates pattern, structure, and interrelatedness. The recognition that the whole ensemble is "very good" indicates a sense for the additional excellence involved in the world as a patterned whole. The parts coalesce so that, "severally good, they are exceedingly good altogether."[46] There are fullness, coordination, and unity in

46. Indeed, as Augustine understood it, the seventh day intimates "the Sabbath of eternal life," when we may rest in God and God in us. Augustine, *Confessions*, 379, 373–74.

the entire organism or body that surpass the parts; indeed, God "the almighty craftsman" is responsible for the natural order.[47]

Thomas Aquinas, with the assistance of Aristotle's understanding of causation, claimed that God is the exemplar cause, the artist who gives definite shape and form to material. He noted that God the Creator is "the molder . . . of heaven and earth." The "divine wisdom is the cause of the variety in things," and indeed the one God arranges and governs not only natural matters but also human affairs.[48] Calvin, for whom nature is "the order prescribed by God," said that God "daily discloses himself in the whole workmanship of the universe." God is the great "Artificer" who orders the motion of the stars, and the "skillful ordering of the universe is for us a sort of mirror in which we can contemplate God, who otherwise is invisible."[49] Indeed, as he introduced the book of Genesis, Calvin said, "Let the world become our school if we desire rightly to know God."[50]

These affirmations encourage us to envision creation as a world, ensemble, or realm of divine orderings that manifests the divine goodness and wisdom, and the importance of this point will become clearer if I repeat that, for Origen of Alexandria, the material world is largely the result of a fall. Origen maintained that all creatures emanate or proceed from the One as eternal rational natures endowed with freedom. Creatures are essentially dependent, incorporeal, and rational souls. With the exception of the Word and Spirit, however, they become negligent. Therefore, they gradually sink to lower levels of existence and take on bodies "suitable to the regions to which they descend; that is to say, first ethereal bodies, then aerial. And when they reach the neighborhood of the earth they are enclosed in grosser bodies."[51] It is then the work of the Word or the Son in conjunction with the Spirit to return fallen, rational, and incorporeal souls to the One. In this sense, all things proceed from and return to God. We have *exitus et reditus*, or the trajectory of exit and return, as a kind of extended cosmological commentary on Revelation 1:8.

Origen's highly Neoplatonic articulation of this pattern makes for a comparatively distant relationship between God the Father (the One, or the monad) and the multiplicity, dynamism, and temporality of the world. In fact, the material and temporal world functions as a temporal repository for eternal souls that

47. Augustine, *On Genesis*, trans. Edmund Hill, OP, and Matthew O'Connell, vol. 13 of *WA*, 60, 114.

48. *The Sermon-Conferences of St. Thomas Aquinas on the Apostles' Creed*, trans. Nicholas Ayo, CSC (Notre Dame: University of Notre Dame Press, 1988), 37; Aquinas, *ST* 1a.47.1 (p. 95).

49. Calvin, *ICR* 1.5.5; 1.5.1.

50. Calvin, *Commentaries on the First Book of Moses Called Genesis*, 60.

51. Origen, *On First Principles*, trans. G. W. Butterworth (Gloucester, MA: Peter Smith, 1973), 40–41.

can be discarded once they are returned to the One, and this attenuates the sense in which Origen can portray the varied and interrelated ensemble of the natural world as the manifestation and disclosure of a skillful and benevolent divine ordering.[52]

Creation as Habitat

Since the time of Augustine, Aquinas, Luther, and the rest, however, a variety of modern scientific findings, theories, and perspectives have greatly expanded and complicated our picture of the cosmic ensemble. This becomes apparent as soon as we pause to consider creation as *habitat*. I have noted that, in Genesis 1, the ensemble of interrelated realities is structured or formed so that the patterned whole is habitable and sustaining. Martin Luther had this in mind when he likened God's making of the world to the building of a house. On the third day, wrote Luther, "after He has prepared the roof of the building, namely, the heaven, and has added light," God "also gets ready a piece of ground, and brings forth the earth, fit for the habitation and activity of mankind." This is "the first part of the house," and, indeed, the construction of the entire dwelling expresses "the divine solicitude and benevolence toward us." For Luther, "when man is created, he finds a ready and equipped home," God having furnished the "kitchen and provisions" when the earth brings forth vegetation. The Bible "teaches that God created all these things in order to prepare a house and an inn . . . for the future man," and thus, "after everything that belongs to the essence of a house is ready, man is brought, as it were, into his possession."[53]

Luther's image of creation as a house certainly envisions the world as sustaining habitat, but from a contemporary point of view at least two things are missing. The first is an appropriate sense of scale, a modern feel for the vastness of the cosmos as well as for the complexities of the elements and interrelationships that go into making creation habitable. We share Luther's recognition that, when it comes to life, the earth is a precious dwelling place, a gift. At the same time, however, contemporary knowledge invites us to form a view of a radically expanded creative system, one in which—astrophysically and astrochemically speaking—the sun and Earth develop from the big bang and cosmic dust, and in which life on Earth unfolds from geophysics and geochemistry. It invites us

52. H. Paul Santmire, *The Travail of Nature: The Ambiguous Ecological Promise of Christian Theology* (Minneapolis: Fortress, 1985), 72.

53. Luther, *Lectures on Genesis 1–5*, vol. 1 of *LW*, 35–39, 47. Calvin also says that, when God gathers together the waters under the sky so that dry land appears, "the waters by their departure have given a dwelling place to man" (Calvin, *Commentaries on the First Book of Moses Called Genesis*, 81).

to envision a vast and expanding creation, currently more than some twenty-eight billion light-years in diameter, in which the sun and Earth and moon and stars are situated and in which seemingly inert elements, distributed over cosmic distances and interacting over both cosmic and evolutionary time frames, turn out—at least in some locations (and remarkably)—to be fertile. Measured against this picture, Luther's image of creation-as-house is too small. It needs to be radically contextualized in order to take into account a vastly expanded set of realities and relationships; otherwise, it needs to be drastically enlarged toward genuinely cosmic dimensions.

A second thing missing is the concept of ecosystem. It is true, of course, that the elements of Luther's house cohere to form a sustaining dwelling, but the house he describes finally has a single owner, for whom it has been expressly built, and who takes sole possession once the master builder has completed it. By contrast, the concept of ecosystem points to interrelationships and functions, to "processes that link the many living, or biotic, components to the non-living, or abiotic, components" in a common web.[54] Emphasis falls on how the system operates as a whole, that is, on its major functional aspects—the transformations of energy and the cycling of chemical elements that occur, its food webs, and so on. Moreover, the dynamic interactions and processes of a given web or system (say, a pond) do not center on any single organism or species (say, a carp). When we consider Earth as an ecosystem, then, we cannot finally say that it is home to one species more than to all others, and we do not estimate the many functions and the various species only with respect to the survival and the flourishing of another single species. This is one reason why even a contemporary person who is squeamish about most insects may find it strange that Luther insists that "harmful worms or vermin, such as toads [and] flies . . . were brought into being," not during the six days of creation, but "later out of the cursed earth as a punishment for sin, to afflict us and compel us to call upon God."[55] Luther's image of creation-as-a-house-for-humans is finally too invested in a dichotomy between humans and the rest of nature, and it is also too anthropocentric.

Calvin's anthropocentric tendencies come to the fore in his comments on humans being given dominion in Genesis 1:28. "And hence we infer what was the end for which all things were created; namely, that none of the conveniences and necessities of life might be wanting to men. In the very order of creation

54. "The Concept of the Ecosystem," Regents of the University of Michigan, accessed June 19, 2012, www.globalchange.umich.edu/globalchange1/current/lectures/kling/ecosystem/ecosystem.html.

55. Luther, *Lectures on Genesis 1–5*, 54. Calvin says similar things about "fleas, caterpillars, and other noxious insects" in *Commentaries on the First Book of Moses Called Genesis*, 104.

the paternal solicitude of God for man is conspicuous, because he furnished the world with all things needful, and even with an immense profusion of wealth, before he formed man. Thus man was rich before he was born."[56] As an alternative to these tendencies in a number of classical theologians, see H. Paul Santmire's discussion of "an ecological reading of biblical theology" that is "predicated in the assumption of a divine and human concomitance with nature, rather than a divine and human disjunction from nature."[57]

Creation as a Vast Cosmic Ecology

To use the word "ecology" in this way is to stretch it beyond its more usual and stricter meanings in the context of evolutionary biology on Earth. Thanks to the Greek root *oikos* (home, household, habitation), the image of all creation as vast ecology retains something of Luther's emphasis on a dwelling place, a formed environment within which we humans live, move, and find ourselves sustained. However, if we take seriously the emphasis that terms such as "ecosystem" and "ecology" place on common webs, dynamic interactions, energy transfers, and the like, as well as the stunning enlargement of our modern picture of cosmos, then we avoid the blatant anthropocentrism of Luther's notion of all creation-as-a-house expressly built for humans.

None of this means that humans are left behind. Creation as cosmic ecology is compatible with Aquinas's claim that God arranges both nature and human affairs, and with Calvin's appreciation of the significance for humans of God's skillful ordering of sun, moon, stars, and seasons—as well as the fruitfulness of Earth.[58] It is compatible with Calvin's claim that God instituted marriage as a primary community of companionship and care, as well as civil government to maintain justice and human well-being.[59] It is also compatible with something like Emil Brunner's ideas about "certain natural constants" that guide human life.[60]

We should recognize, of course, that modern sciences, cultural studies, and social movements have made us increasingly aware that the patterns of nature

56. Calvin, *Commentaries on the First Book of Moses Called Genesis*, 96.

57. Santmire, *The Travail of Nature*, 189–90.

58. Calvin, *ICR* 1.5.2; 1.5.5; 1.16.2; See also Calvin's comments on Ps. 104 in *Commentary on the Book of Psalms*, 1143–71.

59. Calvin, *ICR* 2.8.41; 4.20.1, 3; Calvin, *The Epistles of Paul the Apostle to the Romans and to the Thessalonians*, trans. Ross Mackenzie, vol. 8 of *Calvin's New Testament Commentaries: A New Translation*, ed. Thomas F. Torrance and David W. Torrance (Grand Rapids: Eerdmans, 1973), 281.

60. Brunner, *Dogmatics*, 2:25–26; Brunner, *Justice and the Social Order*, trans. Mary Hottinger (London: Lutterworth, 1945), 120, 127, 133.

and society are not static but dynamic. Nature has a history—and so do cultures. Temperature ranges and seasons on Earth, forms of government, marriage, and family vary, change, and develop in different places and over time. Thus, while Calvin himself appreciated that appropriate forms of government sometimes differ according to circumstances, we are now acquainted with political and cultural varieties of which he was not aware.[61] Brunner counted among the created constants we are called to uphold "monogamous permanent marriage," as well as the family with "a certain hierarchy of organization" in which "the husband is the head of the wife."[62] We have good reasons not only to criticize aspects of Brunner's understanding of marriage and family but also to allow for greater variation and flexibility in these institutions than he did.

Even so, we continue to discern given patterns and relationships on which we depend for quite significant possibilities. That is, within the vast cosmic ecology of articulated relationships, operations, and interactions, we may distinguish certain relevant wholes or "neighborhoods," and within our own neighborhood we find natural orderings, cultural patterns, and social contexts of responsibility that are requisite or at least critical for human living.

James M. Gustafson points to experiences highlighted in the early chapters of Genesis, experiences of time (day and night), space (land, waters, sky), animal and plant life, distinctive human capacities, human possibilities to work and cultivate what is given, marriage and family, moral accountability and guilt, capacities to develop culture, arts, and technology. "In all these experiences, human beings are depicted in interrelationship with nature and with other persons, responding to possibilities given in the world. There is a strong sense of dependence on what has been given prior to human intervention into the world, of interdependence of aspects of the world, of the capacities to develop what is given, of appropriate relations of things to each other, as well as of man's accountability for being properly related to what is given and for relating things properly to each other."

Today it is true that we locate our surroundings (or particular cosmic locale) within a stunningly vaster cosmic context than Genesis did. But our surroundings—their patterns and articulations—continue to evoke feelings and sensibilities of dependence, gratitude, and possibility. Thus, within our particular subsystem of the cosmic ecology, "we also depend upon and respond to many things that are given to us both as limits and possibilities for our species." Although we understand some of them differently, like those persons depicted in

61. Calvin, *ICR* 4.20.

62. Brunner, *Dogmatics*, 2:25–26; Brunner, *Justice and the Social Order*, 127–28.

early chapters of Genesis, "we need to discover the limits and the boundaries which we overstep only to our peril and the peril of the world around us."[63]

We should keep in mind five additional things about the image of creation as a vast cosmic ecology. First, it intimates *mystery* as well as dynamic interconnections and patterns. There is much we do not know about the whole vast cosmic ecology, its dynamic interactions, processes, tendencies, and ends. Indeed, as we discover black holes, antimatter, and the like, and as our procedures for detecting stars and planets improve, it is apparent that we are unsure just what the *whole* cosmic ecology is. When we study processes that link biotic and abiotic components in common webs, we select a relevant whole, subsystem, or locale. We focus on the "local ecosystem" of a particular planet, specific sea, or geological mass. But at the same time, we also recognize that we cannot adequately tell the story of how a selected ecosystem has come to be apart from reference to its wider situation and larger context, as when we talk about the formation of Earth or the possible impact of meteors on evolutionary sequences of life on Earth. We understand many very important things (though not nearly everything) about our own cosmic neighborhood, but we also realize that it is situated within a whole cosmos that remains beyond our comprehension.

Second, the cosmic ecology is *dynamic*. There may have been times when the order of things appeared to be entirely stable and static, but this is not now a plausible view. We know that the many systems and subsystems, from ponds to oceans and planets, involve continual interactions and energy transfers. We know that new astrophysical forms—for example, stars and planets—coalesce over time. We know that new species of plants and animals emerge on Earth, while others go extinct. The many subsystems, interrelationships, and realities of the cosmic ecology are always *in process*. There are important continuities: forms emerge and persist for significant periods of time. But there is also continuing development and change, as any careful student of persons, institutions, societies, species, ponds, oceans, planets, planetary systems, stars, galaxies, and so on will surely know. Cosmic ecology entails significantly stable interrelationships, systems, and forms but also movement, transition, and emergence.

Third, in our studies of particular ecosystems, we recognize that the many interdependencies, processes of interaction, energy transfers, and the like involve important *sustaining features* but also *tensions and conflicts*. The sustaining features of the cosmos considered as God's cosmic reign are underscored by the idea of cosmic ecology as habitat or dwelling as well as by the idea of sustaining patterns and orderings in the lives and histories of many species, including our own. I shall return to these features when I discuss divine providence. Never-

63. Gustafson, *ETP*, 1:237, 238.

theless, we also note quite significant tensions and conflicts. The movements of tectonic plates that are critical to the formation of Earth's planetary habitat sometimes exact a terrible toll in earthquakes and tidal waves. The food chains in many ecosystems we are aware of routinely involve levels of predation that entail disturbing instances of suffering. Lions may lie down with lambs in God's peaceable kingdom, but here and now they hunt and often brutally slaughter their prey. Not that this particular feature of divine providence would surprise many biblical writers.

> Young lions roar for their prey,
> seeking their food from God. (Ps. 104:21)

Evolutionarily speaking, we recognize that diseases may serve to cull populations and thus hold them in balance with their environments, but this does not deny the often terrible suffering of diseased individual organisms and communities. Within the sequence of life on Earth, entire species rise and fall: 90 percent of all species that have lived on Earth are now extinct. We also know that events within and beyond solar systems may dramatically and violently alter entire planetary ecosystems with catastrophic consequences for many of the populations they support, for example, meteors and their devastation of dinosaurs on Earth. For these reasons and more, we should not romanticize the interdependencies, interactions, and transfers that characterize the cosmic ecology. All is not unambiguous sustaining harmony, and there is room in creation piety for anxiety and fear.

Fourth, the vastness, mystery, and intricacy of the many interrelationships and processes intimated by the idea of creation as cosmic ecology help us regain an appreciation for great themes, texts, and sensibilities of creation piety in the Bible, which some other images and views—for example, creation as a house exclusively for humans—may obscure.

> "Where were you when I laid the foundations of the earth? . . .
> Can you bind the chains of the Pleiades,
> or loose the cords of Orion?" (Job 38:4, 31)

The Lord's answer to Job out of the whirlwind more than suggests that God's creation is vast and not simply centered on us. It expresses a sense of awe and radical dependence. This same text intimates mystery:

> "Where is the way to the dwelling place of light,
> and where is the place of darkness?" (Job 38:19)

A point that needs to be underscored here is that, for creation piety, the idea of ecosystem helps us uncover some aspects of Genesis 1:1–2:4a and its premodern sensibilities that Luther's more cozy and anthropocentric image of creation as house tends to obscure. Moreover, Psalm 104, "the most extended explication of God's work of creation outside of Genesis," points toward ecosystem, rather than a merely mechanical and inert environment, when it portrays God as stretching out the heavens, building a world, and ordering a dominion of sun, thunder, rain, valleys, hills, and more that furnishes food, habitat, and times for living things.[64] "In the poetic portrait of the world in vv. 10–23, everything has its provender, its place, and its time. Everything coheres. All are interrelated in the great web of the works of the Lord. To watch the wild animals, to enjoy a glass of wine, to see birds building nests, or observe the rhythm of the passing of day and night is to sense and wonder and revel at the wisdom of it all." Life forms are integrated into a "great process of making and supporting" where the human species is one among others, and "our similarities to the animals indicate how much we are part of the world."[65]

> Yonder is the sea, great and wide,
>   creeping things innumerable are there,
>   living things both small and great.
> There go the ships,
>   and Leviathan that you formed to sport in it. (Ps. 104:25–26)

Finally, then, the image of creation as cosmic ecology helps to shape and express piety's sense of the *distinctive role of humans*. The vast cosmos clearly is not centered in us, or even on the particular solar system in which Earth is located. Nevertheless, we humans have a special position and worth. We are stewards or *distinctively equipped participants*, and our recognition of this fact elicits in us senses of both possibility and responsibility. We may use our considerable powers of understanding and intervention in a way that reflects our awareness of the worth both of human beings and of the larger welter of interdependent interrelationships on which we and all other creatures depend. Our persistent failure to do so is in fact a distinctively human *irresponsibility*. And if contemporary political and ecological indicators are accurate, it is a failure for which we are now being judged and for which we may continue to be judged far into the future.

64. Patrick D. Miller Jr., "The Poetry of Creation: Psalm 104," in Brown and McBride, *God Who Creates*, 87.

65. Mays, "Maker of Heaven and Earth," 84, 85.

Proposition #29 The created world is good.

This statement has bases in a range of human experiences and sensibilities evoked in the midst of cosmic ensemble—experiences and senses of the fittingness of things, their complementarities and contrasts, rhythms and patterns, interrelationships, proportions, and beauty. Consider a breathtaking coastline, mountains and valleys, stars in the nighttime sky, a porpoise, flowers, grackles, and the human body. Appreciate the routinely extraordinary capabilities of creatures—the bird's flight, our own flights. Marvel at Chicago's skyscrapers along the lakefront, a parent's care for his child, an exquisite mosque, Mozart's music, a bird's song, a good friend, an Italian meal, a Scottish folk song, the artistry of Christian Ronaldo as he approaches an opponent's goal, a young child, the elegance of a mathematical equation. All these things have their places within the cosmic ecology.

As Augustine enumerated the Creator's blessings, he extolled human capacities of mind that make for wisdom, virtue, arts, industry, theater, cooking, musical instruments, and song. He wondered at our sense organs and the symmetry of the human body. Then he turned to the rest of creation—"with all its beauty and utility."

> Shall I speak of the manifold and various loveliness of sky, and earth, and sea; of the plentiful supply and wonderful quantities of light; of sun, moon, and stars; of the shade of trees; of the colors and perfume of flowers; of the multitude of birds, all differing in plumage and in song; of the variety of animals, of which the smallest in size are often the most wonderful—the works of ants and bees astonishing us more than the huge bodies of whales? Shall I speak of the sea, which itself is so grand a spectacle, when it arrays itself as it were in vestures of various colors, now running through every shade of green, and again becoming purple or blue? Is it not delightful to look at it in storm, and experience the soothing complacency which it inspires, by suggesting that we ourselves are not tossed and shipwrecked? What shall I say of the numberless kinds of food to alleviate hunger, and the variety of seasonings to stimulate the appetite which are scattered everywhere by nature, and for which we are not indebted to the art of cookery? How many natural appliances are there for preserving and restoring health! How graceful is the alteration of day and night! How pleasant the breezes that cool the air! How abundant the supply of clothing furnished us by trees and animals! Who can enumerate all the blessings we enjoy?[66]

66. Augustine, *The City of God*, trans. Marcus Dods (New York: Random House, 1950),

And there is an additional experiential warrant: a sense beneath or behind our experiences of all these things, a sense of existence or of being and participating in world, a sense of being present in the midst of encounters with realities that engage our attention and draw us out. Call it a sense that it is compelling and good to be.

In a Christian frame of reference, these experiences and sensibilities both come to expression in and are shaped by a signal creedal affirmation about God and its corollary about the world. The good and faithful God is "maker of heaven and earth"; therefore, creation is good. Augustine again makes an especially trustworthy guide. Creation, he says, is good because "the cause of created things, whether in heaven or on earth, visible or invisible, is nothing other than the goodness of the creator who is the one true God, and there is nothing that is not either himself or from him."[67] Likewise, Calvin insists that there is no evil nature in the entire universe. Why? Because "from the beginning nothing at all has existed in which God has not put forth an example both of his wisdom and his righteousness."[68] Therefore, persons of piety "should daily exercise themselves, to consider the infinite goodness, justice, power, and wisdom of God" in this magnificent theater of God's glory.[69]

The Nicene Creed calls God the Father Almighty "the Maker of heaven and earth, *and of all things visible and invisible*." This is another way to emphasize that there is nothing God didn't make. When I first encountered that formula, I suspect that I thought the Nicene fathers were simply covering all their bases by saying, in effect, "Just in case there are also things unseen, well, God made them, too." But Thomas Aquinas was probably closer to the Nicene Creed's early meaning when he noted a dispute over the status of things visible. Manichaean dualists, said Aquinas, believed that visible and material things were created by a bad God or devil, and thus they attributed to the good God "the creation of invisible things only."[70] Some believed that lower animals and life-forms that cling to the soil and occupy lower regions of the world were built into the fabric of the universe by a hostile intelligence. And this belief, Augustine confessed to his Maker, contributes to a worldview in which "people do not find your crea-

22.24 (p. 854). Commenting on Gen. 1:31 ("God saw everything that he had made, and indeed, it was very good"), Calvin remarks on the symmetry of God's works taken together as a whole (Calvin, *Commentaries on the First Book of Moses Called Genesis*, 100).

67. Augustine, "The Enchiridion on Faith, Hope, and Charity," in *On Christian Belief*, trans. Edmund Hill, OP, et al., vol. I/8 of *WA*, 278.

68. Calvin, *ICR* 1.14.3.

69. Calvin, *Commentaries on the First Book of Moses Called Genesis*, 106.

70. *The Sermon-Conferences of St. Thomas Aquinas on the Apostles' Creed*, 37–39.

tures pleasing."[71] Those who see creation through God's Spirit, Augustine said, see it differently, and created things thus arouse their delight.

Taken together, the experiential warrant and the creedal affirmation indicate that we are to regard creation as the bestowal, or good *gift* and blessing, of the faithful and good God. This articulates a fundamental pattern for a theology of grace: God gives; creatures receive. In fact, within the frame of creation piety, the first gift that creatures receive is the good of their existence in God's good world. That they are and that they are in God's good world, therefore, constitute their first debt. A salient and also subtle point that often evokes both thankfulness and praise is made memorably enough by a well-known hymn: "For the wonder of each hour, of the day and of the night, hill and vale and tree and flower, sun and moon and stars of light, Lord of all to thee we raise this, our hymn of grateful praise."[72]

Good in Its Parts and as a Whole

That the created world is good means that the cosmic ecology is good both in its parts and as a whole. Thus, according to Genesis 1, God saw that the works of each day—for example, light, sky, land, seas, vegetation, creatures that swarm in the waters—were good, and at the close of the sixth day, "God saw everything that he had made, and indeed, it was very good" (Gen. 1:31). Following Augustine once more, we should say that the several realities are good individually, but there is an additional goodness in the relationships, the interactions, and the orderings that constitute the ensemble. This is why the whole creation is *very* good.[73] Jonathan Edwards claimed that excellence is a matter of symmetry, proportion, relationship, and agreement: "One alone, without any reference to any more, cannot be excellent; for in such a case there can be no manner of relation . . . and therefore, no such thing as consent." Indeed, what we call a single reality, being, or creature—for example, a tree—is excellent "because of a consent of parts, or some consent of those in that being that are distinguished into a plurality some way or other."[74] The creation is therefore excellent due to the consent of its related parts.

Parts and their interrelationships in wider wholes and ensembles are good in an *aesthetic* sense. A branch of a large water oak outside my office window is

71. Augustine, *Confessions*, 375.

72. "For the Beauty of the Earth," lyrics by Folliot Sandford Pierpont, in *The Presbyterian Hymnal* (Louisville: Westminster John Knox, 1990), #473.

73. Augustine, *Confessions*, 377.

74. Jonathan Edwards, *Scientific and Philosophical Writings*, ed. Wallace E. Anderson, vol. 6 of *WJE*, 6:337.

beautiful (and itself consists of related parts), but there is an additional beauty when I see it as a part of the entire tree, and when I view the tree together with the equally large willow oaks and maples in my field of vision, the play of light and shade on the ground beneath them, the luminous background of blue sky and wisps of cirrus clouds above. Then I see the branch and the water oak in relationship; I see them as parts of a wider scene of objects, colors, textures, and movements. "Every beautiful body," says Augustine, "conveys the same message, for a body consisting of beautiful limbs is far more beautiful than its component parts individually, because though each one has its own loveliness, it is only through their exquisite coordination that the whole organism attains its perfection."[75] Creation shows forth not only divine workmanship but also divine artistry.

Elaborating on proposition #28 above, I obviously should also say that, within the ordered cosmic ecology, parts in their interrelationships are good in a *functional* sense. They are good for one another and also for wider systems in that they contribute to one another's well-functioning and also to the well-functioning of the ensemble. The bee pollinates as it moves from flower to flower to transfer pollen. The pollinated plant bears fruit. A bird eats the fruit, flies away, and excretes the seed, having transported it to another location. The seed takes root and grows; the plant flowers and makes seeds, and so on. In this sequence, we recognize that flower, bee, and bird are linked by mutual utility. Again, we also have noted given patterns and orderings in our experience that form conditions for human life and flourishing, such as marriage and family, the cooperative organization of labor, and schemes of civil government. These are good for humans and their communities.

As I noted earlier, the sun and Earth developed from the big bang and cosmic dust, and life on Earth from geophysics and geochemistry. In its earliest years, the solar system was "a vast cloud of gases held together by gravity; at the center, the blinding yellow globe of the young sun; and surrounding the sun, an iridescent halo of ice crystals and rocky grains, drifting slowly in planetary orbits." Therefore, the idea of creation as vast cosmic ecology clearly also allows us to say that nonliving things, such as gravity, heat, gases, ice, and cosmic dust, are good for us and for other forms of life, since without them there is no habitat.[76] It points toward quite substantial and functional senses of "good-for-ness." (As I also noted above, this same idea indicates that the isolated goods of individuals, species, and subsystems are not guaranteed. It highlights sustaining interrelationships, but it also discloses terrible, often routine and disturbing instances

75. Augustine, *Confessions*, 374.
76. Jastrow, *Until the Sun Dies*, 55.

of suffering and catastrophe. So, we recognize "good-for-ness" within the vast cosmic ecology, and we take delight in it at the same time that we refuse falsely either to domesticate or romanticize the interdependencies and harmonies. In face of cosmos, it is perhaps appropriate to recall Rudolf Otto's insistence that the holy is mysterious, daunting, aweful, good, and even fearful.)[77]

Aesthetic and functional senses of goodness may be combined. Edwards's writings on insects and spiders furnish one example. The Puritan remarked on "the exuberant goodness of God" in providing creatures with extraordinary means not only for their sustenance but also for their recreation and pleasure. He pointed especially to the movement by bridging and ballooning of the kinds of spiders that live in forests and bushes, and sometimes pass from one plant to another by sailing through the air on strings of web.[78] Edwards's focus was on how contrivance and function communicate God's wisdom, but his descriptions of "shining webs and glistening strings" indicate that an aesthetic sensibility and appreciation were also close at hand. Or consider the art of naturalistic illustration that has played so great a role in biology, medicine, and botany, and that owes much to the woodcuts, engravings, and watercolors of Albrecht Dürer. Here it seems that art and science, as well as our appreciations for the beauty and function of things and their component parts, can hardly be separated at all.[79] An exhibition at the Tang Teaching Museum of Skidmore College in Saratoga Springs, New York, explored the social, scientific, and artistic aspects of ten "Molecules That Matter" (e.g., aspirin, penicillin, DNA, Prozac), and it tried to help people "appreciate not only the utility, but also the beauty of these molecules."[80]

Good in God's Sight

Clearly, then, we may speak of the "goodness" of both abiotic and biotic elements without claiming that their value is only for us. We may apprehend their *aesthetic* excellence even when, functionally speaking, some constituents threaten our own good—for example, a menacing storm. We can appreciate the *functional* excellence or goodness of certain constituent elements, for example, a "thin" atmosphere and low temperatures, for a subsystem or a planet that does not include us. We can appreciate how some constituents may have been good for a

77. Rudolf Otto, *The Idea of the Holy: An Inquiry into the Non-Rational Factor in the Idea of the Divine and Its Relation to the Rational,* trans. John W. Harvey (London: Oxford University Press, 1958).

78. Edwards, *Scientific and Philosophical Writings,* 6:40, 157, 158.

79. Martin Kemp, "Science in Culture," *Nature* 420 (December 19, 2002): 744: www.nature.com/nature/journal/v420/n6917/full/420744a.html.

80. Fiona Case, "Molecules That Matter," *Chemistry World,* December 2007, 50.

system that, for billions of years past, did not include us—for example, our solar system. We may speculate how still others will be good for a system that, billions of years hence, may not include us. In a theological frame of reference, however, and particularly as we take into account imaginative resources and narrative suggestions made in Genesis, a number of psalms, and elsewhere in Scripture, we should take a further step. The Creator stands in relationship to all things; and all things have their places in God's vast created ensemble. The many components of the ensemble are excellent as they stand in relationship to one another, and also as they stand (both individually and collectively) in relationship to God and God's purposes. Theologically speaking, we should say that, within subsystems, constituent elements are good both aesthetically and functionally in relationship to each other and in relationship to the wider subsystem. They are good both aesthetically and functionally with respect to the entire cosmos—a whole that, as we attend to interrelationships within selected subsystems, we do not entirely comprehend. And, both as parts and as a whole (that we do not entirely comprehend), creation is good and has worth in relationship to the deity (a reality we also do not entirely comprehend). In sum, nothing that is, whether abiotic or biotic, is axiologically inert, negligible, or profane.

This brings us to a critical image. What can it mean for piety to say that creation is "good in God's sight"? In Genesis 1:1–2:4, it says that God saw that particular works of creation were good—for example, light, waters, sky, birds—and that, at the end of the sixth day, "God saw everything that he had made, and indeed, it was very good." "Good in God's sight": here we take our experiences of seeing and even of contemplating, appreciating, and evaluating things in "our mind's eye" as an analogy for God's relationship to the world and its component parts.

God's appreciation for the goodness of light in Genesis 1:4a is especially interesting. I observed earlier the aesthetic excellence and the functional "good-for-ness" of component parts in relationship to other things in ensemble and cosmic ecology. We certainly appreciate this about light, as it contrasts with darkness, makes shapes and colors vibrant, and is functionally good for many creatures and wider systems. But in Genesis 1:4a, the cosmic system does not yet exist, and there is as yet no created thing other than light. Indeed, we are also told that God saw that the light was good even before it was separated from the darkness. Therefore, "the light is good simply because God regards it as good."[81] God's seeing or regarding may very well involve an appreciation for the aesthetic excellence of particular relationships and the functional good-for-ness of particular things in relationship that we also appreciate. Augustine's ruminations

81. Westermann, *Genesis 1–11*, 113.

about the sea and its many shades of green, as well as the vision in Psalm 104 of creation as a wondrous network of gifts (including habitations and a sustaining food chain), are eloquent testimonies to that. But here in Genesis 1:4a there are as yet no "mundane" relationships, no relationships of light to other created things within the cosmic ensemble for God to appreciate. God's seeing that light is good in Genesis 1:4a is thus not entirely like our own seeing. We encounter a difference in the divine "perspective" or "point of view," an added valence or dimension of divine appreciation.[82]

We encounter the difference once more and quite significantly when we read "God saw everything he had made, and indeed, it was very good." Certainly, we may *imagine* that the many relationships that constitute creation or cosmic ecology—all of reality—are aesthetically excellent when taken as a whole. We may also imagine that the entire system is aesthetically excellent with respect to something beyond it. But we have neither experience nor genuine comprehension of such things. In what relationship, for what or for whom, can *all* that is or the entire creation be good functionally? "One cannot say for man, because man is part of it." For the same reason, one cannot say for the solar system, the Milky Way, or black holes. Neither should we simply say "for God," since in the Genesis narrative and elsewhere in Scripture, when God creates, God gives, blesses, and bestows. God's work of creation, then, is at least in some sense good for others or for creatures. But again, the creatures are parts. If God sees that the *whole* creation is very good, then God sees that it is simply aesthetically excellent as a whole or is functionally good as a whole for what God intends it (or for some comprehensive end). The Creator, therefore, "sees" and "appreciates" that the entire creation is good in a manner that can be neither reduced to nor equated with what is good in our own view or in our own sight. This difference in perspective, this different relationship or context in which God "sees" that the entire creation is good, is critically important.

> What is good is good in the eyes of God: *God* looks at what is created, and *God* says of it that everything is very good. The priestly tradition is thereby saying that this goodness in creation is not something that man notices in the works of God; it is not a judgment that man exercises. This sentence that runs

82. The book of Judges is not concerned with the goodness of creation but with conquest and apostasy. Even so, it points to differences between the way things sometimes appear in the sight of Israel and the way they appear in God's sight. When the people do what is right in their own eyes, very often they do what is evil in the sight of the Lord, for example, worshiping Baal and hence failing to praise the God of the covenant (Judg. 2:11–12; 10:6; 17:6; 21:25). So here, too, God's seeing and our seeing are not always alike; indeed, there are sometimes rather sharp disjunctions.

> through the chapter—that the works of creation are good—will not disappear just because in the eyes of man there is much in the works of creation that is not good, much that is incomprehensible, much that appears savage and senseless. This sentence is pronounced despite such negative experience and judgment of the world, despite the never-ending questions about the why of creation, about the meaning.[83]

We are ready now to entertain a proposal about the goodness of the entire creation in God's sight. In Genesis 2:1–3, the whole work of creation, all that is, the vast cosmic ecology is good for the purpose intimated by the seventh day—the hallowed day of worship. God's chief end in creating the world, the end for which the whole creation is good, is Sabbath, the praise for God's surpassing greatness that occupies not just Israel but also angels, sun, moon, firmament, and indeed all that is mentioned in Psalms 148 and 150.

Allow me to elaborate. We catch glimpses of beauty and goodness in our many experiences of the fittingness of things, their complementarities, rhythms and patterns, interrelationships and proportions in the midst of the cosmic ensemble. I say "glimpses" partly because these experiences neither gainsay nor cancel out our many negative, sometimes fearful, and genuinely disturbing experiences and judgments. I say "glimpses" also because we never really comprehend the whole and because we comprehend no relationship in which the whole stands to some further reality or end that will comprehensively define what it is good for. Nevertheless, the glimpses are real enough, and the fact remains that (as a Calvin-conflated-with-an-Edwards might put it), almost wherever we cast our eyes in this magnificent theater, we have many, many experiences of things and relationships that intimate excellence.

The proposal that I am making here, with the help of Genesis, is that beyond these many glimpses there is a fuller and more comprehensive excellence that God "sees." This is the excellence of the many interrelated works of creation participating in the hallowed day, the excellence envisioned in Psalms 148 and 150 of the entire creation praising its Creator. All things—sun, moon, stars, heavens, waters, sea monsters, fire, hail, snow, frost, wind, mountains, hills, trees, wild animals, cattle, creeping things, birds, young and old, men and women, and even, in Saint Francis's poetic meditation on Psalm 148, Sisters Earth and Death—all effectively praise God. All participate in existence. And all—and don't forget the galaxies, nebulae, molecules, and antimatter we now know to add to the list—are parts of creation's single ensemble of praise. Piety's inkling is that this is what the creation or cosmic ecology is for.

83. Claus Westermann, *Creation*, trans. John J. Scullion, SJ (Philadelphia: Fortress, 1974), 61.

Classical Reformed theology claims that the chief end for which God created the world is God's own glory, and hence that the chief end of the creature is to glorify and to praise God. I agree, but I hasten to note two things. First, praising God is not a foreign requirement superimposed on the creature but what the creature is built for. It is the creature being most truly itself, the creature exercising its own created excellence, something like a horse galloping or a hawk gliding. This is why, following the Westminster Shorter Catechism, we may say that our chief end is not only to glorify but also to *enjoy* God. Second, as Edwards insisted, God's glory (which finally also lies beyond our comprehension) is neither isolated nor exclusive but expansive. It is the characteristic exercise of the really real as it overflows and goes out to create. It is God being God, and it is this expansive exercise that both makes possible and elicits the joyful exercise of existence in which all participate.

The proposal is not entirely rational. With piety, it takes a step that goes beyond our tally of the many glimpses. The step is not really a judgment that the sum total of our glimpses of excellence and goodness, when weighed in the balance, outweighs the sum total of our experiences of senseless suffering, tragedy, and despair. Instead, it is a step suggested by imaginative and mythopoeic resources that both express and sculpt a deep and emotionally resonant sense beneath and behind our many experiences and glimpses of the many excellences. It is a routinely extravagant step encouraged by the symbolic idea of creation as it shows forth and shapes our deep feeling of being and participating in the world, our deep sense that it is compelling and good to be in God's world.

Finally, we cannot help but acknowledge an important practical corollary. To say that God sees the goodness of the many interrelated works of creation participating in a single ensemble of praise is to say that God appreciates the goodness of all things and that everything in its time, place, and interrelationships has value or worth in God's sight. Piety senses or apprehends this somewhat in and through its many glimpses of excellence and goodness, and especially in the sense that it is compelling and good to be. The practical point, then, is simply that all things have worth in relationship to God. We do not construct this worth or bestow it; it is something given that we are called upon to acknowledge. And this recognition or acknowledgment, in turn, is part and parcel of Christian humanism. Since human beings are good in God's sight, human beings also have a value or worth that cultures and nations neither construct nor bestow. This, too, is something we are simply called upon to acknowledge.

Chapter Four

The Dynamic Continuation of the World: Cosmic Passage

Generally speaking, classical Christian theology takes creation to mean that God makes the world. Providence, which is sometimes called "preservation," comes from the Greek *pronoia* and the Latin *provideo* and *providere*, meaning foresight, foreknowledge, to care for, and to make provision for. Providence signifies that God upholds the world and governs it.

Proposition #30 Creation and sustenance go together.

There are reasons to distinguish between creation and continuation: creation implies calling into being, whereas providence points to the sustaining and governing of things. Princeton theologian Charles Hodge therefore claims that "creation and preservation differ, first as the former is the calling into existence what before did not exist; and the latter is continuing, or causing to continue what already has being." Second, says Hodge, when God creates, something that did not exist is simply brought into being, and so there is no cooperation. But in the course of nature and history, God's providence *concurs* with the operations and activities of already existing created realities, for example, natural forces and human agents.[1]

On the other hand, there are also reasons to associate creation and providence rather closely. "I believe in God the Father Almighty, maker of heaven and earth." As I noted earlier, the word translated in the creed as "almighty" is *pantokratōr* (Nicene Creed) or *omnipotens* (Apostles' Creed), and more accurately means "all-governing" or "all-ruling."[2] Therefore, the first article of the creed claims that the maker of heaven and earth is the living and dynamic God who presently rules and

1. Charles Hodge, *Systematic Theology* (Peabody, MA: Hendrickson, 1999), 1:578.

2. See, for example, J. N. D. Kelly, *Early Christian Creeds*, 3rd ed. (New York: Longman, 1972), 132–34, 215–16, 369.

governs. John Calvin claimed that "we see the presence of divine power shining as much in the continuing state of the universe as in its inception," and that, "unless we pass on to his providence . . . we do not properly grasp what it means to say: 'God is creator.'"[3] The God who creates is not a distant or unengaged originator; the same God creates, maintains, governs, and directs. Providence or divine sustenance indicates continuous divine activity, even continuous sustaining creativity.

Because they wished to emphasize God's sovereignty and to deny that any created reality continues to exist of itself, some Reformed theologians spoke of providence as a continuing creation. "There is a single divine act by which God creates the world and determines its government. That is why Providence may be conceived as a continuous world-creation."[4] Friedrich Schleiermacher maintained that, since neither the Apostles' Creed nor the Creed of Constantinople (which we often call the Nicene Creed) says anything definite about the manner of creation that might help us distinguish God's creating from God's sustaining, the full effect of the first article is simply to declare that "nothing, no point of space and no point of time, should be exempted from the Divine All-Sovereignty." Therefore, he claimed that, in church teaching, the two doctrines of creation and providence explicate a single original expression of the relationship between the world and God, namely, "that the world exists only in *absolute* dependence upon God," a claim that accorded with his understanding of the core of Christian piety. Indeed, as Schleiermacher thought, "there is no sufficient reason" to retain a division between the two "instead of the original expression which was so natural."[5]

Hodge objects to this line of thinking, claiming that it collapses creation and providence or continuation in a way that finally denies the concurrence and efficacy of created realities or second causes. He believed that the undifferentiated and absolute dependence of things on the divine all-sovereignty amounts to a pantheism in which the concurrent operations of created realities are neglected in favor of the assumption that "God is sole cause of all things."[6]

In any case, Reformed confessional documents clearly place creation and providence in close proximity. The Heidelberg Catechism's exposition of the first article of the Apostles' Creed notes that "the eternal Father of our Lord Jesus Christ, who out of nothing created heaven and earth with all that is in them . . . also upholds and governs them by his eternal counsel and providence."[7] Heinrich

3. Calvin, *ICR* 1.16.1.

4. Heinrich Heppe, *Reformed Dogmatics: Set Out and Illustrated from the Sources*, ed. Ernest Bizer, trans. G. T. Thompson (Grand Rapids: Baker Books, 1978), 251.

5. Schleiermacher, *CF*, #36 and #37 (pp. 142–45) (emphasis added).

6. Hodge, *Systematic Theology*, 1:578–80, 594.

7. The Heidelberg Catechism, in *BOC* 4.026 (p. 62).

Bullinger's Second Helvetic Confession treats "the Providence of God" *before* "the Creation of All Things," an order that underscores our present experience, that the all-governing deity we now encounter in the course of things is the Creator and originator.[8] The Westminster Confession of Faith says: "God, the great Creator of all things, doth uphold, direct, dispose, and govern all creatures, actions, and things . . . by his most wise and holy providence."[9] The statement of the Scots Confession, characteristically brief, makes a good summary: "We confess and acknowledge one God alone . . . by whom we . . . believe all things in heaven and earth, visible and invisible, to have been created, to be retained in their being, and to be ruled and guided by his inscrutable providence."[10]

The position I am developing here is informed by these traditional reflections and, like them, also holds creation and providence in close proximity. I maintain that, for Christian piety, the world in its constitution may be described as a dynamic "cosmic ecology"; in its continuation, it may be termed "cosmic passage." God, the all-governing maker of heaven and earth, is the maker of cosmic ecology and sustainer of cosmic passage. At all points, then, piety senses that the world depends on and is subject to the masterful divine creativity.

Proposition #31 The world and its ordering processes continue.

John Calvin offered a basic statement of the doctrine of providence: "God by his power nourishes and maintains the world created by him, and rules its several parts by his providence."[11] Somewhat similarly, the Reformed Scholastic Johannes Wollebius said that God's providence is "that work by which God not only preserves his creatures, but governs all things."[12] The world in its several parts—the world as dynamic ensemble and cosmic ecology—continues because the God who creates also nourishes, maintains, and rules. God creates and sustains; God governs what God makes; God provides. Our primary business here is with a corollary of these statements. God upholds and governs; therefore, the world continues, and its dynamic processes and structures continue.

Thomas Aquinas claimed that God is in all things as the agent that causes them to be: "And God is causing this effect in things not just when they begin to exist, but all the time they are maintained in existence, just as the sun is light-

8. The Scots Confession of 1560, in *BOC* 5.029–5.032 (pp. 100–101).

9. The Westminster Confession of Faith, in *BOC* 6.024 (p. 178).

10. The Scots Confession of 1560, in *BOC* 3.01 (p. 33).

11. Calvin, *ICR* 1.16.1.

12. John W. Beardsleee III, ed. and trans., *Reformed Dogmatics: Seventeenth-Century Reformed Theology through the Writings of Wollebius, Voetius, and Turretin* (Grand Rapids: Baker Books, 1977), 58.

ing up the atmosphere all the time the atmosphere remains lit."[13] Without God sustaining them in existence by the continuing exercise of God's power, things could not continue even for a moment "but would fall away into nothingness."[14] Created existing beings "participate" in being only so long as God *continually and actively* causes them to do so. Something like this is also what the writers of the Scots Confession have in mind when they say that all things are "retained in their being" by God's providence.[15] The claim that all things continue means that the created ensemble persists by divine power.

Another dimension of the traditional doctrine is that, as Aquinas also noted, natural and human affairs are "arranged" and "have a determined pattern."[16] If creation is not haphazard, neither is the continuing world. Instead, the continuing world is an articulated set of dynamic relationships, operations, and interactions. There are dependable and regular patterns in both nature and society of the kind mentioned in Psalm 104 or intimated in Genesis 2:24 and Exodus 20. As we noted earlier, Calvin, for whom nature is "the order prescribed by God" and for whom God "meets us in the fabric of the world," pointed to regularities of sun, moon, stars, and seasons, as well as to the fruitfulness of the earth.[17] He also claimed that God instituted marriage as a principal office of human society for companionship, and civil government in order to maintain justice and "for the wellbeing of mankind."[18] All this, for Aquinas, is counter to mere chance, a point that Calvin also emphasizes: Aquinas takes the providence of the omnipotent God to mean that "there is no such thing as fortune or chance."[19]

Over against Deist notions that God created the world, gave it laws of nature, and thereafter does not interfere, Tillich claims that "continuous creativity" is "the only adequate understanding of preservation." This, he says, was accepted

13. Aquinas, *ST* 1a.8.2 (p. 113).

14. Aquinas, *ST* 1a.104.1 (p. 39).

15. The Scots Confession of 1560, in *BOC* 3.01. Louis Berkhof also says that preservation has reference to the being of all things (Berkhof, *Systematic Theology*, new edition containing the full text of *Systematic Theology* and the original *Introductory Volume to Systematic Theology* [Grand Rapids: Eerdmans, 1996], 167).

16. *The Sermon-Conferences of St. Thomas Aquinas on the Apostles' Creed*, trans. Nicholas Ayo, CSC (Notre Dame: University of Notre Dame Press, 1988), 29–33.

17. Calvin, *ICR* 1.5.2; 1.5.5; 1.16.2; Calvin, *Commentary on the Book of Psalms*, trans. James Anderson, vol. 4 in *Calvin's Commentaries*, Calvin Translation Society (Grand Rapids: Baker Books, 1998), 143–71.

18. Calvin, *ICR* 2.8.41; 4.20.1, 3; Calvin, *The Epistles of Paul the Apostle to the Romans and to the Thessalonians*, trans. Ross Mackenzie, vol. 8 of *Calvin's New Testament Commentaries: A New Translation*, Thomas F. Torrance and David W. Torrance, gen. eds., 12 vols. (Grand Rapids: Eerdmans, 1972), 281.

19. *The Sermon-Conferences of St. Thomas Aquinas on the Apostles' Creed*, 29–33.

by Luther and radically formulated by Calvin. Nevertheless, he continues, there is a difference between "originating and sustaining creativity," since "the latter refers to the given structures of reality."[20] We should emphasize not only that human affairs are arranged but also that the arranging and the ordering (gerunds both) *continue*. Hence, God not only creates but also *continues* to arrange and order, continues to dispose in ways that preserve and provide and sustain. As the psalmist says,

> The trees of the LORD are watered abundantly. . . .
> You have made the moon to mark the seasons;
>   the sun knows its time for setting.
> You make darkness, and it is night,
>   when all the animals of the forest come creeping out. . . .
> When the sun rises, they withdraw
>   and lie down in their dens.
> People go out to their work
>   and to their labor until the evening. (Ps. 104:16–23)

A third point is that the traditional symbol of providence implies *guidance*. As the Scots Confession has it, "all things in heaven and earth" are not only created; they are also "ruled and guided by [God's] inscrutable providence . . . for such end as his eternal wisdom, goodness, and justice have appointed."[21] Calvin, of course, maintains that all things and events are determined in accordance with God's will and purposes. The Westminster Confession of Faith likewise claims that God upholds, directs, disposes, and governs "all creatures, actions, and things, from the greatest even to the least, by his most wise and holy providence." Indeed, God orders and governs all (including the sins of angels and people) "to his own holy ends."[22] For Berkhof, one meaning of providence (versus fortune and chance) is that things are guided or directed to their appointed end.[23] Divine guidance means that people and all other mundane causes and agents are "moved," "induced," and "led" to operate and to act in ways that uphold divine purposes and plans.[24]

20. Paul Tillich, *Reason and Revelation, Being and God*, vol. 1 of *Systematic Theology* (Chicago: University of Chicago Press, 1951), 262.

21. The Scots Confession of 1560, in *BOC* 3.01.

22. The Westminster Confession of Faith, in *BOC* 6.024; 6.027.

23. Berkhof, *Systematic Theology*, 166–67.

24. Hodge's claim that God's providence concurs with the operations of created things accords with the insistence of Reformed theologians generally that the reality and efficacy of mundane causes and agents are neither denied nor neglected. For example, the Westminster

Providence and Experience

The world continues to exist, its dynamic patterns and orderings continue, and many things are guided or disposed toward appropriate ends. That is a brief account of the basic three-dimensional grammar of the idea of providence as it bears on the world. Let me emphasize here that each dimension both emerges from and interprets important aspects of people's experiences. The idea that things and processes (the entire ensemble) continue because they are preserved correlates with the feeling or sense that not only is the origin of things and world contingent, so is their continuation, or the "on-going-ness" of the entire (and particular) set of interrelationships and interactions we call the world. Wondering humans not only ask, "Why is there something rather than nothing?" but also, "Why do things continue?" After all, they might not. For many people and communities, the "on-going-ness" of things or of the world of dynamic patterns and interrelationships, and not just its origin or beginning, points beyond itself. It implies mystery as well as a sense of dependence. Classical theology both underscores and interprets this wonderment when it says that the world continues because it is continually held up by the exercise of divine power.[25]

In our interactions with objects and others in nature and society, we encounter patterns, dynamic arrangements, and orderings—rather than simple randomness. We find that we rely on processes and relationships that are not of our own making, and the significance of this fact provokes reflection. Call it an inkling of sustaining arrangement that correlates with senses of dependence and gratitude. James Gustafson expresses it this way:

> If the sun's temperature were higher or lower by a relatively insignificant degree, the conditions necessary for life on this planet would not exist. Con-

Confession of Faith maintains that, with respect to God, the first cause, "all things come to pass immutably and infallibly." But even this confession also affirms that divine providence orders things "to fall out according to the nature of second causes." That is, divine providence does not violate the integrity of created realities (the Westminster Confession of Faith, in *BOC* 6.025). I discuss the subject of human agency in prop. #38 below. Thomas Aquinas quotes Dionysius approvingly: "To ruin the nature of a thing is not the work of Providence." He takes this to mean that "the effect of divine providence is for a thing to come about not just anyhow but in its own proper style, necessarily or contingently as the case may be" (Aquinas, *ST* 1a.22.4 [p. 103]). Wollebius says simply that "the providence of God does not destroy secondary causes, but upholds them" (Beardslee, *Reformed Dogmatics*, 59).

25. Indeed, Jonathan Edwards thought that the bodies of things are made up of atoms and that "the constant exercise of the infinite power of God is necessary to" keep the atoms from flying apart and thus to "preserve bodies in being" (Edwards, *Scientific and Philosophical Writings*, ed. Wallace E. Anderson, vol. 6 of *WJE*, 214).

> tinuities in the genetic code make possible the replication, generation after generation, of creatures with the capacities we call human. A natural "food chain" sustains not only human life but all other forms of life on this planet. There are orderings of human relationships, varied in their particular forms, but nonetheless operative, that must be complied with for the biological, educational, and social nourishing of human young.

According to Gustafson, "an ordering process in a whole range of life in the world continues to be a warrant for an attitude of piety on the part of many persons and communities." Thus piety includes a sense of dependence that backs the symbol of God as Creator, even as the same sensibility is also thematized, interpreted, and shaped by this symbol. Similarly, our reliance on "the continuation of the ordering of the universe, of life on this planet, and of human relationships" evokes a sense of gratitude and thanksgiving in persons and communities.[26] Indeed, within the thicket of orderings and interrelationships, persons and communities sometimes feel upheld, supported, or even cared for. This knot of feelings and sensibilities elicits the symbol of God as sustainer and provider, and at the same time it is interpreted, sculpted, and perhaps also heightened by this symbol.

But that is not all. Individuals and communities sometimes also apprehend directives, purposes, and guides in the midst of their interactions with ordering processes that characterize our world. They perceive a dynamic pattern or government in and through the many prerequisites for the world of nature and for human societies to survive and flourish.

Consider the practice of caring for dependent children. All known human societies and cultures uphold it to some degree, although there are, of course, significantly different ways of caring for children. The practice has bases in the distinctive features and pace of the biological development of human offspring, and it is one that promises important benefits, including the education of young people into a community's particular social pattern and cultural heritage. Indeed, failure to care adequately for children can have seriously deleterious consequences: poor education, the disruption of a community's cultural heritage, an erosion in the felt obligation to respect and care for elders, and (in extreme instances) disease, physical endangerment, and death. Similar points can be made about maintaining truthful and equitable courts of law. As with caring for dependent children, particular societies and cultures institutionalize the judicial function in different ways. But, once again, there are considerable benefits to communities that uphold tolerably just and truthful courts of law, and there are also rather steep costs where communities rely on means for settling disputes

26. Gustafson, *ETP*, 1:239–40.

that are widely thought to be arbitrary, deceitful, and unjust. Caring for children and maintaining equitable institutions for settling disputes are practices that help to make human communities possible. They are practices that ensure goods of principled social cooperation. Indeed, they appear to be among the requisites for the survival and well-being of human communities.[27]

For many persons and communities, felt senses of guidance, sustenance, responsibility, and direction emerge in conjunction with their experiences of the benefits associated with upholding practices such as these, as well as with their experiences of the costs associated with failing to do so. These sensibilities and others like them furnish additional backing for the symbol of God as provider, sustainer, and governor. Moreover, the symbol also interprets and sharpens the imperative mood of such intimations of guidance and direction, because now they are associated with the source that bestows the good gift of creation itself. Religious individuals and communities often come to feel that the divine governance impinges on them and that it guides and directs, not only because it furnishes sustaining possibilities but also because it sets limits and requirements that people and communities ignore at their peril. The divine governance moves, induces, leads, and lures individuals and communities to act in certain ways.

Particularity and Plurality

At this point (as at others), we should note the importance of our current intense recognition of historical particularity and cultural plurality. The recognition has roots in voyages of discovery, for example, Chateaubriand's encounter with native tribal cultures in Louisiana, rather than with the "natural (culture-free) man" he may have expected to find outside the confines of European civilization. It is strengthened today by globalized travel, communications, and economies. For our purposes in this book, the crucial point is that a contemporary sense of divine orderings and action guides needs to account for the fact that we now have knowledge and experiences of cultures and societies that many classical theologians could scarcely imagine. We are (or should be) more keenly aware than they were that elaborated moral norms, practices, institutions, and laws are responsive not only to specific circumstances but also to a bewildering variety of cultural heritages. Therefore, we need to recognize that requisites for human survival and well-being take many different forms. For example, the need for

27. Arthur Dyck, *Rethinking Rights and Responsibilities: The Moral Bonds of Community* (Cleveland: Pilgrim, 1994), 123–49; Dyck, *On Human Care: An Introduction to Ethics* (Nashville: Abingdon, 1977), 93.

tolerably fair and equitable means of settling disputes remains relatively constant across human societies; but it is also clear that particular conceptions of justice vary widely and that judicial practices and institutions are differently structured and articulated. They are at least partly socially constructed. Even within the same cultures, orderings of basic human relationships—for example, parents and children—alter and develop over time.

The Decalogue and Natural Law

I will have more to say about the Ten Commandments in part 3 of the present system. Here, let me simply echo the frequent insistence of some classical Christian theologians that, especially when it comes to duties toward other people, the Decalogue is in accordance with the natural law known to all.

Thomas Aquinas said that "all the moral precepts of the Law belong to the law of nature." This is true because "the moral precepts are concerned with right conduct, which is what conforms with reason, and, further, every judgment of human reason derives, in some way, from natural reason." Indeed, "the natural reason of every man" recognizes a number of the precepts contained in the Decalogue straightaway, for example, "Honor your father and your mother," "Do not kill," and "Do not steal."[28] Martin Luther believed that God reawakens our knowledge of the natural law, "which even heathen, Turks, and Jews have to keep," through the law of Moses given to Israel and through preaching based on this law.[29] Similarly, Calvin claimed not only that the natural law is inwardly impressed on human hearts and testified to by human consciences, but also that "the Lord has provided us with a written law to give us a clearer witness of what was too obscure in the natural law, shake off our listlessness, and strike more vigorously our mind and memory."[30]

Proscriptions against murder, stealing, and adultery indicate important conditions for the survival and well-being of human societies. So does the command not to bear false witness, which functions to safeguard the judicial process.[31] So does the command to honor parents, which helps to ensure continuity across

28. Aquinas, *ST* 1a.100.1 (pp. 59–61).

29. Luther, "Admonition to Peace: A Reply to the Twelve Articles of the Peasants in Swabia," in *Selected Writings of Martin Luther, 1523–1526*, ed. Theodore G. Tappert (Philadelphia: Fortress, 1967), 327; Paul Althaus, *The Ethics of Martin Luther*, trans. Robert C. Schultz (Philadelphia: Fortress, 1972), 27–28.

30. Calvin, *ICR* 2.8.1.

31. See Patrick D. Miller, *Deuteronomy* (Louisville: Westminster John Knox, 1990), 93; Luther, *Sermons I*, ed. and trans. John W. Doberstein, vol. 51 of *LW*, 158.

generations. In this way, one may argue that persons and communities generally recognize the validity of all five of these norms. Indeed, some years ago, in his philosophical introduction to ethics, Arthur Dyck included a discussion of "the ancient code of the Mosaic covenant, for which there are counterparts in other religions and cultures." He justified the inclusion by saying that it introduces readers to constraints that safeguard associations that "are requisite to there being any form of community or cooperative action among people."[32]

We should say that, within the frame of Christian sensibility, the Decalogue articulates norms and practices appropriate to or fit for humans. At a significant level of generalization, it indicates patterns that, when they are given historically and culturally particular expressions and institutionalizations, both protect and enhance human societies. Piety adds to these observations the feeling that the divine ordering or governance, which yields norms such as these, also continues to sustain, guide, and direct.

Proposition #32 We have a place and a time within a vast *cosmic passage.*

John Calvin could write that, since "we know that the universe was established especially for the sake of mankind, we ought to look for this purpose in his governance also." Indeed, he said, "God's providence especially relates to men."[33] But today we have good reasons to review statements such as these with a critical eye.[34]

Cosmological Implications of Modern Knowledge

The cosmological implications of modern scientific findings, theories, and perspectives not only have an impact on the idea of creation, they also back important challenges to many traditional conceptions of providence. Consider space. Earlier Christians sometimes pictured themselves at the center of a comparatively cozy cosmos made up of three parallel planes: heaven above, Earth in the middle, and hell, or the "underworld," below. Over the centuries, however, scientific theories and findings have contributed to a vastly different outlook. The Copernican, heliocentric theory of the universe displaced Earth and human beings from the center of the planetary system—a sufficiently disturbing occur-

32. Dyck, *On Human Care*, 98–99.

33. Calvin, *ICR* 1.16.6; see also *ICR* 1.14.22.

34. In what follows, I draw freely and extensively from my article "Which Way Is Up?" *Interpretation: A Journal of Bible and Theology* 59, no. 4 (October 2005): 374–81.

rence to have contributed to Galileo's later troubles with the church. What's more, our displacement has only been radicalized by the stunning expansion in our picture of the cosmos courtesy of calculations concerning its expansion from a big bang, as well as findings by means of telescopes, satellites, and space probes. The distances are staggering, and the cosmos that we envision today no longer seems cozy so much as unimaginably vast.

Consider time. Our forebears sometimes found it plausible to figure the age of the earth in handfuls of thousands of years. Indeed, biblical chronology was once a popular pursuit, and Bishop James Ussher's work, published in the 1650s, rather famously fixed the date of creation at October 23, 4004 BCE. But there were many others. For example, the Venerable Bede (d. 735) wrote a chronology that set the date of creation at 3952 BCE, and some fifty years after Ussher's chronology, Isaac Newton set it at 3998 BCE. Today our calculations need to take into account evolutionary biology and geology, not to mention theories and findings concerning the origins of matter, stars, and planets. As a result, we now speak of years in the billions: the current scientific consensus is that the earth is roughly 4.6 billion years old, and the entire cosmos is roughly 14.7 billion years old. To picture this temporal expanse and our place in it, George Fisher, my geologist friend from Johns Hopkins University, suggests that we convert the billions of years of cosmic history into a more familiar distance. Suppose, then, that we "locate" the big bang on a South Pacific island near the eastern coast of Australia, and then travel toward Richmond, Virginia. Human history would begin only a few yards away from the door of my old office in Richmond.

There is also the question of where we fit in the sequence of things on Earth. Many of our predecessors assumed that a great chasm divides humans from animals, plants, and natural environments. Thomas Aquinas thought that the image of God in humans is the rational soul and that, while we share this intellectual and spiritual endowment with the angels, there is nothing like it among the animals.[35] Even more radically, perhaps, the Enlightenment philosopher René Descartes argued that humans are endowed with rational souls and emotions but that animals are mere mechanisms without either feeling or thought.[36] By the mid-nineteenth century, there had emerged in the West an outlook that we might call "industrial humanism." Two of its great representatives, Adam Smith

35. Aquinas, *ST* 1a.90.2 (pp. 7–9); 1a.93.2–3 (pp. 53–59).

36. Mary Midgley says that Descartes's complete identification of the human soul and consciousness with reason led him "to conclude that animals could not be conscious at all, and were in fact just automata" (Midgley, *Animals and Why They Matter: A Journey around the Species Barrier* [New York: Penguin, 1983], 11; Midgley refers to *Discourse on Method*, part 5 in *Philosophical Works of Descartes*, trans. Elizabeth S. Haldene and G. R. T. Ross [Cambridge: Cambridge University Press, 1969], 1:115–18).

and Karl Marx—the one capitalist and the other communist—harbored significant disagreements. But they agreed that human beings alone act to purpose, whereas nonhuman nature is merely arbitrary and amounts to inert raw material for human production. In 1936, Emil Brunner wrote: "Man is something other than animal, as animal is something other than plant" (thus recalling an earlier classifying scheme that Charles Darwin himself had argued against).[37]

Today a number of findings and ideas point in a different direction. Human life depends on the formation and distribution of carbon, oxygen, and other elements, as well as electricity, water, and temperatures that fall within certain ranges. This is also true of the other life-forms we know of. The MRI (magnetic resonance imaging) allows us to obtain detailed information about brain functions, and it is not unusual for scientific papers to be delivered on neural correlates of consciousness. The Human Genome Project has enabled biologists to observe that we share upwards of 98 percent of our genetic material with other species. (As it turns out, among nonprimates, we are particularly close to rodents.)[38] Many people in our society today think that animals are sufficiently similar to humans to suffer terribly from the usual conditions under which they are farmed and slaughtered (a conviction that leads some to be vegetarians or lobby for a differently organized and more "humane" agricultural industry). A number of researchers and philosophers now believe that the image of an evolutionary tree or ladder with humans at the top overstates both the directionality of evolutionary processes and the differences between humans and other species. They thus prefer to picture us in the upper reaches of a less hierarchical bush.[39] Furthermore, of course, one of the great lessons of modern geology and evolutionary biology is that nature is not static. It has a history; in fact, human history may be regarded as a short part of this longer story.

The result is an outlook that is quite different, not only from the theologies and philosophies of past millennia but also from the industrial humanism that predominated in many circles just a century ago. True, we humans exercise dis-

37. Emil Brunner, *Our Faith*, trans. John W. Rilling (New York: Scribner's Sons, 1954), 35. In saying this, he harked back to an earlier classifying scheme that Darwin himself argued against. "Some naturalists," Darwin wrote, "from being deeply impressed with the mental and spiritual powers of man, have divided the whole organic world into three kingdoms, the Human, the Animal, and the Vegetable, thus giving to man a separate kingdom" (Darwin, *The Descent of Man, and Selection in Relation to Sex* [Princeton: Princeton University Press, 1981], 186).

38. National Institutes of Health, "Scientists Compare Rat Genome with Human, Mouse," news release, March 31, 2004, https:\\www.genome.gov/11511308/2004-release-scientists-compare-rat-genome.

39. Mary Midgley, *Beast and Man: The Roots of Human Nature* (Ithaca, NY: Cornell University Press, 1978), 160–61.

tinctive capacities of intervention and reflection, but we are not beings entirely set apart, surrounded by a foreign, inert world. We are living organisms that have emerged from and are enmeshed within a vast, interconnected ecology. We do have distinctive capabilities, and arguably with these capabilities also come distinctive responsibilities. But neither the planetary ecology nor the evolutionary sequences of life on Earth seem centered on us humans alone.

Suppose, then, that we assume—as I expect we must—that within a Christian frame of reference the great God of glory intimated by the Bible and theological tradition is indeed Lord of the entire cosmos. Recalling the Nicene Creed, we say that God is the *all-governing* maker of "all things visible and invisible." Taking into account the kinds of scientific findings and ideas I have just outlined, we should affirm that the space God orders and brings into being is the vast cosmic span of stars and planetary systems, billions of galaxies, black holes, and nebulae. The time that God governs is the immense history of the cosmos. The sequence of life on Earth that God sustains is the comparatively lengthy and incomplete saga of molecules, bacteria, plants, dinosaurs, humans, birds, insects, and viruses interacting with somewhat stable—but also evolving and sometimes catastrophically malleable—environmental conditions. Does it make sense, then, to insist that we humans, who inhabit a small blue planet in an obscure corner of a galaxy, are the crown of all creation? Does it make sense to maintain that humans and their fate compose God's chief end and primary concern?

The case against that is rather strong, and it is partly a matter of proportion. All the world may be a stage, but isn't God's cosmos, as we have come to fathom it, a rather outsized stage for the drama of human life and history? On a stage so vast, might there not be other dramas, realities, and developments of equal or even greater importance that have taken place, are taking place, or have yet to take place? Aren't we saying that the cosmos and even planet Earth were around for billions of years before humans appeared on the scene? Aren't we also saying that different species have emerged on Earth, survived and flourished for a time, and then gone extinct? Isn't it possible, or perhaps even likely, that the human species also will come to an end well before the cosmos does?

Of course, even when faced with modern pictures of a vast cosmos, as well as of life on Earth characterized by ecological interrelationships and interdependencies, there has been at least one way for people to continue to place themselves at the center of the picture. "Yes," we might say, "the cosmos is indeed vast. But it appears to be mostly cold, dark, and inhospitable. When it comes to life—and especially to the conscious and comparatively intelligent life of our own species—we simply have no evidence that there is anything like it anywhere else. Moreover, precisely because we are intelligent, we are able to appreciate God's cosmos as no other creatures can. We seem fashioned to appreciate it, and it seems fashioned to be appreciated by us. Indeed, our recent probes, studies, and explorations of everything from deep space to intricate ecologies and firing neurons are rather good examples of our distinctive capacity for appreciation."[40]

This is where some recent findings come in. We now know that many meteors and space objects are made up partly of ice. Simple organic chemicals have been detected in interstellar clouds of dust and gas, and organic substances have been found in meteorites.[41] There is ice on the south pole of Mars. There is also evidence that in the past there has been water on the Martian surface. But indeed, where there's ice and where there once was water, there may also have been a biosphere.[42]

Discoveries such as these prompted Olivia Judson, an evolutionary biologist, to warn that rock samples containing Martian microbes and bacteria might pose hazards on Earth. Remember what happened when the Spanish brought smallpox and measles to the New World; recall also the consequences of transporting starlings to North America.[43]

None of this means that Mars or any other planet we know of either has supported or does support life in anything like the variety and developed forms present on Earth. But Mars is incredibly nearby—at least in cosmic terms. Moreover, meteors and other bearers of organic substances might have seeded other planets. Hence, if there is or was another biosphere in our immediate neighborhood, and if there may be many others scattered near and far, might it be that some have, do, or will support life in something like the variety and complexity that Earth does? But if this is true, then the cosmos is not simply cold, dark, and inhospitable; it may even be somewhat fruitful. And if this is true, when it comes

40. This echoes the "Anthropic Principle" affirmed by some scientists, philosophers, and theologians. John Polkinghorne favors a "strong" formulation, "which alleges that the universe must be capable of evolving life," and also suggests teleology or design. What he thinks of prospects for life elsewhere is difficult to determine, although he says that "the unambiguous discovery that life independently arose on Mars, or elsewhere in the galaxy, would provide vindication of those of us who feel that the universe is seeded with life" (Polkinghorne, *Science and Theology: An Introduction* [Minneapolis: Fortress, 1998], 36–40).

41. See, e.g., Sid Perkins, "Unprecedented Organic Meteorite," *Science News* 175, no. 13 (June 2009): 14.

42. I can't help but note that London bookmakers started taking bets during the early 1960s at 100 to 1 on whether life once existed on Mars. In response to various findings, Ladbrokes, a well-known establishment, cut the odds to 50 to 1 in August 1996, and to 16 to 1 in January 2004. On March 3, 2004, the day after NASA announced that the rover *Opportunity* had found evidence that there once was surface water on the planet, Ladbrokes quit taking bets (Marshall Poe, "Life on Mars: The Odds," *Atlantic Monthly*, June 2004, 49).

43. "Some Things Are Better Left on Mars," *New York Times*, April 19, 2004, A25.

to life and perhaps even appropriately appreciative and intelligent life, it's not necessarily all and only about us.[44]

This can be an unsettling thought. We seem chronically to assume that we are at the center of things, and our assumption seems partly due to our finite perceptual equipment. (Stand up, open your eyes, turn around in a circle, and you will be at the center of all you see.) In addition, more than a few theologians—among them some at the generally progressive Second Vatican Council—have pictured "the world as the theatre of human history."[45] Of course, one might read the biblical narrative as ineluctably human-centered. Within days of creating light, God makes humans. With the appearance of Adam and Eve, history becomes the story of human salvation, and humans are present on Earth right up to the apocalypse.

One sophisticated theological version of this perspective begins with the idea that God creates the cosmos so that God can redeem, and then (rather quickly) equates or limits redemption to the redemption of humans. Karl Barth, the most important Protestant theologian of the twentieth century, explained it this way: creation is the external basis for God's covenant of redemption with human beings. "The purpose and therefore the meaning of creation is to make possible the history of God's covenant with man which has its beginning, its centre and its culmination in Jesus Christ."[46] Or again, "the whole cosmos was precisely created that in it there might be this event and revelation—that man might be what he is by the grace of God and for the grace of God."[47] In short, then, from the big bang to the present day and beyond, across the virtually unfathomable span of space, replete with almost countless stars and planets, the entire cosmos was created so that we humans could be saved by the grace of God in Jesus Christ. But if I am correct, this is just the sort of misproportioned theologizing that cannot stand in the face of our current understandings of cosmic space and time, the evolution of life on Earth and the possibilities for life elsewhere.

44. When it comes to the question of life elsewhere, we can only speculate. Still, not only London bookmakers but also some scientists believe the odds in favor have improved. Michael W. Werner of NASA's Jet Propulsion Laboratory says, "The number of potential Earthlike planets in the galaxy is greater than we previously imagined." Some also think recent advances in planet detection bode well for finding habitable planets. See *Science News: The Weekly Magazine of Science* 165, no. 23 (June 2004): 355; see also *Science News* 167, no. 25 (June 2005): 387.

45. "Pastoral Constitution of the Church in the Modern World," in *Vatican Council II*, vol. 1, *The Conciliar and Post Conciliar Documents*, ed. Austin Flannery, rev. ed. (Northport, CT: Costello, 1975), 904.

46. Barth, *CD* III/1:42.

47. Barth, *CD* III/1:67.

Rethinking Our Theatrical Imagery

Let me begin to sketch an alternative theology of divine governance by rethinking our theatrical imagery. If all the cosmos is a stage, then it is far too vast and complex for us to plausibly consider it the stage for human history alone. Indeed, given the vast expanse of cosmos, the staggering cosmic time frames, the astounding number of stars, planets, and meteors, the gases, chemicals, ice, and dust scattered through space, and so forth, perhaps the appropriate analogy is not a single stage but a world with many different venues, theaters, stages, and shows in many regions, cities, hamlets, and towns. Some productions may be located in the same city or even the same neighborhood and district, and they seem sufficiently near one another to share the occasional set design, orchestra, or even actor. Some, although they take place in the same town, remain almost wholly unrelated because they run during different seasons or even different eras. Others take place simultaneously but in regions or cultures of our imaginary world so far removed from one another that they never come into contact.

We may suppose that there are dramas (or local sequences and lines of development) on all these stages.[48] For those of us looking for signs of life, some of these sequences may seem a tad boring and inactive (something like Andy Warhol's famous film of the Empire State Building in which, after a few hours, a bird flies by). But, of course, even lifeless venues might include chemical and volcanic developments. Some stages, in addition to our own planet Earth, might very well support more lively dramas. And we cannot rule out the possibility that some of these livelier dramas have supported, do now support, or will (at some time in the future) support life-forms that we might deem intelligent.

Now, concerning this picture of the cosmos, we cannot say that we humans are at the center, and we cannot say that the entire cosmos was constructed for the benefit of humans alone. We cannot say that the idea of God and God's providential ordering leads us to focus only on the evolutionary-historical trajectory on planet Earth. Indeed, when we contemplate the many, many venues present in the cosmos, we cannot say that the idea of God—God's providential ordering or holistic cosmic activity—focuses our minds entirely on trajectories that are

48. Gordon D. Kaufman notes that there are multiple trajectories at different places in the cosmos, though in constructing his very interesting and important understanding of God and a universe characterized by "serendipitous creativity," I think he concentrates his attention too quickly on what takes place in the evolutionary trajectory on Earth. In turn, he too quickly assures us that "the divine activity is moving toward a *humane order*" and that the word "God" focuses our minds on the "growing unity of *directedness toward the human*" that he believes to be characteristic of the particular evolutionary-historical trajectory in which we find ourselves (Kaufman, *IFM*, 281, 283, 317, 337, 349).

moving toward the human or even the humane. What we can say is that we humans have a "place and time" within the local sequence or line of development on Earth. Here, in the midst of this particular planet's dynamic ecology, we have a habitation. As we say this, we need not deny that there are other ecologies, sequences, and lines of development very different from the one in which we find ourselves. We need not insist that there are no others like our own. And we need not insist that, once sprung, our species necessarily will continue to flourish until entropy finally brings the cosmos to a close. Indeed, that particular insistence seems entirely excessive. We need not claim that the human species necessarily will continue right up to the end of planet Earth. (After all, we have quite a ways to go before our species gets as long in the tooth as the dinosaurs did, though we do have many more ways than they did to hasten our own demise.) What we may hope for is not that the human species will continue for all time, but that it may have, as they sometimes say about plays in New York, a good run.

When one considers the multitude of factors and relationships that had to come together for our species to emerge and then also continue for a time, "a good run" is no small testimony to the sustaining qualities of God's cosmic reign and the place of humans in it. Depending on what counts as a relevant line of development on Earth in which to place the human species, the phrase "a good run" may indicate anywhere from 120,000 to 2 billion years—a period that dwarfs the few thousand years of human history portrayed in the Bible. And clearly there may be additional impressive testimonies to the sustaining qualities of God's reign strewn throughout the cosmos. Therefore, it should not be too difficult to retrieve (and perhaps also enhance) at least some of what was meant by classical doctrines of providence and preservation.

Theologically speaking, the symbol of the divine governance gathers the many stages, trajectories, forces, interdependencies, relationships, and events into a single dynamic movement. It suggests to piety a regimen or reign that includes the very many and indeed virtually countless venues and sequences other than our own. It indicates that the particular ecology and dynamic trajectory on Earth in which we find ourselves is one among very many, a part within the continuing, developing, and vast cosmic ecology. And it indicates that, within this encompassing passage or movement, we humans—as a species, as communities, and as persons—have a place and a time.

Some Characteristics of Cosmic Passage

The encompassing passage is *mysterious*. We do not know why it is, and we do not know that it is all that is. We do not know all that it entails, and we find it difficult even to picture or imagine. We are not entirely clear about its emergence. (What was "before" the big bang? Is the cosmos that proceeds from the big bang part of a larger movement?) We are unclear about its end. (What comes "after" or "lies beyond" the arc, edge, or limit of cosmic expansion?) We have not yet mapped and discovered let alone understood nearly all the local venues, trajectories, and sequences involved (organic or not). We do not know how the many venues, sequences, and forces relate to one another and to the larger whole. We do not know just how or why they may be influenced, deflected, or terminated. We do not know how many others may emerge. And we do not know precisely where or to what ends each trajectory is heading.

For us humans, the image or thought of this vast and encompassing cosmic passage is *decentering* and *displacing*. Certainly, the earthly geological-evolutionary-historical sequence of which we are a part does not appear to be at Earth's center. By many astrophysical measures, it does not appear to be especially prominent either. Moreover, even within our particular planetary sequence, we need to take into account the many interdependencies, or the planetary ecology that we may now be called upon to oversee or manage but that also is clearly not centered simply on us. Of course, there are also the many wider interrelationships and interdependencies in which our solar system and Earth participate, which influence the course of things on Earth, and which we neither control nor entirely understand.

The cosmic passage is *creative*. Within this movement, stars are born, planetary systems coalesce, and organic substances emerge. Within the geological-evolutionary-historical trajectory on Earth, life emerges, species rise, organisms become more complex, and consciousness develops. Organisms are endowed with generativity. People, cultures, and institutions emerge. That is, at very many points in the cosmic passage, we note the rise or emergence of something new, something more than the mere extension of what already is, something different from the simple persistence of factors, processes, relationships, and realities already in place. The origin of cosmic ensemble is a fundamental point of creativity. But there are many others: the emergence of chemical elements; the formation of galaxies, stars, and planetary systems; the emergence of life and the organic from the inorganic; the rise of new life-forms and species within the evolutionary sequence on Earth (and perhaps elsewhere); the emergence of the human species with its distinctive (and also evolving) consciousness and capabilities; the rise of new cultures and institutional forms in human history; and the births and historic formations of specific persons. Points of formation and emergence such as these suggest, as Kaufman has also noted, that the universe itself may be regarded as "a serendipitously creative process or movement," and the rise of "human historical existence" may be seen "as a significant expression of the serendipitous creativity manifest in the cosmos as a whole."[49]

The cosmic passage *continues* and *sustains*. Within its purview, stars and planetary systems not only emerge but perdure for billions of years. Conditions for life on Earth, such as atmospheric composition, temperatures, and genetic codes, hold steady within certain ranges for significant periods of time; enduring institutional forms shape and support human social possibilities. Moreover, within the geological-evolutionary-historical sequence on Earth, the somewhat stable ecological interdependencies on which species depend, as well as certain social and institutional requisites for human communities, furnish bases for senses of guidance and direction. Generations succeed one another. The histories of peoples, cultures, and nations transpire. Composers write symphonies and street-corner players strum ballads. Lawyers litigate and mechanics repair. I teach. My colleague enjoys his young children. You read this book.

But the cosmic passage is also *destructive*. Galaxies collide, stars expand, and worlds end. Meteors strike planets and sometimes drastically alter the conditions on which species depend. Species emerge but also compete. Predation makes for both survival and suffering. Microbes infect. Species go extinct. Communities emerge, cooperate, compete, go to war, and occasionally commit genocide. Empires fall. Tectonic plates move, mountains quake, and cities collapse. Individuals are born, are sustained for a time, and die. Families emerge, care for children and loved ones across generations, and then fade away. Massive starvation and disease take their tolls. Cultural artifacts are produced, developed, preserved, and lost. Much of this is necessary, no doubt, if certain trajectories and lines of development, both organic and otherwise, are to continue. But even as this thought can comfort us, it also indicates that there are significant disjunctions between the wider movements of venues and contexts, not to mention tensions between the overall movement of the whole and the goods of specific species, communities, and individuals. And all the while, the encompassing cosmic passage continues as the total context and movement, the dynamic whole from which things emerge and into which they perish and pass away.

In sum, the cosmic passage is the process within which are situated all the sublines, trajectories, venues, and events. It is the encompassing movement within which are situated the geological, evolutionary, and historical sequences in which we find ourselves on Earth. It is the reality within which, when we look to the more immediate and particular sequences in our own experience, we discern preconditions and requisites for the survival and well-being of humans and their societies. We might diagram it like this: cosmic passage > the

49. Kaufman, *IFM*, 279, 284; see also chap. 6, prop. #45.

many sublines, trajectories, and venues of the cosmos > trajectories and lines of development on Earth > human histories and preconditions and requisites for human survival and well-being. This is the vast, intricate reality within which we live and move in all our many interactions. We live, act, and respond within the stream of cosmic passage precisely as we interact with the many particular objects and others in our place and time. Or, to put it differently, we are situated within dynamic reality in its vastness, we are surrounded by it, and we participate in it. Thus do our many particular interactions and experiences have immediacy at the same time that they point toward something more, something underlying and transcending, something ultimate and mysterious.

A point worth emphasizing is that we cannot speak of a still frame at the cosmic (or indeed at any other) level of the vast reality in which we are situated. There is a passage or movement of the whole. There are also more particular movements and trajectories of specific galaxies and planets, life on Earth, peoples and their communities and cultures, in all of which novelties emerge, new realities are born, and then also dissipate and cease. There is a continuing and creative—often a surprising, destructive, and unfinished—character of things.

This is part of what it means to say that, for creation piety, the world is historical. It is in process—unfolding, unfinished. We cannot know all outcomes on either macro or micro scales. Although we can predict the courses of some things with varying degrees of probability, in many respects the future remains opaque, and it does not yet appear what shall be.

The symbols of divine governance, continuation, and sustenance direct piety's attention toward this encompassing reality by interpreting the nexus of relationships, realities, interdependencies, patterns, processes, and occurrences within the purview of divine agency and creativity. They encourage us to ask what comes to us—and indeed to all creatures—in and through this expansive matrix. Not surprisingly, then, for religious persons the symbol of divine providence and the realities that it intimates, gathers, and interprets evoke a slew of interrelated affections that are critical for piety or for a basic disposition toward the world. Discernments of divine governance in the midst of cosmic passage link to senses of dependence and displacement. They instill awe and fear. They evoke thankfulness and gratitude for the gifts of existence and continuing sustenance. They point to patterns and interrelationships that support possibilities and limits for our lives and also elicit a sense of guidance and direction.

And especially, as we find ourselves within the most powerful commercial, media-capable, and military society on Earth, another point worth emphasizing is that nations and empires rise and fall. They do not control all relevant outcomes and thus cannot ensure their indefinite survival. For piety, this is a corollary of the vision of history, as well as of the feelings of dependence and contingency that come to expression in and are shaped by the symbol of divine providence. Egypt, Assyria, Babylon, Rome, America—all are contingent. Not one of them is eternal.

Bernard Meland uses the term "Creative Passage" to evoke "the nexus of relationships" that "is given with existence" and from which "come resources of grace that can carry us beyond the meanings of our own making, and alert us to goodness that is not of our own willing and defining." Within this Creative Passage, "the passage of [human] history" occurs in its many streams and cultural currents. For Meland, Creative Passage is the "objective aspect" of "the stream of experience." It points to "an ultimate reference in the way traditional metaphysics used the term 'being' or 'ground of being.'"[50]

My use of the term "cosmic passage" signals appreciation for Meland's proposal. I think he is largely correct to associate the reality of God with this encompassing passage. I think he is also correct in his reluctance to offer a complete metaphysical definition of God and his preference for attending to the work or activity of God in relation to the world and ourselves. As Meland develops his theology, however, he links "Creative Passage" very closely with growth and human creativity and fulfillment. To be sure, he also recognizes that "the creative passage of events must issue in destruction and suffering," but this is destruction that accompanies growth and is for the sake of creativity.[51]

On this score, Meland's proposal owes much to Henry Nelson Wieman's idea that God is the source of human good.[52] My first response to Wieman's idea is also appreciative. We can say that God is the source of human good in the sense that humans have a place and a time in the encompassing creation that God governs and upholds, and that they do well to adjust themselves to requisites for human life and well-being as these are discernible in patterns of divine governance. But, of course, such a vision of the whole does not identify God's purposes or the passage of reality with what is good for humans alone. Indeed, it does not identify the good of the whole creation that God upholds with the isolated needs and goods of any particular species or individual organism. Nor do we need to gloss over very significant tensions and disjunctions between processes and events that contribute to the good of wider systems and ecologies and at least some quite defensible understandings of the needs, interests, and goods of particular species and creatures. The meteor showers that

50. Bernard Meland, *Fallible Forms and Symbols: Discourses on Method in a Theology of Culture* (Philadelphia: Fortress, 1976), 151–52.

51. Bernard Meland, *Seeds of Redemption* (New York: Macmillan, 1947), 68, 63.

52. Meland, *Seeds of Redemption*, 54; see also Henry Nelson Wieman, *The Source of Human Good* (Chicago: University of Chicago Press, 1946).

apparently struck and then darkened the earth some millions of years ago, thus rendering our planet inhospitable to dinosaurs, may be said to have contributed to the wider evolutionary process. But surely those meteor showers were not good for the dinosaurs. The Lisbon earthquake was a result of the movement of tectonic plates, without which the earth could not be the supportive habitat that it is, but the earthquake advanced neither the growth nor the creativity of those who perished.

Although the passage of reality is creative and sustaining, I also believe that the term "*cosmic* passage" intimates such disjunctions in a way that the term "creative passage" may not. Properly understood, the image evokes gratitude and thankfulness, but it also expresses and sculpts a sense for the dwarfing vastness of reality and its dynamic movement. Therefore, it checks excessively optimistic and easy assurances that the overall movement of things always upholds the good, the creativity and fulfillment of any particular species or creature, including humans.

As I have noted earlier, it's true that Calvin said that the universe was established especially for the sake of humankind. Even so, he also claimed that the world is the magnificent theater, not of human history, but of God's glory. Indeed, he said, "Wherever you cast your eyes, there is no spot in the universe wherein you cannot discern at least some sparks of his glory."[53] Having undertaken studies of insects, Jonathan Edwards could extol spiders as "wondrous animals . . . from whose glistening webs so much of the wisdom of the Creator shines."[54] Edwards claimed, in rather typical Calvinist fashion (but also in a distinctively creative fashion for a Calvinist), that God's chief end in creating the world is God's own glory, and that genuine piety hinges on a sense of the divine excellence. In short, both theologians thought that we are equipped to appreciate a world that is *not* centered on us, and both believed that the Bible supported them on this point.[55] These are the theological perspectives regarding creation and continuation that need to be retrieved and developed in conjunction with the implications for piety of modern cosmologies and scientific findings. Even if it no longer seems plausible to insist that we humans occupy center stage, even if it appears that the Lord of the cosmos rules venues and has purposes beyond our imaginings, something like the God-centered vision promoted by Calvin and Edwards remains a live option.

53. Calvin, *ICR* 1.5.1; 1.5.5.

54. Edwards, *Scientific and Philosophical Writings*, 154, 169.

55. Edwards, *Scientific and Philosophical Writings*, 353. Edwards believed that "to find out the reason of things in natural philosophy is only to find out the proportion of God's acting."

An Unscientific Postscript for a Scientific Age

This brings us to an unscientific postscript for a scientific age:

> O LORD, our Sovereign,
> how majestic is your name in all the earth! . . .
> When I look at your heavens, the work of your fingers,
> the moon and the stars that you have established;
> what are human beings that you are mindful of them,
> mortals that you care for them?
> Yet you have made them a little lower than angels,
> and crowned them with glory and honor.
> You have given them dominion
> over . . . sheep and oxen,
> and also the beasts of the field,
> the birds of the air, and the fish of the sea. . . . (Ps. 8)

Psalm 8 is among the best-known psalms in the Bible. It begins by directing our attention to the only God, the sovereign whose name is majestic, and whose glory is set above the heavens. It then turns our attention to the magnificent night sky, to the moon and the many stars in sight. It acknowledges that all this falls within the purview of the Creator's reign. Only then, after having surveyed this spacious expanse, does the psalm raise the question of human beings. In the midst of the splendor of the heavens, the moon, and the stars, what are human beings that they, too, should be objects of divine care and concern?

This is old—even ancient—poetry, and it conveys an old and even ancient piety. As I have noted, it supposes a rather quaint and outmoded picture of the cosmos. Whoever wrote it did so without benefit of either evolutionary biology or modern ecological studies. Nevertheless, even in an age of astrophysics, many of the psalm's more important features seem intensified rather than rendered obsolete.

Look out into the night sky. We know that only a minute fraction of the stars, planets, and other objects is visible to our eyes. There are galaxies and nebulae and black holes beyond our ability to depict them. If today's calculations are correct, the whole thing has been expanding from a single point for billions of years. What might be "beyond" or "before" that point seems genuinely difficult to say.[56] But, in any case, on a clear night, perhaps the first thing to be said is

56. See, for example, Willem Drees, *Beyond the Big Bang: Quantum Cosmologies and God* (La Salle, IL: Open Court, 1990), 41–75.

that the panoramic view remains truly magnificent. Now focus on the light of a single star. It has traveled an enormous distance, quite possibly having left its point of origin thousands of light-years ago. And, of course, the light from this particular star has traveled not only toward us but also in other directions. It appears, has appeared, and shall appear in the night sky of other planets and worlds as well.

When, as contemporary persons of piety we look out at these things, we, too, may be moved to ask questions. What are human beings that they have a place and a time in this vast and intricate cosmos, that they have emerged from an almost unfathomable set of interrelationships, interdependencies, and interactions, and that they have continued to be sustained for generations? And yet they are endowed with distinctive, even wondrous, capacities and powers of intervention. They are able to manage and to reshape plants, animals, and even their planetary habitat. They can probe spiders' webs. They can appreciate the stars. "O Lord, our Sovereign, how majestic is your name in all the earth!"

Proposition #33 The image of cosmic passage is compatible with a robust understanding of divine governance, but it encourages us to remain agnostic about what some theologians have meant by particular and special providence.

The image of cosmic passage helps us to portray the divine governance in relation to us and to our world as the dynamic movement and development of a vast cosmic ecology. The movement encompasses a multitude of realities, interdependencies, forces, and relationships, and it also includes many local sequences or lines of development, such as the geological-evolutionary line of development on Earth.

Patterns

Within this encompassing cosmic passage, then, we discern significant interdependencies and patterns. Some of these constitute physical and biological conditions for life generally and for human life in particular, as well as requisites for human societies and their well-being. Many of the interdependencies and physical and biological conditions for life that we are aware of have been discovered only recently, for example, astrophysical relationships and events critical to the formation of the star we call the sun and the planets that orbit it or the various ecological systems on Earth. So we may reasonably expect our knowledge in this regard to be emended and increased quite significantly in the future. Many of the requisites for human societies and their well-being have long been recognized by different human communities, for instance, the need for institutions whose purpose it is to adjudicate disputes fairly, though we now recognize greater historical and cultural variability and development in them than traditional societies and classical thinkers did. Therefore, we have reason to expect clarifications and emendations of our knowledge in this area as well.

Theologically speaking, piety associates these interdependencies and patterns, these conditions for life and requisites for human well-being, with the divine governance mediated to us in cosmic passage. Persons of piety infer from them certain rather general purposes or directives to which we do well to conform: proscriptions against murder and a strong bias against killing, care for dependent children, honoring debts to parents, and the maintenance of fair and just institutions and laws. Guided by these inferences, they discern that, in certain instances, God is acting to bring about certain ends. In our current circumstance, for example, we may sense that the environmentally degrading consequences of many human activities express the judgment of God on our destructive and ungrateful failure to act as responsible stewards of this very good world. The complexities of such discernment should not go unnoticed. Though it is based on justifiable revulsions at polluted rivers and countrysides, it also combines observations about requisites and conditions for life with an interpretation of our current circumstance, as well as a theology of creation (perhaps as cosmic ecology).

Consider, for example, Martin Luther King Jr.'s insistence that, in the United States of America during the 1950s and 1960s, God was acting to release African Americans from the bonds of discrimination. King's thorough, eloquent, and powerful interpretation of circumstances may be regarded as a case for discerning what God was enabling and requiring. It had a basis in persistent moral sensibilities that were pained, offended, and outraged by unjust practices, laws, and sufferings. But it also included an analysis of the nation's history, its founding impulses, subsequent course, and recent practices, as well as a theological reading of God's demand for justice in Amos and the prophets and in Jesus's reconciling message of the kingdom and the beloved community.[57]

The notable complexities indicate that such cases, urgent as they often are, also need to be appropriately measured and careful in the inferences they make, especially when it comes to specific instances and occurrences. By itself, for example, the discernment that certain forms of marriage and family are among the requisites for human societies does not mean that there cannot be significant variability among marriages and families even within the same society, let alone

57. *A Testament of Hope: The Essential Writings of Martin Luther King, Jr.*, ed. James Melvin Washington (New York: Harper & Row, 1986), 12–20, 43–53, 217–20, 289–302, 507.

across societies and cultures. And certainly, by itself, it does not mean that we know it to be a part of the divine plan for person X to marry person Y, or even for person X to marry at all. That stable genetic codes are among the conditions for human life and flourishing does not mean that they cannot vary or be disrupted. It certainly does not indicate that we know it to be a feature of the divine plan that person Q should suffer a severe and debilitating genetic malformation, and it is not an argument against gene therapy. These observations and others like them encourage persons of piety to be appropriately circumspect in their claims for discerning the activity and purposes of God in situations and events. In classical theological terms, these observations and others like them lead us to affirm God's providence but also to remain agnostic about what some theologians have called particular and special providence.

A Calvinist Vocabulary

Just what this means will become clearer if we explore the somewhat technical vocabulary that Calvinist theologians developed in order to talk about providence. The basic tenet, as the seventeenth-century Scholastic Johannes Wollebius put it, seemed straightforward enough: God's providence governs "all things from the greatest to the least."[58] The complexities—partly due to the emergence of modern science—were in the details. And it was in order to grapple with these details that various writers tarried over the claim that the ordinary workings of the universal and encompassing divine governance are general, particular, and special. Often they also distinguished these ordinary workings from miracles.

For example, Charles Hodge argued that the same divine agency controls all things in a way that respects secondary causes and that may also be understood with respect to regular laws. The operations of nature, as well as of all events, he said, "are due to the efficiency of physical forces; but those forces, which are combined, adjusted, and made to cooperate or to counteract each other, in the greatest complexity, are all under the constant guidance of God, and are made to accomplish his purpose." The distinction Hodge drew between general and special providence, therefore, does not refer to any difference of God's agency in the production of effects but only to the kinds of effects produced. We speak of general providence with reference to general effects, "such as the orderly motion of heavenly bodies, or the support and regular operations of the laws of nature." We speak of special providence, said Hodge, with reference to definite and "special effects." Indeed, the reality of special providence is why people who

58. Beardslee, *Reformed Dogmatics*, 59.

are sick or in danger pray to God for help, although it "does not suppose that God sets aside or counteracts the laws of nature; but simply that He controls them and causes them to produce whatever effects He sees fit." Citing the Westminster Confession of Faith, Hodge noted that all this is "ordinary providence." In addition, he maintained, there are also *miracles*—for example, the raising of Lazarus from the dead—that neither in whole nor in part are brought about by natural causes but instead are "due to the simple word, or volition, or immediate agency of God."[59]

Similarly, Augustus Hopkins Strong claimed that providence is both general, having to do with movements of planets and destinies of nations, and particular, having to do with specific events and "what seem to us the minor affairs of nature and of human life." (Would we, with our expanded modern view of the cosmos, draw the distinction in quite this way?) Special providence, Strong said, refers to instances of particular providence that make a "peculiar impression upon us." Even so, God's general, particular, and special providence is all of one piece because it "works in the realm of nature and through natural laws." This, he maintained, distinguishes it from "miracles and works of grace," which are "supernatural acts, not to be explained from antecedent natural causes."[60]

Now, according to Louis Berkhof, the *denial* of special providence is not simply a refusal to recognize that some particular events make peculiar *impressions* upon us. It is rather a denial of particular providence altogether, or the position that God administers the world under a fixed system of general laws but does not control "the details of history, the affairs of human life, and particularly the experiences of the righteous." That is, for those who deny special providence, God is either unconcerned with "the smaller things of life" or unable to control them "since the laws of nature bind His hands."[61] Strong also noted: "Many who acknowledge God's control over the movements of planets and the destinies of nations deny any divine arrangement of particular events." This, he thought, is not the classic Deist view that "the universe is a self-sustaining mechanism" that God has "left to a process of self-development." Yet it is "a form of deism, which holds that God has not wholly withdrawn himself from the universe, but that his activity within it is limited to the maintenance of general laws."[62] My own position—namely, that divine ordering and purposes are expressed in certain

59. Hodge, *Systematic Theology*, 1:608, 609, 618. The relevant passage from "Of Providence," chap. 5 of the Westminster Confession, is this: "God, in his ordinary providence, maketh use of means, yet is free to work without, above, and against them, at his pleasure" (*BOC* 6.026).

60. Augustus Hopkins Strong, *Systematic Theology: A Compendium and Commonplace Book*, 6th ed. (New York: A. C. Armstrong and Son, 1899), 213, 215.

61. Berkhof, *Systematic Theology*, 168–69.

62. Strong, *Systematic Theology*, 204, 213.

interdependencies and patterns of cosmic ecology and cosmic passage, but that we need to be circumspect in building our cases for discerning God's purposes in particular instances and events—does not really correspond to the positions criticized by Strong and Berkhof, partly because the patterns and orderings I have in mind are not a fixed system of general laws.

What's at Stake Practically

Much of what is at stake here, practically and pastorally, will become apparent if we return to Calvin's *Institutes*. The Genevan Reformer did not use the terms "general," "particular," and "special" with reference to providence, but he maintained that God governs all events in the sense that God "directs everything by his own incomprehensible wisdom and disposes it to his own end."[63] Calvin also criticized the view that God sets things in motion, but that "all things, either of themselves or by chance, are borne whither inclination of nature impels" (1.16.5). This, he said, leaves no place for God's favor and God's judgments, and it runs counter to Scripture's claim that "not one drop of rain falls without God's sure command" (1.16.5). By contrast, he claimed, God determines all natural occurrences as well as seemingly fortuitous events, such as a branch breaking and hitting a passing traveler. "No wind ever arises or increases except by God's express command," and by God's special favor, some are barren whereas others conceive (1.16.7).

Calvin upheld this position, not against modern Deism (which had not yet emerged) but against a Stoic conception of fate. "What then? you will ask. Does nothing happen by chance, by contingency? I reply: Basil the Great has truly said that 'fortune' and 'chance' are pagan terms, with whose significance the minds of the godly ought not to be occupied" (1.16.8). Indeed, Calvin went so far as to issue God what amounts to a metaphysical blank check. God's providence, he said, "is the determinative principle of all things in such a way that sometimes it works through an intermediary, sometimes without an intermediary, sometimes contrary to every intermediary" (1.17.1).[64]

This is the portrait of divine hyperagency that many have come to expect from

63. Calvin, *ICR* 1.16.5. Hereafter, references to the *Institutes* will appear in parentheses in the text.

64. As far as I can tell, Calvin's principal example of God working apart from intermediaries derives from the fact that, in Gen. 1, there is light and there are plants *before* God creates the sun and the moon. "Moreover, it did not happen fortuitously that herbs and trees were created before the sun and moon. We now see, indeed, that the earth is quickened by the sun to cause it to bring forth fruits; nor was God ignorant of this law of nature, which he has since ordained:

Reformed theologians. Unlike any other agent, God's actions are never thwarted or even deflected from their intended purposes by other realities, the actions of other agents, etc. Unlike any other agent, God may circumvent all other agents and causes. Unlike other agents, the omnipotent and omniscient God determines all outcomes, so that, at some level, every outcome must accord with God's purposes and intentions. Thus, for Calvin, unlike those Stoics who extolled fortune, the world was suffused with purpose (1.16.2; 1.16.8).

A frequent objection to this portrait is that it appears to undermine the efficacy and integrity of mundane causes and agents. Calvin, however, was convinced that his claim for divine determinism does not lead to quietism, that human responsibility remains, and that it remains important for us to exercise prudence in our daily lives (1.17.4). Essentially, he let these affirmations stand side by side: God determines all, mundane causes operate, and human agents are responsible.[65]

Very many subsequent Reformed theologians said something similar. For example, the writers of the Westminster Confession of Faith maintain that, while God's decree causes "all things to come to pass immutably and infallibly," God orders all things "to fall out according to the nature of secondary causes, either necessarily, freely, or contingently." It affirms further that God ordinarily makes use of means, "yet is free to work without, above, and against them, at his pleasure." It also claims that God has endowed the human will with natural liberty and that people are not forced to do good or evil.[66]

Schleiermacher should be distinguished from this grouping because he did not issue God the same metaphysical blank check that Calvin and Westminster did, and he saw no reason to interpret a fact or event in such a way that its dependence on God "excludes its being conditioned by the system or Nature."[67] However, he did claim that, in the creed, "God is regarded as the sole Determinant" (146). For Schleiermacher, the religious self-consciousness that places "all that affects or influences us in absolute dependence on God, coincides entirely with the view that all such things are conditioned and determined by the interdependence of Nature" (170). The divine causality equates with natural causality in scope, but it is distinguished from natural causality in kind, as the former is timeless (or eternal) and omnipresent while the latter is temporal and spatial (201). Schleiermacher, accordingly, developed a view of the divine omnipotence

but in order that we might learn to refer all things to him, he did not make use of the sun or moon" (Calvin, *Commentaries on the First Book of Moses Called Genesis,* 82).

65. See also chap. 6, prop. #44.

66. The Westminster Confession of Faith, in *BOC* 6.025–6.026; 6.059.

67. Schleiermacher, *CF*, #47 (p. 178). Hereafter, page references to this work will appear in parentheses in the text.

that allows for natural causality of all kinds to operate according to its own laws; there is no reason to choose between the two as if they were competitors. "Rather, everything is and becomes altogether by means of the natural order, so that each takes place through all and all wholly through the divine omnipotence, so that all indivisibly exists through the One" (212). So, for Schleiermacher, too—though he sees no need to ensure the divine omnipotence by claiming that God's agency operates apart from or contrary to intermediaries—the divine causality is all-determining, natural causes operate, and human agents remain responsible.

Charles Hodge, as I have noted above, worried that some Reformed portraits of divine sovereignty merged "all efficiency in God," in effect denying the efficacy of second causes, destroying human freedom, and making God "in reality the only Being in the universe."[68] His concern, whether or not we share it, remains instructive, since it shows that, with the Reformed tradition in Christian theology, we often find ourselves at least on the verge of a pantheistic monotheism that, for many, has quite troubling implications.[69] The question I should like to press here, however, is more expository than metaphysical. Why was Calvin willing to embrace a portrait of providence that runs the risk, at least in the judgment of many, of denying the efficacy of second causes and damaging the integrity of human agency? In particular, what was *the point in piety* that he was trying to articulate and protect?

Calvin answered these questions in some remarkable passages of the *Institutes* on "God's providence as solace of believers." The Christian heart, he said, has this assurance: "God's singular providence keeps watch to preserve it, and will not suffer anything to happen but what may turn out to its good and salvation." This is why Calvin rejected "the opinion of those who imagine a universal providence of God, which does not stoop to the especial care of any particular creature." Indeed, it is a matter of utmost importance "that we recognize this special care toward us."[70] The existential upshot, then, is that Calvin's understanding of providence equips the faithful to be grateful for favorable outcomes, patient in adversity, and free from worry about the future (1.17.7). Consider his memorable argument that, without certainty about God's providence, life would be unbearable:

> Innumerable are the evils that beset human life; innumerable, too, the deaths that threaten it. We need not go beyond ourselves: since our body is the receptacle of a thousand diseases—in fact holds within itself and fosters the causes

68. Hodge, *Systematic Theology*, 1:615–16.

69. See chap. 1, prop. #13.

70. Calvin, *ICR* 1.17.6. Hereafter, references to this work appear in parentheses in the text.

> of diseases—a man cannot go about unburdened by many forms of his own destruction, and without drawing out a life enveloped, as it were, with death. For what else would you call it, when he neither freezes nor sweats without danger? Now, wherever you turn, all things around you not only are hardly to be trusted, but almost openly menace, and seem to threaten immediate death. Embark upon a ship, you are one step away from death. Mount a horse, if one foot slips, your life is imperiled. Go through the city streets, you are subject to as many dangers as there are tiles on the roofs. If there is a weapon in your hand or a friend's, harm awaits. All the fierce animals you see are armed for your destruction. But if you try to shut yourself up in a walled garden, seemingly delightful, there a serpent sometimes lies hidden. Your house, continually in danger of fire, threatens in the daytime to impoverish you, at night even to collapse upon you. Your field, since it is exposed to hail, frost, drought, and other calamities, threatens you with barrenness, and hence, famine. I pass over poisonings, ambushes, robberies, open violence, which in part besiege us at home, in part dog us abroad. Amid these tribulations must not man be most miserable, since, but half alive in life, he weakly draws his anxious and languid breath, as if he had a sword perpetually hanging over his neck?
>
> You will say: these events rarely happen, or at least not all the time, nor to all men, and never all at once. I agree; but since we are warned by the examples of others that these can also happen to ourselves, and that our life ought not be excepted any more than theirs, we cannot but be frightened and terrified as if such events were about to happen to us. (1.17.10)

For Calvin, then, knowledge of divine providence relieves the godly person from extreme anxiety and fear. It delivers her from the dread of fortune and chance into the solace of God's safekeeping, because she knows that no harm can befall her except as God, her faithful benefactor, gives it occasion. In short, it underlies the assurance of the saints (in Ps. 118:6) that "the Lord is my helper" (1.17.11). This is why "ignorance of providence is the ultimate of all miseries," and why "the highest blessedness lies in the knowledge of it" (1.17.11).

You and I may be tempted to regard these sentiments as especially alarming survivors of a bygone piety, but I expect that, if we substitute the words "jumbo jet" for "ship" and "automobile" for "horse," the basic message will seem quite contemporary. Really, almost anyone of a certain age who reflects on the unexpected death of a friend and then also contemplates the diseases and conditions that his own physician may soon detect in him will understand Calvin's point. Indeed, I can recall a comparatively recent and vivid statement of piety very much like the one Calvin described. It came in an interview with the former president of Egypt, Anwar Sadat, which was recorded after the president had made peace with Israel and was under constant threat; it was aired just after he had been assassinated while reviewing Egyptian troops. The correspondent asked Mr. Sadat whether, in light of his many dangerous enemies, he was sometimes fearful and afraid. The president said no, and he added that, as a person of faith, he believed his life was in Allah's hands, that when and how he died was entirely a matter of his sovereign maker's choosing. His job was simply to do what he believed was right.

Other than assurance and release from extreme anxiety, however, Calvin's radical insistence on special providence had somewhat limited practical and pastoral implications. When, for example, he spoke of the fatherly care demonstrated by God's sustaining providence, Calvin frequently referred to regular processes within the order of nature, such as the role of the brightness and warmth of the sun in nourishing plants, and the power to procreate—which many would associate with workings of general providence. Moreover, Calvin reminded his readers that just why certain events and occurrences take place often eludes us. "Let us imagine," he wrote, "a merchant who, entering a wood with a company of faithful men, unwisely wanders away from his companions, and in his wandering comes upon a robber's den, falls among thieves, and is slain." Calvin had no doubt that the merchant's "death was not only foreseen by God's eye, but also determined by his decree." But "as far as the capacity of our mind is concerned," the entire episode seems fortuitous because, though we deny that fortune rules the world, "the order, reason, end, and necessity of those things which happen for the most part lie hidden in God's purpose, and are not apprehended by human opinion" (1.16.9).

A Proposal

We are ready now to say what it means for piety to associate divine governance with dynamic interdependencies and patterns of cosmic passage and yet remain agnostic about particular and special providence. It does not mean *denying* that God's governance has to do with specific events or their arrangement. Indeed, it seems clear that patterns, processes, and conditions having to do with the formation of galaxies, the sun's temperature, Earth's distance from the sun, genetic codes, human social well-being, and the like do indeed influence specific conditions and events, such as a given storm, an individual's mental acumen, a particular family, a court case, or a social reform movement. And, as I have noted above, persons of piety may draw inferences about divine purposes from interdependencies and patterns in cosmic passage; they may also, in circumspect fashion, make cases for particular discernments about what God enables and requires in certain circumstances—for example, Martin Luther King Jr.'s arguments about discrimination and the civil rights movement in the United States. To remain agnostic about particular and special providence means, instead, that we also recognize that there is much we do not know. It means that, in our own judgment, we do not have sufficient information or warrants at our disposal to make definite claims about specific divine purposes, intentions, whys, and wherefores in very many particular events.

Agnosticism about particular and special providence also means, I believe, that we do not have sufficient knowledge to make especially compelling arguments for complete determinism. The philosopher Mary Midgley notes that Bertrand Russell defined determinism as follows: "Given *the state of the whole universe throughout any finite time*, however short, every previous and subsequent event can theoretically be determined as a function of the given events during that time." Midgley continues: "Unless you think it conceivable that anybody should be given that, determinism remains something highly theoretical and remote."[71] I agree.

The position I am advocating here—an affirmation of divine governance and continuance coupled with agnosticism about particular and special providence—is compatible with James M. Gustafson's departure from the assumption "that the divine intention directs all particular events, and that consequences can thus be attributed not only to the moral responsibility of agents but also to the specific intentions of the Deity to punish and to reward particular persons and communities."[72] Interestingly, it is also something like Calvin's position when we emphasize his insistence that the whys and wherefores of specific events "for the most part lie hidden in God's purpose, and are not apprehended by human opinion."

A pious agnosticism about particular and special sustenance obviously cannot reduplicate Calvin's assurance that everything that befalls us is determined by the singular will of the God who intends our salvation. But to be fair, systematically considered, Calvin's own position hardly banishes all anxiety either. After all, Calvin's God may very well visit upon people some extremely bad things, as the illustration of the merchant's murder clearly shows. Therefore, it seems reasonable, given Calvin's view, for pious people not only to be prudent but also somewhat anxious and concerned about the things that may befall them on a journey, not to mention the potential consequences for their dependents and loved ones. We may also recall that, for Calvin, God does not simply and effectively intend

71. Midgley, *Beast and Man*, 64. Midgley quotes Bertrand Russell, "On the Notion of Cause," in Russell, *Our Knowledge of the External World* (London, 1914), 221 (Midgley's italics).

72. Gustafson, *ETP*, 1:246.

salvation for all. This is an unavoidable consequence of Calvin's affirmation of double predestination and, especially when coupled with the insistence that God sometimes determines that bad things happen to people, it also seems able to provoke no small degree of pious tension (if not also despair).

Now for an extended illustration. On September 24, 1757, the Reverend Aaron Burr, president of the College of New Jersey (and father of the American politician by that same name), died following a fever that appears to have begun intermittently during his trip to Philadelphia in late August. He was survived by his wife, Esther Edwards Burr, and their two children. Shortly thereafter, the trustees of the college chose Rev. Burr's father-in-law, Jonathan Edwards (the sole founder of the college who remained), as his successor. Among other things, Edwards was concerned that, as president, he might have little time to write; but after reflecting, praying, and consulting for some time, Edwards accepted the position. He moved from Stockbridge, Massachusetts, to Princeton in January 1758. There, in the midst of a smallpox outbreak, he was inoculated on February 23. The inoculation was to precipitate a mild case of the disease that the patient would survive, having built up immunity or at least a resistance. Sereno E. Dwight tells us that at first "Edwards had it well," but that he subsequently died (at age fifty-five) on March 22, 1758, after pustules in his throat prevented medicines from being administered for the treatment of fever. Edwards's wife, Sarah Pierpont Edwards, had not yet moved to Princeton, and she was informed of her husband's death in a letter from his physician, William Shippen. She then sent a brief letter to her recently widowed daughter, Esther. Mrs. Edwards wrote: "What shall I say? A holy and good God has covered us with a dark cloud. . . . The Lord has done it. He has made me adore his goodness that we had him so long."[73] Esther never read her mother's letter. She and her children had also been inoculated when her father was, and she seemed perfectly recovered. But then she "was suddenly seized with a violent disorder" that may not have been related to her inoculation at all, and she died on April 7, 1758, at the age of twenty-seven. Sarah Edwards moved to Philadelphia in September in order to care for her orphaned grandchildren; but shortly after that she "was seized by a violent dysentery" and died on October 2, 1758.

I recall here the sobering calamities that struck the Edwards and Burr families in a year's time (1757–1758) in order to try my hand at answering Sarah Pierpont Edwards's question. Though she put it and answered it as a bereaved participant, I approach it as a mere observer more than 250 years later. What shall I say?

Certainly, according to my understanding of God's governance manifest in

73. Sereno E. Dwight, "Memoirs of Jonathan Edwards, A. M.," in *The Works of Jonathan Edwards* (Edinburgh: Banner of Truth Trust, 1834), 1:clxxix.

cosmic passage, there are good reasons to be thankful for the gifts of life and of life together that are sustained in God's world. (We should note that Jonathan and Sarah Edwards appear to have enjoyed an unusually close and happy partnership.) There are good reasons to mourn so many premature deaths, as well as their painful and tragic consequences; there are also reasons to note that no one's life is entirely secure and that, inexorably, death comes to us all. What I cannot say of Jonathan Edwards's death and the circumstances surrounding it, at least not with the same specificity, assurance, and literal sense that Mrs. Edwards did, is that "the Lord has done it." Nor can I say that about the deaths of Rev. Burr, Esther Edwards Burr, and Mrs. Edwards herself.

What, then, of Mrs. Edwards's rather eloquent statement, that a "holy and good God has covered us with a dark cloud"? This seems intentionally and wisely metaphorical. My theology does not encourage us to see a single and clear divine why or wherefore through the tangle of decisions, actions, and medical interventions. But there is nothing in her letter to indicate that Mrs. Edwards did either. On the other hand, I cannot say what I think Mrs. Edwards firmly believed, namely, that God intentionally willed both her and her daughter to be widowed, as well as her daughter's children to be orphaned and then left without the care of their grandmother. I can agree, of course, that her husband's death covered his family like a dark cloud. And I can also say that his death took place in the cosmic ecology and passage, or the ordering of the good and great God who creates and redeems. I can say the same thing about Esther's subsequent death, though I do not know what Mrs. Edwards had to say on that occasion, and I do not know how she might have regarded her own death as she tried to care for her daughter's children. (Were these also dark clouds that one expects to dissipate eventually, as storms generally do?) Finally, Mrs. Edwards and I agree that the divine governance—sustaining though it often is—can also be quite severe, and that it did not guarantee all relevant aspects of the happiness and well-being of either herself or her family. We also agree that, since the Creator is the Redeemer, the dark cloud of her husband's death (as well as the perhaps even thicker darkness of her daughter's death) was neither the only nor the last word.

I do not know what one or another pastor may have said and done following the deaths of Jonathan and Esther; cultural expectations and pastoral practice have no doubt changed rather dramatically since that time. In any case, some pastoral implications of my own theology largely accord with the actions of a friend of mine who is a pastor in Texas and who visited us in North Carolina with his daughter. She was a high school senior, and they were on an exploratory tour of colleges. We had a pleasant dinner, some wine, and good conversation. The next morning my friend told me that he had received a phone call later in the evening. A parishioner in her early fifties had died suddenly of a brain aneurysm. He had, in fact, spoken with her just the day before about her father, a man in his seventies and also a church member, who was still mourning the death of his beloved wife, which had occurred only a few months earlier. My friend's plans changed. When my friend told his daughter, she said, "Oh, Daddy, sometimes your job is so hard," and gave him a hug. After breakfast, he took her to the campus they were scheduled to visit, having arranged for her to travel from there to the home of friends in Maryland, where they both had intended to relax for a few days with family and friends. Then he filled up the tank of his Ford van and began the very long drive back to Texas.

My friend returned, of course, to be a pastor to the family and friends of the woman who had died, and he was especially concerned about her aging father. Would the latter, he wondered, ever be able to come to terms with the deaths of his wife and his daughter in such rapid succession? My friend returned to be intentionally present with persons in grief. He returned to hold hands and hug people in tears, to make arrangements for and to perform the funeral and the burial, and to make sure that other members of the congregation were organized to help as well. He drove back to Texas to give thanks for the woman's life and to mourn her death, to affirm the resurrection and to say that God is Redeemer. He returned to help a particular Presbyterian church demonstrate that it continues to be a community of care, and that, however fragmentarily, it embodies God's grace. But he did *not* return to tell people that we know just why the woman's untimely death had taken place or that it was God's intention to leave her father without both his wife and his daughter in so short a time. In all these ways, his pastoral practice accorded with what I have said here about divine governance and cosmic passage.

Proposition #34 The images of creation as cosmic ecology and of divine governance and sustenance manifest in an all-encompassing cosmic passage have implications for a view of redemption.

I will treat eschatology (or the question of the end) in detail in part 3 of the present system, where, among other things, I shall also interpret the great symbols of the kingdom, life eternal, and new creation with respect to a world picture in which the end of humanity need not be the end of Earth's ecology, the end of Earth and our solar system need not be the end of the Milky Way, and the end of the universe need not be the end of all. Let me simply note here that, for piety, ideas of governance and providence give us pictures or visions of the sweep of things, as well as inklings about redemption and the end toward which things tend or incline.

When Calvin assures his readers that "God's singular providence watches over the welfare of believers" and will allow only those things to happen that "may turn out to [their] good and salvation," a certain reading of the end comes into view.[74] When Martin Luther King Jr. said that the long arc of the universe bends toward justice, he linked the struggle for civil rights in America with a view of the great sweep of history.[75] Similar points can be made even about theologies in which present principalities and powers are radically fallen, mired in destructive tendencies, and marginally aligned with divine governance only insofar as they serve to restrain even greater evils. In this case, emphasis falls on disjunctions between current history and the divine purpose disclosed in the countercultural career of Jesus. This emphasis, in turn, often is coupled with the claim that, in the end, God will work a great reversal and bring in a kingdom or state of affairs that is radically different from present realities.

Ideas of governance or sustenance connect present circumstances and events with the tendency or flow of things because they collect the many processes, realities, and events into a single divine movement. They help persons of piety to situate and construe particular processes and events within an encompassing pattern, trajectory, and direction. The symbolic idea of divine governance implies that particulars have their place within a longer story. It requires, as Ernst Troeltsch points out, a teleological view, or, in more traditional terms, the view that divine providence moves toward salvation.

Reenvisioning Destiny

Troeltsch also recognized an important relationship between our religious sense of destiny and the modern concept of nature, and here he sounds a revisionary note:

> The modern view of nature consists essentially in this insight: that our fate is dependent on the entire context of the far-flung causal nexus of reality . . . now we are aware of the general interconnectedness of things. . . . If, millions of years ago, the earth had veered in a slightly different direction, we would not be sitting here today. God has put me in this place where I stand today, but not directly; it is only as the result of and as part of the all-encompassing context of reality. Whether this all-encompassing context is open or closed, we cannot think about our destiny except in terms of the interconnectedness of the whole. Nothing stands in isolation.[76]

74. Calvin, *ICR* 1.17.6.

75. King, *A Testament of Hope*, 230.

76. Ernst Troeltsch, *The Christian Faith*, translated with an introduction by Garrett E. Paul (Minneapolis: Fortress, 1991), 209.

If this is so (and I believe it is), then the destiny of humans cannot be abstracted from the vast nexus of interrelationships and interconnections. It cannot be abstracted from cosmic passage. Theologically speaking, redemption cannot be conceived as a transaction between God and humans for which the rest of nature or the cosmos has little or no relevance. Or, to put this point another way, once they are joined with what Troeltsch calls "the modern view of nature," creation and governance point to a universal and cosmic horizon (all of nature or the cosmos) for reflections about redemption.

The French paleontologist and Roman Catholic priest Teilhard de Chardin understood this. In his terms, "the enrichment and ferment of religious thought in our time has undoubtedly been caused by the revelation of the size and the unity of the world around us and within us."[77] The modern picture of a vast cosmos and of the interconnected evolutionary sequence of which we are a part raises the distinctive—and once again the religiously and spiritually charged—question of our place and significance: Where do we humans fit into the great sweep of things? Or, in Teilhard's words, "How does the human world itself appear within the structure of the universe?" His answer is: "As a zone of continuous spiritual transformation," in which the self-conscious and social human microcosm assimilates the realities and forms of the world, and there occurs a decisive cosmic in-folding, or convergence.[78] Of course, this view, in turn, fits with an inkling of the end and redemption.

Teilhard observed that, when we focus on "the Immense," the stars and galaxies are "the natural sidereal unit" (102–4). Planets are secondary; they are *not* where the important action is. Indeed, in this perspective, here on Earth "we strut for a tiny moment on a tiny stage" (108). But if we focus on "centered complexity," then a very different picture emerges (109–11). Now, Teilhard insists, we discern an "ascending movement towards higher consciousness" that takes in or appreciates other things, and so we confront "a complete reversal of values and perspective" (112). Now we glimpse a final purpose for which the planet Earth is crucial, for here on Earth the ascending movement of consciousness reaches its critical development. "Tiny and isolated though it is, [Earth] bears clinging to its flanks the destiny and future of the Universe," and the significance of the human species becomes clear (114). "Life is the spearhead of evolution" on Earth, and, within this evolutionary sequence, the reflective consciousness or intelligence that emerges with humans (and which, for Teilhard, is separated

77. Pierre Teilhard de Chardin, *The Divine Milieu* (New York: Harper & Row, 1960), 45.

78. Teilhard de Chardin, *The Divine Milieu*, 124–25; Teilhard de Chardin, *The Future of Man*, trans. Norman Denny (New York: Harper & Row, 1969), 233–34. Hereafter, page references to *The Future of Man* appear in parentheses in the text.

by a barrier from the unreflective) can be recognized as "a unique and privileged value" (226–28). Indeed, Teilhard believes that reflective and intelligent human consciousness culminates in a social or collective reflection, a single center that embraces all the individual units on Earth. A cosmic coiling, folding-in, or convergence takes place in the microcosm of collective human consciousness (230–31).[79]

The great threat to this culminating convergence, then, is not the death of the individual but death on a planetary scale, and thus the loss of humanity's collective reflective consciousness. The end of Earth's habitability thus threatens to paralyze the forces of vitality. In the face of this threat, Teilhard proposes a *telos*, or end, that embraces reflective consciousness, of which humankind becomes increasingly aware through a mystical sensibility. "Is it not conceivable that Mankind, at the end of its totalisation, its folding in upon itself, may reach a critical level of maturity where, leaving Earth and stars to lapse slowly back into the dwindling mass of primordial energy, it will detach itself from this planet and join the one true irreversible essence of things, the Omega Point?" (127).

There are notable similarities and differences between Teilhard's view and the vision of cosmic passage that I am developing here. Both pictures introduce a universal or cosmic horizon for redemption. Somewhat like Teilhard, I note the turn to life (as well as the implied fertility of the inorganic). I affirm the development of reflective consciousness as an important point in the passage of things, and I agree that reflective humans are distinctively equipped to appreciate the cosmos (a nod to the human mind as microcosm).

Teilhard's evolutionary vision is important because it connects humanity with the considerably wider, longer, and dynamic development of nature and cosmos, and, from my perspective, this is all to the good. Nevertheless, his vision is too closely tied to the sequence of life on Earth, and it focuses on an overly unilateral and monodimensional trajectory toward intelligent human life. This seems problematic because of the similarities between humans and other animals, possible mass extinctions, the extensive history of the cosmos both before and (potentially) after humans, and the almost countless local venues and trajectories strewn throughout the galaxies. Again, I suspect—as I think Darwin and others would as well—that the barrier Teilhard sees between unreflective and reflective consciousness is overstated and too severe. I am also uncertain whether or not there may be life-forms on other planets, at least some of which are also equipped distinctively to appreciate and take in the cosmos.

These differences make for differences in the kind of cosmic horizon that

79. For Teilhard, at the center of this process of "hominisation" is the church as a mystical superorganism (231–32).

my notions of creation and governance contribute to piety's inklings of end and redemption. I believe that we are caught up in a vast cosmic passage that contains many distinguishable sublines and subtrajectories. The cosmic passage, then, is a larger movement with a place and a time for us and for other creatures on Earth. We participate in this larger movement, and our emergence is an important expression of the divine creativity manifest in cosmic passage. But there are no guarantees either that we are at the center of it all or that there will always be a place for one or another species, including our own.

We cannot be certain, in my view, about the end toward which we are moving within the particular subline of development on Earth, let alone the end of the entire cosmic process. We cannot be certain that human reflective consciousness is at the heart of it all, or even whether the emergence of multiple versions of reflective consciousness, including the human, is at the heart of it all. Accordingly, in my view, statements about the sweep of things as well as about the end toward which things incline ought to allow for large doses of mystery and even agnosticism; ruminations about precisely where we fit should, in the end, be tempered by the recognition that we are participants in an enormously longer story of an enormously vast ensemble. But one thing is certain. The cosmic horizon for redemption contributed by the images of cosmic ecology and cosmic passage encourages us to ask how an idea or notion such as new creation may extend well beyond the human. Indeed, it encourages us to recognize that God's own glory, the image so often proposed as a representation of the *telos* of things by Reformed theologians, is not merely coterminous with human fulfillment; it also intimates genuine incomprehensibility. In these ways, the theology I am developing here accords with a sharply *theocentric* piety.

Chapter Five

Created and Sustained Human Life

Within the frame of theocentric piety, humans are not a fundamentally different category from the world. They are not beings either accidentally or maliciously cast into an alien reality. Humans are distinctive creatures. As *creatures*, then, they belong to a wider category that includes all other created things; therefore, they are like or similar to other things. The human species is a part of the wider cosmic ensemble and passage, and human life is distinctive and peculiar. As *distinctive* creatures, humans possess a knot of capacities, needs, affections, tendencies, relationships, and responsibilities that are not entirely duplicated elsewhere. In short, humans are distinctive parts of God's good creation.

In this chapter I will consider the mystery, blessing, sociality, capability, personality, and purpose of human life. These rubrics do not exhaust the reality of human life in a theological frame of reference; rather, they indicate salient features that come into view when we regard human life in the context of the world as cosmic ecology and cosmic passage—and in relationship with God as Creator. Additional characteristics come to the fore when we consider human life in relationship with God as Judge and Redeemer.

Proposition #35 Created and sustained human life is mysterious.

One challenge for contemporary religious sensibility is how to apprehend the mystery of life at a place and time where we can explain very much about it, from bone structure to brain lobes, neurons, psychological needs, and genetic endowments. Indeed, making allowances for what one means by "produce," the possibility that we will produce human life in a laboratory cannot be dismissed. But the mysterious quality I have in mind here does not refer to a lack of knowledge that will be filled in later by further investigation and reflection. Gordon Kaufman says that we live in the face of mystery, and he means, in part, that we live with a sense of our own finitude, limitedness, and relativity. We are "aware that at virtually every point of our being and action we are dependent on and relative to what is beyond us, not under our control."[1] This is one reason why we encounter facts, experiences, and questions that provoke wonder.

The awareness Kaufman speaks of seems almost unavoidable when we consider ourselves and our identities. Part of our fascination with a good biography or a novel such as *Great Expectations* is that it probes the many twists and turns by which characters become who they are. An extended (though now neglected) masterpiece is C. P. Snow's set of eleven novels entitled *Strangers and Brothers*, which follows the life of a single character, Lewis Eliot, from childhood and adolescence in early-twentieth-century England, through young adulthood at Oxford, adulthood in the service of the British government and involvement in atomic energy projects during World War II and the Cold War, to a literary life in old age. Why has he been matched with these particular companions, circumstances, and challenges? How have they shaped him? Might he have been matched with others and thus been differently shaped and formed? When an accomplished narrator tells his or her own story, as in a Dickens novel or Snow's sequence, there is always something irreducible and elusive in the telling. There are also a coming to terms with and consenting (or not) to the person one has become.

That there is something irreducible and that we should need to come to terms with the persons we have become make sense when we consider the many contingencies. How have I become this particular person, constituted and formed by this particular genetic endowment, family, society, and history? Why is this specific identity mine? Questions such as these arise because, while we certainly influence the kinds of persons we become by our own actions and decisions, much also depends on matters beyond our control.

How and why am I who I am? That question betrays an inkling that the particular bundle of abilities, limits, inclinations, dispositions, memories, and so on that makes up me might not be configured just as it is. My identity might have been differently formed. I might not be as I am. Indeed, *I* might not be at all.[2] Once I begin to trace things out, once I come to acknowledge the many astrophysical, geological, biological, and social factors—the historical contexts and occurrences that go into making me who I am—then I see that who I am, my very self, points beyond itself toward myriad realities. How and why am I *me*? In all likelihood, my explanation for myself remains woefully incomplete. But even an incomplete explanation indicates that my life and my identity depend

1. Kaufman, *IFM*, 6.

2. Langdon Gilkey, *Maker of Heaven and Earth: A Study of the Christian Doctrine of Creation* (Lanham, MD: University Press of America, 1985), 20–21, 25, 31.

on a variety of factors, realities, and conditions. I am ineluctably embedded in the sense that my life is inexplicable apart from interconnections with persons, events, and realities beyond my own control or anyone else's. My life and my self, therefore, both depend on and refer to considerably more than me. Creation piety shapes and expresses the sense that I am embedded in and dependent on Something More.

Some years ago, my son Albert came home from middle school with an assignment. The idea, I think, was to get fourteen-year-olds to discover that their parents had lives even before they had children. In any case, my son had been directed to ask Pamela and me about something important that took place before he was born, and he settled on the question of how we first met. He asked it at the dinner table. Pam and I explained to him that we had met when I moved in next door to where she was living with two friends on Floyd Avenue in Richmond, Virginia. We explained further that our meeting had depended on a number of factors. Pam had moved to Richmond to attend Virginia Commonwealth University (VCU) and decided to stay in Richmond after graduating from there. I had moved to Richmond to teach at Union Theological Seminary. Had she not attended VCU, or had the seminary not offered me a job, or had I not accepted it, or, indeed, had the seminary not been moved from Hampden Sydney to Richmond in the 1890s, Pamela and I almost certainly would never have met. The same would be true if Pam and her friends had chosen a different apartment, or I had rented a different apartment.

Albert paused and then said, "Well, Dad, I guess I would have had a different father then." We tried to explain that he might have missed the full force of what we were saying. I said that, given what we know about genetics, early childhood, and their relationship to personal identity, "if your mother and I had never met, you would not have been." And, in fact, we can extend that sort of realization considerably further to include observations about how Pamela's parents met and how mine did, larger political, social, and economic histories and patterns in North America, the development of the human species, life on Earth, the formation of Earth, various forces and events that have gone into making the cosmos what it now is, and so forth.

I want to underscore here simply that people wonder, and wondering people sometimes discover that their lives are inexplicable apart from connections with other persons, events, conditions, and realities beyond their control or anyone else's. If Forest Ray Nester hadn't gotten shore leave in May 1952, spied an attractive girl named Barbara Ann Young on the bus outside Roanoke, and returned that evening with his brother Cletis to track her down by knocking on doors, there would have been no Pamela Elise Nester for me to marry (and, once again, no Albert). The wonder provoked by our awareness of this fact is a personal and existential equivalent of the wonder provoked by questions such as "How and why is there something rather than nothing?" or "How and why is there this particular world rather than another?" As human beings, we can ask ourselves, "What does it mean that I am in *this* particular world at this particular place and time?" or even, "What does it mean that *I* might not have come to be at all?"

We may experience similar wonderment at the compelling presence of other people and of particular realities, situations, and circumstances. We find ourselves drawn out by our encounters with this particular person here and now, this particular countryside, society, or institution. These realities do much to define our experiences. We are embedded with them. They are *copresent* with us, and what is present—whether positive or negative, threatening or promising—captures our attention. It has thickness and facticity. Of course, we also understand that many of the realities present to us need not be. We can remember a time when some were not. We can imagine circumstances in which some others would not be. A person, countryside, or society may be compellingly present to me now, but if some things had gone differently, it might not be. Suppose, for example, that my major professor in graduate school had been felled by disease as a child or killed during World War II. Then much of my formative training would have been different, and you might very well not be reading this particular book. Suppose the glaciers had formed and receded differently than they did in what is now northern New Jersey. There would have been no Palisades Cliffs near my hometown overlooking the Hudson River and Manhattan. Like the shock of my own contingency, these observations lead me to realize that the presence of particular others also depends on a welter of factors and conditions and is therefore also contingent.

Well, so what? You and I may strive to eliminate daydreams. With some success, we may restrict our attention to the projects over which we exercise larger measures of control and to the things we in fact do know and comprehend. Wonderments of the kind I have mentioned may be minimized or even suppressed. But the questions, mysteries, and wonderments can always return. And when they do, we recognize that human life (mine and yours) does not explain itself. Instead, it refers to and points beyond itself. It gives rise to wonder and mystery. It raises the question of whence.

The explicit theological point is that human life refers to and implies the wider cosmic ecology and cosmic passage within which are situated all the local ecologies, venues, and histories. I am reminded of Langdon Gilkey's claim that we are living symbols of the divine presence and activity.[3] Augustine, in

3. Langdon Gilkey, *Through the Tempest: Theological Voyages in a Pluralistic Culture*, ed. Jeff B. Pool (Minneapolis: Fortress, 1991), 57–60.

his *Confessions*, rather famously said, "Our hearts are restless until they rest in you." For piety, the inherent theological reference of the human heart suggested by the good bishop is a distinctive form of the inherent theological reference of the creature, and it is also part of the point of Anselm's famous ontological argument. Anselm, we may recall, was interested in "the awakening of the mind to the contemplation of God." In a sense, he aimed to make explicit the sense of relatedness or of pointing that Augustine articulates at the outset of *Confessions*.[4] For Anselm, "that than which nothing greater can be conceived" must also be thought of as existing, and this amounts to the claim that, if one can think of anything at all, then one must also be brought to the point of thinking about (or contemplating) the existing God. But this means that the thinking human mind inevitably implies, refers, and points. Just as, for Augustine, the feeling human heart inevitably implies, refers, and points. Just as, we might say, self-aware and contingent human life inevitably implies, refers, and points. Theologically speaking, this implying, referring, and pointing is part and parcel of what it is to be a human being who participates in the world that God creates and sustains. It is part and parcel of what it means to be self-aware and situated in the welter of interdependent conditions, processes, and interrelationships of cosmic ecology and cosmic passage. Created and sustained human life is embedded, dependent, and self-aware. And this is why there is no human life that does not intimate, imply, or ponder the mysterious ground of contingent realities (whether or not one calls this ground "God" or simply remains silent).

Proposition #36 Created and sustained human life is a gift.

We take a further step when we consider the blessing and the gift of life. I can *imagine* a time when I was not, as well as a time when I will no longer be, but I cannot *remember* a time when I was not. Human life, in my most fundamental experience of it, is always already there physically, mentally, and emotionally. In a contemporary American idiom, we sometimes speak of a person "inventing" or "reinventing" herself, meaning that she has altered her practices, habits, and style to become a different kind of actor, tennis player, entrepreneur, or what have you, in ways that may also change how others perceive her. We may refer to someone as a "self-made man" to emphasize that he has worked hard, perhaps in the face of significant obstacles, to obtain his current position (i.e., he didn't merely inherit it). Strictly speaking, however, we have no experience of bringing about our own lives, no experience of self-creation. We experience our lives as

4. Anselm, *Proslogion*, in *A Scholastic Miscellany: Anselm to Ockham*, ed. and trans. Eugene R. Fairweather (New York: Macmillan, 1970), 70, 74.

given. And, as we have seen, we know that we depend for both our emergence and our continuation on a multitude of astrophysical, geological, genetic, social, and historical factors beyond our control.

We also experience human life as given in another and related sense. We can make use of it; we can do things with it; we can exercise human capacities. In fact, the capabilities of humans are both distinctive and impressive. We can cultivate abilities and pursue goals; we can participate in societies and institutions; we can enter into personal relationships. We can cooperate with others to build cities and produce or operate technologies. We can unravel genomes, and we can reduce our planet to nuclear winter.

We shall also have the opportunity to observe soon enough the important limits we humans experience. We can intervene in nature and in history, but we are unable to anticipate all relevant outcomes and consequences. (Remember the decisions of the Spanish and the Portuguese to colonize South America, the decision to introduce starlings to North America, or Lyndon Johnson's decision to escalate American involvement in Vietnam.) There also appear to be certain requisites for human flourishing, such as the maintenance of tolerably just institutions for adjudicating disputes, which we ignore at our peril. It thus seems altogether too strong to say that human life is given to us simply to do with as we please. Nevertheless, when we consider the gift of human life and its many capabilities, we appropriately conclude that there is a quite significant and comparatively extraordinary range of things that humans can do.

Even so, in its "givenness," human life (mine, yours, the life of the species) is much like some other forms of life. Other animals also depend for their emergence and continuation on a multitude of cosmic, geological, genetic, and historical factors beyond their control. Rats, horses, chimpanzees, for example, are also given certain capabilities and possibilities together with rat life, horse life, and chimp life. Indeed, many of the factors on which they depend not only are analogous to and overlap with those on which we depend; they are largely the same. All depend on the same astrophysical and geological factors that make carbon-based life possible; animals on Earth share 98 percent of their genetic material.

Our biologically based emotional constitution is distinctive and also susceptible to cultural formation; but the biologically based emotional constitutions of some other species also seem susceptible to social formation. At an appropriate level of generalization, we may speak of certain more or less common patterns of primate behavior.[5] It is true, of course, that speech and language constitute impor-

5. For a nontechnical account, see Frans de Waal, *Our Inner Ape: A Leading Primatologist Explains Why We Are Who We Are* (New York: Riverhead, 2005).

tant human excellences. But if we do not concentrate on syntax alone and instead look to broader patterns of communication, including gestures and signs, then this distinction also appears as one of degree rather than kind.[6] When it comes to the "givenness" of life—as already there, as dependent on very many factors, and as given capacities—no great chasm separates us from other animals.

Considered within the framework of a theocentric piety, human life in the midst of cosmic ecology and passage is a *gift of God the Creator and Governor*. Thus do we find Augustine, in the *Confessions*, speaking of "your gift of being."[7] John Calvin notes that "the mighty gifts with which we are endowed are hardly from ourselves" and that "by these benefits . . . we are led as by rivulets to the spring itself," or to God as the fountain and source of every good.[8] The theological language of gift places human life into the context of *all* God's gifts or of God's entire creation. It emphasizes that we humans share the gift of life with other creatures and that we experience the gift of life in the setting of the everyday orderings of God's world. It also emphasizes another point: the fact that we are and that we live constitutes, as it were, our first debt. Moreover, this recognition, this experiential apprehension of life as a gift, is taken to evoke in us a correspondent attitude and affection. It heightens our sense of gratitude.

Genesis 1 associates creation and the gift of life with God's *blessing*. The words of blessing in 1:28, "Be fruitful and multiply," indicate that humans are endowed with generativity, as are the birds and the creatures of the waters "of every kind" that God blesses using these same words in 1:22. Therefore, "every genus and species of creation can 'bring forth,' according to its kind."[9] Again, in Genesis 1:11, the earth "puts forth" (or as some would translate it, "greens forth") vegetation, plants, and fruit trees of every kind with their seeds. The earth is fertile, viable for life, and for their part, plants with their seeds have the capacity to generate more vegetation. In short, life always continues, a point that is driven home after the flood (Gen. 8:17; 9:1, 7), when God repeats the same words of blessing that we find in Genesis 1:22 and 1:28 to Noah, his sons, and their wives, and to every living thing that is with them. Moreover, the blessing anchored in Genesis 1:28 subsequently works itself out in the *sequence of generations* recounted in the genealogies. This sequence reminds us of our kinship in biological life with other species. It suggests our experience of the *stream* of life.[10] In addition, generations

6. See Mary Midgley, *Beast and Man: The Roots of Human Nature* (Ithaca, NY: Cornell University Press, 1978), 203–51, 258, 321–51; see also de Waal, *Our Inner Ape*, 188.

7. Augustine, *Confessions*, trans. Maria Boulding, OSB, vol. I/1 of *WA*, 342.

8. Calvin, *ICR* 1.1.1.

9. Walter Brueggemann, *Theology of the Old Testament: Testimony, Dispute, Advocacy* (Minneapolis: Fortress, 1997), 529.

10. Eccles. 3:18–20 mentions another reminder of this kinship: we are like animals in that we meet the same fate in death and return to dust.

are the means by which God's blessing comes to Israel (through Abraham) and then (through Israel) to "all the families of the earth" (Gen. 12:3).

The blessing of life helps to elaborate the giftedness of life by pointing to additional goods, for example, embodied sexuality and offspring. These are goods that people experience in distinctive fashion and that clearly also are features of the lives of other species. Moreover, in our own highly social species, as also in some others, embodied sexuality and offspring intertwine with the further goods of intimate and mutual companionship, gratification, and play. They involve the needs of cooperation in caring for children, as well as for the possibility of personal relationships across the generations and the sense of what these intergenerational relationships may bring for the continuing stream of life.

The Bible scholar Claus Westermann makes a further point. As it is presented in the Old Testament, "the blessing is not a matter of the extraordinary times when, for example, one experiences deliverance, but rather of the daily flow of daily life." The gift of life is something that the creature experiences in everyday physical existence and the continuation of life from one generation to the next. It relates to the course of life "from day to day and year to year."[11] Accordingly, the gift of life is one that we do not experience only on one or another isolated occasion. It is a gift that we generally experience as a steady current and in gradual processes, such as the maturing of certain capacities; the birth of a child and his continuing physical, mental, and emotional growth into adulthood; or a couple's enduring relationship of mutual help and care. It is a gift that we sometimes too easily overlook but that we may often observe in the daily activities of other animals round about us, the seasonal migrations of birds, the seasonal changes in the trees, and so on.

For creation piety, the gift of life means that our relationship with God embraces the continuing and often ordinary flow of life. Our relationship with the divine is not restricted to matters of "salvation"; it is also resident in the everyday. Again, the gift "is given to a person as a living being with all other living beings together."[12] Thus, the relationship between God and the human being is not restricted to the latter's life within a particular historic community; it expands to include her membership in the human race. Indeed, it extends beyond that to her place within the world of living beings and even the cosmic ecology and passage of all things that owe their life and their being to the one who creates and sustains.

Obviously, the idea of God's blessing and gift of life does not guarantee flourishing or even survival to persons and other living things. It cannot be reduced to

11. Claus Westermann, *Elements of Old Testament Theology*, trans. Douglas W. Stott (Atlanta: John Knox, 1982), 103.

12. Westermann, *Elements of Old Testament Theology*, 112.

a moralistic doctrine of compensation in which God blesses only the righteous or God-fearing and withdraws the blessing and the gift from the unrighteous. It hardly guarantees the ethical rationality of life in God's world—a point made by the books of Job and Ecclesiastes. We might rather observe that the blessing and the gift of life, while quite generally experienced, are also indiscriminate and gratuitous, and that God "makes his sun rise on the evil and on the good, and sends rain on the righteous and on the unrighteous" (Matt. 5:45). The blessing and gift of life intimate the world as an order of grace.

This brings us to another main theological point: the recognition that life is a gift evokes in us (or at least should evoke in us) a certain attitude, affection, or emotion. Martin Luther makes the claim with characteristic vigor as he exposits the Apostles' Creed: "The first article teaches that God is the father, the creator of heaven and earth. . . . This article teaches that you do not have your life of yourself, not even a hair. . . . Do not let us think that we have created ourselves, as the proud princes do."[13] Rather than pride, the recognition and the experience of life as God's gift ought to evoke in us emotions of gratitude, thankfulness, and humility. Calvin thinks that it is true piety when people "recognize that they owe everything to God." The difficulty, of course, is that, like Luther's proud princes, we too often prove to be cosmic ingrates.[14]

You may have seen an interview on television with a victorious sprinter following an especially important race, where the commentator asks an opening question, and the athlete begins by saying, "First, I just want to thank God. . . ." Public testimony of this sort was not an especially prominent feature of the piety in which I was raised. But the athlete is profoundly correct, theologically speaking, to acknowledge that, though she worked very hard, in the wider context of cosmic passage she is not responsible for the genetic and biological bases of her physical abilities. She is not responsible for the presence of her coaches and the quality of the training they have given her while they were employed by institutions that, in turn, were supported by other persons and communities over time. She is not responsible for the training that her coaches received from other coaches at similar institutions. Nor is she responsible for the nurture and support she has received from family and friends. All these things and more have played a part in her accomplishment. She has benefited from them all, and so she is appropriately grateful, even if she cannot name a particular person or group of persons who are entirely responsible for them all.

We might say that, for persons of piety, God's creation itself is "doxology-evoking," an unmistakable point of Psalm 148, as it enlists humans together with

13. Martin Luther, *Sermons I*, ed. and trans. John W. Doberstein, vol. 51 of *LW*, 162–63.
14. Calvin, *ICR* 1.2; 1.5.4.

all other creatures in a universal hymn of praise. Or consider the opening lines of John Milton's rendition of Psalm 136. The psalm itself opens this way: "Oh, give thanks to the Lord, for he is good, for his steadfast love endures forever." Milton renders it this way: "Let us with a gladsome mind, praise the Lord who is so kind: for God's mercies shall endure, ever faithful, ever sure." A "gladsome mind" is one inclined to give thanks, one filled with gladness and gratitude. And within the frame of the theological vision I am presenting here, the significance of the affirmation that human life in the midst of cosmic ecology and passage is a gift of God the Creator will not be appreciated until we understand it in conjunction with corresponding attitudes, emotions, or affections of thankfulness, gratitude, and humility that prepare people to use their gifts toward praise and willing service.

Proposition #37 Created and sustained human life is socially inclined, institutionally sustained, and socially conditioned.

We experience created and sustained human life as a gift, as something always already there and endowed with capacities and possibilities. Of course, it is also true that we always experience life together with other realities and companions. We also experience it in the midst of relationships, interrelationships, and interdependencies with persons, things, organisms, communities, and conditions. In this sense, though clearly not in some other relevant senses, we are never alone, never isolated. We are always *situated.*

This observation coheres with the ideas of cosmic ecology and cosmic passage, and it comes through clearly enough in texts such as Genesis 1:1–2:4 and Psalm 104.[15] The Bible indicates that, within the local venue that we call Earth, humans (plural, and both male and female) are located within an articulated set of relationships, interdependencies, and processes. We interact with light and darkness, sea, sky, and land, with plants, animals, one another, and God. In addition, as the biblical narrative unfolds, persons and communities find themselves situated within a field of divine governance that includes sun, moon, stars, plants, animals, other individuals, peoples, nations, empires, and so on.

We live in context. This basic point is made in very many places besides the Bible, and most notably perhaps by Darwinian theorists. We are enmeshed in both nature and society, so that our capacities, possibilities, and limits depend on interrelationships and interactions in both arenas.

15. See chap. 3, props. #28 and #29.

Humans Are Socially Inclined

The religious, practical, and moral significance of the situation of life, as we may call it, becomes clearer when we observe that humans are *socially inclined*. This, in fact, is a large part of what we mean when we say that humans are social; it also comes to expression in the mythopoeic literature of the Bible. Thus, having been informed almost rhythmically by Genesis 1:1–2:4 that, at the close of each day, God saw that what God had made was "good"; and after having been told in Genesis 1:31 that God surveyed all that God had made during the first six days, "and indeed, it was very good"; in Genesis 2:18, after having formed the human from "the dust of the ground," God makes a jarring assertion: "It is *not* good that the human should be alone." Why not? Because the human needs a "helper" (*'ezer*, a comparatively rare Hebrew word that should not immediately be taken to imply subordination, since it is sometimes used to refer to God as our helper and deliverer) and a "partner."[16] Therefore, God forms from the ground every animal and bird in an effort to keep the human company and thus spare the first earth-creature the bad fate of being alone; but among these additional creatures "there was not found a helper as [the human's] partner." Then the almighty maker of heaven and earth, having proven, poetically enough, unable to make another human from scratch, fashions a second one from the flesh and bone of the first. This *wo*man is "at last" the true helper, partner, and companion required for the man.

Just about every word of this text has been fought over, and I cannot rehearse here the history of its interpretation and misinterpretation. But I should make a few elementary observations. In Hebrew, *Adam* is not simply a proper name, like Joe or Fred. It means humankind. We are thus entirely within our rights to refer to the first creature God fashions from the ground in Genesis 2:6 simply as the human or the human being. Woman (*'ishshah* in Hebrew) is presented in Genesis 2:23 as a wordplay on man (*'ish* in Hebrew); interestingly and appropriately, gender does not appear in the text until Genesis 2:22, when both the man and the woman are present.[17]

Taken as a whole, then, Genesis 2:5–25 encourages piety to acknowledge that humans, both male and female, are made to participate in mutual relationships of

16. See Pauline A. Viviano, "Genesis," in *Collegeville Bible Commentary*, ed. Dianne Bergant, CSA, and Robert J. Karris, OFM (Collegeville, MN: Liturgical Press, 1989), 42; Christiana De-Groot, "Genesis," in *IVP Women's Bible Commentary*, ed. Catherine Clark Kroeger and Mary J. Evans (Downers Grove, IL: InterVarsity Press, 2001), 6.

17. Note, too, that when the woman is brought to him and he first sees her (naked, as we learn from v. 25), the man is *very* impressed. He thus speaks approvingly, and *in poetry* (v. 23), a point that would seem appropriate to make at many weddings.

help, responsibility, and care. The text claims that apart from these relationships, which are required in order for there to be any human society at all, the good creature called humankind is incomplete.

Indeed, a striking feature of Genesis 2:5–25 is that, while the creation of the man and the woman clearly is critical for procreation, children, and the continuation of the species (remember the blessing of generativity in Gen. 1), emphasis falls on the companionate *relationship* of mutual responsibility and care. There is no mention of children. The emphasis was not lost on some Puritans and other classical Protestants, who did not portray marriage primarily as an arrangement to procreate without excessive lust, but as a covenantal relationship of mutual help, responsibility, and care, *among* the significant but hardly requisite purposes, two of which are procreation and raising children.[18]

We might say that humans are naturally inclined toward social relationships and interactions. This is a feature of the way the Bible says they are put together, created, or assembled, and this, in turn, is why it is not good for the original human to be alone. Commenting on Genesis 2:18, Calvin thus notes God's design of the world so that "there should be human beings on the earth who might cultivate mutual society between themselves." Indeed, with the relationship of Adam and Eve, "God begins . . . at the first step of human society, yet designs it to include others, each in its proper place. The commencement, therefore, involves a general principle, that man was formed to be a social animal."[19] Other biblical passages and themes have similar implications. At Sinai, for example, God's people are bound to God and to one another by a covenant of mutual responsibility; the apostle Paul claims that the faithful are united as members of Christ's body.[20] Covenant community and the church as Christ's body are appropriate means for holding socially inclined humans in relationship with the God of grace.

18. See, e.g., Richard Baxter's *A Christian Directory; or, A Sum of Practical Theology, and Cases of Conscience*, vol. 1 of *The Practical Works of Richard Baxter* (Ligonier, PA: Soli Deo Gloria, 1990), 1:431–57. Might one argue that, within the context of a companionate relationship of mutual affection, responsibility, and care, sex has multiple functions, including the establishment and maintenance of deep emotional and personal bonds, psychic-physical gratification, and play? For Puritans and other classical Protestants, that would seem to have gone at least two words too far. But surely not for a contemporary theology that means to take account of more recent studies of the "natural" functions of sex for a social species, as well as to build on the claims that created and sustained human life is socially inclined and that marriage is, first and foremost, a companionate relationship.

19. John Calvin, *Commentaries on the First Book of Moses Called Genesis*, trans. John King, vol. 1 of *Calvin's Commentaries*, Calvin Translation Society (Grand Rapids: Baker Books, 1998), 128.

20. Richard T. Ely, "Social Christianity," in *The Social Gospel in America, 1870–1920*, ed. Robert T. Handy (New York: Oxford University Press, 1966), 235–41.

Again, the basic point is not at all exclusively biblical. Instead, the Bible is commenting on and theologically depicting a rather generally available bit of human knowledge and experience. Therefore, Aristotle notes in his *Nichomachean Ethics* and in his *Politics* that humans are socially inclined and political animals bound together in different sorts of associations and communities—from families to villages and states—by feelings of friendship. "No one," he says, "would choose the whole world on the condition of being alone, since man is a political creature and one whose nature is to live with others."[21] Or, in a statement that might be taken to set the stage for later investigations in sociobiology, the great philosopher intones: "Man is more of a political animal than bees or any other gregarious animals."[22]

Centuries later, Charles Darwin maintained that humans are social animals who take pleasure in one another's company, feel sympathy with others, and perform mutual services. Humans, he said, tend to be faithful to comrades and loyal to their groups—qualities emphasized today by some primatologists in their reflections about humans and higher apes.[23] This social feeling, as it is often called, is fundamental for the formation and continuation of communities. Why? Because their survival depends on their ability to successfully negotiate the possibilities and challenges of their environments, including competitions with other communities and groups of the same species. And the ability of communities to do this depends, in turn, on individuals who cooperate effectively to obtain food, raise offspring, and protect the group from threats. Simply put, "evolution favors animals that assist each other if by doing so they achieve long-term benefits of greater value than the benefits derived from going it alone and competing with others."[24] "Selection favors what is useful to the group," and, among humans, it favors socially cooperative tendencies fueled by social feeling.[25]

From a Darwinian perspective, then, the roots of human morality lie in needs for social organization and cooperation. Empathy, reciprocity, kindness, gratitude, courage, prudence, and the like are needed for the welfare of the tribe

21. Aristotle, *Nichomachean Ethics*, trans. W. D. Ross, in vol. 2 of *The Works of Aristotle*, Great Books of the Western World, vol. 9 (Chicago: Encyclopedia Britannica, 1952), bk. 9, chap. 9, p. 423.

22. Aristotle, "Politics," trans. Benjamin Jowett, in vol. 2 of *The Works of Aristotle*, bk. 1, chap. 2, p. 446.

23. Charles Darwin, *The Descent of Man, and Selection in Relation to Sex*, introduction by John Tyler Bonner and Robert M. May (Princeton: Princeton University Press, 1981), 84–85; Frans de Waal et al., *Primates and Philosophers: How Morality Evolved*, ed. Stephen Macedo and Josiah Ober (Princeton: Princeton University Press, 2006), 15.

24. De Waal et al., *Primates and Philosophers*, 13.

25. Midgley, *Beast and Man*, 132.

or the general good and well-being of the community.[26] Indeed, says Frans de Waal, a sense of fairness "starts with resentment if you get less, then moves to concern about how others will react if you get more, and ends with declaring inequity a bad thing in general."[27] The generally distributed bit of human moral wisdom called the Golden Rule, therefore, has its roots in conflict avoidance and the need for social cohesion and solidarity.[28] And the emergence of *conscience*, or the ability to recognize moral norms, such as fairness, and apply them to one's own actions, as well as the emergence of a sense of obligation, depends not only on capacities for memory and reflection but also on our specific social ties and interactions within our particular groups as well as our loyalties to our own groups.

The close connection between moral sensibility and solidarity, or group cohesion, has important implications. One is that human morality does not emerge from isolated self-interest or simple egoism; it is, in fact, bound up with our capacities to recognize and participate in social relationships and interdependencies.[29] Another is that the extension of human social sympathies and moral sensitivities beyond the bounds of smaller groups and tribes toward larger communities (not to mention their extension toward all humans, other species, or even a wider ecology) turns out to be no easy task.[30] Emotion is critical for our own definitions of our communities of moral concern, but our social sympathies and emotions are not easily enlarged.

Political communities acknowledge these facts when they, persistently and sometimes rather strenuously, present themselves and the things they stand for as objects of devotion or causes capable of binding people together. This was certainly true when I grew up in northern New Jersey during the 1950s and 1960s. Considerable time and energy were expended in the form of history courses, pledges, flags, movies, monuments, and field trips, in order to make Moira Mackenzie, Alden Iwahashi, Andy Mendez, John Javna, Carol Hajinilian, Michael Prigoff, Brian Mahoney, Chris Menotti, Varhum Anhilian, and me into more or less loyal Americans. And never more so than on the Fourth of July, when many of us rode our bicycles decorated with red, white, and blue crepe-paper

26. Darwin, *Descent of Man*, 95; de Waal et al., *Primates and Philosophers*, 13.

27. De Waal, *Our Inner Ape*, 220.

28. In this, de Waal is once again elaborating on Darwin, who wrote that "the social instincts—the prime principle of man's moral constitution—with the aid of active intellectual powers and the effects of habit, naturally lead to the golden rule . . . and this lies at the foundation of morality" (Darwin, *Descent of Man*, 106).

29. Indeed, philosopher Midgley says flatly, "Egoism is not a plausible account of motivation" (Midgley, *Beast and Man*, 122).

30. Darwin, *Descent of Man*, 100–101.

streamers, and equipped with baseball cards fixed by clothespins to our fenders so that they would protrude into the spokes of the wheels and make noise as they snapped back and forth. Our destination? Downtown Tenafly to see the parade, hear Sousa marches, and spend our dimes at ice-cream stands. But the really big event came hours later: a fireworks display put on by the police department at Roosevelt Commons, a show that self-consciously rehearsed the plot of "The Star-Spangled Banner" and filled the nighttime sky while we watched, seated on blankets with our families. It was political liturgy, and was at least partly successful as a vehicle for extending our social feelings and loyalties beyond our ethnic and religious groups to the nation, its citizens, and its welfare.

In any case, the expansion of our communities of loyalty and moral concern remains a fragile, often labor-intensive, enterprise. We are able to include outsiders only with difficulty because the building blocks of human sociality and morality are so thoroughly bound up with our loyalties to our own particular groups. It is generally true that socially inclined humans have the imaginative capacity to put themselves in another's place as well as the emotional capacity to be affected by the emotional states of others. Even so, the same feelings of group solidarity and loyalty that enable us to develop these capacities and their attendant moral sensibilities anchor especially heartfelt obligations to our own specific groups that we may not feel toward others. They may also be coupled with loathing for out-groups; indeed, loathing or hatred for out-groups—for instance, another tribe, nation, or race—often enhances the felt cohesion and self-worth of our in-groups. Moreover, as human history so frequently attests, out-group loathing may be heightened and manipulated for just this purpose. "It's a trick," says de Waal, "as old as man, but the psychology [which we share with some other primates] may in fact precede our species."[31]

The dynamics of in-group and out-group psychology in the formation of human social inclination and morality lead de Waal to conclude that "moral systems are inherently biased toward the in-group." I would rather say that these dynamics exert regular pressures on our social feelings, moral sensibilities, and reflections. This is true because tendencies toward in-group identification and bias are by-products of the specific social loyalties and feelings needed for the emergence and formation of our moral sensibilities and ideas.[32]

An important theological conclusion at this juncture is that created and sustained humans are socially inclined creatures endowed with a distinctive knot of morally relevant capacities and sensibilities that have emerged from evolutionary and social processes. These may themselves be construed as gifts bestowed by

31. De Waal, *Our Inner Ape*, 141.
32. De Waal et al., *Primates and Philosophers*, 163, 165.

the divine governance at work on cosmic ecology and cosmic passage that help to preserve persons and societies, for which we may be appropriately thankful, and that form significant bases for our senses of responsibility and obligation. A piety shaped and expressed by images of God as Creator and Provider thus stands in close connection with an inventory of morally relevant sensibilities and capacities that have biological bases but are socially elicited and formed by interactions within our particular groups. These sensibilities and capacities include social feelings of pleasure in the company of others, as well as feelings of empathy, solidarity, and group loyalty. They also include an imaginative capacity to identify with others, a sense of fairness, aversion to gross suffering and inequity, and conscience. While these capacities and sensibilities have biological bases, they are socially elicited and formed by interactions within our own particular groups.

Calvin says similar things in his *Institutes*, where he claims that, "since man is a social animal, he tends through natural instinct to foster and preserve society," and that we are endowed with a sense of equity and fair dealing. However, he also acknowledges that our moral judgment often falters when it comes to matters in our own interest.[33] This last point properly belongs to the doctrine of sin, which we shall not treat in earnest until part 3. In any case, what I have added here is a more developed account of the social formation and development of sensibilities like the ones Calvin mentioned, but hence I have also introduced the additional worry that human moral judgments often are skewed by loyalties to our in-groups.

Institutions Sustain by Furnishing Critical Goods

Now for a second point. Certain basic institutions *sustain* socially inclined humans by furnishing goods that are critical for their well-being. In many modern societies, for example, we find nuclear families, business corporations, democratic states, schools, colleges and universities, symphonies, churches, synagogues, and mosques. These institutions structure certain relatively independent arenas or spheres of human life and activity, for example, family, economics or work, politics, art, science, education, and religion.[34] They also have distinguishable purposes: business corporations produce wealth, schools educate, sym-

33. Calvin, *ICR* 2.2.13; 2.2.23.

34. For a helpful recent discussion of these matters by an important social theorist, see Niklas Luhmann, *The Differentiation of Society*, trans. Stephen Holmes and Charles Larmore (New York: Columbia University Press, 1982).

phonies play music, and so on. We recognize that without these structures and orderings, our lives would be impoverished—indeed, in some instances, even imperiled. Therefore, it is not uncommon to read statements in the Christian tradition to the effect that our well-being depends as much on families, businesses, governments, and the like as it does on food, air, and water.[35]

The insight that follows close behind is well stated by Max L. Stackhouse: certain "quite stable functional requirements of human living . . . demand participation in and maintenance of some viable institutions."[36] This is partly what Calvin means when, in his commentary on Genesis 2, he claims that, by divine design, the making of Adam and Eve, or "the first step of human society," includes other steps "each in its proper place." Among other things, the Genevan Reformer believed that God institutes family and civil government for our good, and that each has its own appropriate end or purpose.

These matters came in for considerable discussion among Protestant theologians and ethicists in Europe during the mid-twentieth century. Emil Brunner developed the (somewhat Lutheran) idea that "state, church, family, labor, and culture are 'orders of creation,' by which God sustains human life against the destructive forces unleashed by human sin." This enabled Brunner to develop a critique of totalitarian states that emerge, he said, when "federalism," or "the building up of the community from below, has vanished." The proper role of the state, according to Brunner, is to organize and unify more primary forms of community. The family is "the primal community" or "the root and prototype of every community," and it performs profound companionate and nurturing functions that cannot be undertaken by another institution. Economic associations, which also exist prior to the state, are essential "for the purpose of coping with material life."[37] These basic structures, then, each derive their own "law-like authority from their roles in preserving the order of God's creation," and thus furnish guides and limits for ordering human societies.[38] In his *Ethics*, Dietrich Bonhoeffer, whose reflections must always be read in conjunction with his active and principled opposition to Nazism, described "divine mandates" of work, marriage, church, and government. The mandates, which he thought were learned from the Word of God, are definite forms in which God commands and

35. Calvin, *ICR* 4.20.3.

36. Max L. Stackhouse, "Public Theology and Political Economy in a Globalizing Era," *Studies in Christian Ethics* 14 (2001): 70–71 (quoted by Robin W. Lovin, *Christian Realism and the New Realities* [Cambridge: Cambridge University Press, 2008], 81).

37. Emil Brunner, *Justice and the Social Order*, trans. Mary Hottinger (London: Lutterworth, 1945), 120–22.

38. Lovin, *Christian Realism and the New Realities*, 77–78.

preserves human beings. Most often, the roles and directives they uphold cohere and interrelate. Occasionally, however, they may oppose one another.[39]

Karl Barth's appreciative if also critical treatment of these proposals comes in his *Church Dogmatics* III/4. Barth appreciated them as attempts to bring divine commands or imperatives into connection with our actual existence, but he worried that Brunner's orders were derived from "something akin to the familiar notion of a *lex naturae* which is immanent in reality and inscribed upon the heart of man, so that it is directly known by him."[40] Can sinful humans in history truly and authentically know valid moral norms in this way? Are not the orders and imperatives we identify finally arbitrary, obscure, and unreliable? Barth's estimate of Bonhoeffer's mandates is more positive, since these are institutions of the reality of Christ that we learn from Scripture. "They do not emerge from reality; they descend to it" (22). But Barth also wondered whether Bonhoeffer's four or five mandates (and no others) occur so evidently and regularly in the Bible. Does there remain, then, in Bonhoeffer's proposal—as in Brunner's—an uncritical reliance on something akin to natural law? In response, Barth identified four lines in the structure of man as God's creature that constitute spheres of divine commanding and human action: the human as (1) a being in history, (2) a being in encounter with other humans, and (3) a material organism who is (4) allotted a fixed span (43–55). He then reflects at length, for example, on divine commanding and human obedience in the differentiated relationship between male and female as the first and typical sphere of fellow humanity (2 above), as well as on the relationship of parents and children (117). Barth also wrote extensively on respect for life, the protection of life, and vocation, but he did not introduce a list of four or five institutions that correspond to the ones offered by Brunner and Bonhoeffer.

In my judgment, the best option here is a kind of middle position. Brunner and Bonhoeffer were correct, I think, to mention the kinds of institutions that they did. They were also correct to acknowledge something akin to the notion of natural law. Even so, I am not entirely free of some of the concerns that Barth articulated.

Basic institutions that order activities within certain arenas or spheres do indeed furnish goods that are critical for our well-being. Moreover, we generally are aware of these institutions and at least some of the benefits they bring, and so we also have some sense of the obligations and demands they entail. We

39. Dietrich Bonhoeffer, *Ethics*, trans. Reinhard Kraus, Charles C. West, and Douglas W. Stott, vol. 6 of Dietrich Bonhoeffer Works (Minneapolis: Fortress, 2005), 68.

40. Barth, *CD* III/4:20. Hereafter, page references to *CD* III/4 appear in parentheses in the text.

don't need to read the Bible to find out about these things, though reading the Bible may reinforce our awareness. It is true that there is no universal agreement on how the orders, spheres, or mandates should be named. It is also true that theologians have provided a number of different lists. Nevertheless, as Robin W. Lovin notes, the basic idea is clear.

> Human beings, with their irreducibly different goods and goals, need several quite different settings in which to work together on lasting goals. The state, with its laws, courts, legislatures, and administrative agencies, is one such institution. The world of work is another. We need employers, labor unions, professional associations, stock markets, banks, and a myriad of other institutions to maintain the productive process and give people a way to participate in it. Intimate relationships with family form yet another area of life, one that is the most important for many people, and one that requires support by and protection from government and the world of work. Education serves the needs of both state and business, but it is also different from either of them; and it requires support from other institutions that maintain cultural heritages and encourage artistic creativity. The church and other religious institutions relate closely to family and to education, but they also supply spiritual needs that also affect how we relate to work and to government.[41]

James M. Gustafson notes that the basic institutions—for example, family, business, government—are not natural in the sense that human processes of reproduction are, because the forms they take and the ways in which their purposes are enacted are the result of historical and cultural developments and the actions of many individuals. I agree. At the same time, he also notes—appropriately, I think—that they do in fact meet basic human needs.[42] Most of the time we benefit from basic institutions in fundamental ways, and precisely because we recognize that we do, we also feel obligations to participate in them, maintain them, and enhance them. In fact, as we participate in these institutions and take up specific roles or positions, we encounter specific obligations and responsibilities as parents, children, employers, workers, judges, lawyers, and so on. This is how people generally discern obligations and specific lines of responsibility in connection with their participation in basic institutions.

Consider our families. By and large, they help to sustain us physically and emotionally in critical ways. They furnish contexts of companionship, nurture, affection, and responsibility in which we exercise and develop important social

41. Robin W. Lovin, *Christian Ethics: An Essential Guide* (Nashville: Abingdon, 2000), 106.
42. Gustafson, *ETP*, 1:219.

skills and sensibilities. Our families are enormous contributors to the kinds of persons we become. At least, we acknowledge much of this most of the time. We are grateful to parents, siblings, aunts, uncles, grandparents, spouses, children, and so on, as well as to our family "community as a whole." We also recognize that this community, its structures, expectations, and activities, also benefits others whom we care about, for example, our siblings and our children. And this is why we often feel a responsibility to participate in our families, as well as to uphold dependably our particular familial roles, say as parents, children, or siblings. We recognize and are grateful for the special relationships of interdependence and the benefits they bestow on us as well as others; therefore, we feel that the familial relationships in which persons participate bring with them specific duties and obligations. Our "knowledge" of these obligations and demands (a knowledge, incidentally, that connects "is" and "ought") is not the product of a rigorous logical argument; it is an affectively charged discernment.

Theologically speaking, then, we should say that the divine governance and sustenance are mediated to us in and through basic institutions, such as family, business, and government. The divine governance generally sustains us in these institutions as distinguishable contexts for responsibility. People of theocentric piety thus also feel obligations to participate in these contexts and, through their participation, to discharge faithfully their specific lines of responsibility, for example, as parents, construction workers, citizens, teachers, and so forth.

But Barth is also right to worry that we may become overconfident in our knowledge of the obligations and demands we encounter in this way. Though in some respects it anticipates our later discussion of sin in part 3, we also need to note here important ambiguities in our experiences of sustenance through basic institutions. Indeed, the entire dynamic of basic institutions, the benefits and essential goods they furnish, plus the sense of gratitude and obligation we feel, can be fraught with complications and corruptions. Families thus generally sustain, but they often do so ambiguously and problematically. Even the parenting of good parents reflects not only their affection and commitment to their children but also their limited knowledge, as well as their anxieties and insecurities. What's more, not all parents are especially good ones; some are irresponsible or even abusive. Similar things can be said about the ways spouses interact with and care for each other, and about the ways grown children interact with and care for aging parents. This is why, at least for some individuals, the dynamic of sustenance and felt obligation is significantly qualified or even breaks down. It is true that culturally specific forms of and attitudes toward family life—its structures, expectations, and responsibilities—can support serious and systematic injustices and abuses, especially toward women and children. This can also qualify the sense of gratitude and obligation that people feel. In some instances, the myriad ambiguities and the unjust and destructive tendencies may elicit indifference, a sense of betrayal, or even hatred. These emotions, in turn, may motivate us to reject particular families—and perhaps to alter or reject specific cultural forms of the basic institution.

Our experiences of other basic institutions can be similarly ambiguous and problematic. Particular states and governments help organize and support important commercial and educational enterprises. They uphold tolerably just courts of law and maintain dependable orders and restraints. But they may also legitimate or commit significant injustices against particular persons and groups (more frequently than we care to admit). Totalitarian states sometimes absorb all other basic social spheres into a single oppressive order. And, of course, there are also failed states and governments that—whether due to poor design, the malice and incompetence of leadership, lack of resources, competing ethnic, ideological, or religious factions, or some combination of all these things—fail to furnish even the most fundamental services and guidelines, leaving whole populations to descend into anarchic strife and chaos. In these and in other instances, the relationships between basic institutional orderings, important or essential goods, feelings of gratitude, and feelings of obligation and responsibility are strained, disrupted, or destroyed. A social covenant is broken.

With these statements we have already begun to explore a third point: created and sustained human life in the midst of cosmic ecology and passage is *socially conditioned*. This is not so much explicitly affirmed or stated in biblical texts as it is reflected by them. Accordingly, we read in the Confession of 1967 of the Presbyterian Church (USA): "The Scriptures," which attest to God's Word, "are nevertheless the words of men, conditioned by the language, thought forms, and literary fashions of the places and times at which they were written. They reflect views of life, history, and the cosmos which were then current."[43]

The more general point, of course, is that human knowledge and experience—including moral sensibilities and ideas—are historically and socially conditioned. This need not mean that there are no commonalities, no more or less stable institutional prerequisites for human living, and no generally apprehended and distributed bits of human moral wisdom. There are commonalities, and our previous discussions of basic institutions, a sense of fairness, the Golden Rule, and the like are intended to make just that point. But it is also true that we never have access to these commonalities apart from the specific language, traditions, institutions, and patterns of interaction current in our own time and place. We never know and discern them apart from the historically particular images, symbols, and ideas of our particular cultures.

43. The Confession of 1967, in *BOC* 9.29.

We may affirm, I believe, a more or less commonly distributed sense of the demand for justice, an inkling of fairness, and also a revulsion at gross and destructive injustices. These sensibilities can push us to recognize claims for justice made by others who differ from ourselves even across social and cultural boundaries. They are bound up with a knot of emotions and reflective capabilities that we have discussed earlier and for which there is some evidence in other primates as well, and in a theological frame of reference, they may be regarded as significant indicators of responsibility and obligation before God. Indeed, my own understanding of our human sense for justice has something in common with that of the philosopher Michael Walzer, who observes that, when marchers in Prague in 1989 were televised carrying signs that simply said "Justice," "I knew immediately what the signs meant—and so did everyone else who saw the same picture." Walzer does not presume that he, the marchers, and other television viewers would agree on a fully elaborated conception of justice. Even so, he claims that "what they meant by the 'justice' inscribed on their signs . . . was simple enough: an end to arbitrary arrests, equal and impartial law enforcement, the abolition of the privileges and prerogatives of the party elite—common garden-variety justice."[44] What Walzer calls "common garden-variety justice" is not, at least in my judgment, best described as a concept so much as a sensibility—that is, a sense for the demand of justice.

But the aspect of this emotional and imaginative knot that we call a sense of fairness or a sense for the demand of justice is insufficient of itself to order any particular community, society, or institution. It needs to be given expression in maxims such as the Golden Rule or to each his due, and these, in turn, need to be elaborated if they are to inform (both positively and critically) any actual community, institution, or developed body of law. Particular socially instantiated norms of justice, for example, liberal democratic ideas of equal opportunity, and particular laws and systems of laws, for example, the Civil Rights Act and the US criminal code, cannot simply be read off from an entirely clear human moral sensibility. They necessarily are devised in ways that reflect particular social histories and specific cultural images, ideas, and resources.[45] They are at least partly socially constructed.

In addition, as I have already noted, and as I will have occasion to elaborate on when we treat the human fault in part 3, our moral sensibilities, including

44. Michael Walzer, *Thick and Thin: Moral Argument at Home and Abroad* (Notre Dame: University of Notre Dame Press, 1994), 1, 2.

45. Douglas F. Ottati, "What Reformed Theology in a Calvinist Key Brings to Conversations about Justice," *Political Theology* 10, no. 3 (2009): 457–58, 463.

our sense of justice, may be stunted, skewed, and rendered ambiguous by inordinately constricted loyalties and commitments to in-groups.

Even so, when combined with salient facts surrounding the circumstances in Prague, as well as with some of our own experiences of moral judgment and even outrage, our generally distributed moral sensibility, or what Calvin called our sense of equity, can be enough to enable us to understand what the marchers' signs meant. It can also be enough, when combined with our own ordinary experiences and social histories (and whether we are Christians or not), to launch a meaningful critique of the tyranny to which Czechs were subject in 1989.

We also need to accord full weight to the observation that the basic institutions that order and uphold more or less stable requirements for human living take significantly different forms in history. Although it is not an especially scriptural point, this may also be illustrated biblically, for example, by the transition from the somewhat charismatic political system of judges to the kingship in 1 and 2 Samuel, as well as by the rise of the priesthood and temple-centered cultic observance. Consider, for example, different forms of family and household that have emerged in different societies, whether they have been structured by norms of polygamous and monogamous marriage, whether or not they also have discharged certain economic functions, and so on. As Stackhouse notes, while "some economic organization is always present for production, distribution, and consumption," the modern corporation "is not a 'natural' institution" because significantly different economic institutions emerge in different societies, and it is thus not "found in every society."[46] The different forms that basic institutions take and the different ways in which these forms structure particular roles and positions—for example, parent, child, CEO, shareholder—are yet another reason why the moral demands and obligations that people encounter as they participate in basic institutions may differ across societies and cultures. Note, for example, that there is also a contemporary debate in many modern societies in the West concerning same-sex unions and marriages.

In fact, not only do the shapes or forms of basic institutions change, so do their numbers, contours, roles, and importance. Indeed, whether or not certain basic institutions emerge as differentiated and relatively independent forms at all, and thus, whether or not it makes sense to speak of some activities as taking place in quite different social settings or spheres, depends on a society's historical development and total dynamics. Hence Niklas Luhmann observes that the necessity of grasping economics as a differentiated sphere of human activity arose only when, "in the course of modern times, production . . . became independent

46. Max L. Stackhouse, "The Moral Roots of the Corporation," *Theology and Public Policy* 5, no. 1 (Summer 1993): 29.

of the household and dependent on the market."[47] This also seems true of the rise in modern times of schools that are largely independent of the household and the need for grasping education as a differentiated enterprise. For these reasons, even as we acknowledge that certain institutions and spheres are *basic* because they meet important human needs, we also recognize that they are *hardly invariant*, and we hesitate to call any particular forms or even any specific number and configuration of them *natural*.[48]

Theologically speaking, then, if we are to point to basic institutions and contexts of responsibility as elements of creation and governance or preservation, if we are to integrate functional social requirements for human life with cosmic passage and with the divine governance and its moral demands (as I believe we should), we need to allow for commonalities and particularities, stability and dynamism, structure and change. That's why, rather than adopting the inert-sounding language of divine orders to describe basic institutions, we would be wise to speak, as Gustafson does, of order*ings* and the order*ing* processes.[49] The intention of this vocabulary is to relinquish neither the basic insight that there are institutional prerequisites for human well-being nor the fact that the basic institutions themselves develop and take different historical forms. The root word "order" indicates organization and structure, while the gerund form "ordering" indicates that the organizations, structures, and social processes involved are not static. Socially inclined and sustained humans experience ordering processes, orderings bound up with basic institutions that are comparatively stable, but nonetheless also dynamic features of human life in God's world. Therefore, we need not picture ourselves set adrift in a sea of discrete occasions and entirely unconnected demands. On the other hand, taking up at least one of Barth's worries, there are also good reasons to conclude that we cannot read off from the structures of the basic institutions in our experience entirely clear and stable directives that will lead us to unambiguously correct moral judgments. As persons of piety, we consult the basic institutions, roles, and lines of responsibility in which we participate as well as the obligations we feel them eliciting as part of a more fragile process of discerning what the God who creates and governs may be enabling and requiring us to do in our own place and time.

47. Luhmann, *The Differentiation of Society*, 199–200.

48. Not surprisingly, then, different theologians and political theorists offer different lists of basic institutions, as well as of estates, orders, spheres, or arenas of human social life. See Lovin, *Christian Ethics*, 105–7; Lovin, *Christian Realism and the New Realities*, 79; Max L. Stackhouse, "Christian Social Ethics in a Global Era: Reforming Protestant Views," in *Christian Ethics in a Global Era*, ed. Max L. Stackhouse et al. (Nashville: Abingdon, 1995), 26–33. See also Michael Walzer, *Spheres of Justice: A Defense of Pluralism and Equality* (New York: Basic Books, 1983).

49. Gustafson, *ETP*, 1:241.

Proposition #38 Created and sustained human life is capable and responsible.

Humans are capable; they can influence and alter situations and realities. However, in this they are not unique. Microbes consume oil, algae produce oxygen, squirrels gather nuts, and birds build nests. The ability to alter and influence is a feature of life interacting with environments. Nevertheless, the powers of intervention that humans wield are comparatively impressive. Both with respect to their purposefulness and their effect, they dramatically outstrip those possessed by other creatures on Earth. This is not to say that other animals cannot act purposefully to alter things or conditions. A strong argument can be made that the differences between humans and other animals in this regard are of degree rather than kind (in fact, Darwin and others have made just that argument).[50]

Distinctive Powers and Capacities

However, this does not deny the fact that human powers and capacities for purposeful intervention are *distinctive*, and that people are distinctively capable creatures. Recall a significant feature of the first chapter of Genesis. Humans are not only blessed with generativity, as are other animals (and plants), but they are also told to "fill the earth and subdue it; and have dominion over the fish of the sea and over the birds of the air and over every living thing that moves upon the earth" (1:28). Today, as I have observed elsewhere, we should rather say that humans occupy a special position as stewards, managers, and caretakers of planet Earth. But even if one favors these less hierarchical and monarchic concepts, the quite significant fact remains that, in the Bible, this charge is given to no other species.[51]

50. Darwin, *The Descent of Man*, 51–62; Midgley, *Beast and Man*, 203–51.

51. Could this distinctive capacity or ability of humans to "have dominion" over (or to manage) other created things be the *image of God* in humanity? The ideas that humankind is created "in God's image" and that humankind is to "fill the earth and subdue it" and also "have dominion over" the animals are certainly in close proximity in Gen. 1:26–30. Gerhard von Rad claims that "the statement about the image of God in man contains no direct explanation about the form which specially constitutes it; its real point is rather the purpose for which the image is given to man." And this purpose, he says, concerns the status of the human "as lord of the world." There is a "lordship of man" that "extends over the world" and relates especially to humanity's "function in the non-human world," where it transmits God's "supreme dignity" (Gerhard von Rad, *The Theology of Israel's Historical Traditions*, vol. 1 of *Old Testament Theology*, trans. D. M. G. Stalker [New York: Harper & Row, 1962], 144, 146, 147). But see also earlier remarks about the image of God in humans and Claus Westermann's comments on Gen. 1:26–30, cited in chap. 3, prop. #28.

Human capacities of intelligence and reflection, language and communication contribute to levels of social cooperation and technological accomplishment without parallel among other species we know of. We can envision certain goals and outcomes, and, to the extent that our knowledge at the time allows, we can cooperate to bring them about. This rather generally recognized point comes to expression even in a text such as Genesis 11, a composition that brings together quite ancient thematic elements of different origin to comment on the beginnings of civilization.[52] Here we read that "the whole earth had one language and the same words" and settled together on the plain of Shinar to build a city and "a tower with its top in the heavens" (Gen. 11:1, 4). The Lord goes down to investigate what the people have built and then returns to the heavenly retinue to sound an alarm. "Look, they are one people, and they have all one language; and this is only the beginning of what they will do; nothing that they propose to do will now be impossible for them. Come, let us go down, and confuse their language . . . , so that they will not understand one another's speech" (11:6–7). Then "the LORD scattered them abroad from there over the face of all the earth, and they left off building the city. Therefore it was called Babel, because there the LORD confused the language of all the earth" (11:8–9).

This story mixes motifs of scattering people and confusing their language, and one of its basic messages is that, when humans understand each other, are united, and working together toward common ends, they are capable of things that need to be prevented. This is a subject to which I will return in part 3 of the present system—in the discussion of sin and human fault. What I want to emphasize here is simply that the Lord's trepidation in Genesis 11:6, even if it does seem to be mythic hyperbole to claim that people might be able to do *anything* they propose, amounts to a recognition of exceptional human capability, and especially of technical capacities that follow on human cooperation. Heavenly worries emerge when *humans* communicate and cooperate purposefully, but not when ants, fish, birds, or any other creatures act (whether cooperatively or otherwise).

Much of this and more should be apparent to anyone who has looked down on the checkerboard pattern of Indiana farmland from a jet at thirty thousand feet. The myriad and distinctive human capacities on display in this experience include the impressive levels of reflection, communication, and cooperation needed to design a jet, build it, fly it, and service it. Exceptional cooperative and technical capacities also are involved in the airports, airlines, and national

52. Gerhard von Rad, *Genesis: A Commentary*, trans. John H. Marks, rev. ed. (Philadelphia: Westminster, 1972), 148; Claus Westermann, *Genesis 1–11: A Commentary*, trans. John J. Scullion, SJ (Minneapolis: Augsburg, 1984), 539, 545, 547.

system of flight controllers that organize and enable the entire enterprise. Birds fly, but usually not at thirty thousand feet and never at 600 miles per hour. They do not carry 150 passengers plus luggage and cargo, and they don't organize reservations, ticket counters, in-flight services, and maintenance schedules; nor do they procure fuel on worldwide markets, and so on.

The topography of Indiana is another impressive indicator of distinctive human powers. From thirty thousand feet it looks like a checkerboard, though, of course, it was once covered with trees. It looks as it does today because people cleared it as they cooperated to engage in large-scale agricultural ventures. They have made use of various seeds (some of them genetically modified) and used various technologies, fertilizers, machinery, and more. They have delivered produce to markets, reinvested profits, devised government agricultural services and price supports, and developed agricultural schools and laboratories. Farming obviously has come a long way since the invention of agriculture, but note that ancient agriculture, or what sometimes is called "the agrarian revolution," was itself a fundamental feat of civilization. Remember, too, that Adam was created—so the story goes—partly because "there was no one to till the ground" (Gen. 2:5).

When we consider life in relationship to God, or within the frame of theocentric piety, it makes good sense for us to be grateful for the distinctive capacities and powers we wield. It makes sense to be thankful for their excellent exercise, say, in designing and constructing a useful and perhaps also beautiful building or bridge. More generally, it makes sense to be thankful for their exercise in the development of agricultural practices and technologies, as well as technologies and practices in other areas. Humans don't always seem like much when set against the majestic glory of the heavens or the great cosmic sweep of things; but when it comes to their exceptional powers of intervention, the psalmist says:

> You have made them a little lower than angels,
> and crowned them with glory and honor. (Ps. 8:5)

Indeed, exceptional capacity is one reason to recognize the special dignity of the human.

Moreover, as humans are good creatures, piety acknowledges that the exercise of the distinctive capacities and powers with which they are endowed is thus also good. We are not called to refrain from exercising them or to stifle human creativity. We are fitted to undertake the venture of created and sustained human capacity. In fact, one quite important way that the divine providence and preservation are mediated to us is in the exercise of human capacities for reflection, social cooperation, purposeful activity, and technological development—as any religiously sensitive and reflective beneficiary of modern agriculture and modern medicine must surely realize.

Capacity Implies Distinctive Responsibility

At the same time, capacity implies responsibility. Just because humans have distinctive powers of purposeful intervention and understanding, they also have distinctive responsibilities. Humans can relevantly feel responsible and be held responsible for significant features of the current topography of Indiana, for decisions about land use, and for patterns of agricultural, industrial, and residential development. Beavers cannot. As is illustrated by recent agreements in California, Michigan, and Ohio, humans—when they farm—may be held responsible for how they treat chickens, pigs, calves, and other animals.[53] We may also be held responsible for environmental effects of flying jets and burning fossil fuels. To the extent that we understand their effects, the same may be said for how we deploy a slew of recent advances in weapons technologies, urban planning, plastics, electronics, genetic engineering, and so on.

We sense that we are responsible *for* these things because we are able to bring them about and because we understand many of their consequences. But *to whom* or *to what* are we responsible for the exercise of our distinctively purposeful and effective powers of intervention?

One answer, clearly, is that particular persons, communities, and organizations are responsible *to* other persons, communities, and organizations whose interests and well-being feel the impact of their actions. Decatur's Garage, an automotive shop in Richmond, Virginia, is responsible to neighborhood residents for how it disposes of used engine oil. Petroleum companies are responsible for safely extracting oil and natural gas from their offshore wells. When British Petroleum spilled millions of barrels of oil into the Gulf of Mexico in 2010, the corporation was understood to be responsible *to* individuals and businesses for damages caused by its operations. This is why there were so many (hotly debated) efforts to devise an equitable process by which individuals and businesses could make financial claims against the company.

Can we say that British Petroleum—and by extension the wider community of those who consume fossil fuels—was also responsible to the other species and to the low-lying estuaries that were damaged by the spill? I recall an imaginative cover of the *New Yorker* magazine that portrayed a balding executive being sworn

53. Wayne Pacelle, "A Tale of Two States," *A Humane World* (Kitty Block's blog), October 2, 2009, http://hsus.typepad.com/wayne/2009/10/michigan-ohio.html.

in to testify before a panel made up of a pelican, a dolphin, a shorebird, a duck, and a fish.[54] Of course, there can be no such panel. But might we, in addition to a bit of dark humor, also see in that cover an attempt to raise consciousness about our responsibilities to other species?

Many people today feel as though we are responsible to other species, and they have reasons for this feeling. For example, as any attentive dog-owner knows, it is possible—at least within limits—for humans to empathize with a member of another species, and vice versa, to be disturbed when a member of another species experiences pain, to delight in the playfulness of another species, and so on. Studies in genetics continue to indicate that life forms on Earth are near relatives. (It was recently reported that the boule gene responsible for sperm production probably emerged 600 million years ago and is present in almost every animal on Earth, from sea urchins and fruit flies to people.)[55] What's more, we're all in the same boat—ecologically speaking. Thus, especially given what we now know about our common biological heritage, as well as about our common dependencies on and vulnerabilities within natural ecologies, we may be moved to feel a sense of solidarity with other living things.

The theological vision I am developing here supports these and other similar sensibilities. Our known and also felt dependence on and participation in the wider and interdependent whole of cosmic passage (or God's good creation) encourage us to extend social feeling beyond the bounds of our own species. Creation piety renders us susceptible to feeling both gratitude and responsibility toward the good world of nature that the good God orders and makes and in which we live and move, even if it may not require us simply to equate our obligations to other animals with our obligations to humans.

Two items in that last sentence deserve some elaboration. First, a person whose theological vision is shaped by the image of God as Creator and Sustainer may be disposed toward reverence and thanksgiving for nature and for nonhuman creatures. Indeed, if creation piety encourages us to be drawn out toward the divine as we encounter the world of nature, then, despite the dispiriting objections of some uncompromising narrative theologians, might we not also allow ourselves to introduce the world of nature into worship and prayer? We may at least hope so.

Second, we need not simply choose between (a) putting all obligations to humans and to other animals on a par and (b) denying that we have any obligations to other animals. There are other options. For example, the primatologist Frans de Waal claims that our moral sensibilities inherently favor our in-groups

54. *New Yorker*, June 7, 2010.

55. *Science News*, August 14, 2010, 14.

(our family, our community, our species), indeed, *should* favor them because "loyalty is a moral duty." He goes on to say: "Animal rights advocates sometimes downplay this tension between loyalty and moral inclusion even though their own behavior tells a different story. . . . One cannot silently practice loyalty to the innermost circles (e.g., by accepting for oneself and one's family medical treatments developed on animals) while vocally denying that these circles take priority over other forms of life."[56]

Let me also underscore a slightly different theological point. When we consider ourselves in the context of cosmic ecology and cosmic passage, we see that we humans are intertwined with all other things in a single, universal, and dynamic web of creation with God at its head. We also understand that the distinctive capacities and powers we wield come to us—are bestowed on us—by means of relationships, orderings, and processes at work in God's cosmos. That is, they are *gifts* for which we should be grateful, unless we wish to become cosmic ingrates. Moreover, in our gratitude we quite appropriately feel responsible *to* the giver of these gifts *for* the ways we use them *in* the world that the giver creates and sustains. This brings us full circle to an image I introduced earlier with reference to Genesis 1:28. People are equipped to be stewards or managers of planet Earth, and persons of piety appropriately feel responsible *to* the God who creates and sustains the world *for* their stewardship and their management.

Limitations

We sometimes characterize persons and communities in the modern world as "playing God." This expression has a range of meanings. Sometimes it means that we now have technical capabilities in areas, such as medicine, that our forebears did not, capabilities that alter matters of life and death in ways they regarded as the province of God alone. This seems true enough. Occasionally, the implication is that we have developed the basic powers and capabilities that many traditions classically attributed to God; but this is not, strictly speaking, true. Modern

56. De Waal et al., *Primates and Philosophers*, 165. De Waal's position is quite compatible with the judgment that we have obligations to animals, and that the precise obligations we have toward them depend in part on what we know of their needs, vulnerabilities, and so forth, as well as on just what, in given instances, we are trying to accomplish. One may agree with de Waal and also believe that, in work with nonhuman subjects, we should pay attention to economies of experimental design (and not use more animals than we need to). One may also question whether certain lines of research on animals should be discontinued. (De Waal himself mentions hepatitis C research on chimpanzees.)

humans are, in fact, neither omnipotent nor omniscient. Their quite significant capacities and powers of intervention are also *limited*.

Although we—in modern cultures—are able to alter some things, you and I are largely shaped and constrained by actions and conditions, including aspects of our own biological, psychological, and social makeups, that are in place prior to our actions and efforts. When we do act, we respond to actions, forces, and events that impinge on us. We always act in context. Therefore, as both individuals and communities, we find ourselves in the midst of things, enmeshed in welters of interrelationships, set within dynamic situations made up of forces and conditions, including other agents. Thus, whenever we act, we *inter*act with other agents and realities in the midst of a field of interactions and interrelationships. Of course, once we have acted, our responses are, in turn, deflected and turned, subjected to additional influences and conditions, including the subsequent actions of others. We are contingent beings who are never simply independent, or on our own, and whose actions and interventions depend on prior, present, and subsequent conditions.

When we act, we also draw on distinctive capacities for reflection. We interpret the actions, events, and realities that impinge on us, and we anticipate replies and reactions to our responses. Human agents are responders, and responders are not mere reactors. They draw on interpretive, reflective, and imaginative capacities in order to devise readings or interpretations of the actions, events, and realities that impinge on them; they also draw on these same capacities in order to envision subsequent events and replies to their own actions.[57]

These reflective readings or interpretive visions help guide agents' understandings of the appropriate actions they may take. For example, federal, state, and local government agencies may respond to the devastation caused to the city of New Orleans by Hurricane Katrina in 2005, and to the Eastern Seaboard by Hurricane Sandy in 2012, in accordance with readings of the conditions that bring about such storms, predictive judgments concerning the sort of levee system that will mitigate or prevent severe flooding, and judgments about how to improve plans for emergency relief. Or the European Union may respond to the actions of Iran in accordance with a reading or interpretation of international political circumstances, including Iran's current intentions, and also in accordance with a reading or interpretation of Iran's anticipated replies to different actions the EU might take. Human responders "place" the actions, events, or realities that impinge on them within an interpretation or vision of the context in which they occur and into which their replies may or may not "fit."

57. Here I am drawing on H. Richard Niebuhr's groundbreaking work in *The Responsible Self: An Essay in Christian Moral Philosophy* (Louisville: Westminster John Knox, 1999), 47–68.

Although they may exercise significant influence over events, when persons and communities interact with other agents and realities in continuing and dynamic contexts of interrelationships and conditions, they often do *not* control all relevant outcomes. This is true because outcomes depend on so many factors in addition to their own interventions and intentions. Moreover, our interpretations of conditions—of the multitude of actions, processes, and realities in play—sometimes fail to take into account all relevant factors. No significant human undertaking, from planning a mission to the moon to administering a university, from developing antibiotics to raising a child, is thus without risk, and every significant undertaking eventually may require that we respond to unanticipated occurrences and unintended consequences. Attentive, experienced, and wise persons and communities know these things; nearly every airline passenger does, too, at least in the back of her or his mind. And so does nearly every farmer (not to mention nearly every alert coach, politician, and preschool teacher). In large part, this is what we mean when we say that human powers of intervention, while distinctive and impressive, are also limited. It is also part of the reason why, though capable human agents have weighty and important responsibilities, their responsibilities are not unlimited.

Another reason we recognize that human powers of intervention are limited is that, when we act successfully to bring about particular results, we find ourselves having to cooperate with what we are able to apprehend or discern about how the world is being ordered. Thomas Aquinas had this in mind when he said that, properly speaking, God alone creates; we work with given materials, as when a carpenter fashions a bench out of wood.[58] Or we might say that the sculptor needs to work with and consent to the properties of the marble that he chisels. Aquinas's premodern statement needs to be emended, however, to reflect our more developed abilities to alter important conditions. James Gustafson puts it this way:

> Whether the focus of attention is on human genetics, psychology, or nutrition, the sciences inform us regarding the ordering conditions and laws. While we can, in modern cultures, intervene in these processes to alter them, we still consent to them in a significant measure, cooperating with them as they are given. If a chromosomal defect cannot be corrected, we can consent to it (not merely resign ourselves to it) and participate in the development of a limited natural capacity. If we understand the chemical components that make for high yields of food grains, we consent to that, and we augment the yields by,

58. Aquinas, *ST* 1a.45.2 (pp. 31–34); *The Sermon-Conferences of St. Thomas Aquinas on the Apostles' Creed*, trans. Nicholas Ayo, CSC (Notre Dame: University of Notre Dame Press, 1988), 38–43.

> in a sense, cooperating with the necessary conditions. The conditions both limit possibilities and make possible our cooperation with them for some developments.[59]

Similar things may be said of our abilities to build dependable jets, and so on. We need to design wings, calculate engine thrusts, and the like in accord with what we know about aerodynamics. Hence, not just any kind of wing or any kind of engine will do. This is a limit. But if we cooperate with what we know about aerodynamics, then we can build planes that fly. This is a possibility.

It is worth emphasizing a few points here with some care. People learn much about what it is to be human as they exercise their capacities for intervention in the midst of practical interactions. They learn something of their own distinctive possibilities and limits from the pliability and resistance they encounter in their interactions with animals, plants, rivers, and so on. They also learn that their own capacities for intervention dramatically exceed those of other animals on Earth. And as they interact with other persons and communities, they learn additional things about their possibilities and limits. In all these interrelationships and interactions, then, they learn that they live and move within the margins of significant dependencies, possibilities, limits, vulnerabilities, and risks. Therefore, in a sense, we might say they encounter the human in their practical interactions with persons, animals, plants, and things.

Pretty regularly, however, and especially as their practical encounters are informed by evolutionary biology, sociobiology, and the like, people also learn something more. They learn not only that their field of social interaction extends well beyond the human but also that nonhuman life, ecologies, and so forth exercise capabilities that are at least distant analogues to their own and in the midst of similar (indeed, often the same) dependencies. That is, they encounter in the nonhuman—in their interactions with animals, plants, rivers, and the like—a circumstance like their own, say, in the arduous southern flight of a flock of birds in autumn as they travel to supportive habitats for the winter, or in the care of a lioness for her cubs (see, e.g., Ps. 104). We might say that they encounter not only the human but also the *creaturely* in the midst of their practical interactions. And they see that "the creaturely" is a category that applies not only to other animals, plants, and things but also to themselves. In response, they may (appropriately) feel empathy and solidarity with the nonhuman as well as the human.[60]

59. Gustafson, *ETP*, 1:241.

60. What do we learn about both our humanity and our creatureliness when our actions and interventions destabilize natural conditions and systems on which we and many other creatures depend and then perhaps also provoke new stabilities that may fail to support (at least

In summary, human agents wield significant but also limited powers of intervention. There are important conditions that they sometimes cannot alter. There are also important factors that they sometimes are unable to interpret and envision either adequately or accurately. Moreover, even when they are able to alter situations and realities successfully, their possibilities for doing so continue to depend in some significant measure on their consent to ordering conditions and processes that are given. When these facts are regarded with the aid of images of God as Creator and Provider (or governor) and ourselves as inhabitants of God's world, they underscore what we might call the *secondariness* of human life and action. They encourage persons of piety to see how human powers and responsibilities are limited. And just here, piety also comes across a warrant for a certain quality or manner in our interactions with others: the sense that, for better or worse, persons and communities sometimes are enmeshed in circumstances, conditions, and events beyond their doing and undoing. This is true of oneself as well as of other persons and communities. And this sense of solidarity in contingency (a sensibility that, as I have noted above, may also be extended to other living things), this recognition that none of us is master of his or her own destiny or fate, furnishes a basis for a host of affections—from gratitude, anxiety, and sorrow to sympathy, empathy, joy, and care.

Responsive Participants

As agents enmeshed in conditions and interrelationships, humans respond to actions and influences of other agents and realities that impinge on them. They exercise considerable and distinctive powers of intervention, and they have weighty and distinctive responsibilities, but they hardly control or entirely grasp all that goes on. Strictly speaking, then, at least within the frame of theocentric piety, people apprehend themselves neither as creators nor as cocreators. They

---

with the same facility) humans and some other forms of life? We might say that, in instances such as these, we experience the rebuke of nonhuman nature (though it seems worth pointing out that very often many, if not most, of the deleterious consequences are experienced by nonhuman nature). The pollution of a river and the consequences for fishes and plants is an example. In any case, this is a profound and increasingly common kind of encounter that capable humans have with nonhuman nature. I shall have more to say about this in part 3, when I discuss misdirected human agency, sin, and judgment. Nevertheless, one thing we do learn is that it is not possible to separate nature and humanity—or the nature that is not us from the nature that is us. Such experiences call into question once again "a 'mastering' humanity," and they help us see that "we come to understand ourselves as creatures in the middle of a world of creatures." See Peter Scott, *A Political Theology of Nature* (Cambridge: Cambridge University Press, 2003), 228, 258.

see themselves as situated and responsive participants in cosmic ecology and cosmic passage—or in God's world.

Proposition #39 Created and sustained human life is personal.

I noted earlier that human life is mysterious, partly because, at virtually every point, our lives and actions are dependent on things beyond ourselves that we do not control, and here I want to suggest that the multitude of factors that make possible and shape our lives also indicate that we are particular individuals and persons. Take, for example, the development of our solar system, the genetic sequences of primates, the history and institutional patterns of my society and communities, the decisions of my parents, and my own particular experiences and actions. When I consider my own life, I am aware that all these processes, dependencies, and contingencies—all these particulars, each of which might have been otherwise—contribute to something ineluctably particular that also might have been otherwise, namely, the specific knot of abilities, qualities, limitations, reflections, emotions, tendencies, memories, and anticipations that is me. Each of the processes, dependencies, or contingencies, the sum of which is finally under the control of no particular person, institution, or community, has a hand in the production, the sculpting, of a specific individual, a person. Each contributes to the emergence of a distinctive reality, of something new that was not already present before, namely, a particular person. Theologically speaking, we become the particular individuals we do as we live and move within the wider, impressively intricate and dynamic context of realities, relationships, and conditions that make up cosmic passage.

We Apprehend Ourselves as Persons Narratively

I also noted earlier that this helps to explain our fascination with a good biography or novel. There is something irreducibly particular if also elusive that may emerge in the telling, namely, a rendering of a specific person. It also helps explain a point that has been made by developmental psychologists, such as Erik Erikson. You and I make choices, but neither our choices nor our personal identities are entirely under our own control. As a stage of development, therefore, maturity often calls for the acceptance of oneself and one's life, or a coming to terms with the person one has become via biology, family, community, accident, intentional choices, accomplishments, and unintended consequences.[61] In any

61. For Erikson, this is part and parcel of the difference between integrity and despair. See Erik H. Erikson, *Identity: Youth and Crisis* (New York: Norton, 1968), 139–40.

event, you and I are particular persons and individuals, and we apprehend that we are as we construct, consider, and construe the stories or narratives of the quite specific constellations of realities, circumstances, and events that help to constitute us—and as we come to terms with the persons we have become.

Emphasis on narrative and personal identity is a postmodern commonplace. Years ago, the theological ethicist H. Richard Niebuhr noted the importance of recitals of events for the identities of persons and communities.[62] Among contemporary theologians/ethicists, no one has done more to emphasize and develop this point than has Stanley Hauerwas: "What is required for our moral behavior to contribute to a coherent sense of the self is neither a single moral principle nor a harmony of the virtues, but, as I have already said, the formation of character by a narrative that provides a sufficiently truthful account of our existence."[63]

We Apprehend Ourselves as Persons Practically

We not only apprehend that we are persons *narratively and developmentally*; we also sense it *practically*. We act and—as we have seen in proposition #38 above—we sometimes are able to alter outcomes and to bring about specific consequences. That is, we experience ourselves as agents with powers of intervention, intentions, and purposes in the midst of conditions, situations, and realities. And this experience, in turn, raises the question of responsibility. When I act in ways that help bring about certain consequences and then also recognize that (within limits, no doubt) I might have acted otherwise, I feel responsible, and I realize that others may fairly hold me accountable as well.

Suppose, then, that I am teaching a course at a college. I am aware that I do not control all that happens in the class. Factors over which I have comparatively little control, such as the attitudes and abilities of my students, the ethos of my college, and the library's holdings, also enter in. Even so, I write my own syllabus. I decide which materials my students will read, when and how they will discuss them, what sorts of opportunities they will have for integrating and reflecting on what they read, and so forth. I thus feel a significant measure of responsibility for how the course proceeds and for what my students learn. The point I want to underscore here is precisely that *I* feel that *I* am responsible. As I engage in the

62. H. Richard Niebuhr, "The Story of Our Life," in Niebuhr, *The Meaning of Revelation* (Louisville: Westminster John Knox, 2006), 23–47.

63. Stanley Hauerwas, *A Community of Character: Toward a Constructive Christian Social Ethic* (Notre Dame: University of Notre Dame Press, 1981), 136.

practical business of teaching, I feel that I am a relevant center of decision, intention, purpose, and action. I feel, in short, that I am a *person* who decides, intends, purposes, and acts, and that important features of the course and how it proceeds may thus relevantly be laid to my account. Similar things may be said about my regard for the intentional acts of others. Partly because of my experience of my own powers of intervention, and partly because the intentional and purposive actions of others—such as my students—sometimes limit, augment, and deflect my powers of intervention, I assume—and indeed often feel—that they are also persons. I assume and feel that they also are relevant centers of decision, intention, purpose, and action, and that at least some consequences and occurrences that flow from what they do may properly be laid to their accounts.

All of this is to say that, in our practical experiences, our intentional actions and interactions sometimes make us feel responsible, and responsibility, in turn, underscores the fact that we are more or less centered persons who fairly may be held responsible. Or, put more simply, our experience of agency implies personality.

Here, again, we run across a bit of general wisdom concerning human life and experience in the world that comes to expression in the Bible, though it is not exclusively biblical:

> Thus says the Lord:
> For three transgressions of Israel,
>   and for four, I will not revoke the punishment;
> because they sell the righteous for silver,
>   and the needy for a pair of sandals—
> they who trample the head of the poor into the dust of the earth.
> (Amos 2:6–7a)

According to this oracle of the prophet Amos, God holds Israel responsible as a community of personal agents—or of relevant centers of decision, intention, purpose, and action—who might have done otherwise. In fact, at some level, the assumption that humans are responsible agents or centered persons who choose seems basic to the very idea of covenant. Therefore, after having commanded Moses to present the law and make a covenant with the Israelites, the Lord says through Moses in Deuteronomy 30:19: “I call heaven and earth to witness against you today that I have set before you life and death, blessings and curses. Choose life so that you and your descendants may live.”[64]

64. Walther Eichrodt, for whom covenant was the basic element of Old Testament theology, claims that, in the Hebrew concept, the covenant, a gift of God’s grace, is a two-sided

A similar idea plays a critical role in Immanuel Kant's philosophical ethics. Kant maintains that humans are autonomous agents. This is why he writes that, in politics and morality, we should use neither ourselves nor other persons as mere means to our subjective ends. "Act always so that you treat humanity whether in your person or in that of another always as an end, and never as a means only."[65] Indeed, the twentieth-century Christian ethicist Albert C. Knudson associates this particular formulation of Kant's categorical imperative with the affirmation of the sacredness of personality, an idea that Knudson also took to be the ground for the ideal of brotherly love.[66] So did Martin Luther King Jr.[67]

We Apprehend Ourselves as Persons in the Midst of Encounters

We should note that encounters with others sometimes disclose personality. We understand *existentially* that we are persons in the midst of meetings with others. The Hasidic philosopher Martin Buber makes this point most forcefully. Buber maintains that living relationship is the fundamental fact of human existence. It is, he claims, only when we step into I-Thou relations—or relationships characterized by mutuality, directness, presentness, intensity, and ineffability—that we become conscious of ourselves as persons. This is how I can directly know what is special to me. Indeed, for Buber, "it is only within this relation," says one commentator, "that personality and the personal really exist."[68] Thus do mutuality and reciprocity serve as "the door into our existence," or into our genuine appreciation for our own personal existence, though "full mutuality is not inherent in men's life together." It is not something we can guarantee or produce in a

---

relationship that lays claim to the whole person and calls for a human contribution. In the terms I am developing here, it thus assumes that humans are responsible agents or persons. The covenant, says Eichrodt, expresses the divine will or the divine demand, and it calls for obedience and a readiness to submit. It is "bound up with certain conditions," even if, as the concept develops over time, God will not allow God's sovereign benevolence "to be vitiated, however great man's faithlessness might be" (Eichrodt, *Theology of the Old Testament*, trans. J. A. Baker [Philadelphia: Westminster, 1961], 1:37–44, 457, 458).

65. *Kant's Political Writings*, trans. H. B. Nisbet, edited and introduced by Hans Reiss (Cambridge: Cambridge University Press, 1970), 18–19.

66. Albert C. Knudson, *The Principles of Christian Ethics* (New York: Abingdon-Cokesbury, 1933), 78–79, 132.

67. *A Testament of Hope: The Essential Writings and Speeches of Martin Luther King, Jr.*, ed. James M. Washington (New York: HarperOne, 1991), 118–19.

68. Martin Buber, *The Knowledge of Man: A Philosophy of the Interhuman*, trans. Maurice Friedman and Ronald Gregor Smith, edited and introduced by Maurice Friedman (New York: Harper & Row, 1965), 12.

surefire way by effort or manipulation. “It is a grace, for which one must always be ready and which one never gains as an assured possession.”

True mutuality, Buber says, may emerge via the relationship of a genuine educator with her student, provided the educator meets the student again and again as her partner in relationship, and provided she does not know the student as a “sum of mere qualities, strivings, and inhibitions,” but is aware of “him as a whole being” and affirms “him in his wholeness.” Not that Buber restricts to humans alone the Thou of the “I-Thou” relationship we enter into. Thous may also include animals and objects of nature. A tree, in its living wholeness, may hence deny itself to “the mere investigator” but disclose itself “to the glance” of one who steps into relationship with the tree as Thou.[69]

We should note, therefore, that for Buber it is possible to have a personal relationship with a nonpersonal reality—a tree, mountain, countryside, or the panoply of stars in the night sky—a point that will be important when we consider ways in which we apprehend and articulate our relationship with God. However, what I should emphasize here is Buber's fundamental claim: I may be afforded the apprehension of myself as self, as person, or as I in the midst of compelling relationships with persons or things as thous, or as whole, unified, and reciprocal beings. This, he insists, is simply fundamental and basic to human life and existence. It is not the terminus of an argument but a report of what we may experience. Is it also an element, assumption, or presupposition of covenantal thinking? Might it also be, as Buber himself occasionally says, an assumption or presupposition of love?[70]

There is also a related point. In our interactions and relationships with others, the reality of *their* persons is sometimes disclosed to *us*. I sense, in my meetings and encounters with another person, that I am in the presence of a centered agent or a self who is more than a list of qualities, parts, and characteristics. I sense the person—or even what we sometimes call her or his spirit. Who someone is may be unthinkable apart from attending to parts and influences, particular characteristics and conditions that contribute to his or her identity, but his or her person does not reduce to these things. The whole person is more than a sum of parts, and this occasionally comes through in our living and emotionally resonant relationships. No doubt, this is less a matter of science than of sensibility. But think of a good friend, a parent, or a spouse who is no longer living. You and I sometimes say that a particular action or expression is “just like” him or her. What do we

69. Martin Buber, *I and Thou*, trans. Ronald Gregor Smith (New York: Scribner's Sons, 1958), 131, 126.

70. Maurice Friedman, *Martin Buber: The Life of Dialogue*, 3rd rev. ed. (Chicago: University of Chicago Press, 1976), 49, 138.

mean when we say this, and how does the acknowledgment feel? Might it not awaken in us an inkling of the person, a sense of the embodied and centered self we once encountered, and who, while brought to mind by a specific gesture or act, nevertheless cannot be reduced to a bundle of specific acts and gestures?

The sense of a person that I am suggesting here is admittedly fragile. It may be neglected, and one wonders whether, especially in some modern contexts, it is not quite regularly suppressed. In any case, whether it emerges through an appreciation for mystery and story, experiences of practical responsibility, or existential encounters, it departs from a merely technical sensibility that reduces all experiences and realities to a single, calculable, and utilitarian surface. It entails passions and emotions that often seem out of place in the cool, empty world of entirely instrumental, means-ends reasoning. Quaintly and even hauntingly, but nonetheless quite definitely, it rejects the iron cage of a merely technical empiricism in favor of a suppler and less manipulable attentiveness to the depths of life and experience. And this is why, though in many ways a sense of the person may be as ordinary as your next conversation, it also seems appropriately associated with the reflections of a Hasidic mystic.[71]

Persons before God

We can summarize these reflections by paying attention to Psalm 139:

> O Lord, you have searched me and known me. . . .
>
> Where can I go from your spirit?
> Or where can I flee from your presence?
> If I ascend to heaven, you are there;
> if I make my bed in Sheol, you are there.
> If I take the wings of the morning
> and settle at the farthest limits of the sea. . . .
>
> For it was you who formed my inward parts;
> you knit me together in my mother's womb.
> I praise you, for I am fearfully and wonderfully made. . . .

71. "Genuine conversation, and therefore every actual fulfillment of relation between men, means acceptance of otherness. . . . Opposed to this effort is the lust to make use of men by which the manipulator of 'propaganda' and 'suggestion' is possessed. . . . Human life and humanity come into being in genuine meetings" (Buber, *The Knowledge of Man*, 69).

These verses portray the psalmist's sense of self as creature, of being fashioned in and enveloped by the deep mystery of the God who creates. The writer develops theological reflections "in the sphere of the reality of God in which he sees his whole life to be embedded."[72] The person of the psalmist finds that he is always already in the presence of God. And this relationship, from which he cannot escape, signals the constancy and depth of his sense that he is a person before God; God is always standing in relationship to him already.

At another and related level, this is also just the point driven home by the literary form of the psalm. The psalm is an address, and thus it presupposes a person who addresses an Other. It is a prayer, and so it presupposes a person, a particular and more or less centered self who prays to an Other. It presupposes a speaker, a personal creature capable of directing words and thoughts to an Other. "God is Thou to the psalmist's I. The psalmist speaks about self by speaking to God and speaks about God by speaking as a self. God and self are thus inextricably the subject of the psalmist's language."[73]

A similar point comes to poignant expression in the longer theological tradition, especially among Augustinian theologians. Consider Anselm's *Proslogion*, in which he famously presents his ontological argument for the existence of God. The title of the treatise is "An Address," and, among other things, the text itself is in significant part a personal address to God. Like Psalm 139, it is really almost in the form of a prayer. "And so, O Lord, since thou givest understanding to faith, give me to understand—as far as thou knowest it to be good for me—that thou dost exist, as we believe, and that thou art what we believe thee to be." Indeed, Anselm began his treatise by quoting (inexactly) Psalm 27:8: "I seek thy face; thy face, Lord, do I desire," and the reference here to a face-to-face encounter expresses the personal and relational tone of much of what Anselm writes.[74]

The affirmation is clearly also fundamental with respect to theological ethics. For persons of piety, God stands in relationship to human beings, and human beings are persons of dignity and worth because they stand in personal relationship with God. This relational and theological inkling of the ineluctably personal is something both "prior to" and "independent of" whatever status and rights governments may or may not confer upon people. And it points to a fundamental conviction: all human government is limited government, called

72. Arthur Weiser, *The Psalms*, trans. Herbert Hartwell (Philadelphia: Westminster, 1962), 801–2.

73. James L. Mays, *Psalms*, Interpretation: A Bible Commentary for Teaching and Preaching (Louisville: John Knox, 1994), 427.

74. Fairweather, *A Scholastic Miscellany*, 73, 70.

on to recognize and acknowledge something that is given, namely, the value of the human person, which it does not control and should not manipulate.

Proposition #40 Created and sustained human life is historical.

People of piety recognize that created and sustained humans who are social, capable, responsible, and personal also are radically situated within a web of circumstances, interrelationships, agents, and events. They are aware that while they are agents equipped with significant powers of intervention, neither individuals nor communities are able to control all relevant outcomes. They acknowledge feelings of uncertainty and risk that accompany virtually every human action and project—from raising a child to leading an army.

Perceived risk and uncertainty are evoked by experiences of changing conditions, processes, and interrelationships, as well as of the unanticipated actions of others that often impact our own lines of activity and thus shape our own possibilities and limits. A young woman decides to attend Davidson College, but she can neither know nor accurately anticipate just who her classmates will be, precisely which professors she will study with, or the exact financial condition of the college during her time there—and just how these factors will influence the course of her education. The citizens of a nation, even of a quite powerful one, cannot know just how the welter of geological, oceanic, climatic, geopolitical, and global economic circumstances and events will limit or enhance their country's possibilities. Both students and nations clearly are able, at least within the limits of their knowledge and capabilities, to respond and adapt to changing conditions. They can influence their futures to some degree, but they are keenly aware that they cannot determine them.

For creation piety, our activities and interventions are enclosed within cosmic passage and its countless dynamic processes, interrelationships, structures, and occurrences. On the one hand, this means that past processes and events profoundly shape our present possibilities and limits (though the ways in which we respond to what we are given are also influenced by just how we interpret the past and envision the future). At the same time, however, our "embeddedness" in cosmic passage is a basis for the sense that our ongoing personal, social, economic, political, and environmental interactions are unfinished and significantly—if not also largely—unpredictable. This, too, is part of what it means for persons of piety to say that created and sustained human life is historical. Thus, where conditions and events change in ways that are favorable and sustaining, for example, by means of a medical intervention or a new political movement, we have existential and experiential bases for feelings of thanksgiving and gratitude. Of course, it also follows that the contingent, unfinished, and largely unpredictable character of history forms an existential and experiential basis for anxieties and insecurities on the part of both individuals and communities.

This much seems tolerably clear, I think, from what I have already said about human life, cosmic ecology, and cosmic passage. Capable persons, communities, and institutions are able to investigate, interpret, respond, and influence, and thus they are not simply set adrift without resources. Even so, they are hardly in control, and pretty often they may feel as if they are largely along for the ride. But now it is time to note something further: the unfinished and humanly unmanageable dimensions of history can also be existential and experiential bases for the *hope* that currently destructive, oppressive, and unjust structures and conditions may be changed, and that we may be afforded opportunities to participate in a different and more positive circumstance. No human power, no matter how venerable or ancient, is eternal; within the purview of cosmic passage, all are subject to change at the behest of circumstances, agents, processes, and events beyond their control. Accordingly, Rome may be called Babylon, and while there clearly are multiple meanings to this striking apocalyptic image, we should not miss the hope expressed in Revelation 18, when the present power is symbolized by a past and fallen empire.

A realistic assessment of human capacities for intervention—as well as their limits—can contribute to reformist and even revolutionary commitments. For, if it is true that those in dependent and oppressed conditions wield genuine though limited powers and hence cannot determine their own futures, it is also true that, within the purview of cosmic passage, very powerful structures, classes, communities, and regimes do not control all relevant outcomes. In addition, there is the perennial and significant tendency of grossly unjust and inhumane circumstances to provoke revulsion, denunciation, and opposition among individuals and groups.

Robin W. Lovin notes that, on this score, the Christian realism of Reinhold Niebuhr and others was sometimes caught up short, and perhaps even degenerated into an unwarranted pessimism about possibilities for change.

> Any assessment of the social situation that does not take hope into account is unrealistic, and it will eventually experience the disconfirmation that comes to all unrealistic expectations, whether the expectations are set too high, or—as in this case—too low. . . . On the basis of twentieth-century realism's estimates, we should still be waiting for the end of legal segregation, especially in those parts of the country where it was honored by long custom and local expectations had adjusted to it. Martin Luther King's crusade should have stalled out against massive white resistance. The "velvet revolution" at the end of the 1980s should have been crushed, as was the earlier uprising in Hungary in the

1950s. The Berlin Wall should not have fallen, and Nelson Mandela would in all likelihood have died in prison.[75]

As it is shaped and expressed by the theology presented here, piety's hope for something different and better often combines two things: a sense for the unfinished, contingent, and humanly unmanageable character of history within the dynamics of cosmic passage, and an awareness of the persistent disjunction between grossly destructive, unjust, and oppressive circumstances and generally distributed senses of fairness, solidarity, and responsibility. Indeed, as I have noted, the persistent disjunction makes for right revulsions and outrage that can become bases for critical denunciations and negations of what is, as well as for imaginative visions of what may be. This is a socially critical and hopeful dimension of theological humanism. Hope is born of the recognition of unmanageable process and passage, plus moral revulsion or negation, plus the suggestion that, as capable and responsible agents, we may find ourselves equipped both to pursue and participate in better possibilities and states of affairs.[76]

Proposition #41 The chief end, calling, or vocation of created and sustained human beings in the midst of cosmic ecology and passage is to participate in true communion with God in community with others.

The well-known first question of the Westminster Shorter Catechism, when the language is updated, reads as follows: "What is the chief end of the human being?

75. Robin W. Lovin, "Christian Realism: A Legacy and Its Future," *Annual of the Society of Christian Ethics* 20 (2000): 14.

76. I shall return to questions of social criticism and hope in part 3—with the help of a doctrine of sin, as well as christological and eschatological resources. But allow me to make a note here of some agreements and disagreements between this position and Rubem Alves's some years ago in *A Theology of Human Hope*. Alves describes a divine politics of liberation in which suffering and hope born of negation are integral to a dialectical thrust toward a new future in a history of creation that remains unfinished. He complains that Jürgen Moltmann's God of the future makes for too much discontinuity with history. He also rejects "the autonomy of human activity" that grounds "the hope of humanistic humanism" in favor of a possibility for human action created by grace (Rubem Alves, *A Theology of Human Hope* [St. Meinrad, IN: Abbey, 1975], 143–44). My understanding of human agency, moral sensibility, and cosmic passage supports Alves's criticism of Moltmann as well as his recognition of the importance of negation for hope and his rejection of autonomous human activity as the ground for hope. Somewhat similar to Alves, I look to the divine dynamism to furnish possibilities for human activity. But whereas Alves speaks of humans as cocreators in cooperation with God to bring about the future, I picture persons and communities as distinctively capable, responsible, situated, and limited participants in the midst of history and cosmic passage.

The chief end of the human being is to glorify God and enjoy God forever." John Calvin's Geneva Catechism opens similarly: "What is the chief end of human life? To know God."[77]

We Pursue Ends

What these questions and answers mean will become clearer if we recall that humans are responsible agents. Although we neither anticipate nor control all relevant circumstances and outcomes, we nevertheless exercise distinctive powers of intervention in conjunction with our emotional constitutions and our capacities for interpretation and reflection. We respond intentionally to other people, realities, and events. We make plans and undertake projects. We pursue goals and objectives. We act purposefully to alter conditions and to pursue particular ends.

Suppose I purchase a train ticket for a trip to see a friend. Although I generally enjoy train rides, I value this one largely as a means of transportation that enables me to visit my friend. Were there to be a drop in airplane fares or the price of gasoline, I might travel by air or by car. The visit is the end I had in mind when I compared prices, phoned Amtrak reservations, and woke up early enough to catch the 6:30 train. Or, looking at it another way: I may want—and also, within a specific social frame of reference, need—money, and thus may go to some lengths to obtain it, such as getting and keeping a job. More likely than not, however, the money is not itself the end or objective in which my desire comes to rest. I want or need money *for* something else, somewhat like wanting or needing a train ticket in order to visit my friend. Money is a subordinate end, something I value and aim at, not on its own account but on account of further ends, such as supporting my family or gaining social prestige.

Someone might say, on the above evidence, that I am the kind of person who buys train tickets and holds a job. These statements would be true enough, but they would neglect more basic ends (for example, visiting a friend, supporting my family) that disclose deeper wants, needs, loyalties, and desires. They would miss the more fundamental ends that disclose my purposeful patterns of activity or even my practical orientation in life.

In any case, the ends we pursue are many, and they reveal what we care about; they disclose our purposes and trajectories in life. They are variously related,

77. The Shorter Catechism, in *BOC* 7.001; *Our Confessional Heritage: Confessions of the Reformed Tradition with a Contemporary Declaration of Faith* (Atlanta: Materials Distribution Service of the PCUSA, 1978), 19.

and some seem more basic than others in the sense that they are especially important to us and more nearly define our orientations and practical stances. When the catechisms ask, "What is the *chief* end of human life?" they are asking whether there is an overall end, aim, or pursuit that defines—indeed, should define—the orientation, stance, and trajectory of human life. Similarly, as the American essayist and poet Wendell Berry asks, "What are people for?" Berry asks his question in the interesting, biblically inspired context of reflections on farming, agribusiness, the dignity of human employment, and our responsibility as stewards.[78] The classical catechisms put their question even more generally: What is the ultimate end that human life serves or should serve? What is human life for?

We should also be clear at the outset that the answers the classic catechisms give do not reduce people to mere means. Why? Because the chief end of glorifying and enjoying God forever is one in which people participate. Once we understand that by "knowing God" Calvin meant an existential understanding of a relationship with the divine that neither falters nor fails, we recognize that the same thing is also true of the answer to the opening question of the Geneva Catechism. My train ticket is indeed merely a means to the end of my visit with my friend; it does not participate in my visit itself. I might be able to exchange it for a plane ticket, and I will certainly discard it once my journey is done. Hence my train ticket does not relate to my visit with my friend in the same way that the catechism understands people to relate to the chief end of knowing, glorifying, and enjoying God. The closer analogy is between my friend's relationship to our visit and the relationship of people to the chief end of glorifying God. My friend is not merely instrumental to our visit; he participates in it and helps to constitute it.

Now for another layer of meaning. The chief end of human life signals a fitting occupation because it indicates not only a goal but also an appropriate activity or participatory practice. It points to a calling or vocation for which humans are suited. We have already reviewed some characteristics of human life that, theologically speaking, indicate the calling or vocation for which we are suited. For one thing, as I noted in proposition #35 above, human life does not explain itself. It raises the question of *whence*. It implies and points to Something More, and so the vocation for which we are suited will presumably also reflect this reference. As we saw in proposition #36, the "givenness" of human life suggests that life is a blessing or a gift that we share with other creatures, and this recognition, in turn, is "doxology-evoking." It disposes humans toward willing praise and service. The catechisms thus claim that the ultimate calling of the human includes a doxolog-

78. Wendell Berry, *What Are People For?* (New York: Farrar, Straus & Giroux, 1990), 123–25.

ical dimension. Humans are socially inclined and sustained. They are, as we saw in proposition #37, emotionally suited for social relationships and interactions in communities of loyalty and moral concern. They are sustained by certain basic institutions, and, within these institutions, they undertake specific practices, obligations, responsibilities, and roles. Moreover, as I observed in proposition #39, humans are persons, and persons exist in genuine meetings, encounters, and relationships. The catechisms thus conclude that the chief vocation of humans entails fundamental encounters and relationships.

In summary, the classical catechisms ask not only whether there is a final goal but also whether there is an ultimate occupation, role, or vocation appropriate to mysterious, given, doxology-evoking, social, and personal human life. They ask whether there is a general human calling that gathers up and encompasses our many other responsible relationships, roles, and activities. They ask whether there is something we either are doing or should be doing in all of our many doings. They answer that there is, and they specify this chief calling or vocation as participation in a perduring relationship with the divine—or as the knowing, glorifying, and enjoying of God.

Our Chief End and Calling in the Midst of Cosmic Ecology and Passage

At this point, then, we ask the question of the classical catechisms: "What is the chief end and calling of human life?" We ask it primarily with reference to the world as creation and God as creator. What are humans for when they are envisioned and understood in relationship to the God who creates and provides? Our answer at this juncture will be largely a function of the basic understanding that humans are distinctive creatures set within the vast cosmic ecology and passage, its subsystems, and its lines of development. In the present age at least, the gift of human life is particularly an opportunity or even an invitation to participate distinctively within the geological-evolutionary-historical sequence of things on Earth.

What is the chief end and vocation of human life? My own answer is: "To participate in true communion with God in community with others." There are important similarities and differences between this answer and the classical answers, though I expect many of those similarities and differences may be subtler than they first appear. It is true, for example, that the phrase "true communion with God in community with others" is more explicitly social than "glorifying God and enjoying God forever," or than "knowing God." Nevertheless, like my preferred phrase, the classical answers clearly suggest that created and sustained humans are suited for relationship with God, and if we ask what kind of a life glorifies God and reflects genuine knowledge of God, we begin to move into the realm of society and ethics. I contend that people who are in "true communion with God" also "know" God in the existential sense that Calvin appears to have in mind at the beginning of the Geneva Catechism and also at the beginning of his *Institutes of the Christian Religion*. Those people stand within a worshipful community or congregation, and in so doing they also stand in a personal and worshipful relationship to God that involves a distinctively human appreciation for the excellence of the Creator, or the deep source and ordering power on which creation depends. Moreover—and in ways that accord with the substance of the Westminster Shorter Catechism—true communion with God intimates doxology because it indicates participation in a worshipful *congregation* of all things that is occupied with both the praise and the enjoyment of the deity.

Nonetheless, it is also true that the more explicitly social tenor of the phrase "true communion with God in community with others" picks up some important biblical emphases. "I shall be your God and you shall be my people": the idea of covenant points to our dual relationship with God and with companions. Covenant with God establishes community. Just as God's relationship to self and to others is a matter of faithfulness, so the connections and relationships among humans under God become a matter of keeping faith with others before God.[79]

H. Richard Niebuhr has noted that many commandments in the portion of Exodus sometimes called "the Book of the Covenant" link loyalty to God with loyalty to neighbors and companions. The link is apparent, he said, "in the characteristic concern for the weak and distressed. Foreigners, widows, orphans, the poor, and even animals in distress are to be the objects of a human care that is demanded in the name of justice." Furthermore, "the seventh day of rest is to be observed not for reasons of ritual but 'that your ox and your ass

79. One thing it means, in a number of Protestant traditions, is to regard marriage as a covenantal relationship of mutual help and care. Indeed, the "vow and covenant" binds married persons in a "life together," and the language of the vows themselves indicates that they are mutual promises to be faithful and loving partners. The language quoted comes from the "Order for the Solemnization of Marriage," in *The Book of Common Worship* (Philadelphia: Publication Division of the Board of Christian Education of the PCUSA, 1946), 184, 187, and is similar to language found in "The Form of Solemnization of Matrimony," in *The Book of Common Prayer according to the Use of the Protestant Episcopal Church in the United States of America* (New York: Harper & Brothers, 1952), 303. The mutual promise is clearly articulated in "Christian Marriage: Rite I," in *The Book of Common Worship* (Louisville: Westminster John Knox, 1993), 845–46.

may have rest, and the son of your bondmaid, and the alien may be refreshed'" (Exod. 23:12). Therefore, "ritual and justice in the courts, Sabbath observance, and economic practices are all parts of one common life in a community consisting of man, his neighbors, and the Deity, bound together in mutual duties and obligations."[80] There is, in addition, the matter of what the story of God's covenant with Noah, every living creature, and the earth itself may contribute to our sense of keeping faith with others. In any case, however, the general point is fundamental. When understood as "true communion with God in community with others," the chief end and calling of the human being has an explicit social and ethical dimension.

We may also note that true communion with God in community with others is part and parcel of knowing ourselves as creatures, or as persons who stand in relationship with the Creator precisely as members of creation or cosmic ecology. To know oneself as a creature, then, is to know oneself in relation to God the Creator and as a participant in a wider whole. Once again, Wendell Berry makes a trustworthy guide: "The more coherent one becomes within oneself as a creature, the more fully one enters into the communion of all creatures."[81] This is worth emphasizing. Within the geological-evolutionary-historical sequence on Earth, humans are creatures equipped to participate distinctively in interrelationships with one another and with nonhuman life-forms and realities, whether these interrelationships are characterized by active interventions, mutual faithfulness, or an almost aesthetic quality of attention and appreciation. At the same time, humans within this sequence are also equipped to offer the deity a distinctive form of worship and praise keyed to a sense for the excellence of God and the world.

Community with others is not only a matter of our sense of our shared contingency and dependence, or the realization that we are all in the same boat and, at least at some levels, similarly vulnerable. The consequences of our actions and interventions for other persons and things also contribute to our understanding that we are linked together in a common web of *inter*relationships and *inter*actions. Feelings of connectivity and community also emerge in meetings and encounters where we apprehend persons, animals, and plants in their integrity and wholeness. Again, as I have noted in chapter 3, proposition #29, and in proposition #37 above, feelings of connectedness and linkage sometimes accompany an appreciation for the compelling ensemble of a landscape or the beauty of a nighttime sky. With respect to our communion with God and the question of

80. Waldo Beach and H. Richard Niebuhr, eds., *Christian Ethics: Sources of the Living Tradition* (New York: Ronald, 1955), 20–21.

81. Berry, *What Are People For?*, 11.

how the worship and praise offered by humans is both typical of creatures and distinctively human, consider the literary composition we call Psalm 148, where sun and moon, mountains, cedars, wild animals, cattle, birds, and people are all invited to praise God. In the psalmist's world it is *creaturely* to be invited to praise God; but among creatures on Earth it is distinctively *human* to write a psalm of praise and to observe all things praising God.

The end or calling of true communion with God in community with others indicates piety's sense that, as created and sustained participants, we humans are *ec-centric.*[82] We are selves whose conscious identities develop in the midst of social meetings and relationships, and so we are appropriately oriented not merely toward ourselves but also toward others and toward an Other. We are agents who regularly interact with others. We are appreciators (scientists, artists, contemplators, musers, and what have you) who take in things beyond ourselves. Our creaturely equipment and circumstance endow us with capacities for attentiveness and interrelationship within situations and contexts that are not centered on us. This is a part of what is at stake in the idea that we humans are equipped and called to be *stewards* of God's earth rather than simply to possess it as an item whose worth is exhausted by our own purposes, ends, and designs. As a designation of our chief end and vocation, the phrase "true communion with God in community with others" emphasizes the *relationship* and *adjustment* of persons and communities to realities beyond themselves. It is intended to express and also shape piety's feeling for ourselves as creatures or members of the encompassing society of creation, a sense that turns us toward the universal community of things with God at its head.

How We Participate in the Wider Cosmos

I have noted earlier, however, that this encompassing society, this cosmos in which we find ourselves, is incredibly vast. It contains virtually countless lines of development in addition to the geological-evolutionary-historical sequence of things on Earth. We are, of course, still learning about this. For example, recently developed methods allow us to detect many more planets orbiting other stars than we were able to detect previously, and additional methods of detection will probably be developed in the future. There is much about our cosmic context that we do not yet know, perhaps much that humans shall never know. Still, we do know that a number of cosmic venues and events, such as the development

82. This is the major theme of David H. Kelsey, *Eccentric Existence: A Theological Anthropology*, 2 vols. (Louisville: Westminster John Knox, 2009).

of our sun and meteor showers, are rather directly implicated in the conditions that have made possible the particular sequence on Earth in which we participate. We also know that many cosmic phenomena are almost incredibly distant. Thus, if it sometimes seems difficult to speak of the chief end and vocation for which humans are suited within the geological-evolutionary-historical sequence on Earth—and it does—it is considerably more difficult to identify the chief end and vocation for which humans are suited within this vastly wider context. How may we think of ourselves as participating distinctively in true communion and community within *that* frame of reference?

When it comes to the cosmos as a whole, the idea of humans as stewards or managers—an idea entirely appropriate with respect to Earth—seems misplaced. Given the vast distances and time frames of cosmic ecology and passage, it is difficult to see how individual humans, human societies, or even the entire human species may intervene significantly and influentially in vast portions of the creation. We may manage, sculpt, adjust, and enhance particular societies and ecosystems on Earth, for example, by making high-quality health care more broadly available or by monitoring patterns of development and water usage in arid terrains. We may alter the ecosystem of our planet as a whole by precipitating global warming from carbon emissions or by engineering a cooler Earth via carbon dioxide removal. We may even impact geological and chemical developments on other objects and planets in nearby space by way of our rockets, probes, radio waves, and so on. It thus seems clear that, among other things, our chief end and vocation entails an active responsibility and care for significant ecologies and contexts. But it is difficult to see just what our distinctive powers of intervention might ever mean for stars and planets in very far-off galaxies. An Associated Press story of October 21, 2010, notes the claim of astronomers associated with the Paris Observatory that a small smudge in a photo taken by the Hubble Space Telescope may be the image of a galaxy from 13.1 billion years ago, a time when the universe was just 600 million years old. What's more, the astronomers believe that, by this time, it has probably already merged into bigger neighbors.[83]

All of this suggests that, when we consider cosmic realities located rather decisively beyond the geological-evolutionary-historical sequence on Earth, our chief end, purpose, or calling to participate in true communion with God in community with others seems less a matter of our distinctive powers of intervention and more a matter of our distinctive capacities for appreciating the vast cosmos in which we have a place and a time. To an extent, this suggestion

83. Seth Borenstein, "Astronomers Say They've Found Oldest Galaxy Yet," *Charlotte Observer*, October 21, 2010.

fits with the classical theme of the human as microcosm: we "take in" a larger field of events, relationships, and realities (the macrocosm), and so become a microcosmic representation or appropriation of things. That is, humans stand in community with creation as they appreciate and take in features of the cosmos beyond themselves, perhaps also realizing that there are further reaches of the cosmos that will always remain mysterious to us and beyond our reach. In doing so, humans also find themselves in true communion with God.

We should also note, however, that the microcosm theme has sometimes been presented in an egregiously anthropocentric way. For example, the conservative Roman Catholic Peter Kreeft says: "When we offer ourselves to God, we offer up the whole universe in our body, for our body is a 'microcosm,' a little cosmos, the universe in miniature." Kreeft integrates that idea, in turn, with the idea that we are "the priests of the whole creation." Indeed, since "we are the bridge between matter and spirit," which is a somewhat Teilhardian thought, "nature becomes humanized in us." Then, as the pivotal point of all things, "we become divinized in Christ." This understanding of the microcosm theme is compatible with the claim that the human creature, or the part of creation who asks the question about the purpose of creation, is itself the very point and purpose of creation. "The galaxies are only the stage, the setting for the play; we are the actors." Or again: "Human nature is the best of all God's creations. . . . The worth of a single human being is more than that of all the galaxies."[84]

In my view, this last point is misplaced and misleading. Are we presented with choices where this is the issue? Moreover, what if we were? If we say that a single human is worth more than all the galaxies, aren't we saying that she or he is worth more than the very galaxy of which she or he is a part, and without which she or he would not exist? Are we thus saying that, at least in some sense, she or he is worth more than herself or himself? Might we also be saying that, if there are other intelligent and feeling (perhaps even humanlike) life-forms elsewhere, this one person is necessarily worth more than all of them? I am puzzled about why we would find it necessary to make determinations such as these. Perhaps I could be persuaded that we must if I were convinced that we alone are the fulcrum and the priests of all creation. But I'm not.

By contrast, the theocentric piety I mean to explore here emphasizes that we humans take in and appreciate features of a cosmos that we participate in but that is not centered on us. Therefore, I do not say that we humans take in the whole or entire cosmos; indeed, I consider that highly unlikely. Neither do I say that humans alone are necessarily the sole species equipped to take in, appreciate,

84. Peter Kreeft, *Catholic Christianity: A Complete Catechism of Catholic Beliefs Based on the* Catechism of the Catholic Church (San Francisco: Ignatius, 2001), 58–59, 53, 57.

or represent significant dimensions of the cosmos. I am comfortable with the affirmation that other creatures are also equipped to offer up and return praise to God. Indeed, I think Psalm 148 says as much. I am also quite comfortable with the idea that there may be creatures that offer up and return praise in ways that, when compared with our own, seem similarly extensive and microcosmic. Who knows? Perhaps when compared with theirs, our ways of returning praise will seem less encompassing.

So, compared to Kreeft's theology, my understanding of "true communion with God in community with others" clearly *displaces* humans from the center of things. But I should hasten to emphasize that it also *repositions* them as good creatures with distinctive capacities in God's world. It repositions humans not as the point of everything or even as the exclusive priests of the entire cosmos, but as distinctive and worthy *participants* who, in the providence of God, are called to take up a covering purpose and vocation that orient them toward compelling and worthy realities that extend beyond themselves.

Living in the Face of Mystery

One last note. Similar to expressions such as "knowing God" and "the glory of God," the phrase "true communion with God in community with others" points to a vague and not entirely comprehensible reality. Who can fully know or comprehend the deity who "dwells in unapproachable light, whom no one has ever seen or can see" (1 Tim. 6:16)? We do not comprehend everything about the deity with whom we are in communion. We also do not entirely understand the many objects, interrelationships, and realities that make up the cosmic passage or community of all creation.

This is as it should be. When we consider it in the frame of theocentric piety, it is appropriate that created and sustained human life—life that refers beyond itself and finally does not explain itself—be lived toward a reality that it does not entirely comprehend and that can be described only symbolically and vaguely. In part 3 of this present system, as I explore the human fault, I will emphasize that, when persons and communities believe that they comprehend the ultimate point and purpose of life entirely and without ambiguity, they become caught up in idolatry. They fall victim to the conviction that their own particular and partial understanding and representation of this chief end and purpose is entirely adequate and right, and that all other understandings are either deficient or simply wrong. Those familiar with the history of human religious, moral, and political convictions will recognize that a train of deleterious consequences often follows, a train that often does significant and even violent harm to genuine community and care. For now, I simply note that when, in piety, created and sustained life is oriented appropriately toward an ultimate reality that remains incomprehensible, it becomes a journey into the Real, a living in the face of mystery.

Chapter Six

God the Creator

We turn now to a discussion of God as Creator and Provider in relationship with the world as creation and ourselves as creatures. The words "in relationship" are crucial: the task here is not to speak of God or the divine nature as it is or may be "in itself," but only as persons of piety understand the divine in conjunction with their interactions with things. The phrase "the world as creation and ourselves as creatures" is also important because our focus here is on the deity in relationship to the cosmic ecology and passage as well as to ourselves as distinctive participants in it. Further statements about God in relationship to humans as sinners and the world as it is subject to the consequences of human corruption will come in part 3, as will statements about God in relationship to the world and ourselves as renewed beneficiaries of redeeming grace.

Proposition #42 Theological language is peculiar because God is not an object alongside other objects—and is not knowable as other objects are knowable.

Christian churches and communities address God and talk about God. They do so as they invoke and pray and preach and sing. They do so as they glorify and thank and praise God, and as they ask God for guidance and forgiveness. They refer to God as the holy one on high, heavenly father and king, creator, ruler, judge, loving parent, and redeemer. They call God almighty, infinite, eternal, compassionate, faithful, gracious, and immortal. It is not unusual—in fact, it is quite typical—for Christian churches and communities to address God and talk about God in these and other ways, and most often they do so without waiting for theories of theological language. Nevertheless, a recurrent claim of Christian piety and tradition is that the divine is an odd reality and that our theological language is peculiar.

If you run across the following sequence of nouns or noun phrases—rock, car, tree, God, frog, beaver dam, galaxy, and corporation—the one that does not belong is God. Why? For one thing, you and I interact with many objects, forces, and realities—persons, communities, institutions, plants, gravity, oxygen, animals, earth, stars, and more—that we can point out, measure, and also distinguish from one another. We can define these things with significant degrees of precision. Theologically speaking, we may perhaps also claim that their pattern and arrangement suggest divine sustenance and care, or that God sustains and cares through persons, communities, plants, oxygen, stars, and so on. And, as we say these things, we indicate that, in our experience, the deity is finally unlike a chemical element, a plant, gravity, or a community of persons in that we cannot simply point it out. God is not an object alongside other objects that we can measure, distinguish, and define with precision. Instead, the divine is a reality that we sense *in and through* our interrelationships and encounters with other things. The idea that the deity is intimately connected with our encounters with other things but not identical to any other thing is signaled by the fact that, for piety, the reality of God is always mediated to us through something else.[1] The relationship between the deity and the medium through which we apprehend or experience it is dialectical: the two are positively intertwined, but they are never simply equated.

Biblical Roots

Not surprisingly, then, there is a long tradition of circumspection in Christian circles about our encounters with and knowledge of God. The tradition has biblical roots. For example, the book of Exodus portrays the Israelites' experience of God in their escape from Egypt, their wilderness wanderings, and their formation as a nation. The text suggests congruence between the divine and Israel's emotionally charged experience of these events when it intimates that their particular pattern indicates that God is faithful and liberating. But difference and dissimilarity are also assumed. The escape from slavery is not God; the wanderings in the wilderness are not God; and the formation of the Israelite nation is not God either. For piety, then, knowledge of God in the exodus event requires that we hold together in a dialectical relationship of similarity and difference the deity, the escape, the wanderings, and the constitution of Israel. The opening chapters of Genesis suggest that we encounter divine wisdom and sustenance in a regular sequence of day and night, trees with fruits and seeds in their kind, and

1. John E. Smith, *Experience and God* (New York: Oxford University Press, 1968), 52–53, 68–98.

cattle in their kind. Of course, for contemporary persons of piety, as well as for the writers of Genesis long ago, the divine wisdom and sustenance are not exhausted by these regularities, and God is not day, night, an olive tree, or a cow.

A related theme—that God remains other, mysterious, and at least in some sense beyond our comprehension—also comes to expression in a number of biblical passages. In Exodus 33:20–23, for example, the Lord says: "You cannot see my face; for no one shall see me and live." Instead, God makes arrangements for Moses to glimpse God's back (or God's "back parts," as the King James has it) from a cleft in the rock. The opening verses of Psalm 97 portray God as the sovereign king of all the earth who is surrounded by clouds and thick darkness; John 1:18 claims that "no one has ever seen God"; and, as I have noted above, 1 Timothy 6:16 says that God "dwells in unapproachable light."

The divine oddity, as we might call it—the dialectical relationship of the mysterious divine object to ordinary and mundane things in our experience—encourages us to understand our theological language (or talk about God) in a peculiar way. Suppose we say, "The Lord is my rock and my refuge."[2] The word "rock" is a metaphor: God is not really a stone; rather, the metaphor suggests a kind of immovable dependability that we may associate with God. Even so, while the dependability we ascribe to God in this way may be similar to the dependability of the rocklike refuges in our experience, it also differs from the dependability of mundane things. (We presume, for example, that the security available in God, unlike the security of rocklike refuges, is not limited to a specific place or location.) Suppose we read that, "like a mother who will not forsake her nursing child, [and] like a father who runs to welcome the prodigal home, God is faithful."[3] This statement points to a similarity between the faithfulness of God and the faithfulness of a nursing mother or of a welcoming father. The statement affirms that God really is faithful. But it does not require us to affirm that the divine faithfulness is simply identical to the faithfulness of loving parents, which in our experience sometimes extends no further than their own biological offspring.

The oddity of the deity and its consequences for our talk about God are also signaled by the account of the disclosure of God's name in Exodus 3:13–15.

> But Moses said to God, "If I come to the Israelites and say to them, 'The God of your ancestors has sent me to you,' and they ask me, 'What is his name?'

2. "The LORD is my rock, my fortress, and my deliverer, / my God, my rock in whom I take refuge, / my shield, and the horn of my salvation, my stronghold" (Ps. 18:2).

3. "A Brief Statement of Faith," in *BOC* 11.3. The "Statement" here makes use of images presented in Isa. 42:14–16; 49:14–15; 66:13; and Luke 15:11–32.

> what shall I say to them?" God said to Moses, "I AM WHO I AM." He said further, "Thus you shall say to the Israelites, 'I AM has sent me to you.'" God also said to Moses, "Thus you shall say to the Israelites, 'The LORD (YHWH), the God of your ancestors, the God of Abraham, the God of Isaac, and the God of Jacob, has sent me to you': This is my name forever, and this my title for all generations."

The name YHWH, often translated into English as LORD, occurs in Hebrew Scripture more than 6,800 times. Its origin is uncertain, though partly on the basis of Exodus 3:13–15, some say it derives from a form of the Hebrew verb "to be." In any case, it is so sacred that Jews traditionally do not pronounce it but say the name Adonai (or "my Lord") in its place. YHWH is sometimes called the Tetragrammaton because it is composed of four letters. Only the vowel markings added by later scholars render it pronounceable as Yahweh, and thus we may wonder what it means to claim that the divine name and title "for all generations" was delivered in a form that is unpronounceable.[4]

Negative Theology

These and other biblical passages and themes have played an important role in the development of "negative theology," so called because of its insistence that, in the final analysis, the terms and concepts we use to refer to God must be negated or denied. John of Damascus (c. 675–749), for example, claimed that the divine "essence and nature is absolutely incomprehensible and unknowable." Indeed, for John, who, in "An Exact Exposition of the Orthodox Faith," began his ruminations about God's incomprehensibility by citing John 1:18, the deity is "above all existing things, nay even above existence itself," and so also "above knowledge." Consequently, there are some terms we use in speaking of God that have entirely negative force. "For example, when we use the term darkness . . . we do not mean darkness itself, but that He is not light but above light: and when we speak of Him as light, we mean that He is not darkness."[5]

The Damascene drew on the broadly influential reflections of a sixth-century Christian philosopher called Pseudo-Dionysius. As God is not a being among

4. Leo G. Perdue, "Names of God in the Old Testament," in *The HarperCollins Bible Dictionary*, ed. Paul J. Achtemeier (San Francisco: HarperSanFrancisco, 1996), 548–49.

5. *St. Hilary of Poitiers: Select Works and John of Damascus: Exposition of the Orthodox Faith*, ed. W. Sanday and S. D. F. Salmond, vol. 9 of *A Select Library of Nicene and Post-Nicene Fathers of the Christian Church*, ed. Philip Schaff and Henry Wace, 2nd ser. (Grand Rapids: Eerdmans, 1989), 4.

beings but is beyond all existence and knowledge, Dionysius maintained that, when applied to God, our symbols and concepts, which inevitably are drawn from the realm of being and existence, must always be negated. He insisted that even the highest concepts, such as oneness, divinity, goodness, and being, must finally be negated, as must "even the names of Father, Son, and Spirit." Indeed, "in the very end, even the denials are denied. . . . Negation is negated, and the human mind, befuddled, falls silent." There is nothing more to say. "Only silence."[6]

Dionysius's ideas emerge in the insistence of the medieval mystic Meister Eckhart that we must finally let go of every concept of God. Indeed, Eckhart uses various rhetorical and linguistic strategies as "pointers toward a horizon that continually eludes us," or as ways of "suggesting what lies beyond speech."[7] Thomas Aquinas is not as negative: he emphasizes that our language reaches out to God, and he also claims that "He Who Is" is the most appropriate name for the deity.[8] Even so, and perhaps through the instruction of Albert the Great, Dionysius's theology also exerted an influence on Aquinas's understanding of theological language.

For Aquinas, God remains incomprehensible because, while our words and concepts are both serviceable and meaningful, they do not entirely define or circumscribe the deity. His position follows from his understanding of the relationship of God with the world. Finite things, for Aquinas, have their being by participating in "He Who Is," and thus there is a fundamental connection between them and the deity. The deity causes creatures to be. This allows us, when speaking of God, to make analogical use of words we use in speaking of mundane realities. That is, there are both congruence or proportion and incongruence or disproportion when we compare these words as they are used in speaking of mundane realities and as they are used in speaking of God. Suppose we were to say, then, that Socrates is wise and good and that God is wise and good. Aquinas maintained that, in referring to Socrates and to God, we do not use the words "wise" and "good" equivocally, but we also do not use them univocally. That is, we do not use them in ways that are simply opposed; neither do we use them in ways that are simply equivalent. Instead, we use the words *analogically*, or in a way that lies somewhere between simple opposition and simple equivalence, and that admits both similar-

6. Paul Rorem, *Pseudo-Dionysius: A Commentary on the Texts and an Introduction to Their Influence* (New York: Oxford University Press, 1993), 213.

7. See Bernard McGinn, "The God beyond God: Theology and Mysticism in the Thought of Meister Eckhart," *Journal of Religion* 61, no. 1 (January 1981): 1–19. McGinn says that Eckhart used various strategies "for suggesting what lies beyond speech," and these strategies are "pointers toward a horizon that continually eludes us" (11).

8. Aquinas, *ST* 1a.13.11 (pp. 91–93). Hereafter, page references to this work appear in parentheses in the text.

ity and difference. We use the same words in different senses. God really is wise and good. At the same time, however, it is impossible to use these words in the same sense of both God and Socrates. Why? Because Socrates is a creature, creatures are God's effects, and creatures fall short of what is typical of their cause. Creatures are not "the same kind of thing as the cause," and so they represent it inadequately (1a.13.5 [p. 63]). The goodness and wisdom of God are perfect, but the goodness and wisdom of creatures are not. "Thus words like 'good' and 'wise,' when used of God do signify something that God really is, but they signify it imperfectly because creatures represent God imperfectly" (1a.13.2 [p. 55]).

But what about "He Who Is"? Surely, for Thomas, this most appropriate name, or title, for God left all negativity and imperfection behind. Perhaps—but it is instructive to consider *why* Aquinas believed "He Who Is" to be the most appropriate name. One reason was that, unlike the words "human," "rock," and "angel," which signify particular forms in existence, "He Who Is" does not signify any particular form among existent forms—but simply existence itself. And this is appropriate, said Thomas, because "the existence of God is his essence," and "this is true of nothing else." Again, any other name we might choose will necessarily be less general and more restrictive. But "in this life," claimed the Seraphic Doctor, "our minds cannot grasp what God is in himself. Whatever way we have of thinking of him is a way of failing to understand him as he really is. So the less determinate our names are and the more general and simple they are, the more appropriately they may be applied to God" (1a.13.11 [p. 91]). Finally, "He Who Is" is an expression whose tense "signifies being in the present and this is especially appropriate to God, whose being [unlike the finite being of any creature] knows neither past nor future" (1a.13.11 [p. 93]). Therefore, each of the reasons why "He Who Is" is the most appropriate name for God points to the peculiarity of the divine object and underscores the fact that we never really entirely grasp the deity.

Nevertheless, Aquinas says, the name "He Who Is" emphasizes that God communicates existence to all things, so that finite things share in existence even if they do not have existence in the same way that "He Who Is" does. For this reason, "God," a word that, unlike the word "existence," can properly be used of no other being, is more appropriate when we want a term that indicates that the divine nature is incommunicable and shared by no other being. But then Thomas adds the following sentence: "Even more appropriate [than the word 'God' for usage in this manner] is the Tetragrammaton, which is used to signify the incommunicable and, if we could say such a thing, individual substance of God" (1a.13.11 [p. 93]). That is, when it comes to signifying the incommunicable divine nature that is shared by no other being, the Tetragrammaton has the advantage of being unpronounceable, and thus presumably preserves our appreciation for the inadequacy of our language in the face of divine mystery.

Gregory P. Rocca explains that "Thomas weaves his negative and positive theology together, precisely because [he believes that] *only that interweaving* can do justice to the fact that the church must speak and praise, must invoke and love and follow God *who just is* the Mysterious and Incomprehensible One who escapes and is never caught by our ideational and conceptual schemes." In short, Thomas is engaged in the project of "speaking the Incomprehensible God."[9]

Reformed Protestants have also participated in this longer tradition of circumspection about our knowledge of God. Discussing the Trinity, for example, John Calvin notes that "we ought to play the philosopher soberly and with great moderation. . . . For how can the human mind measure off the measureless essence of God according to its own little measure . . . ?"[10] The Reformed Scholastic Johannes Wollebius claims that "the essence of God is incomprehensible to us"; at the same time, he notes God's intimate connection with and difference from all finite things. "God," he says, "is wholeness from all points of view: the whole in himself, the whole in all things, the whole in every particular thing, the whole beyond everything."[11] A bit of negative theology pokes through again in the first paragraph of the Scots Confession of 1560, which notes that God is "infinite, immeasurable," and "incomprehensible." Citing Romans 11:33 and Psalm 145:3, the Westminster Confession of Faith also says that God is "incomprehensible." Indeed, the following summary statement by the twentieth-century Dutch Reformed theologian Louis Berkhof seems entirely accurate. "Reformed theology holds that God can be known, but that it is impossible for men to have a knowledge of Him that is exhaustive and perfect in every way. To have such a knowledge of God would be equivalent to comprehending Him, and this is entirely out of the question: '*Finitum non posit capere infinitum.*' Furthermore, man cannot give a definition of God in the proper sense of the word, but only a partial definition."[12]

The classic posture of Reformed piety with respect to the divine oddity, our knowledge of God, and our God-talk is well represented in the hymn "Immortal, Invisible, God Only Wise," written by the Scottish Presbyterian minister and poet

9. Gregory P. Rocca, OP, *Speaking the Incomprehensible God: Thomas Aquinas on the Interplay of Positive and Negative Theology* (Washington, DC: Catholic University Press of America, 2004), xvii, 353.

10. Calvin, *ICR* 1.13.21.

11. John W. Beardslee III, ed. and trans., *Reformed Dogmatics: Seventeenth-Century Reformed Theology through the Writings of Wollebius, Voetius, and Turretin* (Grand Rapids: Baker Books, 1977), 39.

12. Louis Berkhof, *Systematic Theology*, new edition containing the full text of *Systematic Theology* and the original *Introductory Volume to Systematic Theology* (Grand Rapids: Eerdmans, 1996), 30. Berkhof also says that God is "the Incomprehensible One" (29).

Walter Chalmers Smith in 1867 (and based on 1 Tim. 6:16).[13] The hymn's first verse opens with two negatives: unlike you and me—or indeed most things we experience—God is immortal (i.e., not mortal) and invisible (i.e., not visible). The hymn praises "God only wise," thus indicating that, while we sometimes call other persons wise, the divine wisdom is unlike and radically surpasses our own. So much so, in fact, that when we compare the two, God alone is wise. Again, if we use the word "wise" to refer to persons and then also to God, we use it in different senses. Returning to the text of 1 Timothy, the second line of the first stanza says that the only wise God is "in light inaccessible hid from our eyes," so that, unlike other things in our experience, we cannot directly see or observe God. There is incongruity between the "most glorious" transcendent God and our finite capacity to perceive, grasp, know, and comprehend. Nonetheless, the first two lines of verse 3 point (almost pantheistically) to the intimate connection between God and creatures.

> To all, life Thou givest, to both great and small;
> In all life Thou livest, the true life of all.

The hymn as a whole, then, insists not only on the deity's transcendence but also on God's immanence. We encounter God—or should we rather say, we are grasped by God—as the true life of all and so also the depth of our own life. The hymn points to piety's experience of God through other things, and it offers a poetic statement of the idea that God is not an object alongside other objects, as well as the further implications of this idea for our knowledge of God and our God-talk.

Somewhat like Thomas Aquinas, the twentieth-century Lutheran theologian Paul Tillich regards the statement "God is being-itself" as "a nonsymbolic statement" that "means what it says directly and properly."[14] Tillich maintains that all finite beings have a double relationship to being-itself, or the infinite power of being (1:235, 237). They participate in it; otherwise, they would not *be*. At the same time, however, the infinite power of being lies beyond all finite beings. The deity, or being-itself, is thus both immanent and transcendent, both intimately present in every finite being and thoroughly beyond every finite being.

This *analogia entis* makes it possible for finite things to point to God, or for a seg-

13. I quote from the text as revised and published in *The Presbyterian Hymnal* (Louisville: Westminster John Knox, 1990).

14. Paul Tillich, *Reason and Revelation, Being and God*, vol. 1 of *Systematic Theology* (Chicago: University of Chicago Press, 1951), 238. Hereafter, page references to this work appear in parentheses in the text.

ment of being—human fatherhood, for example—to symbolize the infinite whole. Therefore, we may use terms other than "being-itself" to refer to God. Thus, unlike the term "being-itself," the religious symbol "father," which takes a part of being as an analogy for the deity, is "double edged": it points toward the infinite, which it symbolizes, and also toward the particular finite thing, human fatherhood, through which it symbolizes the infinite (1:240). Consequently, when we call God "Father," God "is brought down to the human relationship of father and child," and the human relationship is now understood to have a sacramental and holy depth.

Not surprisingly, then, Tillich also insists that being-itself is an odd or peculiar reality because it "cannot be understood as the existence of a being alongside others or above others" (1:235). Accordingly, he is at pains to distinguish his position from a type of theism that sees God as a self related to a world, an ego related to a thou, or a cause related to its effect. In these instances, Tillich complains, God is indeed reduced to one being alongside others, but the true God, who is the depth of life and reality, transcends this God. And thus we may speak of the God above the God of theism, or "the God beyond God."[15]

A Proposal

My own understanding of theological language owes a good deal to Friedrich Schleiermacher's claim that the attributes we ascribe to God do not denote something special in God per se but in our consciousness of God in relation to us and to the world.[16] In my judgment, the words Christian communities use to talk about God, such as "creator," "judge," "rock," "fountain of goodness," and "deliverer," are symbols. They express and also shape our encounters with objects as well as our affective responses to them. And they express, shape, and encourage the distinctive step of religious piety and sensibility, or affection, from the many objects in our experience to Something More, or to an object beyond. That is, religious symbols "take" our perceptions of various objects and interrelationships, as well as our affective responses to them, as referring to the deity and thus, at least implicitly, they assume that our experiences of the reality of God are always at the same time experiences of other things.

Consider once again the exodus account of the Israelites' escape from Egypt, their wilderness wanderings, and their constitution as a nation. These occurrences and events, as well as the Israelites' emotional responses to them (such as awakened senses of liberation from oppression and of new possibilities), are expressed,

15. Paul Tillich, *The Courage to Be* (New Haven: Yale University Press, 1952), 186, 188.
16. Schleiermacher, *CF*, #50 (p. 194).

interpreted, and shaped by mythopoeic resources portraying Moses, Pharaoh, the ten plagues, crossing the Red Sea, following pillars of cloud and fire, gathering manna from heaven, and receiving commandments at Sinai. The narrative complex as a whole supports statements about God, such as "God is a faithful deliverer." This statement (as well as others like it) is not about God as God is or may be "in Godself," but about God in relationship to Israel and to the world of Israel's experiences. It is a symbolic statement that ancient Hebrews did not presume to convey all there is to know about the deity. How could it convey that if God is also the unpronounceable I AM? In fact, other biblical texts express, interpret, and shape Israel's emotional responses to being cut off from significant possibilities in events such as the exile, and portray the deity as judge. For the religious community, the statement "God is a faithful deliverer" points toward a deity or divine reality that, in the emotionally freighted experiences of Israel, is also more than a faithful deliverer, that remains mysterious, and that they never entirely comprehend.

Theological language, then, speaks of the divine as persons of piety apprehend it via emotionally freighted encounters with worldly realities. Its vitality depends on its ability to evoke both the connection and the distinction between the divine and our mundane encounters. God-talk indicates the mysterious presence of God that constitutes the true depth of life and of mundane objects and occurrences, but it also indicates the transcendence and mystery of the Other whom we never entirely know or comprehend. Vital God-talk is evocative and symbolic. Like some works of art, it helps us apprehend and construe realities and events freshly and with new vision.[17]

To put this point differently, symbolic theological language refers to both God and the world. It furnishes patterns or schemes of interpretation that encourage us to ask about our emotionally freighted encounters with mundane realities, the deity, and the adequacy of the proposed patterns or schemes for bringing out the relationship between them. Symbolic God-talk functions as a hypothesis that encourages us to inquire about our encounters with mundane realities, about the all-encompassing divine reality, and about a proposed relationship between them. This is how it precipitates interaction between persons and the divine object that we may apprehend in and through other objects. This is how it facilitates conversations among people about how to understand and interpret the divine object that is mediated to us by way of our experiences of other objects. This is the way it portrays how God relates to all that is not God.[18]

17. See William Stacey Johnson, ed., *H. Richard Niebuhr: Theology, History, and Culture* (New Haven: Yale University Press, 1996), 22. For much of what I say here, I am indebted to Niebuhr's discussion in his Cole Lectures, entitled "Toward New Symbols."

18. David H. Kelsey, *Eccentric Existence: A Theological Anthropology*, 2 vols. (Louisville:

Therefore, when a Christian community says that God is a faithful deliverer, it recalls, among other things, a traditional proposal made in the book of Exodus about the relationship between divine reality and the Israelites' escape from Egypt, their wilderness wanderings, and their constitution as a nation. It also proposes a current discussion about God as deliverer. It encourages its members—people whose imaginations and sensibilities already have been prompted and shaped by rituals and sermons and studies connected with the book of Exodus—to ask whether and to what extent this relationship makes sense of other encounters and occurrences as well. To the extent that it suggests to these people fruitful interpretations of emotionally freighted events and occurrences in their current experience, such as the civil rights movement of the 1950s and 1960s in the United States, the symbolic statement that God is a deliverer gains for them a measure of confirmation. It portrays God and the way God relates to things that are not God. To the extent that it seems inadequate to occurrences and realities that the community currently encounters, its members may enter into conversations about how to understand God in other ways as well. For example, they may also ask about ideas of God as judge, and how they connect with proposals about the relationship between the deity and mundane occurrences such as the exile. Indeed, the felt inadequacy to certain occurrences and events of the image of God as faithful deliverer, especially if they determine that it cannot be integrated with other symbols, such as God as judge, may lead some members of the community—or perhaps even the community as a whole—to reject this image altogether.

Piety's God-talk loses its vitality when symbol and deity merge. Then we no longer ask whether and how our symbol is adequate to different and continuing encounters, as well as to a divine reality that is more than our particular symbols convey and that finally remains beyond our comprehension. Then our language ceases to indicate disjunction and to evoke wonder; it ceases to point beyond itself, and it ceases to be symbolic. Then we understand our words as vessels that contain and convey all that needs to be known rather than as instruments for exploration and discovery. Indeed, as our words, their adequacy, and their function no longer are in question, we now may use them to assert and proclaim in a way that discourages further questions and the search for additional symbols. We reduce our words to technical terms that signify things completely known.

My own judgment, then, is that good theological language has a profoundly self-negating dimension, that it tries to put us in touch with what finally re-

Westminster John Knox, 2009), 1:9, 19, says that primary theology considers whether any given ecclesial practice "is in fact appropriate in that place and time as a response to the particularities of God's ways of relating to all that is not God."

mains beyond our words. Communities that understand this refuse to be satisfied with the God they have thought of. They acknowledge, at least implicitly, the peculiarity of their God-talk and also understand that this acknowledgment preserves an appreciation for the incomprehensible deity. They recognize that good theological language conveys both similarity and difference. They fear that even our most carefully formulated and cherished concepts of God may become idols; so they remain aware that genuine God-talk points to the God beyond our concept of God.

The opening lines of Martin Luther's famous hymn that is based loosely on Psalm 46 illustrate this:

> A mighty fortress is our God, a bulwark never failing;
> Our helper he amid the flood of mortal ills prevailing.

The hymn is not concerned with God as God is or may be in Godself, but with the God who relates to us as "our helper"—an expression connected with the idea of God as redeemer. The word "fortress" is a metaphor: communities who sing Luther's hymn generally do not believe that God is literally a big castle. What, then, shall we say about the next phrase, "a bulwark never failing"? Surely, it expresses a sense of divine dependability as well as a kind of spiritual or existential security with respect to our dependable helper. But it also indicates the peculiarity of God-talk. Along these lines, I am reminded of a very pleasant vacation with my family some years ago in the Borders region of Scotland. We explored a number of picturesque but ruined castles, the remnants of an earlier and failed Scottish border policy that tried unsuccessfully to keep out the English, ruins that thus underscore a significant fact. You and I encounter many bulwarks that can fail and eventually do, but "a bulwark *never* failing" is beyond the pale of our ordinary experiences. It is, in fact, a bit of explicitly self-negating theological language. In Luther's hymn, it encourages us to realize that, when we refer to God as "our helper . . . amid the flood of mortal ills," we are using the word "helper" in a sense that ultimately differs from the ways we ordinarily use it. The deity, who is our helper, is like some other helpers in our experience; but that deity is also both unlike and beyond them, just as a "bulwark never failing" also points beyond our usual ideas about bulwarks (even in Scotland). And so, though the ecclesial practice of hymn singing itself contains no developed theory of theological language, there are hymns that participate in the longer tradition of circumspection about our knowledge of God and our God-talk.

Proposition #43 Creator and Sustainer or Governor are symbols that point to God with respect to the constitution and continuation of the world.

Christian communities symbolize God as Creator with respect to the constitution of the world, and as Sustainer (or Provider) with respect to its dynamic continuation. These symbols function as elements of a wider vision of God, the world, and ourselves, where specifications of any one basic term are understood in relationship to specifications of the others. For example, to specify what it means to call human beings contingent, finite, capable, and good creatures, we explore their possibilities and limits as they depend on God the Creator for their existence in the created world. Piety does not speak of humans in themselves or in isolation, but in relationship with God and the world. To specify what it means to call the world a contingent, subsistent, and good creation, we do not speak of the world in isolation but in relationship to the Creator on which it depends and in relationship to ourselves as creatures. Similarly, when we explore what it means to call God "Creator," we note that the existence and constitution of the world as creation and humans as creatures depend on God as their source; when we explore what it means to call God "Provider," we note aspects in which humanity and the world continue to be sustained. That is, we do not speak of God *a se*, or in isolation, but in relationship to cosmic ecology and cosmic passage, or in relationship to the existence, constitution, and continuation of the world and ourselves.

The following propositions, therefore, engage in a semipoetic exercise of elaborating symbols and arranging them into patterned relationships to one another. In particular, I investigate two basic images that, when taken together, further specify what it means to call God "Creator" and "Governor." They are source and ordering power. I will portray God as source (and ground) in connection with the sensed dependence, incompleteness, mystery, and reference of humanity and world. I will portray God as ordering power in connection with the dynamic and dependable arrangements, tendencies, interdependencies, and trajectories that we encounter in the world. I will also note that these images help to specify what it means to call God "giver and bestower," and that these terms correlate with a sense of gratitude for human life and the world as gifts.

Finally, I shall also ask what these reflections indicate about the divine disposition, what they suggest about the purposes of God, or, if you will, about theocentric piety's sense for the *tendency and trajectory of the Real*. But I must repeat that good theological language contains profoundly negative elements. There is much that we do not know and cannot fathom, and the images of creator, provider, source, ordering power, and bestower ultimately portray the world and humanity in relationship to the vague circumambient *all*. They picture the world and ourselves as subsistent realities predicated on a mysterious reality.

Proposition #44 God is Creator.

For people of piety, life and the world do not explain themselves.[19] In part, this is because we find ourselves, thanks to the many interrelationships and contingencies of astrophysical and geological developments, genetics, family, society, and history, set within specific contexts and endowed with certain capabilities. Our situation prompts us to ask questions and to wonder. Why do I find myself in this particular context? What are the factors, events, and configurations that go into making me who I am? In this way, life in the world points beyond itself. It is inexplicable apart from reference to wider realities; it refers to and implies the vast cosmic ecology and passage within which we ourselves—as well as all the local venues, dynamics, and histories—are situated.

To persons of piety, this wider reference also prompts further questions and suggests Something More. Why is this vast and dynamic cosmic ecology and passage patterned or articulated as it is? Why does it proceed as it does? Why is there any context (or anything) at all? Why does the context in which we find ourselves continue? This is where a great symbol comes in, one that is largely shared, if also somewhat differently developed, by the several Abrahamic faiths. To say that God is Creator means that we ourselves and all other things are contingent and derivative. The symbol of creator, at least as the creed develops it, means that the deity is the almighty, all-governing, or all-ruling maker of heaven and earth. That is, it refers to the deity involved in creation and continuation, or both the making and the governing of world. It draws out and shapes our apprehension of the mystery, contingency, and "ongoingness" of life and world. It suggests that the vast cosmic ecology and passage have their basis in deity and that life and world are thus always before God.

The fundamental idea/sensibility is that, as all-governing maker of heaven and earth, the deity is the deep ground and source of cosmos and life, as well as the ordering power at work throughout cosmic passage. We are—and all is—because God is. To say this, to say that God is the source and ordering power, lends to life and the world a peculiar significance. For persons of piety, then, my life and yours, the world as cosmic ecology and its many interrelationships, contingencies, processes, and events proceed from Something More. They subsist in something greater. They have a coherence and depth that are not self-contained. They are connected with a ground. The many circumstances, realities, persons, processes, and occurrences of cosmic ecology and passage—the molecules and stars and communities and evolutions and insects and vast expanses and lakes

19. See chap. 3, prop. #27, and chap. 5, prop. #35.

and seas, and so on—have a referential valence and a depth in the *real*, on which all depend. They are realities in relationship. And, once we have said this, piety then also turns around and says something additional and dynamic about the real that these realities are related to. The many realities, cosmic ecology, and cosmic passage are based and grounded elsewhere, and the elsewhere thus bases, grounds, connects, orders, and relates. The ground of realities—the "really Real," if you like—tends, acts, or moves to become the basis for cosmic ecology and passage, or for the world. God ventures, God creates.

Biblical Depictions

The Bible depicts this venture in various ways. Genesis 1 portrays a creating by word or command in conjunction with a number of separations and gatherings. For example: "And God said, 'Let there be a dome in the midst of the waters, and let it separate the waters from the waters'" (1:6). Waters under the sky are then gathered into seas, and dry land appears (1:9). Here the act of creation gives shape and form to an already present, watery, and formless void. The divine creativity sculpts; it operates with purpose and plan (or "wisdom," as Calvin calls it) that are displayed in the constitution of the world as an articulated whole and circumstance for life.[20] Creation is depicted as a deliberative action that fashions a habitat and environment. The world or cosmos that God creates displays orderings and patterns. In the terms I am developing here, much of Genesis 1 portrays God ordering an articulated and dynamic cosmic ecology. Isaiah 29:15–16, Isaiah 45:9–13, Jeremiah 18:1–6, and Romans 9:20–21 present an image of the divine potter who works with unformed clay. A similar motif—creation as cosmic fashioning—comes through in the Yahwist text of Genesis 2:7, where God forms the human from the dust of the earth. Elsewhere in the Bible, and in a more workmanlike manner, God builds the heavens: Psalm 8 depicts the heavens as "the work of your fingers"; Psalm 19 says "the firmament proclaims his handiwork"; and in Psalm 104:2 and Isaiah 40:22, God stretches out the heavens like a canopy or a tent.

We should note that the dynamic cosmic ecology and passage, with its patterns, interrelationships, processes, and orderings, its light and darkness, topographies, and plants and animals in their kinds (Gen. 1), also *bestows*. It makes possible life and relationships and motility, and thus we recognize that the divine dynamic that comes to expression in cosmic ecology and passage is itself a bestowing and a giving. That is, the ordering and constructing work of creation

20. Calvin, *ICR* 1.5.2–3.

is itself a bestowal; God the Creator is giver and bestower. Indeed, this is a part of what the Christian community means when it says that the great God who creates is the good God of grace. The Creator, as Calvin says, is "the fountainhead and source of every good."[21] It is also true that cosmic ecology and passage shapes our possibilities and limits. Humans have their place and vocation within it: their lives take shape within its natural processes and social patterns, and thus the forming, constructing, and ordering Creator is responsible for an articulated human situation or environment that directs human lives along certain lines. Among other things, then, creation also directs life into certain channels of activity and responsibility, and, as ordering power, the deity is also the director. For persons of piety, the God of grace who creates, the source and ordering power, also directs, guides, and commands.

In addition, however, God's act of creating by word in Genesis 1 not only separates, gathers, and organizes already present stuff; God also speaks things into existence.[22] For example, "Then God said, 'Let there be light'; and there was light" (1:3). Or, alternatively translated, "Then God said, 'Let the light appear'; and light appeared." Here we encounter an imperative form of the verb "to be"—"to become," or "to appear." The act of creating light, while associated with its separation from darkness and the organizing of day and night, is thus not simply equated with acts of separation and organization. God bestows not only schema and form but also existence, or becoming; God speaks light into being. Similarly, we read in Psalm 33:9:

> He spoke, and it came to be;
>   he commanded, and it stood firm.

To these passages we may add 2 Maccabees 7:28: "I beg you, my child, to look at the heaven and the earth and see everything that is in them, and recognize that God did not make them out of things that existed."

Yet another critical passage is John 1, where a key point is that the redeeming Word that comes into the world in Jesus Christ was also active in creation. Here, in verse 3, we encounter a form of γίνομαι, a verb generally meaning "to make," which is capable of a range of meanings in different contexts, such as "to be born

21. Calvin, *ICR* 1.2.1–2.

22. See chap. 3, prop. #28. This is also a point emphasized by many theologians, such as Robert W. Jenson, who affirm that God creates *ex nihilo*. In fact, Jenson says, "Genesis' reference to emptiness and formlessness, and the darkness and 'waters' of chaos, is not to a *presupposition* of creation but to the *inconceivable beginning* of creation, made inconceivable by the absence of presuppositions" (Jenson, *The Works of God*, vol. 2 of *Systematic Theology* [New York: Oxford University Press, 1999], 11).

or produced," "to come about or occur," "to be established," "to happen," or "to take place." This is also the verb that was used in the Septuagint translation of Genesis 1 to indicate that God's commands came to pass: "Then God said, 'Let there be light'; and there was (καὶ ἐγένετο) light," and it was with conscious reference to this translation of Genesis 1 that γέγονεν made its way into John 1:3. Not surprisingly, then, this verse can be variously translated. Compare "All things *came into being* through him, and without him not one thing *came into being*" (NRSV) with "All things *were made* through him, and without him *was not anything made* that was made" (RSV).

Consider, too, Romans 4, where emphasis falls on the life-giving promise of God to Abraham and then also to gentiles in Jesus Christ. Paul views the justification and rightwising of persons in God's gracious gift of redemption as a bestowal of new life or a kind of resurrection. And he says this about the promise to Abraham:

> For this reason it depends on faith, in order that the promise may rest on grace and be guaranteed to all his descendants, not only to the adherents of the law but also to those who share the faith of Abraham (for he is the father of all of us, as it is written, "I have made you the father of many nations")—in the presence of the God in whom he believed, who gives life to the dead and *calls into existence* the things that do not exist. (Rom. 4:16–17)

The verb translated here as "calls into existence" is the present tense of καλέω, meaning to call, name, or address, though it can also be used as an equivalent of the verb "to be." That the latter translation of καλουντος is appropriate for verse 17 is indicated by Paul's reference to things that are not and things that are (τὰ μὴ ὄντα ὡς ὄντα). Is this Paul's attempt to pick up the imperative "Let there be . . ." and God's act of speaking things into existence in Genesis 1? In any case, by using καλέω here and in this way, Paul associates the act of redemption, or of giving life to the dead, with the idea that God calls into existence what was not. If we recognize, as both John and Paul do, that the God who redeems creates, and vice versa, then Romans 4:17 indicates that the deity who creates also calls things into existence. And if this is true, then God the Creator not only bestows patterns, interrelationships, processes, and orderings, but also existence itself.

Jürgen Moltmann notes that, in the New Testament, testimony to creation is bound up with "the kerygma about resurrection" and the Spirit. "In these God's creative activity is understood eschatologically as καλεῖν (to call to life), as ἐγείρειν (to raise) and as ζωοποιεῖν (to make alive)." Indeed, "when quickening and resurrection are described in the categories of divine creative activity, it is because this event is supposed to correspond to creation in the beginning (Rom. 4:17; 2 Cor. 4:16)."[23]

Theologies of Creation

Given the multiple ways in which the Bible depicts the venture of creation, it is not surprising that Christian theologians have constructed different theories. Augustine framed the dominant doctrine of classic Christian orthodoxy in the West while arguing against Manichaean dualism; God created the world out of nothing (*creatio ex nihilo*), an affirmation that was upheld by later thinkers, including Aquinas and Calvin. The basic idea here, as it shaped and expressed creation piety, was that all that is depends radically on the good God alone. In creation God was the sole source of all existence; the divine creativity was in no sense deflected or constrained by the characteristics of some preexistent stuff that God did not create. Therefore, creation (indeed, for Augustine, whatever is) is good. This idea, in turn, was often paired with an insistence that God alone is responsible for all that comes to pass, or that providence and the divine governance represent a continuing exercise of creativity, which, while perhaps distinguishable from *creatio ex nihilo*, nevertheless also brings things to pass apart from significant constraints.[24]

23. Jürgen Moltmann, *The Future of Creation: Collected Essays*, trans. Margaret Kohl (Philadelphia: Fortress, 1979), 123.

24. The close relationship between creation *ex nihilo* and a certain conception of providence is illustrated by the work of the nineteenth-century Princeton theologian Charles Hodge. Hodge claims that, according to Scripture (including Gen. 1), there is "an immediate, instantaneous creation *ex nihilo* by the simple word of God," by which the world is called into existence. However, he also says that there is "a mediate, progressive creation, the power of God working in union with second causes." This mediate exercise of divine creativity is similar to the divine providence or preservation, where the divine cooperates with things that already exist. Providence, or preservation, is thus *not* simply a continuous creation from nothing, as some Reformed theologians wrongly suppose. Indeed, such a doctrine, Hodge complains, destroys all continuity in existence, effectively denies second causes by making God "the sole agent and the sole cause in the universe," and also tends toward pantheism. Thus, when it comes to God's providential governing of things, Hodge maintains that God, who brings second causes into being, preserves them, excites them to act, and directs them to predetermined ends. At the same time, Hodge is careful to leave room for *miracles*, which, following the Westminster Confession, he defines as events that take place in "the external world" and "are produced or caused by the simple volition of God, without the intervention of any subordinate cause." He continues: "The original act of creation, in which all cooperation of second causes was impossible" because it was immediate and from nothing, belongs to this same class. See Hodge, *Systematic Theology: In Three Volumes* (Grand Rapids: Eerdmans, 1977), 1:557, 578, 579, 600,

Modern scholarship led the twentieth-century Reformed theologian Emil Brunner to recognize that the idea of creation by ordering or sculpting preexistent stuff is the gist of many ancient creation myths and that there are also traces of it in Genesis 1. Nevertheless, he insists that *creatio ex nihilo* is the predominant New Testament concept, and that it is clearly indicated by such passages as Hebrews 11:3 and Romans 4:17. *Creatio ex nihilo*, he says, is a way of claiming that "God is the One who determines all things and is determined by none," and that the world has its foundation and origin in God alone. There is no additional force or preexisting reality whose purposes, tendencies, or characteristics might limit God's options, so to speak. "God assumes complete and sole responsibility for the existence of the world." Brunner goes on to say that, in the subsequent history of agents and things, God limits Godself in order to work through and with what God has created, though Brunner also claims that God sometimes works miracles, apparently reversing this self-limitation in order to act immediately and apart from the ordinary processes and course of created things.[25]

Note three signal implications of the *ex nihilo* formula: (1) It affirms that God is the sole source of existence and not just its organizing principle. What God does in creating is radically different from what people do when they "fashion" objects from materials that are already there. The divine act of bringing things into being is thus unique. (2) "Since all creation comes from God's will as its source," creation is good and "nothing in existence can be intrinsically evil." (3) Since God is able to determine everything about it, the world brought into existence by God is intelligible and purposive.[26] In addition, we should note that the portrait of divine power entailed by the *ex nihilo* doctrine intensifies the wrenching question of evil and suffering. If God is all-powerful, all-determining, and also good, then every evil that befalls good creatures must be divinely determined. Eschatologically speaking, this portrait of divine power also furnishes

618. Somewhat similarly, though without the clarifying language of causes, Jürgen Moltmann claims that Israel's understanding of "the divine creation of unexpected and unmerited salvation in history" is of a piece with the idea of *creatio ex nihilo* and the liberty of the Creator in creating without presuppositions. The doctrine of creation, he says, connects with a view of the "total process of divine creative activity" in history and at the end (see Moltmann, *The Future of Creation*, 118, 119–20).

25. Brunner, *Dogmatics* (Philadelphia: Westminster, 1952), 2:9–10, 156. For Brunner, the question is bound up with "the personal idea of God" and "the divine freedom over all causality, over all necessity." See also *Dogmatics*, 2:20, 172–75, 190–92. "God *limits Himself* by creating something which is not Himself, something 'over against' Himself, which he endows with a relative independence. Thus it is God Himself who creates this limitation—hence He is also free to remove it" (Brunner, *Dogmatics*, 1:251).

26. Langdon Gilkey, *Maker of Heaven and Earth: A Study of the Christian Doctrine of Creation* (Lanham, MD: University Press of America, 1985), 51–58.

grounds for a sure and certain conviction that the saving purposes of the all-powerful God cannot fail.

As we have seen, however, Genesis 1 does not present the later *ex nihilo* doctrine. "Nowhere in the seven-day scheme of Genesis 1 does God create the waters; they are most likely primordial."[27] In fact, the chapter depicts uncreated chaos as the backdrop for God's creative work.[28] The Jewish theologian Jon Levenson thus suggests that, when viewed in the wider context of other ancient literature, such as the Babylonian *Enuma Elish* and the Egyptian "Hymn to Aten," as well as in connection with other biblical passages and later theological tradition, Genesis 1 plays a part in a longer development of a magisterial idea of divine sovereignty.[29] But this clearly is not the same thing as claiming that we find unambiguous support for a strict *ex nihilo* doctrine either in Genesis or in many other biblical passages.

An alternative doctrine put forward by process theologians portrays God as the preeminent creative principle who lures or persuades realities that retain their own relatively independent and also occasionally resistant measures of creativity.[30] Process thinkers say this position is more adequate to biblical portraits of the divine creativity and God's subsequent providential activity. Moreover, as John Cobb notes, "the notion of *creatio ex nihilo*, if that means creation out of *absolute* nothingness," renders God the "absolute controller."[31] By contrast, process theism does not reduce everything that comes to pass to God's own act; therefore, it allows us to portray the relative independence and creativity of things other than God, including human agents. It also opens a way to explain

27. Jon D. Levenson, *Creation and the Persistence of Evil: The Jewish Drama of Divine Omnipotence* (San Francisco: Harper & Row, 1988), 5.

28. B. W. Anderson, "Creation," in *The Interpreter's Dictionary of the Bible* (Nashville: Abingdon, 1962), 1:778.

29. Levenson, *Creation and the Persistence of Evil*, 65.

30. Classically, some Christian theologians aligned their doctrines of creation with Neoplatonic ideas concerning the procession of immaterial souls from an utterly transcendent one, and the subsequent sculpting by a demiurge of forms and bodies from a preexistent material that offers some resistance to and places some limits on its work. Origen of Alexandria's portrait of the procession of souls from the One and their subsequent fall into material represents a modification of this kind of Neoplatonic scheme.

31. John B. Cobb Jr. and David Ray Griffin, *Process Theology: An Introductory Exposition* (Philadelphia: Westminster, 1976), 65; see also John B. Cobb Jr., *A Christian Natural Theology* (Philadelphia: Westminster, 1965), 203, 226–27. Is hypertheism an inevitable implication of the Westminster Confession when it says, "God from all eternity did . . . freely and unchangeably ordain whatsoever comes to pass," even if it also claims that violence is not thereby done to the will of creatures "nor is the liberty or contingency of second causes taken away, but rather established" (*BOC* 6.014)?

the persistence of evil as the result of a resistance or recalcitrance among creatures that God cannot entirely determine or control.[32]

So, for example, Lewis S. Ford conceives of creation in terms of persuasion. "God proposes and the world changes." The emergence of the genuinely new requires divine initiative. God constantly introduces, and the divine creativity is not simply a recombination of the old but a novel structuring of possibilities. Nevertheless, there must be a fusion of novel form with inherited matter and the self-creative decision of the creature, and it is conceivable that the vast multiplicity of actualities will elect to frustrate the divine aim. Pursuing this model, Ford says that "the eight consecutive acts of divine speech" in Genesis 1 "schematically represent the untold multiplicity of divine urgings whereby God shaped this world, originally without form and void, into that which we may celebrate as a fit habitation for man." He also claims that God's providential governing follows this same pattern. "From the standpoint of divine persuasion, providence is simply another way of looking at God's guidance of the historical process already manifest in creation."[33]

There is, I believe, much to be said in favor of this line of thinking. It points up important difficulties in much classical theologizing. For example, the *ex nihilo* doctrine does seem less than adequate to the full field of biblical portraits. Moreover, definitions of miracle such as the one offered by Brunner threaten to establish a hypertheism, in which the principle of divine activity and power displaces, absorbs, or even negates the efficacy of all other powers and realities, including human agents.[34] Nevertheless, as we have also seen, in addition to the divine sculpting or fashioning motif, which seems basically compatible with process theism, there are biblical passages, including Genesis 1:3, Psalm 33, John 1:3, and Romans 4:16–17, that depict divine creativity as a calling into existence. Moreover, even if we note the preexistence of a watery void in Genesis 1, the

32. David Ray Griffin notes that, "while Whitehead does not reject divine providence altogether in order to solve the problem of evil (as have thinkers such as Richard Rubenstein), he does consistently reject the traditional notion of 'unqualified omnipotence,' which is 'accompanied by responsibility for every detail of every happening' (*Adventures in Ideas*, p. 217)." Whitehead "grounds this rejection on the metaphysical position that creative power is inherent throughout the realm of actuality" (Griffin, *God, Power, and Evil: A Process Theodicy* [Philadelphia: Westminster, 1976], 281).

33. Lewis S. Ford, *The Lure of God: A Biblical Background for Process Theism* (Philadelphia: Fortress, 1978), 23, 119, 21, 22. Or, as Griffin puts it, "God's power is persuasive, not controlling" (*God, Power, and Evil*, 276).

34. This third objection is something like Hodge's worry that portraits of God as the sole agent and cause compromise the efficacy of second causes. See also my earlier remarks about special providence in chap. 4, prop. #33.

text does not indicate that God is bound or limited by it.[35] Levenson, who notes the preexistence of the waters as well as significant nuances and developments in the biblical portraits of God's creating activity, thus says that Genesis 1 depicts "the uncompromised mastery of YHWH."[36]

Some Critical Points

An important exegetical fact is that the variety of biblical depictions of creation, as well as their comparatively nontechnical, poetic, and wide-ranging vocabularies, can be made to fit one or another fully developed metaphysical model only with significant difficulty. Walter Brueggemann notes that, in the course of its testimony, Israel appealed to all the models of creation that were already available in the ancient Near East.[37] Moreover, if some important New Testament passages either point to or contain the *ex nihilo* idea, there are others, such as Hebrews 1:2, where creation is mentioned but the *ex nihilo* idea is not so clearly suggested. No single, philosophically precise articulation of creation emerges in the Bible.

The diversity of expression and poetic imprecision we find in Scripture need not undercut Augustine's chief concern in his debates with the Manichees. Biblically speaking, to affirm that the good and masterful God of grace creates the world means that the world is good—an affirmation made prominently and repeatedly in Genesis 1 despite the text's metaphysical ambiguities. In addition, not only proponents of the *ex nihilo* doctrine but also some process theologians affirm that God the Creator is the source of the world and ground of being, as well as the ordering power that fashions an articulated and dynamic world. As John Cobb modifies Alfred North Whitehead's philosophy, for example, God causes new occasions to come into being when old ones have perished, and "we know God . . . as ground of being, the ground of purpose, and the ground of order."[38] Therefore, the comparatively poetic vocabulary of a passage such as

35. Anderson, "Creation," 1:778.

36. Levenson, *Creation and the Persistence of Evil*, 3, 65. Levenson claims that, in Genesis and elsewhere, the Bible makes magisterial claims for the subordination of all else to the creator God that go well beyond what we find in the Babylonian *Enuma Elish*, where Marduk, who must defeat other gods, also has his mastery conveyed to him by other members of the pantheon.

37. Walter Brueggemann, *Old Testament Theology: Testimony, Dispute, Advocacy* (Minneapolis: Fortress, 1997), 146, 148, 158.

38. John B. Cobb Jr., *A Christian Natural Theology Based on the Thought of Alfred North Whitehead* (Philadelphia: Westminster, 1965), 227; see also Cobb, *God and the World* (Philadelphia: Westminster, 1969), 64–65. Schubert M. Ogden claims that "the real motive of the traditional doctrine," the denial "against all forms of metaphysical dualism, that there is any

Genesis 1 (with its intimation of divine mastery), the *ex nihilo* doctrine, as well as certain understandings of process theism all preserve a signal feature of creation piety. All encourage us to construe human life and the world as good gifts that appropriately evoke gratitude and thanksgiving as well as a disposition to care for the gifts we have been given.

However, there are further considerations. Process theologians repeatedly claim that the classical *ex nihilo* doctrine depicts God as "absolute controller," and that this, in turn, supports a divine determinism that undercuts the efficacy of other agents and causes. This is a serious charge, especially for those of us who work within the Reformed subtradition in Christian theology. The Westminster Confession rather famously claims that "God from all eternity did . . . freely and unchangeably ordain whatsoever comes to pass"—yet so as neither to violate "the will of creatures" nor take away "the liberty or contingency of second causes."[39] Although Reformed theologians have made considerable efforts to render these affirmations intelligible and mutually consistent, one wonders whether they have entirely succeeded.

For theology as a practical wisdom that shapes and expresses Christian piety and sensibility, one critical question is whether the *ex nihilo* doctrine finally issues in an unfaithful or perhaps even debilitating quietism that undercuts our sense of responsibility. The answer here, I think, is no. Theologians from Calvin to Edwards and Schleiermacher to Barth have articulated "both/and" positions something like the one espoused by Westminster. (God determines all, and mundane causes and agents also operate and act.) Their reflections introduce significant theoretical ambiguities into higher levels of metaphysical reflection, but they need not—and, in fact, historically they *have not*—led to quietism. Consider, for example, Calvin's emphasis on sanctification and moral striving, the activist bent of much Puritan piety, and what sometimes has been called the "world formative" impulse of Reformed Christianity.[40] But another question does expose significant practical difficulties. Do depictions of God as absolute controller, with their implication that God purposefully determines all that comes to pass, have deleterious consequences for piety and pastoral care?[41]

The idea that God specifically, self-consciously, and intentionally determines all the particular occasions of suffering and destruction that befall specific com-

being or principle save God alone which is the necessary ground of whatever exists or is even possible," also is "an essential implication" of process theism (Ogden, *The Reality of God and Other Essays* [New York: Harper & Row, 1977], 62–63).

39. *BOC* 6.014.

40. See John W. de Gruchy, *Liberating Reformed Theology: A South African Contribution to an Ecumenical Debate* (Grand Rapids: Eerdmans, 1991), 18.

41. See chap. 4, prop. #33.

munities and creatures—from the accidental deaths of children to debilitating diseases, earthquakes, highly destructive storms, and episodes of mass starvation—is a dark and, pastorally speaking, highly problematic side of hypertheism. Even if one maintains, as Calvin does, that we often cannot be certain of God's purposes and intentions, this idea regularly encourages pious people to believe that their own failings, whether or not these failings bear any relationship to the situation at hand, have somehow called forth divine retribution. Often enough, it also leads others to judge that those who suffer gratuitously deserve their sufferings at the behest of the all-determining and just God. The effect is to undermine the solidarity of tragic, innocent, and gratuitous suffering in which so many creatures participate, and which constitutes a primary basis for feelings of empathy and care. This, in fact, is the mistake that Job's friends make when they unwisely break their silence, and it should be rejected.

Uncompromising *ex nihilo* doctrines, especially when they underwrite divine determinism, may also threaten to render exceedingly sure, certain, and definite piety's passionate hopes for new creation. For example, they fail to preserve the tension and the risk of waiting in hope for what we do not see (Rom. 8:22–25) and what, to us anyway, hardly seems inevitable.[42] Again, when combined with specific readings of divine purposes and intentions, portraits of divine agency and power that accompany *ex nihilo* doctrines often support interpretations of the eschaton, the end and *telos* of all things, that are considerably more definite than our knowledge of cosmic passage allows.

When we think of God as process theists do, says Cobb, "the problem of evil does not disappear . . . but it loses much of its force."[43] This observation forms the background for a critical question about process theism. Does it threaten to dismiss too easily the wrenching tensions of persistent suffering, injustice, and evil in God's world?

Here, I think, an accurate answer needs to be carefully calibrated. Although it need not do so, the idea that persuasive divine power always acts to contribute to the creativity of creatures might mask an existentially troubling feature of cosmic passage. Many of the same processes, points, and patterns in which we discern the divine creativity, such as the emergence of species that compete successfully in a given environment, or the movements of tectonic plates so essential to our geological habitat, also entail significant suffering and destruction. This is why,

42. We may also wonder how they can be adequate to the flexibility and even uncertainty intimated near the end of the book of Revelation by portraits of "the kings of the earth" weeping and wailing at Babylon's demise, being cast together with the beast into the lake of fire, and then also bringing their glory into the new Jerusalem (Rev. 18:9–10; 19:19–20; 21:24).

43. Cobb, *God and the World*, 64.

by many measures, the divine creativity is not always positive or even benign, and why it is possible to lament being caught up in it for ill.

Consider an argument made by David Ray Griffin in *God, Power, and Evil: A Process Theodicy*. For Griffin, God does not absolutely determine any particular event and so is never "fully responsible for the details of events that occur." Even so, "God is clearly responsible . . . for all of the evil of discord in the world . . . in the sense of having urged the creation forward" to states where discord and suffering are felt with greater intensity. That is, God's decision to stimulate greater complexity not only makes possible richer and more intense forms of experience but also risks possibilities for more intense and greater suffering. Was, then, the decision to lure creation forward at such a cost the decision of a good God? After all, "if God had ceased stimulating novelty prior to the advent of life, there would be no pain in the world. If God had rested content with the state of creation prior to the emergence of animals with central nervous systems, the intensity of pain would have been low. Or if God had even ceased stimulating the development of mentality before the rise of rational creatures, the planet would have been spared its most intense horrors."

Griffin notes, however, that leaving things in a state of banal simplicity is not especially good either. Moreover, on any of these scenarios, not only would there have been no Hitler and no Auschwitz, there also would have been no Jesus, Gautama, Socrates, Michelangelo, Florence Nightingale, Gandhi, and so on. He therefore concludes that the decision to lure creation beyond chaos and triviality was indeed worth the risk, and that, while responsible for the suffering and evil that ensue, God is "not indictable" because the conditions for the possibilities of greater complexity and intensity "are necessarily [also] the conditions for the possibilities of greater suffering."[44] The God who is not an absolute controller, but who always labors to enhance the creativity of creatures, is therefore good.

Griffin's argument does *not* deny the key disturbing feature of cosmic passage, at least as this feature may be understood within the framework of a process theology. The same divine creativity that enables good to emerge also risks increased suffering. Nevertheless, for piety's sake, it also seems important to point out that his argument leaves Job in something like the position he occupies in the canonical tale. In fact, by many measures, it leaves the core of Job's existential predicament intact. True, from Griffin's perspective, God cannot be charged with absolutely controlling or determining all that has happened to Job. Even so—also from Griffin's perspective—Job has been caught up undeservedly for ill and beyond his doing and undoing in circumstances and events of cosmic

44. Griffin, *God, Power, and Evil*, 300, 308, 310.

passage. Job recognizes that the deity is powerful, good, and significantly beyond our comprehension. It may also comfort Job to realize that, metaphysically speaking, sufferings such as his own and very many more are simply the price that some creatures must pay if God is to move the things forward. Existentially, however, this hardly renders Job entirely without justification when he curses the day he was born.

A More Rough-and-Ready Vocabulary

Considerations such as these make me reluctant to relinquish a more rough-and-ready vocabulary. Theologically, I think that what can and should be said—even if it finally must also be said symbolically and rather poetically—is this: the almighty God, maker of heaven and earth, is the source of creation, or of cosmic ecology and cosmic passage, as well as the ordering power responsible for its dynamic patterns, continuing processes, and interrelationships. Masterful divine creativity calls things into existence, and it also orders, sculpts, and presents possibilities. Amidst the articulated interrelationships and interdependencies, the creative orderings manifest in astrophysical, geological, biological, and historical processes both enable and limit the creativity of creatures. (Think, for example, of how genetic patterns and mutations both enable and curtail the possibilities of particular individuals.) Within these orderings, the regular, foreseen, experienced, and sometimes quite impressive consequences for many creatures of certain lines of activity and inactivity (such as caring or not caring for their young, upholding or failing to uphold institutions that adjudicate disputes fairly, and protecting or polluting natural environments on which they depend) also allow us to say that the divine creative ordering manifest in cosmic passage encourages, discourages, directs, limits, and calls forward. The symbol of God as Creator therefore expresses and sculpts a piety attuned to constraining as well as persuasive exercises of cosmic passage, even if it need not require an affirmation of all-determining and absolute divine control.

When we compare it with proposals generated by some *ex nihilo* and process doctrines, this comparatively piecemeal language fails to banish some significant ambiguities. For example, it does not allow us to say with certainty whether the world did or did not proceed from absolutely nothing. Practically speaking, however, I believe that these are ambiguities that communities of piety both can and do live with. Indeed, by eschewing certain highly developed, comprehensive, and definite discourses, the comparatively rough-and-ready idea of masterful divine creativity respects the long tradition of circumspection about our knowledge of God and our theological language. It tries to avoid the tendency of too many theologians to utter things too wonderful for themselves that they do not know or understand (Job 42:3).

Consider, for example, Jürgen Moltmann's elaboration of his understanding of creation in his Gifford Lectures. God is all in all, Moltmann claims. Making use of the Jewish doctrine of *zimsum*, he then also asserts that, if God is to create *ex nihilo*, there must be a prior self-limitation or withdrawal by God in order for the primordial space or nothingness to emerge. "God makes room for his creation by withdrawing his presence." This "self-restriction" or even "self-humiliation" precedes God's creative activity. Self-humiliating love thus grounds the divine creativity, and it is "the beginning of that self-emptying of God that Philippians 2 sees as the divine mystery of the Messiah." Even to create, then, God takes the form of a servant. Whereas the initial creation is without preconditions, the new creation is the "laborious creation of salvation out of the overcoming of disaster" that emerges from the history of God's suffering. Still, the initial creation is the beginning and the promise of redemption from the nothingness of death and annihilation. As a consequence, even in the face of the annihilating nothingness of negation and death, even in the face of senseless suffering and murder, there is no suppression of the annihilated. Hope is founded on "the miracle of God's new creation" in resurrection, since neither annihilation nor the end of the world can set limits on the God who creates out of nothing.[45]

This very powerful statement places the *ex nihilo* doctrine near the center of Moltmann's eschatological theology of divine suffering and hope. From the perspective of theology as practical wisdom, however, it also prompts critical questions. What is the status of the comparatively speculative dimensions of Moltmann's discourse? Can we ever know whether or not the world proceeds from nothing? What counts for and against his reflections about God's self-limiting and restricting withdrawal into God's self as the precondition for the divine creativity? Will the biblical passages to which he refers actually bear the weight of these reflections?

Consider, too, a basic feature of John Cobb's metaphysics. Creativity, he says, is a basic characteristic of all reality, and indeed, "that apart from which nothing can be . . . whatever *is* is a unit of creativity." All reality, for Cobb, as for Whitehead, is made up of units of creativity, and "God is also an instance of creativity." "*How* an occasion becomes" or develops—the trajectory it takes up in its situation amidst other occasions and their becoming—"is finally determined by its own decision." That is, once an occasion and its trajectory is in place, no factor or influence, including God, can absolutely control how it becomes or develops.

45. Jürgen Moltmann, *God in Creation: A Theology of Creation and the Spirit of God* (Minneapolis: Fortress, 1993), 87, 88, 90, 92.

What, then, of the emergence of a new occasion and its trajectory in the first place? Cobb says, "*That* a new occasion occurs at all cannot be determined by itself" because its new trajectory, which must emerge out of the old but not merely repeat the old, does not yet exist. Therefore, the new occasion needs to be furnished an initial aim or opportunity for self-actualization that, in turn, it can decide to modify and variously pursue in relation to other occasions. This initial ideal aim is what God contributes. Indeed, according to Cobb, without it, given Whitehead's metaphysics, the genuinely new (in distinction from a simple recombination of the old) cannot emerge. Thus, in the emergence of a truly new occasion, "the decisive factor is God." God determines *that* a new occasion occurs. Precisely *how* a new occasion shall occur, however, depends not only on God but also on the multitude of other influential occasions in its environment as well as on its own creative decision as to how it will combine these influences and respond to them. Even so, God's determination "is far from irrelevant to *how* [an occasion] shall occur," since "God offers to every occasion an ideal opportunity for its self-actualization or satisfaction."[46] And these are the reflections that warrant Cobb's willingness to call God the ground of being as well as the ground of purpose and order.

This argument makes room for the integrity of agents and realities other than God, and it offers a self-consistent view of the divine creativity interacting with other creative realities. It also allows us to say that God calls new things into existence. Even so, Cobb's position entails some rather speculative ideas that provoke critical questions. (1) It denies that there might have been an initial point at which the stuff of cosmic passage came into being out of nothing, but can we ever have enough information to decide this with definiteness? (2) It speaks of all occasions of reality as having or making their own "decisions," but does this vocabulary indicate an overreliance on the experience of human agents as the model for all creativity? (3) It pictures the deity rather closely on the model of a self-conscious human agent who makes deliberate and intentional decisions, such as the one described by Griffin to risk heightened suffering and pain in order to pursue possibilities for greater complexity, but do we have sufficient warrants for portraying God in this way?

God creates. The almighty maker of heaven and earth calls forth and orders the world of interdependencies, processes, and creatures, and, as is emphasized by the doctrine of providence, God's ordering activity continues. Among other things, this amounts to a disclosure of purpose or trajectory. God calls into existence and orders the world or cosmos in order to create a dynamic and articulated cosmic ecology that reflects the divine wisdom and glory and is very

46. Cobb, *A Christian Natural Theology*, 210, 226.

good in God's sight. And, in piety's view for God's good creatures who are living, acting, and interacting in the midst of things, this is a fundamental grace—a giving and bestowing of good gifts. That we are, and that we are endowed with significant capabilities in the context of God's good world, is our first debt. This is why the basic utterance of creation piety, "God creates," contains within itself the recognition of oneself and others as beneficiaries. It portrays a circumstance that elicits thanksgiving, gratitude, and loyalty to God and the things of God (or the dynamic cosmic ecology and passage in which we live and move).

Masterful divine creativity comes to especially impressive expression in points and processes where, as I have observed above, we discern the emergence of something more and something new, such as the big bang, the formation of galaxies and planets, the emergence of the organic from the inorganic, the rise of new species, the birth and formation of a human person, and the like. These are points and processes (both extraordinary and ordinary) in which we discern an extravagance, or the advent of things that represent something more than and something different from the persistence of relationships, things, processes, and capabilities already present. Must we, then, conceive of these points and processes—such as the quintessential creative act as portrayed by proponents of the *ex nihilo* doctrine—as instances where realities are created from *nothing*, or wholly apart from relationships, realities, and processes that already are? No, they may very well involve dynamic combinations and alterations of things that already exist.

Remember, even when it comes to the big bang, we simply don't know whether there was something before or what that something might have been. Neither do we know whether there have been multiple big bangs or whether there are multiple universes, and so on. Indeed, according to one current scenario put forward by scientists, the known universe is one of a number of patches that inflate or bubble out of a multiverse; according to another, the big bang may have been one of a number of collisions or a cycle of contractions and bounces that release energy and from which galaxies and other cosmic structures form.[47]

May these points and processes be described as the creation of things that did not exist? Certainly, and I expect that it may be worthwhile to ponder the possible relationship between the emergence of life and the organic from the inorganic and Paul's insistence in Romans 4:17 that God "gives life to the dead and calls into existence the things that do not exist." (This is a subject to which I shall return in part 3, as I consider the topics of redemption and new life.)

Where, then, may we encounter the masterful Creator? The short answer is everywhere, but this can be further specified and detailed. We encounter God as

47. Ron Cowen, "Pre-Bang Branes and Bubbles," *Science News*, April 23, 2011, 22–23.

source or ground and ordering power in our engagements with and appreciation for the world as cosmic ecology and passage. We discern divine wisdom in nature and also in basic institutions and practices that make for human well-being. Hence Calvin noted that the world of objects, realities, interdependencies, and processes constitutes the theater of God's glory. Abraham Joshua Heschel noted our "radical amazement" at the divine presence in the encompassing reality of creation.[48] In addition to the way of engagement with and appreciation for the world, there is also (as has been repeatedly claimed in history) the way of introspection. The theater of divine glory includes the galaxies and stars and clouds and trees and leaves and molecules and seas and mountains and cultures and societies, but it also includes our selves and our capacities. Here, too, we encounter traces of masterful divine creativity, wisdom, and glory that evoke wonder and amazement, as well as senses of dependence, gratitude, and direction. Of course, without focusing on specific sinews, organs, appendages, thoughts, and abilities, we may simply be struck by the fact of our existence. There, in the depths of the mysterious and compelling fact and feeling that we are, piety finds itself in touch with the masterful deity who speaks light into being.

Proposition #45 God is Sustainer.

People of piety are struck not only that the world, or cosmic ecology, is, but also that it continues. Moreover, they realize that there are features of the dynamic continuation of cosmic ecology, or cosmic passage, that sustain them, and that neither its continuation nor our continued participation in it is their own doing. The symbol of God as Sustainer draws out and shapes their wonderment and gratitude by construing the deity as ground of the vast, intricate, dynamic, and sustaining cosmic passage. The tradition thus maintains not only that God creates but also that God governs, sustains, and provides.

Creation and Governance

We note, once again, the close relationship between creation and the continuing process, or governance. In a contemporary frame of reference, we recognize that the forming, ordering, and sculpting creativity portrayed in Genesis 1 takes place over quite significant time frames, that is, from the beginnings of cosmos to the geological formation of Earth, to the emergence of plants, animals, and humans. Theologically speaking, the formation of galaxies, planetary systems,

48. Abraham Joshua Heschel, *God in Search of Man* (New York: Harper & Row, 1966), 46.

and our solar system and the emergence of organic molecules, proteins, plants, and animals (including us) are instances of creativity and bringing about things that were not, but they are also instances of continuing dynamism, governance, sustenance, and providence.

Consider a recent—and, at present, more or less standard—scenario for the formation of our solar system. (1) A universe expanding from the big bang contains clouds of hydrogen, deuterium, and helium that become the birthplaces for a first generation of stars when gravitational forces contract them, release energy, and raise internal temperatures. Atomic collisions then produce nuclear fusion in the interior of the stars. When rates of the nuclear generation of energy and its loss balance, there is a stable period. Once the stores of hydrogen are depleted, stars contract again, temperatures rise, and additional chemical elements are formed. When the nuclear fuel is used up, the central cores collapse; the collapses then reverse in supernova explosions that eject elements into space. (2) A next generation of stars incorporates these elements, and successive cycles of star births and deaths produce additional elements needed for planets and also for life. (3) Interstellar clouds that form are made up of gases and particles, and when densities increase, the clouds form into disks. (4) In the disk that becomes our neighborhood, a protosun emerges at the core of a large solar nebula of gases and particles. The solar nebula is an energetic environment where gases and dust form small condensates. These, in turn, coalesce to form objects centimeters broad. In the midplane of the nebula, swirling objects form a disk where there are many collisions and, as a result, meter-sized boulders aggregate. These also collide and form planetesimals, which are meters to tens of kilometers across. The planetesimals then aggregate into protoplanets whose gravitational pulls attract atmospheric gases. (5) Smaller bodies continue to fall onto protoplanets, evidence for which is preserved in the cratered surfaces of the moon, Mercury, and Mars. In the last stages of planetary formation there are giant collisions that alter orbital inclinations and tilt axes of inner planets, and one such collision ejects material from Earth that forms the moon.[49]

> You stretch out the heavens like a tent. . . .
> You set the earth on its foundations. (Ps. 104:2b, 5a)

According to this scenario, the creative ordering poetically portrayed as divine workmanship in Psalm 104 takes place over billions of years. The psalmist

49. Alan W. Schwartz and Sherwood Chang, "From Big Bang to Primordial Planet," in *Life's Origin: The Beginnings of Biological Evolution*, ed. J. William Schopf (Berkeley: University of California Press, 2002), 48–64.

joins these verses with others that refer to the gushing forth of springs that give drink to wild animals, to the cedars where birds nest, to mountains that are home to goats, and to alternations of darkness and light that regulate activities of animals and humans alike. And this seems appropriate because we cannot separate the divine providence signaled by the continuation of Earth's sustaining habitat from the formation of the heavens and the accretion of Earth. Consider again the words of the creed: "I believe in God the Father, almighty (or all-governing), maker of heaven and earth." Current views of the formation of the cosmos, solar system, and Earth give us good reason to recall Schleiermacher's observation that this first article refers to God appropriately and, when compared with much later theology, also rather unself-consciously, in a single expression: the all-governing maker of heaven and earth is both Creator and Governor, or Provider.

Cosmic Passage and Emergence

My concern here is to show how recent reflections may help us identify certain dynamics of cosmic passage and to note how these dynamics, in turn, may help persons of piety picture the continued divine ordering and creativity.

J. William Schopf, a paleobiologist, says that we can construct a "fairly clear" and plausible "six-part scenario" of how life began. The first two steps have been detailed above: (1) chemical elements are produced in stars, and (2) our solar system forms; then (3) simple organic compounds build up in Earth's oceans; (4) they link to form more complicated organic compounds; (5) multicomponent and information-containing compounds arise; (6) "the aggregation of living cells" occurs. Schopf notes, however, that the details of this scenario remain unclear. "We cannot . . . estimate the likelihood of these steps," and we don't know whether the origin of life was rapid and easy or long, difficult, and improbable.[50]

Scenarios such as this one lead the biochemist Pier Luigi Luisi to claim that increasing molecular complexity is "accompanied by the onset of novel properties—up to the point where self-reproduction and eventually life itself arise." To describe this process, Luisi makes use of the philosophical idea of *emergence*, which, he says, refers to the advent of novel properties that cannot be described in terms of initial constituents. An example is the formation of water from its atomic components. "The collective properties of water are not present in hydrogen and oxygen; so the properties of water can be viewed as emergent

50. J. William Schopf, "When Did Life Begin?" in Schopf, *Life's Origin*, 158.

ones."[51] That is, while the atomic structure of water consists of the basic components of hydrogen and oxygen, the properties of water cannot be reduced to the properties of hydrogen and oxygen. A new relatedness of parts gives rise to properties that cannot be deduced from the properties of the components. "At each level of increasing complexity" from atoms and molecules to an entire organism, "there are novel properties that cannot be described in terms of the lower constituents." Thus, "the properties of a rose, or any other living organism, cannot be interpreted on the basis of atoms and molecules" (119). Luisi claims that "life itself can be seen as an emergent property" (126), and he applies the idea of emergence to the organization of components into more complex patterns, structures, or systems in crystallization and protein assembly under thermodynamic control; virus assembly and anthill formation under genomic, enzymatic, and evolutionary control; and even the formation of human social systems, such as companies, families, and tribes. What becomes increasingly clear, then, is that the idea of emergence is inextricably linked with the idea of ensembles or wholes—from water to viruses to societies—that result from the arrangement of component parts but that also appear to be something other and more than the sum of their parts. Indeed, Luisi notes that some cognitive scientists now apply the idea of a collective ensemble without a localized center to the "I," or the formed self that emerges from feelings, memories, and thoughts organized into a pattern (109–10, 124–25).

The application of the idea of emergence to this wide range of phenomena yields a nonreductive view of the formation of complex wholes and novel or new realities; it suggests a nonreductive naturalism. This view, if we resist the temptation to develop it into an entirely detailed and comprehensive map of reality, can help us portray dynamics of cosmic passage. Within its frame of reference, the formation of first-generation stars, evolving galaxies, and nebulae may be understood as the emergence of new ensembles. The formation of our solar system is the emergence of a system or an ensemble that was not previously present and that supports habitats that its component parts did not. Earth's planetary ecology and the more local ecologies of rivers and valleys are natural systems with characteristics that do not reduce to the properties of their component parts. Consciousness can be described as an emergent property of certain organisms.

The formation of a human community or a culture may also be viewed as the emergence of an ensemble with properties or characteristics that were not

51. Pier Luigi Luisi, *The Emergence of Life: From Chemical Origins to Synthetic Biology* (Cambridge: Cambridge University Press, 2006), 112, 114. Hereafter, page references to this work appear in parentheses in the text.

previously present. Here, as in the story of the beginnings of the people of Israel, individuals, families, and tribes (or smaller ensembles) combine to constitute a more complex social entity. Their coming together depends on historical vitalities and occurrences that fashion the original core of the community but are controlled by no single individual or tribe. Indeed, Israel, the historic entity that results and perdures over generations through peril and promise, turns out to be something more and something other than any of its original leaders and architects intended or expected. This is why the story mentions a wide variety of factors, including oppression at the hands of an imperial overlord, liberating escape, wilderness wanderings, conquests, and settlements, as well as the emergence of specific institutions, traditions, rituals, and codes that help to organize life at the same time that they carry social memories and also express common loyalties and agreed-upon rules. Moreover, as was the case with Schopf's six-part scenario for how life began, we find it exceedingly difficult to estimate the likelihood or probability of these steps and events. There are contingencies that we cannot eliminate.

All this suggests certain dynamics of cosmic passage. I have mentioned one repeatedly already: new ensembles or wholes emerge, and their emergence expresses genuine creativity and even extravagance, since it is not possible to deduce their emergent properties from the properties of the initial components. Luisi and others point to certain molecules or the emergence of life. Analogously, in the historical sequences and events in which we participate, outcomes, circumstances, and realities routinely emerge that participants neither intend nor predict. There is also "reciprocal causation." Components interact and influence one another, but so do parts and wholes, components and ensembles. Thus, if particular ants build a colony, the mutual relationships and patterns of the colony also influence the behavior of individual ants. A person's consciousness and mental capacities depend partly on hydration, heart, and circulatory system, but her conscious decision to run a long distance also affects her hydration, heart, and circulation. Behaviors of particular families influence broader social practices, norms, and expectations, but broader practices, norms, and expectations also influence the behavior patterns of specific families. Reciprocal interactions and influences indicate a second dynamic. Ensembles (stars, planetary systems, ecologies, organisms, communities, and so on) continue. Moreover, their continuation is neither stasis nor still life, but a period of balance and equilibrium during which comparatively constant processes, interrelationships, and patterns endure. A third dynamic is that, over time, ensembles destabilize and dissipate; critical interrelationships, processes, and patterns deteriorate, alter, and cease.

With this in mind, we may say that the dynamics of cosmic passage manifest creativity. Creativity is most apparent to us, perhaps, when we consider the particular geological-evolutionary-historical sequence or line of development in which we participate, for example, when we consider the emergence of life or perhaps the course of a particular people or culture. Yet it is manifest in all the vast array of trajectories and sequences throughout cosmic passage. Critically, the dynamics of cosmic passage also entail significant stabilities, equilibria, and balances that allow stars, planetary systems, habitats, species, organisms, and societies to exist and persist. Nevertheless, the dynamics do not come to rest here. The destabilization and dissolution of systems and ensembles, such as particular stars, ecosystems, organisms, and colonial empires, furnish compounds and building blocks for additional ensembles, such as planetary systems, new organisms, and political communities. The upshot is that the overall cosmic passage not only includes a vast array of emergent ensembles at different stages of formation and relative stability, and it not only includes virtually countless trajectories and lines of development at different locales; it also includes regular processes and episodes of dissolution and destruction as the condition for further emergences. So, for example, the sustaining institutions and communities that emerge in human history, such as specific forms of family and forms of government, all eventually degenerate, destabilize, and fail. There is also good reason to believe that the entire geological-evolutionary-historical sequence of which we are a part eventually will also fall victim to destructive instabilities. As one astronomer puts it, "The death of the sun around five billion years from now will incinerate the inner planets, evaporate the outer ones and gradually disperse the resulting detritus of heavy elements back into the interstellar medium."[52]

Because of the virtually countless local trajectories strewn throughout the cosmos, the fact that the specific local line of development in which we participate on Earth continues to develop, and the likelihood that the ensembles and interrelationships that sustain this particular line will also destabilize and dissipate, we may well hesitate to identify the dynamics of cosmic passage with a creativity that is paradigmatically disclosed in a trajectory directed toward the human. I prefer to say instead that the dynamics of cosmic passage manifest creative orderings characterized by serendipitous contingencies, emergences, reciprocal influences, constancies, instabilities, destructions, further emergences, and so on. These orderings are manifest in far-flung galaxies (at last count, 200 billion or so) and also in our own Milky Way. Within their purview, we humans have a place and a time. Indeed, within our local sequence on Earth, creative orderings—with their many contingencies, emergences, reciprocal influences, stabilities, and instabilities—have given rise to sustaining interdependencies and relationships such as those mentioned by Psalm 104: springs that give drink to

52. James E. Geach, "The Lost Galaxies," *Scientific American* 304 (May 2011): 53.

wild animals, cedars in which birds nest, mountains where goats reside, and alternations of night and day that regulate activities of humans and other animals. Moreover, at multiple points in human history, such as the emergence of Israel or the development of modern medicine, these factors have contributed to something more and different from what the human actors, leaders, and inventors involved either expected or intended. To call God "Governor" and "Provider" is to construe the deity as the ground of dynamic orderings and processes such as those that direct, provide, and sustain. And yet, as many biblical narratives and much classical theology also make clear, there is more to be said. The dynamics of cosmic passage involve more than emergences, new ensembles, and persistent sustaining stabilities; they also entail *endings*, something to which I shall return when discussing eschatology in part 3.

Gordon D. Kaufman offers an important theological reflection on serendipitous creativity, a theme that he draws in part from nonreductive accounts of the evolutionary process and in part from an interpretation of human history.[53] Kaufman speaks of a "serendipitous universe," and he associates God with the serendipitous (and "munificent") creativity that originates the universe (281, 296). More specifically, "the symbol 'God'" points "to that trajectory of cosmic and historical forces which, having emerged out of the ultimate mystery of things, is moving us toward a more truly human and ecologically responsible mode of existence" (347–48). The word "God" focuses "our minds on this growing unity of *directedness toward the human*," which faith discerns "amid all the enormous diversity of cosmic powers and movements" (348–49).

As I have mentioned above, in chaper 4, proposition #32, I think that Kaufman moves rather too quickly from the enormous diversity of powers, movements, and trajectories to the specific local trajectory in which we find ourselves, and that this, in turn, has led him to construct a portrait of divine creativity that is overly focused on the human. I agree with Kaufman that the word "God" can express "the profound meaning of the situatedness of human life in the world," but I understand that situation or context somewhat (and significantly) differently than he does (339).

A Unifying Reign, or Trajectory

The mythopoeic resources of the Bible and Christian tradition encourage people of piety to acknowledge that the many creative orderings constitute a single

53. Kaufman, *IFM*, 262, 268, 275. Hereafter, page references to this work appear in parentheses in the text.

overall government or reign of the one God. Within this frame of reference, the many interdependencies and interrelationships are linked within a single extensive fabric, matrix, system, or process. That is, the symbolic idea of divine governance, when developed in a monotheizing and monotheistic key, construes the many ensembles and trajectories as elements of a single ensemble and trajectory. "World-as-a-whole" comes into view because the one God renders the many others a *uni*verse, the circumambient all.

This single and unifying reign, trajectory, or governance is what I have represented as an ordering discernible in the dynamics of cosmic passage that is creating, sustaining, and directing. There is, I repeat, genuine mystery here. There is much we do not know about the end or goal toward which these dynamics tend; nor do we have an entirely clear understanding of how they came to be. Even so, as I have also emphasized repeatedly, at different levels of generalization, we can identify significant patterns, such as emergence-stabilization-dissipation, comparatively stable processes and interactions critical to Earth's ecology, and basic institutions and practices that contribute to human well-being.

These patterns indicate how the divine creating, sustaining, and directing/ordering (or governance) operate *in and through* the many objects, processes, interrelationships, and agents. Thus, for example, when we turn to biblical accounts of the exodus, we need not choose between divine creativity, sustenance, and direction and the agency of Pharaoh. They interpenetrate and operate in the same events. Isaiah's oracle can refer to Assyria as the rod of divine anger that will spoil and plunder even as it acknowledges that commanders and kings also act (Isa. 10:1–11). When Martin Luther King Jr. discerned the living God at work in the struggle for civil rights, he had no reason either to deny or overlook the many individuals, political parties, institutions, and historical prejudices and commitments that were active and influential. The divine ordering is mediated through other things: it operates in molecules, supernovae, gushing streams, persons, communities, and events.

This affirmation does not require that we write out a metaphysical blank check of the kind Calvin did when he claimed that God may act through, apart from, and even contrary to every mundane cause and intermediary. Nor does it require us to affirm a complete divine determinism, as did both Calvin and Schleiermacher. The divine ordering that piety discerns comes to expression and is manifest in the dynamics of other things, and so we should say that an instance or experience of the divine ordering is always at the same time an instance or experience of something else, for example, a supernova, a stream, a historical movement, a community, or an institution.[54]

54. This is roughly the equivalent of John E. Smith's insistence that "the encounter with

Once again we enter murky waters. Some classical Reformed theologians developed the idea of concurrence, which Louis Berkhof defined as "the co-operation of the divine power" with mundane powers or agents.[55] A process theologian might describe this as the deity luring, persuading, or influencing mundane occasions, their "decisions" and directions. Partly because I conceive of theology as a practical wisdom, I think there is much to be said for Ernst Troeltsch's warning against speculation concerning the *concursus divinus*: we cannot say precisely how it works.[56]

The Deity at Work in Cosmic Passage

How, then, shall we conceive of the deity or the divine at work in the vast cosmic passage of which we are only partly aware? The dominant model in the longer biblical and theological tradition is the image of God as a personal agent: the deity is at work in all things as a personal actor, much like a human individual. The processes and events of nature and history are then taken to express the self-conscious intentions and purposes of God, much as our own actions sometimes express our deliberate intentions and purposes as well as our choices of particular means to achieve them. The biblical theology movement of the mid-twentieth century emphasized this model. In fact, George Ernest Wright looked on biblical theology as the recital of God's acts in the events of history.[57] The theological ethicist H. Richard Niebuhr portrayed God similarly as the one who is acting in all events that impinge on us.[58]

This basic image, then, is drawn from our experience of ourselves as actors in relationship to other persons, objects, and realities, but even as it is used in the Bible and subsequently developed by classical theologians, the model often portrays God as a rather odd or peculiar agent. We have had occasion to note the peculiarity of Genesis 1:3: "Then God said, 'Let there be light'; and there was light." No human agent is able to speak realities into being; no human agent is

---

God is direct but not immediate. . . . All initial encounter with God is mediated," and thus "there is *no experience of God that is not at the same time experience of something else*" (Smith, *Experience and God*, 150).

55. Berkhof, *Systematic Theology*, 171–73.

56. Troeltsch, *The Christian Faith*, translated with an introduction by Garrett E. Paul (Minneapolis: Fortress, 1991), 211, 215.

57. G. Ernest Wright, *The God Who Acts: Biblical Theology as Recital* (London: SCM, 1952).

58. H. Richard Niebuhr, *The Responsible Self: An Essay in Christian Moral Philosophy* (Louisville: Westminster John Knox, 1999), 126; see also H. Richard Niebuhr, *The Meaning of Revelation* (Louisville: Westminster John Knox, 2006), 23–47.

able to utter a verbal command that then is enacted without someone performing physical actions. The majesty and the peculiarities of the text go together. Again, we are not entirely surprised to find Job admitting,

> "I have uttered what I did not understand,
> things too wonderful for me, which I did not know." (Job 42:3)

The image of God as personal agent often is paired with a stiff dose of negative theology.

Consider, too, Jonathan Edwards's claim that God is the "Supreme moral agent." Somewhat like humans, according to Edwards, God exercises "faculties" of understanding and will, though Edwards is also careful to note that our language is ill adapted to "express things existing in the mind of the incomprehensible Deity." Like Calvin, Edwards portrays God as a hyperagent who determines all, though Edwards's rather more refined agent model allows him to comment on God's "excellent disposition" to communicate and diffuse Godself.[59] Indeed, a perceptive commentator notes that, for Edwards, "God is inherently a tendency toward an increase or enlargement of God's own being."[60] And we should observe that the language of tendency, while closely connected with Edwards's understanding of personal agency, seems also to pass beyond it. That is, tendencies may also be associated with nonpersonal realities, as in the sentence, "The weather tends to be hot and humid in North Carolina during the month of August."

In any case, to cohere with our experiences of the dynamics and creative orderings of cosmic passage, the personal agent model would need to be modified significantly. What we need is a model that allows us to speak of broad purposes and directions that we discern in orderings, processes, and events of nature and history but also reflects the fact that we do not have warrants sufficient to claim immediate and self-conscious divine intentions at work in particular occurrences and events. (What we need is an image or model that is compatible with the rejection of unqualified claims for divine hyperagency.) James M. Gustafson outlines a modified agent model for God in his *Ethics from a Theocentric Perspective*. He notes that, in some moral philosophy, animals have purposes but not deliberate intentions; that is, they are not thought to deliberate about specific ends and the means of fulfilling them in the way that humans do. The point, I take it, is not that this necessarily constitutes an accurate description of animal agency (which, after all, may well be quite varied), but to show that ideas

59. Jonathan Edwards, *Ethical Writings*, ed. Paul Ramsey, vol. 8 of *WJE*, 166, 376, 433.

60. Sang Lee, *The Philosophical Theology of Jonathan Edwards* (Princeton: Princeton University Press, 1988), 184.

or models of agency need not be based only or exclusively on the activities and capabilities of humans.[61]

Gordon D. Kaufman, after having worked extensively with agent models in *God the Problem*, rejects them in his magisterial book *In Face of Mystery*. He notes serious problems with the symbolism of a personal agent as applied to God, among them that (1) it can support a terrifying portrait of an authoritarian and all-powerful ruler, (2) it envisions a dualistic cleavage between God and creation, (3) it has serious problems in our time with basic intelligibility, and (4) it has become dangerous religiously, sometimes legitimating authoritarianism and sanctioning holy wars.[62] Instead, as I have noted above, Kaufman prefers the nonpersonal symbolism of serendipitous creativity manifest in history. Symbolic ideas such as "Creator" and "Lord," he says, should be interpreted as poetic metaphors that refer to this underlying reality, dynamic, or process. Thus, rather than speak of the acts, intentions, and purposes of God, Kaufman speaks of directions and trajectories that we may identify in the processes of the cosmos and human history.

In my judgment, these lines of reflection are helpful and also complementary. Gustafson's modified agent model and Kaufman's nonpersonal symbolism are attempts to refer to a process or governing that we experience but do not entirely comprehend, and yet within which we discern significant interdependencies, orderings, conditions for possibilities, and directions. Both try to do this in ways that avoid problematic features of some more traditional conceptions of God as a (hyper)personal agent. Both point to encounters with a dynamic divine reality that is intimately connected with and manifest in cosmic passage. Therefore, I believe that people of piety may use both kinds of symbolism—a modified agent with broad purposes and an ordering process or dynamic that manifests certain trajectories or directions—as we endeavor to portray the living and mysterious God.

Proposition #46 God is the *Real*, whose fundamental tendency or trajectory is to ground, instigate, and shape a process of reality that we encounter as a dynamic order of grace, and that pushes us toward an *ec-centric* orientation in life.

It is time to tie together some points about a contemporary Christian vision of God with respect to the constitution and continuation of the world.

61. Gustafson, *ETP*, 1:270–73.
62. Kaufman, *IFM*, 270–72.

God Is the Real

People informed by contemporary scientific findings and views understand that we are situated within a vast cosmos, and they also discern signal patterns and orderings, such as astrophysical dynamics that make for our solar system, comparatively stable environmental ecologies on which we and other species depend, and social requisites for humans and their well-being. Christians approach this understanding and these discernments with a particular piety (or sensibility and imagination) shaped by the symbols of God as Creator and Sustainer or Governor that depict the deity as the source and ordering power that bears all things. When they do so, they may envision the divine as the dynamism in cosmic ecology and passage, its many different interrelationships and lines of development, and they may also construe some of the signal patterns, processes, and interrelationships that they encounter as orderings or trajectories of the deity. Or, in short, they may envision God as the Real that bears cosmic ecology and passage, the fundamental reality we encounter in the many processes, patterns, and realities of nature and history. This, to recall the first sentence of the Scots Confession, is the one God we confess, acknowledge, serve, worship, and trust.[63]

The Encompassing Tendency of the Real Bears on Us as a Dynamic Order of Grace

Do we discern and encounter a single more general and coherent tendency or trajectory of the Real that encompasses the many processes, patterns, and trajectories? A number of classical theologians have believed so, and some, such as Edwards, have said that the general tendency of the Real is to overflow, to go out from itself, to create and hold things in relationship to itself. I agree. When persons of piety envision it with the aid of the symbols of God as Creator and Sustainer, the fundamental dynamic of the Real is to "realify" (or to ground, instigate, and shape) the process of reality. This is the divine venture, or what the deity does. Just as the tendency of the sun and stars is to emit energy, just as the hawk tends to soar, and just as the seed's highest capacity is to sprout, to "realify" is the excellent tendency and exercise of the Real. It is the Real being the Real, or God being God.

The "realifying" tendency at the heart of things, then, is roughly equivalent to what Edwards called the propensity of the divine being to flow out, expand, and

63. The Scots Confession of 1560, in *BOC* 3.01.

diffuse itself.[64] What we understand of this encompassing propensity and how it bears on all things, what we know of the regimen or pattern that traditional Protestants called God's universal reign, remains partial and incomplete. There is much that we do not know, and perhaps much we shall never know, about many of the local venues and lines of development in addition to our own that are in motion throughout cosmic passage. Even so, the patterns and dynamics we do discern are compatible with a symbolic description of the divine governance or process of reality suggested by texts in the Bible and tradition. We live and move within a *dynamic order of grace*.

A fuller exposition of this statement must wait for the exploration of the idea of redemption in part 3, but here let me note a salient feature: the Creator and Governor bestows gifts of life, existence, capacity, and world. For piety, the order of grace in which we find ourselves is one in which benefits and blessings are distributed indiscriminately. The sun rises on the evil and on the good; rain falls on the fields of the righteous and on those of the unrighteous (Matt. 5:45), and this discernment of fundamental gratuity appropriately evokes within us a sense of dependence and gratitude. (Certainly, as Paul mentions repeatedly, it also indicates that we have little reason to boast.) But that is not all; we also find that burdens are often distributed indiscriminately: "Again, I saw that under the sun the race is not to the swift, nor the battle to the strong, nor bread to the wise, nor riches to the intelligent, nor favor to the skillful; but time and chance happen to them all" (Eccles. 9:11). The dynamic order of grace that we encounter is one in which creatures and communities often are caught up, both for good and for ill, in circumstances, situations, and processes beyond their own doing and undoing. Therefore, our glimpse of or brush with the Real as it impinges on us not only evokes a sense of dependence and thanksgiving, it also elicits feelings of solidarity with others in contingency and in undeserved sufferings as well as benefits. It impresses on us the fact that we are all in the same boat, and this apprehension, as I have mentioned previously, forms a basis for extending sympathy, empathy, and a disposition to care.

It is also true that the ordering of things sometimes brings destructive outcomes when we fail to respect and uphold basic interdependencies, institutions, and practices, such as environmental balances, tolerably just courts of law, and caring for dependent children. Even here, however—as the christological pattern will help us appreciate more profoundly—there is fundamental gratuity. Often enough, due to unforeseen consequences and events, as well as the resilience of people, communities, and natural habitats, more than a few deleterious outcomes fail to materialize. Again, while suffering for the sins of the guilty sometimes

64. Edwards, *Ethical Writings*, 433, 435.

falls on the guilty themselves, quite often it falls disproportionately on the undeserving, for example, other species caught up in our environmental profligacy, persons unjustly tried and sentenced, and neglected and abused children.

There are further features of the dynamic ordering of grace that people of piety discern with the aid of the symbolism of creation and providence. For example, we attend to and sometimes even are fascinated by compresent persons, plants, planets, institutions, coastlines, valleys, stars, or what have you. We find them compelling. This attentiveness is largely bestowed on us; it has bases in the evolutionary development of our perceptual equipment, our sexuality, communal interactions, and social feelings, as well as in the repeated practical recognition that we must cooperate with other agents and powers to achieve important ends and that we ignore relevant forces at our peril. The point I wish to emphasize here, however, is simply that, within the dynamic order of grace, we are indeed equipped with a deep-seated attentiveness to the world beyond ourselves. Moreover, our attentiveness intertwines with senses for the beauty of things as well as their mutual utility—or good-for-ness. The excellences, proportions, and intricacies of a leaf, a tree, or a forest capture our attention. We appreciate that supernovae are essential for the formation of planets and that the bee is good for the flower. We are amazed by a moving symphony or a gracefully turned double play.

Another feature is our ineluctable embeddedness within wider interrelationships, processes, and contexts. Our lives, our capacities, and even our identities are inexplicable apart from interconnections with and references to ever wider social and natural contexts and, finally, to the encompassing context of cosmic ecology and passage (see chap. 5, prop. #35). When we apprehend this, we recognize that we are not self-made and that much is bestowed upon us through a dizzying array of processes and interrelationships. This recognition, in turn, elicits a sense of dependence but also senses of interconnectedness, mystery, and wonder. Moreover, we are also drawn to exercise the capacities and capabilities—whether mental or physical—with which we are endowed. Pretty often, in fact, we relish them as we exercise them, and as we exercise them, we feel a sense of possibilities and perhaps also a sense of responsibility for their appropriate development and use.

As I have observed repeatedly, the order of grace is one in which we discover certain requisites or conditions for human well-being, among them the practice of caring for dependent children, as well as the maintenance of basic institutions, such as family and courts of law. Our apprehensions of these things elicit senses of obligation and direction. Moreover, in concert with the imaginative capacity to put oneself in another's place, the emergence of social feeling, and some acquaintance with one's own interests and needs, our social interactions are also closely associated with the emergence of conscience and a sense of fairness. Again, existential encounters impress us with the fact that created and sustained human life is ineluctably personal, and that, as persons, we stand in relationship to God and others. I have observed, too, that when estimated in the wider compass of our creatureliness and shared contingency, our capacities for attention and interaction, as well as the many interrelationships and interdependencies within which we function, the chief end or calling of created and sustained human life is to participate in true communion with God in community with others.

The Dynamic Ordering of Grace Pushes Us toward an Ec-centric Orientation in Life

Prominent features of the order of grace, our apprehensions of them, and the sensibilities that they evoke move us in an admittedly general but nonetheless discernible direction. To acknowledge that much has been bestowed on us, to recognize our solidarity in contingency, to be attentive to compresent persons, planets, plants, and institutions, to be struck by the beauty and utility of a molecule, or to be amazed by a graceful athlete, to sense our deep embeddedness in cosmic passage, to exercise given capacities for intervention, to conscientiously put ourselves in others' places, to encounter other persons, and to recognize the chief end of true communion within community—all these things draw us out toward others and toward the world. All push toward an expansive sensibility, engagement, and participation.

Evolutionarily speaking, of course, we must also note that the emergence of social feeling in humans, on which the development of conscience and moral sensibility depends, is closely intertwined with dynamics of in-group affection and out-group loathing.[65] This is a point to which we shall return in part 3. For now, however, it is enough to emphasize (1) that in-group and out-group dynamics do in fact support the development in humans of moral resources that are extendable beyond one's initial in-group, and (2) that within the more general ordering of grace, there are multiple dynamics and forces that work to extend them.

In summary, the propensity of the dynamic order of grace in which we live and move is to render human life *ec-centric*, or to orient us not only toward ourselves but also toward others in God's encompassing creation. This being-carried-and-pushed-and-lured-beyond-ourselves indicates the general shape

65. See, e.g., Frans de Waal, *Our Inner Ape: A Leading Primatologist Explains Why We Are Who We Are* (New York: Riverhead, 2005), 136–43, 223–25.

of human life when it is attuned to the divine ordering of grace, or what I shall identify in chapter 9 below as the ethos or spirit of creation. It is something like what Jonathan Edwards calls true virtue and H. Richard Niebuhr calls the universal loyalty that accompanies radical monotheism.[66] It signals a piety, a deep disposition and orientation in living that is adjusted to and corresponds with the tendency and trajectory of the Real.

66. "True virtue most essentially consists in benevolence to Being in general" (Edwards, *Ethical Writings*, 540). H. Richard Niebuhr speaks of a "loyalty to all existents" that extends beyond all closed societies (*Radical Monotheism and Western Culture, with Supplementary Essays* [Louisville: Westminster John Knox, 1993], 33, 35–37).

PART III

Redemption

Chapter Seven

Jesus Christ and the Covenant of Grace

In Jesus Christ, we come to know the God of grace. The God of grace whom we encounter and apprehend is the Creator-Redeemer who is gracious to us and to others, and by disclosing the gracious Creator-Redeemer, Jesus Christ fulfills the covenant of grace. Moreover, a number of images and symbolic ideas in the New Testament, including incarnation as well as the notion that Christ is the image or icon of God, may be understood to express and shape piety's apprehension of the divine excellence or gratuity in Jesus as the Christ. That God is the God of grace is one way to summarize the upshot of Jesus's teaching and embodiment of the kingdom as well as of his crucifixion and resurrection and our dying and rising with him. Again, piety's apprehension in Christ of the God of grace is an existential knowledge that entails assurance; as Calvin says, it does not flit about in the top of the brain, but by the work of the Spirit takes root in the depth of the heart.[1] At the outset, however—as we embark on Christology proper or discourse and reflection about the Christ—the very basic and simple statement is the most critical one: in Jesus Christ we come to know the God of grace.

Proposition #47 God the Redeemer is God the Creator, and this equation has important consequences for the way we understand both redemption and creation.

This sentence is the mirror image of proposition #1 in part 1, and so my exposition here can be brief. In part 1, I emphasized that because God the Creator is identified with the Deliverer and Redeemer—as in Psalm 124:8,

> Our help is in the name of the Lord,
> who made heaven and earth—

1. Calvin, *ICR* 3.2.36.

there is a redeeming, renewing, or salvific dimension to the divine dynamic at work in creation and preservation. This in fact is also a feature of the early creeds and their close association of the Creator who makes all things with the Reconciler and the Sanctifier. Among other things, what emerges is a theology that shapes and expresses a piety or deep-seated disposition for which creation is not merely a prerequisite for redemption. Redeeming and renewing grace is embedded in the existence, constitution, and continuation of world. The nebulae, galaxies, geosphere, biospheres, societies, and histories are not merely a neutral backdrop or stage for human activity and purpose. They are the Creator-Redeemer's cosmos of grace, a matrix of interrelations, processes, and events in which we encounter a renewing and redeeming trajectory.

Now in part 3 we turn around to emphasize the related and reverse point: God the Redeemer is God the Creator. Redemption therefore concerns nothing less than creation. Thus, in John 1 we are told that the Word or principle of redemption, in whom is life and who became flesh, was in the beginning, and that nothing was made or came into being without the Word. This close association of redemption with creation—an association that no world-denying spiritual dualist would countenance—lends to redemption the universal horizon of all things.

Consider, for example, the Christ hymn in Colossians 1:15–20.

> He is the image of the invisible God, the firstborn of all creation; for in him all things in heaven and on earth were created, things visible and invisible, whether thrones or dominions or rulers or powers—all things have been created through him and for him. He himself is before all things, and in him all things hold together. He is the head of the body, the church; he is the beginning, the firstborn from the dead, so that he might come to have first place in everything. For in him all the fullness of God was pleased to dwell, and through him God was pleased to reconcile to himself all things, whether on earth or in heaven, by making peace through the blood of his cross.

Note the parallelisms. Christ is the firstborn of all creation through whom and for whom all things (*ta panta*) have been created, and in whom all things hold together. Christ is also firstborn from the dead, the one through whom God reconciles all things to Godself. Eduard Lohse adds that, "although there is no mention of it, it is presupposed here that the unity and harmony of the cosmos have suffered a considerable disturbance, even a rupture."[2] Things threaten to

2. Eduard Lohse, *Colossians and Philemon*, trans. William R. Poehlmann and Robert J. Karis, Hermeneia (Philadelphia: Fortress, 1971), 59.

burst apart. The Christ event that erupts into the history of the Christian community heals the wound and restores the coherence. It signals a cosmic reconciliation of all things to God, and so redemption strains toward the universal scope of creation.

The close link between Creator and Redeemer therefore impacts how Christian piety regards both creation and redemption. Redemption, as we emphasized in part 1, lends a renewing dynamic to creation and providence (or to cosmic ecology and cosmic passage). At the same time, and as we emphasize now, creation lends a capacious horizon to redemption, a point that comes to articulation in Paul's striking motif of "new creation," and also in the image in Revelation 21 of a new heaven and a new earth in which all things are made new.[3] Grace abounds.

Proposition #48 The event of Jesus Christ points to a Trinitarian dynamic.

The New Testament presents the event of Jesus Christ in an expansive compass that extends in two "directions."[4] The genealogy in Matthew 1 extends the event of Jesus Christ "backward" to God's covenant with Abraham, while the genealogy in Luke 3 extends it to Adam and the creation. Texts such as the account of Pentecost in Acts 2, Paul's account of new life in Romans 8 ("For all who are led by the Spirit of God are children of God," v. 14), and his statements about spiritual gifts and participation in the one body of Christ in 1 Corinthians 12 extend the event of Jesus Christ "forward" toward renewal in the Spirit. The logic of these symbolic statements is clear. The event of Jesus Christ fulfills God's promise to Abraham, through whom all people shall be blessed, as well as the promise inherent in the creation of the world and human beings. And it does so by its close associations with the Spirit, the reversal of Babel's confusion, and the emergence of new life in a community called church that goes to all nations.

The two-way extension is a primary reason why the Christian community speaks of the event-of-*redemption*-in-Jesus-Christ that discloses the God of grace who extends a saving relationship or participation to all. That is, the one extension or expansion connects Jesus with the Creator, who chooses and delivers Israel. It links Jesus with God's gathering and election of a people into redeeming relationship with Godself following the misdirection of creation in the cycle of corruption and violence described in Genesis 4–11. The other extension—toward

3. Paul works with the motif in 2 Cor. 5, Gal. 6, and Rom. 8. See David L. Bartlett, "Creation Waits with Eager Longing," in *God Who Creates: Essays in Honor of W. Sibley Towner*, ed. William P. Brown and S. Dean McBride Jr. (Grand Rapids: Eerdmans, 2000), 229–50.

4. See chap. 1, prop. #14.

the Spirit—links Jesus to a decisive expansion of this covenant to the graceful gathering of all nations into the people of God.

Taken together, as we noted in part 1, these expansions point to a Trinitarian dynamic of which Jesus Christ becomes the fulcrum. The covenanting Creator and God of Israel, the reconciliation accomplished in Christ, and the renewing work of the Spirit all exhibit the same movement or trajectory toward redemption. And, indeed, the event of Jesus Christ cannot be adequately understood unless both of these references, extensions, or expansions are taken into account.

Proposition #49 Jesus Christ fulfills the covenant of grace.

The extensions or expansions point to what John Calvin understood to be the *one* covenant of grace by connecting reconciliation and renewal in Jesus Christ with the Creator, who covenants with Israel and also with the Spirit and the church. Here, Calvin built on Paul's idea that, in Christ, the blessing of Abraham, which remains with the Jews, comes also to the gentiles, who, by the Spirit, now are adopted as God's children (Gal. 3:6–14; 4:1–7). Indeed, says Calvin, it is by Christ and the Spirit that we are "reckoned members of his [Abraham's] tribe" and so become "children of God."[5]

Biblical Themes

The scriptural bases for these ideas will become apparent if we return to the fact that when we open a Bible to the New Testament, the first thing we see is a genealogy (or family tree) of "Jesus the Messiah, the son of David, the son of Abraham" (Matt. 1:1). That the New Testament begins this way is, of course, a result of the complex and somewhat political history of the formation of the canon, but it is also a theologically articulate result. It is as much as if, with the help of those who later decided on the canon, the writer or writers of the Gospel of Matthew were saying, "Listen. We are going to tell you about a very important person—Jesus the Messiah—and if you want to understand what we say, you can't just consider him apart or alone. You need to look at him in the context of the longer story of God's promises to Israel, from Abraham forward."[6]

5. Calvin, *ICR* 2.10.1–2, 11.

6. Among other things, of course, this is to insist that the Hebrew Scriptures are indispensable for understanding the New Testament. The Confession of 1967 of the Presbyterian Church (USA) says that "the Old Testament is indispensable to understanding the New, and is not itself fully understood without the New." *BOC* 9.28.

The genealogy's somewhat artificial arrangement into three groups of fourteen generations each (1:17) also highlights important theological claims. (In fact, only thirteen generations are recounted in the third group.) Jesus is the descendant of Abraham (the first group), the one with whom God covenants to make a great nation (Israel), and in whom "all the families of the earth shall be blessed" (Gen. 12:2–3). He descends from the one with whom the people of God was begun, a people that, by God's own free election or choosing, enjoys a sometimes rocky but nevertheless steadfast relationship with God. Again, as descendant of David (second group), the Messiah inherits the promise of the kingship or of God's anointed one, and thus of God's holy and just reign over the many peoples and nations (Isa. 2:2–4). These lines of descent are legacies of a divine faithfulness that has continued from the deportation to Babylon forward despite the faults and vacillations of God's people (third group). Indeed, this rather stylized beginning to the Gospel of Matthew accords with its ending, where the risen Christ commissions his disciples to "go . . . and make disciples of all nations," thus fulfilling the blessing of all the families of the earth by receiving all peoples into God's people. As far as the Gospel of Matthew is concerned, with the coming of Jesus the Messiah, God's gracious covenant with Abraham radiates into the entire world.

This is a basic outline, but there is considerably more to be said. If you went to Sunday school and were anything like me when I did, I suspect that when the teacher drew attention to a genealogy, you may have taken it as a bad sign: ". . . and Hezron, the father of Aram, and Aram the father of Aminadab, and Aminadab the father of Nahshon. . . ." Was our teacher really about to make us memorize this polysyllabic tongue twister? But it turns out that my anticipated drudgery obscured a fundamentally positive significance of genealogies in the Bible. "Be fruitful and multiply" is God's blessing of generativity and life in Genesis 1:22 and 1:28, and so, every subsequent genealogy, no matter how taxing to memorize, both recalls and embodies this blessing, this basis for life's continuing possibilities.

Indeed, that the Gospel of Matthew opens with a genealogy from Abraham forward links the coming of Jesus the Messiah rather explicitly with the blessing of life. How so? Because the way forward to Abram and Sarai, following the death-dealing cycle of violence and misdirection that introduces civilization in Genesis 4–11 and that terminates in Babel, is yet another genealogy, yet another chronicle of the continuation of life from generation to generation. And, in fact, by means of two further genealogies, Abram finally is connected to Noah and then to Lamech and the cycle of violence that engulfs humanity after Cain, and then also to Eve, Adam, and the blessing of created life itself. These mythopoeic narratives therefore insist that, even as all else fails (from deterrent schemes of vengeance to a primordial flood and the restarting of humanity and world with a clean slate), the blessing to be fruitful and multiply that was given at the creation to humans and other creatures continues. The blessing of generativity and life continues, if not quietly then at least somewhat prosaically and despite humanity's recurrent and destructive misdirection; and with this blessing, the gracious possibility that humans and world may be rightwised also continues. At the outset of Matthew's Gospel and of the New Testament itself, then, a genealogy that expresses the continuing blessing of life introduces the gracious fulfillment of new life.

This also helps us to make a theological connection between the genealogy of Jesus in Matthew and the one in Luke, which goes back not to Abraham but to "Enos, son of Seth, son of Adam, son of God" (Luke 3:38).[7] Mythically and symbolically, we are being told here that Jesus represents a second chance for humanity, a new period, or a new beginning in history—in Paul's terms, a "second Adam"—the rightwising fulfillment that makes all things new. The Creator goes out to make all things and hold them in relation to Godself—this, as we noted at the close of part 2, is the divine tendency. Now, in Christ, this same God (following Paul's vocabulary in 2 Cor. 5:19) reconciles all things to Godself, and so the fundamental excellence or tendency of the divine becomes clear. Now, the Messiah, who descends from Abraham and even from the first human, reveals the promise resident in the act of creation itself, namely, that *the great God of glory who creates is the good God of grace who redeems.*

The Covenant of Grace

The classical Reformed idea of the one covenant of grace suggests all this and more. Although for Calvin, in one sense at least, there are an "old covenant" made with the patriarchs and described in the Old Testament and another made later in the New Testament, he also insists, "in substance and reality . . . the two are actually one and the same."[8] Indeed, "all men adopted by God into the company of his people since the beginning of the world were covenanted to him by the same law and by the bond of the same doctrine as obtains among us."[9]

A primary reason is this: the covenantal relationship made with the patriarchs

7. This, despite the fact that Joseph A. Fitzmyer, SJ, is quite correct to say that, in Matthew and in Luke, "the New Testament has preserved for us two strikingly different genealogies of Jesus, which resist all harmonization." See *The Gospel according to Luke (I–IX): Introduction, Translation, and Notes* (Garden City, NY: Doubleday, 1981), 496.

8. Calvin, *ICR* 2.10.2.

9. Calvin, *ICR* 2.10.1.

and the one made in the New Testament are both established by the free mercy and grace of God alone. Calvin underscores this point by quoting Leviticus 26:12, "I . . . will be your God, and you shall be my people." Israel's adoption, Calvin insists, is gratuitous. Thus, "he is our God on this condition: that he dwell among us"—that is, on the condition of God's own free choosing.[10] Note that here Calvin makes no distinction between the patriarchs and his own community. In addition, Calvin claims, similar signs accompany the Old and New Testaments, for example, circumcision and baptism, Passover and the Lord's Supper.[11] Indeed, as we noted above, for Calvin, "to be children of God, we must be reckoned as members of his [Abraham's] tribe" (2.10.11).

What, then, is the role of Christ? Here too Calvin emphasizes God's free grace and promise. Thus, the Jews "had and knew Christ as Mediator, through whom they were joined to God and were to share in his promises" (2.10.2). Again, "the Old Testament was established upon the free mercy of God, and was confirmed by Christ's intercession" (2.10.4). Or, again, "the salvation revealed in Christ [is] the manifestation of the promises that the Lord had formerly made to Abraham and the patriarchs" (2.10.4). For Calvin, Christ is the mediator through whom all (both Jews and gentiles) are joined to God and become members of God's people. These convictions lead the Genevan Reformer to ask some rather striking questions. "Who, then, dares to separate the Jews from Christ, since with them, we hear, was made the covenant of the gospel, the sole foundation of which is Christ? Who dares to estrange from the gift of free salvation those to whom we hear the doctrine of the righteousness of faith was imparted?" (2.10.4).

Thus, for Calvin, the differences between the two covenants do not detract from their essential unity but "pertain to the manner of dispensation rather than to . . . substance" (2.10.1; 2.11.1). They amount to pedagogical adjustments, expedient accommodations to different ages or times (2.11.13–14). Calvin lists five such differences, though in many respects they boil down to two: the New Testament is clearer when it comes to matters such as the future life and the relationship between law and freedom, and with the New Testament all the nations have been called into covenant with God (2.11.1–12). And, in fact, as Jan Rohls points out, Reformed confessions generally follow Calvin, "defining the relation

10. Calvin, *ICR* 2.10.8. In his *Commentaries on the Last Four Books of Moses Arranged in the Form of a Harmony*, trans. Charles William Bingham, in *Calvin's Commentaries*, Calvin Translation Society (Grand Rapids: Baker Books, 1998), 3:212–24, Calvin treats Lev. 26 together with Deut. 28.

11. Calvin, *ICR* 2.10.5; 2.10.8; 2.11.23. Hereafter, references to this work appear in parentheses in the text.

between the Old and New Testament in such a way that the substantial identity of the covenant of grace comes clearly to expression."[12]

The Scots Confession of 1560 rather strikingly outlines some possible implications of these ideas. Its fourth chapter, "The Revelation of the Promise," says, "after the fearful and horrible departure of man from his obedience," God "did seek Adam again, call upon him, rebuke and convict him of his sin, and in the end made unto him a most joyful promise, that 'the seed of the woman should bruise the head of the serpent.'"[13] That is, Genesis 3:15 signals a graceful promise, and with this promise, the Scots supposes, God recruits humanity to God's cause over against the devil. "This promise was repeated and made clearer from time to time; it was embraced with joy, and most constantly received by all the faithful from Adam to Noah to Abraham, from Abraham to David, and so onwards to the incarnation of Christ Jesus; all (we mean the believing fathers under the law) did see the joyful day of Christ Jesus, and did rejoice."[14]

This single and continuing relationship, repeated and clarified "from time to time," is the one covenant of grace. It includes Christian followers of Jesus Christ, but also Hebrew patriarchs and prepatriarchal ancestors who lived prior to God's call to Abraham, for example, Adam and Noah, and who antedate even anything recognizable as Judaism. The graceful promise or covenant forms the basis for the people of God, the church, or in Scottish dialect, the Kirk. Therefore, following chapter 4, "The Revelation of the Promise," but *before* the sixth chapter, "The Incarnation of Christ Jesus," comes chapter 5, "The Continuance, Increase, and Preservation of the Kirk." This is its first sentence: "We most surely believe that God preserved, instructed, multiplied, honored, adorned, and called from death to life his Kirk in all ages since Adam until the coming of Christ Jesus in the flesh."[15] The Kirk, then, is coterminous with the people of God and has its historical beginning, not with the incarnation and not even with Abraham, but with God's gracious promise to the first human beings. Thus, according to the Scots, there is no "Christians only" sign over the door of the Kirk, and there has never been a person or generation of persons for whom God was not the God of grace.

12. Jan Rohls, *Reformed Confessions: Theology from Zurich to Barmen*, trans. John Hoffmeyer (Louisville: Westminster John Knox, 1998), 89. The one exception is the Erlanthal Confession, which, "picking up on Melanchthon, explicitly speaks not only of two testaments but also of two covenants: the Old Testament covenant of law and the New Testament covenant of grace."

13. *BOC* 3.04.

14. *BOC* 3.04. The theology of this passage also accords with the genealogical implications discussed above.

15. *BOC* 3.05.

Further Intricacies

We have to do here, of course, with theological reflections on some rather rich mythopoeic material, and there are further intricacies worth probing. For example, the Westminster Confession of Faith spoke of a covenant of works, first made with Adam on "condition of his personal obedience," and then of a second "covenant of grace . . . differently administered in the time of the law, and in the time of the gospel."[16] The latter covenant, whereby Jesus Christ and the Spirit offer salvation to sinners, was limited in its efficacy to the elect, or to those predestined by God's eternal decree to everlasting life.[17] (By logical implication, this was also the case for Calvin, who believed God's free mercy to be illustrated when God gives to some people what God denies to others.)[18] Westminster therefore summarized the justification of sinners by God's free grace as follows: "God did, from all eternity, decree to justify the elect, and Christ did, in the fullness of time, die for their sins and rise again for their justification: nevertheless they are not justified until the Holy Spirit doth, in due time, actually apply Christ unto them."[19] The claim is that Christ died for the sins of the elect rather than for the sins of all, and that the Spirit, by its quickening power, activates in the elect the effects of Christ's atonement.

Louis Berkhof, the early-twentieth-century systematician at Calvin Seminary, follows a good many Reformed scholastics when he elaborates these ideas by maintaining that the covenant of grace between God and the elect has its eternal basis in a counsel or covenant of redemption. Here, "the Father is the originator, the Son the executor, and the Holy Spirit the applier."[20] The Father freely, mercifully, and out of love elects to save those whom he wills. The Son promises to render "satisfaction" for their sins, thus furnishing the "juridical foundation" for the covenant of grace (267). (His atonement is therefore "particular" rather than "universal," because, by the Father's decree of election, it is limited only to some [268–69].) Finally, the covenant is fully realized in the elect by "the effective application of the Spirit" (278). The eternal counsel, therefore, makes possible the covenant of grace in history as "a relation of friendship" freely established by God with fallen man in Genesis 3:15 and definitely contracted in Abraham, but never meant to include all people (270, 273, 275).

16. *BOC* 6.038; 6.039; 6.041.

17. *BOC* 6.016–6.018; 6.039.

18. Indeed, Calvin wrote, "the very inequality of grace proves that it is free" (*ICR* 3.21.6).

19. *BOC* 6.071.

20. Louis Berkhof, *Systematic Theology*, new edition containing the full text of *Systematic Theology* and the original *Introductory Volume to Systematic Theology* (Grand Rapids: Eerdmans, 1996), 266. Hereafter, page references to this work appear in parentheses in the text.

The basic content of the covenant of grace, says Berkhof, is the electing promise of God in Genesis 17:7 ("I will establish my covenant between me and you . . . to be God to you and to your offspring after you") as well as the faithful response of God's people (277). This covenant is eternal and unbreakable because "God remains forever true" (278). Despite what some heretics (and even Lutherans!) mistakenly teach, it is particular and not intended for realization in the lives of all. It remains essentially the same in its two dispensations, the one in the Old Testament and the other in the New. Nevertheless, there are multiple "revelations," disclosures, or iterations of the covenant of grace in the Old Testament.

The initial disclosure recorded in Genesis 3:15 points to the friendship that God reestablished almost immediately with fallen humanity; enmity between the serpent and the woman signals that God has become humanity's confederate or partner in the struggle with Satan (294). The covenant with Noah constitutes a second iteration, which, Berkhof admits, is very general or even all-inclusive but consists only of earthly benefits (294). Nevertheless, like the later covenant with Abraham, the covenant with Noah originates in the grace, unmerited favors, and blessings of God that were forfeited by sin.

Of all the disclosures of the covenant of grace in the Old Testament, says Berkhof, the most normative for the New Testament is the covenant with Abraham. Here, again, he is following a good deal of classic Reformed theology (which, in turn, made use of the apostle Paul's reflections in Romans 4 on the faith of Abraham). Berkhof claims that, unlike Genesis 3:15, the covenant with Abraham is a definite transaction, and so marks the "formal establishment" of the covenant of grace as well as of an "institutional church" (296). Again, although it is not as general or inclusive as the covenant with Noah, the covenant with Abraham bestows clearer spiritual benefits. The later Sinaitic covenant is essentially the same as that established with Abraham, but it differs somewhat because it is a truly "national covenant" and introduces the law in several aspects (moral, civil, and ceremonial) as the rule of service and life (298).

The dispensation in the New Testament, says Berkhof, "will continue until the return of Christ, when the covenant of grace will be realized in a life of intimate communion with God" (300). Although it is essentially the same as the dispensation in the Old Testament, the new dispensation also differs in three ways. First, it is universal because it extends to the elect of all nations. (Berkhof claims, in fact, that the promise God made to the first humans in Genesis 3:15 originally was also universal in this sense; "particularism," or the limitation to one people, began with Abraham but was not intended to be permanent.) Second, the New Testament dispensation places greater emphasis on the gracious character of the covenant. Third, it brings richer blessings than did the Old Testament dispensation.

Critical Observations

What shall we make of the subordination of the covenant of grace to the dual decree of election? This, after all, is the crux of the persistent limitation of the covenant of grace at the hands of classical Reformed theologians. It is true, of course, that much like other Reformed thinkers, Berkhof says the New Testament dispensation is universal because it overcomes the Old Testament's limitation of the covenant of grace to a specific people. But we should not let this claim pass without observing that, according to Berkhof and the rest, even in Jesus Christ, the covenant remains particular, in the sense of being limited to the elect. Moreover, Berkhof's insistence that universality distinguishes the New Testament dispensation tends to obscure significant universal dimensions of the Old Testament iterations.

For example, if one allows the somewhat creative Reformed interpretation of Genesis 3:15 to stand, then, as Berkhof also notes, God's agreement with the first humans implies a horizon considerably broader than any particular nation. Again, not only for our own purposes here but also for the sake of an appropriate reading of the Gospel of Matthew, we note that, according to Genesis 12:3, in Abraham "*all* the families of the earth shall be blessed." The covenant with Noah is even more sweeping, since it clearly harkens back to the blessing of generativity given to creatures in their kinds in Genesis 1. It is a covenant "between me [God] and you [Noah] and every living creature that is with you, for all future generations," a "covenant between me [God] and the earth" (Gen. 9:12–13). Moreover, we also glimpse elements of an expansive horizon in the election and mission of Israel to all nations mentioned in some psalms and prophetic writings.

Questions arise when we look at the event of Jesus Christ in the context of these earlier iterations. Does the dispensation of the covenant of grace in Jesus Christ and the New Testament really fulfill the earlier universalizing trajectories? Rather than say Christ fulfills the covenant with Abraham in whom all families shall be blessed, should we say instead that in Christ some members of many families are blessed? Should we say that in Jesus Christ God's grace is shown to be less extensive than the promise to Adam intimates or implies? Are we bound to admit that it is not nearly as inclusive as the covenant with Noah and every living thing?

It seems apparent, then, that classical Reformed theologians failed to ask certain questions with sufficient force. Why are *none* of the iterations of the covenant of grace in the Hebrew Scripture simply and entirely particular? Why is a universalizing and inclusive element and energy persistently present? Should we not be encouraged to attend with greater rigor (and also joy) to this persistent energy and element, especially when we look upon it in the light of universalizing texts in the New Testament? What if we believe the fulfillment of the covenant of grace to be indicated by texts such as Colossians 1:20, "and through him God was pleased to reconcile to himself all things"—where "all things" translates *ta panta* and thus signifies the whole universe or cosmic collective? What if we believe it to be indicated by 2 Corinthians 5:19, "in Christ God was reconciling the world to [Godself]," where "the world" translates *kosmos*?

We may enlist in our effort (at least temporarily) no less a Reformed theologian than Karl Barth, who regarded reconciliation in Jesus Christ as the fulfillment of the covenant of grace "between God and *man*."[21] Barth emphasized that, when God speaks to "Noah and his sons" in Genesis 9:1, 8, this refers to the whole of humanity after Noah, both before and outside Abraham. The race as a whole is therefore in covenant, and this, Barth insisted, is the outer circle of which the relation with Israel forms the inner circle (27). Hence, "creation is the outward basis of the covenant," and "the fall does not take place outside but within this special relationship" (27)—an idea that moves an important step beyond even typical Reformed interpretations of Genesis 3:15.

Again, Barth noted, when the Old Testament speaks of the election and call of Israel, or the saving relationship inaugurated at Sinai, it "never has any hesitation in allowing figures from outside, from the nations . . . to enter the inner circle: Melchizedek . . . Jethro the Midianite . . . Balaam . . . Rahab . . . Ruth . . . to mention only a few out of a list which is remarkably continued in the New Testament" (27–28). Moreover, the covenant with Israel is not an end in itself but has a representative significance as a sign and a witness to all people. Thus, Zion is the site for a redemptive event of universal significance in Isaiah 25:6–8, where "the Lord of hosts will make for all peoples a feast of rich food" and "well-aged wines," and "will wipe away the tears from all faces." In Isaiah 49:6, Israel is given "as a light to the nations," and Isaiah 52:13–15, said Barth, points to an eschatological event where the nations finally understand the meaning of the presence of Israel among them (29). In fact, the Day of Yahweh, a day when the covenant finds fulfillment in Israel's judgment and redemption, is also the day of redemption for all nations. This, Barth admitted, may not be the broadest line in the Old Testament, but it is at least an unmistakable one, whose significance is heightened all the more by universalizing descriptions in the New Testament of reconciliation in Jesus Christ (31).

21. Barth, *CD* IV/1:22 (emphasis added). Hereafter, page references to *CD* IV/1 appear in parentheses in the text.

Stepping beyond Barth

Barth lifted up certain witnesses, including, curiously, the Noachian covenant with its references to "every living creature," as indicators of a covenant of grace that extends to the whole of *humanity*. But, having identified in at least some New Testament witnesses to reconciliation in Christ a bolder trajectory toward expansion than even the expression "the whole of humanity" implies, we may now raise additional questions. Why did Barth himself not go further? Especially in the light of witnesses to a new creation, to a new heaven and earth, and to the reconciliation in Christ of "all things" and the "cosmos" to God, why did he not take an additional step? Is the outer circle of the covenant of grace really restricted to humanity? Is the reconciliation of humans an end in itself? If it is, then why should the creation or the whole created universe wait in hope to be set free from bondage to decay and to enter upon the freedom and glory of the children of God (Rom. 8:19–23)?

Barth was certainly right to question and overcome the limitation imposed by Reformed orthodoxy on the covenant of grace when it gave priority to theological speculations concerning the eternal decree over the good news of reconciliation in Jesus Christ. He did so because he believed instead that, following the doctrinal formula of Chalcedon, the good news of the gospel must be that human nature, or the being of humans, has been reconciled to God in Jesus Christ. And this insistence allowed him to see the covenant of grace with new eyes. But now we must also ask whether a similarly speculative idea—namely, the Chalcedonian two-natures formula itself—kept Barth from appreciating a more radical point. Do not the persistently expansive iterations of the covenant of grace suggest that, despite recurrent human failings, it is and will be the covenant of the effective grace *of God*? Do they not therefore suggest a circle or horizon that extends not only beyond any particular nation but also beyond humanity?[22] Indeed, especially when we consider them from the vantage point of fulfillment by the reconciliation in Jesus Christ of *ta panta* to God, do they not intimate a truly (and unambiguously) universal covenant of grace? Does reconciliation in Jesus Christ, by overcoming the rupture, hurt, or wound in *ta panta*, therefore disclose the original and basic divine dynamic in creation itself?

22. For Barth, creation is the external basis for God's covenant of redemption with human beings. "The purpose and therefore the meaning of creation is to make possible the history of God's covenant with man which has its beginning, its centre and its culmination in Jesus Christ." Or, again, "the whole cosmos was precisely created that in it there might be this event and revelation—that man might be what he is by the grace of God and for the grace of God." *CD* III/1:42, 67.

If so, then our brief study has wrested from Reformed ruminations about mythopoeic representations of the one covenant of grace an important result. The covenant of grace fulfilled by reconciliation in Jesus Christ is in some sense coextensive with creation itself. It clarifies, sharpens, and re-presents the promise inherent in God going out from Godself to create and hold all things in relation to Godself. And this clarification, in turn, elaborates the meaning of some rather fundamental statements about God. God the Creator is God the Redeemer. The great God of glory who creates is the good God of grace who redeems. God is the faithful God of grace who creates and renews *all* things. This is what is displayed and comes to expression in the event of Jesus Christ, and this is also what comes to expression in creation. This, to borrow a phrase from Jonathan Edwards, is a disclosure of *the divine excellence*, and this excellence, rather than a limiting decree, forms the basis for the covenant of grace and finally also for creation itself. Moreover, it also forms the appropriate theological frame within which to consider the event of redemption-in-Jesus-Christ and sin or the human fault.

What's New?

What, then, does the disclosure in Jesus Christ add? Much of the answer waits for an extended consideration of the particulars of Jesus's life, ministry, death, and resurrection. But here we may at least say that it does not add a fundamentally different content. Certainly it does not present a reversal of previous iterations, as is sometimes claimed by those who contrast Judaism as law with Christianity as grace, gospel, and forgiveness.[23] This much is clear from the genealogies in Matthew and in Luke, and it indicates a point on which the classical Reformed idea of the one covenant of grace was certainly right. In substance, the dispensation in Jesus Christ and the dispensation in the Hebrew Scriptures are one and the same.

Then again, for the gentiles, or at least for very many outside of Israel, there is in the gospel a message, when compared with the previous dispensation, an opening and therefore something other and something more than an exact or simple repetition. There is a gospel that for many amounts to a clarifying *re-presentation*, a distinguishable iteration in the light of which something crucial becomes clear. There is a portrayal of the divine excellence that grasps many beyond Israel because it makes clear that God is gracious to many beyond Israel. Moreover, to be grasped by this re-presentation is in fact to encounter, *perceive*,

23. See chap. 2, prop. #20 on anti-Judaism, where I elaborate this same point in another context.

or apprehend the God of grace who is gracious to us, and, as we may say following Barth, the apprehension that the God of grace is gracious to us "is itself grace."[24] The clearer apprehension by one or another people of the God of grace *in relation to themselves* is itself grace. The apprehension in Jesus Christ by one or another people that God establishes a relationship with creation that neither falters nor fails but instead finally drives toward the reconciliation and renewal of all things, including themselves, is itself grace.

This apprehension and its re-presentation in the New Testament shape and express piety's sense that, in relation to God, life and existence are good and worthwhile. In saying this, we do not derive the event of redemption-in-Jesus-Christ from creation, or vice versa. Creation and redemption are mutually clarifying. They point to the same thing, namely, the God of grace in relation to which we sense that it is good to be. This is the true light, relationship, or perspective for which every creature is claimed, and when it radiates or shines out into the world, this too is grace.

Parenthetically, then, it was not only a mistake for the older Calvinist theology to speculate that, in the eternal counsel of redemption, the Son's promise of atonement is limited by the Father's decree of election, it was also a mistake to speculate at all about a pact or a counsel of redemption between Father, Son, and Spirit in order to render God gracious or merciful. God is always and already the God of grace. God *is* gracious, and this excellence is already present from the very first. Creation and redemption (and the covenant of grace) illustrate and disclose this excellence, though neither is the basis for it. Instead, this divine excellence, this gracious tendency to create and renew that establishes and continues the relationship between God and all things, is itself the basis or the ground for creation and redemption.

An Expansion and a Revision

Jesus Christ fulfills the covenant of grace. To make this point I have expanded and therefore also revised a traditional Reformed idea. Let me pause now to review just how I have done so.

I accept some rather basic traditional outlines. From Calvin, I take the point that the primary covenantal relationship made with the patriarchs and the one made in the New Testament are both established by the free grace of God. This is why Calvin attaches such importance to Leviticus 26:12, "I . . . will be your God, and you shall be my people." Israel's adoption is gratuitous, and gratuitous

24. Barth, *CD* IV/1:45.

adoption means that here we have a true covenant *of grace* in the sense that it depends first of all and finally, not on the actions of humans, but on God's own choosing and election, or on grace alone.

Grace alone; this, for Calvin, is what is efficient and salvific. Clearly, it is *appropriate* for human agents and communities to respond to God's grace, but the existence and efficacy of the covenantal relationship do not depend on our response. That relationship does not depend on works. Instead, its sole condition is that God chooses to "dwell among us." So, when we turn in a later chapter to the question of grace and works, we shall note the extraordinary fittingness of good works in response to grace. Indeed, we may also say that gratitude for God's gracious gifts impels and drives one to respond with works of love, and that it is therefore possible to speak here of an imperative or even a kind of necessity.[25] But we shall not say that good works are necessary for saving grace; saving grace is logically prior and also sufficient. Thus, one basic feature of the Reformed idea of the covenant of grace is that it points to *the God of grace* who freely or gratuitously chooses to be in relationship with whom and what God wills.[26]

I also accept a capacious claim articulated so forthrightly by the Scots Confession, namely, that the one covenant of grace includes Hebrew patriarchs and matriarchs as well as Adam, Noah, and others who antedate Judaism. This is why the Scots also includes them in the Kirk, thus in effect distinguishing the true Kirk and its members from historic Christianity, since it also includes persons who did not acknowledge Jesus in their lifetimes. Biblically speaking, of course, all people are descended from Adam and Noah as their fathers. The point the Scots makes here therefore tends toward Karl Barth's insistence that the "outer circle" of the covenant of grace is all humanity, rather than all Christians who profess Jesus as Lord or even a religiously diverse group called the elect who are distinguished from the reprobate by an eternal decree.

Only two points remain to complete my expansion or revision of the scope of the covenant of grace beyond even Barth's idea. First, the iteration of the

25. Thus, the Heidelberg Catechism says, "it is impossible for those engrafted into Christ through true faith not to produce fruits of gratitude," but this refers to what I would call an impulsion of gratitude. See "The Heidelberg Catechism," *BOC* 4.064. See also Douglas F. Ottati, "Learning Theological Ethics through the Heidelberg Catechism," *Acta Theologica* (2014, Supplement 20): 148.

26. This, incidentally, is also why the chapter of the Westminster Confession of Faith on effectual calling says, "Elect infants, dying in infancy, are regenerated and saved by Christ through the Spirit, who worketh when, and where, and how he pleaseth. So also are all those other elect persons who are incapable of being outwardly called by the ministry of the Word" (*BOC* 6.066). That is, persons may be saved by grace even if they have not consciously responded to God's free grace.

covenant of grace with Noah is not simply between God and Noah, or even between God, Noah, and all of Noah's descendants. "As for me, I am establishing my covenant with you and your descendants after you, and with every living creature that is with you. . . . I have set my bow in the clouds, and it shall be a sign of the covenant between me and the earth" (Gen. 9:9–13). *The "outer circle" of the covenant extends not simply to all humanity but to all living creatures and even to the earth.* This accords in spirit with texts such as Colossians 1:20, where the suggestion is made that, through Christ, "God was pleased to reconcile to himself all things (*ta panta*), whether on earth or in heaven." It accords also, I think, with the cosmic scope of redemption intimated by Paul's image of "new creation" and by the apocalyptic image of "a new heaven and a new earth" that we find in Revelation.[27]

Second, because, as Berkhof says, the iterations of the covenant with Abraham and at Sinai have the character of "definite transactions," some may object to my expansion on the grounds that God establishes the covenant of grace only with sentient and intelligent humans who can enter into an explicit transaction and respond to it. But this objection is itself called into question by the passages above when they refer to "every living creature," a "new creation," and "a new heaven and new earth." And, as I have indicated, it is also called into question by the Reformed insistence that a response is not a condition for the efficacy of the covenant. I conclude, then, that the one covenant of grace, with its many iterations and emphases, is best regarded as a way of pointing to the apprehension or idea that the true God is the God of grace. I conclude, further, that the divine tendency of this gracious God is to create, and thus freely bestow existence and life on all things, and then also to redeem in a cosmic scope that affects not only humans but also all living and material creation.

I should add that this expansion and revision of the covenant-of-grace image is consonant with the stunningly expanded and intricate vision of the story of life offered by the contemporary field of study called astrobiology. This multidisciplinary inquiry underscores the importance for life of elements generated by the big bang and early-generation stars, close relationships and connections between the inorganic and the organic, varieties of microbial life, and relationships between human life and other forms of life. It also treats life as a planetary process and points to possibilities for life beyond Earth.[28] To extend the scope

27. See Bartlett, "Creation Waits with Eager Longing," and John T. Carroll, "Creation and Apocalypse," in Brown and McBride, *God Who Creates*, 232, 237, 242–43, 250, 255–56, 258–59. See also Joseph A. Fitzmyer, SJ, *Romans: A New Translation with Introduction and Commentary* (New York: Doubleday, 1993), 505–6. See also chap. 3, prop. #26.

28. Ximena C. Abrevaya et al., "The Astrobiology Primer v2.0," *Astrobiology* 16, no. 8

of the covenant of grace and the meaning of Jesus Christ in the manner I have suggested helps us to envision the God of grace in relation to this expansive and complex cosmic context.

Excursus on the Image of God

This is a good place to note the collective testimony of Genesis 1 and 2 that God fashions *adam*, the human being, from the dust of the earth and then breathes life into his nostrils, but that this earth creature—humanity—both male and female, is also made in the image of God. There are both commonality and distinction here. Thus, in Genesis 2, not only the human being but also "every animal of the field and every bird of the air" is fashioned out of the ground. All are earth creatures, limited, tethered to the soil from which they were made, dependent on physical, biological, organic, and abiotic stuff. Even so, God brings the other creatures to the man to see what he will call them (and thus also classify them). In Genesis 1, all creatures, including humans, are placed within a wider world of orderings and relationships that they do not control and on which they depend. All must adjust or somehow fit in with an environment replete with seas and land and skies. All receive the blessing of generativity in their kinds. But only humans are said to be made in God's image.

The image of God—it is not easy to say just what this means. Genesis 1:26 and following are frustratingly nonspecific, and through the centuries different writers have said that one or another human quality or capacity, such as reason or the ability to manipulate and master the earth, constitutes the image of God in humans. For example, Thomas Aquinas cites Augustine in support of the claim that "man's eminence [lies in the fact], that God made man after his own image in so far as he gave him an intelligent mind, which is where he surpasses the animals." Aquinas also associates reason with the dominion of humans or their ability to hold sway over other things.[29] The twentieth-century Bible scholar Gerhard von Rad argues that "the purpose of this image of God in man" is bound up with the "lordship of man," which "extends over the world and not, for example, just over animals."[30] More recently, however, and inspired partly by Karl Barth, Claus Westermann insists that, in Genesis 1:26, 27, no peculiar

(2016): 562–63; Eric Smith and Harold J. Morowitz, *The Origin and Nature of Life on Earth: The Emergence of the Fourth Geosphere* (Cambridge: Cambridge University Press, 2016), 1–13.

29. Aquinas, *ST* 1a.93.1–4 (pp. 49–61); 1a.96.2 (pp. 127–29).

30. Gerhard von Rad, *The Theology of Israel's Historical Traditions*, vol. 1 of *Old Testament Theology*, trans. D. M. G. Stalker (New York: Harper & Row, 1962), 147–48.

quality of humanity is meant. Instead, the text is speaking about the action and purpose of God in creating humans. The human person can take a stand before God and can be responsible before God because all humanity, all persons, are created to correspond to God. They are created so that something may happen between them and God.[31]

According to B. A. Gerrish, for Calvin, the image is to be found in the "unimpaired use and ordering" or integrity of Adam's created powers, which are vitiated where we do not thankfully acknowledge God's gifts. This definition, in turn, fits with the idea that "the image is like a *reflection* in a mirror. All of God's creatures are mirrors of God's glory; humans are distinguished by their ability to reflect the glory of God in a conscious response." People reflect "the bountiful Creator in the act of thanksgiving, which defines, for Calvin, the attitude of *pietas* to God."[32]

I find this account of the image suggestive, and propose that the human earth-creature made from dust images or mirrors the divine glory, and that human life and the human spirit therefore point beyond themselves. Humanity stands before God in a distinctive fashion so that people may image or reflect the gratuitous excellence of God by apprehending it and then also offering an explicit or conscious acknowledgment in worship and in life. This idea supports the priestly contention that, among creatures, people participate in the seventh day or Sabbath self-consciously, linguistically, and liturgically. People may call upon God's *name*, and people may also consciously try to live faithfully in relation to God. Here, too, however, we also need to reckon with both commonality and distinction. According to Genesis 1:1–2:4, not only humans but all creation tend toward Sabbath rest, and elsewhere in Scripture it is clear that our imaging, mirroring, or reflecting of the divine graciousness is not without parallels and analogies among other creatures.

Consider, for example, Psalm 148, a text constructed with explicit reference to Genesis 1. The psalm is itself a part of a liturgy in which the worshiping community calls on the *name* of the Lord as no other creature we know of can (v. 13), and yet it also calls all creatures or creations, including nonliving ones such as snow, frost, and wind, to praise God. Thus, the first part of the psalm (vv. 1–6) extends the call to worship to all things in heaven, for example, angels, sun, and moon, and it also says that these things should praise God because they

31. Westermann, *Creation*, trans. John J. Scullion, SJ (Philadelphia: Fortress, 1974), 56; Westermann, *Genesis 1–11: A Commentary*, trans. John J. Scullion, SJ (Minneapolis: Augsburg, 1984), 150–58.

32. B. A. Gerrish, *Christian Faith: Dogmatics in Outline* (Louisville: Westminster John Knox, 2015), 65.

have been brought into being by God's creative word. We might say that their existence itself is therefore articulate testimony to the gratuitous excellence of the God who creates. The second part of the psalm (vv. 7–14) invites all things on Earth to praise God. The longer list of invitees includes all people (princes, rulers, young, old, men, women) together with hills, cedars, and cattle. Then, the final verse introduces the children of Israel, the liturgical community that worships and exalts God's name.

Taken as a whole, the psalm suggests that humans image and reflect the divine not only in explicit services of worship, as no other creature we know of does, but also in "their very being and doing," as in fact all other creatures do.[33] Like the existence of all other creatures, the very existence of humanity, the very reality of being human, is itself testimony to the gratuitous excellence of the God who creates and redeems. Unlike many other creatures, however, human beings may also consciously acknowledge that this is so. And, in fact, this distinctively reflective imaging of the divine includes the imaginative and poetic possibility of envisioning all things mirroring the divine glory in their being and doing, which is precisely what Psalm 148 does.[34]

A parenthetical question that arises here is whether the difference is one of degree or kind, and almost immediately we are drawn into complex discussions about human consciousness in relation to other animals and creatures. In a number of respects—one being self-reflexiveness—human consciousness seems highly distinctive, if not unique. But to say this we need not suppose that analogous things never happen with respect to elephant consciousness, dog consciousness, etc. As the philosopher Mary Midgley notes, when we look at animals, "there is a lot of uniqueness around."[35] Some writers, especially ones who want to emphasize the language of soul, stress "the great fact of human ex-

33. James L. Mays, *Psalms*, Interpretation: A Bible Commentary for Teaching and Preaching (Louisville: John Knox, 1994), 444–45.

34. Again, these ideas are not novel. Although Aquinas insists that humans alone possess God's image, he also says that there is in all creatures "some sort of likeness" to God, some sort of "print" in them of their divine cause, insofar as they are and are alive. Calvin calls the universe "a sort of mirror in which we can contemplate God," who is otherwise invisible, and also "a spectacle of God's glory." Commenting on Ps. 148, he also writes of "this symphony" of praise that all would hear "were they at all attent upon considering the works of God. For doth not the sun by his light, and heat, and other marvelous effects praise his Maker? The stars when they run their course, and at once adorn the heavens and give light to the earth, do they not sound the praises of God?" See Aquinas, *ST* 1a.93.2 (pp. 53–55); Calvin, *ICR* 1.5.1; 1.5.5; John Calvin, *Commentary on the Book of Psalms*, trans. James Anderson, vol. 5 in *Calvin's Commentaries*, Calvin Translation Society (Grand Rapids: Baker Books, 1998), 304–5.

35. Mary Midgley, "On Being Anthrozoon," *Minding Nature* 5, no. 2 (September 2012): 11.

ceptionalism" and seem committed to a sharp and dramatic difference of kind.[36] However, it also seems possible to say that human mind is an emergent property of the human brain.[37] Indeed, I think it may be best simply to say that humans are social animals with a distinctive knot of capabilities, many of which are variously shaped both socially and experientially.

This proposal will allow for vigorous acknowledgments and investigations of human spirituality. It is also compatible with the idea that, to make sense of humans and their experiences, we need to make use of multiple and complementary forms of description offered by a plurality of disciplines and perspectives, including sociology and literature, but also biology.[38] This does not decide once and for all the question of whether the human difference is one of degree or kind. But I suspect the difference between differences of degree and differences of kind (or qualitative differences) does not remain stable across different discourses and descriptions. And the question—"Different in degree or kind?"—looks to me like a problem not worth solving in a totalizing way. In any case, what I have said here about the image of God in humans does not require that we do so.

As I understand it, the distinctively human mirroring or imaging of the divine excellence includes an apprehension of one's own relationship with the God who goes out to create, hold all things in relation to God, and to redeem. It includes an apprehension or knowledge of oneself as a participant in the gratuitous excellence of deity, as well as a correspondent sense for one's kinship with all other creatures under God, or with all those whose very being and doing participate in and reflect the divine glory.

Indeed, we might say that humans may recognize themselves as creatures that participate in the interdependent vector or dynamic of life. They may come to see themselves as creatures that depend upon and emerge from cosmic and natural processes beyond their doing, social creatures that depend on one another. That is, they may consciously regard and see themselves as participants who are "drawn out" by and toward others and by the excellence of things. They are endowed with a distinctive capacity to "go out from themselves," to consciously appreciate the awe-inspiring circumambient world, to live a good life together with others, and thus to consciously reflect the divine tendency or glory to go out from Godself to create and redeem.

36. Marilynne Robinson, *Absence of Mind: The Dispelling of Inwardness from the Modern Myth of the Self* (New Haven: Yale University Press, 2011), 133.

37. See chap. 6, prop. #45. See also Pier Luigi Luisi, *The Emergence of Life: From Chemical Origins to Synthetic Biology* (Cambridge: Cambridge University Press, 2006), 109–10, 124–25.

38. David Fergusson, *Faith and Its Critics* (Oxford: Oxford University Press, 2009), 69, 115.

The traditional Christian idea that the *imago* in humans is tarnished or obscured and therefore in need of renewal and restoration expresses piety's judgment that, when mired in sin and corruption, people neither apprehend nor reflect the divine excellence clearly. The participatory and ec-centric vector or tendency of created and interdependent human life is therefore obscured. As sinners, people do not perceive what the divine excellence means for their relationship with God and for their kinship with others, and so they do not reflect this excellence in their relationships with God and others. Instead, they become constricted, curved in upon themselves. This idea of the *imago* also coheres with the conviction that many persons come to perceive or apprehend the divine excellence—their relationship to God and their kinship with others—in Jesus Christ, the kingdom-minded person-for-others.

Sensing the Gratuitous Heart of Reality

If this is at all correct, then theological reflections about the covenant of grace help to shape and express a sense of the divine, and, specifically, a sense for the divine gratuity that lies behind and beneath both creation and redemption and that is critical for grasping the divine excellence as well as the capacity of humans to reflect it. Somewhat like Edwards, we might call this a sense and taste for the divine excellence, an appreciation for the beauty or loveliness of the divine that does not reduce to its "profitableness" or utility for us, a spiritual sensation that encourages a certain temper of mind and heart.[39] It is, at one level, a perception of the divine tendency or trajectory at work in existence and in the renewal of things, an apprehension that is closely intertwined with our feeling that it is good to be, with our feeling for the preciousness of our own life as well as our sense for the precious value of all finite things. It is the religious apprehension that all is gift, all the consequence of a mysterious graceful donation, and that, likewise, the continuation and renewal of all are also graceful donation.

This sense and taste for the divine excellence sculpts and supports feelings of dependence, gratitude, repentance, possibility, and assurance. It is basic or fundamental for a thankfully and hopefully realistic piety or disposition. In short, it is a consciousness of the deep gratuity at the heart of reality that disposes human life ec-centrically toward God and others. And this, together with our appropriate response to it, is in fact just what has been tarnished and now stands in need of rehabilitation and renewal.

39. Jonathan Edwards, *Religious Affections*, ed. John E. Smith, vol. 2 of *WJE*, pt. 3, I, pp. 201–8; pt. 3, II, pp. 240–47.

Proposition #50 Jesus is the Christ, the living Word and wisdom of God in a human life.

For Christian communities, the event of redemption in Jesus Christ constitutes the paradigmatic proposal for picturing God, the world, and ourselves.[40] It is the single most important clue to the deity as well as to a faithful life, or to patterns of interaction and affection that are responsive to the divine.

The New Testament makes this point by connecting the man Jesus with a number of basic images or symbolic concepts. Consider again the rich theological statements presented in the genealogies in Matthew and Luke. Matthew indicates that Jesus Christ is the son of David, the Messiah-King who fulfills the covenant with Abraham, in whom, according to Genesis 12, all the families of the earth shall be blessed. Thus, at the close of this gospel the risen Christ sends his disciples to all nations, in effect opening up the covenantal people of God to all. The genealogy in Luke 3 presents Jesus Christ as the second Adam in whom all humanity is presented with a new possibility for a truer and more genuine life, and, fittingly, at the conclusion of Luke-Acts, Paul the apostle preaches unhindered at the center of the known world.

Davidic Messiah-King and second Adam—both of these symbolic themes interpret Jesus; both construe him as the answer to the question of the blessing of humanity and its renewal or re-creation. They also connect with the image of reconciliation that we shall discuss shortly. Jesus Christ reconciles people to God and one another, and so renews corrupted humans. Davidic Messiah-King and second Adam—both are ways of saying why we should pay special attention to the story of this person, Jesus of Nazareth, who is critically important for the story of God and God's people and, indeed, for the story of all humanity.

Another way to indicate this is to associate Jesus with the symbolic idea of the Christ or the Messiah. *Jesus is the Christ* or the Messiah, and, as the twentieth-century theologian Paul Tillich noted, the Christ is "a figure with a function."[41] Or, as Calvin might have said, Christ signifies an office. "The Christ," then, is not a surname like Smith, Iwahashi, or Obama but a title, something like "apostle," "king," or "Mr. President." This comes through in the early expression "Christ Jesus," which Paul sometimes uses in his letters (e.g., Rom. 8:39; 1 Cor. 1:1). To say "Christ Jesus" is something like saying "the apostle Paul," "King David," or "President Obama." It is to identify the man Jesus of Nazareth with a specific and symbolically resonant title. When we say Jesus Christ, we are interpreting Jesus.

40. See chap. 1, prop. #14.

41. Paul Tillich, *Existence and the Christ*, vol. 2 of *Systematic Theology* (Chicago: University of Chicago Press, 1957), 97–98.

We are saying, in effect, that Jesus is the Christ or the Messiah. We are saying that Jesus of Nazareth occupies the *office* and performs the function of the Christ or the Messiah. The Christ is the title of God's anointed one who stands in a special relationship with God and God's people. The Christ is the Messiah, the one who proclaims the advent of God's kingdom and in whom that kingdom is made manifest.[42] Jesus Christ is the one in whom God's kingdom has drawn near, and so, with him, a new state of things has been inaugurated.

As we shall see, these ruminations about the Christ or the Messiah accord tolerably well with what many scholars take to have been the message of the *historical* Jesus of Nazareth. It accords especially well, I think, with important recent discussions about the Jesus of history and just how much we know about him.[43] Even so, the famous twentieth-century New Testament scholar Rudolf Bultmann makes a basic point on which there is broad consensus among historians to the present day: Jesus comes preaching the kingdom.[44]

Consider the Lord's Prayer as it appears in Matthew and in Luke. The texts differ, and the probability is that neither goes back in its entirety to the historical Jesus.[45] Nevertheless, Jesus's historic emphasis on God's kingdom comes through. "Thy kingdom come" tells us that Jesus's prayer places all within the context of God's in-breaking reign or rule, a state of affairs in which God's will shall be done on earth as it is in heaven. Jesus is the one who proclaims that the kingdom is at hand, the one whose life and ministry embody the kingdom. Jesus is the Christ or the Messiah, the one who teaches and inaugurates the kingdom in what he says, does, and endures. Therefore, to know God's kingdom purpose, we must attend to the specifics of Jesus's life, ministry, death, and resurrection.

A good many texts in the New Testament present Jesus this way, and the point I wish to make here is simply that, when Christians look to Jesus *as the Christ or the Messiah*, they look with an expectation that they will find out what God's kingdom is like. They look with an expectation that they will find out that God's fundamental aim or purpose is bound up with a reign, rule, or state in which

42. Douglas F. Ottati, *Jesus Christ and Christian Vision* (Louisville: Westminster John Knox, 1996), 17.

43. See, for example, Marcus Borg and N. T. Wright, *The Meaning of Jesus: Two Visions (Plus)* (San Francisco: HarperOne, 2007); John Dominic Crossan, *The Historical Jesus: The Life of a Mediterranean Jewish Peasant* (New York: HarperCollins, 1991); N. T. Wright, *Simply Jesus: A New Vision of Who He Was, What He Did, and Why He Matters* (San Francisco: HarperOne, 2011). These and other recent works are discussed in chap. 8.

44. Rudolf Bultmann, *Theology of the New Testament*, trans. Kendrick Grobel, vol. 1 (London: SCM, 1952), 33.

45. Robert W. Funk, Roy W. Hoover, and the Jesus Seminar, trans. and commentary, *Five Gospels: The Search for the Authentic Words of Jesus* (San Francisco: HarperSanFrancisco, 1993), 148, 325.

the last shall be first and the poor and the marginalized blessed, in which people shall have life eternal, etc. This reign, rule, or kingdom expresses the divine will. Moreover, since God's will is to bring about the kingdom, a human life truly fitted to the divine tendency or dynamic is one turned toward or adjusted to God's kingdom purpose.

> "Blessed are you who are poor,
> for yours is the kingdom of God." (Luke 6:20)

This sentence expresses Jesus's kingdom-mindedness. It is a statement of God's kingdom purpose, and, as such, it also points to what a human life adjusted in attitude and action to that purpose is like, what participatory life attuned to the interdependent dynamic of God's reign is like. It helps to express and to sculpt a set of attitudes, a way of living, and a Christoform piety that entails a sense of solidarity with others as well as a heightened concern for the destructive injustices and deprivations so often suffered by the poor.

Jesus is the Christ. To connect the meaning of this sentence with the theology I have been developing here, return momentarily to the observation that the Gospel of Matthew presents Jesus as the Davidic Messiah-King who fulfills the covenant with Abraham and opens the people of God to all and to the observation that the Gospel of Luke presents Jesus Christ as the one who renews all humanity. In Tillich's terms, these are ways of saying that the Christ is the one who brings a new state of things.[46] Or, as we might say, the Christ brings the kingdom, the new state of things promised by the divine tendency or dynamic at work in all things.

Consider now a powerful image or symbol in the hymn-like prologue to the Gospel of John that also interprets and draws attention to Jesus. Jesus is the Word of God that became flesh or a human being who lived among us. Later church councils at Nicea and Chalcedon elaborate this motif metaphysically. But if we go back behind this subsequent doctrinal development and try, for the moment at least, to stick more closely to the terms of the Johannine text, then the affirmation that the Word became flesh and lived among us means that Jesus is the enfleshed Logos or Word of God.

The term "Logos" both can and has been understood in relation to Greek philosophical texts to indicate the principle of reality, and I agree it may be argued exegetically that here, in this particular figure, we encounter the agent and dynamism of the Real. But, of course, in the context of the New Testament, Logos or Word of God also has Hebrew antecedents, such as the speech, message, or

46. Tillich, *Existence and the Christ*, 97.

Torah of God. The Torah is the law that comes to expression in the Pentateuch and the prophets, and which the psalmist calls my joy and my delight (Ps. 119). The Torah expresses the divine justice and mercy that make for peace and well-being or shalom—"the webbing together of God, humans, and all creation in justice, fulfillment," and flourishing.[47] It is the living law, wisdom, will, presence, and purpose of God that pertain to every dimension of human life.

Or, again, we may observe that the hymn with which the Gospel of John begins draws on an old legacy, a "profound and melancholy myth regarding wisdom." Divine wisdom creates the world and is at God's side from the beginning, but humans shut themselves off from it.[48] So, if we describe it apart from the two-natures and metaphysics talk of the later councils, the "enfleshment" or incarnation motif points to the creating, life-giving, and rightwising wisdom and will of the deity in a human life. Jesus, as Hans Küng says, is the Logos of God in person, the Logos as a mortal man. Becoming flesh or becoming human means that, in this person, God's life-giving and rightwising Word, wisdom, will, and love took on human form.[49] Or, as I prefer to say, that Jesus Christ is the enfleshed Word means that the living dynamic, excellence, or trajectory of God is displayed in the man Jesus as his human life adjusted to, fitted to (or was in appropriate reflective relation with), this dynamic excellence.

Let me emphasize the claims in John 1 that this living wisdom, word, or will of God was in the beginning with God, that through it all things came into being, and that without it nothing came into being. In the terms I am developing here, this is mythopoeic language that aligns the enfleshed Word with the divine going-out, the trajectory or tendency by which all things were created. It therefore aligns the man Jesus with the "realifying" dynamic of the Real. What it trains us to see when we look to Jesus Christ or the Word of God "enfleshed," then, is a person who discloses the fundamental divine dynamic and excellence at work in all creation, as well as the other-directed and ec-centric dynamic of a human life adjusted to or in appropriate relationship with that dynamic.

All this and more is meant when we say that, for the Christian community, Jesus as the Christ is the paradigmatic disclosure of God's living wisdom, will, and purpose as well as of human life in appropriate relation to God. The Christian community looks to this enfleshed Word for knowledge of the divine propensity and purpose as well as knowledge of human life in faithfully responsive relation

47. Cornelius Plantinga Jr., *Not the Way It's Supposed to Be: A Breviary of Sin* (Grand Rapids: Eerdmans, 1994), 10.

48. Ernst Haenchen, *John 1: A Commentary on the Gospel of John Chapters 1–6*, trans. Robert W. Funk (Philadelphia: Fortress, 1984), 102.

49. Hans Küng, *Credo: The Apostles' Creed Explained for Today* (New York: Doubleday, 1992), 60–61.

to God. Jesus as the Christ, in his kingdom-mindedness and his enactment of God's will for the kingdom, is the great clue to the divine excellence or dynamic always at work in cosmic ecology and cosmic passage, as well as to a pattern of human affect and action (or a life) conformed to this dynamic. In Jesus as the Christ, the Word, wisdom, or divine excellence at work in creation and redemption is enfleshed or made manifest in a human life adjusted or conformed to that excellence. Jesus as the Christ, the one in whom God's kingdom draws near, constitutes the great clue to knowledge of God and ourselves that has come to Christians in their history. He is the Logos of God made manifest in the life and ministry of a man from Nazareth.

Excursus on Christology and History

This is a good place to offer some initial if also quite general remarks about portraits of Jesus in the New Testament, Christology, and modern historical studies.

The New Testament contains different literary compositions, for example, gospels, letters, an apocalypse. These compositions, in turn, also contain different sorts of texts, for example, narratives, sayings, pastoral advice, moral exhortations, hymns, and creedal summaries. Not all writings in the New Testament are directly concerned to portray Jesus as the Christ—for example, the narrative presented in the book of Acts largely interprets the emergence and progress of the mission of the apostles and the early church. But a good many texts are, and one question that has arisen during the modern period in the West is, "How do the portraits of Jesus that we find in the New Testament relate to recent critical attempts to get at the historical Jesus, his message and mission?"

Clearly, the two are not the same. For one thing, while the New Testament furnishes sources for modern historical investigations and reflections into Jesus's life, message, and mission, contemporary historians work with other sources and information as well, for example, the noncanonical Gospel of Thomas, other literature from the area at the time (such as the Dead Sea Scrolls), archaeological digs and investigations into then-current social and cultural practices and conditions. Moreover, the New Testament literature and modern historical investigations into Jesus have different aims or objectives. Modern historical investigations aim to construct critical estimates of what took place, that is, what Jesus said and did, what happened to him and to his disciples, and under what conditions. In a sense, they try to get at the historical figure back behind the New Testament texts and to which these texts point. By contrast, New Testament texts themselves often contain religious and theological representations of the meaning or significance of Jesus Christ constructed by early Christians and their communities. An illustration is the difference between the historical judgment that Jesus was executed on the cross and the theological statement that the cross is the wisdom of God.

Consider the rather peculiar literary compositions we call gospels. They are not conventional or complete biographies but narrative presentations that concentrate on the significance of Jesus's life, ministry, death, and resurrection. They might very well be described as *written preaching*.[50] (Hence the word "gospel" means "good news.") They are not neutral investigations so much as attempts by committed followers of Jesus Christ to proclaim his significance or meaning for the church. The gospels are faithful witnesses, rather than dispassionate or detached accounts. They make theological statements about the significance of Jesus for understanding God, the world, and ourselves.

Moreover, as they make their theological statements, both the Gospels and other New Testament compositions make use of mythopoeic images and ideas. We have already noted, for example, how Jesus may be understood as "the Christ," and it should be emphasized that "Christ" and "Messiah" are theologically suffused symbolic concepts. I have also suggested that genealogies of Jesus in Matthew and in Luke are best read not as historical records of his family tree but as theological statements that Jesus fulfills the covenant with Abraham and that he represents the renewal of all humanity. As we proceed, I shall also comment on mythopoeic ideas of Jesus's spiritual conception, his divine sonship, his office as "high priest and perfect sacrifice," his resurrection, ascension, and return in judgment.[51]

Here, however, we do well to keep in mind a significant point that is sometimes lost on modern believers. The Gospels, just because they are the written preaching of early communities, proclaim Jesus of Nazareth; they interpret him, construe him, and present him. Thus, while the gospel preacher-writers may not share modern historians' objectives and canons of evidence, neither do they intend simply to construct Jesus out of whole cloth. Their preaching points beyond

50. Karl Barth noted that the Bible bears witness. "It is itself the deposit of what was once proclaimed by human lips. In its form as Scripture, however, it does not seek to be a historical monument but rather a Church document, written proclamation." *CD* I/1:102.

51. Can historical investigations into the life of Jesus challenge Christian faith and piety? We should be mindful, of course, that historians who investigate the mission and message of Jesus often disagree, that different information comes to light from time to time, and that one or another interpretation may always be mistaken. Nevertheless, the answer is, "Yes, historical investigations may challenge Christian piety." This is especially the case for those forms of piety that do not recognize that (1) many New Testament texts are theological statements (written preaching) that interpret the meaning of Jesus as the Christ for faith rather than try to present simple historical reports, and (2) that biblical texts often make use of mythopoeic language.

itself. So far as the Gospels are concerned, then, we encounter Jesus of Nazareth in their preaching or proclamation only when we understand the relationship of testimony to that about which it testifies, only when we understand it as preaching and proclamation that point to Jesus rather than as Jesus himself. The Gospels therefore do not discourage interest in and attention to the Jesus of history; they authorize it.

How, then, may we preserve a balance of interpretive testimony and historical reference? A liberal Protestant theology of the sort I am presenting here tries to do this by recognizing the importance of *both* the portraits of Jesus presented in the New Testament *and* historical reflections about the Jesus of history. It affirms that the New Testament portraits present indispensable christological images, symbols, and ideas. But it also recognizes that historical work helps us to see more clearly the theological character of the New Testament portraits as well as their use of mythopoeic language. It also recognizes that historical studies may alert us to disjunctions between what we know of the Jesus of history and certain aspects or dimensions of the New Testament portraits. We learn, for example, that the Gospel of John retrojects conflicts and concerns of a later circumstance into its portrait of Jesus and his followers in relation to "the Jews," and that this may distort important aspects of the meaning of Jesus's message and ministry.[52] We also learn, however, that John Dominic Crossan's historical claims about Jesus's practice of "open commensality" point to significant continuities between the Jesus of history and episodes in the Gospels that portray him as a religious leader who associates with outcasts.[53]

I do not claim a complete and detailed correspondence between one or another historical study of Jesus and the Christology I shall present in the pages that follow. Nevertheless, I do presume that there was a person, Jesus of Nazareth, whose life, ministry, and fate precipitated and provoked New Testament portraits of him as a religious leader who was appropriately responsive to the divine. I also claim that the christological statements I develop in conjunction with these portraits stand in meaningful continuity with important things we can know of the historical figure of Jesus, his message and mission. If, for example, it could be shown that my later statements about Jesus as a God-centered figure whose ministry and message focused on the kingdom cannot take into account a number of important critical investigations into the Jesus of history, then I would need to revise them.

Obviously, since Christians continue to interpret the New Testament and since historical investigations and reflections also continue, this possibility (and

52. See chap. 2, prop. # 20.

53. Crossan, *The Historical Jesus*, 261–64.

others like it) can never be ruled out in principle. In fact, however, as things now stand, there are rather broad but nonetheless quite important points of continuity between certain aspects of the New Testament portraits on which I shall draw and what more than a few historians claim about the Jesus of history. For example, Jesus was a Palestinian Jew who preached a prophetic message of the nearness of God's kingdom that called people to repent and called into question important social practices and powers. His teachings, which emphasized radical devotion to God, love of neighbor, and love of enemies, drew on previous Jewish traditions, although occasionally they also departed from some. In the course of his ministry, he associated with the poor and with outcasts, and engaged in the practice of regular common meals. He had followers and was understood by some to be a healer. He also provoked opposition and was crucified by Roman authorities.[54]

In sum, as a *liberal* theologian, I intend to work with current historical and biblical scholarship rather than dismiss it on dogmatic grounds; I will therefore try to present a Christology that is sensitive to both New Testament texts and recent historical work. I intend to indicate how my statements take into account key New Testament images and ideas. I will note places where my Christology entails claims about Jesus, his message and ministry, that relate to the work of some recent historians. I also will point out features of the New Testament portraits that, in my judgment, are best read as symbolic and mythopoeic texts that make important theological points—for example, genealogies of Jesus, narratives of his spiritual conception, his resurrection, and his ascension—and that may not require many of the historical claims that some may associate with them.

Here, I cannot endorse the more definite separation of the Christ of faith and the "so-called historical Jesus" favored by some theologians. I agree that the Gospels tell us what Jesus meant to early Christian communities in an effort "to kindle the same faith in us."[55] But I also think their written preaching points beyond itself to a historical figure. And I hasten to add that our own theological interpretations of how Jesus as the Christ articulates and embodies the message of God's kingdom can be significantly enriched and, at points, also emended by investigations into the Jesus of history as well as the historical circumstances of the early Christian communities. Theologically speaking, however, Jesus as the Christ discloses the gracious tendency of God and God's kingdom, as well as the ec-centric trajectory in human life that is appropriately responsive to it.

54. See Ottati, *Jesus Christ and Christian Vision*, 67, 69.

55. Gerrish, *Christian Faith*, 137, 160. Following Schubert M. Ogden, Gerrish insists that "the gospels tell us what Jesus meant to the first generation of believers in order to kindle the same faith in others."

Proposition #51 Jesus Christ is reconciler.

What do Christians see when they look to this enfleshed Word and divine excellence, this paradigmatic clue to knowledge of God and ourselves? To outline an answer, I want to reflect on the theological image or summative pattern of *reconciliation* that Paul presents in 2 Corinthians 5:18: God "reconciled us to [Godself] through Christ, and has given us the ministry of reconciliation." Let me also stress two related moments or movements. (1) The Christ, who welcomes tax collectors, sinners, and (really) all kinds of people, points to God's generous and gracious acceptance and so to the restoration and renewal of our relationship with God. (2) The Christ, the person for others who teaches us to love our enemies, and whose mind and attitude we in turn should adopt (Phil. 2:1–5), points to the renewal and restoration of our relationships with others. Thus, the work of reconciliation in Christ addresses and overcomes a double alienation or division—of people from God and of people from others. And this is how the image or pattern of reconciliation also approximates Jesus's message of the kingdom as a reign or state of affairs in which persons participate in true communion with God in community with others.

Beyers Naude, a Reformed minister who spoke and labored against apartheid in South Africa, makes the basic point quite clearly. "If God in Christ has enacted the great Reconciliation between Him and us then we begin to realize that all human relations are thereby affected and transformed. A new quality and content, a new spirit and approach thus become part of all our relations."[56] Our reconciliation in Christ to God entails a change in our relations with others, and so it approximates Jesus's message of and commitment to the kingdom. The Spirit, in turn, continues the work of reconciliation by gathering the church, a community in which, however fragmentarily, diverse and often divided people are reconciled to God and to one another.

An Inexhaustible and Multifaceted Theme

The New Testament uses two words meaning reconciliation: *katallassō* (Rom. 5:10; 1 Cor. 7:11; 2 Cor. 5:18–20) and its intensified form, *apokatallassō* (Eph. 2:16; Col. 1:20, 22). Both convey a sense of alteration or change, as well as the restoration of broken relationships. For example, with respect to humans relations, Matthew 5:24 directs one to be reconciled with one's brother or sister before

56. "From the Archives: Reconciliation," in *The Legacy of Beyers Naude*, vol. 1 of *Beyers Naude Centre Series on Public Theology*, ed. L. D. Hanson (Stellenbosch, South Africa: Sun, 2005), 140.

leaving a gift at the altar. First Corinthians 7:11 recommends that a wife who is separated from her husband either remain unmarried or else reconcile with her husband, and 2 Corinthians 5:18–20 uses this same word (*katallassō*) to speak of God reconciling persons and the world to Godself through Christ. Colossians 1:20 says, "God was pleased to reconcile" all things to Godself.

The general background in the Hebrew Scriptures for these ideas lies in the deity's covenant with Israel, which constitutes and sustains the people in communion with God and community with one another. The covenant, that is to say, holds God's people in relationship with Godself and also spells out terms for true relationships and a genuine or flourishing community among God's people. Reconciliation, then, is one way of speaking about God's overarching end or goal in the covenant of grace. And, in the New Testament, the ministry of Jesus as the Christ may be looked upon as the culmination of "God's search for reconciliation" or true communion in community.[57]

The Confession of 1967 of the Presbyterian Church (USA) says, "God's reconciling work in Jesus Christ and the mission of reconciliation to which he has called his church are the heart of the gospel in any age."[58] We can outline one way in which this is true by reviewing how H. Richard Niebuhr understands Jesus Christ as reconciler in connection with the idea of covenant. For Niebuhr, covenant thematizes our dual relationship with God and companions. This is why he claims that the idea of covenant signals a triad.[59]

God

Self Other

Where God is regarded as the Creator who stands in relation to all, then, the field defined by self and others, the covenant community of self and companions, God's kingdom or reign, extends to all creatures. This is the true communion with God in community with others for which we were created.

The problem of human existence, for Niebuhr, is the disruption of relation-

57. L. William Countryman, "Reconcile," in *The Westminster Theological Wordbook of the Bible*, ed. Donald E. Gowan (Louisville: Westminster John Knox, 2003), 412–23, says "the terminology" of reconciliation, although "rare in the Scriptures of Israel . . . represents something central . . . God's determined and unflagging effort to restore a relationship of friendship with the creation, not least the human creation, despite our own tendency to sabotage it."

58. *BOC* 9.06.

59. H. Richard Niebuhr, *The Responsible Self: An Essay in Christian Moral Philosophy* (Louisville: Westminster John Knox, 1999), 86–87.

ships within this universal community of all persons and creatures with God at its head. As sinners, we live apart and curved in upon our isolated interests, and therefore become estranged from God and others. We move beyond egoism by identifying ourselves with a partial community, such as the nation or the race and its exclusive cause. But, unlike the community of all creatures with God at its head, these partial communities, such as the nation or the race, leave many others out of account. We therefore divide ourselves from outsiders (or the members of other communities) at the same time that we extend our interests and responsible relationships to our own limited community.

Jesus Christ reconciles people to God and also challenges them to take up with him the ministry of reconciliation. His reconciling cause, says Niebuhr, is "the establishment of friendship . . . between the power by which all things are and this human race of ours," a friendship that necessarily also entails reconciling people to one another and to their world.[60] This is how Jesus's message of the kingdom accords with the reconciling image. Thus, by reconciliation, Niebuhr means an adjustment to God and God's universal reign by which our lives are disposed by love of all creation, all things, or all being in relation to God rather than by loyalty only to ourselves and to our partial causes and closed societies.[61]

Niebuhr goes on to say the reconciliation theme "has more aspects than have been dreamed of in our theologies."[62] Its symbolism points to the depth of the human condition as well as to the persistence of the God of grace. It affirms the gracious heart of reality; it intertwines with the work of Christ (or what he says, does, and endures) and its cruciform, self-emptying pattern, with what this work discloses about the divine and about ourselves, and with how this disclosure alters persons.

This same complex theme is basic to Reformed theology and may be traced in the work of other theologians as well. For example, when Calvin writes about Christ as Mediator, he emphasizes a particular function, work, or task. We were, he says, estranged from God; our iniquities were "like a cloud cast between us and him."[63] Jesus Christ fulfills "the office of Mediator" by serving "as the intermediary to restore peace," or bring together in a renewed relationship those who have been separated and alienated.[64] Calvin thus highlights the theme of the restoring of a broken covenant or community and thereby a change of situation or circumstance. With Jesus Christ, a dispute is mediated, an obstacle, grievance,

60. H. Richard Niebuhr, *The Responsible Self*, 43–44.
61. H. Richard Niebuhr, *The Responsible Self*, 144.
62. H. Richard Niebuhr, *The Responsible Self*, 44.
63. Calvin, *ICR* 2.15.1.
64. Calvin, *ICR* 2.15.5.

or estrangement is overcome, and people are altered. "What the Mediator was to accomplish," Calvin writes, "was no uncommon thing. His task was so to restore us to God's grace as to make the children of men, children of God."[65]

The mediation is costly; the reconciler suffers. Here, Calvin turns to Paul. Christ was "put forward as a sacrifice of atonement by his blood" (Rom. 3:25).[66] He

> emptied himself,
> taking the form of a slave . . .
> he humbled himself
> and became obedient to the point of death—
> even death on a cross. (Phil. 2:7–8)

Like others in the West, then, Calvin claims that Jesus dies for our sins. Much might be said about this.[67] Among other things, and as the Confession of 1967 indicates, classical theologians made use of a variety of images and ideas, for example, ransoming a captive, priestly sacrifice, defeating the devil, and satisfying divine justice, in order to explain it. But for now it is enough to note a basic and broadly shared dimension of Christian piety: Jesus's crucifixion is bound up with passionate feelings of sorrow and remorse at persistent human corruption and injustice, an inkling of judgment, and nevertheless and beyond tragedy, also a heartfelt hope. This is why, for persons of Christian piety, there are fundamental lessons to be learned about God and ourselves at the foot of the cross.

Note an asymmetry in much of what Calvin says about reconciliation in Jesus Christ. *We* are restored to God's grace, but it is *not* that suddenly, with Christ's mediatorial work, "God begins to love those whom he has hated." Indeed, according to Calvin, God has not changed. We are reconciled to the God who *already* loves us and "with whom we were enemies on account of sin." Therefore, "the work of atonement" does not establish God's love but instead derives from it and discloses it.[68] The *a*symmetry indicates that God remains steadfast before, during, and after Christ's reconciling work. What Christ's reconciling work discloses about the divine has always been the case, namely, that God is the God of grace.[69] But it is through Christ's costly work, and largely (for Calvin) by means

65. Calvin, *ICR* 2.15.2.

66. Calvin, *ICR* 2.16.5.

67. See chap. 8 below.

68. Calvin, *ICR* 2.16.4.

69. The same asymmetry is also characteristic of much classical Reformed theology. "Christ is the mediator of the covenant of grace, insofar as he appears as reconciler. One would [however] . . . be completely misguided if one thought that God's mind first had to be changed, in order for God then to be favorably inclined toward humanity." Zwingli therefore claims

of his sacrificial suffering, that sinners are altered or changed by being brought around or adjusted to what God is and has always been. And, as Calvin makes clear in his discussion of repentance and our regeneration by faith, the alteration of sinners comes to expression in a different disposition not only toward God but also toward others.[70]

When Barth expounds the doctrine of reconciliation, he sounds similar notes, complete with allusions to the parable of the prodigal son. As sinner, the human being "does not find . . . fulfillment . . . in participation in the being of God by the gift of God. Instead, he aims at another salvation which is to be found in the sphere of his creaturely being and attained by his own effort."[71] This is how the sinner becomes curved in upon himself or herself, misguided, and diminished. This is how the good human creature becomes a "lost son in a far country."[72]

Reconciliation, for Barth, is the grace of God as "a sheer Yet and Nevertheless," or as God's refusal of humanity's defection and of its skewed attempt to wrongly determine, misdirect, and diminish itself.[73] Moreover, this redemptive event, this fulfillment of the covenant of grace, brings genuine renewal, since "we are awakened to our truest being."[74] The human who turned away toward diminishment and nothingness is, by the grace of God, not nothing. Instead, by the grace of God, a fellowship is resumed, and humanity is divinely altered.[75]

In both instances, then, the reconciliation of persons with God also entails their alteration. Sinners are changed. They become regenerated children of God

---

that God sends the Son into the world "to be an expression and revelation of God's goodness (*bonitas*)." Or, again, the French Confession insists, "Christ's sacrifice does not reconcile God to the world, but the world to God." See Rohls, *Reformed Confessions*, 90–91. However, Rohls also points out that this view "sometimes is supplemented by the contrary idea that God is reconciled by Christ's sacrifice," an idea we also find in Zwingli as well as in the Latin text but not in the Scottish dialect text of the Scots Confession. The word in brackets is mine.

70. Calvin, *ICR* 3.3.

71. Barth, *CD* IV/1:10.

72. Barth, *CD* IV/1:11.

73. Barth, *CD* IV/1:11.

74. Barth, *CD* IV/1:14.

75. Barth, *CD* IV/1:79–80, 89–91. We could also review the theme in others. For example, Emil Brunner says that, in Jesus Christ, God restores communion between Godself and sinners who were alienated from God; people thus become new creatures "who know for themselves what it is to be children of God." This, in fact, is much of what Brunner means when he calls Christ the Mediator. See Brunner, *Dogmatics*, 2:336. See also Brunner, *Dogmatics*, 2:306, 337, and *Our Faith*, trans. John W. Rilling (New York: Scribner's Sons, 1936), 85. Or, to mention a theologian who is not Reformed, Paul Tillich insists that the Christ brings a new state of things. For Tillich, the Christ mediates in the sense that he reunites what is estranged. The Christ reconciles as the one who represents God to humans and also shows what God wants humans to be. See Tillich, *Existence and the Christ*, 93, 119, 169.

(Calvin). They are awakened to their truest being (Barth). That is, the first moment of reconciliation, namely, the overcoming of the alienation and estrangement of people from God, necessarily is interconnected with a second, namely, overcoming the alienation or estrangement of people from others.

One way to underscore this interconnection is to say, as Paul does in 2 Corinthians 5, that Christ's reconciling work calls persons to an expansive ministry of reconciliation. This is also a focal point of two recent Reformed confessions. One, the Confession of 1967, adopted by the Presbyterian Church (USA), I have mentioned already; the other is the Belhar Confession, adopted by the Dutch Reformed Mission Church in South Africa in 1982. Reconciliation in Christ, says the Confession of 1967, calls us to be reconciled to God and one another.[76] Christ's reconciling work unites persons into a community of reconciliation, a covenantal people of God that opens to all and which, in turn, is sent into the world to engage in a mission of reconciliation. Or, again, the Confession says that true humanity is realized in the one who "expressed the love of God in word and deed and became a brother to all kinds of sinful men."[77] At one and the same time, Jesus's reconciling activity sets us right with the deity by disclosing God's love, demonstrates what it is to be truly human, and commissions God's "reconciling community."[78] Belhar affirms that "Christ's work of reconciliation is made manifest in the Church as the community of believers who have been reconciled with God and one another," and that God "has entrusted to his Church the message of reconciliation in and through Jesus Christ."[79]

The Confession of 1967 then proceeds to offer an interpretation of four then-current and alienating divisions that are thrown into sharp relief when the church views the world through the lens of reconciliation. (1) "God has created the peoples of the earth to be one universal family," and God's reconciling love in Jesus Christ, which overcomes barriers and boundaries, calls people to receive and uphold one another as persons.[80] This highlights the divisive issue of discrimination based on racial or ethnic difference. (2) The mediator who restores peace commends to the nations the search for peace, particularly in an age of highly destructive weapons that risk "the annihilation of mankind."[81] (3) Jesus's identification "with the needy and exploited" makes "the cause of the world's poor the cause of his disciples," and it encourages the church to engage

76. *BOC* 9.06–9.07.

77. *BOC* 9.08.

78. *BOC* 9.10.

79. Piet J. Naude, *Neither Calendar Nor Clock: Perspectives on the Belhar Confession* (Grand Rapids: Eerdmans, 2010), 219, 222.

80. *BOC* 9.44.

81. *BOC* 9.45.

in economic affairs, to denounce and work to overcome "enslaving poverty in a world of abundance."[82] (4) The emphasis on relationships of mutual care, responsibility, and respect that characterizes new life in Christ highlights alienation and anarchy in sexual relationships, the exploitation of sexual symbols, and the importance of caring for children.[83] Belhar uses biblical images and terms to underscore the church's ministry in the world. "The Church is called to be the salt of the earth and light of the world," and "the Church is called blessed because it is a peacemaker." Moreover, it says, God's people should "live in a new obedience which can open new possibilities of life for society and world." Indeed, the credibility of the gospel is undermined "when it is proclaimed in a land which professes to be Christian, but in which the enforced separation of people on a racial basis promotes and perpetuates alienation, hatred, and enmity."[84]

Here we should note, especially in light of recent discussions surrounding truth, reconciliation, and justice in South Africa and elsewhere following periods of severe civil conflict, that the social criticisms in the Confession of 1967 and in Belhar, as well as the references to reconciled community and new social possibilities, indicate an enduring connection between reconciliation and justice.[85] Reconciliation points to right relationships and restored community, and thus to prophetic notions of justice that emphasize social well-being.[86] But relationships are not right and communities remain unrestored—they are, in fact, distorted and malformed—where they exclude persons and groups from political participation, deprive persons of resources needed to live humanly, and are characterized by domination and exploitation.

Aware that in the present age God's creation is despoiled and that traces of the kingdom seem present in human societies only by fits and starts, the Confession of 1967 closes with a section on "the fulfillment of reconciliation,"[87] which makes explicit a theological equation suggested by this proposition and the previous one. *The kingdom may be understood as the fulfillment of reconciliation, the culmination of the covenant of grace and of covenant community.* Thus, despite chronic

82. *BOC* 9.46. Indeed, "a church that is indifferent to poverty, or evades responsibility in economic affairs, or is open to one social class only, or expects gratitude for its beneficence makes a mockery of reconciliation and offers no acceptable worship to God" (9.46).

83. *BOC* 9.47.

84. Naude, *Neither Calendar Nor Clock*, 221.

85. For a discussion of these connections, see Nigel Biggar, "Making Peace or Doing Justice: Must We Choose?," "Conclusion," and "Epilogue: Burying the Past after September 11," in *Burying the Past: Making Peace and Doing Justice after Civil Conflict*, ed. Nigel Biggar, expanded and updated ed. (Washington, DC: Georgetown University Press, 2003), 3–24, 307–24, 325–30.

86. See chap. 8 below.

87. *BOC* 9.53–9.55.

strife and corruption, the Confession points to a rightwising completion of God's redeeming will that includes the whole of human social life as well as the natural environment. Why? Because, in light of the reconciling divine trajectory and excellence disclosed in Jesus Christ, it *hopes* for the culmination and completion of God's reign or kingdom. Indeed, it is "with an urgency born of this hope" that the church undertakes its ministry of reconciliation, and so "applies itself to present tasks and strives for a better world."[88]

A Proposal

"In Christ God was reconciling the world to [Godself]" (2 Cor. 5:19). This simple and elegant statement of the gospel points to one who lived and died and rose again for the cause of reconciling people to God, one another, and their world. It construes the event of Jesus as the Christ, or what Jesus Christ says, does, and endures, through the symbolic lens of reconciliation. It indicates that the trajectory or dynamic of God's reconciling activity comes to expression in the pattern of a person for others, a ministry that crosses boundaries and breaks down barriers by eating and drinking with outcasts, tax collectors and sinners; by healing the sick; and by blessing the poor. Christ the reconciler fulfills the covenant of grace; he proclaims and embodies the kingdom, by opening the covenant community to all or to the entire world and "not counting their trespasses against them" (2 Cor. 5:19).

Now for the big claim: *This is how Jesus as the Christ clarifies the dynamic ordering of grace. This is how he discloses the renewing tendency of the Real. This is how the Word manifests the redemptive dimension of the "realifying" excellence of God. This is how the Christ discloses the God of grace. This is the Logos of God displayed in a mission and in a human life.* Jesus the reconciler points to and embodies the kingdom or the overcoming of estrangement by the establishment and renewal of true communion with God in community with others. He points beyond tragedy and misdirection to the renovation of a fellowship for which we, as social creatures who participate in the myriad interrelations of cosmic ecology and cosmic passage, have been fitted and sustained all along. In doing so, the reconciler reveals that, despite our misguided and persistent turning away from God and one another, God goes out to make us new and ec-centric creatures. God goes out to renovate and re-create a broken society. God goes out to bring in God's kingdom, and thus a new possibility emerges.

People are altered in Christ because, here, they are brought to the realization

88. *BOC* 9.55.

that the gratuitous and overflowing tendency of the Real, which creates and sustains, also renews and redeems. In Christ, people discern the divine excellence, the gratuitous divine dynamic that creates and sustains but also overcomes estrangement and makes for new community. They see, in short, that the Creator of all is also the Redeemer, and with this discernment, they come to their truer selves and are gripped by a new vision. They recognize themselves and others as valued participants in the expansive divine trajectory of cosmic passage. They are adjusted to Reality, to God and neighbor, or to God and all things in relation to God, and they envision an emergent kingdom, a beloved and universal community, which, although clearly not yet realized, nevertheless seems on its way.

Or, again, we might say that, by means of the Christic pedagogy and with the aid of the Spirit, persons who had become curved in upon themselves, as well as their closed in-groups and partial causes, are set right with the Real. They are brought to a sense for the divine excellence, a realization of what is already always the case, namely, that the gratuitous tendency or dynamic of the divine is to hold them as well as all others in relation to Godself. This sensibility is deeply affecting, and as Edwards notes, it is as different from what many people often experience as the sweet taste of honey is from the ideas people get of honey by only looking on.[89] Among other things, it brings with it a feeling of assurance and even, to draw upon an older vocabulary, a feeling of blessedness. I *am* a child of God; we *are* children of God, valued participants gratuitously held in a "realifying" dynamic that reconciles and renews.

This is the discernment that (also with the aid of what Christians call the Spirit) changes people. Clearly, it involves me, but despite the rhetoric of some evangelical conversion preachers, it never involves *only* me and it always also involves others (even nonhuman others). It entails the conviction that true piety or religion finally is about our participation in God's kingdom or in a divinely gathered community of all things rather than simply about my own individual and isolated salvation. By means of the christological pattern, we learn to regard ourselves and our communities, as well as other peoples and communities, as participants in the single covenant of grace and epic of all creatures in relation to God and one another from creation to the end. That is, the discernment in Christ of the gratuitous and reconciling divine dynamic or excellence establishes what we might call a *nonexclusive* and *shared* friendship with the Real that both elicits and demands an expanded and capacious sympathy for others, a feeling of solidarity too often subordinated to our diminished and closed-society causes and affections. This expanded and capacious affection, now released from subordination and diminishment, is what Edwards describes as true virtue or

89. Edwards, *Religious Affections*, pt. 3, I, pp. 205–6.

benevolence to being in general, and it manifests itself in a quest for new community. Or, again, says the nineteenth-century American Horace Bushnell, in Christ we are brought to a new reigning love, "so that life proceeds from a new center."[90] Those who have been reconciled and now feel themselves to be God's children also feel called to overcome damaging separations and divisions that estrange them from other people as well as from the natural world. In short, they respond to the reconciling divine dynamic by imitating it in their own lives; they are called to a kingdom-minded ministry of reconciliation.

The renovated and renewed community that thus begins to emerge and be seen is, in fact, fragmentary and sporadic. It is on the way rather than fully present. "In our biographies as in our human history the process of reconciliation has begun; at no point is it complete."[91] Nevertheless, and quite importantly, the renovated and renewed community that is on its way is something more and something different than the *status quo ante*. In the shadow of the cross, it is a society of those who bear the negative wisdom and insight of having lived in the destructive shadows of division. It is a society made up of persons and communities who have experienced the forces of estrangement but now feel compelled to try another way. In the light of resurrection, despite setbacks and despite the tentative character of the emergent possibilities, it is also a community whose hopes run toward eschatological and extravagant depictions of a new heaven and new earth.

A Cosmic Resonance and Reference

This account of how Jesus as the Christ reconciles people both to God and to the world of interdependent and interrelated creatures and realities in which they participate presses toward the universal because it claims that the Christ discloses the gratuitous divine dynamic that encompasses all things. The event of redemption-in-Jesus-Christ has a cosmic resonance and reference because his reconciling pattern represents human life fitted to the contours of the divine dynamism. Indeed, we should say the manifestation in the event of Jesus Christ, or in his life and ministry, of a manner of life truly adjusted to the Real *bears the contours of the Real*, similar to how an impression corresponds to the contours of a stamp (only in this instance both stamp and impress are living and dynamic).[92] This comes to expression in the Greek phrase *charaktēr tēs hypostaseōs autou* used

90. See chap. 2, prop. #22.

91. H. Richard Niebuhr, *The Responsible Self*, 144.

92. Here and in the next two paragraphs I borrow extensively from my book *Jesus Christ and Christian Vision*, 107–9.

with reference to Jesus Christ in Hebrews 1:3, where *charaktēr* may be translated as impress, imprint, reproduction, or representation, so that the phrase might be rendered "an impression or representation of God's nature or reality."

Colossians 1:15 says Jesus Christ is the icon, image, or likeness of the invisible or unseen God (*hos estin eikōn tou theou tou aoratou*). This expression connects with the further claim that "in him all the fullness of God was pleased to dwell, and through him God was pleased to reconcile to himself all things" (Col. 1:19–20). Jesus Christ is the image or likeness of God in a manner that discloses the dependence on God of the whole creation, its ordering, continuing sustenance, reconciliation, and renewal. We might say that, because he is the *charaktēr* or *eikōn* of God, knowledge of Jesus Christ is also knowledge of God in the fullness of God's dynamic relatedness to all things.

As we noted earlier, we may also speak of Jesus Christ as the wisdom, Word, or Logos of God through whom all things were made and by whom all things are renewed (John 1:3). The Logos image points to continuity between redemption-in-Jesus-Christ and the entire creation. Yet its force is not only to tell us that the covenant between God and God's people in Jesus Christ refers to a wider whole inclusive of all things; nor is it only to suggest that what is disclosed in Jesus Christ about authentic human existence is of a piece with the tendency of all things under God. It is also to assert that the way of God with the world that comes to us in Jesus Christ discloses the dynamic divine reality as it always already stands in relation to all things. In my terms, Jesus Christ discloses the excellence of the God of grace at work in creation and redemption or the divine dynamic at work in all things. In this sense, one who has seen this man has seen the Father. The incarnational element or accent in my proposal, and about which I shall say more presently, is the affirmation that here the dynamic reality and power of God are manifest in Jesus's particular life, ministry, death, and resurrection. In Christ the reconciler, people encounter human life in appropriately responsive relation to God as well as the dynamic excellence of the God who always stands in relation to all.

Return now to the image of creation as a vast cosmic ecology and passage that includes virtually countless galaxies, stars, and planets, each with its own scenario, sequence, and line of development. As I indicated in part 1 of this systematic, on this view, the particular ecology and dynamic trajectory of atmosphere, geology, biology, and human societies in which we find ourselves on Earth is one among very many planetary trajectories. (The Milky Way alone, for example, contains more than 100 billion planets.)[93] If we think of Earth as a stage or a venue on which a drama or a play transpires, we must therefore also recognize that the cosmos contains a virtually countless number of stages and venues on which

93. Michael D. Lemonick, "The Dawn of Distant Skies," *Scientific American*, July 2013, 46.

a virtually countless number of dramas and plays also transpire. Significantly, however, nothing we have said here about the cosmic resonance and reference of redemption-in-Jesus-Christ excludes the possibility of other manifestations and disclosures of the gratuitous dynamic of the Real within other scenarios, sequences, and lines of development.[94] In fact, and as is implied by a capacious Reformed claim for a covenant of grace that includes figures such as Adam and Noah, it does not exclude other manifestations of the gratuitous divine excellence in other histories and traditions on Earth. Jesus Christ brings knowledge of God through acquaintance with the manner of a human life and ministry fitted to the dynamic excellence of God. This seems an especially effective way for humans to discern the trajectory of the Real and its significance for them. Still, there may be other ways for people in other traditions and historical sequences, and certainly the communicative appropriateness or articulateness for us of the manifestation of God in Jesus as the Christ also leaves open the question of how the same dynamic divine excellence might be disclosed to other creatures on other worlds.

This line of thinking accords in spirit, I believe, with a feature of classical Reformed Christology that emerged in (often polemical) conversation with Lutherans. The Lutheran theologian Martin Chemnitz (1522–1586) claims that, by virtue of the hypostatic union, the divine majesty (certain attributes of the divine nature, including omnipotence, omniscience, and ubiquity) was communicated to the human nature. By contrast, the Reformed scholastic Francis Turretin (1623–1687) explains that, while attributes of the divine nature and the human nature were both communicated to Christ's person, divine properties such as ubiquity, omniscience, omnipotence, and the power of making alive were not transfused into the human nature of Christ. Neither were properties of the flesh communicated to the Logos. For this, says Turretin, would have resulted in a leveling of the two natures and a consequent destruction of Christ's genuinely finite humanity as well as of his infinite deity. The Logos, he maintains, was indeed united with humanity and the flesh. Being infinite, however, it was neither circumscribed nor encompassed by human nature and the flesh.

The disagreement here over how the Word became flesh can be traced to the earlier reformers. Luther, while making a devotional point about the Eucharist, stresses "the incarnate God" defined in Jesus Christ, and he maintains that, as of the incarnation, Word and flesh are so united that the eternal Son or Logos is never apart from the flesh—"wherever you place God for me, you must also place the humanity for me."[95] By contrast, when it comes to eucharistic piety, Calvin

94. See also Tillich, *Existence and the Christ*, 100–101.

95. Martin Luther, "Confession concerning Christ's Supper, 1528," in *Word and Sacrament III*, ed. Helmut T. Lehmann, trans. Robert H. Fischer, vol. 37 of *LW*, 218–19.

prefers to speak of the spiritual or mystical presence of the Word in the practice of the sacrament, and he embraces an understanding of its presence and efficacy that is not restricted to the human nature. Calvin explains his position this way.

> They thrust upon us as something absurd the fact that if the Word became flesh, then he was confined within the narrow prison of the earthly body. This is mere impudence! For even if the Word in his immeasurable essence united with the nature of man into one person, we do not imagine that he was confined therein. Here is something marvelous: the Son of God descended from heaven in such a way that, without leaving heaven, he willed to be borne in the virgin's womb, to go about the earth, and to hang upon the cross; yet he continuously filled the world even as he had done from the beginning.[96]

Calvin thus affirms that the redemptive principle or God the Son is manifest in the man Jesus but not encompassed by the man Jesus. The Word became flesh and dwelt among us, and yet the Word also continues its active reign beyond the flesh of the man Jesus. This is what the Lutherans called the *extra calvinisticum*, or a certain something extra among the Calvinists: the doctrine that, before, during, and after the incarnation, the eternal Son, Logos, or second person of the Trinity continues his operations also beyond the flesh (*etiam extra carnem*) of the man Jesus.[97] As the nineteenth-century Reformed theologian I. A. Dorner explains, the Logos "also eternally is and remains omnipresently active outside the humanity and its limitation."[98]

Theologians concerned to advance the conciliar Christology may debate whether the Lutheran or the Calvinist position gives the better expression to the orthodox doctrine of incarnation.[99] (Does the Lutheran position tend toward

96. Calvin, *ICR* 2.13.4.

97. Whether this is as innovative as some Lutherans sometimes claimed is a matter of debate. In *CD* I/2:169, Barth says the Calvinists reverted to an earlier tradition in order to meet the innovation introduced by Luther and his followers. E. David Willis argues that Calvin's Christology is truly catholic in the sense that it continued a line of thinking found in theologians as diverse as Peter Lombard, Thomas Aquinas, Augustine, Origen, Theodore of Mopsuestia, Athanasius, and Cyril. He therefore concludes that, rather than an *extra calvinisticum*, it would be more appropriate to speak of an *extra catholicum* or an *extra patristicum*. See Willis, *Calvin's Catholic Christology: The Function of the So-Called* Extra Calvinisticum *in Calvin's Theology* (Leiden: Brill, 1966), 60. See also Aquinas, *ST* 3a.10.1.

98. I. A. Dorner, *A System of Doctrine*, trans. Alfred Cave and J. S. Banks (Edinburgh: T&T Clark, 1882), 3:242–43.

99. See Rowan Williams, "Religious Experience in the Era of Reform," in *Companion Encyclopedia of Theology*, ed. Peter Byrne and Leslie Houlden (London: Routledge, 1995), 576–93. My own judgment is that the different positions (Does the Lutheran one end in Eutychianism?

Eutychianism? Do the Reformed tend toward Nestorianism?) However, I am content simply to point out that, for the Reformed theologians, the activity of the redemptive divine principle (the Son or the Logos) cannot be confined to the flesh of the man Jesus (or, as we might say, to the historical Jesus of Nazareth). Calvin, Turretin, and Dorner obviously do not operate in an intellectual milieu where it is known that water is distributed throughout the universe and that there are billions of planets as well as other venues—for example, moons, some of which may now support life—that may have supported life in the past or may support it in the future. But we do, and as it happens, one may build on their christological ruminations in order to claim that there may be other manifestations and disclosures of the gratuitous divine dynamic within other scenarios and lines of development in God's cosmos.

Should we speak of "multiple incarnations"? For example, Thomas O'Meara notes, "the history of sin and salvation recorded in the two testaments of the Bible is not a history of the universe: it is a particular religious history on one planet." He then says, "the divine generosity that led once to the Incarnation in earth suggests there might be other incarnations—many incarnations and in various species, many creatures touched in one or another special metaphysical way by a person of the Trinity."[100] Again, Timothy Pawl notes that Thomas Aquinas thinks it "possible for there to be multiple incarnations by different Divine Persons," and he argues, contra Brian Hebblethwaite's objections, that this possibility is consistent with the Christology of the first seven ecumenical councils.[101] Ilia Delio, OSF, argues that, relying on Duns Scotus and Bonaventure, we see the incarnation pointing to "a pattern of divinization that renders creation complete" and "reflects the fecund, self-communicative love of God." Thus, "on an extraterrestrial level . . . Christ may assume another form integral to that creation by which that creation may be spiritually complete in its relationship with God."[102]

Partly because I find the metaphysics of the conciliar Christology itself exces-

Does the Reformed position tend toward Nestorianism?) indicate ambiguities in the conciliar Christology itself with respect to the metaphysics of natures.

100. Thomas F. O'Meara, OP, "Christian Theology and Extraterrestial Intelligent Life," *Theological Studies* 60, no. 1 (March 1999): 28. Andrew Davison, Starbridge Lecturer in Natural Sciences and Theology at Cambridge, makes an especially good guide to such ideas. See "Christian Systematic Theology and Life Elsewhere: A Study in Suitability," *Theology and Science* 16, no. 4 (2018): 447–61.

101. Timothy Pawl, "Thomistic Multiple Incarnations," *Heythrop Journal* 57 (2016): 364; Timothy Pawl, "Brian Hebblethwaite's Arguments against Multiple Incarnations," *Religious Studies*, FirstView Article, February 2015, 2–9.

102. Ilia Delio, OSF, "Christ and Extraterrestrial Life," *Theology and Science* 5, no. 3 (2007): 261.

sively speculative as well as biblically insecure, especially when it comes to the metaphysics of natures, I favor other, more reticent formulations—for example, in Jesus Christ, we come to know the God who creates to be the God of grace who is our sure redeemer. As I think and shall argue, Jesus's teaching and embodiment of the kingdom, or Christ's prophetic and royal offices, disclose this. Christ's priestly office, that is, Jesus's crucifixion and resurrection, our dying and rising to new life, and the gathering of the church, does, too. And this is also, in my judgment, an appropriate conclusion to draw from the *symbolic idea* or *metaphor* of incarnation.

I therefore think we should be willing to say that God is the God of grace, not just in Palestine during the first century, not just in one or another historical-religious sequence on Earth, and not just on planet Earth. God is the God of grace who is present and active everywhere. But in saying this we do not therefore necessarily also claim to comprehend all there is to know about the God of grace who creates and redeems. There are things we do not know about the economy of God's grace in the cosmos, though there may very well be—indeed, it would seem fitting and appropriate for there to be—redeeming presences and encounters beyond our capacities to imagine.

In any case, as I think, the interdependence of things within the vast cosmic ecology and passage means that, at some level, the divine excellence or the gratuitous dynamic of the Real intersects with all things. All things participate in the divine excellence, and we may therefore suppose a cosmic dimension not only to the reconciling trajectory that comes to us in Jesus as the Christ and the knowledge that God *is* the God of grace, but also perhaps to the estrangement or rupture that it addresses. Thus, if there have been, now are, or shall be species other than ours in which there was, is, or shall be a similar rupture or alienation, then they need not be without reconciling disclosures/manifestations of divine gratuity. That is, the reconciling manifestation/disclosure of the gratuitous divine excellence in one place indicates the fittingness or appropriateness of its manifestation and disclosure in other places as well. The appearance of Jesus the reconciler in our own historical continuum on Earth both indicates and presupposes that God is gracious in relation to the entire cosmos.

The Reconciler Also Judges

Just here we verge upon articulating a truly universal and cosmic triumph of grace, and so, just here we need to underscore the shadow reality that accompanies any discussion of reconciliation from the start. If Christ discloses the reconciling divine trajectory in and for the world, and if this dynamic, in turn, appropriately calls forth a ministry of reconciliation in and for the world, then it must also be that there is a problem. *It must also be that the world stands in need of reconciliation.*

The basic biblical plotline is tolerably clear. Having made humankind on the sixth day, "God saw everything that he had made, and indeed, it was very good" (Gen. 1:31). We humans are good creatures who participate in a good creation. We are fitted for a good life together in the midst of cosmic ecology and passage, a life in which we may deploy our considerable though hardly unlimited powers and capacities in responsible interrelations with God and others. Nevertheless, it is also true that "there is no one who is righteous. . . . All have turned aside. . . . All have sinned and fall short of the glory of God" (Rom. 3:10, 12, 23; cf. Pss. 14:1–3; 53:1–3).

What this rupture or corruption may mean for other creatures in sequences or lines of development elsewhere in the cosmos is difficult to say. For humans on Earth it means that, with far-reaching and deleterious consequences, persons and communities chronically deploy their powers, capacities, and gifts in order to divide and destroy. There is a persistent human fault. Our isolated and partial interests skew our practical reasoning. We love the wrong things, or else the right things wrongly; we fail to uphold responsibilities to others and, too often, our social and political relationships are inequitable and unjust. There is no person, community, or institution that is exempt from sin's effects, and we therefore find ourselves adrift in cycles of fragmentation, conflict, massive suffering, and violence in which the true communion with God and community and neighbor, for which we are fitted, is broken.[103]

Such a world stands in need of reconciliation because it stands in need of love of God and neighbor or of an expansive and ec-centric redirection of affection, sensibility, and practice. It stands in need of a new quality of attentiveness to the needs and worth of others as well as new community overcoming division. It stands in need of loyalty to the universal commonwealth of all persons, animals, plants, and things in their appropriate interrelations with God and with one another. It stands in need of true communion with God in community with others. And, of course, such a world is a hard and difficult place just because it is not much open to these things. All too often people seem hell-bent on going straight the other way. This is an important, sobering, and, one is tempted to say, empirically verifiable fact. The media offer distressing and daily testimony: economic exploitation, political oppression, corrupt governments, ethnic hatreds, genocidal wars, terrorist attacks, increasingly sophisticated weapons and

103. Douglas F. Ottati, *Reforming Protestantism: Christian Commitment in Today's World* (Louisville: Westminster John Knox, 1995), 66–68.

weapon systems, starvation, child abuse, racism, xenophobia, homophobia, the rapacious destruction of Earth's natural environments, and much more.[104]

This is why the new sight or new vision that comes to persons in Christ is not simply positive. Like the poet W. H. Auden, who was driven to reflect by the horrors and destruction of World War 2, a Christ-formed piety sees that humanity is not capable of extricating itself from its predicament on its own.[105] A Christ-formed piety sees the emergent and as yet fragmentary kingdom and community of reconciliation beset on all sides. It recognizes that diminishment, death, destruction, and conflict often rule the day. It knows that those who hope also have reasons to weep and lament. And so, it is neither merely nor falsely optimistic. It is hopeful but also realistic.

Now, for such a piety, and as the second article of the creed appropriately insists, Christ the reconciler is our *judgment* as well as our hope. The Christ reveals that we are caught up and entangled in a difficulty. He points to a threatening circumstance from which we need to be delivered. The reconciling Word made flesh reveals not only the grace of the divine but also the persistent and extraordinary distance of humans from the divine.[106] Jesus as the Christ provokes a vision of true humanity and he rightwises and redirects life, but therefore (and at one and the same time) he also accuses and convicts. The one who teaches love of God and neighbor, and love of enemies, the one who fulfills the covenant of grace, who attends especially to the vulnerable, and who therefore embodies the kingdom by crossing barriers and boundaries marks off a true way in life that also throws our human fault into sharp relief. He underscores the high, ec-centric, other-directed, and equitable calling and possibility of the human under the influence of grace, but thereby also our dire need for rehabilitation and renewal. As Judge, the Savior who, with the aid of the Spirit, enables and renews also accuses all of falling short.

This indicates a related aspect or dimension of the divine dynamic. The reconciler who accuses and convicts discloses God as Judge; he points to the tendency of the divine excellence and ordering of grace to bring death and destruction when we bring it upon ourselves. He underscores destructive consequences of the diminishment and maladjustment of persons, communities, and institutions. He illumines the terrible and nightmarish price of the human fault; indeed, as the crucified one, he also experiences and embodies it. In this

104. Douglas F. Ottati, *Hopeful Realism: Reclaiming the Poetry of Theology* (Cleveland: Pilgrim, 1999), 106–7.

105. See, for example, Auden's "New Year's Letter (January 1, 1940)," in his *Collected Longer Poems* (New York: Random House, 1969), 77–130.

106. Reinhold Niebuhr, "A Christmas Service in Retrospect," in *Essays in Applied Christianity: The Church and the New World*, ed. D. B. Robertson (New York: Meridian, 1959), 31–33.

sense, we note that not only the image of God as Reconciler and Redeemer but also the image of God as Judge correlates with the Christic pattern. The symbolic idea of God as Judge arises with the recognition that, with dire consequences and at a terrible cost, we often fail to employ our powers appropriately and to uphold our responsibilities; it therefore shapes and expresses feelings of remorse, dissatisfaction, and repentance at what we have become. The wisdom of the cross demands that such feelings be acknowledged rather than neglected or suppressed; the emergence in us of renewed life and humane possibility requires that we both acknowledge and turn away from destructive inattention and injustice. As the first sentence, together with the haunting music, of John Sheppard's masterpiece, *Media Vita*, makes clear, "In the midst of life we are in death."[107]

Hope

The mission of reconciliation and its drive toward the kingdom of true communion in community presuppose the dynamic ordering of grace that impinges upon us in cosmic ecology and cosmic passage (and that was one of the main concluding themes of part 2). It accords, for example, with our abilities to attend to excellences of the world beyond ourselves and even beyond our species. It draws on our solidarity with others in contingency, vulnerability, and undeserved suffering as well as in undeserved benefits. It furthers the extensive sympathy and disposition to care elicited by the apprehension that we are all in the same boat, and it deploys senses of fairness and justice that point to preconditions for right relationships and social well-being. Again, and as I have emphasized here in part 3, a commitment to reconciliation and the kingdom presupposes that we and all other creatures are valued participants in the reconciling and renewing trajectory of the Real. It emerges with a discernment in Christ that calls God's children to work to overcome separations and estrangements in a quest for renovated and rightwised community.

Then too, and as I have just now indicated, the mission of reconciliation also presupposes that humanity stands in need of reconciliation because, caught in

107. John Sheppard (c. 1515–c. 1559) was an English composer of church music. His *Media Vita* is music for the text of "the *Nunc dimittis* at Compline on major feast days in the two weeks before Passion Sunday." See notes by Peter Phillips to the recording of Sheppard's work by the Tallis Scholars, Gimell Records (1989). See also prop. #54 below on crucifixion, judgment, and the right nightmare.

the grips of a persistently skewing tendency and power, persons and communities both manufacture and suffer chronic fragmentation and conflict. It presumes that we stand accused and convicted, and it presupposes God as Judge. Here we come across an apprehension that intertwines with feelings of sorrow, remorse, and lament—affections that may contribute powerfully to piety's reconciling commitment but that also may foster a deep pessimism or even despair that renders reconciling practices precarious.

Personally, I have no small sympathy with those engulfed by pessimism and despair; all the more reason, I expect, why I now underscore a further point. When persons of piety survey a world marked by diminishment, injustice, conflict, and death, they nevertheless also *hope*. They continue to look for enlargement, reconciliation, the kingdom, and renewed life. Their hope is founded partly on the fact that persons and communities neither anticipate nor control all relevant possibilities, and that, even in the midst of fragmentation and destruction, occasions of grace and good abound. Perhaps I am acquainted with the routinely moving fidelity of a husband who draws on unanticipated and untested resolve to care for his wife through years of degenerative illness. Perhaps we find that, once a city reins in profligate development and pollution, a damaged ecosystem recovers. Perhaps we know a movement that emerged in dire circumstances and came to pursue a course of nonviolent and costly resistance in order to witness to the possibility of a less fragmented and more just society. Perhaps we anticipate a time when our own society and culture may push toward a more equitable and compassionate reception of immigrants and refugees. These are occasions of grace, and they are both heartening and inspiring. Piety's hope takes root, persists, and grows stronger because, in the light of Jesus as the Christ and despite the shadows of destruction, it takes these occasions to indicate the power and presence of something more. Hope takes root, persists, and grows stronger because, encouraged by the pattern of Jesus Christ, piety takes an extravagant step. It "sees," posits, imagines, and senses a gratuitous *tendency*. Therefore, even in the midst of less promising and oppressive circumstances, it affirms that something else is nevertheless possible. It construes intermittent occasions of grace as traces of the redeeming and renewing trajectory and excellence of the Real. It envisions them as indicators that the arc of the cosmos, despite human recalcitrance and our frequent inability to make out its curvature, bends toward reconciliation, kingdom, and redemption.[108]

108. This is a modification of a favorite line of Martin Luther King Jr. See *A Testament of Hope: The Essential Writings of Martin Luther King, Jr.*, ed. James Melvin Washington (New York: Harper & Row, 1986), 230.

Excursus on Christological Doctrine

We are ready now to locate my Christology more firmly in relation to some biblical and traditional benchmarks. And the first thing to note, I think, is the variety of christological images and strands one finds in the New Testament. A divinity school professor of mine counted on the order of fourteen to seventeen different Christologies in the New Testament. To mention a few, Jesus is portrayed as the messianic king in the line of David, God's Son or agent, the Son of Man who will return in judgment at the eschaton, the second Adam who represents a chance for the renewal of humanity, the image or icon of the invisible God, the Lamb, and the enfleshed preexistent Word or Logos.

The Nicene Creed (325 CE) and the Chalcedonian Definition (451 CE) develop this last image with the aid of Hellenistic philosophical concepts from beyond the Jewish religious milieu in which Christianity emerged. Nicea says that "our Lord, Jesus Christ . . . is true God from true God . . . of one Being with the Father." Chalcedon develops this statement further into the two-natures formula: "our Lord Jesus Christ" is "of one substance with the Father as regards his Godhead, and at the same time of one substance with us as regards his manhood." These statements combated other interpretations that were also put forward using Hellenistic concepts, such as the idea that Jesus was a divine being who appeared in human form but was not genuinely human (docetism), and the idea that he was an intermediate being who, strictly speaking, was neither God nor man (Arianism).

Must we agree that Jesus is God in the rather hard-and-fast metaphysical sense of the conciliar Christology? Historians alert us to the fact that, as a devout Jew, the Jesus of history is unlikely to have claimed that he was God. For example, Ulrich Luz says, "Jesus accepted that he was the one who one day would be installed by God as the heavenly Son of Man and would judge."[109] Geza Vermes says the historical Jesus was "a charismatic prophetic preacher and miracle-worker, the outstanding 'Galilean Hasid,'" and he also wonders whether the man from Nazareth would have reacted to Ignatius of Antioch's second-century allusion to Jesus as "our God" with "stupefaction, anger, or grief."[110]

109. Ulrich Luz and Axel Michaels, *Encountering Jesus and Buddha: Their Lives and Teachings*, trans. Linda M. Mahoney (Minneapolis: Fortress, 2006), 130.

110. Geza Vermes, *The Religion of Jesus the Jew* (Minneapolis: Fortress, 1993), 5. Vermes, *Jesus the Jew: A Historian's Reading of the Gospels* (London: Collins, 1973), 213. See also Marcus Borg's contention that "the pre-Easter Jesus was not God," and that "Jesus stands" in a tradition of Jewish figures, including Moses and Isaiah, "for whom God, the sacred, was an experienced reality." *Jesus: Uncovering the Life, Teachings, and Relevance of a Religious Revolutionary* (New York: HarperOne, 2007), 109, 117.

What of the New Testament texts and the theologies they offer? B. A. Gerrish notes that "in the Gospels Jesus does not claim to be God, but to be sent by God. 'Why do you call me good? No one is good but God alone' (Mark 10:18). '[W]hoever welcomes me welcomes not me but the one who sent me' (Mark 9:37)."[111] To this we may add the testimony of the demons in Mark 1:24 who know Jesus and who, as Jesus drives them out, identify him not as God but as "the Holy One of God."[112] Again, as presented in Matthew and in Luke, the Lord's Prayer, or "Our Father," seems at home within Judaism, and here Jesus does not teach his disciples to pray in his own name. Bruce Chilton says the Synoptic Gospels portray Jesus as the kingdom's herald and advocate, the Son of Man or agent of redemption who will return to Earth and vindicate his followers.[113] Vermes says none of the Synoptics tries to equate Jesus as the Son of God with God proper. "Indeed, it is no exaggeration to contend that the identification of a contemporary historical figure with God would have been inconceivable to a first-century Palestinian Jew."[114] Furthermore, in the Gospel of John, when he tells the disciples that he is going away and that the Father will send the Advocate, the Holy Spirit, "in my name," Jesus rather famously says, "You heard me say to you, 'I am going away, and I am coming to you.' If you loved me, you would rejoice that I am going to the Father, because the Father is greater than I" (14:28).

This, of course, does not settle the broader question of whether other New Testament texts attribute deity to Jesus, and to address this question Gerrish offers a brief and quite helpful survey of passages sometimes taken to state explicitly that Jesus is God. He notes, for example, that passages in Revelation distinguish the Lamb from angels and also portray the Lamb and the Father receiving adoration together (5:13; 7:10), though "the distinction between God and his messiah is plain (11:15; 12:10)."[115] Colossians 2:2, Gerrish says, presents Christ as God's mystery rather than simply as God, and, we may add, a distinction between Christ and God follows from the claim in 1:15 that Christ is the image or icon of the invisible God. Romans 9:5 is a problematic verse that may be rendered in different ways.[116] Hebrews 1:8, "But of the Son he says, 'Your throne, O God, is forever and ever,'" is grammatically ambiguous and also may be translated, "God

111. Gerrish, *Christian Faith*, 142.

112. See also Adela Yarbro Collins, *Mark: A Commentary*, ed. Harold Attridge (Minneapolis: Fortress, 2007), 172.

113. Bruce Chilton, *Pure Kingdom: Jesus' Vision of God* (Grand Rapids: Eerdmans, 1996), 135–38.

114. Vermes, *The Religion of Jesus the Jew*, 212.

115. Gerrish, *Christian Faith*, 142.

116. Compare "to them belong the patriarchs, and from them, according to the flesh, comes the Messiah, who is over all, God blessed forever. Amen" (NRSV) with "Theirs are the patri-

is your throne." Moreover, other passages in Hebrews that designate Jesus "the apostle and high priest of our confession" (3:1), "the pioneer and perfecter of our faith" (12:2), and "the great shepherd of the sheep" (13:20) do not indicate Jesus's deity. Gerrish says "tandem expressions," for example, "so that the name of our Lord Jesus may be glorified in you, and you in him, according to the grace of our God and the Lord Jesus Christ" (2 Thess. 1:12, and similar statements in Titus 2:13 and 2 Pet. 1:1), most likely distinguish Christ from God. This seems true, too, of 1 Corinthians 8:6, "yet for us there is one God, the Father, from whom are all things and for whom we exist, and one Lord, Jesus Christ, through whom are all things and through whom we exist," as well as of John 17:3, "And this is eternal life, that they may know you, the only true God, and Jesus Christ whom you have sent." Gerrish also says, "most commentators think it improbable that the statement in 1 John, 'He is the true God' (1 John 5:20) refers to Christ."

The NRSV renders John 1:1–2, "In the beginning was the Word, and the Word was with God, and the Word was God. He was in the beginning with God." Gerrish notes, however, that "in the Greek there is no definite article with *theos* ('God'), and some scholars argue that a more correct rendering of *theos ēn ho logos* would be 'the Word was divine' (James Moffatt's translation)."[117] Indeed, Ernst Haenchen translates John 1:1 as follows: "In the beginning was the Logos, and the Logos was with God, and divine [of the category of divinity] was the Logos."[118] In any case, the question of the divinity of the logos or the Word in the opening verses of John is therefore somewhat complicated.[119]

Gerrish also notes that one reading of John 1:18 "has the remarkable expression *monogenēs theos*, the 'only begotten God.' But again there is disagreement, and the RSV follows the alternative reading *monogenēs huios*, 'only [or only

archs, and from them, in natural descent, sprang the Messiah. May God, supreme above all, be blessed for ever. Amen" (NEB).

117. Gerrish, *Christian Faith*, 143.

118. Haenchen, *John 1*, 108.

119. Rudolf Bultmann argues that the alternation in John 1:1–2 between "the Word was in the beginning with God" (implying preexistence but also distinction), "the Word was God or divine" (implying a kind of identification), and "He was in the beginning with God" (distinction again) expresses a paradoxical yet important idea. "The Father and the Son are one (10:30), and yet the Father is greater than the Son (14:28). . . . Whoever encounters the revelation, really encounters God . . . [but] God is only encountered in the revelation, when it is understood that it is his *revelation*." This leads him to interpret John's prologue in a manner that bears a striking similarity to the *extra calvinisticum*. Here, Bultmann says, as in the Hebrew Scriptures, "the belief is that God works in the historical event, and yet is not limited to this event, not identical with it, but stands beyond it as God." Rudolf Bultmann, *The Gospel of John: A Commentary*, trans. G. R. Beasley-Murray, R. W. N. Hoare, and J. K. Riches (Philadelphia: Westminster, 1971), 34–35.

begotten] *Son.*'" In fact, then, says Gerrish, "the sole place in the New Testament where everyone agrees, Jesus is incontestably called 'God'" is John 20:28, when "Thomas addresses the risen Jesus as 'My Lord and my God.'" But some also suggest that this is a "Christian retort to the insistence of Emperor Domitian (51–96 CE) that *he* should be addressed as 'lord and god,'" and, however one adjudicates this question, one also needs to ask how Thomas's exclamation squares with the repeated subordination of Jesus to the Father in John's Gospel.[120]

Gerrish concludes his survey by noting that pictures of the postresurrection Lord in the New Testament often "add the vision of *a preexistent being* subordinate to God." Moreover, there are passages in the New Testament, such as "Thomas's obeisance before the risen Lord," where we see "some foreshadowing of the shift from the primitive Christian confession 'Jesus is Lord' (1 Cor. 12:3; 2 Cor. 4:5; cf. Luke 2:11) to the Nicene Creed's 'true God from true God.'" But the foreshadowing is neither consistent nor overwhelming, and thus the sheer variety of Christologies in the New Testament "urges caution in pronouncing the charge of heresy on deviations from catholic dogma."[121]

My basic position may be stated quite simply—in Jesus Christ, we come to know the God of grace. This, I think, is the upshot of a number of christological images and strands in the New Testament, as well as of gospel portraits of what Jesus says, does, and endures (which we shall review in the next chapter). Knowledge of the God of grace who is our sure Redeemer—this is a fundamental, relational, and experiential apprehension of Christian piety. When Christians encounter Jesus as the Christ, this is how they apprehend the maker of heaven and earth to whom they are indebted at every turn. There are other ways to get at this same theme. Colossians 1:15–16 claims that Christ is the image or icon of the invisible God and that in or by him "all things in heaven and on earth were created." In John 1, the preexistent divine wisdom and agent in creation becomes enfleshed to bring to people grace and truth or true knowledge of God. The conciliar formulae develop this last christological strand with the aid

120. Gerrish, *Christian Faith*, 143–44.

121. Gerrish, *Christian Faith*, 144. In *The Religion of Jesus the Jew*, 213, Vermes is more strident, and he almost reduplicates Adolf von Harnack's negative judgment that Hellenistic speculation represents an intrusion on the gospel and results in christological formulas that do not fit the Jesus Christ of the gospel. "When Christianity later set out to define the meaning of *son of God* in its Creed, the paraphrase it produced—'God of God, Light of Light, true God of true God, consubstantial with the Father'—drew its inspiration, not from the pure language and teaching of the Galilean Jesus, nor even from Paul the Diaspora Jew, but from a Gentile-Christian interpretation of the Gospel adapted to the mind of the totally alien world of pagan Hellenism." See also Adolf von Harnack, *History of Dogma*, trans. Neil Buchanan (New York: Dover, 1961), 4:106; *What Is Christianity?* trans. Thomas Bailey Saunders (New York: Harper Torchbooks, 1957), 235.

of a quite specific metaphysics of divine and human natures. But I think my own statements—that in Jesus as the Christ the gratuitous divine excellence at work in creation and redemption is displayed in a human life; that his true life is the light that enlightens people—are at least as closely related to the Johannine text as is the two-natures doctrine. Moreover, my admittedly less precise and more symbolic formulations can accommodate the piety-meanings of other New Testament images and strands without claiming that all must converge on the Chalcedonian Definition.

Unlike Christologies that try to further the Chalcedonian metaphysics, my formulations do not require me to give a hard-and-fast interpretation of God's nature (is it, for example, impassible?), of the human nature "assumed" by the Word (is it a general human nature, a general rational nature, *sarx*, etc.?), or how their properties are shared (are omniscience and ubiquity communicated to the human nature?). Neither do my formulations require me to decide whether it is the Word rather than the human nature that forms the center of the incarnate person, whether a nature even can be truly human if it does not form its own personal center, etc. I am relieved of having to answer these questions and others like them because I regard incarnation talk as one of a number of possible and also largely symbolic ways of articulating piety's apprehension that, in Jesus as the Christ, we know the God of grace. This formulation does not protect all that the ancient (and especially the Alexandrian) Christology means for some strands of ancient Christian piety. For example, it does not protect the conviction that the salvation of humans is a process of "divinization" that hinges on the hypostatic union of the divine and human natures. But it does recognize that, in Christ, we apprehend the true disposition or excellence of God, as God always stands *in relation* to all.

My claim that the life and ministry of Jesus as the Christ are fitted to the divine and therefore disclose the divine tendency or excellence follows the general lead of Friedrich Schleiermacher, who holds that the perfect and constantly potent God-consciousness of Jesus yields a new and ideal spiritual life. Indeed, he says, "to ascribe to Christ an absolutely powerful God-consciousness" that determines the shape of his life, "and to attribute to Him an existence of God in Him, are exactly the same thing."[122] Whether this last claim ventures a step too far will depend on just what one means by "an existence of God in Him," but I agree with the basic point that the Christ, the one who displays the new or true human life, also discloses the divine.

Donald Baillie articulates a similar position in his little book *God Was in Christ*. Jesus Christ, he says, was a person perfectly receptive to God's grace, and this receptivity yielded a life and ministry pleasing to God. Indeed, this grace,

122. Schleiermacher, *CF*, #94 (pp. 386–87).

says Baillie, on which Jesus's obedient human choices were wholly dependent, "was nothing short of an incarnation."[123] Consider too Paul Tillich's claim that the Christ represents essential humanity, humanity in relation to God, or what God wants humanity to be, rather than humanity skewed, warped, and estranged from God. The Christ therefore not only displays what (theologically speaking) is truly human; he also manifests the endemic and eternal relatedness of God to essential humanity, or "the divine presence in essential manhood."[124] This, says Tillich, may be called an incarnation in the qualified sense that "God is manifest in a personal life-process as a saving participant in the human predicament."[125]

My own understanding of what classical theology often calls "the person of Christ" is that, for the Christian community, the reconciling event of Jesus as the Christ displays a pattern or manner of life appropriately adjusted to the divine. Christ's ministry and mission are fitted to the dynamic reality of God, or, as Richard R. Niebuhr says, Jesus as the Christ is "a God-shaped man."[126] Jesus's ministry centers on his message of the kingdom and his enactment of it in reconciling actions and practices that challenge and overcome barriers and boundaries. This pattern displays the divine excellence as well as the basic skein or trajectory of a human life authentically fitted to the divine excellence. It bears the impression or imprint of the divine (Heb. 1:3). We may therefore say that Jesus as the Christ is the living Torah, icon, wisdom, or Word of God manifest in a person precisely because his manner of life and his ministry are authentically conformed to God's will. He who has seen him therefore has seen the divine tendency and excellence.

How this stands in continuity with much of the New Testament can be seen if we recognize that the Gospels (and especially the Synoptics) portray Jesus as the Christ or Messiah who proclaims and enacts the kingdom of God. The figure of Jesus in the Gospels teaches and enacts a pattern of affection and action that points uncompromisingly to God's purposes as these purposes come to expression in the divine kingdom or reign.[127] Or, to put this somewhat differently, Jesus's *theocentric kingdom piety* disposes and shapes the reconciling pattern of his ministry and mission, and so, in turn, the reconciling pattern of his ministry and mission displays his theocentric kingdom piety and conforms to God's kingdom purpose.

Why do Jesus's ministry and message take on this specific manner, cast, or

123. D. M. Baillie, *God Was in Christ: An Essay on Incarnation and Atonement* (New York: Scribner's Sons, 1948), 130–31.

124. Tillich, *Existence and the Christ*, 94, 96.

125. Tillich, *Existence and the Christ*, 95.

126. Richard R. Niebuhr, *Experiential Religion* (New York: Harper & Row, 1972), 124, 130.

127. This is substantially the position I outlined in *Jesus Christ and Christian Vision*, 50–72.

temper? How and why should this particular figure come to be gripped so radically by a theocentric kingdom piety as to represent it so thoroughly and decisively? To answer questions such as these, one may speculate about the myriad biological, historical, and cultural factors that formed him. In the providence of God, one might say, these specific factors, which clearly lie quite beyond the control of any person or community and certainly beyond the control of the man Jesus of Nazareth, combined to yield this result. Perhaps, like Baillie, we shall say Jesus's exceptional receptivity to grace was itself the product of a prevenient grace at work in and through these factors, so that, in Augustine's arresting phrase, Jesus Christ—at least in the view of many Christians—is "the brightest illustration of grace."[128] Or perhaps we shall turn to mythopoeic portraits of his spiritual conception and the descent of the Spirit in the form of a dove at his baptism. In any case, the Gospels present Jesus as a person whose life and ministry are gripped by theocentric kingdom piety, who therefore displays what human life in appropriately responsive relation to God is like, and thus also discloses the gratuitous excellence or dynamic of the Real, or of the Creator-Judge-Redeemer. Early Christian communities depicted Jesus this way, and with the help of texts they left behind, later Christian communities continue to view or construe him similarly.

This is a way of saying how the event of redemption-in-Jesus-Christ constitutes the paradigmatic disclosure for picturing God and ourselves. Is it also an appropriate way to specify the meaning of the word "incarnation"? Yes, if we understand incarnation as a symbolic concept that expresses and shapes the sense that, in Jesus as the Christ, we apprehend and encounter the excellence of the God of grace, an excellence that is at work in bringing things into existence and in bestowing new and renewed life. Yes, if we understand incarnation to indicate the contours of the divine excellence in a human life conformed to it. But certainly not in the sense of the classical two-natures doctrine taken as a substantive metaphysical specification of how humanity and divinity coinhere in Christ's person.

On my view, which is partly indebted to christological hints in James M. Gustafson's *Ethics from a Theocentric Perspective*, one may say that the Christ incarnates theocentric piety and devotion, and that, through the gospel accounts of his life and ministry, we see and know something of the divine reign or dynamic of the Real as it impinges upon us.[129] Somewhat similarly, H. Richard Niebuhr holds that Jesus Christ incarnates "radical faith" in "the Lord of heaven and earth as fatherly goodness toward all creatures." This faith, says Niebuhr, comes to expression in Jesus's "acts of healing as well as in teaching, in his interpretation

128. Augustine, *De praedestinatione sanctorum* 1.15, cited by Baillie, *God Was in Christ*, 118.
129. Gustafson, *ETP*, 1:276.

of the historic moment in which he lives and in the leadership he seeks to give to his people, in his relations to national enemies and to the morally rejected."[130] But these statements do not repeat the conciliar Christology. I do not regard this as disqualifying, and, as I indicated earlier, I also think such statements accord more closely with a variety of New Testament symbols, including the symbol of the enfleshed Word or Logos in John 1, than we often recognize.

The two-natures doctrine formulated at Chalcedon was the fruit of controversy and compromise. The fathers operated within quite specific political and intellectual limits, and the Definition they furnished hardly settled all speculative questions about the relationship between the divinity and humanity of the incarnate Christ.[131] If anything, it provoked additional questions and speculations. Schleiermacher was therefore quite correct to complain that, in its persistent efforts to elaborate on the celebrated formula, subsequent orthodox Christology became excessively subtle and scholastic, "overloaded with a multitude of distinctions" that have little to do with living Christian piety and affection.[132]

This may be one reason why, some centuries before Schleiermacher, Calvin and other French-Swiss reformers refused to sign the Nicene Creed as a test of orthodoxy at Lausanne and elsewhere in disputations with Peter Caroli. They affirmed the piety or religion of the early church symbols, and therefore were quite willing to recite them in worship, but they did not think that all subsequent church confessions and theological statements should be bound to a specific formula of words. In particular, they did not want to be required to repeat what seemed to them the rather speculative terms *persona* and *trinitas*.[133] Centuries later, Reinhold Niebuhr made a similar point as he recalled a Christmas service. Niebuhr said he believed the Christmas story but that, in the Nicene Creed, the poetry of religion had been transmuted into dogma—"'very God of very God, begotten not made.' I want to raise some questions about that. But why bother? The choir is singing it to an E flat tune by Eyre. . . . The alchemy of the service has changed what was once poetry and has been made into dogma back into poetry again."[134]

130. H. Richard Niebuhr, *Radical Monotheism and Western Culture, with Supplementary Essays* (Louisville: Westminster John Knox, 1993), 42. See also H. Richard Niebuhr, *Christ and Culture* (New York: Harper & Row, 1951), 27.

131. Ottati, *Jesus Christ and Christian Vision*, 23–35.

132. Schleiermacher, *CF*, #95 (p. 390). Similarly, B. A. Gerrish notes that Calvin, who regarded the Trinity "chiefly as a *defensive* doctrine," worried about excessive speculation, especially when it comes to terms such as *hypostasis* and *personae*. *The Old Protestantism and the New: Essays on the Reformation Heritage* (Chicago: University of Chicago Press, 1982), 206.

133. W. Nijenhuis, "Calvin's Attitude towards the Symbols of the Early Church during the Conflict with Caroli," chap. 4 of his book *Ecclesia Reformata: Studies on the Reformation* (Leiden: Brill, 1972), 73–96.

134. Reinhold Niebuhr, *Essays in Applied Christianity*, 30.

Rather than a univocal statement about the metaphysics of incarnation, I think one may argue that the Chalcedonian Definition is best understood as a fractured dogma, a semisymbolic statement that points to the paradigmatic character of the event of Jesus Christ.[135] The compromise formula framed by the fathers guarded against certain misconceptions. Indeed, the less speculative and more practical upshot of the two-natures formula is that it furnishes Christians who encounter Jesus Christ in the Bible, and in preaching, teaching, worship, and prayer, with a kind of guiding framework. It tells them to look to Jesus as the Christ for their basic and heartfelt knowledge of God and of humanity. Here, in my terms, they apprehend the divine excellence and dynamic of the Real, the God of grace to which every person is called to conform, and here they see how persons may be truly responsive to the Real. What Jesus Christ says, does, and endures therefore discloses the excellence or dynamism of the Real that creates, judges, and redeems at the same time that it discloses a manner in life that is appropriately responsive to the divine dynamism. For the Christian community, Jesus as the Christ is the paradigmatic disclosure of the reality of God and of human life in appropriate relation to God.

This christological grammar, I think, is the key point of the classical two-natures doctrine. It encourages us to look to Jesus as the Christ to find out what God and human life in relation to God are like. It tells us that the event of Jesus as the Christ is the great clue to knowledge of God and ourselves. But I am not inclined to repeat either the metaphysics of the two-natures doctrine or the scholastic subtleties to which later tradition was driven in order to maintain it. Indeed, if one understands Christian theology the way I do—as a practical wisdom that shapes and expresses a particular piety and possibility in life—then one may very well prefer to affirm the paradigmatic character of Jesus as the Christ in a manner that relinquishes Chalcedon's more speculative language and conceptuality. I think the basic accomplishment of Chalcedon's doctrine should be recognized. But I also think that the vital interpretive point (not unlike the one made by the French-Swiss reformers at Lausanne and elsewhere) is to recognize and respect piety's apprehension of the God of grace in a personal life fitted to the divine reign without reifying the classical doctrine's technical vocabulary.

135. Ottati, *Jesus Christ and Christian Vision*, 44–49.

Chapter Eight

The Truth, the Way, and the Life

We turn now to consider the reconciling event of Jesus Christ in greater detail, and the basic statement I shall use to guide our consideration is this: Jesus as the Christ teaches the truth, embodies the way, and empowers the life. He teaches the truth about God's reign or dominion and about human life in God's world. He marks off or displays a way or a manner in life that coheres with the truth, and so guides or governs faithful living. He empowers this life by his sacrifice on the cross, resurrection, and continuing presence, and so enables people to walk in the way or live in a manner aligned with the truth. Put differently, the particulars of Jesus's message, ministry, and crucifixion/resurrection define the reconciling event and illumine the contours of the divine excellence as well as a manner of living that fits with and reflects that excellence. This, broadly speaking, is my shorthand understanding of the pattern of Jesus as the Christ, the Word of God—what H. Richard Niebuhr called revelation, the event that precipitates a reinterpretation of life and experience in relation to God, or "the intelligible event which makes all other events intelligible."[1]

Proposition #52 Jesus as the Christ teaches the truth.

Like the images of Christ as prophet, king, and priest that we find in Calvin's *Institutes of the Christian Religion*, my shorthand points to three elements: *teaching-instruction*, *governance-guidance*, and *sacrifice-atonement*.[2] Especially in the light of modern biblical scholarship, however, it is important to recog-

1. H. Richard Niebuhr, *The Meaning of Revelation* (Louisville: Westminster John Knox, 2006), 69.

2. See Calvin, *ICR* 2.15.1. In what follows more generally here and in the next two propositions, I am elaborating a schema from my earlier book *Jesus Christ and Christian Vision* (Louisville: Westminster John Knox, 1996), 37–39, 73–95.

nize that the images of the one who teaches the truth, embodies the way, and empowers the life intersect and overlap. Jesus teaches, for example, not only by what he says but also by his actions and his sufferings; his teaching-instruction, governance-guidance, and sacrifice-atonement intertwine. Each symbol, each shorthand expression, points to the same figure, the same integral event; indeed, my interpretation of Jesus as the Christ and his significance for Christian piety will remain incomplete until all three elements are explored.

One additional note before we turn to the specific proposition at hand: we have no unfiltered or direct access to what Jesus as the Christ says, does, and endures. Jesus, unlike Paul, was not a writer who left a collection of letters, and so the gospel writers, working decades after Jesus's death, could only draw on sayings sources and other traditions about Jesus, some of which were based in memories and statements of his earliest followers. What the gospel writers, in turn, produced are theologically suffused narrative portrayals that are organized and integrated by varied interpretative images and ideas, for example, Jesus as Davidic-Messiah King who opens the people of God to all nations (Matthew), Jesus as a messianic exorcist and healer locked in a decisive conflict with the demonic (Mark).

The situation is not entirely different when we consider portraits of Jesus offered by recent scholars.

> For E. P. Sanders: Jesus was an eschatological prophet who anticipated the restoration of Israel and the end of the old world order. For Burton Mack: Jesus was a sage resembling the ancient Greek and Roman Cynics in his teaching and lifestyle. For Elizabeth Schussler Fiorenza: Jesus was a prophet and messenger of Sophia God who sought the renewal of Israel as the holy people of God. For Marcus Borg: Jesus was a charismatic healer and holy man, a sage and social prophet. For John Dominic Crossan: Jesus was a Mediterranean Jewish man of the artisan class, who rejected the current world order. For Bart Ehrman: Jesus was an apocalyptic prophet who announced the cosmic destruction of the present world order and the establishment of a new physical world paradise with human co-regents.[3]

These portraits are disciplined by modern historiographical methods, meticulous attention to a variety of ancient texts, and recent studies of ancient cultures. Very often, they help us to see more clearly the theologies of the canonical Gospels and to better understand the sociocultural context for Jesus's own teaching and

3. Charles W. Hedrick, *The Wisdom of Jesus: Between the Sages of Israel and the Apostles of the Church* (Eugene, OR: Cascade, 2014), 179.

activity. They also help us to get back behind certain features of the canonical portraits, such as a tendency to retroject into the life and teaching of Jesus certain tensions between Christians and Jews that can only have arisen later when the communities became differentiated, as well as a tendency, in the light of later institutional restrictions, to downplay the role of women within the early Jesus movement. Even so, the earliest available sources remain sparse and the reliable details about Jesus's life comparatively few, with the result that recent scholarly portraits are constructed around interpretative images that integrate different judgments about the earliest traditions.

I repeat: we have no unfiltered or direct access to what Jesus says, does, and endures. This is true when we consult the Gospels and when we consult contemporary scholars. And it is one reason why there is still much to commend Albert Schweitzer's negative judgment from so many years ago: the Jesus of history remains enigmatic and especially liable to being constructed in the image of his interpreter's preferences.[4] The theologian and the believer confront multiple scholarly portraits, many interrelated, but most also characterized by different emphases and nuances. And, while one may offer reasons for preferring one portrait to another, as well as for drawing on particular features of different portraits, one cannot reduce the plurality to a single, agreed-upon, and detailed picture.

In any case, the reflections I offer here on what Jesus as the Christ says, does, and endures are something of a hybrid. I make use of recent historical scholarship but am not simply trying to get at the historical Jesus. I employ biblical and traditional theological symbols but am not trying simply to explicate traditional christological doctrine apart from historical and exegetical evidence. Why? Because Christian theology is reflection in the service of Christian piety, and, for persons of Christian piety, Jesus as the Christ is a person, but also an image and a pattern that help to give form and meaning to their experiences. As anyone who has sung "O Come, O Come Emanuel" during a liturgically literate Advent service must surely know, the one who discloses the reality of God and of human life in responsive relation to the divine remains a symbolically elaborated historical figure.[5] Accordingly, I shall note how my reflections intertwine with and benefit from the work of historians and biblical scholars, though I will not assume that

4. Albert Schweitzer, *The Quest for the Historical Jesus: A Critical Study of Its Progress from Reimarus to Wrede*, trans. W. Montgomery (New York: Macmillan, 1968), 398–403. Indeed, Charles W. Hedrick concludes, "given the nature of the sources and the orientation of the interpreter, almost any image of Jesus seems possible." See *The Wisdom of Jesus*, 179.

5. In *The Responsible Self: An Essay in Christian Moral Philosophy* (Louisville: Westminster John Knox, 1999), 157, H. Richard Niebuhr writes, "for Christians it is at least as important to reject the thought that Jesus Christ is only an historical figure as it is to deny that he is only a symbol." I agree.

their scholarship is either neutral or incorrigible. (Indeed, at points, I will simply note what I consider to be illuminating differences and disagreements among interpreters without resolving them.) I will also explore narratives, sayings, and mythopoeic texts in the New Testament that are not confirmed as historical by life-of-Jesus research. These too are often theologically highly significant.

Teacher

That Jesus taught is noncontroversial, but there is no complete agreement on precisely what Jesus said and did, just how many teachings on his lips in the New Testament are traceable to the historical Jesus, and so on. For example, "Love your enemies" is attested in Matthew, Luke, and the hypothesized common sayings source Q.[6] Many historians, including most who participate in the Jesus Seminar, believe Jesus said this or else something very much like it. However, they are not convinced that he uttered all the lines that make up the Lord's Prayer in Matthew 6, though many think he probably said things like what we read in much of the prayer. Comparatively few participants in the seminar think Jesus said that the Golden Rule summarizes the law and the prophets, but some think the Golden Rule itself accords with some of Jesus's own ideas.[7] By contrast, Hans Dieter Betz is inclined to accept not only "Love your enemies" as an authentic teaching of the historical Jesus but also a good deal of the Lord's Prayer. He also thinks that, though it did not originate with Jesus, Jesus probably taught the Golden Rule.[8]

Even so, here we encounter a general point on which the historians and the Gospels basically agree: Jesus teaches. Thus, the Gospel of Mark, our earliest narrative source for the life of Jesus, portrays him as one who teaches in parables to large crowds beside the sea and also explains his parables and their purpose to his inner circle of disciples (1:27; 4:1–34). It also tells us that Jesus "went about among the villages teaching (*didaskein*)" (6:6b), and that, when he went to the region of Judea and beyond the Jordan, "crowds again gathered around him; and, as was his custom, he again taught them" (10:1). The Gospel of Luke portrays

6. For a reconstruction and interpretation of Q, see Burton L. Mack, *The Lost Gospel: The Book Q and Christian Origins* (New York: HarperOne, 1993).

7. Robert W. Funk, Roy W. Hoover, and the Jesus Seminar, trans. and commentary, *The Five Gospels: The Search for the Authentic Words of Jesus* (San Francisco: HarperSanFrancisco, 1993), 145, 148, 155.

8. Hans Dieter Betz, *The Sermon on the Mount: A Commentary on the Sermon on the Mount, Including the Sermon on the Plain*, ed. Adela Yarbro Collins, Hermeneia (Minneapolis: Fortress, 1995), 309, 311, 349, 390–91, 515.

a scene (that clearly is not historical but forms a part of the gospel's prelude to Jesus's ministry) in which the young Jesus's parents find him in the temple sitting among teachers listening, asking questions, and amazing those who hear him with his understanding (2:46–47). Like Q, Luke collects some of Jesus's sayings in a single sermon, the so-called Sermon on the Plain (6:17–49). It also tells us that, when his disciples ask him to teach them how to pray, Jesus says the Lord's Prayer (11:1–4). The Gospel of Matthew collects sayings in the Sermon on the Mount—an oration that, like the sermon in Luke, many scholars believe also draws on the Great Sermon in Q. The sermon in Matthew opens by noting that Jesus "went up the mountain . . . began to speak, and taught them, saying . . ." (5:1–2). It closes with the observation that "he taught them as one having authority," rather than as a mere scribe (7:29).[9] Again, in John 1:38, we read that two of the Baptist's disciples follow Jesus and then say to him, "'Rabbi' (which translated means Teacher), 'where are you staying?'"

Performative

Jesus taught, but what kind of a teacher was he? Calvin, who regards Christ as the law's best interpreter, says that, as prophet, Jesus teaches "perfect doctrine," but this expression evidently does not signify merely intellectual instruction.[10] Quoting Isaiah 61:1–2 (cf. Luke 4:18), Calvin believes the Spirit anoints Christ to his prophetic office "to preach to the humble . . . to bring healing to the brokenhearted, to proclaim liberation to the captives . . . to proclaim the year of the Lord's good pleasure." The prophet-teacher instructs but also proclaims and heals. That Calvin understands Jesus's teaching to be more than intellectual is also apparent when he discusses self-denial, suffering, and bearing the cross

9. When opponents address Jesus as teacher in Matthew, the term often is used mockingly. Consider a series of episodes narrated in chapter 22. The Pharisees try "to entrap him," saying, "Teacher, we know that you are sincere, and teach the way of God in accordance with the truth, and show deference to no one. . . . Tell us, then, . . . is it lawful to pay taxes to the emperor, or not?" (vv. 15–17). Next, the Sadducees, who believe there is no resurrection of the dead, ask Jesus whose wife a woman shall be in heaven if she has been married in succession to seven brothers on earth (vv. 23–28). Then, "When the Pharisees heard that he had silenced the Sadducees, they gathered together, and one of them, a lawyer, asked him a question to test him. 'Teacher, which commandment in the law is the greatest?'" (vv. 34–36). In each instance, detractors try to throw Jesus off his game and demonstrate that he is not really a true or profound teacher after all, but Matthew's Jesus refuses to be duped, and offers true and profound answers, which indicate that he is indeed a genuine teacher. So, for the Gospel of Matthew the ambiguity and tension over calling Jesus "teacher" finally serve to emphasize that Jesus is in fact the teacher par excellence.

10. Calvin, *ICR* 2.8.7; 2.15.3.

as aspects of the Christian life.[11] The same point emerges in Calvin's discussion of Christ's instruction, since he also says that, as prophet, Jesus brings healing, proclaims liberation, and teaches self-denial. In short, we see that "the sum of doctrine" Jesus has given contains "all parts of perfect wisdom."[12]

Enlightenment and liberal thinkers, it is often said, reduce Jesus to little more than a teacher. Perhaps Francis Greenwood Peabody, an American exponent of the Social Gospel who wrote about "the teaching of Jesus" in relation to "the Social Question" and to "Christian character," is a candidate for this dubious distinction.[13] Perhaps Immanuel Kant's Enlightenment, rational, and moral religion is.[14] Certainly Thomas Jefferson's *Life and Morals of Jesus of Nazareth Extracted Textually from the Gospels in Greek, Latin, French, and English* qualifies. Literally a cut-and-paste job, "Jefferson's Bible," as it came to be called, tries to distill the sublime and benevolent code of a great moral reformer by excising miracles, superstitions, and apostolic misconceptions Jefferson thinks unsupportable through reason.[15] Gone, for example, is Jesus casting out an unclean spirit in Mark 1:21–28 (par. Luke 4:31–37). Gone too is Matthew 11:18–19: "For John came neither eating nor drinking, and they say, 'He has a demon'; the Son of Man came eating and drinking, and they say, 'Look, a glutton and a drunkard, a friend of tax collectors and sinners!'" What emerges is Jesus the (more or less enlightened and presumably also sober) moral philosopher.

By contrast, Søren Kierkegaard insists that we obscure or even nullify the venture of genuine discipleship when we reduce Jesus to a didactic teacher of

11. Calvin, *ICR* 3.8.

12. Calvin, *ICR* 2.15.3.

13. Francis Greenwood Peabody, *Jesus Christ and the Social Question: An Examination of the Teaching of Jesus in Its Relation to Some of the Problems of Modern Social Life* (New York: Macmillan, 1903), 1–75. Among other things, Peabody believes the teaching of Jesus has a "quality of comprehensiveness," or an "extraordinary capacity for new adaptations" (73). See also Peabody, *Jesus Christ and Christian Character* (New York: Macmillan, 1905), 1, 7, 71.

14. Kant refers to Jesus as "the Teacher of the Gospel" in his *Lectures on Ethics*, trans. Louis Infield (New York: Harper & Row, 1963), 72, and also in *Religion within the Limits of Reason Alone*, trans. Theodore M. Greene and Hoyt H. Hudson (New York: Harper & Row, 1960), 155, 189, but the emphasis of his rational religion, with its concept of radical evil and divine grace, lies elsewhere. For an interpretation that makes this clear, see Allen W. Wood, *Kant's Moral Religion* (Ithaca, NY: Cornell University Press, 1970).

15. This will be apparent from even a short glance at the table of contents of Jefferson's Bible. See *The Jefferson Bible: What Thomas Jefferson Selected as the Life and Morals of Jesus of Nazareth* (Thousand Oaks, CA: Lakewood, 2011). See also Elizabeth Campbell, "Thomas Jefferson: Religion, Politics and *The Life and Morals of Jesus of Nazareth*," in *The Jefferson Bible* (Lakewood, 2011), 8–10; Harry R. Rubenstein and Barbara Clark Smith, "History of the Jefferson Bible," in *The Jefferson Bible: The Life and Morals of Jesus of Nazareth Extracted Textually from the Gospels in Greek, Latin, French, and English* (Washington, DC: Smithsonian, 2011), 20.

merely intellectual doctrine. "He never lectured," says Kierkegaard, "neither did He seek to prevail upon anyone by reasons" or proofs. "His teaching in fact was His life" (including his sacrifice and sufferings), which, for Kierkegaard, presents an absolute requirement that resists convenient accommodations to common sense.[16] In short, when we turn to Jesus, teaching, practice, and endurance interpenetrate in ways that challenge and disturb our more conventional notions of instruction. Jefferson's portrait of the reasonable moral reformer is precisely the denial of destabilizing presence Kierkegaard feared when the man from Nazareth is reduced to a soothing intellect. For Kierkegaard, the problem is not just that interpreters such as Jefferson reduce Jesus to little more than a teacher, but also that they badly misconstrue the sort of teacher Jesus was.

Kierkegaard's insistence suggests the profundity of some classical themes, and it also anticipates a point pressed by the contemporary Bible scholar John Dominic Crossan. Jesus not only announces the kingdom or reign of God; he also practices it by his unsettling healings, exorcisms, and table fellowship with outcasts. Crossan therefore opens his book *The Historical Jesus: The Life of a Mediterranean Jewish Peasant* with the following rather arresting sentence: "In the beginning was the performance; not the word alone, not the deed alone, but both, each indelibly marked with the other forever."[17]

Sapiential

The unsettling character of Jesus's performance intersects with another emphasis of recent scholarship, namely, that his teaching was sapiential. Consider the ending of the Sermon on the Mount in Matthew 7:24–27: "Everyone then who hears these words of mine and acts on them will be like a wise man who built his house on rock. The rain fell, the floods came, and the winds blew and beat on that house, but it did not fall, because it had been founded on rock. And everyone who hears these words of mine and does not act on them will be like a foolish man who built his house on sand. The rain fell, and the floods came, and the winds blew and beat against that house, and it fell—and great was its fall!" The characters of the wise (or prudent) man and the foolish one in Matthew 7:24–27 (par. in Luke 6:47–49 and in Q) are also traditional in Egyptian and Jewish wisdom literature,[18] and the passage links the teaching of Jesus with the image of

16. Søren Kierkegaard, *"For Self-Examination" and "Judge for Yourselves!" and Three Discourses*, trans. Walter Lowrie (London: Oxford University Press, 1941), 200, 197.

17. John Dominic Crossan, *The Historical Jesus: The Life of a Mediterranean Jewish Peasant* (New York: HarperOne, 2005), xi.

18. Betz, *The Sermon on the Mount*, 558–63.

human lives as houses built by Wisdom in Proverbs (9:1–6; 14:1–2; 24:3–4). Some years ago, Reginald Fuller regarded the parable of the wise and foolish builders as an authentic teaching of Jesus, while Hans Dieter Betz thinks this unlikely. Still, the gist of the final lines in Jesus's sermon is clear—one must both hear and practice Jesus's precepts[19]—and the effect is to construe what Jesus says in Matthew 5–7 as instruction in a wise rather than a foolish manner of living.

Again, when John's disciples question Jesus in Matthew 11, Jesus tells them to return to the Baptist and tell him what they see. He then enters into a comparatively lengthy discourse about the Baptist and himself in which, even as he contrasts his own style of mission (eating and drinking with all the wrong people) with John's asceticism, he notes that both have been rejected. Finally, Jesus asserts, "Yet wisdom is vindicated by her deeds" (11:19), or in the Lukan parallel, "Nevertheless, wisdom is vindicated by all her children" (7:35). Among other things and somewhat like Jesus, the feminine figure of Wisdom to whom Jesus alludes teaches her hearers how to live correctly and how to walk in the ways of God's commandments. She too admonishes people not to "forget my teaching," to "accept my words," and to "be attentive" (Prov. 3:1; 4:1, 10; and 5:1). Moreover, Luke 7:35 depicts Jesus as the last in a series of Wisdom's envoys or children; Matthew 11:19 suggests he may be Wisdom's definitive emissary.[20]

Jesus's sayings often seem imprudent, for example, "Do not worry about your life, what you will eat or what you will drink, or about your body, what will you wear" (Matt. 6:25), and Marcus Borg sees Jesus as a teacher of *subversive* wisdom of the sort we find in Job and Ecclesiastes. Jesus, says Borg, presents an alternative way of seeing reality and of living that undercuts more conventional postures and attitudes.[21] He teaches a "narrow way" in life that contrasts with the broad and conventional way centered on status, family, and wealth. Jesus's alternative path is centered on the compassionate God; it leads out of "the disease of common human life," and therefore also entails repentance, a turning, or a reorientation.[22]

"Blessed are the meek, for they will inherit the earth" (Matt. 5:5) or

> "Blessed are you who are poor,
> for yours is the kingdom of God." (Luke 6:20)

19. Reginald H. Fuller, "Matthew," in *Harper's Bible Commentary*, James L. Mays, gen. ed. (San Francisco: Harper & Row, 1988), 960–61; Betz, *The Sermon on the Mount*, 560.

20. Fuller, "Matthew," 964.

21. Marcus Borg, *Meeting Jesus Again for the First Time: The Historical Jesus and the Heart of Contemporary Faith* (New York: HarperOne, 2005), 69–95.

22. Borg, *Meeting Jesus*, 192, 205–23.

Betz notes that, while we have no complete collection of ancient beatitudes and no entirely satisfactory classification of their literary forms and styles, the broader genre ordinarily is associated with wisdom teaching. The oldest examples, he says, are associated with mystery cults and are sayings to be chanted or recited from memory, for example, a quotation in the *Homeric Hymn to Demeter* from the mysteries of Demeter and Persephone at Eleusis, "Happy is he among humans on earth who has seen these mysteries."[23] In some Jewish texts, says Betz, for example, 2 Enoch, beatitudes "are part of the literary effort to create, or recreate an apocalyptic vision in the imagination of the reader,"[24] and a number of Jesus's beatitudes appear to function similarly. In addition, among Greek philosophers, including Epicurus, beatitudes sometimes serve as succinct introductory principles for collections of ethical maxims, and Betz believes that, in their own ways, those in the Sermon on the Mount and the Sermon on the Plain also "follow this convention."[25]

What, then, can it have meant in Jesus's time and place to utter blessings on the poor, the hungry, the meek, and the peacemakers? Crossan thinks the implications are clearly subversive; Jesus proclaims a "sapiential Kingdom" that "looks to the present rather than the future and imagines how one could live here and now within an already or always available divine dominion." Jesus proclaims and performs "a here and now Kingdom of the nobodies and the destitute" as an alternative to the present social order.[26]

Prophetic

We may also, I think, characterize Jesus's teaching as prophetic. Classical Protestants, who associate Jesus's prophetic office with his teaching, tend to view the prophets as advocates of Mosaic law. The early-twentieth-century proponent of the Social Gospel, Walter Rauschenbusch, adds a socially critical note that is largely absent from both classical Protestant and Enlightenment estimates of Jesus by aligning Jesus's preaching of the kingdom with the "ethical monotheism" of the prophets.[27] Jesus's prophetic message of the kingdom, says Rauschenbusch, "involved a thorough regeneration and reconstruction of social life" that authorize a special concern for the poor and oppressed, as well as solidaristic

23. Betz, *The Sermon on the Mount*, 94, 97, 99.

24. Betz, *The Sermon on the Mount*, 102.

25. Betz, *The Sermon on the Mount*, 105.

26. Crossan, *The Historical Jesus*, 292.

27. Walter Rauschenbusch, *Christianity and the Social Crisis* (Louisville: Westminster John Knox, 1991), 1–43, especially 26, 53, 71.

commitment to the common good.[28] And, indeed, here the alignment of Jesus with the prophets comes within range of a theme emphasized by more recent liberation theologians: Jesus's preaching of the kingdom, says Rauschenbusch, "implies a revolution of the human world."[29]

Gerhard von Rad points out that what is specifically "prophetic" is more complicated than early Protestants imagined, and that "there were different kinds of prophets and different kinds of prophecy."[30] Moreover, the question of what counts as prophetic has become more complicated since von Rad, Rauschenbusch, and even most liberation theologians wrote. For example, Crossan identifies different types of first-century prophets in and around Palestine. He distinguishes popular prophets, who were illiterate and dreamt of a transcendental and violent overthrow of overlords, from millennial prophets, both scribal and oracular, whose unarmed enactments of millennial visions could disrupt normal social activities and were sometimes misunderstood by authorities. Crossan then argues that John the Baptist was a millennial prophet but that Jesus does not fit the categories. Why? Because Jesus regarded God's kingdom or reign as nonviolent, as involving human collaboration, and as already present among us.[31]

Interestingly, however, Borg describes Jesus's alternative way as one of both personal transformation and active nonviolent resistance to the sociopolitical domination system in Palestine. This is how Borg understands Jesus's entrance into Jerusalem on Palm Sunday and Jesus's "disruptive act" in the temple.[32] Moreover, in actions such as these as well as in a number of sayings, Borg claims, "Jesus resembles the prophets of the Jewish Bible, especially those who challenged the monarchies of ancient Israel in the decades before their destruction."[33] Citing Mark 6:4 and Luke 13:33, he notes that Jesus may have thought of himself as a prophet, and that, in any case, the Gospels certainly claim that some people saw Jesus this way. "But whether or not Jesus thought of himself as one," says Borg, "the category of prophet provides a lens through which to see a significant

28. Rauschenbusch, *Christianity and the Social Crisis*, 143.

29. See, for example, Leonardo Boff, *Jesus Christ Liberator: A Critical Christology for Our Time*, trans. Patrick Hughes (Maryknoll, NY: Orbis, 1978), 72.

30. Gerhard von Rad, *The Theology of Israel's Prophetic Traditions*, vol. 2 of *Old Testament Theology*, trans. D. M. G. Stalker (New York: Harper & Row, 1965), 3, 7. However, one may wonder whether von Rad's brief characterization of classical Protestant ideas about the prophets is entirely adequate. For example, what Calvin means by Jesus's prophetic office seems broader than expositing the law. See above.

31. Crossan, *The Historical Jesus*, 158–67; Crossan, *The Greatest Prayer: Rediscovering the Revolutionary Message of the Lord's Prayer* (New York: HarperOne, 2010), 88–92.

32. Marcus J. Borg, *Jesus: Uncovering the Life, Teachings, and Relevance of a Religious Revolutionary* (New York: HarperOne, 2006), 226–27, 235.

33. Borg, *Jesus*, 240.

portion of his mission and message."[34] Like earlier prophets, Jesus "indicted the powerful and wealthy in the name of God and God's passion for justice."[35]

I agree, and would only add this. While Borg's more recent interpretation differs from the earlier, somewhat simpler accounts of the prophetic dimension of Jesus's message and mission offered by Rauschenbusch and others, in many respects the two are not so very far apart. Jesus upholds Torah, resists the dominant unjust social and political system, and furnishes an alternative vision of life together under God in the kingdom.

The Kingdom

This brings us to a key theme. Rauschenbusch sees a revolutionary attitude in Jesus's commitment to God's kingdom—a symbol the American reformer takes to authorize religious concerns for society, politics, and the poor.[36] The kingdom, says Rauschenbusch, which "continued to be the centre of all [Jesus's] teaching as recorded by the synoptic gospels," was integral to "the social Christianity of Jesus."[37] Indeed, he says, "the fundamental purpose of Jesus was the establishment of the kingdom of God, which involved a thorough regeneration and reconstitution of social life."[38] Rudolf Bultmann, the great twentieth-century New Testament scholar, notes that to get at the message *of* Jesus we need to go back behind the early Christian communities' proclamation *about* Jesus, and he also thinks the kingdom lies at the center of Jesus's own preaching, "The dominant concept of Jesus' message is the Reign of God. Jesus proclaims its immediately impending irruption, now already making itself felt."[39] However, Bultmann does not associate Jesus's proclamation of the kingdom with an explicit commitment to structural social reform, so much as with an eschatological and ethical divine demand that protests against legalism as well as merely cultic piety, and so also calls for repentance.

A subsequent generation of Bible scholars largely followed Bultmann's lead. Thus, Norman Perrin says, "Jesus appeared as one who proclaimed the Kingdom; all else in his message and ministry serves a function in relation to that

34. Borg, *Jesus*, 240.

35. Borg, *Jesus*, 241.

36. Rauschenbusch, *Christianity and the Social Crisis*, 44–92.

37. Rauschenbusch, *Christianity and the Social Crisis*, 54; Rauschenbusch, *Christianizing the Social Order* (New York: Macmillan, 1913), 48–68.

38. Rauschenbusch, *Christianity and the Social Crisis*, 143.

39. Rudolf Bultmann, "The Message of Jesus," in *Theology of the New Testament*, trans. Kendrick Grobel, vol. 1 (London: SCM, 1951), 4.

proclamation and derives its meaning from it."[40] Perrin thinks Jesus believed that God's decisive act of salvation is now at hand, and that the new age of God's reign presents "the challenge of the forgiveness of sins and the offer of the possibility of a new kind of relationship with God and with one's fellow man."[41] Somewhat similarly, Joseph Fitzmyer notes that, "in the Lucan Gospel . . . Jesus is the kingdom-preacher par excellence," and that, though there are distinctive nuances, "the Lucan Jesus proclaims . . . what the Markan and Matthean Jesus does."[42]

More recent New Testament scholars sometimes point to additional themes and metaphors connected with Jesus's message and mission. For example, N. T. Wright, who regards the kingdom of God as "the great slogan for [Jesus's] whole project," associates it with a new exodus, as well as with a sovereign reign of Jesus over the world that operates through us, exalts the humble, and sends the rich away empty.[43] Borg, as we have seen, recognizes the kingdom as a key element of the portrait of Jesus offered by the Synoptic Gospels but also emphasizes Jesus as a wisdom teacher who proclaimed an alternative vision of the compassionate God that comes to expression in healings, exorcisms, and common meals.[44] Crossan stresses this last point as well, namely, Jesus's open commensality, or his leveling practice of table fellowship with anyone and everyone, including outcasts and undesirables.[45] In addition, he points to another metaphor for God and God's rule in Jesus's sayings, and, most notably, in Jesus's prayer to Abba Father—God is the good "Householder of the world house" who creates, protects, provides, and is especially concerned for members of the household who are weak, disabled, ill, and poor.[46] Even so, for Crossan, "household" does not displace "kingdom," and he continues to regard the latter term as especially important for contrasting the ruling style of God with violent human empires.

40. Norman Perrin, *Rediscovering the Teaching of Jesus* (New York: Harper & Row, 1967), 54.

41. Perrin, *Rediscovering*, 107. Perrin also suggests that, since Bultmann demythologized the symbolic language of the kingdom to refer to a divine demand and crisis of decision, whereas Rauschenbusch "fully accepted the ancient myth," they represent diametrically opposed hermeneutical options. Perrin, *Jesus and the Language of the Kingdom: Symbol and Metaphor in New Testament Interpretation* (Philadelphia: Fortress, 1976), 198.

42. Joseph A. Fitzmyer, SJ, *The Gospel according to Luke (I–IX): Introduction, Translation, and Notes* (Garden City, NY: Doubleday, 1981), 154.

43. N. T. Wright, *Simply Jesus: A New Vision of Who He Was, What He Did, and Why He Matters* (New York: HarperOne, 2011), xii, 59, 66, 219–20.

44. Borg, *Jesus*, 146–50, 157–60, 175.

45. Crossan, *The Historical Jesus*, 261–64, 266–76. But note that Perrin also offers an extended discussion of Jesus's table fellowship with undesirables in connection with Jesus's proclamation of God's kingdom and mercy. Perrin, *Rediscovering*, 102–8.

46. Crossan, *The Greatest Prayer*, 40–52.

To a significant extent in Crossan's view, the themes of kingdom and household interpenetrate and overlap. Thus, he notes that, in Israel's experience, "the notion of 'household' extended" not only from the peasant's farm to God's world as house but also to "the king's land as house, since the king was the divinely appointed householder of God's land."[47]

My own judgment is that, both performatively and verbally in the New Testament, Jesus teaches about many things. He addresses marriage and divorce. He instructs his disciples to love their enemies, as well as where and how to pray and fast. He welcomes little children. He sends followers out to villages and towns with instructions on how to respond to different receptions. He comments on Caesar and paying taxes and about trusting God rather than being anxious. He blesses the poor. He makes an oddly royal entrance into the capital city at the time of the most important national religious observance. He repeatedly eats and drinks with tax collectors, sinners, and other undesirables. With some frequency, his sayings and parables feature slaves, householders of substantial means, managers, vineyard owners, agricultural workers, and shepherds.

All this contributes to Jesus's vision of God and God's purposes. All this contributes to his *theology*. So, there is considerable richness here, and it would be an open mistake, for example, *not* to ask what it means theologically when Jesus claims that God cares for birds and lilies, addresses God as Abba Father and teaches his disciples to do likewise, and tells parables that liken the kingdom to a king who gives a wedding banquet but also to a householder giving a great dinner (Matt. 22:1–14; Luke 14:15–24). It therefore simply will not do to say that Jesus's message is *only* about the kingdom. Neither will it do to overlook the fact that his statements about God and God's reign do not always rely on royal or political symbols.

Nevertheless, once we note the many topics Jesus connects to his theological vision, and once we make allowance for different interpretations of just what Jesus means by the kingdom—whether it is future or present, whether people collaborate in its coming, whether it directly engages social structures or is mostly a matter of existential self-understanding, etc.—it seems fair to note a loose consensus among interpreters that extends from the Social Gospel, to Bultmann, and right up through a good many contemporaries. *God's kingdom or reign forms a focal point for what Jesus says and does as well as for his theological vision.*

Bruce Chilton notes that, in the Synoptic Gospels, Jesus is the kingdom's herald and advocate.[48] To the general reader this will seem apparent from the preliminary summary of Jesus's message in Mark 1:14–15, which presents Jesus's

47. Crossan, *The Greatest Prayer*, 81.

48. Bruce Chilton, *Pure Kingdom: Jesus' Vision of God* (Grand Rapids: Eerdmans, 1996), 135.

preaching of the kingdom in connection with repentance or a turning and transformation. "Now after John was arrested, Jesus came to Galilee, proclaiming the good news of God, and saying, 'The time is fulfilled, and the kingdom of God has come near; repent, and believe in the good news.'"

Consider also the Lord's Prayer. Rauschenbusch says that, to pray it rightly, we should recognize that communities and institutions more interested in ecclesiastical ritual and individual salvation than in the prayer's own rather straightforward social meaning have misinterpreted it. The Lord's Prayer, he insists, is a kingdom prayer, and when we say "Thy kingdom come," we pray for "the divine revolution."[49] Even if one thinks this characterization may be complicated by observations such as Crossan's about God as Father and Householder, it nevertheless seems plain that Jesus's prayer joins "our Father" with the "kingdom." In fact, Crossan himself regards the prayer as "a beautiful summary of the themes and emphases in Jesus' vision" of the sapiential, present, and subversive "kingdom of God."[50]

Here, I think the Brazilian liberation theologian Leonardo Boff makes an especially good guide. Boff recognizes the existential shock of "Abba" Father and notes that "we may not have the courage to call God by such a familiar name."[51] Yet he also claims that, "with the supplication 'thy kingdom come' we get to the very heart of the Lord's Prayer" and "are confronted with the ultimate intention of Jesus."[52] Indeed, he says, in a phrase that retains the symbol's political relevance, the kingdom "signifies a total revolution of structure." But, for Boff, this does not mean the kingdom is a stand-alone metaphor, and, he says, "the figure of speech" often used to define its content "is that of the house or city of God, where persons sit down to eat and drink."[53]

The clear implication, then, is that God's kingdom, rule, or imperial reign is a bit odd. It is something like the human reigns and kingdoms with which we are familiar, but it is also unlike them. Indeed, to attach the kingdom image to the Creator/Redeemer of all, "the Alpha and the Omega" who governs Israel and the nations with true justice, is to extend the image temporally, expand it spatially, and also intimate a divine transformation of politics.[54]

49. Walter Rauschenbusch, *Prayers for the Social Awakening* (Boston: Pilgrim, 1910), 18–19.

50. Crossan, *The Historical Jesus*, 294.

51. Leonardo Boff, *The Lord's Prayer: The Prayer of Integral Liberation*, trans. Theodore Morrow (Maryknoll, NY: Orbis, 1983), 21. Though we should also note Geza Vermes's caveat that, in Jesus's time and place, "Abba" still does not carry the degree of familiarity that the word "daddy" does in contemporary American English.

52. Boff, *The Lord's Prayer*, 54.

53. Boff, *The Lord's Prayer*, 58–59.

54. On the peculiarity or oddity of God talk, see chap. 6, prop. #42.

Temporal extension means the divine administration is past, present, and future, that it was in the beginning, is now, and ever shall be. Thus, a general claim on Jesus's lips in the New Testament is that the kingdom is at hand and yet also coming. For those with eyes to see, it is (in some sense) already here, but it also points to a changed future. Scholars debate the appropriate tenses and their interrelations. Have the gospel writers or later theologians softened Jesus's radically apocalyptic visage by intimating that the kingdom is a present possibility? Or have they tried instead to apocalypticize Jesus's message of a present reality in which the faithful participate? My concern is simply that the oddness of the temporal extension does not escape us. Because it is the reign *of God*, the divine imperial rule extends to the culmination of history, whereas the reigns or administrations of earthly emperors and kings clearly do not. No human empire, not even Rome, either extends to or controls an indefinite future. All are contingent and insecure; all finally fall.

This is a primary point of the apocalyptic vision in Revelation 18, where Rome is called Babylon. Despite Rome's powers and pretensions, it is no more eternal than Babylon was. "God is the one who 'builds' and 'plants' but who also 'plucks up' and 'breaks down,' 'destroys' and 'overthrows,' as Jeremiah notes (1:10), the relativizer of everything human and finite."[55] Talk about the reign or kingdom *of God* therefore *relativizes* the kingdoms. It temporalizes them, puts them in their places, and indicates that they are not ends in themselves.

Recent scholarship emphasizes that the divine rule in Jesus's teaching is not only or simply an eschatological and future reality. Consider Luke 17:20–21 (par. Thomas 113):[56] "Once Jesus was asked by the Pharisees when the kingdom of God was coming, and he answered, 'The kingdom of God is not coming with things that can be observed; nor will they say, "Look, here it is!" or "There it is!" For, in fact, the kingdom of God is among [or within] you.'" Crossan thinks this aphorism stems from Jesus's polemic *against* John the Baptist's vision of a future apocalyptic kingdom. He therefore takes it to bolster his claim that the historical Jesus taught a sapiential kingdom of nobodies, beggars, and peasants as a *present* ethical realm and a style of life for now rather than a reality that is not yet.[57] But whether or not Crossan is correct in his judgment about the Jesus of history, the Gospels clearly depict Jesus combining tenses. That is, the Jesus

55. Kaufman, *IFM*, 312.

56. The saying in Thomas reads as follows. "His disciples said to Him, 'When will the Kingdom come?' (Jesus said,) 'It will not come by waiting for it. It will not be a matter of saying "Here it is" or "There it is." Rather, the Kingdom of the Father is spread out upon the earth, and men do not see it.'" Ron Cameron, ed., *The Other Gospels: Non-Canonical Gospel Texts* (Louisville: Westminster John Knox, 1982), 37.

57. Crossan, *The Historical Jesus*, 283, 292.

of the New Testament proclaims a kingdom or rule of God that has both present and future relevance.

> "Blessed *are* the meek,
> for they *will* inherit the earth." (Matt. 5:5)

> "Blessed *are* you who are poor,
> for yours *is* the kingdom of God." (Luke 6:20)[58]

Accordingly, Betz insists that the beatitudes in Matthew and in Luke have both eschatological and "this-worldly implications," and that "it is a fundamental mistake to favor either their future aspect or their present pronouncement."[59] I agree, and would simply add that Jesus's language in the Gospel of John also indicates future expectations already under way: "The hour is coming, and now is here . . ." (4:23; 5:25). Perhaps we may say that, whereas Queen Elizabeth's reign began in 1952 and that, before then, the British monarch was her father, King George VI, there is no time at which the reign of God is not. It is therefore, in some sense at least, always present.

Spatial extension means that the divine rule encompasses all things. Human rulers influence and oversee particular communities, institutions, and territories, and they also depend for their legitimacy and coherence on social and cultural conditions they do not control. Moreover, they are subject as well to the actions and purposes of other powers and regimes. Biblically speaking, however, God rules over all, over cultural and social conditions as well as over "the nations." This is why we encounter declarations that indicate the large and international horizon of Yahweh's governance.[60]

> The LORD, the Most High, is awesome,
> a great king over all the earth. (Ps. 47:2)

Or, again,

> Say among the nations, "The LORD is king! . . .
> He will judge the peoples with equity." (Ps. 96:10)

58. The emphasis is mine.

59. Betz, *The Sermon on the Mount*, 96.

60. Walter Brueggemann, *Theology of the Old Testament: Testimony, Dispute, Advocacy* (Minneapolis: Fortress, 1997), 492–93.

Human regimes, especially in antiquity, do not govern the regularities, events, and interdependencies of nature and the cosmos. (In fact, neither do today's governments, though we are increasingly aware that their actions and policies may have significant effects on natural habitats and systems.) For this reason, the course of nature and the cosmos discloses comparatively little about the aims and practices of human empires. But things stand differently with the divine rule. The heavens are the Lord's handiwork (Pss. 8:3; 19:1), God establishes the mountains and also waters the earth (Ps. 65), and God makes provision for birds, lions, sea monsters, and humans (Ps. 104). Thus, in Matthew 5:45, when Jesus observes that "your Father in heaven . . . makes his sun to rise on the evil and on the good, and sends rain on the righteous and on the unrighteous," we encounter a theology of God's governing activity in creation—one that accords with passages in Job and Ecclesiastes as well as with the poetic vision of God's reign articulated in many psalms.

The reign of the Creator/Redeemer is expansive as no human rule is or ever can be because it encompasses all of human history as well as the vast cosmic ecology and cosmic passage within which all creatures live and move.[61] Similar things may be said about the expansion of the divine Householder's administration to the entire world as house, or of the vision of God's establishment of a worldwide banquet for all the peoples in Isaiah 25:6. An expansive sense of God-ruling emerges also in eschatological visions of the coming kingdom in the Apocalypse of John not only as a new city but also as a new heaven and earth or a renewed creation.

Finally, the divine kingdom or rule also symbolizes a transformation of politics. God loves justice (Isa. 61:8; Pss. 37:28; 99:4). The Bible does not contain a full theory of justice but insists, more practically, that God loves the presence of equity in social relations and of a judicial system that secures justice for the wronged.[62] Even so, a predominate claim is that the justice God loves has as its end shalom, or a social well-being and flourishing that deliver, save, and vindicate the oppressed. Israel's particular experience of salvation in its deliverance from Egypt and its constitution as a nation play a significant role here. And, all of this lies behind a peculiar emphasis of God's law: the tendency to single out for special attention the poor, the widow, the orphan, and the resident alien, or what Nicholas Wolterstorff calls "the quartet of the vulnerable."[63]

61. For more on this, see chaps. 3 and 4.

62. Nicholas Wolterstorff, *Justice: Rights and Wrongs* (Princeton: Princeton University Press, 2008), 81–82, 86.

63. Nigel Biggar, ed., *Burying the Past: Making Peace and Doing Justice after Civil Conflict*, expanded and updated ed. (Washington, DC: Georgetown University Press, 2003), 12.

> You shall not wrong or oppress a resident alien, for you were aliens in the land of Egypt. You shall not abuse any widow or orphan. If you do abuse them, when they cry out to me, I will surely heed their cry; my wrath will burn, and I will kill you with the sword, and your wives shall become widows and your children orphans. If you lend money to my people, to the poor among you, you shall not deal with them as a creditor; you shall not exact interest from them. (Exod. 22:21–25)[64]

The assumption here is that those at "the bottom of the social hierarchy are especially vulnerable," largely because they tend to be abused and treated unjustly by the rich and those in positions of power. And, as may be seen in Isaiah 1:17 and Psalms 103:6–7 and 147:6, "the prophets and the psalmist [also] do not argue the case that alleviating the plight of the lowly is required by justice. They, too, simply assume it."[65] So does Jesus, when he says,

> "Blessed are you who are poor,
> for yours is the kingdom of God." (Luke 6:20)[66]

In fact, once we grasp that his teaching is not only verbal but also performative, we see that when Jesus touches and heals the leprous and unclean, the blind, the possessed, and the paralyzed, and then also makes a regular practice of eating and drinking with "irreligious tax-collectors and predatory profiteers," he is at pains to expand the list of the downtrodden, the outcast, and the marginal.[67] Ditto when he eats with women and instructs them, when he interacts with gentiles and Samaritans, and when he welcomes children. All these, according to the gospel portraits of Jesus, are to be lifted up and rendered valued participants in the shalom of God's reign, and this, quite plainly, is something other and something different than politics and empire as usual.

Note too that Yahweh's international rule, which directs the nations toward peace and shalom, is more a matter of the law, to which *both* Israel and the nations will be held to account, than of the imperial rule of one nation over

64. See also Exod. 23:6–9; Deut. 24:17; 27:19.

65. Wolterstorff, *Justice*, 75–76. The word in parentheses is mine.

66. "Jesus took for granted the prophetic sensibility to injustice—that is, took for granted the fact that the fate of the vulnerable low ones is to be interpreted in terms of justice rather than charity and that they are to have priority in the struggle against injustice." Wolterstorff, *Justice*, 117.

67. Wolterstorff, *Justice*, 127–28; Oliver O'Donovan, *The Desire of Nations: Rediscovering the Roots of Political Theology* (Cambridge: Cambridge University Press, 1996), 98.

others. Yahweh may choose that one or another superpower govern for a time, and in Israel's experience, this seemed to have been the case. But, again, world powers rise and fall. Moreover, they also are to "govern within the bounds of Yahweh's mandate,"[68] and they too will be judged with equity. Thus, biblically speaking, it would be a mistake to think God's international rule means simply the elevation of one or another world empire. There is, in fact, no single nation or empire that mediates the divine ruling over all. Internationally—and partly due to Israel's experiences of ascendant empires—"Yahweh reigns" can never be simply identified with one or another historical regime.

Oliver O'Donovan therefore observes quite helpfully that "Yhwh's world order was plurally constituted. World-wide empire was a bestial deformation."[69] And just here, it seems appropriate to recall a curious feature of the later chapters of the Revelation of John. "The beast and kings of the earth with their armies" are decisively defeated and destroyed in 19:17–21. But then, in 21:23–26 we read that the nations will walk by the light of the glory of God and the kings of the earth will bring their glory into the new Jerusalem—where, as it turns out, no one of them reigns supreme. Call it a mythical expression of the transformation of politics.

Love God, Your Neighbor, and Even Your Enemies

As we turn now to a prominent line in Jesus's teaching, keep two basic points in mind. First, his teaching is a matter of actions and practices as well as words, and his words take a variety of verbal or literary forms, such as beatitudes, exhortations, and parables. Second, the basic trajectories and themes in Jesus's teaching, from blessing the poor and lowly to casting out demons, healing the sick, and eating and drinking with outcasts and undesirables, need to be understood in connection with the kingdom as the focal point of his message and ministry.

The Law

God's reign, as both Israel and Jesus understand it, is in large part a matter of *law*. Indeed, the law, an indispensable element of Israel's salvific transition from Egyptian slavery to a nation, makes possible human flourishing or a good life together before God; it promises a society of equity, compassion, and justice. But, of course, the law in its entirety is quite complex. It includes the Ten Commandments and very much more—from codes having to do with worship and holiness

68. Brueggemann, *Theology of the Old Testament*, 518.
69. O'Donovan, *The Desire of Nations*, 68, 72.

to statutes concerning lawsuits, marriage, liability, the treatment of slaves, and bribes, to penalties for certain crimes and demands for the proper treatment of the poor, the orphan, the widow, and the stranger. The law in its entirety, then, can be difficult to grasp and to remember, which is why people need instruction in its primary pattern, principle, or trajectory.

John P. Meier says that "it is Torah and Torah alone that puts flesh and bones on the spectral figure of Jesus the Jew."[70] That is, if we expect to meet a *Jewish* Jesus, which is finally and in fact the only Jesus we have, then we shall not understand him either sympathetically or adequately apart from his interpretation of Torah or the law. And, indeed, the Gospels portray Jesus as a teacher who is much concerned with the law and who summarizes its basic principle with a *dual* command to love God and neighbor. The summary, which appears in Matthew 22:35–40 and Mark 12:28–34, links two basic principles embedded in the Torah: the *Shema Yisrael* in Deuteronomy 6:5, "You shall love the LORD your God with all your heart, and with all your soul," and Leviticus 19:18b, "you shall love your neighbor as yourself."[71]

The verse from Leviticus figures prominently in rabbinic discussions and debates—just the sorts of debates about legal and behavioral matters we should expect Jesus the teacher and leader of a Palestinian Jewish movement to have engaged in.[72] Just who counts as one's neighbor? Should the admonition to love your neighbor be tied to Leviticus 19:18a, "You shall not take vengeance or bear a grudge against any of your own people"? Or should it be understood in the more capacious frame of Leviticus 19:34, "The alien who resides with you shall be to you as the citizen among you; you shall love the alien as yourself, for you were aliens in the land of Egypt"?[73]

70. John P. Meier, *Law and Love*, vol. 4 of *A Marginal Jew: Rethinking the Historical Jesus* (New Haven: Yale University Press, 2009), 648.

71. Members of the Jesus Seminar are divided over whether early Christians simply assigned the dual commandment to Jesus or assigned it to him because he agreed in substance with other interpreters, such as Rabbi Hillel, though many think the dual commandment contains ideas like Jesus's own. See Funk, Hoover, and the Jesus Seminar, *The Five Gospels*, 237. And, of course, we needn't find it either strange or insignificant if and when different teachers agree.

72. See Bruce Chilton, "Jesus, the Golden Rule, and Its Application," in *The Golden Rule: The Ethics of Reciprocity in World Religions*, ed. Jacob Neusner and Bruce Chilton (New York: Continuum, 2008), 78–79. See also John P. Meier, *Companions and Competitors*, vol. 3 of *A Marginal Jew: Rethinking the Historical Jesus* (New York: Doubleday, 2001), 339–40.

73. There is much to consider. For example, the list of persons in Lev. 19:9–18 that Israel is to care for is quite extensive, and, in the NRSV, includes "the poor" (vv. 10, 15), "the alien" (v. 10), "a laborer" (v. 13), "the deaf" (v. 14), "the blind" (v. 14), "anyone of your kin" (v. 17), and "any of your people" (v. 18). Rabbi Akiba claims that the fundamental law of Israel should be defined

But a Samaritan . . .

The Gospel of Luke portrays Jesus telling the parable of the Good Samaritan as a kind of commentary on the dual commandment, and here I want to review what this parable indicates about the law and God's reign. But remember, parables are short, often jarring, and somewhat open-ended narrative metaphors or similes that often are susceptible to more than one interpretation.[74] "Just then a lawyer stood up to test Jesus. 'Teacher,' he said, 'what must I do to inherit eternal life?' He said to him, 'What is written in the law? What do you read there?' He answered, 'You shall love the Lord your God with all your heart, and with all your soul, and with all your strength, and with all your mind: and your neighbor as

---

by the comparatively restrictive sense of Lev. 19:18, where the neighbor may be understood as "anyone of your people." But Ben Azzai objects, saying, "When God created man he made him in the likeness of God (Genesis 5:2). Therefore, 'you should not say "Since I despise myself, let my fellow be despised with me; since I am cursed let my fellow be cursed with me."'" That is, as Samuel Ballentine explains, "Ben Azzai recognizes 'a creational foundation for loving one's neighbor as oneself.' The 'failure to love others is equivalent to saying that neither they nor we have value in the eyes of God,' but this, in light of the fact that every human 'bears "the likeness of God,"'" is clearly incorrect. Samuel E. Ballentine, *Leviticus* (Louisville: John Knox, 2002), 165–66.

Similarly, Jacob Neusner notes that the rabbis debated the question of just who counts as one's neighbor in Lev. 19. Should one prioritize verse 18a or verse 34? The latter might easily be linked with the idea in Genesis that the Israelites are related to all peoples through Adam and Eve. Jacob Neusner, "The Golden Rule in Classical Judaism," in Neusner and Chilton, *The Golden Rule*, 57–59.

74. Consider, for example, the parable of the mustard seed in Mark 4:30–32. "He also said, 'With what can we compare the kingdom of God, or what parable will we use for it? It is like a mustard seed, which, when sown upon the ground, is the smallest of all the seeds on earth; yet when it is sown it grows up and becomes the greatest of all shrubs, and puts forth large branches, so that the birds of the air can make nests in its shade.'"

When I was young, I heard these lines interpreted with an emphasis on how, from humble beginnings, the mustard seed becomes the greatest plant. Hence the kingdom of God is something like a modest but also highly successful investment that becomes the richest prize of all. But Crossan contends that the mustard plant was a weed, which, just because its seed is so small, inadvertently makes its way into farmers' seed bags. Once sown, it grows rapidly into a large invasive bush that crowds out the desired crop. To make matters worse, birds nest in it, and no farmer wants a field populated by hungry birds. On this reading, the kingdom is not like a wise investment so much as an unintended and invasive plant that disrupts a farmer's field. Crossan, *The Historical Jesus*, 237. My point is simply that, as we look at the story of the Good Samaritan, we need to be alert to different possible readings.

Note, too, that Joseph A. Fitzmyer, SJ, thinks the story of the Good Samaritan should not be classified as a parable in a strict sense, but regardless of how we resolve the question of its literary form, it still seems susceptible to multiple interpretations. *The Gospel according to Luke (X–XXIV): Introduction, Translation, and Notes* (Garden City, NY: Doubleday, 1985), 883.

yourself.' And he said to him, 'You have given the right answer; do that and you will live'" (Luke 10:25–28).

The lawyer is a contentious challenger. He does not really think Jesus is a reliable teacher, and this is why he wants to *test* Jesus. When he asks his first question, Jesus asks him what the law says, and then the lawyer (not Jesus) delivers the dual commandment. Jesus says this is the right answer, the correct summary of the law, and he tells the lawyer to do as it says. "But wanting to justify himself, he asked Jesus, 'And who is my neighbor?'" (v. 29).

The lawyer is not yet satisfied, and he asks a second question meant to indicate how smart or wise he is, by showing that his question is profound and not so easily answered as Jesus has implied. After all, the dual commandment requires some further definition of neighbor if it is to be followed and understood. It requires further commentary on what neighbor means.

Jesus responds to this second question by telling the parable of the Good Samaritan, in which a man is beaten by robbers and left on the side of the road. Respected members of society, a priest and later also a Levite, pass him by. "But a Samaritan while traveling came near him; and when he saw him, he was moved with pity" (v. 33), and helped him.[75]

The episode has curious features. For one thing, Jesus does not really answer the lawyer's second question, "And who is my neighbor?" Is this because he thinks the question is really just an attempt to limit those we consider to be our neighbors and thus to exclude some people from the scope of moral concern? Is it because, even though Jesus's story originally was not connected with it, the writer of Luke wants to frame the compassionate Samaritan as an answer to the question about Leviticus 19:18b debated by rabbis? In any case, rather than answer the question, Jesus tells a story, and he follows his story by asking the lawyer, "Which of these three, do you think, was a neighbor to the man who fell into the hands of the robbers?" (v. 36). The lawyer answers correctly: "The one

75. We are not told why the priest and the Levite pass him by. Possibly they are on their way to Jericho to perform religious rituals and think that the man is dead. If so, then touching his corpse would render them ritually "unclean" and make it more difficult to complete their task. So, Fitzmyer, *The Gospel according to Luke (X–XIV)*, 883. That is, they may have ceremonial reasons for not going over to investigate the man's condition and perhaps also help, and, if so, what we have here may be a polemic against overemphasizing cultic observance. Then again, maybe they are afraid. Maybe they don't stop for fear that the man's attackers are still nearby and have left the beaten man there in order to lure passersby into a trap. What is certain, however, is that once the two pass him by, the situation of the beaten man seems dire indeed. Martin Luther King Jr. offers this interpretation as he argues for "a kind of dangerous unselfishness" and in favor of helping Memphis sanitation workers in his last speech, "I Have Seen the Promised Land," in *A Testament of Hope: The Essential Writings of Martin Luther King, Jr.*, ed. James Melvin Washington (New York: Harper & Row, 1986), 284–85.

who showed him mercy (or kindness, *eleos*)" (v. 37), and then Jesus tells him to go and do likewise. (That is, to be or to prove to be a neighbor is to have mercy on and to help anyone in need.)

Second, the beaten man remains unidentified. Perhaps he is a generic everyman, but he might also be a Jew, a Roman, a Samaritan, or what have you. If he is a Jew, as seems likely given the road's location, then the Samaritan who fulfills the law by proving to be neighbor not only helps a person in need but also helps a member of a religious and ethnic group that despises Samaritans.[76] That is, if the beaten man is a Jew, then the Samaritan who proves to be neighbor also loves his enemy.

Third, it is the quality of divine mercy or compassion (*oiktirmon*) that furnishes the theological ground in Luke 6 for Jesus's admonition to "love your enemies, do good to those who hate you, bless those who curse you, [and] pray for those who abuse you" (vv. 27–28). Jesus says, "If you do good to those who do good to you, what credit is that to you? For even sinners do the same" (v. 33), and then asserts, "The Most High . . . is kind (or good) to the ungrateful and the wicked. Be merciful, just as your Father is merciful" (vv. 35–36). Thus, it may be that the Samaritan proves to be neighbor by acting with a kindness analogous or in some sense correspondent to the kindness, goodness, mercy, or compassion with which God reigns.

In any case, Jesus's story features two highly respected members of Jewish society passing by the beaten man, and it casts a despised Samaritan in the role of the one who upholds the law and imitates God's righteousness. In fact, the story forces the lawyer, who is a Jew, to admit that a hated Samaritan is the exemplary figure. The Samaritan, himself a despised person in the lawyer's view and also in the view of others who may hear Jesus's parable, is here lifted up as the example of true righteousness, compassion, and love. And, at the close of the story, the Jewish lawyer who wants to know what he must do to live well before God is told to go and imitate a *Samaritan*!

76. In the eyes of Jews in Jesus's time, Samaritans practiced the wrong religion and were not to be trusted. The feeling was mutual, as is illustrated by Luke 9:51–56, where a Samaritan village refuses to receive Jesus and his disciples, who, we need to remember, are themselves Jews. Indeed, the ancient historian Josephus notes a series of violent encounters between Jews and Samaritans during the first half of the first century.

The story does not elaborate on the identity of the beaten man. Perhaps, since he is without his clothes and badly beaten, one cannot tell whether he is Jewish, Roman, or a member of some other group. Perhaps, in Jesus's story, the beaten man is supposed to be a nondescript and generic "everyman." On the other hand, perhaps he is a Jew—as most travelers on this particular road would be—and therefore it seems unnecessary to identify him as such. In any case, traveling alone down the road to Jericho proves a treacherous business, and by the time others see him the man is in bad shape.

Therefore, and perhaps in more ways than one, Jesus's story "subverts the negative stereotyped identity of the Samaritan and throws the conventional distinction between 'us' and 'them' into question." Indeed, if the beaten man is a Jew, then Jesus's story tells of an exemplary person who crosses the long-standing gulf between Jews and Samaritans in order to love his enemy and so perform a reconciling act in a divided land. Either way, but especially on the second reading, Jesus's story brings into view "the possibility of another kind of social world."[77]

Pause now for a brief thought experiment. Suppose the man the Samaritan helps is a Jew. Will either he or the people who hear Jesus's story appropriately appreciate the Samaritan's act? Will his act turn people toward a different, new, more inclusive, and more humane community? Will it actually reconcile?

Certainly, both he and we may hope so, but Jesus's story simply doesn't say. The matter is left hanging because, like God's mercy to the ungrateful and the wicked, the appropriateness of the Samaritan's act does not hinge on this possibility. The Samaritan does what one ought to do in order to prove neighbor. And, as is the case with loving neighbors and enemies more generally, there can be no guarantee that doing what one ought to do will win them over and convert them to a new form of life and community. The risk that this may not happen must simply be borne. And this, at least, is one way to teach the truth about God's kingdom or reign—to show that it calls for risky acts that point in the direction of a different kind of social world we cannot guarantee.

But no matter how one interprets the parable, "Love your enemies" remains a signal feature of Jesus's teaching, and in the Gospel of Matthew Jesus supports this admonition somewhat differently than he does in Luke.

> "You have heard that it was said, 'You shall love your neighbor and hate your enemy.' But I say to you, Love your enemies and pray for those who persecute you, so that you may be children of your Father in heaven; *for he makes his sun rise on the evil and on the good, and sends rain on the righteous and on the unrighteous*. For if you love those who love you, what reward do you have? Do not even the tax collectors do the same? And if you greet only your brothers and sisters, what more are you doing than others? Do not even the Gentiles do the same? Be perfect, therefore, as your heavenly Father is perfect." (Matt. 5:43–48)

Jesus's teaching about the law radicalizes the idea of who counts as the neighbor one should love. Thus, in the rabbinical debate over the heart of the Torah, he sides with those who argue for a more expansive understanding of Leviticus

77. Funk, Hoover, and the Jesus Seminar, *The Five Gospels*, 324.

19:18a through the lens of Leviticus 19:34. Moreover, theological ethicists sometimes point to "Love your enemies" as the distinctive pinnacle of Jesus's ethic. Most Bible scholars attribute it to Jesus, and many also think he taught something like the creation theology in Matthew 5:45–46.[78]

What I want to emphasize here is that, in Matthew, the admonition to love your enemy is presented as a standard for being like God the Creator. The Creator, says Jesus, does not dispense gifts of sun and rain only on those who love God or do as God wills. Instead, the deity dispenses gifts indiscriminately and gratuitously to all. Indeed, as Betz notes, "God bestows the benefits of . . . creation continuously on the good and the bad," though "the assumption is . . . that God's enemies will *not* appreciate [God's] benefits."[79] Or, to put this another way, God's reign or kingdom is a reign of grace, and to be like God, to live in a manner that corresponds to the divine excellence, we should love not only those who love us; we should also love our enemies. Our regard for others should be as indiscriminate and capacious as the Creator's gifts, and it should therefore extend even to enemies. That is, we should be attentive and gracious to others; we should in short reflect the divine going-out toward others.

A Theocentric Radicalization of Love of Neighbor

The argument I have been pursuing thus far, albeit somewhat indirectly, and with the aid of the Gospels of Matthew and Luke, is that Jesus's admonition to love your enemies finally represents a theocentric radicalization of the admonition to love your neighbor that corresponds with God's reign of grace. Let me make this point explicit now with the help of what some classical theologians say about the connection between love of God and neighbor.

Thomas Aquinas claims we ought to love our neighbor under the aspect of God, "for what we ought to love in him is that he be in God."[80] John Calvin says the command to love the neighbor is like the command to love God because, in order for people to love their neighbors, devotion to God must first displace their self-centeredness and inordinate self-concern.[81] Jonathan Edwards makes a similar point when he says that devotion to God, which is based not in God's utility for us but in a sense or perception of the divine excellence, overcomes the

78. Betz, *The Sermon on the Mount*, 309; Funk, Hoover, and the Jesus Seminar, *The Five Gospels*, 145–47.

79. Betz, *The Sermon on the Mount*, 323–24.

80. Aquinas, *ST*, vol. 34, *Charity*, 2–2.25.1.

81. John Calvin, *Harmony of the Gospels Matthew, Mark and Luke and the Epistles of James and Jude*, vol. 3, trans. A. W. Morrison, in *Calvin's New Testament Commentaries: A New Translation*, ed. David W. Torrance and Thomas F. Torrance (Grand Rapids: Eerdmans, 1963), 36–39.

principle of self-love and turns one's heart toward others. "Love of God," says Edwards, "is the foundation of gracious love to men" because hearts and minds that are opened toward God are no longer centered exclusively upon themselves. Others are then loved because "they have the nature or spiritual image of God; or because of their relation to God as his children, as his creatures, as those who are beloved of God, or those to whom divine mercy is offered, or in some other way from regard to God."[82]

We might say that love of God seems indissolubly united with the disposition to love one's neighbor because respect for God's reign entails loyalty to the creatures that God creates and upholds, or the others to whom God shows mercy and benevolence by bestowing upon them the gifts of existence. That is, Jesus authorizes his expansive interpretation of the law by appealing to the divine benevolence. Just as God the Creator indiscriminately dispenses gifts of sun and rain to all, or to both the evil and the good, so should we be merciful and benevolent to all. Theologically speaking, then, when carried to its appropriate and radical conclusion, love of neighbor extends even to enemies. Why? Because even if someone is my enemy in the context of one or another particular social commitment (say to my family, my nation, or my religious group), in the context of God's universal reign over all things, my enemy is my companion in creation (or existence) and thus my neighbor.[83] That is, our love of God finds in the Creator-Redeemer the one who points back again to creatures.[84] In the context of God's universal reign, all are fellow creatures, companions in creation. Considered in relation to God—a truly inalienable relation—all have worth and all are neighbors.

82. Edwards, "Charity and Its Fruits," in *Ethical Writings*, ed. Paul Ramsey, vol. 8 of *WJE*, 133–34.

83. H. Richard Niebuhr, *Radical Monotheism and Western Culture, with Supplementary Essays* (Louisville: Westminster John Knox, 1993), 34.

84. If we make allowances for the anthropocentric tint of his theology that we noted earlier, Karl Barth also says something like this. "It is no accident," he says, that Jesus summed up the law and the prophets in this "two-fold law of love." For Jesus, love of God and love of neighbor, while not identical, are conjoined. The one or single "two-fold" love required of persons "has reference to God, but also to the neighbor." It has both dimensions. "It finds in the Creator the one who points to this creature, fellow-man. And it finds in this creature, fellow-man, the one who points to the Creator." *CD* III/2:216–17. My statement here also is intentionally broader than Aquinas's claim that "'neighbor' cannot be understood to include irrational creatures, because they do not share man's rational life. . . . Yet they can be loved from charity as good things we wish others to have, in that by charity we cherish this for God's honor and man's service. Thus does God love them by charity." *ST* 2–2.25.3.

A Pattern, a Vision, and a Piety

Return now to our basic proposition. What is the truth that Jesus teaches? Essentially, that God's kingdom or dominion is a reign of justice and grace in which all have value. Moreover, there is a discernible pattern here. The divine reign relativizes present reigns and rules because no human reign endures forever and none extends to the cosmos at large. Indeed, as a reign that pursues shalom and is especially concerned for those at the bottom of social hierarchies, one that displays and commends loving neighbors and even enemies in the risky pursuit of reconciliation and new community, the kingdom that Jesus teaches and proclaims also critiques every human reign and rule. More positively, Jesus presents a kingdom-minded vision, one that provokes a distinctive piety or a knot of affections and dispositions characterized by an ec-centric and passionate responsibility and care for others. It symbolizes and points to an emergent, elusively present but also transcendent transformation of politics that corresponds to our true and ec-centric calling, which is already but also not yet, a historical possibility that nevertheless also lies beyond human history.

My fuller account of how Jesus's entire performance, or what he says, does, and endures to shape the visions and pieties of Christians and their communities, also draws on the substance of propositions 53 and 54 below. (It can only be a product of the complete christological shorthand.) But here I want to emphasize once more at least this: Jesus's teaching or vision of God's reign promises a reinterpretation of life partly because it suggests a particular understanding of the human and of a good society. The vision of God going out to create and sustain, to dispense benefits gratuitously to all, and to lift up the marginal and the vulnerable in the renewed and radically inclusive community of the kingdom evokes and shapes a specific piety and orientation in life. It provokes a sense that the expansive calling or vocation of human beings, one which is reflective of and correspondent with the divine tendency, is to love God, neighbor, and even enemies, or to pursue true communion with God in community with others. Indeed, for Christian piety, this new Jerusalem, this radical, beloved, and reconciled society of persons, communities, and creatures no longer separated, alienated, or estranged, is the chief end of the human being.

Proposition #53 The ministry and mission of Jesus as the Christ embody and display a way or a manner in life that accords with the truth.

This is the second proposition having to do with what Jesus as the Christ says, does, and endures. Jesus teaches the truth, but he also marks off a manner in life that accords with the truth. He does so by his practices and actions, by means of the particular pattern of his life and ministry, which is attuned to God's imperial reign and kingdom purpose. The way in life he thus embodies and displays fits with the truth about God and God's realm or reign of grace. It fits with and is responsive to the divine excellence.

Or, again, Jesus as the Christ embodies and expresses a manner of living oriented by *theocentric piety*, by a dominant devotion to God's reign as Creator-Judge-Redeemer and its attendant sensibilities. He not only proclaims the truth about God and God's reign and gives verbal instructions about dispositions, purposes, and actions that accord with it; he also displays in his life, practices, and ministry the trajectory of that reign as well as appropriate dispositions, purposes, and actions. He expresses theocentric piety in his obedience to God's in-breaking imperial reign by accepting outcasts, blessing the poor, healing the sick, casting out demons, welcoming little children, and so on. As a result, his life and ministry communicate a discernible stance, manner, or way in life that consents to God and God's kingdom-purpose.[85] In short, Jesus as the Christ enacts the kingdom. "For that reason, Jesus' teaching was not only a matter of making statements. . . . He also engaged in characteristic activities, a conscious performance of the kingdom, which invited Israel to enter into the reality that he also portrayed in words."[86]

The classical theological tradition connects these affirmations with the image of Christ as king. Jesus as the Christ is the one who rules or governs the faithful, sharing what he has received, and clothing them with righteousness. Jesus as the Christ marks off a path or a way that guides the life of faithfulness both inwardly and outwardly. In this role, he relates to others as leader to followers, pathfinder to travelers. Thus, Philippians 2:5 rather famously exhorts the faithful to "let the same mind be in you that was in Christ Jesus," a line Calvin takes as an admonition "to have the same attitude that was in Christ."[87] Richard R. Niebuhr notes that the Greek word *archēgos*, used with reference to Jesus by the writers of Acts and Hebrews, seems well suited to suggest this confluence of embodiment and governance.[88] The term may be translated into English as "pioneer." In its wider

85. The point is something like H. Richard Niebuhr's contention that Jesus displays many radical virtues or excellences of character, for example, love, hope, obedience, and humility, but that these are intelligible only within the frame of his devotion and loyalty to God. *Christ and Culture* (New York: Harper & Row, 1951), 14–29.

86. Chilton, *Pure Kingdom*, 100.

87. John Calvin, *The Epistles of Paul the Apostle to the Galatians, Ephesians, and Colossians*, trans. T. H. L. Parker, in *Calvin's New Testament Commentaries: A New Translation*, ed. David W. Torrance and Thomas F. Torrance (Grand Rapids: Eerdmans, 1965), 246.

88. Richard R. Niebuhr, "Archegos: An Essay on the Relation between the Biblical Jesus Christ and the Present-Day Reader," in *Christian History and Interpretation: Studies Presented to John Knox*, ed. W. R. Farmer, C. F. D. Moule, and Richard R. Niebuhr (Cambridge: Cambridge University Press, 1967), 84, 87.

meaning, it signifies one who begins something and also supplies the impetus—the originator, founder, guide, captain, leader, prince, or ruler. Jesus as the Christ is God's representative or vicegerent, the one who recapitulates and fulfills the true office or function of the leaders and kings of Israel who were anointed to direct, protect, and rule God's people.[89] Jesus as the Christ displays a manner of life that guides the faithful.

The Gospel Narratives and the Jesus of History

As we explore this claim, we need to keep in mind that while the Gospels certainly contain teachings, they are also *narratives* that portray a person, his characteristic purposes, attitudes, and actions. They are literary compositions that render a figure.

They are also rather tightly *focused*. The gospel narratives concentrate on Jesus's ministry, a period of not more than a few years, and so the pattern of purposes, attitudes, and actions the Gospels portray is almost exclusively with reference to his public mission. Again, they are also comparatively *sparse*, as can easily be seen if one compares them, for example, with something like Robert A. Caro's *The Passage of Power*, a volume that covers a period of about four years in the life of Lyndon Baines Johnson and runs over six hundred pages![90] The Gospels operate with narrative economy; when they portray Jesus healing the sick and eating with tax collectors and sinners on two or three occasions, they suggest that these are recurrent and characteristic practices.

Finally, and as we noted earlier, the focused and sparse compositions we call gospels are theologically freighted attempts to present committed accounts of Jesus as the Christ for early Christian communities. They are "written preaching" rather than modern attempts at historical reconstructions. They are literary works that commend Jesus as God's representative, the Messiah, Christ, or Son in whom God's kingdom has drawn near. Their portraits of Jesus's characteristic practices and actions are integral to their theological interpretations of his significance and to their understandings of the message of the kingdom.

Not surprisingly, then, when we ask about the manner of living that Jesus embodies and displays, we can rely on no simple or complete correspondence

89. Indeed, N. T. Wright recently has devoted a book to explaining what it can mean to say that Jesus is king and that God rules through the human beings God has rescued. See *Simply Jesus*, 206–29.

90. Robert A. Caro, *The Years of Lyndon Johnson*, vol. 1, *The Path to Power* (New York: Vintage Books, 1990); vol. 2, *Means of Ascent* (New York: Vintage Books, 1991); vol. 3, *Master of the Senate* (New York: Vintage Books, 2003); vol. 4, *The Passage of Power* (New York: Vintage Books, 2013). The four volumes run well over two thousand pages.

between the symbolically and theologically elaborated figure in the Gospels and modern historical accounts of Jesus's life. Indeed, when we turn to the relationship between the gospel narratives and historical judgments about specific points in the life of Jesus, as well as about recurrent patterns in his activities, many of the same cautions we noted with respect to the authentic sayings of Jesus bear repeating. The Gospels organize their portraits around varied interpretative images, for example, Jesus as Davidic-Messiah King, and recent scholarly portraits also are constructed around interpretative images that integrate judgments about early resources and traditions, for example, Jesus as eschatological prophet. Reputable scholars disagree, and though they make use of resources in addition to the New Testament Gospels, the available resources are also rather limited.[91]

Moreover, when it comes to the early textual sources available for historical investigations into Jesus's life and ministry, the New Testament Gospels are especially prominent. The oldest text that narrates Jesus's life and ministry is the Gospel of Mark, from the mid to late 60s. The Gospels of Matthew and Luke depend rather heavily on Mark's narrative frame, though they also expand upon it, mainly by including many more sayings and by adding infancy narratives that serve as prologues to their stories of Jesus's ministry. Thus, the Gospel of Mark opens with the proclamation of John the Baptist, and, in fact, following their prologue-like birth and infancy narratives, both Matthew and Luke also begin their accounts of Jesus's ministry with the proclamation of John the Baptist (Matt. 3:1–3; Luke 3:1–3).[92] And, of course, the Gospel of Mark—composed some decades after Jesus's death—is also written preaching, a thoroughly theological document, rather than a strict attempt at a neutral or dispassionate account.[93]

The lone non-Christian reference to Jesus from the first century is exceedingly brief, and comes from Josephus's *Jewish Antiquities*, written at Rome around 90 CE. As reconstructed by John Meier from the received text, which many scholars believe to have been altered by later Christian writers, it reads as follows:

91. See prop. #52 above.

92. Indeed, Joseph A. Fitzmyer, SJ, believes that Luke originally began with what reads like a formal opening in what is now its third chapter—"In the fifteenth year of the reign of Emperor Tiberius, when Pontius Pilate was governor of Judea, and Herod was ruler of Galilee . . . the word of God came to John son of Zechariah" (Luke 3:1–2)—and that the narrative in chapters 1–2 was added later. Fitzmyer, *The Gospel according to Luke (X–XIV)*, 310–11. The Baptist's testimony also follows the poetic prologue of the Gospel of John (1:19).

93. Scholars interested in the teachings of Jesus work with sayings found in the Gospels of the New Testament (especially the "Synoptics," Matthew, Mark, and Luke), the hypothesized common sayings source drawn upon by Matthew and Luke called Q, and the Gospel of Thomas, a nonnarrative collection of 114 sayings written about 115 CE that may contain some material as old as what we find in the canonical Gospels. Judgments about which sayings originate with Jesus benefit from comparing these texts and also asking how they relate to material attributed to other figures, for example, Hillel, in other ancient texts.

> At this time there appeared Jesus, a wise man. For, he was a doer of startling deeds, a teacher of people who received the truth with pleasure. And he gained a following both among many Jews and among many of Greek [meaning 'Gentile,' that is, non-Jewish] origin. And when Pilate, because of an accusation made by the leading men among us, condemned him to the cross, those who had loved him previously did not cease to do so. And up until this very day, the tribe of Christians (named after him) has not died out.[94]

Given the nature of the sources, then, we never have the Jesus of history simply apart from the theologically freighted testimonies of the Gospels. We do not (and indeed really cannot) reconstruct the historical Jesus of Nazareth apart from the gospel narratives. With this in mind, let me hazard a minimal outline of some aspects of the ministry of Jesus on which many historians and New Testament scholars would agree and that are relevant to our present proposition.

Jesus was a Palestinian Jew and formally uneducated member of a lower artisan class who appears to have been a follower of John the Baptist (thus baptized by John). His eventual style of ministry involved frequenting villages and towns as well as common meals, and it contrasted with John's wilderness asceticism. Some regarded him as "a doer of startling deeds," including healings and other wonders. He taught, and like John's public activity, Jesus's kingdom-centered message and performance generated tensions with established religious and political authorities (though one needs to be careful about gospel portrayals of his relations to Jewish religious authorities, since these often reflect later tensions and polemics that emerged as Christian groups became differentiated from Jewish communities). Jesus's public career generated a following or a popular movement—a kind of Jesus movement among first-century Palestinian Jews—and many of those who participated in it were at the margins of respected society. He was involved in an altercation in and around the temple at Jerusalem, and subsequently was crucified, a Roman method of public execution reserved for those deemed political opponents. As Josephus notes, and as the New Testament indicates, many of his followers nevertheless remained committed to him; some claimed that, after his execution, he appeared to them.[95]

Even on the basis of this slender sketch, we may emphasize a basic connection between the New Testament and research into the historical Jesus. The Gospels

94. John Meier, *The Roots of the Problem and the Person*, vol. 1 of *A Marginal Jew: Rethinking the Historical Jesus* (New York: Doubleday, 1991), 61, and quoted by Borg in *Jesus*, 30.

95. To corroborate elements of this outline, see Hedrick, *The Wisdom of Jesus*, 186–89; Wright, *Simply Jesus*, 85, 91, 95, 105–6; John Dominic Crossan, *Jesus: A Revolutionary Biography* (San Francisco: HarperCollins, 1994), 44–48; Crossan, *The Historical Jesus*, xiii; Borg, *Jesus*, 259–60.

portray Jesus calling disciples, attracting a large number of followers and hearers, sometimes being called "King of the Jews," and being crucified by Roman authorities. Thus, just as, more or less in accord with the gospel portraits, historians generally agree that the Jesus of history did indeed teach, they also generally agree, more or less with the Gospels once again, that the Jesus of history led a popular movement, that some regarded him as the Messiah or Israel's anointed leader, and that he was executed under Pontius Pilate in a manner reserved for political enemies of the empire. This falls far short of what is needed for a modern biography, but it constitutes a narrative and historical thread from which the longer theological tradition wove the tapestry of the kingly image.

The Jewishness of Jesus

Focus now on an obvious but underappreciated point: Jesus was a first-century Palestinian Jew. Neglecting and, at times, almost suppressing this fact is a staple of the Christian forms of anti-Judaism and anti-Semitism I discussed in part 1, and that go hand in glove with overly sharp separations from Judaism of the New Testament and indeed from Christianity itself.[96] Here, however, let me emphasize that neglecting the significance of the Jewishness of Jesus leads to a misunderstanding of Jesus and his message.

It is not enough merely to note that Jesus was a Jew; what needs to be recognized is how his Jewishness and his Jewish context inform and illumine his teachings and actions. Geza Vermes notes, for example, that Jesus was a Galilean. That is, Jesus hailed from a region from which a number of revolutionary movements had emerged, and he was of a population that more "orthodox" Pharisees and rabbis in Jerusalem regarded as boorish and religiously uneducated.[97] John P. Meier adds that Jesus and the Pharisees "were competing to influence the main body of Palestinian Jews and win them over to their respective visions of what God was calling Israel to be and to do."[98] One point that follows is that Jesus may have become politically and religiously suspect partly because of his Galilean heritage.[99] Another quite significant matter we have already encountered is that, as a teacher-leader preaching to crowds and disciples, Jesus, like the Pharisees, takes part in halakic (or legal and behavioral) debates about the Torah.[100] Accordingly, the gospel of Jesus Christ cannot be divorced from his

96. See above, and also chap. 2, prop. #20.

97. Geza Vermes, *Jesus the Jew: A Historian's Reading of the Gospels* (London: SCM, 2001), 26–38.

98. Meier, *Companions and Competitors*, 339.

99. Vermes, *Jesus the Jew*, 39.

100. Meier, *Companions and Competitors*, 340.

interpretation of the law because we cannot separate the Jesus of the Gospels or of history from debates about and interpretations of the law. And, indeed, as we have seen and shall continue to see, Jesus's interpretation of the law and behavioral codes makes a critical contribution to our understanding of his message and performance.[101]

Another important point, which connects with the theme of Christ as King, is this. For Jesus the Jew and his first-century Palestinian audience, a range of meanings were likely to have been associated with calling Jesus "lord." As Vermes notes, "in Jewish Aramaic the designation '(the lord)' is appropriate in connection with God, or a secular dignitary, or an authoritative teacher, or a person renowned for spiritual or supernatural force." We know that "Jesus is lord" constitutes an early Christian confession. However, given the Palestinian Jewish background, we should keep in mind that the field of meanings for "lord" is comparatively fluid and open. "Everything tends to suggest that from a purely linguistic point of view Jesus could have been both addressed and described as 'lord' in a number of senses."[102]

The Messiah—King and Son of God

The image of Christ the King owes much to the longer theological and scriptural traditions of Israel. This is especially apparent in the genealogies and birth narratives presented in Matthew and in Luke. The Matthean theology, signaled immediately by the gospel's first sentence, portrays Jesus as the Davidic Messiah-King who fulfills the blessing of all families of the earth made through Abraham—"An account of the genealogy of Jesus the Messiah, the son of David, the son of Abraham" (Matt. 1:1). In fact, one commentator calls Matthew 1:1–17 "the Royal Genealogy."[103] Additional royal elements emerge in Matthew's account of the birth of the Messiah, which includes the visitation of the wise men or astrologers, who search for "the child born king of the Jews" by following his rising star (a narrative detail that suggests cosmic recognition) and also bringing precious gifts fit for a king. In Matthew 28, these and other royal elements are joined with the blessing through Abraham once again when the risen Lord commands his followers to go to all nations.[104]

The Lukan genealogy presents Jesus as "son of Adam, son of God," and the

101. See prop. #52 above.

102. Vermes, *Jesus the Jew*, 100.

103. Douglas R. A. Hare, *Matthew* (Louisville: Westminster John Knox, 2009), 5, 13.

104. "The special relation of Jesus to David and Abraham is a pre-Matthean insight, for it is attested in the Pauline letters of the 50s (Rom 1:3; Gal 3:16)," and Matthew has woven these themes together to appeal to his mixed community of Jewish and gentile Christians. See

significant differences between it and the one in Matthew point to their different theological functions.[105] Thus, if the earlier theology represented by Paul claims that the Christ "was descended from David according to the flesh and was declared to be Son of God with power according to the spirit of holiness by resurrection from the dead" (Rom. 1:3–4), a major point of Luke's later infancy narrative is that Jesus was already Son of God according to the spirit from birth. That is, here we see a backward extension of Son of God language from resurrection to conception and birth.[106] This, of course, is *not* to deny that Jesus is the Davidic Messiah-King, and the longer story of Jesus's conception and birth in Luke also contains unmistakably royal and Davidic elements. Indeed, the two motifs are combined in the birth announcement of the angel Gabriel in Luke 1:32–33.[107] Mary's child "will be great, and will be called the Son of the Most High [Son of God motif], and the Lord God will give to him the throne of his ancestor David [Davidic Messiah-King motif]. He will reign over the house of Jacob forever, and of his kingdom there will be no end" (Luke 1:32–33).[108]

In addition, there is the juxtaposition of the emperor Augustus (high) and the infant Jesus (low) in Luke 2:1–7.[109] Augustus sends out a decree (for which, incidentally, there is no historical evidence) that requires "the whole world" to be registered and therefore also requires Mary and Joseph to travel to Bethlehem, where Mary delivers her vulnerable infant wrapped in rags. The result? Augustus has now been conscripted into God's plan.[110] As Calvin puts it, "God's amazing providence" reveals "itself in the fact that a dictator's bidding pulls Mary away from her home in fulfillment of prophecy." God does in fact employ "that very tyranny in the redemption of His people. For the Governor (or whoever was Caesar's minister), in fulfilling his commands, is God's secret herald, summoning Mary to the place divinely appointed."[111] Thus, an angel visits shepherds to tell them "a Savior, who is the Messiah, the Lord" is born in the (royal) city

---

Raymond E. Brown, *The Birth of the Messiah: A Commentary on the Infancy Narratives in the Gospels of Matthew and Luke*, new updated ed. (New Haven: Yale University Press, 1993), 68.

105. Brown, *The Birth of the Messiah*, 84; Fitzmyer, *The Gospel according to Luke (X–XIV)*, 308.

106. James D. G. Dunn, *Christology in the Making: A New Testament Inquiry into the Origins of the Incarnation* (Philadelphia: Westminster, 1980), 256.

107. Fitzmyer, *The Gospel according to Luke (X–XIV)*, 335–37.

108. The words in brackets are mine.

109. A point emphasized classically by Martin Luther and also by Reinhold Niebuhr, *Essays in Applied Christianity*, ed. D. B. Robertson (New York: Meridian, 1959), 29–30, and recently elaborated in detail by John Dominic Crossan.

110. Fitzmyer, *The Gospel according to Luke (I–IX)*, 393.

111. John Calvin, *A Harmony of the Gospels Matthew, Mark, and Luke*, trans. A. W. Morrison, *Calvin's New Testament Commentaries: A New Translation*, vol. 1, ed. David W. Torrance and Thomas F. Torrance (Grand Rapids: Eerdmans, 1972), 71.

of David (2:11), and accompanying the angel is a multitude of heavenly beings singing glory to God (2:8–14). Moreover, at the close of Luke's Gospel and at the beginning of Acts, it will be Mary's child, rather than Augustus, who is carried up into heaven to share in the divine imperial rule (Luke 24:51; Acts 1:9).

The genealogies and infancy narratives in Matthew and in Luke, which, as we have noted, have no parallel in Mark, function as prologues to their accounts of Jesus. They set an interpretative frame or perspective for what comes afterward. And, when we read them this way—as important *theological* statements rather than as historical reports—what we find are sophisticated interpretative images of Jesus as the Davidic Messiah-King and Son of God who fulfills the blessing of all nations through Abraham and whose kingdom will be without end. Thus, as Raymond E. Brown notes, the genealogies "tell us nothing certain about [Jesus's] grandparents. The message about Jesus, son of Joseph, is not that factually he is also (grand)son of either Jacob or Eli (Luke) but that theologically he is 'son of David, son of Abraham' (Matthew), and 'Son of God' (Luke)." [112]

When we look into precedents for this imagery in the Hebrew Scriptures, we find that the Davidic kingship and divine sonship motifs intertwine. Walter Brueggemann observes that the Torah was the most comprehensive mode of mediation between Yahweh and Israel, that it pertained to every sphere of life, and that it set forth definite commandments and conditions, but that the Davidic kingship also came to function as a mode of mediation. Thus, Nathan's promise in 2 Samuel 7:12–16, which parallels Gabriel's announcement in Luke 1:32–33 that Jesus shall reign forever, declares "Yahweh's unqualified grace" in connection with the Davidic kingship. Psalm 89 reiterates the assurance.[113]

> I have exalted one chosen from the people.
> I have found my servant David;
> with my holy oil I have anointed him. . . .
> Forever I will keep my steadfast love for him,
> and my covenant with him will stand firm.
> I will establish his line forever. . . .
> If his children forsake my law
> and do not walk according to my ordinances . . .

112. Brown, *The Birth of the Messiah*, 94. Hare, *Matthew*, 5, says that the Matthean genealogy supplies an initial definition of who Jesus is that will be elucidated in the subsequent gospel story.

113. Brueggemann, *Theology of the Old Testament*, 605; Fitzmyer, *The Gospel according to Luke (I–IX)*, 338.

> and do not keep my commandments,
> then I will punish their transgression . . .
> but I will not remove from him my steadfast love. . . .
> Once and for all I have sworn by my holiness;
> I will not lie to David.
> His line shall continue forever. (Ps. 89:19–36)

Brueggemann says, "this is an extraordinary declaration, a genuine *novum* in Israel's faith" because here "the conditional 'if' of the Mosaic Torah (Exod. 19:5–6) is overridden, and David is made a vehicle and carrier of Yahweh's unqualified grace in Israel," rather than simply on the condition that his ancestors keep God's commandments.[114]

Now consider Psalm 2, the immediate context for which was the royal court. Kings quite likely were made kings or anointed and enthroned with the following formula:

> I will tell of the decree of the LORD:
> He said to me, "You are my son;
> today I have begotten you." (Ps. 2:7)

The psalm thus joins together the Davidic King motif and the Son of God motif. Indeed, "the basic event at an accession," says Gerhard von Rad, "was the incorporation of David's descendant into a filial relationship with Jahweh."[115] The "begetting" here is clearly metaphoric, and as Brueggemann notes, "son of God" is "an exalted political title" that "does not concern any ontological claim or metaphysical status."[116] Again, enthronement is also a prominent theme in Psalm 110, where "the LORD" assures "my lord" (the king) of victory and protection in words that anticipate Jesus's ascension to God's right hand.

114. Brueggemann, *Theology of the Old Testament*, 605. Gerhard von Rad agrees with the prophecy of Nathan, that a "great new thing" takes place, namely, "an everlasting covenant with David." *The Theology of Israel's Historical Traditions*, vol. 1 of *Old Testament Theology*, trans. D. M. G. Stalker (New York: Harper & Row, 1962), 310–11.

115. Von Rad, *The Theology of Israel's Historical Traditions*, 320.

116. Brueggemann, *Theology of the Old Testament*, 606. See also James L. Mays, *Psalms*, Interpretation: A Bible Commentary for Teaching and Preaching (Louisville: John Knox, 1994), 47. "In Psalm 2 the king is reporting the content of a decree or protocol that presumably has been given or read to him earlier in the proceedings. The decree interprets the rituals of installation as a divine 'begetting' of the king as son of God. . . . Sonship is created by sacral-legal action."

> The LORD says to my lord,
> "Sit at my right hand
> until I make your enemies your footstool." (Ps. 110:1)

Another strand in the Hebrew Scriptures qualifies the royal ideology by insisting that the kingship is subordinate to Torah and by pressing kings to obey it. Solomon is therefore evaluated in 1 Kings according to whether or not he has kept the statutes of Torah (e.g., 1 Kings 11:9–11), and in his farewell address, Samuel, whose ambivalence to the kingship reflects commitments to the older tribal confederacy, insists that both the people and the king fear God and obey the commandments, or else "you shall be swept away, both you and your king" (1 Sam. 12:25).[117] The tension between the royal ideology of unconditional acceptance (really a kind of divine right of Israelite kings) and this Deuteronomistic strand in which the kingship is evaluated by the higher standard of Torah underscores the theme of the kingship and justice. Justice becomes not only the obligation of individual kings but also the criterion by which the institution of the kingship itself may be judged. Thus, Psalm 72:1–4, 12–14:

> Give the king your justice, O God. . . .
> May he judge your people with righteousness,
> and your poor with justice. . . .
> May he defend the cause of the poor . . .
> who have no helper.

So, too, Jeremiah's exhortation to the "King of Judah sitting on the throne of David" to "do no wrong or violence to the alien, the orphan, and the widow, or shed innocent blood in this place. . . . If you will not heed these words, I swear by myself, says the LORD, that this house shall become a desolation" (22:2–5).[118]

Here the overall view is that the monarchy as an institution must be committed to justice. Moreover, in this frame of reference, the destruction of the Northern Kingdom and the later exile of Judah to Babylon are the consequences of a failed monarchy, as is clear from the conclusions of 2 Kings and 2 Chronicles.[119] The claim of the Deuteronomist strand is that "power—political, eco-

117. Brueggemann, *Theology of the Old Testament*, 606–11.

118. Years ago, Brevard S. Childs, who claimed an approach to Scripture that takes seriously the canonical shape of the text, saw Jeremiah within the Deuteronomistic tradition of "preachers of the law." *Introduction to the Old Testament as Scripture* (Philadelphia: Fortress, 1979), 353.

119. "In the fifth month, on the seventh day of the month—which was the nineteenth year of King Nebuchadnezzar, king of Babylon—Nebuzaradan, the captain of the bodyguard, a servant of the king of Babylon, came to Jerusalem" (2 Kings 25:8).

nomic, military—cannot survive or give prosperity or security, unless public power is administered according to the requirement of justice."[120] The kings did not comply with the divine will promulgated by Moses, and the catastrophes of 722 and 587 BCE are to be understood in this light.[121]

Hope for the coming Messiah-King—the expectation of a good and faithful king—arises out of the strands of political theology surrounding the kingship because, despite the catastrophes of 722 and 587, Israel continues to hope for a king who will not fail to do God's will. This Davidic hope is also the context in which to understand the image in Zechariah 9–10 of the humble ruler riding on a donkey. Here, as in Psalm 2, the Messiah-King is very much a human agent, and "'Son of God' . . . is a royal, liturgical title, reflecting no ontological linkage to Yahweh."[122] This expectation is then applied to Jesus in the New Testament, and quite prominently in the genealogies and the conception and infancy narratives in Matthew and in Luke. In fact, the point of including the exile in the Matthean genealogy may well be to indicate that Jesus reverses and overcomes the kingship's spectacular failure—the kings of Israel and Judah often did what was evil in God's sight, but Jesus as the Christ will live and rule in accord with Torah.

Excursus on the Spiritual Conception of Jesus

Recent Bible scholars often prefer to speak of Jesus's spiritual, virginal, or miraculous conception rather than his "virgin birth," partly because, while Matthew and Luke emphasize that "the child conceived . . . is from the Holy Spirit" (Matt. 1:20), they say nothing about the manner of Jesus's delivery, which was sometimes elaborated in later Mariology. Thus, Marcus Borg and John Dominic Crossan write, the "virginal *conception* of Jesus should not be confused with the Roman Catholic doctrine of his virginal *birth*—with Jesus coming from Mary's womb like sunlight through the glass of a medieval cathedral window."[123] Douglas R. A. Hare refers to "Matthew's story of the miraculous conception ('virgin birth' is the traditional but less accurate designation)." In his comments on Matthew 1:18–25, Calvin basically agrees. "Matthew does not here expound the place or the manner of Christ's birth, but describes how His heavenly conception was disclosed to Joseph."[124]

A tendency toward the increasing elaboration of Mary's virginity and purity takes root early in Christian tradition. It is visible, for example, in the Infancy Gospel of James (c. late second century), which portrays Mary's special birth—announced by a heavenly messenger—to a childless couple, her childhood spent in the temple, Joseph as an old widower

120. Brueggemann, *Theology of the Old Testament*, 614, 615.

121. Von Rad, *The Theology of Israel's Historical Traditions*, 339, 343.

122. Brueggemann, *Theology of the Old Testament*, 617–18.

123. Marcus J. Borg and John Dominic Crossan, *The First Christmas: What the Gospels Really Teach about Jesus' Birth* (New York: HarperOne, 2007), 111.

124. Hare, *Matthew*, 9; Calvin, *A Harmony of the Gospels Matthew, Mark, and Luke*, 1:61.

who is reluctant to take a young woman into his house, and a high priest who devises a test to confirm the claim of Joseph and Mary that she has not had sex with any man. Again, and unlike the canonical Gospels, this text also says that Jesus is Mary's only child and assigns Joseph's other children to his previous marriage. Mary therefore remains a virgin before, during, and after Jesus's conception.[125] (Some believe that later understandings of the doctrine of the virgin birth may also obscure interpretative ambiguities surrounding the quotation in Matthew 1:23 from the Septuagint translation of Isaiah 7:14, "Look the virgin shall conceive." For example, the Hebrew text of Isaiah refers to a "young woman.") More importantly, perhaps, the Hebrew Scriptures sometimes refer to "the virgin Israel" (2 Kings 19:21; Isa. 37:22; Amos 5:2), and it is possible that, in Matthew 1:23, "Mary represents Virgin Israel, who cannot bring forth the Messiah without God's direct intervention."[126]

In any case, the writers of the Gospels of Matthew and Luke narrate a spiritual and virginal conception of Jesus, and it is not immediately apparent that they mean this only symbolically. At the same time, we should also keep in mind that "the modern intensity about historicity was not theirs. For them, the primary import of the virginal conception was theological, and more specifically, christological."[127] Theologically speaking, as we have noted, one way to regard the Lukan account of Jesus's spiritual conception is as a further development of the Pauline idea of Jesus's divine Sonship articulated in Romans 1:3–4. The Matthean account of the spiritual conception of the Davidic Messiah-King who fulfills the promise and blessing through Abraham may be viewed as a further development of the royal theologies of enthronement in which the king is begotten (or adopted) as Yahweh's son. And, of course, there are also important royal elements in Luke.

Note too that there is no explicit reference to the virginal conception in the New Testament outside of the infancy narratives. Mark uses the phrase "son of Mary" (6:3) but never mentions Joseph by name, and presents a portrait of strained relations between Jesus and his family that is not entirely positive. Some say John 7:41–42, where people in a crowd question whether the Messiah can come from Galilee rather than Bethlehem, indicates that the writer knew of Jesus's virginal conception. But "in summary evaluation of the evidence," even a comparatively conservative Roman Catholic commentator such as Brown concludes "that it is perfectly proper to speak of the silence of the rest of the New Testament about the virginal conception." This silence, of course, need not mean that no New Testament author other than the writer(s) of Matthew and Luke "knew of the virginal conception, or that the historicity of the virginal conception is thus disproved."[128]

Could the idea of Jesus's spiritual and virginal conception have emerged for theological

125. Ronald F. Hock, *The Infancy Gospels of James and Thomas: With Introduction, Notes, and Original Text Featuring the New Scholar's Version Translation* (Santa Rosa, CA: Polbridge, 1995), 6–7, 11–12, 14–15, 24–25.

126. Hare, *Matthew*, 10–11.

127. Brown, *The Birth of the Messiah*, 517.

128. Brown, *The Birth of the Messiah*, 518–21.

reasons? Some scholars think so. For example, Borg and Crossan claim that other ancient accounts of divine conceptions shed light on the theologies of the gospel conception narratives. They note that, in the Hebrew Scriptures, we find narratives in which, by divine help, barren women conceive, that is, Sarah and Hannah. They also point to other ancient accounts of divine and special conceptions that bolster claims for the importance of certain figures, for example, Alexander and Augustus (who was regarded as son of Apollo). By describing Jesus's conception as divine *and virginal*, say Borg and Crossan, Matthew and Luke intentionally exalt it over the accounts of other special conceptions in the Old Testament, "and especially over that of Caesar Augustus." Indeed, they say, the birth of John the Baptist in Luke to aging parents (and one of them, Elizabeth, a barren mother) tracks special births in Hebrew Scriptures and indicates that the Baptist is the last of the prophets before God does something really new with Jesus, whose conception, unlike John's, is also of the Spirit and virginal.[129] If this line of reflection is correct, then the development of a *theological idea* may explain why Matthew and Luke, as well as the traditions they worked with, contain narratives of a spiritual and virginal conception.

Brown clearly thinks otherwise. He wonders whether early Christians would really have known of stories of divinely engendered births "in *world religions* (the Buddha, Krishna, and the son of Zoroaster), in *Greco-Roman mythology* (Perseus, Romulus), in *Egyptian and Classical History* (the Pharaohs, Alexander, Augustus), and among famous *philosophers or religious thinkers* (Plato, Apollonius of Tyana), to name only a few." Moreover, he says, if early Christians did know of these claims, they very well may *not* have wanted to fashion their accounts of Jesus's conception after them. Finally, he asks, Are any of these other births "really parallel to the non-sexual virginal conception of Jesus described in the NT"? (After all, even Isaiah 7:14, in the Hebrew at least, does not really speak of a virginal conception.) Brown therefore finds that the case for the narratives of Jesus's conception having been modeled on other accounts of special conceptions in the ancient world at large and in Jewish sources in particular is not strong.[130] At the same time, he notes that difficulties attend claims for some, possibly historical and independent, bases for the gospel accounts, for example, a preserved family tradition. He therefore concludes that "the *scientifically controllable* biblical evidence leaves the question of the historicity of the virginal conception unresolved." But he adds that he would shock scholars who dismiss the virginal conception "by affirming that I think that it is easier to explain the NT evidence by positing historical basis than by positing pure theological creation."[131]

Neither Borg and Crossan nor Brown assumes the accounts of Jesus's spiritual and virginal conception are simply *modeled* on other claims or stories of special divine births.

129. Borg and Crossan, *The First Christmas*, 123.

130. Brown, *The Birth of the Messiah*, 522–24.

131. Brown, *The Birth of the Messiah*, 525–28. By "scientifically controllable," Brown means evidence of the transmission of traditions concerning the virgin birth.

They agree too that, by claiming Jesus's conception to have been *both miraculous and virginal*, Matthew and Luke take an important step beyond other stories. Borg and Crossan see this additional step as an explicit (and perhaps deliberate) attempt by the gospel writers or their sources to distinguish Jesus from the rest. Brown sees it as an indicator that early Christians, who probably did not know of claims for special births beyond their Jewish context, passed on and elaborated accounts of Jesus's conception that are finally quite distinctive and may have a historical basis.

Brown makes the further point, with which Borg and Crossan presumably also would agree, that while Matthew and Luke "presuppose a biological virginity," this "is not the main point of their affirmation." Indeed, he says, the creedal affirmation of the virgin birth "is not primarily a biological statement" but a theological one.[132] Then Brown says some things that Borg and Crossan might not. The virginal conception, he says, "was primarily an extraordinary action of God's creative power, as unique as the initial creation itself (and that is why all natural science objections to it are irrelevant, e.g., that not having a human father, Jesus' genetic structure would be abnormal). It was not a phenomenon of nature; and to reduce it to one, however unusual, would be as serious a challenge as to deny it altogether."[133]

These points are essentially textual and theological. Nevertheless, we should note that (1) claims for the historicity of Jesus's virginal conception finally outrun merely textual evidences, and (2) a theological understanding of Jesus's conception that does not reduce to a natural phenomenon but requires him to have been conceived without the participation of a human male still entails a strange biological occurrence.

To clarify some points, it may be helpful to compare Brown's position with what Karl Barth says in *Church Dogmatics* II/1. Barth says the miracle of Christmas is Jesus's conception by the Holy Spirit or his birth of the Virgin Mary.[134] He notes that the miracle is not expressly mentioned in the Gospels of Mark and John, that Paul and the Catholic Epistles betray no acquaintance with it, that after their childhood narratives Matthew and Luke never expressly return to it, and that the kerygmatic summaries in Acts do not mention it (175). Still, he claims that the words of the creed, *natus ex Maria virgine*, refer to an event that occurs in the creaturely world but "cannot be understood in continuity with the rest that occurs in this world." This event, he says, is a sign of the *vere Deus vere homo* that also eliminates docetic Christologies, which affirm that Jesus is divine and only appears human, as well as Ebionitic Christologies, which regard Jesus as a divinely adopted human (177, 181, 183). Indeed, Barth links the virgin birth with the empty tomb: the two belong together as "a single sign" that describes and marks off the existence of Jesus Christ as "that human

132. Brown, *The Birth of the Messiah*, 529.

133. Brown, *The Birth of the Messiah*, 531.

134. Barth, *CD* II/1:173. Hereafter, page references from *CD* II/1 will be given in parentheses in the text.

historical existence in which God is Himself" (182). Moreover, says Barth, *conceptus Spiritu sancto* is not a natural possibility to be understood by means of biological speculation but a miraculous sovereign act "not in any way analogous to the effects of creaturely *eros*." Yes, Jesus has no human father, but this does not mean that the Spirit "does what the human male does" (200, 201).[135] Or, again, Barth says, "'born of the Virgin Mary' means born as no one else was born, in a way which can as little be made clear biologically as the resurrection of a dead man, i.e., born not because of male generation but solely of female conception" (185).

Barth's claims for Jesus's resurrection are similar, and Van A. Harvey notes that they are difficult to reconcile when it comes to judgments about the event's historicity. Barth says that Jesus's resurrection is a historical event in ontic and noetic reality but that, in the nature of the case, it cannot be understood in continuity with other such events. Harvey objects that this raises an issue of consistency. Barth "has . . . exempted himself from any possibility of assessing the historical truth of his claims." He "claims all of the advantages of history but will assume none of its risks."[136] My point here, however, is simply that Barth's claims for Jesus's virgin birth quite clearly entail a strange biological occurrence, namely, "birth without previous sexual union between man and woman." This lack, says Barth, is precisely what distinguishes the birth of Christ.[137] And it is just this lack—quite apart from what some may regard as theologically unwarranted speculations about the genetic endowment of a person conceived by the Holy Spirit, etc.—that one is forced to regard as historically implausible.

This underscores a basic problem with any claim for the historicity of Jesus's spiritual conception and virgin birth, but I also have a second reason for introducing Barth's position here, namely, his very clear understanding of the *theological* significance of Jesus's conception and birth. Barth forthrightly views the virgin birth through the spectacles of the two-natures doctrine of the incarnation promulgated by the early councils. He says that Jesus's special birth—precisely because of the lack of participation of a human male in his conception by a human female—is a biological sign of *vere Deus vere homo*. But what we have said earlier about links between the royal idea of divine sonship in the Hebrew Scriptures and the genealogies and the narratives of Jesus's conception and birth in Matthew and Luke indicates that there are weighty reasons to question this way of reading the New Testament texts.

135. Barth also rejects parallels between Jesus's special conception and similar-sounding "heathen" legends in which "the divine agents . . . are definitely not God in the full and strict sense of the word" but gods who represent human hypostatizations of natural and historical forces (*CD* II/1:197).

136. Van A. Harvey, *The Historian and the Believer: The Morality of Historical Knowledge and Christian Belief*, with a new introduction by the author (Urbana: University of Illinois Press, 1996), 157, 158.

137. Barth, *CD* II/1:190.

Subsequent ecumenical councils of the church give ontological status to the idea of divine sonship by means of the *homoousios* formula. But it is not at all clear that the writers of the New Testament regard the idea metaphysically, and the transmutation of the royal political title "Son of God" into an ontological claim certainly goes well beyond the Hebrew Scriptures.[138] The ontological interpretation is in fact a later Hellenistic development/interpretation that owes a good deal to a different intellectual-cultural milieu. Its emergence may not be incongruous with the trajectory of some New Testament interpretations of Jesus as the divine wisdom, the one who reveals the character of God's creative power and God's redemptive power. (Consider, for example, 1 Corinthians 1:24 on Christ crucified as the wisdom of God, and its further development in texts such as the hymn of Colossians 1:15–20.)[139] Certainly, to later Hellenistic circles the ontological idea seemed a possible interpretation of John 1. But, biblically speaking, it is also important to observe that the later ontological idea (two natures hypostatically united in one person) clearly operates with comparatively alien concepts in a highly distinctive vocabulary.

Not surprisingly, when this later Christology becomes the authoritative template for interpreting the narratives of Jesus's conception and birth in Matthew and in Luke, the effect is to displace other possible readings that are closer to the language, images, and conceptualities of the narratives themselves, for example, that Jesus is the Messiah-King who truly embodies and expresses Torah. Moreover, the metaphysical pressure imposed by the later doctrine clearly encourages rather serious misinterpretations of key New Testament images and terms, as when one or another classical theologian says that Christ is called Son of Man according to his human nature and Son of God according to his divine nature.[140] The premature displacement and misreading of alternative christological images and reflections in the New Testament, in turn, contribute to a tendency to limit current options. The church of today, presented with an interpretation of the Bible that seems simply to endorse the language and conceptualities of the church councils, is all the more strongly bound to a particular formula of words—*vere Deus vere homo*—at places and times when other words and ideas might as easily or even more effectively sculpt and express a genuine and true Christian piety.

In any case, I regard the narratives of Jesus's spiritual conception and virgin birth as imaginative mythopoeic discourses that make important theological points. The spiritual conception and birth narratives are, in my judgment, ways of articulating and emphasizing the special importance of Jesus for Christian piety. There are, of course, many other ways of doing this as well, many of which are to be found on the pages of the New Testament, for example, a genealogy presenting Jesus as son of David and son of Abraham, portraits of the Spirit descending like a dove at Jesus's baptism, the claim that Jesus is the Son of

138. Brueggemann, *Theology of the Old Testament*, 621.
139. Dunn, *Christology in the Making*, 211.
140. Calvin, *ICR* 2.14.6.

> Man ascended to the right hand of the Power, or the claim that he is the reflection of God's glory and an exact imprint of God's very being. These need not be competing traditions or ideas, and, as Eduard Schillebeeckx notes, the fashioning of an adequate Christology does not mean that we must ascribe all of them to Jesus at once.[141] Neither must a given Christology simply repeat one or another New Testament image or concept. But it is critical (and also somewhat freeing) to recognize that there are multiple ways in which the New Testament points to Jesus as God's emissary or Son, a claim made with reference to resurrection in Romans and, as we have seen, with reference to royal or kingly ideas in the distinctive prologues to the Gospels of Matthew and Luke, and which may or may not call forth ontological elaborations.

The Way of Christ the King

How, then, does this particular king act? What does he do? How does he behave? There is much to say on this score, but surely, as the Gospels tell their stories, one of Jesus's recurrent practices is eating and drinking with the wrong people.

Consider the relationship between Jesus's style or manner of ministry and asceticism, or a life defined by austerity and abstaining from pleasure. It is true that, in the Gospels of Matthew and Luke, Jesus rejects temptations in the wilderness by saying, "One does not live by bread alone," and by refusing Satan's offer of "all the kingdoms of the world and their splendor" (Matt. 4:1–11). Jesus refuses to become a simple materialist, and he refuses to become Caesar. But this does not mean that his life and ministry are characterized by extraordinary austerity—as can be illustrated by differences in style between Jesus and John the Baptist.

Luke 5:27–39 reads as follows:

> [27]After this he went out and saw a tax collector named Levi, sitting at the tax
> booth; and he said to him, "Follow me." [28]And he got up and left everything,
> and followed him. [29]Then Levi gave a great banquet for him in his house; and
> there was a large crowd of tax collectors and others sitting at the table with
> them. [30]The Pharisees and their scribes were complaining to his disciples,
> saying, "Why do you eat and drink with tax collectors and sinners?" [31]Jesus
> answered, "Those who are well have no need of a physician, but those who are
> sick; [32]I have come to call not the righteous but sinners to repentance." [33]Then
> they said to him, "John's disciples, like the disciples of the Pharisees, frequently
> fast and pray, but your disciples eat and drink." [34]Jesus said to them, "You
> cannot make wedding guests fast while the bridegroom is with them, can

141. Eduard Schillebeeckx, *Jesus: An Experiment in Christology*, trans. Hubert Hoskins (New York: Seabury, 1979), 53.

> you? [35]The days will come when the bridegroom will be taken away from them, and then they will fast in those days." [36]He also told them a parable: "No one tears a piece from a new garment and sews it on an old garment; otherwise the new will be torn, and the piece from the new will not match the old. [37]And no one puts new wine into old wineskins; otherwise the new wine will burst the skins and will be spilled, and the skins will be destroyed. [38]But new wine must be put into fresh wineskins. [39]And no one after drinking old wine desires new wine, but says, 'The old is good.'"

This passage has parallels in Matthew 9:9–17 and Mark 2:13–22, and, for our purposes, it is worth dwelling on some details. In verses 27–28, Jesus calls Levi, a tax collector, to follow him, and Levi does. Tax collectors are reviled in Jesus's time and place; hence the phrase "tax collectors and sinners." They collect taxes for a government in league with an occupying power. What's more, their practices and relations with gentiles render them ritually unclean, and many of them are also dishonest. And, here in Luke, as if it isn't enough that Jesus calls a passingly traitorous and untrustworthy tax collector to be a disciple, Levi the tax collector then throws a party in Jesus's honor with a large crowd of tax collectors and other undesirables, and Jesus and his disciples attend. They sit or recline (*katakeimenoi*) at table together, as those with some wealth do, and they enjoy a sumptuous banquet financed by questionable means. At this point the Pharisees complain to Jesus's disciples, "Why do you eat and drink with tax collectors and sinners?" Jesus himself answers, saying he does so because he has come to help those who need help and to call them to repentance.

The Pharisees then say that John the Baptist's disciples don't behave like this. In fact, John's disciples frequently fast and pray just as the disciples of the Pharisees do. So, what's up with *your* disciples? Jesus says, "Look, wedding guests don't fast while the bridegroom is still present. They celebrate. They'll have occasion soon enough to fast when the groom is taken away." Then follow some sayings about old and new garments and old and new wine, the basic point of which is that the old and the new don't go together.[142] For good measure, Luke adds that those who have drunk the old wine never really like the new wine anyway. They just go around saying that the old stuff was better. Small wonder, then, that more conventional religious teachers and their pupils (both the Pharisees and John and his followers) are disturbed at the party behavior of Jesus and his disciples. They prefer the old wine and the old ways.

The contrasting styles of Jesus and John come up again in Matthew 11:16–19, which has parallels in Luke 7:31–35 and in Q. John sends messengers to ask Jesus,

142. These also have a parallel in the noncanonical Gospel of Thomas 47.

"Are you the one who is to come, or are we to wait for another?" Jesus then tells John's messengers to go and tell John what they hear and see—"the blind receive their sight, the lame walk, lepers are cleansed, the deaf hear, the dead are raised, and the poor have good news brought to them." There follow some verses in which Jesus says that John is more than a prophet; he is a messenger sent ahead to prepare the way. Nevertheless, says Jesus, there is a gulf between John and the new aeon, a gulf so wide that "even the least in the kingdom of heaven is greater than" John. In short, John is Elijah, the one who prepares the people for God's kingdom or reign. Anyone who has ears should listen.

And, then, as if to scold his hearers, Jesus says this:

> "But to what will I compare this generation? It is like children sitting in the marketplaces and calling to one another,
>
> > 'We played the flute for you, and you did not dance;
> > we wailed, and you did not mourn.'
>
> "For John came neither eating nor drinking, and they say, 'He has a demon'; the Son of Man came eating and drinking, and they say, 'Look, a glutton and a drunkard, a friend of tax collectors and sinners!' Yet wisdom is vindicated by her deeds."

So, in Jesus's judgment, at least as he is portrayed here, the generation that should listen to John and to Jesus really doesn't. When the messengers of God's kingdom play music, they refuse to celebrate and to dance. When the messengers wail, they refuse to mourn. This generation is recalcitrant and resists the message of God's reign no matter how it is presented and no matter who presents it. Thus, when John came *as an ascetic*, clothed with prickly camel's hair, subsisting on bugs and wild honey, as Mark 1:6 puts it, or fasting, and "neither eating nor drinking," as our text in Matthew puts it, those who were supposed to listen said he was a nut or that he had some kind of a demon. And when Jesus the antiascetic comes, behaving in the exact opposite manner—that is, eating, drinking, and celebrating—well, they don't like that either. Then they say, "Look, he's a glutton and a drunkard, a friend of tax collectors and sinners. Who in their right mind would listen to him?" There is, in short, no way to please these people. Even so, says Jesus, true wisdom proves herself by her deeds. And, in this case, the deeds of true wisdom—indeed, the wisdom of God—are to eat, drink, and be merry with tax collectors and sinners.

One need not believe that the sayings in Matthew 11:16–19 are authentic historical sayings of Jesus in order to think, as Crossan does, that Jesus quite consciously adopted a style of mission different from John's, and that the "difference between John and Jesus was discerned and expressed in the tradition" in scenes like this one and the banquet at Levi's house.[143] And, for our purposes, this difference is the main thing. John is an ascetic in the wilderness. The intentional and noticeable *style* of his mission is one of extreme austerity and denial. By contrast, the quite intentional and noticeable *style* of Jesus's ministry and mission is "semiurban party animal." As a matter of explicit principle and intent, Jesus and his disciples frequent villages, towns, and cities. They make a point of eating, drinking, and celebrating with all the wrong people, and, when others criticize them for it, Jesus defends these practices as deeds of divine wisdom.

Consider also some additional passages. In Luke 14:13, Jesus says to his host at yet another meal, "When you give a banquet, invite the poor, the crippled, the lame, and the blind." In Luke 9:10–17 and parallels, the disciples want to send away a crowd near Bethsaida because there is nothing for them to eat. Jesus tells the disciples to feed the crowd from a paltry supply of five loaves and two fish, and it turns out there is enough for everyone to eat their fill with twelve baskets to spare. We commonly call this "the feeding of the five thousand," but we might as easily call it "the banquet for five thousand," or even "the picnic party for everyone."

Again, the first miracle Jesus performs in the Gospel of John is during a wedding celebration at Cana, where Jesus's mother tells him the hosts have no more wine—the party is therefore about to come to a halt. Jesus tells the servants to fill six stone water jars, each with a capacity of 20 or 30 gallons, with water. Then he turns all that water into wine—wine so good that the steward says the bridegroom has reversed common custom and served the very best wine last. No ascetic, Jesus saves the party by manufacturing between 120 and 180 gallons of the finest wine available.

The difference in style between Jesus and John indicates a significant and illuminating pattern of Jesus's ministry and mission. Jesus eats and drinks with all the wrong people. He enters into table fellowship with them. Now, in Jesus's time and place, to enjoy a good meal, good wine, and conversation together is to forge a bond, to form a living community. (It's not so different in our own time and place, either. Go to the same school, work together on the same floor—these experiences may make someone your acquaintance. Invite them home for dinner and wine at your own table. Now they're your people.) That is, by eating and drinking with the wrong people, Jesus befriends them, he invites them into a new community of nourishment and fellowship and celebration and life.

What we have here, then, are not a few isolated occurrences but the portrait

143. Crossan, *The Historical Jesus*, 259; Funk, Hoover, and the Jesus Seminar, *The Five Gospels*, 180.

of *an intentional mission strategy*. Jesus's open commensality, as John Dominic Crossan calls it, is not just the practice of eating and drinking with people; it's the practice of eating, drinking, and celebrating *randomly* with *everyone*.[144] Jesus's manner of ministry intentionally *transgresses* the usual niceties, discriminations, and divisions of stature, class, and religion that characterize respectable society. It *welcomes*, and it seeks new community overcoming divisions. This is how it points to something new.

Crossing Barriers and Boundaries

Jesus's antiascetic table fellowship and open commensality has a certain energy and direction. It mixes things up and overcomes the usual divisions. It turns things upside down and accepts the unacceptable. Interestingly, as they are presented in the Gospels, his exorcisms and healings display a related pattern.

Just after Jesus has called his first disciples, the Gospel of Matthew makes a general statement. "Jesus went throughout Galilee, teaching in their synagogues and proclaiming the good news of the kingdom and curing every disease and every sickness among the people" (4:23). Consider, too, the sequence early in the Gospel of Mark on which this statement in Matthew is based. John the Baptist is arrested, and Jesus begins his public ministry by announcing that the kingdom is at hand. Jesus calls Simon, Andrew, James, and John to follow him. Next, he casts out an unclean spirit from a man in the synagogue at Capernaum, and as he does so, the unclean spirit acknowledges Jesus as the holy one of God. At Simon's house, he cures many who are possessed and heals many who are sick. Then Jesus preaches throughout Galilee, cleanses a leper, and heals a paralytic. Next, he calls Levi, the tax collector, and, as we have seen, has dinner with his disciples and "many tax collectors and sinners" at Levi's house, and then defends the practice.

Thus, in Matthew and in Mark, driving out demons, curing, and healing the paralyzed and the sick are features of Jesus's public performance on a par with his teaching and preaching. Ched Myers says Jesus's inaugural exorcism in Mark 1:21–28 is bound up with the question of his authority as both a teacher and a leader in the struggle with demonic and destructive forces. The exorcisms and healings show that Jesus's astounding messianic mission represents a challenge to established scribal and religious authorities.[145] The "Holy One of God" exercises his authority in areas of life and religious responsibility reserved for others; thus, he teaches as one with authority and he commands even the unclean spirits.

144. Crossan, *The Historical Jesus*, 261–64.

145. Ched Myers, *The Binding of the Strong Man: A Political Reading of Mark's Story of Jesus* (Maryknoll, NY: Orbis, 1988), 141–43.

We should add that the portraits of Jesus's healings and exorcisms express an intimate connection between proclaiming the kingdom, freeing the possessed, and making people well. Here is a king who not only eats and drinks with tax collectors and sinners but also subverts religious establishments and holiness codes as he heals the sick and casts out debilitating demons.

When some people hear this, their first impulse is to demonstrate that the exorcisms and the healings attributed to Jesus actually happened. Others find exorcisms and healings strange and implausible, whether they purportedly take place in ancient Galilee or present-day Tennessee. Here, however, I am uninterested either in proving or disproving the historicity of particular exorcisms and healings attributed to Jesus. My aim is simply to emphasize some features of the gospel stories and then ask what these features have to do with the manner of ministry of Christ the king and the good news that he brings.[146] "A leper came to him begging him, and kneeling he said to him. 'If you choose, you can make me clean.' Moved with pity, Jesus stretched out his hand and touched him, and said to him, 'I do choose. Be made clean!' Immediately the leprosy left him, and he was made clean" (Mark 1:40–42).[147]

Jesus cures all sorts of people in the Gospels, many of them poor and destitute. His cleansing of a leper in the first chapter of Mark is presented as an act of touching one who is ill and therefore outcast. Indeed, in ancient Israel, lepers and others suffering from skin diseases are separated, sometimes banished, and also required to warn others of their presence by crying out. Their diseases of disfigurement are thought to be contagious and to render them ritually unclean and capable of polluting others.[148] Those whose leprosy fades or disappears may be returned to normal social interactions, but purity codes require that "a priest must preside over ritual cleansing."[149] So, drama builds as the leper kneels before Jesus and says, "*If* you choose, you can make me clean." The kneeling posture and

146. My comments are, I believe, without prejudice to the historicity of the gospel accounts in the sense that I judge myself to be in no position to deny that, behind and beneath some of the stories, there may be rather widespread experiences of exorcisms and healings that many ancients understood in spiritualist terms. This will not be too difficult to grasp if you have attended some contemporary Pentecostal services where people sometimes seem gripped by affectively intense patterns of behavior from which they are freed or released by the touch of an "apostle" thought to wield a countervailing spiritual power or authority. A contemporary observer may very well choose to interpret these occurrences in social psychological terms. But at least some people even today—notably many of the participants in these services—deploy the idiom of possession, spiritual conflict, and cleansing. And we should remember that the former "scientific" vocabulary was unavailable to Palestinians in Jesus's time.

147. There are parallels in Matt. 8:1–3 and Luke 5:12–13.

148. See, for example, Lev. 13:45–46; 2 Kings 7:3–10; and 2 Chron. 26:19–21.

149. Myers, *Binding the Strong Man*, 152–53.

the statement express confidence in Jesus's power to heal and to sanctify, but the conditional clause also implies a question. Might Jesus have reasons to choose *not* to make the man clean?

The answer, of course, is yes. He might be repulsed by the man's disfigurement, by his ritual uncleanliness, and by the possibility of contracting his condition. He might also defer to the ritual purity codes and the exclusive role they establish for priests in declaring that a person is clean. But our verses from Mark insist that Jesus *does* choose to make the leper clean, that he reaches out to touch the leper, and that he makes him clean. That is, in cleansing the leper Jesus crosses a social, cultic, and even visceral boundary in order to touch and to heal a disfigured outcast. Having both made and declared the man clean, Jesus then sends him off with a stern warning to "say nothing to anyone" and to show himself to the priest so that his cleanliness may be officially acknowledged.[150]

In Matthew 8:5–10, the cleansing of the leper is followed by a Roman centurion asking Jesus to heal his servant, who is lying at home paralyzed. Jesus offers to "come and cure him," but the centurion replies, "I am not worthy to have you come under my roof. . . . Only speak the word and my servant will be healed." Besides, says the soldier, I am accustomed to the orders of persons in authority, including my own, being carried out. As the story is told, emphasis falls on the centurion's great faith, on his confidence in Jesus's great authority and that Jesus need only, as it were, give the order. Moreover, this particular scene, which is presented also in Luke 7:1–10 and bears similarities with one in John 4:46–54, clearly serves to advance Matthew's interest in supporting the church's mission to the gentiles, and so it may not be historical. But note, once again, a pattern that depicts a manner or mode of operating: Jesus acts as one with authority, and he crosses yet another barrier in order to help yet another "wrong person," this time an officer in an occupying military force.

Decisive things about the manner of Christ the king are depicted by the practice of eating and drinking with the wrong people and also by the practices of casting out demons, making people well, and healing and caring for them even across significant barriers and divisions. Jesus as the Christ challenges established practices, boundaries, codes, and authorities. He overcomes established divisions and alienations. Jesus as the Christ acts like a king, and like a good king, he exercises his authority to protect his people and to share benefits with them. But then it must also be said that scenes where Jesus engages in table fellowship with tax collectors and sinners, scenes where he touches and cures the

150. Myers notes in *Binding the Strong Man*, 153, that it is almost as if the leper who approached Jesus says, "You could declare me clean if only you would *dare*," and then Jesus does dare.

disfigured, ill, paralyzed, and possessed, scenes where he challenges established expectations, structures, barriers, boundaries, and codes in order to welcome persons and to make them well portray him as a peculiar king indeed.

Benevolence, Reversal, Reconciliation, and Renewal

With this peculiarity in mind, consider now the parable of the workers in the vineyard in Matthew 20:1–15, which has no parallels, though the statement appended to it about the last and the first in 20:16 has parallels in Mark 10:31, Matthew 19:30, Luke 13:30, and Gospel of Thomas 4:2–3. A number of scholars believe "the repetition of the owner's activity and the play on words and themes are evidences of oral transmission," and that Matthew 20:1–15 goes back to the Jesus of history.[151]

The parable likens "the kingdom of heaven" or God's imperial reign to a landowner who hires laborers early in the morning, agreeing with them to pay the usual daily wage. At nine, he sees others idle in the marketplace and agrees to pay them whatever is right. At noon and at about three o'clock, he does the same, and at about five o'clock he sends others out to work in his vineyard. When it comes time to be paid, the owner tells his manager to pay the workers, beginning with those hired last, and *all*—those who had gone out at five o'clock, those hired at midday, and those who had gone out early—are to receive the same daily wage. Those who had gone out early then complain that those who have worked only one hour receive the same compensation that they do. The proprietor replies, "Friend, I am doing you no wrong; did you not agree with me for the usual daily wage?"

Some Christian theologians read the parable as a statement about the different ways and times that Jews and Christians receive salvation. Thus Calvin, who thinks *all* are saved by grace alone, notes an interpretation with which he disagrees: "at the first hour the Jews were called for an agreed wage, in that the Lord promised them eternal life on condition that they fulfilled the Law, whereas in the calling of the Gentiles there was no agreement."[152] We find an interpretation something like this in no less an authority than Augustine. Righteous or just men, such as Abel and Noah, says the good bishop, "were called, so to say, at the beginning of the day. . . . Other just men, Moses and Aaron . . . were called, you could say, about noon. . . . After them the holy prophets, called as it were

151. Funk, Hoover, and the Jesus Seminar, *The Five Gospels*, 225.

152. John Calvin, *A Harmony of the Gospels of Matthew, Mark, and Luke*, trans. T. H. L. Parker, in *Calvin's New Testament Commentaries: A New Translation*, vol. 2, ed. David W. Torrance and Thomas F. Torrance (Grand Rapids: Eerdmans, 1975), 265,

in the afternoon." But "all Christians, called at the equivalent of 5 o'clock," will receive "the happiness of this resurrection" at the same time that these others do. And, since "those first people receive it after so long, and we after a short time, although we all receive it together, still we seem to have received it first because our reward hasn't been so long in coming."[153]

If, however, the basic parable itself goes back to Jesus, and thus to a time *before* significant differentiation between Jewish and Christian communities, then it must also be amenable to other interpretations. Borg says that Jesus's peasant audience may have heard it as an indictment of the domination system and wealthy landowners who did not act as the vineyard owner does.[154] This seems entirely possible, even plausible, though the likening of the kingdom to the landowner's behavior in 20:1 suggests that the negative judgment may have been joined with a positive statement concerning the divine reign. Thus, another recent commentator, Douglas R. A. Hare, thinks the climax of the parable occurs in 20:15, which underscores the vineyard owner's generosity and his decision "to pay his workers not on the basis of their merits but on the basis of his own compassion." This indicates that "underlying the parable is the Old Testament conception of God as the Creator who is *good* . . . generous to all."[155] And, of course, this is the same creation theology to which Jesus also appeals in Matthew 5:45, when he notes God's gifts of sun and rain to both the just and the unjust in order to bolster his teaching that we should love our enemies. In any case, especially when read in the context of the peculiarity of Jesus's kingship and style of mission, the parable of the workers in the vineyard may be regarded as a positive statement about the benevolent and gracious divine rule or administration that, in some significant measure, also challenges and undercuts more usual commercial and economic expectations and behavior. That is, it may be read as a statement of the divine excellence.

Hare is correct, I think, to emphasize that what is striking about the parable is the benevolence, generosity, or grace of the vineyard owner. This is what seems odd and what contrasts with ordinary practice and expectation. The landowner chooses to pay each an equal wage, and as his reply in verses 13–15 makes clear, his generosity or grace does *not* contravene justice in the form of the agreement he made with those who went out first.

Another well-known parable—that of the prodigal and his brother—also emphasizes the compassion and benevolence of its central figure in a manner

153. Augustine, *Sermons III (51–94) on the New Testament*, trans. Edmund Hill, OP, vol. III/3 of *WA*, 410.

154. Borg, *Jesus*, 182–83.

155. Hare, *Matthew*, 230–31.

that challenges ordinary expectations. So much so that some prefer to call it the parable of the loving father.[156] Moreover, this parable also has no parallels, and a number of scholars think it also goes back to the Jesus of history.

As it appears now in Luke 15, the story of the loving father is one of three parables introduced by the following sentences: "Now all the tax collectors and sinners were coming near to listen to him. And the Pharisees and the scribes were grumbling and saying, 'This fellow welcomes sinners and eats with them'" (15:1–2). All three parables, then, are presented in response to the now-familiar complaint by more conventional religious authorities about the style or manner of Jesus's public performance. Joseph Fitzmyer believes that, originally, the three were not a single unit but were later sculpted to contribute to the common "Lucan theme of God's love and mercy for sinful human beings and of Jesus' call for repentance and conversion."[157]

The first parable (vv. 4–7) asks, "Which one of you, having a hundred sheep and losing one . . . does not leave the ninety-nine in the wilderness and go after the one that is lost until he finds it?" Then it switches to the third person, and observes that, when he finds the sheep, he rejoices, goes home, and "calls together his friends and neighbors, saying to them, 'Rejoice with me, for I have found my sheep that was lost.'" There follows an interpretative comment: "Just so, I tell you, there will be more joy in heaven over one sinner who repents than over ninety-nine righteous persons who need no repentance." If we regard this last sentence as a Lukan addition and read the parable apart from it, the text exhibits a template or pattern—lost, found, celebrate—that we observe also in the body of the second parable. Here a woman with ten silver coins loses one and searches carefully until she finds it. Then she "calls together her friends and neighbors, saying, 'Rejoice with me, for I have found the coin that I had lost.'" Again, there follows an interpretative comment: "Just so, I tell you, there is joy in the presence of the angels of God over one sinner who repents."

Despite the interpretative comments on the lips of Jesus in 15:7 and 15:10, it is not easy to see how these first two parables emphasize repentance. A sheep and a coin may be lost and then found, and surely, when they are found, we may understand their owners celebrating with others. But does either a sheep or a coin repent? Moreover, the theme of repentance, while present in the parable of the loving father and his lost son, seems especially complicated there.

Here is the story.

"There was a man who had two sons." The younger asked his father for his inheritance, and so the father divided his property between them. The younger

156. Fitzmyer, *The Gospel according to Luke (X–XIV)*, 1083.
157. Fitzmyer, *The Gospel according to Luke (X–XIV)*, 1071, 1075.

son then traveled to a distant land where he squandered what he had, ended up destitute, and with a job feeding pigs. "But when he came to himself," he remembered that his father's hired hands had enough to eat whereas he was dying of hunger. He resolved to return to his father and say, "I have sinned against heaven and before you," admitting that he was no longer worthy to be called his father's son and should be treated instead like a hired hand. "But while he was still far off, his father saw him and was filled with compassion," and "ran and put his arms around him and kissed him." The son then launched into his planned confession, but his father cut him off, telling his servants to bring out the best robe and put it on the young man together with a ring and sandals. Then the father also told his servants to kill the fatted calf so that all may "eat and celebrate; for this son of mine was dead and is alive again; he was lost and is found!"

There follows a second part of the story. The elder son returned from working in the field, heard music and dancing, and asked a servant what was going on. Told that his brother had returned and his father had killed the fatted calf, the elder son became angry and refused to go in and join the celebration. His father then came out to plead with him. But the elder son rebuked his father, saying that he had worked obediently for years, without his father giving him so much as a young goat to celebrate with friends. And yet, he continued, when this profligate son returns, the father kills the fatted calf. "Then the father said to him, 'Son, you are always with me, and all that is mine is yours. But we had to celebrate and rejoice, because this brother of yours was dead and has come to life; he was lost and has been found.'" With that, the parable ends rather abruptly, without any interpretative comment.

Note some salient features. When the younger son calls for his inheritance early, by the standards of his time (as well as of many other times) he commits an offense. Then he separates himself from his father by going to a far country. When the elder son gets angry and refuses to go in to the celebration, his reaction is perhaps understandable. But when he rebukes his faithful father, he also commits an offense, and, in another fashion, he also separates himself from his father. Again, when speaking to his father, the elder son refers to the profligate as "this son of yours," whereas, speaking to the elder son, the father calls the profligate "this brother of yours."

One reading of the parable that we find in Augustine's sermons aligns the elder brother with "the people of the Jews," as well as with some other people who had come to Christ early on. These "couldn't stomach it that the Gentiles" should come to the church, receiving "saving baptism" or feasting on the fatted calf while they are still sinners—that is, without first working in "the Father's fields," or "without the imposition of any of the burdens of the law" and "without the pain of physical circumcision."[158] This obviously is constructed to fit the circumstances of later missions like those we find in Paul and in Luke-Acts. The Puritan theologian Jonathan Edwards also says that, like "Christ's eating with publicans and sinners . . . the parables of the lost sheep, piece of money, and prodigal son" are "figurative of the calling of the Gentiles."[159] Once again, however, if the parable goes back to the Jesus of history, to a time before the differentiation of his followers from Jewish communities and also before the calling of the gentiles, there is reason to think it may be read quite differently.

Let me suggest two additional interpretations. The first reads the three parables in Luke 15 as a single literary unit sculpted in defense of Jesus's table fellowship with sinners. The general defense is that, as God's emissary, Jesus has a mission to find the lost, to reclaim persons as belonging to God or as heirs to God's kingdom, and that, when the lost are found, there is heavenly celebration and rejoicing. This is why Jesus is the sort of king who eats, drinks, and celebrates with the wrong people—a practice that crosses barriers and boundaries and that also challenges the conventional practices of both the Pharisees and John's disciples (Luke 5:27–39 and pars.).

As we noted earlier and as seems clear from 15:7 and 15:10, Luke also wants to emphasize that Jesus calls sinners to repentance, though in the first two parables the theme seems a bit forced, and in the third, it appears to be considerably more complicated than 15:7 and 15:10 indicate. True, the prodigal comes to himself and resolves to return to his father and confess his fault. But no one explicitly calls him to repent, and his father is not much interested in hearing his confession. Perhaps he remembers his father's generosity and love, and this is what "calls" him to repent. In any case, the parables of the lost sheep and the lost coin may be said to defend Jesus's open commensality and its challenge to established expectations. The parable of the loving father may be said not only to defend this strategy but also, through its portrait of the father's unconditional love and extravagance and its portrait of the elder brother, to show us *why* Jesus's ready acceptance of sinners and outcasts troubles more conventional religious groups.

A second interpretation is more open-ended and existential. It takes its cue from the judgment that the parable of the loving father originally was unconnected with the first two and may in fact go back to Jesus himself. It was suggested to me, not by a Bible commentary, a sermon, or a theological treatise, but by the following story told at the close of Tobias Wolff's novel *Old School*.

158. Augustine, *Sermons on the New Testament (94A–147A)*, trans. Edmund Hill, OP, vol. III/4 of *WA*, 158.

159. Edwards, *Notes on Scripture*, ed. Stephen J. Stein, vol. 15 of *WJE*, 58.

Dean Makepeace (Arch to his friends) had grown into the life of a prep school in the eastern United States. He loved literature, he loved to teach, he cared about the boys, and his own life was set to the rhythms of the place. But there was also a problem: students had got the impression that Arch was friends with Ernest Hemingway, in part because both had served with the Red Cross, both had been wounded, and, as a result of his injuries, Arch walked with a limp and a cane. He did not correct their mistake; to some extent it increased his standing and authority with the boys. Then, in 1960, the school invited Hemingway to visit campus in the spring of the next year, and Arch's soon-to-be-exposed deception weighed upon him.

As a result, when it came time to expel a young plagiarist, Arch couldn't. He felt that he himself was guilty of a greater falsehood and had been in violation of the honor code for years. He went to the headmaster, a longtime friend, and resigned, though the headmaster thought the infraction minor and tried to convince him to stay. Arch left but soon fell into a depression. He realized that, in leaving the school, he had left himself, that his sense of being a distinctive and valuable person "was conferred upon him by others, by their knowing and cherishing him," and that, "unrecognized, he had become a ghost, even to himself."[160] He had thrown away his good life because it was imperfect, marred by a flaw, but now he missed the routines and the noise and the smell and the manners and the seasons of the school, and he wanted it all back. He wanted his life back. So he wrote a friend at the school saying he had made a terrible mistake in leaving and would return if he could. His friend spoke to the headmaster, and the headmaster wrote back, saying he had listed Arch "as absent on leave," hired a replacement only for the year, and hoped Arch would return to teach. Indeed, his same apartment would be available, only Arch mustn't confuse the boys by attempting "to set the record straight" about Hemingway, who, in any case, had died before he was to have visited the campus.

Arch returned to campus while the faculty was enjoying its annual opening-of-school reception in the garden of the headmaster's house. Here are the novel's last lines.

> As he came in under the rose-covered trellis someone yelled Arch! *Ecce homo!* And every head turned.
>
> Arch stopped and looked down the garden to where the headmaster stood by the drinks table with another master. The headmaster said, Late for his own funeral! and everyone laughed, then he put his glass down and came toward Arch with both hands outstretched. Though the headmaster was the younger

160. Tobias Wolff, *Old School: A Novel* (New York: Vintage Books, 2003), 191.

> man, and much shorter, and though Arch was lame and had white stubble all over his face, he felt no more than a boy again—but a very well-versed boy who couldn't help thinking of the scene described by these old words, surely the most beautiful words ever written or said: His father, when he saw him coming, ran to meet him.[161]

The story of Arch suggests that the story of the prodigal has to do with the recovery and renewal of a relationship. Luke 15:11–32 differs from the first two parables because here what's lost is a person, a son, with important and also strained relationships with father and elder brother and home. And so, when he becomes lost, he loses these life-defining relationships. He loses himself—as is implied by the evocative statement in 15:17 that "he came to himself" (*eis heauton de elthōn*), which would be badly out of place with reference to a sheep or a coin.

Within pages of his claim that Luke 15:11–32 concerns the calling of the gentiles, Augustine makes another point. Before returning home, says Augustine, the prodigal first returns to himself, and he finds himself in a sorry state.[162] He comes to a true self-knowledge and recovers himself. Other commentators make a similar point when they say the prodigal comes to his senses and that this entails his remorse and regret at what he has done to his father.[163] Or, viewing the parable through the lens of Arch's story, perhaps we should say that, in returning to himself, the prodigal realizes that he is dying apart from home and the father who cherishes him. He wants to live again. So he resolves to return and, as he comes to this resolution, he acknowledges his fault and accepts his life and his self even though they are seriously flawed.

But of course, he rather desperately needs one thing more if he is to regain himself and his life. He needs to be accepted and welcomed home despite his fault; he needs to be reconciled with his father and reintegrated into the relationship and community that sustain his life. This, however, cannot be earned, it can only be bestowed, which is why the father's unwavering and extravagant love is crucial. And, indeed, his father's running to meet him expresses the father's initiative and marks the beginning of his extravagant, life-renewing welcome.

That the father celebrates when the son returns is also crucial, and for some of the same reasons that Jesus eats and drinks with the wrong people. The celebration—the sustenance of the common meal, the table fellowship, and the welcome—is life giving; it reestablishes relationship and community. Not the initial, somewhat taken-for-granted-and-naïve-community that may have existed

161. Wolff, *Old School*, 195.

162. Augustine, *Sermons on the New Testament (94A–147A)*, 155.

163. Fitzmyer, *The Gospel according to Luke (X–XIV)*, 1088.

before the breach and before the estrangement, but a reconciled community, a community that recognizes the younger son to be flawed but accepts him anyway, a community that includes a son who knows himself to be flawed, knows he has been restored by the grace of his loving father, and perhaps therefore is now better equipped to bear the faults in others.

Which brings us to the elder brother. What may we make of him? Will he also come to himself? Will he also come to acknowledge his fault, and having been moved by his father's unwavering grace and acceptance, go in to the celebration and reenter his life and community? The parable doesn't say; it simply leaves us with the father's imperative insistence, "But we had to celebrate . . ."

If we regard this text as an insight into Jesus's theology, either because it does go back to Jesus himself or because it goes back to an early tradition that captures something of the manner of his ministry and preaching, what might it mean? Perhaps something like this. God is like a loving father who accepts the lost. Therefore, God's faithful emissary, the one enthroned as God's king and son, the one who undertakes his mission in the service of God's reign or kingdom, goes out to the outcast, the abhorrent, the separated, the alienated, and the estranged *and calls and accepts them*. He reintegrates them into the community of God and neighbor—into the life for which they have been created and sustained all along—by sharing meals together and celebrating. Indeed, when the public performance or mission of Christ the king is appropriately and passionately understood, this reconciling welcome home, this renewal of relationship and communion with God and neighbor—the very practice and behavior that undermines and challenges more ordinary and conventional expectations and practices—is precisely what is life giving and salvific. It is that which parabolically points to or enacts the kingdom and the divine excellence.

What King Is This?

I want to turn now to the story of Jesus's entrance into Jerusalem. That Jesus got into trouble and was executed there are important points on which historians and the Gospels generally agree. This need not mean, of course, that the narratives we have in the Gospels are entirely historically accurate. Indeed, it is clear that, just at this point, the gospel writers are working hard to frame theological interpretations of the significance of Jesus, his trial, and crucifixion. Thus, for example, the Gospel of Mark seems constructed so that it is before Pilate that Jesus finally claims to be the Messiah. Again, elaborating on Mark, the Gospels of Matthew, Luke, and John all link Jesus's triumphal entry into Jerusalem to the victorious humble king riding into Jerusalem on the foal of a donkey in Zechariah 9:9. Perhaps Jesus intentionally (and provocatively) tried to enact the passage from Zechariah, though the reference very well may be an interpretative addition.

The primary question I should like to raise here, however, is largely theological and not simply a matter of historical accuracy. What does the story of Jesus's entrance into Jerusalem indicate about the manner of Christ the king?

To approach this question, it seems important to observe that, when it comes to Jesus, people often see what they want to see. Albert Schweitzer made this point about scholarly studies, but his troubling conclusion also applies to more popular portraits.[164] Consider, for example, a recurrent American tendency to see Jesus as a master of commerce and industry. During the 1920s, an executive named Bruce Barton wrote a book called *The Man Nobody Knows: A Discovery of the Real Jesus* in which he claimed that Jesus was "the founder of modern business," a kind of prototype for Henry Ford. Jesus, said Barton, "picked up twelve men from the bottom ranks of business and forged them into an organization that conquered the world."[165] Laurie Beth Jones's book *Jesus CEO: Using Ancient Wisdom for Visionary Leadership* presents an entrepreneurial portrait for the 1990s. Like Barton, Jones says Jesus was particularly adept at developing the talents of his "staff." Jesus, says Jones, "trained twelve human beings who went on to so influence the world that time itself is now recorded as being before (B.C.) or after (A.D.) his existence." But Jones adds a more contemporary note: Jesus's "Omega management style incorporates and transcends the best of Alpha (masculine) and Beta (feminine) leadership styles," and this "leadership style was intended to be put to use by any of us."[166]

OK, when it comes to Jesus, people often see what they want to see, and in America this means that, with some regularity, Jesus has been portrayed as a successful businessman, CEO, or chairman of the board. But, of course, this cannot be what most people have wanted to see in Jesus, since the modern corporation is a comparatively recent invention. Most people at most places and times simply would have no idea what a CEO is. Success of the kind that people emulate and respect was therefore pictured in other ways. And, very often, successful leaders as well as their coveted qualities of power, prestige, and nobility were understood in *royal* terms. The great successes were emperors, princes, and kings.

The gospel writers narrate a royal scene, a king's entrance into Jerusalem, and, of course, Jerusalem is not just any place.[167] Jerusalem is the capital city, the city

164. Schweitzer, *The Quest for the Historical Jesus*.

165. Bruce Barton, *The Man Nobody Knows: A Discovery of the Real Jesus* (Indianapolis: Bobbs-Merrill, 1924), 23.

166. Laurie Beth Jones, *Jesus CEO: Using Ancient Wisdom for Visionary Leadership* (New York: Hyperion, 1995), xiii–xiv.

167. Marcus J. Borg and John Dominic Crossan, *The Last Week: What the Gospels Really Teach about Jesus' Final Days in Jerusalem* (New York: HarperOne, 2006), 5.

where Pilate the Roman prefect now governs, and the city where kings David and Solomon once reigned. Jerusalem is the *holy* city, the home to the sacred temple, the national shrine. What's more, as the Gospels portray it, when Jesus enters into Jerusalem, he receives a hero's welcome. Crowds line the street and shout,

> "Blessed is the king
>   who comes in the name of the Lord!
> Peace in heaven,
>   and glory in the highest heaven!" (Luke 19:38)[168]

That is, they quote a verse from Psalm 118, and they combine it with words that the multitude of angels sang out at Jesus's birth in Luke 2:14.

In fact, as we have seen, Jesus's birth as portrayed in Luke also has its share of royal elements. For one thing, Jesus is not born just anywhere. He is born in Bethlehem, the city of David, the hometown of Israel's greatest king, and an angel announces Jesus's birth by saying it is good news to all the people. Not to be outdone, the Gospel of Matthew says that King David is Jesus's ancestor through Joseph. It also says that wise men (or astrologers) came from the East bearing gifts in treasure chests in order to pay homage to the child born "king of the Jews" (2:1–2, 11).

So, when Jesus rides into Jerusalem with joyful crowds lining his path, it is definitely a royal scene—one that reprises Zechariah 9:9–10, where the humble king who shall command peace to the nations enters Jerusalem riding on the foal of a donkey. It is, in many respects, exactly what many people have wanted to see. Here is Christ the king, the descendant of mighty David, the savior whose birth was announced by angels, entering the capital city in triumph.

But on closer inspection, a number of things seem out of kilter. In fact, the whole business has been a bit strange from the beginning. An angel and even a choir of angels announce Jesus's birth, but only to a few shepherds (Luke 2:8–14). Matthew and Luke say that Jesus is descended from Israel's greatest king, David, but they also say he was born out of wedlock, and Luke says he was laid in an open trough for feeding animals. The royal entrance seems equally strange. There is no prince's army and no marching band. There is no flashy stallion, no elegant saddle, no red carpet, and no royal coat of arms. No party of dignitaries

168. The crowds say somewhat different things in different gospels, though in all, they elaborate on Ps. 118, and in all, the royal overtones are unmistakable. "Blessed is the one who comes in the name of the Lord! / Blessed is the coming kingdom of our ancestor David!" (Mark 11:9–10). Matthew also mentions David. In John 12:13, the crowd shouts, "Hosanna! / Blessed is the one who comes in the name of the Lord— / the King of Israel!"

comes out to greet Jesus and hand him the keys to the city. (These sorts of things might have been appropriate for Pilate's imperial military procession into the city, which Borg and Crossan claim took place during the same week.)[169] Jesus rides into town on a young borrowed donkey (Matt. 21:1–7). He sits on the cloaks of his disciples, and the crowds throw their cloaks in his path. (Matthew and John add that the crowds break off branches and throw them on the ground, too. Hence, Palm Sunday.) The whole thing is almost a spoof of a royal procession. Borg and Crossan, contrasting it with Pilate's military procession into the city to preserve order during a festival celebrating Israel's liberation from an earlier empire, say it's a peasant procession. Or, perhaps, following the lead of the gospel texts, we should say that it's *a royal-procession-with-a-difference*.

Not only is Jesus's entrance into Jerusalem portrayed as somewhat provocative and bizarre—the ramshackle entrance of a beggar king, a rabble-rousing leader, having yet another good time with crowds of peasants. But as far as the Gospels are concerned, and as they amply foreshadow, Jesus is entering the royal city not to be enthroned in a palace but to be arrested, unjustly condemned, beaten, mocked, and crucified. In fact, in Luke's Gospel, as he comes near the city, Jesus weeps over it, claiming that its enemies "will crush you to the ground," and then rides his borrowed donkey straight to the national shrine, the temple, the central place of established cultural and religious meaning. There the instigator of the street people drives out the people who collect money and donations in order to support the temple and its religious services. He then proceeds to set up shop, teaching in the temple for days.

N. T. Wright says that this stakes "an implicitly royal claim: it was kings, real or aspiring, who had authority over the Temple." David planned the temple; Solomon built it; Hezekiah, Josiah, and Judah cleansed it; and Zerubbabel and Herod the Great rebuilt it.[170] Jesus at the temple is emphatically provocative, and his provocation gets him into real trouble. Not too long afterward he will be betrayed and arrested, and one of the principal charges against him will be that he proclaimed himself to be king of the Jews. While he is hanging on the cross, soldiers will mock him, saying, "If you are the King of the Jews, save yourself!," and over him someone will affix a sign reading, "This is the King of the Jews" (Luke 23:37–38).

And then, to look ahead, yet another strange thing happens. Sometime after his death, Luke says that this rabble-rousing, bizarre, and civilly disobedient royal pretender appeared to his followers, that they were gathered into a new community and empowered to undertake a mission, and that *this* is the person God raises up into glory at God's right hand, a leader who is both an anti-king and a king.

169. Borg and Crossan, *The Last Week*, 2–3.
170. Wright, *Simply Jesus*, 127.

Now consider once again *the really big claim*. Here is the Word and wisdom of God in person. This provocative preacher who receives praise from peasants is the true light that enlightens the world (John 1:9), the intelligible event that precipitates a reinterpretation of God and humanity and world. This anti-king who is nevertheless true is the decisive clue to God's kingdom or reign and thus also to human existence.

What can it mean? Images multiply here for good reason, and perhaps none of us can be entirely sure. But we do know this: the Gospels picture Jesus as a king who is not a king who is a king. That is, when it comes to Jesus, the Gospels don't want to make it too easy for us to see what we want to see. They want us to catch a glimpse of something different. And, in this respect, the story of Jesus's entrance into Jerusalem is a tradition (in my judgment and in the judgment of many others, also largely historical) that discerns and dramatizes Jesus's peculiar ministry or public performance and its challenge to prevailing structures and authorities. Jesus is a king with a difference. This is how the Gospels summarize his manner of ministry that transgresses usual divisions and discriminations in order to seek new community. This is how they depict the one who eats and drinks with tax collectors and other undesirables and who subverts religious establishments as he exorcises and heals. This is how they understand the one who embodies God's grace and acceptance of the lost in a reconciling and salvific welcome. Jesus as the Christ is the king who reconciles.

The Manner Embodied and Displayed by Jesus's Ministry and Mission

Jesus's performance—his mission, practices, and teaching—embodies and displays God's kingdom as a reign of grace. To use Origen of Alexandria's striking term—one emphasized also by Stanley Hauerwas—Jesus as the Christ is the *autobasileia*, or the kingdom in person.[171] In him the kingdom is a divine reign or government that welcomes all—the outcast, the vulnerable and the marginal, the tax collector, the afflicted and the Roman occupier, the Jew and the gentile—into a beloved community or a renewed communion with God in community with others. Moreover, as portrayed in the Gospels, the kingdom in him is emergent. It is already, and so discernible "among you" and in certain attitudes and actions. It is not yet, and so also in conflict with present attitudes and orders. It is present but also on the way, and indeed, the considerable tensions between the *autobasileia* and current expectations and structures will lead to Jesus's crucifixion.

The manner of Christ the king—the pattern of ministry and mission that co-

171. Stanley Hauerwas, *The Peaceable Kingdom: A Primer in Christian Ethics* (Notre Dame: University of Notre Dame Press, 1991).

heres with and displays the truth of God's kingdom or reign—has characteristics that finally identify Jesus as an alternative king.

- It is marked by an expansive disposition to love God, neighbor, and even enemies.
- It crosses barriers and boundaries to help and to heal.
- It is specially concerned for the vulnerable.
- It forgives and welcomes the alienated and estranged.
- It pursues reconciliation, or renewed community and life together.

Here we should pause to consider how this way of Christ the king helps to shape and sculpt a historically and specifically Christian piety that is also somewhat distinct. We should emphasize that the pattern provokes and commends certain sorts of affections and actions.

Christian affections, especially as I have developed them in this volume, clearly include dimensions of what we may call a creation piety. So, for example, Christian piety, as it both comes to expression in and is shaped by certain biblical texts and theological images and ideas, cannot be described adequately apart from gratitude to God in response to gifts of existence and life in the midst of a sustaining environment. It also includes feelings of solidarity with other creatures, both human and nonhuman, with which we share certain limitations, needs, and vulnerabilities, for example, needs for nurture and care, susceptibilities to time and chance (as Eccles. 9:11 puts it). The point I wish to emphasize here is that, among those who participate in communities of faithfulness and worship that take the manner of Christ the king to display the integral pattern or skein of human life conformed to God and God's kingdom, there are also somewhat more specific and historically Christomorphic affections. Thus, if my account is at all correct, the specific manner of Christ the king shapes and provokes a willingness or disposition to stand with and care for the marginalized—the poor, the sick, the stranger. This clearly accords with Jesus's message of the kingdom as I have described it in the previous proposition. Again, we should also observe that the pattern or manner of Christ the king shapes and provokes a disposition and a willingness to cross barriers and boundaries and so to restore relationships and community by welcoming (and even celebrating) the stranger, the alienated, the prodigal, and the lost.

These and other Christomorphic affections display a particular piety and disposition, and they support what we may call "the politics of Jesus," a pattern of actions, practices, and attitudes, or a total complex of relations and affections, that comes to expression in Jesus's performance.[172] Recall Paul's admonition to

172. Among Christian ethicists, the phrase "the politics of Jesus" is associated with John

the faithful in Philippians 1:27 to live in a manner worthy of the gospel; whether or not he was familiar with narrative portraits of Jesus like those we have in the Gospels, his descriptions certainly cohere with them. Among other things, for Paul, a style or way of living worthy of the gospel requires patience and even suffering. It is a manner in life that takes up the same mind that was in Christ Jesus, looking not to one's own interests but to the interests of others, and so it necessarily stands in a measure of tension with the present age (whether in the ancient Mediterranean or contemporary North America). Or, again, in 2 Corinthians 5:18–19, Paul makes use of the image of reconciliation to summarize the gospel. In Christ, God reconciles the world to Godself. In Christ, God reconciles a world that has turned away from God and is opposed to God. In Christ, God loves enemies, "not counting their trespasses against them." This is the gracious divine pattern.

Consider these themes and images in the light of Jesus's practice (the *autobasileia*'s practice) of eating and drinking with wrong people, or of accepting tax collectors and sinners into communion. Consider them in the light of the loving Father who welcomes the prodigal home. This is the good news of the gospel, the special pattern that illumines—that in Christ God reconciles the world to Godself without counting their trespasses against them. Moreover, to respond appropriately, to live in a manner worthy of this gospel, says Paul, means to take up the message and ministry of reconciliation as our own, to become "ambassadors of Christ," or, as we might say, to love even enemies, not counting their trespasses, and so to witness to the possibility of a different, more humane world. And, indeed, just here we may suggest a broader claim; this is *a historically particular piety and manner in life that consent to God*, a manner in life whose temper, demeanor, and direction are fitted to the trajectory of the Real or to the reign of the Creator-Judge-Redeemer. This is the ec-centric and other-regarding pattern in mission and ministry that performs the kingdom, that enacts or participates in a divine and gracious excellence, and that also displays a manner in life that corresponds to this excellence.

Proposition #54 The crucifixion and continuing presence of Jesus as the Christ empower a manner or way in life that aligns with the truth.

Howard Yoder's excellent and important book by that title, *The Politics of Jesus: Vicit Agnus Noster*, 2nd ed. (Grand Rapids: Eerdmans, 1994). Though Yoder understands the significance of Jesus's politics differently than I do, he also associates it with an orientation or stance that continues to be relevant for Christian ethics and that comes to articulation in Paul with reference to justification, becoming a new creature in Christ, and the invitation to Jews and gentiles to become parts of a new community.

This is the third statement about what Jesus Christ says, does, and endures, or what classical theology calls the work of Christ. The first—Jesus as the Christ teaches the truth—points to his teaching and instruction, and it concerns what classical theologians sometimes call Christ's prophetic office. In his message of the kingdom, Jesus as the Christ teaches the truth about God's reign of grace; he presents the divine tendency, trajectory, or excellence as well as an expansive calling, vocation, or direction in life that conform to that excellence. The second—the ministry and mission of Jesus as the Christ embody and display a way or a manner in life that accords with the truth—points to his governance and guidance, or Christ's kingly office. In his ministry and mission, Christ the (alternative) king performs God's kingdom or reign of grace as he crosses barriers and boundaries to welcome, exorcise, challenge, and heal; he displays and enacts the divine excellence in a manner of ministry and mission that accords with that excellence. Now we turn to the third statement, or what some call Christ's priestly office.

A scriptural image intertwined with this third idea comes from Hebrews, and it combines priestly and royal images. Jesus Christ is the high priest and perfect sacrifice now enthroned at God's right hand. He sanctifies somewhat like Jewish priests who offered the blood of goats and bulls to purify those who were defiled. Unlike the offerings of the priests, Christ sanctifies once for all and wins a permanent victory (Heb. 1:3–4; 4:14; 7:1–3; 9:11–14, 26; 10:10–14). Again, in Revelation 1:5–6, Jesus Christ is "the ruler of the kings of the earth" who "freed us from our sins by his blood, and made us to be a kingdom [of] priests."

Thus, for example, commenting on Hebrews 1:3–4, which he takes to have been written by Paul, Calvin says, "by His death [Christ] has reconciled us to the Father, and put an end to the old sacrifices." He also says that, in 4:14–16, Paul shows the benefits Christ's "priesthood has brought," which include freeing us from sin and opening the way to God "to all who trust in the mediation of Christ." In commentary on 7:1–3, Calvin asserts that Christ is a king not only because he exercises a just rule, as others do, but also because he "communicates to us the justice of God." Indeed, Christ makes "it possible for us to be accounted righteous by a free act of reconciliation" and is called "king of righteousness because of what he does in imparting righteousness to all his people."[173]

With respect to the Christ event, the current proposition concentrates on crucifixion, resurrection, and ascension, and what comes to the fore is a pattern or shape of this event and its redemptive relationship to sinners. How does

173. Calvin, *The Epistle of Paul to the Hebrews and the First and Second Epistles of St. Peter*, trans. William B. Johnson, in *Calvin's New Testament Commentaries: A New Translation*, ed. Thomas F. Torrance and David W. Torrance (Grand Rapids: Eerdmans, 1963), 9, 54, 56, 88–89.

Jesus as the Christ enable sinners (who are curved in upon themselves and in bondage to inordinate self-concern, who are chronically confused in their loyalties, disoriented in their lives, and misdirected in their living) to be gripped by devotion to God and God's kingdom, or to the supreme cause and reality that govern all things? How does this event save people from their sins, move them toward reconciliation, and turn them from sinful corruption and set them on the way to God's kingdom? How does it contribute to an "enlargement of hearts," the regeneration of persons, and the emergence in them of a new spiritual sense and holy disposition of heart?[174] How does it enable people to be motivated by the excellence of God and of Jesus Christ rather than simply by private or restricted interests?

Part of the answer in the experience of the Christian community is that the event of Jesus as the Christ does these things in conjunction with *the power of the Spirit*, and we keep this in mind as we proceed. Note too that a discussion of the Spirit, regeneration, and the church follows. But here in proposition #54 we focus on a particular pattern of the Christ event and how its features empower and provoke a redemptive change.

Jesus as the Christ teaches the truth, embodies the way, and empowers the life. Note once more that, like the traditional metaphors of prophet, king, and priest, the three dimensions/images signaled by my symbolic shorthand interpenetrate and overlap. For example, Jesus teaches the truth about God's kingdom and human life conformed to it not only in what he says but also by what he does, by the characteristic actions and practices of his ministry and the manner in life they embody and display. Again, his teaching and performance—in parables, healings, table fellowship, etc.—also precipitate changes of heart and mind, and in this sense they too empower renewed life. So we are not surprised to find that Christ's last sufferings, death, and resurrection not only provoke and empower people to take up a manner in life that accords with the kingdom, they also help to teach the truth about God's gracious reign and to display the pattern in life that accords with the divine excellence.

Biblical Texts

Jesus was arrested and crucified. He was tortured and killed. These facts constituted a fundamental challenge, and early Christian communities felt the need to interpret them. Why did God's Messiah, a figure of royal victory, suffer? Why

174. Douglas F. Ottati, *Jesus Christ and Christian Vision* (Louisville: Westminster John Knox, 1996), 86.

did he die a criminal's death? Why were the authorities motivated to put him to death? Isn't his death a final rejection and repudiation of his authenticity?

Christian preaching, instruction, and worship addressed questions such as these from the very first, and so multiple oral, liturgical, and written traditions emerged that were drawn upon by both Paul and the canonical Gospels. But these so-called primitive traditions were not simple historical recollections. In them, the process of theological interpretation and reflection had already begun.

Early Kerygma and Paul

Paul draws on short summaries of the gospel, and at least one pre-Pauline tradition affirms God's "exaltation of Jesus to heavenly status as a sequel to his death on a cross, but without any mention of resurrection."[175] In Philippians 2:6–11, the hymn Paul quotes moves from Christ's humility and obedience "to the point of death" directly to his enthronement, when "every knee should bend" at Jesus's name and "every tongue should confess" that he is Lord. There are also ambiguous references in the New Testament to Christ sacrificing himself and apparently entering "once for all into the Holy Place" simply in virtue of his sufferings (Heb. 9:12, 24–26).

But consider also Paul's quite important statement to the Corinthians: "I handed on to you . . . what I in turn had received: that Christ died for our sins in accordance with the scriptures, and that he was buried, and that he was raised on the third day in accordance with the scriptures, and that he appeared to Cephas" (1 Cor. 15:3–5a). Here the apostle transmits a creed-like summary that had been handed on to him, one based on the early preaching and worship of the church that later also developed the narrative tradition we see in the four Gospels, and one that clearly includes resurrection.

The early statement refers to "major events that gave life to the Christian church"—from Christ's death to his being seen by Cephas. After this point, Paul adds a list of further witnesses, which he also received, and which he introduces by *eita*, "then," *epeita*, "thereafter," and *eita*. With *eschaton de pantōn*, "and last of all," he adds his own witness.[176]

By saying that Jesus's death was "in accordance with the scriptures," the early tradition *interprets* Jesus's death as a saving event, rather than a rejection or re-

175. Fitzmyer, *The Gospel according to Luke (X–XXIV)*, 1534.

176. Joseph A. Fitzmyer, SJ, *First Corinthians: A New Translation with Introduction and Commentary*, Anchor Yale Bible (New Haven: Yale University Press, 2008), 541–42. Some scholars also include 5b, "then to the Twelve," in the original tradition that mentions Cephas. See Hans Conzelmann, *1 Corinthians*, trans. James W. Leitch (Philadelphia: Fortress, 1975), 248–63.

pudiation.[177] Jesus's death is a feature of God's redemptive work. This same line of interpretation is developed further by the claim that, after he was buried, "he was raised on the third day," a phrase that occurs in other New Testament texts as well and may designate "the time of the first appearance(s)."[178] Fitzmyer says it counts the day of Jesus's death and burial, an intervening day, and the first day of the week, which is "the day of the discovery of the empty tomb," though Conzelmann says the phrase antedates "the tomb legend."[179] In any case, the force of the expression is that Jesus's death and burial are properly understood only in connection with "he has been raised" (by God) also "in accordance with the scriptures."

The ancient formula says nothing about "the nature of Christ's resurrection, whether or not it involved *sōma*, 'body.'" Neither does it say explicitly that Jesus was raised "from the dead," *ek nekrōn*. These are features of Paul's interpretation later in the chapter, and interestingly, "no NT text describes Jesus' resurrection itself as a perceptible event, such as Luke does for Christ's ascension (Luke 24:50–51)."[180]

For this ancient summary, then, Jesus's death is not a stand-alone occurrence but an event in connection with his resurrection and appearances. It is linked with God lifting up Jesus in victory, a divine raising-up and exaltation. (This also is a primary point of the early tradition to which Paul refers in Romans 1:4.) That is, for this very early tradition of the Christian community, Jesus's execution is in the *sequence* of crucifixion-resurrection-appearances, and this sequence, in turn, determines the true meaning of his death. Jesus as the Christ, the crucified but lifted-up and exalted one, is then seen by Cephas, the most prominent leader of the early church.[181]

How does Paul *interpret* this early gospel summary? Note that he works with its *complete* pattern or sequence. Thus, most often, when Paul refers to "Christ crucified," he does not mean to indicate only Jesus's execution; "Christ crucified"

177. Conzelmann, *1 Corinthians*, 255.

178. Conzelmann, *1 Corinthians*, 256.

179. See Fitzmyer, *First Corinthians*, 547–48; Conzelmann, *1 Corinthians*, 256.

180. Fitzmyer, *First Corinthians*, 548.

181. With this appearance and those that follow in 1 Cor. 15, Conzelmann says, "the idea is that the exalted Lord appears on each occasion from heaven." *1 Corinthians*, 256. Fitzmyer adds that, translated literally, 5a does not say "and he appeared to Cephas" but "and he was seen by Cephas." "The strange use of the aor. pass. of the Greek *horao*, 'see,' as a way of saying 'he appeared' is a Hebraism preserved in the" Septuagint, where it indicates that God "revealed his nature to the extent that the beholder was capable of seeing." *First Corinthians*, 549. Does this usage intimate a bit of negative theology, that is, that no one who sees the risen Lord sees all? In any case, the early idea seems to be that the risen Christ was disclosed in a manner fitting the (limited?) capabilities of the various witnesses.

refers to the one who is raised up and exalted, and then seen by his disciples. The overall pattern, then, is not one of death and defeat but one of suffering, death, victory, and new life, and, for Paul, when it is understood in this context, Christ's death brings benefits.[182]

Paul's explanations of *how we benefit* from Christ's death include three intertwined and prominent motifs. First, in 1 Corinthians 15 the apostle regards God's raising up of Jesus from the dead in an eschatological perspective as "the first fruits" of the general resurrection of the dead. "Christ the first fruits, then at his coming those who belong to Christ. Then comes the end, when he hands over the kingdom to God the Father" (15:23–24). In this connection Paul enters into reflections about a spiritual body (*sōma pneumatikon*), claims that "flesh and blood cannot inherit the kingdom of God," and claims that, on the last day, "the trumpet will sound, and the dead will be raised imperishable, and we will be changed" (15:50, 52).[183]

It is not easy to know just what Paul means by a "spiritual body," though it is clear from 15:44, 50 that this is not a "physical body." Perhaps the expression represents a bald dualism of matter and spirit, but if so, why does Paul speak of a "spiritual *body*"? Why not simply say, "it is sown a physical body, it is raised a spirit"?

Partly because the Apostles' Creed refers to *carnis resurrectionem*, which, literally translated, is "the resurrection of the flesh," a number of theologians also make relevant comments. The expression pretty clearly opposes later spiritual dualists who denigrated life in the body and thought of life eternal as a matter of immaterial spirit. Nevertheless, to some classical theologians it also seems at odds with 1 Corinthians 15. Thus, Luther says that, when Germans "hear the word 'flesh,' we immediately think that what is being spoken of is flesh in a meat market," but that "what the Hebrews called 'flesh,' we call 'body.'"[184] And indeed, "the resurrection of the body" is the conventional translation of the phrase that is used in the churches. The contemporary South African theologian John de Gruchy articulates a variant of this second idea. "The 'resurrection of the body,'" he says, "is not to be understood in a crude, literal sense; it refers to the reconstitution of our personhood in relation to others in ways that we cannot even begin to imagine." And it upholds "the most enduring qualities" of being human:

182. Calvin saw this lesson also in the Apostles' Creed. "So then, let us remember that whenever mention is made of his death alone, we are to understand at the same time what belongs to his resurrection." Again, whenever Christ's resurrection "is mentioned separately from death, we are to understand it as including what has to do especially with his death." *ICR* 2.16.13.

183. Compare this with Paul's earlier understanding of these matters in 1 Thess. 4:13–18.

184. Luther, *Sermons I*, trans. and ed. John W. Doberstein, vol. 51 of *LW*, 168.

"an everlasting protest against meaninglessness and despair," and "love as an affirmation of the human against its denial."[185]

If we allow that, for Paul, "the flesh" often refers to a wrong and destructive orientation of the human person while "the spirit" designates a renewed and appropriate manner of living, another, related point comes to the fore.[186] Paul's expression may refer to an appropriately oriented and sanctified self that takes up the meaning and importance of embodied disposition and desire without itself being "flesh and blood."[187]

However we resolve this question, the benefit, as the apostle intones, quoting Isaiah 25:8, is that death is defeated.

> "Death has been swallowed up in victory.
> Where, O death, is your victory?
> Where, O death, is your sting?"
> The sting of death is sin, and the power of sin is the law. But thanks be to God, who gives us victory through our Lord Jesus Christ. (15:54b–57)

A second motif: in Romans Paul connects Christ's death and resurrection with another benefit, the disclosure of God's righteousness and our justification through faith apart from law. He begins by saying that, since all sin and fall short, none obtains right relationship with God, and none obtains righteousness or justification, by means of works or moral performance. Rather, all "are now justified" and obtain right relationship with God "by [God's] grace as a gift" (3:24).

Abraham becomes our predecessor and father in this because, before there were Sinai and the law, he stood in right relationship and in covenant with God. (In Galatians 3:17, Paul says the law came 430 years after Abraham.) Thus, Abraham was counted upright, not because he fulfilled the law but because he had faith in the God who promised him a son, though he and Sarah were unable to have children. And, just here, Paul quotes Genesis 15:6, "Abraham believed God, and it was reckoned to him as righteousness" (Rom. 4:3). That is, Abraham had faith in the God who gives life, and so "calls into existence the things that do not exist" (4:17). Abraham trusted the God who creates, the deity who freely bestows blessings of existence and life, to give him and Sarah a son. And, of course,

185. John de Gruchy, *Confessions of a Christian Humanist* (Minneapolis: Fortress, 2006), 208–9.

186. See, for example, Rom. 8:1–17 and Gal. 5:16–26.

187. See Michael Welker, *God the Revealed: Christology*, trans. Douglas W. Stott (Grand Rapids: Eerdmans, 2013), 132.

Abraham is the beginning of the covenant for Israel. The right relationship with God in which Abraham stands by his faith in the God who creates defines the covenant of grace that forms the foundation for the people of God.

"Now," says Paul, "the words, 'it was reckoned to him,' were written not for his sake alone, but for ours also. It will be reckoned to us who believe in him who raised Jesus our Lord from the dead" (4:23–24). Why? Because we now experience the God who gives life and brings into being things that were not—we now experience the God who creates and bestows the blessings of existence and life—in the one who was crucified, dead, buried, and then raised up. Moreover, since Paul and others now bring this good news to those beyond Israel, the Scripture, which says that all the nations are blessed in Abraham, is now fulfilled (Gal. 3:8).[188]

Jesus's death and resurrection display the sovereign grace or gratuity of the God who creates and gives life. They show forth the unconditional gift, the bestowal of life, and the acceptance of people into a right relationship that will not fail that is characteristic of the God who gives life. They reveal that God *is* the God of grace. That is, in Christ's death and resurrection, people experience the God who bestows life and new life; they experience the Creator who is also the Redeemer. By the gift of faith or trust in the God who gives existence and life and who raises up Jesus, they are counted or reckoned righteous. They perceive that they are placed in right and reconciled relationship with God; they sense that they are accepted, that they stand in God's grace, and that they participate in God's kingdom or realm of grace.

Here we encounter as profound a theological reflection as can be found in the Bible. Luther saw in it what he regarded as the quintessential point of the gospel: the radical teaching that sinners are justified by grace through faith rather than by any act or effort or work of their own.[189] In Jesus Christ, the righteousness of God, unlike human righteousness, is sheer gospel, free grace and acceptance. Or, as we might summarize Paul's argument here, in God's redemptive economy, Abraham's faith in "the God . . . who gives life to the dead and calls into existence the things that do not exist" (Rom. 4:17b) was credited to him as righteousness. This confidence in the God who gives life now is "specified in our faith, which experiences the God who gives life in the raising of Jesus from the dead."[190] By faith or confidence in the God who does this, uprightness before God will also

188. See also Gen. 12:3; 18:18; and 22:18.

189. Luther, "Preface to the Epistle of St. Paul to the Romans," in *Martin Luther: Selections from His Writings*, ed. John Dillenberger (Garden City, NY: Doubleday, 1961), 19–34.

190. Joseph A. Fitzmyer, SJ, *Romans: A New Translation with Introduction and Commentary* (New York: Doubleday, 1993), 290.

be credited to us, so that we are reconciled with God, so that we too share in God's promise and are located in the covenant and realm of grace, not by our works or performance but by sheer gift. Jesus's death and resurrection display the sovereign grace and faithfulness that characterize the God who creates, and that Abraham held in hope. And, since through faith we are justified and rightwised with the God who gives life, we are at peace with God by our confidence in the grace God has extended to us. We are reconciled to God by the grace of God shown forth in Christ's death and resurrection.[191]

For this reason, we need not vouchsafe ourselves; we need not endeavor to secure our worth by our own works, or by our own strength, performance, and effort. Our worth, value, or justification is God's free gift. This is Christ crucified, the power of God and the foolishness of God that are wiser than human wisdom (1 Cor. 1:24–25). This is how Christ's death benefits us.

Now for a third motif, which some may regard as an extension of the second. Dying and rising with Christ, our old orientations or old selves are put to death and we are lifted up to a new orientation and new life. We become new creatures, or as Paul says in 2 Corinthians 5:17, "there is a new creation." This is so because, as sinners who are alienated and separated from the God of grace, we are captivated by the law and in bondage to the notion that we must rightwise ourselves by our own merits and efforts. We become curved in upon ourselves. We walk according to the flesh, commending ourselves, anxious and insecure about our own meaning and worth, and prone to press our own interests. But by faith in the sovereign grace and power of the God who creates and raises Christ from the dead, we obtain new orientation or new life.

Indeed, just because we are freed from the inordinate preoccupation and concern to justify ourselves, we are enabled to look to the interests of others and to have "the same mind . . . that was in Christ Jesus" (Phil. 2:5). In Romans 6:4, Paul describes it this way—"we have been buried with him [Christ] by baptism into death, so that, just as Christ was raised from the dead by the glory of the Father, so we too might walk in newness of life." Baptism reprises in our own lives the basic kerygmatic sequence: death, burial, and resurrection. By dying with Christ and sharing in his death, the old orientation, or the sinful flesh, is put to death (Col. 3:1–5). And, buried with Christ in baptism, "you were also raised with him through faith in the power of God, who raised him from the dead (Col. 2:12). We therefore participate in new life.

A more detailed description of renewed life waits for our later discussion of justification and sanctification. Suffice to say here that it is a life of love, care, responsibilities, and works—only now these proceed from a graced and animating center, rather than from a preoccupation with my self, its meaning and worth.

191. Fitzmyer, *Romans*, 393.

Thus Paul argues once again that Christ's death is no defeat or rejection of his lordship. Indeed, when it is properly understood in sequence with God's raising up of Jesus, and in conjunction with our own participation in Christ, it is the power and wisdom of God that bestow renewed and true life.

Passion Narratives

Turn now to the Gospels. Here we encounter what commonly are called *passion narratives*, Christ's passion being a term from the later Latin that refers to his suffering and endurance over the last days in his life as commemorated during Holy Week and ending with Good Friday. Rather than terse creed-like summaries, now we confront connected stories that, roughly speaking, narrate events from Jesus's arrest to his crucifixion and death, for example, Mark 14:1–16:8.

The narratives are comparatively lengthy and frequently foreshadowed—so much so that the nineteenth-century scholar Martin Kähler famously characterized the Gospels as "passion narratives with extended introductions."[192] Indeed, "all four canonical Gospels . . . have a passion narrative with a certain striking similarity (betrayal of Jesus by Judas, Last Supper with the disciples, arrest in an outdoor area outside the city, Peter's denials, and interrogation before a high priest, an appearance before P. Pilate, being led off to death, crucifixion, title on the cross, death, burial)." This similarity, "scarcely manifest elsewhere in the Jesus-story," suggests that the writers of Matthew, Mark, Luke, and John had access to a comparatively fixed group of passion stories,[193] though not all to the same ones.

The passion narratives not only present a connected account of events from Jesus's arrest to his crucifixion, they also situate this account within a broader story of his mission and his entry into Jerusalem. This placement, in turn, allows the gospel writers to answer questions that Paul's interpretations of early formulas did not. Why, for example, did established authorities oppose Jesus and want to execute him?

Thus, the narrative in Mark begins in 14:1 with religious authorities "looking for a way to arrest Jesus by stealth and kill him" without disturbing the Passover festival, and it follows a number of important scenes.

- Jesus enters Jerusalem to the shouts of crowds (11:1–10).
- He purges the temple, overturning tables and seats, teaching, and not allowing "anyone to carry anything through the temple" (11:15–16).
- Priests, scribes, and elders question Jesus's authority to do these things

192. Martin Kähler, *The So-Called Historical Jesus and the Historic Biblical Christ* (Philadelphia: Fortress, 1964), 80n11.

193. Fitzmyer, *The Gospel according to Luke (X–XXIV)*, 1360.

(11:27–28), and then he tells a parable "against them" in which wicked tenants first beat a vineyard owner's emissaries and then, when the owner sends his beloved son, kill him (12:1–12).

- Jesus answers tense questions about paying taxes to Caesar and about the resurrection that are intended to entrap him and expose him as a false teacher, and then he gives an important summary of the commandments (12:13–27).
- He denounces the scribes for taking in contributions money that widows need to live and for saying long prayers for the sake of appearances (12:38–40).
- He foretells the destruction of the temple as well as persecutions of his followers (13:1–13), and he asserts that, in days of sacrilege and suffering, the Son of Man will come on the clouds with great power (13:14–27).

So, by the time we are told of the plot to kill Jesus in 14:1, and of his subsequent betrayal, arrest, and questioning before the council of priests, elders, scribes, and Pilate, this much is already crystal clear. *There is significant and even lethal tension between Jesus and the authorities over his commandeering of the temple and his teachings.*

Mark depicts soldiers, bystanders, and priests mocking Jesus just before and during his crucifixion. In 15:33, a world-enveloping darkness falls on the scene of Jesus's death from noon until three in the afternoon, a darkness of judgment that may evoke the vision in Amos of God's wrath on the last day or perhaps simply express the significance of Jesus and his death as a turning point in salvation history.[194] There follow Jesus's last words, "My God, my God, why have you forsaken me?" (15:34), a cry of dereliction that quotes Psalm 22:1a and is probably a Markan elaboration of Jesus's wordless cry in 15:37.[195] Psalm 22 is an individual lament in which one who suffers derision and hostility pleads for deliverance—"Why are you so far from helping me, from the words of my groaning?" (Ps. 22:1b)—though by its close, God hears and rescues the (now grateful) afflicted one. Commentators emphasize that, as we interpret Mark, the victorious ending of the psalm should not take priority over the distressed beginning, especially since it is the beginning alone that Jesus quotes. Here, consistent with the

194. Joel Marcus, *Mark 8–16: A New Translation with Introduction and Commentary*, Anchor Bible (New Haven: Yale University Press, 2009), 1062.

195. Adela Yarbro Collins, *Mark: A Commentary*, ed. Harold W. Attridge (Minneapolis: Fortress, 2007), 753.

scene at Gethsemane in 14:32–42, Mark depicts an anxious and distressed Jesus who experiences "the terror of death in the core of his being."[196]

Mark's passion narrative looks to be based on an earlier account that may have ended with 15:38 and the tearing of the temple curtain from top to bottom as a sign that the presence of God is no longer enclosed or restricted to that place. The evangelist then appears to have altered this earlier tradition by adding items, including the story of the empty tomb, either from another source or by his own composition.[197]

Matthew and Luke exhibit significant dependence on Mark as well as some emendations and elaborations that they either obtained from other sources or composed themselves.[198] For example, Matthew adds verses to the scene of Jesus before Pilate, which say that Pilate's wife is warned in a dream, that Pilate finds Jesus innocent, and that the crowd especially wants Jesus crucified and also accepts responsibility for his execution. Indeed, in Matthew 27:24b–25, Pilate says, "'I am innocent of this man's blood; see to it yourselves.' Then the people as a whole answered, 'His blood be on us and our children!'" The clear (and historically questionable) function of these additions is to exonerate Pilate, the representative of Roman authority, and transfer responsibility for Jesus's execution to the people of Israel.[199]

Luke makes insertions into a block of Markan material.[200] For example, "the order of Jesus' interrogation before the Sanhedrin is inverted: in Mark 14 Jesus is interrogated (55–64a), mistreated (64b–65), and denied by Peter (66–72); but in Luke 22 Jesus is first of all denied by Peter (54c–62), mistreated (63–65), and finally interrogated (66–71)."[201] Unlike the other Gospels, Luke breaks up Jesus's trial before Pilate with an account of a hearing before Herod Antipas.[202] After the third time Peter denies Jesus, Luke alone says, "The Lord turned and looked at Peter" (22:61). Unlike Matthew, which repeats Jesus's last words from Mark, Luke 23:46 replaces Jesus's cry of dereliction with an expression of trust and

196. Collins, *Mark*, 753. Marcus, *Mark*, 1063, suggests that, for Mark, Jesus in his agony and fear may have suffered a sudden satanic assault, something like a man possessed.

197. Collins, *Mark*, 626, 638, 781; Raymond E. Brown, *The Gospel according to John (XIII–XXI): Introduction, Translation, and Notes*, Anchor Bible (New Haven: Yale University Press, 1970), 788–89.

198. Collins, *Mark*, 625.

199. Hare, *Matthew*, 316–17.

200. Fitzmyer, *The Gospel according to Luke (I–IX)*, 67.

201. Fitzmyer, *The Gospel according to Luke (I–IX)*, 71.

202. On the possible reasons for this, see Fitzmyer, *The Gospel according to Luke (X–XXIV)*, 1478–80.

dedication, "Father, into your hands I commend my spirit." Again, Luke's account of Jesus's death follows a special tradition when the centurion says, "Certainly this man was innocent" (23:47b). By contrast, in Mark 15:39 the centurion says, "Truly this man was God's Son!"[203]

The Johannine passion narrative appears to draw on Mark but also on an extensive independent tradition, and it therefore departs more strongly from Mark and the general template of the Synoptics.[204] Thus, for example, in Mark and the Synoptic Gospels the Last Supper is a seder or Passover meal with the disciples and Jesus is crucified the next day. In John, Jesus's last meal is on the evening before the day of preparation for the Passover meal, Jesus is crucified on the day of preparation, and the Passover meal itself was to be eaten after Jesus's crucifixion (13:1; 18:28; 19:14). Again, in John, Jesus is not questioned before the entire Sanhedrin or council, as in the Synoptics, but simply appears before the high priest. The lines of questioning also differ—in John, the high priest asks Jesus "about his disciples and about his teaching" (18:19); in the Synoptics Jesus is asked whether he is the Messiah (Matt. 26:63; Mark 14:61; Luke 22:67). Jesus's cry of thirst captures a note of agony, though his last words in John 19:30, "It is finished," seem less a cry of desolation than an expression of victory and the completion of a mission.[205]

The Empty Tomb, the Appearances, and Jesus's Resurrection

Each gospel joins the passion narrative with Jesus's resurrection. Mark connects the passion with intimations of resurrection by means of the empty tomb, a story that may have been composed in order to express the proclamation of Jesus's resurrection. Thus, when the women enter the tomb, a young man in a white robe tells them, "He has been raised; he is not here" (16:6). This, says Adela Yarbro Collins, is a disappearance story in which the discovery of Jesus's absence points to his resurrection without depicting the event directly.[206] The effect is to emphasize more strongly than did Mark's early source Jesus's divine elevation and vindication. In Mark, the divinely appointed Messiah, who has battled against dark and demonic forces from the very beginning of his ministry, becomes the divinely vindicated Messiah "translated to heaven whence he will return in glory as the Son of Man."[207]

203. Fitzmyer, *The Gospel according to Luke (I–IX)*, 67; Fitzmyer, *The Gospel according to Luke (X–XXIV)*, 1520.

204. Brown, *The Gospel according to John (XIII–XXI)*, 791; Collins, *Mark*, 625.

205. Brown, *The Gospel according to John (XIII–XXI)*, 930–31.

206. Collins, *Mark*, 779–81.

207. Collins, *Mark*, 639.

The original text of Mark alludes to an appearance at Galilee in 14:28 and 16:7 but does not narrate it. Another and longer ending to the gospel furnishes a firmer link to the rise of the church. It adds accounts of appearances of Jesus to Mary Magdalene and to two disciples—neither of whose reports are believed by his mourning disciples. Then, Jesus also appears "to the eleven themselves as they were sitting at the table," upbraids them "for their lack of faith," and tells them to "proclaim the good news to the whole creation" accompanied by signs and wonders. Having spoken these things, Jesus "was taken up into heaven" and enthroned "at the right hand of God." The disciples then go out to proclaim "the good news everywhere" (16:9–20).

All the other Gospels contain the empty tomb story. Each also narrates appearances, though not the same ones, and the variety indicates that the need for a single continuous story of all reported appearances did not emerge.[208]

Matthew 28:16–19 narrates the appearance at Galilee intimated in Mark. Here the eleven go "to Galilee, to the mountain to which Jesus had directed them," where Jesus comes to them and delivers what often is called the Great Commission: "All authority in heaven and on earth has been given to me. Go therefore and make disciples of all nations, baptizing them in the name of the Father and of the Son and of the Holy Spirit, and teaching them to obey everything that I have commanded you. And remember, I am with you always, to the end of the age."

The effect here, somewhat as with the longer ending to Mark, is to narrate an explicit beginning of the story of the church's mission, which is undertaken by the authority of the risen Lord and accompanied by his presence. Moreover, the highly influential Matthean text also connects the church's mission to baptism in the three names, and, by sending the disciples to "all nations," it links the event of Jesus as the Christ (as was implied in Matthew's opening genealogy) to the fulfillment of the promise given to Abraham. Now membership in God's people, or a saving relationship to the gracious Creator, is open to all.

Luke narrates two appearances of the risen Jesus. The first (24:13–35) is the longest appearance story in the New Testament. Here the risen Jesus comes near two disciples while they are walking on the road from Jerusalem to Emmaus and talking about "all these things that had happened." He asks them what they are discussing, "but their eyes were kept from recognizing him" (24:16). One of the two wonders that the stranger doesn't know what has taken place in Jerusalem, and says, "Jesus of Nazareth, who was a prophet mighty in deed and word," was "condemned to death" and crucified. The same disciple then expresses his profound disappointment, saying, "But we had hoped that he was the one to redeem

208. Fitzmyer, *The Gospel according to Luke (X–XXIV)*, 1535.

Israel." He also reports that "some women of our group" found his tomb empty and said they had "a vision of angels who said that he was alive."

Jesus responds, "Oh how foolish you are," and he exclaims that, in accord with the Scriptures, it was "necessary that the Messiah should suffer these things and then enter into his glory." He interprets for them all things about himself in the Scriptures, *but still they don't recognize him*. Finally, they invite the stranger to stay with them, and "when he was at the table with them, he took bread, blessed and broke it, and gave it to them. Then their eyes were opened, and they recognized him; and he vanished from their sight." The two disciples remark how their hearts burned as he interpreted the Scriptures to them. They return to Jerusalem to "the eleven and their companions," who are saying, "The Lord has risen indeed, and he has appeared to Simon," and the two then also tell of their experience "on the road, and how he had been made known to them in the breaking of the bread."

This "appearance story par excellence" contains a number of theological motifs,[209] among them the following. (1) The risen Lord comes to the disciples, teaching them "according to the scriptures." (2) What he teaches, namely, that the Messiah who redeems and is glorified must also *suffer*, revises popular expectation, and it also furnishes a direct theological answer to the question, "Why was Jesus executed as a criminal?" (3) The risen Jesus is made known to his disciples—they see and recognize him—in the eucharistic breaking of bread at table, and (4) this and other appearances ignite the church.

The second story (24:36–49) narrates an appearance in Jerusalem that takes place as the two disciples who were on the Emmaus road are talking to "the eleven and their companions." The risen Lord says, "Peace be with you," but the group is frightened, thinking he may be a ghost, and so, to demonstrate otherwise, Jesus invites them to touch and see his hands and feet. He eats broiled fish in their presence and then instructs them in the Scriptures, taking special care to point out that "it is written . . . the Messiah is to suffer and to rise from the dead on the third day, and that repentance and forgiveness of sins is to be proclaimed in his name to all nations, beginning from Jerusalem" (24:46–47). Then Jesus leads them "out as far as Bethany," blesses them, withdraws, and is "carried up into heaven" (24:51). The disciples and their companions worship him and return "to Jerusalem with great joy" and also praise God in the temple (24:53). Thus, once again, there are eucharistic overtones; once again, Jesus appears to disciples (or to the church), teaching from the Scriptures about the suffering Messiah.

These appearance stories and the subsequent story of Jesus's departure into heaven (or his ascension) also make a transition to the story of the church in

209. Fitzmyer, *The Gospel according to Luke (X–XXIV)*, 1557–58.

Acts, which, following an introduction to Theophilus, begins with an account of Jesus's ascension as well as the return of the eleven to Jerusalem, where Peter speaks before a group of about 120 and Matthias is chosen to replace Judas. The appearances ignite the church. Moreover, rather than Caesar Augustus, who rules the world at Jesus's birth (Luke 2:1–7), it is Jesus, the alternative king and Messiah who suffers and proclaims an alternative rule, who is lifted up and enthroned at God's right hand. Indeed, Acts will end with Paul preaching unhindered in Rome, the capital of the empire, or with the message of Jesus preached on Caesar's home turf.

A significant feature of the passion narrative in John is that, in accord with the Fourth Gospel's tendency to emphasize Jesus as king of the Jews, Jesus is lifted up and enthroned on the cross itself. Thus, not only does Pilate ask Jesus, as he does in the other Gospels, "Are you the King of the Jews?" (John 18:33; Matt. 27:11; Mark 15:2; Luke 23:3), he also asks, again, "So you are a king?" (John 18:37). Moreover, in John's narrative, Pilate has the inscription "Jesus of Nazareth, the King of the Jews" put on the cross *in three languages*: Hebrew, Latin, and Greek. The statement of the Roman charge against Jesus therefore doubles as a proclamation of his true identity that goes forth from the cross in the language of Israel as well as the most prominent languages of the Roman (and gentile) world. Christ the crucified King is universal, the logos or wisdom of God that suffuses creation. Jesus is the light of the entire world.

John's version of the empty tomb story emphasizes Simon Peter and another disciple running to the tomb after Mary Magdalene's report that Jesus has been taken, "and we do not know where they have laid him" (20:2). Four appearances follow.

The first is to Mary Magdalene as she stands weeping at the tomb. Two angels ask why she is weeping; she answers, because "they have taken away my Lord." Then Jesus, standing beside her unrecognized, also asks why she is weeping, and, after she responds, he says to her, "Mary!" She now turns and says to him "in Hebrew, 'Rabbouni!' (which means Teacher)." The risen Jesus tells her not to hold on to him, since he has not yet ascended to the Father. Mary then goes to the disciples, announces that she has seen the Lord, and tells them what he said to her (20:11–18).

The second appearance takes place in Jerusalem that same evening, "the first day of the week" (also the traditional day of resurrection and the day of Christian worship). Jesus enters a locked house where the disciples are meeting and says, "Peace be with you," shows them his hands and his pierced side, and the disciples rejoice. Jesus again says, "Peace be with you," and then he tells them, "Receive the Holy Spirit. If you forgive the sins of any, they are forgiven" (20:19–23). But Thomas doubts, and so, "a week later" (also on the day of Christian worship),

Jesus appears again to the disciples and asks Thomas to touch his hands and side. Following these appearances, a first ending to the gospel in 20:30–31 says that, while Jesus performed many other signs for the disciples, these three have been written so you may come to believe "that Jesus is the Messiah, the Son of God," and also have life in his name.

Next follows a fourth, more elaborate appearance story in 21:1–23 set not in Jerusalem but by the Sea of Tiberias in Galilee, where the disciples are fishing but catching nothing. Jesus stands on the shore and tells them to cast their net on the right side of the boat, at which point there are so many fish that the disciples are unable to haul them in. Simon Peter swims ashore first, while the others come later in the boat with their net. They see a fire with fish on it and bread. Then, in a eucharistic scene of a common meal, Jesus takes the bread and fish and gives it to them. He instructs Peter to "Feed my lambs," "Tend my sheep," and "Feed my sheep." He also refers to Peter's future martyrdom and says, "Follow me."

As in the other Gospels, the appearances in John mark the beginnings of the church and also characterize its continuing experience of the risen Lord as well as its mission. So, for example, the appearance to Mary Magdalene emphasizes that she recognizes the risen Lord as her *teacher* once he calls her by name. The next two focus on the disciples being commissioned to forgive sins and also coming to believe that Jesus has indeed been raised. Both also take place on Sunday, or the day of Christian worship. The fourth story points to the disciples as "fishers of men" or to the church's Christ-empowered mission to gather followers, the eucharistic presence of the risen Lord to the church, and the special role of Peter and the disciples as ministers who feed Christ's followers.

A second ending to the gospel then says that, if Jesus wills, the disciple who reclined next to him at the supper, and also asked who would betray Jesus, may yet remain until Jesus returns. "This is the disciple who is testifying" in this gospel, though there are also many other things that Jesus did (21:24–25).

Historical Information

Because the Gospels sometimes draw on different "primitive" traditions, Matthew, Luke, and John may contain historical information that Mark doesn't, even though the text of Mark was composed earlier. Given the strongly theological and interpretative nature of the texts, however, the question of to what extent and degree we may regard the passion and resurrection narratives in the Gospels as historically accurate needs to be approached with caution. Nevertheless, the following basic points seem to me to be historically secure.

Jesus's trial and execution took place in Jerusalem near Passover, though there is no agreement as to the precise day. Essentially, there were significant tensions between Jesus and established religious authorities (priests and scribes) having to do with his teaching and behavior in and around the temple. These tensions threatened social order and tranquillity at a critical time of year, that is, a festival celebrating Israel's escape from slavery and its eventual constitution as an independent nation, and so provincial civil authorities also became involved.

Jesus was arrested and appeared before Pilate, though priests and religious authorities probably collaborated. The concern during his appearance before Pilate was largely political, that is, that Jesus claimed to be "King of the Jews," or that he was a messianic pretender whose message and movement might destabilize established order. This having been confirmed to Pilate's satisfaction, Jesus was beaten and crucified.[210]

Thus, Collins notes that Jesus was tried and executed by Roman authority in the manner reserved for political threats.

> Historically speaking, Pilate alone had responsibility for the execution of Jesus. . . . A likely scenario is that Jesus was arrested by a troop of Jewish temple police and taken to the house of the high priest, Caiaphas. There he was interrogated. Afterward, he was taken to Pilate with a report that he was stirring up the people. Pilate decided the matter in a *cognitio extra ordinem*, an informal legal proceeding often used by Roman governors in cases involving provincials. He came to the conclusion that Jesus was deserving of death on account of *seditio* (sedition or revolt). So he had Jesus whipped and then handed over to his soldiers for execution.[211]

Crossan offers a somewhat different reconstruction.

> Jesus was arrested during the Passover festival and those closest to him fled for their own safety. I do not presume at all any high level consultation between Caiaphas or Pilate about or with Jesus. They would no doubt have agreed before such a festival that fast and immediate action was to be taken against any disturbance. . . . I doubt very much if Jewish police and Roman soldiery needed to go far up the chain of command in handling a Galilean peasant. . . .

210. Collins, *Mark*, 748, says that the inscription in Mark, "the King of the Jews," could have been words placed on a placard to indicate the crime of which Jesus was convicted. However, it is more likely, she says, that they represent a theological interpretation and apologetic in the pre-Markan narrative. It accords with Pilate's question in 15:2, as well as with the mocking of the soldiers in 15:18, and is placed as a parody that "unwittingly expresses the truth that Jesus is a king" (and an odd one at that).

211. Collins, *Mark*, 699–700.

> It is hard for us to see the casual brutality with which he was probably taken and executed.[212]

As we estimate the historicity of the resurrection narratives, we need to remind ourselves that there are New Testament passages, for example, Philippians 2:6–11 and Hebrews 9:12, 24–26, that move directly from Jesus's suffering to his exaltation, without mention of resurrection. Resurrection was therefore not the only way early Christians articulated God's endorsement and exaltation of Jesus.

In the Gospels, Jesus's resurrection and exaltation form a presupposition for experiences of the risen Lord among his followers. If we also consider Acts and Paul's letters, these experiences include trance-like visions. Crossan, who tellingly entitles a chapter "How Many Years Was Easter Sunday?," takes the main point to be that the Jesus movement did not stop with his death but that his followers felt empowered by Jesus's continuing presence.[213] The resurrection, we might say, is not narrated in the New Testament but pointed to as a kind of an inference from appearances, visions, and personal faith.

Bultmann claims that the cross and resurrection are inseparably united, and that both are made present through the church's preaching. We come to believe in the saving efficacy of the cross because Christ meets us in the word of preaching. "The real Easter faith is faith in the word of preaching which brings illumination. If the event of Easter Day is in any sense an historical event additional to the event of the cross, it is nothing else than the rise of faith in the risen Lord. . . . The resurrection itself is not an event of past history. All that historical criticism can establish is the fact that the first disciples came to believe in the resurrection."[214]

For John Hick, "the term 'resurrection' has been used throughout Christian history to refer to the transitional event or events in virtue of which the Jesus movement survived the death of its founder. . . . Precisely what this transitional event was we cannot now discern with confidence."[215] His "preferred conjecture" is that there were experiences "of seeing Jesus after his death, an appearance or appearances which came to be known as his resurrection."[216]

212. Crossan, *Jesus*, 152.

213. Crossan, *Jesus*, 159–62.

214. Rudolf Bultmann, *Kerygma and Myth: A Theological Debate*, ed. Hans Werner Bartsch (New York: Harper & Row, 1961), 42. See also Bultmann, *Faith and Understanding*, ed. Robert W. Funk (Minneapolis: Fortress, 1987), 177.

215. John Hick, *The Metaphor of God Incarnate: Christology in a Pluralistic Age* (Louisville: Westminster John Knox, 1993), 23.

216. Hick, *The Metaphor of God Incarnate*, 24. John Shelby Spong suggests that Simon Peter had a "vision of Jesus alive" as many as six months after Jesus's crucifixion. The vision, he says,

What shall we make of the appearances? Are they visions, or perhaps even hallucinations? Are they encounters, and, if so, is Jesus present physically or in spirit?

Michael Welker notes that, taken at face value, the appearance stories in the Gospels and the story of Paul's experience on the Damascus road in Acts narrate encounters with the risen Lord. And, in these stories, the risen Lord takes a variety of forms, for example, eating and drinking, passing through locked doors, vanishing from sight, etc. The forms are, in some degree, discontinuous with the pre-Easter Jesus—hence the women and the disciples sometimes don't recognize him. But there is also sufficient continuity for them finally to recognize the risen Lord as the same person or patterned identity, for example, as the teacher and the crucified one. Indeed, they recognize him especially in eucharistic scenes with the breaking of bread or eating of fish.[217]

What seems the case to me is that, when they had lost him through crucifixion and death, the disciples encountered the deep strangeness and assurance of grace in Jesus's abiding presence among them, and the spirit-inspired impetus to participate in a renewed life in community in his name.[218] Appearances, visions, and encounters were taken to testify to the fact that Jesus has been raised or exalted by God and therefore that he continues to be available and present to the faithful. The disciples continued to experience Jesus as the one who instructs or teaches, leads, and empowers or delivers. This is what gathered disciples together as members of Christ's body in the world. These instances of "a real mystical presence," as we might call it, form the reality that lies behind the disappearance narrative of the empty tomb as well as the claim that he has been raised.[219]

Crucifixion and Atonement

Contemporary believers often have difficulty integrating the crucifixion into their theologies, and this is as it should be. Jesus's crucifixion is a brutally vio-

---

occurred in Galilee, where Simon witnessed to other disciples who also saw the risen Jesus. This is the experience behind the resurrection idea. At the Feast of Tabernacles, they gathered in Jerusalem to share their faith, and so the Easter story unfolded in this context. Thus, writes Spong, "the truth of Jesus alive and available created the narratives and the legends" (Spong, *Resurrection: Myth or Reality? A Bishop's Search for the Origins of Christianity* [San Francisco: HarperSanFrancisco, 1994], 259–60).

217. See Michael Welker, *God the Revealed: Christology*, trans. Douglas W. Stott (Grand Rapids: Eerdmans, 2013), 118–26, as well as a more extensive discussion of these matters below in chap. 12.

218. See chap. 9 below, "The Spirit and the Church."

219. The expression is drawn from Reformed eucharistic theology.

lent event in which he suffers unjustly at the hands of established authorities, and is mocked by soldiers and crowds. The church's early kerygma, Paul's vivid interpretations, and the subsequent formation of the passion narratives all testify that Christians have found it difficult to come to terms with Jesus's crucifixion from the very beginning.

For some recent theologians, the difficulty centers on interpretations of Jesus's execution as a saving sacrifice that satisfies or appeases God's wrath against sinners. The critique is that this celebrates divine injustice, violence, and abuse. "And when parents have an image of God righteously demanding the total obedience of 'his' son—even obedience unto death—what will prevent the parent from engaging in divinely sanctioned child abuse? The image of God the father demanding and carrying out the suffering and death of his own son has sustained a culture of abuse and led to the abandonment of victims of abuse and oppression. Until this image is shattered it will be almost impossible to create a just society."[220]

The basic objection is to Anselm of Canterbury's theory of the atonement, or his understanding of how, through Christ, people and God are reunited and brought back together following their estrangement due to sin.[221] The claim is that, though Anselm may intend to underscore a theology of grace, his atonement theory conjures up a picture of a cruel and monstrous God.

Nevertheless, the death-crucifixion of Jesus, which finally should not be isolated from resurrection and appearances, remains an essential feature of the reconciling or saving Christ event and has been regarded as such from the beginnings of the Christian movement. Theologies that neglect Jesus's crucifixion and its salvific significance cannot be adequate to the early kerygma, Paul, or

220. Joanne Carlson Brown and Rebecca Parker, "For God So Loved the World?" in *Christianity, Patriarchy, and Abuse: A Feminist Critique,* ed. Joanne Carlson Brown and Carol R. Bohn (New York: Pilgrim, 1989), 9. See also Dolores S. Williams, *Sisters in the Wilderness: The Challenge of Womanist God-Talk* (Maryknoll, NY: Orbis, 1993), 161–70. Again, see Carter Heyward, *Saving Jesus from Those Who Are Right: Rethinking What It Means to Be Christian* (Minneapolis: Fortress, 1999), 122: "The cross has nothing whatsoever to do with a deity who, in the image of a father, would hand his son over to be crucified. Such a strange notion of God could only have arisen, as it did, in the midst of a patriarchal, feudal culture of static hierarchical relationships." Or, again, "The deep roots in Christianity of a psychosexual spirituality that links sex and violence are being cultivated to this day by a twisted understanding of atonement that is assumed by most Christians to be right and central to Christian faith" (175–76). Much of what I say about critiques of Anselm, and about Barth and Calvin, is a reworking of things I wrote in *Theology for Liberal Presbyterians and Other Endangered Species* (Louisville: Geneva, 2006), 12–15.

221. Keep in mind, however, the asymmetry noted earlier. It is not that God is changed or reconciled to sinners; sinful people are changed or reconciled to God.

the passion narratives in the Gospels; they fail to interpret the idea of a suffering Messiah. Classical theologians, including Anselm, generally recognize this, and thus, despite the very serious ambiguities and shortcomings in how they do so, it seems worthwhile to sort through some details of their understandings of atonement and election.

In Anselm's satisfaction theory, humans owe God perfect obedience but instead have fallen into sin and offended the justice and infinite honor of God. They therefore find themselves in an untenable situation. Humanity has offended God, and so humanity must satisfy the debt, but finite and fallible humans are unable to do so. God can satisfy the debt, but, of course, the debt is owed not by God but by humanity. Enter Jesus Christ, the God-human who, by his obedience unto death on the cross, satisfies the divine justice in our place.[222]

Note that Anselm tries to demonstrate the appropriateness or intelligibility of the two-natures Christology by showing that it addresses the experientially resonant problem of sin and forgiveness. Hence the title of his treatise: *Cur deus homo?* His logic is that, if we understand sin in such and such a manner, then the two-natures doctrine makes sense as a necessary feature of redemption. Presumably, however, if one does not view sin as an offense against God's infinite honor, or if one does not hold to the two-natures doctrine, the logic of Anselm's demonstration falters.[223]

Even so, it seems worth pondering how Anselm's images finally operate. God is the offended party, and humanity, the offender, must repay its offense but cannot. God the Son does. But, of course, for Western orthodoxy, which Anselm affirms, the Son is of the same being as the Father. (Augustine, in fact, regarded the "persons" of the Trinity as subsistent relations within the one God.) So it is just as accurate to say that, for Anselm, the offended party, God, makes reparations on behalf of the offender, humanity. The offended party takes up the cause of the offender and satisfies the offender's debt.

This, we should recognize, is strange justice; in fact, on most definitions it is hardly justice at all. It is grace, and even if we have good reasons to think that Anselm's legal terms are not the best available ones with which to express divine forgiveness, what pokes through his intentionally fractured juridical metaphors is a glimpse of the God of grace.

Perhaps only a glimpse, however, if we accept Karl Barth's criticism that An-

222. Anselm of Canterbury, "Why God Became Man," in *A Scholastic Miscellany: Anselm to Ockham*, ed. and trans. Eugene R. Fairweather (New York: Macmillan, 1970), 100–183.

223. Presumably, too, the criticism that any portrayal of Jesus's execution as a saving event must mean that God, in effect, executes Jesus, or requires him to be executed, also loses much of its force if one either revises or rejects a strict agent-model for God. See chap. 6.

selm has not gone far enough. Why must God's honor be satisfied at the terrible price of Jesus's unjust execution? Is the satisfaction of divine justice really the best way to interpret the cross? Again, is the Christ event, and specifically the crucifixion, merely the fulfillment of a precondition that enables God to be gracious, or is it itself an event that communicates and re-presents the God of grace to us?[224]

Calvin's approach to the atonement points the way to this criticism largely because it intensifies the emphasis on a gracious God by placing atonement in the context of the doctrine of election. The Reformer's basic logic goes like this. God has resolved in eternity (and, indeed, before the foundations of the earth) to redeem sinners. It therefore follows that God cannot actually have been hostile to sinners before the moment of Christ's sacrifice. Indeed, it must rather be the case that God already loves sinners even before Christ's sacrifice takes place. "For how could he have given in his only begotten Son a singular pledge of his love to us if he had not already embraced us with his free favor?"[225]

For Calvin, then, and despite the ambiguities of his double predestinarian scheme that we noted earlier, the single most important thing we learn in Jesus Christ is that the great God who creates and governs is also the good and faithful Redeemer.[226] Indeed, God loves us even while we are sinners; otherwise God would not furnish the Son as the remedy for our sin. "For God so loved the world . . ." (John 3:16). Thus, in Calvin's theology, Christ's work of atonement does not establish God's love; it derives from God's love. "The fact that we were reconciled through Christ's death must not be understood as if his Son reconciled us to him that he might begin to love those whom he had hated."[227] God is not first our Creator and Judge and then later our Redeemer. The doctrine of election means that there never was a time when God was not our faithful Redeemer. Christ's atoning work vividly portrays and impresses upon us what was

224. This last question is my way of formulating Barth's point in my own terms. His formulation is as follows: "To this view [that God can only forgive on the fulfillment of a prior condition for God's forgiveness]—in addition to the objections which Anselm himself raised and gave a not very satisfactory answer—we may have to raise the following questions. Is the incarnation of God, which is the goal of the whole sequence of Anselm's thought, really no more than the fulfillment of a prior condition which enables God to forgive in a manner worthy of Himself? Is it not the real accomplishment of His pure and unconditional forgiveness, His forgiveness *sola misericordia*?" Karl Barth, *CD* IV/1:486–87. The words in brackets are mine.

225. Calvin, *ICR* 2.16.2

226. Calvin defines the faith that comes to us in Jesus Christ as "a firm and certain knowledge of God's benevolence toward us." In addition, while he admits that, when it comes to knowledge of God, the books of philosophers are sprinkled "with droplets of truth," he also insists "they never even sensed that assurance of God's benevolence toward us (without which man's understanding can only be filled with boundless confusion)." *ICR* 2.2.18; 3.2.7.

227. Calvin, *ICR* 2.16.4.

always the case. It discloses what was already true, but what we, in our sin and misdirection, were unable to discern, namely, that the almighty power that brings into being all things and also upholds them is the God of grace, who redeems even chronically corrupted sinners.[228]

A Proposal

I shall try to uphold this affirmation in a manner that reflects my earlier review of the kerygma, Paul's interpretations of it, and the passion narratives in the Gospels. So, for example, I think it theologically crucial to regard the crucifixion and the appearances, or the cross and Jesus's resurrection/exaltation, as aspects or dimensions of a single event. When we do so, then the crucifixion-resurrection of Christ indicates God's vindication of Jesus, his message and mission following the gruesome tragedy of his execution. The appearances or postresurrection encounters are the great clue here, and as Rosemary Radford Ruether notes, they enable the disciples "to repudiate the possibility that the Crucifixion signaled the failure of Jesus' mission or his rejection by God," and instead to reinterpret his mission in terms of redemptive suffering.[229]

Apprehending the God of Grace

Paul's interpretation of the early kerygma illumines one way that Jesus as the Christ empowers a manner or way in life that aligns with the truth and with his alternative kingship. According to the apostle, in Jesus's crucifixion-resurrection-exaltation, we experience and apprehend the God of grace who bestows existence and life as free gifts. In Christ's death and resurrection we encounter the God of grace who "calls into existence the things that do not exist" (Rom. 4:17). That is, in my terms, the crucifixion-resurrection-exaltation of Jesus as the Christ re-presents the divine excellence manifest in creation, or the excellence of the

228. "However much we may be sinners by our own fault, we nevertheless remain his creatures. However much we have brought death upon ourselves, yet he has created us unto life. . . . Therefore, by his love God the Father goes before and anticipates our reconciliation in Christ. Indeed, 'because he first loved us' (1 John 4:19), he afterward reconciles us to himself." Calvin, *ICR* 2.16.3.

229. Rosemary Radford Ruether, *Sexism and God-Talk: Toward a Feminist Theology*, with a new introduction (Boston: Beacon, 1983, 1993), 122. See also Welker, *God the Revealed*, 126. "These varied and differing witnesses point to a complex historical event, a new reality; the persuasion that Jesus had died and that his mission and person had failed is replaced by a grounded conviction of his living presence."

God who bestows existence and life, and which excellence we who live and exist therefore always already experience. We encounter this excellence in the gift of a place and a time in God's world, but now, in the crucifixion/resurrection sequence, we also apprehend it beyond tragedy and alienation through the experience of participating in renewed life.

I repeat: this excellence, or God's going out to bestow existence and life, is the same excellence that suffuses creation, only now we encounter it in re-creation and renewal, or in new possibility both in the midst of and emerging from fragmentation, conflict, and tragedy. The fundamental content, then, is the same as in true knowledge of God as Creator, but now it is re-presented in and beyond alienation and destruction as knowledge of God the Redeemer. Christian piety experiences the divine excellence in the gifts of created life and existence, and also in the gift of renewed life overcoming alienation and destruction. God the Creator is God the Redeemer, and vice versa; God is the God of grace whose excellence it is to go out to create and uphold and renew.

Crucially, when we apprehend this, we also apprehend that we ourselves are included among the things that God creates, upholds, and renews. This pointedly personal perception of grace is itself grace. The apprehension in Jesus Christ that the God who bestows life and who calls into existence things that are not establishes a relationship that neither falters nor fails but drives toward the reconciliation and renewal of all—including ourselves—is itself grace.[230]

This apprehension furnishes a warrant for piety's feeling for the preciousness of our own life as well as for the value of all finite things. The knowledge in Christ that God the Creator is God the Redeemer (and vice versa) shapes and expresses piety's sense that, in relation to God, life and existence (mine but also yours and indeed the lives and existences of all) are good and worthwhile. Here we come across the discernment that all creation is gift, all the consequence of a mysterious and graceful donation, and that, likewise, the continuation and renewal of life and existence are also graceful donation.

At one level, reconciliation, or the alteration of sinful humanity that overcomes our alienation and estrangement from the divine purpose and trajectory, simply means the resumption of fellowship between persons and God by means of the internalization of this discernment. The encounter in Christ with the gratuitous divine dynamic changes people because persons assured that God is gracious to them need not endeavor to secure their own worth by their own accomplishment. Persons who sense the gratuitous heart of reality are therefore relieved of the anxieties of having to demonstrate their own value and of demanding that others demonstrate theirs.

230. See chap. 7, prop. #49.

This deep sensibility and assurance, in turn, encourage a kingdom-minded commitment to reconciliation, which seeks to overcome the destructive divisions that alienate us from others. The practical upshot is a ministry or mission that pursues renewed relationship and community with the others whom God also values. Moreover, when pursued by sinners, or by those who bear the marks of having lived in the destructive shadows of inordinate self-concern, pride, sloth, estrangement, and division, when pursued on the other side of injustice, diminution, fragmentation, and conflict, this reconciling mission differs from the *status quo ante*. Christian piety's experience of reconciliation, its encounter in Jesus as the Christ with the excellent gratuity of God, lifts up life so that, as Horace Bushnell says, life may proceed from a new reigning center.[231] The experience of being raised up into this animating affection amounts to participation here and now in a renewed and true life, and it calls for a mission of reconciliation that strains toward the shared well-being and shalom of the alternative king who heals the sick and attends especially to the poor, the widow, the orphan, and the stranger. Piety's encounter with the gratuitous divine excellence in the crucifixion-resurrection of Jesus as the Christ disposes persons to live along a different line.

The emergence in us of this affection and practical commitment corresponds with another Pauline theme: Christ's death-resurrection-exaltation is *salvific* because, in some sense, we participate in it. We die and rise with Christ. We participate in Christ's death and in his new, resurrected life. The old person and its misdirected trajectory or stance are put to death, and we rise to a new manner of life characterized by love of God and neighbor rather than by inordinate self-concern. (This is part of the reason why Jesus as the Christ, the person-for-others who embodies a manner and trajectory in life that accords with the truth, is our judge as well as our savior: when looked upon in relation to our sinful misdirection, salvation and new life necessarily imply a sharp and judging disjunction.) Even so, assured by our encounter with the divine excellence, we are freed from the obsession to justify ourselves and vouchsafe our own worth, and we are enabled to look to the interests of others, or to have "the same mind . . . that was in Christ Jesus" (Phil. 2:5). Calvin says this means coming to have the same attitude that was in Christ Jesus.[232] What emerges, I think, is the possibility of a kenotic redirection of persons. Perhaps we should call this entire transition, from the death of the old person to the emergence of the new, the resurrection in Christ

231. Horace Bushnell, *The New Life* (London: Richard D. Dickerson, 1885), 69.

232. Calvin, *The Epistles of Paul to the Galatians, Ephesians, Philippians, and Colossians*, trans. T. H. L. Parker, in *Calvin's New Testament Commentaries: A New Translation*, ed. Thomas F. Torrance and David W. Torrance (Grand Rapids: Eerdmans, 1972), 246.

that we can experience.[233] It indicates that God remains faithful, that, in the face of alienation and misdirection, God continues to pursue God's kingdom, and so, it nourishes hope for a better and truer life in relation to God and others.[234]

A Dangerous Memory, the Right Nightmare, and a Persistent Hope and Accompaniment

To the early kerygma and Paul's theological interpretations of it, the passion-resurrection narratives add an explanation of *why* Jesus was executed and *how* (nevertheless in and beyond tragedy and loss) he ignites the church. The theological importance is difficult to overestimate.

For one thing, the Gospels foreshadow tensions between Jesus and established authorities, for example, Herod's intentions and actions in Matthew 2, and they anticipate his crucifixion and resurrection, for example, the predictions in Mark 8:31, 9:31, and 10:33–34 that the Son of Man must be condemned and killed but will rise again. Thus, a basic answer of the passion narratives to the question of why certain people wanted Jesus executed is that lethal tensions reached their boiling point at Jerusalem near the time of the Passover festival, when the priests and Pilate found Jesus's message and activities in and around the temple dangerously threatening and destabilizing. This is why Pilate had Jesus executed as a political criminal, a messianic pretender, or "the king of the Jews."

The appearance narratives claim that, following the crucifixion, God exalts Jesus, and that Jesus's unexpected and strange but continuing presence gives rise to the church. The risen Christ, as they portray him, differs from the pre-Easter Jesus but finally is the selfsame crucified one (John 20:20, 27). Jesus's followers continue to encounter and also to recognize him (eucharistically) in common meals (Luke 24:30–31, 35; John 21:13). Again, Jesus continues to teach

233. H. Richard Niebuhr says something like this in *Faith on Earth: An Inquiry into the Structure of Human Faith*, ed. Richard R. Niebuhr (New Haven: Yale University Press, 1989), 97. "This is the resurrection of Christ which we can experience. In and through his betrayal, denial, and forsakenness, we are given the assurance that God keeps his promises. In and through and despite this we hear him, we accept him as God's word to us that God is faithful and true, that he does not desire the death of the sinner, that he is leading his kingdom to victory over all evil, that we shall not die but live, that the last word to us is not death without ending, but life everlasting."

234. All of this also accords (at least somewhat) with Paul's ruminations about resurrected bodies. One recognizes that in 1 Cor. 15 the apostle is struggling with a mystery and, as Fitzmyer says, perhaps not very successfully. Yet whatever else *soma pneumatikon* may mean for Paul, it clearly indicates that the sinful, misdirected person signaled by "the flesh" does not inherit (or come into) the kingdom; the reoriented and renewed person who lives by the spirit does.

(Luke 24:27), and he continues to lead by sending his disciples on a mission to the world (Matt. 28:16–20; Mark 16:15; Luke 24:47).

The execution by established authorities of the kingdom-minded one who teaches God's alternative reign where the poor are blessed and love of neighbor extends even to enemies, who enacts this reign by healing the sick, eating and drinking with outcasts, and pointing to a reversal of present practices—this, to recall Johann Baptist Metz's political theology, is *a dangerous memory*, one of suffering, danger, and peril that highlights "deadly conflict between God's promises and a history that is dominated by man's alienated desires and interests."[235] Metz notes that "danger and peril are found everywhere in the New Testament," but surely we may also emphasize that Christian liturgies rekindle "the *memoria passionis*" whenever, in accord with the passion narratives, the celebrant says, "On the night that he was arrested . . ." Thus, one thing Jesus's resurrection and appearances mean is that he continues to be present as the crucified one, the alternative teacher and king who suffers unjustly at the hands of the main social systems of his day. This historically particular and dangerous memory continues to shape a socially critical and subversive dimension of specifically Christian piety.

Now consider two related points. (1) The *memoria passionis*, the memory of the execution of the kingdom-minded one, empowers regeneration and repentance because it constitutes the right nightmare, one that brings with it an appropriate sorrow and revulsion. (2) The *memoria passionis*, the right nightmare and remembrance of the suffering victim, provokes lament and complaint and so also empowers the church to accompany those who suffer.

The philosopher Cora Diamond points out that, in *A Christmas Carol*, Charles Dickens's Scrooge does not move simply and directly from a miserly and selfish spirit to a felt solidarity with others. He does not respond to mere exhortations. Instead, the enlargement of Scrooge's heart, or his reorientation, depends on his being blessed with the right nightmares, the basic content and function of which are signaled early in the novella by the dark but also penetrating account of the meaning of Christmas given by Scrooge's nephew. The old man has just responded to his nephew's "Merry Christmas" by saying that keeping the holiday hasn't done his nephew any good, and then his nephew says this.

> There are many things from which I might have derived good, by which I have not profited . . . Christmas among the rest. But I am sure I have always thought of Christmas time, when it has come round . . . as a good time: a

235. Johann Baptist Metz, *Faith in History and Society: Toward a Practical Fundamental Theology*, trans. David Smith (New York: Seabury, 1980), 203–4.

> kind, forgiving, charitable, pleasant time: the only time I know of, in the long calendar of the year, when men and women seem by one consent to open their shut-up hearts freely, and to think of people below them as if they really were fellow-passengers to the grave, and not another race of creatures bound on separate journeys.[236]

The result of Scrooge's nightmares, according to Diamond, is that he gains an understanding of himself as mortal or as being "bound towards death."[237] (Indeed, near the close of his visit from the "Ghost of the Future," a trembling Scrooge, who has been brought face-to-face with his own gravestone, claims that he is no longer the man he was.) And his new self-understanding entails a sense for others as his "fellow passengers to the grave" rather than as alien creatures "bound on separate journeys," a sense that enables him to respond to the vulnerabilities and sufferings of others.[238]

For Christians, the cross functions similarly. It is the great occasion of the kingdom-minded one suffering unto death that hangs over all the many occasions of suffering, injustice, and oppression that continue to be the wages of sin in our history. The innocent one who was crucified at Calvary suffered the consequences of the sins of others. This is the great parable or discerning lens through which Christians look at the world. Jesus's crucifixion is the occasion of innocent suffering that hangs over all the many occasions of innocent suffering that continue to be the wages of sin in our history, and it enables us to reinterpret them. When we look through this lens, then we discern the many other Calvaries both great and small that clutter the horizons of our world. We see the innocent suffering still on account of the sins of the guilty—for our sins—on many an obscure hill. And in this suffering we see the cross.[239]

Rather than minimizing the question of God's righteousness in the world, when understood in this way, the crucifixion accents and intensifies it. For, here, piety discerns that the kingdom-minded one who is crucified suffers as a consequence of *our* sins. Good Friday liturgies therefore may include reproaches in which, taking the part of the divine, a liturgist reads statements such as these.

236. Charles Dickens, *A Christmas Carol* (New York: Puffin, 1984), 7.

237. Cora Diamond, "The Importance of Being Human," Royal Institute of Philosophy Supplement: 29, *Human Beings*, ed. David Cockburn (Cambridge: Cambridge University Press, 1991), 49–51.

238. Dickens, *A Christmas Carol*, 7. The phrases I quote in this sentence are part of the rather dark but also penetrating account of the meaning of Christmas that Scrooge's nephew gives as he invites his uncle to a party.

239. Ottati, *Jesus Christ and Christian Vision*, 87.

> I gave you a royal scepter,
> and bestowed the keys of the kingdom,
> but you have given me a crown of thorns.
> I raised you on high with great power,
> but you have prepared a cross for your Savior.
> I sent the Spirit of truth to guide you . . .
> but you continue to quarrel and divide . . .
> and you have prepared a cross for your Savior.

And, the congregants reply:

> Holy God,
> holy and mighty.
> Holy and Immortal One,
> have mercy upon us.

Again, partly by means of the alchemy of the liturgy, this historically specific memory becomes a discerning lens through which we look at ourselves and our world. Looking through this lens, we see, as H. Richard Niebuhr once noted during the Second World War, other Calvaries that mark our alienated world. Through the interpretative spectacles of the revelatory image, Niebuhr says, it is plain that suffering "for the sins of a nazi party and a Hitler falls on Russian and German soldiers, on the children of Cologne and Coventry, on the Finns and the French."[240] We therefore see on many hills, both prominent and obscure, the innocent—the kingdom-minded as well as the vulnerable, the outcast, and the poor—suffering still due to the sins of the guilty.

With this in mind, consider the following comment on Johann Sebastian Bach's *St. Matthew's Passion* by the American philosopher Josiah Royce. At the Last Supper, "Christ has just said: 'One of you shall betray me.' And they all begin to say . . . 'Is it I? Is it I? Is it I?' And then there begins the chorus of 'the Believers'; ''Tis I, *My* sins betray thee, who died to make me whole.'" The effect, says Royce, is that "an old story of the past retold" becomes the listener's own.[241] What I wish to emphasize is this: now I see that the kingdom-minded one as well as the vulnerable ones he would lift up into the shalom of God's kingdom suffer as a consequence of *my* sins. Now we see that Jesus was crucified not only at the hands of those who put him to death in Palestine centuries ago, but also "at the

240. H. Richard Niebuhr, "War as Crucifixion," in *War in the Twentieth Century: Sources in Theological Ethics*, ed. Richard B. Miller (Louisville: Westminster John Knox, 1992), 65.

241. Josiah Royce, *The Problem of Christianity* (Chicago: University of Chicago Press, 1968), 167.

hands" of the power of sin in our history that continues to infect our hearts. Bach is therefore quite correct to put the words "'Tis I, *My* sins betray thee" into the recurrent chorus of "the Believers."

This is the right nightmare, and, to all but the hardest of hearts, it is a power able to work a change of heart, a power able to turn people from the way of inordinate self-concern toward the way, the truth, and the life marked off by Jesus as the Christ. This is the right nightmare, a vision that moves people to repent because it punctuates and underscores and will not let them turn their gaze from the sight of sin's tragic consequences, namely, the suffering of the kingdom-minded one and the poor, the weak, the sick, the widow, the orphan, and the stranger to whom the kingdom belongs. This is the right nightmare, a bad dream that discloses a disturbing and fundamental ordering and pattern in our moral experience.[242] "Out of such despair," says Reinhold Niebuhr, "contrition is born; and of contrition faith is conceived; and in that faith there is 'newness of life,' which is to say 'power.'"[243]

Or, again, we may say that the execution-crucifixion of Jesus as the Christ, the kingdom-minded one, mediates a perception of the *malum* or of the tearing of life's fabric that the philosopher Hans Jonas tells us is basic to the emergence of responsibility and the idea of the good. Jonas writes, "As long as [a] danger is unknown, we do not know what to preserve and why. Knowledge . . . comes . . . from the perception of what to avoid. This is perceived first and teaches us, by the revulsion of feeling which acts ahead of knowledge, to apprehend the value whose antithesis so affects us. We know the thing is at stake only when we know that it is at stake. Because this is the way we are made: the perception of the malum is infinitely easier to us than the perception of the bonum."[244]

The *memoria passionis* brings with it an appropriate revulsion, one that feels the grossly destructive violations—the mother holding her starving child, the terrorist bomb that explodes on a busy sidewalk, the most recent attempt at ethnic cleansing, the dead fish floating in a putrid harbor—and so apprehends the value of the kingdom in its antithesis. The *memoria passionis* brings with it the appropriate revulsion at the *malum*, the tearing and grossly destructive violation of the divine excellence. We are turned or empowered only as those who suffer and are revolted at injustice and destruction, as those who long for something different, and so, in some significant measure, and as Albert Camus's

242. H. Richard Niebuhr, "War as Crucifixion," 63–70.

243. Reinhold Niebuhr, *NDM*, 2:61.

244. Hans Jonas, *The Imperative of Responsibility* (Chicago: University of Chicago Press, 1984), 27.

character in *The Plague*, Dr. Rieux, might put it, protest and fight against the world as we find it.[245]

What needs emphasizing here is that, for the faithful, not only does the cross illumine current situations, but contemporary experiences also contribute to the meaning of the cross. Believers are able to discern the meaning of Jesus's sacrifice with greater clarity through the tragic suffering of others in their own times and places. Present experiences are not only like Jesus Christ; as they are reinterpreted and redescribed in the light of the cross, they demonstrate the same dynamic.[246]

Hope

Somewhat paradoxically, then, we must also note that, when combined with Jesus's resurrection-exaltation, the right nightmare brings *persistent hope*. This is so partly because the exaltation of the kingdom-minded one, or his ascension to God's right hand, symbolically indicates that deity vindicates Jesus and his mission. It expresses the apprehension that, though apparently cut down and defeated in history, Jesus's teaching, manner, and power, rather than, say, Caesar's, accord with the true peace of God's reign. It insists that Jesus as the Christ, the kingdom-minded one who attends to the vulnerable, remains the true criterion of human life, history, and society under God.

How so? If the right nightmare and appropriate revulsion function in something like the way I suggest, then the *memoria passionis*, with its vector toward contrition and remorse, is itself a feature or an aspect of saving grace and possibility because it changes the meaning of our sin and the tragic suffering it causes. Ordinarily, our sins and the misdirected or constricted hearts (the loyalties, attitudes, purposes, dispositions, and intentions) they express build up a misshapen social ethos and become embedded in customs, institutions, and expectations. These structures, in turn, help to shape the emotional constitutions of others, and thus engender skewed affectivities and manners of living in others. They build up structural and suprapersonal forces of evil whose destructive malice threatens chaos and despair. This is what Friedrich Schleiermacher calls "the corporate dimension of sin," and it is, therefore, not too much to say, with him, that sin is "in each the work of all and in all the work of each."[247] There is in

245. Albert Camus, *The Plague*, trans. Stuart Gilbert (New York: McGraw-Hill, 1948), 116.

246. Douglas F. Ottati, *Meaning and Method in H. Richard Niebuhr's Theology* (Washington, DC: University Press of America, 1982), 82–87.

247. Schleiermacher, *CF*, ##69–72. Walter Rauschenbusch, who quotes Schleiermacher on this point, refers to a "solidaristic conception of sin," which he also sees in the work of Albrecht Ritschl. Rauschenbusch, *A Theology for the Social Gospel* (Louisville: Westminster John

this sense a socially embodied power of sin at work in the world, or, to employ a more ancient vocabulary, a "reign" or a "kingdom" of sin and evil. This is, at one level, precisely what the cross emphasizes and underscores. Nevertheless, when encountered and interpreted with the aid of the right nightmare and appropriate revulsions, our sins and the innocent suffering they cause become occasions for repentance, a change of heart, and hope. They are enlisted in the service of regeneration. For persons of piety, the cross turns sin's power against itself because the very occasions that otherwise help to build up and contribute to sin's kingdom are transformed into occasions for revulsion and remorse. Sin's solidaristic dominion becomes a house divided; Christ's victory in defeat turns the very fact of sin and its infectious power toward repentance, reconciliation, and renewed life.

Thus, in the view of Christian piety, there is a deep structure in things that can bring fellowship and new possibilities out of the destructive consequences of sinful misdirection and inordinate self-assertion. Piety does not say that therefore sin ceases to exist, only that its power and dominion are dealt a serious blow. It does not say that therefore we see divine righteousness and justice vindicated, only that we glimpse emergent traces of an alternative kingdom, reign, or excellence. And yet this is why, even in the face of seemingly intractable conditions of alienation, corruption, injustice, and destruction, Christian piety hopes nevertheless for a truer life and better circumstance by way of repentance and reconciliation.

Consider this same dynamic now not only with respect to the many "Calvaries" of World War Two and the children of Cologne and Coventry mentioned by H. Richard Niebuhr, but also with respect to the thousands of lynchings of African Americans in the United States during the nineteenth and twentieth centuries.[248] The Harlem Renaissance poet Countee Cullen writes these lines in "The Black Christ," which portrays a lynching and was published in 1929.

Knox, 1997), 93. Gustavo Gutiérrez is concerned that theology spell out "structures of sin" in the current economic order, or the "aspects of our socio-economic structures [which] create and maintain unjust inequalities," among them "the fact of, . . . and the justifications of, the primacy of profit and the absolute character of the market." Gustavo Gutiérrez and Gerhard Ludwig Muller, *On the Side of the Poor: The Theology of Liberation*, trans. Robert A. Kreig and James B. Nickoloff (Maryknoll, NY: Orbis, 2015), 100–101.

248. The exact number is not known. See Angela D. Sims, *Ethical Complications of Lynching: Ida B. Wells's Interrogation of American Terror* (New York: Palgrave Macmillan, 2010), 77. See also "The Waco Horror," an account by a special agent of the NAACP, in *Witnessing Lynching: American Writers Respond*, ed. Anne P. Rice and Michele Wallace (New Brunswick, NJ: Rutgers University Press, 2003), 150, which contains a table of "Colored Men Lynched by Years" from 1885 to 1916, and records a total of 2,843.

How Calvary in Palestine
Extending down to me and mine,
Was but the first leaf in a line
Of trees on which a man should swing
World without end in suffering
For all men's healing, let me sing.[249]

The crowds, the public gatherings that accompanied the "strange and bitter crop" noted by Cullen, Billie Holiday, and others, may indicate an even closer parallel to Christ's crucifixion than is the case with some other "Calvaries."[250] (Surely, the *intention* of the public spectacles, namely, to reaffirm established white supremacy and to terrorize and keep another people "in their place," also contributes to the likeness.)[251] In any case, Cullen's "The Black Christ" revisits a theme that he explored in an earlier poem published in 1922 and whose title, "Christ Recrucified," makes what for Christian piety is surely a crucial connection.[252] Langston Hughes's 1922 poem "Christ in Alabama," which ends with the lines "Ni**er Christ, On the cross of the South," does, too.[253]

James H. Cone says, "the cross is a reminder that the world is fraught with many contradictions—many lynching trees," an observation that, when it comes to the brutal murders of African Americans in the United States, is absent from the writings of white American theologians from Edwards and Rauschenbusch to Reinhold Niebuhr.[254] The critical matter is that "the cross and the lynching tree interpret each other," and that they be remembered together. Apart from

249. *Countee Cullen: Collected Poems*, ed. Major Jackson (New York: Library of America, 2013), 162.

250. The opening verse of "Strange Fruit," written by Abel Meeropol in 1937 and sung by Holiday and others, is "southern trees bear strange fruit, blood on the leaves and blood at the root, Black bodies swinging in the Southern breeze, Strange fruit hanging from the poplar trees." As Cullen notes in his stunning poem, which he "Hopefully" dedicates "to White America," the lynching party "dragged" their victim "out to be, Queer fruit upon some outraged tree." *Countee Cullen*, 162, 183. The parallel is also made with some frequency by drawings, lithographs, and paintings included in antilynching exhibitions of 1935 and reviewed in Dora Apel, *Imagery of Lynching: Black Men, White Women, and the Mob* (New Brunswick, NJ: Rutgers University Press, 2004), 83–131.

251. Apel says, "in the South, lynching evolved into a semiofficial institution of terror against blacks" that bolstered white rule (*Imagery of Lynching*, 23).

252. *Countee Cullen*, 238.

253. Rice and Wallace, *Witnessing Lynching*, 269.

254. James H. Cone, *The Cross and the Lynching Tree* (Maryknoll, NY: Orbis, 2011), 161. Clearly, too, the disproportionate numbers of African American men who continue to be incarcerated in the United States (and also to be subject to the death penalty) raise important and related questions.

the lynching tree, the cross is in danger of succumbing to false pieties. "Yet the lynching tree needs the cross, without which it becomes simply an abomination. It is the cross that points in the direction of hope." (Cone also says when he heard and read of the torture and abuse at Abu Ghraib prison in Iraq, he "thought about lynching.")[255] Indeed, he claims, only when the evils of the cross, the lynching trees, and the many "Calvaries" are taken and remembered together is there hope "beyond tragedy."[256] We might also note that, following the lynching, Cullen's "The Black Christ" goes on to depict a resurrection appearance framed by the doorway of the house from which the victim was dragged, as well as a change in the tree from which he was hung.

> For there he stood in utmost view
> Whose death I had been witness to;
> But now he breathed; he lived; he walked. . . .
>
> But where had swayed that misery
> Now only was a flowering tree
> That soon would travail into fruit.[257]

All this, I think, gestures toward an image and idea of atonement that focus on Christ's suffering endurance. The revelatory occasion in which the kingdom of God draws near imparts the power to change hearts, and so it alters the situation of misdirected humans. For Christian piety, Christ's suffering does not eliminate sin's tragedy; neither does it make sin or tragedy good, but it points to new possibilities. Now sin and the consequent suffering of the kingdom-minded, the vulnerable and the innocent, compose a moving, costly, and tragic occasion for the possibility of renewed life. Now suffering and death need not be the only or the last word. Now, through cruciform spectacles, we glimpse possibilities for renewal beyond tragedy. The redemptive power of Christ's suffering is that it lends transformative force to other occasions of unearned and unjust suffering. This, finally, is the "awe full" and also awful mystery of the cross. To those who

255. Cone, *The Cross and the Lynching Tree*, 161, 164.

256. Cone, *The Cross and the Lynching Tree,* 167. I take Cone's point to be similar to the one I am making here. Apel makes a related point about the ways in which we remember images when she notes that the gruesome photos of lynchings were intended to bolster the commitments of those who participated in lynching bees. The later appropriation of these photos "by the intended victims," she says, "subverted their purpose of valorizing whiteness and vilifying blackness by transforming the photographs into weapons against the terror of white supremacy" (*Imagery of Lynching*, 43).

257. *Countee Cullen*, 191.

are perishing it is dark folly, but to persons of piety it mediates a divine power made perfect in weakness that calls into existence things that are not.

This picture of atonement, or the reconciling of persons to the divine excellence, purpose, and reign, retrieves elements of a number of classical statements, though it does not repeat any single classic articulation of that doctrine. I underscore the suffering of the kingdom-minded one due to our sins but do not duplicate Anselm's emphasis on the penal satisfaction of divine honor. I emphasize a personal bond of affection by indicating how Christ's suffering elicits a change of heart, but, unlike Abelard, I link this elicitation to nightmares and revulsions. I affirm something like Luther's focus on "Christ's work as a conflict and triumph," or the conquest of sin and the devil through Christ the victor, but in order to do so I deploy a corporate or solidaristic notion of sin developed by leading liberal theologians during the nineteenth and twentieth centuries. In fact, my interpretation, with its emphasis on the continuing suffering of the kingdom-minded and the vulnerable due to sins of the guilty, like H. Richard Niebuhr's vision of "war as crucifixion," would not be possible without Horace Bushnell's work on "the vicarious sacrifice." The claim that Jesus's crucifixion can alter the meaning of our sin and its tragic consequences owes much to this American theologian, who delivered his manuscript on Christ's work to his publisher as the nation mourned Lincoln's death.

The Civil War, Bushnell dared to think, "could be good in some way akin to the way in which Good Friday was good."[258] Anyone who has seen the casualty statistics as well as the photos of fighting men and of fields filled with corpses from that war must surely find this a chilling sentence. And so, just here it seems especially important to comment on Jesus's last words in Mark 15:34 and Matthew 27:46: "My God, my God, why have you forsaken me?"

Jürgen Moltmann's profound and highly revisionist Trinitarian meditation on Jesus's cry of dereliction in *The Crucified God* rightly emphasizes agony and abandonment. God suffers, says Moltmann. Indeed, suffering, death, and hope are taken up into the Trinitarian history of God, so that God the Trinity—the Son suffering abandonment and pain, and the Father suffering the death of the Son—becomes, in Alfred North Whitehead's phrase, "the fellow sufferer who understands."[259] Moreover, Moltmann says that events of human suffering in history, for example, Auschwitz, affect God, and that the divine pathos sup-

258. Sidney E. Ahlstrom, *A Religious History of the American People* (New Haven: Yale University Press, 1972), 686.

259. Jürgen Moltmann, *The Crucified God: The Cross of Christ as the Foundation and Criticism of Christian Theology*, trans. R. A. Wilson and John Bowden (New York: Harper & Row, 1974), 255–56.

ports a form of human life that sympathizes with those who suffer.[260] Still, he also recognizes that even if "Auschwitz is taken up into the grief of the Father, the surrender of the Son and the power of the Spirit," this "never means that Auschwitz and other grisly places can be justified." Only eschatologically, "only with the resurrection of the dead, the murdered and the gassed, only with the healing of those in despair . . . only with the annihilation of death" will sorrow turn to eternal joy.[261]

My own speculative reticence also leads me to note Hans Küng's insistence that "the cross is not the symbol of the 'suffering,' 'screaming God,' . . . but the symbol of humanity suffering the distress of death."[262] On the cross, the one commissioned by God, the kingdom-minded one, suffers innocently due to the sins of many. Like Reinhold Niebuhr and James H. Cone, I want to affirm a message of hope in tragedy that is illumined by the crucifixion-resurrection-exaltation sequence and does not devolve into a false optimism.[263] I want to affirm a victory in defeat that points to new possibilities for reconciliation and life that track the emergent reality of the kingdom. Indeed, I see a kind of analogy between this and what I said in part 2 about cosmic passage and the emergence of new ensembles and realities from component parts, at least some of which parts result from the dissipation and dissolution of previous ensembles.

What must not be lost sight of, however, is that, while they furnish a ground for persistent hope, the Word and its basic pattern of new possibilities emerging out of tragedy, defeat, and destruction do not erase tragedy, defeat, and destruction. There is always a bad and sometimes an overwhelming remainder. I am enough of a dipolar theist to affirm a divine creativity that is not all-controlling; thus, I do not find God indictable for suffering and evil. But even a less-than-all-controlling divine creativity that somehow manages to turn forces of sin and destruction toward emerging possibilities nevertheless leaves something like Job's existential circumstance in place. Perhaps, in a larger scheme of things that we do not entirely comprehend, the sufferings of creatures who feel intensely and that accompany destruction, dissolution, injustice, and death are a kind of price paid for the emergence of new possibilities. But this will not and should not keep either Job or us from faithfully speaking the anguish of our spirits and truthfully complaining in the bitterness of our souls (Job 7:11).

Similarly, we may say that possibilities for renewed life, community (or

260. Moltmann, *The Crucified God*, 272.

261. Moltmann, *The Crucified God*, 278.

262. Hans Küng, *Credo: The Apostles' Creed Explained for Today* (New York: Doubleday, 1992), 87.

263. Reinhold Niebuhr, *Beyond Tragedy: Essays on the Christian Interpretation of History* (New York: Scribner's Sons, 1937), 18–21.

church), and even life eternal emerge from Jesus's crucifixion-resurrection-appearances. But his cruciform suffering, abandonment, and agony remain, and indeed the pattern as a whole—the emergence of new possibilities from tragedy and defeat—also calls for lament and complaint. This is one reason why the words from Psalm 22:1 on the lips of the crucified Christ in Mark and in Matthew are theologically and humanly appropriate and profound, even (and perhaps especially) if we also note the trajectory toward deliverance later in the psalm. "My God, my God, why have you forsaken me?" As we have seen, the gospel traditions vary at this point, and Jesus's last words in Luke and in John appear to express trust in God and the completion of his mission. But if we keep these variants as well as their theological significance in mind, we may also say that we have systematic reasons here to focus on Christ's last words in Mark and in Matthew. Like Job's anguished protests concerning everything from the unearned and overwhelming nature of his own sufferings to the injustice and violence of the wicked—but now on the lips of an actual and executed person—Jesus's cry of dereliction remains a passionate prayer that voices an agonized complaint, and that, as in the book of Lamentations, also presumes a continuing relationship with the divine.

Küng calls Jesus "the image of the sufferer par excellence," and he contrasts this image, as presented in Grunewald's Isenheim Altarpiece, with portraits of Gautama Buddha as the Enlightened One.[264] He also says that, in "the suffering and dying 'servant of God' (cf. Isa. 52:13–53:12), the man of grief from Nazareth," we find no entirely satisfying theoretical solution to the problem of suffering. I agree. Jesus as the Christ, the crucified and remembered victim whose cry of dereliction gives haunting voice to lament and complaint, provokes a response to the problem of suffering that moves along more practical and pastoral lines.

Accompaniment

And this brings us, I think, to the second and related feature of the dangerous memory and right nightmare: the remembrance of the suffering victim empowers Christians to accompany those who suffer. The issue here is largely one of discernment. When we remember and commemorate them Christianly in the context of the *memoria passionis*, when we envision them in the frame of the right nightmare, then we see that the many "crucified victims of history" are Christ's companions.[265] We see that they inhabit the place or the space of the

264. Küng, *Credo*, 55–56.

265. Roberto S. Goizueta, *Christ Our Companion: Toward a Theological Aesthetics of Liberation* (Maryknoll, NY: Orbis, 2009), 18.

crucified one; they walk where Jesus walked. Indeed, as Roberto S. Goizueta points out, very often, whether at the hands of isolating and alienating poverty and injustice or at the hands of debilitating and isolating vulnerability and disease, this is a place or a space apart, an abandonment, a being-cut-off like "the abandonment experienced by Jesus on the cross."[266]

Thus, we should say that the agonized crucified one encourages those who suffer to voice their own expressions of lament and dissatisfaction and agony. We may say, too, that when people suffer unjustly or die alone and in agony, Jesus has been there, insisting that, despite everything, even though "God does not preserve us from all suffering," God may nevertheless be addressed as hiddenly present.[267] After all, the one who says "My God, my God, why have you forsaken me?" still addresses "my God." In this sense, the sufferer is neither simply nor merely alone. Now, perhaps even in the vision of the suffering victim, the dangerous memory illumines and underscores the crucified one as the suffering companion to whom God remains strangely present.

That God remains present, and perhaps hiddenly and strangely so, need not mean that God is the power or agent determining the circumstance and its outcome. It need not mean that, were we to know more, there would be a clear divine "intention" to be read off of every event. We need, I think, to appreciate dimensions of divine presence that do not reduce to determining will, biblically and liturgically aided inklings that may furnish comfort to those who suffer even in instances of forsakenness and abandonment. If we do, then we may also repeat the Apostle's stirring affirmation that "neither death, nor life, nor angels, nor rulers, nor things present, nor things to come, nor powers, nor height, nor depth, nor anything else in all creation, will be able to separate us from the love of God in Jesus Christ our Lord" (Rom. 8:38–39).[268]

But this stirring message of divine presence and love needs at least a partial, practical, and pastoral embodiment in the midst of trying and destructive realities by the church as Christ's body, now in the form of the companion who has been there, now in the form of a caring community that accompanies and does not abandon wounded sufferers and victims. It needs enactment now in the form of a companion that does not minimize loss and fear, now in the form of a community and institution that remembers and laments and protests undeserved suffering and, wherever possible, also struggles against it. The cross encourages

266. Roberto S. Goizueta, *Camineros con Jesus: Toward a Hispanic Theology of Accompaniment* (Maryknoll, NY: Orbis, 1995), 180.

267. Küng, *Credo*, 92.

268. See my earlier discussion of Sarah Edwards's interpretation of the death of her husband in chap. 4, prop. #33. Does she imply, perhaps, that God is present as a determining power or intentional agent because her Calvinism keeps her from imagining other possibilities?

Christians to adopt a robust and pastoral stance of accompaniment or companionship that begins to overcome alienating barriers, boundaries, and separations. It encourages them to cultivate a "'being with' people in difficult and threatening circumstances" that does not presume to resolve every difficulty and threat, and does not presume to "do for" those who often suffer in contexts that we may "hardly begin to understand."[269]

Goizueta says this is a step toward liberation, since accompaniment begins to restore persons from dehumanizing abandonment to genuine relationship. "Suffering shared," he says, "is already suffering in retreat." Certainly, we may hope so. Minimally, we may say that accompaniment is an appropriate step toward reconciliation and true community taken in hope by a ministry of reconciliation.

The church may foster a piety that senses the presence of the God of the crucified one with those who walk the path he did. Indeed, it seems possible to be a Christ to the neighbor only when one begins to see Christ in and with one's neighbor's vulnerabilities and sufferings. "For I was hungry and you gave me food, I was thirsty and you gave me something to drink, I was a stranger and you welcomed me, I was naked and you gave me clothing, I was sick and you cared for me, I was in prison and you visited me" (Matt. 25:35–36).

Easter

On Easter Sunday, of course, we are also and joyously compelled to acknowledge something more, but not, I think, the intellectual speculations of some theologians and philosophers about the possible metaphysics of Jesus's resurrected body. These speculations—insistences that Jesus's resurrection body "was physical (i.e., it took up space, could be located, could be seen under certain conditions, etc.), but also in some sense supernatural (which accounts for the 'spiritual' motifs in Paul and some of the appearance stories in the Gospels)," and the like—risk leading piety astray toward a somber and anxious emphasis on right belief. They threaten to turn Easter Sunday into a spiritual test, a reminder that things will go well for you if only you believe the right stuff about Jesus's resurrected body.[270] No. On Easter, or so it seems to me, we are called to acknowledge the triumph expressed in a passive construction.

269. C. Matthews Samson, "The Martyrdom of Manuel Saquic: Constructing Maya Protestantism in the Face of War in Contemporary Guatemala," *Social Sciences & Missions* 13 (October 2003): 63.

270. Stephen T. Davis, *Risen Indeed: Making Sense of the Resurrection* (Grand Rapids: Eerdmans, 1993), 58–59. See also Douglas F. Ottati, *Hopeful Realism: Reclaiming the Poetry of Theology* (Cleveland: Pilgrim, 1999), 63.

When, in Mark 16, Mary Magdalene, Mary the mother of James, and Salome go to Jesus's tomb "very early on the first day of the week, when the sun had risen," a young man in a white robe tells them not to be afraid. Then he says, "You are looking for Jesus of Nazareth, who was crucified. He has been raised; he is not here. . . . Go, tell his disciples and Peter that he is going ahead of you to Galilee; there you will see him." The passive construction "he has been raised" invites the question, "Raised by whom?" And the answer here, as in Paul, is that God, the almighty maker of heaven and earth, has raised Jesus. Therefore, Jesus's resurrection tells us some things about God.

- God endorses Jesus of Nazareth, the one who has been crucified. *The victim becomes the victor*. Together with the ascension, then, God's raising of Jesus means that God exalts the one of low birth who proclaimed a kingdom that reverses current orders, the one who taught love of neighbor and even enemies.
- God's raising of Jesus means that Jesus is going ahead of you to places where you shall see him. The crucified one whom God raised is going ahead of you to appear and be present in faithful community, worship, the Lord's Supper, etc., and so to empower you to take up the renewed and true life in relation to God and neighbor.
- Recall, too, that the Gospels place Good Friday and Easter in the context of Passover, the celebration of God's deliverance of Israel from Egypt. Thus, the events of Good Friday and Easter and Jesus's subsequent appearances constitute the gathering of the church as an expansion or an opening of God's deliverance to "all nations" (Matt. 28:19) or even "the whole creation" (Mark 16:15). Or, again, in Pauline terms, they are the events in which we participate as we die and rise with Christ. They signal that God overcomes alienation and unjust and destructive forces of human history to bring about new possibilities, renewed life, and new community.

So, on Easter Sunday, the Christian community celebrates the triumph of God's faithfulness and grace in the continuing presence of the kingdom-minded one as well as our participation in it. Easter, the day of resurrection, is, in the words of the hymn, a "triumphant and holy day." It is a day on which we pray that God will bring new life where we are worn and tired; solace, reconciliation, and forgiveness where we are hurt and where we have wounded others; renewed love and affection where we are hard-hearted; freedom for good and for justice where we have been imprisoned by our constricted interests and destructive practices.

In Sum . . .

To return at last to our proposition, by his crucifixion and continuing presence, Jesus as the Christ empowers a way in life that aligns with the divine excellence, or with his proclamation of the kingdom as well as with the alternative manner of his performance, ministry, and mission. His cross—as both dangerous memory and right nightmare—illumines. It becomes a revelatory and intelligible event. It hangs over other occasions when the kingdom-minded and the vulnerable suffer consequences of the sins of others (including our own), and so, by his costly sacrifice, he enables sinners to reinterpret, repent, and walk in a newness of life that, among other things, gives voice to agony and complaint, and also endeavors truthfully to accompany those who suffer and lay sick and dying. This newness of life is true and eternal. It mirrors the God of grace, the excellent gratuity of the one who, even in the midst of suffering and alienation, bestows possibility and life and calls into existence things that are not.

The New Testament scholar Willi Marxsen says the words "Jesus is risen" essentially mean "the cause of Jesus continues; or in the words of the hymn, 'still he comes today.'"[271] I agree, but the basic argument of this chapter compels me to add that still he comes today as a patterned and articulated presence or identity in the instruction, preaching, sacraments, and mission of the church. Still he comes today as the crucified one who teaches the truth of God's kingdom and who embodies and empowers a renewed manner in life that accords with the truth. His continuing presence has a decisive impact on the shape of Christian piety, and it illumines the world.

271. Willi Marxsen, *The Resurrection of Jesus of Nazareth*, trans. Margaret Kohl (Philadelphia: Fortress, 1970), 138–41.

Chapter Nine

The Spirit and the Church

The Holy Spirit belongs together with Jesus as the Christ in the economy of redemption. This is clear from the third article of the Apostles' Creed, which aligns the Spirit with "the holy catholic Church, communion of saints [or those who are being sanctified], the forgiveness of sins, the resurrection of the body, and the life everlasting." The Nicene Creed adds rather importantly that the Spirit is "the giver of life." We therefore turn now to the Spirit, the giving and renewing of life, and the gathering of the church.

Proposition #55 The Spirit gives and renews life.

Orthodox Calvinists sometimes distinguish general and special operations of the Spirit, the former having to do with the life of the natural creation and the latter with redemptive new life.[1] We have reason today to contemplate the possibility that God's Spirit may bestow life rather regularly in the cosmos and also well beyond the confines of planet Earth. This, at least, is a potential implication of recent conjectures by astrobiologists that life may be a widely distributed development of cosmic chemistry.[2] In any case, the traditional affirmation is that the Spirit gives *and* renews life. We might say that God's Spirit or breath bestows living dynamism or the energy of interdependent life at the creation, and that it bestows true life through baptism, participation in the church, the communion of saints, and the life everlasting. Because sin is a falling away from the truth and the life that befits us, when the Spirit bestows true life, it also renews life;

1. Louis Berkhof, *Systematic Theology*, new edition containing the full text of *Systematic Theology* and the original *Introductory Volume to Systematic Theology* (Grand Rapids: Eerdmans, 1996), 426.

2. Ximena C. Abrevaya et al., "The Astrobiology Primer v2.0," *Astrobiology* 16, no. 8 (2016): 562–63.

the Spirit restores us to the end, calling, and manner of living for which we have been fitted and sustained all along.

Some Initial Reflections

Classical thinkers often align the Spirit especially with sanctification—the basic idea being that, with respect to "the order" of "the external operations of the persons of the Trinity" in the world, the person of Spirit is specifically concerned with making holy, the person of the Father especially with creation, and the person of Son especially with reconciliation. Even so, of course, because for orthodoxy the three persons are one divine being, these works are performed in such a way that they are "none the less common to the three persons."[3] Martin Luther claims in commentary on the Apostles' Creed that the third article is about the Holy Spirit, and that the "office" or function of the Spirit "is to make holy or vivify."[4] The Spirit, says Luther, sanctifies, and the process or work of sanctification extends from our baptism or entrance into the people of God to its completion with "the life everlasting." For Luther, then, the third article of the creed has wide-ranging sacramental, ecclesial, and eschatological dimensions, and it is not, as some early theologians feared, simply a hodgepodge list of things that for one reason or another failed to make it into the first two. It names matters especially connected with the Spirit's particular function or purpose.[5]

3. Heinrich Heppe, *Reformed Dogmatics: Set Out and Illustrated from the Sources*, ed. Ernst Bizer, trans. G. T. Thompson (Grand Rapids: Baker Books, 1978), 116.

4. Martin Luther, "The Creed," in *Sermons I*, ed. John W. Doberstein, vol. 51 of *LW*, 166.

5. J. N. D. Kelly says that, when initially formulated, the third article of the Roman Creed consisted of "a string of miscellaneous credenda," and that "it occasioned embarrassment in certain quarters to find a series of lesser items ranged alongside the Person of the Holy Spirit." But Kelly also says "certain thoughts, we may be sure . . . were present in the believer's mind as he stepped down to the waters of baptism. He could scarcely forget . . . that it was the Holy Spirit Who sanctified the faith of the community and enlightened it with knowledge of the truth. It was the Spirit too, he had been taught, . . . Who had been active in the ancient prophets. . . . It was the Spirit Who filled the Church, Who guaranteed immortality and eternal life, Who gave efficacy and power to the sacraments, and Who could be bestowed upon him," renewing him "in the great process of baptism which he was now undergoing." *Early Christian Creeds*, 3rd ed. (New York: Continuum, 2006), 152, 155. On balance, Luther takes up this second interpretation.

In a later Reformed scholastic and somewhat technical vocabulary, the matters listed in the third article are, as to their manner, the "personal" or "proper" operations or works of the Spirit. This accords with "an order of operations" among the persons of the Trinity: the Father creates or inaugurates things, the Son reconciles or redeems, and the Spirit consummates, sanctifies, or regenerates. Though it should be remembered that, for the scholastic orthodox

Translated as literally as possible into English, *Credo in Spiritum Sanctum* means "I believe in the Holy Spirit." "Ghost" is an older and by now rather unhappy English translation of *Spiritum*. The Spirit is not an apparition or a magical being of an animistic sort. It is not the kind of thing contacted in a séance, or that occasionally appears on late-night TV and in more than a few Hollywood movies. Indeed, Hans Küng notes that, according to Pope Benedict XIV (1745), the Spirit can only be depicted symbolically in the form of a dove. It is God's invisible yet powerful activity or influence.

The Hebrew word *ruach*, which has parallels in a number of ancient and modern languages, signifies wind, breath, or a movement of air. It is the "'storm' of God which moves over the waters" in Genesis 1.[6] In Genesis 2:7, once "the LORD God formed man from the dust of the ground, and breathed into his nostrils the breath of life . . . the man became a *living* being." Here, in a verse that reflects a longer ancient tradition and prehistory concerning the creation of humans as well as other creatures out of the earth, God's Spirit enlivens.[7] It bestows the life principle that renders beings living, and, indeed, Psalm 104 claims that when God withdraws God's breath, creatures die. In Genesis and also in Psalm 104, God's breath enlivens humans as well as every animal in the wider context of the whole creation and its interdependent orderings. They are enlivened to live and move or to participate in this ordered and interdependent environment. The Greek word *pneuma* was used for the Hebrew *ruach* in the Septuagint, and so has a similar range of meanings in that translation. In the New Testament, *pneuma* often refers to a living power of God that grasps persons inwardly and renews their lives in a manner that contrasts with the corrupted misdirection of life called "the flesh."[8] Biblically speaking, then, the Spirit is a dynamic and creative force, an energizing and moving divine presence intimately associated with life-giving dimensions of both creation and redemption.

The preposition "in," which occurs at the beginning of each of the three articles of the creed, also deserves comment. Rufinus insists that it goes with the

---

theologians, every personal or proper operation or work of one person of the Trinity is also, by definition, a "common operation" or work of all since the three are one God, deity, or divine being. See Heppe, *Reformed Dogmatics*, 115, 116, 118.

6. Hans Küng, *Credo: The Apostles' Creed Explained for Today* (New York: Doubleday, 1992), 123–24.

7. Claus Westermann, *Genesis 1–11: A Continental Commentary*, trans. John J. Scullion, SJ (Minneapolis: Augsburg, 1984), 204–7; W. Sibley Towner, *Genesis* (Louisville: Westminster John Knox, 2001), 77.

8. Küng also notes that, during the seventeenth century, Pope Urban VIII banned artistic representations of the Spirit in human form and a century later Pope Benedict XIV decided that the Holy Spirit may be depicted in the form of a dove, and that this decision was reaffirmed by the Roman Holy Office in 1928. *Credo*, 124–25.

Holy Spirit rather than with the other items listed in the third article.[9] Calvin concurs. "We testify that we believe *in* God because our mind reposes in him as truthful, and our trust rests in him." To say "*in* the church," he claims, "would be as inappropriate as" to say "'*in* the forgiveness of sins' or '*in* the resurrection of the body.'"[10] This accords with a distinction in English between "believing *in*" someone or some idea and "believing *that*" something exists, that it is or was the case. Believing *in* suggests an investment of trust and confidence. Thus, I *trust* and *have confidence* in the Creator, who bestows life and existence. Indeed, I rely on my Creator. I *trust* and *have confidence* in Jesus Christ, who reconciles by teaching the truth, embodying the way, and empowering the life. And, when I recite the creed, I affirm that I *trust* and *have confidence* in the Spirit to render us living and to make us holy, to vivify, to sanctify, to inaugurate, and to bring to completion not just any life pattern or direction in life but true life.[11]

The Spirit Orients and Directs

God, Christ, and Spirit (2 Cor. 13:13)—for the Christian community, these three belong together because historic and experiential Christian piety links the trajectory of the all-governing Creator, the Christ or wisdom and will of God in person, and the Spirit or power that gives and renews life. To live truly in response to the Creator's governance in nature and history—to be genuinely, existentially, and practically responsive to it—one may take up the ec-centric manner in life disclosed in Jesus as the Christ. And to take up this ec-centric manner in life requires that we be turned, that our minds and hearts be reoriented and enlarged by the work of the Spirit.

Accordingly, the Spirit is not an inchoate animating energy. Reformed theologians, such as Louis Berkhof, therefore say it originates, maintains, develops, and guides.[12] The key point for our purposes is that the Spirit energizes and also orients. It moves people in a manner and direction that accord with the gracious divine trajectory in creation and redemption; it enlivens them in a manner that accords with the pattern, activity, life, and ministry of Jesus as the Christ. Indeed, the divine Spirit renders creatures living and breathing beings, which, if

9. Kelly, *Early Christian Creeds*, 152.

10. Calvin, *ICR* 4.1.2.

11. Somewhat like Rufinus, Küng, *Credo*, 132, makes the point that, in the Apostles' Creed, the preposition "in" does not precede "the holy catholic church," thus indicating that we trust in the Spirit and only derivatively or secondarily in the church. Perhaps we should say we trust that the church is among the media through which the Spirit sanctifies and regenerates.

12. Berkhof, *Systematic Theology*, 426.

we recall Psalm 148, are to praise and glorify God as they live and breathe. From the hand or the breath of the Creator, as it were, their living creaturely dynamic has a doxological tendency and direction.

Or, again, in John 14:26 Jesus says the helper, or "Advocate, the Holy Spirit, whom the Father will send in my name, will teach you everything, and remind you of all that I have said to you." Paul claims in 1 Corinthians 12–13 that the Spirit of God apportions appropriate gifts or charismata, culminating in the gift of love, to those who participate in Christ's body or the church. As it sanctifies and enlivens, the Spirit moves people in the way of Christ, and, when he discusses life in the Spirit in Romans 8, Paul associates "the Spirit of Christ" and "the Spirit of God" quite closely.

First Peter makes similar points. The "Spirit of Christ" within the prophets, which testified in advance to Christ's sufferings, is associated here with "those who brought you good news by the Holy Spirit sent from heaven" (1:11–12). The claim, then, is that, taught by the Spirit, the faithful are to trust in God, hope in God, and have genuine love for one another (1:21). According to Calvin, this is because the perfection of the faithful consists in love, though "nothing is more difficult than to put our mind to love our neighbors."[13] First Peter says we are to live as free people who do not use their freedom as "a pretext for evil" but to serve God (2:16), and that Christ serves as our example even in suffering (2:21). "In short," says Calvin, "it is a free servitude, and a serving freedom."[14] A Christian life of freedom in the Spirit takes the Christlike form of love, and thus, Calvin says, 1 Peter also details "one of the duties of love," or hospitality (4:9), even as it admonishes the faithful to "serve one another with whatever gift each of you has received" (4:10).[15]

A critical matter, then, is that, by referring to this pattern, direction, or way, we may distinguish the *Holy* Spirit from other energies, forces, or spirits—say from the spirit of sexual dominance that orients some people, or from the spirit of one or another commercial enterprise, nation, or political movement. Calvin therefore insists, "Word and Spirit belong inseparably together." The true Spirit is "the Spirit of Christ," and it does not orient and direct us in just any manner or way whatever, but in ways that accord with directives and patterns we find in Jesus as the Christ and that are "commended by the gospel."[16]

13. John Calvin, *The Epistle of Paul the Apostle to the Hebrews and the First and Second Epistles of St. Peter*, trans. William B. Johnston, *Calvin's New Testament Commentaries: A New Translation*, ed. Thomas F. Torrance and David W. Torrance (Grand Rapids: Eerdmans, 1963), 252.

14. Calvin, *Hebrews*, 272.

15. Calvin, *Hebrews*, 304.

16. Calvin, *ICR* 1.9.1–3.

A hymn by Isaac Watts well describes the role of the Spirit in the affectively charged and reorienting renewal of persons.

> Come, Holy Spirit, heavenly Dove,
> with all thy quickening powers,
> kindle a flame of sacred love
> in these cold hearts of ours.[17]

Represented classically in the form of the dove that descends at Jesus's baptism and that is symbolic of divine communication and empowerment, the Spirit quickens and enlivens. It warms our cold hearts by kindling a sacred love in them. Or, as the last stanza says, into our hearts it sheds "abroad a *Savior's* love" (emphasis added). The love or affection that the Spirit kindles in us has its originating pattern in Christ. As it gives and renews life, the Spirit's enlivening powers redispose, redirect, and reorient persons' affective and motivating centers with a Christlike affection and in a Christoform shape and direction.

Again, this is why Paul stresses in Galatians 5:13–15 that we are called to freedom in Christ not in order to use our freedom "as an opportunity for self-indulgence, but through love [to] become slaves [or servants] to one another." For, he continues, "the whole law is summed up in a single commandment, 'You shall love your neighbor as yourself.'" His admonition in 5:16 to "live by the Spirit" rather than "gratify the desires of the flesh" follows directly on the heels of this recommendation. Why? Because, for Paul, life in the Spirit has a different emotional dynamic, pattern, and norm than does the self-indulgent orientation of "the flesh." Life in the Spirit takes up a Christoform disposition characterized not by self-preoccupation and inordinate self-interest but by the true, other-directed summary and fulfillment of the law. Works of the flesh include idolatry, enmity, strife, jealousy, anger, and dissension; "by contrast, the fruit of the Spirit is love, joy, peace, patience, kindness, generosity, faithfulness, gentleness, and self-control" (5:22–23). This, then, is how sinners are placed or located in Christ. "Those who belong to Christ Jesus have crucified the flesh with its passions and desires" (5:24). Their old selves, their previous orientations, "the flesh," have died, and they themselves have been raised or remade for a new (and ec-centric) life of love in the Spirit. Moreover, as a number of commentators stress, for Paul, love

17. *Glory to God: The Presbyterian Hymnal* (Louisville: Westminster John Knox, 2013), #279. Watts's hymn, originally entitled "Breathing after the Holy Spirit; or Fervency of Devotion Desired," illustrates his concern for lively affective religion, and the idea that "the Spirit kindles our love for God by making us aware of God's saving love for us and, thus, enables us to sing his praise." Graham Beynon, *Isaac Watts: Reason, Passion, and the Revival of Religion* (London: T&T Clark, 2016), 2, 9–11, 163.

is not one virtue among others but an affection that embraces the other virtues, which he sometimes lists as concrete ways in which love may be expressed.[18]

All this needs to be kept in mind as we read Galatians 5:25, a verse that, according to Hans Dieter Betz, "contains [Paul's] ethic in a nutshell."[19] "If we live by the Spirit, let us also be guided by the Spirit" (alternatively, "let us walk by the Spirit," "let the Spirit also direct our course," or "let us follow the Spirit"). Enlivened by the Spirit, we are not to become "conceited, competing against one another, envying one another" (5:26), but we are to "bear one another's burdens, and in this way . . . fulfill the law of Christ" (6:2).

Paul makes similar points in Romans 8 when he explores how the Spirit of God empowers the new life of the Christian. Those who live according to the flesh, he says, are hostile to God and to God's law; they do not love God and neighbor but are self-preoccupied or self-centered. But now Christ has rescued human beings from enslavement to sin and the flesh, and has enabled them to live "according to the Spirit" (8:5). In fact, the Spirit is "the vivifying power of the risen Christ himself (1 Cor. 15:45)," and "thus 'God's Spirit' has also become for Paul 'Christ's Spirit.'"[20] It is this Spirit (of God and of Christ), now dwelling in the Christian (Rom. 8:9–11), that shapes her or his life, so that, in this respect at least, the idea of law may now be applied to the Spirit, that is, "the law of the Spirit of life" (8:2).

Paul offers a series of instructions in Romans 12 that outline more concrete dimensions of new life in the Spirit. Transformed by the indwelling Spirit, Christians are to offer their lives as a kind of worship and to renew their minds or whole way of thinking (12:1–2). They should live together as one body in which the many members use their varied gifts—prophecy, ministry, teaching, leadership, etc.—for all (12:6–8). They are to love one another with mutual affection (12:10), rejoice in hope, be patient in suffering, and persevere in prayer (12:12).

18. See Victor P. Furnish, *Theology and Ethics in Paul*, 3rd ed. (Louisville: Westminster John Knox, 2009), 88. Charles Cousar, *Galatians* (Atlanta: John Knox, 1982), 139–40, cites Furnish, and claims that, for Paul, love is not one virtue among the others, for example, patience, but "the sum and substance of what it means to be a Christian." Indeed, says Cousar, Rom. 13:8–10 suggests that Paul may very well regard love as both the summation and the completion of the law. "For the one who loves another has fulfilled the law. . . . Love does no wrong to a neighbor; therefore, love is the fulfilling of the law" (131).

19. Hans Dieter Betz, *Galatians: A Commentary on Paul's Letter to the Churches in Galatia* (Philadelphia: Fortress, 1979), 293.

20. Joseph Fitzmyer, SJ, *Romans: A New Translation with Introduction and Commentary* (New York: Doubleday, 1993), 480. See Rom. 8:9–11. This, according to Fitzmyer, when in 1 Cor. 15:45 Paul says that the last Adam has become "a life-giving Spirit." Joseph Fitzmyer, SJ, *First Corinthians: A New Translation with Introduction and Commentary*, Anchor Yale Bible (New Haven: Yale University Press, 2008), 591–96.

They should contribute to the needs of others in the community and also "extend hospitality to strangers" (12:13). Indeed, says Paul, in words reminiscent of the teachings of Jesus, "Bless those who persecute you. . . . Rejoice with those who rejoice, weep with those who weep. . . . Do not repay anyone evil for evil. . . . Live peaceably with all." He also quotes Proverbs 25:21–22, "'If your enemies are hungry, feed them; if they are thirsty, give them something to drink.'" In this way, he admonishes the faithful to "overcome evil with good" (Rom. 12:20–21) by being compassionate and refusing to promote evil or to become like those who injure—a way that, in fact, has been taken up by a number of nonviolent protests and movements.[21]

Calvin on the Holy Spirit and Faith

Calvin develops many of these ideas systematically. The Holy Spirit, he says, is called "the 'Spirit of sanctification' [cf. 2 Thess. 2:13; 1 Pet. 1:2; Rom. 1:4] because he not only quickens and nourishes us by a general power that is visible in the human race and in the rest of the living creatures, but he is also the root and seed of heavenly life in us."[22] So, the Spirit is the source of life in creation and also the source of heavenly life. The Spirit is the source of the life of living creatures as "a general power," and it is "the root and seed" of new or heavenly life in us because it is "the bond that unites to Christ," or "the secret energy . . . by which we come to enjoy Christ and all his benefits."[23] Apart from participation in the Spirit, "no one can taste either the fatherly favor of God or the beneficence of Christ."[24]

Calvin's basic point is that "faith is the principal work of the Spirit." That is, the Spirit is "the inner teacher" by which the promise of grace and mercy in Jesus Christ "penetrates into our minds, a promise that would otherwise only strike the air and beat upon our ears."[25] Faith is a kind of knowledge. More specifically, for Calvin, it is a "higher knowledge," rather than a more common human sense perception, and it persuades us that "God is faithful."[26] Or, again, in commenting on Ephesians 1:3, Calvin says, "the Spirit seals the truth of the gospel on your

21. Fitzmyer, *Romans*, 659. Karl Barth says, "the being and work of Jesus Christ . . . must now be understood as the being and work of his Holy Spirit," and that here we have to do with "the subjective apprehension of the reconciliation of the world with God made in Him." *CD* IV/1:147.

22. Calvin, *ICR* 3.1.2.

23. Calvin, *ICR* 3.1.1.

24. Calvin, *ICR* 3.1.2.

25. Calvin, *ICR* 3.1.4.

26. Calvin, *ICR* 3.2.14.

hearts."[27] The Spirit "confirms" us in the gospel promise of divine mercy and salvation. "The true conviction which believers have of the Word of God, of their own salvation, and of all religion, does not spring from the feeling of the flesh, or from human and philosophical arguments, but from the seal of the Spirit who makes their consciences more certain and removes all doubt."[28]

In this way the Spirit makes preaching, or the presentation of the truth of the gospel of Christ, efficacious. And this, returning now to Calvin's discussion in his *Institutes*, is "the chief hinge on which faith turns: that we do not regard promises of mercy that God offers as true only outside ourselves, but not at all in us; rather that we make them ours by inwardly embracing them. Hence, at last is born that conscience which Paul elsewhere calls 'peace'" (Rom. 5:1).[29]

Calvin can therefore say that "the Word of God is not received by faith if it flits about in the top of the brain, but when it takes root in the depth of the heart."[30] The salvific pedagogy of the Spirit entails both the illumination of the mind and the conviction or confirmation of the heart. "Each . . . is the work of the Spirit,"[31] but the latter is more difficult to accomplish. Indeed, "if it is true that the mind's real understanding is illumination by the Spirit of God, then in such confirmation of the heart his power is much more clearly manifested, to the extent that the heart's distrust is greater than the mind's blindness. It is harder for the heart to be furnished with assurance than for the mind to be endowed with thought."[32]

Calvin defines faith as "a firm and certain knowledge of God's benevolence toward us, founded upon the truth of the freely given promise in Christ, both revealed to our minds and sealed upon our hearts through the Holy Spirit."[33] The Spirit, then, is critical for our "knowledge of God's benevolence toward us" because, as our inner teacher, it dispenses a heartfelt apprehension or assurance; it convinces us that, in Jesus as the Christ, God is gracious *to us*. And, in doing so, the Spirit makes possible what, from the very beginning of his *Institutes*, Calvin regards as true religion or piety—"that reverence joined with love of God which a knowledge of his benefits induces."[34] God is, and has always been, "the

27. John Calvin, *The Epistles of Paul the Apostle to the Galatians, Ephesians, Philippians, and Colossians*, trans. T. H. L. Parker, *Calvin's New Testament Commentaries: A New Translation*, ed. Thomas F. Torrance and David W. Torrance (Grand Rapids: Eerdmans, 1965), 131.

28. Calvin, *Galatians*, 131.

29. Calvin, *ICR* 3.2.16.

30. Calvin, *ICR* 3.2.36.

31. Calvin, *Galatians*, 132.

32. Calvin, *ICR* 3.2.36.

33. Calvin, *ICR* 3.2.7.

34. Calvin, *ICR* 1.2.1.

fountain of every good," but it takes the event of Jesus Christ coupled with the persuasive pedagogy of the Spirit for us to recognize and acknowledge this fact. Once we do, we are freed *from* inordinate concern for ourselves, or what in our fallen state Paul identifies as the basic dynamic of "the flesh," and we are freed *for* a faithful obedience in Christ that looks to the interests of others and bears one another's burdens.

Thus, when Calvin comments on the regenerate life in Romans 12, he says that, by appealing to Christians "to present [their] bodies as a living sacrifice," Paul means "we must cease to live to ourselves" and instead devote ourselves to God's service. Our former life must "be destroyed in us" so "that we may be raised up to a new life,"[35] and this new life has a definite pattern, that is, being members of one body, loving one another with mutual affection, relieving "our needy brethren."[36] Indeed, the new life also entails extending hospitality toward strangers, and this, says Calvin, is partly due to their heightened vulnerability. "For these are the most destitute of all, since they are far away from their own kindred. . . . We see, therefore, that the more a man is disregarded, the more attentive we ought to be to his wants."[37] And, of course, to do and to see these things is to be made holy, to be involved via the Spirit in the process of sanctification.

The Spirit and a Sense of the Divine Excellence

A feature of Calvin's pneumatology, then, is that anyone who is alive (anyone who breathes the breath of life) has an experience of the Spirit as the source of life in creation, or as a general power in the human race and the rest of living creatures. Especially in our own time, as we become increasingly aware of the cosmic, chemical, planetary, evolutionary, and ecological interdependencies and complexities of life, this ought not to be passed over too lightly. There is, in the ordinary but also routinely magnificent experience of living, a quickening and enlivening, an energy and dynamism that is of the Spirit, if only we are able to attend to it and discern it.

A second feature of Calvin's doctrine is that anyone who has genuine faith or piety has a heartfelt experience of the Spirit as "the root and seed" of new life. Thus, despite what some contemporaries may say or imply, experiences

35. John Calvin, *The Epistles of Paul the Apostle to the Romans and to the Thessalonians*, trans. Ross Mackenzie, *Calvin's New Testament Commentaries: A New Translation*, ed. David W. Torrance and Thomas F. Torrance (Grand Rapids: Eerdmans, 1973), 263–64.

36. Calvin, *Romans*, 273.

37. Calvin, *Romans*, 273.

of the Spirit are not confined to dramatic episodes and occurrences of glossolalia or prophecy. Indeed, for Calvin, the heartfelt fulcrum of our experiences of the Spirit as giver of both life and new life is an apprehension, appreciation, or sense of the divine beneficence. This is the "knowledge" that can move us to live our lives as a kind of worship and to extend our affections and attention toward others. This is the Spirit that sanctifies, pushing us toward a Christoform and ec-centric pattern of living partly by relieving us of the need to secure our own worth.

Turn now to another Reformed theologian. Jonathan Edwards, in the midst of religious revival, writes in his *Treatise on Religious Affections* as a pastor concerned to distinguish true religion or piety as the work of the Spirit. At one point, he notes a "natural gratitude [that] may be the foundation of a sort of love to God in many ways."[38] This gratitude is finally sinful or corrupted, a sort of gratitude that springs up in persons from the reception of outward benefits and from "a false notion of God" as one who "loves them above most in the world, and has engaged to improve all his infinite power and wisdom in preferring, dignifying, and exalting them, and will do for 'em just as they would have him" (244, 245). There is, however, also "a gracious gratitude," which differs rather sharply from all this, and has a different foundation in those who are being sanctified by the Spirit. These people, whom Edwards calls the saints, "do not first see that God loves *them*, and then see that he is lovely; but they first see that God is lovely, and that Christ is excellent and glorious; their hearts are first captivated with this view, and the exercises of their love are wont from time to time, to begin here . . . and then consequently, they see God's love, and great favor to them" (246). Thus, "in a gracious gratitude," people are affected with "the attribute of God's goodness and free grace, not only as they are concerned in it, or as it affects their interest, but as a part of the glory and beauty of God's nature" (248). This is a gratitude that, for Edwards, arises "primarily from the excellency of divine things as they are in themselves" (249). Or, again, for "the love of the true saint, God is the lowest foundation," but "the hypocrite lays himself as the bottom of all, as the first foundation . . . and even his acknowledgment of God's glory itself, depends on his regard to his private interest" (246).

The distinction, for Edwards, is crucial. Genuine love of God finds God inherently lovely; false love of God finds God lovely primarily and perhaps only because God is thought to have utility for the self and its interests. Gracious gratitude sees the excellence of God's great works of creation and reconciliation; corrupted gratitude is affected by God's grace only as we ourselves are concerned

38. Edwards, *Religious Affections*, ed. John E. Smith, vol. 2 of *WJE*, pt. III, II, p. 244. Hereafter, page references from this work will be given in parentheses in the text.

in it. How does Edwards's distinction square with Calvin's insistence that the principal work of the Spirit is faith and that faith and piety are founded on the heartfelt knowledge of the divine benevolence and of God as the fountain of every good?

My two favorite Reformed theologians may not be saying precisely the same thing here, but before we conclude that they differ irreconcilably, we should recall that, despite his emphasis on the divine benevolence, Calvin's more general ruminations about the sovereign God clearly do not commit him to the idea that God guarantees the good in all relevant respects either for humans generally or for the saints in particular. There is ample room in the Reformer's theology for an apprehension of God that includes elements of sublimity, awe, mystery, and fear, and it would be a mistake to think that, for Calvin, we should love God only because God has utility for us. Consider, for example, his insistence that "the Holy Spirit aids right prayer" partly by tempering our emotions, and that, when we pray, we should be "moved by God's majesty" and "not . . . ask for more than God allows."[39] Then, too, while Edwards points to a form of gratitude that is not based primarily in God's utility for us, he also recognizes the divine benevolence.

In addition, Calvin and Edwards offer similar portraits of the ec-centric orientation in life that results from the Spirit's pedagogy and sanctifying work. Calvin describes this orientation as one of self-denial in the service of God, a form of living that takes up the disposition or attitude we see in the mind of Christ. This, as we have seen, is how he interprets Paul's admonition in Romans 12:1 to present ourselves to God as a living sacrifice. The indwelling Spirit renews our minds so that we subordinate self-concern to God's will, have reverence for others, and make use of our gifts for the neighbor's benefit.[40] Edwards calls the orientation that results from the Spirit's work "true virtue," a "benevolence to being in general" that goes beyond all partial loves to self and limited communities, such as the family or the nation.[41] It is true that, for Edwards, some less extensive loves, devotions, and moral sensibilities have something of true virtue in them, to the extent that they carry us beyond mere regard for ourselves toward attentiveness to and mutual service of some others. They move in the same direction as true virtue, though they do not extend as far; love of family and love of nation count as examples. Moreover, like true virtue, they may also restrain wickedness. "So, natural affection, love to our party, or to particular friends, tends to keep us

39. Calvin, *ICR* 3.20.5–6. Indeed, he complains that "many rashly, shamelessly, and irreverently dare importune God with their improprieties and imprudently present before his throne whatever in dreams has struck their fancy." *ICR* 3.20.5.

40. Calvin, *ICR* 3.7.1–5.

41. Jonathan Edwards, *Two Dissertations, Dissertation II: The Nature of True Virtue*, in *Ethical Writings*, ed. Paul Ramsey, vol. 8 of *WJE*, chap. 1, p. 540.

from acts of injustice towards these persons. . . . Pity preserves us from cruelty."[42] But there is also in true virtue, says Edwards, a more radical enlargement of chronically constricted human hearts and sensibilities, so that our affections now extend to God and the things of God, or to all things.[43]

Parenthetically, in his later *Lectures on the Essence of Religion*, the nineteenth-century philosopher Ludwig Feuerbach claims that when confronted with a threatening world, persons and communities are rendered anxious and insecure. They therefore imagine a personal being who transcends the world and possesses supernatural powers. As they conceive it, this imaginary being, in turn, saves them from the world's threats, grants them their desires and wishes to flourish, and thus relieves them from anxiety and insecurity.[44]

The existential dynamic that Feuerbach identifies sometimes ensnares people in what amounts to a sort of magic—practices (and perhaps even formulas of words) that are thought to encourage or constrain God (or the gods) to act on their behalf. Perhaps someone will pray in order to encourage or constrain God to heal a person who otherwise would die. Perhaps a prominent figure will argue that America will enjoy safety and prosperity if only Americans believe in God and go to church. Maybe a preacher will tell his hearers in Houston and around the world that God wants them to be wealthy and successful.

Edwards would agree that this sort of piety or religion really does amount to the projection onto an imaginary god of our heartfelt preferences and desires. Calvin might add that this is how we fashion God "according to our own presumption."[45] In these cases, there is no genuine encounter with a reality that pushes back; finally, all that we encounter are our own wants and desires writ large. The difference, of course, is that Feuerbach thinks this is the only sort of religion there is, whereas Calvin and Edwards think there is an alternative.

42. Edwards, *True Virtue*, vol. 8 of *WJE*, chap. 7, p. 616.

43. Edwards, *True Virtue*, chaps. 4–7, pp. 575–618. Similarly, H. Richard Niebuhr points to "radical monotheism," a sort of faith or piety that values whatever is because it entails loyalty to the universal community of beings with God at its head. *Radical Monotheism and Western Culture, with Supplementary Essays* (Louisville: Westminster John Knox, 1993), 31–37. See also H. Richard Niebuhr's chapter entitled "Introduction to Biblical Ethics," in *Christian Ethics: Sources of the Living Tradition*, ed. H. Richard Niebuhr and Waldo Beach (New York: Random House, 1988), 34–35.

44. In this way, the "feeling of anxiety, of uncertainty, this fear of harm that always accompanies man, is the root of the religious imagination." Ludwig Feuerbach, *Lectures on the Essence of Religion*, trans. Ralph Manheim (New York: Harper & Row, 1967), 40. Quoted by Van A. Harvey, *Feuerbach and the Interpretation of Religion* (Cambridge: Cambridge University Press, 1995), 182.

45. Calvin, *ICR* 1.4.1; 1.4.3; 1.11.8.

A Contemporary Restatement

I am ready now, with appropriate caution and within rather important and intractable limits, to make my own proposal. Return, first of all, to a point made above by Hans Küng, and one that fits with the negative dimension of theology I discussed in part 2.[46] Pope Benedict XIV claimed that the Spirit, a kind of dynamic and divine impetus, influence, force, communication, and living power, was to be represented only symbolically in the form of the dove that descends on Jesus at his baptism in the Gospels. There is wisdom in Benedict's reticence, and so what I say here will retain an indirect and symbolic cast, even an air of imprecision or ambiguity.

One basic point is that the Spirit renews life by rendering compelling and attractive to us the patterns or dynamics of the God of grace and of Jesus as the Christ. This is the Spirit working as our inner teacher; this is its saving pedagogy—to seal in the heart what Calvin calls the "higher knowledge" of God's faithfulness and benevolence so that it does not merely "flit about in the top of the brain." This is also what Edwards calls a new spiritual sense, a taste for the excellence of God and Christ that the "natural" or corrupted person finds difficult to grasp or understand because it does not reduce to the fulfillment of our own wants and desires. The excellence of God and Christ—a phrase that refers to the bestowal of existence and dynamic life in the whole creation, to sustaining orderings whose regular functions sometimes also bring suffering and destruction, and to a process of redemption marked by the right nightmares and revulsions as well as the death of the old person and the emergence of the new—is sure and true. But it does not reduce to utility for us. This is why the Spirit's work, or the proper illumination of mind and heart, is so difficult: it entails an assurance of God's goodness that concerns us but not only or even preeminently us. We want a god who will protect and guarantee the goods we desire, but we meet a God whose gracious tendency displays an excellence or glory that extends far beyond our regard for ourselves and our private or isolated goods and interests. That is, to modify Edwards's quote, the Spirit's illumination traffics in something other than "a false notion of God" as one who "loves us above most of the world, and has engaged to improve all his infinite power and wisdom in preferring, dignifying, and exalting us, and will do for us just as we would have him."

Another way to put this is to say that the Spirit, which in-spires all living creatures to praise God (Ps. 148), is also an inner and redemptive pedagogue that brings about in us *a correction or transformation* of vision and affection. The Spirit enables us to appreciate and discern the excellence and the beauty

46. Chap. 6, prop. #42.

of what we may call the *Divine Project*—the creation, sustenance, and renewal of an entire and vast cosmos of which we are finally only a part.[47] Indeed, the Spirit enables us to appreciate and discern the excellence of a divine endeavor that entails the cruciform death of our old selves even as it brings about the emergence of the new. What the Spirit enables in us, then, is an appreciation for being a participant in the cosmos and of having a place and a time, rather than being the one thing God loves above all else. This, in turn, constitutes the deep foundation for a gratitude that is not constricted but proper, gracious, and capacious. It is also the basis for a kind of peace, assurance, and rest that derives from the heartfelt knowledge of participating in Something More and Something Greater—the Divine Project or even, as the hymn says, the divine "re-creation of the new day."[48] The Spirit enables us to discern the excellence of the God of grace, whose tendency it is to bestow existence and life on all things and gather them up into the Divine Project. *Consequently*, as Edwards says, we see God's great love to us, since, by the grace of God, we certainly also participate in the Divine Project.

To get at another important dimension of this discernment, ponder Job 38, where God answers Job "out of the whirlwind." For much of the epic poem, Job has been asking for an opportunity to contend with God over the clear injustice of his own plight as well as many of the wider injustices in the world. But now God changes the subject by asking a series of questions in chapters 38 to 42. "Have you commanded the morning since your days began? . . . Have you entered into the springs of the sea, or walked in the recesses of the deep? . . . Where is the dwelling place of light? . . . Can you draw out Leviathan with a fishhook, or press down on it with a cord?" The effect is to humble Job, and some commentators emphasize that God does not really respond to either Job's questions or his plight, but merely pulls rank and even diminishes Job. Here, however, I want to focus on a feature of the initial verses of chapter 38.

> Then the LORD answered Job out of the whirlwind:
> "Who is this that darkens counsel by words without knowledge?
> Gird up your loins like a man,
> I will question you and you shall declare to me.

47. What I mean here is something like what Augustine does near the end of his *Confessions*, trans. Maria Boulding, OSB, ed. John E. Rotelle, OSA, vol. 1 of *WA*, 375–76. He says, while the Manichees view the world in the conviction that it was put together by "a hostile intelligence," those "who see creation through your Spirit" see "that everything is good which in any degree has being."

48. Eleanor Farjeon, "Morning Has Broken," in *The Hymnbook* (Richmond, VA: Presbyterian Church in the United States, 1955), 389.

> Where were you when I laid the foundation of the earth?
> Tell me if you have understanding.
> Who determined its measurements—surely you know!
> Or who stretched the line upon it?
> On what were its bases sunk,
> or who laid its cornerstone
> when the morning stars sang together
> and all the heavenly beings shouted for joy?" (38:1–7)

William Blake renders the scene recounted by the second half of the last question (v. 7) in an unforgettable block print that shows the morning stars and the heavenly beings celebrating against a blue background. Why are they singing and shouting for joy? The answer is that they have just now seen the commencement of the Divine Project. They have just now witnessed the beginning of the creation; they have just now been issued the divine invitation to participate in the whole, dynamic, and interdependent ensemble. And so, here we see portrayed yet another basic dimension of the participatory energy of created life and existence, namely, a genuinely appreciative and often irrepressible joy and delight at being a part of the cosmos.

In any case, the constricted person, curved in upon her or his isolated interest, may not experience this sense, taste, or emotion. Edwards claims, "the natural man discerns nothing of it, (1 Cor. 2:14) any more than a man without the sense of tasting can conceive of the sweet taste of honey; or a man without the sense of hearing can conceive of the melody of a tune; or a man born blind can have a notion of the beauty of the rainbow."[49] The "new sense" for the excellence of divine things expands anxious, constricted selves. It frees us from having to prove our selves and our worth, it frees us to appreciate the excellence of a created ensemble that is not centered on us, and it does not reduce to utility for us. It is a new sight or new vision that appreciates the excellence of a kingdom in which the vector of new and true life is to look to the interests of others, and to love even enemies. So the Spirit now becomes, as it were, the corrective spiritual lenses that enable us to see excellence and glory in the Divine Project, in the dynamic of crucifixion and resurrection, and in the reorientation that characterizes renewed life and the kingdom. Edwards says this is the work of the Spirit of God in regeneration, and that "the giving of this new sense, with the blessed fruits and effects of it in the soul, is compared to a raising of the dead, and to a new creation."[50]

With this in mind, return to the idea that, in the midst of creation's interde-

49. Edwards, *Religious Affections*, 208.
50. Edwards, *Religious Affections*, 206.

pendent orderings, the Spirit bestows the participatory energy of life. The orderings obviously are interconnected in natural and social networks and ecologies, for example, valleys, oceans, families, societies. These, in turn, also are interconnected within broader environments. All living things, including humans, are parts of these wider wholes, networks, and ecologies. Ultimately, they participate in the whole interdependent ensemble. The energy or élan of living things is, in this sense, a participatory one. The vibrancy and movement of life is always situated, and, in its situation, it always points to a wider ensemble or set of realities, relations, conditions, and orderings. Recent astrobiologists emphasize this situated, interrelated, interdependent, and participatory character of life when they claim "life is a planetary process."[51] In any case, the energy of created life or its élan has a participatory trajectory that tends toward relatedness and keeps the individual from referring only to itself, and it is what Christians call the Spirit that gives or bestows created life with this participatory energy.

What the Spirit Is

The Spirit may be described in nonpersonal terms as a divine energy or force that we never encounter or experience by itself or in isolation from all else but always in conjunction with, always mediated in and through, other objects, realities, and processes. An experience of the reality of the Spirit is therefore at the same time an experience of something else, and indeed, these other things—these media—are what allow us to speak of a discernible pattern, form, and content. The basic analogy I have in mind is between the Spirit and *the ethos of a community*, a vitality, an animating principle or power that has a describable pattern and trajectory, and so may energize, sculpt, and orient in specifiable ways, but that we always experience in and through particular structures, interactions, customs, persons, and processes. We experience the Spirit as something akin to an energizing and impelling ethos.

Consider the media through which we experience the Spirit as represented in some biblical texts. We surmise from Genesis 1 and 2, as well as from classical theology, that the Spirit has to do with the animating breath of God, the bestowal of life and vitality in creation. This, says Calvin, is "a general power" in humans and the rest of living creatures. And we should observe that God's creative and energizing activity in Genesis is itself characterized by orderings and interrelations that render the elements of creation (light, land, plants, animals, humans,

51. Eric Smith and Harold J. Morowitz, *The Origin and Nature of Life on Earth: The Emergence of the Fourth Geosphere* (Cambridge: Cambridge University Press, 2016), 2–5. Indeed, Smith and Morowitz say, "life is defined by participation in the biosphere" (591).

etc.) somewhat and also significantly self-sustaining, regenerating, and interdependent.[52] (You may remember this the next time you observe a bird singing, foraging for food, etc. At some level, we share a common energy.) In Genesis, however routinely or improbably, life on Earth, both human and otherwise, emerges in the midst of things, both inorganic and organic. Humans and other living creatures are commissioned with powers of movement and generativity. They are enmeshed in orderings, processes, and social relations, and, as we are now increasingly aware, their activities, including agriculture, help to shape their planetary environment.

We might say, in a more contemporary vocabulary, that the multitudinous media in and through which we encounter and experience the general power of God's life-giving Spirit include the chemical and physical elements, the genome sequences and sustaining social relationships, the institutions, practices, and activities, etc., by which we are brought forth, sustained, and shaped for living together. Moreover, the ethos that comes to expression in the interrelations, powers, and processes portrayed in Genesis and elsewhere in the Bible is one of *participatory interdependence*. People and other creatures are not made to be alone, but to live in relation with other persons, animals, plants, etc. The Spirit of God, the ethos of the cosmos, is an energy that enlivens and forms creatures, including humans, as participants with distinctive powers of movement and interaction—in fact, if we consult Psalm 104, with participatory powers or capacities that are appropriate to their places within the larger, wider, and dynamic whole. This accords with the basic dynamic of God the Creator I noted at the close of part 1; it pushes creatures outward, it orients us ec-centrically toward God and others.

The world as God creates and sustains it, then, is a matter of relationships, interactions, and orderings. We may observe that even the most elementary particles do not exist independently as isolated entities, and the same is true for plants, animals, and humans. Particles and parts exercise their vitalities in the midst of things and are characterized by an ineluctable connectedness. Indeed, as William P. Brown says, "the process is the point."[53] The elements or parts of creation are neither powerless nor slavish; they share a level of power that is acknowledged and employed within the world and its interdependent interrelations. We experience the Spirit, in and through various media, as an enlivening

52. William P. Brown, *The Ethos of the Cosmos: The Genesis of Moral Imagination in the Bible* (Grand Rapids: Eerdmans, 1999), 15–17, 48. I have found the title of Brown's book as well as its argument suggestive, though the use of the phrase "the ethos of the cosmos" to refer to the Spirit is my own.

53. Brown, *The Ethos of the Cosmos*, 47.

vitality, an influence, power, wind, breath, or élan of interconnected and participatory movement, activity, and creativity.

Viewed in a Christian frame of reference, however, the participatory tendency or energy of human life is now corrupted and constricted. Human life is now less than true. Yes, its participatory energy points beyond the individual alone toward families, tribes, nations, and other communities, but human life is now truncated and skewed, so that its participatory reference or pointing is diminished and falls short. Certainly, and as Edwards notes, even in this corrupted and diminished state, we see something of true and participatory attentiveness to others in the devotions to limited and partial communities that ordinarily characterize human life. Love of family, tribe, or nation often carries people beyond simple egoism, or beyond a literal devotion to and care for *only* oneself. Such devotions routinely support significant service to and care for at least some others, and they also may restrain cruelties and injustices. At the same time, however, and with a train of deleterious consequences, this too limited or constricted participatory tendency and trajectory often also results in a kind of in-group preference or collective egoism that devalues and even despises others beyond our partial and limited communities of concern. Our ordinary human visions, devotions, and patterns of attentiveness therefore need to be expanded.

In Genesis, the story of humanity therefore soon takes a salient turn toward corruption, isolation, and alienation. Humans turn away from the skein of interdependent interconnection and participation within which and for which they are created and sustained. They take a wrong turn that comes to vivid expression in Cain's haunting question, "Am I my brother's keeper?" (Gen. 4:9). A cycle of recurrent violence, misdirection, and corruption therefore characterizes the story in Genesis of the emergence of human society and civilization, and it betrays a deep and persistent fault, an isolating and alienating constriction of the human that brings with it a train of destructive existential, social, and environmental consequences. A claim of the New Testament is that the reconciling, regenerating, and renewing event-of-Jesus-as-the-Christ addresses this fault.

This is why, when it comes to redemption, the Holy Spirit is, in a Christian frame of reference, not only the giver of life but also the renewer of life or the Spirit of regeneration and sanctification. It is also the Spirit of Christ or of the more radically other-directed ethos of Jesus as the Christ. As the Spirit of Christ, it focuses, clarifies, renews, re-presents, and intensifies the participatory ethos of creation. It enlarges the participatory trajectory and tendency of human life by eliciting a new sense for the excellence of participating in the divine ensemble, a vast project that affords us a place and a time but is not simply centered on us and our partial communities. Following Augustine, then, we may say that this new sense enables persons to delight in the excellence of the wider ensembles, to discern that, while the individual parts are good, together and coordinated in ensemble they are *very* good.[54] Again, to employ a Pauline vocabulary, the advent of this sensibility means the crucifixion of the old or constricted self and the resurrection or emergence of a renewed and enlarged participatory self. It means being re-turned and reoriented toward the encompassing excellence of God's reign or kingdom, and it means the emergence of a new identity and renewed self-understanding.

As the ethos and pattern of Jesus as the Christ, the Spirit focuses, specifies, and intensifies the participatory energy of life in the cosmic ensemble. Here we find that the Spirit is a Spirit of freedom characterized not by self-indulgence but by service in the Christlike form of love. Here we find a Spirit that encourages us to "bear one another's burdens, and in this way . . . fulfill the law of Christ" (Gal. 6:2). Here, rather than spirits or ethoi of dominance, conquest, or manipulation, we encounter a Spirit that encourages us to contribute to the needs of brothers and sisters and also to practice "hospitality to strangers."

In the pastoral logic of the Epistles, it therefore follows that this Spirit of freedom that is bound up with Christ is also bound up with the ethos of the body of Christ—with a church in which each member is invited to "love one another" (1 John 3:11) and to exercise her or his particular gift or "manifestation of the Spirit for the common good" (1 Cor. 12:7). The Holy Spirit, the ethos of participatory created life and the ethos of Christ, shapes the ethos of the church or the body of Christ that comes to expression in and through its members, their interrelations, their practices of worship, study, mission, and so on. The Spirit of Christ energizes, forms, and informs a church that, however symbolically and fragmentarily, points beyond itself to the true communion with God in community with others that reflects the participatory dynamic of created life and the life-restoring salvific pattern and message of Jesus as the Christ or his kingdom-mindedness.

The Spirit and the Kingdom

Consider now the close connection between Spirit and kingdom. The Spirit prepares people for the kingdom;[55] this, after all, is a part of the meaning of regeneration and the bestowal of renewed life as people are adopted as God's children. The Spirit moves people toward a manner of living embodied in Christ, a life oriented toward the interests of others in a community of mutual love and service. It turns people toward love of God and neighbor, or toward loyalty to

54. Augustine, *The Confessions*, vol. 1 of *WA*, 373–74, 377.

55. James D. G. Dunn, *Pneumatology*, vol. 2 of *The Christ and the Spirit: Collected Essays of James D. G. Dunn* (Grand Rapids: Eerdmans, 1998), 133.

and communion with God in community with others. The Spirit makes effective the call to repentance (the crucifixion of the old self and the emergence of the new) and the kingdom. The Spirit instigates a new identity in Christ. This much is clear from Paul's admonition to "live by the Spirit" (Gal. 5:16) in a Christoform disposition, a willingness to "bear one another's burdens, and in this way . . . fulfill the law of Christ" (Gal. 6:2).

Again, in the Gospels, the divine Spirit, the breath of truly participatory and ec-centric life, anoints Jesus the alternative king who preaches and performs the kingdom. The risen Jesus teaches about the kingdom, and when the apostles ask whether this is the time when he "will restore the kingdom," he tells them they "will receive the power when the Holy Spirit has come upon" them (Acts 1:6–8). James D. G. Dunn concludes that the Spirit's presence is the "already" of the kingdom in the midst of you, and the inadequacy of humanity's recognition of and obedience to the Spirit means that the kingdom is "not yet."[56] All this accords with Calvin's claims about the Spirit of sanctification and the subordination of self-concern to God's will, as well as with Edwards's reflections about a true virtue and "benevolence to being in general" that go beyond partial loves to limited communities and so anticipate the kingdom. The communion of the Holy Spirit (2 Cor. 13:13) represents a confluence of "vertical" and "horizontal" relationships; the true communion with God in community with others displayed in Jesus as the Christ, in the Word, and fragmentarily anticipated in the church or the body of Christ, a "treasure in clay jars" (2 Cor. 4:7). Indeed, the Spirit that prepares people for and turns them toward the kingdom is therefore also the ethos of the new and alternative politics of Jesus.

Testing the Spirits

The association of the Spirit with the participatory energy of created life, Jesus as the Christ, the church as Christ's body, and the kingdom indicates how we may "test" the spirits or ethoi to determine which are holy. Does a particular piety or skein of affections, its prominent dispositions and practices, represent the participatory élan and joy of interdependent created life? Does it represent the ethos of Jesus as the Christ with its allegiance to the maker of heaven and earth, its concern for the neighbor (and most especially, the plight of the vulnerable), its welcoming practice of eating and drinking with everyone, and its healing touch? Does it build up and promote a community of mutual love, care, and service? Does it accord with the alternative ethos of God's coming reign?

Edwards notes important ambiguities as he negotiates religious revival. "'Tis

56. Dunn, *Pneumatology*, 138.

no sign that affections have the nature of true religion, or that they have not, that they have great effects on the body," or "that persons did not make 'em themselves, or excite 'em of their own contrivance."[57] Likewise, "it is no sign that religious affections are truly holy and spiritual, or that they are not, that they come with texts of Scripture, remarkably brought to the mind," that "they dispose persons . . . to be zealously engaged in the external duties of worship," or "that they make persons exceedingly confident" and assured of divine favor.[58] Instead, the Puritan pastor maintains, "gracious and holy affections have their exercise and fruit in Christian practice," and "Christian practice or a holy life . . . is *the chief* of all the signs of grace."[59] That is, the Holy Spirit disposes persons toward a gracious gratitude and faith and toward a true life of benevolence and building up community in mutual service, and so this disposition becomes the chief sign of its presence. But even this, according to Edwards, must remain a fallible test, since "the *witness* or seal of the Spirit consists in the *effect* of the Spirit of God in the heart," and external appearances give us no sure and direct access to persons' hearts.[60] To this, we may add that overly scrupulous and specific tests and determinations often are mistaken because, under varied and shifting circumstances, the many attitudes and practices associated with the ec-centric energy of created and graciously renewed life may be manifest in myriad ways and myriad combinations as well as with different relative emphases.

Paul admonishes the faithful to live "in a manner worthy of the gospel of Christ" (Phil. 1:27), and so the dispositions and practices that furnish evidence of the working of the true Spirit of God are those that accord with the Word. Calvin, too, is explicit; "the Holy Spirit is recognized in his agreement with Scripture."[61] Spirit and Word, or divine energy and the message of the gospel, go together because the Spirit of Christ does not inspire and guide persons and communities in paths that are opposed to the Word. Those who forsake this test, says Calvin, invent "new and unheard-of revelations" because "they have drunk of another spirit than that which the Lord promised his disciples" (*ICR* 1.9.1). Obviously, as Paul notes and as we have just noted above, the Spirit gives different gifts to different people, and the ethos of creation, Christ, and the body of Christ often come to fruition among persons in individual ways. When it comes to judging the spirits, it therefore makes good sense to exercise caution. Nevertheless, when we estimate the spirits of various movements, including those of Aryan and white

57. Edwards, *Religious Affections*, 131, 138.

58. Edwards, *Religious Affections*, 142, 163, 167.

59. Edwards, *Religious Affections*, 383, 406.

60. Edwards, *Religious Affections*, 420, 454.

61. Calvin, *ICR* 1.9.2. Hereafter, references from this work will be given in parentheses in the text.

supremacist groups that appropriate Christian symbols, as well as the spirits of allegedly clashing civilizations, quite traditional tests are as important today as they have been in any age. Roughly speaking, the question is whether the persons, communities, and movements in question represent genuine internalizations of the interdependent and participatory ethos of creation and the ethos of the gospel (or of Christ, the body of Christ, and the kingdom).

Appropriate Regard for Self

Now, for an additional note—though classical statements sometimes obscure it, there is room here for proper or appropriate self-regard. Hence, Calvin emphasizes "the denial of ourselves" as "the sum of the Christian life," and he claims that "the Christian philosophy" subjects itself to the Spirit and so "subordinates our self-concern . . . to God and his commandments" (*ICR* 3.7.1–2). He also insists, however, that God's gifts are distributed "for our good," and that they are used properly when they are "referred to that end to which the author himself created and destined them for us" (3.10.2). Thus, in Christian freedom, says Calvin, "we should use God's gifts for the purpose for which he gave them to us, with no scruple of conscience, no trouble of mind" (3.19.8).

These admonitions cohere because Calvin assumes that we often rush into a self-love that flatters and takes pride in ourselves, judges others to our own advantage, and despises "all others in comparison" (3.7.4). The denial of our misguided self-concern in devotion to God "gives us the right attitude toward our fellow men" because it undercuts this inordinate form of self-love and redirects us toward God and God's purposes. Indeed, having denied ourselves "in the service of the Lord," our proper love of neighbor is not merely a response to her or his merits or attractions (3.7.1).

> Say, "He is a stranger"; but the Lord has given him a mark that ought to be familiar to you, by virtue of the fact that he forbids you to despise your own flesh [Isa. 58:7, Vg.]. Say "He is contemptible and worthless"; but the Lord shows him to be one to whom he has deigned to give the beauty of his image. Say that you owe him nothing for any service of his; but God, as it were, has put him in his own place in order that you may recognize toward him the many and great benefits with which God has bound you to himself. Say that he does not deserve even your least effort for his sake; but the image of God, which recommends him to you, is worthy of your giving yourself and all your possessions. Now if he has not only deserved no good at your hand, but has also provoked you by unjust acts and curses, not even this is just reason why you should cease to embrace him in love and to perform the duties of love on

> his behalf [Matt. 6:14; 18:35; Luke 17:3]. You will say, "He has deserved something quite different of me." Yet what has the Lord deserved? (3.7.6)

We are, in fact, given gifts to use for our neighbor's benefit as we participate in the world of interdependent interrelations with others who bear our same flesh as well as the divine image. Commenting on the sixth commandment, then, Calvin mentions the image of God and our common humanity once again as he claims not only that all injury to our neighbor is forbidden to us but also that we are commanded faithfully to employ anything of use to us in saving our neighbors' lives, warding off anything harmful, and lending a helping hand (2.8.39–40).

This means, in effect, that we may have legitimate regard for ourselves in at least two related senses.

1. We should value ourselves as *participants* whose gifts of intellect, affect, and will may be cultivated, developed, and deployed in the various callings or lines of responsibility in which we stand. Calvin mentions our callings as magistrates and heads of households, and, if we consult the Puritan literature of practical divinity, we may add as parents, children, teachers, physicians, or what-have-you (3.11.6).[62] So, for example, if you are a physician, it is a matter of moral importance that you be a good one who has cultivated and continues to cultivate appropriate capacities of intellect and habits of practice. (The same thing is true of auto mechanics. When parents load their kids in the car to take a trip, they depend on the competence of the person who repaired the brakes.) We therefore both may and ought to cultivate the capacities or gifts we have been given in order that we may fulfill the general calling to glorify God by serving others and the "public" good of God's reign or kingdom. And we also have good reason to take appropriate satisfaction and delight in their exercise.

2. Since, like our neighbors, we too are made in God's image and we too are participants in the Divine Project, an appropriate respect and regard for ourselves also means that we may gratefully make use of and enjoy the many benefits God dispenses. In gratitude, "If we ponder to what end God created food, we shall find that he meant not only to provide for necessity but also for delight and good cheer. Thus the purpose of clothing, apart from necessity, was comeliness and decency. In grasses, trees, and fruits, apart from their various uses, there is beauty of appearance and pleasantness. For if this were not true, the prophet would not have reckoned them among the benefits of God, 'that wine gladdens the heart of man, that oil makes his face shine' [Ps. 104:15]."[63] The main principle

62. Douglas F. Ottati, *Reforming Protestantism: Christian Commitment in Today's World* (Louisville: Westminster John Knox, 1995), 117–25.

63. Calvin, *ICR* 3.10.2.

here is that these are gifts and goods to be delighted in and enjoyed, though, in the light of our inveterate tendency toward inordinate self-interest and self-love, Calvin also thinks we need to be reminded that they are not to be abused, "coveted too greedily," "proudly boasted of," or "lavishly squandered."[64]

I agree, but note that the corruption to be avoided is not an appropriate self-regard or sense of self-worth but what we might call an inordinate self-regard or a constricted self-love and self-concern. Calvin's theology of regeneration is quite compatible with an appropriate regard and respect for oneself that supports the cultivation and exercise of good capacities among participants in God's world, and it is also entirely compatible with an appropriate enjoyment of and delight in the many attractive gifts that God may shower upon us. Moreover, as I shall discuss in more detail on the topic of sin, there clearly is also such a thing as an insufficient or inadequate regard for oneself that may lead one to participate deficiently in God's world of responsibilities and good gifts.

Proper self-regard, in my own estimate at least, counts as an important gift of the Spirit. It accompanies and contributes to the ec-centric, enlarged, and participatory life toward which the Spirit, as both a general creative power and a catalyst of renewal, orients us in the midst of our many interdependent interrelations with others. It contrasts with an inordinate self-regard or self-love that too often accompanies the lesser spirits of our partial and closed communities and that leads us to contract and pull away from others, or even to denigrate and despise them. It contrasts with the inordinate self-regard and self-preoccupation that accompany alienating spirits and that undermine or diminish the good and abundant life of true communion with God in community with others for which we are created, sustained, and redeemed. It also contrasts with a deficient self-regard and self-confidence that sometimes dispose people—especially the victims of neglect and oppression—to overlook their free gifts and capacities, and thus to participate deficiently in God's world or even to disengage from that world. Proper self-regard is a feature of a Spirit-empowered conversion toward relationality, mutual interdependence, and service, and away from prideful individual and group egoism.[65] Indeed, a genuine or true love and regard for one's expansive, enlarged, and participatory self include a *joi de vive* that gratefully acknowledges having been invited to the party of existence, that discharges responsibilities, and that delights in God's many benefits without destructively coveting, hoarding, spoiling, or depleting them.

64. Calvin, *ICR* 3.19.9.

65. Rosemary Radford Ruether, *Sexism and God-Talk: Toward a Feminist Theology*, with a new introduction (Boston: Beacon, 1993), 161–64.

Community

It remains now only to state the obvious. At the same time that the Spirit, or the ethos of God and Christ, renews the participatory energy and direction of life, it also gathers a community. Schleiermacher saw that a specific historic piety or skein of religious affections forms a basis for a fellowship or religious communion because similarly pious people will associate their shared pattern of religious emotions with the same occasions.[66] To this we may add, as after a fashion Schleiermacher also did, that the community-forming impulse will be especially strong when the occasion that shapes the particular skein or pattern of piety in question is the reconciling event of Jesus Christ, and when the Spirit that orients is the Spirit of Christ.[67] For, in this instance, the pattern of religious affections disposes persons to reestablish relationships and also to contribute to the needs of others in community. As Paul says, it disposes them to "bear one another's burdens" (Gal. 6:2), to "rejoice with those who rejoice, weep with those who weep" (Rom. 12:15), and, in short, to live together as one body in which the many members use their varied gifts for all. Indeed, as soon as one understands the basic vectors and dimensions of renewed life, one sees that it does not take place apart from community. One sees that the Spirit—the ethos of interdependent and participatory created life, the gospel, and the kingdom—brings together a particular historic community even as it renews and sanctifies, and this, in fact, is the substance of our next proposition.

Proposition #56 The Spirit gathers the church and sends it on its mission.

The third article of the creed links the Holy Spirit with the church. The Spirit, the giver of life and renewed life, *sanctifies* people; it makes them holy partly by means of the church, its fellowship and sacraments. Spirit, church, and the redirection, reorientation, and rehabilitation of life in Christ go together. One encounters this insistence at many places in the New Testament, including quite prominently, in Paul's letters. "In the Spirit," says the apostle, "we were all baptized into one body" with many members (the church). As members of this community, we receive gifts of prophecy, tongues, and, preeminently, love (1 Cor. 12–14; Gal. 5:13–14); we look to the interests of others, take up collections for those in need, etc.

Now in this proposition we turn to a related point emphasized in early chapters of Acts: the Spirit gathers the church and launches its mission. As we do so, we shall elaborate the following statement. The Spirit—the participatory energy

66. Schleiermacher, *CF*, #6 (p. 29).
67. Schleiermacher, *CF*, #121 (pp. 560–65).

of life manifest in the interdependent cosmos, an energy that is both focused and clarified by the other-directed ethos of Jesus as the Christ—issues in a community drawn from the entire human race that finds itself impelled to undertake a mission of reconciliation.

Pentecost

Consider the coming of the Spirit at Pentecost. The scene in Acts follows the reconstitution of the full complement of twelve disciples—Matthias, having been chosen after prayer by lots, and hence (presumably) by the divine itself, to replace Judas the betrayer (1:12–26)—as a preparation to go to the twelve tribes of Israel. The mission radiates from Jerusalem to all Judea and Samaria, and then turns to evangelizing the known world, thus including Jews, Samaritans, and gentiles. It reconstitutes Israel as the people of God, and then, later in the book of Acts, it adds persons drawn from all families and nations. This is the expansive missionary witness in which, according to Acts, Peter eventually comes to participate (10:23–11:18), and which Paul's journeys do so much to promote.[68]

Acts 2:1–13 introduces this witnessing mission with a gift of the Spirit at the pilgrim feast of Pentecost (fifty days after Passover) when devout Jews "would seek to celebrate in Jerusalem."[69] Tongues like fire appear among Jesus's followers, one tongue resting on each of them, so that "filled with the Holy Spirit," they are enabled "to speak in other languages, as the Spirit gave them ability" (2:4). Indeed, each devout Jew, "from every nation," also hears Jesus's followers speaking in his own native tongue. Is this related to the phenomenon of speaking in tongues that Paul mentions in his letters? Perhaps, but Joseph Fitzmyer says Luke-Acts modifies "the usual expression by adding 'other' because of his concern for the universal scope of the salvation the apostles were about to

68. Luke Timothy Johnson says that Acts 10–15 narrates stages of a church discussion concerning the admission and status of the gentiles during which Peter comes to understand that the message of God to the children of Israel "already bore" an "implicit message of peace and reconciliation between peoples," and that, "in principle . . . the extension of the mission to the Gentiles is a continuation of Jesus's own mission." *The Acts of the Apostles*, Sacra Pagina, vol. 5 (Collegeville, MN: Liturgical Press, 1992), 16, 195. Harold Attridge notes that Acts "seeks to legitimate a social body comprising both 'Jews' and gentiles, and that, in Acts, it is the Spirit that validates 'acceptance of the gentiles' (10:1–11:18)." *Acts: A Commentary* (Minneapolis: Fortress, 2009), 21–22, 23–24. Acts presents Paul's expansive mission as his response to an explicit commission by the risen Lord: "Go, for I will send you far away to the Gentiles" (Acts 22:21). See also Acts 26:17–18.

69. James D. G. Dunn, *The Acts of the Apostles* (Valley Forge, PA: Trinity Press International, 1996), 24.

proclaim."[70] Luke Timothy Johnson notes that the expression *heterais glōssais* stresses communicative rather than ecstatic dimensions of their speech.[71] So, at this juncture, what Acts portrays is not really so much glossolalia in need of interpreters as a miracle of speaking and hearing multiple languages, or a miracle of international and even universal communication.[72]

If we regard it within a broad biblical compass, the symbolism here suggests that, in gathering the church and sending it on its mission, the Spirit reverses the dispersion of humanity and the confusion of human languages narrated in Genesis 11. Recall the scene there: all the earth travels to Shinar and tries to build a city with a tower reaching to the heavens. Salient themes are especially well articulated by Gerhard von Rad in his commentary on Genesis and in his *Old Testament Theology*. The tower of Babel episode comes near the completion of a cycle of stories concerning sin breaking into the world and spreading "like an avalanche." This cycle, which von Rad regards as something akin to wisdom literature in the profound reflections it offers on the human condition, portrays "a chain of events"—from the disobedience of Adam and Eve to Cain murdering Abel, the song of Lamech, the marriages of the angels to the daughters of men and a resultant race of demonically violent supermen, and the drive of early civilization to build the tower. These events, in which people chronically overstep limits and boundaries, and the last of which clearly involves the deployment of technological capabilities by an urban civilization, largely contradict God's created orderings and subvert the calling of humans to ec-centric interrelations with God and others. They lead to the alienation and estrangement of people from God and also from one another, and they are presented as "a road which" humanity took, and whose consequences humans finally could not undo.[73]

We shall consider the sequence or cycle in Genesis once again and in additional detail in our discussion of human sin and corruption in chapter 10. A key matter to emphasize here is simply that the scattering of the peoples into different nations and cultures as well as the confusion of their languages are presented as consequences of humanity's attempt to "make a name for ourselves" (Gen. 11:4), or its attempt at the godlike intensification of itself through the cooperative construction of the tower. The divine response is to disperse and confuse in order to

70. Joseph A. Fitzmyer, SJ, *The Acts of the Apostles: A New Translation with Introduction and Commentary* (New Haven: Yale University Press, 1988), 239.

71. Johnson, *The Acts of the Apostles*, 42.

72. See also Attridge, *Acts*, 63–64.

73. Gerhard von Rad, *The Theology of Israel's Historical Traditions*, vol. 1 of *Old Testament Theology*, trans. D. M. G. Stalker (New York: Harper & Row, 1962), 154, 158, 164; von Rad, *Genesis: A Commentary*, trans. John H. Marks, rev. ed. (Philadelphia: Westminster, 1972), 152. Von Rad also notes that Shinar indicates Babylon in Gen. 10:10; 14:1, 9, in *Genesis*, 148.

restrain. God reckons that a divided and mutually uncomprehending humanity is at least a humanity held in check, one less likely to cooperate in such sweeping enterprises and therefore also less likely to accelerate the cycle of violence and disorder. One might debate just how effective this strategy finally proves to be; for one thing, the subsequent history of the nations certainly makes it clear that the resultant divisions and conflicts also have their price. Fortunately, however, the catastrophe is not final, which is why the saving history (the remedy) begins with the call of Abraham in Genesis 12 and God's plan "to bless 'all the families of the earth through Abraham.'"[74]

An important theme of my earlier christological discussions is that Jesus as the Christ fulfills this blessing (and hence the covenant of grace). With the Spirit's gathering of the church in the early chapters of Acts, we encounter the related claim that, in some sense, Babel's dispersion and confusion are now reversed. Indeed, as we find them in Luke-Acts and elsewhere in the New Testament, the portraits of mutual understanding and cooperation in the Spirit differ from the skewed spirit of cooperation and achievement in the land of Shinar portrayed in Genesis 11. Now, in the power of the Spirit—the participatory energy of interdependent life as well as the ethos of Jesus-as-the-Christ—mutual understanding comes linked with a common commitment and renewed life. Leonardo Boff therefore observes that, according to the symbolism of Pentecost, "the message of the Church is . . . destined to reestablish the primitive unity of the human race and the mutual accord between human beings" in the shalom of God's reign.[75] We might say that, at Pentecost, those who are gathered into the Jesus movement understand the gospel, and each in his own language, because they are joined together in the same mind or attitude that was in Christ Jesus and that attends to the interests of others. Indeed, this feature of salvation from alienation and division fits with the idea that, in Christ, there is a new social organism, a community that takes up a different form of life together, one characterized by mutual concern rather than the effort to "make a name for ourselves."

Acts 1 goes to some lengths to situate the emergence of this community and its mission at Pentecost in *continuity* with Jesus's ministry, message, appearances, and ascension as recounted in the Gospel of Luke. Thus, following his sufferings,

74. Von Rad, *The Theology of Israel's Historical Traditions*, 164; *Genesis*, 152–55.

75. Leonardo Boff, *Church, Charism, and Power: Liberation Theology and the Institutional Church*, trans. John W. Diercksmeier (New York: Crossroad, 1985), 150. Boff claims, "It was also the belief at the time that the confusion of languages created by humanity's pride (see Gen 11) would be abolished and overcome. It was to be a time of reconciliation and fraternal communion. Language would no longer be cause for separation or misunderstanding. In narrating the Pentecost event, Luke has the Spirit descend as tongues of flame. All are present: Arabs, Jews, Romans, and so forth, understanding Peter's words in their own tongue."

the risen Jesus appears to the apostles "during forty days," speaks to his followers about God's kingdom rule, and tells them they will "receive the power of the Holy Spirit." He commissions them to become his "witnesses in Jerusalem, in all Judea and Samaria, and to the ends of the earth," and then he is "lifted up" on a cloud into heaven (Acts 1:1–11).

Fitzmyer says Jesus's exaltation or ascension marks off the period of Jesus from the period of the church empowered by the Spirit whose coming the risen Christ announces.[76] One might posit significant discontinuity here, for example, Jesus preaches the kingdom and then the church preaches Jesus, or the Spirit displaces Jesus as the focal point for the new community. For Luke-Acts, however, the fact that the church's witness points to Jesus as the Christ, his ministry, his message, and his crucifixion-resurrection indicates that there is no fundamental break or disjunction. So does the fact that the witnessing church not only preaches and delivers a verbal message but is also formed by the Spirit in such a way as to adopt a manner of life together characterized by common prayer and mutual care. The verbal proclamation and style of living belong together as integral aspects of the kind of association or community (*koinōnia*) that offers a genuine witness to Jesus as the Christ in the power of the Spirit. Indeed, taken together, the church's proclamation, its manner of life (a living in the Spirit that is always the opposite of what Paul understands to be living in the flesh), and its mission characterize a witness that stands in continuity with Jesus's kingdom-mindedness.[77]

Consider, for example, the clearly idealized portrait of the Jerusalem community in Acts 2:42–47. The Spirit brings about a community that distributes possessions and goods to all who have need, a community that fulfills prominent ancient ideals of friendship and unity, and so will have been taken to realize "the highest aspirations of human longing."[78] Or, again, the passage shows "the early Jesus movement in Jerusalem as a utopian community in which an entire society operates like a band of friends (or an extended family) by eliminating the barriers imposed by the unequal distribution of wealth."[79] This story of the

76. Fitzmyer, *The Acts of the Apostles*, 194, 208–9. Harold Attridge says that, for Luke-Acts, "Jesus was a human being, a prophet, exalted by God to the divine realm, an action that made the universal gift of the Spirit possible." *Acts*, 23.

77. Thus, the narrative arc of Acts, which presents the movement of the church's witnessing mission from all of Israel to all the earth, ends with Paul "proclaiming the kingdom of God and teaching about the Lord Jesus Christ" unhindered and "with all boldness" at Rome, the political and economic center of the Mediterranean world (Acts 28:31).

78. Johnson, *The Acts of the Apostles*, 61, 62. Indeed, in *Critias* Plato portrays early Athens as a community that held possessions in common.

79. Attridge, *Acts*, 90. See also Acts 4:32, "Now the whole group of those who believed were

church's founding, in turn, functions as "a foil to the scandal and squabble to be recounted in Acts 5 and 6."[80] But it could not function this way if it were not also understood to indicate that the Spirit's formation of the church has a discernible pattern or content; moreover, there is also some evidence in Paul for the sharing of possessions (Gal. 2:10; 6:10; 1 Cor. 16:1–4; 2 Cor. 8–9). The idealized portrait indicates that, when it is genuinely gathered and formed in the Spirit, true Christian community entails attention to apostolic teaching, common prayer and celebration of the Lord's Supper, care and concern for one another, and welcoming new members. This distinctive pattern of life together recalls important elements of the reconciling mission and alternative politics of Jesus and the kingdom.

All of which is to say that the Spirit enables or empowers a life of true communion with God in community with one another. It elicits a social space, reality, and form of life together that re-present genuine reconciliation, or the confluence of "vertical" and "horizontal" relationships meant to characterize created life, God's covenant with Israel, Jesus's insistence on love of God and neighbor, his message of the kingdom, as well as any proper celebration of the Lord's Supper. It is true, of course, that even at their best, the churches we experience approximate this reality and Christoform manner of life together only fragmentarily.[81] Corruption takes its toll. Even so, as far as Acts 2 is concerned, the Spirit-elicited manner or pattern remains integral to the fellowship and mission of the churches, or to their kingdom-minded witness to Jesus as the Christ.

Some Classical and Contemporary Reflections

Pause now to ponder some classical and more recent Protestant reflections. The Heidelberg Catechism (1563), according to one of its principal authors, maintains that the substance of our comfort in life and in death is that "we are Christ's and through him reconciled to the Father."[82] Strictly speaking, however, the catechism does not take the activity that reconciles and brings renewed life to be simply a matter of Christ's atoning work. It is true that, according to the catechism's substitutionary soteriology, "without any merit of my own, out of sheer

of one heart and soul, and no one claimed private ownership of any possessions, but everything they owned was held in common."

80. Fitzmyer, *The Acts of the Apostles*, 268–69.

81. Somewhat similarly, Jürgen Moltmann notes that, as "an anticipation" of the kingdom, the church is "not yet a fulfillment" but only "a fragment of the coming whole." *The Church in the Power of the Spirit: A Contribution to Messianic Ecclesiology*, trans. Margaret Kohl (Minneapolis: Fortress, 1993), 193.

82. *The Commentary of Zacharias Ursinus on the Heidelberg Catechism*, trans. G. W. Willard (Cincinnati: Bucher, 1851), 19.

grace, God grants and credits to me the perfect satisfaction, righteousness, and holiness of Christ, as if I had never been a sinner." It is also true that "all I need to do is accept this with a believing heart."[83] But it is the Spirit that produces this faith or acceptance in me. It is the Spirit that creates in us a wholehearted trust in God's free forgiveness (*BOC* 4.021). Thus, in addition to Christ's atoning work per se, "the Spirit is given to me, so that, through faith, he makes me share in Christ and all his benefits" (*BOC* 4.053). The turning of persons to the divine in the confidence that the gracious God values them therefore involves two related moments: Christ's atoning work and the Spirit's engrafting of persons into Christ (and thus into Christ's body or the church) through faith (*BOC* 4.064). This is how we are reconciled, redeemed, and renewed. This is how, according to the catechism, we become forgiven children who recognize God as our faithful Father.[84]

In the catechism's terms, then, as the Spirit participates in the work of redemption, it also gathers the church. The church in the power of the Spirit is *old* and it *endures* because—as the catechism says—it is gathered, protected, and preserved "from the beginning of the world to its end." The church is a feature of the gospel message or word of assurance because it is an ancient and enduring community of persons who know they stand in relationship with God, and of which, by grace and the Spirit, "I am and always will be a living member" (*BOC* 4.054). Moreover, just because it is old and endures, just because, in some sense, it is the community of the one covenant of grace that extends from Adam to the end, just because it is gathered in a manner that fulfills the promise that in Abraham all families of the earth shall be blessed, and just because it is gathered in accord with a great commission to go to all nations, the church is also something *new*. Why? Because, says the catechism, it is gathered "out of the entire human race" (*BOC* 4.054). We might say that, like the reconciler who crosses barriers and boundaries, and unlike very many other human communities, the church in the power of the Spirit is gathered from and goes to all families, tribes, ethnic

83. *BOC* 4.060. Hereafter, references to this document will be given in parentheses in the text.

84. Does the Heidelberg Catechism commit an "Anselmic error" by making satisfaction of the divine justice the precondition for divine mercy? Jan Rohls, *Reformed Confessions: Theology from Zurich to Barmen*, trans. John Hoffmeyer (Louisville: Westminster John Knox, 1998), 91–94, says it modifies Anselm so that Christ's death does not satisfy God's honor but God's justice. Eberhard Busch, *Drawn to Freedom: Christian Faith Today in Conversation with the Heidelberg Catechism*, trans. William H. Rader (Grand Rapids: Eerdmans, 2010), 96–97, assures us that, in the catechism, "it is not that *God* must clear things up with God's own self. *We* have to be cleared up," although "it would be *unmerciful* if God were not at the same time just." Even so, one remembers that, when it comes to the sovereignty of grace, Karl Barth thought Anselm did not go far enough. Does the catechism wholly escape Barth's concern?

groups, and nations. In this sense, it is not, or at least it *ought* not to be, bound by a spirit of tribalism. It is not, or at least *ought* not to be, defined by the recurrent in-group/out-group or us-versus-them tendencies of human communities that so often issue in conflict as well as in claims for the superiority and righteousness of our own group and the inferiority of others. It is, or at least *ought* to be, defined by another energy and Spirit.

Let us repeat again that corruption unfortunately and persistently takes its toll. A popular hymn, quoted by Martin Luther King Jr. in a sermon at Montgomery, Alabama, on "loving your enemies," nevertheless makes a salient point: "In Christ there is no east or west, in him no south or north."[85] Or, as the apostle says, in Christ there is no male or female, Jew or gentile, slave or free. The Heidelberg Catechism insists that, in the communion of saints, we share in a fellowship and manner in life with persons gathered from the entire human race, and that this fellowship and manner obligate all to use their gifts "readily and joyfully for the service and enrichment" of others (*BOC* 4.055). That is, it understands "the holy catholic church"—the church formed in the energy of the Spirit—to approximate what King might have called a community of reconciliation.[86] Or, again, as two more recent documents put it—the Confession of 1967 of the Presbyterian Church (USA) and the Belhar Confession adopted by the Dutch Reformed Mission Church in South Africa in 1986—the church is a community in which persons "have been reconciled with God and one another."[87] Commenting on Belhar, the South African theologian Piet J. Naude says, "the unity of the church," a body that brings together people who have been divided and often also in conflict, is "a manifestation of Christ's reconciliation."[88]

The modern statements then proceed to emphasize what Paul mentions in 2 Corinthians 5, namely, that this gathered community, which embodies a reconciling trajectory precisely because its members are "called from the entire human family," is itself also entrusted with the message and mission of reconciliation. For King, this meant, among other things, that the church should uphold the worth of persons in God's sight, witness to justice, and criticize injustice in the service of restoring a broken but beloved community.[89] The Confession of 1967 critiques then-current circumstances through the spectacles of reconciliation and highlights four alienating divisions: (a) the fragmentation of the human fam-

85. *A Testament of Hope: The Essential Writings of Martin Luther King, Jr.*, ed. James Melvin Washington (New York: Harper & Row, 1986), 58.

86. King, *A Testament of Hope*, 6–8, 12–15.

87. Piet J. Naude, *Neither Calendar Nor Clock: Perspectives on the Belhar Confession* (Grand Rapids: Eerdmans, 2010), 219–10; *BOC* 9.07; 9.20.

88. Naude, *Neither Calendar Nor Clock*, 8.

89. King, *A Testament of Hope*, 18–20, 122.

ily by racial prejudice and discrimination, (b) war in an age of weapons that risk "the annihilation of mankind," (c) "enslaving poverty in a world of abundance," and (d) confusion and exploitation in sexual life that diminish relationships of mutual responsibility and care.[90] Belhar affirms that God's people should "live in a new obedience which can open new possibilities for society and world," and that the credibility of the gospel is undermined "when it is proclaimed in a land which professes to be Christian, but in which the enforced separation of people on a racial basis promotes alienation, hatred, and enmity."[91]

Gathering and Sending, Ec-centric Piety, and the Sacraments

In my judgment, a deep theological point that lies behind and beneath these statements and others like them is this: The Spirit, which, as we recall, is the energy and ethos manifest in participatory created life and in Christ the reconciler, gathers the church from the entire human race as a community of reconciliation that brings together people who often have been divided and in conflict. It gathers them into a community of common prayer and mutual care, and it impels the church to take up a mission of reconciliation to the entire human race. The impulsion amounts to a necessity of consonance or fittingness. The Spirit sanctifies; it orients and directs persons to take up the ec-centric manner of living manifested in Jesus as the Christ, *and this ec-centricity fittingly comes to expression in a life together, a life in which persons attend to and serve one another, welcome newcomers, and engage in a mission of reconciliation to the wider world.* As Barth says, here, in this historic community, we encounter a subjective apprehension of and awakening to the reconciliation of the world with God in Jesus as the Christ. Here the reality of Jesus Christ becomes the work of the Spirit awakening and building up the community, quickening it and pointing it beyond itself.[92]

Gathering and sending constitute integral features of the reconciling dynamic of the church in the power of the Spirit. The church gathers in the power of the Spirit. It assembles as an association and community of common worship, mutual communication, care and concern. It assembles in Christ as a community of reconciliation. The church disperses in the power of the Spirit. It goes out into the world equipped with the message that all have worth in relation to God, that all therefore are to be treated justly and with respect, and that, by the grace of God and on the other side of forgiveness and contrition, alienation and conflict may

90. *BOC* 9.43–47.
91. Naude, *Neither Calendar Nor Clock*, 221.
92. Barth, *CD* IV/1:147–53.

be mitigated or even overcome in a renewed life together. The church disperses and goes out into the world to undertake its mission of reconciliation.

Or, again, as it sanctifies, the Spirit reorients and directs, and so enables persons to take up the ec-centric manner of life manifested in Jesus as the Christ. This reorientation toward ec-centricity yields a distinctive community of mutual concern and service, one characterized by hospitality to strangers and a bias toward welcoming inclusion that, when drawn from the entire human race—from peoples historically alienated from one another and in conflict—is itself a community of reconciliation. And, at the same time, this reorientation toward ec-centricity, the energizing and impelling ethos of this community, appropriately yields a ministry and mission of reconciliation in the world. The Spirit, the ethos of the gospel and the kingdom, brings together the historic Christian community or the church, and also sends it out on its mission to the world. It accords also with the ethos of creation; we are, as Calvin says, born to help one another.[93]

This indicates yet another basic dimension of specifically Christian piety: a sense of having been called and empowered to participate in a community of reconciliation that brings together people in common prayer and mutual care and that pursues a mission of reconciliation in the wider world. This particular historic aspect of ec-centric Christian piety is responsive to the story of the church in Acts as well as to various portraits of the Christian community in the Pastoral Epistles. It encourages people to envision themselves as participants in an inclusive, welcoming church that crosses barriers and challenges injustices as it witnesses to and hopes for God's renewing possibility and kingdom purpose.

As a Reformed theologian and a Presbyterian, I should note, following the Scots Confession of 1560 on the Kirk at least in part, that we are engrafted by grace into the body of Christ and so into the people of God, which extends from Adam and Abraham to the end.[94] There are a basic assurance and calling here, since to be a member of the people of God is to stand in a gracious relationship with God and others within a community of reconciliation that neither falters nor fails. Luther has the note of assurance clearly in sight when, in commentary on the third article of the Apostles' Creed, he says, "There is a holy group and a congregation made up only of saints. And you too are in this church; the Holy Spirit leads you into it."[95] (This is a point worth remembering the next time you see tombstones in a churchyard. There, symbolically at least, are gathered still the communion of saints in that particular place and congregation.) In any case, there is a basic assurance as well as a basic calling—you are a saint who, by the

93. Calvin, *ICR* 3.7.5–7.

94. *BOC* 3.04–3.05.

95. Luther, *Sermons I*, ed. and trans. John W. Doberstein, vol. 51 of *LW*, 167.

grace of God and the power of the Spirit, perseveres, and who therefore is also sent into the world as an alternative and persistent reconciling presence.

If this is at all correct, then the church cannot be a community of reconciliation in Christ and the Spirit without also engaging in a kingdom-minded ministry and mission of reconciliation in the world that is both critical and hopeful. The church cannot first concentrate on getting its internal dynamics together and then, only later, go out to minister to the wider world. As a matter of felt piety and as a necessity of consonance, it can only attempt both together as aspects of the same living and social reality.

With this in mind, let me bring this proposition to a close by briefly observing that the reconciling dynamic of the church in the power of the Spirit also has important sacramental implications.

"Go therefore and make disciples of all nations, baptizing them in the name of the Father and of the Son and of the Holy Spirit" (Matt. 28:19). Biblically speaking, baptism is tethered to the church's reconciling mission. The church baptizes as it goes to all nations in order to gather the people of God from the entire human race, and so bring together into its unity people who have been scattered, divided, and often in conflict. The church baptizes as it crosses barriers and boundaries in order to extend the community of common prayer and mutual care. In a Reformed Protestant frame of reference, moreover, whether we baptize infants or adults, the sacrament signals the entrance of persons into the one covenant of grace. It enacts their acceptance or adoption by grace and in the power of the Spirit as God's children and members of God's family. It enacts a word of assurance because it symbolizes their unshakeable worth in God's sight, and their participation in a saving community with the God of grace and with others that will neither falter nor fail. And, in these senses, it intimates the kingdom.

The Lord's Supper has its Christian background in Jesus's table fellowship, his open commensality or practice of eating and drinking indiscriminately with everyone—tax collectors, sinners, etc. This practice, which in the Gospels routinely runs afoul of established religious sensibilities and cultural expectations, is one way that Jesus as the Christ enacts the true communion with God in community with others that characterizes both covenant and kingdom. Indeed, Jesus himself defends the practice to both Pharisees and followers of John the Baptist (Mark 2:18–22 and pars.), and Luke 15 has him telling the parables of the lost sheep, the lost coin, and the lost son in response to the criticism that he welcomes sinners and eats with them. So, when we once understand that the Supper is based in an intentionally reconciling mission strategy by means of which Jesus accepts tax collectors and sinners and restores them to relationship with God and also to relationships with one another, we see that, in the power of the Spirit of Christ, this sacrament, too, ought to be characterized by welcoming inclusion. Indeed, as the South African theologian Robert Vosloo points out, for Michael Welker and for others, "Holy Communion is an event of unconditional acceptance or hospitality."[96] Welker emphasizes quite helpfully that those who participated in the Last Supper from which the sacrament derives "were Judas, 'who betrayed Him,' Peter, 'who denied Him,' and the disciples, 'who abandoned Him and fled.' They all participated fully in 'the night of betrayal.' Thus one can argue that Jesus' pre-Easter practice of table-fellowship, which demonstrated acceptance of the community's enemies and sinners, 'reaches its apex in Jesus' celebration of the last supper.'"[97]

Even so, and just at this point, churches often succumb to practices that diminish and divide. A classic example, drawn once again from the Scottish background of my own Presbyterian tradition, is the practice of "fencing the table," so that only those deemed worthy, on doctrinal and also moral grounds, can partake of the Supper. Indeed, Scottish communities, for which, alongside Word and sacrament, ecclesiastical discipline was a third note of the true church, sometimes dispensed tokens that admitted only the right people to the Lord's Supper.[98] In more recent times, Presbyterian churches have extended their understanding of who may participate in the Supper to all baptized and confirmed members of the congregation, all baptized and professing Christians, and even to baptized children who are not yet confirmed but are able to understand the meaning of the sacrament. Still, though the overall liberalizing trajectory of these notions is positive, it seems to me that, when measured against Jesus's practice, they remain overly restrictive. The strange and also reconciling discipline of the gospel of grace is to welcome everyone, even, and perhaps especially, when the community is under pressure not to do so.

I therefore find myself in agreement with Jürgen Moltmann's insistence on "the open feast."

> Because this fellowship comes into being on the basis of Christ's unconditional and prevenient invitation, the fellowship will be an open one. It cannot limit Christ's invitation on its own account. Everyone can participate who wants to participate in the fellowship of Christ. The communion is the answer to Christ's open invitation . . . it is not the feast of the particularly righteous, or

96. Robert Vosloo, *Reforming Memory: Essays on South African Church and Theological History* (Stellenbosch, South Africa: African Sun Media, 2017), 251.

97. Vosloo, *Reforming Memory*, 245. Vosloo quotes from Michael Welker, *What Happens in Holy Communion?* (Grand Rapids: Eerdmans, 2000), 72.

98. *BOC* 3.18.

> the people who think they are particularly devout; it is the feast of the weary and heavy-laden, who have heard the call to refreshment.
>
> As a feast open to the churches, Christ's supper demonstrates the community's catholicity. As a feast open to the world it demonstrates the community's mission to the world. As a feast open to the future it demonstrates the community's universal hope.[99]

In the light of the reconciling trajectory of Jesus as the Christ, the gospel of grace, and the Spirit's gathering and sending, the ecclesiastical discipline that should be practiced, especially as we celebrate the Supper, is a discipline of radical welcome and inclusion.[100]

Proposition #57 The church that the Spirit gathers and sends is a community of worship.

The power of the Spirit, or the participatory energy of interdependent life and the ec-centric ethos of Jesus-as-the-Christ, gathers and sends the community called church. This means, as we have seen, that the church is a community gathered out of the entire human race, a community that reflects the boundary- and barrier-crossing impetus of the kingdom-minded one who reconciles, and a community entrusted with a ministry of reconciliation. It means that, at a basic or even foundational level, the church will be characterized by two inextricably intertwined vectors of life, namely, radical dependence on God and interdependence with others. It embodies the theological truth that created human life refers or points to God and to others—for example, as we exercise our created powers and capacities, we encounter God as the Creator, source, and

99. Moltmann, *The Church in the Power of the Spirit*, 259–60.

100. Here we run up against a basic point about the means of grace and discipline as Ernst Troeltsch understood them to function in church- and sect-type ecclesiastical organizations, and, unsurprisingly, there is much to consider. Ponder a point Lewis S. Mudge makes in *The Church as Moral Community: Ecclesiology and Ethics in Ecumenical Debate* (New York: Continuum, 1998), 20: "Ask any group of Christians on what grounds, if any, they would be prepared to refuse Eucharistic fellowship with some other Christian group. Moral issues are the ones most likely to be named. For one group the issue could be racism. For another it could be ordaining gay and lesbian persons." Or, again, the feminist theologian Letty M. Russell makes use of "the black church tradition" to argue for an understanding of "the welcome table" over against "the old patriarchal fencing of the table by excluding those who are not members in good standing." She wants to remove fences "so that all may bring their gifts to the table and seek to discern the presence of Christ in their midst." On the other hand, she also argues for "fencing the table with justice." See *Church in the Round: Feminist Interpretation of the Church* (Louisville: Westminster John Knox, 1993), 146–47.

fountain of existence, and we encounter the many conditions and creatures in the midst of which we live and move. Indeed, apart from these encounters or references beyond ourselves to God and the wider field of creation, we humans are inexplicable. But the two intertwined vectors come to expression also in a series of covenants that link persons before God in responsible interrelations with one another. We see them again when Jesus-as-the-Christ teaches love of God and neighbor, welcomes all into a renewed and reconciled community, and proclaims a kingdom in which the nations and peoples before God live together justly and peaceably. And, now, we take a step further when we acknowledge that, in the power of the Spirit, the church as *a community of worship* embodies and expresses this same dynamic. The Spirit gathers and sends a community that intimates, however fragmentarily and partially, the life of true communion with God in community with others, and the confluence of these "vertical" and "horizontal" relationships largely defines public worship.

Word

The community called church embodies this dynamic as it gathers to hear God's Word in the power of the Spirit. For now, in the light of the event of Jesus-as-the-Christ, the Scriptures become the saga of the divine excellence that goes out from itself to create, judge, and redeem. The Bible becomes the story of good, capable, and social creatures gone awry, alienated and separated from God and others but nevertheless, and by the grace of God, reconciled to God and one another. The Scriptures become the classic account of dependent and interdependent life in community created, lost, and restored. In this sense, the gospel, the Word that comes to us in and through the many words of Scripture, though thoroughly acquainted with chronic human misdirection and tragedy, is finally and fundamentally a Word of promise and grace.

Here we may enlist the help of John Calvin himself, who, in the opening sentences of his *Institutes*, famously says true wisdom consists in the knowledge of God and of ourselves. To make a long story very short, Calvin insists that we shall have no true knowledge, either of God or of ourselves, unless and until we understand God to be the author and fountain of every good.[101] We must know God's benevolence toward us, and in our present state this knowledge is available to us only in God's freely given promise of grace in Jesus Christ. This promise is the heart of the gospel, and it comes to us in Scripture. To grasp it is to be assured of God's graciousness toward us, and, as we have seen, this assur-

101. Calvin, *ICR* 1.2.1–2.

ance, which is as much a matter of the heart as of the brain, is the work of the Spirit.[102] In fact, true religion or saving faith is the end to which we ought to relate Scripture's contents.

There is more to the Scriptures than God's free promise of grace in Jesus Christ, but for true piety and saving faith this is the point on which all others hang. Calvin therefore points to "the word of life" or the "word of faith" in the living words of Scripture that "shows forth Christ."[103]

> Faith is certain that God is true in all things whether he command or forbid, whether he promise or threaten; and it also obediently receives his commandments, observes his prohibitions, heeds his threats. Nevertheless, faith properly begins with the promise, rests in it, and ends in it. For in God faith seeks life: a life that is not found in commandments or declarations of penalties, but in the promise of mercy, and only in a freely given promise. . . . The apostle, therefore, bears witness to the gospel: that is the word of faith [Rom. 10:8].[104]

For the Reformer, it is crucial that in our reading of Scripture we look for the gospel. Thus, when as a feature of its faithful witness the church points to the Bible, it also does more than simply point to the Bible. It witnesses to the gospel, to God's free promise of grace, to the word of life within the living words of Scripture. And, as Calvin well knew, for many readers of Scripture as well as for more than a few Christian communities, this word of grace remains distressingly obscure.

This does not mean that the word of life is the only thing in Scripture, or even the only important thing. It means rather that, when we read the Bible through the spectacles of true piety, this word configures the words. This word of grace and reconciliation shapes our understanding of the commands, the prohibitions, the lesser promises, and the threats. This norm configures our reading and interpretation. Stated in my terms, when we read, exposit, and hear the words of the Bible in the power of the Spirit (in the power of the dependent, interdependent, and participatory impulse of good created life and of the welcoming and ec-centric ethos of Jesus-as-the-Christ), there emerges a reconciling promise of acceptance and true community. Read in this fashion, the Bible helps us to envision God-before-life as the excellent and gracious Creator, Judge, and Redeemer—the reality that goes out from itself to create good life together, redirect alienated and corrupted human life, and finally reconcile and renew what has become fragmented and flawed. And so, as it is read in this fashion, the Bible

102. Calvin, *ICR* 3.2.6–7, 33–36.
103. Calvin, *ICR* 1.7.1; 1.9.3.
104. Calvin, *ICR* 3.2.29.

also helps us to envision human-life-before-God—humans as good, capable, dependent, and interdependent creatures, who are mired in sin or a radical fault and its severely destructive consequences, but who nevertheless also are graced with reconciling and renewing possibilities for true communion with God in community with others.

The first segment of the Service for the Lord's Day of the Presbyterian Church (USA) is entitled "Gathering," and it enacts this very pattern just before the service turns to a second segment entitled "The Word." "Gathering" includes the following elements: a Call to Worship, an Opening Prayer, a Hymn of Praise, a Prayer of Confession, a Pardon, and the Peace. The sequence summarizes the pattern of God-before-life and life-before-God. Thus, the Call to Worship—with sentences such as "Our help is in the name of the Lord who made heaven and earth" or "This is the day the Lord has made; let us rejoice and be glad in it"—the Opening Prayer, which ordinarily is one of adoration, and the Hymn of Praise all enlist the good human creature in doing what it has been created to do, namely, praise and adore God, the source and fountain of all good gifts. The Prayer of Confession and the Pardon enact the dynamic of sin or human fault and redeeming grace and forgiveness. Worshipers here encounter the gracious God, who as Judge redirects and calls them to confess their sin before God and one another. Here they meet the gracious God who empowers repentance, and who also assures them of their acceptance. Here they encounter the God who in Christ reconciles sinners to Godself. Next, they may hear the law or a summary read, for example, "Let each of you look not to your own interests, but to the interests of others" (Phil. 2:4)—not as an accusation but as a gift to guide and encourage a good life together. Finally, the Peace—the moment in the service where persons in the congregation (who have just now confessed their sins against God and one another) exchange signs of Christ's peace—enacts symbolically and fragmentarily the promise of renewed life and reconciled community.[105]

In sum, by the time it turns to "The Word," the Presbyterian service has already shaped our identity and expectation by articulating in the power of the Spirit a rather full theology of grace. Who are we who have gathered to hear the Scriptures read and interpreted? The threefold answer is that we are good, dependent, and interdependent creatures who receive copious gifts and whose purpose it is to commune with God in community with others. We are sinners mired in corruption and alienation from God and neighbor. We are beneficiaries of grace and forgiveness who are guided by the Spirit of interdependent life and

105. *Book of Common Worship*, prepared by the Theology and Worship Ministry Unit for the Presbyterian Church (U.S.A.) and the Cumberland Presbyterian Church (Louisville: Westminster John Knox, 1993), 46, 48–59.

of Jesus-as-the-Christ toward new community. The service therefore instructs us in what Calvin calls "the Christian philosophy" not with syllogisms but experientially (and liturgically).[106] By means of worshipful enactment, it instructs us in what to look for as the Scriptures are read and interpreted. It encourages us to listen for the epic of redemption, for the story of good creatures gone awry but nevertheless renewed and reconciled by the God of grace and in the word of gospel.

A last note about worship, the Spirit, and the Word—the service directs the preacher to say a Prayer for Illumination before the Scriptures are read and "their message is proclaimed in a sermon" or in some other form. Here is a sample: "Lord, open our hearts and minds by the power of your Holy Spirit, that as the scriptures are read and your Word is proclaimed, we may hear with joy what you say to us today. Amen."[107] Why say this prayer now? Answer: the prayer indicates that, despite the preacher's extended and ordinarily quite necessary studies, despite the congregation's Christian education and good attention, and despite the well-conceived liturgical sequence leading up to "The Word," neither preacher nor hearers simply determine whether the words of Scripture will be articulated and received as the Word of life and grace. This rather depends on whether our hearts and minds are opened by the Spirit, on whether the words of the Bible are interpreted and heard in the power of the Spirit—in the interdependent and participatory ethos of created life and the ec-centric trajectory of Jesus-as-the-Christ. This rather depends on whether the Bible is interpreted and heard in the true ethos of a community of mutual care gathered and sent as a fragmentary but nonetheless articulate embodiment of and witness to reconciling and renewing possibilities for true communion in community.

Sacrament

Consider now the third part of the Presbyterian service, entitled "The Eucharist." A sacrament, in Augustine's influential view, is a visible sign and seal of an invisible grace. Churches and denominations long have discussed and debated whether and how Christ is really present and whether and how Christ nourishes and supports us in the Supper. Though I have no desire to continue the classical debates, which often become quite technical, let me say that, overall, I side with Calvin, who, rather than offer a metaphysical explanation, claims that Christ is really spiritually or mystically present by the power of the Spirit that "towers

106. Calvin makes this observation about prayer. See *ICR* 3.20.1.

107. *Book of Common Worship* (1993), 60, 62.

above our senses."[108] In my view, where two or three are gathered together in his name, the Christ is spiritually and mystically present. Where the Spirit—the ethos of Christ's ec-centric and kingdom-minded ministry and message—gathers a community, the Christ is present. Where, in the power of the Spirit, the church's preaching proclaims that Word of life, grace, and the gospel, the Christ is present. (Indeed, I also take this as a significant clue to the manner of the risen Lord's presence in the disciples' post-Easter encounters with him.)

What makes the Eucharist special is that here the Christ is present at a common meal after the fashion and in the memory of Jesus's banquet practice and his last supper with the disciples. The Supper, then, is a visible sign or symbol—a common meal and a visible Word of grace—that, rather than being empty, invites our participation in and encounter with the reality of eating and drinking with everyone in Christ's name, and the sequence of Jesus's crucifixion and resurrection.[109] Christ is the host, and in this common meal, this celebration, we are fed, nourished, and restored. How so? Well, for one thing, we apprehend anew the nightmare of Christ's crucifixion, the execution of the kingdom-minded one, and we anticipate that we shall sit at table together in God's kingdom.[110] For another, and as I hope is apparent in proposition #56 above, we are accepted as participants in the community of those who are reconciled to God and one another. Like the prodigal welcomed home, we go in to join the celebration. We liturgically enact and, in turn, are nourished by participating in the reconciled reality of true communion with God in community with others.

I was once asked by a member of a class at a church in Macalester, Oklahoma,

108. Calvin, *ICR* 4.17.10. For an excellent review of the various positions, see B. A. Gerrish, "The Lord's Supper in the Reformed Confessions," in *Major Themes in the Reformed Tradition*, ed. Donald K. McKim (Grand Rapids: Eerdmans, 1992), 245–58. For an important discussion of the ambiguity of the word "sacrament," see Wolfhart Pannenberg, *Systematic Theology*, trans. Geoffrey Bromiley, vol. 3 (Grand Rapids: Eerdmans, 1997), 336–69.

109. Note the distinction that Calvin draws between an empty symbol and one that shows forth the thing signified; *ICR* 4.17.10–11. For Calvin, this means that in the bread and wine there is shown to us Christ's "very body and blood, in which he fulfilled all obedience to obtain righteousness for us." I would prefer to say that the common meal is a symbol that enlists our participation in the realities of Christ's banquet practice, crucifixion, and resurrection.

110. Luke 13:29, "Then people will come from east and west, from north and south, and will eat in the kingdom of God," is a part of the "Invitation to the Lord's Table" in the Presbyterian Service for the Lord's Day. See *Book of Common Worship* (1993), p. 68. The relationship between the Supper as an anticipatory sign of the coming reign of God and the mutual fellowship of all who share the meal is an important theme in Wolfhart Pannenberg's discussion of the Supper. See *Systematic Theology*, 3:286, 290, 325. On 328, he also says, "the celebration of the Lord's Supper" lays on members of a single congregation but also on various local congregations "the duty of mutual fellowship."

what Jesus looked like. Of course, we have no photograph. Was he short, tall, or of medium height? Thin or stocky? Did he have a prominent chin, forehead, or nose? What color was his hair? We do not have in the Gospels even an approximate physical description. The long history of artistic depictions of Jesus is itself, among other things, an exercise in cultural reception and theological reflection. On the one hand, the many, almost endlessly diverse portraits help people to encounter the Christ or identify with him in different ways. At the same time, they also should discourage us from concluding that, on the basis of his physical appearance, some of us are closer to Jesus than others. (Lest you mistakenly conclude that this last possibility seems unlikely, you may wish to review Rosemary Radford Ruether's argument against the traditional Roman Catholic idea that only men can be priests because the Savior was a man.)[111]

In any case, I think the answer to the question put to me in Oklahoma is this (and it also follows from the idea that the sacrament is a true visible symbol that participates in and mediates to us the reality of the thing signified): though we have no historical physical description, we don't lack a definitive picture. Jesus-as-the-Christ looks like Eucharist or like Lord's Supper. He looks like and is mystically or spiritually present in a meal together celebrated in this name to which persons from the entire human race are invited, and in which, by the power of the Spirit and in full recognition of crucifixion and apparent defeat, we enact and embody the reconciling gift of true communion with God in community with others.

Jesus-as-the-Christ, the event of reconciliation, aims at overcoming the alienation, separation, and breach that the human fault brings into our relationships with God and with one another. It aims at healing the disruption of life's inherent "vertical" and "horizontal" references beyond ourselves to God and to one another, but its effects remain partial, ambivalent, and hidden. In the life of the church and by the power of the Spirit, the new life and new community of God's kingdom are present only in the form of a sign, and especially at the heart of the church's worship "in the celebration of the Supper."[112]

111. Ruether, *Sexism and God-Talk*, 116–38.

112. Pannenberg, *Systematic Theology*, 3:369. In a statement before its closing part, entitled "The Fulfillment of Reconciliation," the Confession of 1967 captures much of what I intend here. "The Lord's Supper is a celebration of the reconciliation of men with God and with one another, in which they joyfully eat and drink together at the table of their Savior. Jesus Christ gave his church this remembrance of his dying for sinful men so that by participation in it they have communion with him and with all who shall be gathered to him. . . . They rejoice in the foretaste of the kingdom which he will bring to consummation at his promised coming, and go out from the Lord's Table with courage and hope for the service to which he has called them." *BOC* 9.52. Compare this also with the following suggested "Prayer after Communion"

Let me add a very brief statement on baptism. This is a visible sign and living symbol of entrance into the covenant of grace. Baptism articulates an extraordinarily excellent and also happy point because it ritually and liturgically enacts a relationship with the gracious God that, since the beginning of humanity, neither falters nor fails. It acknowledges that the God of grace knows us before we know God. The God of grace always already stands in relation to all, and so always already counts all as God's own. Where people are baptized with water in the power of the Spirit, they are engrafted and accepted into the people of God, into the reality of true communion with God in community with others that extends—if we rely, once again, on a strained but nevertheless true Reformed exegesis of Genesis 3:15—from the first human pair forward. Again, we need to acknowledge that ambiguities abound and that the full reality is here present largely in the form of a sign. Moreover, with the acknowledgment of this excellent inclusion comes the very great responsibility of witnessing to the God of grace and to the reconciled and true community of the kingdom in a fragmented world. But first, and in the power of the Spirit, perhaps we should focus on the extraordinary and happy fact of a gracious God.

in the Presbyterian Service for the Lord's Day: "Loving God, we thank you that you have fed us in the Sacrament, united us with Christ, and given us a foretaste of the heavenly banquet in your eternal kingdom. Send us out in the power of your Spirit to live and work to your praise and glory." *Book of Common Worship* (1993), 76.

Chapter Ten

Human Life: Sin and Regeneration

Having reviewed the event of Jesus as the Christ as well as the Spirit's bestowal of life and renewed life, we are ready now to consider humanity under the aspect of redemption—human life characterized by the dynamic of corruption and renewal, or of sin, forgiveness, and regeneration. The ecumenical creeds contain no article dedicated to sin. Indeed, describing the work of the Spirit in the third article, the Apostles' Creed mentions "the *forgiveness* of sins," and the Nicene Creed mentions "one baptism for the *remission* of sins" (emphasis added). Sin, that is to say, goes together with grace, and it remains a largely unstated presupposition of the reconciling work of Jesus Christ as well as the sanctifying work of the Spirit. The first article entails the idea that human beings are good and dependent creatures endowed with significant capabilities, but redemption in Christ and the Spirit (the overall point of the second and third articles) furnishes a solution to a problem. It indicates that there is something humans need redeeming from.

This is the implication, too, of a confident sentence in the Gospel of John, which, in the RSV translation I first learned, reads as follows: "The light shines in the darkness, and the darkness has not overcome it" (John 1:5). It is to this darkness or to the presupposed misorientation and chronic corruption of persons that we initially turn our attention here. Even so, in order to offer a full picture of human life under the aspect of redemption, and in order to be guided by the creed, we have (in the previous chapters) proceeded from, and must now also keep in mind, and make our way toward the major premise. The light shines, and so the good human creature is not only corrupted and mired in sin but also reconciled and regenerated.

Proposition #58 People stand in need of rehabilitation and renewal because they are mired in and diminished by a persistent fault.

A text that looms large in this regard is Romans 5: we have peace with God and are reconciled to God by God's love and grace in Jesus Christ.[1] For Paul, the event of Jesus Christ reconciles and renews; it overcomes alienation and reverses a degenerative condition. Hence, he says, it is through Jesus Christ, while we were still weak and ungodly sinners, that we "have obtained access to this grace in which we stand" (5:2). Some chapters later he also says it is by the Spirit of God and of Christ that we obtain true life as God's children (8:9–17).

Paul devotes a good portion of Romans 5 to a telling and extended parallel between two figures: Adam and Christ. Calvin comments that here the apostle presents "a comparison of opposites," since "a clearer realization of what we possess in Christ can come only when we have been shown what we have lost in Adam."[2] And, indeed, for Paul Adam is disobedient, Christ obedient. "Adam and Christ," says Joseph Fitzmyer, "are type and antitype."[3] The former's "baleful influence has affected all human beings, making sinners of them all," whereas Christ brings grace and peace.[4] But this also means, and as David L. Bartlett notes, that "Adam and Christ are opposite, but not equal. . . . They are not equal because what Christ does is so much greater than what Adam does."[5]

It is worth quoting the passage at some length.

> [12]Therefore, just as sin came into the world through one man, and death came through sin, and so death spread to all because all have sinned. . . . [15]But the free gift is not like the trespass. For if the many died through the one man's trespass, much more surely have the grace of God and the free gift in the grace of the one man, Jesus Christ, abounded for the many. [16]And the free gift is not like the effect of the one man's sin. For the judgment following one trespass brought condemnation, but the free gift following many trespasses brings justification. . . . [18]Therefore just as one man's trespass led to condemnation for all, so one man's act of righteousness leads to justification and life for all. [19]For just as by the one man's disobedience the many were made sinners, so by the one man's obedience the many will be made righteous. [20]But law came in, with the result that the trespass multiplied; but where sin increased, grace

1. Joseph A. Fitzmyer, SJ, *Romans: A New Translation with Introduction and Commentary* (New York: Doubleday, 1993), 393; Luther, *Lectures on Romans*, ed. Hilton C. Oswald, vol. 25 of *LW*, 285; Calvin, *The Epistle of Paul the Apostle to the Romans and to the Thessalonians*, trans. Ross Mackenzie, *Calvin's New Testament Commentaries: A New Translation*, ed. Thomas F. Torrance and David W. Torrance (Grand Rapids: Eerdmans, 1973), 104.

2. Calvin, *Romans and Thessalonians*, 111.

3. Fitzmyer, *Romans*, 406.

4. Fitzmyer, *Romans*, 407.

5. David L. Bartlett, *Romans* (Louisville: Westminster John Knox, 1995), 58.

abounded all the more, [21]so that, just as sin exercised dominion in death, so grace might also exercise dominion through justification leading to eternal life through Jesus Christ our Lord.

Calvin comments, "sin has spread to all" from Adam, but not in such a manner that there is "no fault of our own" since, as 5:12 affirms, "all have sinned." We share in Adam's fault, says the Reformer, due to "the natural depravity . . . we bring from our mother's womb." This depravity "does not produce fruits [or sinful acts] immediately," though eventually and inevitably it does. Nevertheless, even before we act, our depravity is "before God, and deserves his punishment. . . . We have . . . all sinned, because we are all imbued with natural corruption, and for this reason, are wicked and perverse."[6]

What Calvin means by "*natural* corruption" is a misalignment of our created nature that we contract even before we act and that both disposes us toward and brings forth sinful acts. He can therefore also say that, with respect to our creation by God, "sin is not our nature but its derangement." The vitiation that comes upon humanity "did not flow from nature" but "is an adventitious quality which comes upon man" by Adam's disobedience "rather than a substantial property which has been implanted from the beginning." For Calvin, then, "we call it 'natural'" not because it is created but so "no man may think that anyone obtains it through bad conduct, since it holds all men fast by hereditary right."[7]

The Fall and Original Sin

This, says Calvin, is "original sin." At his creation, Adam "received for his posterity as well as for himself the gifts of divine grace." Indeed, in himself, the first human contained all of human nature, and so "by falling from the Lord, in himself he corrupted, vitiated, depraved, and ruined our nature—having lost the image of God,"[8] or the proper alignment of our faculties, especially of understanding and will. This must therefore be restored in Christ.[9] Thus, for Calvin, a corrupted and misaligned nature has descended from Adam to us. "His sin is the cause of our sin," since it results in a perverse disposition, inclination, or tendency that has become "natural and innate in us" and then produces sinful acts.[10]

6. Calvin, *Romans and Thessalonians*, 111–12. The words in brackets are mine.
7. Calvin, *ICR* 2.1.10; 2.1.11.
8. Calvin, *Romans and Thessalonians*, 111–12.
9. Calvin, *ICR* 1.15.3–4, 6–8.
10. Calvin, *Romans and Thessalonians*, 115. See also *ICR* 2.1.8.

According to Calvin, then, Adam fell from a state of grace into sin, and thereafter all humans were entangled in sin with the consequence that all are subject to death. People are plagued by a persistent fault that brings about works of the flesh and are therefore other than they were created to be. By contrast, "grace," which comes to us in Jesus Christ, "means the pure goodness of God, or his unmerited love" that relieves our misery. The free gift, unlike "the effect of one man's sin," is the fruit of God's mercy, and it is "the reconciliation by which we have obtained life and salvation. It is also righteousness, newness of life, and every other similar blessing."[11]

Calvin learns much of this by reading Paul in the light of Augustine, who, in his *City of God*, maintains that "the whole of human nature" existed in Adam and was therefore vitiated by his sin. Created human nature, says Augustine, was altered so that man "suffered in his members the warring of disobedient lust, and became subject to the necessity of dying."[12] This vitiated and altered nature—both misdirected and subject to death—is what humanity was made "not when created" but when Adam sinned, and it was then "transmitted by the woman to posterity" by "ordinary generation."[13]

As Augustine understands it, then, God created the human being upright and with a good will, and "the first evil will, which preceded all man's evil acts," is therefore a "falling away from the work of God." The transition is from a "right will," or "well-directed love" oriented toward the truth and toward God, to a "wrong will," or "ill-directed love" that is oriented not toward God and God's glory but toward ourselves.[14] The deep origin of our evil will or ill-directed love, says Augustine, is pride, or a "craving for undue exaltation," an inner turning away from God, the highest and unchangeable good, toward oneself.[15] This inward turning toward self in pride, he says, is what makes Adam and Eve "listen with pleasure to the words, 'Ye shall be as gods.'"[16]

The Fall diminishes us because the first humans turn from the capacious and true good of God and all things in their appropriate relations with God,

11. Calvin, *Romans and Thessalonians*, 115.

12. Somewhat notoriously, Augustine goes on to say that the "disobedient lust" mentioned here was "a new motion of their flesh," which was not under their control (422), as it would have been before the Fall. A lustful and involuntary movement of bodily members therefore now accompanies sexual intercourse, which persons regard as shameful and so hide from "the public eye." *The City of God*, trans. Marcus Dods (New York: Random House, 1950), 13.13 (p. 422); 14.23–26 (pp. 465–68, 470–76).

13. Augustine, *City of God* 13.6 (pp. 414, 416).

14. Augustine, *City of God* 14.11 (p. 457).

15. Augustine, *City of God* 14.13 (p. 460).

16. Augustine, *City of God* 14.13 (p. 461).

toward the narrowed sphere of their own isolated selves and interests. They do not thereby become "absolutely nothing," says Augustine, but, having turned away from God, they become curved in upon themselves. They are diminished because their being becomes "more contracted than it was" when they remained devoted to "Him who supremely is."[17] Sin acts as an astringent. Using the terms I have been developing in this systematic, we should say that, as sinners, humans are turned in on themselves, and so their orientation or stance in life, when measured by the broader, ec-centric, and Christoform standard of love of God and neighbor, is inappropriately diminished, narrowed, or constricted.

Calvin, though he does not merely repeat Augustine, essentially agrees. The deep "root of the Fall," he says, was "unfaithfulness," or an inward turning aside from God's word and promise. "Thereafter ambition and pride, together with ungratefulness arose, because Adam by seeking to be more than was granted to him shamefully spurned God's great bounty." Indeed, "to have been made in the likeness of God seemed a small matter to a son of earth unless he also attained equality with God."[18] The sinner, for Calvin, is a cosmic ingrate.[19] In any case, according to both Calvin and Augustine, it is an ill-directed love, a narrowed and disoriented will or capacity for choosing, that ensnares all human agents and renders them "corrupt trees" that produce bad fruits or evil actions.[20]

Grace Abounds?

Tough stuff, and so we should probably pause here to remind ourselves that sin and grace go together. This, in fact, is a feature of Reformed liturgies where a Call to Confession typically indicates not only that we are sinners but also that God is merciful, and where an Assurance of Pardon follows a Corporate Prayer of Confession.[21] It is also a major implication of the parallel Paul draws between Adam and Christ. Nevertheless, when Calvin comments on Romans 5, he fails to make this point as forcefully as he might.

17. Augustine, *City of God* 14.13 (p. 460).

18. Calvin, *ICR* 2.1.4.

19. In addition, while Calvin agrees with Augustine against Pelagius that original sin is not transmitted by imitation, rather than specify, as Augustine does, that it is transmitted by physical generation, he claims that Adam lost God's gifts "both for himself and his descendants" by divine ordinance. Calvin, *ICR* 2.1.7.

20. Augustine, *City of God* 13.11; 14.14 (pp. 422, 457).

21. *Book of Common Worship*, prepared by the Theology and Worship Ministry Unit for the Presbyterian Church (U.S.A.) and the Cumberland Presbyterian Church (Louisville: Westminster John Knox, 1993), 18, 20–21. See Douglas F. Ottati, *Theology for Liberal Presbyterians and Other Endangered Species* (Louisville: Geneva, 2006), 26–28, and also chap. 9, prop. #57.

Beginning with Romans 5:15, says Calvin, Paul corrects a misimpression one might receive from his earlier statements. Now, Paul makes it clear that Christ and Adam are not *matching* opposites. For one thing, the condemnation following Adam's trespass is a matter of justice, whereas the free gift is a matter of grace. For another, the grace of Christ overcomes the sin of Adam, and it also overturns the curse of Adam (or death) because "Christ surpasses Adam."[22] This, finally, is the source of our full assurance and gratitude.

Calvin then notes two additional differences, which "the apostle omitted" because his present argument did not require them. The first, he says, concerns Paul's understanding of grace. "We are condemned by Adam's sin not by imputation alone, as though we were punished for another's sin," but because, due to our corrupted nature, we, too, are infected and therefore guilty before God. By contrast, "the righteousness of Christ restores us by a different means." We are counted righteous not "because we have righteousness within us, but because we possess Christ Himself." That is, "the gift of righteousness . . . does not signify a quality with which God endows us," but rather "the free imputation of righteousness."[23]

A second, related difference is this. "The curse, which we derive from Adam, is conveyed to us by nature," and thus, says Calvin, "includes the whole of mankind," but to "participate in the grace of Christ, we must be engrafted into Him by faith." Thus, "the mere fact of being a man . . . is enough to entail participation in the wretched inheritance of sin," but "it is necessary . . . to be a believer in order to enjoy the righteousness of Christ."[24]

The meaning of this last point comes through in Calvin's comments on Romans 5:18, which he translates as follows. "So then as through one man's trespass the judgment came unto all men to condemnation; even so through one act of righteousness the free gift came unto all men to justification of life."[25] Calvin's interpretation? "Paul makes grace common to all men, not because it in fact extends to all, but because it is offered to all. Although Christ suffered for the sins of the world, and is offered by the goodness of God without distinction to all men, yet not all receive Him."[26] Calvin, that is to say, systematizes Romans 5 so that the "for all" or the "to all human beings" in verse 18 accords with "the many" mentioned elsewhere in the chapter. In Christ, grace effectively abounds for many but not for all. Indeed, for both Calvin and Augustine, Christ's benefit

22. Calvin, *Romans and Thessalonians*, 116.

23. Calvin, *Romans and Thessalonians*, 116–17.

24. Calvin, *Romans and Thessalonians*, 117.

25. Compare this with the NRSV: "Therefore just as one man's trespass led to condemnation for all, so one man's act of righteousness leads to justification and life for all" (Rom. 5:18).

26. Calvin, *Romans and Thessalonians*, 117–18.

is, at least in its effect, less extensive than Adam's curse. Sin is universally effective, but saving grace is not, either because, while offered to all, it is sometimes spurned or because it is intentionally withheld from some.[27]

There is, however, another way to read Romans 5:6–21. Begin with translations of 5:18 that differ somewhat from Calvin's. "Therefore just as one man's trespass led to condemnation for all, so one man's act of righteousness leads to justification and life for all" (NRSV). "So just as through one trespass condemnation came upon all, through one act of uprightness justification and life came to all human beings" (Joseph Fitzmyer).[28] Or, even my own intentionally quite rough translation: "So, just as through one transgression (or wrong step) to all human beings punishment, so also through one righteous act (or step) to all human beings acquittal (or justification) and life." The point is that each of these translations ties justification (or acquittal) and life directly to all human beings.

Next, rather than try to make the "all human beings" of 5:18 cohere systematically with "the many" of 5:15 and 5:19, we might observe instead a persistent rhetorical energy and theological exuberance that emerge at certain points in Paul's writings. We see it, for example, in 1 Corinthians 15:28, where the apostle exclaims, "all things are subjected to [the Son] . . . so that God may be all in all"—an expression that intimates redemption for all people or God's coming redemptive relationship with all things.[29] Again, consider 2 Corinthians 5:17–19: "So if anyone is in Christ, there is a new creation . . . everything has become new! All this is from God, who reconciled us to himself through Christ, and has given us the ministry of reconciliation; that is, in Christ God was reconciling the world to himself" (where "world" translates *kosmos*). Or, again, we see it in Romans 8:18–21: "I consider the sufferings of this present time are not worth compar-

27. Do Calvin's comments on Romans finally differ on this point from his position in the *Institutes*? In the latter, he says that "faith is the principal work of the Holy Spirit," "a firm and certain knowledge of God's benevolence toward us . . . both revealed to our minds and sealed upon our hearts through the Holy Spirit," and that "repentance is God's free gift" whose efficacy depends upon "the Spirit of regeneration" (*ICR* 3.1.4; 3.2.7; 3.3.21). Indeed, "whomsoever God wills to snatch from death, he quickens by the Spirit of regeneration," even as God hardens the reprobate (3.3.21). Thus, in the *Institutes* at least, those who do not receive Christ do not receive him because God does not will them to do so, and therefore it becomes difficult to distinguish the genuine offer of grace from its effective extension. This, in fact, is the line of thinking that led some later Calvinists to maintain that God's grace is "irresistible," and then to affirm Christ's *limited* atonement. See, for example, the Westminster Confession of Faith in *BOC* 6.071.

28. Fitzmyer, *Romans*, 405.

29. David L. Bartlett, "Creation Waits with Eager Longing," in *God Who Creates: Essays in Honor of W. Sibley Towner*, ed. William P. Brown and S. Dean McBride Jr. (Grand Rapids: Eerdmans, 2000), 242–43.

ing with the glory about to be revealed to us. For the creation waits with eager longing for the revealing of the children of God; for the creation was subjected to futility, not of its own will but by the will of the one who subjected it, in hope that the creation itself will be set free from its bondage to decay and will obtain the freedom of the glory of the children of God."

Thus, as David Bartlett notes, sometimes redemption and new creation seem "a gift for the faithful and sometimes a promise for all humankind, even a promise for the whole cosmos."[30] And, especially if we recognize the direct ascription of acquittal and life to all human beings in Romans 5:18, we may note that a similar rhetorical energy builds toward theological exuberance in Romans 5.

> Much more surely . . . will we be saved through him. . . . Much more surely, having been reconciled, will we be saved by his life. . . . Much more surely have the grace of God and the free gift in the grace of the one man, Jesus Christ, abounded for the many. . . . Much more surely will those who receive the abundance of grace . . . exercise dominion. . . . Therefore just as one man's trespass led to condemnation for all, so one man's act of righteousness leads to justification and life for all. (5:9–18)

So, there is reason to favor a reading of Romans 5 that leaves more room for Paul's occasional exuberance than does Calvin's more systematizing interpretation. What if, by fits and starts, Paul strains toward a truly radical and magnificent idea? What if, in Jesus Christ and the Spirit, we should discover that God simply *is* the God of grace who is gracious to you and to me and to all creation?

Humanity Entangled in Sin

In any case, even as we reflect on a primary text taken by important classical theologians to point to original sin, we may (and should) remind ourselves that sin and grace go together. What, then, of the claim that all have become entangled in sin? Fitzmyer notes that while the doctrine of original sin is for the Western theological tradition "the *sensus plenior* of Paul's teaching in Romans 5:12–21," the apostle himself "does not explain how the baleful effect of Adam takes place," and "he makes no mention of sin's hereditary character (as Augustine did later)."[31] Moreover, the idea that Adam falls from grace and thus "loses a supernatural status" is an Augustinian teaching difficult to square with Genesis 3.[32] Nevertheless,

30. Bartlett, "Creation Waits," 250.
31. Fitzmyer, *Romans*, 407.
32. Fitzmyer, *Romans*, 409.

the view that all are entangled in corruption seems biblically appropriate if one reads the Genesis story of the early history of humanity in the light of something like Paul's claims about sin, reconciliation, and redemption.

> They have all gone astray, they are all alike perverse;
> there is no one who does good, no, not one. (Rom. 3:12; Ps. 14:3)

Genesis 3:1–11:9 may be read as the story of the emergence of an evident and persistent human fault. This should be plain to anyone who has read the very impressive section entitled "The Incursion and Spread of Sin" in Gerhard von Rad's *Old Testament Theology*.[33] Let me summarize.

The story of humanity begins with Adam and Eve in the garden where, after Adam has named the animals and been introduced to Eve, a serpent, who is "more crafty than any other wild animal that the LORD God had made," asks the woman whether there is any tree in the garden from which God has forbidden the humans to eat. She says we may eat of the fruit of all trees but one, and that, if we touch it, we shall die (a pretty good reason to leave it alone). "But the serpent," who knows how to pique human interest, says "to the woman, 'You will not die . . . but you will be like gods.'" This prospect is sufficiently tempting that the woman and her husband eat, thus transgressing the boundary God has set.

As it happens, the humans do not die, though, depending on your theology, they do not quite become gods either. Instead, God expels them from the garden. But, then, another boundary is crossed. The first human pair becomes the parents of the first murderer and the first murder victim. Cain kills his brother, Abel (4:8), and God sentences the murderer to wander. Cain then laments that he cannot bear the punishment because (though, according to the story thus far, he and his parents are the only humans on Earth) "anyone who meets me may kill me." But the Lord says, "Not so," promises that anyone who kills Cain will suffer sevenfold vengeance, and puts a mark on Cain so that no one who comes upon him will kill him (4:15).

This is God's deterrence-vengeance scheme to restrain violence and to prevent further killing, and, as anyone who has lived in New Jersey and in Chicago knows, it is not unlike the strategies gangs employ to protect their members. With Lamech's speech in 4:23–24—

> If Cain is avenged sevenfold,
> truly Lamech seventy-sevenfold—

33. Gerhard von Rad, *The Theology of Israel's Historical Traditions*, vol. 1 of *Old Testament Theology*, trans. D. M. G. Stalker (New York: Harper & Row, 1962), 154–65.

we see that the scheme fails. What's more, the cycle of human violence intensifies even further; it spirals out of control to the point where the Nephilim, or warriors of renown (the offspring of sons of God and the daughters of men), are on the earth. God is not pleased. Seeing, then, "that the wickedness of humankind was great . . . and that every inclination of the thoughts of their hearts was only evil continually, . . . the LORD was sorry that he had made humankind on the earth," and therefore resolved to "blot out from the earth the human beings . . . together with animals and creeping things and birds of the air" (6:5–7).

This admittedly seems unfair to the animals, but the basic point is clear: since "the earth was corrupt in God's sight, and . . . filled with violence" (6:11), God once again allows the waters to cover the earth, even the "high mountains" (7:19). God spares Noah, "a righteous man, blameless in his generation" (6:9) (as well as his family), directs Noah to make "an ark of cypress wood" (6:14), and to bring pairs "of every living thing, of all flesh" (6:19) into the ark. When the flood subsides, Noah, his family, and the creatures they have brought on to the ark are therefore ready to repopulate the earth. Moreover, God, who covenants with Noah and every living creature never again to flood the earth and destroy all flesh, now replaces the earlier deterrence-vengeance strategy with a virtually Hammurabian code or law, and also repeats the blessing of generativity given with the creation in Genesis 1:

> "Whoever sheds the blood of a human,
>   by a human shall that person's blood be shed;
> for in his own image
>   God made humankind.
>
> And you, be fruitful and multiply, abound in the earth and multiply in it." (9:6–7)

OK, now that God has hit the reset button, we begin again with a blameless man, Noah, and his descendants. The history of humanity starts afresh. And what happens? Within a few generations, the basic fault—a tendency to overstep limits or boundaries—is back. The whole population of the earth, speaking the same language, migrates to the land of Shinar, settles there, and resolves to cooperate in the building of "a city, and a tower with its top in the heavens" (11:4). (Recall that in Genesis 3 the desire to be like gods, or to be something other and more than they are, is what set humans on the wrong trajectory to begin with.) The Lord comes down to see what mortals have built, notes that this is only the beginning of what they will do, resolves to confuse their language (presumably with the aid of other divine beings) so that humans will not understand one another, and then scatters humankind "over the face of all the earth" (11:8). Why? Because when human beings cooperate and communicate, bad things can happen.

What we have here, fast on the heels of the creation stories in Genesis 1 and 2, is a mythopoeic narrative of the beginnings of human civilization that has been knitted together from a series of older stories and tales, for example, the first murder and a failed deterrent strategy; an ever-increasing spiral of violence; warriors of renown; heavenly dissatisfaction; the great flood, and a divine promise that "the waters shall never again become a flood to destroy all flesh"; the building of the first great city with a tower that reaches into the heavens; the confusion of human languages; and the scattering of humankind. It's pretty negative, and von Rad concludes, "The story of the Tower of Babel is therefore to be regarded as the end of a road upon which Israel [I would say humanity] stepped out with the Fall, and which led to more and more serious outbreaks of sin."[34] An unmistakable point of the connected narrative is this: humans chronically overstep created limits to try to become like gods. The consequences are highly destructive, and, indeed, it is as if humans are in the grips of a corrupting fault that renders them violent and prone to evil. And the fault doesn't go away.

This has the feel of hard-won wisdom. In our experience, persons and communities do indeed have distinctive capabilities that are on display in the great technical accomplishments of agriculture, urban societies, and more. At the same time and in the midst of their considerable accomplishments, however, they also seem plagued by proclivities toward chronic corruption and persistent violence, tendencies that wise persons and good societies anticipate and endeavor to restrain.

Proposition #59 Sin's corruption is multifaceted, radical, and universal.

The extended narrative in Genesis 3:1–11:9 suggests that the story of persistent corruption is the story of "every person" and of every human community. Much Christian theological tradition, especially in its Protestant varieties, elaborates further: the corruption is multifaceted, radical, and universal. For example, the Westminster Confession of Faith says that people become "wholly defiled in all faculties and parts of soul and body."[35] Or, consider a segment of a corporate prayer of confession that appears in the Episcopalian Book of Common Prayer and also the Presbyterian *Book of Common Worship* (1947): "We have followed too much the devices and desires of our own hearts. We have offended against

34. Von Rad, *The Theology of Israel's Historical Traditions*, 163. The words in brackets are mine.

35. *BOC* 6.002.

Thy holy laws. We have left undone those things which we ought to have done. And we have done those things which we ought not to have done; And there is no health in us."[36]

We might say that, as befits their significant, even wondrous, powers and capacities, humans are equipped for conscious, intentional, and creative interrelations with God and others. The human fault is a corruption of what we are equipped to be, a turning away from God and others, a diminution of the abundant and good life that befits us. Especially when viewed in the light of redemption in Jesus as the Christ and the Spirit, humans are equipped to be faithful and creative participants; we are fitted for an ec-centric existence of covenantal relationships of attentiveness, fidelity, and responsibility with God and others. We are fitted for the true communion with God in community with others that characterizes the kingdom. Sin means that, although we are equipped for this distinctive, truly grand, and glorious vocation, we are chronically confused, misoriented, and misdirected in the ways we live and move and deploy our powers. We are in the grips of a corrupting tendency, an impelling influence that keeps us from living a truly good and abundant life. Sin means the diminution of life in its fullness, or the way toward death.

Paul Tillich writes of "man's estrangement from God, from men, from himself."[37] We might call this an estrangement of persons from God, from others, and so also from their own best and true life possibility. Gustavo Gutiérrez points to "the fundamental alienation, the root of a situation of injustice and exploitation" that has both personal and collective dimensions. Sin, says Gutiérrez, may be understood as a basic "breach of friendship with God and others."[38] In the terms I am developing here, this breach of friendship is itself a turning away from the ec-centric, good, and abundant life for which we are equipped and sustained. It is the fundamental alienation from true communion with God in community with others. Leonardo Boff writes of "disgrace" as a "closing in upon oneself" that constantly threatens the drive toward openness and communion inherent in grace.[39]

Generally speaking, the varieties of destructiveness in human interrelationships, as well as in human relationships with nonhuman life-forms and realities,

36. *The Book of Common Worship Approved by the General Assembly of the Presbyterian Church in the United States of America and the Presbyterian Church in the United States* (Richmond, VA: John Knox, 1946), 21.

37. Paul Tillich, *Existence and the Christ*, vol. 2 of *Systematic Theology* (Chicago: University of Chicago Press, 1957), 47.

38. Gustavo Gutiérrez, *A Theology of Liberation: History, Politics, and Salvation*, trans. Sister Caridad Inda and John Eagleson, 15th anniversary edition with a new introduction (Maryknoll, NY: Orbis, 1988), 100–101, 103.

39. Leonardo Boff, *Liberating Grace*, trans. John Drury (Maryknoll, NY: Orbis, 1979), 4–5.

are truly protean. Sin's corruption is multifaceted, and it therefore seems important to resist its reduction to a single term. We need to keep before us "the many ways we go astray" in order to find and create "a variety of ways to combat these destructive powers," and also to "point toward the multifarious ways God graces the world."[40] We need a broad and extensive portfolio.

James M. Gustafson notes that the longer theological tradition has identified at least four interrelated facets of the human fault.[41] Two are direct corruptions of affect. *Idolatry*, a corruption of confidence and loyalty, is a matter of placing our confidence and loyalty in inappropriate objects, or of misplaced degrees of confidence in and loyalty to otherwise proper objects such as race or nation. *Concupiscence* indicates a corruption of love and desire. Wrongly ordered loves and desires orient persons toward inappropriate ends or toward the right ends wrongly, such as health, wealth, and power. In matters of the heart, then, we often devote ourselves to the wrong things, or to the right things with either excess or defect.

Two further facets of sin, though they are not directly matters of corrupted affect, have their roots there. *Corrupt rationality*, says Gustafson, refers to "the wrong depiction and interpretation of the particular 'world' that attracts our attention and that evokes our activity." Wrong confidences, loyalties, and loves skew our rational interests so that our interpretations of contexts and circumstances in which we participate often are slanted and incomplete. Finally, *disobedience* indicates a related corruption of our moral interests. Skewed devotions and depictions encourage us both to transgress and to participate deficiently in personal and social relationships of obligation and responsibility.

Gustafson also points out how these varied facets of sin may be joined together by means of the Augustinian and Edwardsian metaphor of *contraction*. The deep root of the human fault is a contraction of the human spirit. As sinners, we shrink from the devotion to God that can enlarge us toward a genuine comprehension of and participation in the community of all things in their mutual interdependence and common dependence on God. Our souls become narrowed as we turn from God toward ourselves and toward our isolated or partial communities. Consequently, idolatry may be understood as a contraction of human trust and loyalty, concupiscence as a contraction of human loves and

40. Mary Potter Engel, "Evil, Sin, and Violation of the Vulnerable," in *Lift Every Voice: Constructing Theologies from the Underside*, ed. Susan Brooks Thistlewaite and Mary Potter Engel (San Francisco: Harper & Row, 1990), 164. See also Susan Brooks Thistlewaite on the differences that both gender and race make in understanding sin and its characteristic forms in her *Sex, Race, and God: Christian Feminism in Black and White* (New York: Crossroad, 1989), 77–91.

41. Gustafson, *ETP*, 1:293–306.

desires, corrupt rationality as a constriction of human vision, and disobedience as a contraction of our moral interests and responsibility.

Radical and Universal

Sin's multifaceted corruption is radical and universal. From the perspective of an Augustinian Christian wisdom, it infects all our capacities, as well as every aspect of human society, so that the entire human project is unavoidably skewed. And, indeed, though aspects of the traditional doctrine of sin frequently are misunderstood, and though some theories associated with it have proved exegetically untenable, these basic affirmations continue to furnish an illuminating commentary on the human condition.

Sin is radical because it is a matter of actions, and inactions, of things done and left undone, and yet, fundamentally, it is more than a matter of discrete external deeds. As Jonathan Edwards notes, sin is an active and persistent tendency, a disposing alignment of our powers, or an orienting impulsion.[42] It has to do not only with the surfaces of life but also with its depth and personal center. Sin is not just a matter of the hands, the feet, and the mouth; it is more than a matter of words and deeds. It is a matter of mind and heart and will, so that no aspect of human life is exempted from sin's effects.

It therefore is not the case, as rationalists occasionally imply, that only the emotions and passions are disordered and that our reasoning capacity can be trusted to hold them in check and bring them to appropriate order. Neither is it the case that only our reasoning is distorted, and that our deepest affections or our hearts remain reliable guides. As Augustine insisted contra Pelagius, our capacity for choice is perversely misdirected because the right will or well-directed love has been transmuted into the wrong will or ill-directed love. Peel away our actions and our habits, and you will find not a neutral capacity for good and evil but a corrupted elective capacity enslaved to wrongly biased affections.[43]

Even so, the radicality of sin does not mean the utter destruction of human capacities and powers, or that we are unable to accomplish anything of value and significance. To the contrary, traditional Reformed orthodoxy insists that, even after the Fall, people retain significant intellectual, moral, and technical abili-

42. Edwards, *Original Sin*, ed. Clyde A. Holbrook, vol. 3 of *WJE*, pt. 1, chap. 1, sec. 2, pp. 120–27.

43. J. Patout Burns, ed. and trans., *Theological Anthropology* (Philadelphia: Fortress, 1981), 12–19, 72, 74–77.

ties.[44] Both Calvin and Edwards, boosters of the notion of total depravity though they are, recognize in persons the continuation of impressive abilities in the arts and sciences, as well as certain basic social affectivities and a rudimentary sense of justice or fairness.[45] Moreover, these continuing abilities are seen as evidences of God's preserving care that remain essential for the levels of personal, social, and moral flourishing that humans generally are able to attain.

The rather more subtle meaning of sin's radicality is more disturbing. Humans wield significant abilities and powers, so that evidences of creativity, achievement, and even heartfelt sensitivity abound. Many parents love and care for their children; many citizens contribute to relatively just and flourishing societies; and many businesspeople and workers labor to fashion productive institutions and systems of economic interdependence. Physicists harness the atom, and biologists unlock the secrets of genetics; advances in electronic communications, artificial intelligence, and human enhancement abound. Nevertheless, even our most impressive achievements, both as individuals and as communities, are corrupted by sin's constriction. Caring parents sometimes neglect and inappropriately manipulate their children, and then again, there are many parents who participate deficiently in or even flagrantly violate important familial obligations. Comparatively just and prosperous societies harbor discriminatory and destructive ethnic and racial prejudices; most societies regard foreign societies and groups largely through the spectacles of their own partial interests; and, of course, many societies are neither comparatively just nor prosperous. Our global economy is littered with notorious imbalances, injustices, and ecological disasters. The deep ambiguity of human scientific and technical achievements is one of the more profound lessons of modern history.

The goods that individuals and communities endeavor to secure and protect—flourishing families, economic success, and national security—ordinarily remain partial, and, more often than not, our partial goods conflict with the partial goods pursued and protected by others. This is part of the meaning of finitude. The radicality of sin indicates that our impressive powers and abilities may be turned toward terrible injustice and terrifying evil as we pursue inordinate desires (How much wealth and power are enough?) and also struggle to protect and enhance our partial goods in the face of significant competition and conflict. The radicality of sin points to a world of human accomplishment and achievement that is also a world of destructive perversions, fragmentations, and conflicts.

Sin's radical corruption is also universal. No person or aspect of society is

44. Calvin, *ICR* 2.2.12–2.2.24.

45. Calvin, *ICR* 2.2.13; Edwards, "The Nature of True Virtue," in *Ethical Writings*, ed. Paul Ramsey, vol. 8 of *WJE*, 569–70.

exempted from sin's effects. It is not the case, as reformers sometimes imply, that a particular leader, community, movement, or institution is free from constricted rationality, devotion, and responsibility. There is no sin-free society; our lives as individuals and in families, in voluntary associations and in nations, all are infected by sin's corrupting tendency. Indeed, as Augustine pointed out, the universality of sin puts the lie to a pious refusal to admit that the church, too, like other institutions and groups, is subject to sin's effects.[46] The universality of sin means that we confront corrupting tendencies in every aspect of every human society and group. It is a confession of universal misorientation that cannot be and ought not to be reduced to an ideology of Christian superiority.

Here, again, the historic wisdom of Christian believing may be misconstrued. Sin's universality does not mean that every social and institutional arrangement is ineluctably futile, or that some social and institutional arrangements are not preferable to others. For one thing, though no society is sin-free, some structures are better able than others to restrain corruption and to encourage more genuine participation. Calvin therefore insists that, while appropriate forms of government often depend on historical circumstances, "a system compounded of aristocracy and democracy" (or what we might call a representative democracy) "far excels all others." Why? Because the wills of kings often disagree "with what is just and right," and it is also rare for kings "to have been endowed with such great keenness and prudence, that each knows how much is enough." The conclusion? "Men's fault or failing causes it to be safer and more bearable for a number to exercise government, so that they may help one another, teach and admonish one another; and if one asserts himself unfairly, there may be a number of censors and masters to restrain his willfulness."[47]

The universality of sin therefore makes it appropriate to adopt certain social principles and strategies. For example, in the light of human tendencies both to

46. In letters directed against the Donatists, Augustine accuses his opponents of "impious schism" and also of expelling people from their communion without sufficient reason. At one point, he says, "even well-known wrongdoers in the church do not harm its good members," and elsewhere he notes that the sacraments remain holy. *Augustine: Political Writings*, ed. E. M. Atkins and R. J. Dodaro (Cambridge: Cambridge University Press, 2001), 137–38, 141–42. Peter Brown says that the Donatists represented the last of the earlier church as a disciplined alternative to the dominant society, whereas Augustine was interested in a church that reaches out into the society and invites the world into itself. *Augustine of Hippo: A Biography* (Berkeley: University of California Press, 1969), 212–25. Herbert A. Deane, *The Political Idea of St. Augustine* (New York: Columbia University Press, 1963), 183, articulates the standard theological view that Augustine "leveled a fundamental attack on" the Donatists' "conception of the church of the pure and their view that the validity of the sacraments depended upon the moral purity of the individual priest or bishop who administered them."

47. Calvin, *ICR* 4.20.8.

neglect and to transgress relations of mutual trust and accountability, it seems appropriate, in family and in church, as well as in economic and political communities, to adopt a *constitutional principle* whereby there are institutionalized clear and binding statements of commonly accepted and mutual responsibilities, for example, wedding vows, business contracts, political charters. The *principle of participation and the dispersal of power* assumes that perennial human tendencies toward self-aggrandizement and injustice are enhanced by concentrations of power in the hands of a few, for example, a king, an executive, a president, and that representative structures, for example, a parliament, a shareholders meeting, a faculty senate, check and balance the exercise of power by enfranchising the participation of a greater number of interested parties. Finally, *the principle of plurality* disallows monolithic and authoritarian hierarchies. It requires that basic social institutions and associations, for example, civil government, business corporations, and religious associations, remain relatively independent of one another, and thus encourages their mutual restraint and participation.

There may, of course, be other ways of limiting corruption and enfranchising more genuine participation. My point is simply that the affirmation of sin's universality underscores the ambiguities present in every human society, even as it rejects all counsels of quietism and despair. No society is sin-free. None avoids sin's constriction and its pernicious consequences. Therefore, none can be affirmed as good without qualification, and none should be exempted from criticism. Nevertheless, the affirmation of sin's universality encourages us to adopt realistic and responsible social strategies that take into account sin's pervasive contraction of the human spirit, as well as admittedly limited, but real, possibilities for fairness and justice.

Original?

Should we also say that sin's multifaceted, radical, and universal corruption is original? The answer, I think, depends on what we mean by calling it that. As we have seen, for traditional orthodoxy, original sin sometimes means that all of human nature was contained in the first human pair, that this nature, in turn, was vitiated or misaligned when Adam and Eve sinned, and that a vitiated or misaligned nature has been passed on from them to all subsequent humans. Somewhat notoriously, Augustine also claims that, when the whole of human nature was vitiated by the first sin, there emerged in the first pair a "disobedient lust" or "a new motion of their flesh" that was beyond their control. Thereafter, this involuntary movement of bodily members accompanies sexual intercourse, and so, by the lust or disordered desire associated with intercourse, the vitiation of nature is passed on to subsequent generations.[48] Calvin does not subscribe to this rather elaborate theory of transmission, though he too regards sin as an inherited depravity. For him, this inheritance means that we *are* sinners, that sin is present in us from birth, and that we are therefore justly condemned by the deity.

There are difficulties here. Augustine's theory of transmission may have some basis in a kind of Platonic dualism, but it is exegetically far-fetched, and it also undermines the goodness of sex and created bodily life. Again, even apart from Augustine's speculations, the basic idea of an inheritance, though it implies an entanglement from which we cannot easily extricate ourselves, fails to indicate any sense in which persons who come after the original pair participate in the emergence of their own sinful propensity. But it is also true that, apart from any explicit theory of transmission, it seems difficult to fathom what it means to say, as Calvin does, that sin's corruption "holds men fast by hereditary right."[49]

I read the story of the first human pair, as well as the extended story of the beginning of human civilization, mythically and symbolically. As does Reinhold Niebuhr, I think these texts indicate that sin's corruption is unavoidable, and that every person and community participates in its emergence. This is so because the human fault has a basis in the finite condition of persons and groups that is artfully indicated by the stories of the serpent and of the tower of Babel. My initial aim here is to describe this condition with reference to the radically situated circumstance of human agents. Following that description, I turn to the role of anxious agency in the emergence of corrupted affect, corrupted rationality, and disobedience or corrupted responsibility.

The Anxieties of Radically Situated Agents

Why are people tempted? Why are they susceptible to sin and corruption? Genesis 3 portrays a talking serpent luring them with the prospect of becoming like gods. But it is not too difficult to outline a more discursive theological answer: *persons and groups are tempted to sin and corruption by the anxieties that accompany radically situated agency*.

You and I have capacities to act and to intervene. We are agents; nevertheless, we do not act in a vacuum but in contexts. That is, we find ourselves in the midst of things, enmeshed in welters of interrelations, set within dynamic situations made up of other agents, circumstances, and conditions. This is a central idea of H. Richard Niebuhr's influential book *The Responsible Self*: whenever

48. Augustine, *City of God* 14.17–26 (pp. 465–68, 470–76).
49. Calvin, *ICR* 2.2.22.

we act—whether as persons or as communities—we *inter*act with other agents and realities in the midst of a field of interactions and interrelations.[50] Human agency, then, is both shaped and constrained by actions and conditions (among them important aspects of the agent's own makeup) that are prior to its exercise. We respond to actions, forces, and events that impinge upon us. Moreover, our responsive actions and their consequences are themselves then deflected and turned, subjected to additional influences and conditions, including the subsequent actions of others.

Niebuhr also observes that *human agents interpret.*[51] They act or respond in accordance with their interpretation(s) of the actions that impinge upon them and also in accord with their interpretation(s) of anticipated replies to their responses. Human responders, then, are not mere reactors. They draw upon interpretive, reflective, and imaginative capacities in order to devise a reading of the actions that impinge upon them, and they also draw upon these same capacities in order to envision subsequent replies to their own actions. These imaginative readings or interpretative visions, in turn, help to guide agents' understandings of the appropriate or fitting actions they might take. Thus, one nation responds to the actions of another in accord with its reading or interpretation of the circumstances, including the other's intentions, and so also in accord with its reading or interpretation of the other's anticipated reply. That is to say, responsible agents "place" the actions that impinge upon them within an imaginative interpretation or picture of the context in which they occur and into which their replies may or may not "fit."

Now, if persons and communities interact with other agents and realities in continuing and dynamic contexts of interrelations and conditions, then, while they may exercise significant influences over events, they do *not* control all relevant outcomes. This is so because outcomes depend on very many factors in addition to their own interventions and intentions. Attentive, experienced, and wise persons and communities recognize that this is so. Moreover, if persons and communities respond to actions and circumstances in accordance with their imaginative interpretations of their wider context, then false interpretations support inappropriate responses. For example, nation A's response to the action of nation B is informed by a misinterpretation of the political dynamics of the international community, nation B's capabilities as well as its intentions, and so nation A's response is out of kilter with the wider circumstance. It doesn't really fit.

This is one reason why, for H. Richard Niebuhr, the primary practical ques-

50. H. Richard Niebuhr, *The Responsible Self: An Essay in Christian Moral Philosophy* (Louisville: Westminster John Knox, 1999), 56–61.

51. H. Richard Niebuhr, *The Responsible Self*, 61–63.

tion raised by responsible agents is not "What is my goal or ideal?" but instead "What is going on?"[52] A responsible self—one who recognizes *the radically situated character of agency*—knows that relevant outcomes finally are determined not merely by what one has in mind but by a blooming and buzzing cacophony of factors, including one's own action. She therefore places a premium on the interpretation of circumstances that an idealist (as well as an ideologue) often fails to appreciate. Like a good politician, she knows that important goals and objectives occasionally must be reconsidered and revised in the light of circumstances and events, possibilities and limits. Or, to put this same point another way, in the light of H. Richard Niebuhr's basic understanding of radically situated human agency, idealism has two related drawbacks. First, it pays too much attention to the agent's own goals and ideas and too little attention to what is going on because, second, it harbors an overly robust idea of what human moral agents can accomplish. This is why Niebuhr insists that, in the final analysis, humans are not *makers* who fashion or produce ends (circumstances, states of affairs, and histories) that mirror their objectives and ideals, so much as situated *answerers* who need to take into account a plurality of factors that lie beyond their control in order to try a response that is both possible and appropriate.[53]

52. H. Richard Niebuhr, *The Responsible Self*, 63.

53. This line of thinking coheres with important features of Reinhold Niebuhr's Christian realism. Robin W. Lovin, *Reinhold Niebuhr and Christian Realism* (New York: Cambridge University Press, 1995), 29, therefore notes "an attentiveness to all of the forces at work in a situation," including configurations of power and interest in Reinhold's writings. See also Reinhold Niebuhr, "Augustine's Political Realism," in *Christian Realism and Political Problems* (New York: Scribner's Sons, 1953), 119–20. Reinhold Niebuhr, says Lovin, in *Christian Realism and the New Realities* (Cambridge: Cambridge University Press, 2008), 8, cares deeply about moral norms and ideals, but he also advocates an "eyes-open, feet-on-the-ground, common sense" demeanor that "pays attention to what is going-on and is not misled by vain hopes and fears." This is why, although Reinhold never relinquishes the language of moral ideals and although he continues to believe that ideals pull our choices in a certain direction, he also consistently claims that the enactment of moral ideals is no simple possibility. In fact, he persistently criticizes those he regards as naïve idealists, whether they favor sentimental prescriptions for social harmony that underestimate class conflict and racial prejudice or "schemes of an ideal world order" that overestimate the capabilities of current international associations, neglect the importance of balancing powers, and generally have little relevance to actual circumstances, dangers, and duties. See also Reinhold Niebuhr, *The Children of Light and the Children of Darkness: A Vindication of Democracy and a Critique of Its Traditional Defense* (Eugene, OR: Wipf & Stock, 2006), 86–190; *The Irony of American History*, with a new introduction by Andrew J. Bacevich (Chicago: University of Chicago Press, 2008), 2. See also Reinhold Niebuhr, *An Interpretation of Christian Ethics* (New York: Seabury, 1979), 23, for a passage quoted by Lovin in *Reinhold Niebuhr and Christian Realism*, 5–6. Indeed, Niebuhr says in "The Illusion of World Government," in *Christian Realism and Political Problems*, 16–18, that "virtually all arguments for world government rest upon the simple presupposition that

The fact that human agents are radically situated constitutes a basic aspect of finitude that naïve idealism fails to take seriously enough. Under the influence of the Spirit, this basic fact points to interdependent interrelations as well as other features of our human situation that indicate that our lives are ineluctably social and intertwined with others, and so it may encourage us to take up an ec-centric existence. The critical point for my purposes here, however, is that it also illumines dynamics of finitude, anxiety, and sin, and so it suggests why we are susceptible to corruption. Here's how.

As agents endowed with significant capacities for knowledge and imagination, we regularly find that the things we value and care about—our lives, projects, accomplishments, and relationships—are set within a world of changing circumstances, the unpredictable actions of others, and unanticipated consequences. This observation is fundamental. We find, in a word, that the things we value are *contingent*, and that there is no human action—from launching an invasion to raising a child—without risk. Moreover, precisely because we recognize that they are vulnerable and at risk, we labor to secure the things we value—our families, our work, or our nation—and their enduring meaning against a world of uncertainties. We sense that we lack control, and, indeed, rendered anxious by our lack of control, we often set out to increase it. And just here our imaginative capacity makes a signal contribution; for no matter how many uncertainties and threats we are able to mitigate and address, we can always envision more. The lives, loves, accomplishments, and relationships of self-aware and radically situated agents must therefore always remain insecure in the face of felt contingencies.

The alchemy of human spirit and emotion is such that, rather than encouraging us to admit the futility of securing our own life's meaning, the heightened anxiety that accompanies our knowledge of contingency and threat ensnares us in a great suppression. Just because we know our life to be ultimately threatened, just because we know the meaning of our activities and relationships to be insecure, we redouble our efforts to secure them. According to Reinhold Niebuhr, then, we attempt to suppress our fundamental anxiety at contingency by amassing power and trying to control circumstances.[54] We try to become something other and greater than we are equipped to be. We try, as Genesis says, to become like gods. And though our striving often is destructive, though it is frequently costly both to ourselves and to others, this does not deter us, because no matter how much power we accumulate, we nevertheless imagine further

---

the desirability of world order proves the attainability of world government"—but this simply goes to show that they are based on an illusion.

54. Reinhold Niebuhr, *NDM*, 1:186–203.

threats. This is sin as inordinate self-assertion or as pride. Lamech therefore boasts to his wives,

> If Cain is avenged sevenfold,
> truly Lamech seventy-sevenfold. (Gen. 4:24)

Inordinate self-assertion is a primary temptation of the powerful—say an empire, or a superpower. A community grows increasingly anxious as the threats it envisions multiply, and so it tries to alter threatening circumstances by exercising its economic, political, and military might. It is moved to take action, and its actions occasionally may lead to substantially creative and positive results. But no matter how successful the community may be at reducing important threats, additional perils and anxieties remain. It realizes that it is never entirely secure from all possible threats. And, indeed, just because it is sufficiently powerful to pursue its interests with few restraints and with little need to negotiate, it is pulled toward unilateral efforts to *guarantee* its security. This, however, is not a possibility, and in fact the community's unilateral designs often threaten other powers and thus actually plant seeds of additional insecurity. Nevertheless, and often at its own expense as well as the expense of others, the community overreaches. It finds itself, for example, engaged in ill-fated and unilateral wars and occupations even as it shirks international norms by abusing prisoners beyond the reach of public scrutiny.

There is, as Reinhold Niebuhr also indicates, another possibility (though he develops it less thoroughly in his writings).[55] We may try to suppress our anxiety by losing ourselves in lesser, more easily secured objects of desire, such as possessions, food, drink, or TV, and thus withdrawing from riskier activities and involvements in a threatening world. We attempt to insulate ourselves, and perhaps we also grow numb. Now the problem is not inordinate self-assertion but rather deficient participation in our many relationships and responsibilities. This also takes a toll on us and on others, on our families, our allies, and so on. Even so, in the face of mounting insecurities and anxieties, we are drawn to opt out, to rid ourselves of discomfort and ambiguity by relinquishing our more challenging

55. For important feminist discussions of Reinhold Niebuhr on sin, see, for example, Valerie Saiving Goldstein, "The Human Situation: A Feminine View," *Journal of Religion* 40 (1960): 100–112. Reprinted in *Womanspirit Rising*, ed. Judith Plaskow and Carol Christ (San Francisco: Harper & Row, 1979), 25–42. Mark Douglas and Elizabeth Hinson-Hasty, "Revisiting Valerie Saiving's Challenges to Reinhold Niebuhr: Honoring Fifty Years of Reflections on 'The Human Situation: A Feminine View,'" a roundtable discussion in the *Journal of Feminist Studies in Religion* 28, no. 1 (Spring 2012): 75–131. Rebekah Miles, *The Bonds of Freedom: Feminist Theology and Christian Realism* (Oxford: Oxford University Press, 2001).

duties and cares. This is what the classical theological tradition calls sin as sloth. Reinhold Niebuhr discerns it in recurrent American impulses toward isolationism, though one might easily draw illustrations from other, more personal areas of life, for example, slothful behavior to dull the anxieties of a failing marriage. The point is that sloth amounts to an attempt to avoid the risks and anxieties of action and assertion by renouncing the responsibilities of agency and power.

Anxiety and the Corruption of Affectivity, Rationality, and Responsibility

Return now to the facets of sin mentioned earlier. How do the anxieties that accompany situated agency contribute to corruptions of affectivity, rationality, and responsibility?

Begin with affectivity. Both as individuals and as communities enmeshed in a cacophony of events and interrelations, we want, need, and are devoted to many different objects, causes, and ends, for example, self-esteem, professional success, the good of the nation, the good of our local community, nurturing and educating children, etc. To live coherently, we must prioritize, organize, and balance our many desires, confidences, and loyalties. Which ends are truly desirable? Which causes are worthy of devotion? Do my several ends and causes cohere? Can I organize them in a more or less stable pattern? Here the unavoidability of corruption means that, in the midst of anxiously negotiating the many challenges, contingencies, and threats, we chronically prioritize, organize, and balance our trusts, commitments, desires, and loves inappropriately, or in ways that diminish, skew, and subvert the good and ec-centric life. Anxious for our own security, we often invest our confidences as well as our loyalties in the wrong things, and in the right things inordinately or wrongly, for example, professional success and the nation. Too often, the causes to which we devote ourselves are unable to lend life meaning. Too often, we become mired in defensive patterns or stances in life as we attempt to protect our partial and insecure causes, confidences, and goods.

To recall Augustine's phrase, we become curved in upon ourselves. We find pleasing those things that are favorable to our isolated wants, needs, and desires and to our partial communities, even when they are at the expense of others. We leave undone those things that are helpful for other persons and groups. Our inordinate attachments to our own desires and to the interests of our limited communities render us disloyal to the wider community of God and neighbor, and so, here, the human fault means the unavoidable constriction and misorientation of our hearts.

Again, the social and natural worlds in which we live and move confront us with multitudes of realities, events, and interrelations. We are unable to attend to everything at once, and so if we are to negotiate our environments, we need to read or interpret our circumstances. We select certain occurrences and relationships for heightened attention and emphasis, and we make use of certain images or patterns to configure our field of vision. Think, for example, of driving down a crowded city street to work. Very many things take place in your surroundings—a bird perches on a branch, cars pass in and out of the lane on your left, a jet passes overhead, smoke rises from a chimney, a man picks up a paper from his doorstep, a traffic light turns yellow, buses traverse an overpass, a colorful billboard appears, a cyclist pedals on your right, a pedestrian on the sidewalk is wearing a stocking cap with a Phillies logo on it, another has on horn-rimmed glasses. If you aim to arrive at work without incident, you cannot pay equal attention to all these things; you need to attend selectively to appropriate items and occurrences, and you need to arrange them by means of a helpful organizing image—say the pattern of one driver in the midst of many trying to negotiate rush hour traffic (rather than the image of a NASCAR driver trying to best her opponents).

The situation is similar with respect to our practical reasoning about circumstances calling for moral involvement. Confronted with complex situations, we need to select for attention the appropriate items, interrelations, and occurrences, and also organize them into a vision, as we consider where to locate a factory, how to fund public education, and how to care for aging parents. Here the unavoidability of sin means that, in the midst of our anxious involvements with the encompassing world, we not only attend selectively to some factors rather than and more than others, and we not only organize them into an imaginative pattern, but our selections and depictions often are skewed, controlled, and warped by inordinately partial interests and purposes. Indeed, our interpretations or depictions of the circumstances and contexts calling for action tend to leave out of account or de-emphasize those interrelations, items, and consequences of less significance to us but of more importance to others. For example, I recall reading in a Richmond, Virginia, newspaper some years ago that good industrial sites along the James River are ones with good drainage. I also recall reading that the toxic effects on the river as well as Chesapeake Bay of kepone released by a chemical plant at Hopewell in 1975 would last for years. We fail to envision our interactions within the context of an expansive and encompassing web of interrelations under God, and sin therefore also means the repeated constriction, skewing, and confusion of our anxious practical reasoning.

In the midst of our many interactions and involvements, we also confront a number of interdependent relationships of responsibility and trust, for example, to family, friends, clients, students, coworkers, voluntary associations, civil communities, etc. Not all of these depend equally on our direct participation, and we clearly cannot be actively engaged in all of them at once. Thus, it is both basic and important for us to rank and to weigh our varied responsibilities, and also to monitor and modify them as circumstances change. The unavoidability of sin means that, being anxiously concerned for our many causes and ends, and often also inordinately partial in our depictions of contexts, we not only rank and weigh our responsibilities, but the moral interests in terms of which we rank and weigh them often are skewed. As noted above, both as individuals and communities we often participate deficiently in or else overreach and transgress important relationships of accountability and trust. Frequently we lack both the commitment and the attention required by our interactions and involvements with others, and therefore we fail to be fully responsive to the broader community of God and neighbor. Too often we are untrustworthy, deceptive, and unjust. Here sin means the unavoidable constriction and misdirection of human responsibility.

In short, the anxieties that accompany situated agency tempt and lure persons and groups toward corrupted affectivity, rationality, and responsibility. This dynamic has consequences for our theological estimate of human nature, if, by the "nature" of human agents, we mean their deep-seated orientation and interactive propensities. These, when properly adjusted, ought to make for an ec-centric manner of existence aligned with the kingdom and the life pattern of Jesus as the Christ. That they do not leads us to the conclusion that humans are "corrupted goods," entangled in a chronic and often destructive misalignment of nature.[56]

Social

Add now a signal contribution of liberal theologians who try to revise and reconstruct the doctrine of original sin rather than reject it. Their basic insight is that sin has important social and institutional dimensions. Friedrich Schleiermacher therefore notes that sin's derangement is both received from others and also our own. Whether we regard sin as guilt, as a state, or as a disposing spirit (an ethos), there are a definite solidarity and interdependence, so that it is "in each the work of all and in all the work of each." Sin, Schleiermacher says, has a "corporate character."[57] Albrecht Ritschl claims that our sinful actions also produce sin in others. Though the inheritance model is flawed, says Ritschl, there are forms of "sinful federation"; it makes sense to speak of "common sin"; and the idea of a "kingdom of sin" articulates what is true in the traditional "hypothesis of original sin."[58]

56. Calvin, *ICR* 2.1.10.

57. Schleiermacher, *CF*, #71 (p. 288).

58. Albrecht Ritschl, *The Christian Doctrine of Justification and Reconciliation*, ed. and

Rauschenbusch, who read both Schleiermacher and Ritschl quite carefully on this point, acknowledges that "original sin is partly social."[59] Indeed, he says, "that sin is lodged in social customs and institutions and is absorbed by the individual from his social group is so plain that any person with common sense can observe it."[60] Sinful corruptions become embodied in cultural artifacts and attitudes as well as in institutional structures. "The laws, institutions, doctrines, literature, art, and manners" that entire classes "have secreted have been social means of infection which have bred new evils for generations. . . . This is what the modern social gospel would call the Kingdom of Evil."[61]

The American reformer has in mind such things as idealizations of intoxication and militarism. These, he says, are embodied in social customs, in songs and in symbols, and then sanctioned, supported, and perpetuated by influential social and cultural authorities due to their profitableness, etc. This is why Rauschenbusch speaks of "super-personal forces of evil"—communities, institutions, or "combinations," such as political parties, corporations, churches, and governments—that may wield a powerful and negative moral force not only over their members but "through their influence in the general social life."[62]

We may link these insights with our earlier analysis of the facets of sin. Various forms of *idolatry*, such as nationalism and racism, amount to truncated and inordinate confidences in and loyalties to causes that are less than ultimate and that skew attitudes and responsibilities. These may become embodied in the language, practices, and atmospheres (or disposing spirits) of particular communities and cultures. If they are, then subsequent generations are socialized into the language, practices, and dispositions that carry the specific idolatry or misplaced devotion in question. They are raised and nurtured in it. Again, as almost any professor at an elite liberal arts college must surely know, *concupiscence*, perhaps in the form of inordinate (and often also personally destructive) desires for wealth, commercial success, and recognized achievement, can be embodied in the practices, language, and ethos of educational institutions. The idealization and inculcation of these desires and aims are profitable. Institutions that embody and transmit them garner significant financial support, because parents will pay high tuitions and fees to have their children attend schools that help them to be

---

trans. H. R. Mackintosh and A. B. Macaulay (Clifton, NJ: Reference Book Publishers, 1966), 338–39, 343–44.

59. Walter Rauschenbusch, *A Theology for the Social Gospel* (Louisville: Westminster John Knox, 1997), 61. See also 92–94.

60. Rauschenbusch. *Theology for the Social Gospel*, 60.

61. Rauschenbusch, *Theology for the Social Gospel*, 81.

62. Rauschenbusch, *Theology for the Social Gospel*, 71–73. See also 62–67.

successful, corporations will support institutions whose graduates are keen to climb corporate ladders, etc.

Similar points can be made about sin as *corrupted rationality*. Constricted fields of attention and skewed patterns of practical reasoning sometimes are embodied and transmitted by particular political ideologies and honored professions and professional associations. Consider, for example, Wendell Berry's complaint that professional education and language de-emphasize local affections, contexts, communities, histories, and responsibilities as they focus attention on selected classes of problems and tasks, and also organize one's vision by means of professional standards and the image of a successful career.[63] Again, constricted patterns of responsibility, or sin as *disobedience*, may be embodied in and transmitted by accepted laws and practices, for example, segregationist codes and customs or cultural idealizations of competitive advancement and success. Add to these malformations things such as the skewed portraits of so-called toxic masculinity often proffered by athletic associations, television advertising, and films.

With these observations, we arrive at the more recent insight into *structural dimensions of sin* developed by a number of liberation and feminist theologians. Rosemary Radford Ruether says "sexism as sin" centers on a "distorted relationality" that truncates the humanity of both sexes, as women are reduced to body-objects for male use and masculinity becomes connected with violence and hierarchy.[64] These distortions have systemic, historical aspects carried by institutions, customs, and cultural images that, in turn, shape the lives and attitudes of women and men across generations. Somewhat similarly, in his 1984 book *Black and Reformed*, the South African theologian Allan Boesak describes racism as both idolatry and "a *system* of domination" upheld by apartheid-era laws, economic institutions, political parties, and churches—a system that involves the direct dehumanization, oppression, and exploitation of more than 80 percent of the nation's population.[65]

Leonardo Boff says evil has the characteristics of a dynamic structure that organizes institutions and creates scenarios or situations that shape agents, their possibilities, and their limits. As the combination of circumstances in which we find ourselves and which envelops us, says Boff, the sin of the world "is perpetuated by actions that survived their perpetrators in the form of institutions,

63. Wendell Berry, *Life Is a Miracle: An Essay against Modern Superstition* (Washington, DC: Counterpoint, 2000), 77, 93, 130–31, 137.

64. Rosemary Radford Ruether, *Sexism and God-Talk: Toward a Feminist Theology*, with a new introduction (Boston: Beacon, 1993), 174. See also 175–83.

65. Allan Boesak, *Black and Reformed: Apartheid, Liberation, and the Calvinist Tradition*, ed. Leonard Sweetman (Maryknoll, NY: Orbis, 1984), 110–12.

prejudices, moral and legal standards, and social customs."[66] The historical situation then "becomes a matter of destiny for those born into it"; they become its victims as they are socialized into it.[67] "The link between the personal and the structural levels" therefore cannot be overlooked, and this leads Boff, not unlike Rauschenbusch, to claim that true representatives of the gospel "can no longer rest content with a conversion of the heart and personal holiness on the individual level." Indeed, "structural sin takes on even more subtle forms when it is introjected into the minds and hearts of the oppressed themselves. Then they unconsciously accept the values of the prevailing system and the human image advocated by imperial governments and their agents."[68] Structural embodiments of sin make for "a kind of sinister solidarity in the evil that rankles humankind, throughout history."[69]

Corrupted Conscience or Moral Sense

This is also a good place to reflect further on how sin's corruption gains a foothold in the formation of moral sensibility and concern. The idea that people are endowed with a social and moral sense is, of course, a very old one, and Calvin draws on an already venerable tradition when he says that "man is by nature a social animal" who tends to foster and preserve society through natural instinct. Indeed, he believes this social sense to be closely associated with moral notions of fairness and equity.[70] Rauschenbusch holds that people are endowed with a social instinct or impulse of affection that binds them together in relations of mutual interdependence. This comes through, he thinks, in sexuality, family life, neighborhood, and nation.[71] He equates this social impulse or "fellow-feeling" with love as "the force that draws man and man together," and "runs through all our relations and is the foundation of all our institutions."[72] Love (or social instinct), according to Rauschenbusch, is "the central law of life" that makes

66. Leonardo Boff, *The Lord's Prayer: The Prayer of Integral Liberation*, trans. Theodore Morrow (Maryknoll, NY: Orbis, 1983), 111–12.

67. Boff, *The Lord's Prayer*, 112.

68. Leonardo Boff, *Liberating Grace*, trans. John Drury (Maryknoll, NY: Orbis, 1979), 85.

69. Boff, *The Lord's Prayer*, 112.

70. Calvin, *ICR* 2.2.13. See also his comments on Gen. 2:18 in *Commentaries on the First Book of Moses Called Genesis*, trans. John King, vol. 1 in *Calvin's Commentaries*, Calvin Translation Society (Grand Rapids: Baker Books, 1998), p. 128.

71. Walter Rauschenbusch, *The Social Principles of Jesus* (New York: Methodist Book Concern, 1916), 17–30.

72. Walter Rauschenbusch, *Christianizing the Social Order* (New York: Macmillan, 1913), 262.

for solidarity and fellowship. "Love binds together; hate and anger cut apart."[73] Love is the basic society-making quality, and Jesus intensifies love, by both his teaching and example. "The chief law of Christianity does not contradict the social nature of man but expresses and reinforces it."[74]

If we excise the christological references, some evolutionary biologists speak in similar terms. Charles Darwin argues that the moral sense in humans represents a development of social instincts, feelings, and dispositions, and that it has analogues in the instincts, feelings, and dispositions of other social animals. He claims that social impulses lead an animal to take pleasure in the society of its fellows, to feel sympathy with them, and to perform various services for them. When these impulses are combined with memory, or images of past actions and motives, it becomes possible for an animal to feel satisfied or dissatisfied with past actions. That is, social impulses or instincts plus memory yield conscience and moral judgments. The process may be aided by language, so that the community's wishes can be expressed, and also by habits strengthening patterns of action that adhere to the community's wishes and judgments. "A moral being," says Darwin, "is one who is capable of comparing his past and future actions or motives, and approving or disapproving them," and conscience represents a knot of social impulses, memory, and reflection.[75]

Within a Darwinian frame of reference, feelings of social sympathy begin with near relations, that is, parents, offspring, and siblings, and then may be extended to a larger group. Social virtues are those the group recognizes as most important, for example, cooperation, mutual aid, refraining from violence and murder—norms that often apply only to behavior within one's own social group. The foundation of morality, then, is neither selfishness nor utility but instincts for the general good of one's community, the general *good* (rather than simply the general *happiness*) being "defined as the means by which the greatest possible number of individuals can be reared in full vigor and health, with all their faculties perfect, under the conditions to which they are exposed."[76]

There is variability among humans, and, in the struggle for existence, some fare better than others. But note that, for Darwin, the struggle selects among

73. Rauschenbusch, *Social Principles of Jesus*, 19.

74. Rauschenbusch, *Social Principles of Jesus*, 25. Or, again, "the social mission of Christianity is to make this natural instinct strong, durable, pure, holy, and victorious over all selfish and hateful passions. The spirit of Christ allies itself with all other social forces that make for love. It is at enmity with anything that checks love or propagates hate" (Rauschenbusch, *Christianizing the Social Order*, 262).

75. Charles Darwin, *The Descent of Man, and Selection in Relation to Sex* (Princeton: Princeton University Press, 1981), 88.

76. Darwin, *Descent of Man*, 97–98.

social animals for the strongest communities, and thus also for individuals who are beneficial for the survival of their communities. Among humans, then, evolution selects not for the bellicose and the recalcitrant, nor even for the mightiest individuals, but for those whose sensibilities and abilities contribute to the general good and survival of the community. Morality enters into the equation because community survival and the general good are linked to cooperative social qualities and intellectual powers.

Theologically speaking, there is a fair amount of good news here. We might say that humans are *not* wholly given over to misdirection. As good and social creatures, they generally retain some social or community feeling for others. Indeed, Calvin adds, they also retain a vestigial sense of fairness, equity, or justice that, however imperfectly, helps them to frame functioning societies.

Note, too, that the contemporary primatologist Frans de Waal develops this line of reflection when he argues that "human morality elaborates upon preexisting tendencies" visible in primates.[77] Among higher apes, he says, individuals sometimes imaginatively adopt the viewpoint or interests of another in order to engage in "targeted helping," or "altruistic behavior tailored to the specific needs of the other in novel situations" (32). For example, when an older female chimp is unable to move the requisite number of tires in order to obtain water collected in the bottom of one particular tire, a young male chimp moves the tires, collects the water, and delivers it to her. Again, de Waal says chimpanzees need to gauge how others are feeling in order to negotiate power struggles and maintain coalitions. This is one reason why, among chimps, a leader does not simply take all the best food but shares it with members of his governing group. Chimps also display comparatively advanced forms of "reciprocal altruism," for example, "adults were more likely to share food with individuals who had groomed them earlier" (43).

A key point is that there are evolutionary reasons why the capacities involved in morality develop among social species, and that their development is very much "an in-group phenomenon." De Waal says, "community concern" becomes visible among apes when females bring together males after a fight, or when high-ranking males "stop fights with others in an evenhanded manner, thus promoting peace in the group." Such behaviors indicate that group members have a stake in a cooperative atmosphere; they have much to lose if their communities splinter. Furthermore, says de Waal, "enmity toward outsiders" is "the most potent force" in bringing about "a sense of community" because "it forces unity

77. Frans de Waal et al., *Primates and Philosophers: How Morality Evolved*, ed. Stephen Macedo and Josiah Ober (Princeton: Princeton University Press, 2006), 181. Hereafter, page references from this work will be given in parentheses in the text.

among elements that are normally at odds." This, too, he says, may be observed among chimps in the wild (54). It also helps to explain why "universally, humans treat outsiders far worse than members of their own community; in fact, moral rules hardly seem to apply to the outside. . . . Morality likely evolved as a within-group phenomenon in conjunction with other typical in-group capacities, such as conflict resolution, cooperation, and sharing" (53).

The first loyalty of the individual, according to de Waal, is to self and kin, but this loyalty may be expanded. Indeed, "the biggest step in the evolution of human morality was the move from interpersonal relations to a focus on the greater good." This step has roots in the individual's appreciation for the stake she has in a cooperative community that protects its members from significant external threats. "In the course of human evolution," then, "out-group hostility enhanced in-group solidarity to the point that morality emerged" (54). Thus, "morality has evolutionary ties to our basest behavior—warfare. The sense of community required by the former was provided by the latter" (55). De Waal claims that "morality evolved to deal with the own community first, and has only recently begun to include members of other groups, humanity in general, and nonhuman animals" (163). It comes with an inbred distinction between "us" and "them," or between in-group and out-group, as well as with a persistent loyalty and bias toward our innermost circles. Indeed, de Waal argues that we not only *are* biased in favor of the innermost circles (ourselves, our family, our community, our species) but that we *ought* to be. "Loyalty is a moral duty" (165).[78]

Focus now on a particular dynamic and some of its implications within the Augustinian theological frame of reference I am developing in this systematic. Moral sensibility or concern that is restricted to my own in-group—when compared with the ec-centric stance in life we find in Jesus Christ and the Spirit—represents a constriction of loyalty or devotion intertwined with constricted practical reasoning and constricted patterns of responsibility. Moreover, I become inordinately loyal to my own group and deficiently concerned for others beyond it partly because—due to its cooperative practices and the protections it offers from external threats—belonging to the group reduces my anxiety over dangers to me and to the things I value.

Taking a cue from the evolutionary biologists, we might say that a tendency toward constriction has a basis in the process of human moral development.

78. He makes this argument over against the moral philosopher Peter Singer. For his part, Singer thinks "concern for judgments made from the perspective of an impartial spectator" arises with our human capacity to reason, which no ape matches (de Waal et al., *Primates and Philosophers*, 144–45). "Reason," he says, "is like an escalator—once we step on it, we cannot get off until we have gone where it takes us" (146)—in this instance to a place where moral judgments are universalized and moral concern extends even beyond our species to other animals.

You and I are equipped with feeling for our fellows, and also with an ability to imagine what the interests and aims of others are like. In addition, we internalize the interactive patterns or ethos of our society and the norms associated with them, which we may use to judge our own actions and the actions of others. (This much seems clear from the work of moral philosophers, such as David Hume and Adam Smith, especially when it is supplemented by a social theory of human agents.)[79] The evolutionary biologists add one more rather crucial thing: the emotional capacities, imaginative capacities, and patterns of interaction so important to our developed moral sensibilities are drawn out, elaborated, formed, and internalized by means of our interactions within near kin groups and communities. What some call our moral sense—a confluence of capacities to "feel with" others, imaginatively "identify with" others, and internalize interactive patterns—emerges in and through our interactions with siblings, relatives, and friends. This is where our moral sensibility is first practiced; this is where it initially emerges, and this is why it is fraught with ambiguities.

Let me illustrate. There is a good ice-cream shop about five miles from where I live in North Carolina. If you sit on a bench outside, you can see railroad tracks as well as the backs of older brick buildings that house businesses on Main Street. The view is almost urban, and it reminds me of Philadelphia, which is why, on a sunny afternoon, Pam and I were in line behind a young girl, who looked to be about twelve or thirteen, and her younger sister, who looked to be about five. The older girl ordered two cones, and then, as the attendant was turning to scoop the ice cream and without consulting the younger girl, she said her sister would like extra sprinkles on her cone, and asked if that would be OK. The attendant smiled, said it would be fine, and then produced two cones—one with extra sprinkles.

The episode shows the older sister's social feeling, imaginative capacity, and internalized pattern of responsibilities operating (rather impressively) with respect to her younger sister. It may also be an instance in the formation of the younger girl's ability to discern the benefits of a cooperative community. But it also illustrates the point that development of emotional and imaginative capacities crucial for morality is an in-group phenomenon, and there is nothing to guarantee that, growing up in the piedmont of North Carolina (or almost anywhere else in the United States for that matter), one or both of the girls might not turn out to be racist. Part of the reason is that our moral sensibilities are intertwined with in-group loyalties and preferences as well as with out-group aversions. We find it comparatively easy to feel with, identify with, and act in accord with internalized patterns of responsibilities toward people in our

79. See, for example, H. Richard Niebuhr's reflections about conscience in *The Responsible Self*, 75–79.

own group, but comparatively difficult to feel with, identify with, and act in accord with patterns of internalized responsibilities toward those who are not. This is so partly because particular bonds of affection and mutual service—the very interactions and relationships that draw us out from ourselves to become morally responsible—also lead us to become especially comfortable with and biased toward members of our own groups. This dynamic is a feature of moral development in every generation. It can be heightened by out-group aversions. And, indeed, as the history of "southern strategies" in American politics shows, it is a dynamic that may be manipulated and exploited in every age, as well as one that may contribute to racist loyalties, patterns of practical reasoning, and responsibility embodied in cultural images, codes, and institutional structures passed on to subsequent generations.[80]

A Sickness of Soul

Suppose now that we turn the screw once more. What if, even in the midst of our constricted devotions and communities of concern, our inordinate desires, our truncated visions, and our skewed responsibilities there remains in us an inkling that it's all wrong? Perhaps this amounts to a residue of regard for the many and expansive interrelations in which we participate with others—a remainder of the spirit or ethos of participatory interdependence that characterizes created life.[81] Perhaps my community maintains a respect and regard for what H. Richard Niebuhr called a "transcendent reference group," for example, Abraham Lincoln, Martin Luther King Jr., Nelson Mandela, that helps to define its ethos and what it stands for by pointing to a cause beyond itself and beyond the bounds of my specific ethnic group.[82] Perhaps one will argue in a somewhat Kantian vein, as the philosopher Peter Singer does, that when it comes to estimating our own actions, the capacity to reason pushes people, at least sometimes, to adopt the perspective of an impartial observer.[83] In any case, if in the light of one or another of these things I judge my act to be wrong, destructive, mean-spirited, and irresponsible, the problem becomes partly internal.

My act points to something deeper and more fundamental. And the deep problem I have is not only with one or another bad act but also with what comes to expression in my bad acts. The deep problem I have now is with myself, with

80. See, for example, Angie Maxwell and Todd Shields, *The Long Southern Strategy: How Chasing White Voters in the South Changed American Politics* (New York: Oxford University Press, 2019).

81. See chap. 9.

82. H. Richard Niebuhr, *The Responsible Self*, 85–86.

83. De Waal et al., *Primates and Philosophers*, 140–58.

my orientation and tendency or trajectory as a person. In the light of an inkling of a broader and participatory interdependence, my internalized image of my community's transcendent reference group, or the viewpoint of an impartial spectator, I become dissatisfied with myself, with the knot of devotions, desires, views, and habits that sets my direction. There is a struggle within me. I am divided from my own best vision and possibility. At some level, I dislike, reject, and perhaps even hate myself. We say that conscience condemns. I accuse myself, and at the same time I feel, perhaps, that I am judged from beyond myself.

Call this a state of guilt and self-recrimination, a discomfiting and even tormenting condition in which I am at odds with myself, divided against myself, or alienated from myself.[84] Perhaps I realize that, even in some of my best and most attentive moments as a parent, I pushed and cajoled my children into certain activities in order to satisfy expectations and desires for my own success. But, of course, such inner struggles may also become features in the life of a community. (Perhaps its stories of past valor and honor conceal its persistent and violent repression of an enslaved people.) It may be that conflicted self-realizations such as these will encourage persons and communities to adopt postures that are less self-righteous and more self-critical. But the state of guilt, self-recrimination, and inner division—a kind of sickness of soul—seems a further dimension of malformation and corruption, a perversely productive contagion that may also drive intensified efforts to deny and suppress the wrong.

The net effect, often enough, is that we "double down." We try to justify ourselves by claiming that our misshapen devotions, desires, and patterns of activity are necessary, good, and true after all. We bolster and intensify false depictions of the policy or the act, for example, "The city we bombed was a den of combatants." We concoct ideologies that commend the deed, for example, "*We* really are superior and good; *they* really are subhuman, incorrigibly evil enemies of the good." We legitimate and defend overt idolatries, for example, devotion to "my superior race," devotion to "my country right or wrong" and no matter at what cost to others.

Not surprisingly, the doubling down intensifies both the fault and its destructiveness. It may also intensify our inner conflict, self-dissatisfaction, self-alienation, and hatred. And, at some level, it becomes easier and more acceptable to be cruel than to admit our flaw. The divided and alienated self or the self-accusing community build and preserve their self-justifying rationalizations with intricacy and care in order to keep from having to admit their fault and keep from being beset or even overrun by guilt. These self-justifying rationalizations, for example, appeals to the superiority of "the American free enterprise system,"

84. Paul Tillich, *The Shaking of the Foundations* (New York: Scribner's Sons, 1948), 157–59.

may even become pillars of meaning for our way of life, and as alienated, self-accusing persons and communities we therefore lash out with special virulence at those who would expose our cover-ups and threaten our manner of living. Where the malformation is communal, in addition to constricted affections, practical reasoning, and patterns of responsibility, powerful undercurrents of self-accusation as well as intense self-justifying rationalizations may become inscribed in the living cultural heritage and its structural features.[85]

Should we conclude, then, by affirming the doctrine of original sin? Not, I think, if by that term we mean a single act of the first pair, a onetime fall from grace that corrupts human nature and then, by some hereditary mechanism tied to sexual passion, is passed on to subsequent generations. Those ideas have run their course. But we may very well read the early chapters of Genesis as an instructive tale concerning every-person and every-human-community. We may very well affirm a multifaceted corruption of affect, practical reasoning, and responsibility as well as a recurrent sickness of soul exposed by comparison with the ec-centric life represented and commended in Jesus Christ and the Spirit. And we very well may affirm that persons and communities are drawn into these malformations by anxieties that accompany situated agency as well as by institutionalizations of skewed devotions and desires, and constricted patterns of reasoning and activity that are inscribed in our cultural heritages and passed down from generation to generation. People stand in need of rehabilitation and renewal because they are mired in and diminished by a persistent fault. Sin is radical. It infects affect, practical reasoning, and patterns of responsibility, as well as the depths of self-judgment and regard—no dimension of the agent is free from sin's effects. Sin is universal. No person, community, or institution is sin-free. None is righteous, all are entangled, and all fall short of the kingdom and its glory.

Proposition #60 For those who embrace the Word of the gospel, there is a transition from a previous constricted orientation to a new and ec-centric manner of life in Christ and the Spirit, and this transition is called regeneration.

We turn now to the remedy for sin's constriction. People encounter the Word of Christ and the Spirit through the church, its preaching, worship, teaching, fellowship, ministry, and mission. And if, as I have argued in proposition #59,

85. Which goes some way toward explaining the portrait of African Americans in D. W. Griffith's 1915 film *The Birth of a Nation*, as well as portraits of Native Americans and Hispanics in more than a few American cowboy movies of a certain era.

sin is both radical and universal, then, at the point when they encounter Christ's ec-centric manner in and through the ethos and practices of the church, they are already entangled in manners or forms of living that, by comparison, often seem constricted, corrupted, and skewed.

What happens next? Many different things—some may opt to retain or pursue other manners in life based in other loyalties and linked with other patterns of responsibility, for example, one or another sort of patriotism or various sorts of nonreligious humanism. Others may try to combine one or another of these forms of life with ec-centric elements they discern in Christ and the Spirit, for example, a drive to reconcile persons and communities in conflict. In neither case need persons simply reject or think ill of the pattern or loyalty they encounter in Christ and the Spirit. To the extent that their preferred loyalties or additional patterns have ec-centric dimensions, they may in fact even admire and think well of it. Again, some who encounter the Word, among them Jews, Muslims, and Buddhists, do so having already taken up manners of life that may be similarly ec-centric. Then, again, in many contemporary environments, some may simply ignore the Word altogether; others, for example, Friedrich Nietzsche or Ayn Rand, may definitively reject and criticize its primary disposition and trajectory.

This is not all. Some people apparently are affected by the gospel message, the ec-centric pattern of life, and the kingdom-centered devotion displayed in Jesus as the Christ but also find that they are not drawn into the regular life of a congregation. This seems true today for at least some people Robert Bellah and others describe as "spiritual but not religious."[86] Still others, who are significantly affected by the Word of the gospel, the kingdom-minded devotion, and the ec-centric manner of life it presents, will become active participants in the life of the church.

In any case, regeneration—the transition from an old manner in life to a new or renewed one in Christ and the Spirit—often entails contact with and participation in the church, though it is not always clear what sort or degree of contact and participation. Theologically speaking, the phenomenon/process involves conversion or repentance, *a turning* away from the old and toward the new. Reformed theology, moreover, holds that this transition as a whole has two aspects: justification, or a changed relationship to God that initiates the turning, and sanctification, or a continuing process of formation in renewed and ec-centric life.

The main topic in the present proposition is regeneration, or the broader

86. Robert Bellah et al., *Habits of the Heart* (Berkeley: University of California Press, 1985).

term associated with the transition to a new manner of life. Its salient aspects—justification and sanctification—will occupy us in propositions #61 and #62.

Reformed Tradition

Calvin considers "regeneration by faith" in his *Institutes* on the heels of his discussion of faith as "the principal work of the Spirit." The Reformer associates regeneration, which "has its foundation in the gospel," with repentance, or a "true turning of our life to God" that "consists in the mortification of our flesh and of the old man, and in the vivification of the Spirit."[87] The first movement is a turning away from evil and the old person. The second is a turning toward good that also involves the awakening or resuscitation of the new person that tracks Paul's understanding of rebirth in Christ (Rom. 6:6).

We are unable to accomplish these things on our own. "Repentance is a singular gift of God," and so the efficacy of our conversion or turning "depends upon the Spirit of regeneration."[88] Even so, says Calvin, this Spirit-led turning away from inordinate desires, impulses, and interests remains incomplete. Though the dominion of sin over believers' lives is broken, vestigial influences continue, and so it is important to reject all illusions of perfection. That is, conflict between misdirected flesh and the spirit persists; the sanctification of the faithful can only be a work in progress. Repentance, whose fruits are piety toward God and charity toward neighbor (or what I have called an ec-centric existence), is lifelong, and it involves an inward change of heart as well as changes in outward behavior. We might say the core of the person—her or his fundamental love and devotion—needs recentering, even as her or his disposition and characteristic pattern of responsibility also need redirecting. And in this regenerating process, for Calvin, the precepts and duties of the law continue to restrain and to guide.[89]

Having made these points, the Reformer next criticizes the understanding of penance put forward by medieval scholastics. (They teach improperly that compulsory confession before a priest is divinely ordained and that the priest has the power of the keys to absolve sins. They also introduce a "foolish distinction" between venial and mortal sins. Indeed, those who claim that indulgences distribute Christ's merits teach "errors so foolish" that they "are fit to be treated by drugs for insanity.")[90] Calvin then outlines the life of a Christian, saying that

87. Calvin, *ICR* 3.3.2, 5.
88. Calvin, *ICR* 3.3.21.
89. Calvin, *ICR* 3.3.16.
90. Calvin, *ICR* 3.4.4, 6, 14–15, 19–20, 28; 3.5.1.

while philosophers exhort people to live in accord with nature, here Christ is the pattern.[91] "The Christian philosophy" therefore subordinates self-concern to God and God's commandments. It issues in a reverence for others that depends not on their merits but on their value as creatures made in God's image, and it also helps us to bear adversity at God's hand with patience and obedience (though, like Jesus and unlike Stoics, Christians express their pain and sorrow).[92] Finally, Calvin includes a "meditation on the future life" as well as a chapter on how to use and enjoy the gifts of this life and how to discharge our assigned stations or callings—all this *before* considering justification (our reconciliation to and acceptance by God) and sanctification (its continual progress).[93]

Heinrich Bullinger's Second Helvetic Confession (1566) has a similarly experiential emphasis. It describes repentance as "the recovery of a right mind in sinful man awakened by the Word of the Gospel and the Holy Spirit, and received by true faith." The sinner, says Bullinger, "acknowledges" his corruption, "grieves from his heart," and "confesses" his sins "before God with shame." And, then, "zealously" considering "the amendment of his ways," he constantly strives "all the rest of his life."[94]

The experiential note sometimes seems muted, though not lost, in the writings of later Reformed scholastics, who associate regeneration with the effectual calling of the elect. Wollebius briefly mentions regeneration, repentance, conversion, and the like in conjunction with sanctification in his *Compendium Theologiae Christianae* (1626), though, he says, the meaning of the terms is ambiguous and may also apply to gifts that precede justification. He also says the special calling of the elect entails both "the enlightenment of the mind" and "the change of the heart of stone into flesh, or turning man to obedience."[95] During the mid-seventeenth century, Voetius claims, "regeneration is God's action in elect sinners . . . by which He . . . turns them from corruption to new life (or holiness), that they may henceforth live unto God." Near the turn of the eighteenth century, Johann Heidegger says, "completed calling" is that by means of which "man becomes a new creature in the realm of grace" through "the Spirit inwardly renewing, enlightening, bending, drawing, founding, consolidating,

91. Calvin, *ICR* 3.6.1–3. See also James M. Gustafson's chapter "Jesus Christ, the Pattern," in *Christ and the Moral Life* (Chicago: University of Chicago Press, Midway Reprint, 1976), 150–65.

92. Calvin, *ICR* 3.7.6; 3.7.10; 3.8.1–4.

93. Calvin, *ICR* 3.9.1–6; 3.10.1–6.

94. *BOC* 5.093.

95. Johannes Wollebius, *Compendium Theologiae Christianae*, in *Reformed Dogmatics: Seventeenth-Century Reformed Theology through the Writings of Wollebius, Voetius, and Turretin*, ed. and trans. John W. Beardsleee III (Grand Rapids: Baker Books, 1977), 159.

strengthening, [and] sealing." He claims, too, that, "in regeneration . . . the old man is discarded, and then the new man is put on," but that "war with relics of the old Adam" continues, and so regeneration is never perfect in this life.[96]

For Friedrich Schleiermacher, who tracks Calvin's discussion rather closely and who also views Christian theology as piety teaching, the experiential element is quite strong. Regeneration becomes the turning point at which continuity with the old life ceases and the new life begins to be in process. It is an assumption into living fellowship with Christ that has two aspects: justification, or a person's changed relation to God, and conversion, or a changed form of life. The two aspects happen together and are inseparable.[97] Conversion, or the subjective occurrence, is a change of heart, which entails regret or mortification (awakened by the vision of Christ's perfection) as well as faith or the joyful appropriation of Christ's blessedness (vivification or revival).[98] The church and its socializing practices are critical, though basically, Schleiermacher says, the same thing happens to us that happened to the first disciples. "The constant factor is above all the divine power of the Word—taking the expression in its widest sense—by which conversion is still effected and faith still arises. The difference is simply that the self-revelation of Christ is now mediated by those who preach Him."[99]

The nineteenth-century Americans Charles Hodge and Robert Lewis Dabney are hardly followers of Schleiermacher! If the experiential dimension in their theologies seems somewhat stronger than among the scholastics, perhaps this is due to the prominence of evangelicalism and revivalism in figures such as Charles Finney, whose positions Hodge criticizes in some detail. In any case, the Princetonian describes regeneration as "a new life" or "new form of life," which, while hard to define, is the birth of a new person or new man and involves intellect (spiritual illumination and new views of truths), will (new voluntary exercises), and new feelings or affections.[100] Dabney associates regeneration with conversion, repentance, and "godly sorrow." He also claims that the Spirit "renovates the mental vision," as well as motives and dispositions that "determine the moral purpose."[101] The insistence of both writers that regeneration entails enlighten-

96. Quoted by Heinrich Heppe, *Reformed Dogmatics: Set Out and Illustrated from the Sources*, ed. Ernst Bizer, trans. G. T. Thompson (Grand Rapids: Baker Books, 1978), 518, 525.

97. Schleiermacher, *CF*, #107 (pp. 478–79).

98. Schleiermacher, *CF*, #108 (pp. 480–85).

99. Schleiermacher, *CF*, #108 (p. 490).

100. Charles Hodge, *Systematic Theology: In Three Volumes* (Grand Rapids: Eerdmans, 1977), 3:8–11, 16, 33–36.

101. Robert Lewis Dabney, *Syllabus of the Course of Systematic and Polemic Theology Taught*

ment, new hearts, and a renewing of wills accords also, as Hodge points out, with the portrait of effectual calling in the Westminster Confession of Faith.[102]

A Proposal

My own understanding of regeneration incorporates elements of all these positions and is rooted in what I have said earlier about Jesus as the Christ as the one who teaches the truth, embodies a manner in ministry and in life that accords with the truth, and empowers this life by his death and resurrection. It coheres as well with my account of sin as corrupted affection, rationality, and responsibility.

To review, *sin as constricted affectivity* means that we inappropriately prioritize, organize, and balance our trusts, commitments, loves, and desires. We devote ourselves to partial causes and goods, for example, our nation, our ethnic group, that finally are unable to sustain meaning and that mire us in self-serving and defensive postures and patterns in life. We are, in Augustine's famous phrase, "curved in upon ourselves," caught up by inordinate attachments to our isolated personal interests and to our limited communities. Moreover, there are important structural dimensions; constricted affectivities, for example, nationalism and racism, become embodied in the language, practices, and atmospheres of our communities and cultures into which subsequent generations are socialized. Inordinate and often destructive desires for wealth, commercial success, recognized achievement, etc., are inscribed in the practices, language, and ethos of varied institutions.

Sin as corrupted practical rationality or vision highlights our tendency to select and depict inappropriately circumstances and situations calling for moral involvement. Our visions and depictions of contexts are inordinately partial to our own interests. Animated by partial devotions and inordinate desires, we leave out of account and neglect interrelations, items, and consequences of less or little significance to us but of more importance to others. Here, too, we encounter structural dimensions that help to define persons' social and cultural situations. Constricted fields of attention and skewed patterns of practical reasoning sometimes are imprinted in and transmitted by political ideologies, as well as by patterns of professional training that encourage us to focus on certain standardized problems and tasks and to neglect other things.

---

in Union Theological Seminary, Virginia, 5th ed. (Richmond, VA: Presbyterian Committee of Publication, 1871), 560–61.

102. Hodge, *Systematic Theology*, 3:30.

Finally, *sin as contracted or corrupted responsibility* names our tendency to rank and weigh our responsibilities in accord with skewed and inordinately partial interests. We participate deficiently in and also overreach and transgress important relationships of accountability and trust. As both individuals and communities, we are mired in misdirected patterns of responsibility, and we fail to be fully responsive to the broader community of God and neighbor. Moreover, these patterns may be inscribed in and transmitted by accepted laws, practices, and attitudes, for example, segregationist codes or problematic idealizations of gender identities.

These three aspects or dimensions indicate that sin is radical because it influences and infects aspects of our persons that are critical for our practical stances or manners of life: affect or emotion, intellect or practical vision, and will or responsibility. In fact, they correspond roughly to the three aspects of regeneration, or of the transition from the old person to the new, outlined by virtually all the Reformed theologians mentioned above. Again, I have also emphasized that the typical formation of our moral sensibilities and concerns often leaves us with tendencies toward in-group favoritisms and out-group aversions, and that we often are at odds with ourselves or our own conscientious judgments as to what is just and fair. Taken together, the three aspects of sin occasioned by anxieties of situated agency as well as their structural manifestations, the formation of our moral sensibilities in own groups, and the self-alienating or accusing dimensions of conscience form a kind of dominion or kingdom of sinful corruption and misdirection. They constitute a force that leads us to retreat from more expansive and capacious possibilities for participation in God's vast, intricate, and interdependent world.

A basic theological judgment, then, is that people become less than they can and ought to be. They are entangled in a fault, held in bondage to the power of sin, contracted and diminished by a persistent astringent. Arraigned against this extensive, highly effective force and dominion are the ec-centric trajectory of interdependent life in God's world (the ethos or Spirit of creation) and the Word of the gospel that is mediated to us by the church through its practices and activities in the power of its ethos or Spirit. The mediation of this Word, a Word that reprises and intensifies the ethos of the cosmos, is the work of the Spirit of regeneration. It comes to us, strikes us, and works in us a transition and renewal that we cannot accomplish on our own.

This transition may be further described and clarified if we correlate features of the Word with prominent aspects of sin or the human fault. As I understand it, the Word of the gospel is the event of Jesus Christ that fulfills the covenant of grace. Jesus as the Christ—the one who teaches the truth, embodies a manner in life that accords with the truth, and empowers this life by his crucifixion and resurrection—is the Word inscribed into the structures and practices of the church, or its preaching, worship, teaching, fellowship, ministry, and mission. Chapter 8, "The Truth, the Way, and the Life," outlines specific contents of this Word, and so, here, a brief summary may suffice.

The Word of the gospel *teaches the truth about God's kingdom*. It illuminates and presents a new view of an expansive reign of prophetic justice and grace (shalom) in which all have worth, and in which the poor and the vulnerable are blessed. This reign entails a distinctive practical visage and moral norm. Paul therefore reminds us to look to the interests of others; Jesus commands us to love our enemies. The message of the kingdom undercuts our usual practices and also suggests alternatives, for example, the parable of the laborers in the vineyard in Matthew 20. From the outset of the Gospels, the kingdom-centered vision of Jesus as the Christ calls us to repent of our usual commitments and manners of living. It encourages and demands the redirection of our more usual aims and politics because it puts forward God and God's kingdom as an alternative and expansive focal point for constricted human confidences and devotions. It is a kind of good news that challenges myopic visions bounded by the causes of partial classes and communities.

Again, the Word etched into the practices and the ethos of the church *embodies and displays a kingdom-shaped manner of ministry and life* marked by an expansive disposition to love God and neighbor, care for the vulnerable and the poor, and cross barriers and boundaries in order to help, heal, and reconcile. It involves new practices and a new pattern of responsibility. Jesus as the Christ accepts and welcomes the alienated and estranged—a major point of his "open commensality" as a strategy for pursuing renewed community and life together. When the prodigal returns, a community of grace has to celebrate and thereby enact a renewed and reconciled life together. Thus, the way inscribed in the practices and the ethos of the church contrasts quite sharply with many of our more usual and constricted ways, where we eat and drink only with our own people, fail to cross barriers, and forget to celebrate. Reinhold Niebuhr therefore rightly reminds us that Jesus Christ is our judge as well as our savior. Then again, the inscribed patterns of the Word also point in hope toward a saving, more capacious, and inclusive loyalty and performance.

Jesus as the Christ, the Word of the gospel, also *empowers the way or manner in life* that accords with the divine excellence of the kingdom as well as with the direction displayed in his ministry and mission. The Word precipitates new feelings and affections. It enables repentance by furnishing us with the right nightmare and the right revulsion—the execution of the kingdom-minded one at the hands of the power of sin in our history, a power that remains effective in us still, which is why, at Good Friday service today, the congregation, taking the part of "the people" in the story of Jesus's trial and execution, was directed to say, "Crucify him! Crucify him!" Again, the Word also precipitates a resurrection and renewal we can experience by joyfully placing us in the presence of the Creator/Redeemer who brings into existence things that are not, even new life out of suffering, tragedy, and death.

A basic aim of the church's preaching, worship, teaching, fellowship, ministry, and mission is to bring about a confrontation or encounter with the Word of the gospel. The effect of this encounter, as the Reformed theologians describe it, is a turning or transition from the old person to the new, a change of orientation, direction, or stance in life that flows from alterations in vision (intellect), responsibility (will), and affect (heart). That is to say, in the power of the Spirit, when people malformed by sinful constriction and misdirection are effectively confronted with the Word of the gospel (including the law and the many iterations of the covenant of grace), the effect is repentance or conversion. And, of course, the transition engenders a piety marked by a heartfelt sense of regret, remorse, and contrition.

Quite a strong statement of these themes comes from the twentieth-century American H. Richard Niebuhr, who associates the turning and conversion of our religious lives through Jesus Christ with the meaning of revelation. Niebuhr notes that, very often, we are guided by imaginative visions that place us at the center of things. But the Word displaces constricted visions focused on images of our selves and our own communities as central reference points and protagonists in favor of visions focused on Jesus as the Christ and the God of grace. It brings new light and precipitates new sight, a new vision in which all creatures, including ourselves, simply and by grace have value and worth before a gracious God rather than due to their own isolated excellences or achievements. It therefore allows us honestly to face the moral law and its radical requirements, and also to bring to light our own chronic shortcomings and failings. It encourages us to construct critical histories of our selves and our communities in the knowledge that we need no longer endeavor to secure our worth by our own pretensions.[103]

Niebuhr claims, too, that in the midst of our devotion and loyalty to the many objects that occupy our lives—families, careers, wealth, nations, etc.—we search for a deity that will unify them all in a summative pattern, thus ensuring the meaning, unity, and coherence of our plural aims, activities, and pursuits. However, the God of Jesus Christ is not only the source of the many unities and goods in our experience but also their enemy when we chronically (and inordi-

103. H. Richard Niebuhr, *The Meaning of Revelation* (Louisville: Westminster John Knox, 2006), 49–72, 90.

nately) elevate them into false gods and centers of value. The kingdom-minded one points to a God whose purposes cannot be domesticated or simply identified with our partial and provisional objects of devotion and desire, a God who therefore "demands the reformation of every particular idea of unity we have." Again, says Niebuhr, the deity we anticipate and seek is powerful, even omnipotent, like the powers of our world raised to the ultimate degree, and thus a god whose help we try to enlist in order to protect the things we value and love from many threats, both real and imagined. And, indeed, the one to whom Jesus prays is the all-governing Lord of heaven and earth, the life-giving and death-dealing power who bears all things and brings them to pass. But Jesus Christ reveals that this power is "made perfect in weakness." He discloses deity exercising "sovereignty more through crosses than through thrones"—a disclosure that begins "a revolution in our power thinking and our power politics."

Finally, says Niebuhr, we believe that deity must be good, and we seek a cherished good on which to center our lives that will also protect and nurture all our other cherished goods. We worship and pray to a good god who will preserve the other objects we adore, such as self, wealth, family, nation, and race, a good that fulfills *our* quests to protect the other goods and gods that we already love. We seek a good to protect our own goods and are met instead by a good that seeks us and values us with a goodness that empties itself. The God revealed in Jesus Christ is "a goodness that is all outgoing, reserving nothing for itself." This disclosure convicts us "of having corrupted our religious life through our unquenchable desire to keep ourselves with our love of our good in the center of the picture." Thus, for Niebuhr, this encounter with and conversion to God in Jesus as the Christ amounts to what the New Testament calls *metanoia*. It is a lifelong turning or "permanent revolution" of love, life, and soul. This, he says, "is what we mean by revelation," and it precipitates the lifelong process of repentance and regeneration.[104]

The forces arraigned against renewed and true life—wrongly configured devotions and desires, confused visions, and corrupted patterns of responsibility, all mediated by warped social structures and cultural images—are indeed deep and formidable. They compose a veritable kingdom of evil. But we do not tremble for the prince of darkness. For arraigned against him is the unlikely but strangely effective power of Word and Spirit.

Proposition #61 Before God, sinners may know themselves to be accepted and to have worth by grace through faith. This is justification.

104. H. Richard Niebuhr, *The Meaning of Revelation*, 96, 98, 99.

We are ready now to explore this permanent revolution further. Justification and sanctification name salient aspects of a continuing transformation from contracted to capacious life, from constriction to an ec-centric manner in Christ and the Spirit. Calvin speaks rather helpfully in this regard of "a double grace."[105] *Justification*, he says, is reconciliation to and acceptance by our "gracious Father" through Christ. *Sanctification* is the Spirit-led course of our regeneration and renewal. Our focus here is on the former; sanctification will be the primary topic in proposition #62.

Justification, for Calvin, is the acceptance with which God receives us into God's favor, not counting our sins for Christ's sake. We are reckoned or counted righteous on account of Christ's righteousness, a righteousness we grasp hold of through faith.[106] Christ's work does not alter or change God's demeanor; instead, it expresses God's essential and constant graciousness or benevolence. This is what faith apprehends in the Word of the gospel. The Genevan Reformer therefore describes "the order of justification" presented in Scripture as follows. "God deigns to embrace the sinner with his pure and freely given goodness" but finds in the sinner only a "miserable condition to prompt Him to mercy." Undeflected and undeterred by this condition, God "seeks in himself the reason to benefit" humanity. "Then God touches the sinner with a sense of [God's] goodness in order that [the sinner], despairing of his own works, may ground the whole of his salvation in God's mercy."[107] Barth puts it this way. Left to his own autonomy and devices, the sinner *chooses* to sin, *chooses* death and nonexistence. But the gracious God ignores and overrides the sinner's choosing, and so, by the grace of God and despite its choosing, humanity is not nothing.[108]

Salvation, that is to say, is therefore entirely "the free work of God," a grace we receive or obtain "by faith," so that "here is nothing of our own."[109] The sinner grasps God's graciousness and thus also her own acceptance through faith, through an existential and assuring knowledge given by the Spirit that takes root in the heart. Hence Calvin's definition of faith: "a firm and certain knowledge of God's benevolence toward us, founded upon the truth of the freely given promise in Christ, both revealed to our minds and sealed upon our hearts through the Holy Spirit."[110]

105. Calvin, *ICR* 3.11.1.
106. Calvin, *ICR* 3.11.2.
107. Calvin, *ICR* 3.11.16.
108. Barth, *CD* IV/1:90.
109. John Calvin, *The Epistles of Paul the Apostle to the Galatians, Ephesians, Philippians, and Colossians*, trans. T. H. L. Parker, *Calvin's New Testament Commentaries: A New Translation*, ed. Thomas F. Torrance and David W. Torrance (Grand Rapids: Eerdmans, 1965), 144. Calvin is commenting on Eph. 2:8–10.
110. Calvin, *ICR* 3.2.7.

These reflections largely elaborate Luther's less systematic lead. For Luther, the person is caught in an existential bind. Her conscience, which apprehends the moral law, accuses her, and so it presses her to obtain righteousness by means of her own good works in accordance with the law. That is, her conscience commends what is finally only reasonable, namely, that to be worthy or righteous in her own sight and before God, she must fulfill the law by her own efforts. But the law makes demands, such as "Do not covet," which, when we are honest, we find ourselves unable to fulfill.[111] The sinner's conscience is therefore rendered uneasy; it plagues her with the entirely reasonable judgment that she is unworthy and deserves God's wrath. What's more, by desperately trying to become righteous in order to commend herself, she becomes entangled in a further self-deceiving counsel of despair. For the law, after all, does not require that we work obsessively in order to commend ourselves, but that we love God and neighbor.

The one thing needed for "Christian life, righteousness, and freedom," says Luther, the one thing needed to address the anxious trial of our accusing conscience, is "the Word of God as gospel." This Word "reveals to the conscience that which the conscience can never tell itself—that God offers mercy to those who feel their sins and God's wrath."[112] And so, it is by faith that we grasp or accept the Word of grace: "God is merciful. . . . [God] freely blesses us undeserving ones" and "gives us the forgiveness of sins."[113] The Word of Life that brings this blessing is the gospel of God's Son, Jesus Christ, and it is to this Word that faith clings.

Now, Luther thinks the devil does not rest but instead continues to make use of the accusing conscience to torment us. Even so, "a faithful man by faith alone in Christ, may raise up himself and conceive such sure and sound consolation, that he" need "not . . . fear the devil, sin, death, or any evils." Indeed, though "the devil set upon him with all might and main, yet he conceiveth good hope," and dares to say, "Sir Devil I fear not thy threatenings and terrors, for there is one whose name is Jesus Christ, in whom I believe; he hath abolished the law, condemned sin, vanquished death, and destroyed hell; and he is thy tormenter . . . for he hath bound thee and holdeth thee captive, to the end that thou shouldest no more hurt me, or any that believeth in him." Now, "this faith," says Luther, "the devil cannot overcome, but is overcome by it."[114] The first hymn I learned

111. Luther, "The Freedom of a Christian, 1520," in *Career of the Reformer I*, ed. Harold J. Grimm, vol. 31 of *LW*, 348.

112. Randal C. Zachman, *The Assurance of Faith: Conscience in the Theology of Martin Luther and John Calvin* (Minneapolis: Fortress, 1993), 69.

113. Luther, *Selected Psalms I*, ed. Jaroslav Pelikan, vol. 12 of *LW*, 324.

114. Luther, "A Commentary on St. Paul's Epistle to the Galatians, 1531," *in Martin Luther: Selections from His Writings*, ed. John Dillenberger (Garden City, NY: Doubleday, 1961), 124.

summarizes the point rather nicely: "The prince of darkness grim, we tremble not for him; His rage we can endure, For Lo! His doom is sure; one little word shall fell him."[115]

Luther insists that we are justified, we are reconciled to or rightwised with God by faith alone rather than by any good work or accomplishment. Faith, which "is something that is done to us rather than something that we do," transcends human reason, competence, and conscience in order to cling to the Word of grace.[116] "This is the work of the Holy Spirit on the heart of man."[117] Reason and conscience, says Luther, "cannot put the sinner before a gracious and forgiving God"; only faith, as "the work of the Spirit," can.[118]

Parenthetically, though a fuller discussion of good works, the law, etc., waits for proposition #62, we should also note Luther's claim that he does not reject good works. The Bible, he says, contains both commandments, which we cannot satisfy, and promises of grace. The person who holds fast to the gospel promises "with a firm faith" has no need of works or the law to be justified. "He is free from law" in the sense that, before God, he enjoys an inner liberty with respect to his worth and salvation.[119] Hence, "a Christian is a perfectly free lord of all, subject to none." At the same time, the faithful Christian continues to live in the midst of multiple outward relationships and responsibilities. "Here, the works begin; here a man cannot enjoy leisure." But the forgiven sinner knows that his justification does not depend on these works, and so his inability to fulfill the law need not torment him. He therefore performs his works out of gratitude and spontaneous love in obedience to and praise of God in Christ, who accepts him (faults and all) by grace alone. He offers his works, says Luther, as we may imagine that Adam and Eve in paradise, who had no sin and no need of being justified by works or the law, offered theirs—freely, simply to please God, and not to obtain righteousness. Thus Luther claims he does not reject good works but only rejects the false notion that righteousness is to be sought through them.[120]

115. "A Mighty Fortress Is Our God," in *The Hymnbook* (Richmond, Philadelphia, Pittsburgh, and New York: Presbyterian Church in the United States, Presbyterian Church in the United States of America, United Presbyterian Church of North America, Reformed Church in America, 1955), 87.

116. Luther, *Lectures on Genesis, Chapters 6–14*, ed. Jaroslav Pelikan, vol. 2 of *LW*, 267.

117. Luther, *Commentaries on 1 Corinthians 7, 1 Corinthians 15, Lectures on 1 Timothy*, ed. Hilton C. Oswald, vol. 28 of *LW*, 69.

118. Luther, *Lectures on Genesis, Chapters 6–14*, 267. See also Luther, *Selected Psalms I*, 324.

119. Luther, "The Freedom of a Christian, 1520," 349.

120. Luther, "The Freedom of a Christian, 1520," 363. The point remains basic for Lutheran theology and piety, though the Augsburg Confession (1530) states it a bit more formulaically. "Men cannot be justified [obtain forgiveness of sins and righteousness] before God by their own powers, merits, or works; but are justified freely [of grace] for Christ's sake through faith."

Augustine

Luther's idea may look as if it suddenly burst upon the scene, but actually it was a long time in the making. Much early Christian literature, for example, the Didache, tends to present Christian faith as a choice between a way of darkness, immorality, and death, on the one hand, and a way of light and righteous faithfulness, on the other.[121] To a significant degree, early Mediterranean monasticism represents an intensification of this idea. And so, one is not surprised to find Pelagius, an Irish monk, setting about the task of improving what he takes to be the lax spiritual and moral atmosphere at Rome during the late fourth century. The influential spiritual guide begins workshops by telling participants about the "strength" of human nature, and the great and good things we may accomplish.[122] He counsels his charges to aim high—to engage in right actions and practices according to the lawful standard of the gospel—and so break through the accumulated sinful habits that have encrusted their wills. That is, Pelagius represents a later articulation of what we might call the "Christianity of the Two Ways"; he tries to found spiritual communities in which the discipline of the monastery may be practiced by all.

By the time Augustine comes across Pelagius's teachings, the good bishop has already opposed the Donatists, a Christian party in northern Africa that maintained that the church is holy because and so long as its leadership remains righteous and faithful. Augustine insists, by contrast, that the holiness of the church lies not in its spiritual and moral perfection but in the grace of God dispensed in its sacraments. He claims that the church is more like a hospital for sinners than a gymnasium for accomplished spiritual and moral athletes, and so one is not surprised that he also comes to oppose Pelagius.

So also the Formula of Concord (1576), which affirms, "God remits to us our sins of mere grace, without any respect of our works." And "faith alone is the means and instrument whereby we lay hold on Christ our Redeemer in the word of the gospel" (*The Creeds of Christendom, with a History and Critical Notes*, vol. 3, *The Evangelical Protestant Creeds*, ed. Philip Schaff and David S. Schaff, 6th ed. [Grand Rapids: Baker Books, 1998], 10, 116). On the Reformed side, Heinrich Bullinger's Second Helvetic Confession (1566) claims, "solely by the grace of Christ and not from any merit of ours . . . we are justified," and "we receive this justification, not through any works, but through faith in the mercy of God and in Christ." The Westminster Confession of Faith (1647) claims that those whom God effectually calls receive and rest on Christ and "his righteousness by faith; which faith they have not of themselves, it is the gift of God." Indeed, "faith, thus receiving and resting on Christ and his righteousness, is the alone instrument of justification" (*BOC* 5.107; 5.109; 6.068; 6.069).

121. "The Didache: Teaching of the Twelve Apostles," in *The Apostolic Fathers*, trans. Francis X. Grimm, Joseph M.-F. Marique, SJ, Gerald G. Walsh, SJ (Washington, DC: Catholic University of America Press, 2008), 171.

122. Pelagius, "Letter to Demetrias," in Burns, *Theological Anthropology*, 40.

Essentially, Augustine claims, we do not possess free and healthy wills that have merely become encrusted with or submerged by removable layers of bad habits. Peel away the layers and you shall find a fundamentally disoriented will or capacity for choosing in bondage to something deeper, namely, wrong loves or a corrupted heart. That is, for Augustine, the basis for our identities and practical orientations lies deeper than our wills and our own choices. Who we are is in large part a matter of what we love or desire, but we do not choose our loves; instead, our loves befall us. A corrupted or sinful heart either loves the wrong things altogether or else loves the right things wrongly, for example, fame, companionship, wealth. Its inordinate desires and disordered loves, in turn, disorient and misdirect the will, so that, when a sinner does as she pleases, she freely chooses wrongly.

Augustine maintains that this deep-seated corruption cannot be corrected by a person trying really hard to do otherwise. Why? Because the effort of a misdirected will can only yield further misdirected choices. If we are to be rehabilitated, then, we need something more than heroic effort and discipline (or a further reliance on our misshapen selves). We need a more radical medicine, a new fundamental love or disposition, a new heart given to us by grace and the Spirit that can redirect our wills. Then (and only then) God or the true good becomes pleasing to us. Then (and only then), when we do as we please, we choose God (or the true good) and also are able to reorder our other desires (for companionship, wealth, etc.) in accord with that primary devotion.

Not surprisingly, Augustine also envisioned the monastic life differently than did Pelagius and many others. The point of being a monk, for Augustine, is *not* to earn exceptional merits before God either for oneself or for the church by means of an especially rigorous discipline or obedience. Instead, the point is to live a rigorous life of service to God and to others *out of gratitude for the gift of grace and the Spirit.*[123]

Luther and Calvin

One way to understand Luther's idea of grace alone is as an intensification of Augustine's anti-Pelagian stance. For Luther, you and I do not prove or earn our worth before God by our accomplishments or achievements. Instead, we are

123. This was a reinterpretation of monasticism that troubled monks from Hadramentum when, upon visiting another monastery in northern Africa, they ran across a manuscript of Augustine's with which they were previously unfamiliar. See Rebecca Harden Weaver, *Divine Grace and Human Agency: A Study of the Semi-Pelagian Controversy* (Macon, GA: Mercer University Press, 1998).

saved by grace alone. Our salvation isn't earned; it is simply bestowed upon us by God as a free gift.

Even so, Luther does not repeat Augustine. Consider a key phrase: justification by grace through faith. Justification, for Luther, introduces an intensified forensic note not found in Augustine. It refers to being accepted, counted, or deemed righteous in God's judgment or sight despite our actual sins and fault. We are, according to Luther, at the same time both justified (or counted righteous) and sinners.[124] And we are justified or counted righteous *by grace*, or by God's unmerited favor and free gift. For Christ's sake, God is gracious to you and to me; for Christ's sake, God gives us a break by not holding our sins and faults against us. Finally, this takes place *through faith* in Jesus Christ and his victory over sin and death. Through faith in Jesus Christ we gain access to God's grace and acceptance. *Then* (and only then) the circle of misshapen choices and desires may be broken, and out of gratitude for God's free acceptance our faith and trust may become active in works of love—*not*, let it be said, in order to gain merit or special favor, but simply in response to the prior fact that God first loves us.

We should also say what Luther does not mean. He does not mean that we obtain God's grace as a result of trying really hard to believe. That, in fact, would turn faith into a meritorious work of credulity. Luther thinks the faith through which we gain access to God's free acceptance is itself a gift of the Holy Spirit. So here, according to Luther, is the very good news of the gospel: *in Christ and through faith, God simply is gracious to you and to me, and there is nothing we need to do to make this so.*

Parenthetically, we may note that Luther also does not regard the monastic life as especially meritorious. If you are a monk trying to do good in order to gain special merit either for yourself or for the church, he has a word for you: "Stop!" And so Luther did when he left the cloister and married a nun, Katharina von Bora (a genuinely countercultural move), in order to live in the midst of interdependent interrelations in which to serve others rather than be set apart in a special holy and "righteous" community.

Calvin follows Luther in many of these respects, though he has no personal experience of the monastery, and he places more emphasis on sanctification. We are justified or reckoned righteous in Christ, meaning, he says, that we are acquitted of guilt "as if" our innocence were confirmed.[125] We are sanctified, reborn in Christ, and elevated to newness of life in the Spirit; and we are thereby turned in service toward God and neighbor, though it is also true that we re-

124. Luther, *Lectures on Galatians (1535), Chapters 1–4*, ed. Jaroslav Pelikan, vol. 26 of *LW*, 232.
125. Calvin, *ICR* 3.11.4.

main sinners.[126] So, for Calvin, too, faith and the life of faith depend entirely on God's grace.

Where Luther and Calvin Go Wrong

Luther's idea of grace alone is, I think, unquestionably superb, but Luther himself fails to follow through its implications for Christian missions to the Jews. Early in his career, he argues toleration because he believes that, with the Protestant rediscovery of the gospel, the Jews may convert. By the 1530s and 1540s, however, and particularly as he believes that the last judgment is near and the devil will be unleashing his strongest attacks on the church, the German Reformer regards Jewish resistance to the gospel as a stubborn, blasphemous, and intolerable apostasy. As I noted above in chapter 2, proposition #20, in his tract *On the Jews and Their Lies* (1545) he argues that, out of devotion to "our Lord," the faithful should set fire to synagogues and schools, and Jews' houses should also be destroyed. (Instead they can live in barns.) Their prayer books and sacred writings should be confiscated; rabbis should be "forbidden to teach . . . on pain of loss of life and limb"; safe conduct for Jews on the highways should be withdrawn; and young Jews should be forced to earn their living at menial labor. However, since even these measures cannot guarantee that Jewish blasphemies will cease, the only solution is to expel the Jews from "our country."[127]

This is a wrong turn. One reason Luther's treatise rings hollow as a witness to the gospel of grace and acceptance is that it recommends a series of deeds that are unjust, mean-spirited, horrifying, and violent, deeds that have an influential place in an evil and genocidal history of sinful, often explicitly Christian, misdirection. Another reason, and one I have discussed elsewhere, is that it fails to pursue the thoroughgoing reconception of evangelism required by the logic of grace alone.[128] Here, however, let me simply ask this. If faith in the gospel is itself the free gift of grace and the Spirit, then how is it that the failure of Jews to convert is due to their blasphemous stubbornness and recalcitrance? How is it their fault if they do not receive the Spirit's gift? In the final analysis, the good news of grace and the gospel not only gives us no reason to boast (as Paul reminds his readers continually), but it also keeps us from concluding that, when persons and communities fail to embrace the gospel, it must literally be their own damned fault.

126. Calvin, *ICR* 3.3.9–10.

127. Luther, *The Christian in Society IV*, ed. Franklin Sherman, vol. 47 of *LW*, 268–72, 285–88.

128. See Ottati, *Theology for Liberal Presbyterians*, 49–61.

Calvin's understanding of Judaism and of the Jews as God's people differs rather sharply from Luther's, partly due to his insistence that the election of God is "without repentance." The covenant with Israel, for Calvin, is a dimension of the one covenant of grace, and so God's blessing remains with the Jews.[129] Nevertheless, and as every student of doctrine knows, there is another side to Calvin's doctrine of election, namely, the claim that, before the foundation of the world, God predestines "some to salvation, others to destruction" (*ICR* 3.21).

There is nothing the reprobate can do to alter their fate, but to those who find this unjust, Calvin responds that God's will is "the highest rule of righteousness," and so "whatever he wills . . . must be considered righteous" (3.23.2). Calvin's fuller defense of the doctrine points to experience—we see, for example, that, "though the voice of the gospel addresses all in general . . . the gift of faith is rare" (3.22.10). It acknowledges mystery—as Augustine noted, "we cannot comprehend" why God created persons who are simply bound for destruction (3.23.5). And it appeals to God's inscrutable discrimination—the fact that God "does not . . . adopt all . . . but gives to some what he denies to others" illumines God's mercy (3.21.1). "The very inequality of his grace proves that it is free" (3.21.6).[130]

This, I think, is another wrong turn. Precisely in an effort to stress God's sovereign grace, Calvin fashions an understanding of predestination that calls into question whether God really is gracious at all. One basic vector of Calvin's theology is that we know ourselves as well as others to be valued creatures in relation to the God who bestows gifts as Creator and Redeemer; God's gracious regard for humans and for other creatures therefore endues them with worth. But does a gracious God create good, distinctively equipped humans capable of mirroring the divine, creatures God loves and values but who are also, by a divine and eternal decree that takes priority over both creation and redemption, bound only and necessarily for eternal alienation and torment?

Reformed orthodoxy repeats Calvin's doctrine. Thus, for example, the Westminster Confession of Faith states the doctrine of double predestination quite clearly. "By the decree of God, for the manifestation of his own glory, some men

129. Calvin, *ICR* 4.16.14. Hereafter, references to this work will be given in parentheses in the text. See also Calvin's comments on Rom. 11:29: "The counsel of God, by which He has once condescended to choose them [the Jews] for Himself as a peculiar nation, stands firm and immutable." Calvin, *Romans and Thessalonians*, 257.

130. Calvin insists on this doctrine, which he admits "human curiosity" may render "confusing and even dangerous," and which he warns should not be pursued without restraint partly because he finds it in some (not very highly developed) New Testament passages. More systematically, he thinks it shows that God's justification of sinners, as also God's election of Israel, is by grade and without deference to merits or demerits. See especially the way he interprets certain passages in the Gospel of John (*ICR* 3.22.7).

and angels are predestined unto everlasting life, and others foreordained to everlasting death." It also does not shy away from the ready implication, namely, that, in Christ, God's redeeming grace is limited to the elect.[131] But the most important Reformed theologians of the nineteenth and twentieth centuries reject this. Friedrich Schleiermacher says that doctrine leaves Christian piety beset by contrary emotions: gratitude for one's own blessedness and ever-renewed sadness for all those who are lost. He also notes that to say God creates one segment of humanity for redemption and another for destruction threatens to introduce a Manichaean cleavage at odds with piety's conviction that God sends God's Son out of love for the entire world.[132]

Karl Barth claims that, in the light of God's act in Christ, we see that God's sovereign deity includes his humanity or free love and affirmation of man.[133] Inspired by passages such as Colossians 1:20, where the event of Jesus Christ presses toward the reconciliation of all, Barth says we see that in the covenant of grace (as it comes to expression in God's promise to Noah, God's promise to Abraham, and elsewhere) the whole of humanity, rather than only a part of it, is the outer circle of which the relation with Israel forms the inner circle.[134] The implications, as Barth well knows, are far-reaching and profound. "Would that Calvin had energetically pushed ahead on this point in his Christology, his doctrine of God, and his teaching non predestination, and his ethics! His Geneva would then not

131. *BOC* 6.016; 6.071.

132. Schleiermacher, *CF*, #120 (p. 558). It is a cleavage potentially at odds also with Calvin's own affirmation that God finds something to love in fallen humanity. Arguing that God's love precedes our reconciliation in Christ and that, therefore, the work of atonement derives from God's love, Calvin says, "All of us . . . have in ourselves something deserving of God's hatred. With regard to our corrupt nature and the wicked life that follows it, all of us surely displease God, are guilty in his sight, and are born to the damnation of hell. But because the Lord wills not to lose what is his in us, out of his own kindness he still finds something to love. However much we may be sinners by our own fault, we nevertheless remain his creatures. However much we have brought death upon ourselves, yet he has created us unto life" (*ICR* 2.16.3, 4). Moreover, it threatens the integrity of Christian ethics because it calls into question a primary feature or vector of a renewed, regenerate, and sanctified manner of life. To be perfect as our heavenly Father is, says Jesus, we should love our enemies (Matt. 5:43–48). At best, however, Calvin's God seems to love only some of God's enemies. Thus the doctrine of double predestination threatens to undercut love of neighbor, or what Edwards called a true virtue that extends to all beings. H. Richard Niebuhr also claims that, in their eschatologies, Augustine, Calvin, and others fall into an inappropriate dualism. See *Christ and Culture* (New York: Harper & Row, 1951), 215–18.

133. Karl Barth, *The Humanity of God*, trans. John Newton Thomas (Richmond, VA: John Knox, 1960), 51.

134. Barth, *CD* IV/1:51.

have become such a gloomy affair."[135] Indeed, the practical import only becomes more intense given Barth's own encounter with a genocidal National Socialist ideology that denied the dignity and worth of humans as humans, rather than, say, only as members of one or another ethnic or national community.

What lies behind and beneath the Reformers' wrong turns, I think, is a failure to appreciate the truly radical nature of their idea. Grace alone, I believe, inevitably points to the fundamental apprehension that God simply *is* the God of grace whose will or dynamic tendency is to bestow existence, life, and renewed life. Let me underscore this point by suggesting how my interpretation of Romans 4 differs from the ones offered by Luther and Calvin.

In Romans, Paul recognizes that the law is the standard for right conduct within Israel's covenant with God. The law, given at Sinai and including both moral and ritual requirements, is a basic institution that constitutes Israel as God's people. But, says Paul, *before* there was the law, *before* the Ten Commandments were given at Sinai, Abraham, the father of Israel, was already in right relationship with God, already justified in God's sight. And so, the question arises: If Abraham did not obtain his justification before God by fulfilling the law, by acting well, or by his own accomplishment, then how did he come to stand in right relationship with God? Paul's answer: Abraham trusted that, when he and Sarah could no longer expect to have a child, God would give them a son. He trusted further that, through this unlikely son, the people of God would come to be and "all the families of the earth" would be blessed. And, says Paul, Abraham's faith or trust that God would do this "was reckoned to him as righteousness" (4:22).

The Reformers say Paul presents Abraham as an example, pattern, or mirror of righteousness for all, and I agree.[136] The difference comes in how we understand 4:16–17: "For this reason it depends on faith, in order that the promise may rest on grace and be guaranteed to all his descendants, not only to the adherents of the law but also to those who share the faith of Abraham (for he is the father of all of us, as it is written, 'I have made you the father of many nations')—in the presence of the God in whom he believed, who gives life to the dead and calls into existence the things that do not exist."

According to Luther, Abraham trusts that God is *sufficiently powerful* to do as God has promised, an emphasis that follows from 4:20–21, which says that Abraham "gave glory to God, being fully convinced that God was able to do what he had promised." Calvin, commenting on 4:16, says Abraham's faith is "based on the goodness of God alone," and that "nothing is set before faith but mere grace" or

135. Barth, *The Humanity of God*, 49.

136. Luther, *Lectures on Romans: Glosses and Scholia*, ed. Hilton C. Oswald, vol. 25 of *LW*, 85; Calvin, *Romans and Thessalonians*, 82.

gratuitous favor. But commenting on 4:17, he says that, since there was at present no token of God's promise, "it was hence necessary for him [Abraham] to raise up his thoughts to the power of God, by which the dead are quickened."[137]

I want to place the emphasis elsewhere. God's promise/act is not simply to give Abraham a son, Isaac, but through Isaac also to make Abraham the father of a people more numerous than the sands and to bless all the families of the earth. Thus, in Paul's telling of it, I think, Abraham did not trust *only* in God's power, he also trusted in *God's gracious disposition to himself and, ultimately, to all.* Abraham trusted that, through Isaac, the God "who gives life to the dead and calls into existence things that do not exist" would bring about the covenant of grace and renewed life, a blessing to all nations. Abraham trusted that resident in the God who creates, who brings things into existence and bestows life, is the gracious divine disposition to do so, and he trusted that this God would *continue* to exercise this same gracious disposition. Abraham's confidence is that the Creator who graciously bestows existence and life is also the Redeemer who graciously reconciles and renews. In short, his faith is that it is simply who God is, God's character, or the divine tendency to be the God of grace who bestows gifts of life, existence, and renewed life. And now, says Paul, we encounter this same God and excellent divine tendency through faith in Jesus Christ; now we apprehend this same God and divine excellence bringing about new life and new creation through Jesus's ministry, suffering, death, and resurrection.

What, then, shall we say? Simply this: that the great God of glory who creates is the good God of grace who reconciles, redeems, and re-creates. This is who God has been, is, and shall continue to be. For this reason, when we know who God is, we also know that we are accepted and stand in right relationship with God by grace alone. God is not first a powerful agent and then, secondarily, one who decides to be gracious or not in order to demonstrate that God is powerful, discriminate, and free. The very good news of the gospel is really quite different and very much better than this: *God simply* is *the God of grace who is gracious to you, to me, and to all creatures.*

137. Calvin, *Romans and Thessalonians*, 173, 175. Calvin says, further, "the character of the divine calling is, that they who are dead are raised by the Lord, that they who are nothing begin to be something through his power. The word *call* ought not to be confined to preaching, but it is to be taken, according to the usage of Scripture, for raising up; and it is intended to set forth more fully the power of God, who raises up, as it were by a nod, whom he wills" (175).

Reinterpreting Justification by Grace through Faith

This sets the stage for what can now be a comparatively short constructive statement. It sometimes happens that persons ensnared by the anxiety of situated agency; caught in patterns of corrupted devotion, vision, and responsibility; and gripped by despairing self-accusation or even sickness of soul nevertheless grasp their worth and acceptance, not in what they have done or achieved, not in their good reputations or in the approbation of their fellows, but in the Word of the gospel. They sometimes grasp their worth and acceptance in the portrait of the kingdom-minded one who blesses the poor, heals the sick, and sits at table with tax collectors and sinners. They sometimes see it in the crucified and resurrected one who crosses barriers and boundaries in order to pursue renewed community, and who invites them to participate in a renewed and resurrected life. And this, in fact, is what people have longed to see and to hear, their justification or reconciliation to God.

We say they are justified by grace because what the faithful glimpse in the Word of the gospel is the divine excellence, the fundamental dynamic of the deity who is gracious to all and to us, the gratuitous divine tendency to create, sustain, and renew. God's essential and constant graciousness—this sovereign grace, this unfathomable mystery and excellence within which we live and move—is what justifies and accepts. In our anxiety, corruption, and self-accusation, we neglect or forget this divine excellence, and then fearfully, perhaps also furiously, we try to justify ourselves and to vouchsafe our own worth, very often at the expense of others. But the God disclosed in Jesus as the Christ does not neglect or forget us. Like a gracious father who welcomes the prodigal home, God accepts, reconciles, and bestows worth on sinners simply by being gracious, simply by exercising God's own characteristic tendency and excellence, simply by being the God "who gives life to the dead and calls into existence things that do not exist."

We say justification is *through faith* because persons who recognize or acknowledge their acceptance *rely* on the gracious divine tendency displayed in Jesus as the Christ. Faith knows and trusts that, resident in the God who creates, the God who brings all things into existence and who bestows life, is the gracious disposition to reconcile and renew. Faith knows and trusts that God simply *is* the God of grace. As the Heidelberg Catechism says, faith is "wholehearted trust" that the "Spirit creates in me through the gospel." Its substance is that, "not only to others, but to me also God has given" the gift of forgiveness and righteousness "out of sheer grace."[138] Emil Brunner, the *other* twentieth-century Swiss Reformed theologian, notes that, in faith, we entrust ourselves to the God

138. *BOC* 4.021.

disclosed in Jesus Christ. Faith, he says, apprehends in Christ "the end of all our self-redeeming activity," and the end of all our anxious, insatiable, and never-ending self-commending.[139] This is why, occasionally and in addition to senses of awe, remorse, gratitude, and direction, Christian piety also may be characterized by a feeling of peace.

Here, my position comes closest to Paul Tillich's claim that "it is as though a voice were saying: 'You are accepted . . . by that which is greater than you. . . . Do not seek anything; do not perform anything; do not intend anything. Simply accept the fact that you are accepted! If that happens to us, we experience grace.'"[140] For my part, I would say simply accept the fact that God *is* the God of grace and that God will be God. In that acceptance there is assurance, as well as the courage to participate in situations replete with promises and risks.

Why this should be so will be apparent if we remind ourselves of two classical Protestant ideas. One is Calvin's insistence, at the outset of his *Institutes*, that knowledge of God and knowledge of ourselves go together. They are correlative. Thus, if we know God to be the fountain of every good, then we also know ourselves to be beneficiaries of divine gifts. Again, if we know that God is the God of grace, then we know ourselves to be graced and to have worth in relation to God. Our worth is grounded in God being God. This theologically objective ground is what vouchsafes assurance. We have trust and confidence that God will be God, the God disclosed in Jesus as the Christ who is faithful and brings into existence things that are not.

The worth of others has the same ground. All have worth before the God of grace. Martin Luther King Jr. puts it this way: "In the final analysis, says the Christian ethic, every man must be respected because God loves him. The worth of an individual does not lie in the measure of his intellect, his racial origin, or his social position. Human worth lies in relatedness to God. An individual has value because he has value to God."[141] And, just here, in addition to the sense of assurance, we see another reason to participate in promising and threatening circumstances: namely, because others are worth the commitment, the risk, and the engagement.

Now, for a second classical notion that bolsters participatory engagement—Luther's insistence on *simul iustus et peccator*.[142] I have worth in God's sight and

139. Emil Brunner, *Our Faith*, trans. John W. Rilling (New York: Scribner's Sons, 1954), 95, 97–98.

140. Tillich, *The Shaking of the Foundations*, 162.

141. King, "The Ethical Demands for Integration," in *A Testament of Hope: The Essential Writings of Martin Luther King, Jr.*, ed. James Melvin Washington (San Francisco: Harper & Row, 1986), 122.

142. "Thus a Christian man is righteous and a sinner at the same time, holy and profane, an

you do too, even though both of us are chronically subject to corruption and misdirection. The God of grace is gracious *not* because we somehow merit or deserve grace by our performance, but simply because that is the deity's own tendency or disposition. This is why, when confronted with our defection and constriction, God remains undeterred and, as it were, seeks in Godself the reason to benefit the deflected creature. By grace alone God accepts you and accepts me as flawed but beloved and good creatures.

This undercuts the anxiety of situated agency decisively. Here there is an assurance of worth *in spite of our flaws*. Thus the reconciled and renewed community before God is like reconciled community in the parable of the loving father and the prodigal. It is a community beyond naïveté and false optimism in which both parent and child are aware of the latter's fault, a community into which the child is accepted anyway and just as he comes to himself and so acknowledges and accepts that his life is flawed. Brunner therefore says that faith apprehends in Christ "the end of all our self-redeeming activity," the end of our anxious, never-ending, and misdirected self-commending and self-aggrandizing. It issues in a newfound freedom, a participatory courage that does not masquerade as (illusory) perfection.

Simil iustus et peccator. Especially in the light of this last point, and on the heels of our reflections on Jesus as the Christ, the Spirit, and the ec-centric manner or vector in life appropriate to humanity, we need to reckon with a felt dissonance and conflict. Christian teaching maintains that persons and communities often are divided and at odds with themselves. They acknowledge the goodness and appropriateness of the way of Christ and the Spirit, they acknowledge felt obligations to attend to the needs and well-being of others, but they also recognize how often they fail to follow in the way or uphold their obligations. They also know they do not do the good that, at some level, they want to do, and so, when they review their lives and their actions, they find themselves beset by sorrows and regrets. This is one reason why Christian worship ought not to neglect the dynamic of sin and grace.

Happily, in my view at least, the orders of worship or liturgies devised by a number of churches enact this very dynamic. Thus, the Episcopal orders for Daily Morning Prayer and Evening Prayer contain "general" confessions followed by Declarations of Absolution, or Remission of Sins. Sin and grace go together. The General Confession addresses our "almighty and most merciful Father." Worshipers acknowledge their fault in straying from God's ways. They recognize publicly that they are corrupted sinners who betray the good life for which they

enemy of God and a child of God. None of the sophists will admit this paradox, because they do not understand the true meaning of justification." Luther, *Lectures on Galatians*, 232–33.

are fitted. They acknowledge God as Judge. But they also encounter the heart of the gospel. God is holy but also merciful. And so, following the Prayer of Confession, the Absolution and Remission of Sins is also pronounced. It is proclaimed that God refuses to abandon even sinful betrayers, that sinners encounter God-in-Christ as their sure redeemer, and so they also know themselves to belong to the God of grace.[143]

The piety that is sculpted and comes to expression here acknowledges fault, regret, and remorse, but it also includes a sense of absolution, and thus also a sense of possibility. Worshipers confess that they *are* sinners, but then the Declaration of Absolution also underscores a leading affirmation of a theology of grace. We are forgiven, pardoned, or justified; we are saved from our sin and its destructive consequences, not by means of our own actions or because we deserve to be—not through any merit of our own—but solely by the free gift of divine mercy. *Sola gratia*.

Why the Reinterpreted and Revised Idea Is Relevant, Even Subversive

I have debated whether to move directly from this last statement to proposition #62 and the theme of sanctification or to include here a short account of how justification by grace alone critiques and perhaps also subverts some basic aspects of many contemporary cultures. I have opted for the latter course. So, briefly and also somewhat sermonically, here goes.

Properly and, as I think, also radically understood, the contemporary and social relevance of grace alone is evident for at least two related reasons. First, it points to the unshakable basis for a truly *theological* humanism. Second, it claims that persons have worth quite apart from their accomplishments or achievements.

Christian theological humanism emerges from the conviction that God simply *is* the God of grace. Theologically, and as we have noted earlier, if one loves the God of grace, one is disposed to love one's neighbors, or all the creatures to which God is gracious (which is, in fact, *all* creatures). Carried to its appropriate and radical conclusion, then, the conviction that God is the God of grace means that love of God entails love of neighbor and even enemies. Considered in relation to this God—a truly inalienable relation—all are rendered valuable.

143. *The Book of Common Prayer and Administration of the Sacraments and Other Rites and Ceremonies of the Church* (New York: Harper & Brothers, 1952), 6–7, 23–24. The Methodist and Episcopalian services include similar patterns.

In our own place and time as in many others, some people, including proponents of crusading religion, nationalism, racial discrimination, and clashes of civilizations, fail to discern that the worth of persons is nonnegotiable and secure. For the Christian humanist, however, the question is *not* whether *we* shall bestow worth on different persons and groups but only whether we (our communities, religious associations, societies, and governments) shall *recognize* and *acknowledge* what is always already the case. People have worth not only as Christians or Germans or Americans or Caucasians or Muslims or what-have-you. In God's sight, *humans as humans have worth*, and we therefore have moral duties to all, including to our adversaries.

The radical conviction that God simply *is* the God of grace who is gracious to all forms the deep foundation for a Christian humanism that finds itself at odds with the in-group/out-group impulses of closed society commitments that so often animate nations, religious communities, and cultures (whether traditional or secular). Where it is not compromised or watered down, this theological humanism resists even the most ingenious arguments for targeting noncombatants, whether they are in skyscrapers or in villages, as well as for torturing prisoners, whether at home or abroad. It strives for justice for all, and it attends especially to the vulnerable and the oppressed. Today it must also condemn unrestrained violence, every instance of indiscriminate bombing and every terrorist attack. It stands with the people of Aleppo and Kabul and Homs and New York and Manchester and London.

This brings us to a *subversive* element. America and the West today are often occupied by conflicts between varied in-groups, cultures of incivility marked by suspicion, discrimination, and Islamophobia. This is why they desperately need persons to witness to a truer humanism. But there is more.

Competitive capitalist and commercial environments finally devalue people when they insist that the worth of individuals is a matter of merits and achievements. A progressive, somewhat classist variety of this insistence often appeals to beneficiaries of elite educations who favor a kind of careerist/intellectual "meritocracy" and tend to look down on the rest. A conservative laissez-faire variety values those who make money and become "successes"—so much so that a recurrent weakness of American politics is to overestimate the transferability of competence in business and finance to almost every other aspect of life and culture, including cultural and political leadership.

And there are quite personal implications. If you are a young professional, working hard at your career and trying to raise your family, you may have received the impression, or even heard people say, that to have worth you must compete and achieve and succeed. You may have encountered the idea that, in order to be worthy or even to justify yourself, you need to make money and be recognized as an accomplished professional. But don't believe it. By the light of the very good news of the gospel and the strange logic of grace alone, you have worth in God's sight whether or not you turn out to be a recognized success.

Perhaps you are a high school student working hard to get good grades, so that you can go to a good college, so that you can get a good and meaningful job, and so that you can win approval of teachers and parents and peers. From time to time, maybe you get anxious because somewhere you've gotten the impression that you matter and make a difference only if you succeed, only if you become one of the educated elite. But don't believe it. Remember the very good news of the gospel and the strange logic of grace alone: you are valuable in God's sight whether or not you get good grades or high scores on standardized tests. You have worth, and your worth is not something that you need to manufacture or bring about by your own actions and achievements. You have worth, and your worth in God's sight is something inalienable that you just can't shake. No school, no business, no profession, and no social clique can take it away.

Or maybe you are closer to my age, and as you look back you sometimes wonder whether you lived up to your potential, whether you might have done better, whether you could have been more important, prominent, and worthy if only you had accomplished more and made fewer mistakes. Well, that's as it may be. But don't believe it. Remember the very good news of the gospel: you have worth in God's sight, and that is true whether or not your past accomplishments seem appropriately impressive by your own estimate or anyone else's.

Now for one more thing—a consciousness-raising exercise that I think evangelists, such as the late Billy Graham and others, too rarely have asked their hearers to try.[144] You have worth in God's sight. As Tillich used to say and as I have repeated, you are accepted. That is a feature of the good news of the gospel of grace. But now, take a moment to look around a public space, perhaps your own congregation, and, in your mind's eye, also imaginatively envision the many other people around your community, nation, and world. When you and I do this, we see Hispanics, Arabs, blacks, whites, Asians, women, men, Jews, Muslims, Hindus, Sikhs, gays, heterosexuals, the intelligent, the not-so-intelligent, the successful, the busted, the brave, the not-so-brave, and more. We may wonder sometimes whether all these others have truly made positive contributions, whether all these others have done enough to prove their value and their worth, and thus to deserve our good will and attention. But don't believe it. Don't be

144. For an insightful critique of revivalist emphases on individual conversion, see Reinhold Niebuhr, "Proposal to Billy Graham," in *Love and Justice: Selections from the Shorter Writings of Reinhold Niebuhr*, ed. D. B. Robertson (Louisville: Westminster John Knox, 1992), 154–58.

fooled by prejudices, manipulative politicians, or fears of those who are different. In light of the very good news of the gospel and the strange logic of grace alone, these other persons and groups have been called into existence and given the great and good gift of life by the God who creates and redeems. They, too, have a place and a time; they, too, have value in God's sight.

Five hundred years on, the Protestant churches and educational institutions that trace their heritages back to the Reformation of the sixteenth century in Europe show considerable signs of wear and tear. It is difficult to know just how many will survive current trends toward secularity and postdenominational Christianity. But in any case, grace alone—the basic material principle of the Reformation—shouldn't be abandoned or left behind. It's a keeper. It ought to be retrieved and radicalized as the basis for a truly Christian humanism and for a fundamental critique of contemporary cultures.

Proposition #62 By the grace of God and in the power of the Spirit, people may be caught up in a lifelong process of rehabilitation, regeneration, and renewal. This is sanctification.

Sin is radical and universal. Nevertheless, grace abounds. Thus far we have explored the meaning of the first sentence and a part of the second. Sin, or the human fault, is radical. Affect, practical reasoning, and patterns of responsibility are all subject to sin's corrosive and corrupting effects. Sin, or the human fault, is universal, and there is no sin-free person, community, or institution. Nevertheless, before God, people are caught up in regeneration—a permanent revolution. Constricted and skewed though they are, they also may know themselves and others to be accepted and have worth before the God of grace. This is justification, the topic of proposition #61. Now, we turn to a second dimension of grace abounding: those who are justified may be caught up in a Spirit-led and Spirit-inspired course of renewal. This is sanctification.

According to classical Reformed theology, sanctification, like justification, is a matter of grace alone. The Spirit, says the Scots Confession, "sanctifies us . . . and brings us into all truth by his own working." Or, "to put this even more plainly; as we willingly disclaim any honor and glory for our own creation and redemption, so do we willingly also for our regeneration and sanctification. . . . He who has begun the work in us alone continues us in it, to the praise and glory of his undeserved grace."[145] Westminster adds that while sanctification remains imperfect in this life, its effects are "throughout the whole man."[146] In my terms,

145. *BOC* 3.12.
146. *BOC* 6.076.

sanctification is growth in ec-centric existence under the impact of piety and by the power of the Spirit, or the ethos of the cosmos and of the Christian community. It influences the entire agent, and, as I noted earlier in proposition #60 with respect to regeneration, it refers to a renewal of constricted or corrupted affectivity, vision, and responsibility. Here let me emphasize three additional and related points. Sanctification entails an alteration in our more usual motives for being moral, an intensification of our more usual interpretations of moral law, and an impetus toward forgiveness and reconciliation.

An Alteration in Our Motives

The Heidelberg Catechism (1563) treats good works, the commandments, and prayer in its third part under the rubric of thankfulness. The basic idea is that our redemption and renewal by grace and the Spirit (and apart from any merits of our own) call forth a thankful response. Grace evokes gratitude, and gratitude disposes us to act. We are to "show ourselves grateful to God for his goodness," and so glorify God with our whole life.[147] What I want to underscore now is that this dynamic yields a distinctive reason of heart and mind for being moral, and that it also suggests that piety may yield additional reasons.[148]

Particularly in contemporary American society, but not, I think, only there, one often hears that those who do good prosper, that virtue makes us stronger as individuals and as a nation, that virtue brings happiness, and that salvation is a reward for being good. These are among the more common motives/reasons mentioned for being moral and upholding our responsibilities. To a degree, they reflect the incursion into the moral life of market forces and a market mentality, though there are clearly also other factors and commitments at work. In any case, claims such as these practically become "common sense" in a society that seeks to legitimate personal fulfillment, commercial success, and national might. Moreover, each entails the rather thinly veiled assumption that morality is an effort to gain or secure something for ourselves. Each assumes that moral sensibility serves to secure our own life and its meaning against threats to prosperity, happiness, strength, or what-have-you. And each is a variant on the idea that self-interest is the primary reason of mind and heart for engaging in a life of moral seriousness.

But question 86 of the Heidelberg Catechism says something rather different.

147. *BOC* 4.086.

148. James M. Gustafson, *Can Ethics Be Christian?* (Chicago: University of Chicago Press, 1975), 82.

We should "do good works . . . so that our whole lives may show that we are thankful to God for his benefits." In a broad theological compass, this statement needs to be understood with reference to both redeeming grace and created gifts. For the catechism, it emerges in conjunction with the claim in question 1 that Christ "makes me wholeheartedly willing and ready . . . to live for him."[149] Gratitude or thankfulness for the gift of redemption in Christ is a primary reason for being moral; it is a feature of piety, a sensibility of persons touched by grace that disposes them to take up a new and ec-centric direction in life.

Consider, too, question 64: Does the teaching that good works merit nothing "make people indifferent and wicked"? This echoes a Reformation-era criticism of grace-alone Protestants, and if the only engine for moral seriousness were our commitment to our own self-realization and fulfillment, the answer would surely be yes. The catechism, however, answers no, because "it is impossible for those engrafted into Christ through true faith not to produce fruits of gratitude."[150] Why? The South African theologian Piet Naude says this is because a kind of necessity accompanies grace. "The faithful *must* bear fruit. . . . The impossible possibility is to receive God's grace—to see God's openheartedness in Christ—and then to close one's own heart to structural injustice and to talk easily about love without corresponding deeds."[151]

For the catechism, the "must" emerges as a function of gratitude, and the broader claim is that a perceived debt of gratitude can effectively orient and direct the agent. The imperative, that is to say, is one of piety and consonance or fittingness. "Freely you have received; freely give" (Matt. 10:8 NIV). If this exhortation holds, then piety's sense of gratitude has imperative dimensions that ground a command in the "is-ness" of experience. Since you have freely received and are thankful, *it is fitting or consonant* that you freely give. "Out of a sense of gratitude should come a sense of justice. Having received, a people should not take more than is their due; they should not deprive others of life's resources. . . . God has freely given life to us; we, in thankfulness to him, are concerned for others' well-being as he has been concerned for ours."[152]

Here, then, we encounter a religious reason of mind and heart to attend to others' needs and interests, as well as the implication that religious bases for

149. *BOC* 4.001.

150. *BOC* 4.064.

151. Piet J. Naude, *Neither Calendar Nor Clock: Perspectives on the Belhar Confession* (Grand Rapids: Eerdmans, 2010), 207. Jan Rohls, *Reformed Confessions: Theology from Zurich to Barmen*, trans. John Hoffmeyer (Louisville: Westminster John Knox, 1998), 133, notes that, for Reformed confessions, "one cannot say that we are justified *without* good works, although we are not justified *on the basis* of good works."

152. Gustafson, *Can Ethics Be Christian?*, 101.

moral seriousness do not reduce to self-realization or self-love. Indeed, we need not limit *all* religiously connected reasons of mind and heart for engaging in lives of moral seriousness *only* to gratitude. Like the catechism, we may also appeal to other aspects of piety or heartfelt sensibilities, say, of remorse or of hope. So, for those who are gripped by regenerative piety and feel remorse for irresponsible past actions and their deleterious consequences, it is fitting to endeavor not to repeat those actions in the future. Or, having been inspired with hope for God's kingdom and its excellence by Jesus's message and performance, having been gripped by kingdom piety, it is fitting or consonant for us to work for a more just and humane society. Sanctification, or growth in ec-centric existence by the power of the Spirit, entails an alteration in and a broadening of some of our basic sensibilities and so also of our more usual reasons for being moral. (It therefore also suggests a related, more theoretical conclusion, namely, that "rational self-interest" plays too central a role in some other forms of ethics.[153] For, if it is true that gratitude, as well as other sensibilities and emotions, may be an effective engine of moral seriousness, then forms of ethics, whether religious or not, that focus entirely on self-realization and self-regard miss or reduce the true emotional depth and complexity of human agency.) But the immediate point is simply that sanctification or growth in ec-centric existence involves a change in our sensibilities and also in our more usual motives for leading lives of moral seriousness.

Interpreting and Reinterpreting Moral Norms and Commands

The changed motives go together with a reinterpretation of moral norms and commands. According to Calvin and other classical theologians, the entire law is not written in any one place. Different parts of it appear at different locations in Scripture, for example, the Decalogue, Leviticus, and the Sermon on the Mount. Again, the law as it is written in Scripture overlaps with dictates of conscience and reason. Thus we find a prohibition against killing in Exodus 20:13, Deuteronomy 5:17, and also in the natural law or generally distributed moral sense of humankind.[154] Furthermore, Jesus's radicalization of this prohibition is also a feature of God's law, for example, "Do not be angry with your brother" and "Love your enemies" (Matt. 5:22, 44).

153. Gustafson, *Can Ethics Be Chrsitian?*, 164.

154. Calvin, *ICR* 2.2.13, 23. Aquinas, *ST* 1a2ae.100.2–3.

The Commandments as Moral Requisites for Human Community

Traditionally, the Ten Commandments are said to consist of two "tablets" or "tables" that Moses brought down from Mount Sinai, the first having to do with duties toward God, and the second with duties toward other people. The moral philosopher Arthur Dyck views the second as "moral bonds" that are "requisites of community," and, if we understand humans to be ineluctably social, we may view them as moral requisites for human life.[155] This view accords with what Calvin regards as the crucial preface or introduction to the commandments in Exodus 20:2, "I am the LORD your God, who brought you out of the land of Egypt, out of the house of slavery," as well as with the longer plotline of the book of Exodus that these words summarize. The escape of Israel from slavery in Egypt, the wilderness wanderings, and the eventual constitution of Israel as a *nation* with its own equitable laws to guide and maintain its own distinct cultural life are the primary saving act of God in the Hebrew Scriptures. Moreover, when the commandments are interpreted within this salvific sequence of deliverance, they are regarded in piety not as random authoritative demands but as a great and good gift intimately connected with the gift of life itself. Why? Because the law enables a good life together in community, and, since humans are social creatures, without community they do not live.

Dyck encourages us to engage in a thought experiment. "Recently escaped slaves" find themselves in "a vast and barren land" (127). What would you advise them to do? Develop a police force to keep people from each other's throats? But this requires an organized government, and an organized government presupposes a society. Perhaps they should agree on some rules, but why should they not quarrel over what the rules should be? Some will say it is in their self-interest to have rules, even a matter of life and death. But, says Dyck, different people find themselves interested in many different things. Why not expect some among this group to deviate from what we deem "rational" self-interest? "We find ourselves spinning around the circle largely created by Hobbesian assumptions. No morality without a government, and, at the same time, no government is created without morality" (131). We need to answer a prior question about the bases for forming and sustaining communities. Warring sensibilities and self-interest are not enough.

Dyck claims instead "that every individual was conceived, born, and nurtured in a community," and that we need to focus on why this is so necessary. For example, families provide care for children, and the community allows for this

155. Arthur J. Dyck, *Rethinking Rights and Responsibilities: The Moral Bonds of Community* (Cleveland: Pilgrim, 1994), 125–49. Hereafter, page references from this work will be given in parentheses in the text.

care by protecting people from injury and preventing killing, and by figuring out how to share resources (132). He therefore recommends that the escaped slaves engage in some consciousness raising about known requisites for a community. He outlines the avoidance of killing as one requisite and illustrates its importance with a story of people planning to climb a treacherous mountain. Would you make the climb with someone who, the previous evening, said he does not regard human life as an especially important value? The point, of course, is that communities presuppose that people generally place a high value on human life, and not just their own. Dyck next adds requisite restraints against stealing "those goods necessary for life and self-respect, such as food and clothing." Then he underscores the expectation that people will speak truthfully; otherwise, they could not discuss and attempt to agree on anything (139).

Dyck follows up these observations by reviewing a history of Alton, New Hampshire, which says that, for the initial settlers, the family was crucial, and that these "family oriented pioneers 'felt the need of banding together TO FORM A COMMUNITY'" (141). That is, from the very beginning there are families needing support rather than simply isolated individuals at one another's throats. "Communities in the form of kinship relations are a given for those who are thinking about beginning a community beyond the family." This allows Dyck to comment on the importance of "honoring parents," since "no community exists and persists without an honored, recognized past," and because honoring parents is an affirmation of the nurture without which there is no life (142). He then notes that parents need to be in stable sexual relationships, otherwise children will not be predictably cared for and parents will not predictably share their own lives and experiences with their children and with one another.

The illuminating suggestion is that we may understand the situation of the escaped Hebrew slaves whose story is told in Exodus to be something like this. The Mosaic covenant and the Ten Commandments have to do with moral bonds that are requisite for the formation and maintenance of a community (153). Dyck, as I have noted, applies this mode of interpretation to the "second table" of the commandments, or that portion traditionally viewed as having to do with duties to our neighbors. But, after a fashion at least, we may also extend it to the "first table," traditionally understood as having to do with duties to God.

To see how this is so, keep in mind some elementary theological reflections on idolatry and its consequences. Idolatry is the fashioning of a god in our own image or presumption. To paraphrase Calvin, we imagine a god in our minds and then fashion a likeness or representation of it with our hands.[156] The idol is the product of our wants, desires, and preferences, and it embodies, guarantees,

156. Calvin, *ICR* 1.11.8.

and legitimates them. It is a false deity whose purposes may be defined or manipulated to accord with our own interests and aims. But, of course, this ruins the "objectivity" of the deity's ethical demands in the sense that they no longer stand "over against" us and our wishes. (Perhaps, after all, we should refrain from killing and be truthful only when it suits us. Perhaps a community should uphold impartial courts of law only when it wishes to.) Often enough, the purposes of such a god are simply identified with those of our own group or nation and its typical interests and practices—a temptation to which, as the prophets saw, Israel and other nations succumb repeatedly. Idolatry, in short, results in a loss of divine transcendence, and this leads to an erosion of norms and values, such as the worth of persons and justice (especially for the vulnerable), that might otherwise enable us occasionally to take a critical view of our own desires, as well as of our own group or nation, its conventional interests, morality, and practices.

These reflections address the basic substance of the commandments in Exodus 20:1–7—we are to have no other gods, to fashion no idols, to refrain from worshiping idols, and to refrain from (wrongfully) using the name of the Lord to constrain God's help or favor. They are relevant too for 20:8–11, which joins the Sabbath of the true God with appropriate treatment of others by enjoining a day of rest for "you, your son or your daughter, your male or female slave, your livestock, [and] the alien resident in your towns." Regardless of our personal interests and preferences as well as those of our community and nation, these Sabbath injunctions are not to be abridged. Indeed, the strictures in the first table protect theological objectivity, thus lending an uncompromising weight or gravity to the moral requisites articulated in the second. They function, among other things, as a down payment on the integrity of the second table. Or, to put this same point another way, piety regards the requisites articulated in the second table as genuine *requirements* for human life set by the one true God whose purposes and judgments will not be manipulated or compromised by our egocentric interests and conventional cultural practices.

The Sixth Commandment

Now consider the sixth commandment in some detail. Literally translated, Exodus 20:13 and Deuteronomy 5:17 say, "You shall not *kill*." The NRSV translates, "You shall not *murder*," probably to render these verses consistent with the fact that in Israel some violations of law, as we see already in Exodus 21, were punishable by death. Still, it is not entirely apparent that the Ten Commandments are either a summary of Israelite law or the foundation principles from which the rest are properly derived. And so, one might argue to let stand the tension between the literal translation of the command, "Do not kill," and some practices in ancient Israel (and elsewhere) precisely in order to call the latter into question.

Calvin, as we have seen, approaches the Decalogue as a synecdoche, a part that stands for a larger whole. Thus, when he considers the sixth commandment as well as others, he identifies a broader purpose, connects the command with further and like prohibitions, and also indicates that it correlates with positive duties. "The purpose of this commandment is: the Lord has bound mankind together by a certain unity; hence each man ought to concern himself with the safety of all." He continues, "all violence, injury, and any harmful thing . . . are forbidden to us." Moreover, we are to employ all means that may save our neighbors' lives or make for their peace; if there is anything harmful, we are "to ward it off," and where "they are in danger," we should "lend a helping hand." Forbidden too, due to Jesus's Great Sermon (Matt. 5:22) and 1 John 3:15 ("All who hate a brother or sister are murderers"), is any inward anger or "murder of the heart." Indeed, "if we do not wish to violate the image of God, we should hold our neighbor sacred" and "cherish his as our own flesh."[157]

The Heidelberg Catechism makes similar points. It intensifies the prohibition against killing with respect to both external actions and internal attitudes and emotions. "I am not to belittle, hate, insult, or kill my neighbor—not by my thoughts, my words, my look or gesture, and certainly not by actual deeds—and I am not to be a party to this in others; rather I am to do away with all desire for revenge."[158] Indeed, "by forbidding murder God teaches us that he hates the root of murder: envy, hatred, anger, vindictiveness."[159] The catechism then turns to positive duties and virtues that correlate with the prohibitions. "Is it enough if we do not murder our neighbor in any such way? No. By condemning envy, hatred, and anger, God wants us to love our neighbors as ourselves, to be patient, peace-loving, gentle, merciful, and friendly toward them, to protect them from harm as much as we can and to do good even to our enemies."[160]

The catechism presents *a radicalization of moral law and its standards* rather than an entirely new ethics—after all, as far as classical Reformed theology is concerned, the basic norms are present in the commandments and also overlap with our general sense of natural equity. And this, essentially, is what H. Richard Niebuhr has in mind when he says that revelation in Jesus Christ does not give us a new ethics so much as it precipitates "a revolutionary understanding and application" of standards we already recognize by revealing God to be the

157. Calvin, *ICR* 2.8.39.
158. *BOC* 4.105.
159. *BOC* 4.106.
160. *BOC* 4.107.

source of the moral law.[161] We might say that the law becomes intensified when piety recognizes that our transgressions break not merely moral standards of conscience or of our own society or even of life but break the standards of the inescapable, righteous, and faithful God. A more extensive application of the law therefore also becomes necessary because the source of moral standards now is perceived to be the universal God who stands in relation to sparrows, to lilies, and, indeed, to all creatures and things. No longer restricted to an in-group or closed society, such as our nation or race, under the impact of theocentric piety, our moral reverence, concern, and benevolence must now extend even to our enemies, nonhuman life, and all created existents.[162]

An Impetus toward Forgiveness

One result of this view is that those formed in Christian piety stand rather radically accused because our lax, narrowing, and self-serving interpretations of moral values, standards, and conventional laws are exposed by the divine law's intensified and extended standards. Accusation, in the frame of Reformed Christian piety, is finally *not* the principal purpose of the law; furnishing positive guidance for a good life is. Nevertheless, the accusatory note plays an important role, and, in particular, we should not let the radicalized interpretation of the law pass by without observing how accusation connects with forgiveness.

Writing in the mid-1930s, Reinhold Niebuhr notes "the cruelty of self-righteous people," and he claims that, for Jesus, "the self-righteousness of the righteous" has both religious and moral connotations. They are "proud in the sight of God"; they are also "merciless and unforgiving" to other people. In fact, says Niebuhr, "their pride" is "the basis of their lack of mercy."[163]

Niebuhr turns to the contemporary relevance of these points by exploring the tendency of moderns to impart universal pretensions to their social interests and objectives. Disingenuous and manipulative political rhetoric is surely a factor in this, but the rhetoric succeeds, says Niebuhr, partly because, to a significant degree, both leaders and citizens are prone to conflate their partial interests with almost "every conceivable universal value," from "Kultur," democracy, and freedom to justice and the classless society. "The consequence is that" many

161. H. Richard Niebuhr, *The Meaning of Revelation*, 90.

162. For H. Richard Niebuhr, moral reverence and concern now extend even beyond the boundaries of life to the universal community of existents in relation to God. See *Radical Monotheism and Western Culture, with Supplementary Essays* (Louisville: Westminster John Knox, 1993), 31–39.

163. Reinhold Niebuhr, *Interpretation of Christian Ethics*, 139.

moderns "fight for their causes with a fury of which only those are capable who are secure in the sense of their righteousness."[164] The pathos of modern political spirituality lies in the belief that we justify ourselves by our lofty, universal, and correct causes or commitments. This supports a prideful moralism lacking genuine self-criticism and remorse because it fails to discern that all (including us) fall short. It supports a politics without an appreciation for our own participation in the universal human fault. The result is a naïve confidence in our own moral achievements coupled with a merciless condemnation of enemies whose wrong values and commitments render them, unlike us, morally derelict (and perhaps even depraved) in our sight.

Niebuhr believes that forgiveness in an absolute sense, forgiveness as Jesus forgave, is impossible for sinful persons and communities in history, and yet he thinks it possible "to engage in social struggles with a religious reservation," or with an appreciation for our own moral failures that undercuts and mitigates self-righteous pretensions. The religious reservation emerges from our recognition of having failed to satisfy the intensified standard of true morality, and just here lies a ground for an impetus toward forgiveness, namely, "the demand that the evil in the other shall be borne without vindictiveness because the evil in the self is known."[165] Call it a dimension of piety and moral possibility that emerges—however fragmentarily and sporadically—from the dynamic of obligation, remorse, and contrition in the face of the law's radical demands. An impetus toward forgiveness takes root in piety's recognition that I and we share corrupted tendencies, faults, derelictions, and sins with my and our opponents.

This impetus toward forgiveness makes a critical contribution to an ethic of reconciliation, though we should emphasize that it has roots, too, in the positive, if also somewhat aspirational, guides that we find in Jesus's kingdom message and teaching of indiscriminate divine benevolence, his parable of the prodigal son, and his practice of crossing barriers and boundaries to welcome sinners and outcasts. Indeed, positive guidance, or teaching God's will and exhorting and moving us to live in accord with it, is for Calvin the third and principal use of the law.[166] Presented as they are to those who in piety perceive that God is gracious to all and to them, the commandments as well as Jesus's teaching and example not only judge and accuse but also guide persons (quite apart from anxieties about their own worth or anyone else's) toward appropriate attitudes, acts, and practices. They point the way for graced sinners to advance in a good and ec-centric life of attentiveness to God and neighbor.

164. Reinhold Niebuhr, *Interpretation of Christian Ethics*, 137–38.
165. Reinhold Niebuhr, *Interpretation of Christian Ethics*, 137, 141.
166. Calvin, *ICR* 2.7.12.

Much has been written in recent years about possibilities for forgiveness and reconciliation following periods of protracted and quite serious civil conflict in South Africa, Ireland, Latin America, and elsewhere, and this is not the place to review the extensive literature. We should note, however, that this is an arena in which a more or less explicitly Christian theological idea appears to have some public currency, and that serious tensions emerge concerning the demands of justice. Just because in the frame of genuine piety reconciliation aims to heal and to restore life together, it must also mean considerably more than merely forgiving, forgetting, and leaving out justice altogether in the name of political expediency. That, after all, would be self-defeating, since, as Nigel Biggar says, the victims are not able to forget, and grievances without redress fester and infect the social future.[167] On the other hand, neither will it do to equate reconciliation with retribution.

Can justice be understood in a manner that redresses grievances and is also compatible with reconciliation and forgiveness? Recall that biblical traditions value justice as procedural fairness and care for the vulnerable but do not identify justice simply with retribution, associating it instead with shalom or a broad quality of social health and well-being. Biggar makes a move in this direction, proposing that criminal justice is primarily not about retribution and the punishment of perpetrators but is a vindication of victims—both actual and potential—that aims to repair damage and remove threats. Vindication, he says, entails recognizing the injury and acknowledging the dignity of victims, direct support for victims, and establishing who is responsible. He notes, for example, that the Truth and Reconciliation Commission (TRC) in South Africa offered some victims the opportunity to tell their stories publicly and "in the context of a legally authorized, quasi-juridical institution," and thereby "gave them a measure of acknowledgment and validation . . . by the national community."[168] Punishment remains appropriate as a response to a perpetrator of a crime; it asserts fairness by penalties designed to annul advantages seized through a crime, and, where there is a conventional or symbolic proportion between the crime and the penalty, it also expresses the opprobrium of the community. Thus, public confession as a requirement for amnesty applicants to the TRC subjected them to punishment in the form of nationwide exposure. "On the other hand," says

167. Nigel Biggar, "Making Peace or Doing Justice: Must We Choose?" in *Burying the Past: Making Peace and Doing Justice after Civil Conflict*, ed. Nigel Biggar, expanded and updated ed. (Washington, DC: Georgetown University Press, 2003), 5.

168. Biggar, "Making Peace or Doing Justice," 15.

Biggar, "punishment is not retributive in the sense of annulling the crime itself, because"—in any complete sense—"that is impossible."[169]

Somewhat similarly, Desmond Tutu and others put forward the idea of restorative justice.[170] Restorative justice, says Tutu, tries to heal breaches, redress imbalances, restore broken relationships, rehabilitate both victim and perpetrator, and reintegrate them into the community.[171] At the same time, however, he also notes important ambiguities and shortcomings of South Africa's TRC, which attempted to practice restorative justice. For example, reparations were thought to be important, but South Africa lacked the resources and skills to reverse the massive wrongs of the apartheid era. The TRC tried to operate with a wide concept of reparation that favors the reconstruction of society, and it also paid significant though symbolic amounts to victims, but the reparation regime was slow and finally also incomplete.[172] The TRC's work was hampered, too, says Tutu, by a lack of white participation due partly to a lack of white political leadership.

We need to keep in mind that situations of civil conflict and injustice are highly particular and complex, that we cannot offer here a full-fledged investigation and analysis of any specific circumstance, and that responsible investigators and commentators often disagree. Thus, for example, Tutu's participation in and view of the TRC process have drawn significant criticisms—among other things, for being too Christian. Even so, I think it instructive to observe where, in Tutu's view, there is a place for something like forgiveness, and also to note that, in order to identify this place, he poses the following question: "How was it possible for normal, decent, and God-fearing people, as white South Africans considered themselves to be, to have turned a blind eye to a system which impoverished, oppressed, and violated so many of those others with whom they shared the beautiful land that was their common motherland?" Tutu responds by noting the systemic separation of the races and the media portrayals that delegitimated those who struggled against apartheid, as well as the "racial capitalism" of the business sector. Moreover, he also confesses that, at one point during a crisis, he

169. Biggar, "Making Peace or Doing Justice," 10.

170. Desmond Mpilo Tutu, *No Future without Forgiveness* (New York: Doubleday, 1999), 49–65. See also, for example, Jennifer J. Llewellyn and Daniel Philpott, "Restorative Justice and Reconciliation: Twin Frameworks for Peacebuilding," Louise Mallinder, "Amnesties in the Pursuit of Reconciliation, Peacebuilding, and Restorative Justice," and Jason A. Springs, "Doing Justice Differently: From Revolution to Transformation in Restorative Justice and Political Reconciliation," in *Restorative Justice, Reconciliation, and Peacebuilding*, ed. Jennifer J. Llewellyn and Daniel Philpott (New York: Oxford University Press, 2014), 14–36, 138–73, 240–58.

171. Tutu, *No Future without Forgiveness*, 54–55.

172. Tutu, *No Future without Forgiveness*, 60–62, 233.

himself had "been so radically brainwashed" as to accept "a white definition of existence."[173] In short, he underscores the "power of conditioning."

> That is why I hold the view that we should be a little more generous, a little more understanding, in judging perpetrators of human rights violations. This does not mean that we will condone what they and the white community in South Africa did or allowed to happen. But we will be a little more compassionate in our judgment as we become a little more conscious of how we too could succumb as easily as they. It will make our judgment just that little less strident and abrasive and possibly open the door to some being able to forgive themselves for what they now perceive as weakness and lack of courage. It might then persuade them perhaps to be a little more willing to accept accountability. And it might make us say to ourselves as we sit in judgment, "There but for the grace of God go I."[174]

As the son of a Latin American immigrant who grew up in the northeastern United States, has lived below the Mason-Dixon Line for many years, and now teaches in North Carolina at a college founded in 1837, I think I can appreciate Tutu's point. Call it one of the gifts of a seriously flawed and troubling past.[175] I also think it relates rather closely to the fragmentary and sporadic impetus toward forgiveness that takes root, as Niebuhr says, in "the demand that the evil in the other . . . be borne without vindictiveness because the evil in the self is known," with the difference, perhaps, that I also want to plumb the anxieties of situated agents, explore how they corrupt, and emphasize that they render us especially susceptible to practices, loyalties, and ideas—or to forces of social conditioning—that encourage us to idolize our in-groups and partial interests at the expense of out-groups. But if in fact piety perceives that *none*, including us, are righteous, then it simply will not do to condemn violators without an accompanying sense that, under certain circumstances, we ourselves might not behave much differently.

Stephen J. Pope argues that "an ethic of forgiveness can support the political and social goals of reconciliation and restorative justice." He also claims that "distinctly Christian perspectives" may "play a significant role in the broader conversation that takes place within the public life of pluralistic societies."[176] Indeed, "the

173. Tutu, *No Future without Forgiveness*, 218–29, 252.

174. Tutu, *No Future without Forgiveness*, 252–53.

175. I have explored this point, among others, with reference to a particular educational institution in "Theology and Ethics, Then, Now, and In-Between at Union Seminary and Elsewhere," *Interpretation: A Journal of Bible and Theology* 66, no. 4 (October 2012): 383–95.

176. Stephen J. Pope, "The Role of Forgiveness in Reconciliation and Restorative Justice: A Christian Theological Perspective," in Llewellyn and Philpott, *Restorative Justice, Reconciliation, and Peacebuilding*, 174, 193.

capacity for forgiveness, particularly the tendency not to exact revenge, and the desire for reconciliation, are relevant to intergroup relations, even on a larger scale." As an illustration, Pope points to the role reconciliation plays in Martin Luther King Jr.'s "integrationist vision" and the drive toward beloved community.[177]

Clearly, reconciliation and a willingness to forgive are vitally important in other areas of life as well. Pope notes that social scientists and psychologists comment on forgiveness in interpersonal relationships and friendships. For example, he says, the psychologist Michael McCullough describes forgiveness as "a private process of getting over" ill will and "negative emotions," and he connects it with reconciliation as "the restoration of a fractured relationship that happens because the victim has forgiven the offender and because the offender has mended his or her evil ways." Like Pope, I think the limitation of forgiveness to "private" life fails to take into account its implications for relations between communities. But, of course, this in no way implies its irrelevance in interpersonal relationships and smaller-scale communities.[178]

Consider, then, James M. Gustafson's interpretation of marriage and family within the frame of theocentric piety as social wholes and institutions critical for human well-being that powerfully form persons, and also have significant biological bases. Gustafson notes that, here, God enables and requires us as spouses, parents, and children to be stewards of one another's lives. We are called to love in the form of attentiveness and creative fidelity, a norm that often requires discernment, sometimes runs counter to other interests and inclinations, and rarely dispels all ambiguities. (For example, how shall caring parents respect and support children with different temperaments, interests, and abilities?) Moreover, in Gustafson's view, the human fault underscores what any reflective member of a family surely knows: we will not always live up to all our responsibilities as one another's stewards. Thus, while marriage and family, as immediate contexts for living, differ rather significantly from civil society, in a Christian framework we find similar dynamics of piety at work.[179] "Being together in family," says Gustafson, "requires a readiness to forgive and to be forgiven; it requires . . . a humility that can acknowledge fault, a strength that can accuse another and that can take being accused."[180]

177. Pope, "The Role of Forgiveness," 177.

178. Pope, "The Role of Forgiveness," 175.

179. Family and civil society are also clearly interconnected. See Lisa Sowle Cahill, *Family: A Christian Social Perspective* (Minneapolis: Fortress, 2000), 7–16.

180. Gustafson, *ETP*, 2:168.

Liturgical Expressions

The dynamics of piety at work here are features of the Spirit of sanctification, of the participatory ethos of created, interdependent, and interrelated life and the ec-centric ethos of Jesus as the Christ, which is present and active in the Christian community. Nowhere is this more apparent than in some of the church's liturgical forms and patterns of worship. And so, here, let me illustrate this articulated spiritual presence by calling attention to how the piety of sin and grace is both shaped and given expression in a particular subsection of the Service for the Lord's Day of the Presbyterian Church (USA).[181]

The subsection falls in the opening part of the service entitled "Gathering." The gathering of a congregation for worship is itself a theologically articulate act.[182] For when a community of fellowship and mutual concern gathers together to worship, it responds to the ethos of interdependent life and the body of Christ by testifying that we live in relation to God and one another. It assembles before the God who creates, and as it does so, however fleetingly and fragmentarily, it symbolizes and (to some degree) embodies what people are for. It enacts liturgically and at the same time helps to form piety's conviction that humans are not fitted to be merely separate or alone. Rather, we are created, sustained, and redeemed for true communion with God in community with others. The act of gathering or assembling for corporate worship in the ethos or power of the Spirit shapes and expresses piety's kingdom-minded and ec-centric conviction that we are fitted to live in relation with God and others.

Having thus assembled, the congregation is ready to worship, or to do what the good creature in fact is created to do, namely, praise God for God's great and good gifts of existence, capacities, sustenance, and redemption. Gathered gratefully to praise the God of glory and of grace, the giver and fountain of all good gifts whose love is disclosed in Jesus Christ, the congregation is now prompted by the service, as well as the ethos or Spirit that it embodies and represents, to enact our corresponding knowledge of ourselves as God's good dependent creatures distinctively fitted and equipped to worship and to glorify God in a society of praise and mutual concern. This is the basic business of the first subsection of the opening part of the service called "Gathering." Once it has been enacted—and perhaps also brought to completion with the aid of a hymn of praise such as "Immortal,

181. See *Book of Common Worship*, prepared by the Theology and Worship Ministry Unit for the Presbyterian Church (U.S.A.) and the Cumberland Presbyterian Church (Louisville: Westminster John Knox, 1993), 52–57.

182. For a more extended discussion of the theology of the service, which I rely upon here, see Ottati, *Theology for Liberal Presbyterians*, 21–33.

Invisible, God Only Wise"—*then* the congregation is ready to move to a second subsection defined by the Confession of Sin and the Declaration of Forgiveness (sometimes called the Assurance of Pardon). Note the following elements.

Call to Confession
Confession of Sin
  Kyrie Eleison
Declaration of Forgiveness
A Summary of the Law may be included here
The Peace may be included here

We are especially concerned with this portion of the service because it enacts the dynamic of sin and grace. Now, in the power of the Spirit, the service both shapes and expresses our sense of culpability and remorse in the midst of our many interrelations and responsibilities, as well as our felt need for forgiveness. Now, in the power of the Spirit, the service confronts and undercuts our inordinate pride. Now, it directs us to acknowledge publicly and in community that we are corrupted sinners who have betrayed God and one another, and who also remain prone to betray the abundant and good life of true communion with God in community with others that characterizes the kingdom. It directs us to acknowledge, too, that a train of bad consequences accompanies our misdirection and corruption. Thus, in this second subsection, the service sculpts and expresses piety's apprehension of God as Judge.

Nevertheless, sin and grace go together; the divine judgment, which presses us to turn, also participates in the movement toward reconciliation and redemption. And so, following the Kyrie ("Lord, have mercy. Christ, have mercy. Lord, have mercy"), the Agnus Dei ("Lamb of God, you take away the sin of the world, have mercy on us"), or some similar expression, the service hastens toward an explicit proclamation and pronouncement in the Declaration of Forgiveness. "The mercy of the Lord is from everlasting to everlasting. I declare to you, in the name of Jesus Christ, you are forgiven." Now we know that we belong to the God of grace.

For the Service for the Lord's Day, then, there most definitely is confession. We are called to confess, and we actually and publicly do confess, that we have sinned against both God and one another in thought, word, and deed. We confess that we are disobedient and need to repent; that we are misoriented and in need of healing and redirection; that not only have we committed sinful acts but we *are* sinners. Nevertheless, it is also true that there is no confession without assurance and declared forgiveness.

In fact, the service has no place, including the Confession of Sin itself, for dwelling on the human fault apart from the knowledge that God remains both faithful and merciful. This becomes abundantly clear when we review a suggested text for the Call to Confession. "If we say we have no sin, we deceive ourselves, and the truth is not in us. But if we confess our sins, God who is faithful and just will forgive us our sins and cleanse us from all unrighteousness. In humility and faith let us confess our sin to God." Or, again, consider the first sentence of a recommended Confession of Sin: "Merciful God, we confess that we have sinned against you in thought, word, and deed, by what we have done, and by what we have left undone." Indeed, none of the suggested Calls to Confession and none of the Confessions of Sin even hint that sin or the human fault is somehow insignificant or unreal. None imply that sin is merely a superficial condition. To the contrary, they direct us to confess a radical fault that comes to expression in what we think, feel, do, and do not do. Neither do they gainsay or forestall judgment. The service steadfastly refuses any naïvely optimistic celebration of our accomplishments and of the human spirit (a point worth emphasizing in current religious cultures where the language of sin and confession may be tossed aside in favor of a more upbeat and therapeutic tone). Even so, the "theo-logic" of piety represented in these texts is not simply "We are sinners, therefore let us confess," but rather "We are sinners *and* God is gracious, faithful, and merciful; therefore let us confess." Though sin is radical and universal grace abounds, and the service never defines us wholly and exclusively by sin and corruption, we are always also good creatures who live and move in relation to the gracious God.

A summary of the law or of the commandments may follow the Declaration of Forgiveness, and if I may be so bold, I believe this is an option that Presbyterians and Reformed congregations certainly should elect. For then, the service forms us in piety's imperative of consonance; then, the law is presented in its "third and principal use" as a guide to those who have already received the word of grace and therefore are enabled in gratitude fittingly to commit themselves anew to the good and abundant life of love of God and neighbor. That is, when the law *follows* the Declaration of Forgiveness, it does not accuse or condemn so much as it aids and abets graced sinners in the process of sanctification or the positive business of renewed life. And so, here, the service displays the pattern of Christ and the law as an instrument of the Spirit or of the ethos of interdependent life and Christian community, for the purpose of forming persons in an ec-centric piety and trajectory. The congregation may say or hear Exodus 20:1–17, or some shorter summary such as John 13:34, "A new commandment I give to you, that you love one another as I have loved you," or Philippians 2:4, "Let each of you look not to your own interests, but to the interests of others." In any case, the point to be underscored is that by the logic of piety and grace, the law is not a burden unwillingly forced upon us so much as it is our joy and delight. It is a gift in and through which the ethos of the Spirit orders our interrelations with

God and others, and thus marks off the pattern for a good life together, the life for which we have been fitted and sustained all along. (Accordingly, Calvin's Strasbourg Liturgy of 1545 directed the congregation *joyously to sing* both tables of the law following a prayer of confession and an assurance of pardon.)[183]

Next comes the Peace, an important and increasingly popular practice in many congregations today. The people of God, having confessed their sin, having heard a word of grace and forgiveness, and having committed themselves to lawful interrelations characterized by justice and love, now are given an opportunity to greet one another and to share the peace of Christ. They are encouraged to ritually symbolize and enact a restoration of fractured and fragmented relationships, or a renewed life and reconciled community.

Thus, what lies behind the drive toward sanctification, the impetus to forgiveness, reconciliation, and the rest is a basic and deep dynamic of regenerative piety formed in Christ and the Spirit, and it looks something like this. A sense of remorse (or repentance), feelings of humility, and a felt need for forgiveness follow upon a heightened sense of obligation before the intensified law and the kingdom teaching and example of Jesus as the Christ. These sensibilities and feelings come to expression in and are shaped by the Call to Confession and the Confession itself, and here piety grasps God as Judge. But this experience of judgment remains linked with piety's apprehension of God as Redeemer, which evokes senses of gratitude, assurance, and renewed possibilities and is sculpted and expressed by the announcement of grace and forgiveness. There follows, then, in the order and logic of piety, a joyful recommitment to the good life and society, or to the divinely given promise and project of renewed and reconciled community. This comes to expression in the summary of the law and the Passing of the Peace.

Does the strain of piety both articulated and shaped by the Service for the Lord's Day finally celebrate a kind of "cheap grace"? Not, I think, by Dietrich Bonhoeffer's lights at least, since the service most assuredly does not preach forgiveness apart from repentance and is careful to place the Declaration of Forgiveness in sequence with a Confession of Sin.[184] The congregation's repeated enactment of the service, with a Confession of Sin on each Lord's Day, also ensures that no one will receive the misimpression that sanctified living proceeds without fault. But, as I think, anyway, it also should be emphasized—by including more definite directions in the service itself—that the piety expressed here

183. Bard Thompson, *Liturgies of the Western Church* (New York: Meridian, 1971), 198. In Calvin's Geneva Liturgy of 1542, the congregation was directed to sing only the first table.

184. Dietrich Bonhoeffer, *Discipleship*, vol. 4 of Dietrich Bonhoeffer Works, ed. Geffrey B. Kelly and John D. Godsey, trans. Barbara Green and Reinhard Krauss (Minneapolis: Fortress, 2001), 44.

fittingly drives and impels persons toward a recommitment to the law as well as to a symbolic embodiment of reconciled and renewed community.

Proposition #63 The idea of calling and vocation helps to clarify the sanctifying formation of persons and communities toward ec-centric piety and existence in the world.[185]

Sanctification, as we have just now indicated, has multiple aspects or dimensions, for example, a self-critical humility and willingness to forgive, a positive commitment to the law and also to renewed or reconciled community. The idea of calling and vocation introduces yet another, and it has been a subject of immense practical concern to Protestants ever since Luther left the cloister to commend the responsibilities of marriage and the Reformation rejected an exceptional monastic life isolated from ordinary social demands.[186] In its classic Protestant form, it answers the following question: How can the life of production, reproduction, and statecraft, the world of work, family, and civil government, become a locus of faithfulness and the good life?[187]

Notice an expansive drive toward the sanctification of the ordinary. For Protestant piety, especially in its Reformed iteration, the spiritual or sanctified life is not one set apart; neither is it confined to inner feeling. Instead, it is ordinary and mundane human life influenced or transformed by genuine piety and faith-

185. This proposition relies on material in chapter 5 of my *Reforming Protestantism: Christian Commitment in Today's World* (Louisville: Westminster John Knox, 1995), 117–50.

186. Luther tends to view marriage as a divine estate to be contrasted with the false spirituality of the monastic estate. See "The Order of Marriage for Common Pastors," in *Liturgy and Hymns*, ed. Urlich S. Leupold, vol. 53 of *LW*, 112. "When a father goes ahead and washes diapers or performs some other mean task for his child," Luther writes, "God with all his angels is smiling—not because he is doing diapers, but because he is doing so in Christian faith." Again, the estate of marriage "together with all its works, however insignificant, is pleasing to God and precious in his sight. These works are indeed insignificant and mean; yet it is from them that we all trace our origin, we have all had need of them. Without them no man would exist. For this reason they are pleasing to God, who has so ordained them and thereby graciously cares for us like a kind and loving mother." Luther, "The Estate of Marriage," in *The Christian in Society*, ed. Walther I. Brandt, vol. 45 of *LW*, 40, 42–43.

187. On the general importance of these developments, see Charles Taylor, *Sources of the Self: The Making of the Modern Identity* (Cambridge, MA: Harvard University Press, 1989), 20–23, 216–18. On Luther's understanding of vocation, see Gustaf Wingren, *Luther on Vocation*, trans. Carl C. Rasmussen (Philadelphia: Muhlenberg, 1957), viii–ix; and on his judgments about marriage and celibacy, see Lisa Sowle Cahill, *Between the Sexes: Foundations for a Christian Ethics of Sexuality* (Philadelphia: Fortress; New York: Paulist, 1985), 128–31. On the rejection of monasticism and the effort to sanctify all of life, see Douglas J. Schuurman, *Vocation: Discerning Our Callings in Life* (Grand Rapids: Eerdmans, 2004), 5.

fulness. What's more, everyday living is not spiritually inert. In and through our regular converse with others in the world of interdependent interrelations, the Spirit or the ethos of creation helps to draw out and to form true spirituality. Properly understood, true piety and spirituality sanctify the ordinary, and the ordinary helps to discipline and extend true piety and spirituality.[188]

Genuine faithfulness and the good life are therefore defined by the way or manner in which one lives in any and all occupations, offices, and activities. There are antielitist energies here that, under certain circumstances, may nurture a discipleship of equals. What is done in the spirit of service, even the most daily and ordinary tasks, is pleasing to God and glorifies God's name. The sixteenth-century Cambridge theologian and Puritan William Perkins therefore insists that "If we compare worke to worke, there is a difference betwixt washing of dishes, and preaching the word of God: but as touching to please God none at all . . . whatsoever is done within the laws of God though it be wrought by the body, as the wipings of shoes and such like, howsoever grosse they appear outwardly, yet they are sanctified."[189] Of course, insistences such as these both have been and can be misused. Who, we may ask, is likely to be engaged in most ordinary tasks? An affirmation of the sanctified worth of outwardly menial works can be co-opted by an argument for keeping certain people at them. Here, however, I want to focus attention elsewhere: on the sanctification of the ordinary and the mundane disciplining and extension of the spiritual.

Coherence and Complexity

The idea of calling and vocation points to both coherence and complexity. Genuine faithfulness, its kingdom vision and commitment, entails a particular stance or manner of living in the midst of multiple, sometimes conflicting and ambiguous interrelationships and responsibilities. It concerns a sense of purpose amid many purposes and a sense of direction amid many directions. This is why, when it is sculpted and empowered in the ec-centric trajectory of the Spirit, Protestant piety poses the question of calling and vocation in a rather specific

188. Thus, as Robert L. Calhoun notes, "there is no such thing as a profane or merely secular order from which God is absent, and in which God is not to be served." See "Work and Vocation in Christian History," in *Work and Vocation: A Christian Discussion*, ed. John Oliver Nelson (New York: Harper & Brothers, 1954), 108.

189. Quoted from William Perkins, *Works*, in Charles H. George and Katherine George, *The Protestant Mind of the English Reformation* (Princeton: Princeton University Press, 1961), 139. See also Taylor, *Sources of the Self*, 224, where the quotation is put to much the same use as I have made of it here.

fashion. What is the relationship between our chief end and our many other ends? What is the relationship between our basic responsibility and our many other responsibilities? What is the relationship between our fundamental role and our many other roles?

For Perkins, the answer has to do with the relationship of the "common" or "general calling" of every believer to be a Christian and the specific lines of responsibility or "particular callings" in which one or another believer may participate as a parent, a physician, a citizen, a teacher, or what-have-you.[190] The former without the latter threatens to degenerate into an abstract or "churchy" godliness apart from the motility of actual life in the world. The latter apart from the former may degenerate into disconnected bits of activity at crossed purposes, or, worse, into disconnected bits of activity that simply capitulate to spirits or ethoi opposed to Christian faithfulness. In my terms, the idea of calling and vocation indicates that to be caught up in the sanctifying power of the Spirit is to increase or grow in ec-centric existence. It recognizes, too, that an ec-centric manner of living, which looks to the interests of others in the service of God and God's kingdom, necessarily comes to expression in the midst of things and therefore must also be articulated along multiple lines.

The New England divine John Cotton declares, "not only my spiritual life, but even my civil life in the world" and, indeed, "all the life I live" should be impacted by faith. A true Christian, he says, "exempts no life from the agency of his faith," and he claims that, as we pursue our vocations, we serve people by serving God, and we serve God by serving people.[191] Perkins furnishes the following definition: "a vocation or calling is a certain kind of life ordained and imposed on man by God for the common good." We might say that the idea of calling or vocation shows how everyday life in the midst of multiple interdependent interrelations may be ordered and directed toward God and neighbor. It plots how, by means of piety and in the power of the Spirit, the disposition to look to others' interests may be guided along specific channels. This is how it helps us to envision the formation of people in a participatory and ec-centric manner of living; this is how it maps specific parts of the sanctified life-pattern of renewed persons.

A calling or vocation, then, entails a manner of living, abiding, and conversing in the world that serves God and neighbor, and for this reason, not just any line of activity or responsibility will do. Perkins therefore notes that many people, though they may think otherwise, actually have no calling, "as for example such

190. William Perkins, "A Treatise on the Vocations and Callings of Men," in *The Works of William Perkins*, ed. Ian Breward (Appleford, UK: Sutton Courtenay, 1970), 451.

191. John Cotton, "Christian Calling," in *The American Puritans: Their Prose and Poetry*, ed. Perry Miller (Garden City, NY: Doubleday, 1956), 173, 176.

as live by usury, carding and dicing, by maintaining houses of gaming."[192] God is the author of lawful callings, and a calling that does not adhere to the law is really no calling at all. There is, then, *a critical dimension* to the idea of calling and vocation. Again, Calvin notes that not all social stations are legitimate and that "there is no vocation in which a great deal of abuse is not committed."[193]

This is the import of the phrase "for the common good" in Perkins's definition.

> The common good of men stands in this; not only that they live, but that they live well, in righteousness and holiness and consequently in true happiness. . . . Here then we must in general know, that he abuseth his calling whosoever he be that, against the end thereof, employs it for himself, seeking his own and not the common good. And that common saying, "Every man for himself and God for all" is wicked and is directly against the end of every calling or honest kind of life.[194]

Cotton has similar concerns, and he insists that a "warrantable" calling is one we enter into by legitimate means rather than by deceit or the undermining of persons. It is one for which God's providence has prepared us with appropriate gifts of mind and body. Furthermore, it is one "wherein we may not only aim at our own, but at the public good. This is a warrantable calling: 'Seek not every man his own things, but every man the good of his brother' (1 Cor. 10:24); (Phil. 2:4) 'Seek one another's welfare'; 'Faith works all by love' (Gal. 5:6)."[195]

The source of the consistent insistence in these writers that a true calling aims not only at one's own good but also at the common good or the public good is this. Persons in whom the sanctifying power of Spirit, or the ec-centric ethos of interdependent created life and of the body of Christ, is at work are caught up in a life reordered and reformed by devotion to God and to the well-being of God's all-inclusive commonwealth or kingdom. If sin means the diminution of life, grace means its regenerating renewal and enlargement toward the community of all things in relation to God. And these ideas are authorized, in turn, by interpretations of the sweeping epic of the Scriptures, especially the cruciform pattern of love of God and neighbor decisively displayed and disclosed in Jesus Christ.

192. Perkins, "A Treatise on the Vocations and Callings of Men," 447–48.

193. John Calvin, *Treatises against the Anabaptists and against the Libertines*, ed. Benjamin W. Farley (Grand Rapids: Baker Books, 1988), 278.

194. Perkins, "A Treatise on the Vocations and Callings of Men," 449.

195. Cotton, "Christian Calling," 174.

Mingling Practices

Return now to the basic substance of our proposition with these things in mind. How does the idea of calling and vocation help us to understand the world of work, family, and civil government as a locus of faithfulness and a sanctified life? How does it help us to understand the relationship between our chief end and our many other ends, our basic responsibility and our many other responsibilities?

Note once again that, for Perkins, there are two kinds of callings—the calling to be a Christian and the particular callings of "every person of every degree, state, sex, or condition." Perkins says there are four main duties of *the calling to be a Christian*. The first is worship, the invocation of the name of God in Christ, or prayer and thanksgiving in the name of Jesus Christ. The second is to further the good estate of the church by means of prayer, edification, and the appropriate use of our gifts and blessings. Third, by the duties of love, "every man should become a servant . . . unto every man . . . as occasion shall be offered, and for the common good of all men (1 Cor. 9:19; Gal. 5:13)." The fourth duty is that Christians should live in a manner that is worthy of their calling in Christ Jesus; they should walk as those renewed by God's mercy and love (Eph. 4:1–2).[196] *Particular callings*, for Perkins, arise because each basic social context is a body in which different interdependent parts perform certain functions and discharge specific roles. Each is a community, association, or institution in which the responsible exercise of different callings tends to "the happy and good estate of the rest," and even of all persons everywhere (449, 455).

The relationship between the two sorts of callings is crucial. "Every man," says Perkins, "must join the practice of his personal calling with the practice of the general calling of Christianity . . . more plainly, every particular calling must be practiced in and with the general calling of a Christian" (456). In this sense, the sanctification of the ordinary and the mundane disciplining of the spiritual amount to a mingling of practices.

One of Perkins's points is simply that a Christian magistrate, wife, student, soldier, or cobbler should combine or join the practice of his or her personal calling with the four main duties of the calling to be a Christian. This is part of what it means to reorder and reform everyday life. We might say that, for Perkins, the everyday life of a Christian is ordinary-life-with-a-difference. A Christian schoolteacher, for example, should worship in the name of Jesus Christ and also use her or his gifts to further the good of the church. She or he ought to envision

196. Perkins, "A Treatise on the Vocations and Callings of Men," 451–54. Hereafter, page references from this work will be given in parentheses in the text.

the specific lines of responsibility involved in teaching children as occasions to serve others and to further the common good of all. At school and elsewhere, she or he should live in a manner worthy of our calling to Christ Jesus: oriented by one faith, one hope, and one baptism; walking in humility, gentleness, and patience; and forbearing others in love.

This is how the calling to be a Christian sanctifies our more particular and personal callings. Indeed, Perkins is convinced that, when severed from the calling of Christianity, the duties and activities of any particular calling may be transmuted into "a practice of injustice and profaneness" by the astringent of the human fault and sin (456). That is, apart from the practices that orient us toward the chief end of human life (or, as I would say, toward true communion with God in community with others), we chronically abuse our callings. We subvert their genuine purpose and promise by turning them toward partial causes, isolated interests, and goods rather than toward the cause of the kingdom and the public good. Temptations differ. Perhaps some teachers will take their position as an occasion to lord it over their pupils, or to impress others with their knowledge and professional competence.

But, of course, the mingling of practices must also mean that our specific lines of responsibility in the world appropriately shape and inform the calling to be a Christian. This is one reason why churches should reject the notion that someone is "just a schoolteacher." Teaching school is a calling of high worth and good purpose. And, indeed, the responsibilities, practices, and experiences of teaching children may enrich and inform the Christian community's understanding of what it is to truly worship and praise God. Teaching school conscientiously and compassionately is one way that the calling to be a Christian becomes incarnate in concrete life, one way that persons may attend to the interests of others and to the common good. It is a mundane disciplining of the spiritual. Perkins puts it this way: "the general calling of Christianity without the practice of some particular calling is nothing else but the form of godliness without the power thereof" (456–57).

We might say that when the calling to be a Christian becomes detached from the practices of particular callings, the astringent of sinfulness and the human fault is more likely to transmute spiritual practices into covers for an inordinately constricted and interior religiosity.[197] Our spiritual practices may become priestly and cultic in a negative sense, matters of mystic withdrawal and the noise of solemn assemblies that may perhaps legitimate but certainly do not challenge current understandings of everyday life and institutions. Perhaps one pursues a

197. Douglas Schuurman notes how the idea of vocation contrasts with privatized forms of religion favored in some secular contexts. *Vocation*, 8.

spirituality centered on personal wholeness entirely separated from politics and business. Perhaps another orders life exclusively around the church. In either case, the calling to be a Christian remains largely unincarnate. The ordinary is not sanctified; neither is the spiritual truly disciplined by mundane practices.

We should emphasize, too, that, where it is properly practiced and understood, where it has not degenerated into a cover for inordinately constricted interests or ecclesiasticism, the calling to be a Christian takes priority. The orientation toward communion with God in community with others takes priority. The glorification and praise of God take priority. The chief end of human existence becomes the criterion of our many other ends. Our basic responsibility becomes the criterion of our many other responsibilities, our most fundamental role the criterion of our many roles.

Perkins understands this as well. "A particular calling must give place to the general calling of a Christian when they cannot both stand together . . . because we are bound unto God in the first place and unto man under God."[198] This is so because a particular calling that cannot stand together with the general calling to be a Christian is one that does not allow for the increase of love of God and neighbor but instead furthers some inordinately constricted interest or private good. It is a practice out of kilter with the ec-centric movement toward reconciliation and renewal. By structure, design, or intractable circumstance, a calling or practice that cannot stand with the calling to be a Christian seeks an end contrary to the public good and well-being of God's all-inclusive reign and kingdom. By Cotton's reckoning it is unwarrantable, and by Perkins's it really is no calling at all.

Spouses, Parents, Physicians, and Soldiers

For more extended illustrations of Puritan thinking about callings and vocations, let me commend Richard Baxter's *Christian Directory; or, A Sum of Practical Theology, and Cases of Conscience*, published in 1673. This massive work aims to advance the pastoral formation of believers by advising them on the "skillful exercise" of "Christian practice" in their "ecclesiastical, civil, and family relations."[199]

198. Perkins, "A Treatise on the Vocations and Callings of Men," 457.

199. Richard Baxter, *A Christian Directory; or, A Sum of Practical Theology, and Cases of Conscience*, vol. 1 of *The Practical Works of Richard Baxter* (Ligonier, PA: Soli Deo Gloria, 1990), 3, 8. Hereafter, page references to this work will be given in parentheses in the text. Max Weber claimed Baxter's *Christian Directory* "is the most complete compendium of Puritan ethics."

The heart of part 1 of the *Directory*, on "Christian ethics," is a chapter entitled "The General Directions for Walking with God, in a Life of Faith and Holiness." In it Baxter counsels believers, or those who, having access to God in Christ, live to God as their chief end, "in that exercise of grace which is common to all Christians" (62). He then turns to more particular social contexts and relations: part 2 is entitled "Christian Economics" and treats family relations; part 3, "Christian Ecclesiastics," deals with directions to pastors and congregants; it is followed by part 4, "Christian Politics (or Duties to Our Rulers and Neighbors)" (394, 547, 737).

Baxter regards the family as an interdependent society structured by a contract or covenant of marriage that tends toward the public good of God's wider commonwealth. He notes that not everyone is called to marry, there sometimes being advantages for serving God in a single state, especially among persecuted Christians. People are called to marry, says Baxter, only when it is clear that they will better serve God and do good to others in a married state that involves weighty, sometimes wearisome duties to spouse, and (should one be so blessed) also to children (395, 400).

For Baxter, then, marriage and family indicate a particular community and institution that may help those who are suited to marry, as well as their children, to order a life of true communion with God in community with others. It is (or may become) a covenantal society that embodies a genuine mutuality and Christian practice in the midst of a host of more specific aims, roles, and responsibilities. This is why he introduces his discussion with a general principle that accords with piety's apprehension of sin, or the human fault, and grace, or the enlargement of persons toward God and others. "It is the pernicious subversion of all societies, and so of the world that . . . ungodly persons enter into all relations with a desire to serve themselves . . . but without any sense of the duty of their relation. . . . They are very sensible what others should do to them, but not what they should be and do to others. Thus it is with magistrates, and with people, with too many pastors and their flocks, with husbands and wives, with parents and children, with masters and servants, and all other relations" (431).

Present-day readers will not mistake Baxter's treatment of marriage and family for a contemporary one, though he does list twenty-two directions for marital companionship, including mutual duties to "a true entire, conjugal love"; cohabitation; and helping one another in knowledge of God, the rearing of children, worldly business, and works of hospitality (431–38). Duties of parents to children include the dedication of children to God in baptism, their holy education, their

The Protestant Ethic and the Spirit of Capitalism, trans. Talcott Parsons (New York: Scribner's Sons, 1958), 155–56.

training in obedience, their encouragement in appropriate sports and recreations, and the choice of an appropriate calling. Baxter obviously thinks that the relationship of parents and children adheres to a definite hierarchy of authority. Even so, he counsels parents that their discipline should be neither too lax nor too stringent, and that they should make children "perceive that you dearly love them, and that all your commands, restraints, and correction are for their good, and not merely because you will" (449–54).[200]

It is clear from the outset of his directions to physicians in part 4 of the *Directory* that Baxter regards the essential aims of this particular calling to be entirely in accord with the calling to be a Christian, and that he does not intend to meddle in subtleties of medical art. The disclaimer, calculated to ease any offense physicians might take at receiving directions from a theologian, also recognizes the relative independence and integrity of the medical profession and its practices. The pastor's purpose is only to tell physicians "very briefly, what God and conscience will expect from them."

The particular line of service in which a physician stands, says Baxter, has "the saving of men's lives and health" as its chief responsibility. This means, as Cotton might say, that the practice of medicine is a warrantable calling, since it clearly is a specific way of attending to the welfare of others that serves the public good under God. As Perkins would insist, it also indicates that physicians abuse their calling whenever this particular line of responsibility is diminished or displaced by some contrary interest or end. Baxter stresses that where personal gain and professional honor become the physician's first intention, he serves not God and the public good but an isolated personal interest. It follows that a primary test of faithfulness is whether a physician helps the poor as well as those who are able to pay. Another test concerns referrals: where physicians reach the limits of their skills, pride should not prevent them from advising their patients "to use the help of other, abler physicians, if there are any to be had." Finally, due to the "abstruse and conjectural" character of the medical profession, only those

200. On the authority proper to wives within their households, see 439, 449–57. Amanda Porterfield discusses the indirect and direct authority of Puritan women in *Female Piety in Puritan New England: The Emergence of Religious Humanism* (New York: Oxford University Press, 1992), 87–95. One of her points is that their indirect authority was helped by the emotional dependence of Puritan husbands on their wives. Among other things, this may be a result of Puritan emphases on mutuality and companionate relationships that come through in Baxter's text as well. It is clear that a Puritan understanding of marriage as a companionate and covenantal community of mutual affection and care is more amenable to accommodating contemporary arguments for same-sex marriages than are understandings that focus first on procreation, though this is not the place to present the argument in detail. For additional suggestions along these lines, see Ottati, *Theology for Liberal Presbyterians*, 67–71.

possessed of natural strength of intellect and wisdom, significant reading, a great deal of acquaintance with the techniques of able physicians, and considerable experience of their own should venture to practice medicine (771–72).

Some basic contemporary implications of Baxter's directions, which he writes well before the advent of modern, more highly bureaucratized and corporatized medicine, are not too difficult to surmise. Surely a fundamental point is that, whether we are physicians, parents, or mechanics, genuine faithfulness means glorifying God in the midst of our many interrelations with others by joining Christian aims and practices with the aims and practices of particular callings. This is why one should endeavor to understand exactly how a particular profession or line of responsibility contributes to the public good of God's kingdom. Again, we should take care to see that we are appropriately prepared and equipped for the particular line of service in question. (The world doesn't need disinterested parents or incompetent physicians and mechanics.) Care should be taken, too, that our labors do not degenerate into a sinful striving after self-aggrandizement. Given, then, the specific skills and responsibilities of a particular calling—in this case medicine—certain comparatively specific directives follow. For example, "Be ready to commit yourself to long hours of study with able physicians" and "Provide medical care for the poor." By doing these things, we sanctify everyday life and also discipline the spiritual.

Soldiering, for Baxter, represents a harder case. In the end, he rejects unbridled militarism as well as uncritical obedience to king and country. He wants a kind of soldiering that fits with his understanding of the legitimate aims and responsibilities of civil government, that is, to preserve the country and its peace, and to prevent harm to the innocent, whether from anarchy or some rival country. But he also thinks that, too often, military service develops a warrior mentality and temperament contrary to "reason, religion, righteousness, professions, vows, and all obligations to God and man" (777).[201] As if to underscore the point, he ends his subsequent chapter against murder with these sentences:

> The greatest cause of the cruelest murders is unlawful wars. All that a man killeth in an unlawful war, he murdereth; and all that the army killeth, he that setteth them at work by command or counsel, is guilty of himself. And, therefore, how dreadful a thing is an unrighteous war! . . . Thieves and robbers

201. Compare this with the following statement of Martin Luther: "To sum up, we must, in thinking about a soldier's office, not concentrate on the killing, burning, striking, hitting, seizing, etc. This is what children with their limited and restricted vision see when they regard a doctor as a sawbones who amputates, but do not see that he does this only to save the whole body." Luther, "Whether Soldiers, Too, Can Be Saved," in *Selected Political Writings*, ed. J. M. Porter (Philadelphia: Fortress, 1974), 103.

> kill single persons; but soldiers murder thousands at a time: and because there is none at present to judge them for it, they wash their hands as if they were innocent, and sleep as quietly as if the avenger of blood would never come. Oh what devils are those counselors and incendiaries to princes and states, who stir them up to unlawful wars. (778)

What sorts of occupations, roles, or callings might we deem severely corrupted or even unwarrantable and illegitimate today? When Douglas Schuurman considers the question of which forms of paid work may be ruled out, he wonders about jobs that "create goods and services that contribute to the welfare of others, but require work processes and conditions that are dehumanizing and harmful," for example, "labor as it was practiced for some time in sugarcane fields of the Dominican Republic." He also wonders about the moral legitimacy of working for tobacco companies.[202] Perhaps we should add working for manufacturers of chemicals used for lethal injections and for merchants who sell semi-automatic weapons to the public. Surely, we should list soldiering in the service of persistently and grossly unjust and inhumane regimes that routinely torture, terrorize, and target civilians. Judging by the practices and behavior in recent decades of many in the financial industry, the behavior of some involved in drug manufacturing and marketing, and the behavior of executives and media personalities recently exposed by the #MeToo movement, it also seems there are at least as many ways to abuse legitimate callings today as there have ever been.

Indeed, while I was writing this chapter, in June 2018, federal authorities of the United States of America were separating undocumented immigrant families in order to deter others from crossing over the country's southern border. Approximately 2,300 children were split from their parents. President Donald J. Trump apparently halted the practice by executive order on June 20, though a Pentagon spokesperson said the government was preparing to shelter as many as 20,000 migrant children on four military bases, and it remained unclear just what would happen to those children already separated from their families as well as how families and children would be held going forward.[203] Congress, which has failed to address the immigration issue a number of times already, was contemplating a longer-term legal fix.

Footage of crying and distraught children separated from their parents as

202. Schuurman, *Vocation*, 131–32.

203. Micheal Shear, Helene Cooper, and Katie Benner, "Four Military Bases Prepare to Hold 20,000 Children," *New York Times*, June 20, 2018, A1; Micheal Shear, Abby Goodenough, and Maggie Haberman, "In Retreat, Trump Halts Separating Migrant Families," *New York Times*, June 21, 2018, A1, A10.

well as photos of cages in which minors were being detained were broadcast by the Public Broadcasting Service on its nightly *NewsHour* program. Just before the president reversed his preferred policy by executive order under severe public and political pressure, a number of air carriers, including Frontier Airlines, United Airlines, and Southwest Airlines, asked the federal government to stop using their commercial planes for transporting children separated from their families by US immigration authorities. American Airlines issued an extensive statement that included the following: "We have . . . requested the federal government to immediately refrain from using American for the purpose of transporting children who have been separated from their families due to current immigration policy. We have no desire to be associated with separating families, or worse, to profit from it."[204]

The statement may have been precipitated in part by flight crews who were described as "struggling with the question of participating in a process that they feel deeply immoral."[205] Mr. Hunt Palmquist, a Dallas-based flight attendant, posted a statement on Facebook that was published, in slightly edited form, by the *Houston Chronicle*. In it, he describes the disturbing experience of working two flights on which ICE (Immigration and Customs Enforcement) agents accompanied "migrant children (approximately four to eleven years old) who had been separated from their families and were being flown to a 'relocation site.'" He says, "it occurred to me a few weeks later that I might as well have been a collaborator in their transport." And, he concludes, "as a result . . . I have made a decision that if I'm ever assigned to a flight with children who've been separated from their families, I will immediately remove myself from the trip due to the nature of this unconscionable act by my government and my employer's complicity." He adds that he has spoken to other flight attendants who pledged to do the same, and that "this inhumane separation of migrant children from their families is against the morals and principles instilled in me, as well as my religious and spiritual teachings."[206]

I do not know whether Mr. Palmquist is a member of a Christian church. (If he is not and is interested in joining one, I would gladly sponsor him for membership in my home congregation, though he may find the commute to

204. Richard Fausset, "Airlines Ask Government to Leave Them Out of It," *New York Times*, June 21, 2018, A15. The entire American Airlines' statement can be accessed at http://news.aa.com/news/news-details/2018/Statement-on-Recent-Reports-of-Separated-Families/default.aspx.

205. Sara Nelson, international president of the Association of Flight Attendants CWA, as quoted in Fausset, "Airlines Ask Government to Leave Them Out of It," A15.

206. Hunt Palmquist, "Flight Attendant: I Won't Work Flights That Separate Immigrant Kids from Families," *Houston Chronicle*, March 20, 2018.

North Carolina prohibitive. If he is neither a church member nor interested in becoming one, then I am willing to revive Karl Rahner's idea of anonymous Christians.)[207] But I should repeat here that, by the reckoning of William Perkins, John Cotton, and other Puritans, where a particular role or responsibility has been so thoroughly abused as to become incompatible with the calling to be a Christian, then the latter takes priority. Christians have grounds to conscientiously object, and to refuse and decry the practices in question. I agree, and would add that forcibly separating families in order to deter migrants—a practice reminiscent of slaveholding times and the darkest days of the twentieth century—is simply and grossly inhumane. It stands in direct opposition to what Perkins called "the duties of love," and it is also, I think, a perfectly legitimate reason for divine judgment. "Audiant principes, et terrantur."[208]

Protestant Differences

Varieties of Protestantism that affirm a pacifist ethics of radical discipleship and a believer's church as an alternative community within a world that opposes the reign of Christ generally reject the mingling of practices that I have outlined here. Thus, Stanley Hauerwas insists that faithful Christians are formed by participating in the story-formed community called church, and that the church is "a beachhead, an outpost, an island of one culture in the middle of another," a "colony of resident aliens." He also (and I think rightly) criticizes tendencies to equate Christian commitment with American patriotism.[209] But while he discusses "being a parent" as "an office of the [Christian] community for the well-being of children," nowhere does he expound an idea of particular callings, and he understands work largely as a way to earn a living that becomes idolatrous when we attribute to it too great a significance.[210] The Mennonite John Howard

207. Gavin D'Costa says that, for Rahner, the "basic orientation and fundamental decision" of non-Christians may indicate that they accept "the salvific grace of God, through Christ, although they may never have heard of the Christian revelation." D'Costa, "Karl Rahner's Anonymous Christian: A Reappraisal," *Modern Theology* 1, no. 2 (January 1985): 131–48.

208. John Calvin commenting on God's use of unwitting agents to break "the bloody scepters of arrogant kings" and overturn "intolerable governments," which translates as "Let the princes hear and be afraid." *ICR* 4.20.31.

209. Stanley Hauerwas, *A Community of Character: Toward a Constructive Christian Social Ethic* (Notre Dame: University of Notre Dame Press, 1981), 3. See also Hauerwas, *After Christendom: How the Church Is to Behave If Freedom, Justice, and a Christian Nation Are Bad Ideas* (Nashville: Abingdon, 1991), 133–52; Hauerwas, *War and the American Difference: Theological Reflections on Violence and National Identity* (Grand Rapids: Baker Academic, 2011), 13–20.

210. Hauerwas, *A Community of Character*, 173; Hauerwas, *Naming the Silences: God, Med-*

Yoder endorses an ethic of discipleship that commends the radically alternative politics of Jesus, and he regards the idea of particular callings as a compromise with alien moral directives, a feature of an inauthentic morality that amounts to "a divine rubber stamp for the present social order."[211] In effect, both uphold the calling to be a Christian apart from particular callings. Both fear that the idea of particular callings threatens the faithful formation of faithful Christians by giving them over to alien practices and standards.

A broad theological difference accounts for the disagreement. Unlike radical Protestantism, Reformed Christianity affirms that "God's care is a *mediated* care," which can operate in and through the world of associations, institutions, and roles.[212] As we have seen, it also claims that the Spirit (on my reckoning, as the participatory ethos of interdependent life) may operate to form persons even beyond the bounds of the Christian community. It therefore does not view basic institutions in the world simply as principalities and powers opposed to Christ's reign. But even so, the criticisms of Hauerwas and Yoder do in fact point to a risk that Reformed Protestants generally are willing to take. Every sociocultural setting and institution has its own relatively independent commitments, values, aims, offices, and practices. Reformed piety wagers that a stance of critical engagement with or frequent participation in many of society's basic functions and institutions does not inevitably dilute and subvert genuine faithfulness so much as it enriches and empowers an ec-centric manner of existence.

It does not make this wager lightly. It harbors a keen sense for sin's radical and universal corruption of the human project. It recognizes that some offices and roles cannot stand together with the calling to be a Christian, and that, as Calvin says, "there is no vocation in which a great deal of abuse is not committed." It knows too that, at any specific place and time, fundamental subversions of basic moral norms, as well as gross harm to the public good, may require that we refuse to participate in one or another community, institution, or role. Nevertheless, it risks a robust and critical engagement confident that, despite sin's quite radical corruption and despite the persistent ambiguities of human societies and history,

---

icine, and the Problem of Suffering (Grand Rapids: Eerdmans, 1990), 118; Hauerwas, *Suffering Presence: Theological Reflections on Medicine, the Mentally Handicapped, and the Church* (Notre Dame: University of Notre Dame Press, 1986), 39–47, 81–82; Hauerwas, "Work as Co-Creation: A Critique of a Remarkably Bad Idea," in *Co-Creation and Capitalism: John Paul II's Laborem Exercens*, ed. John W. Houck and Oliver F. Williams, CSC (Lanham, MD: University Press of America, 1983), 48.

211. John Howard Yoder, *The Priestly Kingdom: Social Ethics as Gospel* (Notre Dame: University of Notre Dame Press, 1984), 83, 210.

212. Douglas J. Schuurman, "Protestant Vocation under Assault: Can It Be Salvaged?" *Annual of the Society of Christian Ethics*, 1994, 33.

God has been, is now, and will continue to be graciously active in and through the many different social contexts, roles, and powers. It wagers that this is *God's* world, and that in and through its many communities, histories, movements, and institutions, the deity's provident and redemptive care remains at work. All of which is to say that the doctrine of calling and vocation finally expresses a piety that strains to see the kingdom, one that looks for a history of fragmentation and conflict transfigured by regenerative possibility.

Proposition #64 Hopeful realism names the practical stance in the world that comes to expression (among other places) in this understanding of calling and vocation, and that draws on a strain of piety intertwined with the symbolic ideas of creation, sin, and redemption.

Creation, sin, and redemption—these three symbolic ideas are fundamental for a piety that features senses of awe, gratitude, obligation, remorse, possibilities, direction, assurance, and more. In turn, the senses and symbolic ideas support a certain picture of human-life-before-God-and-God-before-human-life. They encourage us to regard ourselves as good, dependent, and capable creatures who are enmeshed in interdependent interrelations with others, and who are distinctively equipped to participate in God's world; to recognize that we are fitted for true communion with God in community with others; to expect diminishment, estrangement, conflict, fragmentation, and death; but nevertheless to look for enlargement, reconciliation, and renewed life.

All this yields hopeful realism, an orienting posture or practical stance that refuses both easy optimisms and cynical pessimisms because it maintains that we know ourselves most truly in relation to God as Creator, Judge, and Redeemer. In this frame of reference, we do not really know ourselves when we concentrate on our abilities and possibilities apart from our limits and our fault. Neither do we know ourselves truly when we focus on our limits and our fault apart from our capacities and apart from the traces of renewing grace that we encounter in God's world. Hopeful realism recognizes the persistently destructive bents as well as the promising possibilities of all persons, communities, and institutions, and it also has confidence that the arc of God's universe bends toward the kingdom. This is why it supports a decidedly worldly sort of Christianity. This is why it subjects all persons, communities, and institutions to criticism even as it affirms them all. And this is why it summons all to repentance as well as to an ec-centric ethic that respects, enhances, and hopes for the good and abundant life of true communion with God in community with others.

The critical point is that the fundamental symbols must be woven together. Creation suggests that, as we exercise our powers and capacities, we encounter God as the good Creator, source, and fountain of existence who orders the interdependent conditions, possibilities, and limits on which we depend. But, taken alone, the affirmation of a good creation misses not only the tragic diminution and perversion of human life and its given possibilities; it also misses the dramatic interaction in human history between destructive misdirection and creative transformation. Sin points to our chronic corruption as well as to our encounters with God as Judge in and through their destructive consequences, and it alerts us to persistent tragedies. Taken alone, however, the doctrine of sin ends in an unrelieved pessimism that fails to apprehend and express the tragedy of life, its continuing possibilities, and—beyond tragedy—its passionate hope. Redemption turns our attention to interactions with God as Redeemer, the gracious bringer of transformation and new life. But apart from creation and sin, redemptive symbols lose their restorative dimensions. They become detached from a sense of possibilities and debilitating threats, and they no longer evoke hope where hope is most severely tested—namely, in a world of fragmentation, conflict, and death. Whenever one or another of these symbols is torn away from the wider poetic fabric, hopeful realism is distorted. Its coherence as a practical stance or posture depends on holding them together in an appropriate balance (as they are, for example, in the Service for the Lord's Day).

Leonardo Boff says we are "simultaneously graced and disgraced," and just because it recognizes the truth of this statement, hopeful realism has two related dimensions.[213] *Responsible realism* correlates with the sense of sin, and its fundamental aim is to restrain evil. As responsible realists, we look upon basic relationships, institutions, and agreements as strategies for preventing and minimizing harm and disorder. Continuing friendships, we think, restrain dishonesty and deception because one fears a loss of credibility and respect. Marriage vows define responsibilities and may illumine betrayals. Business contracts specify legally enforceable obligations. A system of civil laws is a set of restraints backed by penalties. Deterrent forces and threats of retaliation restrain nations from going to war. Responsible realism, then, is an effort to limit and avoid harm in a way that is informed by rudimentary senses for justice, fairness, and accountability.

A basic strategy in this effort is to balance powers, since, within contexts where powers are balanced, persons and groups anticipate that the inordinate pursuit of partial interests by one or another power is more likely to be met by countervailing power. Thus, the ability of labor unions to go out on strike may balance powers of management and capital. Representative and democratic assemblies limit, restrict, and balance the power of single individuals and groups

213. Boff, *Liberating Grace*, 4–5.

in the dynamics of decision making. International alliances and organizations sometimes check the power and influence of individual nations. But even in the midst of their efforts, responsible realists recognize that none of these strategies and structures can guarantee either that harm will be avoided or that justice will prevail. Indeed, almost all the balances and restraints are provisional, all have their shortcomings and ambiguities, and all are subject to subversion and defeat. The intentions behind even carefully structured representative assemblies can be subverted by greed and by the undue influences of concentrated wealth. Corrupt rationality clouds the practical reasoning and judgments of even the most attentive spouses, parents, and children. The responsible realist is not surprised that racism and sexism may exclude entire communities and groups from meaningful economic and political enfranchisement, or that beyond the reach of relatively just laws, corrupted devotions continue to foster climates of exclusion and hate. Neither is he surprised to learn that shifting winds of economic, political, and military interests and strengths can wreck international agreements and assemblies.

The conviction of sin not only motivates the responsible realist to restrain evil, it also supports an attitude of sorrowful vigilance and criticism. The conviction of sin accuses, and so it points to the perils and shortcomings of every strategy that promises balance and restraint. The responsible realist therefore has reason to resist temptations to conservative complacency that often accompany less thoroughgoing realisms.

Creative responsibility correlates with a sense for grace and new possibilities, and its fundamental aim is to pursue good. Now, many of the same basic relationships, institutions, and agreements that may function as restraints also look to be schools that train people in more attentive habits of practical reasoning, enlarged devotions, and truer patterns of responsibility. They appear to be structures of interdependence that guide us toward a better, more ec-centric manner of living.

A basic insight here is that enfranchising persons and groups as participants within interdependent communities and institutions may train them for effective cooperation, since enfranchised participants often must learn how to pursue their own interest in coalitions with others. Participation in families can train people in devotion to the well-being of an intimate community. Business partnerships and contracts can educate us in fairness as well as in attending to what others may need in order to perdure and prosper. Participating in representative and democratic politics can educate persons and groups in deliberative processes that pursue the well-being of a wider society. Participating in international alliances and assemblies may train national communities and their governments in the discipline of identifying mutual interests and pursuing cooperative ventures.

Even so, the convictions that grace abounds and that the arc of the universe bends toward the kingdom encourage the hopeful realist to recognize continued prospects for improvement. The hopeful realist learns to share the visions of visionaries and the hopes of revolutionaries, noting, for example, that persons devoted to their families often fail to take a wider public good into account, that cooperative agreements of labor and capital may advance the welfare of only a part of society, that legislative assemblies often overlook the well-being of non-citizens, and that effective frameworks for international cooperation often favor the interests of some nations at the expense of others.[214]

This is why the conviction that grace abounds not only motivates hopeful realists to pursue good but also nourishes in them an attitude of continuing and hopeful criticism. The conviction of grace brings hope, and its visions of the kingdom point to further possibilities for good beyond every reformation and every improvement. The conviction of grace brings hope, and so the hopeful realist has reasons to resist temptations to complacency with things as they are that accompany less radical visions.

At this hopeful and visionary point, where the temper of creative responsibility threatens to embrace utopian illusion, hopeful realism turns again to the conviction of sin. It recognizes that persons and groups are constricted even in their virtues, and that therefore all the efforts to pursue good and to bring about beloved community cannot guarantee that true virtue and genuine cooperation will prevail. It recognizes that every witness to the cause of God's kingdom is provisional and subject to subversion, if not at the hands of powers that be, then at the hands of new possibilities for constriction. It therefore recognizes that every revolutionary witness to true good must reckon with the possibility of ambiguities, subversions, and defeats. And so, it turns again to the cruciform pattern in the service of God's great cause. Here is a gift to hopeful imagination and to imaginative hope, a defeated service that, beyond destruction and beyond tragedy, proves to be the transformative power of God, a moving occasion whose victory lies in the inspiration of further witnesses great and small. In this recollection, piety finds reason to hope that any and all of the defeated efforts, any and all of the ambiguous and even vanquished witnesses, may yet be taken up into transformative occasions of grace.

214. See, for example, Cahill, *Family*.

Chapter Eleven

The Fragmentation and Renewal of the World: Civil Government, Church, and Sustainability

A general theological picture of the world, its history, and human possibilities and limits emerges from three basic themes of Christian piety. The first is creation. In relation to God as Creator, the world and its history (meaning everything, or the universe including us, and not just us on our own) are good creation. Like other creatures, we find ourselves graced with the gift of life in the midst of a world of sustaining interrelations. Again, we humans are significantly capable but also limited creatures. When we act, we are able to influence but unable either to anticipate or control all relevant outcomes. There are always unanticipated and unintended consequences. This is true whether the project at hand is raising a child or launching an invasion. The outcomes of our activities remain subject to the influences and impacts of other persons and communities as well as the influences and impacts of other, nonhuman factors, for example, environmental interdependencies. We are distinctively capable. However, like all other creatures, we are also enmeshed in wider contexts of interdependent interrelations that we impact but neither determine nor control.

Sin or the radical and universal human fault constitutes a second theme. Our valued projects, wants, desires, and needs are uncertain and at risk in a multivalent and interdependent world, and so we feel threatened and insecure. To this circumstance we often respond in two ways. We may try to avoid anxieties and threats by choosing to focus on less risky and more readily attainable objectives—in some social contexts, shopping and the acquisition of consumer goods. This is sin as sloth, or underparticipation in interrelationships of responsibility and care, and it generally is accompanied by a degree of self-deception, since most of us remain aware that we cannot entirely eliminate our insecurities about more important matters. Or, again, we may try to banish feelings of insecurity by heightening our control. This second strategy—sin as pride and overreach—is also false and self-deceptive, since we know that total control eludes us, and we can always imagine further threats and challenges. This, according to Reinhold

Niebuhr and others, is the temptation to be like gods, and it brings with it a train of bad and unjust consequences for others, as we endeavor to protect ourselves and our limited interests often at their expense. Indeed, sin as pride almost invariably builds resentment and opposition among those whose interests and needs we unfairly slight or deny. As Niebuhr also observes, it therefore sows seeds of self-destruction.

In sum, threatened by persistent risks and insecurities, persons and communities sometimes neglect or suppress important lines of responsibility in which they stand. Alternatively, they often become captivated by corrupted devotions to their own groups and isolated objectives, prone to pursue and to press their partial and inordinate interests at the expense of others. These tendencies, in turn, skew their lines of practical reasoning and their fields of attention when they confront situations calling for moral involvement by highlighting those factors and interrelations that bear upon corrupted interests.

The recognition that we are mired in a radical and universal fault nevertheless supports realism rather than pessimism. Why? For one thing, the doctrine of sin does *not* entail the claim that we are wholly given over to misdirection. As good and social creatures, we retain some social or community feeling for others, as well as an approximate sense of fairness. These may lead us to structure societies with the aim of restraining inordinate interests and gross derelictions—through public agreements and contracts that specify mutual responsibilities, and through checks, balances, and dispersals that aim to deny all power to any single person or group. This suggests a realistic argument in favor of democratic forms. To be sure, in the hands of inordinately self-invested and slothful persons and groups—that is, in human hands—these structures require constant vigilance to operate in ways that are even approximately and tolerably just. Moreover, checks, balances, and dispersals sometimes court inefficiencies or even gridlock. But Mussolini made the trains run on time, and we easily underestimate the value of structured restraints.

Again, those who impose gross iniquities and benefit from them may retain a vestigial sense of justice. They may know and feel themselves to have been unfair, and thus harbor some sense of guilt or remorse. These emotions sometimes lead people to double-down on their injustices and denials. Nevertheless, Martin Luther King Jr. believed that some good remained even among his white opponents. He thought that confrontations with nonviolent resisters, who suffered unjustly and also acknowledged the worth even of their oppressors, might move at least some consciences. One notes, too, that among oppressed persons and communities, a sense of justice makes for deep-seated and enduring resentments, and that therefore, despite what oppressive powers intend, blatantly unjust acts and structures sometimes sow seeds of their own destruction. This is one reason why those who view events from outside centers of power realize that no human agency finally is able to control all relevant outcomes. Thus, even in the midst of seemingly intractable circumstances, there is reason to hope things can be different.

A residual sense of justice, feelings of guilt, remorse, and resentment at injustice—these contribute to our experience of God as Judge. But if this is so, then divine judgment does not simply destroy: it presses persons and communities to repent, to redirect their lives, to change their practices, to turn from their self-centered curvatures, and to take up changed attitudes and commitments. At times, perhaps the suffering of the innocent (say of starving and bombed children in Yemen) due to the sins of the guilty—due to our sins—will, in conjunction with the dangerous memory of crucifixion, constitute a poignant nightmare or right revulsion that will precipitate a change of heart. Or, again, dire and even catastrophic consequences of environmental irresponsibility may press communities to reevaluate.

Just here, we begin to see that judgment may in fact constitute a dimension of renewing grace, and so we arrive at a third basic theme. Renewal and redemption suggest that persons and communities are not fated simply to be consumed by the destructive consequences of their corrupted affections and interests, their skewed lines of practical reasoning, and their corrupted patterns of responsibility. Residual, if also admittedly somewhat corrupted, moral sensibilities may render consciences uneasy in the face of the unjust sufferings of others, and so press persons and groups to attend to and even mitigate grossly destructive conditions. Again, persons and groups may begin to alter their actions and practices when and if they are subjected to consequences of their own doing that seem sufficiently dire for their own needs and interests, for example, the responses of certain communities and government agencies to the toxic effects on humans and wildlife of releasing the pesticide kepone, or chlordecone, into the James River at Hopewell, Virginia, in 1975.[1] Indeed, under certain circumstances, and ordinarily not without important and sustained efforts at reform as well as continuing ambiguities, possibilities may emerge for reconciliation and greater measures of social justice following periods of systemic discrimination and oppression, as happened in the United States in conjunction with the civil rights movement and with the end of apartheid in South Africa. Piety looks for encounters with God as gracious Redeemer. Despite the persistent facts of

1. Allied Chemical Company and Life Sciences Product Company produced the compound at Hopewell. Fishing was shut down for one hundred miles along the James River, and in 2009 the Stockholm Convention banned the chemical's production and use worldwide.

corruption and malformation, its attention also turns toward traces of grace and toward the advent of new possibilities. These traces and possibilities, in an analogy to resurrection, must sometimes emerge from destructive dissolutions and defeats. Even so, the theme of redemption brings hope.

My initial aim in this chapter is to elaborate this view with respect to basic human communities and institutions. Hopefully but also, I think, realistically, piety construes the histories of dynamic, ambiguous, and sometimes quite destructive human communities and institutions bending toward an eschatological and elusive kingdom that is partly within but also finally beyond history. Rather than attempt a comprehensive account of this vision, however, I shall confine myself here to civil government and the church as selected illustrations. Theologically considered, of course, we should not separate human communities, institutions, and their historical possibilities and limits from the wider whole of creation. I shall therefore try to situate my remarks about human communities and institutions by also considering the following question: For what may we hope when we consider the larger environmental challenges we face as embedded participants in Earth's planetary system?

Proposition #65 Civil government is a historical means in and through which God's sustenance and care are mediated to us, but all governments are subject to chronic corruptions, all fall short of the kingdom, and so all stand in need of criticism and reform. Occasionally, they also stand in need of fundamental reconfiguration.

"Give therefore to the emperor the things that are the emperor's, and to God the things that are God's" (Matt. 22:21). "Let every person be subject to the governing authorities" (Rom. 13:1). "And the armies of heaven, wearing fine linen, white and pure, were following him on white horses. From his mouth comes a sharp sword with which to strike down the nations, and he will rule them with a rod of iron; he will tread the wine press of the fury of the wrath of God the Almighty" (Rev. 19:14–15).

Each of these passages is subject to interpretation. For example, it is unclear whether the first leaves much to give the emperor at all, and, in some respects, the last two excerpts seem at odds. I mention them here only to show that Christians have constructed different visions of civil government, the state, and the nations from New Testament times forward. Augustine's comparatively negative view of the state, as an earthly necessity in which we participate "between the times" until we find rest in the city of God, has influenced many Christians in the West. "What," says the good bishop, "are robberies themselves, but little kingdoms?"

> The band itself is made up of men; it is ruled by the authority of a prince, it is knit together by the pact of the confederacy; the booty is divided by the law agreed on. . . . Indeed, it was an apt and true reply which was given to Alexander the Great by a pirate who had been seized. For when the king had asked the man what he meant by keeping hostile possession of the sea, he answered with bold pride, "What thou meanest by seizing the whole earth; but because I do it with a petty ship, I am called a robber, whilst thou who do it with a great fleet art styled emperor."[2]

To outline the more or less Reformed vision I prefer, however, a good place to start is with John Calvin and the Protestant Reformation of the sixteenth century.

Calvin's Reformation Perspective

Calvin published nine editions of *The Institutes of the Christian Religion*, from 1536 until he was satisfied with it in 1559. During those years, the book grew from a comparatively short "movement treatise" to a 1,500-page tome with folio margins intended for candidates in theology at the College of Geneva. However, all editions concluded with a chapter on civil government in which, in the later editions, Calvin contrasted his reflections with those of Peter Rideman, a Hutterite who published his *Account of Our Religion, Doctrine and Faith* in 1545.

One reason Calvin concerned himself with the topic is that the Protestant Reformation destabilized established patterns of political order in much of Europe. In broad compass, the Holy Roman Empire gave way to more recognizably modern nation-states. German princes, anxious for a greater measure of power and authority, cut ties with Rome. City-states emerged in what is now Switzerland at Bern, Zurich, and Geneva (where Protestant refugees from France, including Calvin, swelled the population, and there were predictable tensions between newcomers and German-speaking residents).[3]

Other Protestant writers also felt called upon to interpret civil government, and Rideman's theology, which stresses a holy community that obeys Christ's

2. Augustine, *City of God*, trans. Marcus Dods (New York: Random House, 1950), 4.4, pp. 112–13.

3. For interesting reflections on Calvin's experience as a refugee and an immigrant as well as its influence on his theology and understanding of hospitality, see Robert Vosloo, "On the Displaced Calvin: 'Refugee Reality' as a Lens to Examine Calvin's Life, Theology and Legacy," and "On Calvin and the Mirror of the Stranger: 'Refugee Reality' and the Gift of Recognition," in Robert Vosloo, *Reforming Memory: Essays on South African Church and Theological History* (Stellenbosch, South Africa: African Sun Media, 2017), 175–88, 189–99.

reign, holds possessions in common, and participates in civil society in a comparatively restricted way, offers a rather definite perspective.[4] Civil government, Rideman says, is from God's wrath, an enterprise by which the deity permits the godless to discipline, punish, and restrain the wicked by force. Christ's disciples, on the other hand, put off all worldly glory. "Thus no Christian is a ruler and no ruler is a Christian, for the child of blessing cannot be the servant of wrath." Moreover, "a Christian neither wages war not wields the worldly sword to practice vengeance." Christian citizens pay general taxes but refuse to pay special taxes levied for war. "Neither can they make weapons," sit as judges, or participate in civil courts. In short, for the occasionally imprisoned Protestant radical, civil government "has its place outside Christ, but not in Christ."[5]

The contrast with Calvin is nearly total. The humanist student of law rails against "certain fanatics" who boast that once we are in Christ and "are transferred to God's Kingdom . . . it is a thing unworthy of us . . . to be occupied with . . . vile and worldly cares."[6] He claims that God has established civil government to provide for the public manifestation of religion, and so "that humanity may be maintained among men." Moreover, he says, its function "is no less than that of bread, water, sun, and air." Discussing magistrates, Calvin claims, "God has entrusted to them the business of serving him through their office," and "civil authority is a calling, not only lawful before God, but also . . . by far the most honorable of all callings, in the whole life of mortal men." Indeed, it is the responsibility of the magistrate to represent "some image of divine providence, protection, goodness, benevolence, and justice."[7]

Calvin's view, in short, is that spiritual and civil governments are not antithetical, and that the latter is a means by which God sustains and cares for persons and communities.

> For spiritual government, indeed, is already initiating in us upon earth certain beginnings of the Heavenly Kingdom, and in this moral and fleeting life affords a certain forecast of an immortal and incorruptible blessedness. Yet civil government has as its appointed end, so long as we live among men, to cherish and protect the outward worship of God, to defend sound doctrine of piety and the position of the church, to adjust our life to the society of men, to form our social behavior to civil righteousness, to reconcile us with

4. Peter Rideman, *An Account of Our Religion, Doctrine, and Faith Given by Peter Rideman of the Brothers Whom Men Call Hutterians* (Rifton, NY: Plough, 1970), 43, 89, 92–93.

5. Rideman, *An Account of Our Religion*, 107, 108, 111–14, 105.

6. Calvin, *ICR* 4.20.2.

7. Calvin, *ICR* 4.20.3–4, 6.

> one another, and to promote general peace and tranquility. All of this I admit to be superfluous if God's Kingdom, such as it is now among us, wipes out the present life. But if it is God's will that we go as pilgrims upon the earth while we aspire to the true fatherland, and if the pilgrimage requires such helps, those who take these from man deprive him of his very humanity. Our adversaries claim that there ought to be such great perfection in the church of God that its government should suffice for law. But they stupidly imagine such a perfection as can never be found in a community of men. For since the insolence of evil men is so great, their wickedness so stubborn, that it can scarcely be restrained by extremely severe laws, what do we expect them to do if they see that their depravity can go scot-free—when no power can force them to cease from doing evil?[8]

We need civil government in this life if we are to have functioning and tolerably humane communities. For Calvin, writing during the sixteenth century, this means it should wield sufficient power to restrain human wickedness (a negative function) and also to guide persons in humane living by upholding true religion and civil righteousness (a positive task). But the more general and contemporary point, I think, is that the purpose of civil government is to maintain humane society both by restraining evil and by guiding us toward what is just and good.

Updating Calvin's View

Taking a cue once again from Arthur Dyck, we might update this view as follows.[9] We humans are social creatures nurtured in families that, in turn, depend on wider communities. We therefore participate in myriad social and cultural enterprises, and modern societies include not only individuals and families but also ethnic groups, corporations, classes, religious associations, militaries, schools, etc. These vitalities, as Reinhold Niebuhr calls them, have varied interests in cooperative enterprises and structures, for example, public safety, recognizably fair means of settling disputes, transportation, and care for elders, but each also has its own partial interests and aims, for example, celebrating particular traditions and producing wealth.[10] More than a few also harbor different visions of a good society. Thus, while there is some impetus toward cooperation, there

8. Calvin, *ICR* 4.20.2.

9. Arthur J. Dyck, *Rethinking Rights and Responsibilities: The Moral Bonds of Community* (Cleveland: Pilgrim, 1994), 140–44.

10. Reinhold Niebuhr discusses these vitalities in *NDM*, 2:256–69.

are also considerable tensions, and, often enough, conflicts emerge between the general interest and the more limited interests of particular persons, groups, and institutions. Moreover, mired in the human fault, people tend to favor their own traditions and members of their own groups over others, and, when they are able, all persons, groups, and institutions therefore tend to pursue their partial interests expansively and inordinately. The vitalities, their organizations, and their structures may achieve rough equilibria or balances of power within a particular society, but the equilibria themselves generally remain partial or skewed, often taking advantage of one or another other group and its interests. They are also unstable, liable to degenerate into anarchy, a cacophony of vitalities and interests, or an unregulated and unjust free-for-all.

This is why human societies need organizing structures and powers in order to achieve a workable, somewhat stable, and tolerably just harmony; these structures are what we call civil government. Its purpose, as Calvin notes, is to form our social behavior to civil righteousness as expressed in laws; to restrain the expansive impulses of capable (but also chronically corrupted) persons, institutions, and groups; and to promote peace as well as important cooperative enterprises. The efforts at restraint, formation, and cooperation clearly do not bring in God's kingdom, but they do help to promote comparatively humane societies. Or, to put this same point differently, the function of civil government—especially in modern nation-states—is to organize and maintain a space in which people, as they participate in social and cultural vitalities, can pursue and shape a meaningful and tolerably just and good common life.[11] (If you are having trouble seeing the value of all this, ask a people or community that doesn't have its own nation or government why it wants one, for example, Palestinian Arabs or Turkish and Iraqi Kurds. Alternatively, ponder why the escape of enslaved clans from Egypt and their subsequent establishment as a nation with its own laws, institutions, and customs is the primary saving event of the Hebrew Scriptures.) Nevertheless, and as the Hebrew Scriptures also illustrate, the power that must be accumulated for this organizing task is itself subject to corruption and abuse. Perhaps it will become the arm for one or another vitality and its partial interest at the expense of the poor. Perhaps the organizing political institutions themselves will generate their own oligarchic class. And these are only two ways that civil government and the state may degenerate into injustice and tyranny.

Calvin, who, unlike Rideman, thinks it worthwhile to distinguish between

11. See Michael Walzer, *Just and Unjust Wars: A Moral Argument with Historical Illustrations* (New York: Basic Books, 1977), 54. Martin L. Cook, *The Moral Warrior: Ethics and Service in the U.S. Military* (Albany: State University of New York Press, 2004), 50–52, makes use of Walzer's concept of common life as he argues for the moral foundation of military service.

better and worse forms of civil government, anticipates some of these points. He says many characteristics of appropriate governments depend on circumstances, but because kings very rarely control themselves "so that their will never disagrees with what is just and right," and because some kings are not especially wise, "a system compounded of aristocracy and democracy, far excels all others." That is, "men's fault or failing causes it to be safer and more bearable for a number to exercise government, so that they may help one another, teach and admonish one another; and, if one asserts himself unfairly, there may be a number of censors and masters to restrain his willfulness."[12] In my terms, the Genevan Reformer is, among other things, a responsible realist who regards representative democratic institutions not only as structures that may foster helpful cooperation but also as strategies for restraining inordinate assertions of partial interests.

Reinhold Niebuhr echoes this position during the twentieth century when, in *The Children of Light and the Children of Darkness*, he tries to furnish democracy "a more realistic vindication than is given it by" liberalism's "excessively optimistic" estimates of human nature and history. "Man's capacity for justice," he rather famously says, "makes democracy possible; but man's inclination to injustice makes democracy necessary."[13] Niebuhr's argument has roots in a theological anthropology marked by a strong doctrine of sin. A sense for the persistent corruption of persons and groups bolsters his insistence that, in order to achieve approximate justice, democratic institutions and societies appropriately harness, balance, and restrain chronically inordinate interests and wills to power. Niebuhr claims, in fact, that the doctrine of original sin makes a critical contribution to political thought, and that the absence of anything like it "has robbed bourgeois theory of real wisdom" and doomed liberal progressive views of history to folly.[14] The error of much modern political thinking, then, is that it finally and sentimentally relies on either human capacity or the process of history to transcend the conflicting interests of individuals, classes, and nations. The consequences of "this grave defect in democratic theory" were comparatively innocuous during an earlier period, but during the mid-twentieth century, with the mounting confusions of industrialism, bourgeois commercial individualism (libertarianism), fascism, and Marxist collectivism, says Niebuhr, they threaten to become intensely destructive.[15]

12. Calvin, *ICR* 4.20.8.

13. Reinhold Niebuhr, *The Children of Light and the Children of Darkness: A Vindication of Democracy and a Critique of Its Traditional Defense* (Eugene, OR: Wipf & Stock, 2006), xii–xiii.

14. Reinhold Niebuhr, *The Children of Light*, 16, 31.

15. Reinhold Niebuhr, *The Children of Light*, 40.

The myriad ways in which things may go wrong suggest why, in a Christian frame of reference, it often has been thought important to maintain that political communities and their civil laws depend upon something prior and more fundamental. Thomas Aquinas claims that the laws of the nations elaborate features of natural law available to reason, which, in turn, have their basis in divine law. Thus, the mere enactment of a given law by a civil authority does not guarantee the law's moral legitimacy; natural law and reasoned understandings of justice furnish standards by which to estimate the appropriateness of particular civil laws.

Calvin claims that people are social animals who tend "to foster and preserve society" and who ordinarily agree that "every sort of human organization must be regulated by laws."[16] He also thinks a sense of equity, which comes to expression in maxims such as the Golden Rule and in definitions of justice, such as to each his due, is generally recognized to be the deep criterion or standard for particular constitutions and positive laws.[17] Nevertheless, "men dispute among themselves about individual sections of the law."[18] Indeed, while "some seed of political order has been implanted in all," and while there is a sense of equity or fairness that roughly is the same for all, Calvin does not believe that socially instantiated norms of justice, for example, the Civil Rights Act or the US criminal code, can simply be read off from an entirely clear moral sensibility. These necessarily are devised to take account of particular circumstances. In addition, says Calvin—and this goes to the point about sin—our particular historic elaborations and institutionalizations of justice inevitably are subject to the influences of our own inordinate inclinations, desires, and interests. Amidst the complexities of real conditions and circumstances, then, justice is never elaborated and applied by entirely impartial actors. There is a skewing effect that becomes especially profound when persons and groups elaborate standards that apply to their own projects, affairs, and concerns. Thus, in commenting on the Golden Rule, the Reformer asks a leading question. "Where our own advantage is concerned there is not one of us, who cannot explain minutely and ingeniously what ought to be done. And since every man shows himself to be a skillful teacher of justice for his own advantage, how comes it that the same knowledge does not readily occur to him, when the profit or loss of another is at stake?"[19]

16. Calvin, *ICR* 2.2.13.

17. Calvin, *ICR* 4.20.16.

18. Calvin, *ICR* 2.2.13.

19. John Calvin, *Commentary on a Harmony of the Evangelists, Matthew, Mark, and Luke*, vol. 1, trans. William Pringle, in *Calvin's Commentaries*, Calvin Translation Society (Grand Rapids: Baker Books, 1998), 355. Calvin continues, "What is more, we maliciously and purposely shut our eyes upon the rule of justice, which shines in our hearts. Christ therefore

This roughly indicates why, in our own time, one who shares something like Calvin's theological vision will not be surprised to find appeals to operative conceptions and applications of justice made by business proprietors who reject additional taxation and advocates of higher taxes to improve public schools, by homeowners concerned for property values and by advocates of halfway houses, by Palestinians, Israelis, and so on. As Niebuhr observes, our elaborations and institutionalizations of justice are "the consequence of pressures and counter-pressures" in living communities. They are subject to vital interests and powers that inevitably intertwine with our tendencies "to take advantage of one another, or to be more concerned with our own weal than with that of others."[20] Moreover, as circumstances and interests, vitalities and powers change, our elaborations and institutionalizations need to be renegotiated and adjusted.

This—with an assist from a notable twentieth-century theological ethicist—is substantially Calvin's position on our common human sense of equity, particular historical circumstances, partial interests, and sin. The Reformer neither furnishes nor endorses a special Christian conception of justice. Instead, he shows how a theological anthropology may influence our understanding of a general sense of equity as well as our evaluations of particular conceptions of justice. His claims for a sense of equity, our historical elaborations of it, and the skewing effect of our inordinate interests may be described as a *circumspect* appropriation of the natural law tradition that we find in Thomas Aquinas, Cicero, and others. David Little says that, within the frame of this theology, "natural law will always remain minimal, or, to use Calvin's word, 'vestigial.'"[21] Appeals to our sense of fairness will be suggestive or indicative of concepts and socially instantiated norms that, in turn, must be formulated and argued for and against in the push and shove of politics, culture, and circumstance.[22]

---

shows, that every man may be a rule acting properly and justly toward his neighbor, if he do to others what he requires to be done to him. He thus refutes all the vain pretenses, which men contrive for hiding or disguising their injustice."

20. Reinhold Niebuhr, *NDM*, 2:252, 253.

21. David Little, "Calvin and the Prospects for a Christian Theory of Natural Law," in *Norm and Context in Christian Ethics*, ed. Gene H. Outka and Paul Ramsey (New York: Scribner's Sons, 1968), 196.

22. Similar appeals are present in a number of later Puritans and, perhaps, most notably, in the work of Roger Williams, who, like Calvin, believed that sin clouds our knowledge of moral norms founded on natural law and also skews their application. See James Calvin Davis, *The Moral Theology of Roger Williams: Christian Conviction and Public Ethics* (Louisville: Westminster John Knox, 2004), 64, 103.

Critical Standards

The main point I wish to emphasize here is simply that, despite their differences and nuances, a number of theologians agree that a basic drive toward community with others and a generally available sense or conception of justice furnish criteria by which we may measure, estimate, and criticize the specific laws and practices of particular political communities. Walter Rauschenbusch makes similar points when he says there is "a divine instinct for righteousness within us" (or what we might call a generally distributed moral sensibility) that is "anchored" largely "by the historical experience of mankind." This instinct may shift, and it is also true that, as "history has been written from the point of view of the dominant class and edited to suit their needs," we sometimes have difficulty consulting it with accuracy; nevertheless, it can serve as a helpful guide. A second way of obtaining guidance, says Rauschenbusch, "for those of us who believe in Jesus Christ," is the disclosure of God's will for humanity in him. This involves some "fundamental utterances of the mind of Christ," including the divine worth of individuals and the unity or solidarity of humanity in God's kingdom—notions that help us to see "directions" in which the drive toward community should be guided.[23]

Ideas such as these also come to expression when Martin Luther King Jr. responds to a question raised about the tactic of civil disobedience deployed in the African American struggle for justice and equality:[24] "How can you advocate breaking some laws and obeying others?" King answers by distinguishing just and unjust laws. "A just law is a man-made code that squares with the moral law or the law of God. An unjust law is a code that is out of harmony with the moral law. To put it in terms of Saint Thomas Aquinas, an unjust law is a human law that is not rooted in eternal and natural law" (293). Or, again, a "law which is out of harmony with the moral law is a law which does not square with the moral law of the universe" (49). That is, King insists that actual civil laws, which are formulated, enacted, and enforced in the push and shove of social forces and historical circumstances, point toward something prior and more fundamental, namely, the moral law or law of God. In addition, he also mentions substantive

23. Walter Rauschenbusch, *Christianizing the Social Order* (New York: Macmillan, 1913), 326–28.

24. He does so most famously in "Letter from Birmingham City Jail" but also about eighteen months earlier in an address to the interracial Fellowship of the Concerned defending student "sit-ins" and "freedom rides." See *A Testament of Hope: The Essential Writings of Martin Luther King, Jr.*, ed. James Melvin Washington (New York: Harper & Row, 1986), 43–53, 289–302. Hereafter, page references from this work will be given in parentheses in the text.

criteria for discerning which laws conform to this standard: respect for human personality, and the meaningful participation of all in the enactment of a law.

These criteria are interconnected and have deep theological roots. A just law, says King, "uplifts human personality," whereas an unjust law "degrades the human personality" (49). To be just, therefore, a law or practice cannot distort the soul and damage the person. But segregation does distort and damage by giving "the segregator a false sense of superiority, and the segregated a false sense of inferiority." (King mentions the disappointment and hurt on his eleven-year-old daughter's face when she sees an advertisement for Funtown and he must tell her that she can't go there because she is black.) Again, referring to the Jewish philosopher Martin Buber, King says, "segregation substitutes an 'I-it' relationship for the 'I-thou' relationship, and ends up relegating persons to the status of things" (293). Basic beliefs back these assertions. For one thing, "human worth lies in relatedness to God. An individual has value because he has value to God," and, according to King, *agapē*, or the kind of loving, "redemptive, creative, good will for men" that "Jesus meant when he said 'love your enemies,'" recognizes this (122).

But if this is so, if all persons have worth in relation to God and are called to acknowledge one another's worth, then another basic belief comes into view, namely, that all are bound together in a kind of unity or solidarity. All persons, to allude to John Donne (which King does repeatedly), "are caught in an inescapable network of mutuality, tied in a single garment of destiny" (121–22). All are called to "the great adventure of community," or to "reconciliation and the creation of a beloved community" (8, 12). An unjust law—one "inflicted upon a minority"—disrespects persons by shutting them out of meaningful political participation. This is antidemocratic, but it also goes against the interrelated and interdependent grain of the universe. Indeed, "the cross is the eternal expression of the length to which God will go to restore broken community. The Holy Spirit is the continuing community creating reality that moves through history. He who works against community is working against the whole of creation" (20).

My own understanding of our generally distributed human sense for justice has something in common with that of the philosopher Michael Walzer, who observes that, when marchers in Prague in 1989 were televised carrying signs that simply said "Justice," "I knew immediately what the signs meant—and so did everyone else who saw the same picture." Walzer does not presume that he, the marchers, and other television viewers would agree on a fully elaborated conception of justice. Even so, he claims that "what they meant by the 'justice' inscribed on their signs . . . was simple enough; an end to arbitrary arrests, equal and impartial law enforcement, the abolition of the privileges and prerogatives of the party elite—common garden variety justice."[25]

What Walzer calls "common garden variety justice," in my judgment at least, is better described as a sensibility than as a concept—as a sense for the demand of justice, an inkling of fairness, and also a revulsion at gross and destructive injustices.[26] It is, I believe, bound up with a knot of emotions and reflective capabilities for which there is evidence in other primates as well.[27] These include feelings of mutual dependence, solidarity, sympathy, and caring emotions, an imaginative capacity to identify with others (at least to a degree), and an aversion to gross suffering and inequity. Call these residual manifestations of the participatory and ec-centric vector or tendency of created interdependent human life.

In any case, this other-attentive and other-directed emotional and imaginative knot that we call a sense of fairness or justice is insufficient of itself to order any particular community, society, or institution. It needs to be given expression in maxims such as the Golden Rule or to each his due, and these, in turn, need to be elaborated if they are to inform (both positively and critically) any actual historical community, institution, or developed body of law. Moreover, I agree with the longer Reformed theological tradition that our sense for justice often is rendered ambiguous, stunted, and skewed by constricted social loyalties and commitments as well as by corrupted practices and cultural views.[28] Nevertheless, when combined with salient facts about the circumstances in Prague as well as with some of our own experiences of moral judgment and even outrage, our generally distributed moral sensibility, or what Calvin calls our sense of equity, sometimes can be enough to enable us to understand what the marchers' signs meant. It can push us to recognize claims for justice made by others who differ from ourselves. Occasionally, it can also be enough, when combined with our own ordinary experiences and social histories (and whether we are Christians or not), to launch a critique of the tyranny to which Czechs were subject in 1989.

25. Michael Walzer, *Thick and Thin: Moral Argument at Home and Abroad* (Notre Dame: University of Notre Dame Press, 1994), 1–2.

26. Walter Rauschenbusch writes, "We can gauge the ethical importance of justice by the sense of outrage with which we instinctively react to injustice." *Christianizing the Social Order*, 332.

27. The basic idea of moral sensibility was developed by British moral philosophers, such as Bishop Joseph Butler and David Hume, during the eighteenth century, and then elaborated in a biological direction by Charles Darwin. See my discussions above of Darwin as well as ideas put forward by Frans de Waal. I also think Mary Midgley's treatment of the emotional discussions of humans and other animals in *Beast and Man: The Animal Roots of Human Nature* (Ithaca, NY: Cornell University Press, 1978) remains among the best.

28. See chap. 10.

Residual moral sensibility plus our own experiences and histories plus some information about specific circumstances may in fact furnish points of departure for significant discussions about justice, injustice, tyranny, and fairness among representatives of different communities and cultural traditions. This is not a formula for easy agreements about justice, human rights, and the rest, though it does keep alive the hope that, in the push and shove of politics and history, even corrupted creatures such as ourselves may occasionally take positive steps toward limited, flawed, but also significant accords and agreements.

I should add, however, that, among persons of Christian piety, moral sensibilities are also aided and further developed at least in part by specific resources of Christian tradition. In earlier chapters I explored many of these, for example, the law in Hebrew Scriptures, Jesus's kingdom-mindedness, and Jesus's teachings. These resources furnish additional grounds for raising critical questions about civil laws and current practices, such as widening gaps between rich and poor, unavailable and overpriced health care, and the separation of immigrant children from their families along the US border with Mexico. Teachings about a neighbor love that extends even to aliens and enemies, hope for a divine kingdom characterized by shalom, as well as concern for the vulnerable—these are among the powerful sculptors of Christian moral sensibility. They also suggest that all human governments finally are *limited* in the sense that they are called to recognize and uphold prior norms and sensibilities, such as the worth of persons before God, and the critical importance of attending to the ill, the weak, and the dependent. The nations do not define so much as they acknowledge what counts as true justice, a humane life, and a good society. In piety's view, the God who creates all things, gives breath to the living, judges the nations, and brings in the kingdom is the God of justice and love. This is why all the nations and all the political communities remain subject to criticism. This is also why, under certain circumstances, persons of piety may be called to participate in movements of political reform, civilly disobedient protests, and even revolutions.[29]

Another reason why Christians sometimes participate in these movements is that they live in hope. Cynical and imperialistic realists tend to overestimate the competence of raw power and to underestimate the practical importance of moral legitimacy, as well as the extent to which, given the generally distributed

29. Though the circumstances and options need spelling out, and very often there are significant ambiguities. See Martin Luther King Jr.'s criteria for nonviolently disobeying unjust laws in his "Letter from Birmingham Jail," in *A Testament of Hope*, 289–302. Calvin also alludes to conditions under which "the fierce licentiousness of kings" may be resisted and the commands of rulers may "go unesteemed." *ICR* 4.20.31–32.

ec-centric vector and sense of equity, repressive and immoral regimes provoke deep-seated opprobrium and lasting opposition.

Consider a letter sent by Nelson Mandela from Robben Island Prison to the South African commissioner of prisons on July 12, 1976. It details at some length a host of oppressive conditions on the island, including the censorship of correspondence, the ways in which visits are monitored, the fact that money sent to prisoners often is not received, various unhealthy practices and surroundings, and the failure of the commissioner to visit and personally monitor conditions and complaints. Then come the following passages:

> It is futile to think that any form of persecution will ever change our views. Your Government and Department have a notorious reputation for their hatred, contempt and persecution of the Black man, especially the African, a hatred and contempt which forms the basic principle of a multiplicity of the country's statutes and cases. . . .
>
> It is certainly quite unreasonable for any man to expect our people to whom we are national heroes, persecuted for striving to win back our country, to forget us in our lifetime at the height of the struggle for a free South Africa.[30]

Repression provokes lasting (and sometimes also effective) opposition.

Mandela is not working with Christian symbols, but we may note that, in a theological frame of reference, while persons, communities, and institutions wield significant powers, as limited creatures, they are unable either to anticipate or control all relevant outcomes. This is true, too, for oppressive powers and regimes. And so, even in the midst of difficult and apparently incorrigible circumstances, piety believes things can be different. It hopes and therefore looks for traces of grace in a world governed by a trajectory toward a kingdom of reconciliation, justice, and peace. It knows that sometimes, as persons and groups persist in struggles for justice and for better societies, oppressive regimes falter. It knows that sometimes, though not without ambiguities, setbacks, and persistent challenges, new political possibilities may emerge.

The Demonic

Now explore further a dark possibility with which many in the West had to reckon during the mid-twentieth century: political communities may become

30. *The Prison Letters of Nelson Mandela*, ed. Sahm Ventner (New York: Liveright, 2018), 312, 316. The underlining is in Mandela's handwritten letter.

grossly inhumane and demonic. This possibility is, I think, best understood in direct theological terms. The doctrine of creation indicates that all finite things, due to their dependence upon an Other and their "situatedness" within an interdependent created world, point or refer beyond themselves. They are, that is to say, inexplicable apart from their "vertical" dependence on the God beyond and their wider "horizontal" situation in the midst of interdependent interrelations with others. This is part and parcel of good creation; good creatures gesture and point beyond themselves in their dependence on God and in their interdependence with others. They have an inherent theological valence, impetus, or trajectory toward God and neighbor.

Christian piety therefore maintains that any particular political community is in some sense derivative; it depends upon Something More. It points beyond itself toward all creation under God, God's universal reign, the kingdom, or true communion with God in community with others. This is why, in a Christian theological frame of reference, the moral standing of any political community and its laws, practices, and policies may be estimated in the light of prior and more fundamental realities and values that it is called upon to acknowledge, for example, the worth of persons in relation to God, justice, and the interconnected, interdependent, and communal character of created human life. Demonic political communities deny or invert this reference or pointing. They distort their own inherent referential dynamic because they identify themselves with the holy or the divine. "And," as Paul Tillich notes, "the claim of something finite to infinity or to divine greatness is the characteristic of the demonic." Among the nations, then, the demonic claim amounts to "the self-elevation of one nation over against all others in the name of her God or system of values."[31]

A demonic political community proclaims itself divine, and thereby becomes a living idol. It posits itself in tandem with or in the place of the God beyond, and thus contravenes the first table of the Ten Commandments. All distance and tension between the particular community in question and the transcendent are thereby denied or (allegedly) overcome; the loss of divine transcendence leads to the simple identification of the political group and its partial interests, practices, and prejudices with the ultimate or the divine.

Just because any government's organization of the realm of social vitalities requires a higher plane of moral sanction and necessity than do mere balances of power, says Reinhold Niebuhr, all governments are at least potentially involved in the sin of idolatry and its pretensions.[32] That is, the organizing or

31. Paul Tillich, *Life and the Spirit, History and the Kingdom of God*, vol. 3 of *Systematic Theology* (Chicago: University of Chicago Press, 1963), 102, 103.

32. Reinhold Niebuhr, *NDM*, 2:267.

governing center needs a higher justification than do the many vitalities precisely because it claims to be the principle that checks, balances, and organizes them. The question is, "In the service of what greater value or reality shall we strive for this organization to be achieved?" And the classical answers—the common good, the commonwealth, and the public good—all have a distinctly moral valence.

In any case, absent the distance and tension entailed by the commonwealth's reference beyond itself to things more fundamental and valuable, the actual historical political community or nation alone defines what is right and good. The political community styles itself the transcendent, the prior, the ultimate, and the end. The result is political idolatry, the stunting or short-circuiting of the inherent theological valence of created life—the loss of both divine transcendence and the inherent orientation of the specific political community to a universal community beyond itself. The true deity and its ethical demands no longer stand beyond and over against the political community and its wishes, pretensions, and commands. The political community no longer points beyond itself toward the kingdom of divine justice and shalom. The way therefore is clear for the actual and historical political community to estimate the value or worth of all persons, activities, and groups solely according to whether or not they bolster and support its aims. In short, the nation is no longer "under God"; it *is* god. The relevant measure of good people, good art, religion, business, science, and what-have-you becomes simply and entirely whether or not they serve or glorify the nation and its interests.

Most political communities, as we have noted, are quite complex, and so it is likely that impulses toward political idolatry among a governing elite will be mitigated and opposed by the many social vitalities, their aims and interests. Business corporations and workers tend to resist the notion that the only measure of good business is its contribution to the political community and its aims. What about the wealth of owners, employees, and shareholders? Artists may balk at efforts to direct art to the service of the state (and very well may produce artistic works that undercut some of the state's preferences and directives). Religious associations may criticize the idea that good religion always supports the nation's partial interests. And it is also possible that some of the opposition articulated in these quarters will reflect a residual reference to God and the kingdom beyond.

Societies and cultures often may be accurately described as fields of tension and conflict among many causes and commitments. The possibility cannot be dismissed that, within these fields of conflict, there will emerge a full-blown and demonic inversion of the transcendent reference of dependent and interdependent created life. But neither should we dismiss the possibilities that such inversions will be resisted, or that societies will pursue prospects for a more genuine, and even, as Martin Luther King Jr. would have said, "beloved" community.

Conflicting Dynamics

Let me explore these conflicting dynamics further with the aid of analyses and ideas offered by H. Richard Niebuhr, for whom there can be a similarity between some political communities and what he calls radically monotheistic faith. Radical monotheism, he says, is faith in God as the principle and source of being—a faith that he takes to be expressed in religious language by the first article of the creed, "I believe in God the Father Almighty, maker of heaven and earth." Moreover, says Niebuhr, this faith entails loyalty to the community of all existents in relation to God.[33]

Essentially, I agree, though my own vocabulary differs somewhat from Niebuhr's, and I think there are additional ways in which Christian tradition represents an idea of universal community. When, for example, the Gospels portray Jesus teaching love of God and neighbor (including enemies), this points toward communion with God in community with others, toward a stance in life that responds to the divine excellence and also accords with the kingdom. The Christ or the kingdom-minded one also indicates something like this by his practice of open commensality—welcoming all, including tax collectors and sinners, into a community of reconciliation. Or, again, as I noted earlier when discussing the Spirit and the church, the Eucharist as well as the practice of public worship more generally may be understood as symbolic enactments of true communion with God in community, the promise of a kingdom in which people come from east and west, north and south to sit at table together. But in any case, the main thing is that, for Niebuhr, political communities may point beyond themselves toward the universal community of all things with God at its head, or as we might say, toward the interdependent community of all creation in its dependence on God. It is precisely in the light of this reference or pointing that a given political community may frame and support *a self-critical patriotism or politics*, a view that may estimate the moral appropriateness of its own laws, practices, policies, and attitudes in the light of matters prior and more fundamental, such as the worth of persons and the importance of maintaining interdependent interrelations characterized by fairness and justice.

How, then, does this dynamic reference or pointing take place? Niebuhr says

33. H. Richard Niebuhr, *Radical Monotheism and Western Culture, with Supplementary Essays* (Louisville: Westminster John Knox, 1993), 31–37.

that modern political communities in the West often solicit the loyalty of their citizens to a cause transcending the nations themselves. For example, the United States of America presents itself as a country loyal to the cause of democracy and a democratic commitment to equality. The nation invites the loyalty of its citizens to this transcendent cause and then also to the nation itself as a representative of this cause. In this it is aided by "a transcendent reference group" of figures such as George Washington, Thomas Jefferson, and Abraham Lincoln (and today I think we should add Martin Luther King Jr.) who are taken to point toward, portray, and embody its democratic cause. We might say that, from the perspective of Christian piety, the American political community is well ordered when it upholds an ever-renewed commitment to the democratic cause of equality. This is so because, when it upholds this commitment, there is an element of or an analogy with a theocentric and ec-centric piety. All people have worth, and indeed equal worth, simply because they *are*, simply because they are created equal, or because each lives, moves, and has her being in relation to the source of existence, the God beyond who always already stands in relation to all.

In the push and shove of history, the cause of equality and the political community's commitment to it often are subject to erosion, subversion, and attack. For example, if the community's democratic commitment weakens under pressure from the social vitalities, their aims and interests, then it may maintain that the worth of persons varies according to their contributions to the production of wealth, to advancing the life of the mind, to prowess in athletics, or to furnishing entertainment, making art, or what-have-you. In any case, it will soon become apparent, as Niebuhr says, that people "are unequal in their relations to all the limited gods, all the limited centers of value, and in the contributions they make to all of the exclusive causes."[34] It is possible, of course, that the more powerful vitalities and their causes will be spliced together into limited coalitions of the worthy, but, even so, they can organize no genuine commonwealth.

There is also, as I mentioned above, another totalitarian and therefore also oppressive possibility: the national community may come to identify itself with the transcendent cause. Or, again, perhaps the commitment to equality will be exchanged for an identification of the nation with the cause of one or another ethnic or racial group in opposition to others. The fit may be more than a little uneasy, since now the democratic and expansive cause of equality must be bounded and hemmed in by a limiting and exclusivist loyalty only to those who belong and contribute to the nation. As we have seen, the country then recognizes commerce, art, religion, etc., as good to the extent that they strengthen the nation. It may recognize the worth of citizens and perhaps their right to

34. H. Richard Niebuhr, *Radical Monotheism and Western Culture*, 75.

respect and equal treatment but deny this worth and respect to foreigners and to "strangers" within its gates. Recently, for example, we have been reminded that the transcendent cause of modern liberal democracies may be subverted by closed-society and xenophobic attitudes and policies toward migrants. Given the link between the human fault and the persistence among communities of in-group preferences and out-group aversions, the political serviceability of appeals to such attitudes and ideas is (unfortunately) perennial.[35]

Niebuhr notes similar dynamics in Western scientific and religious communities. The appropriate transcendent cause for the scientific community is truth, and the fidelity of scientists to it, which bolsters the responsibility of truth telling, is one source of the respect in which many of us often hold them. In fact, says Niebuhr, there is something like radical faith operating here. Investigators generally maintain an ec-centric trajectory by honoring the right of persons to the whole truth and thus accurately communicating their findings to the wider community. But just at this point we may also note constricting challenges. Where scientific inquiry is entirely funded by and beholden to partial commercial interests, there may be pressure to suppress certain findings or communicate them only to corporate management. Again, when scientific inquiry is set within a political community that identifies itself and its survival as the ultimate cause, secrecy and deception often thwart the responsibility to communicate findings publicly. But even in these circumstances, there may be some scientists who criticize or reject such pressures in the name of truth.

Religious communities are appropriately configured when they point beyond themselves, by means of transcendent reference groups and ec-centric life in the Spirit, to the one God who holds all things in universal community. In the light of this cause, their expansive purpose becomes something like the increase of love of God and neighbor, or to do justice, show kindness, and walk humbly with God. But, again, where religious worship and practice are set within and bounded by a culture's commercial aims, the community's devotion and mission may be confused with the production and accumulation of wealth. Then it may be thought that good religion is the sort that advances general productivity and perhaps also promises to reward the faithful with financial success. Or, perhaps, as is so often the case, religious practice and devotion are equated with the limited cause of advancing and defending the national community and its partial interests. (I once attended a holiday dinner where someone lamented his pastor's unease when members of his congregation spontaneously stood up in Sunday worship and sang the national anthem. "Doesn't the minister know," asked my companion, "that devotion to God and country is the entire point of

35. See chap. 10.

Christianity?") The expansive character of the church's mission, for example, the increase of the love of God and neighbor, will likely be truncated and diminished accordingly. The explicit equation of national and religious loyalties bodes ill as well for the integrity of Christian ethics, and the way is clear for the church merely to baptize the nation and its partial interests.

The church may also fall victim to more directly ecclesiastical idolatries. Perhaps it will simply identify itself as divine or as an exclusive extension of the divine. "The community that pointed to the faithfulness of the One now points to itself . . . God and church have become so identified that often the word 'God' seems to mean the collective representation of the church. God is almost defined as the one who is encountered in the church or the one in whom the church believes."[36] Perhaps it will directly identify its holy text—the Bible—with the divine, and then elevate itself as the one community or institution that possesses, reads, and understands this text. Either way, the religious community lays exclusive claim to divine greatness, and the way is clear for it to identify its purpose entirely with reference to itself. Now perhaps the mission of the church becomes simply the increase and growth of the church rather than the increase of love of God and neighbor. There is also a corresponding and predictable subversion of a truer understanding of evangelism. One hopes, of course, that even where ideas and pieties such as these do emerge, a remnant will criticize and reject them in the name of devotion to God and the kingdom beyond.

Proposition #66 The church is in, with, against, and for the world.[37]

The church's situation in history is complicated partly because, in piety's view, "world" has multiple meanings. It may refer to God's good creation. For example, a basic claim of John 1:10 is that "the world (*kosmos*) came into being" through the Logos or principle of redemption made flesh in Jesus Christ. Even so, love of the world may indicate a corrupted or stunted affection. Thus, 1 John 2:15–16 says that the love of the Father is not in those who love the world (*kosmos*), a realm of pride in riches and corrupt desires. Or, again, in 2 Corinthians 5:19, the world (*kosmos*) refers to the object of God's act of reconciliation in Christ.[38]

The range of meanings, however, is quite compatible with a relational core

36. H. Richard Niebuhr, *Radical Monotheism and Western Culture*, 58–59.

37. This proposition represents a reworking of chapter 5 of my book *Reforming Protestantism: Christian Commitment in Today's World* (Louisville: Westminster John Knox, 1995), 93–116.

38. Kittle distinguishes three senses in which *kosmos* means world in the New Testament: world as universe or the sum of all created things, e.g., Acts 17:24; world as the abode of people, the inhabited world, or the theater of history, e.g., Matt. 4:8; and world as fallen creation or hu-

theology. God is the Creator and the world therefore is God's good creation; God is Judge and the world is mired in sin; God is Redeemer and the world is the object of redeeming grace. H. Richard Niebuhr wrote penetrating essays in 1935 for a volume entitled *The Church against the World*. But on careful examination, the stance he commends is not nearly as singular as the title suggests, and Niebuhr continued to write about church and world in other terms as well.[39] In any case, here I want to say that the church is in, with, against, and for the world. The church's relationship with and stance toward the world, when considered as a whole, cannot be captured by a single preposition. Multiple valences come into play, so that now one, now another deserves special emphasis.

The Church *in* the World

The church is *in* the world. As a community that the Spirit gathers out of all nations and then also sends to all nations, the church cannot be the church without engaging the world and standing in dynamic relationship with the world. It should not shrink from either the command or the gift of true communion with God in community with others. Then, too, recognition in Jesus Christ of God's reconciling way with the world also issues in the conviction that the church, too, should be in the world, not unwillingly or with a bad conscience, but willingly and with a good and faithful conscience. The church is the church precisely as it reaches out and intentionally mixes into a world of variability and plurality; a world of distinct communities, institutions, and groups; a world of distinctive interests, visions, and practices. In fact, one way the church resists the temptation to turn in on itself and thus diminish or curtail its ec-centric existence is by remaining in converse with the varied and plural perspectives of the world's many ethnic groups, political communities, and economic classes.

Precisely because it is in the world in these ways, the church may endeavor to see itself as others do. It may fail to do so. But its intentional and missionary presence in the world is an indispensable precondition for a church that reflects on its presence and action from beyond the visible boundaries of the church, for a church that is able to learn from others and respond to changing currents.

---

manity and the theater of salvation. *Theological Dictionary of the New Testament*, ed. Gerhard Kittle, trans. Geoffrey W. Bromiley (Grand Rapids: Eerdmans, 1965), 3:883–95.

39. See H. Richard Niebuhr, "The Question of the Church" and "Toward the Independence of the Church," in H. Richard Niebuhr, Wilhelm Pauck, and William P. Miller, *The Church against the World* (Chicago: Willett, Clark & Co., 1935), 1–13, 123–56. These and other essays are reprinted in *"The Responsibility of the Church for Society" and Other Essays by H. Richard Niebuhr*, ed. Kristine A. Culp (Louisville: Westminster John Knox, 2008).

Gustavo Gutiérrez therefore notes that this intentional and faithful presence of the church "implies an openness to the world, gathering the questions it poses, being attentive to its historical transformations."[40]

If the church dwells in the world, then it is also true that the world dwells in the church in the form of cultural practices, insights, and attitudes. The church appropriates (and often also revises) one or another technology, political idea, or educational strategy, etc. So, for example, historic Protestantism is virtually unthinkable apart from the invention of the printing press, and, among other things, the participatory representative structures of more than a few churches seem intertwined with the development of democratic political structures in the West. The world enters into the church primarily in the persons of those members whose sensibilities and abilities, ideas, possibilities, and limits are shaped by constellations of conditions, traditions, and institutions. The world is in the church in the persons of Christians shaped by genotypes, phenotypes, kinship ties, and cultural constructs of gender, as well as by apprenticeships, educations, nationalities, friendships, rivalries, and animosities. There is little use arguing that these factors are either all alike in or make for no differences between Christian communities, say, in São Gonçalo, Brazil, or in Ann Arbor, Michigan. The world is in the church in the persons of Christians who are shaped by their lives in specific places and times, and whose distinctive roles and identities are neither lost nor blotted out in the church.[41]

This is one reason why there is in the church a mélange of memories, hopes, tragedies, experiences, triumphs, failures, and sufferings, a world of ideas, commitments, expectations, customs, languages, and gestures. And, again, this is not only a sociological and historical fact or necessity. It is also an intentional occurrence, a dynamic that the church (and hopefully also its pastoral leadership) embraces as a feature of faithfulness and mission in God's world. Welcoming diverse groups, communities, and cultural identities—welcoming tax collectors, women, children, centurions, and sinners—is one way the church crosses barriers and boundaries in order to suggest a reconciled alternative to a fragmented and conflicted world. It is worth noting, too, that diverse communities, groups, and interests within the church justifiably may criticize the inordinately partial loyalties, visions, and practices that sometimes corrupt and captivate the church. Attending to such criticisms is one way that church attends to the world for the

40. Gustavo Gutiérrez, *A Theology of Liberation: History, Politics, and Salvation*, trans. Sister Caridad Inda and John Eagleson, 15th anniversary edition with a new introduction (Maryknoll, NY: Orbis, 1988), 9.

41. James B. Nelson, *Moral Nexus: Ethics of Christian Identity and Community* (Philadelphia: Westminster, 1971), 217–19.

sake of the gospel, one way it endeavors to determine whether it has allowed an inappropriate and exclusionary commitment to displace loyalty to God and God's expansive kingdom.

The broad refusal to leave the world has important recent consequences. For example, during the twentieth century in North America, a number of Protestant churches altered long-standing traditions that excluded women from ordained leadership. More recently, some have altered their stances toward same-sex marriages and the participation of LGBTQ persons in the life and leadership of the church. These changes call for serious theological reflections about creation and the nature of human sexuality, about marriage as a covenantal community of mutual affection and care, and about the welcoming character of a community shaped by an inclusive kingdom-mindedness. But, like the earlier emergence among Calvinists and Puritans of democratic polities within the church as well as their eventual appreciation for the legal separation of church and state, the changes have been made at least in large part in response to broader social and cultural currents. One thinks of the profound influences on the ethos of North American society of newer post–World War Two patterns of participation in education, professions, and the workplace more generally, of feminism and the women's movement, and of movements for LGBTQ liberation. Some deeper consequences of these currents for almost every aspect of Christian life and theology are now being seen, for example, a fuller appreciation for the deleterious consequences of homophobia, sexism, and abuse; a revised and enhanced appropriation of the contributions of women to our own theological traditions; and more diverse seminary faculties and student bodies.[42]

The Church *with* the World

The church is also (or should be) *with* the world, confessing common faults and sins. This follows from piety's knowledge that sin is radical and universal. The church is aware that all persons, movements, and institutions are called to repentance and that all stand in need of reform. And, aided by the many questions and criticisms posed by the world both within and beyond itself, as well as by a radical view of the law and a hope for God's coming kingdom of justice and

42. Barbara Brown Zikmund, "Winning Ordination for Women in Mainstream Protestant Churches," in *Women and Religion in America*, vol. 3, *1900–1968*, ed. Rosemary Radford Ruether and Rosemary Skinner Keller (San Francisco: Harper & Row, 1986), 339–48. On economic, educational, and political conditions that have helped make the women's movement possible, see Janet Saltzman Chafetz and Anthony Gary Dworkin, *Female Revolt: Women's Movements in World and Historical Perspective* (Totowa, NJ: Rowman & Allanheld, 1986), 101–4.

love, the church certainly has every means at its disposal to apply these insights about sin to itself.

When it does so, the church finds itself accused and threatened partly because it has been infiltrated by worldly interests, affections, and interactive patterns, for example, devotion to race or country, false confidence in the salvific powers of wealth and technology, sexist practices, and so on. But it also finds itself beset by misplaced confidence in and devotion to the church for its own sake, as well as by salvific (and even idolatrous) claims made for ecclesiastical traditions and practices. The church is (or ought to be) contrite, and it is (or ought to be) *with* the world confessing sin in *two* related senses. It should confess its captivity to corrupted sociocultural devotions, desires, images, ideas, and practices that plague the world and then are reduplicated and baptized in the church.[43] But it also should confess that it succumbs to the constricting tendencies of the human fault in distinctly ecclesiastical forms.

The history of the church engulfed by sin is just as important as its history in the world responding to and learning from changing currents and conditions. I noted earlier, for example, that anti-Semitism and anti-Judaism have long plagued the church. Again, as is apparent from the history of colonialism in America and elsewhere, the church frequently has been beset by racism. Here we should underscore that many white Protestants in the United States bear heavy burdens for the participation of their churches in a history of violent, unjust, and hateful treatment of people of color and their communities. This is why one point of continued studies, reflections, and statements about racial justice by predominantly white churches in America ought to be a repentant self-examination. These churches know—or ought to know—that the terrible, persistent, and corrupting power of racism does not reduce to mere ignorance. They also ought to know, as James Cone and others have pointed out, that theological discussions need to be approached with a willingness to learn insights into the gospel from others who remain genuinely "other."[44]

The efforts of some churches to correct past judgments about and attitudes toward scientific inquiries and inquirers furnish examples of churches confessing their occasional captivity to distinctly ecclesiastical forms of corrupting con-

43. *Love and Justice: Selections from the Shorter Writings of Reinhold Niebuhr*, ed. D. B. Robertson (Louisville: Westminster John Knox, 1992), 97.

44. See Gayraud S. Wilmore and James H. Cone, eds., *Black Theology: A Documentary History, 1966–1979* (Maryknoll, NY: Orbis, 1979), 135; Major J. Jones, *The Color of God: The Concept of God in Afro-American Thought* (Macon, GA: Mercer University Press, 1987), 2. On the need for repentant self-examination with respect to race, see Reinhold Niebuhr, *Love and Justice*, 128–29, 153. A troubling feature of Niebuhr's call for repentance in this regard is that he connects it with an unsatisfying gradualism.

striction. These exercises in self-criticism try to expunge myopic visions and corrupt rationalities that result from inappropriate if not also idolatrous conceptions of and commitments to ecclesiastical dogma. Partly due to these efforts, some churches have moved from authoritarian and biblicistic condemnations of evolutionary biology and critical historiography toward sponsoring more open inquiries into the relationship between theology and the sciences and also supporting critical methods of biblical scholarship at church-related educational institutions. Note, too, the statements made by Pope John Paul II about "the Galileo case" before a meeting of scientists at Rome in 1983 to commemorate the 350th anniversary of the publication of *Dialogue on the Two Chief World Systems*. It is sometimes pointed out that there were good reasons why some disagreed with Galileo in 1633. But disagreeing is one thing, and condemning those with whom one disagrees is quite another. John Paul II accordingly acknowledged that "the Church's experience during the Galileo affair and after led to a more mature attitude and to a more accurate grasp of the authority proper to her." Nine years later, the pope made a speech vindicating Galileo and restoring the Renaissance scientist as a faithful Christian.[45]

One is tempted to exclaim, "Just in time!" And yet, publicly confessing historic and recurrent faults may be a step toward health, as at some institutions of higher education in the United States, such as Georgetown University and Davidson College, which have formed commissions on slavery and their own institutional histories. For ecclesiastical institutions, confession also may function to check the hubris of a holiness that sees the church as the locus of all truth and light and views the world as nothing other than error and darkness. Confession and repentance constitute the Christian principle of self-criticism. The church ought to be a community that recognizes this, and its confessions of sin should therefore be understood not only to undercut its own self-righteousness but also to strengthen its sense of solidarity with a fragmented and often beleaguered world.

The Church *against* the World

A Christian piety shaped by the symbols of creation, sin, and redemption issues in no simple endorsement of things as they are. Instead, it presses toward new possibilities. This is part of the meaning of confessing common faults and sins; it also follows from piety's claim that we are created for a good and abundant

45. Robert L. Spaeth, "Trial and Error: Galileo and the Church," *This World: A Journal of Religion and Public Life* 20 (Winter 1988): 104–13.

life of true communion in community, as well as from its hope for the kingdom. If it is to be genuine, then, the church's engagement with the world must also be prophetic. The church is called to denounce the inordinate and destructive narrowness that accompanies stances and practices centered on isolated causes and inordinate interests. This is why, as a matter of its faithful mission, the church is also *against* the world, criticizing idols, constrictions, corrupt practices, and irresponsibility.

Conscientious churches do not shrink from the prophetic task. In our own time, they will attest that all are embedded in a single garment of global interdependence. They will testify that the fates of many increasingly are in the hands of many, and they will insist that this profound interdependence magnifies issues of human responsibility. They will point to the perilous consequences for Earth's planetary system and for future generations of our current practices. (Recently, a number of international and US government agencies have issued increasingly dire warnings about accelerating greenhouse gas emissions and carbon dioxide in Earth's atmosphere, and have also indicated that the window of opportunity to address climate change has nearly closed.)[46] They will point to the inhumane suffering of refugees and innocent migrant children, as well as to other terrible costs of inordinately constricted nations and political communities.

Prophetic criticism may provoke pressure and opposition, but it is also possible that the world of political and economic powers will largely dismiss the nuisance and refuse to take the church seriously.[47] In the latter case, prophetic communities have all the more reason to remain in the world, refusing to leave *it* alone, calling into question business as usual, and remembering that cynical realists often underestimate the practical importance of moral legitimacy as well as the extent to which persistent injustice and wanton destruction may provoke deep-seated opposition. There are also circumstances in which the church's prophetic witness may demand the patient resistance of refusals to cooperate with severely unjust and inhumane attitudes, institutions, and practices. Here, prophetic witness connects with important aspects of the doctrine of calling and vocation discussed in the previous chapter. In extreme instances, it may lead the

46. See, for example, Kendra Pierre-Louis, "Greenhouse Gas Emissions Accelerate like a 'Speeding Freight Train' in 2018," *New York Times*, December 5, 2018. Brady Dennis and Chris Mooney, "'We Are in Trouble.' Global Carbon Emissions Reached a Record High in 2018," *Washington Post*, December 5, 2018, quote United Nations Secretary-General Antonio Guterres as saying, "We are in trouble. We are in deep trouble with climate change," in his remarks at the opening of the twenty-fourth annual UN Climate Conference in Poland.

47. Hans Küng, *The Church*, trans. Ray Ockender and Rosaleen Ockender (New York: Sheed & Ward, 1967), 99–100.

church into a *status confessionis*, and therefore into intentional and fundamental noncompliance with civil policies and governments.

The church *against* the world has a passionate history that stretches back to the earliest Christian communities. Followers of Christ sometimes have suffered explicitly for the sake of upholding a good Christian confession. Consider, for example, the persecutions of Christians at the hands of imperial power in ancient Rome: apostles imprisoned, Polycarp, bishop of Smyrna, burned for refusing to curse Christ and say, "Caesar is Lord." John Fox noted in his *Universal History* that early martyrs, both celebrated and obscure, often took Jesus to be their example, as well as their comforter and Savior.[48] Similar instances during the twentieth century include the struggles of some "confessing Christians" under Hitler and the trials of a number of churches under Soviet rule.[49] Less frequently mentioned are the persecutions of Korean Christians at the hands of the Japanese government and occupying troops during the first half of the twentieth century.[50] In every case, the willingness of governments to engage in systemic and violent persecutions reveals a corrupt politics, if not also political idolatry.

Recent examples also come from Latin America. One recalls, for example, the murder of Archbishop (and now Saint) Oscar Romero in San Salvador, as well as the widespread imprisonment, killing, and expulsion of Jesuits and other priests by totalitarian regimes.[51] In many of these instances there emerges a pattern not unlike the one associated with more purely religious persecutions. Protests against human suffering caused by corrupt economics uncover a corrupt politics that stands behind the economics. The beating and killing of those who protest help to drive home to others how grossly corrupt a given regime has become. The willingness of a regime's leaders to do literally anything in order to suppress protest and preserve their own power undercuts their moral legitimacy.

In our own time and place, the persistence of systemic injustice toward and

48. Robert M. Grant, *From Augustine to Constantine: The Thrust of the Christian Movement into the Roman World* (New York: Harper & Row, 1970), 86; John Fox, *A Universal History of Christian Martyrdom: From the Birth of Our Blessed Savior to the Latest Periods of Persecution* (Philadelphia: Key, Meilke & Biddle, 1832), 5. See also W. H. C. Frend, *Martyrdom in the Early Church: A Study of a Conflict from the Maccabees to Donatus* (Oxford: Basil Blackwell, 1965), 268–302.

49. For illuminating reflections on the latter and some of its lasting effects, see John Burgess, *Holy Rus': The Rebirth of Orthodoxy in the New Russia* (New Haven: Yale University Press, 2017).

50. See Wi Jo Kang, *Religion and Politics in Korea under Japanese Rule*, Studies in Asian Thought and Religion 5 (Lewiston, NY: Edwin Mellen, 1987), 25, 35–39; Donald N. Clark, *Christianity in Modern Korea* (Lanham, MD: University Press of America, 1986), 13–14.

51. Brian H. Smith, "Churches and Human Rights in Latin America," in *Churches and Politics in Latin America*, ed. Danial H. Levine (Beverly Hills, CA: Sage, 1979, 1980), 156, 183–84.

also violence against persons of color indicated by the rates of incarceration for African American men and the recurrence of xenophobic attitudes toward people from Mexico and Central America should come in for special mention. The former continues a line of white corruption and oppression that includes not only slavery but also lynchings and Jim Crow. The latter continues a line of recurrent white prejudice and rejection from early colonial times to the present. And then, there is the continuing and current shameful treatment of Native American tribes.

The church against the world denounces, and in doing so it looks for the good and abundant life of true communion in community for which we are fitted, sustained, and redeemed. By its denunciations and hopes, it testifies to the excellence of the God of grace and the coming kingdom of justice and peace.

The Church *for* the World

A church whose piety is formed through the power of the Spirit and keyed to the symbols of God as Creator, Judge, and Redeemer cannot come to rest only in denunciations and resistance. In the midst of a fragmented and conflicted world, its prophetic vision must also have a constructive dimension. Its passionate witness, emboldened by hope for a new heaven and a new earth (Rev. 21:1), must always press toward new possibilities.

Here, yet another valence of the complex relationship of church and world comes into view. The church is in the world, and it intentionally and pastorally welcomes the world into itself. It is (or ought to be) with the world confessing common faults. As a repentant church, and therefore we may hope in all humility, it also may find itself against the world, denouncing and occasionally resisting corrupted and inhumane practices and demands. But in all these things, it is also fundamentally and finally true that the church is *for* the world.

This follows from piety's apprehension of the divine excellence. The deity, which goes out from itself to create, judge, and redeem, refuses to abandon the world to wayward misdirection and destruction. The God who was in Christ reconciling the world to Godself continues to work for reconciliation, renewal, and the kingdom and its beloved community. The church that proclaims this good news refuses to believe that sin is the last word; it insists that there is always also and decisively a Word of grace.

This is why the church is, or ought to be, a community of hope. Sin means derangement, but grace means rearrangement. Sin means inordinate constriction, but grace means ec-centric enlargement. Sin means broken interrelationships with God and one another, but grace means a divine initiative of acceptance and reconciliation that elicits a new responsiveness to God and neighbor. The church wagers that grace means the turning and rehabilitation of persons and communities, and this wager entails a hope for genuine communion in community. It therefore not only denounces constriction and injustice but it also announces that no person, group, or institution lies beyond regenerating possibilities, and it hopes for a new world.

Enlivened by this hope, Christian communities sometimes point toward and partly embody new possibilities for a more genuine life together. One thinks, for example, of nonhierarchical teachings about mutual service, as well as emphases on hospitality and charitable distributions to the poor in some early Christian communities. By implication, at least, new possibilities for participation surely were presented in ancient communities where "there is no longer Jew or Greek . . . slave or free . . . male and female" (Gal. 3:28). What might it have meant for prospects for new community when the Apostle asked Philemon to receive Onesimus "no longer as a slave but more than a slave, a beloved brother . . . both in the flesh and in the Lord" (Philem. 16)?[52]

There are, of course, also more recent examples. In the midst of myopic and exclusionary societies, churches sometimes structure themselves for inclusion, as did the confessing churches in Germany when they refused to accept "the so-called Aryan paragraph, which called for the exclusion from the church of all Christians with Jewish ancestry."[53] Again, churches sometimes give succor and sanctuary to those who are mistreated and threatened, as a number have for undocumented migrants along the US border with Mexico. This last initiative may be regarded as part of a wider attempt to accompany those who suffer not only in hospitals and prisons but also at border crossings and in refugee camps.[54]

Another example is the reformist posture of black churches in America from the Underground Railroad to the civil rights movement. Here, the efforts of a minority to obtain freedom, justice, and economic opportunity for itself also meant announcing new possibilities for many basic and influential institutions of American society.[55] Note, too, that Martin Luther King Jr.'s realistic strat-

52. Wayne A. Meeks, *The First Urban Christians: The Social World of the Apostle Paul* (New Haven: Yale University Press, 1983), 63–64, 81, 161; Meeks, *The Moral World of the First Christians* (Philadelphia: Westminster, 1986), 113. See also Elisabeth Schüssler-Fiorenza, *In Memory of Her: A Feminist Reconstruction of Christian Origins* (New York: Crossroad, 1984), 205–18. If Schüssler-Fiorenza is correct that the earliest Jesus movement was a "discipleship of equals," then this is another important illustration.

53. "Introduction to the Theological Declaration of Barmen," *Book of Confessions: Study Edition* (Louisville: Geneva, 1996), 303.

54. See chap. 8.

55. C. Eric Lincoln and Lawrence H. Mamiya, *The Black Church in the African American*

egy of nonviolent pressure and resistance also tried to win over opponents in friendship and understanding. Among other things, then, this was a strategy borne by hope and informed by the christological confidence that unearned suffering is redemptive as well as the conviction that God is for the beloved community.[56] We should mention also the involvement of the poor in Christian communities in Latin America that sometimes points toward and prepares for new social possibilities by "developing a vision of faith that encourages people to participate politically."[57] Precisely this, says Gustavo Gutiérrez, is the new and hopeful thing that those who suffer see "germinating in this universe of unmerited afflictions."[58]

Christian piety interprets or construes movements and occurrences such as these as traces of grace, or historical instances where we glimpse the reconciling and renewing trajectory of the Creator, Judge, and Redeemer. In piety's vision, these instances become indicators that point to the curvature of the arc of God's universe, the disposition and direction of the divine excellence. As Reinhold Niebuhr reminds his readers, this should not be confused with excessively optimistic estimates of human nature and accomplishments that rob much bourgeois theory and modern political thought of real wisdom. There is in this strain of Christian piety no sentimental reliance on either human capacity or goodness to transcend the conflicting interests of individuals, classes, and nations.[59] The claim is different: despite sin and beyond tragedy, despite the corrupted intentions and designs of even very powerful human communities and institutions, new possibilities may emerge in the providence of God.

This is partly what it means to say that, in the hopefully realistic view of Christian piety, the arc of the universe is God's arc and that, while we cannot always make out its curvature, it bends toward God's universal kingdom or city. Finally, not without confessing sins and launching prophetic criticisms, and not apart from enduring chastening judgments and passionate sufferings, Christian piety hopes because it believes that the power of goodness is greater than the

---

Experience (Durham, NC: Duke University Press, 1990), 212. The civil rights struggle during the 1960s was, among other things, a fight of a minority movement for a new American society. See Taylor Branch, *The Parting of the Waters: America in the King Years, 1954–1963* (New York: Simon & Schuster, 1988), 413–91.

56. King, *A Testament of Hope*, 5–9, 12, 18, 20, 41–42.

57. Scott Mainwaring, "Brazil: The Catholic Church and the Popular Movement in Noya Iguacu, 1974–1985," in *Religion and Political Conflict in Latin America*, ed. Daniel H. Levine (Chapel Hill: University of North Carolina Press, 1986), 148.

58. Gustavo Gutiérrez, *We Drink from Our Own Wells: The Spiritual Journey of a People*, trans. Matthew J. O'Connell (Maryknoll, NY: Orbis, 1984), 120.

59. Reinhold Niebuhr, *The Children of Light*, 16, 31.

powers of evil. "For God so loved the world . . ." God is for a world reconciled and renewed, for all creatures in their appropriate interrelations with God and with one another.

The promising historical developments, personal hopes, and traces of grace that piety construes as indicators need not bear any direct connection to Christian churches and traditions. Humanitarian works of nongovernmental organizations, such as Doctors without Borders, spring to mind. Or, again, though complexities and ambiguities abound, especially when we estimate the actions and policies of nations, it is difficult not to be impressed by victors sending supplies to former foes under the auspices of the Marshall Plan following World War Two. One may be impressed as well by the willingness of the current German chancellor, Angela Merkel, to take substantial political risks in order to frame a conscientious and welcoming reception of refugees and immigrants.

It is a matter of importance that we not overpromise. All these actions, movements, and groups are subject to criticisms; none brings in the kingdom. None fulfills the promise of true communion in community. Moreover, and as we saw earlier in christological sections of this systematic, the New Testament knows of no resurrection apart from crucifixion. Note, too, for example, that in Memphis during his last speech, Martin Luther King Jr. says not only that he has been to the mountaintop and seen the promised land, but also that he personally may not get there. His more tempered but nonetheless appropriately bold message of hope is rather "that we, as a people will get to the promised land."[60]

In a more personal text, and also apart from Christian overtones and symbols, Nelson Mandela, who was imprisoned for twenty-seven years from 1962 until 1990, keeps hope alive while writing on February 4, 1969, to his daughters Zenani and Zindzi (then ten and nine years old, respectively).

> Zindzi says her heart is sore because I am not at home and wants to know when I will come back. I do not know, my darlings, when I will return. You will remember that in the letter I wrote in 1966, I told you that the white judge said I should stay in jail for the rest of my life.
>
> It may be long before I come back; it may be soon. Nobody knows when it will be, not even the judge who said I should be kept here. But I am certain that one day I will be back at home to live in happiness with you until the end of my days.
>
> Do not worry about me now. I am happy, well and full of strength and hope.[61]

60. King, *A Testament of Hope*, 286.

61. *The Prison Letters of Nelson Mandela*, 63–64.

A letter written twelve days later to his eldest daughter, Makaziwe, then about fifteen years old, takes a different tack in response to hearing about her progress in her studies and her ambition to become a doctor or a scientist.

> Both are strenuous professions and you must work hard and steadily during school terms and have a good rest during school holidays. I see that you are afraid of being kidnapped one day when you have discovered a dangerous drug. Do not worry much, darling, about kidnappers. Their world is getting smaller and smaller and their friends fewer. One day there will be a new world when all of us will live in happiness and peace. That world will be created by you and me; by Kgatho, Zeni & Zindzi; by our friends and countrymen. When you become a doctor or scientist and use your knowledge, training and skill to help your people who are poor and miserable and who have no opportunity to develop, you will be fighting for that new world.[62]

Robin W. Lovin says that, "looking back on the last third of the twentieth century"—at the end of segregation in the United States, the "velvet revolution," the fall of the Berlin Wall, Nelson Mandela's release from prison and the end of apartheid in South Africa—the expectations of some Christian realists were too low.[63] The point of realism is to estimate possibilities and limits accurately, which is a risky business in any era or time. Things change. Revolutions and promising victories may be followed by disappointments and delays, as well as by cruel reversals and defeats. But even if one questions the overoptimism of some liberal progressives and some recent liberationist and feminist theologies, they make an undeniably important point. There is a hopeful dimension of realism in historical life that "only those who view events from outside the centers of power" are likely to provide, namely, a robust sense even in the face of trying and unpromising circumstances that "something else is, nevertheless, possible."[64]

Proposition #67 Current challenges posed by the effects of human activity on our planetary home and by the prospects for sustainability call for both realism and hope.

I turn now to a pressing and illustrative issue. What, in rather broad brush-strokes, does the current challenge of sustainability look like from the viewpoint

62. *The Prison Letters of Nelson Mandela*, 65–66.

63. Robin W. Lovin, *Reinhold Niebuhr* (Nashville: Abingdon, 2007), 66; Lovin, "Christian Realism: A Legacy and Its Future," *Annual of the Society of Christian Ethics* 20 (2000): 14.

64. Lovin, "Christian Realism," 14.

of my theology? I believe an outline of an answer to this question will suggest prominent lines along which my fuller interpretation of prospects for renewal in a fragmented world might move. And, there are two reasons I think this particular illustration apt. First, it accords with my rather strong theological insistence that we understand human life in the wider and interdependent context of planet Earth and the cosmos. Second, it throws into sharp relief my estimate of some practical consequences of our human abilities and limitations, our fault, and grounds for hope.

Let me dwell momentarily on the first point. Earlier in this systematic, I claim creation is a vast cosmic ecology within which we live and move in interdependent patterns and interrelationships. When we act we interact, though we needn't keep the entirety of things in view at once. Indeed, except in more or less symbolic ways, that is impossible for us, and so, in our practical lives, it is entirely appropriate for us to pay special attention to the particular "neighborhoods," relevant wholes, natural orderings, and cultural contexts in which we are more immediately involved. Nevertheless, a robust doctrine of creation lends to Christian piety a profound awareness of our "situatedness" in broader contexts as well as the fact that our actions have consequences for persons, animals, and plants linked together with us in intricate and interdependent systems.

Again, the cosmic ecology within which we live and move is dynamic. Systems and subsystems, from ponds and seas to families, societies, and planets, involve continual interactions and energy transfers. Stars, planets, and civilizations coalesce, vary in their characteristics over time, and die. In fact, I find this dynamism sufficiently prominent to justify talk about the encompassing dynamic stream of things within which we live and move as a vast cosmic passage. The many subsystems, orderings, and interrelationships often remain stable for a time, but they are always also in process. Moreover, we should emphasize that we participate in this stream, and so, while we often depend on the stabilities, alterations, and changes that emerge, it makes little sense to treat them as if they were still-life displays that can never be altered or (occasionally) also improved. Even so, within particular "neighborhoods," ecologies, and systems (both natural and social), we also recognize important sustaining features that remain stable for significant periods, are not of our own doing, and contribute to habitats on which we and other forms of life depend.[65] Thus, in a theological perspective, part of the reason why the challenge of sustainability is so important is that we now are damaging sustaining features in God's good and dynamic creation.

65. See chap. 3, prop. #28, and chap. 4, prop. #32.

The Problem

Begin with an informal inventory. Human activity, especially but not only our continued use of fossil fuels, contributes significantly to global warming, climate change, and environmental degradation. Moreover, many of our most prominent projects—housing, industry, transportation, and agriculture—consume more and more land surface and resources, thus dramatically shrinking habitat for other animals and for plants. Our use of pesticides threatens insect and bird populations on which many plants and animals depend. Garbage sickens our seas. We are fishing a number of marine species to the brink of extinction, killing elephants for their ivory tusks, and driving indigenous peoples from their historic homelands. There is a growing belt of space debris encircling the earth. Small wonder that some commentators picture our presence as an infestation or a disease.

I am not going to present evidence for any of these statements; I simply assume they are true (and that, if they turn out not to be, with a little imagination the broad-brush exercise will still function to illustrate my theological vision in much the same way). I note, too, that some scientists, environmentalists, and ethicists debate whether we now live in the Anthropocene epoch, a term that names us humans as principal drivers of a new geological era following the Holocene, which began about 11,600 years ago after the last glacial period, which, in turn, followed the Pleistocene epoch, or "Ice Age." But we don't have to take a position in this debate to observe the extraordinary and growing influence that humans and their activities are having on the planet.

In our current circumstance, then, many ask whether we can preserve or protect ecological systems. Depending on what one means by preserving and protecting, this may be a comparatively high bar, given our profound influences (some of which, if we are to live at all, seem inevitable) and also the inherent dynamism of systems and ecologies. Another debated term is "sustainability." It points to the possibility that we may achieve a kind of balance in which our activities and use of resources will enhance, or at least not destroy, current and future prospects for meeting human needs and aspirations. A sustainable economy, for example, would be one that incorporates ecological limits and does not regard environmental costs as mere externalities, which can be ignored. There is also the matter of how the environmental costs of various enterprises may be fairly distributed among persons and populations. A sustainable society, then, will order economic and social institutions and practices so that significant natural resources and life-support systems will continue and significant costs and benefits will be equitably distributed.[66] It is possible, of course, to conceive

66. "Restoring Creation for Ecology and Justice," a report adopted by the 202nd General

of this balance in an excessively anthropocentric fashion. That worry may perhaps be mitigated if, instructed by very many scientific findings, more than a few ecological disasters, and a robust doctrine of creation, we emphasize the profoundly interdependent set of ecological interrelations in which we stand with other animals as well as with plants, astrophysical developments, geological processes, chemical processes, and so on. In any case, for my purposes here, I will regard "sustainability" as a word that refers to a balance in our dynamic interrelations with our context on Earth sufficient to avoid catastrophically destructive consequences for the planet's ecology and for ourselves, and also to support our abilities to better meet critical human needs within tolerably just and good societies.

Planetary-Scale Thinking, Human Responsibility and Limits

The next time you fly over the state of Indiana on a clear day, look down at the checkerboard pattern—now also dotted with center-pivot irrigation circles. Beavers affect topography when they build dams, but a large proportion of the surface of Indiana—once covered with forest—appears as it does today due to the highly productive agricultural practices of humans. We also know the water that runs off the fields contains fertilizers and other chemicals used to increase crop yields. Here is an important point. *Our increasing technological and organizational capabilities, in this case industrial-scale farming, and our increasing knowledge of their intricate and far-reaching consequences, for example, chemicals that run off and alter the ecological systems of the Ohio and Mississippi Rivers and eventually wind up in the Gulf of Mexico, also increase or ought to increase our sense of responsibility.* (While we're picking on Indiana, we might also mention pollutants pumped into the air in and around Gary that end up in the lungs of people farther east.)

The basic point in the previous paragraph—our responsibilities increase as our capabilities and knowledge increase—is an entirely conventional one, and it underlies almost every discussion of the challenges of managing our relationships with the environment. Now introduce a more recent line of reflection that we may call planetary-scale thinking. We are increasingly aware that Earth's local and regional ecologies are interconnected and that life regularly impacts and

Assembly (1990), Presbyterian Church (USA) (Louisville: Office of the General Assembly, 1990), 24, links sustainability with stewardship and "the incorporation of earth-keeping into earth management." It also draws on additional biblical images when it maintains that "the steward is a manager, charged with responsibility for tilling and keeping for the sustenance of the household."

shapes Earth's entire planetary system in ways that are critical for life. For example, without gases released by microbes into Earth's atmosphere during its longer history, you and I would be unable to breathe. Again, a high proportion of Earth's soil is actually organic matter. Life doesn't simply adapt to inert environments; it interacts with and also helps to constitute a dynamic environmental system. Life helps to shape the habitat for life. We should therefore acknowledge that (1) there is no life that does not impact Earth's planetary system, and (2) we humans, as well as other forms of plant and animal life, are deeply embedded in Earth's specific interdependent systems that have developed over time partly due to the impacts of different organisms. This knowledge serves to heighten, complicate, and extend our knowledge of the interactions of organisms, including us, with the dynamic and interdependent processes that make up our planetary home. Life, we should acknowledge, is a planetary phenomenon.[67] In my judgment, this also intensifies our responsibility. And it is among the observations that require us to regard sustainability as a complex and ineluctably *global* challenge.

Now add a dollop of astrobiology, the multidisciplinary field that studies the story of life and its distribution in the universe.[68] A basic point here is that, while we have good reasons to focus our attention on Earth as a "neighborhood" or relevant whole, we should not forget that items critical for Earth's story, including the production and distribution of elements critical for life, cannot be separated from the considerably longer and wider story of the universe. Moreover, we cannot be at all certain, given what we know of the size, age, and future duration of the universe, the number of galaxies, stars, and planets it contains, and the distribution of water, that there has not been, is not now, or shall not be life elsewhere.[69]

We therefore reach an important, double-barreled conclusion about human responsibilities and limits. In the light of our increasing capabilities, including space probes, etc., and also our increasing knowledge of Earth as a planetary system interconnected with the wider universe, we obtain *both* an increased sense of our responsibilities *and* an enhanced sense of our dependence and our limits. We have a very significant impact on Earth as a planetary system and its prospects, and we also are embedded in and highly dependent on this same system. It therefore seems appropriate, at least in some sense, to see ourselves as managers or caretakers of planet Earth, and even to speak of "Earth in human

67. Eric Smith and Harold J. Morowitz, *The Origin and Nature of Life on Earth: The Emergence of the Fourth Geosphere* (Cambridge: Cambridge University Press, 2016), 2–5.

68. Ximena C. Abrevaya et al., "The Astrobiology Primer v2.0," *Astrobiology* 16, no. 8 (2016): 562.

69. Abrevaya et al., "The Astrobiology Primer v2.0," 565–73, 613–23.

hands." Nevertheless, our knowledge of how the entire system works as well as of the potential consequences of certain interventions is clearly limited.[70] Theologically speaking, this limitation alone requires us to conclude, despite our increasing knowledge and acumen, that we have not escaped all conditions of creatureliness and finitude. Clearly, and as a number of environmental impacts and disasters indicate, we often become mired in unanticipated and unintended consequences. Moreover—and this next point takes on considerable significance as we estimate our prospects for resolving the multifaceted and global challenge of sustainability—amidst the swirl of interests, aims, ideas, and practices endemic to historical human communities and institutions, our political abilities to organize and pursue fair and wise courses of action seem not only limited but also greatly troubled. Add to the mix the idea that, given our present scientific estimates of its longevity and size, we clearly are not equipped to be managers or caretakers of the entire universe. (Some things are better appreciated than managed, and currently we are in very little danger of reduplicating either the omnipotence or the omniscience attributed to God by some classical traditions.)

Prospects for Sustainability

Return now to the practical challenge. It's complicated, with many dimensions and moving parts. In his encyclical letter *Laudato Si': On Care for Our Common Home*, Pope Francis includes a call for "an ecological conversion," a new lifestyle, spirituality, and education that will critique myths of modernity and support "an 'ecological citizenship.'"[71] (Somewhat similarly, the astrobiologist David Grinspoon writes of a "dramatic moment of awakening," "a new global conversion," and even the project of committing ourselves "scientifically and spiritually" to "creating a sustainable civilization.")[72] Francis also refers to an "integral ecology" that includes not only natural systems but also cultures, and so highlights threats to important human goods like housing, and transportation, as well as justice for the poor and between generations.[73] Again, Francis notes that appropriate lines of action in response to current threats and their global scale

70. See David Grinspoon, *Earth in Human Hands: Shaping Our Planet's Future* (New York: Grand Central, 2016). Grinspoon is aware of limitations in our knowledge that render some possible Earth interventions for addressing global warming, for example, solar radiation management, currently unwise (177–85).

71. Pope Francis, *Laudato Si': On Care for Our Common Home* (Huntington, IN: Our Sunday Visitor, 2015), 137, 140–43.

72. Grinspoon, *Earth in Human Hands*, 459, 462, 468.

73. Francis, *Laudato Si'*, 93–108.

require international dialogues and enforceable agreements, as well as a politics that is not subject simply to an economy for which profit is the sole criterion, and an economy that is not "subject to the dictates of an efficiency-driven paradigm of technocracy."[74] By the pope's reckoning, in short, we need new models of progress and growth, as well as a politics of international cooperation that is responsive to the common good and attentive to scientific findings, grants freedom for the development of capabilities present at every level of society (the principle of subsidiarity), and is also sufficiently farsighted to take long-term futures into account.[75]

Does Francis sufficiently appreciate the difficulties entailed in fashioning a new political order sufficient to meet the sustainability challenge? That is difficult to say. Claiming that "interdependence obliges us to think of *one world with a common plan*," he insists that "a global consensus is essential for confronting deeper problems, which cannot be solved by unilateral actions on the part of individual countries."[76] We urgently need "enforceable international agreements," "global regulatory norms," "stronger and more efficiently organized international institutions," and indeed, "an agreement on systems of governance for the whole range of so-called 'global commons.'"[77] One of Francis's points is that, while nongovernmental organizations, local communities, smaller pilot projects, and changed personal attitudes and habits are genuinely important, the global nature of the problem demands at least some quite significant global approaches. Moreover, global governance in support of sustainable interrelations with Earth's planetary system will require the rethinking of national interests. Francis quotes the following statement by Pope Benedict XVI: "To manage the global economy; to revive economies hit by the crisis; to avoid any deterioration of the present crisis and the greater imbalances that would result; to bring about integral and timely disarmament, food security and peace; to guarantee the protection of the environment and to regulate migration: for all this, there is urgent need for a true world political authority, as my predecessor Blessed Pope John XXIII indicated some years ago."[78]

Anyone familiar with the founding of the United Nations, and the strategies deployed to accommodate world powers as well as the principle of national sovereignty, will be somewhat skeptical, I think, of the prospects for "a true world political authority." Neither are they likely to think the cause of world cooperation will

74. Francis, *Laudato Si'*, 123.

75. Francis, *Laudato Si'*, 128–29.

76. Francis, *Laudato Si'*, 110.

77. Francis, *Laudato Si'*, 115.

78. Benedict XVI, *Caritas in Veritate* (June 29, 2009), chap. 5, para. 67, quoted by Pope Francis in *Laudato Si'*, 116.

be furthered by present international trends toward identity politics and by troubling tendencies, from Rome to Washington, DC, to exclude or even demonize immigrants and refugees. In my theological perspective, these developments are emblematic of countervailing forces intimately connected with the human fault, such as the perennial strength among human communities of inordinately partial interests as well as of recurrent in-group preferences and out-group aversions. Moreover, many of these partial interests, in-group preferences, and out-group aversions are thematized by cultural images and ideas that are then transmitted from generation to generation. There is also a tendency, visible in many corners of the world today, toward ethnic and nationalist idolatries. I therefore think we should be careful not to be beguiled into a naïve optimism.

Still, there are also some important bright spots. Francis mentions current agreements about governance of the oceans, as well as the 1992 Earth Summit in Rio de Janeiro, the 1972 Stockholm Declaration, the Basel Convention on hazardous wastes, the binding convention on international trade in endangered species, the Vienna Convention, and the Conference of the United Nations on Sustainable Development, "Rio+20" in 2012.[79] We might add the nonbinding Paris Accords on climate change, as well as initiatives, such as the European Union Emissions Trading Scheme, that try to join government policies and incentives in ways that make it economically feasible for nations and businesses to limit the release of greenhouse gases. There are also popular movements and demonstrations, such as the "School Strike for the Climate" initiated by Greta Thunberg outside Swedish Parliament in August 2018. Grinspoon notes the good news that "our world is on track to be completely free of polio by the year 2018," and he also mentions as "a hopeful microcosm" progress made protecting the Asian snow leopard by local communities and nongovernmental organizations in Pakistan, Afghanistan, Tajikistan, and China whose efforts draw on satellite-enhanced tracking, sophisticated models, and coordination on the ground.[80] I shall return to some of these strategies and how they relate to theologically recognized grounds for hope. For now, I note that I am inclined to characterize them as traces or sparks of grace rather than as elements of a strong argument for high confidence that our future will be a sustainable one.

I think the piety I have developed in this systematic an appropriate one for faithful living in what Grinspoon calls the "mature Anthropocene"—a phase or period in which we no longer tinker accidentally with planetary evolution but become conscious of the planetary changes we induce.[81] Such a piety ac-

79. Francis, *Laudato Si'*, 111–12, 115.
80. Grinspoon, *Earth in Human Hands*, 467.
81. Grinspoon, *Earth in Human Hands*, 225–26.

knowledges significant human capabilities, limits, and responsibilities; our embeddedness in and dependence upon Earth's planetary system; and possibilities for mitigating climate change by appealing to the partial economic interests of persons and groups (aspects of the idea of creation), as well as our significant and chronic misdirection and irresponsibility (dimensions of the human fault). It therefore entails senses or feelings of dependence, interdependence, possibility, and remorse or regret. It inclines us to acknowledge that a part of our human calling is to be managers or stewards of Earth, but it also entails a spirituality that stresses our solidarity with other creatures, our strong interconnection with Earth, and an inkling for the divine excellence that meets us in and through the natural environment. In addition to management or stewardship, then, another aspect of our human calling is to appreciate with awe, wonder, gratitude, and joy the planetary and cosmic contexts over which we often exert little or no influence and within which we are situated and sustained. Indeed, I suspect that a truthful and appropriate regard for our calling as stewards or managers depends partly on this spirituality (or something like it) as well as on a lively and profound regard for our calling as embedded appreciators.[82]

May we also add to piety's inventory a sense of hope that engages our current circumstance and the challenge of sustainability? I think so.

Let me outline this sense of hope by recounting parts of two discussions about our future prospects for a sustainable civilization between Grinspoon and Frank Rosenzweig, a microbial biologist, at which I was privileged to be present. Grinspoon admits that reasonable people come to different conclusions about the future. He also confesses that he doesn't know what is going to happen, though he tends toward a "pragmatic optimism" that looks to human powers of imagination, abstraction, and foresight to negotiate the Anthropocene in sustainable directions.[83] At points he borrows from Teilhard de Chardin's notion of the Noosphere—a realm of mind or intelligence enveloping Earth—in order to speak of a *Sapieozoic* aeon in which cognitive processes become dominant and global intelligence becomes "a lasting planetary force."[84] He is also willing to contemplate world ships that, over periods of time spanning generations, will transport human communities to exoplanets.[85]

When Grinspoon looks to the future, he sometimes pictures three rough scenarios with the help of three cartoon panels drawn by R. Crumb in 1988 as the "Epilogue" to a series of twelve drawn in 1979 and entitled "A Short His-

82. See chap. 5, prop. #41.
83. Grinspoon, *Earth in Human Hands*, 478.
84. Grinspoon, *Earth in Human Hands*, 230, 271, 275.
85. Grinspoon, *Earth in Human Hands*, 457–62.

tory of America." One of the more recent panels, labeled "Worst Case Scenario: Ecological Disaster," depicts an overheated wasteland of depletion, decay, and abandonment. A second, "The Fun Future: Techno-Fix," shows a clear blue sky with flying disks transporting people across a neat town of manicured lawns, well-maintained roads, and buildings of forward-looking design. The third, "The Ecotopian Solution," features large trees, dirt roads, a vegetable stand, and people walking, riding bicycles, and living in smaller, unobtrusive buildings. Grinspoon's point is that we all want to avoid the first scenario, but that a more realistic picture of a possible and positive future will need to combine features of the last two.[86]

Rosenzweig takes a different tack; he raises a question that should concern all of us. Where are the poor located in these panels? If anything like present social trends continue, he says, any realistic portrait of the future will need to incorporate elements of the "Worst Case Scenario." Recalling a remark made by a young biologist in Canada who came across a butterfly many thought extinct, Rosenzweig uses the metaphor of driving a car down a winding mountain road at a high speed and tapping the brakes to avoid or at least delay going over a cliff. Even so, he says, here too we encounter an element of "pragmatic optimism": in order to keep to the task at hand, we have to believe that humanity will somehow muddle through.

From my perspective, there is much to commend in both sides of the discussion. Crumb's three panels are imaginative pictures or portraits—something like religious visions of human destiny. They are symbolic, perhaps even mythological, and they present channel buoys, warning signs, inspirations, and hopes. I think Grinspoon is right—each of the aspirations expressed in panels two and three is incomplete and needs to be supplemented or corrected by the other. Again, both Grinspoon and Rosenzweig, in the face of having to work and act toward an unknown future, maintain measures of "pragmatic optimism," though I think Rosenzweig's question about the place of the poor and his Camus-like parable about tapping the brakes on a mountain road introduce not only genuinely helpful but also haunting elements.

On balance, what I call hopeful realism yields a view of prospects for sustainability more like Rosenzweig's than Grinspoon's. Consider a brief inventory of theologically supported grounds for hope.

We may hope, I think, that appeals to the consciences and moral sensibilities of persons and communities will have an effect. Theologically, this follows from the creation theme. Humans are good creatures endowed, among other things, with capacities to attend to others. In terms of responses to environmen-

86. Grinspoon, *Earth in Human Hands*, 257.

tal degradation, there is an analogy with the appeal to the consciences and moral sensibilities of opponents and other white Americans that Martin Luther King Jr. believed *nonviolent* demonstrations might make during the civil rights movement in the United States. Sensitive persons, trained in universalizing traditions of philosophies, cultures, and religions, feel some sense of solidarity with and obligation to an inchoate community of all humanity. Given some experiences or knowledge of dire conditions, these sensibilities and their salutary effects may extend to groups other than our own that seem especially vulnerable to effects of climate change, for example, poor communities in coastal regions and subsequent generations. Under the impact of planetary-scale thinking as well as notions of the value, beauty, and interdependence of all creatures, some of these sensibilities may extend to nonhuman nature as well.

Nevertheless, as Calvin insists, our sense of equity falters when we consider and confront our own cases and circumstances. A feature of sin or the human fault is that our partial interests and corrupted devotion often cloud not only our sense for justice but also our moral feelings and affections for others. We are not wholly misdirected, and so appeals to the moral sensibilities of persons and groups with respect to the effects of environmental degradation on others remain important. Even so, these appeals are neither as untroubled nor as effective as we sometimes believe or wish. To continue the analogy above, this, in fact, is why King endorsed a strategy of nonviolent *resistance* that might not only appeal to opponents' residual moral sensibilities but also dramatize the issue of injustice and actively pressure prejudiced, partial, and sometimes also calculating politicians and communities.[87]

Again, government-imposed guidelines and requirements can help to mitigate climate change and environmental degradation. Taxes on gasoline, for example, can reduce consumption. As was indicated by the "yellow vest" protests in France in 2018–2019, however, even when government has the will to impose environmentally beneficial tariffs, care must be taken that financial burdens do not fall disproportionately and unfairly on those least able to afford them.[88] Government standards for fuel consumption or automobile "mileage" also have been helpful, though in the United States a rise in emissions appears to have been driven by low gas prices and bigger cars. Government regulation of carbon emissions, for example, from coal-burning power plants, is another tool, but it often waxes and

87. See "Pilgrimage to Nonviolence" and "Letter from Birmingham City Jail," in King, *A Testament of Hope*, 39, 291–92.

88. Alissa J. Rubin and Sumini Sengupta, "'Yellow Vest' Protests Shake France. Here's the Lesson for Climate Change," *New York Times*, December 6, 2018.

wanes in accord with economic conditions.[89] We may hope deleterious effects of industry will also be mitigated by initiatives that appeal to partial economic interests. For example, the European Union Emission Trading Scheme, which came into existence in 2005, tries to link government policies and incentives in ways that render it in the economic interests of nations and businesses to limit the release of greenhouse gasses. Countries agree on national emission caps that are approved by the EU Commission and then allocate tradable allowances to their industrial operators. The scheme, a prime example of "cap and trade," has been "a crucial cornerstone of the efforts . . . made by EU member states to fulfill . . . targets of the Kyoto Protocol."[90] Commentators disagree about the scheme's precise effects. In 2015, there was evidence that it reduced carbon emissions significantly, did not diminish economic performance, and also helped to spur innovation in clean technologies.[91] This was not enough to keep the world from record levels of greenhouse gas emissions in 2018, though, in fairness, it should also be noted that the biggest polluters were the United States, China, and India, rather than the EU.[92]

So, even apart from more dramatic techno-fixes, such as orbiters to reflect sunlight (which ought not to be discounted, though the global governmental mechanisms to implement them, not to mention the technology itself, remain largely speculative), if we can get our more conventional political-economic acts together, there are promising possibilities.[93] It must also be said, however, that there is no historical instance of the sorts of rapid changes in infrastructure that would be needed to hold global warming to acceptable levels, and, indeed, the UN Intergovernmental Panel on Climate Change said in October of 2018 that, if we are to prevent the worst consequences of climate change, we have about a

89. Dennis and Mooney, "We Are in Trouble." Moreover, significant ambiguities continue to impress. In June of 2019, the *Guardian Observer* ran an article noting environmental progress in Britain, and also that, during the first six months of 2019, fossil fuels produced "less than half of UK electricity for the first time." Jillian Ambrose, "Fossil Fuels Produce Less Than Half of UK Electricity for First Time," *Guardian Observer*, June 21, 2019. Two days earlier, however, the *New York Times* reported that, at the direction of the Trump administration, the Environmental Protection Agency in the United States had completed its plan to keep coal plants open longer and to protect the coal industry. Lisa Friedman, "E.P.A. Finalizes Its Plans to Replace Obama-Era Rules," *New York Times*, June 19, 2019.

90. Ulrich Oberndorfer and Klaus Rennings, "Costs and Competitiveness Effects of the European Union Emissions Trading Scheme," *European Environment* 17 (2007): 1–17.

91. Ralf Martin, Mirabelle Muuls, and Ulrich J. Wagner, "The Impact of the European Union Emissions Trading Scheme on Regulated Firms: What Is the Evidence after Ten Years?" *Review of Environmental Economics and Policy* 10, no. 1 (Winter 2016): 143–45.

92. Dennis and Mooney, "We Are in Trouble."

93. Note, too, the possible, if also controversial, role of nuclear power in reducing carbon and greenhouse emissions.

decade to take unprecedented actions.[94] The historical track record is genuinely troubling. Nevertheless, even as we grapple with admittedly narrow and often corrupted human interests, communities and governments are not simply fated to plunge headlong into disaster. There are prospects for improvement despite our misdirection, and, theologically speaking, the possibility that even our partial interests may be directed toward better ends is a feature of divine sustenance, or what classical thinkers called the doctrine of preservation.

This, indeed, is an appropriate place to note once more that our inabilities to anticipate and control all relevant outcomes may also furnish grounds for hope that things can be different. There is no doubt that, when it comes to mitigating climate change and environmental degradation, we encounter more than a little strategic foot-dragging as well as cynical deceptions in both the political and the economic arenas. But not even the powerful can be certain that such strategies, negative though they may be, will have their intended effects. Brazen injustices as well as the readiness to bring about sickening destruction can prompt deep resentments and determined opposition. Theological realism suggests that destructive injustices cannot prevail indefinitely just because they provoke deep-seated enmity and resistance.

I am convinced, too, that we should reconsider the relevance of the somewhat discredited theological category of divine judgment. As I noted earlier, the basic idea here is not that the trajectories and dynamics of cosmic passage may simply vaporize or destroy. The rather more relational and interactive point is that, in the economy of God's world, the destructive consequences of constricted interests and devotions, skewed lines of practical reasoning, and corrupted patterns of responsibility may sometimes push persons and groups toward repentance and contrition. Intolerable outcomes—the right nightmares and revulsions—may press persons and communities to reevaluate their true interests and to change their ways. We humans sometimes learn best through reflective encounters with disasters we might have avoided, and, theologically, this is to say that judgment can be a dimension of grace. Though surely we may wonder just how many devastatingly destructive disasters finally may be required to constitute a sufficiently "teachable moment" of instructive judgment that can motivate us to change our ways.[95]

94. Dennis and Mooney, "We Are in Trouble"; Chris Mooney and Brady Dennis, "The World Has Just Over a Decade to Get Climate Change under Control, U.N. Scientists Say," *Washington Post*, December 6, 2018. Note, too, that an annual energy review by British Petroleum found that, in 2018, carbon emissions rose at the fastest rate in almost a decade. Jillian Ambrose, "Hopes for Climate Progress Falter with Coal Still King across Asia," *Guardian Observer*, June 16, 2019.

95. With this question in mind, see Somini Sengupta, "The Year Global Warming Turned

Think of it as a sort of cosmic adjustment therapy complete with allusions to crucifixion. At a memorial gathering on Armistice Day in 2018, President Emmanuel Macron of France made a point of distinguishing patriotism from destructive nationalism. This seemed, especially in the then-current context of resurgent nationalism and destructive attitudes toward immigrants and refugees, an attempt to invoke the terror and sacrifice of World War I as a right revulsion. A day earlier, the *Guardian Observer* ran a photo of four Scottish brothers killed in the war, for whom a plaque and a wreath were to be laid, and also noted that their mother never recovered from the loss. Was this a right nightmare? The question, of course, is whether the destructive environmental consequences of our shortsighted and narrow economic interests, our inadequate policies, and our irresponsible habits may function similarly. Might they be looked upon as judgments that prompt us to needed conversions, and so furnish grounds for hope? No doubt, we should join Pope Francis in his call for "an ecological conversion," and his claim that a new lifestyle, spirituality, and education are needed in order to critique excesses of modernity and support "an ecological citizenship."

In any case and in sum, we should also say this. Appeals to moral sensibility, judicious restrictions, strategies aimed at harnessing the engine of our limited and partial interests, the unintended consequences of lethargic and cynical exercises of power and influence, and judgments that may turn persons and communities toward other ways are among the traces of grace for which we may hope.

Theologically speaking, an eschatological dimension begins to come into view. Christian piety looks to sparks and traces of grace, and then, without any-

---

Model into Menace: Crops Fail, Fires Rage and a Scorching Summer Tells Us We're Not Ready," *New York Times*, August 10, 2018, A16. Sengupta reviews current disruptions, including fires in California and Europe, reduced grain harvests in Sweden and El Salvador, and heat-related deaths in Japan. (We may add fires in Australia.) She notes that seventeen of the warmest eighteen years on record have occurred since 2001, and that industrial levels of carbon dioxide grew to record levels in 2017. She also quotes Cynthia Rosenzweig, director of the climate impact group at the NASA Goddard Institute for Space Studies, as saying, "It's not a wake-up call anymore." David Wallace Wells argues that, with respect to climate change, "catastrophic thinking" and "alarmism" are now useful and appropriate. "Time to Panic," *New York Times*, February 17, 2019, in *Sunday Review*, pp. 1, 6–7. See also Christopher Flavelle, "With More Storms and Rising Seas, Which U.S. Cities Should Be Saved First?" *New York Times*, June 19, 2019. Flavelle mentions the high costs of providing even basic storm-surge protection for larger coastal cities like Charleston, Manhattan, and New Orleans, and that it seems unlikely the costs of protecting smaller communities can also be met. Some communities probably will need to be relocated. And, of course, there is also the question of whether and how to meet the costs of protecting coastal cities worldwide, and not only in comparatively wealthy nations.

thing approaching complete empirical confirmation, and claiming to apprehend a curvature or an arc to the trajectory of God's universe, it hopes for something that remains unseen. Its hope clearly does not gainsay possibilities for catastrophe. Moreover, the general biblical expectation that, in order to be truly just, any genuine fulfillment must reverse a good many present structures and practices also intimates something like Rosenzweig's concern that we keep in mind the place of the poor as we reflect on possible futures.

Portraits of a sustainable civilization bear some resemblance to piety's visions and symbols of the end, for example, the kingdom of God, a new heaven and new earth, and the new Jerusalem. They are relevant to historical human expectations, aspirations, and hopes, even though they may also include portraits of judgment, and even though they portray possibilities and circumstances that lie beyond the history we know. I am reminded of comments made by Nadia Sitas, a senior researcher at the Council for Scientific and Industrial Research in South Africa, at a Symposium on Planetary-Scale Thinking held at the Stellenbosch Institute for Advanced Study. Sitas, who has worked with governmental and intergovernmental groups concerned for biodiversity, ecology, and policy, claimed that the idea of sustainability is aspirational, and also said, "most of the global goals [of sustainability] are *not* going to be achieved." She noted, further, that "ten years ago we agreed we didn't want to be where we now are."[96] I expect the sustainable civilization that combines techno- and eco-utopias, and is also a genuine blessing for the poor, the immigrant, the weak, and the sick, is, after all, something like the symbol of God's kingdom. In history, it never entirely arrives, and there are always failings, ambiguities, and injustices to be criticized as well as further hopes to be cherished and pursued. But the symbol helps us to see things truly.

96. The Institute and the Center of Theological Inquiry in Princeton jointly sponsored the symposium, May 28–30, 2018. I took down Nadia Sita's comments in my own notes; any inaccuracy is surely my own.

Chapter Twelve

God the Redeemer

We are in a position now to complete the doctrine of God that drives this systematic: God is Creator, Judge, and Redeemer. This, in my judgment, is the fundamental biblical and symbolic specification of the presiding mystery that envelops life and world. It is a primary theological artifact that expresses and shapes Christian piety's apprehension of the dynamic Something More that we encounter at every turn and in which we live and move. This chapter consists of three propositions that elaborate the third image, God as Redeemer. But before we turn to them, we should remind ourselves of a few salient points concerning God-talk and the threefold schema as a whole.

The first point is that the schema uses mythopoeic discourse to connect the world, human life, and the events of history to Something More, with a presiding mystery in, with, under, but also beyond. This means that its chief symbols are, as Reinhold Niebuhr maintains, always in danger of deceiving.[1] They risk being misread as entirely adequate explanations as they portray the meaningful depth of life, world, and history by making odd and symbolic use of occurrences, stories, and events to intimate that which remains involved in mundane reality but cannot be equated with it.

A second point concerns the relationship between the mythopoeic symbols and some of the affectivities or sensibilities I have associated in this systematic with the religious dimension of our experience.[2] Piety intimates felt encounters with Something More or with an Other in and through our many interactions with objects and others. The traditional language of God as Creator expresses and shapes senses of dependence, thanksgiving, and awe evoked in experiences of contingencies, benefits, gifts, grandeur, and sublimity. Senses of obligation

1. Reinhold Niebuhr, *Beyond Tragedy: Essays in the Christian Interpretation of History* (New York: Scribner's Sons, 1937), 5.

2. See, for example, chap. 1, prop. #5.

and remorse elicited in relationships of responsibility, by requisites for humane community, and by failing to uphold these or to remain steadfast are shaped and expressed by the image of God as Judge. The symbol of God as Redeemer clarifies and expresses inklings of renewing possibilities and assurance elicited by the lifting of diminishing and oppressive conditions as well as by the fact that, despite our shortcomings, failures, and betrayals, we continue to participate in and benefit from persistent openings and excellences. That is, the general sensibilities remain hazy and almost inchoate apart from the historically particular and interpretive key furnished by the biblical and theological tradition and its mythopoeic symbols of God as Creator, Judge, and Redeemer. The symbolic idea of God expresses, clarifies, interprets, and sculpts the additional referential dimension in the experiences of religious persons and communities.

Third, while the schema thematizes and elaborates circumambient reality, it does not dispel the mystery.[3] The three mythopoeic symbols anchor piety's picture of the whole, or of the meaning and dynamics of world-and-humanity-before-God and God-before-humanity-and-world. But they neither univocally describe the entirety nor render it clear and distinct; instead, they point to a reality that finally remains beyond our grasp and control. Unlike the usual technical and commercial vocabularies of modernity, then, piety's symbols push us to depict human life and the world in the context of an overarching and presiding mystery. We do not know all, and, furthermore, the deity is incomprehensibly more than the sum of our knowledge. Piety's symbols thus call for a negative dimension in our reflections or for an awareness of limitations. God will be God, rather than merely our conceptions of God. This must be forthrightly recognized and acknowledged, or else genuine theology is lost.[4]

Fourth, as should also be apparent from my reflections on God as Creator in part 2, I do not think we must choose between nonpersonal and personal images or symbols of the divine.[5] I agree with those who claim that a Protestant and more or less biblical piety emphasizes divine activity and influences in the world and its history.[6] Nevertheless, biblical texts and traditional writers (including

3. Chap. 6, prop. #42.

4. It follows, then, that from the perspective of my theology, the technical and commercial vocabularies of modernity, while often useful, may also become grossly reductive, especially when they are used to depict lived experiences and important emotions and sensibilities. See Douglas F. Ottati, *Hopeful Realism: Recovering the Poetry of Theology* (Cleveland: Pilgrim, 1999), 7–38.

5. Chap. 6, props. #45 and #46.

6. This was a tenet of the biblical theology movement during the mid-twentieth century. See G. Ernest Wright, *The God Who Acts: Biblical Theology as Recital* (London: SCM, 1952). In *The Responsible Self: An Essay in Christian Moral Philosophy* (Louisville: Westminster John

Protestants) often work with a variety of both personal and nonpersonal images of the divine. Thus, Calvin calls God "the fountain of every good" and "the Author of every good."[7] Psalm 23:1 famously refers to the Lord as "my shepherd," and Psalm 42:9 reads,

> I say to God, my rock,
> "Why have you forgotten me?"

Moreover, a number of biblical texts portray God as a rather odd or peculiar agent, for example, one who speaks light into being (Gen. 1:3), and one who acts in and through human agents for good even when they intend to do evil (Gen. 50:20). I think there is genuine wisdom both in the variety of images of God and in the peculiarity of portraits of the divine agent. The deity remains sufficiently mysterious to elude a too definite vocabulary. I also think models of God as a modified agent with broad purposes and as an ordering process or dynamic that manifests certain trajectories or directions are compatible or even complementary, and therefore that piety and theology may use both kinds of symbolism. Indeed, in my judgment, to affirm the God of grace and to say the encompassing tendency of the Real bears on us as a dynamic ordering of grace amount to the same thing.[8]

Fifth, because it is the larger threefold pattern that construes the presiding mystery, the meaning of any one basic image will be badly distorted when and where it is torn away from the others.[9] For example, where it is detached from the symbolic idea of redemption, judgment reduces to destruction apart from prospects for renewal and so ceases to accuse and call for repentance in any practically meaningful way. The symbol of creation, when elaborated without reference to judgment, portrays a world of interdependent interrelations apart from the destructive consequences of sinful and even demonic corruption. Abstracted from the wider pattern of creation and judgment, theologies of redemption naïvely envision possibilities for fulfillment apart from tragedy and misdirection. They fail to foster hope where hope is most severely tested, and they miss restorative dimensions of reconciliation and redemption.

Knox, 1999), 126, H. Richard Niebuhr, who was well versed in the biblical theology of his age, claims that God is acting in all actions that impinge upon you, though he also makes use of nonpersonal terms when he calls God the power of being, etc., in both *The Responsible Self* and *Radical Monotheism and Western Culture, with Supplementary Essays* (Louisville: Westminster John Knox, 1993).

7. Calvin, *ICR* 1.2.1–2.

8. Chap. 6, prop. #46.

9. Chap. 6, prop. #43.

Now for a sixth item: the symbolic portrait of God as Creator, Judge, and Redeemer is also thoroughly relational. Its core statements about or images of the divine invariably intertwine with statements about or images of humanity and world. For example, we do not know what it means to say God is Creator apart from talk about world as good dependent creation and humanity as good, limited, and capable creature. This is another reason why, in this final chapter, as also in others, I am not highly invested in talk about God *a se* (though, when employed judiciously, I am not opposed to it). But the point is reversible and may also be made with respect to my earlier analyses of humanity, history, and world. Theologically speaking, we know these realities more truly in relation to the Creator, Judge, and Redeemer.

A final introductory matter is this. Taken as a whole, the symbolic and relational schema—God as Creator, Judge, and Redeemer—displays the divine disposition, excellence, or dynamic trajectory that sculpts life-before-God into an orientation I call hopeful realism. The threefold divine excellence elicits a practical stance. It prompts a manner of living that gives thanks for gifts of life, capabilities, and interdependencies, expects corruption, contraction, alienation, and death, but nevertheless also continues to look for new possibilities, reconciliation, and life.[10]

Proposition #68 God is Redeemer.

God redeems, but this, of course, is not all.

The Redeemer is the Creator. Biblically speaking, as we interact with the many others, situations, and realities, we find ourselves interacting also with an Other who covenants with Abraham, the God who delivers, constitutes, and saves Israel. But in Israel's mythic poetry, this deity is also the one who governs world and whose dominion we inhabit. This mysterious Deliverer, whose name as Moses receives it cannot be said, and who brings Israel out of Egypt, divides the Red Sea, guides the people through the wilderness, constitutes Israel as a people, and promises them land, is also the Creator who fashions the heavens, spreads out the earth on the waters, and makes the sun and moon to rule over day and night (Ps. 136). The Deliverer, who covenantally constitutes our social life together and our responsibilities, is also the maker who sculpts an encompassing environment of sublimity, sustenance, and interdependence that carries, pushes, and lures us beyond ourselves. This is why Israel sings,

10. Chap. 1, prop. #15.

> Our help [deliverance or redemption] is in the name of the LORD,
> who made heaven and earth. (Ps. 124:8)

The Deliverer is the Creator.

New Testament portraits of the expansive event of redemption in Christ and the Spirit also indicate that the circumambient sovereign mystery who dwells in unapproachable light is the God who creates and redeems. Speaking poetically, and perhaps also quoting a hymn that refers to a process or an event no person possibly could have witnessed, the first chapter of the Gospel of John claims that nothing was made apart from the Logos or principle of redemption that comes to us in Christ. Colossians 1:15, 19–20 says Jesus Christ is "the image of the invisible God" in whom "all things in heaven and earth were created," in whom "all the fullness of God was pleased to dwell, and through him God was pleased to reconcile to [Godself] all things." Paul writes to the church at Corinth that, in Christ, the God who directed Israel through perils and threats was reconciling the world to Godself. Thus "everything has become new" (2 Cor. 5:17). The Spirit discloses this same reconciling and redeeming trajectory when it adopts the world's peoples and nations (many of which chronically are at odds and in conflict) as Christ's brothers and sisters, and hence engrafts them into the one people of God. Christ and the Spirit indicate that the great and presiding mystery—the deity who graciously creates, sculpts interdependent interrelations, and bestows existence, life, and all manner of gifts—is also the gracious God who covenants with Israel, the deity whose purpose is reconciliation, renewal, and a kingdom of justice, shalom, and light. God the Creator is God the Redeemer.

This mythopoeic specification of the divine remains incomplete unless we also observe that redemption is a solution to a problem. Redemption indicates that the world needs redeeming; deliverance indicates that creatures need to be delivered. For Christian piety, then, the world is ruptured, fragmented, mired in corruption, and enslaved to a fault. The Bible therefore depicts a world marked by chronic misdirection and sin. None is righteous, no not one. All fall short of the kingdom and its glory. All must therefore be called to repent. And, indeed, it is just this call to repentance that leads us to a third image: God is Judge.

From piety's perspective, the deity or divine dynamic elicits contrition and repentance in and through the destructive consequences for both others and ourselves of our sinful misdirection. The ready implication of key biblical texts from Genesis 3 to 1 Corinthians 1:26–29 is that whatever eminence we possess, for example, wisdom, might, and nobility, tempts us to pretension, to pretend to be other and more than we are and to exercise our eminence or special power in ways that further our own interests but are unfair to others. Again, the biblical story recounts Israel's persistent and idolatrous attempts to equate its own partial interests with God's will, as well as its chronic injustices toward the poor and the vulnerable. These, in turn, elicit the Lord's insistence that "for three transgressions . . . and for four, I will not revoke the punishment," but also God's promise to raise up ruins and to rebuild and restore (Amos 2:4–6; 9:11, 14). Judgment and a corresponding call to repentance are features, too, of the preaching of Jesus, for example, "The time is fulfilled, and the kingdom of God has come near; repent, and believe in the good news" (Mark 1:15).

Especially in the face of popular misconceptions, we should emphasize that, biblically speaking, God's judgment is not simply destruction as an end in itself. Divine judgments are neither only nor primarily retributive.[11] They issue in calls to repent and change direction; they purify and look toward transformation. This comes through also in apocalyptic visions. Thus the kings of the earth who, together with their armies, are killed and defeated by the rider on the white horse in Revelation 19 subsequently, in Revelation 21, walk by the light of the Lamb and bring their glory into the new Jerusalem. And, in Revelation 22, we read that on either side of the river of the water of life in the city is the tree of life, and that the leaves of the tree of life "heal the nations." Call it a mythopoeic vision of judgment as a transformative aspect or dimension of redemption. The Judge is the Redeemer.

God creates. This elaborates piety's apprehension of the presiding mystery that graciously bestows existence and life in cosmic ecology and passage, and that draws out created life ec-centrically to appreciate a world of interdependent interrelations and to participate in it. God redeems. Now piety depicts the presiding mystery delivering and redeeming skewed and corrupted creatures—judging and eliciting contrition, welcoming persons into new community, and renewing them by expanding their participatory and ec-centric demeanor. God creates. God redeems. Taken together, these statements depict the presiding mystery or depth of reality as *the gracious divine dynamic or the God of grace.*

Jesus as the Christ and the Spirit

Return to the observation that for Christian faith and commitment, the event of redemption in Jesus Christ and the Spirit is the paradigmatic clue to the redeeming trajectory of the presiding mystery. This is where piety discerns most clearly the movement toward welcoming acceptance, new community, renewed life, and the kingdom.

11. See Robert Jenson, *The Works of God*, vol. 2 of *Systematic Theology* (New York: Oxford University Press, 1999), 322–37.

The ministry and message of Jesus focus on the kingdom. The Christ teaches parables of the kingdom, for example, the laborers in the vineyard, and he embodies the kingdom message, for example, eating and drinking with all people, healing, crossing barriers and boundaries to reconcile and establish renewed community with God and others. The Christ accepts the corrupted and misdirected, calls them to repent, and also models an expansive ec-centric manner in life keyed to love of God and neighbor. The Christ crosses barriers and boundaries (cleansing lepers, helping centurions, speaking to a Samaritan woman, etc.) in order to restore true communion and community, and so in this systematic I have emphasized reconciliation and renewed life together. Jesus as the Christ points to God as redeemer, the force or power whose trajectory is toward the kingdom of shalom.

Moreover, in Christ and the Spirit, the new community called church is gathered from all peoples. Here we see the crucifixion/resurrection dynamic, or the pattern of new life in community following tragedy and death that Christian piety takes to be characteristic of the divine and gracious tendency that bears upon us. This is what piety discerns as an articulated movement toward the kingdom in Christ and the Spirit: church and new community emerge/arise out of betrayal, crucifixion, and death. The church becomes a partial, fragmentary symbol of the kingdom (or of the peoples of all nations reconciled into one community). It becomes an integral, if also fragmentary and partial, symbolic embodiment that nevertheless, in the power of the Spirit, manages to point beyond itself toward the kingdom. This is the church as a community of mutual concern and ec-centric mission to the world. Clearly, as we have seen, some of the New Testament portraits of this community are at least partly aspirational, for example, Acts 2:43–47, just because they mean to point beyond the church to a new heaven and earth, or toward the new Jerusalem, though other New Testament portraits seem more realistic, for example, 1 Corinthians. We remind ourselves, as Walter Rauschenbusch rightly insists, that the church is not the kingdom.[12] It is not the new Jerusalem either, and when we confuse the church with these eschatological realities and divine aims, the consequences are destructive and sometimes also demonic. Nevertheless, the church is—aspirationally and, to some extent, actually—a symbol that participates in the reality beyond, to which it points. And so, in addition to Jesus's message and mission, the emergence of the church through

12. Rauschenbusch thinks medieval ecclesiasticism substituted the church for the kingdom of God, thereby putting "the advancement of a tangible and very human organization in the place of the moral uplifting of humanity." *Christianity and the Social Crisis* (Louisville: Westminster John Knox, 1991), 181.

appearances of the risen Lord, both vague and odd and in the ec-centric power of the Spirit, is taken to be an indicator that the presiding mystery redeems.

As we have also seen, when piety looks to the gospel passion narratives, it encounters the right nightmare and the right revulsion, the execution of the inclusively accepting and kingdom-minded one because of the power of our sin. The Christ is arrested and tried. His disciples fall away in a night of betrayal. This nadir of abandonment, suffering, and death starkly portrays the corruption, tragedy, and defeat that greet the Word of God in history. It points toward, underscores, and fixes our gaze on the divine judgment, on the many Calvaries and perennial destructive consequences of sinful misdirection that punctuate human history. The Christ, the kingdom-minded one, comes to his own in order to reconcile and renew and redeem, but the world does not know or recognize him (John 1:10–11). Instead, it executes the Word and wisdom of God and then continues to betray the vulnerable and true. And yet, if we continue to attend to the Christ event in the New Testament, whether by means of visions, eucharistic meals, or proclamation, appearances of the resurrected Jesus nevertheless follow his betrayal, suffering death, and defeat. Still he comes today. The kingdom-minded one continues to be present with and to accompany his disciples. Persons are changed, recommitted to the Christic skein, turned toward the pattern of the kingdom-minded person for others. By the grace of God and beyond tragedy there emerge hope, possibility, and life.

The turning toward renewed (and ec-centric) life in Christ is taken up in the Pauline pattern of persons dying and rising with Christ, of the death of the old person or old manner and orientation in life *and* the birth or emergence of the new person, manner, and orientation in life. This, as we have seen, is regeneration.[13] A key aspect of this transition, especially as described in the later theological tradition, is that, despite our sin and its destructive consequences, we are accepted as valuable or worthy (*justification*). Another is that we begin to be formed or sculpted in Christ and the Spirit (*sanctification*). To this, we should also add the experience of life's ordinary interrelationships and responsibilities moving and directing persons into ec-centric life (*calling, vocation*). There are clearly—and at all these junctures—still fragmentariness, diminishment, and sin. *Simil iustus et peccator*; Luther's dictum remains theologically and existentially accurate. Renewed and sanctified life is a fragmentary symbol that nevertheless participates in and also gestures beyond itself toward a true and eternal life. Piety therefore takes this also to be an indicator that the presiding mystery is Redeemer.

It should be emphasized, once again, that, as many New Testament texts

13. See chap. 10, prop. #60.

including the passion narratives imply, the Redeemer is also our Judge. Judgment is the critical and negating dimension of redemption, new possibility, and renewal. It underscores the gap between us as individuals and as communities and the one who teaches love of God, neighbor, and even enemies, heals the sick, and blesses the poor. Moreover, in piety's view, the suffering of the innocent and kingdom-minded one becomes a synecdoche, standing for, among other things, the destructive consequences of our chronic sinful misdirection. It stands for and points toward our continuing tendency to execute God's wisdom and truth as we press our inordinate interests, overreach in attempts to banish our anxieties, underparticipate in lines and relationships of responsibility, fail to bear the evil in others without vindictiveness because we lay claim to a false self-righteousness, devalue other communities due to our idolatrous devotions to the pretensions of our own, etc. The innocent suffer, and, if we are truthful, our pretensions blind us as well to how our corruptions often sow seeds of self-destruction. Thus, by means of the symbol of judgment, piety expresses a sense of guilt and contrition; it also construes these and other destructive consequences of our misdirection as punishments that may push persons and communities toward repentance and a truer life.

What should not be missed is how this apprehension of a Redeemer who also judges may be extended and developed when communities and persons interpret human life and history. Those who trust in a Redeemer who also judges will be inclined to believe that ideologies of linear and consistent progress toward entirely good lives and societies are shallow and naïve. They will tend to think that naïve optimism about the human prospect routinely underestimates persistent and inordinate human egoism and the consequent need for structures of restraint. They will suspect that naïve optimism tumbles into despair when confronted with the more troubling and intractable aspects of human history. They also are likely to fear that despondent idealists too easily tire of continuing responsibilities, too easily relinquish hope that things can be different, and too often embrace cynical exercises of power that promise to avoid political and social disintegration but fail to uphold the ec-centric insistence on justice and love.

Piety suggests, in short, that much modern culture, politics, and religion prove to be shallow and naïve because they recognize no persistent tension or disjunction between even our highest values and achievements and the person-for-others who embodies the kingdom and the law of love. Just at this point, a tradition that remembers that the Christ accuses supports a clear-eyed view of human history, limitations, and faults without however relinquishing hope. Without the crucifixion, people "are beguiled by what is good in human existence into a false optimism and by what is tragic into despair." Human life remains tragic and self-contradictory, plagued by destructive impulses. This must be clearly recognized, and it is by Christian interpretations of crucifixion and resurrection, atonement and reconciliation. But "the basic message of Christianity is a message of hope *beyond* tragedy." God is Creator and Judge, but not only Creator and Judge. God is also Redeemer. The divine "does not allow human existence to end tragically" but "snatches victory from defeat."[14]

The fundamental idea emerges also when we consider the lone reference to judgment in the Apostles' Creed. The creed's second article affirms that Jesus Christ was conceived by the Spirit and born of Mary, "suffered under Pontius Pilate, was crucified, dead, and buried." It says he descended into hell, rose from the dead, ascended into heaven, and sits on "the right hand of the Father Almighty." And then, finally, it also says, in a phrase that takes up the vivid image of Mark 14:62, "from thence he shall come to judge the quick and the dead."

Luther and others note that the second article as a whole presents an account of the event of reconciliation and redemption.[15] I agree, and therefore also note that we are left with the following question: How does Christ's return to judge the living and the dead form a part of the larger message or theme of reconciliation and redemption?

Calvin offers an important clue when he says, "The Judge is the—Redeemer!"[16] Because this is so, grace triumphs, and piety encourages us to meet our judgment with assurance. Here the Reformer is following Paul. "Who is to condemn? It is Christ Jesus, who died, yes, who was raised, who is at the right hand of God, who indeed intercedes for us. Who will separate us from the love of Christ?" (Rom. 8:34–35). There most certainly is judgment; our misdirection has genuinely grave and destructive consequences. Nevertheless, judgment remains a feature of grace and redemption. The Heidelberg Catechism puts it this way. "Q. How does Christ's return 'to judge the living and the dead' comfort you? A. In all distress and persecution, with uplifted head, I confidently await the very judge who has already offered himself to the judgment of God in my place and removed the whole curse from me."[17] There is, so to speak, a court of divine judgment, but the judge is gracious.

The truth, here expressed in mythopoeic tones, is this. Judgment, which points to a real disjunction and real consequences, cannot simply be passed by; even so, judgment remains a critical and negative part of the larger reality of

14. Reinhold Niebuhr, *Beyond Tragedy: Essays on the Christian Interpretation of History* (New York: Scribner's Sons, 1937), 19, 20 (emphasis added).

15. Luther, "The Creed," in *Sermons I*, ed. and trans. John W. Doberstein, vol. 51 of *LW*, 164–65.

16. Calvin, *ICR* 2.16.18.

17. *BOC* 4.052.

redemption. Even though he apparently is defeated by the powers in history, the uncompromising exponent of love of God, neighbor, and even enemies remains the true and steep standard by which history will be judged. But this true and steep standard is also the one who welcomes all—including tax collectors and sinners—to the feast of true communion with God in community with others. Thus, when measured by this standard, human history will be found wanting, needing to rely on the grace of forgiveness and a discipline of repentance that disallow self-righteousness and inordinate self-regard. And, both fortunately and in fact, the divine judgment—which differs from human judgments—turns out to be mercy. God is Redeemer; God is the God of grace.

For Reinhold Niebuhr, the realistic but also hopeful stance toward human history and prospects that emerges from piety's apprehension of the Creator, Judge, and Redeemer points to illusory elements in other views of history, for example, liberal optimism, Marxist utopianism, and the cynical realism of power politics. Christian believing notes that, periodically, even if not constantly, tragic and self-destructive aspects of human pride and misdirection are borne out in the histories of all individuals, communities, and nations. It notes, too, that, occasionally, even if not consistently, new possibilities for truer life and community emerge following tragedy and misdirection. One might therefore say the gospel is validated negatively to some degree by evidence that both overly optimistic and overly pessimistic worldly wisdoms offer inadequate views of "the total situation."[18] But the ability to be in dialogue with other views and occasionally also to mount trenchant criticisms is not a full-blown apologetic or demonstration of the truth of Christian faith and piety. It is only, but quite significantly, a feature of the church engaging in its interpretative pastoral task as it tries to guide and encourage people in faithful living. It is only, but quite significantly, the effort to invest Christian piety with the measure of intelligibility and, at points, even plausibility, needed to orient and support lives of faithful witness. It is only, but quite appropriately, part of the ordinary business of Christian theology.

In any case, to say that God is Redeemer means that, not without tragedies, sufferings, trials, and setbacks, persons and communities experience possibilities for truer life. They encounter traces of grace, possibilities for forgiveness, renewal, and more genuine life together. To say that God, or the presiding mystery, is Redeemer means that, not apart from judgments and the destructive consequences of misdirection, persons and communities in history may encounter traces of grace, and even the trajectory or arc of the universe toward the king-

18. Reinhold Niebuhr, *Faith and History: A Comparison of Christian and Modern Views of History* (New York: Scribner's Sons, 1949), 165.

dom. They encounter the bestowal of new and renewed possibilities in a world gone awry, and this bestowal promises something more.

The Creator, Judge, and Redeemer Is the God of Grace

God is Creator, Judge, and Redeemer. This threefold statement is finally what we mean by saying that the presiding mystery is the God of grace. In fact, the overall dynamic that it indicates also displays the divine excellence, and it is in response to this excellence that life moves toward ec-centricity and a hopefully realistic demeanor.

Reformed Christianity is a particular subtradition and strain of piety that bears this specification of the divine. True, the images of God as Creator, Judge, and Redeemer are shared by Christian traditions more broadly, and all Augustinian Christian traditions in the West, for example, Catholicism, Lutheranism, Reformed Christianity, and Anglicanism, emphasize the priority of grace. But more strongly than most, Reformed Christianity stresses that these images indicate what Brian A. Gerrish calls "sovereign grace." It upholds a piety that insists that our relationship with God does not depend on what we do, and so it assures us by causing us to look outside ourselves.[19] As I have also indicated throughout this systematic, the Reformed subtradition and strain of piety that bears this specification of the God of grace does not stand still. It develops in conversations with insights offered by biblical scholars, historians, philosophers, scientists, etc., and, as it does so, it sometimes revises key affirmations and beliefs.

To mention one broad development, we have seen that portraits of Jesus as a religious figure whose message and mission are wholly without social and political dimensions are badly out of step with recent biblical scholarship. Profound implications follow for understanding Jesus's commitment to the kingdom, and also for understanding the reign of the Creator-Judge-Redeemer. These sharply undercut and call into question an otherworldly spirituality that focuses on the survival in eternity after death of individual souls or spirits. Kingdom talk is not just, or perhaps even primarily, talk about what transpires on another metaphysical plane.

Or, again, consider the theological implications of two points recently made by multidisciplinary astrobiological inquiries into the emergence and distribu-

19. Brian A. Gerrish, "Sovereign Grace: Is Reformed Theology Obsolete?" *Interpretation: A Journal of Bible and Theology*, January 2003, 45–57. Gerrish also notes Luther's claim in *Lectures on Galatians 1535, Chapters 1–4*, ed. Jaroslav Pelikan, vol. 26 of *LW*, 356, that our witness to the gospel of grace "is the reason why our theology is certain: it snatches us away from ourselves and places us outside ourselves."

tion of life in the universe through a long history of factors and conditions from the big bang to the formation of stars, elements, and planets. One is the idea that *life is a planetary phenomenon*, or that links between life and Earth's environment are reciprocal and extend to the planet as a whole.[20] Earth's habitability, then, is partly due to the influences of life on the planetary environment, for example, microbes and the formation of Earth's atmosphere; the formation of the symbiotic stuff we call soil by decomposing plants, algae, and fungi; the erosion of rocks, etc. Another point emerges from explorations into the distribution of ice and water beyond Earth, planets that may be located in "habitable" zones relative to their stars, etc. (Our recent information is partly the result of improved techniques and methods of detection that have vastly increased the number of known planets, moons, etc.) In any case, multidisciplinary astrobiological studies not only indicate that the story of life on Earth is integrated with the longer story of the universe, but also that life very well may exist elsewhere.

Significant implications follow for a theological picture of creation and the place and responsibilities of humans in it. For example, an intensified sense for the deeply embedded and interdependent character of life on Earth suggests that, at some level, we are indeed made to help one another and contribute to one another's well-being, that *not* impacting our planetary environment is not an option, and that life on Earth cannot be transported elsewhere as readily as we sometimes imagine. It also heightens our sense of dependence on and responsibility for critical planetary systems, other species, etc.

Additional implications concern the scope of redemption, and in a Reformed context, this suggests the need to reconsider the one covenant of grace. As we have seen, the traditional idea is that the covenant has multiple iterations, beginning with Adam and extending through Noah, Abraham, Sinai, and Jesus. Moreover, Reformed theologians subject this idea to significant revisions. Schleiermacher claims that Calvin's idea of a dual decree (double predestination) threatens a Manichaean cleavage, wherein God creates some persons explicitly for damnation and beyond hope of redemption. Barth insists, in opposition to the idea that the covenant is limited by a dual decree, that the covenant's outer circle is all humanity.[21] I think that, under pressures of astrobiological findings and ideas, attending to the covenant with all living things through Noah, as well as to the insistence of passages, such as Colossians 1, that in Christ all things (*ta*

20. See Eric Smith and Harold J. Morowitz, *The Origin and Nature of Life on Earth: The Emergence of the Fourth Geosphere* (Cambridge: Cambridge University Press, 2016), 2–5; David Grinspoon, *Earth in Human Hands: Shaping Our Planet's Future* (New York: Grand Central, 2016), 206–78.

21. See chap. 7, prop. #49.

panta) are reconciled to God, we should now conceive the covenant of grace as extending to the entire cosmos.[22]

Thus, in the light of recent astrobiological findings and ideas, we might not only reconsider possible meanings of biblical depictions of humans and other animals as earth creatures fashioned from the ground but also the possible meanings of biblical symbols of a new heaven and new earth. We might consider, too, how to articulate the claim that the Creator, Judge, and Redeemer is the God of grace across a potentially fertile universe.[23]

All this suggests how *revisionary assimilations* may be set in motion by *both* the interest of Reformed theology in scientific knowledge of the world and the new knowledge and ideas presented by astrobiology. In my judgment, a Reformed theological framework may *assimilate* at least some astrobiological ideas by *selectively retrieving* from its storehouse of resources the symbolic ideas of creation and the covenant of grace. But the retrieved ideas are also revised if one reinterprets the covenant of grace (1) by furthering the expansive trajectory of some Reformed views and rejecting the restricted scope of some others, and (2) by reconsidering certain biblical passages and symbols. That is, Reformed theology may read, interpret, and evaluate astrobiology as an expansive template for reconsidering the sovereign God of grace, and this illustrates some of the complexities in store when we turn to the question of faith and reason in a Reformed frame of reference. These, in turn, might be compared and contrasted with the dynamics of other theological stances, at least some of which, for one or another reason, may be considerably more circumscribed when it comes to considering new knowledge and information.[24]

22. Among other things, I noted earlier that the significantly enlarged canvas on which to portray the idea of redemption suggests the soteriological limitations of the classical claim that the divine and human natures of Christ are united hypostatically. Proponents of a two-natures Christology (of which I am *not* one) may need to say how this claim can be modified to address the possibility of intelligent creatures in other worlds. See chap. 7.

23. Some may object that the covenant theme is ill suited for this purpose, since, in many instances, it entails a kind of agreement between intelligent agents, and not all things in the cosmos are intelligent. But Reformed theology has never really insisted on that point, and instead has claimed that God elects Israel without waiting for a ratifying response, saying in Lev. 26:12, "I . . . will be your God, and you shall be my people" (Calvin, *ICR* 2.10.8). Again, the covenant with Noah and all living things of the earth clearly also extends beyond the realm of intelligent life.

24. Were we to take up this last task, we would need to keep in mind Reformed claims, from the Scots Confession of 1560 and the Westminster Confession of Faith (1647) forward, that church councils and doctrines, while important for handing on the faith, *are fallible and subject to criticism* or revision in the light of (interpretations of) the gospel. Indeed, this claim has also been intensified by the decision of the PC(USA) to maintain a *Book of Confessions*

Future Developments

Reformed theology presents a vision of human life and the world in relation to God. My claim is that this vision is rooted largely in a biblically inspired idea of God as Creator-Redeemer, and that it pictures everything from human capacities, limits, and corruptions to natural environments and institutions in relation to the divine. Interestingly, however, while it is rooted in the particular historical resource we call the Bible, this vision itself, in virtue of its distinctive symbolic content, encourages us to engage philosophical and scientific perspectives on human life and the world. That is, just because God is understood to create and redeem the world, whatever we know about the world is at least potentially relevant for a Reformed theological vision. This engaging or even collaborative disposition, as we may call it, leads to quite significant complexities when we consider the classical question of "faith and reason," and, in a Reformed perspective, it also connects with a notable willingness to consider both assimilations into and revisions of its theological framework.[25]

It therefore seems not only appropriate but somewhat necessary for a Reformed theologian also to be a revisionary theologian. That is, in virtue of its theocentric spine, this particular Christian subtradition remains open to and surely cannot rule out the possibility that it may develop theological statements and expressions of piety that differ appreciably from their Reformed antecedents. Allow me to modify a saying of Count Zinzendorf that Ernst Troeltsch recalls in his essay "What Does 'Essence of Christianity' Mean?" Reformed theology "needs daring and much loyalty."[26] Loyalty in meditation on and devotion to the history of a particular tradition; daring in order to bring forward out of the history a living idea for the present time.

Nevertheless, like any other particular tradition, Reformed Christianity is not infinitely malleable or elastic, and in my judgment the apprehension that the presiding mystery—the Creator, Judge, and Redeemer—is the God of grace also forms its theocentric anchor. Troeltsch ponders the question of whether, in the course of its historical development, Christianity might morph into something else, and rightly observes that there can be no guarantee it won't. He notes, too,

(plural), and its insistence, in the Confession of 1967, that the church confesses its faith in every age. See *BOC* 3.20; 6.175; 9.02–9.03.

25. See Douglas F. Ottati, "A Collaborative Manner of Theological Reflection," in *Theology as Interdisciplinary Inquiry: Learning with and from the Natural and Human Sciences*, ed. Robin W. Lovin and Joshua Mauldin (Grand Rapids: Eerdmans, 2017), 132–60.

26. Ernst Troeltsch, "What Does 'Essence of Christianity' Mean?" in Troeltsch, *Writings on Theology and Religion*, trans. and ed. Robert Morgan and Michael Pye (Louisville: Westminster John Knox, 1990), 176.

that this raises the question of the criteria we should use to determine whether this has taken place. Let me ask some similar if also more specific questions. Might the subtradition we call Reformed Christianity develop historically to the point where it morphs into something else, something that we should no longer call *Reformed* Christianity? If so, what would be the indicators that it has?

Like Troeltsch, I think there can be no guarantee this won't happen. History swirls. But with respect to Reformed Christianity, I think the key criterion to keep in mind is the apprehension, claim, or symbolic idea that the presiding mystery—the Creator, Judge, and Redeemer—is the God of grace.

Important developments in the course of Reformed theology largely bear this out. Revisions to Calvin's predestinarian scheme offered by Schleiermacher and Barth are recognizably Reformed because both also continue to affirm that God is sovereign grace. One may argue, in fact, as I have earlier in this work, that these revisions aim to rescue the affirmation of sovereign *grace* from Calvin's ill-conceived attempt to equate it with arbitrariness.[27] By contrast, Arminianism, or the idea that God elects those whom God foresees shall repent, effectively makes the correct self-determination of our free will the precondition for salvation.[28] It therefore also fails to appreciate sufficiently how the radicality and persistence of the human fault preclude the possibility of effective self-correction. It undercuts *sovereign* grace and turns our attention toward our own efforts and righteousness.

In any case, if we take sovereign grace as our benchmark, then it seems possible to argue that, in some contemporary quarters, Reformed piety and Christianity may have morphed already into something else that is no longer specifically Reformed. This, at least, is an implication of the fact that certain forms of evangelicalism, postdenominational Christianity, and progressive moralism appear to have captured the faith and practice of some Reformed and Presbyterian churches in America. Attention shifts away from a gracious God and toward our merits and accomplishments partly because less than radical and universal estimates of sin diminish our grasp of our need for radically merciful divine grace and acceptance. Thus, rather than the good news of grace and forgiveness, evangelism comes to stress the efforts of evangelists to change persons' minds and the abilities of those whom evangelists address to reform themselves. Theological ethics obscures the quality of mercy or forgiveness, namely, a willingness to bear the evil in the other "without vindictiveness because the evil in the self is known." Why? Because it maintains that the evil in the self may be largely, if not entirely, overcome by our own moral commitment, with the result that persons and groups may press their

27. See chap. 10, prop. #61.

28. See, for example, Robert Letham, "Arminianism," in *Encyclopedia of the Reformed Faith*, ed. Donald K. McKim (Louisville: Westminster John Knox, 1992), 11–12.

own highest values and moral judgments with self-righteous fury.[29] Reformed theological humanism teeters when theology fails to articulate and insist upon the value of all persons in God's sight despite their (flawed) accomplishments and their faults. Call these evangelical, postdenominational, and progressive malformations a new Pelagianism.[30] Whatever we call them, they finally do not support the same contrite and hopefully realistic stance that emerges from the apprehension that the Creator, Judge, and Redeemer is sovereign grace.

I should also mention some current permutations of the classical malformations of the Creator, Judge, and Redeemer idea that I described in part 1.[31] Today there occasionally emerges a privatized and interiorized spirituality that largely separates Christian commitment from the world of institutions and communities, politics, professions, social ethics, etc. True religion then becomes almost entirely a matter of inner spirit and personal subjectivity. This development reflects distinctly contemporary and commercial emphases on individual choices, wants, and desires, though, to some extent, it may also represent a return to older spiritualist dualisms, for example, Gnosticism, that were prominent in the early Mediterranean period. Essentially there is a failure to appreciate that the God of grace is the Creator, and that society, institutions, and life in the body are good created gifts in which we are called to participate faithfully.

Moral dualism, a second malformation, sometimes accompanies contemporary political idolatries and reductive nationalist commitments. In a manner akin to Manichaeanism, inordinate and destructive closed-society loyalties enlist Christian piety in the project of contrasting good in-groups with evil out-groups. There are multiple theological difficulties here, including a disposition to deify our own society. There is a tendency also to sever judgment from redemption, a malformation of the Creator-Judge-Redeemer idea that goes hand in glove with the failure to appreciate that *all* persons and communities, including we ourselves and our own, must finally depend on the radical and redeeming mercy of a gracious Judge.

Today, partly under the impact of darkly troubling cultural trends, pieties also may arise that juxtapose love and grace with law and that falsely oppose Jesus and Judaism. Here, again, theological difficulties abound—a failure to see how the law is a means of grace and a blessing that promises a good life together, a failure to see that Jesus does not abrogate but intensifies Torah, and a tendency to falsely differentiate Jesus from the many currents in the Judaism of his day.[32] Behind and beneath these failures lies an extraordinarily basic difficulty,

29. Reinhold Niebuhr, *An Interpretation of Christian Ethics* (New York: Seabury, 1979), 137.

30. Gerrish does. See "Sovereign Grace," 56.

31. Chap. 2, props. #19 and #20.

32. Charles A. Wilson, *Christological Recommendations*, vol. 2 of *Inventing Christic Jesuses: Rules and Warrants for Theology* (Eugene, OR: Cascade, 2018), 143–46.

namely, a chronic failure to see that the God of Israel and the covenant is also the Redeemer or God of grace and deliverance to whom the kingdom-minded Christ points. Anti-Judaism thus often spawns and gains support from the idea that Christianity and the New Testament have to do with a God of grace, love, and forgiveness, whereas Judaism honors a God of law, wrath, and judgment portrayed in the (superseded) Old Testament. The split between a commanding Judge and a loving Redeemer suppresses or forgets that, properly understood, judgment and redemption go together: the God who redeems judges, and the God who judges redeems.

Proposition #69 God is the answer to the question of hope.

At the end of chapter 11, I surveyed grounds for hope as we confront challenges posed by environmental degradation and prospects for sustainability. My aim there was to illustrate how this systematic, keyed to God as Creator, Judge, and Redeemer, estimates our historical possibilities and limitations as we undertake projects, fashion relationships, and participate in communities and institutions in the face of changing conditions, threats, and uncertainties. I argued that there are significant, though not untroubled, grounds for hopes for sustainability, and also that aspirational portraits of a sustainable civilization seem at least partly eschatological.

The question of hope may, of course, also be raised in a more forthrightly ultimate key. This is so largely because, in addition to the knowledge that our loved ones, our cherished causes and projects, and we ourselves are subject to threats of changing events and conditions, we also know that we, both as individuals and as communities, die. The knowledge and anticipation of death may not be uniquely human;[33] still, when compared to what (little) we know about the mental lives of other animals, it seems at least distinctively so. Our awareness of death sometimes insinuates itself into daily living, and we may imagine our deaths again and again.

For what may we hope as we undertake projects, fashion relationships, and participate in communities and institutions in face of life's uncertainties and our own inevitable demise? For what may we hope after death? For what may we hope with reference to the ultimate destiny of human communities? What is the end or destiny of the cosmos? These questions and others like them verge on the transcendent and beyond. They can be fascinating and arresting, and they may

33. Mary Midgley notes that elephants appear to mourn their dead with ritual patterns, a practice that may indicate a general awareness of death. See *Animals and Why They Matter: A Journey around the Species Barrier* (New York: Penguin, 1983), 9–18.

also threaten debilitating despair. Hence, as Ernest Becker notes in his popular classic *The Denial of Death*, we often devise schemes, ideas, and practices to help us address and perhaps also suppress them.[34]

A personal remembrance may not be out of place. The first time I understood that people, including me, get sick and die, I was about six years old. My aunt Vi, who had been born with a thumb and two fingers on each hand and one leg shorter than the other, died at about age fifty at the home she shared with her partner in Ann Arbor, Michigan. I liked her, and had one of her childhood crutches in my room. (Years later, I learned that, whenever a baby, including me, was born to a family member, Vi called to ask if mother and baby were well—meaning physically well and normal.) When I was told she was very sick, I wrote out and sent to her a copy of the Lord's Prayer. On the evening she died, as well as for more than a few thereafter, the darkness in my room at bedtime in New Jersey didn't become scary, it just seemed thicker, as if it had gained a new advantage. I wondered whether death is like being alone in the dark, and decided on reflection that it probably isn't. Is it not being at all? That seemed more likely but, if so, what's that? Two things I did know were that I wouldn't see Vi again, and that one day I too would die.

For Christian piety, the very human question of hope, when raised in an ultimate key, just as when it is raised in more mundane ones, always takes a specific form. For what may we hope with respect to our destinies and ends in relation to God the Creator, Judge, and Redeemer? This way of putting the question denies none of the threats and anxieties intimated and mentioned above. Persons of piety know that we live and move under physical and social threats; they know, too, that everyone dies, and that no community or institution lasts forever. What signals the distinctive form of the question as Christian piety asks it is the additional sense that "we do not live to ourselves, and we do not die to ourselves" (Rom. 14:7). We live and die ec-centrically and in relationship with the Creator, Judge, and Redeemer.

Pastoral, Political, and Spiritual Dimensions

There are important pastoral dimensions here when we attend to and care for others as they face sufferings, anxieties, fears, and death. How, for example, can a congregation help people cope and live faithfully in the face of these things?

No easy and comprehensive answers, no invariant and surefire techniques commend themselves. But it is worth stressing once again the theological artic-

34. Ernest Becker, *The Denial of Death* (New York: Free Press, 1973).

ulateness of being present with and accompanying those who suffer and undergo trials. Intentional presence and accompaniment mitigate isolation (and, in our own time, too many people who suffer and are sick or dying are left alone, cordoned off in places and spaces separated from others). Practices of intentional presence and accompaniment also embody and express continued community, interrelationship, and life together; they embody a true communion with God in community with others that needn't always be joyful or celebratory in order to be meaningful, pastoral, worshipful, and humane. This bit of wisdom seems an essential aspect of congregational care—from bringing dinners to the bereaved to visiting hospitals and prisons, to more elaborate structures, regimens, and ministries that ensure that the sick, the dying, and the imprisoned are not isolated.

The pastoral task also extends to ensuring that those who suffer social, economic, and political deprivations and injustices are not left isolated and alone. Christological, pastoral, and political overtones merge. In present-day America, for example, the pastoral task will include ministries of intentional presence and accompaniment with victims of abuse as well as with immigrant and migrant populations systematically (and unconscionably) hounded by the federal government and also by some local communities. The circumstance brings to mind an insistence of the Latin American bishops at Medellín: ministry responds to pastoral problems of anxiety, despair, etc., suffered by individuals and families. Behind the pastoral problems, however, lies a corrupt economics that keeps people mired in poverty and powerless, and behind the corrupt economics lies a corrupt politics.[35]

Again, care for the dying brings us face-to-face with the very human grief of separation from cherished persons, projects, and aims. Part of a response here may be found in communities that remember and endure, for example, families, congregations, schools. These offer comfort and continuing possibilities for life together to those who continue to live. Indeed, communities of memory sometimes also furnish significant satisfaction to those who face death. Think, for example, of the satisfaction many take in their children and grandchildren. No doubt, these ongoing social structures and communities need to exert effort in order to remember—by telling stories, memorializing, etc.—and sometimes they fail to do so. But even where communities of memory succeed, there is still the pain of separation that death brings.

Egoism enters in. I do not want to be separated from those I love, and I do not want them to be separated from me. Remembering someone makes me feel

35. See "Medellin Documents: Justice, Peace, Family, and Demography, Poverty of the Church," in *The Gospel of Peace and Justice: Catholic Social Teaching Since Pope John*, ed. Joseph Gremillion (Maryknoll, NY: Orbis, 1976), 445–76.

as if I am not entirely cut off from and am in some sense still with her or him. Anticipating that a community may remember me brings me a measure of comfort. Pastorally and humanly, however, we should also note that not all of this is merely egoistical. If, in some degree, our interrelations with others and with broader causes appropriately orient us beyond ourselves, then their foreclosure cuts against the grain of life's ec-centric reference. Moreover, a scheme that encourages people to participate in affecting interrelations but then also requires them finally and consciously to separate and go down to extinction seems a tall order—one that very well may elicit both lament and complaint. Jacob, after all, is small (Amos 7:2).

As already mentioned, the many-faceted pastoral dimension of accompaniment and care connects also with practical and political concerns. How shall we sustain meaningful and faithful participation in our communities and institutions in the face of suffering, destruction, injustice, death, and the unfinished nature of our involvements? People who live intelligently and honestly know that they live and live together only for a time, and, even then, always in face of death and potential separation. Those who devote themselves to causes, aims, projects, relationships, and communities that transcend and go beyond their own lifetimes surely do so with a nagging sense that progress is neither inevitable nor linear, and that lines of advance may be thwarted and reversed. Illustrations abound: for example, congregations and even entire denominations that flourish for a time and then dissolve, initiatives in higher education that run their course and then give way to countervailing trends, revolutionaries who turn out simply to usher in another repressive regime. Consider, again, the sensibilities, structures, and policies aimed at social equality, the alleviation of poverty, improved access to medical care, and more broadly distributed educational opportunities that emerged in the United States following the Second World War. Americans who grew up during that period may perhaps be forgiven for thinking that general trajectory was normal or even destined to continue. Does the fact that practical, institutional, and political projects rise and fall fatally undermine our committed participation?

This brings us to a spiritual dimension of the question of hope that intertwines with all that has been mentioned thus far but also has a rather definite and distinct accent. How, in the face of the many challenges and anxieties, shall we maintain an integral piety and a felt relationship with the divine? For what may we hope as we live and move and die *in relationship with the Creator, Judge, and Redeemer*? The spiritual note, that is to say, emphasizes our relatedness to God, and it heightens our concern that answers to the question of hope not degenerate into the merely egoistic and therapeutic, that our relationship with God not reduce to a relationship with or ratification of our own wants and desires.

In terms of Western philosophy, the question here is whether Christian piety's felt relationship with God finally falls victim to Ludwig Feuerbach's critique of religion. Does it reduce to the activity of imaginatively constructing a god in the image of our own preferences? Does it amount to little more than a projection of our own devising, which functions (falsely) to reassure us that life is meaningful in the face of a threatening world?[36] A similar concern is not unknown also to classical Reformed theology. For example, Calvin claims that human nature is "a perpetual factory of idols" because the human mind "dares to imagine a god according to its own capacity." He therefore worries that people will let their wishes dictate their prayers, and that they will "ask for, expect, or demand" more than is summarized in the Lord's Prayer.[37]

In response, and as a testament to the existential crises that often accompany the issue of hope, perhaps the first thing we should do is simply repeat that egoism is not the only thing involved in the separation of persons from cherished others and causes. Even so, the danger of formulating an answer to the question of hope that responds simply to self-concern is real. "It always remains hard," says Norman Pittenger, "to learn the lesson that it is God that matters most and that not even our deepest concern for those whom we have loved unselfishly and generously can be given central place."[38] The spiritual dimension of the question of hope emphasizes that, for persons of piety, "it is essential to make sure that it is God, not human desires or wishes or aspirations as they now stand, who is to be 'given the glory,' and it is in God, and in God alone, that we may speak meaningfully of the significance of our existence."[39]

Call this the theocentric criterion of integral piety. It leads one to conclude that there are serious spiritual and theological difficulties with much conventional talk of "life after death" because, in our (quite understandable) concern for our own personal survival and fulfillment, we are prone to forget the importance of "centering upon God."[40] Indeed, some conventional talk seems almost entirely utilitarian, emphasizing the person's own fulfillment rather than a life conformed to the ec-centric vector of love of God and neighbor and to God's kingdom. Note, for example, some of the criticisms of individualist religion made by Walter Rauschenbusch. A piety focused on personal salvation, he says, risks reducing to a "refined egoism" or "egoistic religion" at odds with the more

36. See Ludwig Feuerbach, *The Essence of Religion*, trans. Alexander Loos (Amherst, NY: Prometheus, 2004); Van A. Harvey, *Feuerbach and the Interpretation of Religion* (Cambridge: Cambridge University Press, 1995), 198–228, 281–309.

37. Calvin, *ICR* 1.11.1; 3.20.49.

38. Norman Pittenger, *After Death—Life in God* (New York: Seabury, 1980), 72.

39. Pittenger, *After Death*, 71–72.

40. Pittenger, *After Death*, 72.

forthrightly social hope and commitments of Jesus and the prophets. Rauschenbusch insists that the culmination of our conversion to an other-directed life initiated by Jesus and the Spirit cannot and should not be reduced to this.[41] One wonders, too, whether much conventional talk of life after death, wedded as it is to the notion of just deserts for having lived a faithful and good life, can possibly conform to the affirmation of grace alone. Does talk about eternal rewards simply reduplicate the curse of the law in an eschatological key? In any case, these are some of the challenges that emerge for Christian piety or devotion in relationship to a gracious God who creates, judges, and redeems but does not simply vouchsafe and guarantee some quite important human wants, desires, and needs.

Some Eschatological Views

Against this background, consider some basic eschatological views. These are not clear and distinct ideas so much as vaguer images and symbols put forward by worshiping communities in the push and shove of faithful living. They portray the furthest horizon, but they do so in a manner relevant to and interconnected with lived anxieties, historical challenges, and threats. Thus, near the beginning of the Christian era, hopes for spiritual existence beyond death were gaining ground in Greek mystery religions that addressed anxieties associated with the transitoriness and sufferings of bodily existence. Emerging Jewish hopes for resurrection helped to sustain martyrs of Jewish resistance during the second century BCE.[42]

New Society, New World

One sort of eschatological hope and expectation focuses on the motif of a new society, realm, city, or world under God. As we have seen, a number of passages in the Hebrew Scriptures refer to a future reign of God from Jerusalem and Zion. The notion has political overtones; all the nations stream to Jerusalem to hear the words and judgments of God (Isa. 2:3). There is a coming or future divine reign, a kingdom in which God will judge the nations, and all will walk according to the law. Moreover, when the ideal kingship comes,

41. Walter Rauschenbusch, *Christianizing the Social Order* (New York: Macmillan, 1913), 111–13, 464–65, 473.

42. Maurice Wiles, *Reason to Believe* (Harrisburg, PA: Trinity Press International, 1999), 111.

> The wolf shall live with the lamb,
> the leopard shall lie down with the kid,
> the calf and the lion and the fatling together. . . .
> The cow and the bear shall graze,
> their young shall lie down together;
> and the lion shall eat straw like the ox. (Isa. 11:6–7)

These are features—poetically depicted—of God's glorious new *creation*, genuine politics, and peace; with the deliverance of Israel's righteous, there is also an alteration of reality, a new heaven and earth, in which there is extended longevity and the wolf and the lamb feed together (Isa. 65:17–25). The Quaker minister Edward Hicks rendered the scene more than sixty times in his paintings of "a peaceable kingdom," which sometimes conflated it with William Penn making a treaty at Shackamaxon, Pennsylvania, in 1683 with Chief Tomanend of the Lenape tribe.

As we have seen, a variation of this kind of kingdom hope is also central to Jesus's preaching and performance in the Gospels.[43] The kingdom, which with Christ's coming has drawn near, sometimes is described not only as future but also as present "among you" (Luke 17:20–21). It is a realm of acceptance and reconciliation embodied by Jesus's eating and drinking with tax collectors and sinners (Matt. 9:10–13; Mark 2:15–17; Luke 5:29–32). It is a kingdom in which the poor and the vulnerable are blessed (e.g., Luke 6), a reign of God's justice and shalom, and so also, as the parable of the laborers in the vineyard shows, one that contrasts rather sharply with the present order (Matt. 20).

There is not a great deal of highly developed apocalyptic symbolism on the lips of Jesus in the New Testament, though there are important references to "the Son of Man coming on the clouds of heaven" in Matthew 24:30, Mark 13:26, and Mark 14:62. In the book of Revelation, however, we encounter more detailed and forthrightly apocalyptic images, for example, the Lamb opening the seven seals; the darkening of the sun; stars falling; the trumpets of angels and hail, fire, and blood hurled to the earth; the defeat of the armies of the nations; a new heaven and new earth; and the new Jerusalem coming down from heaven (Rev. 6; 8; 19; 21). A repeated critique of the world's principalities and powers is unmistakable; thus, Babylon, a symbol for the Roman Empire with its claim to be eternal, becomes "a haunt of every foul bird" (Rev. 18:2).

The contrast with present orders comes through, too, in the emergence of a perfected world beyond the negativities of history, where "the home of God is among mortals." There is victory over suffering and fear.

43. See chap. 8, prop. #52.

> "[God] will wipe every tear from their eyes.
> Death will be no more;
> mourning and crying and pain will be no more." (Rev. 21:3–4)

There is also a kind of transformation or regeneration of politics, as on either side of "the river of the water of life" in the new Jerusalem we find "the tree of life with its twelve kinds of fruit . . . and the leaves of the tree are for the healing of the nations" (Rev. 22:1–2). The image of perfection is not elaborated here in the direction of other animals as it is in Isaiah, though, as we have noted, Christian tradition has clearly (and, as I think, also appropriately) sometimes done so, as in Hicks's *Peaceable Kingdom* paintings.

Due partly to Hellenistic influences, but also because established Christianity favored political stability, later church tradition often de-emphasizes the strands of eschatological expectation and apocalyptic imagery that critique present powers and envision a new political realm or creation in favor of a focus on personal survival. Even so, eschatological visions of a new society or realm are prominent from time to time among Christian thinkers and movements that look to reform the church and pursue an alternative society. For example, followers of Montanus, a Christian convert in Asia Minor during the second century, believed that the Paraclete continues to speak through charismatic prophecy, and many also hoped for an imminent second coming of Christ and for the new Jerusalem to descend in Phrygia. Tertullian, the most famous convert to the movement, leaves the Catholic Church in 212–213, and thereafter emphasizes moral rigor, eschews fleeing from persecution, and criticizes the laxity of bishops.[44] Girolamo Savonarola, who enters the Dominicans in 1475, denounces clerical corruption, despotic rulers, and the exploitation of the poor. His early preaching claims that "the Church and Italy must be scourged severely and soon" before it can be reformed. Later, Savonarola says Florence will be "the harbinger of a renovated Church" and the site of the new Jerusalem, and after the Medici are deposed in 1494, he sets up a democratic republic there.[45] Opposed by the duke of Milan, the pope, and a Florentine party, Savonarola was executed on May 23, 1498. (His wooden likeness appears in the chapel of the Waldensian Seminary in Rome.)

Later Marxists are among those who admire Thomas Müntzer, a radical and apocalyptic contemporary of Martin Luther and prominent participant in the

44. See, for example, "Flight in Time of Persecution," in *Tertullian: Disciplinary, Moral, and Ascetical Works*, trans. Rudolf Arbesmann, OSA, Emily Joseph Daly, CSJ, and Edwin A. Quain, SJ (Washington, DC: Catholic University of America Press, 1959), 275–99.

45. Bernard McGinn, ed. and trans., *Apocalyptic Spirituality: Treatises and Letters of Lactantius, Adso of Montier-En-Der, Joachim of Fiore, the Franciscan Spirituals, Savonarola* (New York: Paulist, 1979), 187–88, 272.

Peasants' Revolt in Thuringia. Müntzer's "Sermon to the Princes," in July 1524, claims that the "full and final reformation" is now in process, and that the poor laity are "ready to challenge tyranny." It says too that the then present empire follows Babylon, the Medes and Persians, the Greeks, and Rome. Like its predecessors, this "fifth empire" would rule with force and the sword, though it is actually "patched together with dung," schemes, and hypocrisy. The returning Christ, who is the stone hurled from heaven in Daniel 2, will smash it when he takes the government of the world into his own hands. For this reason, Müntzer counsels the princes of Saxony to hasten to make "God's true unwavering purpose" their own.[46] Not long after this sermon, however, and as the persecuted poor continue to flee the princes and arrive as refugees in various cities and towns, Müntzer turns from his hope for a new type of Christian prince to a more radical vision of the transfer of power to "the common people." He advises those who defend tyrants and rob the poor "not to despise those who are lowly (as you tend to do) for the Lord raises up those who are weak in order to cast down the mighty from their seats."[47] Indeed, on May 15, 1525, Müntzer himself commands local militia under religiously themed banners near Mulhausen, where thousands of peasants and almost none of the better-armed and better-trained princes' soldiers are killed. He is captured in the following days, subsequently tortured, and then executed on May 27.

A different, more aspirational vision of the kingdom that largely eschews violence animates Walter Rauschenbusch's Social Gospel in the midst of industrialization, urbanization, and waves of immigrants in America near the beginning of the twentieth century. Rauschenbusch argues that, as "eternal life came to the front in Christian hope, the kingdom of God receded into the background, and with it went much of the social potency of Christianity."[48] The kingdom hope, he says, needs to be reclaimed by focusing on Jesus and the prophets. He also claims devotion to the kingdom, a social reality that includes economic life, supports "the progressive transformation of all human affairs by the thought and spirit of Christ."[49] The kingdom, for Rauschenbusch, is the truly human society, the common good of humanity, and also the fulcrum of a "revolutionary religion" that redeems persons' minds; it is "always but coming," and yet "every approximation to it is worth while."[50] Once again, as for figures such as Savonarola and Müntzer, social justice and the plight of the common people

46. *The Collected Works of Thomas Müntzer*, trans. Peter Matheson (Edinburgh: T&T Clark, 1988), 226, 228, 244–45, 251–52.

47. *Collected Works of Thomas Müntzer*, 4, 96, 150–51.

48. Rauschenbusch, *Christianity and the Social Crisis*, 162.

49. Rauschenbusch, *Christianizing the Social Order*, 458.

50. Rauschenbusch, *Christianity and the Social Crisis*, 421.

take center stage. But partly because he thinks the costs in suffering to labor and the poor too great, Rauschenbusch opposes apocalyptic, millenarian, and "dogmatic socialist" stances that hope for a deteriorating social circumstance and catastrophe to usher in the new society. Instead, he pursues a spate of more immediate, piecemeal reforms.[51]

Eternal Life

Less immediately political eschatological visions that emphasize a general resurrection of the dead as well as the motif of eternal life also emerge in early Christianity. Consider, for example, Paul's reply to anxieties and questions raised by the church at Thessalonica, where some members of the community have died. Have they therefore missed Jesus's return and the day of salvation? If so, are the dead separated from Christ? Or has the end perhaps already arrived without us noticing, so that now we already live in the new reality?

Paul's reply in 1 Thessalonians 4:13–5:11 adapts and elaborates the Hebrew tradition of the last day of Yahweh, for example,

> Alas for you who desire the day of the LORD! . . .
> It is darkness, not light. (Amos 5:18)
>
> [Yahweh] of hosts has a day
>   against all that is proud and lofty. (Isa. 2:12)

The apostle interprets this as the day of judgment or the parousia of the risen and exalted Christ, and he claims that we who understand it properly have no reason to grieve or mourn the dead as others do who have no hope. The reason is that we believe Jesus died and rose, and so, through Jesus, God will also bring to life those who have died; the same divine power and grace are active in both. Indeed, says Paul, we know from Jesus's own teaching that those who are still alive until the coming of the Lord will have no advantage over those who have died (1 Thess. 4:15).[52] Out comes the apocalyptic imagery: Jesus himself, "with a cry of command," at the archangel's call, and the sound of God's trumpet, will descend from heaven. Those who have died in Christ will rise first. Next, we who are still

51. Walter Rauschenbusch, "Dogmatic and Practical Socialism," in *The Social Gospel in America, 1870–1920: Gladden, Ely, Rauschenbusch*, ed. Robert T. Handy (New York: Oxford University Press, 1966), 308–22.

52. The precise reference Paul has in mind is difficult to determine. Perhaps he is summarizing the substance of what we see in a passage such as Matt. 24:30–31. Clearly, however, he expects the end so soon that some of those to whom he writes will still be living.

alive will be taken up together with them in the clouds "to meet the Lord in the air." That way, Paul says, we will all be with the Lord forever (1 Thess. 4:16–17).

The apostle continues, noting that you (the Christians at Thessalonica) need not be instructed about the dates and times. You know that the day of the Lord is coming like a thief in the night, but because you are in light rather than darkness, it won't catch you by surprise as it will others who will not escape destruction. Stay awake and be sober. Wear faithfulness and love like protective armor and the hope of salvation like a helmet. For God has not destined us to wrath but to salvation through Jesus Christ. Paul proposes this scenario as grounds for the Thessalonians to encourage each other and build up one another. For him, it allows the community to attend pastorally to anxieties surrounding death and to continue to live faithfully.

He develops his reflections further in 1 Corinthians 15, and to see how he does so, let me briefly outline the chapter, which may be read as a kerygmatic premise followed by an argument, an extended exploration, and a pastoral conclusion. Paul begins by reminding the Corinthians of the gospel he proclaimed to them, which they received, and in which they stand. He repeats a formula that summarizes this message, a tradition he received, and then handed on to the community: "that Christ died for our sins in accordance with the scriptures, and that he was buried, and that he was raised on the third day in accordance with the scriptures, . . . and that he appeared to Cephas, then to the twelve." Then Christ appeared to more than five hundred people at once, many of whom still live, then to James, and "then to all the apostles." Paul continues with his own testimony, saying, "last of all . . . he appeared also to me," and therefore, "by the grace of God" I too am an apostle. That is, Paul begins the chapter with a rehearsal of the gospel, the basic kernel of the saving message, or the kerygma.

This forms the basis or premise on which he presents an argument against the claim that there is no resurrection of the dead. His reasoning is this: since God has raised Christ from the dead, there is also a more general resurrection of the dead (15:12ff.). The two events are linked, much as they were in 1 Thessalonians 4:14, and the theological point, once again, is that the gracious God who raised Christ Jesus will also raise the dead through Jesus. To underscore the point in 1 Corinthians, Paul now calls God's raising of Christ from the dead "*the first fruits* of those who have died" (1 Cor. 15:20). He claims further, as he does in Romans 5, that there is a contrasting parallel between Christ and Adam, and as is also the case in Romans, there are universalistic undertones. "For as all die in Adam, so all will be made alive in Christ" (1 Cor. 15:22). It is important to grasp the proper order. First, Christ's resurrection takes place, the first fruits. Second, at his coming, those who belong to him are raised. Third, and finally, comes the end (or the raising of the rest), when Christ, having destroyed every ruler and power, "hands over the kingdom to God the Father . . . so that God may be all in all" (15:23–28). This is the argument that forms the basic theological ground for an answer to the question of hope: through Christ, we may hope for all to be made alive and for God to be all in all.

Paul then adds an extended explanation, about how the dead are raised and about the body in which they are raised. He says that the seeds of wheat or some other grain that one sows in the ground must die before they come to life. Moreover, God gives to each seed its own body, and so there are many different sorts of bodies—of humans, animals, birds, and fish. There are not only earthly bodies, in fact, but also heavenly ones, for example, the sun and moon, each with its own glory. Now comes an application. "So it is with the resurrection of the dead." One sort of body—a perishable and physical body—is what is sown, but it is raised "a spiritual body" (*sōma pneumatikon*). The physical body is first, and then there is a spiritual body, just as "the first man was from the earth, a man of dust," and "the second man is from heaven" (15:47). Then, to emphasize the point, the apostle asserts, "flesh and blood cannot inherit the kingdom of God, nor does the perishable inherit the imperishable" (15:50). At the final trumpet and in a moment "we will be changed," and our perishable body will be raised imperishable and put on immortality. Then death and its sting will be overcome thanks to the grace and power of the God who gives us victory through Jesus Christ (15:54–55).

Paul closes these reflections on resurrection with a pastoral exhortation not unlike the one in 1 Thessalonians 5:13. "Therefore, my beloved, be steadfast, immovable, always excelling in the work of the Lord, *because you know that in the Lord your labor is not in vain*" (1 Cor. 15:58).

Precisely what does the apostle mean by *sōma pneumatikon*, or "a spiritual body," in 15:44, an expression as surprising in the Greek as it is in English? No doubt, we should try to understand it in conjunction with his statement in 15:50: "What I am saying, brothers and sisters, is this: flesh and blood cannot inherit the kingdom of God." Even so, he seems not to articulate a bald dichotomy of matter and spirit as he clearly would have had he said, it is sown a physical body, it is raised a spirit. Paul develops his explanation of spiritual bodies in some detail, and though one may find it muddled and unclear, the details seem at odds with a simple or strict dualism. Why should Paul say so much about various bodies, including those of plants, humans, animals, fish, and birds, unless he is trying to articulate some measure of continuity between created physical bodies and spiritual ones? In any case, one also notes that in 15:51 he exclaims, "Listen, I will tell you a mystery! We will not all die, but we will all be changed." Of course, we might ask, who are "we" who shall be changed, who live for a time in physical bodies and may also put on imperishable ones?

Certainly, the question, "With what bodies do they come?" continues to occupy theologians, and is one to which we shall return shortly. Here, however, let me observe that the Latin text of the Apostles' Creed speaks of *carnis resurrectionem*, literally "the resurrection of flesh." Luther, preaching on the creed, says that when uneducated Germans hear this, they think of meat in a market. Moreover, although Latin has perfectly good words for body, the proper affirmation, Luther insists, is "the resurrection of the body," a phrase that leaves room for Paul's ruminations and that also is used in many English translations.[53] The framers of the Apostles' Creed clearly choose an expression that disallows dualist devaluations of created life in the physical body, but one may wonder whether their vocabulary is entirely appropriate. The Nicene Creed seems less problematic as it speaks instead of "the resurrection of the dead and the life in the world to come." (And, as we noted earlier, since this affirmation comes at the close of its third article, the life to come may be understood as the completion of the Spirit's awakening, vivifying, and sanctifying work.)

Turn now to the more "realized eschatology" put forward by passages in the Gospel of John, where salvation is mostly "vertical" and comes down from above with gifts of light and life.[54] With Jesus "the light has come into the world" (3:19)—an event that separates in the present the children of darkness from those who come to the light. Thus, in John 5:23–24, Jesus says, "Anyone who does not honor the Son does not honor the Father who sent him. . . . Anyone who hears my word and believes him who sent me has eternal life, and . . . has [already] passed from death to life."[55] Or, again, Jesus, "the light of the world" sent from above, discloses the truth and brings eternal life (3:16–21; 8:12). He bestows the power to be born again of the Spirit. Thus, adoption as God's children and heirs of God's kingdom is a gift granted on earth here and now (1:12–13; 3:1–21).

But there are also futuristic elements in the Gospel of John. The complete gift comes after Jesus's ministry with the Spirit, who "will teach you everything" (14:26). Full faith becomes possible after Jesus's resurrection, as persons confess him as Lord and benefit from the eucharistic bread of life and living (baptismal) water in the power of the Spirit (6:22–59; 7:37–39). There is an additional future element even then; after death, there will be a completeness of eternal life, a future vision of glory in the presence of the Father. The gospel also clearly includes apocalyptic imagery. Thus, the dead "will rise again in the resurrection on the

53. Luther, *Sermons I*, 162–69.

54. Raymond E. Brown, SS, *The Gospel according to John (I–XII): Introduction, Translation, and Notes* (Garden City, NY: Doubleday, 1966), cxv.

55. The word in brackets is mine. See also Brown, *The Gospel according to John (I–XII)*, cxvii–cxviii, 214–15.

last day" (11:24), and Jesus, who is the way to the Father, says, "I will come again and will take you to myself" (14:3). Moreover, additional references to a last day of judgment are scattered throughout the gospel (e.g., 5:28–29; 6:39–40, 44, 54; 12:48).

What to make of this? Rudolf Bultmann takes these passages to be later additions that point to important tensions in the theologies of the early church. Consider 5:27–29, where Jesus refers to the Son of Man and the coming hour "when all who are in their graves will hear his voice and will come out." Bultmann sees this as the work of a redactor attempting to reconcile with the then-traditional apocalyptic eschatology of the church "the dangerous statements" in 5:24–25, which claim that eternal life is already present and that judgment comes "wherever and whenever" one hears the word of Jesus.[56] Raymond Brown disagrees. He says the church's eschatology was already moving in nonapocalyptic directions anyway following the destruction of the temple at Jerusalem in 70 CE. The writer of the Gospel of John and others, he says, stressed that the immediate return of Jesus is not needed because of "all that the Christian has already received in JC."[57] There is no need to long excessively for blessings of the future parousia because the two great gifts of divine adoption and eternal life are already given through faith in Jesus, baptism, and the Eucharist. There need be no "indefinite agony" waiting for the resurrection of the dead, since after death there is a continuation of the eternal life already begun, and its continuation brings closer union with Jesus and a vision of God. (This might be read as a fuller response to anxieties like those that emerged at Thessalonica.) Indeed, Brown says the Gospel of John developed over a period of time, which is why we see in it traces of the swinging back and forth over eschatological expectation that took place in the first century.[58]

In any case, later theological iterations of the eternal life motif generally com-

56. Rudolf Bultmann, *The Gospel of John: A Commentary*, trans. G. R. Beasley-Murray, R. W. N. Hoare, and J. K. Riches (Philadelphia: Westminster, 1971), 257–62.

57. Brown, *The Gospel according to John (I–XII)*, cxx.

58. See Brown, *The Gospel according to John (I–XII)*, cxx, who also partly puts it up to Jesus that there are both realized and futuristic elements of eschatology in John. "The recognition that there were both realized and final elements in Jesus' own eschatology means that in the subsequent developments . . . the NT writers were not creating *ex nihilo* theories of realized or of final eschatology, but were applying to a particular situation one or another strain already present in Jesus' thought. And we may add that there were strains of both types of eschatology in the Judaism contemporary with Jesus" (cxvix). More recently John Dominic Crossan claims that Jesus envisioned a present sapiential kingdom that critiques the family, blesses beggars, accepts infants (including girls), entails open commensality and radical equality, and generally disrupts the status quo. See *Jesus: A Revolutionary Biography* (San Francisco: HarperCollins, 1994), 54–74.

bine elements in Paul and John into an amalgam of Hebrew thinking about the last day and the Hellenistic idea of an immortal soul. This can be seen in the theology of John Calvin, for whom "the right longing for eternal life" offers comfort and, indeed, though we are grateful for the benefits of this life, also keeps us from being enmeshed in its vanities, for example, "the empty dazzlement of riches, power, and honors."[59] The human being, says Calvin, consists of a soul ("sometimes called 'spirit'") and a physical body. The soul is "an immortal yet created essence," and the seat of conscience, intelligence, and the *imago Dei*.[60] It survives when freed from the body at death, when it is immediately present with Christ in an "intermediate state." (Hence there is no reason to be anxious about waiting for resurrection on the last day.) Later, at the day of Christ that Paul mentions in 1 Thessalonians 5:23, there is the hoped-for resurrection of our bodies or of "the flesh" by God's omnipotence, and of which Christ's resurrection is the parallel and prototype. The soul is then reunited with its selfsame earthly body, which now has a different and imperishable quality.[61]

We find a similar view in Thomas Aquinas as he interprets "the resurrection of the flesh" (*carnis resurrectionem*) and "eternal life" (*vitam aeternam*) in his sermon-conferences on the Apostles' Creed. The former, he says, concerns the raising of our bodies by the Holy Spirit and its sanctifying power. This we believe because, as Paul points out, Jesus was raised up from the dead. Faith and hope in the resurrection, Aquinas says, "takes away the sadness we bear for those who died." It "takes away the fear of death," so that we will not commit sins out of such fear. Moreover, that we will receive eternal goods for what we do here motivates us to lead a good life and also draws us away from evil.[62]

The resurrected body will be "the same body that now exists both in its flesh and its bones," but in "another condition"—"immortal" and "incorruptible," without use for food or sex, and with integrity or without defect, such as deafness or blindness. Indeed, our bodies rise in "a perfect state," and so everyone will be "thirty-two or thirty-three years of age," since that was Christ's age at his resurrection, and "because those who have not yet come to this [age] have not achieved a perfect state, and older people already have lost it." The bodies of the faithful will shine; they will also be invulnerable, as God will dry every tear

59. Calvin, *ICR* 3.9.1–9.

60. Calvin, *ICR* 1.15.2–3.

61. Calvin, *ICR* 3.25.3, 7. It is interesting to observe that Calvin was not as concerned as Paul was about those who will still be alive at the end, and was more concerned to say there is an intermediate state wherein souls are present with Christ before the general resurrection on the last day.

62. *The Sermon-Conferences of St. Thomas Aquinas on the Apostles' Creed*, trans. Nicholas Ayo, CSC (Notre Dame: University of Notre Dame Press, 1988), 145–47.

and death will be no more (Rev. 21:4). Note, too, that for Aquinas, these will be "spiritual bodies"—meaning not that they will be altogether spirit, but that they "will be totally subject to the spirit." (Does this align with his conviction that they will have no use for food or sex, and thus will avoid sensual disruptions?) In any event, the condition of the damned will be the opposite.[63]

Turning to eternal life, Aquinas says that the soul does not perish with the body but resembles God in its immortality, "whereas in its sensibility" the body "resembles the animals." Eternal life is, first and foremost, life espoused to God or life united with God in perfect vision and worship (or praise). Possessing God will be the perfect and superabundant satisfaction of desire, so that, for example, "if knowledge is yearned for, it will be there most perfect, because we will know there the nature of everything, all truth, and whatsoever we wish to know." There is no complete security in this life, of course, but in eternal life "there is security most perfect," and "no sadness, no labor, no fear [of loss]." Also, says Aquinas, "in heaven there will be every kind of sharing of all goods," and "each one will love the other as oneself."[64]

Much like Calvin, though in a briefer and drier style, the Westminster Confession of Faith, the longtime standard of Presbyterianism, claims that after death, our bodies "see corruption." However, our "souls (which neither die nor sleep), having an immortal subsistence, immediately return to God who gave them" to "behold the face of God in light and glory, waiting for the redemption of their bodies." There is no need for purgatory to further refine or sanctify the elect, and "the souls of the wicked are cast into hell." Those still living on the last day will "not die, but be changed." On that day, too, "all the dead shall be raised up with the self-same bodies . . . although with different qualities," and "shall be united with their souls for ever." All shall also "appear before the tribunal of Christ," which God appoints "for the manifestation of the glory of his mercy in the eternal salvation of the elect; and of his justice in the damnation of the reprobate."[65]

These doctrines function pastorally and practically to deter people from sin, console the godly in adversity, and render them watchful (since they do not know when the end will come).[66] The fuller text of 1647 casts redemption as the gracious and sure result of election working out in effectual calling, justification, adoption, and sanctification. Presbyterian churches in the United States added a chapter on the Holy Spirit as the omnipresent "Lord and Giver of life" in 1903.

63. *Sermon-Conferences of St. Thomas Aquinas*, 149.
64. *Sermon-Conferences of St. Thomas Aquinas*, 153–55.
65. *BOC* 6.177–6.181.
66. *BOC* 6.182.

It indicates that the Scriptures infallibly record "the mind and will of God," and also that, as Comforter, Sanctifier, and the spirit of Adoption, the Holy Spirit "performs all those gracious offices by which [believers] are sanctified and sealed unto the day of redemption."[67]

Funeral Services and Memorials

Funerals and other memorials often are closer to lived piety than are more formal theological statements, and this is a reason to reflect on them here, however briefly. In fact, most of the eschatological ideas we have reviewed appear in funeral and graveside services of the churches. The Episcopalian Book of Common Prayer 1928 (as amended and published in 1952) speaks of "the spirits of those who depart" and "the souls of the faithful" that "are delivered from the burden of the flesh" and now dwell with "joy and felicity" in the presence of God.[68] It speaks, too, of being found acceptable in the Son's judgment at "the general Resurrection of the last day."[69] Like a number of services, it also includes an extensive reading from 1 Corinthians 15:20 and following on the raising of Christ as the first fruits of the general resurrection. Direct references to the kingdom are less prominent in all the services, though the Presbyterian "Witness to the Resurrection" (2018) includes a "Prayer after Communion," which speaks of "a foretaste of the heavenly banquet" that renews "our hope in your everlasting reign where there is no more crying, but only joy."[70]

Something the services add without fail, however, is an explicit mention and remembrance of deceased persons by name. The typical "Service of Death and Resurrection" of the United Methodist Church, which is to "be seen as a part of the larger ministry of the Church at death," includes a section called "Naming," where "the life and death of the deceased may be gathered up in the reading of a memorial or appropriate statement, or in other ways, by the pastor or others involved." A "Commendation" or "Committal" also includes the following. "Receive Name into the arms of your mercy. Raise Name up with all your people . . . that we may enter into your joy in the world to come. Amen." And, further, "Into your hands, O merciful Savior, we commend your servant Name. Acknowledge, we humbly beseech you, a sheep of your own fold, a lamb of your own flock, a

67. *BOC* 6.051–6.054; 6.183–6.186.

68. *The Book of Common Prayer and Administration of the Sacraments and Other Rites and Ceremonies of the Church* (New York: Harper & Brothers, 1952), 334. Similar wording appears also in Burial Rite I of the Book of Common Prayer (New York: Church Publishing, 2016), 488.

69. *The Book of Common Prayer* (1952), 335, 336.

70. *Book of Common Worship: Prepared by the Office of Theology and Worship for the Presbyterian Church (U.S.A.)* (Louisville: Westminster John Knox, 2018), 792.

sinner of your own redeeming. Receive Name into the arms of your mercy. . . . Amen."[71] Almost the same text is one of those suggested for the "Commendation" in the 2018 Presbyterian service.

The practices of naming, remembering, and memorializing are critical for those in attendance. The congregation or community memorializes and remembers the deceased person. It mourns the deceased person, and it commends her or him to God. Saying the name evokes both the deceased person's presence and the deceased person's absence, both our continued relationship with him or her and its interruption or, perhaps, even its close. Anyone who has been to an Irish Catholic wake knows there are other, sometimes less formal but quite effective, ways to remember, commemorate, and commend particular souls. In any case, a gathering at the death of a loved one seems incomplete without practices such as these.

There are, of course, also other memorials. I shall not forget the first time I heard read aloud the names of the members of a synagogue in Richmond, Virginia, who had died during the past week and also the names of those who had died during that same calendar week in previous years. One by one, they are read into the memory of the congregation and also, it seems, into the memory of God. The practice reminds me of plaques I have seen in the sanctuaries of English churches that list the names of members who perished in the Great War. It reminds me of the names of employees of the Pennsylvania Railroad Company who died in the Second World War and are listed on the base of a statue of "The Angel of the Resurrection" at the entrance to Thirtieth Street Station in Philadelphia. It reminds me, too, of the powerful simplicity of the names etched into the black marble wall that makes up the Vietnam Veterans Memorial in Washington, DC.

Surely, a part of the point of the Vietnam Memorial is to etch the names into the memory of the national community and, given the wall's resemblance to a long headstone, perhaps also into the divine memory. People frequently leave sentimental and commemorative items at the memorial. Some take pictures of the name of a loved one; others make pencil or wax crayon rubbings of a name on the wall, presumably to bring them home and to place them in a special album, on a shelf, or in a drawer. There is at the wall, as there also may be at makeshift memorials along roadsides and elsewhere, a power in the particular name at the particular place, a kind of a promise to those who go there of some continuing relationship, presence, or solidarity with the deceased, and also, I think, something very much like a hopeful commendation of the particular person to what lies beyond.[72]

71. "A Service of Death and Resurrection," accessed January 21, 2019, https://umcdiscipleship.org/resources/a-service-of-death-and-resurrection.

72. For a discussion that takes up some of these themes but also moves in some different

Some Recent Theology

A professor of mine at divinity school, Joseph Sittler, used to say that when Paul asks, "With what bodies do they come?" and then answers with "spiritual bodies," or *sōma pneumatikon*, his expression seems a contradictory idea, perhaps even an intentional dodge that cheats the philosophers out of a literal and univocal explanation. There is much to recommend his view, as a brief consideration of some reflections by more recent theologians will indicate.

A turning point occurs when Rudolf Bultmann argues in his *Theology of the New Testament* (1948–1953) that *sōma*, as Paul uses it in a number of passages, should be translated simply "I." "The *sōma* is not something that outwardly clings to a man's *self* . . . man does not *have* a *sōma*; he is *sōma*." For Paul, says Bultmann, "the equation '*sōma* = self, person' hovers in the background."[73] The self is alienated, estranged, and misoriented where *sarx* or the flesh rules, but the Spirit rules the resurrected self, the *sōma pneumatikon*, which hence is appropriately oriented. Thus, while a classical theologian would have said the resurrected body is the selfsame physical body with different qualities, but also that, in life eternal, the saint is completely sanctified, Bultmann says human existence, "both before and beyond death," is somatic, but at the consummation, there is "redemption from the *soma* as ruled by *sarx*."[74] Note, however, that, with Bultmann, while we are speaking of *sōma*, we are *not* now concerned with characteristics of a physical body.

Emil Brunner's position is somewhat similar. In *Our Faith* (1936), a short book pitched as a "simple . . . straightforward account," he says that, in history, the new life in fellowship with God and others in the Spirit "must abide in the old life," in a process of struggle and becoming. By contrast, eternal life after death is "life *with* God, *in* God, *from* God; life in perfect fellowship."[75] Years later, in his *Dogmatics*, Brunner criticizes "'the medieval conception of the resurrection of the body' . . . which has also been inserted into the Apostles' Creed," saying, "Paul's teaching about a spiritual body is in opposition to such a conception. Resurrection of the body, yes: Resurrection of the *flesh*, no! The 'Resurrection of the body' does not mean the identity of the resurrection body with the ma-

directions, see Miles Richardson, "The Gift of Presence: The Act of Leaving Artifacts at Shrines, Memorials, and Other Tragedies," in *Textures of Place: Exploring Humanist Geographies*, ed. Paul C. Adams, Steven Hoelscher, and Karen E. Till (Minneapolis: University of Minnesota Press, 2001), 257–72.

73. Rudolf Bultmann, *Theology of the New Testament*, trans. Kendrick Grobel, complete in 1 vol. (New York: Scribner's Sons, 1951, 1955), 1:194–95.

74. Bultmann, *Theology of the New Testament*, 1:198, 201, 239–46.

75. Emil Brunner, *Our Faith*, trans. John W. Rilling (New York: Scribner's Sons, 1954), 141, 151.

terial (although already transformed) body of flesh; but the resurrection of the body means the continuity of the individual personality on this side, and on that, of death."[76] Indeed, Brunner says, *sōma pneumatikon* is a "paradoxical self-contradictory concept," but what underlies it is "the principle of the individuality of man." It "expresses the wholeness of the person as an individuality created by God."[77] (To this, my former colleague in theology at Union Theological Seminary in Virginia added that the resurrected self is the individual shaped and sculpted by its specific historical experiences and relationships.)

A more recent New Testament scholar, Joseph Fitzmyer, thinks Bultmann's basic equation of *sōma* with self in 1 Corinthians finally incorrect because it fails to take sufficient account of "the dichotomy of body and soul" that "would be a common way of thinking" at Corinth.[78] Indeed, Fitzmyer claims that all attempts to formulate what Paul means, for example, including both the more traditional idea of a body endowed with special qualities and Bultmann's idea of the self, are in vain.[79] "One must remember that Paul has had no personal experience of such a 'body,' and in attempting an apocalyptic description of it, he is content to express it by an oxymoron. It is easier to say what Paul did not mean than to say what he meant: not a resurrected body of flesh; not the earthly body simply endowed with new *dotes*, 'qualities.' All such formulations are in vain. One should learn to live with the oxymoron."[80]

Fitzmyer's negative conclusion holds more theological promise than it first appears. Consider, for example, the position put forward by Norman Pittenger, who draws on process thought in his little book *After Death—Life in God*. Pittenger says that, as a general feature of a process model for God, "God remem-

76. Brunner, *Dogmatics*, 2:372.

77. Brunner, *Dogmatics*, 3:413.

78. Joseph A. Fitzmyer, SJ, *First Corinthians: A New Translation with Introduction and Commentary*, Anchor Yale Bible (New Haven: Yale University Press, 2008), 266, 587.

79. Not that some don't continue to try. Though he is working with many texts in addition to 1 Cor. 15, see, for example, N. T. Wright's contention in *The Resurrection of the Son of God* (Minneapolis: Fortress, 2003), 398, that resurrection is accompanied by a transformation of Jesus's body, and that the body Paul saw in his experience was "still a physical body." According to Wright, the resurrected Jesus appears to others in the Gospels as a human with a body endowed "with properties that are, to say the least, unusual" (605), such as the ability to vanish and to enter through closed doors. This is why friends don't recognize him. Michael Welker criticizes Wright for falling into the trap of "a speculative reconstruction of physical resurrection" (Welker, *God the Revealed: Christology*, trans. Douglas W. Stott [Grand Rapids: Eerdmans, 2013], 131).

80. Fitzmyer, *First Corinthians*, 597. He also includes a short review of other thinkers who regard Paul's expression as paradoxical on 594.

bers," or what happens in creation is taken into "the divine remembrance."[81] The God who creates is in this way "also the chief receptive agency in the creation. Whatever is done, and wherever or by what or whom it is done, makes a difference to God." As creative-responsive love, "God is not only that One who effects things; he is also the One who is affected by things . . . the accomplishments of the created order are received by him into his own life" (61).

The Seder meal at Passover, says Pittenger, illustrates this general idea. Those present remember what the religious tradition says about the event, and in the commemoration something happens: the deliverance is reenacted and made vividly contemporary. Ritually and liturgically, those present become participants in the deliverance. They ask that God remember what was done in the past—at the first Passover—that it be a part of the divine experience. They affirm that these things make a difference *for* and *in* God, and now, "it is *they*, quite as much as their ancestors . . . who know and experience God's arm as 'mighty to save'" (63). The ritual is a way of enacting and symbolizing the idea that God incorporates into the divine life and uses for good what takes place in the historical sequence of which they are a part. This is, in fact, "God's way of securing permanent validity for that which otherwise would be nothing other than an instance of the 'perpetual perishing' which patently marks the world as we know it." And indeed, for Pittenger, symbolic talk of resurrection presents the same basic idea. Those who are "in Christ" are raised up into the divine life where they are remembered and abide forever (64).

Pittenger thus neither repeats nor elaborates the conceptualities offered by Paul and John, but he presents a way of *reconceiving*, with the aid of process thought, "the implicit intention" of "the inherited notions of 'life after death'" (71). Moreover, for him, the fulcrum here is not what we may want, need, or desire, but an understanding of the divine nature or of who God is and the relationship of God to creation. God is *the supremely receptive One* who always and already takes up into Godself whatever happens in creation and history that may be used for good or for the divine aim. All depends on who God is, or on the doctrine of God. We do not know with certainty how this reception is accomplished or just what being taken up into "the divine memory" finally means, but God can and still does use the saints—the memories of them—to further the grand design of God's love. What happens after death thus depends on the inexhaustible divine receptivity. Pittenger puts it this way. "'Lord, in thy mercy, gather into thy purposes the lives of those we remember before thee,

81. Pittenger, *After Death*, 58. Hereafter, page references from this work will be given in parentheses in the text.

that they may not be lost.' These words, to my mind, say all that we can need or want" (76).

We now turn to the position of Maurice Wiles in *Reason to Believe*, a little book that attempts an intelligent but nontechnical interpretation of Christian faith. Wiles notes that Christian hope for life with God beyond death often makes use of "the idea of a non-physical soul as the essential person, which is able to survive bodily death and enjoy immortality free from the restraints of the body," though the close interrelation of the physical and nonphysical aspects of human life makes this "very difficult to entertain." Indeed, he says, that the body is integral to personal being "does nothing to remove the obvious difficulties in the concept of bodily resurrection."[82]

Wiles also notes that we do not know precisely what happened to precipitate the texts concerning Jesus's resurrection. The more important point is that Jesus's resurrection should not be taken on its own, "but as a climactic moment in the wider story of God's dealings with the world." Like Pittenger, then, Wiles thinks the emphasis falls, not on a single event, but on "the broader concept of the character of God." This broader concept, in turn, points to experiences of having "been taken into a relationship with God of such intensity" (presumably, in regeneration and in God's covenantal faithfulness) so "that it is inconceivable to envisage it ever being broken."[83] The conviction "that the final word rests with God rather than death" is "much more broadly based than on a single event in the past," and it "finds . . . powerful symbolic expression in the resurrection of Jesus."[84]

When he comes to the question of contemporary understanding, Wiles points out that humans are complicated organisms in which the physical and the nonphysical are intertwined in ways that remain mysterious. The whole clearly is greater than the sum of its parts, and we indicate this by using words such as "person," "self," and "spirit." "In short, what it is to be a human person necessarily transcends our capacity to understand. It is ultimately and impenetrably mysterious to us." This "fundamentally mysterious nature of the human person" indicates that hopes for life beyond death cannot be ruled out as impossible, "even when we are unable to conceive how such hopes might be fulfilled." Thus, for Wiles, "talk about an immortal soul or resurrected body is as symbolic as talk about the music of heaven or the flames of hell, the second coming of Christ and the final day." It expresses "a faith that the final word lies with God rather than death," and that this "final word involves God's human creation."[85] And so, once

82. Wiles, *Reason to Believe*, 112.
83. Wiles, *Reason to Believe*, 113.
84. Wiles, *Reason to Believe*, 114.
85. Wiles, *Reason to Believe*, 115–16.

again, we arrive at an eschatological statement quite compatible with Fitzmyer's conclusion that Paul's expression, *sōma pneumatikon*, though it points to life beyond death, furnishes us with something far short of a detailed and coherent conception of how this takes place.

The contemporary New Testament scholar Peter Lampe offers an interpretation of Paul that differs from Fitzmyer's as well as from Bultmann's equation of *sōma* with self, but that also has theological promise. Lampe points out that, in 1 Thessalonians 4:17 and 1 Corinthians 15:51–54, Paul considers "those persons who will still be alive at the time of the eschatological *parousia*. In this particular case, the physical bodies . . . will be 'snatched up . . . in the clouds to meet the Lord in the air' . . . and 'transformed' (1 Cor. 15:52)." But, says Lampe, in 2 Corinthians 5:1–4, Paul speaks of what happens when persons die. There he furnishes a description of human longing that uses images and metaphorical statements concerning "the unclothing and clothing of the self." As Lampe translates 5:2–4, in the present body "we groan, longing to be further clothed with our dwelling from heaven," and, indeed, "we groan, being burdened, because we do not want to be unclothed but to be further clothed."[86] Moreover, for Paul, the faithful who have died are with Christ, as is indicated by the phrase "those who have died (or fallen asleep) in Christ" (1 Cor. 15:18). According to Lampe, then, Paul's more complete idea is this: the self, the "me," or the "I" exists in this life with a physical body. For the faithful who die before the last day, however, the "I" or "me" is directly with Christ—"sleeping" until it is joined with an imperishable, transformed, and spiritual body (1 Thess. 4:14; 1 Cor. 15:51–53). Thus, at death, the "I" or "me" (indicated in Paul simply by personal pronouns) exists without the first physical body that is stripped off and also without the spiritual body, which will be given at the resurrection. And in this state, the "I" or the "me" is "with Christ."

Lampe elaborates: "the 'me,' the self" (which does not equate with *sōma*), "continues to exist as a relational entity between death and resurrection." Nevertheless, and quite significantly, "Paul does not spell out in detail how." The apostle is speculatively and theologically reticent—a quality Lampe thinks we do well to emulate. "God is 'faithful,'" says Lampe, "and we will be *with* Christ. These two promises are the only consolation a dying person really needs to know about his or her immediate future."[87]

Michael Welker puts forward a position that fits with Lampe's interpretation. Welker notes important complexities in Paul's statements, and he is critical of

86. Peter Lampe, "Paul's Concept of a Spiritual Body," in *Resurrection: Theological and Scientific Assessments*, ed. Ted Peters, Robert John Russell, and Michael Welker (Grand Rapids: Eerdmans, 2002), 112–13.

87. Lampe, "Paul's Concept of a Spiritual Body," 114.

attempts, such as N. T. Wright's, to speculatively reconstruct Jesus's resurrected body. Indeed, Welker says that, for Paul, a key point is that "the body is a *bearer of revelation* through which Jesus is glorified and can be recognized (2 Cor. 4:10; Gal. 6:17)." This claim, in turn, needs to be understood in conjunction with the wide range of meanings that accrue to the notion of spirit, for example, the mind, the intellect, or the pattern of a group or a person.[88] Thus, for Paul, "in the resurrection of Jesus Christ, we encounter the Spirit in 'bodily' form, as the 'Spirit of Christ' in what is now no longer 'fleshly' continuity with the life of the pre-Easter Jesus." This "self-disclosure of the Resurrected stands in both continuity and discontinuity with his pre-Easter life," and it also stands in continuity and discontinuity "with the activity of the Spirit as attested by biblical traditions."[89]

The resurrection of Christ, for Welker, is the presence of the fullness of his life and his personhood encountered in a variety of appearances in different forms. Moreover, Christ's "transfigured body . . . calls for the participation of the witnesses in the glorified life." Indeed, the witnesses "become 'one with Christ,'" as they do also in the church as Christ's body and in the Eucharist.[90] Welker then turns to other, complementary eschatological symbols. By the divine power of the Spirit, he says, participation in Christ, the resurrected one, allows for participation in eternal life or "the life of the world to come." In Christ, people participate in "the divine power and life that sustains, rescues, and ennobles the creation and will never perish."[91] This is how they participate in God's reign or kingdom.

Fitzmyer's point that it is easier to say what Paul did not mean than what he meant seems, once again, to be respected here. Welker affirms eternal life as life in Christ and in the power of the Spirit without speculating about the composition of resurrected bodies. Moreover, he is also able to envision eternal life in the broader context of the creation, the kingdom, and a world to come.

A Proposal

I am ready now to outline my own position, though I note from the outset that we are dealing here with something that, exegetically and otherwise, seems shrouded both in ambiguity and in mystery. This is one reason, I expect, for the

88. Welker, *God the Revealed*, 137–38. See also Michael Welker, "Flesh-Body-Heart-Soul-Spirit: Paul's Anthropology as an Interdisciplinary Bridge-Theory," in *The Depth of the Human Person: A Multidisciplinary Approach*, ed. Michael Welker (Grand Rapids: Eerdmans, 2014), 45–57.

89. Welker, *God the Revealed*, 142.

90. Michael Welker, "Theological Realism and Eschatological Symbol Systems," in Peters, Russell, and Welker, *Resurrection*, 39.

91. Welker, "Theological Realism," 42.

plurality of theological interpretations both within and beyond the New Testament. It also seems a good reason to offer one's own statements with a measure of humility, and a recognition that the plurality likely will continue.

God is the answer to the question of hope. Among other things, this means the controlling idea is the divine pattern and tendency, or who God is, rather than simply what we may believe we want or need to live "meaningful" lives. For me, as for a number of theologians, the affirmation of life eternal does not stand with Jesus's resurrection taken on its own. The broader and more fundamental answer to the question of hope is the presiding mystery construed as Creator, Judge, and Redeemer, the God of grace who goes out from Godself to bestow existence and life, to challenge corrupting constriction, and to re-turn persons in Christ and the Spirit to an enlarging ec-centricity. All creatures, including we ourselves, have value and worth within the frame of this gracious divine tendency; all are fashioned to participate in a vast network or ensemble of interdependent interrelations that (somehow) is also on its way toward a redemption beyond, which cannot be equated with our present experience.

Humans are physically embodied and also embedded in the planetary home we call Earth. Their embodied embeddedness points to their ineluctable interrelation with Earth and cosmos, and thus to the importance of portraying redemption in a manner that refers not only to us but also to a renewed world or creation.[92] At the same time, it is also true that our lives are mysterious, inexplicable apart from connections with particular persons, events, conditions, sufferings, and realities beyond our control. Our lives are given and doxology evoking, social, distinctively capable and responsible, historical, and personal. This last point—we are, as we often say and as Wiles and others also note, *persons*—means we are self-conscious agents who emerge from but cannot be reduced to the sum of our parts. As distinctively equipped, personal, self-conscious, and reflective participants who appreciate that we live and move in the midst of a vast cosmos, we may in fact also appreciate that we live in face of mystery.[93]

Theologically and biblically, we say that humans are created in the divine image, meaning, I think, that we are equipped to distinctively mirror and reflect the divine or the God of grace. How so? One upshot of almost all we have said—about creation as the gracious bestowal of existence and life, judgment as the right nightmares and influences to encourage us to turn, and redemption or renewal as participation in a true life of attentiveness and love to God and the

92. See, for example, John Polkinghorne's notion of an emergent, new creation in both continuity and discontinuity with the old in "Eschatological Credibility: Emergent and Teleological Processes," in Peters, Russell, and Welker, *Resurrection*, 55.

93. Chap. 5, prop. #35.

things of God, or love of God and neighbor—is that, however imperfectly and fragmentarily, persons of piety know and apprehend these things. They know and grasp that, by grace alone, we are caught up into a defining relationship. Thus, in Psalm 148, while all creatures, including humans, are called to praise God by their very being and doing, we humans are called to do so consciously, reflectively, and liturgically. Indeed, we humans write the psalm precisely because we *may know and acknowledge* that both we and all other creatures mirror the gracious God by our very living and doing. We may consciously envision and appreciate the entire ensemble in relation to God. And it is in this conscious apprehension or acknowledgment that, when compared with other creatures we know, we are *distinctive* in our mirroring or reflecting of gracious deity.

My particular branch of Protestant Christianity calls this never-failing relationship, which often is articulated in terms of creation, judgment, and redemption and of which we humans may be conscious, the one covenant of grace. It includes you, me, and all else. The gracious divine economy or tendency makes for a fundamental relationship that we are called to appreciate and acknowledge in wonder, humility, awe, sorrow, remorse, gratitude, faithfulness, and hope. Now we ask just what form or shape this relationship may take after death or beyond history. But we should be careful to note the most important point: God is the answer to the question of hope. Because the presiding mystery is the God of grace, we have confidence that the relationship established by grace alone neither falters nor fails. Nevertheless, given the longer theological tradition as well as piety's funereal predilections, we ask a further question about the form this relationship may take.

In order to elaborate and refine this further question, return for a moment to Aquinas's claim that "in heaven there will be every kind of sharing of all goods," and that all will love one another. The affirmation is especially important because it points to the fulfillment of sanctification in Christ and the Spirit, or to the completion of created life's ec-centric vector and orientation. And, to my mind, the New England Puritan Jonathan Edwards offers a compelling and instructive statement of this same idea in his sermonic lecture "Heaven as a World of Charity or Love."

Edwards takes 1 Corinthians 13:8–10 as the text for his reflections, which he has in the King James Version as follows: "Charity never faileth: but whether there be prophecies, they shall fail; whether there be tongues, they shall cease; whether there be knowledge, it shall vanish away. For we know in part, and we prophesy in part. But when that which is perfect is come, then that which is in part shall be done away." "Charity or divine love," says Edwards, this "great fruit of the Spirit," is the same affection poured into human hearts when they are born of the Spirit (rather than the flesh) "in the work of regeneration." It will remain after death and the end of the world when all other fruits of the Spirit have failed because "God dwells in heaven and fills it" with "God's glorious presence."[94] And, since God is love, in heaven love "dwells and reigns" in "every heart."[95]

The wellspring or principle of heavenly life therefore amounts to a genuine and universal benevolence, or to what Edwards elsewhere calls a true virtue that extends beyond all partial interests and limited communities, for example, devotion to one's ethnic group or nation. This love is true and neither corrupt nor selfish, because it "aims at no end inconsistent with God's glory and the happiness of the universe." The saints in heaven are animated by the principle of a renewed nature; they "love God for his own sake, and each other for God's sake, and for the sake of the relation that they have to him, and the image of God that is upon them."[96] This is a reason why heaven finally must be a *world* of love rather than simply a state in which discrete, separate, and individual souls enjoy a vision of God. Life eternal is the completion of reconciliation in which all have "the most excellent and perfect behavior . . . toward God and each other."[97]

Let me underscore this point by repeating it in terms I have used throughout this systematic: the kingdom is the fulfillment of true communion with God in community with others, and so also the completion of the vector of true, expansive, and ec-centric (rather than corrupted and contracted) life. This vector emerges with the good, interdependent creation. Though fragmented and corrupted by the human fault, it nevertheless comes to expression in residual social feeling and a sense of equity, in covenantal community, in Jesus's teaching of love of God and neighbor, and in the church as a society of mutual love and care that gathers persons long separated and in conflict. We enact it liturgically in the sacrament of the Lord's Supper. Or, as we might say in Johannine phrases, eternal life, as a life of love born of the Spirit, is a gift granted here and now that is brought to completion in future glory. Only the fulfillment of this now-struggling vector toward ec-centric existence must therefore be understood as a society or realm in which the poor and the vulnerable are blessed, a world in which persons are attentive to neighbors, both human and nonhuman, something like Edward Hicks's *Peaceable Kingdom*, because those who love truly stand in relationships with others. The completion or fulfillment of ec-centric existence drives toward images and reflections like those in Romans 8, where, in addition to humans, the whole universe is involved in the movement toward new creation.[98] Thus, when

94. Edwards, *Charity and Its Fruits, in Ethical Writings*, ed. Paul Ramsey, vol 8 of *WJE*, 366, 387.

95. Edwards, *Charity and Its Fruits*, 373.

96. Edwards, *Charity and Its Fruits*, 374.

97. Edwards, *Charity and Its Fruits*, 383.

98. David L. Bartlett, "Creation Waits with Eager Longing," in *God Who Creates: Essays*

properly refined and elaborated, our further question is this: May we hope for life eternal in a world, kingdom, or society of love?

Such a world, then, would complete or fulfill the ec-centric vector of existence, which is, at present, fragmentary and struggling. And this is why such a world must always be in some sense present but also not yet. In piety's vision, God's kingdom—a world, realm, or city where the poor and the vulnerable are blessed, where all are oriented by love of God and neighbor, where sorrows and tears are no more, and where all creation is redeemed—is a symbol. It points to an eschatological reality that is present in traces but never entirely present, emergent and always future. We catch glimpses of this reality that neither gainsay nor cancel out the many negative, sometimes fearful, and genuinely disturbing occurrences in our experience, glimpses that do not comprehend the entirety of what we hope for but that, interpreted in the light of eschatological symbols and resources, embolden us to hope. May I have recourse to Hicks's painting once again? *The Peaceable Kingdom* appropriately conflates William Penn's treaty with Chief Tomanend in Shackamaxon, Pennsylvania, in 1683 (a trace in history) with a depiction of lion and lamb lying down together led by a little child (a transcendent hope). It joins historical possibility with the hope for a kingdom beyond.

Informed now by Hicks's painting, we ask where we encounter the hoped-for kingdom, the society and creation renewed by the grace of God. The answer? In history as we know it, the beloved community never arrives entirely or complete. But there *are* traces, occasions on which we catch a glimpse, and, for Hicks, we catch a glimpse of the kingdom when Penn and Tomanend reconcile and make peace.

Here, as elsewhere, I think the person of piety knows we are mired in misdirection, tragedy, and death, but she continues to look for instances of redirection, promise, and life. She is a hopeful realist who—now here, now there—glimpses occasional bright spots. Penn and Tomanend make peace. A husband cares for his wife through years of trying and dying illness—a promise splendidly kept. These occasions are fleeting, fragmentary, and often ambiguous. This seems obvious as soon as we consider the longer genocidal history of treaties between Europeans and Native Americans. But then and nevertheless, the hopeful realist does something truly extravagant. Remembering the God of grace disclosed in Jesus's performance, she hopes for something more and as yet unseen. Living in a world of perils and promises, sufferings, brutalities, and possibilities, she hopes for the new-community-overcoming-alienations-divisions-and-conflicts. She hopes for the kingdom beyond.[99]

---

in Honor of W. Sibley Towner, ed. William P. Brown and S. Dean McBride Jr. (Grand Rapids: Eerdmans, 2000), 229–30.

99. *Holy Mountain III*, a painting done in 1945 by the African American World War One

Indeed, hope for this kingdom comes to expression in the initial lines of the Lord's Prayer. We say "*Our* Father," signaling that the God of grace stands in relation to all, and that we have to do here with an intensely important but also nonexclusive relationship. "Hallowed be thy name." Our first petition asks that God's name be held holy, or, in effect, that we shall hold it holy and thus be changed and conformed to God and God's glory. "Thy kingdom come." We pray that God complete and fulfill God's own purpose and aim in a realm of justice and shalom. "Thy will be done, on earth as in heaven." We ask for the transformative sanctification of worldly interrelations, and for a renewed or new world.

What we petition and hope for here is, at best, only elusively and fragmentarily present, but it is relevant nonetheless. The kingdom, embodied in Jesus as the Christ, the kingdom-minded one, remains the true criterion by which human history shall be judged, and this idea receives mythological representation in visions of the parousia: "You will see the Son of Man . . . coming with the clouds of heaven" (Mark 14:62).[100] The kingdom's negative relevance, as we have seen, is that all communities, societies, nations, and institutions fall short; all are subject to criticism. The positive relevance is that the kingdom, city, or world-to-come functions aspirationally and hopefully. It points to what may and should be, and so it helps us to sharpen our practical aims and to live more truly.

We remind ourselves once again, however, that we see only through a glass darkly (1 Cor. 13:12) and that hope for what is seen is not hope (Rom. 8:24). The kingdom is emergent. You and I catch glimpses of it here and now, and sometimes in the unlikeliest places, but it also remains a transcendent reality at the edge of history and beyond. We note that this kingdom hope—unclear though it may be—passes Rauschenbusch's social gospel test because its inherently eccentric vector does not reduce to a "refined egoism" at odds with Jesus and the prophets. It also passes a theocentric test since, unlike much conventional talk of "life after death," it centers on God and God's purposes rather than on individual fulfillment, and as a hope for a *world* to come it presses beyond anthropocentric expectations toward an inkling of renewed creation. But, again, as *hope*, it remains unseen, and so we add this: though piety recognizes the symbolic and even opaque character of its ideas of eternal life in the world to come, it remains steadfast, trusting that, whatever its eventual shape or form, and whether or not it entails our personal survival, the relationship with God

---

veteran Horace Pippin, shows the peaceful beasts and a black shepherd, woman, and child in the foreground, but a tank, foot soldiers, and a figure hanging on a rope from a tree in its dark background—as if to emphasize that the kingdom really is beyond.

100. For a classic statement of this point, see Reinhold Niebuhr, *NDM*, 2:290–94.

neither falters nor fails.[101] Talk about resurrection, about continuing spirits, and selves, or about worlds and kingdoms to come remains opaque. Nevertheless, it articulates Reformed piety's claim that the final word lies with the Creator, Judge, and Redeemer, or with the God of grace, rather than with death. It expresses piety's confidence that God is the answer to the question of hope.

Proposition #70 God is love.

This culminating affirmation nevertheless expresses what is always already the case.

First John delivers the love commandment. For the writer, it is *not* new, since Jesus taught it, and so the community has heard it from the beginning of the Christian movement (2:7). The commandment is "that we should love one another. We must not be like Cain" (3:11–12). Why? Because if the love of God abides in us, then we shall love in truth, we shall walk as Jesus walked (2:6), and this way is diametrically opposed to the way of Cain. At the same time, however, this must also mean that the commandment is always new, always a departure from humanity's chronic fault. "Thus, the author of 1 John sees the life of love in the community as evidence of the eschatological work of God in making all things new."[102] It is part and parcel of the renewal of life via the ec-centric impulse or dynamic of life in Christ and the Spirit (2:8).

There are, in fact, two dueling loves. There is love of the things of the world, or an orientation of the flesh that is self-seeking, overreaching, and represented by Cain, the spiral of violence and wrongdoing in the early chapters of Genesis, etc. There is also the love of God (or the Father), which is outgoing, comes to us, accepts us, and adopts us as heirs and children in Jesus Christ (3:1). If this love of God abides in you, then you too will be outgoing, ec-centric, loving others.

So we begin to see a basic logic. Genuine love is from the God who loves and abides in the Christian community, a new community of mutuality in Christ and the Spirit in which life is renewed. "We love because he first loved us" (4:19). Hence, the repeated address in 1 John, "Beloved . . ." Hence, the claim in 4:21 that "those who love God must love their brothers and sisters also." By contrast, the

101. I agree with B. A. Gerrish, *Christian Faith: Dogmatics in Outline* (Louisville: Westminster John Knox, 2015), 316. "For myself, I think the weight of tradition advises Christians, despite modern skepticism, not to surrender the belief in personal survival too quickly and yet to remain frankly agnostic about its nature and, more important, not to make it the whole of Christian hope for the future."

102. John Painter, *1, 2, and 3 John*, ed. Daniel Harrington, SJ (Collegeville, MN: Liturgical Press, 2008), 179.

way of Cain stands opposed to the love of the God who creates. The way of Cain, as is apparent from the opening chapters of Genesis, stands against the life for which we are created and sustained; it is inhumane.

The writer of 1 John wants readers to "test the spirits to see whether they are from God" (4:1), and, not surprisingly, then, the primary test is whether they lead us to love. There are many spirits, for example, the spirit of empire or of material gain, and each orients or conditions our manner of living. But the true Spirit confesses that Jesus Christ is from God, and it brings a distinct and enduring fruit. "Beloved, let us love one another, because love is from God; everyone who loves is born of God and knows God" (4:7). So, the life of love is appropriate because "love is from God." The next verse goes a crucial step further: "Whoever does not love does not know God, for God is love" (4:8). We know this because "God's love was revealed among us in this way: God sent his only Son into the world so that we might live through him" (4:9). That is, God reveals God's love by bestowing renewed life through Jesus Christ. Jesus as the Christ loves others, and he reveals or discloses that God is love and that to walk in love as he did is true and renewed life.

The text of 1 John concentrates on the demonstration of God's love in Jesus's atoning sacrifice for our sins (4:10), as have many strands in Christian tradition. That is, in terms of the theology I have presented in this volume, emphasis falls on Jesus's crucifixion and resurrection as the right nightmare, and then, beyond sin's destructive death-dealing consequences, on the emergence of new or renewed life. If we also look to the way Jesus walked as the disclosure of divine love and even of the fact that God *is* love, then we may add that Jesus demonstrates God's love also in his acceptance or welcoming of persons in open commensality and in healing, and in every way that he displays the grace of God. The disclosure will also include Jesus's devotion to the cause for which he dies, his kingdom-mindedness, his message that God's kingdom is a just and inclusive reign of wholeness and shalom, a kingdom in which the poor and the vulnerable are blessed and healed, and a reign in which the God of grace values all. That is, Jesus displays the truth that God is love, not only as the crucified and resurrected one who empowers renewed life but also as the one who teaches the truth about God's reign and embodies it.

This, then, is the ground for the new commandment revealed in Jesus Christ, and the content of what is revealed, namely, that God is love. Raymond Brown says the statement "God is love" is not a precise definition but a description of God in relation to humans. Moreover, it "does not mean that there was no divine love before the coming of God's Son into the world"—an important reason to emphasize the affirmation here that God *is* love. God "did not become love" with the coming of Jesus, says Brown, but Jesus as the Christ reveals what God always already is.[103] We might say, following John 1 and the Logos hymn quoted there, that this is what God is from the very beginning.

Again, the disclosure of God's love in Jesus Christ does not contrast with God's character as displayed in the Hebrew Scriptures. The statement "God is love" represents a further elaboration of *hesed*, or God's covenantal love and mercy. The contrast is not with the God revealed in the Hebrew Scriptures but with the (corrupted) love of the world represented by Cain and by others. As Georg Strecker reminds us, God chooses God's people in an unconstrained act of love and saving deliverance from captivity in Egypt. God's *agapē*—and this is the word used for God's love in 1 John—is a descending love, a love that goes out to and seeks others. This same going out, this same unconstrained love, is the basis for creation, and it is identical with the mercy God shows to the whole earth.[104] The claim of God's love, based in the fact that God first loved us, is, in this sense, a claim on all. And among those who live in Christ and the Spirit, "human love is not the cause but the manifestation of being begotten by God."[105]

The statement "God is love" therefore is not describing an inner-Trinitarian relationship among persons of the Godhead but refers to the fact that God is the one who loves in relation to humanity and world. God's *agapē*, or the descending love of God, is present and displayed in creation, in the history of God's dealings with Israel, in Jesus as the Christ, and in the Spirit pouring out the love of God into human hearts and gathering a "communion of those who, as beloved of God, reciprocate that love."[106] God is the ultimate source and ground of loving one another.[107]

Consider now Martin Luther King Jr.'s description of *agapē* among humans as a "disinterested love" in the sense that it does not seek our own good and that it "does not begin by discriminating between worthy and unworthy people, or any qualities

103. Raymond Brown, SS, *The Epistles of John: Translated with Introduction, Notes, and Commentary* (Garden City, NY: Doubleday, 1982), 551. The point is also one on which John Calvin insists. See Calvin, *ICR* 2.16.4.

104. Georg Strecker, *The Johannine Letters*, trans. Linda M. Maloney, ed. Harold Attridge (Minneapolis: Fortress, 1996), 144–48. Strecker refers to Deut. 7:8 and to Pss. Sol. 18:3, which reads, "Thine ears listen to the hopeful prayers of the poor. Thy judgments (are executed) upon the whole earth in mercy."

105. Painter, *1, 2, and 3 John*, 268, 270.

106. Strecker, *The Johannine Letters*, 147–48.

107. H. Richard Niebuhr, *Christ and Culture* (New York: Harper & Row, 1951), 27–29, makes a similar point. Niebuhr's definition of Christ emphasizes the "unique devotion to God . . . which can be symbolized by no other figure of speech so well as by the one which calls him Son of God." This devotion, says Niebuhr, means that Jesus points away from the world toward "the One who creates all worlds, who is Other than all worlds." Nevertheless, "since God is *agapē*," the one who loves God must also point back again toward human beings and the world that God loves. Devotion to the God who is *agapē* always orients life ec-centrically toward others.

people possess." *Agapē*, says King, is "a love in which the individual seeks . . . the good of the neighbor" (1 Cor. 10:24). It is a "'neighbor-regarding concern for others,' which discovers the neighbor in every man it meets," and "therefore . . . makes no distinction between friends and enemies" but "is directed toward both."[108] We might say that, when it abides in us, God's love or *agapē* loosely imitates the God who makes the sun to rise and rain to fall on the evil and the good (Matt. 5:43–45), and, indeed, this is how we may participate in the Divine Project.

Go a step further. King notes that *agapē*, or "the love of God operating in the human heart," is not romantic or merely sentimental, and that it is "more than friendship." It is "understanding, creative, redemptive good will for all men" that aims at reconciliation and restored or beloved community. Thus, "when one rises to love on this level, he loves men not because he likes them, not because their ways appeal to him, but he loves every man because God loves him. And he rises to the point of loving the person who does an evil deed while hating the evil deed that the person does." Indeed, says King, "I'm very happy that [Jesus] didn't say like your enemies, because it's difficult to like some people. Like is sentimental, and its pretty difficult to like someone bombing your home . . . 'threatening your children,' or denying your civil rights."[109]

Now suppose, following 1 John and King, we take this description of the love of God that abides and operates in persons as a clue to God's love for humanity and world. The point then would be that God's *agapē* is not romantic or sentimental, but a matter of creative and redemptive good will that does not discriminate between those who are worthy and unworthy but is directed toward all. God's *agapē* loves creatures while it hates the evil that creatures do.[110] This, we might say, is what comes to expression in the life and ministry of Jesus as the Christ, in his calls to repentance, his welcoming of tax collectors and sinners, and his kingdom-mindedness and devotion, as well as in the cross and resurrection, and in the Spirit pouring out the love of God and gathering a community that reciprocates God's love. Moreover, this same ec-centric vector, this same going out to others, is part and parcel of creation and interdependent life as the divine gift of participation in being, existence, and world. It is part and parcel of redemption or the gift of a good, participatory, and renewed life that, beyond conflict and tragedy, strives for reconciled community, and so fulfills what hu-

108. *A Testament of Hope: The Essential Writings of Martin Luther King, Jr.*, ed. James Melvin Washington (New York: Harper & Row, 1986), 19.

109. King, *A Testament of Hope*, 12, 46–47.

110. Consider Calvin's statement in *ICR* 2.16.3. "But because the Lord wills not to lose what is his in us, out of his own kindness he still finds something to love. However much we may be sinners by our own fault, we nevertheless remain his creatures. However much we have brought death upon ourselves, yet he has created us unto life."

mans are for. It is also the *telos* of judgment or of the negative consequences of sinful constriction that may push persons and communities away from self-seeking toward contrition and the renewal of life's participatory and attentive stance toward others. Not surprisingly, then, the creed presents eternal life as the completion of the Spirit's sanctifying work in bringing about the proper orientation of persons (versus the flesh). We should also add that the kingdom, as a society of love, symbolizes the fulfillment of reconciliation and life together that emerges when life's ec-centric and participatory vector is fulfilled. Both life eternal and the kingdom indicate a movement toward the enlargement of life versus its destructive diminution and constriction.

The basic point I mean to make here, then, is that the divine love closely intertwines with every aspect of piety's experience of the God of grace. It is mediated in and through the graces we encounter as creatures called into existence and sustained in the midst of a compelling creation, as misdirected agents pressed to mitigate our persistently destructive bents and turn toward ec-centric living, and as persons and communities raised up beyond our own doings (and even imaginings) to renewing opportunities for participating in life together in communion and community. Here I am willing to make a metaphysical statement. The God of grace is the tendency of reality to go out to create or bring into existence, to judge, and to renew.[111]

Even so, it is crucial to note that the grace and goodness and love of God are by no means always easily or readily apparent. There are occasions and experiences in which the goodness of God is *not* displayed, but instead darkly obscured by natural and social structures and powers bearing down upon us to elicit intense anxiety, pain, and even despair.

> "For he crushes me with a tempest,
>   and multiplies my wounds without cause;
> he will not let me get my breath,
>   but fills me with bitterness." (Job 9:17–18)

It is a notable feature of Reformed Christian wisdom to insist that God is present here, too—though perhaps hiddenly, sublimely, and or even fearfully so. One thinks of Sarah Edwards's lament at her husband's untimely death: "What shall I say? A holy and good God has covered us with a dark cloud." The divine gov-

111. It is in this sense that I would interpret James M. Gustafson's statement: "I participate in God's love of all that exists; all that exists comes from the amplitude of goodness in God, the ultimate power." See James M. Gustafson, "Participation: A Religious Worldview," *Journal of Religious Ethics* 44, no. 1 (2016): 172.

ernance—sustaining though it often is—does not guarantee all relevant aspects of the happiness and well-being of persons and communities.[112]

Piety does not take this to refute its sense that both God and life are good, though surely the quality of thankfulness is strained, and there is cause for complaint. There are, as all of us should know, the highly destructive and even disastrous evils—the ravages of rampant and debilitating diseases, the torturing oppressions that affect millions. There are also the smaller-scale but nonetheless poignant distresses and defeats that almost every family confronts over time, the debilitating physical and psychological conditions of loved ones, the beloved who suffer and are taken from us. The persons ensnared in and sometimes consumed by these conditions are, of course, not without their abilities to bestow profound affection and happiness and joy on others. I want to say that, somewhat like the troubled, rusting, blighted, but also vibrant New Jersey landscapes visible from some passenger trains, they may retain their compelling dignity, value, and beauty. But there is still reason to lament ("My God, my God . . ."), and I cannot either remove or absolve God from these realities any more than the better biblical and theological traditions do.

Nevertheless, and in sum, the statement "God is love" points to the characteristic exercise of the really Real, to the divine going out as Creator, Judge, and Redeemer, or to the divine tendency that entails an affirmation of the worth of creatures, as we say, "in God's sight." The divine excellence, in turn, is the ground and source of a love among us that attempts (however fragmentarily) to go out and to reconcile what is separated, alienated, and estranged. This is the logic of grace, and it correlates with piety's inkling that in, through, and despite searing trials and sufferings and tragedies nothing separates us from the love of God. Theologically speaking, no created or existent reality is ever entirely alone. To be is to be in relationship with the God who always already stands in relationship to all, and it is good to be because the God of grace is inseparable from creaturely existence.

112. The Sarah Edwards quote is from Sereno E. Dwight, "Memoirs of Jonathan Edwards, A. M.," in *The Works of Jonathan Edwards* (Edinburgh: Banner of Truth Trust, 1834), 1:clxxix, and quoted in chap. 4, prop. #33, where I also note my qualified agreement with Mrs. Edwards.

Epilogue

The Sense the Trinity Makes

Throughout this systematic I maintain that Christian theology is a historically particular and practical wisdom that articulates a vision of God, the world, and ourselves.[1] I say, too, that my theology is Trinitarian because it indicates how God, Christ, and Spirit (2 Cor. 13:13) are interconnected in the experience and life of the Christian community. Even so, my metaphysical reticence leads me to remain agnostic about "internal relations" among three persons within God.[2]

These characteristics of my theology go together. That Christian theology is a practical wisdom points to a deep connection between theology and ecclesial instruction in Christian piety, fidelity, and living. A primary purpose of the church, in my judgment, is to build up the people of God in a life of faithfulness. This, broadly speaking, is its pastoral aim, and Christian theology serves this aim by furnishing a vision or a picture of the many objects and others with which we interact, for example, our children, the nations, and Earth's planetary ecology, with respect to the God disclosed in Jesus Christ. It thereby helps persons and communities to respond faithfully to God in the midst of their interrelations with these many objects and others.[3] Thus, when I look for the sense the Trinity

1. Chap. 1, prop. #1.

2. Chap. 1, prop. #14.

3. Chap. 1, prop. #1. Indeed, just because Christian theology is a practical wisdom that pursues piety's need to envision things in relation to God, I am not at all certain it is a discipline like other modern disciplines. For one thing, its object, that is, God, and other things in relation to God, is peculiar, since the divine is not an object alongside other objects and is not known as other objects are. Peculiarity is signaled, too, by the capacious or panoramic intent of Christian theology, which follows from the conviction that there is nothing that is not related to God in some way, and that seems at odds with the more specialized and discrete aims of modern disciplines, for example, sociology or biology, which focus on specific kinds of information. See Douglas F. Ottati, "A Collaborative Manner of Theological Reflection," in *Theology as Interdisciplinary Inquiry: Learning with and from the Natural Sciences and Human Sciences*, ed. Robin W. Lovin and Joshua Mauldin (Grand Rapids: Eerdmans, 2017), 133–37.

makes, I look for it at the level of faithful living or the ec-centric vector, trajectory, and pattern in life that Christian piety supports.

This puts me at odds with much "mainline Trinitarian theology," which, as B. A. Gerrish points out, "insists that the presence of God in Christ and the church requires us to think of two further eternal hypostases in addition to the Father." Gerrish continues:

> There are ways of interpreting the New Testament in support of this view, including the Pauline testimony to the preexistence of the Son and the Johannine notion of another Paraclete. But orthodox Trinitarianism must be understood contextually, as refutation of particular ancient "heresies," and is not immune to critical questions in another day. To begin with, there are questions about a too literal reading of symbolic and analogical language. Furthermore, although the possibility of distinctions within the Godhead (*Deus in se*) need not be ruled out, the supposed logical inference from what the New Testament says of Father, Son, and Holy Spirit to what "must" be affirmed about an immanent Trinity is not self-evidently convincing.[4]

Gerrish's statements, with which I agree, clearly leave room for other views. Before I outline my own, however, let me also comment briefly on features of a more orthodox argument made by Kathryn Tanner.

Tanner makes a claim with which I basically agree: "the Father is always and everywhere working to bring about what accords with the shape or form of the Son, efforts that are enabled, sustained, and completed in the power of the Spirit."[5] Along the way, however, she also makes statements I find unnecessary about how Word and Spirit go out from the Father and what classical theologians call the order of procession from the Father of the Son and the Spirit. Quite importantly, I think, she also recognizes that, "whatever one's other theological presuppositions, if one does not assume an already developed trinitarian theology, one is hard pressed to get one out of the NT. It is a long and hard theological road from scripture to the Christian ecumenical consensus at Chalcedon."[6] Indeed, she says, "the NT does not . . . contain . . . a very highly developed Trinitarian theology; that only developed centuries later, at least in part because of all kinds of further pressures—theological, political, and so on."[7]

4. B. A. Gerrish, *Christian Faith: Dogmatics in Outline* (Louisville: Westminster John Knox, 2015), 305.

5. Kathryn Tanner, *Christ the Key* (Cambridge: Cambridge University Press, 2010), 195–96.

6. Tanner, *Christ the Key*, 158.

7. Tanner, *Christ the Key*, 149.

What Tanner argues instead is that, if one begins with a developed Trinitarian theology, one may interpret the NT in the light of this later doctrine, especially if one reads it "through the developing sense of the soteriological stakes of belief in Christ." These stakes she aligns with the affirmation that "Jesus achieves for us some sort of deification or enjoyment of divine properties like that of eternal life," and that, to do this, Jesus can be "no mere creature" but must be "of the same divine rank" with the Father.[8]

Tanner's account of salvation and its christological requirements recalls Athanasius. ("But humanity would not have been deified if joined to a creature, or unless the Son was true God.")[9] I agree that the New Testament may be read to affirm that Father, Son, and Spirit are working in the same direction to bring about ec-centric and renewed life but would add that one may read it this way without assuming what, in any case, is *not* articulated so clearly in the New Testament, namely, that God, Christ, and the Spirit are "of the same divine rank." Again, it seems possible to articulate life everlasting as a fruit of God's raising up of Jesus from the dead without also insisting that it amounts to a deification worked by Jesus. Or, to put this another way, I think the gracious all-ruling Father of the universe quite capable of working redemption in and through Christ, Spirit, and church even if neither Christ nor Spirit is *homoousios tō patri*.

Tanner, of course, does *not* logically infer from the New Testament that an immanent Trinity *must* be affirmed. As I understand her, she argues that hers is a possible approach, and also admits (at least tacitly) that there may be others.[10] Suppose, then, that one has less confidence in the ecumenical creeds than Tanner does.[11] If so, then one is likely to be less comfortable than she is in assuming the

8. Tanner, *Christ the Key*, 156.

9. *Athanasius*, edited with introductions by Khaled Anatolios (London: Routledge, 2004), 163. Also, "if the Son was a creature, humanity would have remained none the less mortal and not united with God" (162). These quotations are from Athanasius's *Orations against the Arians*. Or, again, from his "Letter 40: To Adelphius," the Word "became a human being that we might be divinized in him" (238). Anatolios points out that Athanasius's understanding of creation "emphasizes that humanity's vulnerability is due to its origination from nothing," and, among other things, divinization in Christ corrects this (defect?) (65).

10. To her credit in my view, she also connects it with an emphasis on "a form of living in keeping with Christ's" and with service to the world. Tanner, *Christ the Key*, 199, 205–6.

11. A number of Reformed theologians, who tend to regard the councils as important but historically particular and fallible articulations of faith, seem less sanguine about the ecumenical creeds than is Tanner. See E. J. Nijenhuis, "Calvin's Attitude towards the Symbols of the Early Church during the Conflict with Caroli," in *Ecclesia Reformata: Studies on the Reformation*, trans. Mary Foran (Leiden: Brill, 1972), 73–96, and also Friedrich Schleiermacher, *CF*, #170 (pp. 738–42). On the authority of church councils and creeds, see the Scots Confession,

correctness and soteriological necessity of the later two-natures Christology and Trinitarian doctrine, and then interpreting the New Testament in those terms.

A Biblically Initiated Exploration

My own understanding of the sense Trinitarian reflections make begins with the observation that they emerge from a biblically initiated exploration. Early Christians inherited and accepted from Judaism the conviction that God is one creator, governor, and deliverer. Indeed, the Gospels themselves portray Jesus as pointing in his special prayer to "our Father," whose name is to be hallowed and whose kingdom shall come. For Jesus, God is the one who feeds birds and clothes lilies, creates all things, and whose reign is coming to fulfillment. At the same time, however, communities gathered in Christ's name through the Spirit also believed that in Christ, the person-for-others who was crucified and resurrected, "there is a new creation: everything old has passed away; see, everything has become new!" (2 Cor. 5:17). How were they to interpret and make sense of their experience of reconciliation, redemption, and renewal in the context of their monotheistic conviction?

Wrestling with this question, many came to understand Jesus as the Messiah or the Christ, the one who proclaims the advent of God's kingdom and the one in whom that saving reality is made manifest. He is the exalted "Son of Man" who will return with the clouds of heaven (Mark 13:26); the second Adam, who succeeds where the first failed (Rom. 5:12–19; 1 Cor. 15:45); the teacher who delivers perfect wisdom (Matt. 5–7); the pioneer and perfecter of our faith (Heb. 12:2). His cross is the power of God (1 Cor. 1:18). And, as we have seen, this is not all. Images multiply, from "the image of the invisible God, the firstborn of all creation" (Col. 1:15–17), and the one who "was declared to be Son of God with power according to the Spirit of holiness by resurrection from the dead" (Rom. 1:4), to the Logos or Word of God who was in the beginning with God (John 1:1–14).[12]

Again, those who continued to experience the risen Lord sacramentally and otherwise in the church believed that the Spirit endowed Jesus with power and also gathered and energized the church in his name (Matt. 3:13–17; Acts 2:1–21). Believers were baptized into the body of Christ, united with one another, and

BOC 3.20, and the Westminster Confession of Faith, *BOC* 6.175. The latter says: "all synods and councils since the apostles' times, whether general or particular, may err, and many have erred."

12. For interpretations of and comments on some of these images, see chap. 7, props. #50 and #51.

reborn by the power of the Spirit (1 Cor. 12:13; John 3:1–9). By the Spirit Christians received gifts of wisdom, knowledge, faith, healing, discernment, tongues, and the interpretation of tongues (1 Cor. 12:4–11). In the Spirit they were sanctified and justified (1 Cor. 6:11), and they experienced a new life of love, joy, and peace (Gal. 4:6; 5:22–25).

With some frequency, then, the early communities' explorations into experiences of redemption and renewal point to a threefold pattern, economy, or dynamic in their experiences of God.[13] The Creator and Father of the universe as well as of Jesus Christ reigns over all things and meets us at every turn in both nature and history. Jesus the Christ is God's Son, the person who communicates God's grace and acceptance and also embodies and empowers an ec-centric life or existence that accords with God's reign. The Spirit (of God and also of Christ) energizes, inspires, and empowers the new life of community, reconciliation, faith, and love.[14] This threefold pattern or dynamic—articulated symbolically rather than precisely—becomes the impetus for Trinitarian thinking and the touchstone to which the best Trinitarian theology always returns.

The Courage to Live Ec-centrically in God's World

As it spread around the Mediterranean, the Christian movement encountered sharply dualistic belief systems that portrayed humans as immaterial souls bound to physical bodies that mire them in a world of impermanence, change, and suffering. These systems portrayed salvation as the release of the human spirit from its entrapment in the physical body and the material world. For example, Marcion of Pontus, who joined ideas such as these to Christian traditions, taught that the world was made of "beggarly elements." He accepted the redeemer god that he found in some New Testament writings but rejected the Old Testament law and the creator God of Judaism. He claimed that the redeemer remained unknown until Jesus Christ, and he rejected any positive relationship of Jesus Christ with the creator.[15]

In this context, debates concerning the relationship of the Creator, Christ, and Spirit presented sharply contrasting theological visions with definite practical

13. However, there are also some twofold designations, such as the benediction at the close of Hebrews, which mentions "the God of peace" and "our Lord Jesus" (13:20).

14. On Paul's tendency to use the terms "Spirit of God" and "Spirit of Christ" interchangeably, see chap. 9, prop. #55.

15. Jaroslav Pelikan, *The Christian Tradition: A History of the Development of Doctrine,* vol. 1, *The Emergence of the Catholic Tradition (100–600)* (Chicago: University of Chicago Press, 1971), 73.

consequences. If the Creator is bad (or perhaps incompetent) and the created order works against redemption and renewed life in Christ and the Spirit, then piety shuns temporal existence in the material world. If, however, the Creator is also the God of grace who redeems and renews through Christ and Spirit, then the created ordering of the world is gracious, working toward renewed life in Christ and Spirit, and then, too, Christian piety gives thanks for the opportunity to participate in the created world. Few debates have had as many practical consequences for the Christian movement. The orthodox decision to regard the gracious divine ordering as inclusive of the material world—nature, history, the physical body, family, children, commerce, civil government, etc.—to view these realities as parts of a good creation in which loyalty to God's redeeming purpose encourages us to participate, influences every dimension of Christian faithfulness.

Trinitarian believing links the all-ruling maker of heaven and earth with Christ the reconciler and with the sanctifying Spirit. This is why it stands against dualistic theologies of redemption as release from a bad creation. This is why it rejects dualistic rejections of the Hebrew Scriptures as well as dualistic devaluations of life in the world. Trinitarian reflections retain the context of the Hebrew Scriptures and also insist that redemption in Jesus as the Christ and the Spirit cannot be understood apart from this context. Trinitarian reflections assert that the Creator who makes and governs all things is also the Redeemer whose fundamental purpose is not suffering and decay but the renewed and true life of the kingdom that comes to us in Christ and the Spirit. Trinitarian reflections affirm that this world is the good creation of the one most excellent God who redeems.

This, of course, is not all. As I have also emphasized throughout this systematic, Trinitarian reflections—just because they are keyed to the Creator-Redeemer—suppose that there is something we need redeeming from. Therefore, they probe the sinful corruption or fault that captivates persons and communities. They elaborate, too, on how divine judgment, reconciliation, and redemption re-turn, redirect, and reorient corrupted creatures. But, in all of this, they avoid Marcionite dualism, and they continue to regard creation as the good gift of the gracious God.

The salvific dimension deserves to be highlighted. To affirm that the deity is Creator (the one by whose grace all things come to be and are sustained) and also good and graceful Redeemer (whose aim is new life and true life) leads to the confidence that God is faithful. God is not loveless power; God is gracious to and for what God has brought into being. Indeed, God's redeeming purpose is new or renewed being.

This affirmation entails a vivifying assurance and existential self-understanding. It expresses and shapes what Paul Tillich called "the courage to be," or what I would call the courage and resolve to live ec-centrically rather than grudgingly and defensively in God's good world despite the many anxieties, doubts, and fears that beset us.[16] Trinitarian believing articulates and shapes the saving inkling and sense that to be is to live in relationship with the gracious Creator-Redeemer. Therefore it is good to be. Therefore it is appropriate to attend to the many others who also have been called into existence, who also live and move in relationship with the gracious Creator-Redeemer, and with whom we find ourselves standing in interdependent interrelationships.

This sensibility or inkling is saving because it delivers us from the destructive defensiveness of being curved in upon ourselves. (It is also, I think, the basic substance of justification by grace through faith.) In the grips of the human fault, we are estranged, narrowed, and diminished selves whose ways of negotiating life are anxious and alienated. Much classical theology therefore claims that the corrupted self either pridefully relies on its own strength in a world that is often hostile to its inordinate and isolated interests, or else slothfully abdicates responsibility in a threatening world. Either way, the self becomes something other and less than it ought to be. Either way, a train of bad consequences follows. The corrupted person turns in upon himself and shrinks away from an ec-centric existence attuned to participatory interrelations with God and others. But the saving inkling that accompanies Trinitarian thinking—the sense that to be is to be in relationship with the gracious Creator-Redeemer—cuts against the grain of sin's diminishing, alienated, and defensive movement, and intimates a renewing confidence or assurance.

We believe in God the Father, the all-ruling Creator who bestows gifts of existence, life, and sustenance in this good cosmos of interdependent creatures and things. We believe in Jesus as the Christ, the ec-centric person for others, who marks off a manner in life that accords with God's reign, and we trust in the Spirit, who renews ec-centric existence. Creation, reconciliation in Christ, and sanctification in the Spirit all insinuate the knowledge that the self is neither isolated nor separate, but instead a being-in-relation-with-God-and-others. That is why reconciliation and redemption lend persons the courage to live ec-centrically—to recognize and enhance the good and abundant life of true communion with God in community with others for which we are fitted and sustained. And this, in fact, is a large part of the sense that Trinitarian reflections make. They insist that the Creator is the Redeemer we meet in Christ and the Spirit, and vice versa. They insist that the great God of glory is the good God of grace. And, in this insistence, despite the travails and sorrows of life, Trinitarian reflections shape and express the participatory and courageous ec-centricity of saving faith.

16. Paul Tillich, *The Courage to Be* (New Haven: Yale University Press, 1952).

A Threefold Apprehension

Trinitarian reflections continue a biblically initiated exploration. They help to shape and articulate piety's knowledge of God and ourselves and thus empower an ec-centric manner of living. But they also summarize the Christian community's distinctive threefold apprehension of God and ourselves.

Return to the threefold pattern intimated in the New Testament. God the Father is the almighty God whose reign bears all nature and history—cosmic ecology and cosmic passage. This is the all-governing Father of the universe who creates, judges, and redeems. This is the Other, the presiding mystery to which we respond in every dimension of life and whose encompassing reign comes to articulation in Jesus's reconciling way in the world. Jesus as the Christ, the Son, Logos, or wisdom of God embodies and communicates in his ec-centric pattern the reconciling and redemptive reality of the gracious God as well as of human life in appropriately responsive relationship with God and others. The particular manner in life characterized by love of God and neighbor is thus truly fitted to the contours of the divine reign. The new life of faithfulness follows the way or the manner of the person-for-others, and the Spirit, the ec-centric ethos of interdependent life, the Christ, and the church, is the power that vivifies and sanctifies us through inner reorientation and enlargement. The Spirit enables an inward turning toward true communion with God in community with others. In and through its power, we are enabled to take up the manner in life that accords with the reconciling pattern of renewed and true life in the Christ.

These three aspects of piety's experience cannot be simply equated or collapsed. Each is integral to the dynamic trajectory of life-before-God and God-before-life, and this is why Trinitarian theology stands against three kinds of unitarianism.[17]

It stands against a unitarianism of the Father or Creator, the all-governing maker of heaven and earth, that forgets the particularity and personal pattern of Jesus as the Christ, and also forgets to look for an empowering and fundamental reorientation or change in ourselves. This variety of unitarianism often supports a deistic, largely intellectual quest to comprehend the first cause and designer of the world. It emphasizes an ethics of commitment to universal laws of nature, but it balks at following Jesus and at talk of conversion or a change of heart.

There is a unitarianism of the Son that often forgets to appreciate and engage God's dynamic power and presence in the world as cosmic ecology and passage,

17. H. Richard Niebuhr, "The Doctrine of the Trinity and the Unity of the Church," in *Theology, History, and Culture: Major Unpublished Writings*, ed. William Stacy Johnson (New Haven: Yale University Press, 1995), 52–62.

and also often fails to look for continuing repentance and sanctification in the ethos of creation, Christ, and church. Marcion's dualism may be essentially a unitarianism of the Son, or, perhaps, a binitarianism of Son and Spirit. In our own time, the unitarianism of the Son sometimes takes pietistic and ethical forms. As pietism, it tends to center all loyalty, worship, and devotion on Jesus as Savior. As ethics, it often supports a narrow and imitative legalism or discipleship.

There is also a unitarianism of the Spirit that often fails to appreciate and engage God's goodness and presence in the world of nature, social structures, and institutions, and that also tends to neglect the particular personal pattern or identity of Jesus as the Christ. Inner life and spirituality become fundamental, and the truth is sought in an inward awareness. A comparatively amorphous spirituality sometimes results that focuses on experiences of inward healing and renewal. Today, this variety of unitarianism often tends toward a therapeutic stance that views participation in relationships, communities, and institutions largely as a means to personal growth, and that reduces Jesus to a healer or spiritual guide who makes few strident demands.

By contrast, Trinitarian theology points toward the dynamic interrelation of Creator, Christ, and Spirit. It insists that genuine responses to God include a participatory attention to and engagement with God's world, an encounter with the disclosive and ec-centric personal pattern or identity of Jesus as the Christ, and a spiritual turning, reorientation, or enlargement toward ec-centricity in the Spirit. The sense the Trinity makes is this: these three experiences indicate a single divine trajectory in relation to us (or *pro nobis*) that creates, judges, and redeems. They point to a single dynamic excellence that bestows life, re-turns it, and sculpts it ec-centrically, thus raising us up to new possibility. We may affirm all of this and yet remain agnostic about the possibility of distinctions within the Godhead (*Deus in se*). There are some things that remain safely beyond our most refined vocabularies and conceptions.

Select List of Works Consulted

Alves, Rubem A. *Protestantism and Repression: A Brazilian Case Study*. Translated by John Drury. Revised by Jaime Wright. Eugene, OR: Wipf & Stock, 1985.

———. *A Theology of Human Hope*. St. Meinrad, IN: Abbey, 1975.

Apel, Dora. *Imagery of Lynching: Black Men, White Women, and the Mob*. New Brunswick, NJ: Rutgers University Press, 2004.

Aquinas, Thomas. *The Sermon-Conferences of St. Thomas Aquinas on the Apostles' Creed*. Translated by Nicholas Ayo, CSC. Notre Dame: University of Notre Dame Press, 1988.

———. *Summa Theologiae*. Blackfriars Edition. New York: McGraw-Hill, 1964–1981.

Assmann, Jan. *The Search for God in Ancient Egypt*. Translated by David Lorton. Ithaca, NY: Cornell University Press, 2001.

Attridge, Harold. *Acts: A Commentary*. Minneapolis: Fortress, 2009.

Augustine. *The City of God*. Translated by Marcus Dods. New York: Random House, 1950.

———. *The Works of Saint Augustine: A Translation for the 21st Century*. John E. Rotelle, OSA, director. Hyde Park, NY: New City, 1997–.

Baillie, D. M. *God Was in Christ: An Essay on Incarnation and Atonement*. New York: Scribner's Sons, 1948.

Ballentine, Samuel E. *Leviticus*. Louisville: John Knox, 2002.

Barth, Karl. *Church Dogmatics*. Edited by G. W. Bromiley, T. F. Torrance, et al. 14 vols. Edinburgh: T&T Clark, 1936–1969.

———. *The Humanity of God*. Translated by John Newton Thomas. Richmond, VA: John Knox, 1960.

Bartlett, David L. *Romans*. Louisville: Westminster John Knox, 1995.

Baxter, Richard. *A Christian Directory; or, A Sum of Practical Theology, and Cases of Conscience*. Vol. 1 of *The Practical Works of Richard Baxter*. Ligonier, PA: Soli Deo Gloria, 1990.

Beardslee, John W., III., ed. and trans. *Reformed Dogmatics: Seventeenth-Century Reformed Theology through the Writings of Wollebius, Voetius, and Turretin*. Grand Rapids: Baker Books, 1977.

Becker, Ernest. *The Denial of Death*. New York: Free Press, 1973.

Berkhof, Louis. *Systematic Theology*. New edition containing the full text of *Systematic Theology* and the original *Introductory Volume to Systematic Theology*. Grand Rapids: Eerdmans, 1996.

Berry, Wendell. *Life Is a Miracle: An Essay against Modern Superstition*. Washington, DC: Counterpoint, 2000.

———. *What Are People For?* New York: Farrar, Straus & Giroux, 1990.

Betz, Hans Dieter. *Galatians: A Commentary on Paul's Letter to the Churches in Galatia*. Philadelphia: Fortress, 1979.

———. *The Sermon on the Mount: A Commentary on the Sermon on the Mount, Including the Sermon on the Plain*. Edited by Adela Yarbro Collins. Hermeneia. Minneapolis: Fortress, 1995.

Biggar, Nigel, ed. *Burying the Past: Making Peace and Doing Justice after Civil Conflict*. Expanded and updated ed. Washington, DC: Georgetown University Press, 2003.

Boesak, Allan. *Black and Reformed: Apartheid, Liberation, and the Calvinist Tradition*. Edited by Leonard Sweetman. Maryknoll, NY: Orbis, 1984.

Boff, Leonardo. *Church, Charism, and Power: Liberation Theology and the Institutional Church*. Translated by John W. Diercksmeier. New York: Crossroad, 1985.

———. *Jesus Christ Liberator: A Critical Christology for Our Time*. Translated by Patrick Hughes. Maryknoll, NY: Orbis, 1978.

———. *Liberating Grace*. Translated by John Drury. Maryknoll, NY: Orbis, 1979.

———. *The Lord's Prayer: The Prayer of Integral Liberation*. Translated by Theodore Morrow. Maryknoll, NY: Orbis, 1983.

Bonhoeffer, Dietrich. *Discipleship*. Vol. 4 of Dietrich Bonhoeffer Works. Translated by Barbara Green and Reinhard Krauss. Minneapolis: Fortress, 2001.

———. *Ethics*. Vol. 6 of Dietrich Bonhoeffer Works. Translated by Reinhard Krauss, Charles C. West, and Douglas W. Stott. Minneapolis: Fortress, 2005.

Borg, Marcus J. *Jesus: Uncovering the Life, Teachings, and Relevance of a Religious Revolutionary*. New York: HarperOne, 2006.

———. *Meeting Jesus Again for the First Time: The Historical Jesus and the Heart of Contemporary Faith*. New York: HarperOne, 2005.

Borg, Marcus J., and John Dominic Crossan. *The First Christmas: What the Gospels Really Teach about Jesus' Birth*. New York: HarperOne, 2007.

———. *The Last Week: What the Gospels Really Teach about Jesus' Final Days in Jerusalem*. New York: HarperOne, 2006.

Brown, Raymond E., SS. *The Birth of the Messiah: A Commentary on the Infancy Narratives in the Gospels of Matthew and Luke*. New updated ed. New Haven: Yale University Press, 1993.

———. *The Epistles of John: Translated with Introduction, Notes, and Commentary*. Garden City, NY: Doubleday, 1982.

———. *The Gospel according to John (I–XII): Introduction, Translation, and Notes*. Garden City, NY: Doubleday, 1966.

———. *The Gospel according to John (XIII–XXI): Introduction, Translation, and Notes*. Anchor Bible. New Haven: Yale University Press, 1970.

Brown, William P. *The Ethos of the Cosmos: The Genesis of Moral Imagination in the Bible*. Grand Rapids: Eerdmans, 1999.

Brown, William P., and S. Dean McBride Jr., eds. *God Who Creates: Essays in Honor of W. Sibley Towner*. Grand Rapids: Eerdmans, 2000.

Brueggemann, Walter. *Theology of the Old Testament: Testimony, Dispute, Advocacy*. Minneapolis: Fortress, 1997.

Brunner, Emil. *Dogmatics*. Vol. 1, *The Christian Doctrine of God*, translated by Olive Wyon. Vol. 2, *The Christian Doctrine of Creation and Redemption*, translated by Olive Wyon.

Vol. 3, *The Christian Doctrine of the Church, Faith, and the Consummation*, translated by Olive Wyon and David Cairns. Philadelphia: Westminster, 1950, 1952, 1962.

———. *Justice and the Social Order*. Translated by Mary Hottinger. London: Lutterworth, 1945.

———. *Our Faith*. Translated by John W. Rilling. New York: Scribner's Sons, 1954.

Buber, Martin. *I and Thou*. Translated by Ronald Gregor Smith. New York: Scribner's Sons, 1958.

Bultmann, Rudolf. *The Gospel of John: A Commentary*. Translated by G. R. Beasley-Murray, R. W. N. Hoare, and J. K. Riches. Philadelphia: Westminster, 1971.

———. *Kerygma and Myth: A Theological Debate*. Edited by Hans Werner Bartsch. New York: Harper & Row, 1961.

———. *Theology of the New Testament*. Translated by Kendrick Grobel. Vols. 1 and 2. New York: Scribner's Sons, 1951, 1955.

Busch, Eberhard. *Drawn to Freedom: Christian Faith Today in Conversation with the Heidelberg Catechism*. Translated by William H. Rader. Grand Rapids: Eerdmans, 2010.

Cahill, Lisa Sowle. *Between the Sexes: Foundations for a Christian Ethics of Sexuality*. Philadelphia: Fortress; New York: Paulist, 1985.

———. *Family: A Christian Social Perspective*. Minneapolis: Fortress, 2000.

Calvin, John. *Calvin's Commentaries*. 22 vols. Calvin Translation Society. Grand Rapids: Baker Books, 1996.

———. *Calvin's New Testament Commentaries: A New Translation*. Thomas F. Torrance and David W. Torrance, gen. eds. 12 vols. Grand Rapids: Eerdmans, 1972.

———. *Institutes of the Christian Religion*. Edited by John T. McNeill. Translated by Ford Lewis Battles. Louisville: Westminster, 1960.

———. *Treatises against the Anabaptists and against the Libertines*. Edited by Benjamin W. Farley. Grand Rapids: Baker Books, 1988.

Cameron, Ron, ed. *The Other Gospels: Non-Canonical Gospel Texts*. Louisville: Westminster John Knox, 1982.

Camus, Albert. *The Plague*. Translated by Stuart Gilbert. New York: Modern Library, 1948.

Capetz, Paul E. *Christian Faith as Religion: A Study of the Theologies of Calvin and Schleiermacher*. Lanham, MD: University Press of America, 1998.

Chilton, Bruce. *Pure Kingdom: Jesus' Vision of God*. Grand Rapids: Eerdmans, 1996.

Christian, William, Sr. *Meaning and Truth in Religion*. Chicago: University of Chicago Press, 1978.

Cobb, John, Jr. *A Christian Natural Theology*. 2nd ed. Louisville: Westminster John Knox, 2007.

Collins, Adela Yarbro. *Mark: A Commentary*. Edited by Harold W. Attridge. Minneapolis: Fortress, 2007.

Cone, James H., ed. *Black Theology: A Documentary History, 1966–1979*. Maryknoll, NY: Orbis, 1979.

———. *A Black Theology of Liberation*. Philadelphia: Lippincott, 1970.

———. *The Cross and the Lynching Tree*. Maryknoll, NY: Orbis, 2011.

The Constitution of the Presbyterian Church (U.S.A.), Part I: Book of Confessions. Louisville: Office of the General Assembly, 2016.

Conzelmann, Hans. *1 Corinthians*. Translated by James W. Leitch. Philadelphia: Fortress, 1975.

Crossan, John Dominic. *The Greatest Prayer: Rediscovering the Revolutionary Message of the Lord's Prayer*. New York: HarperOne, 2010.

———. *The Historical Jesus: The Life of a Mediterranean Jewish Peasant*. New York: HarperOne, 2005.

———. *Jesus: A Revolutionary Biography*. San Francisco: HarperCollins, 1994.

Cullen, Countee. *Countee Cullen: Collected Poems*. Edited by Major Jackson. New York: Library of America, 2013.

Dickens, Charles. *A Christmas Carol*. New York: Puffin, 1984.

Dorrien, Gary. *The Making of American Liberal Theology: Crisis, Irony, and Postmodernity, 1950–2005*. Louisville: Westminster John Knox, 2006.

———. *The Making of American Liberal Theology: Idealism, Realism, and Modernity, 1900–1950*. Louisville: Westminster John Knox, 2003.

———. *The Making of American Liberal Theology: Imagining Progressive Religion, 1805–1900*. Louisville: Westminster John Knox, 2001.

Dunn, James D. G. *The Acts of the Apostles*. Valley Forge, PA: Trinity Press International, 1996.

———. *Pneumatology*. Vol. 2 of *The Christ and the Spirit: Collected Essays of James D. G. Dunn*. Grand Rapids: Eerdmans, 1998.

Dyck, Arthur. *Rethinking Rights and Responsibilities: The Moral Bonds of Community*. Cleveland: Pilgrim, 1994.

Edwards, Jonathan. *The Works of Jonathan Edwards*. Perry Miller, John E. Smith, and Harry Stout, gen. eds. 26 vols. New Haven: Yale University Press, 1957–2008.

Fergusson, David. *Faith and Its Critics*. Oxford: Oxford University Press, 2009.

Feuerbach, Ludwig. *The Essence of Christianity*. Translated by George Eliot. New York: Harper & Row, 1951.

———. *Lectures on the Essence of Religion*. Translated by Ralph Manheim. New York: Harper & Row, 1967.

Fitzmyer, Joseph A., SJ. *The Acts of the Apostles: A New Translation with Introduction and Commentary*. New Haven: Yale University Press, 1988.

———. *First Corinthians: A New Translation with Introduction and Commentary*. Anchor Yale Bible. New Haven: Yale University Press, 2008.

———. *The Gospel according to Luke (I–IX): Introduction, Translation, and Notes*. Garden City, NY: Doubleday, 1981.

———. *The Gospel according to Luke (X–XXIV): Introduction, Translation, and Notes*. Garden City, NY: Doubleday, 1985.

———. *Romans: A New Translation with Introduction and Commentary*. New York: Doubleday, 1993.

Ford, Lewis S. *The Lure of God: A Biblical Background for Process Theism*. Philadelphia: Fortress, 1978.

Francis. *Laudato Si': On Care for Our Common Home*. Huntington, IN: Our Sunday Visitor, 2015.

Funk, Robert W., Roy W. Hoover, and the Jesus Seminar, trans. and commentary. *The Five Gospels: The Search for the Authentic Words of Jesus*. San Francisco: HarperSanFrancisco, 1993.

Gerrish, B. A. *Christian Faith: Dogmatics in Outline*. Louisville: Westminster John Knox, 2015.

Goizueta, Roberto S. *Camineros con Jesus: Toward a Hispanic Theology of Accompaniment*. Maryknoll, NY: Orbis, 1995.

———. *Christ Our Companion: Toward a Theological Aesthetics of Liberation*. Maryknoll, NY: Orbis, 2009.

Gremillion, Joseph, ed. *The Gospel of Peace and Justice: Catholic Social Teaching Since Pope John*. Maryknoll, NY: Orbis, 1976.

Griffin, David Ray. *God, Power, and Evil: A Process Theodicy*. Philadelphia: Westminster, 1976.

Grinspoon, David. *Earth in Human Hands: Shaping Our Planet's Future*. New York: Grand Central, 2016.
Gruchy, John W. de. *Confessions of a Christian Humanist*. Minneapolis: Fortress, 2006.
———. *Liberating Reformed Theology: A South African Contribution to an Ecumenical Debate*. Grand Rapids: Eerdmans, 1991.
Gustafson, James M. *Can Ethics Be Christian?* Chicago: University of Chicago Press, 1975.
———. *Ethics from a Theocentric Perspective*. Vol. 1, *Theology and Ethics*. Vol. 2, *Ethics and Theology*. Chicago: University of Chicago Press, 1981, 1984.
Gutiérrez, Gustavo. *A Theology of Liberation: History, Politics, and Salvation*. Translated by Sister Caridad Inda and John Eagleson. 15th anniversary edition with a new introduction. Maryknoll, NY: Orbis, 1988.
Gutiérrez, Gustavo, and Gerhard Ludwig Müller. *On the Side of the Poor: The Theology of Liberation*. Translated by Robert A. Kreig and James B. Nickoloff. Maryknoll, NY: Orbis, 2015.
Haenchen, Ernst. *John 1: A Commentary on the Gospel of John, Chapters 1–6*. Translated by Robert W. Funk. Vol. 1. Philadelphia: Fortress, 1984.
Handy, Robert T., ed. *The Social Gospel in America, 1870–1920: Gladden, Ely, Rauschenbusch*. New York: Oxford University Press, 1966.
Harvey, Van A. *Feuerbach and the Interpretation of Religion*. Cambridge: Cambridge University Press, 1995.
———. *The Historian and the Believer: The Morality of Historical Knowledge and Christian Belief*. With a new introduction by the author. Urbana: University of Illinois Press, 1996.
Hauerwas, Stanley. *A Community of Character: Toward a Constructive Christian Social Ethic*. Notre Dame: University of Notre Dame Press, 1981.
Hedrick, Charles W. *The Wisdom of Jesus: Between the Sages of Israel and the Apostles of the Church*. Eugene, OR: Cascade, 2014.
Heppe, Heinrich. *Reformed Dogmatics: Set Out and Illustrated from the Sources*. Edited by Ernest Bizer. Translated by G. T. Thompson. Grand Rapids: Baker Books, 1978.
Heschel, Abraham Joshua. *God in Search of Man*. New York: Harper & Row, 1966.
Hodge, Charles. *Systematic Theology: In Three Volumes*. Grand Rapids: Eerdmans, 1977.
Jenson, Robert W. *Systematic Theology*. Vol. 1, *The Triune God*. Vol. 2, *The Works of God*. New York: Oxford University Press, 1997, 1999.
Johnson, Luke Timothy. *The Acts of the Apostles*. Sacra Pagina, vol. 5. Collegeville, MN: Liturgical Press, 1992.
Jonas, Hans. *The Imperative of Responsibility*. Chicago: University of Chicago Press, 1984.
Kaufman, Gordon D. *In Face of Mystery: A Constructive Theology*. Cambridge, MA: Harvard University Press, 1993.
Kelly, J. N. D. *Early Christian Creeds*. 3rd ed. New York: Longman, 1972.
Kelsey, David H. *Eccentric Existence: A Theological Anthropology*. 2 vols. Louisville: Westminster John Knox, 2009.
King, Martin Luther, Jr. *A Testament of Hope: The Essential Writings of Martin Luther King, Jr.* Edited by James Melvin Washington. New York: Harper & Row, 1986.
Küng, Hans. *Credo: The Apostles' Creed Explained for Today*. New York: Doubleday, 1992.
Levenson, Jon D. *Creation and the Persistence of Evil: The Jewish Drama of Divine Omnipotence*. San Francisco: Harper & Row, 1988.
Lindbeck, George A. *The Nature of Doctrine: Religion and Theology in a Postliberal Age*. Philadelphia: Westminster, 1984.

Llewellyn, Jennifer J., and Daniel Philpott, eds. *Restorative Justice, Reconciliation, and Peacebuilding*. New York: Oxford University Press, 2014.

Lohse, Eduard. *Colossians and Philemon*. Translated by William R. Poehlmann and Robert J. Karis. Hermeneia. Philadelphia: Fortress, 1971.

Lovin, Robin W. *Christian Realism and the New Realities*. Cambridge: Cambridge University Press, 2008.

———. *Reinhold Niebuhr*. Nashville: Abingdon, 2007.

———. *Reinhold Niebuhr and Christian Realism*. New York: Cambridge University Press, 1995.

Luhmann, Niklas. *The Differentiation of Society*. Translated by Stephen Holmes and Charles Larmore. New York: Columbia University Press, 1982.

Luisi, Pier Luigi. *The Emergence of Life: From Chemical Origins to Synthetic Biology*. Cambridge: Cambridge University Press, 2006.

Luther, Martin. *Luther's Works*. Edited by Jaroslav Pelikan et al. American edition. St. Louis: Concordia, 1958–.

Mandela, Nelson. *The Prison Letters of Nelson Mandela*. Edited by Sahm Ventner. New York: Liveright, 2018.

Marxsen, Willi. *The Resurrection of Jesus of Nazareth*. Translated by Margaret Kohl. Philadelphia: Fortress, 1970.

Mays, James L. *Psalms*. Interpretation: A Bible Commentary for Teaching and Preaching. Louisville: John Knox, 1994.

McGinn, Bernard, ed. and trans. *Apocalyptic Spirituality: Treatises and Letters of Lactantius, Adso of Montier-En-Der, Joachim of Fiore, the Franciscan Spirituals, Savonarola*. New York: Paulist, 1979.

Meier, John P. *A Marginal Jew: Rethinking the Historical Jesus*. Vol. 3, *Companions and Competitors*. Vol. 4, *Law and Love*. New Haven: Yale University Press, 2001, 2009.

Meland, Bernard. *Fallible Forms and Symbols: Discourses on Method in a Theology of Culture*. Minneapolis: Fortress, 1976.

———. *Seeds of Redemption*. New York: Macmillan, 1947.

Metz, Johann Baptist. *Faith in History and Society: Toward a Practical Fundamental Theology*. Translated by David Smith. New York: Seabury, 1980.

Midgley, Mary. *Animals and Why They Matter: A Journey around the Species Barrier*. New York: Penguin, 1983.

———. *Beast and Man: The Animal Roots of Human Nature*. Ithaca, NY: Cornell University Press, 1978.

Miles, Rebekah. *The Bonds of Freedom: Feminist Theology and Christian Realism*. Oxford: Oxford University Press, 2001.

Moltmann, Jürgen. *The Church in the Power of the Spirit: A Contribution to Messianic Ecclesiology*. Translated by Margaret Kohl. Minneapolis: Fortress, 1993.

———. *The Crucified God: The Cross of Christ as the Foundation and Criticism of Christian Theology*. Translated by R. A. Wilson and John Bowden. New York: Harper & Row, 1974.

———. *The Future of Creation: Collected Essays*. Translated by Margaret Kohl. Philadelphia: Fortress, 1979.

———. *God in Creation: A Theology of Creation and the Spirit of God*. Minneapolis: Fortress, 1993.

Müntzer, Thomas. *The Collected Works of Thomas Müntzer*. Edited and translated by Peter Matheson. Edinburgh: T&T Clark, 1988.

Myers, Ched. *The Binding of the Strong Man: A Political Reading of Mark's Story of Jesus*. Maryknoll, NY: Orbis, 1988.

Naude, Piet J. *Neither Calendar Nor Clock: Perspectives on the Belhar Confession*. Grand Rapids: Eerdmans, 2010.

Neusner, Jacob, and Bruce Chilton, eds. *The Golden Rule: The Ethics of Reciprocity in World Religions*. New York: Continuum, 2008.

Niebuhr, H. Richard. *Christ and Culture*. New York: Harper & Row, 1951.

———. *The Meaning of Revelation*. Louisville: Westminster John Knox, 2006.

———. *Radical Monotheism and Western Culture, with Supplementary Essays*. Louisville: Westminster John Knox, 1993.

———. *"The Responsibility of the Church for Society" and Other Essays by H. Richard Niebuhr*. Edited by Kristine A. Culp. Louisville: Westminster John Knox, 2008.

———. *The Responsible Self: An Essay in Christian Moral Philosophy*. Louisville: Westminster John Knox, 1999.

———. *Theology, History, and Culture: Major Unpublished Writings*. Edited by William Stacy Johnson. New Haven: Yale University Press, 1995.

———. "War as the Judgment of God," "Is God in the War," and "War as Crucifixion." In *War in the Twentieth Century: Sources in Theological Ethics*, edited by Richard B. Miller. Louisville. Westminster John Knox, 1992.

Niebuhr, Reinhold. *Beyond Tragedy: Essays on the Christian Interpretation of History*. New York: Scribner's Sons, 1937.

———. *The Children of Light and the Children of Darkness: A Vindication of Democracy and a Critique of Its Traditional Defense*. Eugene, OR: Wipf & Stock, 2006.

———. *Christian Realism and Political Problems*. New York: Scribner's Sons, 1953.

———. *Essays in Applied Christianity*. Edited by D. B. Robertson. New York: Meridian, 1959.

———. *Faith and History: A Comparison of Christian and Modern Views of History*. New York: Scribner's Sons, 1949.

———. *An Interpretation of Christian Ethics*. New York: Seabury, 1979.

———. *Love and Justice: Selections from the Shorter Writings of Reinhold Niebuhr*. Edited by D. B. Robertson. Louisville: Westminster John Knox, 1992.

———. *The Nature and Destiny of Man*. Vol. 1, *Human Nature*. Vol. 2, *Human Destiny*. Louisville: Westminster John Knox, 1996.

Nijenhuis, E. J. *Ecclesia Reformata: Studies on the Reformation*. Translated by Mary Foran. Leiden: Brill, 1972.

O'Donovan, Oliver. *The Desire of Nations: Rediscovering the Roots of Political Theology*. Cambridge: Cambridge University Press, 1996.

Origen. *On First Principles*. Translated by G. W. Butterworth. Gloucester, MA: Peter Smith, 1973.

Ottati, Douglas F. *Hopeful Realism: Reclaiming the Poetry of Theology*. Cleveland: Pilgrim, 1999.

———. *Jesus Christ and Christian Vision*. Louisville: Westminster John Knox, 1996.

———. *Meaning and Method in H. Richard Niebuhr's Theology*. Washington, DC: University Press of America, 1982.

———. *Reforming Protestantism: Christian Commitment in Today's World*. Louisville: Westminster John Knox, 1995.

———. *Theology for Liberal Protestants and Other Endangered Species*. Louisville: Geneva, 2006.

Otto, Rudolf. *The Idea of the Holy: An Inquiry into the Non-Rational Factor in the Idea of the*

Divine and Its Relation to the Rational. Translated by John W. Harvey. London: Oxford University Press, 1958.

Painter, John. *1, 2, and 3 John*. Edited by Daniel Harrington, SJ. Collegeville, MN: Liturgical Press, 2008.

Pannenberg, Wolfhart. *Systematic Theology*. Translated by Geoffrey Bromiley. Vol. 3. Grand Rapids: Eerdmans, 1997.

Pelikan, Jaroslav. *The Christian Tradition: A History of the Development of Doctrine*. Vol. 1, *The Emergence of the Catholic Tradition (100–600)*. Chicago: University of Chicago Press, 1971.

Perkins, William. *The Works of William Perkins*. Edited by Ian Breward. Appleford, UK: Sutton Courtenay, 1970.

Peters, Ted, Robert John Russell, and Michael Welker, eds. *Resurrection: Theological and Scientific Assessments*. Grand Rapids: Eerdmans, 2002.

Pittenger, Norman. *After Death—Life in God*. New York: Seabury, 1980.

Rad, Gerhard von. *Genesis: A Commentary*. Translated by John H. Marks. Rev. ed. Philadelphia: Westminster, 1972.

———. *Old Testament Theology*. Vol. 1, *The Theology of Israel's Historical Traditions*. Vol. 2, *The Theology of Israel's Prophetic Traditions*. Translated by D. M. G. Stalker. New York: Harper & Row, 1962, 1965.

Rahner, Karl. *Foundations of Christian Faith*. Translated by William V. Dych. New York: Seabury, 1978.

Rauschenbusch, Walter. *Christianity and the Social Crisis*. Louisville: Westminster John Knox, 1991.

———. *Christianizing the Social Order*. New York: Macmillan, 1913.

———. *Prayers for the Social Awakening*. Boston: Pilgrim, 1910.

———. *The Social Principles of Jesus*. New York: Methodist Book Concern, 1916.

———. *A Theology for the Social Gospel*. Louisville: Westminster John Knox, 1997.

Rice, Anne P., and Michelle Wallace, eds. *Witnessing Lynching: American Writers Respond*. New Brunswick, NJ: Rutgers University Press, 2003.

Ritschl, Albrecht. *The Christian Doctrine of Justification and Reconciliation*. Edited and translated by H. R. Mackintosh and A. B. Macaulay. Clifton, NJ: Reference Book Publishers, 1966.

Robinson, Marilynne. *Absence of Mind: The Dispelling of Inwardness from the Modern Myth of the Self*. New Haven: Yale University Press, 2011.

Rocca, Gregory P., OP. *Speaking the Incomprehensible God: Thomas Aquinas on the Interplay of Positive and Negative Theology*. Washington, DC: Catholic University Press of America, 2004.

Rohls, Jan. *Reformed Confessions: Theology from Zurich to Barmen*. Translated by John Hoffmeyer. Louisville: Westminster John Knox, 1998.

Ruether, Rosemary Radford. *Sexism and God-Talk: Toward a Feminist Theology*. With a new introduction. Boston: Beacon, 1993.

Russell, Letty M. *Church in the Round: Feminist Interpretation of the Church*. Louisville: Westminster John Knox, 1993.

Schleiermacher, Friedrich. *The Christian Faith*. Edited by H. R. Mackintosh and J. S. Stewart. Philadelphia: Fortress, 1976.

Schuurman, Douglas J. *Vocation: Discerning Our Callings in Life*. Grand Rapids: Eerdmans, 2004.

Schweiker, William. *Theological Ethics and Global Dynamics: In the Time of Many Worlds.* Oxford: Blackwell, 2004.

Schweitzer, Albert. *The Quest for the Historical Jesus: A Critical Study of Its Progress from Reimarus to Wrede.* Translated by W. Montgomery. New York: Macmillan, 1968.

Sittler, Joseph. *Evocations of Grace: Writings on Ecology, Theology, and Ethics.* Edited by Steven Bouma-Prediger and Peter Bakken. Grand Rapids: Eerdmans, 2000.

Smith, Eric, and Harold J. Morowitz. *The Origin and Nature of Life on Earth: The Emergence of the Fourth Geosphere.* Cambridge: Cambridge University Press, 2016.

Smith, John E. *Experience and God.* New York: Oxford University Press, 1968.

Strecker, Georg. *The Johannine Letters.* Translated by Linda M. Maloney. Edited by Harold Attridge. Minneapolis: Fortress, 1996.

Strong, Augustus Hopkins. *Systematic Theology: A Compendium and Commonplace Book.* 6th ed. New York: A. C. Armstrong and Son, 1899.

Tanner, Kathryn. *Christ the Key.* Cambridge: Cambridge University Press, 2010.

Teilhard de Chardin, Pierre. *The Divine Milieu.* New York: Harper & Row, 1960.

———. *The Future of Man.* Translated by Norman Denny. New York: Harper & Row, 1969.

Tillich, Paul. *The Courage to Be.* New Haven: Yale University Press, 1952.

———. *The New Being.* New York: Scribner's Sons, 1955.

———. *The Shaking of the Foundations.* New York: Scribner's Sons, 1948.

———. *Systematic Theology.* Vol. 1, *Reason and Revelation, Being and God.* Vol. 2, *Existence and the Christ.* Vol. 3, *Life and the Spirit, History and the Kingdom of God.* Chicago: University of Chicago Press, 1951, 1957, 1963.

Towner, W. Sibley. *Genesis.* Louisville: Westminster John Knox, 2001.

Troeltsch, Ernst. *The Christian Faith.* Translated with an introduction by Garrett E. Paul. Minneapolis: Fortress, 1991.

———. *Writings on Theology and Religion.* Translated and edited by Robert Morgan and Michael Pye. Louisville: Westminster John Knox, 1990.

Tutu, Desmond Mpilo. *No Future without Forgiveness.* New York: Doubleday, 1999.

Vermes, Geza. *Jesus the Jew: A Historian's Reading of the Gospels.* London: Collins, 1973.

———. *The Religion of Jesus the Jew.* Minneapolis: Fortress, 1993.

Vosloo, Robert. *Reforming Memory: Essays on South African Church and Theological History.* Stellenbosch, South Africa: African Sun Media, 2017.

Waal, Frans de, Robert Wright, Christine Korsgaard, Philip Kitchen, and Peter Singer. *Primates and Philosophers: How Morality Evolved.* Edited by Stephen Macedo and Josiah Ober. Princeton: Princeton University Press, 2006.

Walzer, Michael. *Thick and Thin: Moral Argument at Home and Abroad.* Notre Dame: University of Notre Dame Press, 1994.

Weiman, Henry Nelson. *The Source of Human Good.* Chicago: University of Chicago Press, 1946.

Welker, Michael, ed. *The Depth of the Human Person: A Multidisciplinary Approach.* Grand Rapids: Eerdmans, 2014.

———. *God the Revealed: Christology.* Translated by Douglas W. Stott. Grand Rapids: Eerdmans, 2013.

Westermann, Claus. *Creation.* Translated by John J. Scullion, SJ. Philadelphia: Fortress, 1974.

———. *Elements of Old Testament Theology.* Translated by Douglas W. Stott. Atlanta: John Knox, 1982.

———. *Genesis 1–11: A Commentary*. Translated by John J. Scullion, SJ. Minneapolis: Augsburg, 1984.

Wiles, Maurice. *Reason to Believe*. Harrisburg, PA: Trinity Press International, 1999.

Wolff, Tobias. *Old School: A Novel*. New York: Vintage Books, 2003.

Wolterstorff, Nicholas. *Justice: Rights and Wrongs*. Princeton: Princeton University Press, 2008.

Wright, N. T. *Christian Origins and the Question of God*. Vol. 3, *The Resurrection of the Son of God*. Minneapolis: Fortress, 2003.

———. *Simply Jesus: A New Vision of Who He Was, What He Did, and Why He Matters*. San Francisco: HarperOne, 2011.

Yoder, John Howard. *The Politics of Jesus: Vicit Agnus Noster*. 2nd ed. Grand Rapids: Eerdmans, 1994.

Index of Names and Subjects

Abelard, 491
affections, 34–45, 51–56
Alves, Rubem, 7n9, 277n76
Anselm, 238, 274, 476–78, 491
anti-Judaism, 97–103, 348, 424, 705
Apostles' Creed, 148, 157, 168, 194–95, 242, 461, 498–500, 532, 542, 543, 697, 717, 719
Aquinas, Thomas, 15, 26, 32–33, 38, 69–70, 82, 99, 131, 143, 145, 147–48, 151, 167, 174, 177, 180, 186, 196–97, 198–99n24, 202, 204, 265, 292–93, 352, 354, 378, 417, 418n84, 649–51, 719–20
astrobiology, 351, 498, 514, 677
atonement, 475–93
Auden, W. H., 381
Augustine, 3–5, 69, 70, 83, 95, 98–99, 131, 145, 167, 170, 176, 185–88, 237–38, 240, 305, 309, 477, 512n47, 516–17, 539, 546–48, 550, 556–58, 560, 565, 590–92, 643–44

Bach, Johann Sebastian, 485–86
Baillie, Donald, 388–90
Barth, Karl, 20, 75, 81, 95, 106, 109, 112n59, 113n61, 139, 141, 149, 164, 208, 251, 253, 310, 418, 418n84, 433–34, 477–78, 505, 505n21, 529, 529n84, 531, 587, 595–96, 703
Bartlett, David L., 161–62, 544, 550
basic human institutions, 249–58
Baxter, Richard, 113n61, 245n18, 628–32
Becker, Ernest, 706
Belhar Confession, 370–71, 530–31
Berkhof, Louis, 149, 197n15, 198, 220–21, 294, 325, 343–45, 351, 498n1, 501
Berry, Wendell, 279, 282, 569
Betz, Hans Dieter, 396, 400–401, 408, 417, 504
Biggar, Nigel, 614–15
Blake, William, 513
Boesak, Allan, 569
Boff, Leonardo, 406, 526, 554, 569–70, 637
Bonhoeffer, Dietrich, 250–51, 621
Borg, Marcus, 358, 384, 384n110, 402–4, 430, 432–33, 444, 453
Brown, Raymond E., 425–26, 425–26n104, 427, 431–33, 718, 735
Brown, William P., 515
Brueggemann, Walter, 160–61, 309, 408, 427–30
Brunner, Emil, 30–31, 112n59, 147, 151, 169n35, 181, 205, 250–51, 306, 308, 369n75, 598–99, 600, 723–24
Buber, Martin, 271–73, 652
Bushnell, Horace, 374, 481, 491
Bultmann, Rudolf, 358, 386, 386n119, 403, 474, 718, 723, 727

Cahill, Lisa Sowle, 622n187, 639n214
calling, and vocation, 280–87, 622–36
Calvin, John, 12, 15, 18, 21, 49n48, 65n76, 68, 72, 82, 84, 95, 100–101, 109, 111–15, 142, 144, 148, 152, 153, 170–71, 174, 177, 179–80, 181, 186, 195–98, 202, 203, 215, 221–25, 229–30, 240, 242, 245, 249–50, 278–79, 294, 302–3, 310, 317, 324, 338, 340–42, 343, 349, 353–54, 367–69, 376–78, 391, 393–94, 397–98, 417, 420, 426, 443, 457, 461n182, 478–79, 481, 501, 502, 505–11, 514, 519–22, 532, 536–37, 539–40, 545–50, 557–58, 560, 579–81, 587, 592–97, 599, 607, 609, 611, 613, 653, 654,

683, 690, 697, 719–20, 736n105, 737n110, 743n11
Camus, Albert, 486–87
Cannon, Katie G., 107
Capetz, Paul, 13, 16n30, 46n46
Carroll, John T., 162
Chalcedon, 150, 347, 359, 384, 388, 391, 392
Christian, William, Sr., 45n44, 60, 62, 64
Christianity, 74–85; Augustinian, 4–6, 12–14; Protestant, 6–8, 12–14; Reformed, 116–35; social, 124–26
church, 523–42; and theology, 26–27; and world, 661–74
civil government, 640–58
Cobb, John B., Jr., 167, 307, 309, 311, 314–15
Collins, Adela Yarbro, 386n467, 468, 473
Cone, James H., 106, 107n48, 489–90, 492, 665
Confession of 1967, 9n12, 118, 129n97, 164, 254, 338, 366, 370–72, 530
Cook, Martin L., 52, 52n54, 647n11
Cotton, John, 624–25, 628, 634
covenant, 281–82; of grace, 338–61
Crossan, John Dominic, 363, 394, 399, 401–2, 404–7, 413n74, 423n95, 430, 432–33, 438–40, 453, 473–74
crucifixion, 465–68, 472–75, 488–90
Cullen, Countee, 488–90

Dabney, Robert Lewis, 148–49, 581–82
Darwin, Charles, 9, 166, 175, 205, 246, 258, 571–72, 653n27
Decalogue, 219–21
Diamond, Cora, 483–84
Dickens, Charles, 79–80, 483–84
divine excellence, 348, 388, 507–14
divine governance, 194–233; as cosmic passage, 203–33, 325–32; as particular and special providence, 217–29
Dunn, James D. G., 518
Dyck, Arthur, 203, 608–9, 646

Edwards, Jonathan, 34–35, 37, 42, 44, 69, 70, 109, 112, 114, 167, 187, 189, 199n25, 215, 227–28, 310, 326, 328–29, 332, 356, 373, 417–18, 447, 508–13, 518–19, 556–57, 730–31
Edwards, Sarah Pierpont, 227–28, 738–39
Ely, Richard T., 11, 124
emergence, 292, 343–50
emotions. *See* affections
Erasmus, 6, 100n28, 111

Feuerbach, Ludwig, 20–21, 510, 709
Fitzmyer, Joseph, 340n7, 404, 413n74, 414n75, 422n92, 445, 460n181, 467n202, 504n20, 524–25, 544, 549, 724, 727–28
Francis (pope), 678–80, 686
Freud, Sigmund, 20

Gerrish, B. A., 353, 364n55, 385–87, 540n108, 699, 704n30, 734n101, 742
Gilkey, Langdon, 13, 237
God, doctrine of, 153–54, 688–91; incomprehensibility of, 292–96; as Judge, 73–75, 692–93, 695–97; as personal, 325–27; as the Real, 328–32
Goizueta, Roberto S., 493–95
Griffin, David Ray, 308n32, 312–13, 315
Grinspoon, David, 678, 680–82
Gruchy, John de, 19n36, 461–62
Gustafson, James M., 8, 13, 26, 38, 41, 118, 136n106, 181–82, 200, 226, 252, 265–66, 327, 390, 555–56, 617, 738
Gutiérrez, Gustavo, 164, 488n247, 554, 663, 671

Harnack, Adolf von, 387n121
Hartshorne, Charles, 70
Harvey, Van A., 11, 20–21, 434
Hauerwas, Stanley, 50–51, 269, 454, 634–35
Hegel, G. W. F., 102n37
Heidelberg Catechism, 119, 147, 158, 195, 350, 528–30, 598, 605–6, 611, 697
Heim, S. Mark, 123–24
Hick, John H., 122–23, 474
Hicks, Edward, 711–12, 731–32
Hodge, Charles, 144, 153, 194–95, 198n24, 219–20, 223, 305n24, 581–82
Hodgson, Peter C., 150
hope, 31, 34, 40–41, 230–33, 382–83, 636–39, 669–87, 705–34
humanity, in God's image, 352–56

James, William, 34, 35n26, 44–45
Jantzen, Grace M., 68
Jefferson, Thomas, 398–99, 459

Jenson, Robert W., 153, 303n22
John of Damascus, 291–92
Johnson, Luke Timothy, 525, 527n78
judgment, 379–82
justification, 586–93, 598–604

Kant, Immanuel, 8, 20, 271, 398
Kaufman, Gordon D., 9, 25n1, 33n19, 125n91, 139–40, 209n48, 235, 323, 327
Kelsey, David H., xxii, 283n82, 297n18
Kierkegaard, Søren, 398–99
King, Martin Luther, Jr., 117–18, 218, 225–26, 230, 271, 276, 324, 383n108, 414n75, 530, 575, 599, 617, 641, 651–52, 654n29, 658–59, 670–72, 683, 736–37
Kreeft, Peter, 285–86
Küng, Hans, 360, 492–93, 500, 501n11, 511, 527
Kuyper, Abraham, 115

Lampe, Peter, 727
Levenson, Jon, 307, 309
Lindbeck, George A., 54–56
Little, David, 650
Lord's Prayer, 148, 158, 358, 359n97, 406, 753
Lovin, Robin W., 14, 252, 276–77
Luhmann, Niklas, 256–57
Luisi, Pier Luigi, 319–20
Luther, Martin, 15, 100, 104n139, 132, 136–37, 168, 170–71, 178–79, 202, 242, 299, 376, 426n109, 461, 463, 491, 499, 532, 588–93, 596, 599, 622n186, 631n201, 695, 697, 717

Mandela, Nelson, 277, 575, 655, 672–73
Manicheanism, and moral dualism, 89, 93–96
Marxsen, Willi, 497
Mays, James L., 174
Meier, John P., 412, 422–23, 424
Meland, Bernard, 214–15
Metz, Johann Baptist, 483
Midgley, Mary, 204n36, 226, 247n29, 354, 653n27, 705n33
Moltmann, Jürgen, 304–5, 314, 491, 528n81, 534–35
Morse, Christopher, 150
Mudge, Lewis S., 124, 535n100
Muntzer, Thomas, 712–14
Myers, Ched, 440–42
mythopoetic discourse, 48–53, 61, 63, 86, 343, 435–36, 553, 711

Naude, Beyers, 365
Naude, Piet, 530–31, 606
Neusner, Jacob, 413n73
Nicene Creed, 150, 186, 194, 195, 384, 387, 391, 498, 543, 717
Niebuhr, H. Richard, 11, 13, 60–61, 69, 75n97, 95, 114, 157–58, 264n57, 269, 281–82, 325, 332, 366–67, 390–91, 393, 395n5, 420n85, 482n233, 485, 488, 491, 560–62, 575, 585–86, 611–12, 658–61, 662, 689–90n6, 736n107
Niebuhr, Reinhold, 10, 11, 13, 39, 49, 74, 95, 117, 125, 276, 391, 486, 489, 492, 560–65, 584, 603, 612–13, 616, 640–41, 646, 648, 650, 656, 671, 688, 698, 733n100
Niebuhr, Richard R., 35, 37, 389, 420
Nussbaum, Martha C., 36n29, 39

O'Donovan, Oliver, 411
Ogden, Schubert M., 167
Origen of Alexandria, 91, 142, 143, 147, 150–51, 170, 177–78, 454
Ottati, Douglas F., 10n16, 76n100, 96n18, 689n4, 741n3
Otto, Rudolf, 189

Pagels, Elaine, 131–32
Pannenberg, Wolfhart, 540n108, 540n110, 541n112
pantheism, 67–70
paradigmatic proposals, 56–58
Pascal, Blaise, 138–39
Peabody, Francis Greenwood, 398
Peirce, Charles Saunders, 55n59, 63–64, 67
Pelagianism, 96–97, 556, 590–91, 704
Perkins, William, 623–28, 630, 634
Perrin, Norman, 403–4
Pittenger, Norman, 709, 724–26
polytheism, 61–63
Pope, Stephen J., 616–17

Rad, Gerhard von, 352, 402, 428, 525, 551–53
Rahner, Karl, 145, 145n134, 149, 634
Rauschenbusch, Walter, 10, 13, 19–20, 116–17,

401–4, 406, 487n247, 568, 570–71, 651, 653n26, 694, 709–10, 713–14, 733
reconciliation, 365–82, 541–42
repentance, 579–82
Rideman, Peter, 644–45, 647
Ritschl, Albrecht, 92–93, 163–64, 487n247, 567
Rohls, Jan, 341–42, 368–69n69, 529n84, 606n151
Rosenzweig, Frank, 681–82
Royce, Josiah, 485
Ruether, Rosemary Radford, 106, 130, 149–50, 479, 522, 541, 569

sacraments, 531–35, 539–42
sanctification, 604–34
Savonarola, Girolamo, 712–14
Schillebeeckx, Eduard, 436
Schleiermacher, Friedrich, 9, 13, 25n1, 55, 58n61, 59–60, 67n75, 75, 90, 97, 103n38, 142, 144, 148, 151, 152n159, 153–54, 167, 195, 222–23, 296, 310, 319, 388, 391, 487, 523, 567, 581, 595, 703, 743n11
Schuurman, Douglas J., 622n187, 627n197, 632
Schweiker, William, 14, 15n26
Schweitzer, Albert, 395, 451
Scots Confession of 1560, 95, 100n129, 110–11, 134, 147, 196–98, 294, 328, 342, 532, 534, 604, 701n24, 743n11
sensibilities. *See* affections
Sheppard, John, 382
Simons, Menno, 12
sin, 77–78, 83–84, 543–90; as original, 559–77; as sickness of soul, 575–77
Singer, Peter, 573n78, 575
Sittler, Joseph, 723
Smith, John E., 42n42, 45n45
Smith, Walter Chalmers, 294–95
Smith, Wilfred Cantwell, 121–22
spiritualist dualism, 95–97
Stackhouse, Max L., 87n108, 122n83, 127n95, 250, 256
Strong, Augustus Hopkins, 144–45, 149, 220
sustainability, 673–87

Tanner, Kathryn, 76n99, 742–44
Teilhard de Chardin, Pierre, 9, 231–32
Ten Commandments, 148, 607–11, 656
theological language, 288–99, 688–91
theology, 25–26; Christian, 25–31, 80–88; negative, 291–96; systematic, 138–54
Tillich, Paul, 11, 13, 14, 15n27, 29–30, 38, 69, 70, 133, 145, 151, 197, 295–96, 357, 359, 369n75, 389, 554, 599, 603, 656, 746–47
Tracy, David, 11n19, 32n15
Trinity, the, 75–76, 378, 741–49
Troeltsch, Ernst, 8–9, 13, 30, 76n100, 140n115, 165, 230–31, 325, 535n100, 702–3
Turretin, Francis, 153, 376, 378
Tutu, Desmond Mpilo, 615–16

Vosloo, Robert, 533–34, 644n3

Waal, Frans de, 269, 271, 286–87
Walzer, Michael, 255, 652–53
Weiman, Henry Nelson, 8, 214
Welker, Michael, 475, 534, 727–28
Westermann, Claus, 174, 241
Westminster Confession of Faith, 21, 95, 132, 153, 196, 198, 220, 222, 241, 294, 305n24, 310, 343, 350n26, 352–53, 553, 581–82, 701n24, 720, 743–44n11
Whitehead, Alfred North, 31, 70, 309, 315
Wiles, Maurice, 726–27, 729
Williams, Roger, 105, 112, 650n22
Wingren, Gustav, 168–69
Wolff, Tobias, 447–49
Wollebius, 148, 153, 196, 199n24, 580
Wolterstorff, Nicholas, 409–10
wonder, 31–33, 236–38
Wright, N. T., 453, 724n79, 727–28

Yoder, John Howard, 12, 455–56n172

Index of Scripture References

Old Testament

Genesis

1 187, 302, 306, 308, 309, 317, 325, 345, 500, 514
1:1–2:4 49–51, 73, 77, 128, 170–76, 184, 190, 243–44, 353
1:3 303, 308, 325, 690
1:4 190–91
1:6 302
1:9 302
1:11 240
1:22 240, 339
1:26 77, 352
1:27 352
1:28 179, 240, 263, 339
1:31 187, 244
2 352, 514
2:1–3 192
2:4b–11:9 83
2:5 260
2:5–25 244
2:6 244
2:7 302, 500
2:14 171
2:18 244
2:22 244
2:23 244
2:24 197
3 550, 560, 692
3:1–11:9 550–53
3:15 344, 345, 346, 542
4:1–11:9 77, 337, 339
4:9 516
4:24 564
8:17 240
9:1 240
9:7 240
9:8 346
9:9–13 351
9:12–13 345
10 525
11 259
11:4 525
12 357, 526
12:2–3 71, 339
12:3 241, 345
15:5–6 71
15:6 462
17:7 344
22:17–18 71
50:20 690

Exodus

3:13–15 290–91
19:5–6 428
20 197
20:1–17 620
20:2 608
20:13 607, 610
21 610
22:21–25 410
23:6–9 410n64
23:12 282
33:20–23 29

Leviticus

13:45–46 441n148
19:9–18 412–13n73
19:18 412, 416–17
19:34 412, 416–17
26:12 349–50, 701n23

Deuteronomy

5:17 607, 610
6:5 412
24:17 410n64
27:17 410n64
30:19 270

Judges

2:11–12 191n82
10:6 191n82
17:6 191n82
21:25 191n82

1 Samuel

12:25 429

2 Samuel

7:12–16 427

1 Kings

11:9–11 429

2 Kings
7:3–10 441n148
19–21 431

2 Chronicles
26:10–21 441n148

Job 312–13
7:11 492
9:17–18 738
38:1–7 512–13
38:4 183
38:19 183
38:31 183
42:3 313–14, 326

Psalms
2:7 428
8 174, 216
8:3 409
8:5 260
8:5–8 77
14:1–3 380
14:3 551
19 302
19:1 409
22:1 466, 493
23:1 690
27:8 274
33 308
33:9 303
37:28 409
42:9 690
46 299
53:1–3 380
65 409
72 71
72:1–4 429
72:12–14 429
89:19–36 428
96:10 408
97 290
99:4 409
103:6–7 410
104 191, 197, 243, 266, 409, 515
104:2 159, 302, 318
104:5 159, 318
104:10–15 77
104:10–26 184
104:15 521
104:16–23 198
104:21 183
110:1 429
114 159–60
115 159
115:5 158
118 452
118:6 224
121 159
121:1–2 158
124 72, 159
124:8 158, 335, 692
136 72, 243, 691
139 273–74
146 159
146:5–7 158
147:6 410
148 176, 192, 283, 286, 353–54, 502, 511, 720
150 192

Proverbs
8 82
25:21–22 505

Ecclesiastes
3:18–20 240n10
9:11 329, 455

Isaiah
2:2–4 339
2:3 710
2:12 714
7:14 432
10:1–11 324
11:6–7 711
25:6–8 346
25:7 462
29:15–16 302
37:22 431
40:22 302
45:9–13 30
52:12–15 346
52:13–53:12 493
58:7 520
61:1–2 397
65:17–25 711

Jeremiah
18:1–6 302
22:2–5 429
23:3 79n101

Daniel
2 713

Amos
2:4–6 693
2:6 74
2:6–7 270
5:2 431
5:14–15 78
5:18 714
7:2 708
9:5–7 160
9:11 693
9:14 693

Zechariah
9–10 430
9:9–10 450–52

New Testament

Matthew
1:1 338, 425
1:17 339
1:18–25 430
1:20 430
1:23 431
2 48
3:1–3 422
3:13–17 744
3:16 71
4:1–11 436
4:23 440
5–7 400, 744

5:1–2 397
5:5 400, 408
5:22 611
5:24 365
5:43–45 737
5:43–48 416–17
5:45 329, 409, 444
6 396
6:14 521
6:25 400
7:24–27 399
7:29 397
8:1–3 441n147
8:5–10 442
9:9–17 437
9:10–13 711
10:8 606
11 400
11:16–19 437, 438
11:19 400
18:35 521
19:30 443
20 584, 711
20:1–5 443–44
21:1–7 453
22:1–4 405
22:21 643
22:35–40 412
24:30 711
25:31–46 74
25:35–36 495
26:63 468
27 97
27:11 471
27:24–25 98, 467
27:24–27 101
27:25 100
27:46 491
28:16–20 483
28:19 496, 533

Mark

1:6 438
1:10 71
1:14–15 405
1:15 693
1:21–28 398, 440
1:24 385
1:27 396
1:40–42 441
2:13–22 437
2:15–17 711
2:18–22 533
4:1–34 396
4:30–32 413n74
6:3 431
6:4 402
6:6 396
8:31 482
9:31 482
9:37 385
10:2 396
10:18 385
10:31 443
10:33–34 482
11:1–10 465
11:9–10 452n168
11:16 465
11:27–28 466
12:12–27 466
12:28–34 412
12:38–40 466
13:1–27 466
13:24–27 74
13:26 711, 744
14:1–16:8 465–70
14:62 733
15:2 471
15:34 491
16:15 483, 496

Luke

1:32–33 426–27
2:1–2 452
2:1–7 426, 471
2:8–14 427, 452
2:11 387, 427, 452
2:14 452
2:46–47 397
3 337, 357
3:1–3 422
3:22 71
3:38 340
4:31–37 398
5:12–13 441n147
5:27–39 436–37, 447
5:29–32 711
6 415, 711
6:17–49 397
6:20 359, 400, 408, 410
6:27–28 415
6:33 415
6:35–36 415
7:1–10 442
7:31–35 437–38
7:35 400
9:10–17 439
9:51–56 415n76
10:25–37 413–15
11:1–4 397
13:29 540
13:30 443
13:33 402
14:13 439
14:15 405
15 533
15:1–32 445–50
17:3 521
17:20–21 407, 711
19:38 452
22:61 467
22:67 468
23:3 471
23:37–38 453
23:46–47 467–68
24:13–35 469–70
24:27 483
24:30–31 482
24:35 482
24:36–53 470
24:47 483
24:50–51 460
24:51 427

John

1 336, 391
1:1–2 386
1:1–5 161, 543
1:3 303–4, 308, 375
1:9 454
1:10–11 695

1:11–14 744
1:12–13 717
1:14 161
1:18 290, 386
1:32 71
1:38 397
3:1–21 717
3:16 478
3:16–21 717
3:19 717
4:23 408
4:46–54 442
5:4–5 78
5:18 98
5:23–24 717
5:24–25 718
5:25 408
5:27–29 718
6:22–59 717
6:39–40 718
6:44 718
6:54 718
7:37–39 717
7:41–42 431
8:12 717
11:45–53 98
12:48 718
13:1 468
13:34 620
14:3 718
14:26 502, 717
14:28 385
16:7 71
18:28 468
18:28–19:6 98
18:33 471
18:37 471
19:14 468
19:30 468
20:2–21:25 471–72
20:19 98
20:27 482
20:28 387
21:13 482

Acts
1:1–11 526–27
1:6–8 518
1:9 427
1:12–26 524
2 337
2:1–13 524–25
2:1–21 744
2:4 524
2:42–47 527
2:43–47 694
4:32 527–28n79
5–6 528
10:23–11:18 524
17:28 169
28:30 527n77

Romans
1:3–4 426, 431
1:4 505, 744
3:10 380
3:24 462
3:25 368
4 344
4:3 462
4:16–17 304–5, 308
4:17 305, 306, 316, 462–63, 479, 597
4:20–22 596
4:23–24 463
5 161
5:1 506
5:2 544
5:6–21 549
5:9–18 550
5:10 365
5:12–19 744
5:12–21 544–45, 550
5:15 548–49
5:18 548–50
5:19 549
6:4 79, 464
6:6 579
7:6–8:9 72
7:15–24 74
8 161
8:2 504
8:5 504
8:9–11 504
8:9–17 544
8:18–21 549
8:19 162
8:19–23 347
8:22–25 311
8:24 733
8:34–35 697
8:38–39 494
8:39 357
9:5 385
9:20–21 302
10:8 537
11:17 73
11:28–32 100
12 507
12:1 509
12:1–21 504–5
12:15 523
13:1 643
14–17 72
14:7 706

1 Corinthians 150
1:1 357
1:18 744
1:24 435
1:24–25 464
1:26–29 692
2:14 513
6:11 745
7:11 365
8:6 386
9:19 626
10:24 625, 737
12 337
12–13 502
12–14 523
12:1–21 504–5
12:3 387
12:4–11 745
12:7 517
12:13 745
13:8–10 730
13:12 733
15 715–17
15:3–5 459
15:20 721

15:22 161
15:23–57 461–62
15:28 162, 549
15:45 504, 744
15:51–54 727
16:1–4 528

2 Corinthians
4:7 518
4:10 728
4:15 387
4:16 305
5 161, 370, 530
5:1–4 727
5:17 73, 464, 692, 744
5:17–19 549
5:18–19 456
5:18–20 365, 366
5:19 346, 372, 661
8–9 528
13:13 75, 501, 518, 741

Galatians
2:10 528
3:6–14 338
3:8 463
3:17 462
3:28 670
4:1–7 338
4:6 745
5:6 625
5:13 626
5:13–14 523
5:13–6:2 503–4
5:16 518
5:22–25 745
6:2 517, 518, 523
6:10 528
6:17 728

Ephesians
1:3 505
4:1–2 626

Philippians
1:27 456, 519
2 314
2:1–5 365
2:4 538, 620, 625
2:5 420, 464, 481
2:6–11 459, 474
2:7 368

Colossians
1 82
1:3 744
1:15 73, 375, 385, 693
1:15–16 387
1:15–17 744
1:15–20 336–37, 435
1:19–20 73, 375, 692
1:20 346, 365, 366, 595
1:22 365
2:2 385
2:12 464
3:1–5 464

1 Thessalonians 150
4:14 715, 727
4:15 714
4:16–17 715
4:17 727
5:23 719

2 Thessalonians
2:13 505

1 Timothy
6:15–16 286, 290
6:16 290

Philemon
16 670

Hebrews
1:2 309
1:3 375, 389
1:3–4 457
1:8 385–86
4:14–16 457
7:1–3 457
9:11–14 457
9:12 459, 474
9:24–26 459, 474
9:26 457
10:10–14 457
11:13 306
12:2 386
13:20 386

James
4:4 78

1 Peter
1:2 505
1:11–2:21 502
4:9–10 502

2 Peter
1:1 386

Titus
2:13 386

1 John 102, 736, 737
2:6–8 734
2:15–16 661
3:1 734
3:11 517
3:11–12 734
3:15 611
4:1–10 735
4:19 734
4:21 734
5:4–5 78
5:20 386

Revelation
1:5–6 457
1:8 162, 177
4:8 162
5:13 385
6 711
7:10 385
8 711
11:7 162
11:15 385
12:10 385

15:3 162
16:7 162
16:14 162
18 276, 407
18:2 711
19 711
19:6 162
19:7–21 411
19:14–15 643
19:15 162
21 693, 711
21:3–4 712
21:4 720
21:5 162
21:22 162
21:23–26 411
22 693
22:1–2 712

Apocrypha

2 Maccabees

7:28 303